D0764284

PARROTS

A GUIDE TO PARROTS
OF THE WORLD

PARROTS

A GUIDE TO PARROTS
OF THE WORLD

Tony Juniper and Mike Parr

Illustrated by
Kim Franklin, Robin Restall, Dan Powell,
David Johnston, and Carl D'Silva

Yale University Press
New Haven and London

Published 1998 in the United Kingdom by Pica Press (an imprint of Helm Information Ltd)
and in the United States by Yale University Press.

ISBN 0-300-07453-0
Library of Congress Cataloging in Publication Number 97-80504

Printed in Hong Kong.
A catalogue record for this book is available from the British Library.
The paper in this book meets the guidelines for permanence and durability of the
Committee on Production Guidelines for Book Longevity of the Council on Library
Resources.

10 9 8 7 6 5 4 3 2 1

In association with the

AMERICAN
BIRD
CONSERVANCY

CONTENTS

INTRODUCTION

The standard reference guide to the parrots of the world since 1973 has been the splendid *Parrots of the World* written by Joseph Forshaw and illustrated by William Cooper. Now in its third (1989) edition, it remains a widely cited and respected work that is a central point in the literature on the natural history of this fascinating group of birds. The present book was proposed in 1989. Its authors, working then at the International Council for Bird Preservation (now BirdLife International), believed that a volume on parrots that better aided their identification would be helpful in efforts to conserve what has become the most endangered family of birds in the world, particularly given the lack of a comprehensive identification handbook that could be used by customs officers and those concerned with wildlife trade law enforcement. We similarly believed that such a guide would be a helpful point from which to develop a better understanding of the parrots in the wild. For such a familiar group of birds, remarkably little is known about their natural history, and this is sometimes an impediment to conservation action.

Parrots can be extremely difficult to identify in the wild and are sometimes misidentified in trade and captivity. Indeed, the very thin literature on the habits of many parrots is partly attributable to identification difficulties. Many species spend their time in the canopy of dense forest, are green (and therefore invisible), often silent when perched, and almost impossible to catch for ringing purposes. Even if they are caught and marked for study, most species are quite capable of removing a leg ring with their bill. They are mainly glimpsed fleetingly in fast flight before disappearing into or behind foliage.

In this volume we have attempted to assemble a digest of information that will enable birdwatchers, fieldworkers and those involved with parrots in captivity or trade to identify species and races of parrots. The 88 colour plates are backed with a systematic section containing identification tips for use in the field and captivity, a summary of range and conservation status, a summary of present ecological knowledge, and descriptive information on all races. These details have been assembled with identification in mind but are augmented where possible with material on natural history, especially where this has relevance to conservation.

A substantial body of new information has come to light since the third (1989) edition of *Parrots of the World*. This includes such things as Collar *et al.*'s (1992) review of the status of threatened birds in the Americas and Thomas Arndt's photographic monograph *Lexicon of Parrots* (1992-1996), as well as many dozens of contributions in the scientific literature concerning the status, distribution and ecology of previously little known species. A number of other species have been the subject of important taxonomic revisions, such as the black cockatoos *Calyptorhynchus*, or the focus of more intensive field studies, such as the Philippine Cockatoo (69), Red-and-blue Lory (5) and Wallace's Hanging Parrot (192).

ACKNOWLEDGEMENTS

This book would not have been possible without assistance from a wide range of people and institutions. We would like to extend our thanks to Nigel Collar for his patient editing, advice and assistance with reference material, to Christopher Helm and Nigel Redman at Pica Press for their encouragement and support throughout the long gestation of this book, and to Julie Reynolds, Marc Dando and Joe Conneally at Fluke Art who expertly handled the production.

We would also like to acknowledge the invaluable assistance of Carlos Yamashita of IBAMA, Robert Ridgely of the National Academy of Sciences at Philadelphia, Bret Whitney and John Rowlett of Field Guides Inc., Peter Colston, Effie Warr and Michael Walters at the Natural History Museum at Tring, Miguel Lentino at the Colección Ornitológica Phelps, Caracas, Ray Paynter at the Harvard University Museum of Comparative Zoology, Paul Sweet and George Barrowclough at the American Museum of Natural History in New York, the staff at the Zoology Museum of the University of Copenhagen, the South Australian Museum in Adelaide, the Australian Museum in Sydney, the Bombay Natural History Society, the University of Cambridge Zoology Museum and Library, and Richard Ranft and Paul Duck at the Library of Wildlife Sounds of the National Sound Archive, London. Paul Toyne of Parrots in Peril, Mike Crosby, Sue Squire and Alison Stattersfield at the BirdLife International Secretariat in Cambridge, Mike Perrin at the University of Natal in South Africa, Teresa Mulliken at the Wildlife Trade Monitoring Unit in Cambridge, and Phil Angle and Pam Rasmussen and the National Museum of Natural History, Smithsonian Institution, also assisted in various ways.

Thomas Arndt, Thomas Brooks, Neil Burgess, Donald Bruning, Trevor and Moira Buckell, Bruce Beehler, Robin Clarke, George and Rita Fenwick of the American Bird Conservancy, Francis Ferki, Thomas H. Fritts, Elaine and Colin Froggett, David Gibbs, F. Gueigiein, Rod Hall, Simon Harrap, Paul Jepson, Nelson and Marianne Kawall, Adrian Long, Jenny Loughlin, Geoff Masson at Paultons Park, Amber Mierisch, Charlie Munn, Robin and Diane Pickering, Michael Poulsen, Melvyn Risebrow, Harry, Pat and Yvonne Sissens, Mike Reynolds, Paul Wexler at Birdworld, Ashley Whitehouse, Steve Whitehouse and Grant Young also helped us.

Finally, we thank our colleagues at Friends of the Earth and BirdLife International, and our respective families for their support in times of stress, especially Rosemary Powell, Sue Sparkes and Maddie, Nye and Sam Juniper.

STYLE AND LAYOUT OF THE BOOK

The Plates

There are more than 1,000 colour illustrations presented on the 88 plates. These have been prepared from material examined in museum collections, live captive specimens, wild parrots and published and unpublished photographs and videos. They are, we believe, the most comprehensive set of images of parrots compiled in one volume and, in conjunction with the caption texts and main species texts, will help with the identification of all species. They should also help the reader to separate most races and immature birds as well as recognise gender-related differences where they exist.

Perched birds on the same plate are drawn to the same scale in relation to one another. Flying birds are sometimes drawn to a different (usually smaller) scale, but these again are in proportion to one another. On the caption text page opposite each plate the familiar Budgerigar relates the birds illustrated to actual size. Some plates show characteristic vegetation to help bring the parrots depicted more to life.

Numbers

Each species has been designated with a number. These have no biological or taxonomic significance and are simply a means of helping to organise the information presented. Some of the species illustrations fall out of taxonomic sequence (and therefore numerical order) for layout reasons but the numbers provide a rapid means of locating specific text accounts.

Names

The English name of each species is shown in uppercase with the scientific name in bold italics.

Other names

Many parrot species are known by several English names. To assist with identification, alternative names are listed. Some of these are now rarely (if ever) used but references to birds by formerly used names remain in the published literature where they can cause some confusion and where clarity can assist with more rapid and reliable identification. A major source document for alternative names is provided by Lodge (1991). Alternative English names that pertain to subspecies are indicated where these are in use, e.g. the English name of Rajah Lory pertains specifically to *Chalcopsitta atra insignis*. These alternative names of subspecies are set apart by use of semi-colons.

Identification

Notes on plumage, appearance and behaviour relevant to identification are provided. Emphasis is placed on differences (or relative differences) between similar species with overlapping ranges but there is also guidance on discriminating between similar-looking species that commonly appear in captivity. Key points are summarized in the captions that appear opposite the plates.

Voice

This section contains a verbal description of vocalisations based on personal knowledge, published literature and various published and unpublished recordings. Our aim has been to provide a summary of typical sounds most useful to identification. However, particularly with a group of birds for which the words "squawk" and "screech" seem to have been invented, it remains unfeasible to render in words the various timbres, timings and tones that distinguish one parrot call from another.

Distribution and Status

A summary of the geographical distribution of each species is given with an estimate of its abundance. In order to render our descriptions of birds' ranges as transparent as possible, we have sought to cite only place names appearing in the Times *Atlas of the World* (Bartholomew *et al.* 1990). However, for some species, especially those with very limited ranges on islands, etc., it has not been possible to incorporate sufficient detail from maps in that publication and we have resorted to use of place names found only on larger-scale maps.

The Distribution and Status section should be read in conjunction with notes on habitat (see Ecology below) as each species will clearly not occur throughout the range described but only in areas that are ecologically suitable. A review of population trends is offered where possible and we indicate which species are listed in Appendix I of CITES (see below under Conservation) and/or are considered in threat of global extinction with the threat category assigned by Collar *et al.* (1994) according to IUCN (the World Conservation Union) criteria (see Conservation section below).

Ecology

This section summarises the present state of knowledge on parrot habitat preferences, social behaviour, diet and reproductive biology. For species like the Australian cockatoos there is a wide and rich literature. In the case of many others, such as the Blue-fronted (41) and New Caledonian (46) Lorikeets, almost nothing is known, whilst for the majority of species limited field observation supports a rather vague understanding of their natural history. The situation is however rapidly improving with fieldworkers devoting more time (correctly prioritised towards threatened species) to the study of parrots in the wild.

Description

Adult male birds assigned to the nominate race are described in this section with female, juvenile and racial differences expanded on in following sections. Where no gender-, age- or range-related differences are known to exist, the notes in this section apply to both sexes and young birds from all parts of the species's range. For species in which the nominate race occupies a limited range compared to some other subspecies, such as Alexandrine Parakeet (193), we describe a more widespread form since this is likely to be of interest to more users of this guide. Where a race other than the nominate is described, this is indicated at the beginning of the section.

The text is based on our judgement of 'typical' specimens from the material available to us in museum collections and captivity. The descriptions are structured for rapid reference to cover, in order, the head, upperparts, wings, underparts and tail. We have sought to describe intraspecific variation. However, it is unlikely that our summary will prove comprehensive given the sometimes wide variation occurring in some species, such as the Yellow-faced Amazon (336), and the limited number of specimens that we have been able to study for some species (such as those that are now very rare). Bare parts are described from collectors' notes attached to museum specimens, live captive birds, photographs and published sources.

Sex/Age

Plumage and bare part differences that assist in the identification of the sexes or of young birds are included in this section.

Measurements

The biometric data are taken mainly from Forshaw (1989). These suggest that in most species the length of the wing, tail, tarsus and exposed part of the culmen cannot reliably be used to determine gender. We have, therefore, for the sake of brevity, merged the measurements provided for male and female birds into one range for both sexes. For polytypic species measurements are given for the nominate subspecies except where explicitly stated.

Geographical Variation

Many species of parrot demonstrate variation in plumage and other characteristics across their ranges. Where these traits are apparently predictable and stable (i.e. are not random variation), a subspecies or race is denoted through the extension of its scientific name to a trinomial title (see Origins and Classification below). A brief comparison between the race in question and other races (the nominate unless explicitly stated otherwise) follows an outline of its range. This section should be read in conjunction with Distribution and Status. A number of references have been used to identify parrot races including Forshaw (1989), Peters (1961) and various more recent analyses and reviews.

Notes

Uncertainties remain in respect of the taxonomic standing of a number of races, species and genera of parrot. Notes in this section aim to summarise the current state of debate and very briefly to indicate or explain the approach we have taken.

References

For the sake of brevity and continuity, we have referred to source material at the end of each species account rather than citing authors in the body of the text. Whilst some readers may experience frustration in directly matching factual information to specific sources, it is our judgement that the majority of users will prefer the approach we have taken.

Maps

Maps appear next to the main species accounts. These are based on our best judgement of species' distributions derived from knowledge of field sightings, the origin of specimens (where known), the distribution of preferred habitat or altitudinal requirements and comments received. We are especially grateful to BirdLife International for use of the distribution maps developed during the course of their project to map world distributions of all restricted-range bird species and for use of the unpublished distributions produced by Robert Ridgely for South American species. The maps developed by Blakers *et al.* (1984) for Australian species have also been of enormous help in presenting distributions for parrots from that part of the world. We have no doubt that some of the maps will be improved in the light of further field observation. Although the maximum extension of each species's range is depicted, parrots will obviously tend towards their preferred habitat and altitude within the presumed area of occurrence. Maps should therefore be read in conjunction with the notes in the Ecology section for the species in question.

Topography

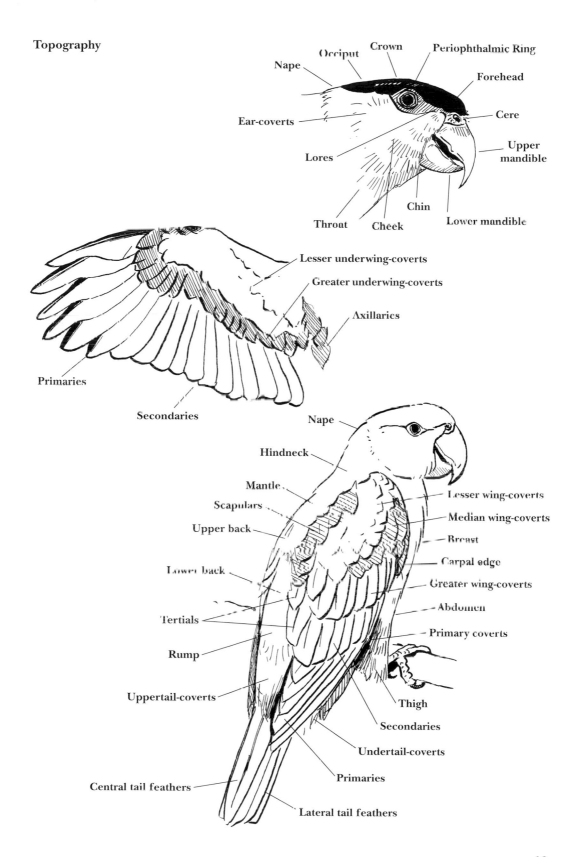

Occiput
Crown
Periophthalmic Ring
Nape
Forehead
Cere
Ear-coverts
Upper mandible
Lores
Chin
Throat
Cheek
Lower mandible

Lesser underwing-coverts

Greater underwing-coverts

Axillaries

Primaries

Secondaries

Nape

Hindneck

Mantle

Scapulars

Upper back

Lesser wing-coverts

Median wing-coverts

Breast

Lower back

Carpal edge

Greater wing-coverts

Abdomen

Tertials

Primary coverts

Rump

Uppertail-coverts

Thigh

Secondaries

Undertail-coverts

Central tail feathers

Primaries

Lateral tail feathers

ORIGINS AND EVOLUTIONARY
RELATIONSHIPS

Early parrot remains are scarce but the few finds so far made confirm the group as ancient. The oldest known evidence for the existence of parrotlike birds dates from a fossil found in southern British Lower to Middle Eocene deposits. This bird, now known as *Palaeopsittacus georgei*, lived about 40 million years ago and, with *Archeopsittacus verreauxi*, another Tertiary parrot known from French upper Oligocene or lower Miocene deposits, shows that the parrots have been around for a very long time. Beyond the few sketchy details and fragmented insights provided by fossils from the Miocene (about 20 million years ago) to the Pleistocene (less than one million years ago), and subfossil remains from the more recent past, little is known about the historical development, distribution or diversity of the parrots.

The evolutionary pathways and selective forces that led to the incredible diversity demonstrated in the parrots today can never be fully understood. These details of biological history are buried in millions of years of adaptive change. The expansion and shrinkage of forested areas caused by climate change, the movement of mighty rivers and the emergence of mountains and islands because of tectonic upheaval and volcanic activity, the chance isolation of founder populations on islands and interaction between the parrots and the millions of other life-forms that have shared their habitats, are just some of the factors that have helped shape the group as we see it today. We recognise 352 species in this volume, although there may only now be 350 as one of those included (Glaucous Macaw, 209) could be extinct and another (Intermediate Parakeet, 198) is, on very recent (as yet unpublished) evidence, a hybrid.

Despite their ancient lineage and radiation into such a wide variety of forms, just about all members of the Psittacidae are instantly recognisable as such. This is despite tremendous variation in size, shape and colour. Some are chunky with short tails and proportionately large bills, the Brown-headed Parrot (162) for example, others are large and comparatively elongated with large heads and long tails such as the large macaws *Ara*, whilst others are small and graceful with long pointed tails (various parakeets). Most show some green in their plumage (especially in the Americas) but cockatoos of the main genera *Cacatua* and *Calyptorhynchus*, in marked contrast, are mainly white or black and crested. The Golden Conure (227) is striking with mainly bright yellow plumage, Lear's Macaw (208) is mainly blue whilst the African Grey (161) is anomalous within the Psittacidae in being mainly silvery grey with a red tail. Some are large and heavy, others smaller than most songbirds. Adult Hyacinth Macaws (207) are over a metre long and weigh over 1,500 grammes and the hefty adult male Kakapo (158) reaches 3,000 grammes, whereas some pygmy parrots tip the scales at just 10 grammes, some 300 times lighter.

In spite of the morphological diversity in the group, the parrots exhibit remarkable structural homogeneity. Several characteristics, such as bill shape, fleshy cere and zygodactyl feet, render parrots instantly recognisable. This is an almost unique circumstance for a group of birds so rich in species. But whilst it is relatively straightforward to assign individual species to the Psittacidae, the apparent absence of closely related groups presents difficulties in identifying the group's ancestral links. Indeed, Beddard, writing in 1898, observed that 'The determination of the affinities of the parrots to other groups of birds is one of the hardest problems in ornithology' (see Sibley and Ahlquist 1990). Matters have not improved much since then. Indeed, the uncertainties that exist over the phylogenetic origins of the parrots are reflected in the fact that a wide range of approaches to their classification has been proposed on the basis of various anatomical and behavioural similarities with other avian groups. For example, Linnaeus concluded in the 18th century that the parrots belonged with the toucans, hornbills, cuckoos, corvines, rollers, orioles, jacamars, starlings, birds of paradise, woodpeckers, hummingbirds and others, whilst in the late 20th century it has been widely held that the parrots are close to pigeons (see for example Forshaw 1989, Sibley and Ahlquist 1990).

Specific structural similarities (perhaps suggesting common ancestry) can be found with many bird groups including (in the case of bills) raptors, (zygodactyl feet) woodpeckers, (tongues) cuckoos and (on the basis of several anatomical and behavioural characters) pigeons. However, these and further similarities with other bird groups are thought to be convergent rather than ancestrally shared, and therefore provide few real clues to the identity of the parrots' closest relatives.

One approach that can help distinguish convergence and true phylogenetic relationships is through the comparison of DNA. Sibley and Ahlquist's (1990) review of evidence based on DNA hybridisation techniques suggests that the parrots are the descendants of an ancient lineage but that they are not especially close to the pigeons and that their affinity with the cuckoos (the most often cited closest group) is at best ambivalent. These authors conclude that the parrots have no close living relatives.

CLASSIFICATION OF THE PARROTS

Most parrots have proportionately large heads, short necks and short legs. The most recognisable feature that places individual species in the parrot family is the characteristic bill. Broad-based with a chisel-shaped cutting edge on the lower mandible and with a wide curve and sharp point on the upper, parrot bills are clearly recognisable but also very variable in size, and to an extent shape. The fleshy cere, which enables some movement of the upper mandible in relation to the skull, is sometimes feathered but in most species bare. The tibia is mostly short and feathered with the tarsus relatively long and covered with small granular scales. When walking on a perch or the ground, parrots show a characteristic swaggering gait. The zygodactyl feet, with two toes pointing forwards and two back, provide a very strong grip and, used with the bill as a kind of grappling hook, enable this largely arboreal group of birds to climb with great agility. Uniquely among birds, the structure of the feet enables many of the arboreal parrots to manipulate food, usually with their left foot. Having said that, one survey of 56 Brown-throated Conures (245) showed exactly half used their left foot and the remainder the right. Species that habitually feed on the ground mostly do not use their feet for feeding.

The feathers of most parrots are rather sparse and hard, and the group is partly defined by the presence of powder down, which in some species (such as the Mealy Amazon, 345) is abundant. Although plumage is highly variable, mainly green parrots are more frequent than other colours, especially in South America. Adult plumage is generally attained between the first and third year. Parrots undergo a complete moult annually with young birds replacing their juvenile feathers before they are one year old. Adults generally undertake a post-breeding moult. Primary feathers are lost in the centre first, then in both directions toward the wing tips and secondaries at the same time, with the secondaries lost from the outside towards the body. Some parrots have exceptionally long tails which take up over half their length (such as the Long-tailed Parakeet, 206), whilst others (such as some hanging parrots *Loriculus*) have tails so short as to be concealed by the tail-coverts. Much of the length of the feather-shafts on the tail feathers of the racquet-tails *Prioniturus* are bare with spoon-shaped tips. The bare shafted tips to the tail feathers of the pygmy parrots assist them in climbing.

All avian classifications include the parrots in the order Psittaciformes. Whilst many authors consider the internal homogeneity of the group to warrant that the entire order also be seen as a single family (Psittacidae), alternative approaches have been proposed. The examination of the parrots provided by Forshaw largely follows (with several important qualifications) Smith (1975), who splits the Psittacidae to four subfamilies comprising various tribes that in turn hold a large number of genera.

Sibley and Ahlquist (1990) review the main proposed treatments but on the basis of comparisons of genetic material conclude that the parrots are probably divisible into several subunits based on geographical groupings. They tentatively suggest that these groupings are based on Africa, the New World and the Australian region. However, their data were insufficient to conclude what the biological groupings within these geographical areas should be, and they retain the parrots in a single family pending more DNA analysis. We follow Sibley and Ahlquist (1990) and Sibley and Monroe (1990) in recognising the single family Psittacidae but expect a strong case for future revision to subfamilies following more DNA-based investigations.

Having recognised the difficulties in correctly assigning subfamilies within the Psittacidae, there are many distinct groups of closely related species in the parrot family that permit the relatively straight-forward identification of genera. Some genera, like the *Amazona* of the New World, are large (31 species), whilst a great many contain only a handful of similar species. There are of course species that cannot be clustered with others, and these are assigned to genera of their own, such as *Strigops* and *Psittrichas*.

The most meaningful unit of classification, however, certainly from ecological and conservation perspectives, is the species. Wilson (1992) provides a helpful summary of the biological species concept concluding that 'a species is a population whose members are able to interbreed freely under natural conditions'. Various behavioural, biochemical and geographical barriers limit breeding between different life-forms but there remains sporadic hybridisation in nature between closely related species. In this regard, the definition of a subspecies (sometimes called a race) is relevant. The question of whether to assign taxa to species or subspecies inevitably occurred several times in our compilation of this work. As mentioned above these issues are dealt with where necessary under the Notes sections in the species accounts.

In general, however, it is the extent of hybridisation along a contact zone that indicates whether two forms are closely related species or races of a single species. If the area of contact produces a high number of hybrid or intermediate forms, then the meeting populations are two races of one species. If it produces few, then they are two species. Hybridisation in captivity is not a good guide to taxonomic status, however, since some of the normal barriers that separate species in nature (especially geographical and ecological) are removed. The 'Adelaide Rosella', often treated as a full species, is an interesting example in which hybridisation between two rosella species (Crimson, 128, and Yellow, 129) has produced two independent populations with separate ranges from the parent species.

Racial (subspecific) differences occur as a result of differing environmental and genetic factors operating within a species's range. Populations separated by a wide river or expanse of ocean, mountain range, or simply long distances on land can differentiate into racial forms because of the appearance in the population as a whole of randomly generated variation or because of different ecological conditions. Some racial differences are clear and tend to be associated with populations that are effectively isolated (on islands for example) whilst others, especially in species with large continental ranges, occur incrementally, with extremes of variation at opposing ends of the range. Such incrementally varying traits are termed clinal, and are often impossible to impose geographic limits on and therefore give names to.

Thus the race or subspecies unit of classification is often not clear, and in many cases has only limited ecological relevance. For instance, some racial traits (especially those linked to random variation rather than adaptation) might break along different geographical lines. In a hypothetical example, the intensity of green on a bird's upperparts may show a north-south difference, whilst the extent of blue on its abdomen may vary east to west. North-eastern birds are dark green with a large blue patch beneath, south-western ones are paler above with limited blue. Variation in these two traits thus gives rise to four possible races, north-east, south-east, north-west and south-west. The addition of one or two more variable traits (for example bill length and tail colour) creates a potentially unmanageable situation that probably occurs in nature more often than is convenient for the clear and consistent description of apparent races (see Wilson 1992).

Whilst we include notes on all apparently valid races, present knowledge of the taxonomic status and distribution of many of these is incomplete.

In the present overview, we have taken for our starting point the treatment (and amendments) of Sibley and Monroe (1990, 1993). In line with several recent authors, we make various minor modifications to their list, in part alluded to by questions raised by Sibley and Monroe themselves. We split the *Ara* macaws into four genera, view the *strenua* form of Green Conure (229) as a race (not a species) but elevate the insular *A. h. brevipes* to a species, and treat *Pyrrhura devillei* as a race of Maroon-bellied Conure (251). We give the name *P. perlata* (not *P. rhodogaster*) to the Red-bellied Conure (252) and *P. lepida* (not *P. perlata*) to the Pearly Conure (253). We resurrect *Psilopsiagon* for two former members of *Bolborhynchus*, and change the name of *Forpus xanthopterygius* to *F. crassirostris* (277). We tentatively regard *Brotogeris chiriri* as a race of Canary-winged Parakeet (283), and merge *Gypopsitta* in *Pionopsitta*. The reasons for these departures are briefly summarised in the Notes section of each relevant account.

Blue-crowned Racquet-tail
Prioniturus discursus

Brown-backed Parrotlet
Touit melanotos

Black-capped Lory
Lorius lory

Sulphur-crested Cockatoo
Cacatua sulphurea

Hyacinth Macaw
Andorhynchus hyacinthinus

Red-breasted Pygmy Parrot
Micropsitta bruijnii

Thick-billed Parrot
Rhynchopsitta pachyrhyncha

Mealy Amazon
Amazona farinosa

Slaty-headed Parakeet
Psittacula himalayana

Budgerigar
Melopsittacus undulatus

Kakapo
Strigops habroptilus

Brown-necked Parrot
Poicephalus robustus

Scale images of a selection of parrot species to illustrate the diversity of sizes and shapes within the family.

NATURAL HISTORY OF THE PARROTS

General Behaviour

Many forest-dwelling parrots awake just before dawn and vacate their roosting site (generally a communal roost outside the breeding season) just before or about sunrise although some depart earlier in total darkness. Birds mainly disperse just above tree canopy height, although some – certain large macaws for instance – travel much higher. Birds mainly first disperse to feeding areas where they spend the first few hours of the day foraging. They then rest or engage in social interaction, bathe or drink. Allopreening and other bonding activities often occur at this time. Birds feed again in the afternoon before gathering into groups for return to their roosting areas. Before settling for the night, parrots often call loudly and engage in intense and excited interaction. The function of such activity may be linked both to the social dynamics of the flock and to foraging effectiveness. The silence of many parrots during most daylight hours, compared to when they are either departing or arriving at their roosting site, is perhaps an anti-predator behaviour. Most species fly on rapid shallow wingbeats but the role and type of flight seen in parrots is highly variable. Some have short rounded wings clearly adapted for flight in foliage, whilst others have long pointed wings adapted for longer-distance or nomadic movements in relatively open country.

Distribution

The parrots are mainly distributed through the tropics and subtropics but some penetrate temperate latitudes and others frequent temperate vegetation at high altitudes within the tropics and subtropics. Thus in South America the Austral Conure (267) ranges throughout Tierra del Fuego in the southern temperate zone to below 54°S (where it is the most southerly of all parrots) and the Antipodes Parakeet (140) and Red-fronted Parakeet (142) co-exist on Antipodes Island in the South Pacific at nearly 50°S. Parrots in the genus *Bolborhynchus* live on the temperate paramo grasslands above the treeline in the Andes, whilst the Kea (76) of New Zealand is frequently found in alpine vegetation and remains on occasion at high altitude after snowfalls. Several *Psittacula* parakeets inhabit temperate vegetation in mountain areas, with the Derbyan Parakeet (203) seen on the Tibetan plateau at 3,300m in midwinter. The occurrence of Alexandrine Parakeet (193) in Afghanistan probably places that species as the most northerly naturally occurring parrot although the Carolina Parakeet *Conuropsis carolinensis* ranged further north in North America until it was persecuted to extinction in the early 20th century.

Parrots become increasingly diverse, however, in tropical and subtropical lowland forested areas, and have speciated most markedly in the New World and Australia, where there are 145 and 59 species representing 25 and 26 genera respectively. For reasons as yet unexplained, the family is relatively poorly represented in Africa and its islands where there are only 23 species in five genera (including the Ring-necked Parakeet, 194, which also occurs in Asia). Within these broad limits, it is lowland tropical forests that are favoured by most species.

A consequence of the large-scale trade in parrots has been the inadvertent (but sometimes deliberate) introduction of species to lands to which they are not native. Up to 27 species of parrot breed as feral birds in North America alone. Feral Canary-winged Parakeets (283) have already been reported as causing damage to mango and other fruit crops in suburban Miami with others, such as Monk Parakeet (269) and Black-headed Conure (247), posing a potential risk as serious crop predators. Feral parrots are established outside their normal range in other parts of the world, too, including the Ring-necked Parakeet, which is present in, among other places, the Arabian Peninsula, UK and Netherlands.

Habitat

Most parrots dwell in forest habitats and are therefore largely or exclusively arboreal. There are, however, exceptions. Some are exclusively terrestrial, such as the Ground Parrot (156) and the flightless Kakapo. Some are specialists of shoreline habitats during at least part of their annual cycles, such as the Orange-bellied Parrot (151) of Australia which feeds on the seeds of halophytic plants outside the breeding season, and the Kermadec island race of Red-fronted Parakeet which is known to include small limpets in its diet. Several more parrot species inhabit grasslands with only light woodland or scattered bushes and shrubs, the Rufous-fronted Parakeet (274) of the Colombian Andes and the Budgerigar (155) and *Neophema* parakeets of Australia, for example.

Within wooded ecosystems, it is generally more humid formations that hold most species, although many of the parrots are found in seasonally dry woodlands, savanna and even arid and semi-arid vegetation. For example, the very dry scrub and thorny woodlands on the Pacific slope of Mexico are home to the Lilac-crowned Amazon (330), while the Lear's Macaw (208) inhabits a dry rugged enclave in the interior of north-east Brazil and the Niam-niam Parrot (165) occurs on the southern fringes of the Sahara.

Forest habitats are obviously dominated by trees and it is upon trees that most parrots rely to provide most of their needs. The most obvious and regular requirement is for food and nearly all parrots rely on various tress to provide their diet. In some cases – for instance, the Thick-billed (225) and Yellow-eared (224) Parrots that respectively need pine trees and wax palms for their food - this requirement is highly specific; but such specialisation is limited to a few situations where certain plants form actual or virtual monospecific stands. Since most parrots nest in tree cavities, old trees with hollows are an essential requirement of their habitat, and in some cases this limits the productivity of populations when the number of breeding pairs exceeds the number of suitable places to lay eggs and rear young. The absence of Monk Parakeets from areas where there are no tall structures (trees or pylons for example) on which to build nests is a good example of how the availability of nest-sites can determine distribution. Additional needs include drinking water (often an issue in seasonally dry forest) and for some parrots access to exposed clay licks where birds take minerals, perhaps to help neutralise plant toxins ingested with their food.

Given that lowland tropical forests hold the greatest diversity of trees (and therefore tree flowers, buds, fruits and seeds) it is to be expected that this is where most forms of parrot are found. Nevertheless, similar species of parrot are commonly not found together and there is little sympatric occurrence among members of the same genus. The Peach-fronted (244) and Cactus (246) Conures are, for example, mutually exclusive: these birds have overlapping ranges but the former inhabits the grassier areas of the cerrado and caatinga woodlands of interior north-eastern Brazil, whilst the latter is mainly found in the woodier portions of the caatinga. Thus at any one locality it is usual to find a community of non-congeneric species showing different-sized bills or foraging strategies. There are of course exceptions. Several species of *Psittacula* parakeet occur together in Asia and several large *Ara* macaws overlap in South America, with no very clear ecological separation in terms of habitat preference or diet.

The association with tree-rich habitats is reflected in the zygodactyl feet of parrots (which are clearly adapted for grasping branches and clambering in foliage), whilst the mainly green plumage of many parrots, enriched with yellow, red, blue and purple highlights, matches the colours of the leaves and flowers in the forest canopies where they dwell.

Susceptibility to low temperatures is clearly not a constraint on the distribution of most species inhabiting tropical and subtropical forests, but in the case of the Purple-bellied Parrot (352) high temperatures do present problems. In captivity, this species demonstrates discomfort about 18°C and this heat intolerance perhaps explains its preference for the forests in the cool and shaded valleys in the foothills of Brazil's eastern coastal mountains.

The extent to which different species can tolerate habitat modification is highly variable. Some have expanded because of reduced tree cover, such as the Peach-fronted Conure and Blue-headed Macaw (220), although most forest-dwelling species have declined in the face of deforestation or forest degradation. Some others, notably in the dry interior of Australia, have benefited from water brought by agriculture to arid areas, even though the agriculture itself has transformed the birds' original habitat.

Movements

Regular large scale seasonal movements in response to altering weather conditions are not necessary for the avian inhabitants of many lowland tropical habitats and long-distance migration is correspondingly rare in parrots. However, the frequent clumping of food sources (such as fruiting trees) does dictate mobility and, under some conditions, seasonal movements, although these might not be predictable between years and instead often involve nomadic travel in response to altering foraging conditions. In this respect, most parrots are neither sedentary nor migratory but mobile within a geographical area that provides for all of the bird's needs, but not necessarily all at once in one locality.

A number of parrots are also nomadic, depending on seasonal availability of water or food. The Budgerigar is perhaps the best known. The Scarlet-chested Parrot (153) is an irruptive breeder, and the enigmatic Night Parrot (157) is also thought to be a nomad. Some psittacine inhabitants of mountainous areas move to lower altitudes during the winter months (certain *Psittacula* parakeets for example). Many others, such as the African Grey, Blue-headed (313), and Eclectus Parrots (111), make substantial daily movements between communal roosting areas and feeding places. Birds are often especially conspicuous morning and evening whilst calling in flight *en route* between feeding and roosting areas. Only a handful of parrot species are migratory in the classic sense. Two *Neophema*, the Orange-bellied and Blue-winged Parrot (148), as well as the lorikeet-like Swift Parrot (154), migrate between Tasmania and the Australian mainland across the Bass Strait, making them the only parrots that undergo regular seasonal migrations across a major body of salt water with almost the entire populations of the first and last of these species making this seasonal displacement.

The nomadic behaviour of many parrots in the post-breeding period of their annual cycle has been subject to very little systematic investigation and may prove to be more structured than is presently understood. Some details of nomadic behaviour suggest that it is primarily young birds that engage in such seasonal wanderings. Although there is no evidence yet to determine the function of such movements, it may be that young parrots gain invaluable knowledge of available food and water sources that may be used later in times of shortage or adverse local conditions.

A few species, such as the Thick-billed Parrot, undertake irruptive movements from core areas of distribution into surrounding areas where favourable foraging conditions are found. In the case of this species at least, irruptive movements are linked to the unpredictable nature of the parrots' main food supply (pine seeds) and the fact that shortages occur in years when trees in its core range produce little or no seed.

Social Behaviour

Most species of parrot are gregarious for at least part of their year and are chiefly encountered in small flocks or at least in pairs. An exception is Australia's Ground Parrot, which is largely solitary. The adaptive significance of the various levels of gregariousness in parrots has been little studied but is probably related mostly to foraging effectiveness and anti-predator defence. Some species 'appoint' sentinels that watch over feeding flocks, and it is probable that communal roosts have at least some anti-predator as well as foraging benefits too.

Social roosting is common in parrots. Some spend the night in the tops of trees on islands in rivers, for example Short-tailed (312) and African Grey Parrots, others in small groups in tree-hollows (e.g. some *Pyrrhura* conures), on cliffs (some macaws) or in communal nests (Monk Parakeet). Some species convene very large night-time gatherings: roosts of Red-spectacled Amazons (328) and Maroon-fronted Parrots (226) hold a substantial proportion of their world populations (if not all in the case of the former). Hanging parrots roost upside-down, as do several lovebirds. The communal roosting of pygmy and fig parrots in cavities in active arboreal termitaria may help to conserve heat. Pairs of some parrots roost in their nest-hole as breeding approaches, presumably as a means of nest-site defence and also possibly to enhance the pair-bond.

In addition to reducing the risk of predation, communal roosting might also enable birds to exchange information about the location of fruiting trees and other patchy food sources. However, work by Chapman *et al.* (1989) suggests that large communal roosts may instead be a mechanism whereby birds more effectively disperse over potential feeding territory. Their observations showed small feeding flocks reluctant to set off from a large roost in the direction of a preceding flock, perhaps indicating a means whereby birds reduce intraspecific competition through effective dispersal.

Various birds of prey appear to be the principal predators of parrots although monkeys, other tree-dwelling mammals and snakes undoubtedly take a lot of eggs and nestlings. When a flock of parrots becomes aware of a potential predator it quickly falls silent before noisily exploding from cover. The sudden noise and movement appears designed to cause temporary confusion.

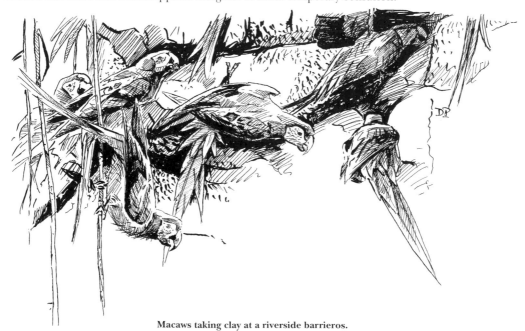

Macaws taking clay at a riverside barrieros.

Diet

Parrots mainly eat plant parts. Seeds, fruits, blossoms, nectar, pollen, buds, leaves, berries, nuts and sometimes bark are the principal known food items. The emphasis on particular plant products varies widely between genera. Some parrots are specialist feeders. The *Anodorhynchus* macaws are structurally adapted (with their massively powerful bills) to exploit various palm nuts, whilst the lories with their 'brush' tongues have evolved to take pollen and nectar. It is believed that the *Hapalopsittaca* parrots of the Andes are specialist feeders on (or at least show a preference for) mistletoe fruits whilst the *Brotogeris* parakeets of South America apparently show an association with trees in the Bombacaceae (although it is not yet known if this preference reflects a trophic relationship). Pygmy parrots feed on lichens taken from tree bark and are adapted to a trunk-hugging lifestyle with stiff projecting shafts from their tail feathers and long curved claws. Others, with long wings, slender pointed tails and streamlined bodies, are adapted for routinely covering long distances in search of grass seeds (*Neophema* and *Psilopsiagon* parakeets for example).

Some others are generalists. With medium-sized all-purpose bills, typical fleshy parrot tongues and the psittacine ability to manipulate food with their feet, they have wide dietary flexibility which sustains some species (such as the Ring-necked Parakeet) over very large and ecologically diverse ranges. The adaptability in feeding habits demonstrated by birds in captivity (denied their normal wild diet) demonstrates a level of behavioural, anatomical and biochemical flexibility that is clearly of great advantage to species inhabiting tropical forest ecosystems where a wide range of feeding opportunities are presented and where adaptability clearly has survival advantages.

Whilst fruits feature in the diet of many parrots, closer examination of some birds' feeding habits has revealed that it is the seeds embedded in the fruit rather than the fruit itself that they are eating. In respect of the lories, it has been widely held for some time that pollen forms an important component of their diet. However, experimental investigations by Brice *et al.* (1989) into pollen digestion indicate that even lorikeets find it difficult to digest pollen grains and that it cannot be an important source of energy or protein. These findings strongly suggest that the importance of pollen is overestimated for birds apparently adapted to exploit it. Why they are so closely adapted to eating it or what comprises their principal source of protein or energy (assuming that the calculations by Brice *et al.* are correct) is not known.

Some species (*Pyrrhura* conures for example) also take a good deal of animal food in the form of insects and their larvae, and there are examples of several species consuming aquatic molluscs (including Golden-winged Parakeet, 287, and Hyacinth Macaw). A wide range of parrots also visit earth banks to take mineral-rich soil where they sometimes congregate in very large numbers. This behaviour is especially noteworthy in Amazonia where many hundreds of parrots from several species attend together at so-called barreiros on river banks in the forest. Visiting clay banks to take mineral deposits clearly serves some very important function, possibly obtaining trace elements, neutralising the toxic effects of poisons ingested with plant foods, or both. A parallel behaviour is perhaps observed in Australian parrots that have been found with charcoal in their stomachs. Many parrots have been found with small stones in their digestive tracts as a means to help grind and digest hard seed food.

The role of parrots as seed dispersers, and therefore as agents in shaping the ecosystems they inhabit, is very poorly known. Whilst many species crush the seeds they eat, birds that take whole berries and small fruits potentially have important dynamic relationships with their habitat. Those that feed on flowers, nectar or pollen undoubtedly play a role as pollinators although for any given parrot species it is not know what precise ecological impact this has compared with the activities of creatures like insects and bats.

Breeding

Parrots are mainly monogamous and, in the case of larger species at least, pair for life. The bond between pairs is constantly reinforced by allopreening and feeding. This strategy is perhaps adaptive, because of the high proportion of learned (as compared to instinctive) behaviour exhibited in parrots: pairs that know each other well and have experience of one another breed more successfully. Most species show no sexual dimorphism and, where this does occur, gender differences are for the most part slight and are seen mainly in plumage rather than size or structure.

There are a few exceptional species that are polygamous. Males of both the Kea and Kakapo of New Zealand sometimes have several female breeding partners. The nocturnal lekking behaviour of the Kakapo, where several males gather at night and make booming calls to attract females, is unique to the group.

Some parrots are territorial whilst breeding and defend at least a small area around their nest. The Purple-bellied Parrot of the Atlantic rainforests of Brazil is highly territorial, with nests generally dispersed around 2km apart. Generally speaking, species living outside the tropics, where food availability is more seasonal, have more defined breeding seasons. Many lories by contrast tend to be opportunistic breeders with the onset of egg-laying determined by the local availability of nectar and pollen on flowering trees. Whilst this is often during the rainiest part of the year, the timing of breeding does vary from year to year. Such opportunistism is facilitated by the parrots' mainly monogamous breeding system with the pair-bond established and the pair ready to commence nesting at any time conditions become suitable.

The vast majority of species are cavity-breeders, with nests located in hollows in trees and palms, either those occurring through, for example, storm damage or ones that have been excavated by other species such as woodpeckers. Most parrots prefer nest-sites as high up as possible. Those species using tree-hollows for breeding often enlarge their nest-cavity with the resulting wood shavings providing a simple platform for eggs. The availability of suitable nest-sites is undoubtedly a limiting factor that determines breeding density. There may be a linkage between the onset of egg-laying and incubation behaviour and the daytime darkness experienced by birds spending time in their nest-hollows. The endocrine changes that occur then may be an important component of the breeding cycle. It is the female of most parrots that spends increasing time in the nest-hollow prior to egg-laying and in nearly all species the female alone incubates. Male birds feed incubating females.

Some parrots excavate holes in arboreal termite nests (some *Brotogeris* parakeets and *Aratinga* conures, for example) and terrestrial termitaria (Golden-shouldered Parrot, 138, Red-faced Lovebird, 172). A few species nest in gaps in masonry (Ring-necked Parakeet and Black-winged Lovebird, 173). Cliff-nesting is observed in several species including the Maroon-fronted Parrot and Lear's Macaw. Some others, such as the Patagonian Conure (249) and some of the *Bolborhynchus* parakeets, dig burrows into banks or cliffs; in the case of the former species these nesting burrows can be up to 3 m long. The Rock Parrot (150) nests only in rock crevices just above the high-tide mark on the south Australian coast. The Ground Parrot lays its eggs in a shallow depression on the ground beneath a bush or tussock.

Very few parrots construct nests although a few do carry nest material into cavities. The Monk Parakeet is unique in the family in building large communal stick nests (in which each pair has its own nest chamber) whilst the lovebirds *Agapornis* are noteworthy for their habit of carrying material to line their nest-chambers (in the case of some species by tucking it into their rump feathers). Some lovebirds (the *fischeri-personatus* complex) and the hanging parrots are also remarkable for the domed grass nests they construct inside their breeding cavities.

Lovebird carrying nesting material tucked in rump feathers.

Whilst some parrots nest in loose colonies (for example some *Psittacula* parakeets) it is very rare for several pairs to share one nest-chamber. In the case of the Golden Conure, however, several females often contribute to a single clutch with 14 young reported from one captive nest. The adaptive significance of this behaviour has not been explored but could include anti-predator advantages or be a response to limited nest-site availability and a means better to retain a nest-cavity in the face of competition from larger or more aggressive species. Some Australian species such as Scarlet-chested Parrot and Budgerigar are irruptive partly in response to rainfall and form nesting colonies in areas where they have been absent for many years.

In common with other cavity-nesting groups, the parrots lay white eggs. Clutch-size is variable with, on average, smaller species producing larger clutches. For example, the Green-rumped Parrotlet (276) lays on average seven eggs and in some years, if conditions are right, will double-brood. The large Imperial Parrot (350) of Dominica on the other hand usually produces one fledgling at most every other breeding attempt and if conditions are not favourable will not breed at all. Differing levels of productivity are clearly of central importance in shaping the resilience of different parrots to negative population pressures.

Young parrots are altricial and born either naked or with only sparse down; they are wholly dependent at first on their parents for food and often for warmth. Most species reach sexual maturity between their second and fourth year with as a general rule maturity reached earlier in smaller species. An extreme case is the Budgerigar, which can attain breeding condition in about six months, apparently an adaptation to the unpredictable ecological conditions that prevail in its range where breeding opportunities must be seized at short notice to be successful. Many juvenile parrots show distinct plumages (generally duller than adults), and are discernibly smaller with darker irides.

Nocturnal Species

Most parrots are diurnal although several are active at night including the Black-lored Parrot (110), which occurs only on the island of Buru, Indonesia, and the Hyacinth Macaw, which can be active when the moon is bright. The Blue-backed Parrot (109) from Sulawesi and the Philippines, and some members of the Pacific genus *Prosopeia*, are active after dark, but the best examples of truly nocturnal species are the amazing Kakapo from New Zealand and the little-known Night Parrot from Australia.

Monk Parakeets at a communal nest.

CONSERVATION STATUS

The parrots possess the largest number of threatened species of any bird family. Collar *et al.* (1994) recognise 90 species at risk of global extinction (see Table 1). The situation in Latin America and the Caribbean is especially serious with 44 species, nearly a third (31%) of the total in that region, considered at risk of global extinction (see also Collar and Juniper 1992, Collar *et al.* 1992). With these dire statistics in mind, it is perhaps fitting that the world's rarest bird (the Spix's Macaw, 210) should be a Neotropical parrot.

Extinct Species

Many parrot species have recently become extinct as a result of human-induced impacts. These species were mainly, but not exclusively, inhabitants of islands.

At the time of the first European expeditions to the Caribbean, a minimum of 28 parrot species lived on the islands there. In the 500 years since then, most have become extinct. These include the Cuban Macaw *Ara tricolor* of Cuba and Hispaniola which was hunted and collected to extinction in the latter part of the 19th century, the amazons of Guadeloupe (*Amazona violacea*) and Martinique (*A. martinica*), and a conure on Puerto Rico (*Aratinga maugei*). Most of those that remain are in danger of extinction with several at critical risk.

Cuban Macaw

Broad-billed Parrot

Carolina Parakeet

Newton's Parakeet

Mascarene Parrot

The Indian Ocean too has seen the untimely departure of a large proportion of its parrot species. The Mascarene and Broad-billed Parrots (*Mascarinus mascarinus* and *Lophopsittacus mauritianus*) of Mauritius disappeared during the first half of the 19th and 17th centuries respectively, whilst two *Psittacula*, the Seychelles Parakeet *P. wardi*, persecuted to oblivion, and Newton's Parakeet *P. exsul* of Rodrigues, extinct for unknown reasons, were lost at about the start of the 20th century.

In the Pacific, the Norfolk Island Kaka *Nestor productus* was hunted to extinction by the early 19th century. The New Caledonian Lorikeet might hang on in New Caledonia whilst several other species of lory have been lost from islands they formerly inhabited and are now at serious risk where they remain.

Whilst most known parrot extinctions have been of island forms, some were inhabitants of continental areas. The Glaucous Macaw has not been seen since 1951 and is now perhaps extinct, probably because of the clearance by farmers of stands of its preferred palm food-plant, whilst the Carolina Parakeet, once widespread in the United States, became extinct during the early part of the 20th century, at least partly because of persecution and collecting.

The disappearance of these birds provides testimony to the folly of humankind's attitude toward its fellow inhabitants of the earth. Whilst the human view of the world has evidently shifted in recent decades to show ever-greater sympathy towards endangered wildlife, the fact remains that a great many more parrot species, unless urgent and decisive action is taken, will soon remain only as distant memories or skins in museum collections.

Norfolk Island Kaka

Threatened species

Collar *et al.* (1994) estimate risk of extinction to different species in several standardised threat categories. The categories used in respect of threatened parrots are Extinct in the Wild, Critically Endangered, Endangered and Vulnerable. Species are deemed Extinct in the Wild when they are known only to survive in captivity or as a naturalised population well outside the past range. Critically Endangered birds face an extremely high risk of extinction in the wild in the immediate future, whilst Endangered species face a high risk of extinction in the wild in the near future. Those categorised as Vulnerable face a high risk of extinction in the medium term. Various criteria linked to population size, vulnerability and the level of threat are used to assign species to these categories. Other threat categories (in addition to those cited above) are used by Collar *et al.* (1994), but these have not been applied to any of the parrots.

The categories used in Collar *et al.* (1994) were subsequently slightly modified but are by and large those now adopted (since 1996) at the global level by IUCN–The World Conservation Union. The threat categories are intended partly to prioritise conservation action with the most threatened in need of most urgent assistance. Species listed by Collar *et al.* (1994) are included in Table 1. These birds are further indicated in the specific species accounts contained in the main body of this book.

Table 1. Parrots under threat of global extinction (from Collar *et al.* 1994). An asterisk indicates listing on CITES Appendix I as at 1997 (for the remaining Appendix I taxa see Table 2 and the later discussion of CITES under Live Bird Trade).

Spix's Macaw
Cyanopsitta spixii

   5 Red-and-blue Lory *Eos histrio* ENDANGERED*
   9 Black-winged Lory *Eos cyanogenia* VULNERABLE
 17 Mindanao Lorikeet *Trichoglossus johnstoniae* VULNERABLE
 21 Iris Lorikeet *Psitteuteles iris* VULNERABLE
 23 Chattering Lory *Lorius garrulus* VULNERABLE
 24 Purple-naped Lory *Lorius domicella* VULNERABLE
 31 Kuhl's Lorikeet *Vini kuhlii* ENDANGERED
 32 Stephen's Lorikeet *Vini stepheni* VULNERABLE
 33 Blue Lorikeet *Vini peruviana* VULNERABLE
 34 Ultramarine Lorikeet *Vini ultramarina* ENDANGERED*
 41 Blue-fronted Lorikeet *Charmosyna toxopei* VULNERABLE
 46 New Caledonian Lorikeet *Charmosyna diadema* ENDANGERED
 47 Red-throated Lorikeet *Charmosyna amabilis* VULNERABLE
 56 White-tailed Black Cockatoo *Calyptorhynchus baudinii* VULNERABLE
 57 Slender-billed Black Cockatoo *Calyptorhynchus latirostris* VULNERABLE
 60 Glossy Black Cockatoo *Calyptorhynchus lathami* VULNERABLE
 64 Yellow-crested Cockatoo *Cacatua sulphurea* ENDANGERED
 67 Salmon-crested Cockatoo *Cacatua moluccensis* VULNERABLE*
 68 White Cockatoo *Cacatua alba* VULNERABLE
 69 Philippine Cockatoo *Cacatua haematuropygia* CRITICAL*
 77 Kaka *Nestor meridionalis* VULNERABLE
 88 Salvadori's Fig Parrot *Psittaculirostris salvadorii* VULNERABLE
 98 Montane Racquet-tail *Prioniturus montanus* VULNERABLE
 99 Mindanao Racquet-tail *Prioniturus waterstradti* VULNERABLE
100 Blue-headed Racquet-tail *Prioniturus platenae* VULNERABLE
101 Green Racquet-tail *Prioniturus luconensis* ENDANGERED
103 Blue-winged Racquet-tail *Prioniturus verticalis* ENDANGERED
108 Blue-naped Parrot *Tanygnathus lucionensis* ENDANGERED
110 Black-lored Parrot *Tanygnathus gramineus* VULNERABLE
112 Pesquet's Parrot *Psittrichas fulgidus* VULNERABLE
121 Superb Parrot *Polytelis swainsonii* VULNERABLE
123 Alexandra's Parrot *Polytelis alexandrae* VULNERABLE
138 Golden-shouldered Parrot *Psephotus chrysopterygius* ENDANGERED*
140 Antipodes Parakeet *Cyanoramphus unicolor* VULNERABLE
141 Norfolk Island Parakeet *Cyanoramphus cookii* CRITICAL*
145 Horned Parakeet *Eunymphicus cornutus* VULNERABLE
151 Orange-bellied Parrot *Neophema chrysogaster* ENDANGERED*
153 Scarlet-chested Parrot *Neophema splendida* VULNERABLE
154 Swift Parrot *Lathamus discolor* VULNERABLE
157 Night Parrot *Geopsittacus occidentalis* CRITICAL*
158 Kakapo *Strigops habroptilus* EXTINCT IN THE WILD*
179 Black-cheeked Lovebird *Agapornis nigrigenis* ENDANGERED

Night Parrot *Geopsittacus occidentalis*

187 Sangir Hanging Parrot *Loriculus catamene* ENDANGERED
192 Wallace's Hanging Parrot *Loriculus flosculus* VULNERABLE
195 Mauritius Parakeet *Psittacula echo* CRITICAL*
198 Intermediate Parakeet *Psittacula intermedia* VULNERABLE
207 Hyacinth Macaw *Anodorhynchus hyacinthinus* VULNERABLE*
208 Lear's Macaw *Anodorhynchus leari* CRITICAL*
210 Spix's Macaw *Cyanopsitta spixii* CRITICAL*
212 Blue-throated Macaw *Ara glaucogularis* ENDANGERED*
213 Military Macaw *Ara militaris* VULNERABLE*
217 Red-fronted Macaw *Ara rubrogenys* ENDANGERED*
221 Blue-winged Macaw *Propyrrhura maracana* VULNERABLE*
224 Yellow-eared Parrot *Ognorhynchus icterotis* CRITICAL*
225 Thick-billed Parrot *Rhynchopsitta pachyrhyncha* ENDANGERED*
226 Maroon-fronted Parrot *Rhynchopsitta terrisi* VULNERABLE*

227   Golden Conure *Guaruba guarouba* ENDANGERED*
230   Socorro Conure *Aratinga brevipes* VULNERABLE
236   Cuban Conure *Aratinga euops* VULNERABLE
237   Hispaniolan Conure *Aratinga chloroptera* VULNERABLE
240   Golden-capped Conure *Aratinga auricapilla* VULNERABLE
248   Golden-plumed Parrot *Leptosittaca branickii* VULNERABLE
250   Blue-throated Conure *Pyrrhura cruentata* VULNERABLE*
257   Santa Marta Conure *Pyrrhura viridicata* VULNERABLE
260   El Oro Conure *Pyrrhura orcesi* VULNERABLE
262   White-breasted Conure *Pyrrhura albipectus* VULNERABLE
263   Brown-breasted Conure *Pyrrhura calliptera* VULNERABLE
274   Rufous-fronted Parakeet *Bolborhynchus ferrugineifrons* ENDANGERED
281   Yellow-faced Parrotlet *Forpus xanthops* VULNERABLE
296   Brown-backed Parrotlet *Touit melanonota* ENDANGERED
297   Golden-tailed Parrotlet *Touit surda* ENDANGERED
298   Spot-winged Parrotlet *Touit stictoptera* VULNERABLE
309   Rusty-faced Parrot *Hapalopsittaca amazonina* ENDANGERED
310   Fuertes's Parrot *Hapalopsittaca fuertesi* CRITICAL
311   Red-faced Parrot *Hapalopsittaca pyrrhops* ENDANGERED
325   Black-billed Amazon *Amazona agilis* VULNERABLE
326   Puerto Rican Amazon *Amazona vittata* CRITICAL*
328   Red spectacled Amazon *Amazona pretrei* ENDANGERED*
329   Green-cheeked Amazon *Amazona viridigenalis* ENDANGERED*
333   Red-browed Amazon *Amazona rhodocorytha* ENDANGERED*
334   Red-tailed Amazon *Amazona brasiliensis* ENDANGERED*
336   Yellow-faced Amazon *Amazona xanthops* VULNERABLE
337   Yellow-shouldered Amazon *Amazona barbadensis* VULNERABLE*
339   Yellow-headed Amazon *Amazona oratrix* ENDANGERED
346   Vinaceous Amazon *Amazona vinacea* ENDANGERED*
347   St Lucia Amazon *Amazona versicolor* VULNERABLE*
348   Red-necked Amazon *Amazona arausiaca* VULNERABLE*
349   St Vincent Amazon *Amazona guildingii* VULNERABLE*
350   Imperial Amazon *Amazona imperialis* VULNERABLE*
352   Purple-bellied Parrot *Triclaria malachitacea* ENDANGERED

Imperial Amazon
Amazona imperialis

It needs to be stressed that these listings are subject to periodic update as new information comes in. The classification of several species listed in Table 1 may not appear consistent with the data available in this book, but this simply reflects changes in knowledge since 1994 when the classifications were made.

Mauritius Parakeet *Psittacula echo*

In addition to the species listed in Table 1, a great many other parrots, perhaps the majority, are in decline and could in the future be included in threatened lists if their circumstances are not addressed. Collar *et al.* (1994), recognising that a number of species are already close to fulfilling the criteria for threat categories, identify a further 40 species in a 'Near-Threatened' category. These species are listed in Table 2. As with Table 1, new (post-1994) information may now render some of these listings inappropriate.

Table 2. Near-Threatened parrots (from Collar *et al.* 1994). Those listed on CITES Appendix I as at 1997 are marked with an asterisk.

8 Blue-streaked Lory *Eos reticulata*
10 Blue-eared Lory *Eos semilarvata*
27 White-naped Lory *Lorius albidinuchus*
38 Palm Lorikeet *Charmosyna palmarum*
42 Striated Lorikeet *Charmosyna multistriata*
48 Duchess Lorikeet *Charmosyna margarethae*
55 Palm Cockatoo *Probosciger aterrimus**
63 Pink Cockatoo *Cacatua leadbeateri*
70 Tanimbar Cockatoo (Corella) *Cacatua goffini**
72 Western Corella *Cacatua pastinator*
76 Kea *Nestor notabilis*
79 Geelvink Pygmy Parrot *Micropsitta geelvinkiana*
90 Blue-rumped Parrot *Psittinus cyanurus*
102 Blue-crowned Racquet-tail *Prioniturus discurus*
194 Yellowish-breasted Racquet-tail *Prioniturus flavicans*
106 Buru Racquet-tail *Prioniturus mada*
113 Crimson Shining-Parrot *Prosopeia tabuensis*
114 Masked Shining-Parrot *Prosopeia personata*
117 Moluccan King-Parrot *Alisterus amboinensis*
119 Olive-shouldered Parrot *Aprosmictus jonquillaceus*
137 Hooded Parrot *Psephotus dissimilis**
144 Yellow-fronted Parakeet *Cyanoramphus auriceps*
152 Turquoise Parrot *Neophema pulchella*
176 Fischer's Lovebird *Agapornis fischeri*
189 Green-fronted Hanging Parrot *Loriculus tener*
191 Yellow-throated Hanging Parrot *Loriculus pusillus*
203 Derbyan Parakeet *Psittacula derbiana*
205 Nicobar Parakeet *Psittacula caniceps*
233 Red-masked Conure *Aratinga erythrogenys*
265 Rose-crowned Conure *Pyrrhura rhodocephala*
268 Slender-billed Conure *Enicognathus leptorhynchus*
284 Grey-cheeked Parakeet *Brotogeris pyrrhopterus*
290 Amazonian Parrotlet *Nannopsittaca dachilleae*
293 Red-fronted Parrotlet *Touit costaricensis*
301 Red-capped Parrot *Pionopsitta pileata**
320 Cuban Amazon *Amazona leucocephala**
321 Yellow-billed Amazon *Amazona collaria*
322 Hispaniolan Amazon *Amazona ventralis*
330 Lilac-crowned Amazon *Amazona finschi*
332 Blue-cheeked Amazon *Amazona dufresniana*

We additionally recommend that the Saffron-headed Parrot (305) be urgently considered for inclusion in future revisions of threatened species lists. It is also worth noting that Collar *et al.* (1994) lumped Great Green Macaw (214) with Military (213), and Uvea Parakeet (146) with Horned (145): since they treat Military as threatened, the Great Green (if 'split' as here) must inevitably be listed as threatened, and since the 'split' Uvea Parakeet is so numerically weak (see account) there can be no doubt that that, too, would have to qualify as a threatened species. We are aware that strong consideration is being given to the splitting of both these forms by BirdLife in its future analyses.

THREATS

The parrots at risk of extinction and those deemed Near-Threatened face a wide range of pressures. In general, however, the principal sources of threat arise from habitat loss and collection of birds for the live bird trade (Collar and Juniper 1992). Some 73 of the 90 species recognised at risk of global extinction are believed to be negatively affected (or potentially negatively affected) by habitat loss, fragmentation or degradation, while 39 are under pressure from trapping to the extent that it may contribute significantly to their extinction, with at least 28 species affected by both pressures.

Habitat Loss

The loss, fragmentation or degradation of habitat is the most serious threat. Some parrots are now confined to small fragments of their original habitat (such as some of the Brazilian Atlantic rainforest endemics, the amazons of the Lesser Antilles and the *Psittacula* parakeet on Mauritius) whilst others are rapidly declining as larger areas of suitable remaining vegetation contract. Birds existing in small populations in restricted areas are at particular risk because of their greater susceptibility to other threats including storms, drought, disease and trapping for the live bird trade.

Outright habitat destruction clearly has most impact but habitat degradation, through the effects of selective logging, heavy grazing or seasonal burning of grasslands, certainly has an impact through loss of nest-sites, direct disturbance, and alterations to the mix of plant species, including food plants. However, the more subtle pressures linked to habitat (especially forest) degradation are poorly documented and the effects undoubtedly vary from species to species and even seasonally within species. A small number of parrots that prefer relatively open habitats in heavily forested regions may have increased in numbers and expanded their range as a result of forest loss or degradation (for example Jandaya Conure, 239, and Blue-headed Macaw), and in Australia some species such as the Galah (62) have benefited from the spread of agriculture and the provision of artificial watering sites for livestock.

The clearance and degradation of tropical forest is the most important manifestation of habitat loss facing the parrots. Estimates of rates of deforestation in the tropics provided by the United Nation's Food and Agriculture Organization in 1993 indicated that there was an acceleration in the area of forest lost during the 1980s, reaching in excess of 150,000km² per year in 1990. This very high figure (encompassing an area of land larger than England and Wales combined) applies to all kinds of tropical forests but the data indicate that the rate of loss was (and still is) on average higher in tropical rainforests. Although the rate of tropical deforestation declined during the early 1990s, further monitoring data published by FAO in 1997 indicate another upward swing in tropical forest loss rates in the mid-1990s. Temperate forests in tropical and subtropical latitudes (such as those in the Andes, South Africa and the Himalayas) continue to decline as well, with forest cover virtually removed in some areas such as the Colombian Andes.

The distribution (as well as the rate) of deforestation is also highly significant. Many species of parrot are restricted-range endemics naturally confined to small areas, often on islands but also within continental land masses (for example Spix's and Lear's Macaws, El Oro Parakeet, 260, and Fuertes's Parrot, 310). Indeed, the majority of them occupy ranges of less than 50,000km², including those inhabiting the eastern coastal forests of Brazil, the Philippine archipelago, several Pacific and Caribbean islands and some islands in the Moluccas. In these and other cases, deforestation has been significant (nearly complete in some Philippine islands and south-east Brazil) or is set soon to be so (such as on the major islands across Indonesia).

The factors behind forest loss vary from place to place. In humid areas, conversion to large-scale agriculture (by fire, chainsaw and bulldozer), clearance by small-scale farmers, large-scale logging, infrastructure development (such as dams and roads) and mining are the principal agents of deforestation. In dry forests, conversion to ranchland, exotic tree plantations and agriculture, overgrazing and excessive fuelwood collection are the principal direct causes behind habitat loss and degradation.

But these visible agents of forest loss are often not the main root causes of deforestation. Macroeconomic difficulties faced by many tropical developing countries are the driving force behind the conversion of forest into 'economically' attractive land-use options as nations struggle to meet repayments on international debts. Many countries have plundered their forests for timber or cleared them away to reach mineral deposits craved by the booming economies of the developed consumer countries. The soils beneath many lowland tropical forests are now employed in the production of tropical agricultural products from palm oil to coffee and pineapples destined for overseas markets where they will earn desperately needed foreign exchange. In many cases, the people who once lived in the forest areas have been displaced by the dollar-earning commodity crops and are forced to engaged in unsustainable slash-and-burn farming elsewhere, thus compounding the problem of forest loss.

In addition to the dire economic circumstances faced by many tropical countries, domestic legislation, poorly targeted economic incentives, official corruption, absence of political interest and inadequate human and financial resources hinder action to halt deforestation. Environmental organisations such as Friends of the Earth and the World Wide Fund for Nature have drawn attention to these issues and, partly because of this, international agreements have been made to address many of the causes of forest loss, including unsustainable logging, unplanned agricultural expansion and the effective safeguarding of at least the most important protected areas. However, much more must urgently be accomplished in practical terms if a large proportion of the parrots (not to mention millions of other species) are not to be committed to oblivion during the coming few decades.

During the 1980s and 1990s the massive wildfires that have swept through the forests in Indonesian Borneo and Sumatra and the Amazon basin of Brazil underline the consequences of poorly enforced measures to achieve sustainable forestry. Driven by policies designed to promote rapid economic growth, countries such as Indonesia and Brazil have found it hard to muster the resources necessary to police the activities of forestry and plantation companies in remote areas. In the case of Indonesia, logging and plantation companies have been held largely responsible for the huge fires that burnt over as much as one million hectares of forest and bush in 1997. Massive economic damage has resulted, with huge costs to tourism, public health and agriculture. Predictably, these costs have been borne by the population as a whole and not by those who have profited financially from the plunder of the forests.

In the face of rapid and sometimes uncontrollable forest loss, adequate and properly resourced protected area networks are an urgent requirement in the battle to conserve biodiversity. Nevertheless, if serious inroads are to be made in slowing and halting tropical deforestation, then the root causes for forest loss must be tackled. These blockages to sustainable forest use are mainly economic, political and social, and will require political action at the national and international level on a scale hitherto unseen. In the meantime, the great many organisations and individuals who devote their energies more specifically to the conservation of parrots must continue with their work undaunted. Were it not for them, the situation faced by many species would be a lot worse. Fire brigade action launched to safeguard the continuing existence of critically endangered birds has undoubtedly so far helped prevent the extinction of, for example, the remaining Caribbean amazons, the Kakapo and Mauritius Parakeet (195), whilst the numbers of others, such as Lear's Macaw, may be boosted in coming years as planned and present conservation initiatives come to fruition.

Although the problems linked to habitat loss and sustainable forest use in the tropics range far beyond the specific issues linked to the conservation of threatened parrots, these birds, as familiar icons of tropical habitats for people the world over, have a special role in the wider battle to save the forests and other threatened habitats. Since the human and ecological tragedy that accompanies the spiral of tropical forest destruction is reflected in the plight of these birds, conservationists should use parrots as a means of generating wider public understanding of the solutions needed to conserve biodiversity more generally. An outstanding example of how parrots can be used to generate widespread public support for conservation more generally can be seen in the efforts of Paul Butler and his co-workers to promote awareness on the plight of the threatened amazons of the Lesser Antilles. In a similar vein, The World Parrot Trust is seeking to establish public support for parrot conservation by stimulating flows of revenue to local forest communities in the Amazon basin by encouraging visitors to go and see wild parrots. Tourism of this kind might add financial value to the parrots and the forest, and thus provide yet another reason for conserving them.

Live Bird Trade

A wide range of human societies from the indigenous peoples of the rainforests to the technologically advanced societies of North America and Europe place a particular value on parrots as pets. These birds' high level of intelligence, potential for tameness (and some would say affection), bright plumage and, perhaps above all, a propensity in many species for uncanny mimicking of the human voice, have led to the parrots attaining unparalleled popularity as cagebirds. Indeed, parrots have featured as companions for people almost as long as recorded history itself, with one species, the Alexandrine Parakeet, named after Alexander the Great who is believed to have kept such birds himself. There is a pre-Christian account (from 400BC) of a captive Plum-headed Parakeet (199) kept by an Indian physician in which the bird's ability to mimic both Indian and Greek words is noted. Later on, the ruling classes of Roman and other European civilisations placed a great value on parrots as colourful talking novelties that conferred great status on their human owners.

Among the treasures brought home by the first European voyagers to the New World were parrots (probably Hispaniolan Amazons, 322) traded from the Carib Indians encountered by the explorers. Since those days, most of the world's parrot species have at some time or other been taken from the wild for a captive existence. Early European travellers to other parts of the tropical world similarly found that the local inhabitants had tamed parrots because of their suitability as pets and soon learned that this group of birds, because of their ease of handling once tamed and their seed-eating habits, could endure long sea voyages and be taken home as novel and valuable souvenirs of far-off lands. Today the trade in parrots is far larger and has a profound impact on many populations and species. Some have been kept so intensively and widely that they are more or less domesticated: the Budgerigar is the outstanding example.

Data collected under the obligations of signatories to the Convention on International Trade in Endangered Species (see below), and analysed by the IUCN's Wildlife Trade Monitoring Unit, reveal the scale and breadth of the trade in parrots (see Mulliken 1995). Between 1980 and 1992, 247 species of parrot were reported in international trade, with 156 of them traded over that period in volumes of more than 1,000 birds annually. Some were traded in huge quantities. For instance, in that 12-year span, 278,000 Senegal Parrots (164), 657,000 Fischer's Lovebirds (176), over 200,000 Ring-necked Parakeets, 158,000 Mitred Conures (232), 406,000 Blue-fronted Amazons (338) and 108,000 White Cockatoos (68) passed quite legally through international borders. Further unknown quantities were undoubtedly moved illegally and therefore not reported in the official statistics. To the officially reported CITES figures and unknown illegal international trade must be added the unmeasured numbers of birds trapped and traded at the national level. In some cases this will be higher than the numbers exported and takes place both legally and illegally. Whatever the total number of parrots trapped and traded, it is clearly vast and taking a toll on wild birds in ways that vary from the negligible to the extremely serious.

Some parrots, especially the larger and long-lived species, like the *Ara* macaws, produce a surviving youngster at most only every other year (and probably less often than that), so that collection of nestlings for trade may eventually lead to rapid population declines when the aged parent stock dies off, leaving nothing to replace it. The destruction of nests (cutting of trees) as a means of obtaining their contents is particularly damaging, as the ability of local populations to reproduce can be completely undermined by great shortages of nest-sites. Because of this biological constraint, trapping for trade has undoubtedly been a negative factor affecting the conservation status of several macaws, amazons and cockatoos, to the extent that several are in danger of extinction principally as a result of this pressure (for example the Hyacinth Macaw, Yellow-headed Amazon, 339, and Yellow-crested Cockatoo, 64). Even for smaller and more prolific species, the impact of trade may be severe. Several species of lorikeet are at risk from trade, including the endangered Red-and-blue Lory which during the 1990s continued to suffer unsustainable levels of illegal capture.

Many governments have recognised the threat posed to parrots through trade and have taken steps at the national and international level to promote the protection and sustainable exploitation of these birds. Several countries (such as Australia and Brazil) have banned the taking of parrots (and other wildlife) for trade whilst others (such as Argentina and Guyana) have introduced quota systems in order to achieve trade levels that are compatible with the long-term survival of wild populations. Whilst these moves are welcome, illegal trade sometimes thrives. For example, although Brazil has ceased the export of birds, the fact that neighbouring Argentina continues to trade means that illegal capture in Brazil can be laundered via Argentina. Although the Canary-winged Parakeet is considered scarce in Argentina, from 1985 to 1990 some 46,522 were exported from there, strongly suggesting illegal capture in Brazil with 'legal' international re-export via Argentina's open borders. A similar situation is thought to prevail in other parts of South America and the world.

At the intergovernmental level, most of the parrots' main range countries are signatories to The Washington Convention on the International Trade in Endangered Species of Wild Fauna and Flora (CITES). This agreement seeks to render the exploitation of wild plants and animals sustainable to the extent that their range and populations are not negatively affected by collecting for international trade. The principles of the treaty recognise the right of countries to exploit their wildlife for economic benefits and establish a framework whereby this might be sustainable. In the case of the parrots, considerable economic potential exists for exporting countries, if only they can achieve the regulatory and practical management structures that reflect the biological capacity of target species. In the case of international trade at least, CITES offers a vehicle to promote this aim.

CITES operates via a permit system linked to several categories of exploitation as expressed by three appendices. Appendix I is for species such as the Hyacinth Macaw, Red-tailed Amazon (334) and Salmon-crested Cockatoo (67) whose trade is banned except under the most controlled circumstances (to take part in recognised international captive breeding programmes, for instance). Appendix II is for species whose exploitation can only proceed according to declared quotas designed to ensure a sustainable offtake. Appendix III is for species whose trade is subject to national-level controls from named countries.

All species listed in Appendices I and II of CITES must be accompanied by an export permit before entering international trade. Those listed in Appendix I must also have an import permit before gaining access to a second CITES country. Species listed in Appendix III are subject to trade controls in one or more range countries and specimens leaving those nations must be accompanied with supporting documentation. Shipments of Appendix III species from other range states must be accompanied with a certificate of country of origin thereby facilitating a monitoring role and aiding conservation action in those countries that have elected to introduce trade controls.

In 1997 47 parrot taxa were listed in Appendix I. These are identified in the Distribution and Status sections of the relevant species accounts, and 38 of them are indicated in Tables 1 and 2; the other nine are Glaucous Macaw and Paradise Parrot (139) (both treated as extinct by Collar *et al.* 1994), Great Green Macaw (treated as a race of Military Macaw by Collar *et al.* 1994), Red-fronted Parakeet (142), Ground Parrot, Scarlet Macaw (215) and Tucuman Amazon (327) (all regarded as at lower risk by Collar *et al.* 1994), and two subspecies, *Cyanoramphus auriceps forbesi* and *Cyclopsitta diophthalma coxeni*. All other species, with the exceptions of the Ring-necked Parakeet, Budgerigar and Cockatiel (75), are included in Appendix II. Traders and keepers of parrots wishing up-to-date details on the CITES status of particular parrots and the legal requirements that accompany such listings should contact their government's CITES Management Authority (usually the national government's environmental department). Failure to comply with CITES regulations can result in the seizure of birds, hefty fines and even imprisonment.

Whilst national-level legal protection and official international trade controls have undoubtedly had a positive impact on the conservation status of many overexploited species, many remain at risk from collecting for trade. This situation not only arises because of legal overexploitation, but from an often thriving illegal trade. For example, the principal threat facing the Hyacinth Macaw and Red-tailed Amazon is illegal taking of birds for covert live bird markets and the same factor is one of the reasons for the near-extinction of the Spix's Macaw.

For those species that remain relatively common in the wild, and where there can be at least in theory a sustainable harvest for trade, a great deal more effort is needed in assessing what levels of exploitation can be sustained. For example, Lambert (1993) presents an approach based on population census, analysis of productivity and patterns of capture to estimate maximum quotas to ensure sustainable harvesting. This effort should be replicated elsewhere to safeguard wild parrot populations not only for their own sake but for their economic potential too. There might also be scope to boost the productivity of some traded species through the provision of nest-boxes and other management tools, but these are rarely used.

Another important aspect of the sustainability equation in respect to the trade in parrots relates to mortality between capture and final delivery to the keeper. Many birds die after capture (a 50% mortality rate is not unusual) from stress, physical damage, disease and starvation. Reducing such terrible wastage is not only necessary to attain the maximum sustainable economic benefit from wild parrots but must be addressed on welfare grounds too. Parrots are intelligent creatures and the suffering many presently endure to become 'pets' should be a disincentive to any animal lover who purchases one from a pet shop, especially at a time when captive-bred alternatives are more widely available (see Captive Breeding below).

But in most instances, sustainable management of wild populations for trade purposes remains a remote possibility. Many countries lack the basic enforcement machinery to ensure that their borders are secure in respect of illegally traded wildlife, and cannot muster the technical expertise required to establish what sustainable trade levels actually are, let alone the management capacity to achieve them. With these practical constraints in mind, and whilst demand for pet parrots remains, including of course for those kept as pets in their own range states, it is unlikely that excessive trade will be brought fully under control. For this reason, some conservationists have sought to reduce demand by drawing attention to alternative sources in the form of captive-bred birds. Whilst this approach is legitimate, it does raise questions over the economic impact on poorer exporter nations. One way of ensuring that both conservation and more immediate economic priorities are advanced would be to breed parrots for export in their range countries. Having said that, a whole plethora of other issues are raised when regulatory bodies seek to ensure that birds in trade are actually captive-bred rather than taken from wild nests (which remains, unfortunately, the cheaper option).

In respect of illegal trade, it seems that, for some collectors craving ownership of rare parrots, the only deterrent against the further depletion of already critically endangered birds is the full force of the law. Whether governments will exercise their legal powers is a different question. The illegal international trade in drugs and arms tend to occupy the attention of intelligence and enforcement agencies more fully than that in rare wildlife, whilst within the exporting countries themselves the general incapacity to act is often matched by the absence of high-level political interest in bringing to book well-organised and amply resourced traders.

Introduced Species
Introduced species cause problems for native wildlife chiefly because of predation and competition for food but also sometimes because of habitat modification and the introduction of disease. At least 10 of the parrot species considered at risk of global extinction face threats from introduced species, mainly

from predators such as rats and cats, but also from competitors for nest-sites and food and potentially from disease. These threatened species are all island-dwelling forms and include the Blue Lorikeet (33), which is now absent from many of the 23 islands from which it was originally recorded owing to predation by rats *Rattus rattus*. The critically endangered Mauritius Parakeet (195) suffers nest predation from both crab-eating macaques *Macaca fascicularis* and rats. This species is additionally at risk from introduced Ring-necked Parakeets which compete for food and nest-sites; moreover, the last fragments of its native forest habitat are at risk from encroachment by introduced plants.

New Zealand's Kaka (77), exploits honeydew the high energy content of which helps to get the birds into breeding condition but this food is now also exploited by introduced wasps and possums and breeding failure and a consequent population crash can be foreseen in the not-too-distant future. Grazing animals may also place pressure on native bird species through the loss of native vegetation. The Socorro Conure (230) is believed to be partly at risk from grazing sheep affecting its preferred native forest, although this pressure is more usually considered a problem of habitat loss rather than one of a damaging introduction of an exotic species.

Almost 90% of the bird species to have become extinct during the past century or so have been island forms. Some continental parrots are also at risk from introduced animals. For example, Spix's Macaw (210) is believed to be partly at risk from competition for nest-sites with introduced African bees, although this is a secondary problem after illegal collection for trade and habitat loss (and merely hypothetical while only a single bird remains in the wild).

Disease transmitted by an introduced to a native species is not yet known to have occurred in parrots, but the potential is considerable. The plight of the highly endangered Puerto Rican Amazon (326), already at risk from introduced Pearly eyed Thrashers *Margarops fuscatus*, which take over parrot nest-sites and kill their chicks, may be deepened by the introduction of disease to its tiny population from non-native Hispaniolan Amazons which now also live on the island.

Persecution and Hunting

The dietary preference of parrots for seeds and fruit brings some species into conflict with people. Maize, rice, citrus fruits, mangos, sorghum, millet, guavas, groundnuts and grapes are among the many economically important crops that are raided from time to time by parrots. Although there has been relatively little systematic investigation into the financial and other impacts of parrots on crops, birds are in many places routinely persecuted as crop pests, even though their actual impact may be light. The damage caused is often enhanced through wasteful foraging practices that involve damage to fruit that is not eaten, thereby ruining far more of the crop than is actually consumed.

Whilst a great many parrots are blamed locally for crop damage, it is relatively few species that cause large-scale damage. Among the most notorious offenders are the Ring-necked (194) and Monk Parakeets, both of which have been the subject of detailed study in respect of their foraging practices and dietary habits. Both cause very serious damage and are subject to widespread and intense persecution.

For these and some other numerous and ecologically durable species, such as the Cactus Conure, Galah and Cockatiel, persecution may have little apparent long term impact on population levels. Others may have suffered in parts of their range, but have not yet reached the stage where the effects place them globally at risk. However, for some more vulnerable parrots, possessing relatively small populations, restricted ranges and low reproductive rates, such as Bolivia's endemic Red-fronted Macaw (217), persecution may be a serious problem. For one species, the Carolina Parakeet, intense persecution is widely held to have played a central role in bringing about its extinction in the early part of the twentieth century.

Many parrots are also hunted for food. In parts of Central and South America for example, where human populations routinely face serious shortages of protein, most of the medium- to large-sized parrots (in common with many other edible mammal and bird species) have been wiped out. For some parrots, hunting may be a serious factor affecting their conservation status. Even Spix's Macaw, despite existing in very low numbers, was within living memory shot for food and probably owes its present critical situation at least partly to hunting.

Some parrots are also subject to traditional uses. The Hyacinth Macaw is taken by indigenous communities in the Xingu region of the Amazon so that its plumes may be used for ceremonial purposes, whilst Pesquet's Parrot (112) is hunted in New Guinea for its red feathers. But since such exploitation has presumably taken place for many centuries, it is in most cases unlikely on its own to pose a serious threat. All the same, the historical harvesting of some *Vini* lories for their plumes by the human inhabitants of their Pacific island ranges evidently led to the local extinction of some and the total extinction of others, known only by their subfossil remains. Where tourist markets are in contact with indigenous communities (such as in the Xingu region of the Brazilian Amazon), the increased trade in traditional artifacts, like head-dresses made from macaw feathers, may turn a once-sustainable activity into a serious negative pressure.

Storms and Climate Change

Several species of parrot, especially those inhabiting islands, are partially at risk from hurricanes. High winds and torrential rain can cause physical damage to birds and loss of food-plants and nest-sites. Birds may be geographically displaced, become more vulnerable to predators (by having to forage in the open) and may be forced to raid crops and thereby come into conflict with people.

All the parrots endemic to the Caribbean islands undoubtedly experience natural population fluctuations as a result of hurricanes, and these birds have behavioural and physiological adaptations that enhance their survival prospects in storm-damaged forests. When they exist in low numbers, however (as the five species inhabiting the Lesser Antilles and Puerto Rico now do), the passage of a hurricane could be a factor leading to their extinction. The Mauritius Parakeet (195) is also at risk from storms although survey work following the recent passage of a severe storm found more birds surviving than had been anticipated.

Changing climatic conditions caused by the build-up of unnatural levels of so-called greenhouse gases (such as carbon dioxide and methane) in the atmosphere as a result of human activities (especially the burning of fossil fuels and deforestation) could affect many species of parrot (as well as just about every other terrestrial higher animal and plant). More extreme weather patterns are expected as the earth's atmosphere warms (on present predictions by about 2.5°C by 2050), including severe storms.

Although some climatologists expect the most marked climate change initially to occur in northern latitudes because of the large landmasses there, tropical zones will still be affected by rising sea levels, more frequent severe weather and longer and more intense droughts, especially in the arid and semi-arid zones.

Species inhabiting low-lying coastal areas (for example the Red-tailed Amazon) and those partially dependent on mangrove swamps will be affected by sea-level rise. Many others (for example Black-cheeked Lovebird, 179) could be affected by more frequent drought conditions. Evidence that the warming atmosphere will lead to the occurrence of more frequent and more severe hurricanes could have serious implications for island-dwelling species such as the Caribbean amazons. The impacts of drought have been graphically demonstrated in the 1980s and 1990s in the massive Indonesian forest fires. The dry conditions that helped to make these fires so devastating might in turn be linked to more frequent, intense and longer-lasting ocean surface warming episodes in the eastern Pacific that may in turn be linked to human-induced global climate change. This periodic ocean warming, the so-called El Niño, is also associated with very stormy and wet weather in South America and droughts in southern Africa. If El Niño's occurrence is seriously affected by climate change, fundamental alterations in the nature of the forest habitats as far apart as East Asia and southern Africa could follow.

CAPTIVE BREEDING

Most parrots species have at some time or other been kept by people. Many have been bred in confinement. The reasons for captive breeding vary. Individual breeders seek a personal challenge from the successful rearing of captive generations. Zoos and other institutions seek to maintain captive populations in order to safeguard against possible extinction in the wild. This breeding is sometimes well coordinated and orchestrated through the use of studbooks and at other times is rather random. Other breeding is undertaken commercially to meet the demands of the pet trade, sometimes to the extent that species have self-sustaining captive populations that no longer need to be augmented with wild-caught birds (for example, Budgerigar, Cockatiel and several species of lovebird).

There are several sets of complex and interrelated issues linked to captive breeding that need to be considered. These relate to the mortality and welfare of trapped and traded birds, the conservation of wild populations, reintroduction and the economic benefits of wild capture and export.

Captive breeding for the pet trade has been advocated as a means to avoid the depletion of wild populations. Since so many birds die or suffer terrible conditions in transit, it is also a means to avoid unnecessary and undesirable pain and suffering. Some of the exporting countries would, however, face economic impacts because demand would be removed for wild-caught birds; but since many former exporting nations have already banned capture and commerce, this question for them is not an issue. For those nations where trade continues, the importing nations could play their most positive role in the conservation not only of the parrots but also of the forests where they live, by cancelling some of these nations' terrible international debts (see Habitat Loss above). This would have a positive economic impact and would not require the liquidation of the forests or the parrots, although practical problems would be faced in its effective regulation.

For those species under very serious threat, captive breeding is sometimes advocated as a means to safeguard a species's existence. There are, however, several very serious drawbacks to this approach. First, some of the species in question are at such low levels that trapping for captive breeding would only worsen their wild status, even if such birds were destined for reputable breeding programmes. Second, captive breeding may do nothing to reduce the potency of the pressures which have rendered a parrot species scarce. Habitat loss, illegal capture or the effects of introduced predators may continue unabated. Even if successful breeding is achieved, there may then be no place to release captive-bred birds to recolonise. Third, reintroduction will not be easy. There are very few examples of successful recolonisation by captive-bred birds or mammals. In the case of parrots, especially the large ones, in which such a large proportion of behaviour is learned, captive birds may quickly starve or be taken by predators. Experiences with the Thick-billed Parrot in Arizona show how difficult successful reintroduction can be (see Snyder *et al.* 1994)

All this is not to say that captive breeding has no place in effective conservation of very rare species. But it must be carefully conceived as part of an overall conservation plan that involves the removal or control of the threats that made the species rare in the first place and be based around clear long-term conservation objectives. It needs to be properly planned, controlled and resourced. It also needs to be politically sound with ownership and legal questions fully clarified. In the absence of proper overall conservation control, the captive population will probably not be effectively managed and difficulties are likely to arise, as with the Spix's Macaw. In those cases where captive breeding has been most promising, it has been carried out under careful control in the range state of the species in question, undertaken as part of a wider recovery programme that includes the management of wild birds. The recovery programmes for the Puerto Rican Amazon, the Mauritius Parakeet and the Kakapo show these characteristics and because of that have a good chance of success.

Under virtually any circumstances, captive breeding of rare and endangered species should be seen as part of a conservation plan that is first and foremost concerned with maintaining a secure and viable population of birds in the wild. Once the wild birds are gone, so has the reason to conserve their habitat, and once the habitat is lost, the birds can never be put back, no matter how successful the captive breeding.

PLATES
1-88

PLATE 1: *CHALCOPSITTA* AND *PSEUDEOS* LORIES

1 Black Lory *Chalcopsitta atra*   **Text and map page 217**

Indonesia in lowland W Irian Jaya including Vogelkop, the Onin and Bomberai Peninsulas, and adjacent islands including Batanta, Misool and Salawati. Habitats include coastal coconut plantations, forest margins and mangrove.

All three subspecies are black with a violet rump and yellowish undertail.

    1a   **Adult** (*atra*; W Vogelkop, Batanta and Salawati) Lacks red markings on thighs and underwing. Head generally all black but can show some red feathers. Misool race similar but with orange-red thighs and forecrown.

    1b   **Immature** (*atra*) Like adult but with white cere and eye-ring.

    1c   **Adult** (*insignis*; E Vogelkop, along the Onin and Bomberai peninsulas, and on Rumberpon) Red markings on face, thighs and wing-coverts.

2 Brown Lory *Chalcopsitta duivenbodei*   **Text and map page 217**

Scattered range through lowlands of N New Guinea from the Memberamo River east to Astrolabe Bay. Open and secondary habitats to 200m.

    2   **Adult** Flight profile typical of the genus, but bright yellow underwing-coverts distinctive. Violet rump. Longer-tailed than Dusky Lory and lacks white rump and yellow or orange on underparts. The two races are doubtfully distinct.

3 Yellow-streaked Lory *Chalcopsitta scintillata*   **Text and map page 218**

Lowlands and hills of S New Guinea east to Port Moresby and in the Aru Islands. Absent from W Vogelkop, meeting Black Lory in westernmost part of its range where the two may occasionally hybridize. Found in a range of habitats from forest to open country.

Typical blunt-headed, long-tailed *Chalcopsitta* flight profile, appearing dark (therefore danger of confusion with Black Lory in west). Mainly green with yellow streaking, red forehead, yellow in base of primaries. Aru race similar to nominate.

    3a   **Adult** (*scintillata*; lowlands and hills of W New Guinea) Underwing-coverts red.

    3b   **Adult** (*chloroptera*; New Guinea to the east of about 142°E) Underwing-coverts green. Less yellow in primaries.

4 Cardinal Lory *Chalcopsitta cardinalis*   **Text and map page 219**

Common large red lory occurring in the Bismarck Archipelago and Solomon Islands. All types of (mainly lowland) wooded habitats, sometimes reaching 1,200m.

    4   **Adult** Entirely red plumage with some darker mottling, and long tail distinctive.

11 Dusky Lory *Pseudeos fuscata*   **Text and map page 225**

New Guinea and the W Papuan islands, frequenting a range of habitats up to 2,400m. Regularly in large noisy flocks.

Orange bill, white rump, twin breast-bands, yellow underwing, pale crown, orange-yellow belly and thighs.

    11a   **Adult** (yellow morph) Both breast-bands yellow.

    11b   **Adult** (red morph) Both breast-bands orange-red.

    11c   **Adult** (intermediate morph) Upper breast-band yellow, lower orange.

    11d   **Immature** Dark bill. Duller plumage.

PLATE 2: *EOS* LORIES

9 **Black-winged Lory** *Eos cyanogenia* **Text and map page 223**

Islands in Geelvink Bay, Irian Jaya, Indonesia. Found in a range of habitats from inland forests to coastal coconut plantations, and around habitation.

9a **Adult** Extensive blue patch on face. All-black wing-coverts.

9b **Immature** Dark margins to mantle and underparts.

6 **Violet-necked Lory** *Eos squamata* **Text and map page 221**

Islands in the N Moluccas and W Papuan group, Indonesia. Coastal habitats and primary forest up to 1,000m.

Dark purplish-blue collar and red face, lacking blue through or below eye.

6a **Adult** (*squamata*; W Papuan islands) Plumage variable, but usually with red crown, narrow purplish collar and red breast.

6b **Immature** (*squamata*) Dark feather-edgings give duller, more uniform but slightly barred appearance.

6c **Adult** (*riciniata*; Morotai, Halmahera, Ternate, Tidore, Moti, Damar, Muor, Widi and Bacan islands) Broader neck-ring extending onto crown. Underparts with more extensive purple and red breast-band, or with entirely purple underparts.

6d **Adult** (*obiensis*; Obi) Purple much reduced. Black scapulars and variable violet-grey collar and crown.

7 **Red Lory** *Eos bornea* **Text and map page 222**

Indonesia in the Moluccas including Buru, Seram and associated islands, also in the Kai Islands. Forest and secondary habitats up to 1,250m.

Entirely red head. Contrasting blue tertials. Sympatric in Seram with Blue-eared Lory but generally at lower elevations (young birds can show some blue on ear-coverts). Some Violet-necked Lories appear mostly red, but lack blue tertials. Seram and Kai races differ only in size.

7a **Adult** (*bornea*; Ambon, Saparua and Haruku) Mostly red with limited black in wing and blue undertail-coverts. Blue in wing restricted to tertials.

7b **Adult** (*cyanonothus*; Buru) Darker red than nominate. Blue extends onto coverts. Broader black edgings to greater coverts.

8 **Blue-streaked Lory** *Eos reticulata* **Text and map page 223**

Tanimbar group, Indonesia. Found in a range of lowland habitats from forest to coconut plantations and mangroves.

8 **Adult** Blue ear-coverts and blue on upper mantle with lighter shaft-streaks. Variegated wing-coverts.

5 **Red-and-blue Lory** *Eos histrio* **Text and map page 220**

Sangir and islands in the Talaud and Nanusa groups, Indonesia, in both forest and cultivated areas, forming large flocks at roosts.

Blue eye-stripe and blue breast diagnostic.

5a **Adult** (*histrio*; Sangir) Variegated wing-coverts. Blue stripe from mantle through eye to crown.

5b **Adult** (*talautensis*; Talaud Islands) Less black in wing-coverts.

5c **Adult** (*challengeri*; Miangas Island, Nanusa group) Blue of eye-stripe does not meet blue of mantle. Narrower breast-band interspersed with red.

10 **Blue-eared Lory** *Eos semilarvata* **Text and map page 224**

Restricted to hill forest on Seram, Indonesia (generally at higher elevations than Red Lory).

10 **Adult** Red mantle. Blue below eye and on lower underparts.

DAN POWELL

PLATE 3: *TRICHOGLOSSUS* LORIKEETS I

13 Rainbow Lorikeet *Trichoglossus haematodus*　　　Text and map page 226

Widely distributed, from Nusa Tenggara, Indonesia, in the north-west extreme of its range to coastal E and SE Australia. Found in a broad range of drier lowland habitats. Twenty races, some of which are very distinctive.

Although races are variable, birds are generally green above, with a yellow-green hind-collar, show a darker head, and have distinctive colourful breast markings. The tail is attenuated, and the underwing is brightly marked with red and yellow. Main forms are illustrated; see main text for less distinctive races.

> **13a** **Adult** (*haematodus*; Buru to W New Guinea) Blue head, green upperparts, yellow collar, orange breast scalloped dark blue, green and yellow belly.
>
> **13b** **Adult** (*mitchellii*; Bali and Lombok) Breast scalloping absent or poorly defined, dark blue belly-patch, darker head.
>
> **13c** **Adult** (*forsteni*; Sumbawa) Like *mitchelli* but with dark blue band across upper mantle.
>
> **13d** **Adult** (*fortis*; Sumba) Yellow breast, green on head, dark green belly.
>
> **13e** **Adult** (*weberi*; Flores) Green with lighter green breast and hind-collar (see also Olive-headed Lorikeet, Plate 5).
>
> **13f** **Adult** (*capistratus*; Timor) Like *fortis* but with more red on breast and greener belly-patch.
>
> **13g** **Adult** (*rosenbergii*; Biak) Heavy breast-barring, broad hind-collar, dark blue belly, orange (not yellow) band through flight feathers.
>
> **13h** **Adult** (*flavicans*; Admiralty Islands) Similar to nominate but distinctive bronze morph illustrated.
>
> **13i** **Adult** (*moluccanus*; E Australia) Bright blue head, breast orange suffused yellow, blue belly-patch.

14　Red-collared Lorikeet *Trichoglossus rubritorquis*　　　Text and map page 229

NW Australia east to Gulf of Carpentaria coast where it approaches (and perhaps meets) the previous species *T. h. moluccanus*. Occurs in riverine woodland and a range of open habitats.

> **14** **Adult** Reddish hind-collar, blue band across upper mantle, dark green belly-patch, broad yellow band on underside of flight feathers.

13a

13a

13c

13b

13b

13d

13g

13f

13e

14

13i

13i

13h

14

DAN POWELL

PLATE 4: *TRICHOGLOSSUS* LORIKEETS II

18 Pohnpei Lorikeet *Trichoglossus rubiginosus* **Text and map page 232**

Restricted to Pohnpei in the W Pacific, where it is widespread and common.

18 **Adult** Unmistakable. Maroon with yellowish tail and olive suffusion on flight feathers.

---

12 Ornate Lorikeet *Trichoglossus ornatus* **Text and map page 226**

Sulawesi and surrounding islands, Indonesia, where common in open habitats including cultivated areas around villages. Also in forest up to 1,000m.

12 **Adult** Similar to Rainbow Lorikeet but with orange chin and throat. Yellow spot to the rear of ear-coverts, no yellow hind-collar; also lacks red underwing-coverts and yellow band through flight feathers of Rainbow Lorikeet.

---

17 Mindanao Lorikeet *Trichoglossus johnstoniae* **Text and map page 231**

Restricted to montane forest above 1,000m on a hlaf-dozen mountains on the island of Mindanao, S Philippines.

Dark mask; red forehead, chin and lores; green crown, yellow wing-bar, green and yellow scalloping below.

17a **Adult** (*johnstoniae*, Mount Apo and neighbouring mountains). Red forehead and face.

17b **Immature** (*johnstoniae*) Duller facial markings.

17c **Adult** (*pistra*, Mount Malindang) Darker blue nape, less red on face.

---

16 Yellow-and-green Lorikeet *Trichoglossus flavoviridis* **Text and map page 230**

Sulawesi and Sula, Indonesia, from lowlands to mountains in a range open and forested habitats. Common.

Both races are generally green with yellow barring below. More distinctive nominate race is less widespread.

16a **Adult** (*flavoviridis*; Sula) Green with yellow head, breast marked brown tending to green scalloping on lower underparts.

16b **Adult** (*meyeri*; Sulawesi) Smaller, with underparts scalloped green and a yellow ear-patch.

---

19 Scaly-breasted Lorikeet *Trichoglossus chlorolepidotus* **Text and map page 233**

Occurs commonly along the eastern seaboard of Australia in a range of habitats including *Eucalyptus* woodland and orchards. It is regularly found in flowering trees in towns.

19 **Adult** Unmarked green head, yellow scalloping on green underparts and mantle. Pinkish red on underwing.

18

18

18

12

12

17c

17b

17a

16a

16a

17a

16a

16b

19

19

DAN POWELL

PLATE 5: *TRICHOGLOSSUS* AND *PSITTEUTELES* LORIKEETS

15 Olive-headed Lorikeet *Trichoglossus euteles*   **Text and map page 230**

Timor and surrounding islands, Indonesia. Occurs in a range of habitats from montane primary forest (up to 2,400m) to cultivated land on more arid islands.

All green with lighter underparts and olive-yellow head, yellow wing-bar and tips to underwing-coverts. No demarcation between breast and belly as in Timor race *capistratus* of Rainbow Lorikeet (see plate 3).

    15a   **Adult** All green with olive-yellow head.

    15b   **Immature** Greener head than adult. From adult Rainbow Lorikeet by brownish bill.

20 Varied Lorikeet *Psitteuteles versicolor*   **Text and map page 233**

Seasonal nomad occurring in a range of wooded and open habitats in N Australia, from around Broome east to the Pacific coast of Queensland.

    20   **Adult** Red crown, white eye-ring, yellow ear-patch, pinkish breast. Plumage with yellow and orange-yellow shaft-streaks. Short pointed tail.

21 Iris Lorikeet *Psitteuteles iris*   **Text and map page 234**

Found in a range of habitats from sea-level to 1,500m on the islands of Timor and Wetar, Indonesia. Uncommon.

Yellowish-green hind-collar, red forecrown, violet-blue ear-coverts, diffuse darker green barring on lighter green underparts.

    21a   **Adult male** (*iris*; W Timor) Red forecrown, less extensive but more obvious barring on underparts than race *wetterensis*.

    21b   **Adult female** (*iris*) Forecrown marked red and green. Yellower cheeks than male.

    21c   **Adult male** (*rubripileum*; E Timor) Little if any blue in crown which can be marked with green at rear. Hind-collar yellower, ear-coverts bluer.

    21d   **Adult** (*wetterensis*; Wetar) Larger. More strongly marked facial pattern. Greener cheeks, more extensive but more diffuse barring below.

22 Goldie's Lorikeet *Psitteuteles goldiei*   **Text and map page 235**

Uncommon nomad in the montane forests of New Guinea including the Huon Peninsula and south-east ranges. Generally 1,000-2,000m, but has been found from sea-level to 2,800m.

Dark green above. Red crown, mauve face with darker streaking. Light yellowish-green underparts streaked dark green. Yellow underwing-bar.

    22a   **Adult male** Bright red crown.

    22b   **Female** Red of crown duller and less extensive, with 'notch' on ear-coverts.

    22c   **Immature** Face pattern duller, crown marked dark blue.

15b

15a

15a

20

20

15a

21b

21a

21c

21a

22a

21d

22a

22b

22c

DavPowell

26 **Purple-bellied Lory** *Lorius hypoinochrous* **Text and map page 239**

Lowlands of E New Guinea and Bismarck Archipelago, in a range of altered habitats unlike the similar, sympatric Black-capped Lory, which is primarily a forest dweller.

Black cap, green wings, red breast, purple thighs, undertail-coverts and belly. Dull red mantle. Like Black-capped, especially its allopatric race *somu*, but with a white, not grey-black cere. Also has a hoarse nasal call unlike the musical notes of Black-capped.

> **26a** **Adult** (*hypoinochrous*; Louisiade Archipelago except Rossel) Black margins to greater underwing-coverts in common with *rosselianus*.
>
> **26b** **Adult** (*rosselianus*; Rossel) Violet markings on lower breast.
>
> **26c** **Adult** (*devittatus*; E New Guinea and Bismarck Archipelago) Lacks black on underwing-coverts.

25 **Black-capped Lory** *Lorius lory* **Text and map page 237**

Seven races throughout the lowlands and hills of New Guinea. Fairly common in primary and well-grown secondary forest to 1,000m, occasionally higher.

All races show a black cap, green wings, red rump, some red below, and a prominent yellow underwing flash. The colour of the underwing-coverts varies by race and age. Races are chiefly distinguished by the extent of purple-blue on the upper- and underparts. All races from Purple-bellied Lory by grey-black, not white, cere.

> **25a** **Adult** (*lory*; W Papuan islands and Vogelkop) Extensive purple-blue markings on upper- and underparts. Red underwing-coverts.
>
> **25b** **Immature** (*lory*) Blue, yellow and black underwing-coverts. Less blue below, narrow blue collar.
>
> **25c** **Adult** (*erythrothorax*; S New Guinea from Onin Peninsula north and east to the Huon Peninsula) More red on breast. Two blue bands on mantle.
>
> **25d** **Adult** (*somu*; southern hill districts of C New Guinea) Red mantle and extensive red on underparts.
>
> **25e** **Adult** (*salvadorii*; N New Guinea from Aitape to Astrolabe Bay) Similar to *erythrothorax*, but with blue-black underwing-coverts.
>
> **25f** **Adult** (*viridicrissalis*; N New Guinea from Humboldt Bay to the Memberamo River) Like *salvadorii*, but blue areas much blacker.
>
> **25g** **Adult** (*jobiensis*; Yapen and Mios Num Islands in Geelvink Bay) Like *salvadorii*, but paler red breast and paler blue mantle-bands.
>
> **25h** **Adult** (*cyanuchen*; Biak in Geelvink Bay) Black of cap meets blue of mantle.

27 **White-naped Lory** *Lorius albidinuchus* **Text and map page 239**

Relatively common throughout its limited altitudinal range from 500 to 2,000m in the hill forests of New Ireland, Papua New Guinea.

> **27** **Adult** Black cap, green wings, red upper- and underparts, white nape.

25a

26b

26a

26a

26c

25a

25c

25b

25h

25d

25e

25f

25g

27

27

DANPOWELL

PLATE 7: *LORIUS* LORIES II

28   Yellow-bibbed Lory *Lorius chlorocercus*   **Text and map page 240**

Found commonly in primary and secondary forest up to 1,000m on islands of the E Solomons.

28a   Adult Black cap, black crescent on neck, yellow bib, blue thighs, white at bend of wing, rose-pink underwing panel.

28b   Immature Yellow bib fainter. Lacks black crescent at side of neck.

---

24   Purple-naped Lory *Lorius domicella*   **Text and map page 237**

Uncommon in the primary and secondary hill forests of Seram, Indonesia, from 400 to 1,000m. No recent records from Ambon although the species was previously recorded there.

24   Adult Black cap with variable purple patch at rear, red underparts, prominent bronze wash on wing-coverts, variable yellow bib, white and violet at bend of wing; tail red, tipped reddish-brown (diagnostic).

---

23   Chattering Lory *Lorius garrulus*   **Text and map page 236**

Restricted to the N Moluccas, Indonesia. Found in primary and mature secondary forests from the lowlands to around 1,000m.

Red head, rump and underparts. Thighs green. Wings green with yellow underwing-coverts and pink panel in primaries. Tail basally red, tipped blackish.

23a   Adult (*garrulus*; Halmahera, Widi and Ternate) Variable yellow mantle-patch suffused slightly with green.

23b   Adult (*flavopalliatus*; Bacan and Obi) More yellow and less green on mantle than nominate.

23c   Adult (*morotaianus*; Morotai and Rau) Small yellow mantle-patch suffused with green.

28b

28a

28a

24

23a

23c

24

23a

24

23b

DAN POWELL

PLATE 8: *PHIGYS, VINI* AND *GLOSSOPSITTA* LORIKEETS

29   Collared Lorikeet *Phigys solitarius*   **Text and map page 241**

Restricted to the Fiji group where it is common in flowering trees in forests and gardens.

> **29**   **Adult** A chunky, compact short-tailed lory with a bright green hind-collar, back and rump; red upper mantle, purple belly-patch and green undertail-coverts.

30   Blue-crowned Lorikeet *Vini australis*   **Text and map page 241**

The only member of its genus not presently classified as globally threatened. Occurs on islands in southern Fiji, Tonga, Samoa and central Polynesia. The species is somewhat nomadic and remains fairly common on some islands. Found in flowering trees in a range of habitats.

> **30**   **Adult** Small green lorikeet. Red throat, elongated blue crown feathers, red and purple belly-patch, yellow undertail.

32   Stephen's Lorikeet *Vini stepheni*   **Text and map page 243**

Only on Henderson Island (Pitcairn group). Found in coconuts and along forest edges.

> **32**   **Adult** Small green lorikeet with red underparts marked with green and purple across breast and purple on belly and thighs. Crown shaft-streaked lighter green. Tail feathers yellow lightly suffused greens with orange spot at base of innerwebs.

31   Kuhl's Lorikeet *Vini kuhlii*   **Text and map page 242**

Confined to the central Pacific Islands of Rimatara (Tubuai Islands), Teraina and Tabueran (Kiritibati). Mainly in coconut palms either around habitation or in forested areas.

> **31a**   **Adult** Small red and green lorikeet with blue nape, purple belly and thighs, bright yellow-green rump and yellowish lateral tail-coverts. Uppertail black tipped green with red innerwebs. Similar to Stephen's Lorikeet, but lacks green markings across breast and has a shorter tail.
>
> **31b**   **Immature** Underparts dark purple, mottled red.

34   Ultramarine Lorikeet *Vini ultramarina*   **Text and map page 245**

Restricted to islands in the Marquesas group, its stronghold being Ua Huka. Apparently less coconut-dependent than the previous species, being found in inland forests as well as coastal areas.

> **34a**   **Adult** Blue crown, blue underparts marked with white on chin and mottle white and slaty-blue on breast, belly and flanks. Upperparts light blue. Bill orange.
>
> **34b**   **Immature** Underparts all black. Dark bill.

33   Blue Lorikeet *Vini peruviana*   **Text and map page 244**

Occurs on a number of island groups in the central Pacific including the Cook and Society Islands and the Tuamotu Archipelago. Dependent on coconuts for feeding and nesting.

> **33**   **Adult** Unmistakable. Dark blue with white face and bib and an orange bill.

35   Musk Lorikeet *Glossopsitta concinna*   **Text and map page 246**

SE Australia and Tasmania in flowering trees in a range of habitats. May form large flocks. Seasonal nomad, especially near range limits.

> **35**   **Adult** Larger than Little Lorikeet without red on chin. Red 'mask', blue crown.

36   Little Lorikeet *Glossopsitta pusilla*   **Text and map page 247**

SE Australia. Habits similar to Musk Lorikeet. Only a single record from Tasmania.

> **36**   **Adult** Small size. Red chin, forecrown and lores.

37   Purple-crowned Lorikeet *Glossopsitta porphyrocephala*   **Text and map page 248**

SE and SW Australia. Seasonal nomad to flowering trees in open woodland, forest and urban areas.

> **37**   **Adult** Red forecrown, purple crown, orange-red on ear-coverts, pale blue below, red underwing-coverts.

29

30

32

30

32

31b

29

31a

34a

35

33

36

35

34b

36

35

33

37

37

DAN POWELL

PLATE 9: *CHARMOSYNA* LORIKEETS I

38   Palm Lorikeet *Charmosyna palmarum*   Text and map page 249

SW Polynesia including Vanuatu, the Duff, Santa Cruz and Banks Islands. Flowering trees in forest, generally above 1,000m but also found in lowlands.

Small green lorikeet with few distinguishing marks except for long yellow-tipped tail; lacks wing-bar.

    38a Adult male Some red feathers on chin.

    38b Adult female Less red on chin, or red absent.

39   Red-chinned Lorikeet *Charmosyna rubrigularis*   Text and map page 250

New Britain, New Ireland, New Hanover, and Karkar Island off north coast of New Guinea. Flowering trees in montane forest generally above 500m.

    39   Adult Red and yellow on chin, red bases to tail feathers, yellow wing-bar, green underwing-coverts, long yellow-tipped tail.

40   Meek's Lorikeet *Charmosyna meeki*   Text and map page 250

Larger islands in the Solomons group. Found in flowering trees in montane forest above 300m.

    40   Adult Indistinct blue crown-patch, olive-brown wash on mantle, long yellow-tipped tail, indistinct yellow wing-bar.

41   Blue-fronted Lorikeet *Charmosyna toxopei*   Text and map page 251

Virtually unknown. Montane forest on the island of Buru only, Indonesia. No recent confirmed records.

    41   Adult Light blue crown, yellow wing-bar, red at bases of tail feathers.

43   Pygmy Lorikeet *Charmosyna wilhelminae*   Text and map page 252

Mountain forests of New Guinea at 1,000-2,000m, from Vogelkop through the central ranges to the Huon Peninsula and south-east ranges.

The smallest lorikeet. Tiny with a short pointed tail. Blue tips to nape feathers, yellow-streaked breast, purple-blue uppertail-coverts.

    43a   Adult male Red rump and underwing.

    43b   Adult female Lacks red markings of male.

    43c   Immature Like female. Young male can show some red.

42   Striated Lorikeet *Charmosyna multistriata*   Text and map page 252

Forests of the central and western highlands of New Guinea above 200m.

    42   Adult Larger than Pygmy Lorikeet. Orange bill with blue-grey base, brown 'mask' and nape (feathers with orange tips), prominent yellow streaking below and less obviously above. Red on vent.

DAN POWELL

PLATE 10: *CHARMOSYNA* LORIKEETS II

44 Red-fronted Lorikeet *Charmosyna rubronotata*   Text and map page 253

Open country and forests of lowland N New Guinea. Also on Salawati and Biak Islands. Less common than Red-flanked Lorikeet and tends to be at higher elevations where the two overlap.

Small green sexually dimorphic lorikeet with red uppertail-coverts and a long yellow-tipped tail. Yellow wing-bar less distinct than in Red-flanked.

    44a   **Adult male** (*rubronotata*; New Guinea and Salawati) Red forecrown, deep blue ear-coverts, red at sides of breast and on underwing-coverts.

    44b   **Adult female** (*rubronotata*) Lacks red on crown, breast and underwing, but red still on uppertail-coverts unlike Red-flanked. Yellow-green streaking on ear-coverts (less distinct than in female Red-flanked).

    44c   **Adult male** (*kordoana*; Biak) Paler and more extensive red on crown, lighter blue ear-coverts. Female like nominate female.

45 Red-flanked Lorikeet *Charmosyna placentis*   Text and map page 254

Ranges from the Moluccas through the Kai, Aru, and W Papuan islands, New Guinea, reaching the Bismarcks and Bougainville in the south-east. Commonest small lorikeet through much of range. Flowering trees in forest, open areas and around cultivation.

Small green sexually dimorphic lorikeet with strong yellow wing-bar. There are five similar races, three in west with blue rumps, two in east with green; all males have obvious red flanks and underwing-coverts.

    45a   **Adult male** (*placentis*; S Moluccas, Kai and Aru Islands, S New Guinea) Red face, flanks, underwing-coverts and marks in tail. Blue ear-coverts and rump.

    45b   **Adult female** (*placentis*) No red markings, ear-coverts with yellow streaks (no blue). Blue rump.

    45c   **Adult male** (*subplacens*; E New Guinea) Rump green, not blue.

47 Red-throated Lorikeet *Charmosyna amabilis*   Text and map page 256

Rain-forest on islands in the Fiji group. Despite being reported as 'not uncommon' on Viti Levu in 1973, and recorded on five separate occasions on Taveuni the same year (Holyoak 1979), there are just a handful of other records this century.

Small green lorikeet with a red throat bordered yellow below, and a long yellow-tipped tail.

    47a   **Adult** Thighs red, strongly defined throat markings.

    47b   **Immature** Duller throat and purplish thighs.

46 New Caledonian Lorikeet *Charmosyna diadema*   Text and map page 255

Only known from two female specimens collected in 1859. It has never been reliably sighted since. Possibly extinct. The only small green lorikeet likely to be encountered in the forests of New Caledonia.

    46   **Adult** Female with blue crown and thighs, red vent and yellow face. Tail feathers marked basally with red and black.

DAN POWELL

48 Duchess Lorikeet *Charmosyna margarethae* Text and map page 257

Solomon Islands, from the lowlands to the hills in forest, woodland, coastal plantations and around villages.

Bright red with black cap, yellow and black collar, green wings, red tail, and striking underwing pattern.

48a **Adult male** Black cap and well defined collar.

48b **Adult female** Yellow sides to rump.

48b **Immature** Lacks black cap, collar poorly defined.

51 Papuan Lorikeet *Charmosyna papou* Text and map page 259

Montane forests of New Guinea from around 1,200m to the treeline. Vogelkop and Huon Peninsula races isolated.

Resembles previous species but tail green above with longer streamers; melanistic morph in eastern populations.

51a **Adult** (*papou*; Vogelkop) Black cap and nape, yellow breast and flank markings, smaller belly-patch than other races, no sexual dimorphism, no melanistic form.

51b **Immature** (*papou*) Shorter tail, yellow wing-bar.

51c **Adult male** (*goliathina*; W and C New Guinea) Lacks black cap and yellow markings on breast and flanks of nominate. Back red and blue. Tail streamers green to yellow, not green to orange-red to yellow as in *stellae*, and longest uppertail-coverts blue, not red.

51d **Adult female** (*goliathina*) Back and sides of rump marked yellow.

51e **Adult male** (*goliathina*, melanistic morph) Red areas replaced with black except back and undertail-coverts, blue rump, duller tail streamers.

51f **Adult female** (*goliathina*, melanistic morph) Undertail-coverts also black; yellow on back replaced by green; blue rump.

51g **Adult** (*stellae*, SE New Guinea) Streamers grade from orange-red to yellow; longest uppertail-coverts red, not blue as in *goliathina*.

51h **Adult** (*wahnesi*; Huon Peninsula) Yellow band across breast.

50 Josephine's Lorikeet *Charmosyna josefinae* Text and map page 258

Montane forests of W and C New Guinea from Arfak Mountains to the Bismarck Range. Mainly lower than Papuan Lorikeet, being commonest at 800-1,200m.

Like Papuan but uppertail red not green, less blue on nape, no melanistic form. Generally red below with belly-patch variable according to race and age. Rump varies according to sex. All with green wings and black nape.

50a **Adult male** (*josefinae*; Vogelkop to the Snow Mountains) Blackish belly-patch, lower back red and blue.

50b **Adult female** (*josefinae*) Lower back yellow, blue and green.

50c **Immature** (*josephinae*) Belly-patch suffused green.

50d **Adult male** (*sepikiana*; mountains of Sepik region and western highlands) Larger belly-patch, grey not lilac markings on black of nape. Female with yellow flanks and lacking green rump shown by nominate.

50e **Adult male** (*cyclopum*; Cyclops Mountains) Lacks belly-patch and nape almost entirely black.

48c 48a 51b 51a 51h

48b

51e

51c 51d 50c

50a

50b

51g 50d

51f

51e 50c

DAN POWELL.

49 Fairy Lorikeet *Charmosyna pulchella* — Text and map page 257

Mountains of New Guinea from Vogelkop to south-east ranges, mainly at 500-1,800m, occasionally to sea-level and 2,300m.

Small lorikeet, red below with yellow breast-streaks, green above, black cap. Green, red and yellow tail is thin and pointed.

49a   **Adult male** (*pulchella*; Vogelkop, central ranges, Huon Peninsula, Owen Stanley Ranges) Dark violet patch on back, sides of back and rump red.

49b   **Adult female** (*pulchella*) Sides of back and rump yellow.

49c   **Immature** (*pulchella*) More yellow on flanks than female, green suffusion on flanks and breast, yellow wing-bar; no yellow breast-streaks or red hind-collar.

49d   **Adult male** (*rothschildi*; Cyclops Ranges and mountains above the Idenburg River) Green suffusion behind yellow breast-streaks, more extensive black cap meeting green of mantle. Female with dark patch on back mottled with green.

53 Yellow-billed Lorikeet *Neopsittacus musschenbroekii* — Text amd map page 262

Mountains of New Guinea from Vogelkop to south-east ranges, generally lower than Orange-billed Lorikeet (1,400-2,500m). Three similar races; Vogelkop population isolated.

Medium-sized green lorikeet, orange-red below, yellow streaking on ear-coverts and crown, pale bill, brownish wash on nape, undertail yellowish, tail with narrow yellow tip, orange-red underwing.

53a   **Adult** (*musschenbroekii*; Vogelkop, where Orange-billed is absent) W and C New Guinea race is intermediate between nominate and *major*.

53b   **Adult** (*musschenbroekii*) Showing variable amount of red below.

53c   **Adult** (*major*; mountains from Sepik region to SE New Guinea) Larger; yellower streaking on face; lighter, less orange-red underparts.

52 Plum-faced Lorikeet *Oreopsittacus arfaki* — Text and map page 261

Three similar races in mountain forests of New Guinea, from Vogelkop to the south-east ranges. Probably the commonest small lorikeet above 2,000m.

Slender green lorikeet with a red undertail, black bill, mauve cheeks streaked with white, red underwing-coverts and yellow wing-bar.

52a   **Adult male** (*arfaki*; Vogelkop) Red cap, reddish flank and belly markings. Snow Mountains race similar but larger with redder tip to the tail.

52b   **Adult female** (*arfaki*) Green crown.

52c   **Immature male** (*arfaki*) Limited red on crown.

52d   **Adult male** (*grandis*; C and E New Guinea) Lacks reddish flank and belly markings.

54 Orange-billed Lorikeet *Neopsittacus pullicauda* — Text and map page 263

Mountains of New Guinea, generally above 2,000m. Absent from Vogelkop.

Smaller than Yellow-billed Lorikeet, greener face with less obvious yellow streaking, tail olive below and lacking yellow tip of Yellow-billed, bill orange, orange-red underwing.

54a   **Adult** (*pullicauda*; Sepik region to SE New Guinea) Red of underparts uniform. Race on the Huon Peninsula and Herzog mountains similar but darker.

54b   **Adult** (*alpinus*; C and W New Guinea) Orange breast contrasts with scarlet belly.

49b

49c

53a

53b

53c

49a

49d

54b

54a

52b

52d

52a

53a

54a

52c

DAN POWELL

PLATE 13: PALM AND BLACK COCKATOOS

55 **Palm Cockatoo** *Proboscer aterrimus* **Text and map page 263**

Ranges through lowland rain-forests of New Guinea, the Aru Islands and the Cape York Peninsula, N Queensland.

Unmistakable. Huge, entirely grey-black apart from pink facial skin and two-tone red and black tongue. Long wispy crest, long tail, broad wings. Three very similar races are currently recognised.

55a **Adult** (*aterrimus*; Aru Islands, Misool, Cape York Peninsula, S New Guinea.

55b **Immature** Some young birds show pale scalloping on the body and underwing-coverts. White eye-ring and tip to bill.

---

60 **Glossy Black Cockatoo** *Calyptorhynchus lathami* **Text and map page 271**

More tied to woodland than other black cockatoos, especially mixed *Eucalyptus* and *Casuarina* forest. E coastal Australia, with three races distinguished on bill size.

Smallest black cockatoo; red tail-patches, huge bill, short rounded crest.

60a **Adult male** All dark, brownish head, unbarred red tail-patches.

60b **Adult female** Variable yellow patches on head, bars in red tail-patches (which look yellower from below), bill slightly paler.

60c **Immature female** No head markings; some yellow stippling on body and wing-coverts.

---

59 **Red-tailed Black Cockatoo** *Calyptorhynchus banksii* **Text and map page 270**

Widespread through N, C and W Australia. Occurrence mainly tied to distribution of riverine eucalypt woodland. Five similar races.

Long tail and wings; tail panel colour varies between sexes. 'Helmet-like' crest. Most racial differences structural, but females in SW Australia and in SE South Australia are more brightly marked.

59a **Adult male** All black except for red tail panels.

59b **Adult female** Upperparts stippled and underparts barred yellow; generally more brownish, tail panels yellow-orange with transverse dark bars.

59c **Adult female** (*naso*; SW Australia) More strongly barred below.

---

58 **Yellow-tailed Black Cockatoo** *Calyptorhynchus funereus* **Text and map page 267**

Wetter areas of E Australia from C Queensland to Tasmania and South Australia. *Eucalyptus* forest.

Long wings and tail, yellow tail-patches stippled brownish-black, yellow ear-coverts, short crest. The southern race, which occurs from E Victoria through S Australia and Tasmania is smaller with a shorter, narrower bill.

58a **Adult male** Dark bill, pink eye-ring, small ear-covert patch, slightly darker below.

58b **Adult female** Paler upper mandible, larger ear-covert patch, grey eye-ring, light scalloping.

---

56 **Long-billed Black Cockatoo** *Calyptorhynchus baudinii* **Text and map page 265**

Recently split from following species based on different bill morphology. Breeds in extreme SW Australia in karri woodland, moving north and east to occupy marri and jarrah woodland.

Long-winged and long-tailed, white tail-patches stippled blackish-brown, white patch on ear-coverts, short crest, scalloped plumage. Upper mandible 15% longer than White-tailed.

56a **Adult male** Pink eye-ring, all-dark bill, smaller ear-covert patch and indistinct pale scalloping.

56b **Adult female** Grey eye-ring, pale bill, larger ear-covert patch, more distinct pale scalloping.

---

57 **White-tailed Black Cockatoo** *Calyptorhynchus latirostris* **Text and map page 266**

SW Australia, in wandoo woodland belt during breeding season, inland of Long-billed Black Cockatoo, but the two species mix in marri and jarrah woodland after nesting.

Identical to Long-billed except upper mandible around 15% shorter.

57a **Adult male**

57b **Adult female**

55a

55b

60a

60c

60b

59a

59b

59c

59a

59b

58a

58b

57a

57b

58b

56b

56a

KWEF

PLATE 14: GANG-GANG, GALAH AND *CACATUA* COCKATOOS

61   Gang-gang Cockatoo *Callocephalon fimbriatum*   Text and map page 272

Coastal SE Australia, breeding in highland forest, dispersing to a range of habitats after nesting.
A grey, Galah-sized cockatoo with fine pale barring and a wispy upturned crest.

61a   Adult male Red head, plain grey tail; looks darker grey than female.

61b   Adult female Grey head, more rusty suffusion below with greenish cast; appears paler grey.

61c   Immature male Some red shows on head from first year.

62   Galah *Eolophus roseicapillus*   Text and map page 273

Common, widespread and increasing throughout Australia. Familiar species, forming large flocks.
Dove-grey upperparts, pink underparts and underwing-coverts, rounded crest.

62a   Adult (*roseicapillus*; N Australia) Greyish-pink eye-ring, whitish crest. A similar but larger
race occurs in E Australia, west to the Eyre Peninsula and C Australia.

62b   Immature (*roseicapillus*) Grey suffusion below.

62c   Adult (*assimilis*; W Australia) Pinkish crest, crusty white eye-ring.

65   Sulphur-crested Cockatoo *Cacatua galerita*   Text and map page 278

Widespread and common in a variety of habitats from rainforest in New Guinea to agricultural lands
and riverine woodland in Australia. Ranges from the W Papuan islands through New Guinea, into N
and E Australia reaching Tasmania in the south-east. Also found in the Kai and Aru Islands.

Familiar large white cockatoo with huge yellow erectile crest, yellow suffusion beneath wings and at
base of tail. Four similar races. Birds in E Australia larger with white eye-rings, birds in N Australia
slightly smaller with bluer eye-rings. New Guinea birds smaller still, with blue eye-rings.

65a   Adult (*galerita*; E Australia and introduced to New Zealand) Large; white eye-ring.

65b   Adult (*triton*; W Papuan islands, New Guinea) Smaller, blue eye-ring.

63   Pink Cockatoo *Cacatua leadbeateri*   Text and map page 275

W and south-central Australia. Widespread in riverine forest and agricultural areas.

Upperparts white, underparts pink including wash on underwing and at base of tail. Long erectile crest
white with red and yellow feather-bases. Race *mollis* has a darker red crest showing little or no yellow,
and occurs in SW Western Australia.

63a   Adult male Less yellow in crest.

63b   Adult female Centre of crest yellow.

64   Yellow-crested Cockatoo *Cacatua sulphurea*   Text and map page 276

Most westerly cockatoo, occurring in a variety of forest and associated habitats in Sulawesi, Nusa
Tenggara and associated islands, Indonesia.

White plumage, yellow crest, yellow wash on ear-coverts, underwing and base of tail, pale bluish-white
eye-ring. Generally smaller than but very similar to Sulphur-crested Cockatoo.

64a   Adult (*sulphurea*; Sulawesi, islands in Flores Sea; introduced to Singapore) Obvious yellow
suffusion on ear-coverts.

64b   Adult (*parvula*; Nusa Tenggara) Little yellow on ear-coverts.

64c   Adult (*citrinocristata*; Sumba) Orange crest.

66   Blue-eyed Cockatoo *Cacatua ophthalmica*   Text and map page 280

Forested lowlands of New Britain and New Ireland.

66   Adult A stocky white cockatoo with a rounded backward-curving crest of white and yellow
feathers. Yellow suffusion beneath wings and tail. Blue eye-ring.

61b 61a
61c
62b
62a
62c

65b 65a
63b 63a
69a
65a
64a
64c
64b
64a
64a
66

K4EF

PLATE 15: *CACATUA* COCKATOOS AND CORELLAS

67   **Salmon-crested Cockatoo** *Cacatua moluccensis*   Text and map page 280

Indonesia on Seram, Haruku, Saparua and Ambon. Highest densities in primary rainforest.

    67   **Adult** Large white cockatoo suffused with pink, especially beneath wings and tail; plumage often ruffled. Large backward-curving white and pink crest.

68   **White Cockatoo** *Cacatua alba*   Text and map page 282

Lowland and hill forest to 600m in N Moluccas, Indonesia. Tolerates secondary growth.

    68   **Adult** Large all-white cockatoo with a yellowish suffusion beneath the wings and tail. White erectile triangular crest.

69   **Philippine Cockatoo** *Cacatua haematuropygia*   Text and map page 283

Previously throughout the Philippines; now only on a few islands (strongholds on Palawan and Dumaran). Mangroves, forest and cultivated areas.

    69   **Adult** Small white cockatoo with a short erectile crest, white-tipped red undertail-coverts and a yellow suffusion beneath the wings and tail.

70   **Tanimbar Cockatoo** *Cacatua goffini*   Text and map page 284

Common in large flocks in forest and open habitats on islands in the Tanimbar group, Indonesia.

    70   **Adult** Small white cockatoo with an erectile crest, pinkish lores, whitish eye-ring, yellow suffusion beneath wings and tail.

74   **Ducorps's Cockatoo** *Cacatua ducorpsii*   Text and map page 289

Widespread in a variety of habitats in the Solomon Islands.

    74   **Adult** Small white cockatoo with a triangular erectile crest, circular blue eye-ring, and a yellow suffusion beneath wings and tail.

73   **Long-billed Corella** *Cacatua tenuirostris*   Text and map page 287

Small area of SE Australia in riverine woodland and farmland.

    73   **Adult** Small white cockatoo, short tail, pointed wings, strong pink suffusion on face and breast, large rounded head with very short crest; more elliptical eye-ring than Little Corella.

71   **Little Corella** *Cacatua sanguinea*   Text and map page 284

Common in large flocks through N and C Australia and S New Guinea. Inhabits forest, open woodland and cultivated areas.

Small white cockatoo with erectile crest, pinkish lores, blue eye-ring with a bulge below the eye, yellow suffusion beneath wings and tail. Four similar races; the W Cape York is like the nominate but smaller.

    71a   **Adult** (*sanguinea*; N Australia) Slight pink on lores, light blue eye-ring.

    71b   **Adult** (*gymnopis*; C, E and SE Australia) Lores strongly washed pink, darker blue eye-ring, ear-coverts slightly washed yellow.

    71c   **Adult** (*transfreta*; New Guinea) Duller yellow suffusion on underwing.

72   **Western Corella** *Cacatua pastinator*   Text and map page 286

Western Australia in two disjunct populations. Frequents *Eucalyptus* woodland and farmland.

    72   **Adult** Small cockatoo with an erectile crest, strong pink wash on lores and sometimes visible pink feather-bases on breast and elsewhere. Elongated upper mandible, blue eye-ring. More widespread northern race is smaller with a shorter upper mandible.

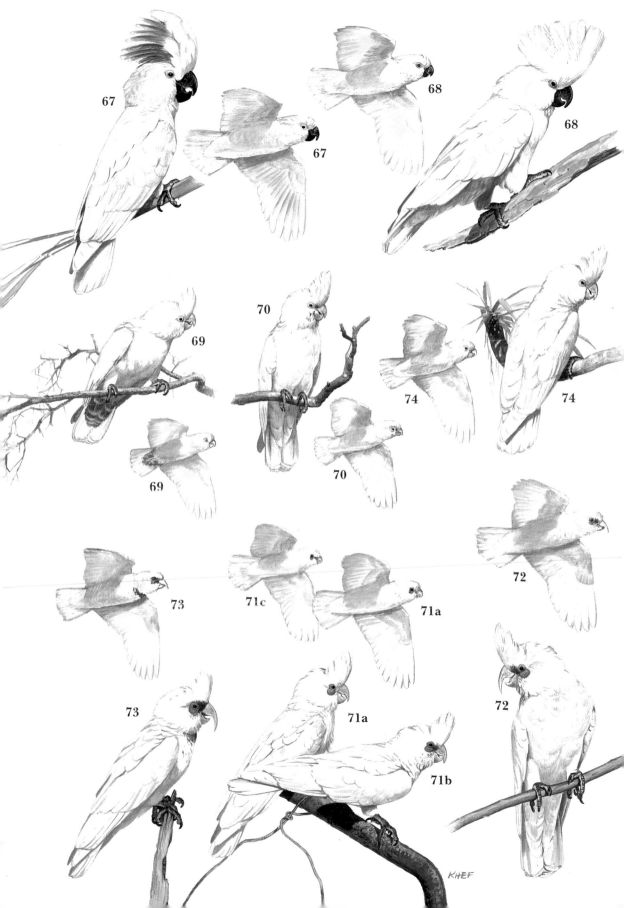

67

67

68

68

69

69

70

70

74

74

71c

71a

72

73

73

71a

71b

72

KHEF

112 Pesquet's Parrot *Psittrichas fulgidus* **Text and map page 322**

Hill forests of New Guinea mainly at 600-1,200m from Vogelkop to the Huon Peninsula and south-east ranges.

Highly distinctive. Exposed facial skin, scalloped breast, red rump, belly and undertail-coverts, wing-flashes and underwing-coverts. Flight with alternate flapping and soaring reminiscent of new world Black Vulture *Coragyps atratus*.

    112a   **Adult male** Red feathers behind eye.

    112b   **Adult female** Lacks red behind eye.

76   **Kea** *Nestor notabilis* **Text and map page 290**

Mountains of South Island, New Zealand, to above the treeline.

Stocky olive-brown parrot, flight feathers washed with turquoise, rusty rump, orange and yellow barring on underwing, elongated upper mandible.

    76a   **Adult** Dark cere. Males have longer upper mandible.

    76b   **Immature** Yellow cere and eye-ring.

77   **Kaka** *Nestor meridionalis* **Text and map page 291**

Native forests of New Zealand; thinly distributed but still fairly common on some offshore islands, e.g. Little Barrier.

A stocky brown parrot, paler cap, reddish hind-collar, rump and underparts, orange-red underwing-coverts, barred underside to flight feathers.

    77a   **Adult** (*meridionalis*; South Island) Brighter, paler cap.

    77b   **Immature** Similar to adult but yellow cere and eye-ring.

    77c   **Adult** (*septentrionalis*; North Island) Duller, especially crown.

158 Kakapo *Strigops habroptilus* **Text and map page 372**

Now only on Maud, Codfish and Little Barrier Islands, New Zealand, where all remaining individuals (except some in captive-breeding programme) have been relocated to prevent predation by introduced mammals.

World's heaviest parrot. Flightless and nocturnal: moss-like pattern above, flattened bill, large feet.

    158a   **Adult** Lighter facial disc, rounded outer primaries, lighter streaked underparts.

    158b   **Adult male** Display in which body is inflated to produce nocturnal booming calls.

    158c   **Immature** Browner facial disc, paler bill, outer primaries pointed and showing light and dark bars of equal widths.

76a

112b

112a

112a

76a

77a

77a

76a

76b

77b

77a

77c

158b

158c

158a

KHEF

80   Buff-faced Pygmy Parrot *Micropsitta pusio*   Text and map page 294

Lowlands of N and SE New Guinea, on some offshore islands, and in the Bismarck Archipelago. Forest and occasionally savanna to 500m.

Tiny, with buff face, including supercilium, blue crown, yellow undertail-coverts, typical *Micrositta* tail and wing patterns. Four similar races.

80a   **Adult** (*pusio*; SE New Guinea and Bismarcks) N New Guinea race similar but darker, especially on face.

80b   **Immature** (*pusio*) Crown washed green, less buff on face.

80c   **Adult** (*harterti*; Fergusson Island) Throat marked with blue. Misima and Tagula race is similar but larger with more yellow below.

78   Yellow-capped Pygmy Parrot *Micropsitta keiensis*   Text and map page 293

W Papuan islands, through Vogelkop, S New Guinea and the Kai and Aru Islands. Forest and second growth, sometimes around habitation.

Tiny stub-tailed green parrot with yellow undertail-coverts and crown and brownish lores. Three similar races.

78a   **Adult** (*viridipectus*; S New Guinea) Bright yellow crown. Nominate (Kai and Aru Islands) is similar but paler.

78b   **Adult male** (*chloroxantha*; W Papuan islands, Vogelkop and Onin Peninsula) Duller crown than previous races. Male with red on underparts.

78c   **Adult female** (*chloroxantha*) Underparts tinged yellow.

79   Geelvink Pygmy Parrot *Micropsitta geelvinkiana*   Text and map page 293

Forest and open areas on the islands of Biak and Numfor in Geelvink Bay.

Green with yellow undertail-coverts, greyish head with a blue crown in all but the male of the Biak race. Slight sexual dimorphism. Two races.

79a   **Adult male** (*geelvinkiana*; Numfor) Blue on crown, orange-yellow in centre of belly.

79b   **Adult female** (*geelvinkiana*) No orange in centre of belly.

79c   **Adult male** (*misoriensis*; Biak) Lacks blue crown, less green around head than Numfor race.

79d   **Adult female** (*misoriensis*) Shows blue crown but lacks orange on belly.

81   Meek's Pygmy Parrot *Micropsitta meeki*   Text and map page 295

Lowland forest and disturbed habitats in the Admiralty and St Matthias groups. Two races.

Male and female similar. Pale bill, scaly yellow and brown head, yellow breast, yellow on underwing-coverts.

81a   **Adult** (*meeki*; Admiralty Islands) Darker facial markings.

81b   **Adult** (*proxima*; St Matthias group) Face paler, yellow frontal area.

80b

80a

80a

80a

80c

78a

78b

78c

78a

79d

79c

79a

79b

81a

81b

81a

KHEF

82   Finsch's Pygmy Parrot *Micropsitta finschi*   **Text and map page 295**

Fairly common in lowland forest on islands in the Bismarck and Solomons groups.

Mainly green, with head and belly markings varying between sexes and races. Five subspecies. Cere pink in male, greyish in female.

82a   Adult male (*finschi*; S Solomons, San Cristobal group) Green crown, blue chin, reddish markings in centre of belly. W Solomons race similar but male lacks red below.

82b   Adult female (*finschi*) Chin pink, lacks red in centre of belly.

82c   Adult male (*aolae*; south-central Solomons) Blue spot on crown, no red below.

82d   Adult male (*nanina*; N Solomons) Blue-tinged crown, no red below.

82e   Adult male (*viridifrons*; Bismarcks) Crown, cheeks and chin blue, sometimes with red below.

---

83   Red-breasted Pygmy Parrot *Micrositta bruijnii*   **Text and map page 296**

The only pygmy parrot above 1,000m in montane forest. Ranges from Buru and Seram, through the highlands of New Guinea to the Bismarcks and some of the Solomon Islands. Locally common.

Marked sexual dimorphism; four largely similar races.

83a   Adult male (*bruijnii*; mountains of New Guinea) Buff crown, pinkish-white cheeks, dark blue breast, flanks and hind-collar, red in centre of belly and on undertail-coverts. Solomons race with more reddish crown and cheeks; Buru and Seram race has a more extensive, darker buff crown.

83b   Adult female (*bruijnii*) Buff forehead, blue crown, white cheeks suffused pink, yellow undertail-coverts.

83c   Immature male (*bruijnii*) Like female but with red markings on underparts.

83d   Adult male (*necopinata*; Bismarcks) Orange-red belly, yellow undertail-coverts.

82a

82b

82c

82d

82e

82a

82a

83d

83a

83a

83a

83b

83c

KHEF

84 Orange-breasted Fig Parrot *Cyclopsitta gulielmitertii*   **Text and map page 297**

Widespread and common through lowlands of New Guinea below 1,000m. Also in W Papuan and Aru Islands.

Small stubby-looking parrot. Seven races. Marked sexual dimorphism and racial variation. Most birds with dark frontal area, distinctive face pattern, orange on breast or face.

84a **Adult male** (*gulielmitertii*; Salawati and W Vogelkop) Buff-yellow face marked with a variable black crescent, blue forecrown, orange breast. Birds in western part of N New Guinea have forecrown black not blue.

84b **Adult female** (*gulielmitertii*) Green breast, black and orange ear-coverts.

84c **Immature** (*gulielmitertii*) Similar to female.

84d **Adult male** (*amabilis*; N New Guinea from Huon Peninsula to Milne Bay) All-yellowish face and breast, black forecrown. Ramu River race similar but with blue forecrown.

84e **Adult female** (*amabilis*) Black forecrown, black facial mark, orange breast.

84f **Adult male** (*suavissima*; SE New Guinea reaching the Purari River in the west) Blue forecrown, whitish cheeks, large black patch on face, wing-bar.

84g **Adult female** (*suavissima*) Blue and orange face, white mark at base of bill and behind eye, orange suffusion on breast.

84h **Adult male** (*fuscifrons*; Fly River to around 138°E) Blackish-brown forecrown, white face with smaller black patch than *suavissima*, less orange on breast. Aru Islands race similar but female with less orange below.

87 Edwards's Fig Parrot *Psittaculirostris edwardsii*   **Text and map page 301**

Common in lowland forests of NE New Guinea.

Small stocky parrot with green crown, darker line from the eye to the nape, elongated yellow ear-coverts tipped blue, red throat and dull violet collar.

87a **Adult male** Red on breast and belly.

87b **Adult female** No red breast and belly; purple collar more extensive.

87c **Immature** Like female; yellowish-green ear-coverts.

88 Salvadori's Fig Parrot *Psittaculirostris salvadorii*   **Text and map page 302**

Replaces Edwards's Fig Parrot in lowland forests of NW New Guinea.

Small stocky green parrot with blue crown and elongated yellow ear-coverts.

88a **Adult male** Scarlet breast-band.

88b **Adult female** Blue breast with some reddish feathers at sides.

84c

84a

84b

84a

84f

84d

84e

84f

84g

84h

87a

87a

87b

87c

88a

88b

KHEF

PLATE 20: DOUBLE-EYED FIG PARROT

85 **Double-eyed Fig Parrot** *Cyclopsitta diophthalma*   **Text and map page 298**

Widespread and common in low- to mid-altitude forest from W Papuan islands through New Guinea and some associated islands to NE Australia.

Small green parrot with eight races, most of which are sexually dimorphic. All share blue in flight feathers, red tertials, yellow flanks; males all show some red on the head.

85a **Adult male** (*diophthalma*; W Papuan islands and NW New Guinea) Red crown, chin and throat, blue mark in front of eye, yellow edge to red at rear of crown.

85b **Adult female** (*diophthalma*) Red cheeks of male replaced by buff.

85c **Adult male** (*coccineifrons*; SE New Guinea from Astrolabe Bay in north to Fly River in south) Darker with more yellow in crown.

85d **Adult male** (*aruensis*; S New Guinea and the Aru Islands) Yellow on crown slight or lacking, mark in front of eye greener than in nominate.

85e **Adult female** (*aruensis*) Lacks red in face; blue crown, lores and upper ear-coverts, mauve-blue sides to throat.

85f **Adult male** (*virago*; Fergusson and Goodenough Islands) Less and paler red on head, mark in front of eye green not blue.

85g **Adult female** (*virago*) Red spot on forecrown, face mainly green with blue on forecrown and blue suffusion on cheeks.

85h **Adult** (*inseparabilis*; Tagula Islands) Head green, forecrown red and blue.

85i **Adult** (*coxeni*; SE Queensland, NE New South Wales) Larger and more yellow-green than nominate. Orange-red cheeks bordered by mauve-blue, red on lores, blue forecrown marked red.

85j **Adult male** (*marshalli*; Cape York Peninsula) Like *aruensis* but mark in front of eye deeper blue.

85k **Adult female** (*marshalli*) Similar to female *aruensis*.

85l **Adult male** (*macleayana*; NE Queensland) Blue around eye, red forecrown, red stripe through ear-coverts.

85m **Adult female** (*macleayana*) Red on face replaced by blue.

85a

85b

85a

85a

85c

85d

85e

85f

85g

85h

85i

85k

85j

85m

85l

KHEF

PLATE 21: LARGE FIG PARROT AND GUIABERO

86   **Large Fig Parrot** *Psittaculirostris desmarestii*   **Text and map page 300**

Forested lowlands of W Papuan islands, W and S New Guinea.

Small stocky parrot with six races. All birds are mainly green with fiery-orange crowns, blue breast markings and blue on flight feathers. Colour of elongated ear-coverts varies with race.

86a   **Adult** (*desmarestii*; N and W Vogelkop) Ear-coverts green streaked orange, blue mark below eye, blue hind-collar.

86b   **Immature** (*desmarestii*) Lacks orange nape; ear-coverts duller.

86c   **Adult** (*intermedia*; Onin Peninsula) Crown more orange, blue collar indistinct or lacking.

86d   **Adult** (*occidentalis*; Salawati, Batanta, opposite coast of Vogelkop, Bomberai Peninsula) Ear-coverts and cheeks orange-yellow, no blue hind-collar. Misool race similar but lacks blue mark below eye in adult (present in immature).

86e   **Adult male** (*godmani*; SW New Guinea) No blue below eye or reddish smudges on breast; yellow hind-collar.

86f   **Adult female** (*godmani*) No yellow hind-collar.

86g   **Adult** (*cervicalis*; SE New Guinea) Head almost entirely orange-red, dark blue collar.

86h   **Immature** (*cervicalis*) Green crown.

89   **Guiabero** *Bolbopsittacus lunulatus*   **Text and map page 303**

Relatively common in lowlands of some Philippine islands. Found in a range of habitats from forest to mangrove and farmland.

Small stocky green parrot with yellow-green rump and dark blue flight feathers. Sexually dimorphic with four similar races.

89a   **Adult male** (*lunulatus*; Luzon) Blue on face and nape, unmarked yellow-green rump. Leyte race similar with darker blue hind-collar. Samar race more yellow-green.

89b   **Adult female** (*lunulatus*) Less blue on face, yellow hind-collar and rump marked with darker scalloping.

89c   **Adult male** (*mindanensis*; Mindanao and Panaon) Darker blue hind-collar; paler head contrasts with darker green of mantle.

86a

86b

86a

86c

86d

86f

86h

86e

86g

89a

89b

89c

89a

KHEF

90   Blue-rumped Parrot *Psittinus cyanurus*   Text and map page 303

Widespread and locally common in lowland forests from Thailand, through Malaysia, Borneo, Sumatra and some offshore islands.

Wings green with blue in flight feathers, reddish shoulder-patch, yellowish margins to wing-coverts. Other characters vary between sexes.

> **90a   Adult male** (*cyanurus*; mainland range and islands except Mentawai group) Red upper mandible, blue head, black mantle, blue rump and underparts, red underwing-coverts. Southern Mentawai islands race similar but larger.
>
> **90b   Adult female** (*cyanurus*) Mainly green with grey-brown head, less blue in rump.
>
> **90c   Immature** (*cyanurus*) Like female but head green.
>
> **90d   Adult male** (*abbotti*; Simeulue) Larger. Green underparts, mantle and rump (suffused turquoise), blue suffusion on face, black hind-collar.
>
> **90e   Adult female** (*abbotti*) Head green.

92   Painted Tiger Parrot *Psittacella picta*   Text and map page 305

High mountains of New Guinea from 2,500 to 4,000m in alpine and montane forest habitats.

This is the large high-altitude tiger-parrot, generally higher than Brehm's with a brighter brown head; red undertail-coverts, barred upperparts and other features varying with race and sex. Three races. Eastern birds with red on rump lacking in Brehm's; female of western race separated from Brehm's by bluish (not olive-brown) ear-coverts.

> **92a   Adult male** (*excelsa*; C New Guinea) Yellow hind-collar, red on rump, unbarred green underparts marked blue on upper breast. Nominate, which occurs in south-east, has warmer brown crown.
>
> **92b   Adult female** (*excelsa*) Lacks yellow hind-collar, cheeks suffused blue, finer barring above, barred underparts.
>
> **92c   Adult male** (*lorentzi*; western highlands) Yellow crescent at side of neck, bluish-green cheeks, no red on rump.
>
> **92d   Adult female** (*lorentzi*) Lacks yellow crescent at side of neck. No red on rump.

90c

90b

90a

90a

90d

90e

92a

92b

92a

92d

92c

KHEF

PLATE 23: TIGER PARROTS

91 Brehm's Tiger Parrot *Psittacella brehmii*   **Text and map page 304**

Mountain forests of New Guinea including Vogelkop and Huon Peninsula where Painted Tiger Parrot is absent. Usually below Painted, at 1,500-2,500m.

Green with an olive-brown head, red undertail-coverts, barred upperparts. Sexually dimorphic and with four similar races.

- **91a**   **Adult male** (*brehmii*; Vogelkop) Yellow crescent at side of neck, unbarred underparts. C New Guinea race similar but slightly larger, more yellowish-green. Huon race paler–headed, less yellowish-green. South-east race with narrower bill.
- **91b**   **Adult female** (*brehmii*) Lacks yellow crescent; barred on breast.
- **91c**   **Immature** (*brehmii*) Orange-red undertail-coverts, slight barring on breast.

93 Modest Tiger Parrot *Psittacella modesta*   **Text and map page 306**

Mountain forests of New Guinea in Vogelkop and central ranges. Absent in south-east and Huon Peninsula where it is replaced by Madarasz's Tiger Parrot. The two are sympatric in C New Guinea, but Modest is usually higher there, 1,700-2,800m.

Small green parrot with olive-brown head and red undertail-coverts. Sexually dimorphic with three races.

- **93a**   **Adult male** (*modesta*; Vogelkop) Male with slight yellowish mottling on head, unbarred underparts; lacks yellow hind-collar of eastern races.
- **93b**   **Adult female** (*modesta*) Breast barred brown and pink, flanks barred green and yellow.
- **93c**   **Adult male** (*subcollaris*; central and east-central highlands) Bright yellow hind-collar. C New Guinea race with broader, duller collar and lighter head. Females of eastern races also with variable yellow on nape.

94 Madarasz's Tiger Parrot *Psittacella madaraszi*   **Text and map page 307**

Mountain forests of New Guinea from west-central highlands to south-east ranges. Also in the Huon Peninsula.

Small, mainly green parrot with red undertail-coverts, male similar to Modest Tiger Parrot, but generally at lower altitudes where the two are sympatric. Sexually dimorphic with four similar races.

- **94a**   **Adult male** (*madaraszi*; SE New Guinea) Olive-brown head and breast; crown and nape mottled yellow. Western race similar but larger.
- **94b**   **Adult female** (*madaraszi*) Underparts green, blue forecrown, nape marked black and pinkish-orange.
- **94c**   **Adult female** (*huonensis*; isolated population in Huon Peninsula) Lacks pink tips to nape feathers. Male with crown more yellowish.
- **94d**   **Adult female** (*hallstromi*; C and E New Guinea) Nape more brightly marked. Male with head darker brown with less yellow.

91a

91a

91b

91c

93a

93b

93c

93a

94a

94b

94c

94a

94d

KHEF

95 Red-cheeked Parrot *Geoffroyus geoffroyi* **Text and map page 303**

Widespread and common in a range of habitats from the Moluccas through New Guinea to the extreme tip of the Cape York Peninsula, N Australia.

Medium-sized green parrot, male with red face and upper mandible, violet crown and nape. Female with black upper mandible and brown head. Underwing-coverts bright blue. Fifteen races.

95a **Adult male** (*geoffroyi*; Timor and Wetar) Red face, violet crown and nape, reddish lesser coverts, green rump. There are a number of similar races: see main text for differences in birds from Flores, the Kai and Aru Islands, S and SE New Guinea, Tanimbar, Huon Peninsula, N Australia, Fergusson, Misima and Tagula.

95b **Adult female** (*geoffroyi*) Brown head.

95c **Immature** (*geoffroyi*) Green head, paler bill.

95d **Adult male** (*cyanicollis*; Morotai, Halmahera, Bacan) Prominent blue collar, brownish wash on mantle, no reddish lesser coverts, underparts tinged blue.

95e **Adult female** (*cyanicollis*) Blue collar.

95f **Adult male** (*obiensis*; Obi) Broader blue collar, reddish patch on back.

95g **Adult female** (*obiensis*) Broad blue collar.

95h **Adult male** (*rhodops*; Ambon, Saparua, Boano, Haruku, Seram, Buru, Gorong, Manawoka) Darker and larger.

95i **Adult male** (*cyanicarpus*; Rossel) No red in lesser coverts, cheeks washed mauve, blue at bend of wing.

95j **Adult male** (*minor*, N New Guinea) Duller red rump than *jobiensis*, but more red in lesser coverts, bronze wash on mantle. Biak and Numfor race similar; see main text for differences.

95k **Adult male** (*jobiensis*; Yapen and Mios Num) Red of rump brighter than *minor*, red in lesser coverts paler, more red on forehead.

95l **Adult male** (*pucherani*; W Papuan islands and Vogelkop) Dark red rump, slight brown wash on mantle, darker blue underwing-coverts.

96 Blue-collared Parrot *Geoffroyus simplex* **Text and map page 309**

Generally common at 800-1,900m in submontane and montane forest in mainland New Guinea.

A medium-sized, fairly nondescript green parrot with blue underwing-coverts. Sexually dimorphic with two races.

96a **Adult male** (*simplex*; Vogelkop) Complete blue collar. Birds in rest of New Guinea have collar duller but more extensive at rear.

96b **Adult female** (*simplex*) Lacks collar; some blue on hindcrown.

96c **Immature** (*simplex*) Green head, pale bill.

97 Singing Parrot *Geoffroyus heteroclitus* **Text and map page 310**

Locally common in lowland and hill forests of the Bismarcks and Solomons.

Medium-sized green parrot with blue underwing-coverts, sexually dimorphic.

97a **Adult male** (*heteroclitus*; throughout range except Rennell Island) Grey collar, yellow head, yellow upper mandible.

97b **Adult female** (*heteroclitus*) Nondescript, grey crown, brownish cheeks, black bill.

97c **Adult male** (*hyacinthinus*; Rennell) Broader grey collar. Both sexes with blue primary coverts and bend of wing.

95c

95a

95b

95f

95g

95d

95e

95i

95h

95j

95k

95l

95l

95l

96a

96b

96c

96a

97a

97a

97b

97c

KHEF

PLATE 25: RACQUET-TAILS I

98 Montane Racquet-tail *Prioniturus montanus*   **Text and map page 311**

Mountain forests of Luzon, Philippines, above 700m.

Smallish green parrot with tail-racquets. Congeners on Luzon are Blue-crowned and Green Racquet-tails: former has a blue crown in both sexes, latter is much more yellowish-green with a blue, not green, uppertail.

     98a   **Adult male** Blue on crown and face, red crown spot.

     98b   **Adult female** Less blue on crown, lacks red crown spot.

     98c   **Immature** Lacks tail-racquets.

---

99 Mindanao Racquet-tail *Prioniturus waterstradti*   **Text and map page 311**

Confined to a small number of forested mountains on Mindanao, Philippines.

Green, bluer on face, olive wash on rump; flight feathers and tail blue below.

     99a   **Adult male** Mainly green with olive rump.

     99b   **Adult female** Like male but with shorter tail-extensions.

---

100 Blue-headed Racquet-tail *Prioniturus platenae*   **Text and map page 312**

Humid lowland forest and nearby cultivated areas of Palawan and associated islands, Philippines.

The only racquet-tail in Palawan.

     100a   **Adult male** All-blue head and obvious wash on underparts, blue underwing-coverts.

     100b   **Adult female** Lacks blue on underparts and less distinct blue suffusion on head. Shorter tail-extensions.

---

101 Green Racquet-tail *Prioniturus luconensis*   **Text and map page 313**

Lowland primary forest and nearby cultivated areas of Luzon and Marinduque, N Philippines.

Most yellowish-green racquet-tail, yellowest on face, bluish uppertail, underwing-coverts yellow-green, lateral tail feathers blue-green, bluish suffusion on underside of flight feathers. Sympatric with Blue-crowned and Montane Racquet-tails.

     101a   **Adult male** Yellowish-green with bluish tail.

     101b   **Adult female** Shorter tail-extensions.

---

103 Blue-winged Racquet-tail *Prioniturus verticalis*   **Text and map page 314**

Lowland forest and associated habitats of Sulu Archipelago, Philippines.

Yellow-green mantle, blue crown, blue wash on primaries, underwing-coverts green. Only member of its genus in range.

     103a   **Adult male** Red crown spot, yellow-green areas brighter.

     103b   **Adult female** No red crown spot, yellow-green areas duller.

98b

99b

98c

98a

99a

100a

101a

100b

101b

103b

103a

DAN POWELL.

104 Yellow-breasted Racquet-tail *Prioniturus flavicans*   Text and map page 315

Forest and trees in cultivated areas of N Sulawesi and nearby islands, Indonesia.

Both sexes with blue crown, light yellow mantle, blue in primaries and on underwing and undertail. Sympatric with Golden-mantled Racquet-tail, but looks heavier in flight. Male also lacks orange hind-collar, and greyish suffusion on mantle and wings. Female Golden-mantled lacks blue crown.

104a Adult male Crown blue, central red spot, mantle ochre-yellow.

104b Adult female Lacks red crown spot, underparts and mantle greener.

104c Immature Lacks tail-racquets.

105 Golden-mantled Racquet-tail *Prioniturus platurus*   Text and map page 316

Throughout Sulawesi and on some associated islands, Indonesia. Humid forest and associated habitats, commonest above 1,000m.

Sexually dimorphic with distinctively marked male showing red and blue crown (red lacking in Taliabu race), orange hind-collar, yellow in secondaries, and grey wash across upperparts. Sympatric with Yellow-breasted Racquet-tail (see above for differences) in N Sulawesi.

105a Adult male (*platurus*; Sulawesi) Red and blue crown with orange hind-collar.

105b Adult female (*platurus*) Lacks hind-collar and crown markings, and the grey wash is less distinct.

105c Adult male (*talautensis*; Talaud) Less grey above, more red and blue in crown.

105d Adult male (*sinerubris*; Taliabu) Lacks red in crown, upperparts less grey, bend of wing suffused violet.

102 Blue-crowned Racquet-tail *Prioniturus discurus*   Text and map page 313

Found throughout most of the Philippines in humid forest and associated habitats to 1,750m.

Green with blue crown, tail blue below and on outer feathers, underwing also marked blue. Sexes alike but female has shorter racquets.

102a Adult male (*discurus*; Jolo, Mindanao, Olutanga, Basilan, Guimaras and Luzon) The race occurring in Negros, Bohol, Samar, Leyte, Masbate and Cebu is similar, but has less blue in the crown. This blue is further reduced in birds from Tablas, Sibuyan and Catanduanes.

102b Adult female (*discurus*) Shorter tail-racquets.

102c Adult male (*mindorensis*; Mindoro) Green forecrown.

106 Buru Racquet-tail *Prioniturus mada*   Text and map page 316

Common in montane forest and nearby cultivation at 1,000-2,000m on Buru, Indonesia.

Sexually dimorphic with distinctive male showing dark blue on crown, nape, mantle and bend of wing. The only racquet-tail in Buru.

106a Adult male Dark blue crown, nape, mantle and shoulder.

106b Adult female Lacks blue on crown, nape and mantle; blue at bend of wing reduced; shorter racquets.

104b 104a 104c 105b 105a 105d 105c 102a 102c 106a 106b 106b 102b

DAN POWELL

PLATE 27: GREAT-BILLED AND BLUE-NAPED PARROTS

107 Great-billed Parrot *Tanygnathus megalorhynchos*   **Text and map page 317**

Moluccas and W Papuan islands, Indonesia. Relatively common in forest and secondary habitats to 1,000m.

Huge red bill, blue rump, wing-coverts boldly marked, with yellow underwing-coverts and tip to tail. Eight similar races which vary in size slightly; Sumba race largest.

107a   **Adult** (*megalorhynchos*; Halmahera, W Papuan islands) Mantle suffused blue, yellow-green below, inner lesser coverts and bend of wing black, yellow margins to median coverts. Buru, Seram, Ambon and Haruku race, and that from Babar and Tanimbar, similar (see main text for differences).

107b   **Immature** (*megalorhynchos*) Wing-coverts less strongly marked.

107c   **Adult** (*djampeae*; Kalao, Tanahjampea) Green primaries.

107d   **Adult** (*floris*; Flores) Underparts greener, less yellowish.

107e   **Adult** (*sumbensis*; Sumba) Darker green head, underwing-coverts greener, darker blue rump.

107f   **Adult** (*viridipennis*; Tukangbesi) Green flight feathers.

107g   **Adult male** (*hellmayri*; W Timor and Semau) Lighter green head, no blue on mantle, bend of wing green, narrower green margins to wing-coverts.

107h   **Adult female** (*hellmayri*) Duller wing-coverts.

108 Blue-naped Parrot *Tanygnathus lucionensis*   **Text and map page 318**

Talaud (Indonesia) and Philippine islands. Introduced to islands off NE Borneo and into N Sabah. Found in second growth and open habitats near forest.

Medium-sized green parrot with a blue crown, large red bill and reddish-brown edgings to wing-coverts.

108a   **Adult** (*lucionensis*; Luzon, Mindoro) Blue on lower back. Polillo race similar (see main text for differences).

108b   **Immature** (*lucionensis*) Less blue in crown, duller wing-coverts.

108c   **Adult** (*talautensis*; throughout range except for Luzon, Mindoro and Polillo) No blue on lower back.

107a

107a

107b

107a

107c

107d

107c

107f

107g

107h

108a

108b

108c

108a

108a

KHEF

PLATE 28: BLUE-BACKED, BLACK-LORED AND ECLECTUS PARROTS

109 Blue-backed Parrot *Tanygnathus sumatranus* **Text and map page 319**

Locally common in lowland and lower montane forest below 800m in Sulawesi, Sangir, Talaud, and the Philippines (where rarer).

No blue on head or in flight feathers; rump and bend of wing blue, underwing-coverts green, upperwing-coverts faintly edged yellowish. Sexually dimorphic with six races.

109a Adult male (*sumatranus*; Sulawesi) Light blue rump, no blue on mantle. Sangir and Talaud races similar (see text account for differences).

109b Adult female (*sumatranus*) Pale yellowish bill.

109c Adult male (*everetti*; Mindanao, Leyte, Samar, Negros and Panay) Iris red. Mantle darker green, suffused blue, darker blue rump. Luzon and Polillo races similar (see main text for differences).

---

110 Black-lored Parrot *Tanygnathus gramineus* **Text and map page 321**

Hill forests of Buru, where it is the only member of its genus. Almost totally unknown and at least partially nocturnal.

110 Adult male Fairly nondescript medium-sized parrot with black line to eye, bluish suffusion on crown. Female with grey-brown bill.

---

111 Eclectus Parrot *Eclectus roratus* **Text and map page 321**

Widespread and common from the Moluccas through New Guinea, Bismarcks, Solomons and into the Cape York Peninsula. Noisy and obvious in a range of habitats from forest to around villages.

Short tail and broad wings. Marked sexual dimorphism. Ten races, with racial differences more marked in females. One race, *westermani*, is known only from captive stock (see main text for description).

111a Adult male (*roratus*; Buru, Seram, Ambon, Saparua, Haruku) Green; red flanks and underwing-coverts, blue bend to wing, dark blue flight feathers, orange iris, red upper mandible tipped yellow.

111b Adult female (*roratus*) Red; purple on mantle, underparts and underwing-coverts, red undertail-coverts, black bill, yellowish iris.

111c Adult female (*vosmaeri*; N Moluccas) Larger with yellow undertail-coverts and broader yellow tip to tail.

111d Adult female (*cornelia*; Sumba) All red except for blue in wing and yellow tip to tail.

111e Adult male (*riedeli*; Tanimbar) Broad yellow tip to tail.

111f Adult female (*riedeli*) Like *cornelia* with yellow undertail-coverts.

111g Adult male (*polychloros*; W Papuan islands and New Guinea) More yellowish-green, green outer margin to outer primaries, narrow yellow tip to tail. Biak, Aru, Australian, and Bismarcks and Solomons races similar (see main text for differences).

111h Adult female (*polychloros*) Purple of upper and underparts bluer, green on outerwebs of primaries. Blue eye-ring.

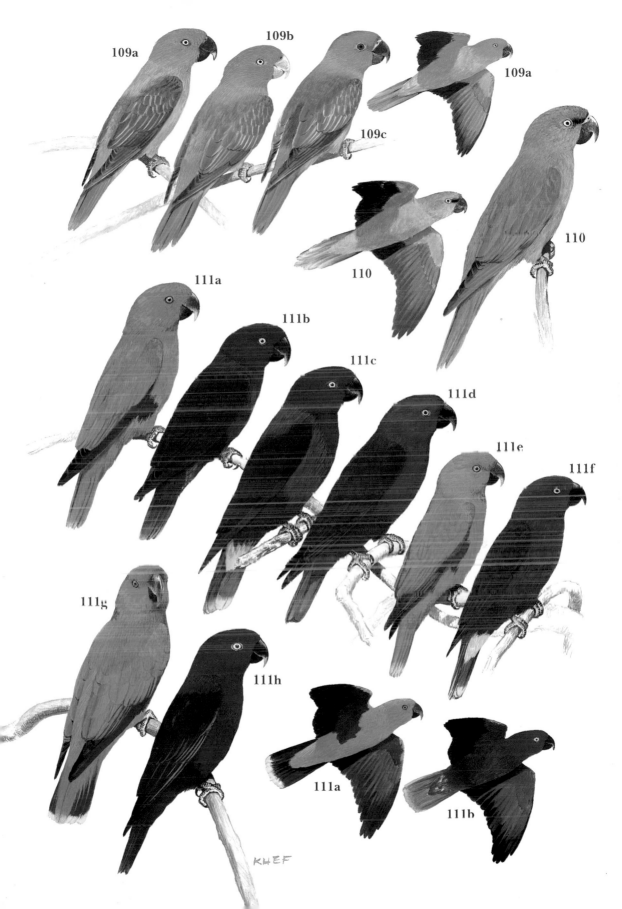

PLATE 29: SHINING AND KING PARROTS

113 Crimson Shining Parrot *Prosopeia splendens*　　　　**Text and map page 323**

Kadavu and Ono islands in the Fiji group. Introduced Viti Levu. Forest, farmlands and near habitation from lowlands to foothills.

113　**Adult** Green above, blue collar, blue in wing and at tip of long tail, red below.

---

115 Red Shining Parrot *Prosopeia tabuensis*　　　　**Text and map page 324**

Mature forest and associated habitats up to 1,750m, straying into village gardens, on Fiji group; introduced Eua, Tonga.

Green above with blue in wing and tail; dark maroon below. Four races.

115a　**Adult** (*tabuensis*; Gau in the Fiji group and 'Eua, Tonga) Few maroon feathers on rump, blue collar. Vanua Levu and Kioa race with broader blue collar and green rump; Taveuni, Qamea and Laucala race lacks blue collar.

115b　**Adult** (*koroensis*; Koro) Blue collar faint or lacking, obvious maroon rump, darker below.

---

114 Masked Shining Parrot *Prosopeia personata*　　　　**Text and map page 324**

Forested interior of Viti Levu, Fiji; occasionally in farmland.

114　**Adult** Green head with black suffusion on face. Yellow and orange below, blue wing-flash, staring red eye.

---

116 Australian King Parrot *Alisterus scapularis*　　　　**Text and map page 326**

Common in forest and associated habitats of E Australia inland to the western slope of the Great Dividing Range.

Medium-large long-tailed parrot with marked sexual dimorphism. Northern race is smaller but otherwise identical.

116a　**Adult male** Pinkish upper mandible and red head, blue where red of nape meets green of mantle, light green scapulars forming 'braces', dark blue rump, tail black above, red underparts, and black-based undertail-coverts.

116b　**Adult female** Black upper mandible and green head and breast, tail green above, green bases to undertail-coverts, pink tips to underside of tail feathers; lacks paler scapulars.

113

113

113

115a

115a

115b

114

114

114

116b

116a

114

116a

116b

KHEF

PLATE 30: KING PARROTS

117 Moluccan King Parrot *Alisterus amboinensis* **Text and map page 327**

Dense forest and occasionally adjacent farmland in Moluccas, W Papuan islands, and W New Guinea, Indonesia. Lowlands to 2,000m.

Long-tailed parrot with brilliant red head and underparts. There are six races.

117a Adult (*amboinensis*; Ambon and Seram) Blue upperparts, green wings, pink webs to outer tail feathers.

117b Immature (*amboinensis*) Green on mantle, brownish bill, pink tips to tail feathers.

117c Adult male (*sulaensis*; Sula Islands) No pink webs to tail feathers, upper mantle green. Peleng race similar but no green on mantle.

117d Adult female (*sulaensis*) Green mantle and green suffusion on breast.

117e Adult (*buruensis*; Buru) Bill completely black, green suffusion on back, pink webs to tail feathers.

117f Adult male (*hypophonius*; Halmahera) Wings entirely dark blue. No pink webs on tail.

117g Adult male (*dorsalis*; W Papuan islands and W New Guinea) Like nominate but lacks pink webs to tail.

118 Papuan King Parrot *Alisterus chloropterus* **Text and map page 328**

N and SE New Guinea in dense forest from sea-level to 2,800m.

A long-tailed, brightly coloured parrot with three races, two of which exhibit strong sexual dimorphism.

118a Adult male (*chloropterus*: SE New Guinea) Red head and underparts, blue rump and nape, black mantle, dark blue uppertail, bright yellow-green flash in wing-coverts.

118b Adult female (*chloropterus*) Green upperparts, head and breast; blue rump, blackish uppertail.

118c Adult male (*callopterus*; C New Guinea) Blue does not extend up nape, more green in mantle.

118d Adult female (*moszkowskii*; N New Guinea) Female largely similar to male, but with green mantle. Male like nominate but with more blue in mantle. Both sexes can show pink tips to tail feathers.

117b

117a

117e

117a

117c

117a

117d

117a

117f

117g

118a

118a

118b

118b

118a

118b

118c

118d

KHEF

119 Olive-shouldered Parrot *Aprosmictus jonquillaceus*   Text and map page 329

Relatively common from forest to savanna and from sea level to 2,600m on the islands of Timor, Wetar and Roti, Indonesia.

Medium-sized green parrot with blue rump and red on wing-coverts.

119a **Adult male** (*jonquillaceus*; Timor and Roti) Blue suffusion on back, blue bend of wing and rump, wing-coverts marked yellow-green and red.

119b **Adult female** (*jonquillaceus*) No strong blue suffusion on mantle; wing-coverts green and red.

119c **Adult** (*wetterensis*: Wetar) Wing-coverts green, not yellowish-green, with less red.

120 Red-winged Parrot *Aprosmictus erythropterus*   Text and map page 329

S New Guinea and N and E Australia, where common in riverine woodland, savanna, farmland and forest edge.

Striking parrot with a blue rump, green head and underparts and red wing markings. Sexually dimorphic with two similar races.

120a **Adult male** (*erythropterus*; E Australia) Black mantle, blue suffusion on nape, red wing-coverts. N Australia and New Guinea race has more blue on crown and nape.

120b **Adult female** (*erythropterus*) No blue on nape; mantle green, less red in wing, rump duller blue. Similar to (allopatric) female Olive-shouldered Parrot, but outerwebs of outer secondaries black not green.

121 Superb Parrot *Polytelis swainsonii*   Text and map page 331

SE Australia (New South Wales and N Victoria), in open eucalypt or riverine woodland.

Smallish long-tailed parrot with marked sexual dimorphism. Breeding habitat varies from east to west. Part of the population is migratory.

121a **Adult male** Brilliant green, yellow face and red band across throat. Elongated central tail feathers with bulbous tip.

121b **Adult female** Mainly green, pinkish-brown suffusion on throat, blue-grey ear-coverts and crown, orange-red thighs, pinkish webs in tail.

122 Regent Parrot *Polytelis anthopeplus*   Text and map page 332

Riverine woodland, farmland and scrub in SE and SW Australia. Bright yellow, green, black and reddish; sexually dimorphic with two races.

122a **Adult male** (*anthopeplus*; SW Australia) Bright yellow; green mantle, reddish inner wing-coverts and tertials, blue-black flight feathers and tail. SE Australian race is similar but brighter yellow.

122b **Adult female** (*anthopeplus*) Like male but greener above and greyer below, pink webs to tail feathers, bend of wing dull blue.

124 Red-capped Parrot *Purpureicephalus spurius*   Text and map page 334

Distinctive parrot of wetter marri forests in extreme SW Australia, entering more open habitats outside the breeding season.

124a **Adult male** Red cap, yellow-green face, green above, dull blue below, brilliant red thighs and undertail-coverts.

124b **Adult female** Similar to male, but slightly duller brownish breast, some green in crown, paler red thighs.

124c **Immature** Green head, duller underparts, wing-bar.

123 Alexandra's Parrot *Polytelis alexandrae*   Text and map page 333

Arid interior of west-central Australia. Nomadic in a range of habitats from sandy desert to riverine woodland in dry areas.

Attractive pastel-hued parrot with extremely elongated tail and spatule tips to primaries in male.

123a **Adult male** Blue crown, pink face, yellow-green wing-coverts, blue rump.

123b **Adult female** Little blue on crown, lacks brighter green suffusion on mantle, dull blue rump, pink webs to tail feathers.

119c

120b

119a

119b

120a

121b

120a

121a

122b

122a

124a

124b

123a

124c

123b

KHEF

PLATE 32: RINGNECKS AND WESTERN ROSELLA

125 Port Lincoln Ringneck *Barnardius zonarius*   **Text and map page 335**

Widespread and common in a range of habitats through W, C and S Australia.

Dark green with a dark blue head, yellow hind-collar, dark blue primaries and whitish outer tail feathers. Three races.

> **125a Adult male** (*zonarius*; C and S Australia) Yellow belly.
>
> **125b Adult female** (*zonarius*) Similar to male but duller.
>
> **125c Adult male** (*semitorquatus*; extreme SW Australia) Larger, green belly, red frontal area.
>
> **125d Adult female** (*semitorquatus*) Similar to male but duller. Most show wing-bars.
>
> **125e Adult** (*occidentalis*; NW Australia) Smaller and paler with a larger, paler yellow belly-patch.

126 Mallee Ringneck *Barnardius barnardi*   **Text and map page 337**

E Australia west of the Great Dividing Range, in arid mallee, riverine woodland and scrubby areas.

Less strikingly marked than Port Lincoln Ringneck. Yellow hind-collar, dark blue-green mantle, red frontal area, wing-coverts marked yellow, yellow belly-patch, bluish cheeks. Two races, and one hybrid population (*barnardi* x *zonarius*) in the Flinders Range region.

> **126a Adult male** (*barnardi*; SE Australia) Dark blue-green mantle, red frontal area, yellow belly marked slightly with orange.
>
> **126b Adult female** (*barnardi*) Generally less strongly marked, greener mantle; normally shows a wing-bar.
>
> **126c Immature** (*barnardi*) Duller with reduced head markings.
>
> **126d Adult** (*macgillivrayi*; interior of NW Queensland and nearby Northern Territory) Much paler, large yellow belly-patch, no red frontal band.
>
> **126e Adult** (*barnardi* x *zonarius*; Flinders Range) Larger yellow belly-patch than nominate *barnardi*, greyish-brown crown, lighter mantle than nominate *barnardi*, less yellow in wing-coverts.

133 Western Rosella *Platycercus icterotis*   **Text and map page 346**

Common in a range of habitats in Western Australia, including towns and suburban gardens.

Bright yellow cheeks, green fringes to dark-centred mantle feathers, males bright red on head and underparts. Females and young with less red. Two similar races.

> **133a Adult male** (*icterotis*; extreme SW Australia) Bright red head and underparts, red fringes to mantle feathers.
>
> **133b Adult female** (*icterotis*) Green mottling on head and green on underparts, especially breast and flanks; wing-bar.
>
> **133c Immature** (*icterotis*) Lacks yellow cheek-patch; some red on underparts; wing-bar.
>
> **133d Adult male** (*xanthogenys*; occurs in drier inland areas of SW Australia) Paler than nominate, with more red edgings on greyer mantle.

PLATE 33: ROSELLAS

128 Crimson Rosella *Platycercus elegans* — Text and map page 339

Widespread in coastal E Australia in forested areas east of the Great Diving Range. Introduced Norfolk Island and New Zealand. Three races; distinctive immature plumage.

128a **Adult** (*elegans*; SE Queensland, E New South Wales, Victoria, SE South Australia) Dark red; blue cheek-patch, black centres to mantle feathers.

128b **Immature** (*elegans*) Mostly green, some red markings; wing-bar.

128c **Adult** (*nigrescens*; NE Queensland) Darker, narrower red margins to mantle feathers.

129 Yellow Rosella *Platycercus flaveolus* — Text and map page 340

Timbered watercourses of SE Australia including NSW, N Victoria and SE South Australia.

129a **Adult male** Pale yellow below, blue cheek-patch, red on forehead, two-tone blue wings, yellow fringes on mantle.

129b **Adult female** Can show wing-bar.

129c **Immature** Generally dull yellowish-green, some red on forehead.

129X Adelaide Rosella *Platycercus elegans x P. flaveolus* — Text and map page 341

Mount Lofty and Flinders Ranges, SE South Australia, including Adelaide.

129x **Adult** Intermediate between Crimson and Yellow Rosellas. Mainly orange-red with yellowish margins to mantle. Two populations, southern birds paler. Considerable variation between individuals.

127 Green Rosella *Platycercus caledonicus* — Text and map page 338

Tasmania and islands in the Bass Strait in a range of habitats from rainforest to montane forest and more open country, orchards and gardens.

127a **Adult male** Red forehead, blue cheek-patch, dark above (green margins), yellow below.

127b **Adult female** Orange wash on breast; can show a wing-bar.

130 Northern Rosella *Platycercus venustus* — Text and map page 342

N Australia in WA, NT, and E Queensland, in savanna, riverine woodland and farmland.

130a **Adult** Black cap, white and blue cheeks, creamy-yellow plumage with black feather centres, pale scapulars forming 'braces', red undertail-coverts, blue in wing and blue-green tail.

130b **Immature** Shows wing-bar, some red flecking on crown.

131 Pale-headed Rosella *Platycercus adscitus* — Text and map page 343

E Australia from Cape York Peninsula south to New South Wales in a variety of habitats from open woodland to farmland and coastal heath.

Pale head, upperparts pale yellow with black feather-centres, blue below, red undertail-coverts. Two races, intergrading where the ranges meet.

131a **Adult** (*adscitus*; Cape York and NE Queensland) Blue on cheek, blue belly, dark scalloping on breast, yellowish rump.

131b **Immature** (*adscitus*) Wing-bar, some red on crown.

131c **Adult** (*palliceps*; NE Queensland south to New South Wales) Light blue wash on rump, white cheek, blue on unbarred underparts extending up to breast, brighter yellow above.

132 Eastern Rosella *Platycercus eximius* — Text and map page 344

SE Australia from SE Queensland through NSW to Victoria, and SE South Australia. Also Tasmania and introduced to New Zealand. Farmland, riverine woodland and suburban gardens.

Brilliant red head, white cheek, scalloped yellow upperparts, green rump and blue-tipped tail. Slight sexual dimorphism; three races.

132a **Adult male** (*eximius*; New South Wales to SE South Australia).

132b **Adult female** (*eximius*) Greener above, especially on nape; wing-bar.

132c **Immature** (*eximius*) Greener on nape and upperparts; wing-bar.

132d **Adult** (*elecica*; S Queensland to New South Wales) Brighter yellow above, blue-green rump.

132e **Adult** (*diemenensis*; Tasmania) Larger white cheek-patch, more red on head and breast.

129x
129x
129c
128c
128a
128b
129b
129c
129a
127a
127b
130b
130a
131a
131b
131c
132a
132b
132d
132e
132c

KHEF

134 Bluebonnet *Northiella haematogaster* **Text and map page 346**

SE Western Australia and SE Australia, in open and riverine woodland, farmland.
Western birds in arid mulga.

Generally greyish-olive; blue face, blue in wing and tail, red and yellow below, blue bend to wing and underwing-coverts. Slight sexual dimorphism; four races.

134a **Adult male** (*haematogaster*; South Australia, Victoria, S New South Wales, S Queensland) Yellow belly marked red, yellow undertail-coverts.

134b **Adult female** (*haematogaster*) Less blue in face; wing-bar.

134c **Immature** (*haematogaster*) Less red below; wing-bar.

134d **Adult** (*haematorrhous*; east-central New South Wales, south-central Queensland) Reddish chestnut wing-coverts, red undertail-coverts.

134e **Adult** (*pallescens*; Lake Eyre region of South Australia) Paler, less red below, more yellowish wing-coverts.

134f **Adult male** (*narethae*; Nullarbor Plain, Western Australia) No red on belly; outer lesser coverts red-orange, red undertail-coverts, male with brighter blue face.

134g **Adult female** (*narethae*) Duller, especially face and wing-coverts.

135 Red-rumped Parrot *Psephotus haematonotus* **Text and map page 348**

Common in drier parts of SE Australia from South Australia through Victoria, New South Wales and S Queensland. Open and riverine woodland, grassland, parks and roadsides.

Smallish, mainly green parrot with brightly marked males and duller females. Two races.

135a **Adult male** (*haematonotus*; SE Australia) Mainly green, yellow belly and shoulder-patch, red rump.

135b **Adult female** (*haematonotus*) Much duller, mainly greyish green, green rump; wing-bar.

135c **Immature** (*haematonotus*) Obvious wing-bar.

135d **Adult male** (*caeruleus*; Lake Eyre Region of South Australia) Paler, less yellow on belly, paler red rump; bluer, especially around head.

135e **Adult female** (*caeruleus*) Generally more greyish than nominate, whitish belly.

134b

134c

134a

134d

134e

134f

134g

135a

135c

135a

135b

135d

135e

KHEF

136 Mulga Parrot *Psephotus varius*   **Text and map page 349**

Widespread and common in S Australia from wheat belt, Western Australia, east to the Great Dividing Range. Dry open woodland and plains.

Small, slender, brightly coloured parrot. Sexually dimorphic.

136a Adult male Yellow frontal band and shoulder-patch, red hind crown, green mantle and breast, red belly, yellow undertail-coverts; light turquoise-green, red and green rump.

136b Adult female Much duller than male; greyish mantle, brownish breast, russet shoulder-patch, belly pale green, paler band on rump; wing-bar.

136c Immature male Like adult male but greyish mantle, lighter rump-band; wing-bar.

136d Immature female Lacks yellow frontal band; duller and more greyish than female, paler rump-band.

137 Hooded Parrot *Psephotus dissimilis*   **Text and map page 350**

W Arnhem Land, Northern Territory, Australia, mainly in open woodland and spinifex grassland.

Male very striking, female similar to Golden-shouldered Parrot.

137a Adult male Black cap, blackish-brown mantle, yellow wing-coverts, red undertail-coverts, bright turquoise underparts.

137b Adult female Generally yellowish-green; bluish cheeks, rump and suffusion on under parts, pink vent and undertail-coverts; wing-bar.

138 Golden-shouldered Parrot *Psephotus chrysopterygius*   **Text and map page 351**

Cape York Peninsula, Queensland, Australia, in mixed open woodland and grassland along edges of partly inundated drainage depressions.

Like Hooded Parrot but male with browner mantle, less yellow in wing, yellow frontal band and red belly, female separable on undertail-coverts.

138a Adult male Bright turquoise below, grey-brown mantle, black cap.

138b Adult female Like female Hooded Parrot, but reddish on belly not undertail-coverts, and greener cheeks.

138c Immature male Shows wing-bar in common with female.

139 Paradise Parrot *Psephotus pulcherrimus*   **Text and map page 353**

Formerly SE Queensland and NE New South Wales. No records since 1927. Occurred in open grassy woodland with terrestrial termitaria.

Blackish crown, reddish frontal band, blue-green rump. Sexually dimorphic.

139a Adult male Black cap, bright red frontal band, turquoise-blue face, more greenish below, red belly, red on wing-coverts.

139b Adult female Buffish face and breast, less red on wing-coverts, less red on belly and forehead; wing-bar.

147 Bourke's Parrot *Neophema bourkii*   **Text and map page 360**

Locally common in drier areas of inland Australia from Western Australia through Northern Territory to Queensland and New South Wales, favouring mulga and *Eucalyptus* woodland and scrub.

A small brownish parrot with pinkish underparts and blue undertail-coverts and wing markings.

147a Adult male Forehead blue, underparts strongly marked pink.

147b Adult female Lacks blue forehead, duller pink below; wing-bar.

147c Immature Duller than female with less pink below; wing-bar.

136d

136b

136c

136a

136a

137a

137b

137a

137b

138b

138c

138b

138a

138a

139b

139a

147b

147c

147a

147b

147a

KHEF

PLATE 36: *CYANORAMPHUS* AND *EUNYMPHICUS* PARAKEETS

140 Antipodes Green Parakeet *Cyanoramphus unicolor*   Text and map page 354

Antipodes Island and nearby islets, in dense tussock, scrub and sedgeland.

140   **Adult** Generally green with brighter green facial area, no red in plumage, blue in flight feathers.

141 Norfolk Island Parakeet *Cyanoramphus cookii*   Text and map page 354

Mount Pitt Reserve, Norfolk Island (Australia). Rain-forest with Norfolk Island pines.

141   **Adult** Like Red-fronted Parakeet, but larger and heavier-billed, with red extending further back on crown, red on ear-coverts forming a patch rather than a continuation of the eye stripe. Red on flanks, blue wing-flash. Female has pale wing-bar (sometimes present in male).

142 Red-fronted Parakeet *Cyanoramphus novaezelandiae*   Text and map page 355

New Zealand and outlying islands. Habitat varies with food availability: forest, tussock scrub and even (in the Kermadecs) intertidal areas.

Green; blue in wing, red crown and eye-stripe, red flank spot. Female has pale wing-bar (sometimes present in male).

142a   **Adult** (*novaezelandiae*; New Zealand, offshore islands and the Auckland Islands) Chatham Island race similar (see main text for differences).

142b   **Adult** (*cyanurus*; Kermadec Islands) More blue in wing, bluish tail.

142c   **Adult** (*hochstetteri*; Antipodes Island) Larger, more yellowish-green, red markings more orange, blue in wing less obvious.

143 New Caledonian Parakeet *Cyanoramphus saisseti*   Text and map page 357

Montane forests of New Caledonia.

143   **Adult** Like Red-fronted Parakeet, but more yellowish-green, notably on underparts and supercilium. Female has pale wing-bar (sometimes present in male).

144 Yellow-fronted Parakeet *Cyanoramphus auriceps*   Text and map page 358

New Zealand and some offshore islands, principally in forest ecosystems, especially beech forests; dense scrub on Chatham Islands.

Like Red-fronted Parakeet but red on head restricted to forehead and lores; yellow crown, blue in wing, red flank spot. Female has pale wing-bar (sometimes present in male).

144a   **Adult** (*auriceps*; New Zealand, offshore islands and Auckland Islands).

144b   **Adult** (orange-fronted morph) Orange (not red) forehead. Crown yellow.

144c   **Adult** (*forbesi*; Chatham Islands) Larger, heavier-billed, brighter green above, more yellowish below, greener face, reduced red on forehead.

145 Horned Parakeet *Eunymphicus cornutus*   Text and map page 359

Humid forest, second growth and savanna woodland on New Caledonia.

145   **Adult** No red flank spot, bright yellowish nape, red forecrown, black in face, wispy backward-pointing crest tipped red, blue in wing.

146 Uvea Parakeet *Eunymphicus uvaeensis*   Text and map page 360

Mature forests on Uvea immediately north of C New Caledonia.

146   **Adult** Like Horned Parakeet, but crest forward-curling without red tips, less black on mainly green face, nape green, not bright yellowish-green.

140

140

141

141

142a

142a

142b

142c

143

143

144c

145

144b

144a

144a

145

146

KHEF

PLATE 37: *NEOPHEMA* PARROTS

148   Blue-winged Parrot *Neophema chrysostoma*   Text and map page 361

Breeds Tasmania and SE Australia, with Tasmanian birds crossing to mainland after nesting. Mainly grassy habitats from sea-level to 1,200m.

> **148a**   **Adult male** Small longish-tailed olive-green parrot with dark blue wing-coverts (more extensive than in Elegant Parrot) and a two-tone blue frontal band which just reaches the eye.
>
> **148b**   **Adult female** Duller; often with a wing-bar.

149   Elegant Parrot *Neophema elegans*   Text and map page 362

Open woodland and savanna in two disjunct populations in SE and SW Australia.

Small olive-yellow parrot, similar to, but brighter than Blue-winged Parrot.

> **149a**   **Adult male** Two-tone blue in wing (less blue than Blue-winged on coverts), blue frontal band passes through eye, more yellowish rump.
>
> **149b**   **Adult female** Duller; often with a wing-bar.
>
> **149c**   **Immature** No frontal band; usually with a wing-bar.

150   Rock Parrot *Neophema petrophila*   Text and map page 363

Breeds on rocky islands, wintering on nearby coast of W and S Australia; rarely more than a few miles from the sea.

The dullest member of the genus, similar to Blue-winged Parrot.

> **150a**   **Adult male** More extensive blue on lores (blue passes through eye), less blue in wing.
>
> **150b**   **Adult female** Less blue in face; sometimes with wing-bar.
>
> **150c**   **Immature** No frontal band; often with wing-bar.

151   Orange-bellied Parrot *Neophema chrysogaster*   Text and map page 364

Nests along forested margin of W Tasmanian coastal plain, migrating north across the Bass Strait to winter on coastal saltmarshes, especially in Port Phillip Bay, Victoria.

Darker and greener than the three previous species with greenish lores (not yellow or blue), orange belly-patch (other *Neophema* species can at times show this feature), tail green above; stocky build.

> **151a**   **Adult male** Greenish lores; orange belly-patch.
>
> **151b**   **Adult female** One-tone frontal band, smaller belly-patch; sometimes with wing-bar.
>
> **151c**   **Immature** Frontal band indistinct; often with wing-bar.

152   Turquoise Parrot *Neophema pulchella*   Text and map page 365

Grassland, scrub, wooded creeks and farmland in Australia east of the Great Dividing Range from Queensland through NSW into Victoria.

Small, brightly coloured parrot, green above, yellow below, with blue face and wing markings. Sexual dimorphism more evident than in previous species.

> **152a**   **Adult male** Reddish inner lesser and median coverts, yellow breast, extensive blue on face.
>
> **152b**   **Adult female** Lacks red in wing-coverts, less (and lighter) blue on face, green breast, whitish lores; wing-bar.
>
> **152c**   **Immature** Like female, but male has more blue on face, and some red in wing-coverts.

153   Scarlet-chested Parrot *Neophema splendida*   Text and map page 366

Arid mallee and mulga, irrupting from Great Victoria Desert region, Western Australia, into other states.

Like Turquoise Parrot, but male has scarlet breast, no red in wing-coverts, lighter blue median and greater coverts, darker blue chin and lores. Female has bluer face and lighter wing-coverts.

> **153a**   **Adult male** Scarlet breast, dark blue in face.
>
> **153b**   **Adult female** Greenish breast, face paler blue; usually with wing-bar.
>
> **153c**   **Immature** Similar to female but less blue on face.

PLATE 38: BUDGERIGAR AND COCKATIEL; SWIFT, NIGHT AND GROUND PARROTS

155   Budgerigar *Melopsittacus undulatus*   Text and map page 368

Widely distributed, and locally abundant in the interior of Australia. Absent from Tasmania and generally from coastal areas, especially the eastern seaboard and Cape York Peninsula. One of the world's most familiar birds; introduced in a number of other countries.

Yellow forehead, scalloped upperparts, green below, underwing-bar, blue tail, purple and black markings on cheek. Caged varieties vary in colour.

    155a   Adult Scalloped upperparts with plain yellow forehead.

    155b   Immature Forehead also scalloped.

---

154   Swift Parrot *Lathamus discolor*   Text and map page 367

Breeds in Tasmania, migrating to SE Australian mainland after nesting. Some birds remain in Tasmania year-round. Breeds in forest; found in flowering trees in a variety of habitats at other times.

Recalls a lorikeet; generally green, with blue in wing, blue forecrown, red and yellow throat, red tail.

    154a   Adult Red underwing-coverts and undertail-coverts. No wing-bar.

    154b   Immature Shows wing-bar.

---

75   Cockatiel *Nymphicus hollandicus*   Text and map page 289

Widespread throughout interior Australia in many habitats.

Slim grey parrot with erectile crest, yellow face, orange ear-covert patch and white wing-flash. A common cagebird bred to various mutations.

    75a   Adult male Yellow face, unbarred rump and tail.

    75b   Adult female Barred tail, rump and underside to flight feathers, duller face.

---

156   Ground Parrot *Pezoporus wallicus*   Text and map page 369

Coastal SW and SE Australia; Tasmania. Heath and sedgeland.

A bright green but cryptically marked parrot that skulks in low-lying vegetation. Very long green tail, obvious wing-bar, reddish frontal area.

    156a   Adult (*wallicus*; SE Australia and Tasmania) South-western race similar with a yellower belly.

    156b   Immature (*wallicus*) Lacks orange-red forehead; brown iris.

---

157   Night Parrot *Geopsittacus occidentalis*   Text and map page 371

Arid interior of Australia; terrestrial, nocturnal and nomadic, at very low densities. Rivals the Kakapo as one of the most difficult birds to see in the world. Very few recent records, all from the Cloncurry region.

    157   Adult Cryptically marked green parrot with an unmarked yellow belly, shorter, browner tail and less distinct wing-bar than Ground Parrot, no red-orange frontal area.

155b

155a

155a

154a

154b

154a

75a

75b

75b

75a

156b

156a

156a

157

157

KHEF

PLATE 39: VASA, BLACK AND GREY PARROTS

159 Vasa Parrot *Coracopsis vasa* **Text and map page 374**

Madagascar and Grand Comoro, Mohéli and Anjouan in the Comoro Islands. Wide range of wooded habitats from forest to cultivated areas with trees.

Large brownish-black parrot with rounded tail and stout pale pinkish bill (dark grey outside breeding season). Larger and paler than Black Parrot, with grey-brown rather than dark brown legs.

159a **Adult** (*vasa*; E Madagascar) Generally brownish-black with a faint paler greyish tinge on upperparts, especially the wings and uppertail. Intermediates with *drouhardi* are found in SW and NW Madagascar. Breeding female (not illustrated) may become bald on head, around eyes and throat, with exposed skin becoming mustard-yellow or orange.

159b **Immature** (*vasa*) From adult by paler grey-brown plumage and paler, less extensive (or even absent) bare skin around eyes.

159c **Adult** (*drouhardi*; W Madagascar) Smaller and paler than nominate. Underparts greyer with undertail-coverts appearing whitish; upperparts show distinct grey-blue tinge. Dark subterminal band on tail.

159d **Adult** (*comorensis*; Grand Comoro, Mohéli and Anjouan in the Comoro Islands) Smaller and paler than nominate but, unlike *drouhardi*, underparts tinged chocolate-brown rather than grey, and undertail-coverts brown (not grey or whitish). Greyer bill.

160 Black Parrot *Coracopsis nigra* **Text and map page 374**

Madagascar, Comoro Islands (Grand Comoro and Anjouan) and Praslin (Seychelles). Variety of wooded habitats.

Almost uniform dark blackish-brown with stout pale bill (darker outside breeding season). More uniformly dark plumage than Vasa Parrot.

160a **Adult** (*nigra*; E Madagascar) Blackish-brown with inconspicuous greyish markings on undertail-coverts and grey outerwebs to primaries. Underside of flight feathers pale grey. Iridescent green sheen during breeding season. Dark subterminal band on tail.

160b **Immature** (*nigra*) Paler than adult with pale undertail-coverts and yellowish tinge on bill and pale grey tips to tail. Buff edges to wing-coverts may separate some immatures.

160c **Adult** (*libs*; W Madagascar) Paler than nominate; underparts browner, upperparts tinted with blue-grey. No dark subterminal band on tail.

160d **Adult** (*barklyi*; Praslin in Seychelles) Greyish-blue reflections in outerwebs of primaries. Some *barklyi* show paler undertail-coverts than body plumage.

161 Grey Parrot *Psittacus erithacus* **Text and map page 375**

West and Central Africa. Mainly in primary and secondary lowland rainforest, forest edge, clearings, gallery forest and mangroves.

Large grey parrot with striking short scarlet tail.

161a **Adult** (*erithacus*; equatorial Africa from SE Côte d'Ivoire to W Kenya, NW Tanzania, S Zaïre and N Angola) Grey with red tail. Silvery belly, underwing-coverts and rump. Breast, mantle and upperwing-coverts slate-grey with primaries very dark grey. Facial area whitish.

161b **Immature** (*erithacus*) Tail darker red towards tip, grey tinge on undertail-coverts and grey iris.

161c **Adult** (*timneh*; West Africa from Guinea-Bissau east to Côte d'Ivoire to at least 70km east of the Bandama River) Darker and smaller than nominate; red of tail more maroon than scarlet. Uppertail-coverts grey tinged with red (not scarlet); upper mandible reddish tipped black.

159a

159c

159b

159a

159d

160a

160a

160b

160c

160d

161a

161c

161c

161a

161b

KHEF

PLATE 40: *POICEPHALUS* PARROTS I

162 Brown-necked Parrot *Poicephalus robustus*   Text and map page 376

Probably occupies three separate ranges in west, south-central and southern Africa. Habitat includes mangroves, riverine woodlands, savanna woodland and montane forests to 3,750m. Nominate race favours *Acacia mearnsii* and *Podocarpus* forest at 1,000-1,700m.

Bulky parrot with top-heavy appearance due to large head and bill and short tail. Bill has long fine tip. Dull olive-brown head and neck, dull green wing-coverts contrasting with grass-green underparts and rump, and orange-red on bend of wing and thighs.

162a **Adult male** (*robustus*; extreme SE Africa mainly in Cape Province, Natal and Transvaal, South Africa) Brown neck and head with large bill distinctive. Brown contrasts with green beneath. Red at bend of wing but not on head.

162b **Adult female** (*robustus*) Usually with well-defined orange-red frontal band.

162c **Immature** (*robustus*) No orange-red markings on wing-coverts or thighs but believed always to show some red on forehead.

162d **Adult male** (*fuscicollis*; Gambia and S Senegal to N Ghana and Togo) Like nominate but head and neck silvery. Broader edges to coverts and scapulars give greener appearance.

162e **Adult female** (*fuscicollis*) Similar to nominate female but with silvery neck and more extensive red on head forming cap.

163 Jardine's Parrot *Poicephalus gulielmi*   Text and map page 378

Disjunct ranges in West Africa, west-central Africa, Central Africa and highlands of East Africa. Mainly sedentary but some local movements. In Kenya and Tanzania frequents montane *Juniperus* and *Podocarpus* forest at 1,800-3,250m; elsewhere confined to lowland, but not necessarily primary, rainforest.

Red or orange markings on forehead, leading edge of wings and thighs. From similar-sized, partly sympatric Brown-headed Parrot by green head and neck, darker green body, relatively small, dark bill and yellow-green rump.

163a **Adult** (*gulielmi*; S Cameroon south to NW Angola and east to Uganda and Rwanda) Fairly large, mainly green parrot with red on head, leading edge of wings and thighs.

163b **Immature** (*gulielmi*) No red on forehead, leading edge of wings and thighs. Sometimes red in underwing-coverts. Feathers on forehead buffish tipped green. Green in plumage slightly paler than adult.

163c **Adult** (*fantiensis*; West Africa from Liberia to Ghana) Forehead, leading edge of wings and thighs orange or orange-red and more extensive than nominate, at least in some birds. Underparts paler green with fewer black markings.

163d **Adult** (*massaicus*; both sides of Great Rift Valley from Mount Elgon, Kenya, south to N Tanzania) Red restricted to forehead. A little paler than nominate with fewer (if any) black markings below.

164 Senegal Parrot *Poicephalus senegalus*   Text and map page 379

West Africa, from Guinea to Cameroon and SW Chad. Mostly sedentary but seasonal visitor especially in north of range in wet season.

Rather small with short tail, grey head and yellow, orange or red belly. Only common short-tailed parrot inhabiting the forest mosaic and savanna woodlands of West Africa.

164a **Adult** (*senegalus*; Senegal to Burkina Faso and N Nigeria, where it intergrades with *versteri*) Mainly green above, silvery head, green breast-patch, mainly yellow underparts and orange axillaries and underwing-coverts.

164b **Immature** (*senegalus*) dull brown head without silvery ear-coverts. Some show extensive green on underparts.

164c **Adult** (*versteri*; Ivory Coast and Ghana to W Nigeria) Orange-red patch on centre of lower breast and belly. Upperparts darker green than nominate.

162b

162a

162a

162d

162c

162e

163a

163a

163c

163b

163d

164b

164a

164a

164c

KHEF

166 Meyer's Parrot *Poicephalus meyeri*　　　　Text and map page 380

Large range in western, central, eastern and southern Africa. Occurs in lowland wooded habitats from dry savanna to riparian woodlands and secondary growth, but avoiding more humid formations. Generally near water; occasionally in suburban areas.

Small. Only parrot in Africa showing combination of extensive blue or blue-green on underparts and blue or blue-green rump on otherwise ashy-brown upperparts.

166a **Adult** (*meyeri*; NE Cameroon to W Ethiopia) Ashy greyish-brown above and on head and neck, with greenish belly tending to blue on breast and rump. Yellow on carpal area, underwing-coverts and thighs and in transverse bar on head.

166b **Immature** (*meyeri*) Generally more greenish-brown than adult. No yellow on crown or thighs and yellow on upperwing surfaces less extensive. Underwing-coverts green and brown with little or no yellow. Underparts more greenish. Iris dark brown.

166c **Adult** (*matschiei*; SE Kenya to N Zambia and E Angola) Green areas bluer than nominate beneath and on rump.

166d **Adult** (*transvaalensis*; N and C Mozambique to NE Botswana and W Transvaal) Paler brown than *P. m. matschiei*, bluer still on rump and below. Yellow on crown often reduced, sometimes lacking.

167 Yellow-faced Parrot *Poicephalus flavifrons*　　　　Text and map page 382

Endemic to the highlands of W Ethiopia. Chiefly in *Juniperus* and *Podocarpus* forests at 1,800-2,900m, mainly in *Hagenia* above 2,900m. Also light woodlands in cultivated country, gallery and riverine forests from about 300m. Sometimes visits urban parks and gardens.

Only medium-sized parrot regularly encountered within most of its restricted highland range. Overlaps with Orange-bellied Parrot in south (Rift Valley) and with Meyer's Parrot in north and possibly south-west.

167a **Adult** Mainly green with striking yellow mask that often shows orange wash. Dark upper, paler lower mandible.

167b **Immature** Like adult but mask dull yellowish olive-green, not yellow.

168 Red-bellied Parrot *Poicephalus rufiventris*　　　　Text and map page 383

NE Tanzania, E and N Kenya into the Horn of Africa in S and E Ethiopia and W and N Somalia. Medium-sized parrot of dry bush and wooded country.

Generally in pairs or family parties where orange belly of adult male is good guide to identity of flock. Particularly swift bullet-like flight just below tree-top level accompanied by shrill screech is characteristic.

168a **Adult male** Deep orange central belly, axillaries and underwing-coverts, pale ash-brown upperparts, green on lower belly and undertail with bright pale bluish rump.

168b **Adult female** Lacks orange beneath except as occasional tinge on belly; grey on breast and green or pale green on belly. Head paler and greyer than male and underwing-coverts grey.

168c **Immature** Similar to female but young males have orange feathers in underwing-coverts and on breast and may show brown markings on breast.

166b

166a

166d

166c

166a

166b

167b

167a

167a

168a

168b

168b

168c

168a

KHEF

PLATE 42: *POICEPHALUS* PARROTS III

169 Brown-headed Parrot *Poicephalus cryptoxanthus* **Text and map page 383**

SE Africa from NE South Africa to E Tanzania (including Pemba and south Zanzibar) and extreme SE Kenya. Occurs Wasiri Island. Sedentary. Wide variety of dry lowland woodlands (except miombo) and riparian forest within forest-savanna, preferring areas with baobabs.

Smallish plain green parrot with greyish-brown head. Bright yellow underwing-coverts visible in flight. From sympatric Brown-necked Parrot by smaller size, no red thighs and wings; from Meyer's by dull green (not blue) underparts and from similar but allopatric Niam Niam Parrot by less extensive brown hood and by yellow underwing-coverts.

> **169a Adult** (*cryptoxanthus*; southern Africa from E Zululand, Swaziland and Transvaal to S Mozambique and SE Zimbabwe) Green beneath, bright yellow underwing-coverts, greyish-brown head and dark tail. Dark upper and paler lower mandible.
>
> **169b Immature** (*cryptoxanthus*) Generally duller than adult with brown iris. Greyish feathers mixed with yellow on underwing-coverts.
>
> **169c Adult** (*tanganyikae*; Mozambique north of the Save River to coastal Kenya) Paler than *cryptoxanthus*. Mantle greener and underparts brighter and 'cleaner' than nominate. Brown 'bib' much smaller than nominate.

---

170 Rüppell's Parrot *Poicephalus rueppelli* **Text and map page 384**

SW Africa from SW Angola to N Namibia. Mainly resident but locally nomadic. Dry woodlands (including *Euphorbia* forests and riverine formations), steppe and thornveld with preference for areas with baobabs, also montane formations in the escarpment region of Namibia. Generally close to water.

Medium-sized dull brownish parrot with bright yellow underwing-coverts. Blue on lower belly and rump (in female), yellow underwing-coverts and thighs, and lack of green in plumage distinguishes it from all other African parrots.

> **170a Adult male** Mainly brownish with grey on head and neck. Bright yellow on leading edge and bend of wing, underwing-coverts and thighs.
>
> **170b Adult female** Like male but lower back, rump, uppertail-coverts, lower belly, undertail-coverts and lower flanks bright blue.
>
> **170c Immature male** Similar to adult female but blue areas less extensive and duller, body plumage paler. Thighs brown. Underwing-coverts and carpal area brown or brownish-yellow; pale margins to wing-coverts.

---

165 Niam-niam Parrot *Poicephalus crassus* **Text and map page 380**

N Central Africa from E Cameroon to SW Sudan. Sedentary with local movements. Wooded savanna, forest-savanna mosaic, moist savannas and riparian woodland up to 1,000m. Commonly near water.

Grass-green short-tailed parrot with olive-brown head, nape and upper breast. Larger than Meyer's and Senegal Parrots. From allopatric Brown-headed Parrot by green (not yellow) underwing-coverts.

> **165a Adult** Green beneath with yellow margins to feathers on belly. Head, throat and upper breast dull olive-brown. Underwing-coverts mainly green. Upper mandible dark grey, lower paler.
>
> **165b Immature** Hood shows strong olive-yellow markings; mantle greener, underparts paler and more yellowish than adult. Innermost secondaries edged yellow. Upper mandible paler than adult, tipped grey.

169a

169b

169c

169a

169b

170a

170a

170b

170b

170a

170c

170c

165a

165b

165a

KHEF

PLATE 43: LOVEBIRDS I

171 Grey-headed Lovebird *Agapornis canus*   **Text and map page 385**

Madagascar, Comoro Islands, Réunion, Rodrigues and Seychelles. Various types of sparsely wooded country and cultivated land to about 1,500m, often near towns, villages and roads.

Only lovebird in range. Noisy flocks in swift twisting flight or feeding on ground in groups.

     171a   **Adult male** (*canus*; Madagascar, except for arid south-west) Green with grey head, nape, throat and upper breast; more yellowish below and brighter on rump. Black underwing-coverts and dark subterminal band on green tail.

     171b   **Adult female** (*canus*) Lacks pale grey hood and has green underwing-coverts.

     171c   **Immature** (*canus*) Grey hood of male suffused with green; bill yellowish, black at base.

     171d   **Adult male** (*ablectanea*; arid south-west lowlands of Madagascar) More green (less yellowish) beneath and grey hood of male darker and bluer than nominate.

     171e   **Adult female** (*ablectanea*) Greener (less yellowish) than nominate.

172 Red-faced Lovebird *Agapornis pullarius*   **Text and map page 386**

Gulf of Guinea islands, C and S Nigeria and Cameroon south to NW Angola and east to Uganda, W Kenya and NW Tanzania. Isolated population in SW Ethiopia. Moist lowland savanna and forest mosaic, riverine woodland, scrub and farmland.

Combination of green upper breast with red (or orange crown, face and throat separates this from other lovebirds.

     172a   **Adult male** (*pullarius*; Guinea and Sierra Leone to Sudan, south to Zaïre and Angola) Bright red forecrown, forehead, cheeks, lores and throat with electric-blue rump.

     172b   **Adult female** (*pullarius*) Head, chin and throat orange bordered yellowish behind.

     172c   **Immature** (*pullarius*) Like adult female but orange on head and throat less bright.

     172d   **Adult** (*ugandae*; Ethiopia, Uganda, E Zaïre, Rwanda, W Kenya and Tanzania) Rump on average paler than nominate.

173 Black-winged Lovebird *Agapornis taranta*   **Text and map page 387**

Highlands of Ethiopia from Eritrea south to Bale including Rift Valley. In montane forest with *Podocarpus, Juniperus*, etc., above 1,800m; grassy savanna lower down. Also cultivated areas and urban fringes.

From other lovebirds by green rump and throat with blackish flight feathers. Only lovebird to manipulate food with foot. Small flocks in tops of trees.

     173a   **Adult male** Red face and forehead, black flight feathers, black underwing-coverts and green tail with black subterminal band.

     173b   **Adult female** Lacks red on head; underwing-coverts sometimes marked green.

     173c   **Immature male** Like female but with more yellowish bill. Young male shows black underwing-coverts with scattered red feathers on forehead.

174 Black-collared Lovebird *Agapornis swindernianus*   **Text and map page 388**

West Africa from Liberia to S Ghana; W Central Africa from S Cameroon and Gabon east to Congo, extreme SW Central African Republic and Zaïre; E Central Africa from Zaïre basin to W Uganda. Lowland evergreen primary and secondary rain-forest, occasionally farmland.

Apart from female Grey-headed, the only lovebird with a wholly green head.

     174a   **Adult** (*swindernianus*; West Africa in Liberia, Côte d'Ivoire and Ghana) Predominantly green with striking bright blue rump and uppertail-coverts. Black nuchal collar bordered yellow behind. Red on base of tail with black subterminal band and green tip.

     174b   **Immature** (*swindernianus*) Like adult but black collar absent, green of head, blue of rump and red in tail duller. Iris brown. Bill pale grey with black spot at base.

     174c   **Adult** (*zenkeri*; Cameroon to Central African Republic) Neck behind black nuchal collar narrowly bordered yellow and then brick-red, extending onto sides of breast.

171c

171a

171b

171d

171a

171b

171e

171a

172a

172c

172b

172a

172d

172a

172a

173a

173a

173b

173a

173a

173c

173a

174a

174b

174a

174a

174a

174c

174a

KHEF

175 Peach-faced Lovebird *Agapornis roseicollis* Text and map page 389

SW Africa from Angola in region of Sumba in belt parallel to coast through Namibia to N Cape Province, South Africa. Usual range within c.400km of Atlantic coast but sometimes further east. Dry wooded country to 1,500m including subdesert steppe, sparse savanna, riverine woodland and cultivated land. Often near water.

Green nape, blue rump and pink face and upper breast separates this from other lovebirds.

175a **Adult** (*roseicollis*; Namibia and N Cape Province, South Africa) Bright blue rump and uppertail-coverts, pink face and upper breast and broad red band on forehead.

175b **Immature** (*roseicollis*) More restricted red frontal band and duller pink face, throat and breast. Base of upper mandible black.

175c **Adult** (*catumbella*; SW Angola) Green, red and pink plumage brighter.

176 Fischer's Lovebird *Agapornis fischeri* Text and map page 390

N and NW Tanzania, Rwanda and Burundi and Ukerewe and Kome islands in S Lake Victoria. Feral in parts of Tanzania and Kenya. Local dry season movements with irruptions in drought years. Wooded grasslands, cultivated country and riverine woodland (not miombo); commonest in *Acacia tortilis* savanna.

From Yellow-collared Lovebird by orange, not yellow, breast, but hybrids confuse matters where feral populations occur together.

176a **Adult** Orange-red face, red bill with white base to upper mandible, white eye-ring, blue rump, brown crown and nape bordered with golden collar.

176b **Immature** Less blue on rump and duller, particularly on collar and head.

177 Yellow-collared Lovebird *Agapornis personatus* Text and map page 390

E and S Tanzania from north of Mount Meru south to Morogoro extending west to Rukwa and Mbeya. Feral populations in Kenya and Tanzania. Well-wooded grasslands with *Acacia*, *Commiphora* and *Adansonia* at 1,100-1,800m. Avoids miombo woodland.

Blackish-brown mask with bold lemon-yellow breast separates this from other lovebirds. Hybridises with Fischer's where feral populations meet.

177a **Adult** Blackish-brown mask with bright lemon-yellow breast and collar with coral-red bill and white eye-ring; otherwise mainly green.

177b **Immature** Similar to adult but head less dark and glossy; yellow collar duller.

178 Nyasa Lovebird *Agapornis lilianae* Text and map page 391

Middle Zambesi valley, including tributary valleys in Zimbabwe and Zambia; separately in NE Zambia in Luangwa valley north to Lundazi; in Malawi around Lake Malombe and in scattered parts of S Tanzania. Birds in S Namibia are escapes. Inhabits mopane and *Acacia* (but not miombo) woodland and riparian forest with preference for areas with fig trees. Mainly in river valleys below 1,000m.

From other lovebirds, including the superficially similar Peach-faced and Fischer's, by combination of orange-red face and throat and green rump and uppertail-coverts.

178a **Adult** Forehead brick-red merging to orange and washed yellowish-green (brown in some individuals) on crown. Lores and cheeks orange-red, paler on throat and upper breast. Yellow patch on back of head and nape, otherwise mainly green.

178b **Immature** Similar to adult but duller with dark suffusion on ear-coverts.

179 Black-cheeked Lovebird *Agapornis nigrigenis* Text and map page 392

From Kafue National Park, SW Zambia, along Zambesi valley to Victoria Falls, Zimbabwe. Mopane and *Acacia* (but not miombo) woodland in valleys at 600-1,000m, favouring fig trees. Also in riparian forests.

Combination of dark face with ochre-yellow nape, green rump and rusty patch on upper breast distinguishes Black-cheeked from other lovebirds.

179a **Adult** Conspicuous blackish-brown face with white eye-ring, ochre-yellow on nape and rusty-orange patch on upper breast. Otherwise mainly green.

179b **Immature** Underparts washed dark green, breast and belly with dark margins.

175c

175a

175b

175a

175a

175a

176a

176b

176a

176a

177a

177b

177a

177a

178a

178a

178a

178b

179a

178a

179a

179b

179a

KHEF

PLATE 45: HANGING PARROTS I

PLATE 45: HANGING PARROTS I

180 Vernal Hanging Parrot *Loriculus vernalis*   Text and map page 393

Widespread from S India and the lowlands of Nepal east to Indochina. Also found on the Andaman and Nicobar Islands. Range of habitats from forest to bamboo, orchards and second growth.

Very small stub-tailed parrot with red rump and bill, blue on chin, all-green head, blue underwing. Sexually dimorphic.

180a   **Adult male** All-green head with blue chin.

180b   **Adult female** Less blue on chin.

180c   **Immature** Lacks blue on chin; rump marked green.

181 Ceylon Hanging Parrot *Loriculus beryllinus*   Text and map page 394

Restricted to Sri Lanka where it is the only member of its genus. Range of habitats up to 1,600m from coastal plantations to forest.

Combination of red crown, orange on mantle and blue throat diagnostic. Sexually dimorphic.

181a   **Adult male** Red crown and orange nape with blue throat.

181b   **Adult female** Duller with less blue on throat.

181c   **Immature** Crown tinged with red, blue throat absent or faint, rump marked green.

182 Colasisi *Loriculus philippensis*   Text and map page 395

Range of forested and more open habitats throughout the Philippines.

Very small green parrot, blue on sides of rump, males with red forehead and bib which vary according to race; females lack red bib but have blue cheeks. Most races with yellowish hind-collar.

182a   **Adult male** (*philippensis*; Luzon, Polillo, Banton, Catanduanes, Marinduque). Red forehead and bib.

182b   **Adult female** (*philippensis*) No red bib; blue cheeks, crown more orange than male.

182c   **Immature** (*philippensis*). No red forehead or bib. Duller rump.

182d   **Adult male** (*mindorensis*; Mindoro) Greener crown, orange mark on nape slight.

182e   **Adult male** (*regulus*; Negros, Panay, Tablas, Romblon, Masbate, Ticao, Guimaras) Red forecrown, yellow crown (less marked in female).

182f   **Adult male** (*chrysonotus*; Cebu) Hindcrown and mantle golden-yellow, slight reddish hind-collar.

182g   **Adult male** (*worcesteri*; Samar, Leyte, Calicoan, Buad, Biliran, Maripipi, Bohol) More red on crown, tending to orange-red at rear with a slight hind-collar; small red bib.

182h   **Adult male** (*siquijorensis*; Siquijor, possibly extinct) Smaller red bib and more red on crown than nominate; no hind-collar.

182i   **Adult male** (*apicalis*; Mindanao, Balut, Siargao, Camiguin, Dinagat) Entire crown scarlet grading to orange on nape and mantle (duller in female).

183 Black-billed Hanging Parrot *Loriculus bonapartei*   Text and map page 396

Replaces Colasisi in the Sulu Archipelago, SW Philippines. Found in dense forest and partially cleared areas.

Like Colasisi but with black bill, red crown grading into orange nape.

183a   **Adult male** Red bib.

183b   **Adult female** No red bib; blue on cheeks.

180a

180b

180c

181a

181b

181c

182a

182b

182c

182d

182e

182f

182g

182h

182i

183a

183b

C.D'S

184 Blue-crowned Hanging Parrot *Loriculus galgulus* **Text and map page 397**

S Thailand through Malaysia, Borneo and Sumatra into extreme W Java where possibly only an escape. Forest and second growth to 1,600m.

Black bill, blue crown-patch, orange wash on mantle, stub tail, red rump; sexually dimorphic.

184a Adult male Red bib, red rump marked above with yellow.

184b Adult female Lacks red bib and yellow on back, blue crown-patch smaller.

185 Sulawesi Hanging Parrot *Loriculus stigmatus* **Text and map page 398**

Common in forest edge and around villages throughout Sulawesi, Indonesia.

The largest hanging parrot; rump and bend of wing red, mantle washed orange.

185a Adult male Red crown, large red bib.

185b Adult female Lacks red crown; red bib smaller.

186 Moluccan Hanging Parrot *Loriculus amabilis* **Text and map page 399**

Forest and secondary growth on the Moluccas and associated islands, Indonesia.

Sexually dimorphic; like Sulawesi Hanging Parrot but smaller, yellow fleck in red carpal mark, red rump, mantle marked slightly with orange.

186a Adult male (*amabilis*; Halmahera and Bacan) Red forecrown.

186b Adult female (*amabilis*) Flecks of red on crown and throat; brown iris.

186c Adult male (*sclateri*; Sula Islands) Larger and longer-tailed with green crown and orange mantle.

186d Adult male (*ruber*; Banggai and Peleng Islands) Like *sclateri* but mantle marked with red.

187 Sangir Hanging Parrot *Loriculus catamene* **Text and map page 400**

Sangir, Indonesia; all types of wooded vegetation including coconut plantations.

187a Adult male Red bib and tips to tail feathers; red crown, red undertail-coverts marked green, and yellow carpal mark.

187b Adult female Lacks red on crown; reduced red bib.

184b

184a

184a

185a

185b

185a

186b

186a

186a

186c

186d

187a

187b

C.D'S

PLATE 47: HANGING PARROTS III

188 Orange-fronted Hanging Parrot *Loriculus aurantiifrons*   Text and map page 400

Lowland forests of New Guinea and some related islands.

Tiny; red rump marked yellow at sides, red bib, black bill.

  188a Adult male (*aurantiifrons*; Misool) Yellow crown, yellow at sides of rump.

  188b Adult female (*aurantiifrons*) No yellow crown; blue on face.

  188c Adult male (*batavorum*; Waigeo and NW New Guinea) Less yellow in forehead.

  188d Adult female (*meeki*; SE New Guinea, Fergusson and Goodenough Islands) Yellowish bases to feathers of forecrown.

189 Green-fronted Hanging Parrot *Loriculus tener*   Text and map page 401

Forest and forest edge of islands in the Bismarck Archipelago, Papua New Guinea.

Tiny; green with an orange-red bib, black bill; the only hanging parrot with a yellowish-green rump.

  189a Adult male Red bib, green face.

  189b Adult female Blue suffusion on face.

  189c Immature Lacks red bib.

190 Red-billed Hanging Parrot *Loriculus exilis*   Text and map page 401

Forests and open country of Sulawesi, Indonesia.

Green with a red rump, red bill; sympatric with Sulawesi Hanging Parrot but much smaller with red (not black) bill, male with green (not red) crown.

  190a Adult male Red bib surrounded with blue.

  190b Adult female Red bib lacking or much reduced.

191 Yellow-throated Hanging Parrot *Loriculus pusillus*   Text and map page 402

Forest and forest edge on Java and Bali, Indonesia.

Green crown and yellow throat in both sexes, slight orange-yellow wash on mantle, red rump.

  191a Adult male Large yellow patch on throat.

  191b Adult female Smaller yellow patch on throat.

192 Wallace's Hanging Parrot *Loriculus flosculus*   Text and map page 402

Locally common in primary montane rainforest on the island of Flores, Indonesia.

Green crown, red bib in male, red bill, orange on nape, orange-red at tips of outer tail feathers.

  192a Adult male Red bib, orange nape.

  192b Adult female Lacks red bib.

188b

188a

188a

188c

188d

188a

189b

189c

189a

190b

190a

190a

192u

191b

191a

191a

192a

192b

C.D'S

193 Alexandrine Parakeet *Psittacula eupatria* Text and map page 403

Afghanistan, Indian subcontinent, Sri Lanka, Burma and Indochina; Andaman and Cocos Islands. Some seasonal movements and local nomadism. Mostly lowland forests and woodlands but also cultivated areas, mangroves and coconuts.

All races large and mainly green with prominent maroon shoulder-patches and large red bill.

193a **Adult male** (*nipalensis*; Pakistan, N India, Bangladesh and Nepal) Black moustachial stripes and rose-pink collar; lores and crown bright green merging to bluish-grey on cheeks, ear-coverts and hindcrown.

193b **Adult female** (*nipalensis*) No black and pink collar markings, generally duller.

193c **Immature** (*nipalensis*) Like female but iris dark and tail shorter.

193d **Adult male** (*eupatria*; peninsular India and Sri Lanka) Smaller and greener than *nipalensis* with hindcrown and cheeks tinged lavender-blue. Black moustachial stripe narrower.

193e **Adult male** (*magnirostris*; Andamans and Cocos Islands) Narrow blue band on hindneck, brighter red shoulder-patch. Larger bill than other races.

193f **Adult male** (*siamensis*; Thailand to Vietnam) Face and neck yellowish with pale blue nape.

194 Ring-necked Parakeet *Psittacula krameri* Text and map page 404

Tropical Africa from Senegambia to Uganda and Somalia, and Asia from W Pakistan to C Burma. Many introduced populations. Mainly sedentary but some movements. Variety of woodland types, e.g. light second-growth moist forest, savanna, riparian forest and gardens. To 2,000m in Africa, 1,600m in India.

Green with large red bill and very long graduated tail. Only *Psittacula* in Africa but wholly or partially overlaps with most congeners in Asia. Green head and lack of shoulder-patches cue identity.

194a **Adult male** (*krameri*; Senegambia to Uganda and Sudan) Front of head bright yellowish-green. Hindcrown, nape and sides of neck pale lavender-grey. Narrow black line on neck becomes broad black stripe on lower cheek and solid black chin. Rose-pink collar. Central tail feathers blue tipped yellow.

194b **Adult female** (*krameri*) Lacks black neck, cheek and chin markings, pink collar and bluish suffusion on neck; has shorter central tail feathers.

194c **Immature** (*krameri*) Like female but bill slightly paler, iris greyish. Male acquires distinctive collar in third year.

194d **Adult male** (*parvirostris*; E Sudan to Somalia) Head and cheeks less yellowish than nominate. Bill smaller and upper mandible brighter red, less blackish towards tip.

194e **Adult male** (*borealis*; N Indian subcontinent and Burma) Larger than *krameri* with wholly red upper mandible. Bluish suffusion on neck.

195 Mauritius Parakeet *Psittacula echo* Text and map page 405

Mauritius. Mainly sedentary but some seasonal movements in relation to food availability.

Bright emerald-green. Darker and more heavily built than introduced Ring-necked but best separated by voice, slower wing-beats and shorter tail. Black bill of female reliable in good light.

195a **Adult male** Mainly dark green. Broad moustachial stripe on lower cheek narrows to form black neck-stripe bordered pink behind and blue in front over ear-coverts and sides of neck. Prominent red upper mandible.

195b **Adult female** Dark green moustachial stripes and no black, pink and bluish markings on sides of neck. Dark green on cheek fades to form yellowish-green collar on hindneck. Black upper mandible.

193d

193a

193c

193b

193e

198f

194a

195b

194c

194a

195a

194b

194d

194e

195b

C.D'S

PLATE 49: ASIAN PARAKEETS II

196 Slaty-headed Parakeet *Psittacula himalayana* Text and map page 406

W Himalayas west to Assam north of the Brahmaputra where it is the only parrot commonly found above 1,350m. Highland forest (denser than close relatives) to about 2,500m in summer.

Mainly green with grey head, orange-red bill and yellow-tipped central tail feathers. Finsch's has bright blue-green ring behind black collar and paler, creamier tips to central tail feathers.

196a **Adult male** Yellow tips to central tail feathers, maroon shoulder-patches.

196b **Adult female** Smaller than male, duller on nape and lacks maroon shoulder-patch.

196c **Immature** Head dull brownish-green becoming slaty-grey after first winter. Dark iris.

197 Finsch's Parakeet *Psittacula finschii* Text and map page 407

E Himalayas to Indochina. Oak, teak, cedar and pine forest, open wooded hillsides and cultivated land with tall trees between 650 and 3,800m.

Green with grey head, black collar, red bill and long pale central tail feathers with dull yellow tips. May overlap with very similar Slaty-headed in west of range.

197a **Adult male** Mainly green with maroon patches on shoulders, emerald on hindneck and dull creamy-yellow tips to central tail feathers.

197b **Adult female** Smaller than male, duller on nape and without maroon shoulder-patches.

197c **Immature** Head dull brownish-green, becoming slaty-grey after first winter. Dark iris.

199 Plum-headed Parakeet *Psittacula cyanocephala* Text and map page 409

Lower Himalayan hills and virtually all Indian subcontinent; Sri Lanka and Rameswaram Island. Favours mosaic of forest and more open country in plains and foothills, locally to 1,500m.

Delicately built, mainly green parakeet with elongated blue central tail feathers tipped white. Yellowish bill.

199a **Adult male** Wine-red face and head with narrow blue band on hindneck. Broad black moustachial stripe becomes narrow black collar bordered behind by bright pale green band on nape and sides of neck. Small maroon shoulder-patches, bluish-green rump.

199b **Adult female** Head dull bluish-grey without black markings. Yellowish on throat and sides of neck, no maroon on wing-coverts and mandibles paler.

199c **Immature** Head greenish sometimes tinged grey. Central tail feathers shorter.

200 Blossom-headed Parakeet *Psittacula roseata* Text and map page 410

E Himalayas to S China and Indochina. Light forest, including savanna, secondary growth, forest edge, clearings and cultivated land. Mainly below 1,500m.

Delicate build. Mainly green with elongated blue central tail feathers with white tips. Small maroon shoulder-patches.

200a **Adult male** (*roseata*; Himalayas from Bhutan to Bangladesh) Face mauve-pink, crown and hindneck powder-blue; broad black moustachial stripe extends to form black collar. Bright green patch on nape.

200b **Adult female** (*roseata*) Head pale bluish-grey, without black markings. Dull olive-yellow patch forms ring around sides of neck.

200c **Immature** (*roseata*) Greenish head, grey tinge to chin and yellowish mandibles until 15 months when both sexes develop plumage similar to female. Males in adult plumage at about 30 months.

200d **Adult male** (*juneae*; Bangladesh to Vietnam) Plumage more yellowish, wing-patch larger, central tail feathers paler blue above.

198 Intermediate Parakeet *P. himalayana* x *P. cyanocephala* Text and map page 408

Now judged to be a hybrid. Range never known; was thought to be from W Himalayas and/or the plains of Uttar Pradesh, India.

Predominantly green parakeet with mauve face and very long blue central tail feathers, tipped yellow. Plumage exactly intermediate between Plum-headed and Slaty-headed Parakeets.

198a **Adult male** Maroon shoulder-patches possibly separate male birds.

198b **Adult female** Possibly lacks maroon shoulder-patches.

196c

196b

197b

197c

197a

196a

199b

199a

199c

200a

200b

200d

200c

198b

198a

C.D'S

PLATE 50: ASIAN PARAKEETS III

201 Malabar Parakeet *Psittacula columboides* Text and map page 411

Western Ghats, India. Mainly in upland evergreen rain-forest but also deciduous forest with bamboo and abandoned coffee and rubber. Often near light cultivation. Mainly at 450-1,000m, exceptionally 60-1,600m.

Dove-grey underparts and mantle contrasting with blue or blue-green rump distinctive. Long blue central tail feathers with pale yellow tips.

> **201a** **Adult male** Grey head and mantle contrasts with blue rump. Red bill, black facial stripes. Some green on face.
>
> **201b** **Adult female** Little or no green on face. Underparts greyish-yellow, yellower towards vent. Less grey on mantle and bill brownish. Shorter tail.
>
> **201c** **Immature** Greyish-green in place of grey plumage of adults. Tail green. Black collar absent.

202 Emerald-collared Parakeet *Psittacula calthrapae* Text and map page 412

S Sri Lanka. Resident in well-wooded country mainly below 1,600m, sometimes to 2,000m. Mostly in Hill Zone but ranges into lowlands, especially in wet forest where found near sea-level.

Grey back, blue rump and shorter tail separates this from sympatric Ring-necked, Alexandrine and Plum-headed Parakeets.

> **202a** **Adult male** Grey head, green face, red upper mandible and black facial stripes. Long central tail feathers blue with yellow tips.
>
> **202b** **Adult female** Duller with blackish mandibles and shorter tail.
>
> **202c** **Immature** Lacks grey plumage of adult and rump is bluish-grey. Recently fledged birds have pink bills which turn black after first moult then red again later in males. From Ring-necked by blue-grey rump and darker green plumage.

203 Lord Derby's Parakeet *Psittacula derbiana* Text and map page 412

NE India (summer visitor, May-Sep), SE Tibet and SW China. Some seasonal altitudinal movements. Mainly highland coniferous, mixed pine-oak or *Rhododendron* forest at 1,250-4,000m, visiting cultivated valleys, especially at harvest.

Largest parrot in range and only *Psittacula* lavender-blue below. Blue tail and black patch on throat. Altitudinally separate western race of Red-breasted Parakeet has paler rosier underparts.

> **203a** **Adult male** Lavender-blue underparts, blue head, no collar but heavy black patch on lower cheek, chin and throat. Black stripe from eye to bill. Bright red upper mandible.
>
> **203b** **Adult female** Black bill.
>
> **203c** **Immature** Head green, lavender underparts paler. Very young bird has pink bill turning black later and then red again in males.

205 Nicobar Parakeet *Psittacula caniceps* Text and map page 414

Nicobar Islands in the Indian Ocean. High rain-forest.

Large, grey-headed, rather dull green parakeet with long graduated tail and heavy black chin-patch. Sympatric Long-tailed Parakeet has red cheeks, dark-green crown, blue rump and blue central tail feathers.

> **205a** **Adult male** Grey head with heavy black patch on chin and throat narrowing to incomplete black collar. Red upper mandible. Black stripe from eye to top of bill striking.
>
> **205b** **Adult female** Black bill.

201c

201b

201a

202a

202b

202c

203c

203b

205b

205a

203a

C.D'S

204 Red-breasted Parakeet *Psittacula alexandri* — Text and map page 413

Lower Himalayas east to SW China, and south-east (including Andamans, Mergui Archipelago) to Indochina and the Malay Peninsula; Indonesia on W Sumatran islands, S Borneo and Java and neighbouring islands. Mainly resident; some local movements. Usually below 2,000m (rarely above 345m in Nepal). All types of forest and wooded areas, but avoids dense evergreen forest in Himalayan region.

Only rosy-breasted *Psittacula*; slower flight than congeners. Head blue-grey with heavy black patches on cheek and chin, narrow stripe from eye to above cere. Long central tail feathers blue. Yellowish patches on upperwing-coverts.

204a **Adult male** (*fasciata*; continental Asia, including Hainan) Upper head pale lavender-grey suffused blue and pink; green tinge around eyes. Lower cheeks and sides of chin black bordered lavender-grey below. Nape bright green. Central tail feathers blue with yellowish tips.

204b **Adult female** (*fasciata*) Breast redder and tail on average shorter. Bill all black.

204c **Immature** (*fasciata*) All-green underparts and crown but may show some pinkish feathers on head. Cheek-patches initially dull brownish-black turning black after first moult. Reddish bill turns blackish (and then red again in mature male). Vague ochre wing-patch.

204d **Adult male** (*alexandri*; Java, Bali and S Borneo) Head bluer than *fasciata* with blue-grey band between black cheek-patches and pink of throat. Bill red. No green tinge around eyes.

204e **Adult female** (*alexandri*) Bill red.

204f **Adult male** (*cala*; Simeulue, off Sumatra) As *fasciata* but belly blue (especially male), breast darker pink and lores and forehead strongly suffused pale blue.

204g **Adult male** (*dammermani*; Karimunjawa Islands, Java Sea) Pink on breast darker than nominate, extending from throat to sides of neck in female. Heavier bill. Bill red (also in female).

204h **Adult male** (*kangeanensis*; Kangean Islands, Java Sea) Head greyer (less blue). Bill heavier than nominate and bill red (also in female).

206 Long-tailed Parakeet *Psittacula longicauda* — Text and map page 415

Bay of Bengal islands east to Greater Sundas. Lowland evergreen forest, mangroves, oil-palm and coconut plantations. Visits parks and gardens in Nicobars.

Mainly green parakeet with grey back and very long tail. From congeners by combination of red cheeks, green crown, pale greyish-green nape and mantle and elongated blue central tail feathers.

206a **Adult male** (*longicauda*; Malay Peninsula east to Borneo and Anambas Islands) Red upper mandible. Crown dark green. Cheeks, ear-coverts and hindneck bright salmon-pink. Lower cheeks and chin black. Nape and mantle pale greenish-grey fading to bright blue on back. Rump and uppertail-coverts green.

206b **Adult female** (*longicauda*) Tail shorter, bill brownish, cheek-patches dark green (not black), paler pink on face, crown darker green.

206c **Adult male** (*modesta*; Enggano off Sumatra) Larger than nominate. Cheeks deep crimson fading to dull pink on neck. Crown browner. Primaries and secondaries green; under parts greener. Pale greenish-blue on back.

206d **Adult male** (*tytleri*; Coco Islands through Andamans south to Ten Degree Channel) Crown pale green with no pink on neck. Hindneck, nape and mantle pale grey fading to pale blue on back.

206e **Adult male** (*nicobarica*; Nicobar Islands) Nape and mantle strongly suffused green (these and crown tinged olive in female). Upperparts more yellowish-green than nominate and washed pale blue; ear-coverts and cheeks deeper red.

204a

204d

204c

204f

204e

204b

204g

204h

206e

206d

206c

206b

206a

C.D'9

PLATE 52: MACAWS I

207 Hyacinth Macaw *Anodorhynchus hyacinthinus*   Text and map page 416

C South America in three main areas (almost exclusively in Brazil): south of Amazon in Pará; interior NE Brazil; pantanal region, extending into adjacent Bolivia and Paraguay. Resident in various habitats rich in nut-bearing palms.

Very large violet-blue macaw with blackish undersides of wings and tail. Birds usually travel lower than other large macaws. Lear's and Glaucous Macaws are more greenish-blue, smaller and with half-moon-shaped paler yellow lappets at base of lower mandible.

> **207**   **Adult** Massive black bill. Bare eye-ring and crescent-shaped lappets bordering lower mandible bright rich yellow.

208 Lear's Macaw *Anodorhynchus leari*   Text and map page 417

Raso da Catarina, NE Bahia, Brazil. Inhabits rugged dry terrain clad with thorn scrub and *Syagrus coronata* palms. Roosts and nests in sandstone cliffs.

Allopatric Hyacinth Macaw is larger and darker with more uniform deep violet-blue plumage and bright yellow crescent-shaped lappets.

> **208**   **Adult** Large and blue, more greenish on head and neck. Half-moon-shaped pale yellow lappets border lower mandible. Bare periophthalmic skin yellow.

209 Glaucous Macaw *Anodorhynchus glaucus*   Text and map page 418

SE South America in N Argentina, N Uruguay, SE Brazil and possibly Paraguay. Almost or actually extinct. Subtropical gallery forests with cliffs, palm-rich savannas.

Hyacinth Macaw is larger and darker with more uniform deep violet-blue plumage and bright yellow crescent-shaped lappets. Lear's is slightly larger and darker.

> **209**   **Adult** Rather turquoise-blue, more greyish on head. Large black bill with very long tail. Half-moon-shaped pale yellow lappets border lower mandible.

210 Spix's Macaw *Cyanopsitta spixii*   Text and map page 419

Lower Rio São Francisco valley, N Bahia, Brazil. Strongly associated with *Tabebuia*-dominated woodland along seasonal creeks in the caatinga zone.

Only blue macaw in tiny range although mainly green Red-bellied Macaw has been confused with Spix's in past. From Hyacinth and Lear's by smaller size, grey head, bare grey loral patch and no yellow lappets.

> **210a**   **Adult** Predominantly blue, lighter beneath. Head greyish and paler than body plumage, sometimes appearing almost white at distance. Very long tail and long narrow wings striking.
>
> **210b**   **Immature** Darker above with bare lores and eye-ring paler. Upper mandible with central longitudinal horn-coloured marking. Tail shorter.

207

208

209

210b

208

210a

209

210a

207

PLATE 53: MACAWS II

211 Blue-and-yellow Macaw *Ara ararauna*   **Text and map page 420**

Tropical lowlands from E Panama and Venezuela to Bolivia and SE Brazil. Generally resident but some seasonal foraging movements. Seasonally flooded and gallery forest, buriti palm swamp, sometimes (in north-west of range) deciduous forest away from water.

Large macaw, blue above, yellow beneath. Much rarer Blue-throated Macaw, sympatric in parts of Bolivia, shows narrow longitudinal yellow stripe on sides of neck, large blue throat-patch and slimmer build, with longer tail and smaller upper mandible.

    211   **Adult** Large with black bill and long tail, ultramarine-blue above, mostly golden-yellow beneath. Bare white facial patch with narrow lines of black feathers, green on forehead and black on throat.

---

212 Blue-throated Macaw *Ara glaucogularis*   **Text and map page 421**

Beni (and possibly N Santa Cruz) department, Bolivia. Seasonally flooded mosaic of savannas, palm groves and low-stature species-poor tropical forest in humid lowlands (200-300m).

May occur in flocks and at roosts with similar, much commoner Blue-and-yellow Macaw (see above for differences).

    212   **Adult** Mainly turquoise-blue above, bright yellow below with broad blue throat-patch and narrow longitudinal yellow stripe on side of neck.

---

215 Scarlet Macaw *Ara macao*   **Text and map page 424**

Middle America from S Mexico to Panama, and tropical South America from Venezuela and Colombia south to E Bolivia. Absent west of Andes. Regular seasonal visitor to some areas. Chiefly in lowland tropical forest and savanna, often near rivers; reaches 1,500m in Costa Rica.

Large, mostly red macaw with long pointed tail and conspicuous bright yellow upperwing-coverts. Widely sympatric Green-winged Macaw is larger, darker red, with green upperwing-coverts and narrow lines of red feathers on otherwise bare facial patch.

    215   **Adult** Red with blue and yellow wings. Bare white face.

---

216 Green-winged Macaw *Ara chloroptera*   **Text and map page 425**

E Panama and South America from Colombia and Venezuela south to N Argentina. Resident in terra firme rainforest, apparently avoiding swampy areas. In south and east of range often in more open or drier forest; to 1,400m in Venezuela.

Despite differences (see above) from widely sympatric Scarlet Macaw, immatures may show some yellowish-green on upperwing-coverts.

    216   **Adult** Large, mostly red macaw with long tail and conspicuous green upperwing-coverts. Bare white facial patch traversed with narrow lines of red feathers.

PLATE 54: MACAWS III

213 Military Macaw *Ara militaris* Text and map page 422

Mexico; Colombia and N Venezuela along E Andes into Ecuador and Peru; east slope of Bolivian Andes and uplands of NW Argentina. Seasonal movements in places. Mainly in wooded foothills from 500 to 1,500m.

From almost identical (probably allopatric) Great Green Macaw by stronger bluish tinge on hindneck, slightly smaller size, smaller and wholly black bill (pale tip to upper mandible in Great Green), slightly darker, more olive-green plumage, dull red (not orange) on base of central tail feathers.

213 **Adult** Large, mostly green macaw with bright red frontal patch, blue flight feathers and bright pale blue rump. Bare pinkish face traversed with narrow lines of blackish feathers. In flight appears vivid turquoise and green from above and green with metallic yellow flight feathers from below.

214 Great Green Macaw *Ara ambigua* Text and map page 423

Lowlands from E Honduras to Panama mostly on Caribbean slope; Colombia west of W Andes; W Ecuador in Guayas and Esmeraldas. Seasonal foraging movements. Mainly in lowland humid forest but also in strongly deciduous formations.

For separation from Military Macaw see above.

214 **Adult** Large, mostly green macaw with bright red frontal patch and blue flight feathers. Bare face traversed with narrow lines of blackish feathers.

217 Red-fronted Macaw *Ara rubrogenys* Text and map page 426

E Andean slope of S Bolivia. Subtropical thorn scrub with cacti, with steep-sided, undisturbed riverside cliffs for nesting (and probably roosting). Often in cultivated areas.

Fairly large, mainly olive-green macaw with orange-red forehead, crown and ear-coverts, olive rump and rather small bare facial patch. Orange-red on underwing-coverts and flanks.

217a **Adult** Orange-red forehead, crown and ear-coverts; orange-red lesser upperwing-coverts form conspicuous shoulder-patch. Flight feathers mostly blue; tail olive tipped blue.

217b **Immature** Less extensive orange-red on head, ear-coverts and wing. Duller with less blue on central tail feathers.

218 Chestnut-fronted Macaw *Ara severa* Text and map page 427

E Panama and widely in South America from Caribbean lowlands of Colombia south to C Bolivia. Forest edge, várzea, palm groves, gallery woodland, savanna; generally avoids terra firme forest.

From sympatric small macaws by combination red underwing-coverts, large white facial patch, chestnut forehead and (except for some red feathers on thighs) wholly green underparts.

218 **Adult** Fairly small green macaw with long pointed tail. Dull brownish-red underside of flight feathers and tail, bluish-green crown, inconspicuous chestnut forehead and large bare white patch on lores and cheeks.

214

213

217a

217b

218

218

214

213

217a

219 Red-bellied Macaw *Orthopsittaca manilata* Text and map page 428

East of Andes from Colombia and Guianas to Bolivia and east to São Paulo, Brazil. Partial migrant at least locally. Dependent on *Mauritia* palms which grow in stands in flooded terrain in dense moist forest, gallery forest and more open savannas and grasslands. Generally below 500m.

Small, mostly green macaw with long pointed tail and swept-back wings giving distinctive streamlined appearance enhanced by small bill, flat back to head and rounded chest tapering sharply back to tail. Birds can appear rather blue in evening light, perhaps explaining confusion with Spix's Macaw.

219 **Adult** Bare yellow facial skin with black bill and blue forehead and crown. Some blue in wings and dull, often inconspicuous reddish belly-patch.

220 Blue-headed Macaw *Propyrrhura couloni* Text and map page 429

W Amazon basin in extreme W Brazil, E Peru and NW Bolivia. Prefers disturbed or partly open upper tropical (foothill) habitats between 150 and 1,550m, mostly at forest edge along rivers, in clearings and in swampy forest areas with *Mauritia* palms.

From sympatric Chestnut-fronted and Red-bellied Macaws by dark bare skin on face, more extensive and obvious blue feathers on head and pale bill. Bare red skin around eyes diagnostic at close quarters.

220 **Adult** Small, mostly green macaw with blue head.

221 Blue-winged Macaw *Propyrrhura maracana* Text and map page 430

E lowland South America in north-east to SE Brazil, E Paraguay and formerly NE Argentina. Probably resident. Tropical and subtropical evergreen and deciduous forest with apparent preference for forest edge or forest close to water. To 1,000m.

From similar Chestnut-fronted Macaw by red forehead, yellowish underside to wings and tail and red belly-patch. From Red-bellied by conspicuous red patch on forehead, red on rump and paler facial skin. Yellow-collared has yellow band on nape. Flight jerkier than other small macaws.

221a **Adult** Mostly green with pointed tail, prominent red forehead and bare yellowish-white face. Bluish head, indistinct red belly-patch and flight feathers blue above.

221b **Immature** Paler blue on head, pale tip to upper mandible and less red beneath.

222 Yellow-collared Macaw *Propyrrhura auricollis* Text and map page 431

NW Argentina, Bolivia, N Paraguay and S Brazil, then separately in W Goiás, NE Mato Grosso and extreme SE Pará, Brazil. Some seasonal movements. Forest, edge, woodland and savanna habitats, remaining common in areas with extensive agricultural development. Mainly below 600m; to 1,700m in Argentina.

Similar to Blue-winged Macaw but distinguished from all small macaws by bright yellow collar and orange on base of uppertail.

222 **Adult** Small, mostly green macaw with conspicuous white facial skin, yellow collar (reddish in immature), yellow on underwings (but mostly blue flight feathers), orange on base on uppertail, blackish forehead, long tail.

223 Red-shouldered Macaw *Diopsittaca nobilis* Text and map page 432

N South America east of Andes from Venezuela south to SE Brazil and west to Bolivia and SE Peru. Introduced São Paulo city. Some seasonal movements. Variety of open wooded habitats with various palms. To 1,400m in Venezuela.

Smallest macaw. From other small macaws by mainly green flight feathers. From similar *Aratinga* conures (especially White-eyed) by conspicuous white skin on lores and upper cheeks.

223a **Adult** (*nobilis*; north of Amazon in S Venezuela, N Brazil and Guianas) Bill all black. Smaller than other races. Bluish forehead, red greater underwing-coverts and red at bend of wing. Underside of flight feathers and tail golden-olive.

223b **Adult** (*cumanensis*; N and E Brazil to south of Amazon) Upper mandible whitish-horn; bluer on head.

223c **Immature** (*cumanensis*) Head all green; lacks red at carpal area of wing.

219

219

220

220

221b

221a

221a

223a

223a

222

223b

222

223a

223c

Aratinga conures are mainly green, medium-sized and long-tailed. Species are largely defined by the distribution and extent of red on head and wings. *Pyrrhura* conures are generally smaller with scaly patterns on neck and breast whilst small macaws are somewhat larger with naked lores and cheeks.

228 Blue-crowned Conure *Aratinga acuticaudata* Text and map page 437

South America in several disjunct populations from Venezuela to Argentina and Uruguay. All kinds of dry and deciduous forest, up to 2,650m in Bolivia.

Blue forehead and crown. Reddish undertail conspicuous as birds alight. Pink upper mandible and pale feet often visible in flight.

228a **Adult** (*acuticaudata*; S South America from E Bolivia to Mato Grosso, Brazil, Paraguay, N Argentina and W Uruguay) Larger than other races with more extensive blue on head and duller underparts.

228b **Immature** (*acuticaudata*) Blue on head restricted to forehead and crown in immatures.

228c **Adult** (*haemorrhous*; north-east Brazil) Both mandibles pale pinkish, underparts brighter green and blue on head more restricted than in nominate.

227 Golden Conure *Guaruba guarouba* Text and map page 436

Lower Amazonian Brazil (south of Amazon). Terra firme tropical rain-forest.

Clear bright yellow plumage of adult unmistakable. Flight feathers green above and dusky yellow on underside.

227a **Adult** Golden yellow with pale bill and green flight feathers.

227b **Immature** Dull olive-brown streaked above with dark green. Head, uppertail and back acquires bright yellow during moult into adult plumage.

242 Olive-throated Conure *Aratinga nana* Text and map page 449

Gulf and Caribbean slope of Middle America and Jamaica. Resident. Mostly forest and forest edge, especially near rivers. Humid lowlands to 1,100m.

Mainly green; brownish and olive beneath with prominent blue band along trailing edge of wing. No red in plumage.

242a **Adult** (*nana*; Jamaica) Fairly dark brown throat and breast.

242b **Adult** (*astec*; Veracruz, Mexico, to Panama) Pale brown underparts.

228b

228a

228a

228c

227a

227b

227a

227b

242b

242a

242b

242b

KHEF

231 Red-fronted Conure *Aratinga wagleri*   Text and map page 439

Andes from Venezuela to Peru. Generally resident. Mainly in humid forest. Needs cliffs for breeding and roosting. Up to 3,000m.

Red crown and forehead, sometimes with scattered red feathers on throat. Red thighs.

231a **Adult** (*wagleri*; north-west Venezuela and W Colombia) Red from forehead to central crown with green above eye.

231b **Immature** (*wagleri*) Red reduced or absent on head.

231c **Adult** (*frontata*; W Ecuador and Peru south to 18°) Red on head extends to behind eyes. Red thighs and red patch at bend of wing in most birds.

232 Mitred Conure *Aratinga mitrata*   Text and map page 441

South-western South America from Peru to Argentina. Mainly dry subtropical vegetation at 1,000 to 2,500m; ranges to 4,000m.

Forehead brownish-red merging to bright red on crown, lores and cheeks. Scattered red feathers on neck and bend of wing, sometimes elsewhere on body.

232a **Adult** (*mitrata*; C and S Peru, C Bolivia south to NW Argentina) Red on head encircles eye. Red thighs.

232b **Immature** (*mitrata*) Less red on head, especially cheeks; brown (not orange) iris.

232c **Adult** (*alticola*; Cuzco region, Peru) Darker; red on head restricted to forehead with scattered red feathers on lores, neck and sides of head. Green thighs.

233 Red-masked Conure *Aratinga erythrogenys*   Text and map page 441

W Ecuador and north-west Peru. Range of arid to humid vegetation types. Sea-level to 2,500m but more usually below about 1,000m.

Striking red head and red underwing-coverts and large red patch at bend of wing.

233a **Adult** Red mask covers head. Solid red underwing-coverts.

233b **Immature** Green head and thighs with only scattered red feathers.

235 White-eyed Conure *Aratinga leucophthalmus*   Text and map page 443

Most widespread *Aratinga*, occurring east of the Andes from Colombia and Venezuela to N Argentina and Uruguay. Range of forest and woodland habitats up to 2,500m.

Conspicuous yellow and red underwing-coverts, bright red on bend of wing.

235a **Adult** Red and yellow underwing-coverts. Red at bend of wing with scattered red feathers on head and neck.

235b **Immature** Fewer red feathers on head, no red at bend of wing and olive outermost greater underwing-coverts.

234 Finsch's Conure *Aratinga finschi* Text and map page 442

SE Nicaragua to Panama. Lightly wooded or open country with scattered trees. Irregular or seasonal in extensively forested areas. Subtropical zone to 1,600m.

Conspicuous red and yellow underwing-coverts and red forehead. Sympatric Olive-throated Conure has blue band on flight feathers and green forehead.

    234a **Adult** Red on forehead and bend of wing, red mixed with yellow on underwing-coverts.

    234b **Immature** Lacks red forehead. Underwing-coverts green with scattered reddish-orange feathers.

236 Cuban Conure *Aratinga euops* Text and map page 444

Remoter parts of Cuba. Mainly resident. Wooded country.

Green with scattered red markings on head and body with red on bend and leading edge of wing. Red and olive-yellow underwing-coverts. Delicate build. No similar species in range.

    236a **Adult** Green with scattered red on head and body.

    236b **Immature** Lacks scattered red feathers. Green and red underwing-coverts, yellowish carpal edge and grey iris.

237 Hispaniolan Conure *Aratinga chloroptera* Text and map page 445

Hispaniola. Natural vegetation from arid lowland forest to palm savanna but prefers upland, including pine-dominated, forest to 3,000m.

Green with conspicuous red underwing-coverts and red leading edge of wing. Scattered red feathers on head, neck or underparts. No similar species in range.

    237a **Adult** Green with red underwing-coverts and leading edge of wing.

    237b **Immature** Underwing-coverts with less extensive red and more green, no red on upper surface of leading edge of wing.

229 Green Conure *Aratinga holochlora* Text and map page 438

From Nicaragua to extreme S Texas, USA. Mainly resident but some movements to e.g. Texas where it is annual visitor. All kinds of wooded habitat except tropical rain-forest. Lowlands to 2,600m.

Fairly large green conure. Green forehead and underwing-coverts with scattered yellow on leading edge of wing.

    229a **Adult** (*holochlora*; E and S Mexico from Nuevo León and San Luis Potosí through Tamaulipas to Veracruz, Oaxaca and Chiapas) Green.

    229b **Adult** (*rubritorquis*; Gulf slope of Central America from E Guatemala to N Nicaragua) Variable-sized patch of orange-red or red on throat of most adult birds.

230 Socorro Conure *Aratinga brevipes* Text and map page 439

Socorro in the Revillagigedo Islands 650km west of Mexico. Native woodland chiefly above 500m but to sea-level where forest remains.

Wholly green long-tailed conure. Only parrot in range.

    230 **Adult** Green.

234a

234a

234b

236a

236a

236b

237a

237a

237b

229a

229a

229b

230

230

KHEF

238 Sun Conure *Aratinga solstitialis*   Text and map page 446

North-eastern South America in the Guianas and N Brazil from Roraima to Pará and E Amazonas. Chiefly in savanna or dry forest with palm groves but also e.g. várzea. Below 1,200m.

Bright yellow with blue and green flight feathers. No similar species in range.

238a **Adult** Yellow with green tail and blue and green flight feathers.

238b **Immature** Duller with yellow on head and body replaced with dull greenish-orange. Lesser and median upperwing-coverts green.

239 Jandaya Conure *Aratinga jandaya*   Text and map page 147

North-east Brazil. Transitional deciduous woodland, cerrado, scrub and where moist forests cleared.

Underparts deep orange-red, yellower towards head. Green upperparts with blue in wing and tail. Yellow crown with red lores, forehead and around eyes. Black bill.

239a **Adult** Head and neck yellow; orange below with green upperparts.

239b **Immature** Yellow head and neck with green markings; paler orange beneath.

240 Golden-capped Conure *Aratinga auricapilla*   Text and map page 447

Interior south-east Brazil. Forest, forest edge and clearings in forest. Lowlands to over 2,000m.

Green with red band on belly. Yellow head and red face. Flight feathers blue with green strip across centres of primaries. Black bill.

240a **Adult** (*auricapilla*; N and C Bahia) Red feathers on rump and back.

240b **Immature** (*auricapilla*) Little or no red on rump, yellow crown duller, red on belly less extensive. Breast greener.

240c **Adult** (*aurifrons*; S Goiás, Minas Gerais and from Espírito Santo to Santa Catarina) Upperparts wholly green with no red on back and upper rump. Breast greener without orange tinge.

244 Peach-fronted Conure *Aratinga aurea*   Text and map page 451

Guianas to E Bolivia and N Argentina. Open wooded habitats below 600m.

Small and mainly green with green and blue head, broad orange frontal band and pale olive underparts.

244a **Adult** Orange skin around eyes.

244b **Immature** Bare periophthalmic patch grey, narrower frontal band, paler bill and grey iris.

238a

238b

238a

238b

239a

239a

239b

240c

240a

240a

240a

240b

240c

240a

244b

244a

244a

KHEF

241 Dusky-headed Conure *Aratinga weddellii*   **Text and map page 448**

W Amazon basin from south-east Colombia to E Bolivia. Nomadic in some parts. Lowland forest to 750m.

Green with grey head. Blue in flight feathers and upperwing-coverts. Conspicuous large bare white patch around eye. Scaly appearance to head.

241   **Adult** Grey head, black bill with contrasting white eye-ring.

243 Orange-fronted Conure *Aratinga canicularis*   **Text and map page 450**

Mainly Pacific slope of Middle America from north-west Mexico to north-west Costa Rica. Lightly wooded country or arid open areas with scattered trees. Lowlands to 1,500m, sometimes higher.

Green with orange-red frontal band extending to lores, blue crown and blue in flight feathers. Pale eye-ring and bill.

243a   **Adult** (*canicularis*; Pacific slope of south-west Mexico through Pacific Central America to north-west Costa Rica) Orange frontal band extends to forecrown. Pale bill.

243b   **Immature** (*canicularis*) Orange frontal patch much smaller; iris brown.

243c   **Adult** (*clarae*; Sinaloa and W Durango south to Michoacán, Mexico) Smaller orange frontal band. Lores blue. Sides of lower mandible dark grey.

245 Brown-throated Conure *Aratinga pertinax*   **Text and map page 452**

N South America, Panama and islands of S Caribbean. All kinds of open country with trees, usually below 1,200m.

Green above with yellowish underparts, blue on crown, dark bill and pale patch around eyes.

245a   **Adult** (*aeruginosa*; N Colombia, north-west Venezuela and upper Rio Branco catchment, Brazil) Yellow belly with orange patch in centre. Blue crown, brown throat. Feathered periophthalmic region orange-yellow.

245b   **Immature** (*aeruginosa*) Greener on head, no orange-yellow around eyes, less orange on belly.

245c   **Adult** (*margaritensis*; Margarita and Los Frailes Islands, Venezuela) More orange-yellow around eye, whitish forehead, cheek and ear-coverts olive-brown with greenish-blue forecrown.

245d   **Adult** (*chrysophrys*; south-east Venezuela, interior Guyana and N Roraima, Brazil) Like *margaritensis* but forehead pale brownish-yellow with smaller orange-yellow eye-patch.

245e   **Adult** (*ocularis*; Pacific slope of Panama) Yellow patch below and behind eye (absent in immature). Forehead and crown green, sometimes tinged bluish.

246 Cactus Conure *Aratinga cactorum*   **Text and map page 453**

Interior north-east Brazil into Rio Grande do Norte and Ceará. Dry, thorny caatinga and heavier cerrado woodlands.

Green with orange-yellow or yellow belly, brown throat and breast with blue flight feathers. Dark bill with pale bare eye-ring.

246a   **Adult** (*cactorum*; E Brazil south of Rio São Francisco) Brownish-grey crown and lores with yellow underparts heavily marked with orange.

246b   **Immature** (*cactorum*) Paler, crown green, upper breast and throat more olive than adults. Iris darker.

246c   **Adult** (*caixana*; NE Brazil on north bank of Rio São Francisco from Bahia to Ceará and Maranhão) Paler, with yellow (not orange) belly.

241

241

243a

243a

243b

243c

215a

245b

245a

245c

245d

245e

246c

246b

246a

246a

KHEF

PLATE 61: MISCELLANEOUS NEOTROPICAL PARROTS I

247 Black-hooded Conure *Nandayus nenday*   Text and map page 454

Pantanal region of upper Río Paraguay basin, with feral populations in Buenos Aires (Argentina) and California (USA). Wanders after breeding. In open country such as cattle rangelands with palms. Lowlands to about 800m.

Dark head and bill, blue breast. Dull brownish-black undersides of flight feathers. Red thighs.

    247a   **Adult** Blue band on breast. Brown or reddish feathers border black hood.

    247b   **Immature** Less blue on throat and upper breast.

---

248 Golden-plumed Parrot *Leptosittaca branickii*   Text and map page 455

N Andes from Colombia to S Peru at 1,400-3,500m (mostly 2,400-3,400m). High-altitude forest, including remnant patches in deforested areas.

Elongated yellow feathers form tufts behind eye; distinctive orange and yellow patch on lower breast. Narrow orange frontal band and orange and yellow lores. Pale bill. Dull reddish undertail.

    248   **Adult** Green with orange band on breast and yellow ear-tufts.

---

224 Yellow-eared Parrot *Ognorhynchus icterotis*   Text and map page 433

N Andes in N Ecuador and W Colombia at 1,200-3,400m (mostly 2,500-3,000m). Wet montane forest in upper subtropical and lower temperate zones.

Similar build to small macaw. Yellowish beneath, green above, with broad bright yellow ear-patches and yellow frontal band. Dark green band on throat contrasts with yellowish underparts. Large dark bill.

    224   **Adult** Yellow face and dark bill. Yellow underparts with green band on throat.

---

267 Austral Conure *Enicognathus ferrugineus*   Text and map page 473

Extreme S South America in Tierra del Fuego north to O'Higgins in Chile and W Neuquén, Argentina. Generally resident. Mostly in wooded country. To 2,000m in north.

Metallic blue sheen on wings. Dull red belly-patch, tail, forehead and lores. Barred body plumage. Dark upper mandible.

    267a   **Adult** (*ferrugineus*; from Aisén in S Chile and from S Chubut in Argentina to Tierra del Fuego) Reddish patch on belly and forehead.

    267b   **Immature** (*ferrugineus*) Duller red on head and duller, less extensive red belly-patch.

    267c   **Adult** (*minor*; Chile from Aisén to O'Higgins and in Argentina from Chubut to Neuquén) Smaller and darker green. Red belly-patch smaller or absent.

---

268 Slender-billed Conure *Enicognathus leptorhynchus*   Text and map page 474

C Chile. Some seasonal altitudinal movements. Forested country to 2,000m in summer.

Bright crimson lores and forehead, dull red tail, blue-green flight feathers and very narrow elongated upper mandible. Austral Conure is smaller, duller and without elongated bill or crimson streak on head.

    268a   **Adult** Dull reddish belly-patch; crimson streak from forehead to behind eyes.

    268b   **Immature** Darker green, less red on face, little or no reddish on belly, shorter upper mandible.

247b

247a

247a

247a

247a

248

248

224

224

267a

267b

267a

267a

268a

267c

268a

268b

268a

RHEF

PLATE 62: MISCELLANEOUS NEOTROPICAL PARROTS II

225 Thick-billed Parrot *Rhynchopsitta pachyrhyncha*   Text and map page 434

Core range in western and C Mexico (Sierra Madre Occidental) with sporadic movements north and south. Resident in core breeding range; pine-seed abundance determines presence elsewhere. Mature upland pine forests. Mostly at 1,500-3,000m.

Like small green macaw with long wings and long wedge-shaped tail, scarlet forehead and stripe over eye, heavy black bill and bright yellow on underwing-coverts conspicuous in flight.

> **225a**   **Adult** Scarlet extends to behind eye, bill black, scarlet at bend of wing.
>
> **225b**   **Immature** Horn-coloured bill, no scarlet feathers behind eye or on bend of wing.

---

226 Maroon-fronted Parrot *Rhynchopsitta terrisi*   Text and map page 435

Confined to Sierra Madre Oriental, Mexico. Upland mixed pine, oak and fir forest. Mainly at 2,000-3,000m.

Like small dark green macaw with long wedge-shaped tail, heavy black bill, red on bend of wing and maroon forehead and stripe over eye. Maroon markings on head may appear almost black in field.

> **226**   **Adult** Maroon forehead, green underwing-coverts.

---

249 Patagonian Conure *Cyanoliseus patagonus*   Text and map page 456

S South America in Argentina, S Uruguay and C Chile. Some seasonal movements, especially in south. Mainly in open grassy country. Lowlands to 2,000m.

Upperparts and long tail dull olive-brown with bright yellow rump and (except for Chilean race) bright yellow belly with reddish-orange patch in centre. Blue flight feathers. Black bill.

> **249a**   **Adult** (*patagonus*; Argentina from N Santa Cruz north to latitude of Buenos Aires and S Uruguay in east and Lake Nahuel Huapi in S Neuquén in west) Bright yellow on belly and rump. Creamy white patches on sides of upper breast.
>
> **249b**   **Adult** (*andinus*; NW Argentina in Catamarca, Tucumán, Salta, La Rioja, San Juan and Mendoza) Lacks bright yellow on belly and pale areas on sides of breast and has duller olive tinged rump.
>
> **249c**   **Adult** (*bloxami;* Restricted range in C Chile) Darker brown upperparts, throat and lower breast and more extensive creamy patches on sides of breast that in some birds merge to form pale breast-band.

---

269 Monk Parakeet *Myiopsitta monachus*   Text and map page 475

East of the Andes from Bolivia south to Patagonia, Argentina. Mostly resident. Dry wooded country mainly below 1,000m, but *luchsi* occurs to 3,000m.

Conspicuous pale grey breast with barring. Pale grey throat and head contrasts with green body and dark underwings. Flight feathers blue. Yellowish band on lower breast. Pale bill.

> **269a**   **Adult** (*monachus*; Argentina in SE Santiago del Estero, E Córdoba, S Santa Fé, Entre Ríos and Buenos Aires; Uruguay) Pale grey extends onto crown.
>
> **269b**   **Immature** (*monachus*) Similar to adults but forehead tinged with green.
>
> **269c**   **Adult** (*calita*; Santa Cruz and Tarija in Bolivia; Paraguay; Formosa, Salta and Jujuy south to Río Negro and possibly Chubut, Argentina) Bluer wings and broader yellow band on breast.
>
> **269d**   **Adult** (*luchsi*; intermontane valleys of E Andes of Bolivia) Brighter yellow lower breast, paler underwings, dark area at base of upper mandible and breast entirely pale grey with no barred effect.

225b

225a

225a

226

226

249b

249a

249c

249a

269a

269b

269c

269d

269a

269a

KHEF

PLATE 63: *PYRRHURA* CONURES I

250 Blue-throated Conure *Pyrrhura cruentata*   Text and map page 457

E Brazil from Bahia to Rio de Janeiro. Resident. Mainly in primary rain-forest or edge, sometimes modified natural forest and areas where tall trees shade cacao. Generally in lowlands below 400m but to 960m in Minas Gerais.

Combination of yellow patches on sides of neck, blue throat and well-defined dark cap bordered blue on nape.

250a   **Adult** Predominantly green with long tail, yellow patches on sides of neck, red on ear-coverts and around eyes, blue throat and upper breast and crimson on rump and belly. Well-defined dark cap. Plumage rather variable with some birds lacking distinct crimson patch on belly.

250b   **Immature** Duller with less red at bend of wing.

251 Maroon-bellied Conure *Pyrrhura frontalis*   Text and map page 458

Coastal SE Brazil from Bahia to Rio Grande do Sul into N Uruguay, N Argentina, Paraguay and SE Bolivia. Resident. Woodland, forest, forest edge with clearings and pantanal habitats. Mainly lowlands to about 1,000m.

Green rump (some reddish-brown on lower back), maroon undertail, brown ear-coverts and greyish neck and breast with scaled pattern lacking any blue. Most conspicuous small parrot over much of range.

251a   **Adult** (*frontalis*; SE Brazil from S Bahia to Rio Grande do Sul and S Mato Grosso) Mainly green with dark face, maroon belly-patch and brown ear-coverts. Tail mainly bronze above with dull red tip, dull maroon beneath. Breast and throat with scaly appearance.

251b   **Adult** (*chiripepe*, C and S Paraguay, N Uruguay and N Argentina) Uppertail wholly olive-green, more yellowish towards tip. Sometimes some orange-red markings at bend of wing, otherwise green.

251c   **Adult** (*devillei*, SW Brazil, SE Bolivia and N Paraguay) Bend of wing and lesser underwing-coverts bright red, greater underwing-coverts yellow. Forehead and crown pale brown. From Green-cheeked Conure by red at bend of wing and red and yellow underwing-coverts.

254 Green-cheeked Conure *Pyrrhura molinae*   Text and map page 461

SW Brazil and NW Argentina to E Bolivia and perhaps extreme S Peru. Some seasonal movements. Dense, often low forests and woodlands with glades. Ascends to mossy cloud-forest on E Andes, reportedly to 2,900m and possibly to treeline.

Mainly green upper- and underwing-coverts, maroon on belly and green rump and cheeks separate this from similar conures. Maroon-bellied has more extensive green on base of uppertail.

254a   **Adult** (*molinae*, highlands of E Bolivia) Scaly breast, brown head, maroon tail and maroon patch on belly. Blue tinge on sides of neck and hindneck. Light grey patch on ear-coverts. Blue in flight feathers with upper- and underwing-coverts mainly green.

254b   **Adult** (*sordida*, yellow morph; S Mato Grosso and Mato Grosso do Sul) Cheek paler than in nominate, red on belly less prominent and pale edging on throat and breast less distinct.

254c   **Adult** (*australis*; NW Argentina and SE Bolivia) Pale margins to throat and breast narrower than in nominate, maroon on breast more extensive with less blue on undertail-coverts.

250a

250a

250a

250b

251a

251a

251a

251b

251c

251c

254a

254c

254b

254a

254a

KHEF

PLATE 64: *PYRRHURA* CONURES II

256 White-eared Conure *Pyrrhura leucotis*   Text and map page 464

Disjunct populations in N Venezuela, NE, central-east and SE Brazil. Some seasonal dispersal to and from deciduous habitats. Forest, edge and clearings with scattered trees. Mostly in lowlands but to 1,700m in cloud-forest in N Venezuela.

Small and delicate with dark head, contrasting white or pale brownish patch on ear-coverts and blue or bluish-green on nape. Pale centres and dark tips to breast feathers give scaly pattern. Bright red patch at bend of wing.

> **256a** **Adult** (*leucotis*; SE Brazil from S Bahia to São Paulo) Dark head with narrow blue forehead, narrow blue band on throat, pale ear-coverts and maroon cheeks, rump and belly.
>
> **256b** **Adult** (*griseipectus*; Ceará, Alagoas and Pernambuco, NE Brazil) Ear-coverts whiter and more extensive. No blue above eyes but blue band on nape more pronounced.
>
> **256c** **Adult** (*pfrimeri*; Goiás, NE Brazil) Similar to nominate but has dull blue crown, nape and back of head. Breast and throat greenish-blue or blue with pale edges. Dark skin around eyes.
>
> **256d** **Adult** (*emma*; N Venezuela from Yaracuy to Miranda) Like nominate but more blue on forehead. Striking white cere and dull white bare periophthalmic skin. Dull yellow subterminal bands to feathers on lower breast. Ear-coverts duller and brownish.
>
> **256e** **Adult** (*auricularis*; Anzoátegui to Sucre and Monagas, Venezuela) Like *emma* but darker green with dark grey cere and periophthalmic skin.

255 Painted Conure *Pyrrhura picta*   Text and map page 462

Disjunct range in S Panama, Colombia, Venezuela and the Guianas, N Brazil south to Goiás and N Mato Grosso, SE Ecuador and E Peru and probably N Bolivia. Some seasonal (altitudinal) movements. Wooded habitats including gallery woodland, mature evergreen forest and cloud-forest. Sea-level to 1,800m in Venezuela.

Striking pale rounded scales or half-diamond-shaped markings on breast, maroon on rump and belly and green underwing-coverts. Pale ear-coverts.

> **255a** **Adult** (*picta*; Guianas and Bolívar and S Delta Amacuro, Venezuela) Forehead, lores, area under eyes and bend of wing dull red. Blue forehead and forecrown. Striking pale buff ear-coverts.
>
> **255b** **Adult** (*lucianii*; W Amazon basin of Brazil on upper Rio Madeira, Rio Solimões and Porto Velho, Rondônia; birds from near Leticia, Colombia, resemble this race) Little or no blue on forehead and forecrown. Some red on lores but little or none on bend of wing.
>
> **255c** **Adult** (*roseifrons*; W Amazon basin in upper Rio Jurúa, Brazil; possibly also in E Peru) Crown and facial area bright red (less extensive in immature). Red on bend of wing reduced in some birds.
>
> **255d** **Adult** (*subandina*; lower Río Sinú Valley, Colombia) Like nominate but narrow brownish-red band on forehead and lores extends to below eyes. Also has bluish-green on cheeks.

252 Crimson-bellied Conure *Pyrrhura perlata*   Text and map page 460

Central-southern Amazon basin of Brazil from W Pará to N Mato Grosso on Rio Roosevelt and Rio Aripuanã; E Bolivia. Mainly lowland terra firme forest but drier formations in N Mato Grosso.

From slightly smaller Painted Conure by red underwing-coverts and underparts.

> **252a** **Adult** Green on back and shoulders; wings mainly blue above; red on underwing-coverts; belly with scaled breast and neck; blue undertail-coverts; maroon tail.
>
> **252b** **Immature** Lower breast and belly green with scattered red feathers. Some with dark margins to scapulars. Green undertail-coverts.

253 Pearly Conure *Pyrrhura lepida*   Text and map page 460

NE Brazil south of the Amazon from Xingu catchment to around São Luis, Maranhão. Lowland terra firme rain-forest, second growth and clearings.

Long-tailed green and bluish-green conure with red or green underwing-coverts. Greyish scaling on neck and upper breast.

> **253a** **Adult** (*lepida*; From Belém and Rio Capim, Pará, east to São Luis, Maranhão) Blue on lower breast, striking pale ear-coverts, blue undertail-coverts, red underwing-coverts and blue lower cheeks.
>
> **253b** **Adult** (*anerythra*; tributaries of the upper Xingu and the left bank of the Tocantins) Leading edge of wing and underwing-coverts green, not red. Less blue and more green beneath.

256a

256b

256c

256d

256a

256e

255a

255b

255c

255a

255d

252a

252b

252a

252a

253a

253b

KHEF

257 Santa Marta Conure *Pyrrhura viridicata*   Text and map page 465

Santa Marta Mountains, NE Colombia. Seasonal altitudinal movements. Cool humid mountain forest, edge, and more open areas with montane shrubs. Chiefly 1,800 to 2,800m.

Only *Pyrrhura* in range. Sympatric Red-fronted Conure is much larger, with more red on head and wholly green tail, flight feathers, wing-coverts and belly.

> **257** **Adult** Red patch on belly often forms distinct broad transverse bar. Orange and red on leading edge and bend of wing and underwing-coverts. Narrow red frontal band.

258 Fiery-shouldered Conure *Pyrrhura egregia*   Text and map page 465

Pantepui region of interior north-eastern South America. Forest, edge and woodlands in precipitous uplands. Occurs from 700 to 1,800m.

Replaced in adjacent tropical lowlands by Painted Conure but may overlap in the upper tropical zone. Painted has maroon on rump, more obvious scaling on breast and relatively small red carpal patch.

> **258a** **Adult** Carpal area, leading edge of wing and underwing-coverts bright orange marked with yellow. Primary-coverts blue (bright yellow in some birds). Brownish crown with broad bare whitish eye-ring. Pale fringes on throat, upper breast and sides of neck give scaled appearance.
>
> **258b** **Immature** Much less yellow and orange on upper and underwing-coverts. Crown green and scaling on breast and sides of neck less pronounced.

259 Black-tailed Conure *Pyrrhura melanura*   Text and map page 466

NW South America in W Amazon basin, S Orinoco catchment and Pacific slope of Andes in SW Colombia and W Ecuador. Lowland tropical rain-forest, wet premontane and cloud-forest. To 3,200m on E Andean slopes.

Leading edge of wing and primary coverts red. Cheek and ear-coverts green. Undertail blackish. Breast green or greyish-green with buff tips giving scaly appearance. Painted Conure has more obvious such scaling and pale ear-coverts.

> **259a** **Adult** (*melanura*; W Amazon basin in Peru, Brazil, Ecuador, Colombia and S Venezuela) Red and yellow primary-coverts, scaly breast and sides of neck, and glossy blackish undertail.
>
> **259b** **Adult** (*souancei*; E Colombia from Macarena Mountains to E Ecuador) Little or no yellow on tips of primary coverts. Wider pale margins to feathers on breast and sides of neck.
>
> **259c** **Adult** (*berlepschi*; Huallaga Valley, Peru, and Cordillera de Cutucú, Ecuador) Similar to *souancei* but with even broader pale margins on breast, less red on leading edge of wing and more pronounced brownish belly-patch.
>
> **259d** **Adult** (*pacifica*; NW Ecuador and SW Colombia) Darker and less olive than other races with grey rather than white periophthalmic skin. Bill blackish and more delicate. No yellow on primary coverts. Pale edges on breast darker and narrower than other races.
>
> **259e** **Adult** (*chapmani*; E slope of upper Magdalena Valley in Central Andes at 1,600-2,800m) Very broad pale (buff) edges on breast extending further onto sides of neck.

260 El Oro Conure *Pyrrhura orcesi*   Text and map page 468

Pacific slope of Andean foothills in Ecuador from El Oro to Azuay. Moist forest in upper tropical zone between at 600-1,300m.

Only *Pyrrhura* in range. Breast scaling almost absent, red on outer upperwing and red forecrown, pale bill.

> **260a** **Adult** Red on forehead and forecrown, virtually no scaling on breast, some blue in primaries. Red on outer primary and median upperwing-coverts.
>
> **260b** **Immature** Less red on head and upperwing.

262 White-breasted Conure *Pyrrhura albipectus*   Text and map page 469

SE Ecuador. Resident. Humid primary forest, perhaps preferring forest along rivers; tolerates some habitat disturbance and partly cleared areas. Mostly 1,400-1,800m.

May be confused with sympatric pale-breasted race of Black-tailed Conure with which it mingles in the Cordillera de Cutucú.

> **262** **Adult** Dark cap, orange ear-coverts, white throat, breast and lower cheeks, red primary coverts and blue primaries. Green on belly and upperparts.

258a

257

257

258a

258b

259a

259a

259c

259a

259b

259a

259d

259e

260b

260a

260a

262

260a

262

KHEF

261 Black-capped Conure *Pyrrhura rupicola*   Text and map page 468

W Amazon basin in Peru, Bolivia and Brazil. Lowland forest.

From Green-cheeked Conure by darker crown and red outer primary coverts but caution needed with wild hybrids.

261a   Adult Mainly green with dark cap and red outer primary coverts and leading edge of wing. Striking scaly pattern on breast. Green uppertail.

261b   Immature Primary coverts and leading edge of wing mainly green with little red.

263 Brown-breasted Conure *Pyrrhura calliptera*   Text and map page 470

E Cordillera of the Colombian Andes. Cloud- and other humid forests. Mainly 1,800-3,000m but sometimes to 3,400m.

Tail proportionately shorter than many other *Pyrrhura* (no congeners in range). Pale yellowish bill; easily recognised by yellow on wings.

263a   Adult Bright yellow and sometimes orange on wing conspicuous in flight. Yellowish bill, scaly brown breast, maroon belly and maroon on tips of mainly green tail feathers.

263b   Immature Upperwing-coverts wholly or nearly all green.

264 Red-eared Conure *Pyrrhura hoematotis*   Text and map page 471

Mountains of N Venezuela from Lara to Miranda. Some local seasonal and daily vertical movements. Montane and cloud-forest with open areas and low scattered trees. Mainly at 1,000-2,000m.

White-eared Conure has pale ear-coverts and more pronounced breast-scaling, and is often at lower altitude.

264a   Adult (*hoematotis*; entire range except Cubrio, Lara) Red ear-coverts, brown forehead and maroon tail (latter conspicuous in flight and contrasts with green rump). Blue in primaries. Indistinct maroon patch on belly. Scaly pattern on breast. Pale bill.

264b   Adult (*immarginata*; Cubrio, Lara) Breast and sides of neck greener with less obvious scaling. No yellowish tips on crown and nape.

265 Rose-crowned Conure *Pyrrhura rhodocephala*   Text and map page 472

Andes of NW Venezuela from Táchira to Trujillo. Daily movements over considerable distances. Mainly in montane humid forest and elfin woodland at 1,500-2,500m.

Only South American Parrot with rose-red cap and white primary coverts; only *Pyrrhura* in range.

265a   Adult Rose-red cap sometimes joins darker red patch on ear-coverts. White primary coverts. Tail light red below, dull red above. Blue primaries. No scaling on breast or neck.

265b   Immature Bluish-green crown with scattered red feathers. Blue primary coverts with greenish base to tail.

266 Sulphur-winged Conure *Pyrrhura hoffmanni*   Text and map page 473

S Costa Rica and W Panama. Mountainous country in montane forests, including in logged areas, secondary growth and partially cleared areas. Mainly at 1,000-2,400m.

Yellow on upperwing largely concealed at rest but conspicuous in flight and may appear as translucent bar when birds pass overhead. Sympatric Finsch's Conure is larger, with red on forehead (not ear-coverts) and no yellow on wings. Orange-chinned Parakeet has shorter tail and green wings and ear-coverts.

266a   Adult (*hoffmanni*; Costa Rica) Mainly green with red ear-coverts and yellow on upperwing. Tail green above, maroon beneath. Underwing mainly yellow.

266b   Immature (*hoffmanni*) Less yellow on head, chest and wing.

266c   Adult (*gaudens*; W Panama) Like nominate but underparts slightly darker, crown and nape with more yellow and varying amount of red or orange-red on tips, red-tipped feathers sometimes extending onto back, throat and breast. Immature *gaudens* very similar to immature nominate.

261a

261b

263b

263a

263a

263a

264a

264b

264a

266a

265a

265b

266a

266b

265a

266b

266a

265b

266a

266c

KHEF

270 Sierra Parakeet *Psilopsiagon aymara*   Text and map page 476

Andes from S Bolivia to N Argentina and perhaps N Chile. Arid shrubby or wooded hills and ravines sometimes to the altiplano; in trees around settlements and agricultural areas. Mainly 1,800-3,400m.

Sympatric Mountain Parakeet occurs higher up and has shorter tail, blue in flight feathers and yellow or green breast.

> 270 **Adult** Elegant, mainly green parakeet with long narrow pointed tail, dark crown and pale grey throat and breast. Flanks and underwing-coverts greenish-yellow. Belly greenish.

271 Mountain Parakeet *Psilopsiagon aurifrons*   Text and map page 477

Disjunctly from N Peru to Argentina and C Chile. Local seasonal movements and perhaps post-breeding nomadism elsewhere. Riparian thickets, thorny scrub, fog vegetation, bushes and cacti on puna, cultivated land. 1,000-4,500m.

For differences from sympatric Sierra Parakeet see above. Andean Parakeet stockier, with broader, less graceful tail and richer green plumage.

> 271a **Adult male** (*aurifrons*; W Peru) Long slender tail and pale pinkish or horn bill. Distinct blue panel on closed wing. Bright yellow breast and/or face. Pale bluish on underwing-coverts and undertail. Whitish cere.
>
> 271b **Adult female** (*aurifrons*) Bright yellow replaced by yellowish-green.
>
> 271c **Adult male** (*robertsi*; one locality in the Marañon Valley, Peru) Yellow restricted to forehead, lores and chin. Yellow patches on chin and head separated by green cheeks.
>
> 271d **Adult male** (*rubrirostris*; Argentina and C Chile) Plumage is greyer and bluer. Pink cere.

272 Barred Parakeet *Bolborhynchus lineola*   Text and map page 478

S Mexico to W Panama and disjunctly in Andes from Venezuela to Peru. Nomadism may link these populations but presence often unpredictable. Mainly in montane forests, 900-2,900m.

Sparrow-sized, mainly green parakeet with short wedge-shaped tail and pointed wings, black patch on shoulders, pale pinkish bill and narrowly barred plumage (only parrot in range with this last feature).

> 272a **Adult** (*lineola*; Mexico to Panama) Bluish-grey forehead, yellowish-green narrowly barred upperparts. Bars on median and greater-coverts bolder, with fainter bars on upperparts and flanks.
>
> 272b **Immature** (*lineola*) Paler with less distinct barring.
>
> 272c **Adult** (*tigrinus*; South America from N Venezuela to Peru) Darker and more heavily barred. Green forehead.

273 Andean Parakeet *Bolborhynchus orbygnesius*   Text and map page 479

NW Peru to Cochabamba and Santa Cruz, Bolivia; west slope of Andes in Peru at least in Lima. Descends to montane valleys after breeding. Mainly in semi-arid upland woodlands. Usually at 3,000-4,000m but recorded over 6,000m.

From southern races of Mountain Parakeet by stockier build, broader tail, darker green plumage and tendency to travel higher. When flushed, birds usually fly only short distance before settling again.

> 273a **Adult** Bright green with blue in flight feathers, pale bill and broad-based pointed tail. Yellower below with bluish tinge to undertail.
>
> 273b **Immature** Shorter tail.

274 Rufous-fronted Parakeet *Bolborhynchus ferrugineifrons*   Text and map page 480

Central Andes of Colombia at junction of Tolima, Quindío, Risaralda and Caldas, and perhaps separately on Vulcan de Purace. Páramo zone in shrubland, sparsely wooded slopes and more open habitats. Mostly at 3,200-4000m.

Only small parrot regularly in high-altitude range. High-wandering Barred Parakeets told by paler bill and black patch on shoulders. Flushed birds fly short distance before settling again.

> 274 **Adult** Small, stocky and dull green with rather short pointed tail. Narrow rufous band on forehead, lores and base of rather bulbous bill. Paler on tail-coverts and yellowish on throat, cheeks and breast. Bluish-green in wings.

270

270

271a

271a

271b

271c

271d

272c

272a

272b

272a

273a

273a

273b

273b

274

274

PLATE 68: *FORPUS* PARROTLETS I

275 Mexican Parrotlet *Forpus cyanopygius* Text and map page 481

W Mexico (including the Tres Marias Islands) east to Durango and Zacatecas. Gallery and deciduous woodland, rather arid scrub, cultivated areas with trees. Mainly in lowlands and foothills but locally to about 1,320m.

Very small, mainly green parrotlet with short tapered tail. No similar species in range.

> **275a Adult male** (*cyanopygius*; Pacific slope from Sinaloa to Colima) Turquoise-blue in wings and on rump. Turquoise on underwing-coverts of male difficult to see in fast flight.
>
> **275b Adult female** (*cyanopygius*) Lacks turquoise-blue markings of male.
>
> **275c Immature male** (*cyanopygius*) As female with some blue feathers in rump and wing-coverts.
>
> **275d Adult male** (*insularis*; Tres Marias Islands) Darker and greyer above with darker turquoise markings. Bluish or glaucous suffusion below. Darker bill.

278 Spectacled Parrotlet *Forpus conspicillatus* Text and map page 484

E Panama and disjunctly in Colombia, including west of Andes in Nariño and through lowland llanos east into Venezuela. Lightly wooded habitats. Chiefly at 200-1,800m.

Mainly green, short tapered tail and pale pinkish bill. Only *Forpus* species in range. Male from Colombian race of Blue-winged Parrotlet by blue at bend of wing and around eyes.

> **278a Adult male** (*conspicillatus*; E Panama and N Colombia) Blue around eyes, on upperwing-coverts, at bend of wing and on rump.
>
> **278b Adult female** (*conspicillatus*) No blue in plumage. More yellowish forehead and beneath, paler green above with brighter, more emerald rump.
>
> **278c Adult male** (*caucae*; SW Colombia) Blue on face confined to line above and behind eyes. More yellowish; less deep blue on wings and rump.

280 Pacific Parrotlet *Forpus coelestis* Text and map page 486

W Ecuador and NW Peru. Mostly in dry wooded habitats, sometimes more humid vegetation. Mostly sea-level to 1,000m, exceptionally to 2,150m.

Small and stocky with short tapered tail. From Yellow-faced Parrotlet by green (not yellow) underparts.

> **280a Adult male** Green; blue on wings and rump and contrasting brown and blue on upperparts of flying male distinctive. Area behind eyes and faint band on hindneck blue. Mainly yellowish-green beneath.
>
> **280b Adult female** Green above with no blue on wings, rump or hindneck, and blue markings behind eyes paler.
>
> **280c Immature male** Similar to adults but paler, especially the brown feathers of young male.

281 Yellow-faced Parrotlet *Forpus xanthops* Text and map page 487

Upper Marañón Valley, Peru. Arid, lightly wooded habitats. Mostly 1,000-1600m, exceptionally 600-2,745m.

Stocky with short tapered tail. Yellow crown and underparts, blue rump in both male and female. Pacific Parrotlet has green (not yellow) underparts and crown.

> **281a Adult male** Greyish-brown upperparts, blue rump and yellow below and on cheeks and crown.
>
> **281b Adult female** Paler and smaller blue patch on rump. Yellow underparts less bright. No blue on upperwing-coverts and fainter blue in flight feathers.

275b

275a

275c

278a

278b

275d

278c

280b

280a

280c

281b

281a

279 Dusky-billed Parrotlet *Forpus sclateri*   Text and map page 485

Interior N South America east of the Andes south to N Mato Grosso and N Bolivia. Lowland rain-forest in clearings, forest edge, riparian growth and secondary habitats. To 1,500-1,800m on east slope of Ecuadorian Andes.

Small and stocky, rather dull and dark (especially nominate) with dark bill. Green-rumped and Blue-winged Parrotlets have paler bills. Amazonian Parrotlet is all green with powdery-blue forehead, lores and crown.

  279a **Adult male** (*sclateri*; S Colombia, W Amazonian Brazil, E Ecuador and E Peru to N Bolivia) Dark grey upper mandible. Dark blue on rump and upper- and underwing-coverts.

  279b **Adult female** (*sclateri*) Lacks blue markings; yellowish on forehead and forecrown contrasting with darker green feathers on hindcrown.

  279c **Immature male** (*sclateri*) Similar to adult but duller.

276 Green-rumped Parrotlet *Forpus passerinus*   Text and map page 482

Guianas west to Colombia and south to Amazon basin, Brazil. Occurs Trinidad, Tobago and Curaçao; introduced Jamaica and Barbados. Perhaps nomadic in some parts. All kinds of wooded habitats except rain-forest and other dense wooded cover. To 1,800m in Venezuela.

Very small, stocky parrotlet, mainly green with short tapered tail, green rump and pale bill.

  276a **Adult male** (*passerinus*; Guianas; also Jamaica and possibly Barbados) Mainly green with turquoise-blue on upperwing, ultramarine on underwing-coverts. Rump brighter green than rest of plumage; only male *Forpus* to show green not blue rump (see *deliciosus* below).

  276b **Adult female** (*passerinus*) Lacks blue markings on wings and shows yellowish forehead. Immature similar to adult.

  276c **Adult male** (*deliciosus*; both banks of Amazon in Brazil from Amapá west to the lower Rio Madeira) Rump with bluish tinge. Blue in secondaries.

  276d **Adult female** (*deliciosus*) Much more extensive yellow on head than nominate with more yellowish undertail-coverts.

  276e **Adult male** (*cyanophanes*; NE Colombia) More extensive blue on wing (forming distinct patch when folded) and on underwing-coverts.

277 Blue-winged Parrotlet *Forpus crassirostris*   Text and map page 483

N Colombia; Amazon basin to N Argentina and Rio Grande do Sul, Brazil. Introduced Jamaica. Dry, fairly open wooded habitats, including cerrado, caatinga, scrubby pasture and riparian woodland. To 1,200m.

Very small, stocky, predominantly green parrot with short tapered tail and blue on upper- and underwing-coverts and rump of male. Female all green.

  277a **Adult male** (*vividus*; N Argentina, Paraguay, E Brazil) Mainly green with rump, upper- and underwing-coverts and secondaries cobalt-blue. Pale bill. Cheeks, ocular area and lores brighter green than body.

  277b **Adult female** (*vividus*) No blue in plumage. More yellowish beneath with yellowish face and ear-coverts.

  277c **Immature male** (*vividus*) Like adult but blue markings of young male mixed with green.

  277d **Adult male** (*flavissimus*; NE Brazil) Paler and more yellowish green with forehead, throat and cheeks yellow.

  277e **Adult male** (*spengeli*; N Colombia) Rump and wing markings turquoise-blue; much paler than nominate.

279b

279c

279a

276e

276a

276b

276c

276d

277a

277b

277c

277d

277e

282 Plain Parakeet *Brotogeris tirica* Text and map page 488

E Brazil from Alagoas to Santa Catarina. Some seasonal movements. Wide range of wooded habitats including partly cultivated country. Lowlands to 1,200m.

Small long-tailed green parakeet with blue in flight feathers, brownish upperwing-coverts, greenish-yellow underwing-coverts and pale bill. No scaled pattern on breast or neck.

282a **Adult** Green with blue primary coverts, other coverts brownish. Long tail, pale bill.

282b **Immature** Little or no blue on primary coverts or in flight feathers.

283 Canary-winged Parakeet *Brotogeris versicolurus* Text and map page 489

East of Andes from C Amazon basin and French Guiana to SE Brazil, Paraguay, Bolivia and Argentina. Several introduced populations in South America and elsewhere. May be migratory in some parts. Wide range of wooded habitats, parks. Chiefly in lowlands.

Small, mainly green parakeet with longish, graduated tail and yellow (in southern races) or yellow and white (in northern race) on upperwing.

283a **Adult** (*versicolurus*; mainly north of the Amazon from French Guiana and Pará, Brazil, to W Amazonia in Colombia, Ecuador and Peru) White flight feathers, yellow greater and primary coverts.

283b **Immature** (*versicolurus*) Yellow edges to secondary coverts and less white on primaries and secondaries.

283c **Adult** (*chiriri*; NE Brazil south-west to S Amazon basin, N Bolivia, Paraguay and N Argentina) Primaries and secondaries green.

283d **Immature** (*chiriri*) Yellow on upperwing-coverts mixed with green.

284 Grey-cheeked Parakeet *Brotogeris pyrrhopterus* Text and map page 490

W Ecuador to NW Peru. Variety of wooded habitats but prefers native deciduous woodland and premontane dry forest. Mainly in lowlands but ranges up to 1,400m.

Only small long-tailed parakeet over most of range. Grey cheeks and ear-coverts, blue crown and reddish-orange at bend of wing and on underwing-coverts. Orange on bend of wing may not be visible when birds perched.

284a **Adult** Grey cheeks, blue crown and reddish-orange underwing-coverts.

284b **Immature** Duller with green crown, blackish upper mandible.

282a

282a

282b

283c

283a

283b

283a

283d

283c

284a

284b

284a

285 Tovi Parakeet *Brotogeris jugularis* — Text and map page 491

Pacific lowlands of S Mexico south to N South America in Colombia and Venezuela. Wanders locally. Wooded habitats, including parks and gardens with large trees. Mainly in lowlands but ranges up to 1,360m.

Small, mainly green parakeet with tapered tail, large bronze-brown shoulder-patch, bright orange-yellow on underwing-coverts. Pale bill. Most conspicuous small parrot in much of range.

285a **Adult** (*jugularis*; Mexico to NW Colombia and Venezuela east to Cordillera de Mérida) Green back, blue primary coverts, bronzy-brown shoulders and orange-yellow underwing-coverts.

285b **Adult** (*exsul*; NW Venezuela and NE Colombia) Greener on undertail-coverts, brown rather than olive on back with smaller, paler orange patch on chin.

286 Cobalt-winged Parakeet *Brotogeris cyanoptera* — Text and map page 492

W Amazon basin in Colombia, Ecuador, Brazil, Peru and Bolivia; also S Venezuela in catchment of upper Orinoco. Seasonally flooded and terra firme forest. Exceptionally ranges over 1,300m.

Small, mainly green parakeet with fairly short pointed tail, yellowish forehead and conspicuously flashing blue wings in flight. Sympatric Tui and Canary-winged Parakeets told respectively by their prominent yellow forehead and yellow or yellow and white on upperwings.

286a **Adult** (*cyanoptera*; all range except upper Huallaga Valley) Mainly green, with cobalt-blue flight feathers and primary coverts. Yellowish forehead and lores, orange chin spot and greyish-horn bill.

286b **Immature** (*cyanoptera*) Duller yellow on forehead and darker and greyer bill than adult.

286c **Adult** (*gustavi*; upper Huallaga Valley, Peru) Greenish forehead and lores, fainter bluish tinge on crown and green outer primary coverts. Bend and edge of wing yellow.

287 Golden-winged Parakeet *Brotogeris chrysopterus* — Text and map page 493

Guianas west to Rio Negro, Brazil, and south to the Rio Madeira in N Mato Grosso. Birds may wander locally. Mainly in lowland rainforest but ranges to at least 1,200m.

Small, stocky and mainly green parakeet with rather short pointed tail, blue primaries and pale bill. Yellow or orange upper primary coverts distinctive.

287a **Adult** (*chrysopterus*; Brazil north of Amazon, E Venezuela and the Guianas) Mainly green with bright orange primary coverts and blue primaries. Dull brown frontal band and chin spot.

287b **Immature** (*chrysopterus*) Green primary coverts.

287c **Adult** (*tuipara*; south bank of lower Amazon) Orange chin spot and frontal band. Paler and more yellowish-green.

287d **Adult** (*chrysosema*; catchment and tributaries of Rio Madeira) Yellow primary coverts, orange frontal band bordered yellowish on forehead and lores. Yellow margins to outer tail feathers.

288 Tui Parakeet *Brotogeris sanctithomae* — Text and map page 494

Amazon basin in Colombia south to Bolivia and separately from around mouths of Rios Negro and Madeira east to east Amazon lowlands. Apparently sedentary. Second growth in rain-forest and at edge of várzea. Lowlands to 300m.

Small, mainly green parakeet with shortish pointed tail, strong yellow patch on forehead and fairly dark orange-brown bill. Green wings.

288a **Adult** (*sanctithomae*; SE Colombia, W Brazil, NE and SE Peru to N Bolivia) Wholly green with bright yellow on forehead and crown.

288b **Adult** (*takatsukasae*; lower Amazon east from around mouths of Rios Negro and Madeira to E Pará and Amapá) Yellow eye-streak extends onto ear-coverts. Yellow on forehead sometimes larger.

285a

285b

285a

285a

286a

286b

286c

286a

287a

287d

287c

287d

287b

288a

288a

288b

PLATE 72: *NANNOPSITTACA* PARROTLETS AND *PIONITES* PARROTS

289 Tepui Parrotlet *Nannopsittaca panychlora*   Text and map page 494

Mainly montane E Venezuela and adjacent W Guyana, also Paria Peninsula and lowlands on Río Ventauri, Venezuela. Mainly in montane moist forest but also lowland rain-forest. Lowlands to 2,200m.

Very small, almost wholly green parrotlet with short square-ended tail, rather pointed wings and yellowish area around eyes. Allopatric Amazonian Parrotlet has blue on head.

> **289**   **Adult** Paler green beneath with yellowish-green on bend of wing and undertail-coverts. Yellow around eyes and greyish bill.

290 Amazonian Parrotlet *Nannopsittaca dachilleae*   Text and map page 495

SE Peru and extreme N Bolivia. May be nomadic. Undisturbed forest near watercourses but avoids dense forest. Lowlands to 300m.

Very small green parrotlet with short square-ended tail, rather pointed wings.

> **290**   **Adult** Powdery-blue lores, forehead and crown, greenish-yellow chin and pale pinkish bill. Pale bare area around eyes.

299 Black-capped Parrot *Pionites melanocephala*   Text and map page 503

North of the Amazon from Peru and Colombia to the Guianas. Nomadic, French Guiana. Tropical forest including both terra firme and várzea, and savanna. Mainly in lowlands but ranges up to 1,100m.

Medium-sized, chunky and short-tailed; only pale-bellied parrot in range. Looks front-heavy in flight with rather short wings.

> **299a**   **Adult** (*melanocephala*; east and south from the Rio Negro, Brazil) Breast and belly yellowish or creamy-white, orange under tail, green upperparts, black cap, yellow throat with apricot on back and sides of neck.
>
> **299b**   **Immature** (*melanocephala*) Brown iris and stronger yellowish underparts with no contrast between undertail and belly.
>
> **299c**   **Adult** (*pallidus*; W Amazonia from Colombia to Peru) Lower flanks, thighs and undertail-coverts lemon-yellow (not orange). Throat yellower.

300 White-bellied Parrot *Pionites leucogaster*   Text and map page 504

South of the Amazon from E Pará, Brazil, to N Bolivia. Mainly in lowland rain-forest in both terra firme and várzea formations. Also in drier forests (where less common) in southern part of range.

Medium-sized, chunky, short-tailed parrot with apricot-orange cap, yellow on throat and sides of neck, white breast and contrasting green upperparts; only white-bellied parrot in range. Similar flight profile to Black-capped Parrot.

> **300a**   **Adult** (*leucogaster*; Maranhão and Pará to Manaus and N Mato Grosso) Green above, white beneath, with green on lower flanks and thighs.
>
> **300b**   **Immature** (*leucogaster*) Duller, especially yellow on face. Dark feathers on cap and darker iris.
>
> **300c**   **Adult** (*xanthurus*; Rio Juruá to catchment of Rio Madeira in Amazonas and Rondônia, Brazil) Yellow thighs, flanks and tail. Yellow and green uppertail-coverts and yellow margins to scapulars.
>
> **300d**   **Adult** (*xanthomeria*; W Amazon basin in Peru, Bolivia and Brazil) Bright lemon-yellow thighs and flanks. Green tail.

PLATE 73: *TOUIT* PARROTLETS I

291 Lilac-tailed Parrotlet *Touit batavica*   Text and map page 496

Guianas to E Venezuela and Trinidad. Some seasonal movements. Forested habitats in both dry deciduous and humid forest. Lowlands to 1,700m.

Small parrot with lilac tail, at distance appearing black and green with pale wing-band.

291   **Adult** Yellowish-green head, dark upperparts and pale powdery-blue breast. Forehead and lores yellow, greater upperwing-coverts yellow.

292 Scarlet-shouldered Parrotlet *Touit huetii*   Text and map page 497

Colombia, Venezuela and the Guianas to E Ecuador and northernmost Bolivia. Chiefly in terra firme forest but also to lesser extent in várzea. Lowlands to 1,200m.

Small, mainly green parrot with striking red underwing-coverts and short square tail. Blue on upperwings, cheeks and forehead, conspicuous bare white skin around eyes and pale yellowish bill. Yellowish undertail-coverts.

292a   **Adult male** Outer tail with red at base and black subterminal band.

292b   **Adult female** Outer tail green with yellowish on innerwebs.

292c   **Immature male** No blue on lores and forehead. Dull red on outer tail.

293 Red-fronted Parrotlet *Touit costaricensis*   Text and map page 497

Costa Rica and W Panama. Cool wet forest in middle altitudes, occasionally to sea-level.

Small, mainly green parrot with short square tail. Red on bend of male's wing prominent in flight from above with yellow inner underwing-coverts conspicuous from below. Red on crown with red streak below eye.

293a   **Adult male** Red on lores, upper cheek and forehead, upperwing and outer underwing-coverts. Inner underwing-coverts yellow. Bill pale horn.

293b   **Adult female** Less red on upperwing-coverts but perhaps more yellow on underwing-coverts.

293c   **Immature** Little or no red on head. Greyer iris.

294 Red-winged Parrotlet *Touit dilectissima*   Text and map page 498

Panama and NW South America east and west of Andes in Colombia, Ecuador and Venezuela. Some seasonal altitudinal movements. Humid and wet forest mainly in uplands to 1,600m.

Small, mainly green, short-tailed parrot with blue forehead, red at base of bill and below eyes. Red upperwing-coverts (in male) and red and yellow underwing-coverts flash conspicuously in flight.

294a   **Adult male** Blue forehead, red beneath and in front of eyes with broad striking red shoulder-patches. Underwing-coverts mainly yellow with some red at leading edge.

294b   **Adult female** Little or no red on upperwing.

294c   **Immature** Like female but little or no blue on forehead or red on face.

291

292b

291

292a

292c

293a

293b

293c

294b

294a

294c

295 Sapphire-rumped Parrotlet *Touit purpurata* Text and map page 499

Mainly Amazon basin in Colombia, Ecuador, N Peru and Brazil east to N Maranhão; also S Venezuela and Guianas. Lowland humid terra firme and várzea and sometimes savanna. Ranges up to 1,200m.

Small, mainly green parrot with square-ended tail, (sometimes indistinct) blue rump, and brown scapulars and tertials forming distinctive V on back. Dark crimson outer tail.

> **295a Adult male** (*purpurata*; SE Amazonas, Venezuela, to the Guianas and E Amazon basin of Brazil) Crimson tail feathers tipped and edged black. Yellowish on flanks. Brownish from forehead to hindneck.

> **295b Adult female** (*purpurata*) Tail feathers (except central pair) with green subterminal band, t ipped black.

> **295c Immature male** (*purpurata*) More yellowish beneath; greenish-olive from forehead to nape and on lower ear-coverts; black on tail confined to tips.

> **295d Adult male** (*viridiceps*; Rio Negro catchment, Brazil, and Venezuela west from Cerro Duida to SE Colombia, N Peru and E Ecuador) Like nominate but with green forehead, crown and hindneck, flanks less yellowish-green, and broad purplish-black edging on outer tail.

---

296 Brown-backed Parrotlet *Touit melanonotus* Text and map page 500

SE Brazil from Bahia to São Paulo. Some seasonal movements (perhaps mainly altitudinal). Humid forest on lower montane slopes mainly at 500-1,000m but up to 1,400m.

Small, mainly green, with short square tail and blackish-brown patch on back. Outer tail red broadly tipped black. May occur with Golden-tailed Parrotlet which has golden tail.

> **296 Adult** Green with pale bill and broad dark patch on back. Red outer tail feathers.

---

297 Golden-tailed Parrotlet *Touit surda* Text and map page 501

E Brazil from Ceará and Paraíba south to São Paulo. Perhaps migratory. Lowland forest but occasionally in adjacent uplands to 800m.

Small, mainly green with short square golden-yellow tail. Dark scapulars form V on back. Yellowish on cheeks, lores and forehead. Brown-backed Parrotlet has red on tail.

> **297 Adult** Golden outer tail feathers. Dark stripes on back.

---

298 Spot-winged Parrotlet *Touit stictoptera* Text and map page 502

Several possibly disjunct populations from C Colombia to N Peru, mainly in E Andes. Tall humid subtropical forest but also in savanna-like woodland and stunted ridge-top growth. Mainly at 1,000-1,700m but ranges from 500 to 2,300m.

Small with short square tail. Plumage mainly green with dark upperwing.

> **298a Adult male** Dull orange on greater coverts. Pale tips to dark upperwing-coverts and scapulars create spotted effect.

> **298b Adult female** Brown lesser and median coverts with broad green margins suggest dark brown spots above. Lacks orange on outer median coverts and has more extensive yellowish on face.

305 Saffron-headed Parrot *Pionopsitta pyrilia*   **Text and map page 508**

E Panama, W and N Colombia, W Venezuela and N Ecuador (one record). Humid and wet forest including rain- and cloud- forest, to 1,650m.

Medium-sized, rather stocky parrot with short square-ended tail. Combination of yellow head, neck and shoulders with red underwing-coverts (conspicuous in flight) and bright green body is diagnostic in range.

305a Adult Head wholly yellow.

305b Immature No yellow on top of head, neck and lesser wing-coverts (instead green). Olive-yellow on face and throat.

---

302 Brown-hooded Parrot *Pionopsitta haematotis*   **Text and map page 506**

Caribbean lowlands of Mexico from Veracruz to NW Colombia. Mainly resident. Dense rain-forest, low elevation cloud-forest, forest clearings with scattered trees and plantations. Lowlands to over 3,000m, Costa Rica.

Medium-sized, stocky parrot with short square-ended tail and owlish expression. Mainly green with brown head and neck and light golden-brown breast. Scarlet patch on sides and base of underwing in flight. Pale bill, white lores and bare skin around eyes contrast with dark head.

302a Adult (*haematotis*; SE Mexico to C Panama) Red ear-coverts.

302b Immature (*haematotis*) Like adult but paler, duller, no red ear-coverts.

302c Adult (*coccinicollaris*; C Panama east to NW Colombia) Lower throat and upper breast marked with red.

---

303 Rose-faced Parrot *Pionopsitta pulchra*   **Text and map page 507**

Pacific slope of Colombia south through Ecuador. Mature wet evergreen forest and edge, including tall secondary growth, plantations and clearings. Mainly in tropical zone but ranges up to 2,100m.

Medium-sized, stocky, mainly green parrot with short square-ended tail and pinkish-rose face. Golden-brown on upper breast extends up to hindneck. Blue on upperwing-coverts. Pale bill.

303a Adult Dark cap and border around pink facial patch. Golden breast.

303b Adult female Golden on cap and around pink facial patch, lacking striking facial contrast of male.

303c Immature Pink on face limited to line above eye and ear-coverts; face otherwise greenish-brown. Greenish on crown and hindneck.

---

312 Short-tailed Parrot *Graydidascalus brachyurus*   **Text and map page 514**

Amazon basin and its major tributaries, extending into French Guiana. Perhaps seasonal visitor to some areas. Lowland tropical rain-forest below about 400m. Mainly in várzea.

Fairly small, plump, mainly green parrot with very short square-ended tail. More yellowish beneath with heavy slaty-grey bill and pale margins to wing-coverts and scapulars. Red at base of leading edge of wing. Frowning appearance from stripe in front of and behind eye.

312a Adult Red on outer tail feathers.

312b Immature No red on outer tail feathers.

305a

305b

305a

305b

302a

302b

303b

302a

302c

303a

303c

303c

312a

312a

312b

312b

304 Orange-cheeked Parrot *Pionopsitta barrabandi* Text and map page 507

Upper Orinoco catchment in Venezuela, W Amazon basin in Colombia, Ecuador, Peru, Bolivia and Brazil to Mato Grosso. Mainly in lowland terra firme forest. Up to about 500m.

Medium-sized, mainly green, rather short-tailed parrot. Orange or yellowish-orange cheek-patch on black hood and bright red underwing-coverts in flight diagnostic.

304a **Adult** (*barrabandi*; S Venezuela, SE Colombia and most of Brazilian Amazon) Yellowish-orange cheek-patch and thighs, yellow at bend of wing and blue primaries.

304b **Immature** (*barrabandi*) Golden-brownish head with more yellowish cheeks, also less yellow at bend of wing, some green feathers in underwing-coverts and yellow on tips of primaries.

304c **Adult** (*aurantiigena*; Bolivia, Peru, Ecuador and catchment of Rio Madeira, Brazil) Cheek, lesser upperwing-coverts, bend of wing and thighs deep orange.

307 Vulturine Parrot *Pionopsitta vulturina* Text and map page 510

E Amazonian Brazil south of the Amazon. Lowland rain-forest in both várzea and terra firme formations.

Medium-sized, stocky, rather short-tailed parrot, mainly green with yellow band around head and neck, and red underwing-coverts. Orange-cheeked Parrot has orange cheek-patch instead of yellow stripe over head and neck.

307a **Adult** Bare black face bordered by striking yellow collar. Red at bend of wing and underwing-coverts. Golden breast and neck with dark margins give scaled appearance.

307b **Immature** Head fully feathered (except for pale eye-ring); greenish on cheek and more olive-yellow on rest of head. Bend of wing and underwing-coverts yellowish-orange. Iris darker.

306 Caica Parrot *Pionopsitta caica* Text and map page 509

SE Venezuela, Guianas and Amazonian Brazil north of the Amazon. Undisturbed lowland terra firme rainforest. Ranges to 1,100m.

Medium-sized, rather stocky parrot with short square-ended tail. Black hood bordered with scaly golden-brown collar is diagnostic in range. Close congeners have red underwing-coverts.

306a **Adult** Black hood, scalloped golden breast contiguous with band on neck. Otherwise mainly green with dark primaries. No red in wings.

306b **Immature** Green on crown with yellowish olive-brown on face. Collar duller with weaker scalloped effect. Iris darker than adults.

301 Red-capped Parrot *Pionopsitta pileata* Text and map page 505

SE Brazil, E Paraguay and NE Argentina. Some seasonal movements and nomadic tendencies. Lowland forest, including *Araucaria*. Ranges up to 1,500m in coastal mountains.

Medium-sized, mainly green parrot with slightly tapered, fairly short tail, blue in wings. Undertail and underwing-coverts bluish-green.

301a **Adult male** Bright red cap extends to below eyes and to ear-coverts.

301b **Adult female** Head mostly green but with rather pale blue on forehead. Smaller than female Purple-bellied Parrot with shorter tail, paler bill.

301c **Immature male** Like female but green or greyish-green ear-coverts and dark patches on base of bill; sometimes with red forehead bordered orange behind.

304a

304b

304c

304a

304a

307a

301c

301b

307a

307a

307b

307a

301a

301b

306a

306a

306b

308 Black-winged Parrot *Hapalopsittaca melanotis*   **Text and map page 511**

High Andes disjunctly in Peru and Bolivia. Perhaps seasonal elevational movements to temperate zone. Humid montane forest. To 3,450m in Peru.

Fairly small and stocky with rather short, slightly tapered tail. Mainly green with large black patches on upperwing and bluish on crown and hindneck. No similar species in range; black wing-patches are reliable fieldmark.

  308a Adult (*melanotis*; Bolivia) Slaty-blue on head tending to lavender-grey on hindneck and throat. Dark patch on ear-coverts. Ochre around eyes.

  308b Adult (*peruviana*; Peru) Head mainly green with dull brownish-orange ear-coverts. Ochre around eyes variable in extent, sometimes reaching forehead.

309 Rusty-faced Parrot *Hapalopsittaca amazonina*   **Text and map page 511**

Andes in Colombia and Venezuela. Wet epiphyte-rich cloud-forest. Chiefly 2,200-3,000m.

Fairly small and stocky, with a rather short, slightly tapered tail and pale bill. Mainly green with red on forehead, cheeks and bend of wing. Yellow lores, golden-brown breast and throat, blue primary coverts and on underwing.

  309a Adult (*amazonina*; E Andes of Colombia south to Cundinamarca and one report from Táchira, Venezuela) Mainly green upperparts. Red on cheeks and forehead with yellowish streaks on lower cheeks and ear-coverts.

  309b Immature (*amazonina*) Head lacks yellow streaks on head, back duller olivaceous, primaries brownish washed bluish, tail duller, more brownish.

  309c Adult (*velezi*; western flank of volcanoes in Caldas and possibly Quindío, Colombia, perhaps extending to head of Magdalena Valley) Similar to nominate but with golden-olive hindneck contrasting with green mantle.

  309d Adult (*theresae*; Mérida and probably Táchira, Venezuela) Similar to nominate but more olive; red on face darker and more brownish.

310 Fuertes's Parrot *Hapalopsittaca fuertesi*   **Text and map page 512**

West slope of Central Andes in Colombia, only known to survive in the Acaime and Cañon del Quindío Natural Reserves, Alto Quindío. Cloud-forest mainly at 2,900-3,150m.

Like Rusty-faced Parrot in shape and size. Mainly green with red on forehead and bend of wing, yellow crown bordered blue behind, yellow on face around eye, blue in wings. Dull reddish tail broadly tipped dark blue. The possibly sympatric *velezi* race of Rusty-faced Parrot has golden-olive hindneck.

  310a Adult Narrow red frontal band bordered yellow and then blue on crown. Yellow face.

  310b Immature Lacks blue and yellow on head.

311 Red-faced Parrot *Hapalopsittaca pyrrhops*   **Text and map page 513**

High Andes of S Ecuador and N Peru. Perhaps seasonal visitor to some areas. Wet upper montane forest. Mostly at c. 2,800-3,000m.

Like Rusty-faced Parrot in shape and size. Mainly green with red on forehead, face, bend of wing and underwing-coverts, blue on upperwing-coverts and flight feathers. Some yellow on ear-coverts and cheeks. No similar species in range.

  311a Adult Red face and forehead. Centre of crown yellow, hindcrown blue. Yellow streaks on ear-coverts.

  311b Immature Reduced red on face.

308b

308a

308a

310b

309b

311a

311b

311a

309a

310a

310a

309a

309c

309d

313 Blue-headed Parrot *Pionus menstruus* Text and map page 515

Costa Rica, Panama and widely in South America south to N Bolivia and SE Brazil. Perhaps wanders outside breeding season, at least in some parts of range. Mainly in lowland forest but in subtropical formations in some parts. Ranges up to 1,500m.

Chunky, medium-sized, short-tailed parrot, mainly green with red vent and blue on head, neck and breast, although these features are sometimes hard to see. One of the most frequent and widespread parrots in lowland South America.

> **313a** **Adult** (*menstruus*; N and C South America east of the Andes from Venezuela and E Colombia to the mouth of the Amazon and N Bolivia) Bill mainly red with dark stripe on length of upper mandible. Head, neck and breast blue with speckled pinkish patch on centre of breast.
>
> **313b** **Immature** (*menstruus*) Mainly green head and breast with scattered blue feathers. Dark edges of feathers on head give speckled effect.
>
> **313c** **Adult** (*reichenowi*; E Brazil) Blue deeper and more extensive with most feathers on underparts showing blue. No red on throat.

317 White-crowned Parrot *Pionus senilis* Text and map page 520

Caribbean slope of Mexico to W Panama. Some local migrations. Mainly humid and wet lowland forest but locally in oak and pine forest, savanna and moist lower montane forests, up to 2,300m.

Medium-sized, short-tailed, stocky parrot with conspicuous white patch on head and throat with speckled brown patches on upperwings. Appears almost black at distance. Most conspicuous and common parrot over much of range. Widely sympatric Brown-headed Parrot has red axillaries and no white on head.

> **317a** **Adult** White crown and throat. Cheeks to hindneck and sides of breast rather dark, speckled blue.
>
> **317b** **Immature** White on head confined to forehead. Head, hindneck and breast otherwise green with pale yellowish margins on cheeks and crown giving pale speckled appearance.

319 Dusky Parrot *Pionus fuscus* Text and map page 522

Venezuela and Guianas east to Amapá, Brazil, and widely in Brazilian Amazon; disjunctly in Sierra de Perijá, Colombia/Venezuela. Regular seasonal movements in some parts. Lowland rain- and humid forest to 1,800m.

Medium-sized, short-tailed, stocky parrot, mainly dull and dark with streaky pale patch on sides of neck, bluish-grey head and browner body. Red patch at base of bill and pale spot on base of dark upper mandible.

> **319a** **Adult** Dark with pale eye-ring, streaky pale patch on neck and ear-coverts, brownish underparts, blue on underwing. Flight feathers blue above.
>
> **319b** **Immature** Green on secondaries and on primary and secondary-coverts. Little or no streaky patch on neck.

315 Scaly-headed Parrot *Pionus maximiliani* Text and map page 517

Central-eastern South America from S and E Brazil to N Argentina. Mainly in lowland dry forest, to about 2,000m.

Medium-sized, stocky, rather dark parrot. Mainly brownish-green with dark blue on throat, pale tip to bill, red vent and blue on side of fairly short square-ended tail. Green wings contrast with duller body.

> **315a** **Adult** (*maximiliani*; NE Brazil south to Espírito Santo) Green with dark markings on feathers to head and mantle giving scaly appearance. Dark blue throat, black lores.
>
> **315b** **Immature** (*maximiliani*) Less extensive blue on throat, less distinct margins on head.
>
> **315c** **Adult** (*melanoblepharus*; central to far SE Brazil and N Argentina) Darker blue on throat and darker above.

313a

313a

313c

313b

319a

313c

319b

317a

317a

317b

315b

315a

317b

319a

315c

316 Speckle-faced Parrot *Pionus tumultuosus* **Text and map page 519**

Andes of Venezuela, Colombia (not West), both slopes in Ecuador to N Peru; separately on east slope from C Peru to N Bolivia. Nomadic. Mainly in humid forest in the subtropical zone in south with northern birds mainly from temperate forest to the páramo, 2,000-3,000m.

Sscruffy-looking, short-tailed, stocky parrot with pale yellowish-horn bill, white around dark eyes, red undertail-coverts. Sympatric Red-billed Parrot has red bill.

316a Adult (*tumultuosus*; C Peru south into Bolivia) Face, head and neck pale vinaceous. Mainly green below with dark bluish-purple band on breast. Speckled appearance from pale tips to feathers on cheeks and ear-coverts.

316b Immature (*tumultuosus*) Green on hindneck and cheeks, and mainly yellowish-green undertail-coverts.

316c Adult (*seniloides*; Venezuela south to N Peru) Head, neck and cheeks pale grey heavily mottled white and pinkish. Large white patch on forehead. Breast and belly greyish-vinaceous with bluish tips on upper breast.

316d Immature (*seniloides*) Head mainly green with some brownish marks on white forehead, white speckles on cheeks.

---

314 Red-billed Parrot *Pionus sordidus* **Text and map page 516**

Uplands of South America from Venezuela to Bolivia. Mainly in various forms of humid forest. Foothills from 200 to 2,850m.

Medium-sized, often scruffy-looking parrot with short square-ended tail. Plumage fairly variable over large range but generally dull brownish or dark green with green flight feathers, red bill and crimson on undertail-coverts. Bare eye-ring fairly pale. Sympatric Bronze-winged Parrot has blue flight feathers and tail, horn-coloured bill and brown upperwing-coverts.

314a Adult (*sordidus*; west-central coastal mountains, Venezuela) Red bill, mainly blue head. Pink centres to feathers on breast. Brown on back with paler margins giving scaly effect. Race *corallinus* has more blue on throat.

314b Immature (*sordidus*) Yellowish-green undertail-coverts with some red markings. Head mainly green. Greyish streak on length of upper mandible. Less striking scaling on upperparts.

314c Adult (*antelius*; east-central mountains, Venezuela) Like nominate but feathers without blue edges on throat or pink centres on breast.

314d Adult (*saturatus*; N Santa Marta massif, Colombia) Darker and greener than nominate with feathers of upperparts lacking paler olive-brown margins. Less green on throat and cheeks. Dark streak on upper mandible.

314e Adult (*corallinus*; Colombia east of Andes, both slopes in Ecuador, east slope in Peru, disjunctly in NW Bolivia) Blue on throat deeper and more extensive than in nominate. Upperparts mainly green, unscaled.

---

318 Bronze-winged Parrot *Pionus chalcopterus* **Text and map page 521**

N Andes from extreme NW Venezuela, Colombia, Ecuador and NW Peru. Nomadic. Humid and wet upland and montane forest. Drier deciduous formations on west Andean slope in Peru. Chiefly 1,400-2,400m.

Medium-sized, short-tailed, stocky parrot, mainly very dark with contrasting pale patch on throat. Red undertail-coverts, pinkish breast, pale bill and bare periophthalmic skin. Underwing-coverts rich ultramarine-blue.

318a Adult (*chalcopterus*; Sierra de Perijá, Venezuela, and Colombian Andes except Nariño) Pale chin-patch bordered pale pink on upper breast. Blue underwing-coverts with bronzy-brown on upperwing. Pinkish eye-ring.

318b Immature (*chalcopterus*) Green head and upperparts, more uniform green below without pale chin-patch.

318c Adult (*cyanescens*; SW Colombia in Nariño, Ecuador and N Peru) Broader blue margins to feathers on breast, belly, mantle and back. Whitish eye-ring.

320 Cuban Amazon *Amazona leucocephala* Text and map page 523

Cuba, Isle of Pines, Great Inagua and Abaco in the Bahamas and Grand Cayman and Cayman Brac in the Cayman Islands. Mostly resident. Range of drier wooded habitats.

Fairly large. Pale bill, white on head, pinkish-red throat and cheeks and vinaceous feathers on belly. Barred pattern on nape, mantle, upperwing-coverts sides of neck and breast. No similar species in range.

> **320a** **Adult** (*leucocephala*; Cuba east of Las Villas Province) Pinkish-red patch from throat to upper breast. Red at base of tail feathers. Distinct vinaceous patch on belly. Dark ear-coverts.
>
> **320b** **Immature** (*leucocephala*) Reduced black edges to body feathers and less vinaceous on belly.
>
> **320c** **Adult** (*hesterna*; Cayman Brac) Smaller and darker than nominate. Mostly with red confined to spot beneath eye and smaller white patch on crown. Belly-patch more extensive and purplish.
>
> **320d** **Adult** (*bahamensis*; Abaco and Great Inagua, Bahamas) Larger than nominate with slaty-blue hindcrown and white on head extending to ear-coverts. Vinaceous feathers on belly reduced or absent, red on undertail less extensive.

322 Hispaniolan Amazon *Amazona ventralis* Text and map page 525

Hispaniola. Introduced Puerto Rico and probably Culebra. Variety of wooded habitats. Sea-level to c. 1,500m.

White forehead and eye-ring, pale bill and dark patch on ear-coverts. Blue flight feathers (including undersides), blue crown and maroon belly-patch.

> **322a** **Adult** White on upper cheek, dark ear-coverts, maroon belly-patch.
>
> **322b** **Immature** Like adult but reduced blue on crown and maroon on belly.

326 Puerto Rican Amazon *Amazona vittata* Text and map page 528

Luquillo Forest, Puerto Rico. Tiny population in montane rainforest at 200-600m.

Medium-small, almost all-green amazon with red forehead and blue on flight feathers. Distinct barred pattern above. Introduced Hispaniolan Amazon has conspicuous white forehead and maroon belly-patch.

> **326** **Adult** Green; red forehead, barred pattern above, blue primaries.

321 Yellow-billed Amazon *Amazona collaria* Text and map page 524

Jamaica. Resident but wanders. Mostly in mid-level wet limestone forest but ranges from sea-level to 1,200m.

Blue on head and wings, white forehead, dark ear-coverts, pinkish throat and yellow bill. Yellowish-green tail (rosy at base) has yellow rim and is often fanned. Sympatric Black-billed Amazon is slightly smaller, with dark bill and darker plumage.

> **321** **Adult** White around eyes and on forehead. Pink throat contrasts with otherwise green underparts. Pale bill and blue crown.

PLATE 81: AMAZONS II

329 Green-cheeked Amazon *Amazona viridigenalis* — Text and map page 531

NE Mexico. Winter wanderer to extreme SW Texas, USA. Tropical lowlands but seasonally to 1,200m.

Red crown, green cheeks and pale bill. Red patch on wing visible in flight. Slightly rounded tail with yellow at tip. Black scaled pattern on upper back. Yellow-cheeked Amazon has blue crown, yellow markings on face and slower, more laboured flight.

329a **Adult** Red forehead and crown. Blue on sides of nape. Red outer secondaries.

329b **Immature** Red much reduced on head.

323 White-fronted Amazon *Amazona albifrons* — Text and map page 526

W Mexico to Costa Rica. Mostly resident but seasonal visitor in some parts. Generally prefers drier wooded habitats but in more humid vegetation where sympatric with Yellow-lored Amazon. To 1,800m.

Mainly green, red around eyes with white forehead. Yellow-lored Amazon has yellow (not red) lores and dark ear-coverts, but these often hard to see.

323a **Adult male** (*albifrons*; Pacific S Mexico into Guatemalan lowlands) Red on face encircles eye. White forehead and forecrown and blue on hindcrown. Red alula and primary coverts.

323b **Adult female** (*albifrons*) Red in wing largely absent.

323c **Immature** (*albifrons*) Like female but with forecrown tinged with yellow. Subadult male often with some green on primary coverts.

323d **Adult male** (*saltuensis*; W Mexico) Plumage strongly suffused with blue. Blue on hindcrown extends to nape.

324 Yellow-lored Amazon *Amazona xantholora* — Text and map page 527

Yucatán Peninsula, Mexico, including Cozumel and N Belize) Tropical deciduous forest, probably avoiding rain-forest. Lowlands.

Mainly green, with short tail, white crown, and broad red patch around eye. For separation from White-fronted Amazon see above.

324a **Adult male** Extensive red on face around eyes, yellow lores, broad white patch on forehead and red on alula and primary coverts. Dark tips to green body feathers creates scalloped pattern.

324b **Adult female** Green wings, less red on face, blue instead of white on forehead and crown, less distinct dark ear-coverts.

324c **Immature** Like female but lores less bright yellow, crown paler blue.

325 Black-billed Amazon *Amazona agilis* — Text and map page 528

C and E uplands of Jamaica. Mainly in mid-level wet limestone forest but also in cultivated plots inside and fringing forest.

Mainly green, small amazon with blue in flight feathers and red primary coverts (partly or wholly green in female). For separation from Yellow-billed Amazon see caption to Plate 80.

325a **Adult male** Red primary coverts, blue on head with dark ear-coverts.

325b **Adult female** Fewer red primary coverts (green instead).

325c **Immature** Similar to adult, but primary coverts green. Also possibly duller on head and without blue suffusion.

329b

329a

329a

323a

323c

323b

323a

323d

323d

325a

325c

324a

324b

324c

325b

327 Tucuman Amazon *Amazona tucumana*　　　Text and map page 529

E Andes of Argentina and Bolivia from Catamarca north to Chuquisaca. Seasonal altitudinal movements. Montane forest with *Alnus* and *Nothofagus*; *Podocarpus* forest in S Bolivia. 1,800-3,050m.

Largely green, stocky, short-tailed parrot with red frontal area and red patch on upperwing. Body heavily scalloped with black. Bill pinkish. Trailing edge of wing deep blue.

327a　**Adult** Red frontal patch and on primary coverts. Yellowish-orange thighs.

327b　**Immature** Green primary coverts, green thighs and yellow flecks in (reduced) red frontal area.

328 Red-spectacled Amazon *Amazona pretrei*　　　Text and map page 530

Rio Grande do Sul, Brazil; very rarely in E Paraguay. Some post-breeding movements. *Araucaria angustifolia* forest in non-breeding season; low open savanna woodland and riverine forests when breeding. Mostly 300-1,000m.

Mainly green, medium-sized amazon with bright red on forehead, face and edge of wings. Pale yellowish bill. Strong dark scalloping on back and underparts. Only parrot in range with extensive red on head and wings.

328a　**Adult male** Red on head extends to mid-crown and below eyes. Red primary coverts, bend of wing, thighs and base of tail.

328b　**Adult female** Much less red on wing with carpal edge and primary coverts mostly green.

330 Lilac-crowned Amazon *Amazona finschi*　　　Text and map page 532

Pacific Mexico from Sonora to Oaxaca. Mostly resident but non-breeding visitor to lowlands. Wooded hills and mountains. Arid or semi-arid scrubby vegetation but with preference for lushly vegetated canyons. Sea-level to c. 2,000m.

Longish, slightly rounded tail. Dark reddish forehead contrasts with pale bill. Combination of dull red forehead, pale green cheeks and lilac or powder-blue crown distinguishes this from all other New World parrots. Red speculum on outer secondaries visible at rest and in flight.

330a　**Adult** (*finschi*; S Sinaloa and Durango south to Oaxaca) Deep red patch on forehead.

330b　**Adult** (*woodi*; SE Sonora, Chihuahua and NE Sinaloa) Body greener (less yellowish).

331 Yellow-cheeked Amazon *Amazona autumnalis*　　　Text and map page 533

Caribbean lowlands of Mexico through Central America to west of Andes in Colombia and Ecuador and north of Andes east into Venezuela. Separately in Brazilian Amazon between Rios Negro and Amazonas. Mainly resident.

Wide range of wooded and open habitats with trees from lowland rainforest to pine woodlands. Sea-level to 1,000m.

Dark horn or grey bill and red frontal area (often hard to see in field). Tail broadly tipped yellowish-green. Red patch on secondaries visible in flight. Partially sympatric Yellow-crowned Amazon has longer tail; Green-cheeked has lavender hindcrown and neck; Mealy is larger.

331a　**Adult** (*autumnalis*; Mexico to Honduras including Bay Islands) Combination of broad red frontal patch on head and lores with extensive yellow patch on cheeks distinctive. Dark horn upper mandible.

331b　**Immature** (*autumnalis*) Little or no yellow on face, reduced red on lores and forehead, brownish iris.

331c　**Adult** (*salvini*; Honduras or Nicaragua to SW Colombia and NW Venezuela) Cheek bright green and base of tail red on innerwebs. Some red feathers on cere. Grey bill. Yellow on cheeks in N Costa Rica (decreasing southwards); some Panama specimens show yellow on lores.

331d　**Adult** (*lilacina*; W Ecuador) Face more uniform and brighter yellowish than *salvini* and red loral patch forms superciliary stripe. Some red feathers on cere. Blackish bill. Crown with red tips.

331e　**Adult** (*diadema*; Amazon basin of Brazil between Rios Negro and Amazonas) Green face. Red on lores and feathered cere darker, forming crimson spot in front of eye. Cheeks with slight bluish tinge. Dark bill.

332 Blue-cheeked Amazon *Amazona dufresniana*   **Text and map page 534**

S and E Venezuela, Guianas and probably Amapá, Brazil. Some seasonal movements. Wooded habitats including rainforest, cloud-forest, savanna woodland and gallery forest. Lowlands to 1,700m.

Fairly large with blue cheeks, ochre lores (appearing as preocular orange spot at distance), yellowish crown. Yellow wing-patch and broad yellowish terminal band to outer tail.

    332a **Adult** Combination of blue cheeks, yellowish-orange wing-patch and ochre lores diagnostic.

    332b **Immature** Less blue on head, duller yellow on crown, smaller ochre patch on lores. Outer tail feathers more pointed.

333 Red-browed Amazon *Amazona rhodocorytha*   **Text and map page 535**

E Brazil from Alagoas to Rio de Janeiro. Mainly in humid lowland rain-forest but also (perhaps seasonally) in inland montane forests to c. 1,000m.

Fairly large amazon with red crown, blue cheeks and red speculum. Tail with red subterminal spots and yellow tips. Orange area on lores. From sympatric Orange-winged and Mealy Amazons by red on head.

    333a **Adult** Red on head from forehead to hindcrown with bright orange on lores. Red on base of three outermost secondaries.

    333b **Immature** Less extensive red on head and tail, and confined to only first two secondaries.

334 Red-tailed Amazon *Amazona brasiliensis*   **Text and map page 536**

São Paulo and Paraná, Brazil. Possibly minor seasonal movements in winter (May-Aug). Lowland coastal forest and wetland habitats. Mostly below 400m.

Fairly large with red forehead and crown and mauve-blue cheeks, ear-coverts and throat. No red speculum. Yellow-tipped tail has broad red subterminal band and blue on base.

    334 **Adult** Tail pattern distinctive. No wing speculum.

335 Festive Amazon *Amazona festiva*   **Text and map page 537**

N South America principally in the Amazon and Orinoco catchments. Mostly resident. Lowland rainforest especially várzea, sometimes in savanna with scattered trees. Ranges up to 500m.

Fairly large amazon with red rump and lower back. Feathers above and behind eyes tinged blue with blue patch on throat. Red lores, frontal band.

    335a **Adult** (*festiva*; Amazon basin) Red rump and lower back. Red on forehead and lores bordered yellowish on forecrown.

    335b **Immature** (*festiva*) Mainly green rump, less blue on head; red on base of innerwebs of some lateral tail feathers.

    335c **Adult** (*bodini*; mainly along Orinoco and its tributaries) Red patch on forehead extends to forecrown. Bill black. More yellowish-green, especially beneath. Lores blackish and cheeks suffused lilac.

346 Vinaceous Amazon *Amazona vinacea*   **Text and map page 550**

E Brazil, E Paraguay, N Argentina. Some seasonal movements. Mixed evergreen forest, often with *Araucaria*. Lowlands to 2,000m.

Fairly large amazon. Breast strongly suffused with vinous-maroon. Upper mandible red with whitish tip. Elongated feathers on nape and mantle subterminally blue tipped black. Red lores, forehead and speculum.

     346a   **Adult** Broad red frontal band. Vinous breast. Cheek tipped yellow.

     346b   **Immature** Breast suffused green, less red on head and bill, no yellow on cheek.

336 Yellow-faced Amazon *Amazona xanthops*   **Text and map page 538**

Interior Brazil from north-east to south and adjacent E Bolivia. Seasonal and nomadic movements. Deciduous woodlands and scrub. Lowlands.

Rather small. Variably extensive yellow on head and underparts. Widely sympatric Orange-winged and Blue-fronted Amazons larger, tend to occur in taller gallery forest and have red speculum.

     336a   **Adult** Yellow head with more orange ear-coverts. Pale bill with grey stripe on upper mandible.

     336b   **Immature** Brown iris. Perhaps less yellow in plumage.

337 Yellow-shouldered Amazon *Amazona barbadensis*   **Text and map page 539**

N Venezuela and offshore islands. Mainly resident. Xerophytic vegetation with cacti and low thorny bushes and trees. To 450m.

Large with yellow head (with forehead very pale or white), thighs and shoulders, heavy pale bill and red speculum. Only large parrot in range. Yellow 'shoulders' and red speculum conspicuous in flight.

     337a   **Adult** Blue subterminal suffusion to feathers on breast and belly probably identifies adults. Crown wholly yellow with no green.

     337b   **Immature** Possibly lacks blue subterminal suffusion to feathers on underparts. Darker green than adults with heavier black margins on mantle. Scattered green feathers on yellow crown.

338 Blue-fronted Amazon *Amazona aestiva*   **Text and map page 540**

Interior lowland South America from NE Brazil to Bolivia, Paraguay and Argentina. Some seasonal movements. Range of wooded habitats and open country with trees. To 1,600m.

Fairly large with extensive yellow on face and head, blue forehead and red speculum. Sympatric Orange-winged Amazon has blue stripe running from base of bill through eye to sides of neck.

     338a   **Adult** (*aestiva*; NE Brazil south to Mato Grosso) Blue cheeks. Red on bend of wing.

     338b   **Adult** (*xanthopteryx*; E Bolivia, Paraguay, N Argentina and extreme SW Brazil) Shoulders and lesser upperwing-coverts yellow perhaps with scattered red feathers. Yellow on head more extensive.

339 Yellow-headed Amazon *Amazona oratrix* **Text and map page 541**

Mexico (including all four Islas Marías) to Belize, E Guatemala and extreme NW Honduras. Feral, Florida and Puerto Rico. Seasonal and dry forests. Lowlands below 500m.

Large with bright yellow head, red speculum with yellow or red and yellow on leading edge of wing.

339a **Adult** (*oratrix*; mainland Mexico) Yellow on head extends to throat and nape.

339b **Immature** (*oratrix*) Little or no yellow on head and little or no red and yellow on wing.

339c **Adult** (*belizensis*; Belize) Less yellow on head than nominate with no yellow on throat. Some birds with green cheeks.

339d **Adult** (*tresmariae*; Islas Tres Marías, Mexico) More extensive yellow on neck and throat. More bluish-green underparts. Odd red feathers in head. Yellow tips to upperwing-coverts, inner secondaries and tail more frequent.

340 Yellow-naped Amazon *Amazona auropalliata* **Text and map page 542**

S Mexico to NW Costa Rica. Resident. All kinds of woodland to 700m.

Large. Bright golden-yellow nape and bright red speculum diagnostic. Variable yellow on forehead.

340a **Adult** (*auropalliata*; Pacific slope of Middle America from Oaxaca, Mexico, to NW Costa Rica) Mainly green with bright golden nape-patch and red on four outer secondaries.

340b **Adult** (*parvipes*; Mosquitia in Honduras and NE Nicaragua) Red feathers at bend of wing.

341 Yellow-crowned Amazon *Amazona ochrocephala* **Text and map page 544**

Panama and South America south to E Brazil and N Bolivia. All kinds of wooded habitat. Often near rivers. Lowlands to 750m.

Large. Yellow on forehead (except W Amazonia) sometimes extends onto lores and around eyes. Red speculum and at bend of wing.

341a **Adult** (*ochrocephala*; E Colombia, Venezuela, Trinidad, Guianas and N Brazil south to lower right bank tributaries of Amazon) Yellow crown, forehead and lores. Red spot on base of upper mandible.

341b **Immature** (*ochrocephala*) Smaller yellow patch on head, orange-red fringes to yellow crown feathers, more pointed tail feathers, brown iris.

341c **Adult** (*xantholaema*; Marajó Island at mouth of Amazon) Yellow on head extends onto hindcrown, lower cheeks and ear-coverts. Often with narrow green frontal band. Bluish tinge on breast.

341d **Adult** (*nattereri*; S Colombia to N Bolivia) Less yellow on head than nominate with green frontal band. Cheeks, superciliary area and lores with blue tinge. No red spot on upper mandible.

341e **Adult** (*panamensis*; Colombia north and west of Andes to W Panama) Bill pinkish-horn, yellow reduced to V-shaped patch on forehead.

342 Orange-winged Amazon *Amazona amazonica* Text and map page 545

Mostly east of Andes from Colombia to SE Brazil. Mainly resident. All kinds of lowland forest and wooded country including rainforest, savanna and other seasonal woodlands. Lowlands to 1,200m.

Medium-sized amazon with yellow and blue on head, orange speculum. Undertail dull orange with green band. Yellow cheek with blue stripe from lores above eye.

342a Adult (*amazonica*; continental South America) Blue stripe on yellow head. Outer three secondaries orange-red forming bright speculum.

342b Adult (*tobagensis*; Trinidad and Tobago) Speculum supposedly on outer four secondaries.

343 Scaly-naped Amazon *Amazona mercenaria* Text and map page 546

Andes from NW Venezuela to N Bolivia. Some elevational or nomadic movements but mostly resident. Hill and mountain forest, 800-3,600m.

Head and neck green with dark tips giving scaly appearance. Red subterminal band on tail and red or maroon on secondaries. Yellow on leading edge of wing.

343a Adult (*mercenaria*; Peru to N Bolivia) Red on outer secondaries forms bright speculum.

343b Adult (*canipalliata*; N Peru to NW Venezuela) Bases of outer secondaries with maroon spots; sometimes scattered red feathers on crown, throat and upper breast.

344 White-faced Amazon *Amazona kawalli* Text and map page 547

Amazon basin in Brazil. Rainforest with apparent preference for river edge and flooded forest.

Fairly large amazon, very similar to sympatric Mealy but patch of bare whitish skin at base of bill, grey eye-ring, red at base of outer tail and no red on edge of wing diagnostic. Red speculum and yellowish-green terminal tail-band.

344a Adult male Possibly has dark lores.

344b Adult female Lores green.

345 Mealy Amazon *Amazona farinosa* Text and map page 548

Middle America from Mexico to Panama and South America in Orinoco and Amazon basins, E Brazil and west of Andes south to Ecuador. Mainly resident but seasonal wanderings in some parts of range. Chiefly in dense humid lowland rainforest but in montane forest to 1,200m.

Large amazon with conspicuous whitish eye-ring. Tail has distal half yellowish with basal portion green. Conspicuous red speculum. Glaucous suffusion on hindneck to back. Dark primaries. Blue trailing edge on secondaries.

345a Adult (*farinosa*; E Colombia, E Venezuela, Amazonian Brazil from Pará to Mato Grosso, E Peru; disjunctly in E Brazil) Most birds have yellow on crown.

345b Immature (*farinosa*) Brown iris.

345c Adult (*inornata*; W Ecuador, W and N Colombia and adjacent Panama, N and W Venezuela) Usually no yellow on crown.

345d Adult (*virenticeps*; Nicaragua to W Panama) Pale blue on crown; no red on leading edge of wing.

345e Adult (*guatemalae*; Veracruz, Mexico, to Honduras) Like *virenticeps* but blue on crown more extensive and darker. Dark bill.

342a

342b

342a

343a

343a

343h

344a

344a

344a

344b

345a

345a

345b

345c

345d

345e

349 St Vincent Amazon *Amazona guildingii*   Text and map page 553

St Vincent. Mature moist forest at 125-1,000m, sometimes cultivated areas.

Large with whitish or pale yellow crown and around eyes with blue on cheeks and hindneck. Tail with blue subterminal band and yellow tip. Flight feathers blue with bright orange-yellow bases. Plumage highly variable, but only parrot in range.

349a **Adult** (green morph) Body plumage and upperwings dark green.

349b **Adult** (brown morph) Body plumage and upperwings rich deep brown.

348 Red-necked Amazon *Amazona arausiaca*   Text and map page 552

Dominica. Rainforest mainly at 300-800m.

Large. Bluish head, red and yellow speculum and bright red patch on throat (and sometimes upper breast). Yellow tip to tail. Sympatric Imperial Amazon larger and darker.

348 **Adult** Blue head, red neck-patch, red and yellow speculum.

347 St Lucia Amazon *Amazona versicolor*   Text and map page 551

St Lucia. Rainforest, sometimes in secondary growth.

Large. Red speculum, bright red patch on throat and upper breast, blue head. Underparts with scattered patches of brick-red. Tail tipped yellow. Only parrot in range.

347 **Adult** Blue head and primaries, red speculum.

350 Imperial Amazon *Amazona imperialis*   Text and map page 554

Dominica. Rainforest, sometimes reaching elfin forest above 1,200m.

Largest amazon. Deep green back, purple head, neck and underparts. Scarlet patch at bend of wing.

350a **Adult** Purplish head and neck.

350b **Immature** Green on crown, nape and lower cheeks.

349a

349b

349b

349a

348

347

347

348

350a

350b

350a

PLATE 88: HAWK-HEADED AND PURPLE-BELLIED PARROTS

351 Hawk-headed Parrot *Deroptyus accipitrinus*   Text and map page 555

N South America east of Andes ranging south to border with N Bolivia. Some seasonal movements. Lowland rainforest appearing to prefer terra firme formations. To 400m.

Elongated neck feathers deep claret-red tipped with bright blue, creating striking scaled effect. Neck feathers sometimes raised to create blue-edged red fan. Resembles small bird of prey when perched.

351a   **Adult** (*accipitrinus*; north of Amazon) Mainly green with pale speckles on dark face with buffy-white cap. Blue tips to claret feathers beneath. Red at base of lateral tail feathers. Grey bill.

351b   **Immature** (*accipitrinus*) Horn-coloured mandible and warm brown iris.

351c   **Adult** (*fuscifrons*; south of Amazon) Forehead and crown brown, lacking buffy-white patch of nominate. No red at base of innerwebs of lateral tail feathers.

352 Purple-bellied Parrot *Triclaria malachitacea*   Text and map page 556

SE Brazil from Bahia to Rio Grande do Sul; twice in Misiones, Argentina. Some seasonal movements reported but these now believed mistaken. Wet lower montane forest with preference for bromeliad-rich stands along watercourses in valleys. Mainly 300-700m (perhaps to 1,000m).

Mainly green with long, rather rounded tail and relatively short wings. Possible to confuse with partially sympatric female Red-capped Parrot which is smaller and has proportionately shorter tail.

352a   **Adult male** Green with large purplish-blue patch on lower breast and belly. Blue tinge on underparts including underside of tail and wings. Pale bill.

352b   **Adult female** No purplish-blue belly-patch.

352c   **Immature male** Less purplish-blue on underparts.

351a

351a

351b

351c

352a

352b

352c

352a

1 BLACK LORY
Chalcopsitta atra   Plate 1

Other names: Red-quilled Lory; Rajah/Raja Lory (*C. a. insignis*)

IDENTIFICATION 32cm. Large blackish lory with a long, rounded tail. In the field, predominantly dark brownish-black plumage and dark violet-blue rump separate this characteristic species from all other lories. Flight silhouette similar to both Brown (2) and Yellow-streaked (3) Lories. Brown is allopatric, occurring only in northern New Guinea. Black overlaps, and may hybridise with Yellow-streaked (race *scintillata*) in the easternmost part of its range, but can be separated by the absence of green in its plumage (poor light can make the two species difficult to separate in flight). All *Chalcopsitta* species can be distinguished in flight from the smaller Dusky Lory (11) and from Rainbow Lorikeet (13) by their rapid shallow wing-beats combined with apparently slow forward progress, making the birds look as though they are working very hard for little return. In captivity, separated from the other all-blackish species, Vasa (159) and Black (160) Parrots, by dark bill, cere and facial skin (adult), and dark-blue rump.

VOICE A high screech or chitter, shriller than any other lory, but not as loud as Dusky Lory or Rainbow Lorikeet. All *Chalcopsitta* species have very similar calls.

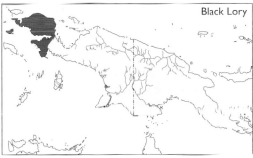

Black Lory

DISTRIBUTION AND STATUS Endemic to western Irian Jaya, Indonesia, including Vogelkop and the Onin Peninsula, as well as on adjacent islands including Batanta, Misool and Salawati. The world population is above 50,000. Small numbers in captivity.

ECOLOGY Black Lories occur in the lowlands, frequenting open habitats such as coastal coconut plantations, savanna, humid forest margins, open grasslands and small scattered eucalyptus groves; they have also been recorded from mangroves and coastal swamp forests. They are sometimes found in large flocks foraging together in flowering trees. Little is known of their reproductive behaviour in the wild, but males in breeding condition have been collected in Apr and Dec. In captivity incubation has been logged at 25 days, with both parents brooding; two eggs are usual, with the young fledging in around 74 days.

DESCRIPTION Rear ear-coverts and nape feathers slightly elongated and attenuated. Plumage generally dark brownish-black with a purplish sheen, darker on the head, which sometimes shows a few red feathers. Lower back through to uppertail-coverts dark violet-blue, extending onto uppertail. Flight feathers and primary coverts blackish-brown; underwing blackish with a slight sheen on the coverts. Underparts with a purplish sheen mainly on the breast and undertail-coverts. Undertail reddish shading through orange-red to yellowish-olive at tips. **Bare parts**: Bill black; periophthalmic ring and cere blue-black; iris orange-red; legs grey.

SEX/AGE Immature has a white periophthalmic ring and cere and a dark brown iris.

MEASUREMENTS Wing 169-193; tail 114-151; bill 20-24; tarsus 22-26.

GEOGRAPHICAL VARIATION Three races.
> *C. a. atra* (W part of Vogelkop, and on Batanta and Salawati)
> *C. a. bernsteini* (Misool) Can be separated from *atra* by its deep orange-red thighs and forecrown.
> *C. a. insignis* (E part of Vogelkop, along the Onin and Bomberai peninsulas, and on Rumberpon Island) A distinctive subspecies sometimes known as Rajah Lory, told from nominate and *bernsteini* by dark red fore-crown, lores, underwing-coverts, bases of flight feathers and thighs, and red markings on throat, flanks, and belly. Head also tinged with greyish-blue.

NOTE A fourth subspecies, *C. a. spectabilis*, is known from a single specimen collected in north west Irian Jaya. The specimen shows characteristics of both *C. a. insignis* and *C. s. scintillata*, and is probably a hybrid between them.

REFERENCES Beehler *et al* (1986), BirdLife (1993), Forshaw (1989), Gyldenstolpe (1955), Lambert *et al.* (1993), Lodge (1991), Peters (1961), Rand & Gilliard (1967), Sibley & Monroe (1990).

2 BROWN LORY
Chalcopsitta duivenbodei   Plate 1

Other names: Duyvenbode's Lory

IDENTIFICATION 31cm. A distinctive large brown lory with a long rounded tail, restricted to northern New Guinea. Combination of dark brown plumage, yellow forecrown, chin, thighs, underwing-coverts, innerwebs of primaries and bend of wing, with violet rump and black bill. Silhouette and flight similar to Black (1) and Yellow-streaked (3) Lories, which are both allopatric. Extensive yellow underwing-flash is obvious in flight. Superficially resembles the sympatric Dusky Lory (11), but is larger and longer-tailed. From adult Dusky by black, not orange bill, uniform brown underparts and violet not buffish white (or yellowish) rump. Immature Dusky has a mostly dark bill, but still shows extensive dappled orange and brown markings below and a yellowish rump. In flight, Dusky Lory also shows a yellow band across the underside of the flight feathers which is lacking in Brown. The flight of Brown Lory is slower than that of Rainbow Lorikeet (13), with more flickering wings.

VOICE Harsh, slightly musical notes together with various hissing and screeching calls, very similar to Yellow-streaked Lory, but weaker and more forced than Dusky Lory or Rainbow Lorikeet.

DISTRIBUTION AND STATUS Endemic to New Guinea, where it is patchily distributed through the northern lowlands ranging from near the Memberamo River in the west to Astrolabe Bay in the east. The world population is greater than 50,000, and there are small numbers in captivity.

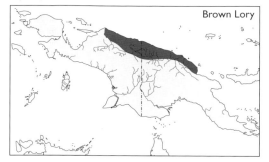

Brown Lory

ECOLOGY Found in the lowlands up to 200m in humid and alluvial forests, in tall secondary growth; along forest margins, and in more open habitats including coastal clearings. Brown Lories frequent the mid- to upper storeys and have been recorded congregating at flowering trees in loose flocks with Rainbow Lorikeets. The birds are most often seen flying in pairs or parties of six to eight birds which roost socially. In display the male swings below a branch to reveal his yellow underwing flash. Little is known of the species's reproductive cycle, but a female in breeding condition was collected in April. Breeding ecology in captivity is very similar to that of the preceding species.

DESCRIPTION Generally dark brown. Forehead yellow blending to greyish-brown on crown with some pale-shafted feathers; hint of violet suffusion on hind-crown and nape where feathers, like rear ear-coverts, slightly elongated with obscure dull yellowish streaking. Lower back and rump violet-blue. Throat and sides of chin surrounding facial skin yellow blending to greyish-brown on cheeks and blackish-brown on upper breast; central breast feathers show faint yellow tips and bases, yellow sometimes extending around upper breast to form incomplete collar. Bend of wing and carpal edge bright yellow extending onto shoulder and underwing-coverts; upperwing-coverts brown with a violet sheen on primary coverts, and flight feathers suffused dark violet with yellow innerwebs to primaries. Thighs orange-yellow. Undertail-coverts dark violet. Uppertail olive-yellow with violet suffusion on feather-centres; undertail olive. **Bare parts**: Bill and facial skin black; iris dark reddish-orange; legs grey-black.

SEX/AGE Sexes alike. Immature shows duller and less extensive yellow facial markings; no pale streaking on nape, and white not black facial skin.

MEASUREMENTS Wing 171-180; tail 117-138; bill 20-23; tarsus 22-25.

GEOGRAPHICAL VARIATION Two races.

> *C. d. duivenbodei* (N New Guinea east to Aitape region)
> *C d. syringanuchalis* (E part of northern New Guinea from the Aitape area to Astrolabe Bay) Doubtfully distinct from nominate. Head and back darker than nominate with a dark violet sheen.

REFERENCES Beehler *et al.* (1986), BirdLife (1993), Coates (1985), Forshaw (1989), Greensmith (1975), Lambert *et al.* (1993), Peters (1961), Rand & Gilliard (1967).

3 YELLOW-STREAKED LORY
Chalcopsitta scintillata   Plate 1

Other names: Greater Streaked Lory, Cream-streaked Lory, Red-fronted Lory (scientific name sometimes spelt *C. sintillata*)

IDENTIFICATION 31cm. A large lory with long, broad, blunt-ended tail. Plumage generally green with a dark head, red forecrown, thighs and base of undertail, and with extensive yellow and orange-yellow streaking on the underparts visible at close range. In flight appears rather long-necked, and in common with other *Chalcopsitta* species has shallow flickering wingbeats and appears to make slow forward progress. In the field the only likely confusion species is the eastern race *insignis* of Black Lory (1) which is partially sympatric (and may hybridise) with nominate Yellow-streaked. Both show a red forecrown and underwing-coverts, but confusion is only really possible if birds are seen poorly in flight, or only in silhouette, when green of Yellow-streaked Lory can appear black. Black can be eliminated by any hint of green in the plumage and a yellow panel across the underside of the central flight feathers.

VOICE Very vocal both in flight and when perched. Two flight calls are described, a multisyllabic buzzy screech, given as a descending series of two to five (mainly three) notes, and a burst of multisyllabic musical twittering notes which vary in length and pitch. Perched birds may call every few seconds with a shorter buzzy squealing *kiss* or *kiss-kiss*. This is sometimes preceded by a variable descending multisyllabic musical call. The voice is generally shrill, buzzy and weaker than in Dusky Lory (11) and Rainbow Lorikeet (13), and suggests the call of Hooded Cuckoo-shrike *Coracina longicauda*.

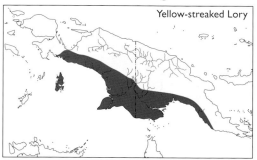

Yellow-streaked Lory

DISTRIBUTION AND STATUS Southern New Guinea from Triton Bay and Geelvink Bay, Irian Jaya, in the west to around Port Moresby in the east. Also found on the Aru Islands. Generally common with a world population over 100,000. There are small numbers in captivity.

ECOLOGY Yellow-streaked Lories occur through the lowlands and hills up to about 800m, occupying a variety of habitats including savanna, forest edge, secondary growth, coconut plantations, gallery forest and mangroves. The birds are gregarious, usually being encountered in pairs or parties of up to several dozen individuals feeding acrobatically on nectar and fruit, or flying high above the forest early in the day. They sometimes feed in the company of other species such as Rainbow Lorikeets and Red-flanked Lorikeets (45), their local abundance being determined by the availability of flowering trees. Favourite species include sago palms and *Schefflera*. Pairs engage in acrobatic aerial and perched displays, and nesting has been recorded in Feb and Sep with a hollow tree being the preferred site.

DESCRIPTION Generally dark vivid green, lower nape and mantle with pale shaft-streaks; rump shaft-streaked brighter green with a light blue suffusion on feather-centres; forehead and lores red; hind-crown, nape, and chin blackish; ear-coverts black; pale green streaking on lower cheeks and around neck; breast suffused purplish-brown marked red at sides and streaked bright orange-yellow and green; belly green, streaked yellow, tending to pale green on lower flanks and vent; thighs red; undertail-coverts bright green. Upperwing-coverts green, shaft-streaked bluish-green at bend of wing; primary coverts green suffused blue; upperside of flight feathers green on outer- and brown on innerwebs; yellow or yellow-orange patch on underside of flight feathers; underwing-coverts red (sometimes showing some green). Basal two-thirds of innerwebs of tail feathers red; distal third dull reddish below and tipped yellow-olive; uppertail appears green when closed. Bill black; periophthalmic ring greyish-white; iris yellow to orange-brown; legs dark-grey.

SEX/AGE Sexes alike. Immature shows less red on forehead, a brown iris, and dusky yellow markings at the base of the bill.

MEASUREMENTS Wing 160-183; tail 96-114; bill 19-23; tarsus 21-24

GEOGRAPHICAL VARIATION Three races, but individual variation is common within all.

C. s. scintillata (Triton Bay and Geelvink Bay, Irian Jaya, east to the lower Fly River, Papua New Guinea)

C. s. chloroptera (intergrades with nominate west of about 142°E, extending east to the Port Moresby region, Papua New Guinea) Can be separated from *scintillata* by green or green and black, not red, underwing coverts (may show some red markings at tips), and by narrower streaking on body feathers. It also shows less yellow on the underside of the primaries, or lacks yellow altogether.

C. s. rubifrons (Aru Islands) Separated from nominate *scintillata* by wider, more orange breast streaks.

REFERENCES Beehler *et al.* (1986), Coates (1985), Diamond (1972), Forshaw (1989), Lambert *et al.* (1993), Lodge (1991), Rand & Gilliard (1967).

---

4   CARDINAL LORY
Chalcopsitta cardinalis   Plate 1

IDENTIFICATION 31cm. A large, long-tailed, entirely red lory. This is the commonest lory in the Solomon Islands. In flight the graduated tail is often fanned, showing a distinctive wedge shape from below. There are no sympatric species likely to present identification problems. In captivity, the longer tail, slender body and absence of clear-cut black tips to the upperwing-coverts and flight feathers, and of blue on the tertials, eliminate Red Lory (7), the other predominantly red species.

VOICE A harsh, rasping, dry repetitious *zheeet-zheeet*, similar in structure to the call of Rainbow Lorikeet (13) but louder and harsher. The shrill, grating voice has also been

described alternatively as a loud bubbling shriek, a coarse shrieking trill and a deep harsh screech. Various chattering calls have also been noted.

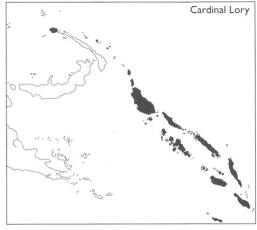
Cardinal Lory

DISTRIBUTION AND STATUS Endemic to the Bismarck Archipelago (Papua New Guinea) and the Solomons. Ranges from New Hanover in the north, through outlying island groups including Tabar, Lihir, Tanga and Feni. The species also occurs on Nissan, Buka and Bougainville (Papua New Guinea), and ranges through the Solomons where it is generally common to abundant, reaching San Cristobal in the south. It has recently colonised Ontong Java atoll which lies around 300km to the north-east of the main Solomons group. The world population is above 100,000. Small numbers in captivity.

ECOLOGY Inhabits mangrove, woodland, coastal coconut palm plantations and humid primary and secondary forest up to 830m on Bougainville and 1,200m on Kolombangara. This is a conspicuous species frequently seen flying swiftly overhead in groups of 5-90 individuals which sometimes move between islands. The birds draw attention to themselves by their noisy chattering and spend much time feeding in the canopy of flowering trees and coconut palms, often in company with the slightly smaller Rainbow Lorikeet. Cardinal Lories feed on pollen, nectar, small berries and fruits. Little is known about their reproductive behaviour but a display which included wing-drooping and flapping was noted in Sep, and mating has been recorded during Aug.

DESCRIPTION Plumage red, brighter on head and darker and duller on mantle, wings and tail. Breast and underwing-coverts tipped buff-yellow producing a lighter scalloped appearance; belly darker with darker feather-bases, giving a slight mottled effect. Bend of wing to median-coverts dark reddish-brown; slight violet suffusion along leading edge of underwing, rest of underwing red. **Bare parts**: Bill coral, lighter at tip and black at base of upper mandible; skin at base of bill black blotched with yellow; periophthalmic ring black; iris dark orange-red; legs grey-black.

SEX/AGE Sexes alike. Immature with lighter red mantle and wings, and a shorter, more pointed tail. The bill is dull orange, strongly marked with black, and the iris is dull yellow.

MEASUREMENTS Wing 174-186; tail 131-155; bill 20-24; tarsus 20-24.

GEOGRAPHICAL VARIATION None.

REFERENCES BirdLife (1993), Cain & Galbraith (1956), Coates (1985), Forshaw (1989), Greensmith (1975), Hadden (1981), Lambert *et al.* (1993), Mayr (1945), Peters (1961), Sibley (1951), Sibley & Monroe (1990).

5 RED-AND-BLUE LORY
Eos histrio   Plate 2

Other names: Blue-tailed Lory, Blue-diademed Lory

IDENTIFICATION 31cm. Red-and-blue Lory is the only *Eos* species occurring on islands between Sulawesi and the Philippines. This is also the only species in the *Eos* group with the combination of a blue eye-stripe and blue breast. Ornate Lorikeet (12) is present on Sangir but is not a potential confusion species.

VOICE Harsh screeches and whistles in flight, but usually quiet while feeding.

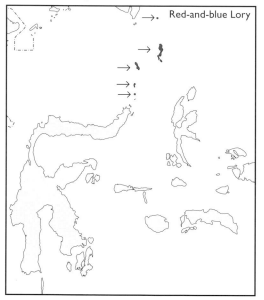

Red-and-blue Lory

DISTRIBUTION AND STATUS Endemic to Sangir, Talaud and the Nanusa Islands to the north-east of Sulawesi, Indonesia. The Sangir race is much reduced. During a 1995 survey small flocks were seen in mixed plantations adjacent to remnant forest around Talawid Atas, and up to 100 birds were thought to be present in the area. This was the first record since 1978, when it was already said to be uncommon. Trapping, compounded by habitat clearance on this and the nearby island of Siau (where the species is probably now extinct), is responsible for the low population. It is not known whether any birds still exist on the tiny island of Ruang to the south of Siau. The main population of Red-and-blue Lory now exists in forested areas of Karakelong Island in the Talaud group, but in recent years probably around 30% of these birds have been trapped and exported, and fewer than 2,000 individuals may now survive there (reported as still common in northern forests in 1995, but less so in the south of the island). Several hundred individuals are still

being trapped on Karakelong each year and sold to traders for sale as cagebirds. The range also includes the island of Salibabu and, although they were not located there during a 1986 survey, one was seen by observers in 1995 and others were heard calling. Locals report that a flock of around 100 birds visits the Gunung Ayambana area on Salibabu each year between Nov and Mar. The species is apparently extinct on Kaburuang, the other island in the Talaud group. Miangas Island, to the north of the main Nanusa group, also holds a population of Red-and-blue Lories, and these birds still occasionally appear in the local trade, although there have been no recent field surveys (Miangas islanders interviewed on Talaud in 1995 had no knowledge of the species). The world population is below 5,000. CITES Appendix I. Recently several hundred individuals have entered the bird trade. ENDANGERED.

ECOLOGY Occurs in forest and cultivated areas. The birds are most commonly seen flying in small groups of up to eight birds between resting and feeding areas. Large numbers (400 or more) congregate to roost and the birds are very vocal at these gatherings. Large flocks have also been seen flying between islands. Their diet includes pollen, nectar, fruit and insects, and they have been recorded feeding on coconut palms *Cocos nucifera* as well as *Ficus*, *Canarium* and *Syzygium*. The nest is a hole high in a large tree where two eggs are laid. Locals suggest that nesting starts between Apr and May, with fledging during Jun and Jul. Trappers also claim however that the breeding season coincides with the main fruiting season between Nov and Dec.

DESCRIPTION Generally bright red and purplish-blue, deeper red on rump. Red forecrown; blue-purple patch on centre of crown; a narrow blue-purple streak from eye through elongated ear-coverts to mantle; nape red. Mantle blue-purple; scapulars black. Flight feathers black with a broad red central band and black shafts; wing-coverts red with black tips; tertials black and red. Underparts red, with broad blue band across breast, thighs dark violet, extending slightly onto flanks, bluish suffusion on undertail-coverts. Uppertail dark reddish-purple, lateral feathers showing red inner- and black outerwebs. **Bare parts**: Bill orange; periophthalmic ring black; iris red; legs grey.

SEX/AGE Sexes alike. Immature mottled grey on breast and head. Blue of head extends to mantle with no red on nape. More black on wings, and tail greyer than in adult; the breast-band is also less well-defined and there is blue scalloping on the underparts.

MEASUREMENTS Wing 160-181; tail 108-131; bill 20-23; tarsus 19-23.

GEOGRAPHICAL VARIATION Three races. On Sangir, escaped *E. h. talautensis* are interbreeding with nominate birds, threatening the genetic integrity of the latter's small population.

> *E. h. histrio* (Sangir, Siau and Ruang Islands, but may be close to extinction on latter two islands)
> *E. h. talautensis* (islands in the Talaud group; escapes also on Sangir) Slightly smaller than nominate, and with less black on wing-coverts and flight feathers.
> *E. h. challengeri* (Miangas Island in the Nanusa group) Slightly smaller than nominate; blue breast-band narrower, and broken by some red markings; blue line from eye does not meet mantle.

REFERENCES Arndt (1992), BirdLife (1993), Bishop (1992a,b), Collar & Andrew (1988), Collar *et al.* (1994),

Forshaw (1989), Lambert *et al.* (1993), Lodge (1991), Nash (1993), Riley (1995), J. Riley *in litt.* (1995), Sibley & Monroe (1990), White & Bruce (1986).

6 VIOLET-NECKED LORY

Eos squamata Plate 2

Other names: Moluccan Red Lory, Violet-headed Lory, Violet-naped Lory, Wallace's Violet-necked Lory

IDENTIFICATION 28cm. Violet-necked Lories are generally red and purple-blue, showing a red face, variable dark violet neck-band and belly with red and black wings, and have dark purplish markings on the underparts in common with Red-and-blue (5) and Blue-eared (10) Lories. There is no range overlap between any of the three, so there is no likelihood of confusion in the field. Violet-necked shows a clean red face, a variable purplish band around throat and a red mantle. Red-and-blue Lory has a purplish-blue eye-stripe, a purplish-blue mantle and black thighs (except immature, which shows some blue). Blue-eared shows no throat or breast band and has a purplish-blue face-patch extending from eye onto ear-coverts and chin. The sympatric Chattering Lory (23) lacks the neck-ring and has green wings and thighs. Violet-necked is also noticeably slimmer-bodied in flight, showing long slim wings; it also generally appears dark red in flight with a red underwing and black-tipped primaries. Chattering Lory shows yellow underwing-coverts and a pinkish-red band across the underside of the primaries.

VOICE A shrill discordant screech similar to the call of Rainbow Lorikeet (13), but less harsh and more musical.

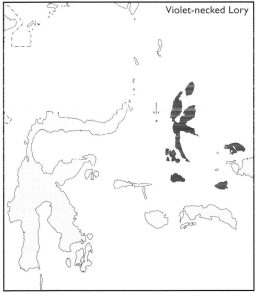

Violet-necked Lory

DISTRIBUTION AND STATUS Endemic to Indonesia on the North Moluccas (Morotai, Halmahera, Bacan and Obi, plus the satellite islands of Mayu, Ternate, Tidore, Moti, Damar, Widi, Muor and Gebe) and the W Papuan islands of Waigeo, Batanta, Salawati and Misool. Fairly common. World population above 100,000; domestic trade in these parrots plus their illegal export to the Philippines is unlikely at present to have a significant detrimental effect on the species.

ECOLOGY A wide-ranging island species found in coconut plantations, mangroves, secondary forest and primary montane forest up to 1,000m. Reports on habitat preference differ, with some observers encountering most birds in disturbed habitats, others finding them mainly in forest. In Halmahera observations in 1987 showed the species to be commonest at 200-300m around 6-8km inland in forest and along forest edge. It is not clear whether these differences relate to seasonal preference or to availability of food. The birds are generally encountered in pairs or small groups of up to ten individuals, with flocks travelling between islands. On Bacan, the species was roughly half as common as Rainbow Lorikeet during field surveys in 1985. The diet includes pollen, fruit, nectar and probably insects. Little is known of breeding ecology, but in captivity incubation has been recorded at 27 days with the chicks fledging in about 80 days.

DESCRIPTION General plumage red; dark violet-blue collar around neck, sometimes broad and well-defined, sometimes narrow and incomplete, or almost absent. Lower scapulars blackish-purple; lesser coverts red; median coverts dull red; greater coverts red with broad black tips and black shafts, innermost entirely black suffused purple; flight feathers black showing a red central bar and black shafts; outermost primaries with black outerwebs; underwing mostly red, with black tips to primaries; tertials black with purple sheen. Abdomen shows purple central blotch with red flanks; thighs red but sometimes with purple-blue markings; undertail-coverts crimson. Uppertail purple-red; undertail brownish-red, innerwebs of lateral feathers red. **Bare parts**: Bill orange; periophthalmic ring grey-black; iris yellow to orange-red; legs grey.

SEX/AGE Sexes alike. Immature with underparts and mantle margined darker, giving a generally duller, slightly barred appearance; may show blue on ear-coverts and crown; green suffusion on wing coverts; iris brown.

MEASUREMENTS Wing 146-153; tail 91-109; bill 18-21; tarsus 19-21.

GEOGRAPHICAL VARIATION Four races.

> *E. s. squamata* (W Papuan islands)
>
> *E. s. riciniata* (Morotai, Halmahera, Ternate, Tidore, Moti, Damar, Muor, Widi, Bacan islands) From nominate adult by more extensive neck-ring extending from upper throat to upper breast (usually also on to crown), and more extensive patch on belly, separated by a red breast-band; some birds with entirely purple underparts. May also show violet-grey crown, red nape and scapulars.
>
> *E. s. atrocaerulea* (Mayu Island in the Moluccan Sea) Similar to *riciniata* but underparts, including thighs, entirely bluish-black; mantle black, washed with blue, blue-black rear ear-coverts; rump darker red.
>
> *E. s. obiensis* (Obi) Adult with black scapulars and variable violet-grey collar. May also show violet-grey crown and red nape.

REFERENCES Arndt (1992), Beehler *et al.* (1986), BirdLife (1993), Forshaw (1989), P. Jepson *in litt.* (1997), Lambert (1993a), Lambert & Yong (1989), Lambert *et al.* (1993), Lodge (1991), Milton (1988), Rand & Gilliard (1967), Sibley & Monroe (1990), Smiet (1985), S. Smith *in litt.* (1993), White & Bruce (1986).

7 RED LORY
Eos bornea **Plate 2**

Other names: Buru Red Lory

IDENTIFICATION 31cm. Entirely red upper- and under-parts apart from blue undertail-coverts with blue and black wing-markings diagnostic. Shows more red than any other member of the *Eos* group. Range overlaps with Blue-streaked Lory (8) which has been introduced to the Kai Islands, and with Blue-eared (10) which is found in the central mountainous belt of Seram (although the highest documented elevation of Red Lory is 1,250m; Blue-eared is rarely found as low as 800m and usually only above 1,600m). From Blue-streaked by lack of blue ear-covert patch, instead showing an entirely red head and mantle, blue on wings and a reddish, not black, tail. Immature Red Lory may show slight blue suffusion on ear-coverts, but no blue mantle-streaks. From Blue-eared, by clean red face without violet-blue face-patch and clean red underparts with blue only on undertail-coverts. Some Violet-necked Lories (6) can show very obscure neck-rings, and superficially resemble Red Lories. Violet-necked can be distinguished by its purplish scapulars, at least some violet on the neck, mantle and belly, and lack of blue tertials. Also in captivity from Cardinal Lory (4) by blue and black wing-markings, and from Crimson Rosella (128) by lack of blue face-patch and clean red mantle.

VOICE A shrill disyllabic screech.

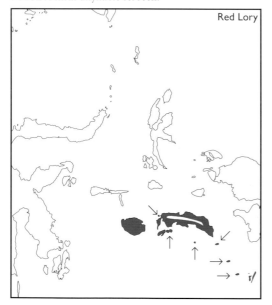

Red Lory

DISTRIBUTION AND STATUS Endemic to Indonesia in the South Moluccas, from Buru in the west through Seram, Ambon, Haruku and Saparua through the small island groups to the east including Gorong, Manawoka, Kasiui, Watubela, Kur, Tayandu and Taam, and thence into the Kai Islands on Tual, Kai Kecil and Kai Besar. Red Lories are common in forested coastal areas of their principal range islands. They were not found on Taam during field observations in 1971, but were still found to be common on small islands of the Kai group in 1981. The species is the commonest parrot on Buru, being encountered frequently in primary, secondary and logged forest at all altitudes. World population greater than 1,000,000. A commonly traded species.

ECOLOGY Noisy and conspicuous, occurring in large groups in plantations near to settlements, in secondary growth, mangroves and also in humid primary forest. Has been recorded up to 1,250m in hills, but generally appears scarcer inland, and in montane and grassland areas. However, on Buru in 1989 its strongest association was with forests on steeper slopes, and it seemed to prefer open-canopy forests, particularly those with recent disturbance. Replaced at higher altitudes in Seram by Blue-eared Lory. Flocks of up to 50 or more birds gather to feed in fruiting or flowering trees such as *Eugenia* and *Erythrina*, sometimes in company with Rainbow Lorikeets (13). Diet includes nectar, flowers and insects. Small fast, high-flying groups sometimes travel between islands. Apparent population fluctuations on certain islands are probably based on the availability of flowering trees. Some nocturnal activity has been noted on moonlit nights. Adults have been seen inspecting tree holes in Seram in Aug, and young birds found in the nest in Dec.

DESCRIPTION Generally bright red with whitish bases to body feathers. Primaries black with conspicuous red central patch; outer primaries with red on innerweb only, inner primaries with red on both webs but black shafts and tips; secondaries red tipped black with a black shaft; greater coverts red with a fine black tip showing more black on inner feathers; lesser and median coverts and bend of wing red; tertials blue. Underwing red with darker tips to coverts and black leading and trailing edge. Undertail-coverts blue. Uppertail reddish-brown; undertail red with browner edges. **Bare parts**: Bill orange; periophthalmic ring greyish-black; iris red; legs dark grey.

SEX/AGE Sexes alike. Immature from adult by red, not blue, undertail-coverts; tertials show greyish edgings with little if any blue showing; ear-coverts suffused with blue (this character appears to vary between populations, but individual variation is also marked); thighs and abdomen may show some blue suffusion; grey-brown bases to body feathers, not whitish as in adult; darker bill.

MEASUREMENTS Wing 159-172; tail 97-122; bill 22-25; tarsus 21-24.

GEOGRAPHICAL VARIATION This species shows some clinal variation with birds increasing in size from Seram east through to the Kai Islands. Four races are recognised here.

E. b. bornea (Ambon, Saparua and Haruku)

E. b. cyanonothus (Buru) Generally much darker red with much more extensive blue wing-markings extending from tertials onto coverts. Broader black edging to outer greater coverts.

E. b. rothschildi (Seram) Similar to nominate but slightly smaller.

E. b. bernsteini (Kai Islands) Adult slightly larger than nominate. Immatures appear to show more extensive blue facial markings. Birds occurring on islands between Seram and Kai are intermediate between *bernsteini* and *rothschildi*.

NOTE Includes Goodfellow's Lory *E. goodfellowi* (Ogilvie Grant 1907), which is now thought to have been an immature *bornea*.

REFERENCES Arndt (1992), BirdLife (1993), Forshaw (1989), Jones & Banjaransari (1990), Holyoak (1970, 1976), Lambert *et al.* (1993), Marsden *et al.* (1997), Poulsen & Jepson (1996), Smiet (1985), Taylor (1990), Walters (1975), White & Bruce (1986).

---

8 BLUE-STREAKED LORY
Eos reticulata Plate 2

Other names: Blue-necked Lory

IDENTIFICATION 31cm. Separated from all other members of *Eos* group by the prominent light blue streaks which extend from the lower nape onto the mantle. If the species still exists in the Kai Islands, where it was introduced, it is sympatric there with Red Lory (7). The present species has a blackish, not reddish, tail, and can also be separated from Red Lory by its blue ear-coverts and characteristic blue streaked mantle. The latter feature also distinguishes it from the other members of the genus encountered in captivity.

VOICE A shrill screech and a high-pitched whistle.

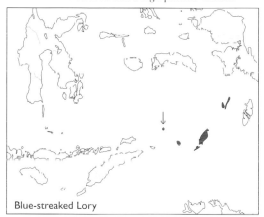

Blue-streaked Lory

DISTRIBUTION AND STATUS Endemic to islands in the Tanimbar group, Indonesia, being recorded from all the islands (Yamdena, Maru and Larat) and also from Babar to the west. It has been introduced to the island of Damar which also lies to the west of Tanimbar, and to Tual, Kai Kecil and Kai Besar to the north-east. There is also a possible record from Wetar. In 1981 it was described as very common on Yamdena, the main island in the Tanimbar group, particularly along the coast. The species has not recently been recorded from the Kai Islands and may now be extinct there. Trade in the species has been very heavy in the past with, for example, 7,669 birds exported in 1983, although this and the effect of deforestation do not seem to be threatening the species's long-term survival at present. World population above 150,000. Previously considered globally threatened, but a 1993 survey showed the population to be larger than originally thought and under no immediate threat. Bred in captivity in a small number of countries. NEAR-THREATENED.

ECOLOGY Little known. The species inhabits mangroves, coconut groves, plantations and secondary forest along the coast as well as primary forest inland.

DESCRIPTION General plumage bright red; blue stripe from eye extending through elongated ear-coverts marked by light blue streaks at tips; mantle red, boldly streaked light blue and marked violet; back and rump red; scapulars marked black. Wing-coverts generally appear variegated black and red; lesser coverts red; median coverts red with black shafts and bases; innermost greater coverts black, outermost with red on outerweb and around tip and margin of innerweb; primaries black with red band across innerwebs, extending onto outerwebs of inner primaries and secondaries; inner secondaries marked yellow on outerweb, innermost red with black shafts; tertials black marked red. Underwing red marked blackish-brown along leading and trailing edges towards tip. Underparts red marked blackish on belly and thighs. Uppertail brownish-black, showing red on innerwebs of lateral feathers; undertail red edged brownish-black below. **Bare parts**: Bill orange; periophthalmic ring black; iris reddish-brown; legs grey-black.

SEX/AGE Sexes alike. Immature with blue mantle streaks replaced by spots; bill brownish.

MEASUREMENTS Wing 156-176; tail 109-138; bill 18-20; tarsus 20-23.

GEOGRAPHICAL VARIATION None.

REFERENCES BirdLife (1993), Cahyadin (1996), Cahyadin *et al.* (1994), Collar & Andrew (1988), Forshaw (1989), Inskipp *et al.* (1988), Lambert *et al.* (1993), Lodge (1991), Smiet (1985), White & Bruce (1986).

---

9 BLACK-WINGED LORY
Eos cyanogenia Plate 2

Other names: Biak Red Lory, Blue-cheeked Lory

IDENTIFICATION 30cm. The only member of the genus *Eos* found on the Geelvink Bay islands, to which it is endemic. Unlikely to be confused with the sympatric Black-capped Lory (25), which shows red underparts, but is short-tailed with a distinct black cap, purple belly and green upperparts. Black-winged Lory can be separated from all other parrots by the combination of red mantle and underparts (except for black thighs), extensive blue face-patch extending from the base of the upper mandible across the entire face and ear-coverts (appearing dark in flight), and black scapulars, coverts and bend of wing, giving a generally black-winged appearance when perched; centre of back also black. From Blue-streaked Lory (8) by lack of obvious light blue streaks on upper mantle and completely black upperwing-coverts. From Violet-necked (6), Red and Blue (5) and Blue-eared (10) Lories by absence of deep violet markings on underparts, and by all-black upperwing-coverts.

VOICE More musical and robust than Rainbow Lorikeet (13). In flight a scolding *schwet schwet*, and while feeding a harsh nasal upslurred *schenh?*, repeated.

DISTRIBUTION AND STATUS Endemic to Biak, Supiori, Numfor, Manim and Mios Num islands in Geelvink Bay, Irian Jaya, Indonesia. In 1982 the species was found to be relatively common on Supiori to around 460m, and on Biak the birds were still common in coastal areas. Numfor has now been almost completely cleared of primary forest, which may have adversely affected the population of this

223

species there. Trapping is also a problem and the status of populations on the other islands is unknown. Hundreds of birds were exported during 1989 and 1990 and it is thought that the population would not sustain this level of trapping in the long term. World population was judged below 5,000 in 1991, but fieldwork in 1997 suggested it might be higher. Small numbers in captivity. VULNER-ABLE.

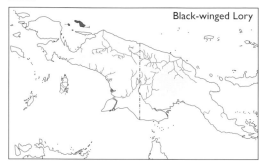
Black-winged Lory

ECOLOGY Found in humid inland forests, along forest edge and in mature second growth up to 460m, as well as in coastal coconut plantations, around villages and in scrubby areas. Apparent differences in abundance between coastal and inland habitats could be seasonal or related to nomadic behaviour. Normally found singly, in pairs, or in small flocks of up to six birds feeding in the canopy or flying swiftly in tight groups below the tree-tops, although flocks of up to 60 birds have been recorded. The birds are colourful, conspicuous, bold and noisy, flying with whirring wingbeats and forming nomadic flocks outside the breeding season. Recorded feeding on red *Loranthus* mistletoe berries and in *Brugiera gymnorhiza* mangrove. Little is known of their breeding ecology, but a possible nest-site in a hole in a tall tree in primary forest was attended by a pair during observations in 1982. Incubation in captivity lasts around 26 days and fledging occurs in around 75 days.

DESCRIPTION General plumage bright red with extensive broad violet-blue face-patch from base of upper mandible back through ear-coverts to sides of nape, also extending above eye; feathers of rear ear-coverts slightly elongated. Nape, mantle, rump and uppertail-coverts red. Upperwing-coverts, scapulars and tertials black; primaries and secondaries red with black shafts and edgings at tips; outerweb black in outermost two primaries; subterminal yellow markings in innerwebs of outer primaries; primary coverts red with black shafts and tips; alula with black shaft and tip; secondaries tipped black with black shafts. Underwing mostly red with black trailing edge. Throat and breast red with slight violet suffusion; thighs black extending to form black flank spots; undertail-coverts red. Tail black, outer feathers with red innerwebs, appearing black from above, red from below with black edges and tips. **Bare parts**: Bill orange; periophthalmic ring and cere black; iris red; legs dark grey.

SEX/AGE Sexes alike. Immature similar to adult but red of upper- and underparts irregularly margined with purplish-black. There is also a green hue to the tips of the black wing-coverts and tertials.

MEASUREMENTS Wing 154-169; tail 91-105; bill 20-23; tarsus 20-22.

GEOGRAPHICAL VARIATION None.

REFERENCES Arndt (1992), Beehler *et al.* (1986), B.M. Beehler *in litt.* (1997), BirdLife (1993), Bishop (1992a), Collar & Andrew (1988), Collar *et al.* (1994), Forshaw (1989), Lambert *et al.* (1993), Lodge (1991), Rand & Gilliard (1967), Sibley & Monroe (1990).

10 BLUE-EARED LORY
Eos semilarvata Plate 2

Other names: Seram/Ceram Lory, Half-masked Lory

IDENTIFICATION 24cm. The smallest member of its genus. The only sympatric *Eos* species is Red Lory (7) which occurs at lower altitudes in Seram. Red Lory is not commonly encountered in mountainous areas, the highest documented records being at 1,250m on Buru, whereas the present species has not been recorded below 800m, and is usually encountered from 1,200m and upwards. From Red by blue face-patch and large purplish-blue abdomen-patch (young Red Lories can show blue on ear-coverts but not also on chin as in this species). Blue-eared Lories are virtually unknown in aviculture, but the species is distinctive, with its unique combination of pure red mantle, nape, crown and breast, with purplish abdomen-patch and undertail-coverts, and a blue face-patch.

VOICE A loud screech.

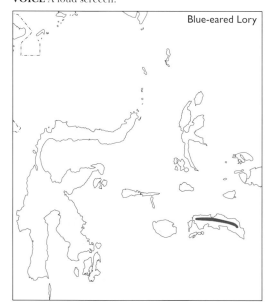
Blue-eared Lory

DISTRIBUTION AND STATUS Endemic to the central mountainous belt of Seram, in the Moluccas, Indonesia. The species was found to be common to abundant between 1,600m and 2,400m during surveys in 1987. World population 5,000-50,000. NEAR-THREATENED.

ECOLOGY Little known, but likely to be similar to other members of the genus. Recorded as low as 800m, but mainly at 1,200m and above. Feeds on flowering trees, including tree-heathers above the tree-line at high altitude. Usually encountered in pairs or small groups. The diet includes nectar and flowers. A pair was seen copulating in Aug after a bowing display when the birds also uttered soft calls.

DESCRIPTION Generally bright red with whitish bases to body feathers. Cheeks, chin and ear-coverts violet-blue with lighter shafts. Primaries black with red band across innerwebs; secondaries red tipped black; tertials black marked blue; scapulars purple-blue. Abdomen and undertail-coverts purple-blue. Uppertail reddish-brown; undertail dull red. **Bare parts**: Bill pinkish-orange; iris orange-red; legs grey-black.

SEX/AGE Sexes alike. Immature generally paler and duller; greyish bases to body feathers; blue face-patch restricted to area around eye and ear-coverts; scapulars brownish-grey edged pale blue; irregular blue margins on abdomen.

MEASUREMENTS Wing 132-145; tail 93-100; bill 18-19; tarsus 16-19.

GEOGRAPHICAL VARIATION None.

REFERENCES Arndt (1992), BirdLife (1993), Forshaw (1989), Lambert *et al.* (1993), Lodge (1991), Taylor (1990), White & Bruce (1986).

---

11   DUSKY LORY
Pseudeos fuscata   Plate 1

Other names: White-rumped Lory, Dusky-orange Lory

IDENTIFICATION 25-28cm. A large stocky lory with a blunt-ended tail, which occurs throughout the lowlands and hills of New Guinea. Colour morphs range from reddish orange to yellow, differing most obviously in the colour of two narrow breast-bands which are separated by a broader, central brown band. All morphs have generally dark-brown upperparts with a whitish rump, a pale crown-patch, reddish thighs and a bright orange bill. In flight, the short, blunt-ended tail eliminates the slightly larger *Chalcopsitta* lories. Brown Lory (2) is superficially most similar, but shows a violet, not whitish, rump, and in flight a large bright yellow flash across the coverts to the leading edge of the underwing, rather than the orange-yellow stripe across the centre of the underwing-coverts and bases of the primaries of the present species. Dusky Lory is larger than the sympatric Rainbow Lorikeet (13), which also has mainly bright green upperparts and a pointed tail. Unlike Rainbow Lorikeets, Dusky Lories tend to congregate in large high-flying flocks. The two species can also be separated on call.

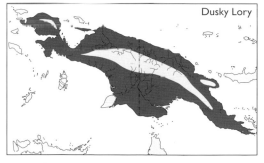

Dusky Lory

VOICE A powerful, shrill, harsh, grating screech. Flocks call continuously and can be located from a great distance, sounding "like a horde of angry giant cicadas". The voice is reminiscent of Rainbow Lorikeet, but is louder, higher-pitched, shorter, more rasping and wheezing and not up-slurred. There is also a more intense alarm call.

DISTRIBUTION AND STATUS Widely distributed throughout Irian Jaya and Papua New Guinea from Salawati in the W Papuan islands to the easternmost mainland. Dusky Lories also occur on Yapen Island in Geelvink Bay, Irian Jaya. The world population is above 100,000. Small numbers in captivity.

ECOLOGY A very gregarious species, often forming large, noisy, high-flying flocks. The birds are highly nomadic and depend strongly on the availability of flowering trees for food: the arrival of a roaming flock is spectacular, the birds sweeping in like an invading force, foraging noisily and aggressively, then departing. It has been suggested that they are partial migrants, and they appear to be absent from parts of the eastern highlands outside the rainy season. Dusky Lories are found in the lowlands and hills to 1,500m, occasionally reaching as high as 2,400m. The birds are frequently seen flying to and from their roosting sites early in the morning or late in the afternoon. More than a thousand individuals sometimes congregate to roost communally, and perform aerobatics as they swoop in to land. They are mainly canopy feeders, foraging in forest, along humid forest margins and in secondary growth, penetrating savanna, plantations and inhabited areas. They especially favour coconut, teak, and *Leucaena* trees (which are used to shade coffee). They feed on flowers and occasionally on fruit and insects, and can sometimes be found in mixed flocks with Rainbow Lorikeets. Little is know of their breeding ecology in the wild, but they tend to choose a high nest-site in a tall tree such as a *Eugenia* or beech. Birds in breeding condition have been collected in Aug and Oct, incubation lasts about three weeks, and the young fledge in around 72 days.

DESCRIPTION Range of colour morphs from reddish-orange to yellow; difference between morphs is most evident on breast with two more or less distinct reddish-orange to yellow bands separated by a broad dark brown band. Intermediate morph shows lower orange band and upper yellow band. Upperparts generally dark brown with brown forecrown and pale crown patch from slightly before eye extending back to nape; hindneck dark brown with buffish or orange collar and orange or greyish scalloping, which extends onto upper mantle and to sides of upper breast; back dark brown; lower back and rump white or buffish-white with dark brown feather-edgings; uppertail-coverts blackish brown. Wings dark brown tinged purplish, with orange-red suffusion on innermost greater coverts and tertials, and orange patch at bend of wing; outerwebs of primaries edged olive; innerwebs of primaries yellow or orange forming band across centre of upper- and underwing. Underwing-coverts suffused orange or yellow. Face dark brown with slight orange suffusion on ear-coverts; throat dark brown; upper breast with narrowish orange or yellow band; broader dark brown band across centre of breast with orange, buffish or greyish feather-edgings giving a scalloped effect; second orange or yellow band on lower breast bordered below with a fairly complete dark brown band; centre of belly yellow or orange with some dark brown markings; flanks dark brown; thighs reddish (even in yellow morph); undertail-coverts violet-black. Tail brownish-olive with orange patches on innerwebs of lateral feathers, undertail more yellowish on outerwebs; central feathers orange broadly tipped purple-brown. **Bare parts**: Bill bright orange; skin orange at base of lower mandible, brown at base of upper; periophthalmic ring brown; iris red; legs dark grey.

SEX/AGE Sexes alike. Immature with less distinctive banding on underparts, appearing generally duller and more uniform; undertail-coverts grey-black; bill brownish-black with yellowish base to lower mandible; iris yellowish-grey.

MEASUREMENTS Wing 148-168; tail 76-89; bill 19-23; tarsus 17-21.

GEOGRAPHICAL VARIATION None recognised here. *P. f. incondita*, which is allegedly brighter and larger, is very doubtfully distinct; its range would cover most of mainland New Guinea.

REFERENCES Beehler (1978b), Beehler *et al.* (1986), B.M. Beehler *in litt.* (1997), Bell (1981), Coates (1985), Diamond (1972), Forshaw (1989), Gyldenstolpe (1955), Peters (1961), Rand & Gilliard (1967), Sibley & Monroe (1990).

12 ORNATE LORIKEET
Trichoglossus ornatus Plate 4

Other names: Ornate Lory

IDENTIFICATION 25cm. General appearance similar to Rainbow Lorikeet (13) but the two species are allopatric. Yellow-and-Green Lorikeet (16) is sympatric but lacks any red in plumage, showing a predominantly yellow head and underparts, barred green. Possibility of confusion slight even with poor views, unless underparts are not seen at all. Smaller and much shorter-tailed than most forms of Rainbow Lorikeet. Can immediately be separated from all races of this species by relatively unmarked reddish-orange chin, throat and face, with reddish-orange markings on nape. Also shows a conspicuous yellow patch on side of nape, and lacks underwing stripe along with pale green hind-collar which are variably present in all races of Rainbow Lorikeet.

VOICE In flight a shrill *kreet...kreet*, a high-pitched *wee-oo-wee*, a variety of whistling notes and a grating screech.

Ornate Lorikeet

DISTRIBUTION AND STATUS Occurs throughout Sulawesi, Indonesia, and on surrounding islands including Sangir, Bangka, Togian, Peleng, Banggai, Muna, Buton and Tukangbesi. Common. World population greater than 50,000.

ECOLOGY Occurs in forest edge, secondary forest, bushy open terrain, cultivated plots and towns, and ranges into upland valleys, but rarely venturing far into primary forest. Chiefly found at 300-500m, occasionally to 1,000m. Birds occur mostly in pairs or small groups, occasionally consorting with Yellow-and-Green Lorikeets. Feeding behaviour is typical of the group and nectar, pollen and fruits make up the bulk of the diet. Little is known of the species's breeding ecology, but individuals in breeding condition have been collected in Sep and Oct. In captivity incubation has been recorded at 27 days with the young fledging in 80 days.

DESCRIPTION Crown and ear-coverts dark purplish-blue; yellow patch at side of nape; variable reddish-orange flecking at back of nape, less extensive in centre; chin, throat, lores and most of face reddish-orange. Upperparts generally bright green with variable yellow flecking on mantle. Blackish tips to primaries and black innerwebs to primaries and secondaries, with fine yellow trailing edge to wing. Underwing black with yellow and green coverts and yellow axillaries. Lower throat and breast heavily but variably barred violet through dark green; rest of underparts green with variable yellow scalloping; thighs yellow-green; belly light green barred darker green; undertail-coverts yellow-green tipped bright green. Uppertail dark green with yellowish tips to outerwebs and yellowish innerwebs to all but central feathers, base of lateral feathers pinkish on innerweb; undertail yellowish with pinkish suffusion at base and greyish tip to each feather. **Bare parts**: Bill orange; iris orange; legs grey-green.

SEX/AGE Sexes alike. Immature with orange nape-markings reduced or absent, bill brownish, breast scalloping less bold and lighter green.

MEASUREMENTS Wing 125-134; tail 70-81; bill 19-20; tarsus 17-19.

GEOGRAPHICAL VARIATION None.

REFERENCES Cain (1955), Forshaw (1989), Holmes & Wood (1979), Peters (1961), Rozendaal & Dekker (1989), Watling (1983), White & Bruce (1986).

13 RAINBOW LORIKEET
Trichoglossus haematodus Plate 3

Other names: Rainbow Lory; Green-naped Lorikeet (*T. h. haematodus*); Mitchell's Lorikeet (*T. h. mitchellii*); Forsten's Lorikeet (*T. h. forsteni*); Edwards's Lorikeet, Blue-faced Lorikeet (*T. h. capistratus*); Weber's Lorikeet (*T. h. weberi*); Coconut Lory, Massena's Lory (*T. h. massena*); Swainson's Lorikeet, Blue Mountain Lorikeet (*T. h. moluccanus*)

IDENTIFICATION 26cm. A widely distributed species, common to abundant throughout most of its range, which spans from Bali and Lombok in the west through many of the Indonesian islands, New Guinea and the Solomons, into eastern coastal Australia. The Rainbow Lorikeet has a number of strongly differentiated subspecies and is sympatric with a number of similar-sized psittacines across its range. The head is generally dark showing more or less blue, the upperparts are green with a paler hind-collar, and the breast is red, orange or yellow, with or without dark barring. The belly varies from green to dark blue-violet according to race. The underwing-coverts are orange-red to yellow and there is a yellow underwing bar. In flight the birds are noisy, and show distinctly pointed tails and wings. The most similar species are Ornate Lorikeet (12) and Red-collared Lorikeet (14). All subspecies of Rainbow Lorikeet (except the anomalous *T. h. weberi*) can be separated from Ornate by the dark chin and throat, and from Red-collared by the green, not reddish-orange nape-band. Subspecies *weberi* is extremely distinct, showing almost entirely green plumage and is more likely to be confused with the allopatric Olive-headed Lorikeet (15), which shows an olive-yellow, not green, head, and uniform yellowish underparts with no demarcation between the lighter breast and darker belly shown by *weberi*. Red-collared Lorikeet may hybridise with Rainbow where captive birds have escaped, and both species have also been recorded on islands in the Torres Strait, where Red-collared is a vagrant. In Australia the sympatric Scaly-breasted Lorikeet (19) has green and yellow underparts and a prominent red underwing flash. In New Guinea this species can be separated in flight from Dusky Lory (11) and the *Chalcopsitta* species by its pointed, not rounded, tail. Rainbow Lorikeet is also smaller than the *Chalcopsitta* lories, but larger than the higher-altitude *Neopsittacus* species. Occasional hybrid Rainbow/Red-collared Lorikeets occur in various parts of the species's range where the latter has escaped.

VOICE A sharp rolling screech, repeated at regular intervals in flight. Also a shrill chattering while feeding, a soft twittering at rest, and a loud, clear musical call. The voice is similar to but slightly deeper than that of Musk Lorikeet (35), which is sympatric in eastern coastal Australia. The call is also louder than that of Yellow-billed Lorikeet (53) and less hoarse and grating than that of Dusky Lory.

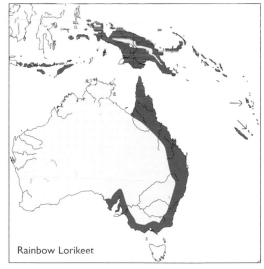

Rainbow Lorikeet

DISTRIBUTION AND STATUS Widespread and abundant. Ranges from Bali in the west, through the Moluccas and New Guinea including many outlying islands, through the Bismarck Archipelago, the Solomon Islands, Vanuatu, New Caledonia, and eastern Australia, where it ranges from islands in the Torres Strait down the Cape York Peninsula to the Gulf of Carpentaria coast at around 140°E, then through eastern coastal areas to Kangaroo Island and the Eyre Peninsula in the south (vagrant inland to the Murray River). The species has been recorded from King Island in the Bass Strait (probably wild birds), but recent records from Tasmania probably refer to escaped cagebirds. *T. h. moluccanus* has also been introduced around Perth, Western Australia, where a small breeding population has become established. The populations in the suburbs of Melbourne and Geelong are wild. This is the commonest lorikeet through much of its range. The world population is in excess of 5,000,000, although populations of some races do give cause for concern (Bali, Lombok, Sumbawa, Tanahjampea, Biak). Heavily traded.

ECOLOGY Commonest in lowlands, but has been recorded up to 2,440m. Occurs in a wide variety of habitats from around settlements to forest, coconut plantations, savanna, eucalypt stands and mangroves. The birds are most often encountered in small noisy groups feeding acrobatically in the canopy or flying overhead, and frequently in mixed flocks with other parrots including Large Fig Parrot (86), Red Lory (7) and Scaly-breasted Lorikeet (19) (has hybridised in the wild). The species feeds mainly on nectar but will also take fruit such as figs, as well as insects, and attends artificial feeding stations. Birds are particularly fond of banksias in coastal Australia, other favourite trees including casuarinas, erythrinas, eucalypts and bottlebrushes *Callistemon* spp. As they are mainly dependent on flowering trees, the birds have to move around, including altitudinally, to find food. Communal roosts may involve many hundreds of birds which wheel acrobatically as they come in to land at dusk. On some of the smaller predator-free Admiralty Islands, Rainbow Lorikeets also roost and nest on the ground. The birds generally nest in isolated pairs in a high, unlined tree-hollow. The display includes some wing-fluttering to reveal the colourful underwing pattern, swinging upside-down, head-bobbing, tail-fanning and bill-fencing. Two to three white eggs are laid and the white downed young hatch in around 25 days, fledging in 7-8 weeks. Breeding has been recorded in most months in Indonesia, New Guinea and northern Australia. In southern Australia breeding takes place between Aug and Jan.

DESCRIPTION Forecrown, face and throat dark bluish-mauve, with lighter blue streaking on forecrown, ear-coverts and lower cheeks; rest of head dark blue with brownish-black feather-bases especially around rear-crown and throat, and with greenish streaking on rear-crown. Upperparts bright green with reddish flecking on centre of mantle (bases to feathers), and a variable, bright yellowish-green hind-collar. Primaries tipped blackish; bright yellow panel on otherwise blackish innerwebs of flight feathers, tending to orange on secondaries; outerwebs of primaries and wing-coverts green; fine yellow trailing edge to wing. Underwing-coverts orange-red; flight feathers greyish-black at tips. Breast, upper belly and upper flanks bright reddish-orange, barred dark blue, tending to green on lower breast (barring appears black from a distance); belly variably marked green centrally, sometimes forming a discrete patch or interspersed with reddish-orange; abdomen and thighs barred green and yellow, with yellow bases; undertail-coverts yellow, tipped bright green. Uppertail green with innerwebs of lateral feathers yellowish; undertail greyish-green on outerwebs, yellow on innerwebs. **Bare parts:** Bill orange-red; iris orange-red; legs grey or greenish-grey.

SEX/AGE Sexes alike. Immature is duller than the adult, with a brownish-black bill and iris and a more pointed tail.

MEASUREMENTS Wing 135-150; tail 93-118; bill 20-23; tarsus 17-20.

GEOGRAPHICAL VARIATION Nineteen races. Two birds supposedly from Spirit Island off Trangan, Aru Islands, were given the name *brooki* on the basis of their large, almost completely black belly-patches, but are probably immature *nigrogularis*.

T. h. haematodus (from Buru through Ambon, Seram, Gorong, Manawoka, Kasiui, Watubela, Tioor, Kur and Tayandu to the W Papuan islands including Misool and Waigeo, islands in Geelvink Bay except Biak, and New Guinea to around 141°E)

T. h. mitchellii (Bali, where rare, and Lombok) Slightly smaller than nominate. Breast-barring absent or very poorly defined; dark blue patch in centre of belly; less yellow on lower abdomen and undertail-coverts than nominate; head dark blackish-brown with grey-green crown and cheek-streaking (blue streaking on forecrown); hind-collar greener and extending further around sides of throat than nominate; upperparts also show less red flecking. From *T. h. forsteni*, which also shows unbarred breast and dark blue patch on belly, by lack of dark blue band on upper mantle. From *T. h. moluccanus* by absence of yellow-orange at sides of breast, darker blue belly-patch and head-streaking greenish not light blue. Immature: dark green abdomen, and yellow suffusion on tips of breast feathers, giving slightly barred orange appearance.

T. h. forsteni (Sumbawa) From nominate by redder, unbarred breast, extensive dark blue patch in centre of belly extending onto abdomen, dark purple-blue band on upper mantle, and largely yellow lower flanks and undertail-coverts with slight green barring. From *T. h. mitchellii* By dark blue band on upper mantle and darker red and completely unbarred breast (head also more strongly streaked violet-blue, rather than green, particularly on forehead and cheeks).

T. h. djampeanus (Tanahjampea) Similar to *T. h. forsteni* but head streaked brighter blue.

T. h. stresemanni (Kalaotoa) Breast orange with virtually no darker edgings; green streaking on rear crown; sides of belly-patch suffused greener than in previous three races; poorly defined blue mantle-band; yellow or orange bases to mantle feathers.

T. h. fortis (Sumba) From nominate by virtually unbarred bright yellow breast with very slight red flecking, large green patch (can be tinged blue-black) in centre of belly extending onto abdomen and tending to barring on the flanks, thighs yellow with some green barring, some green on throat and extensive suffusion on crown and behind eye; lacks red bases to mantle feathers. From *T. h. capistratus* by less red flecking on breast.

T. h. weberi (Flores) Smaller than nominate (male wing 129). Very distinct race with plumage almost entirely green with lighter green breast and hind-collar (may show some yellowish or reddish suffusion on breast and thighs); forehead and lores slightly

suffused turquoise blue; underwing-coverts yellowish-green; head-streaking bright emerald-green. Further research may show that this race should be upgraded to specific status.

T. h. capistratus (Timor) Similar to *T. h. fortis* but more red on breast and greener belly-patch.

T. h. flavotectus (Wetar and Roma) Similar to *T. h. fortis* and *T. h. capistratus* but breast entirely pale yellow (may show light orange suffusion) with very fine darker tips; head with more green and with blue areas lighter; belly-patch entirely green; underwing-coverts bright yellow; no red on mantle.

T. h. rosenbergii (Biak) From nominate by very heavy dark blue barring on breast with only a small amount of reddish-orange visible, very extensive dark blue patch extending from lower breast to abdomen, yellow-green lower flanks and undertail-coverts broadly tipped dark green and very broad greenish yellow hind-collar with sporadic very slight red flecking where it meets mantle and fine red line where it meets the rear-crown. Orange band on underside of flight feathers.

T. h. nigrogularis (Aru and the eastern Kai Islands) From nominate by more orange breast with narrower barring, centre of belly blackish; lighter blue head-streaking. Head darker than in *T. h. caeruliceps*.

T. h. intermedius (considered synonymous with *T. h. haematodus*; said to occur from around the Sepik River in northern New Guinea, ranging east to Astrolabe Bay and south to the upper Purari River and Karimui districts; it also occurs on Manam, and probably on Schouten Islands)

T. h. micropteryx (E New Guinea west to the Huon Peninsula in the north, to around Lake Kutubu in the Central Range and to around Hall Sound in the south; also on Misima Island) Intermediate between nominate and *T. h. massena*. Smaller and paler than nominate with more orange breast and narrower barring.

T. h. caeruleiceps (S New Guinea from lower Fly River to around Hall Sound in the east) Similar to *T. h. nigrogularis* but head entirely streaked with blue. Breast with narrower barring than previous race.

T. h. flavicans (Admiralty Islands including Manus, Lou, Pak, Rambutyo and Nauna, also on New Hanover and, apparently, the Nuguria Group) Similar to nominate but shows some reddish suffusion on vent and thighs. Variable, entire upperparts ranging from bronze-yellow to green (in bronze morph, hind-collar is also yellow); feathers of nape purplish, tipped reddish-brown. Forehead and lores bright violet-blue, rest of head dark purple streaked grey-green in the centre of the crown; red marks at edges of hind-collar.

T. h. nesophilus (Ninigo and Hermit groups) Similar to *flavicans* but upperparts never vary to bronze-yellow.

T. h. massena (islands of the Bismarck sea from Karkar, Bagabag, Crown, Long, Tolokiwa, Umboi, Malai and Sakar in the west through New Britain, New Ireland, the Saint Matthias Group and related islands including the Witu Islands, Lolobau, Duke of York, Tabar, Masahet, Lihir, Tanga, Feni, Nissan, Buka, Bougainville, through the Solomons – including Guadalcanal, Ulawa, Uki and San Cristobal – Torres and Banks Islands to Vanuatu) Similar to nominate but breast-barring narrower and more broadly spaced, red on breast more restricted, not extending down onto flanks or upper belly. Like *T. h. micropteryx* but hind-collar less yellowish. Strong purplish-brown tinge on nape.

T. h. deplanchii (New Caledonia and the Loyalty Islands) From nominate by lighter blue head, greener hind-collar and scarlet-crimson breast with narrower dark barring; light green streaking on rear-crown and sides of head. Narrower breast-barring than *T. h. massena*.

T. h. moluccanus (islands in the Torres Strait, and E Australia from the Gulf of Carpentaria coast at around 140°E through eastern coastal districts including the Cape York Peninsula, south to South Australia where it reaches Kangaroo Island and the Eyre Peninsula; also introduced around Perth, Western Australia) From nominate by more extensive light blue streaking on head; breast bright orange-red with variable yellow suffusion (most extensive at sides) and very slight barring; large violet-blue belly-patch which extends as barring onto lower breast and down onto reddish-orange flanks; some reddish-orange feathers may be present on lower abdomen interspersed with blue; lower flanks green; undertail-coverts yellow broadly tipped green; shows slight, mainly yellow flecking on the mantle with very small amount of red; nape-band narrow and greener than nominate. Underwing-coverts orange-red washed with yellow. Slight blue suffusion on outer primaries. Superficially resembles Red-collared Lorikeet but lacks orange-red hind-collar. Red-collared occurs from Broome in Western Australia east to the Gulf of Carpentaria in the Northern Territory, but is not found on the Cape York Peninsula where *moluccanus* reaches its north-westerly extreme.

REFERENCES Arndt (1992), Beehler (1978b), Beehler *et al.* (1986), Bell (1982), Bowler & Taylor (1989), Blakers *et al.* (1984), T. Bird & *in litt* (1995), Cain (1955), Cain & Galbraith (1956), Coates (1985), Diamond (1972), Draffan *et al.* (1983), Emison *et al.* (1987), Forshaw (1981, 1989), Lambert *et al.* (1993), LeCroy *et al.* (1992), Lodge (1991), Long (1981), MacKinnon & Phillipps (1993), Milton & Marhuti (1987), Peters (1961), Pizzey & Doyle (1983), Rand & Gilliard (1967), Schodde & Tidemann (1988), Sibley (1951), Sibley & Monroe (1990), Slater (1989), Taylor (1990), White and Bruce (1986)

14 RED-COLLARED LORIKEET
Trichoglossus rubritorquis Plate 3

IDENTIFICATION 26cm. Only similar species is Rainbow Lorikeet of the race *T. h. moluccanus*, which meets the range of the present species in northern Queensland. Red-collared can be separated from *T. h. moluccanus* by its orange-red, not green, hind-collar, prominent blue band on mantle, which is marked with orange-red at its lower margin, and greenish-black, not violet-blue, belly-patch. The thighs, vent and undertail-coverts also show more yellow. Escaped cagebirds may occur outside the species's normal range.

VOICE Similar to the previous species.

DISTRIBUTION AND STATUS Ranges from Broome,

Western Australia, in the west, possibly intersecting with Rainbow Lorikeet at around 140°E on the Gulf of Carpentaria coast in northern Queensland. Access problems have made it hard to establish to what degree (if any) the ranges actually overlap, but this species regularly ranges east to Burketown and the lower Gregory River, and has occurred east to Normanton. Vagrant west to the De Grey River, and north to Booby Island in the Torres Strait. It occurs around Darwin and in other urban areas. This is one of the commonest parrots throughout its range.

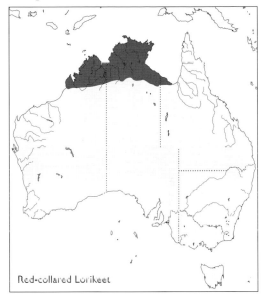

Red-collared Lorikeet

ECOLOGY Occurs in riverine eucalypt woodland, moving to eucalypt and paperbark *Melaleuca* woodland when trees are flowering; also occurs in swamps, scrub, heath and towns. Red-collared Lorikeets feed on nectar, fruit and insects. There are no large-scale seasonal movements but local populations respond to the availability of flowering trees for food. For example on Groote Eylandt, birds congregate to feed on flowering banksias in April and May. The species often feeds in company with Varied Lorikeet (20). Breeding takes place between Mar and Jun. Other aspects of the species's ecology are similar to Rainbow Lorikeet, with which it hybridises, the two forms possibly being conspecific.

DESCRIPTION Head darkish blue heavily streaked bright violet-blue, generally appearing light blue; hind-collar orange-red meeting orange-red of breast; upper mantle with dark violet-blue band showing prominent orange-red markings towards lower margin, extending round sides of throat to meet at centre; lower mantle and rest of upperparts bright green. Wings green with blackish tips to flight feathers; fine yellow margins to primaries and wing-coverts more obvious than in *T. haematodus*; underwing shows broad yellow band on flight feathers (much broader than in *T. h. moluccanus*); underwing-coverts more orange than in *T. haematodus*. Throat and foreneck dark violet; breast orange-red with a few narrow darker edgings; belly-patch dark purplish-black, slightly suffused green; thighs and undertail-coverts yellow marked bright green. Uppertail green with yellow innerwebs and green outerwebs; undertail greenish-olive with prominent yellow innerwebs. **Bare parts**: Bill orange with yellow tip; iris orange-red; legs grey.

SEX/AGE Sexes alike. Immature duller than adult. Hind-collar less distinct and narrower. Bill dark brown with yellow-orange tip. Iris brown.

MEASUREMENTS Wing 141-160; tail 127-142; bill 19-22; tarsus 16-19.

GEOGRAPHICAL VARIATION None.

REFERENCES Blakers *et al.* (1984), Christidis & Boles (1994), Draffan *et al.* (1983), Forshaw (1981, 1989), Schodde & Tidemann (1988), Sibley & Monroe (1990).

15 OLIVE-HEADED LORIKEET
Trichoglossus euteles   Plate 5

Other names: Perfect Lorikeet, Yellow-headed Lorikeet

IDENTIFICATION 25cm. Only all-green lorikeet with a clearly demarcated olive-yellow head. The one similar species is the allopatric Flores race *weberi* of Rainbow Lorikeet (13), which shows an all-green, not olive-yellow, head. Immature Perfect Lorikeet shows a much greener head than the adult, but also has a brownish bill, whereas adult *weberi* shows an orange bill; *weberi* also has a darker green belly whilst Perfect Lorikeet has uniform underparts. Female Red-cheeked Parrot (95) is sympatric in Timor but is green with a demarcated brownish (not olive-yellow) head; Red-cheeked also has a short, blunt-ended tail, a brown bill and blue, not greenish, underwing-coverts. The flight of Olive-headed Lorikeet is swift and slightly undulating.

VOICE A shrill screech lacking the pronounced guttural tones of Rainbow Lorikeet.

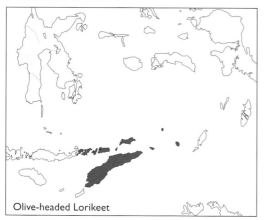

Olive-headed Lorikeet

DISTRIBUTION AND STATUS Endemic to Timor, Nusa Tenggara, Indonesia, and a number of nearby islands including (to the north) Lomblen, Pantar, Alor, Wetar, Roma, Damar, Teun and Nila, and (to the north-east) Kisar, Leti, Moa, Luang and Babar. Commoner than Rainbow Lorikeet on Timor and generally replacing it at higher altitudes. World population greater than 50,000.

ECOLOGY Occurs from the lowlands to 2,400m on Timor, frequenting both primary and secondary forest as well as savanna woodland. Many of the other range islands are arid and the birds have been able to adapt to cultivated

and settled areas. Outside the breeding season flocks of up to 100 can sometimes be seen flying overhead, drawing attention by their shrill calls. Little is known of the species's breeding ecology.

DESCRIPTION Head bright olive-yellow, separated from green mantle and yellow-green breast by a faintly indicated bright green collar; cheeks warmer in tone, crown showing slight green suffusion; throat darker and greener. Upper-parts uniformly bright light green. Upperwing-coverts green; flight feathers blackish on innerwebs, green on outerwebs. Underwing blackish with greenish-yellow coverts. Yellow panel across innerwebs of primaries and secondaries. Underparts generally yellower than upper-parts; upper breast lightly mottled with greyish-brown which blends from throat; belly and undertail-coverts marked green. Uppertail bright green with dark shafts; undertail dull greenish-grey with a yellowish suffusion on innerwebs. **Bare parts**: Bill orange; narrow periophthalmic ring greyish; iris red; legs grey-black.

SEX/AGE Sexes alike. Immature from adult by greener head (with more obvious light shaft-streaks), and brownish base to bill.

MEASUREMENTS Wing 123-134; tail 90-108; bill 14-17; tarsus 15-17.

GEOGRAPHICAL VARIATION Apparent slight plumage differences between eastern and western populations are not sufficient to justify subspecific separation.

REFERENCES Arndt (1992), Forshaw (1989), Lambert *et al.* (1993), Lodge (1991), Mayr (1944), White & Bruce (1986).

16 YELLOW-AND-GREEN LORIKEET
Trichoglossus flavoviridis   Plate 4

Other names: Yellow-green Lorikeet, Sula Lorikeet

IDENTIFICATION 21cm. A mainly green lorikeet with a yellow breast strongly scalloped with green barring. The head is patchy yellow and brown, sharply demarcated from the green mantle by fine brown hind-collar. Overlaps with Ornate Lory (12) in Sulawesi (subspecies *meyeri*) from which it can easily be separated by scalloped yellow-green not reddish-orange breast. Only three other lorikeets show yellow or yellow-green breasts with green barring: Mindanao (17), Iris (21) and Scaly-breasted (19), none of which overlap. From Mindanao by absence of dark mask, and by patchy yellow and brown, not green, crown. From Iris, which shows only very slight breast-barring, by patchy yellow and brown, not red or blue and red, crown. From Scaly-breasted by patchy yellow and brown, not green, head, absence of yellow patch on mantle, and green, not red, underwing-coverts.

VOICE In flight a harsh rasping *dra-dra-dra*. Call is less penetrating than that of Ornate Lorikeet, and more chirrupy and tinkling.

DISTRIBUTION AND STATUS Endemic to Sulawesi and Sula, Indonesia. Common and widely distributed in Sulawesi. World population in excess of 100,000.

ECOLOGY Found from lowland to upper montane rain-forest (from 500 to 2,000m), overlapping with Ornate Lorikeet up to an altitude of 1,000m in Sulawesi (generally it replaces Ornate at higher altitudes). Yellow-and-Green

Lorikeet has also been found in open country particularly when *Erythrina* is flowering, along forest edge and in isolated stands of trees. Occurs in small noisy parties and tends to be shy, keeping to dense foliage and flying off noisily when disturbed. Little is known of the species's breeding ecology.

DESCRIPTION Head dark chocolate-brown with strong olive-yellow suffusion on crown (giving patchy appearance); throat with less pronounced yellow markings producing a lightly barred effect, strongest on sides of lower throat where suffusion forms a yellow patch; yellow of hind-crown sharply demarcated from green of mantle by a fine brown hind-collar. Upperparts uniform bright pale green (venturing to sides of neck) with yellowish-brown suffusion and a few chocolate-brown smudges. Upperwing bright light green on coverts; flight feathers blackish on inner-, green on outerwebs. Underwing-coverts yellowish-green. Flight feathers blackish below. Breast yellow with patchy chocolate-brown suffusion at sides of upper breast, feathers having narrow bright green tips producing a very marked scalloped effect, these becoming broader towards upper belly where yellow merges into a yellow-green suffusion. Undertail-coverts yellow-green tipped brighter green. Uppertail light green with dark shafts; undertail yellowish with grey-brown tips. **Bare parts**: Bill orange-yellow; iris orange-yellow; legs grey-black.

SEX/AGE Sexes alike. Immature with yellow generally replaced by more greenish markings. Tail faintly barred with a darker green tip.

MEASUREMENTS Wing 120-139; tail 92-110; bill 15-17; tarsus 14-16.

GEOGRAPHICAL VARIATION Two races.
    T. f. flavoviridis (Sula: Taliabu, Mangole and Sulabesi)
    T. f. meyeri (Sulawesi) Smaller and shorter-tailed than nominate (wing 96-106; tail 51-65). Crown greyish-green, warmer and yellower towards rear, with a very slight yellow suffusion at forehead; cheeks and throat scaled yellow and dark green; yellow patch on ear-coverts; broad dark green bars on breast; heavy green barring at sides of neck; lower underparts with more

indistinct barring, entire underparts appearing more uniform than nominate, and upperparts darker green. Underwing-coverts bright green.

REFERENCES BirdLife (1993), Forshaw (1989), Lambert *et al.* (1993), Rozendaal & Decker (1989), Watling (1983), White & Bruce (1986).

17 MINDANAO LORIKEET
Trichoglossus johnstoniae   Plate 4

Other names: Johnstone's Lorikeet, Mrs Johnstone's Lorikeet, Mount Apo Lorikeet

IDENTIFICATION 20cm. Range overlaps with several dissimilar psittacines such as Blue-backed Parrot (109) and Guiabero (89), which generally occur at lower altitudes, and the tiny Colasisi (185). Poor views in forest could however present difficulties with the two racquet-tails, Mountain (98) and Blue-crowned (102) (which is generally found at lower altitudes but does occur up to at least 1,750m). This species can be separated from both by the yellow barring on the underparts, the dark mask and the green crown. In captivity it can be separated from the other small allopatric *Trichoglossus* with yellow-barred underparts, Yellow-and-Green (16) and Scaly-breasted (19), by the combination of green crown and dark mask with red markings around forehead, cheeks and chin.

VOICE Flight call a continuous *lish-lish*.

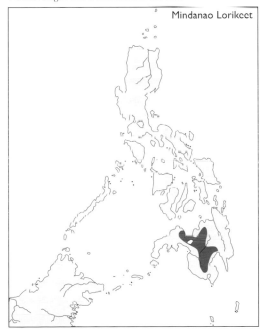

DISTRIBUTION AND STATUS Endemic to Mindanao, Philippines, where it occurs on Mount Kitanglad, around Lake Lanao, Mount Piagayungan, Mount Apo, Mount Matutum, Lake Parker and the Sitio Siete area, and on Mount Malindang. It is generally uncommon, especially on Mount Kitanglad, and forest destruction is affecting its already very limited range. World population below 10,000. VULNERABLE.

ECOLOGY Found from 1,000 to 2,500m on Mount Apo and from 1,000 to 1,700m on Mount Malindang. Mindanao Lorikeets prefer mossy montane forest, but also occur along forest edge and in degraded or logged areas. There is some altitudinal movement with flocks of up to 30 birds roosting at lower altitudes, moving higher during the day to feed on flowering trees and shrubs before returning to the lower slopes at dusk. Little is known of the species's breeding ecology, but birds in breeding condition have been collected between Mar and May. Records of captive breeding indicate that two eggs are laid, incubation lasts about three weeks, and the young fledge from around three weeks to one month later.

DESCRIPTION Lores, ear-coverts and narrow band around nape mauve-brown; centre of crown green; cheeks, chin and forehead heavily spangled with dull pinkish-red; lower ear-coverts greenish-yellow; cheeks lightly scalloped green. Upperparts green. Wings green with black inner-webs to flight feathers, outermost primary with fine yellow outer margin; yellow bar across innerwebs of inner primaries and secondaries; underwing-coverts light green barred darker on carpal edge; wing with fine yellow trailing edge. Underparts yellow-green, strongly barred dark green appearing scalloped; undertail-coverts yellowish-green tipped mid-green. Uppertail green; undertail blackish-green with yellow inner edges to innerwebs. **Bare parts**: Bill orange-red; periophthalmic ring blue-grey; iris red-brown; legs blue-black.

SEX/AGE Sexes alike. Immature has less red on upper ear-coverts. Mask duller behind eye and does not meet at rear of crown. Periophthalmic ring white instead of grey. Bill blackish in juveniles.

MEASUREMENTS Wing 99-116; tail 63-76; bill 12-15; tarsus 13-15.

GEOGRAPHICAL VARIATION Two races.

T. j. johnstoniae (Mount Apo and neighbouring mountains)

T. j. pistra (Mount Malindang) Doubtfully distinct from *johnstoniae*: upperparts slightly darker green, nape-band darker blue, less red on face.

REFERENCES BirdLife (1993), Collar *et al.* (1994), Dickinson *et al.* (1991), duPont (1971), Forshaw (1989), Lodge (1991).

---

18   POHNPEI LORIKEET
Trichoglossus rubiginosus   Plate 4

Other names: Ponapé Lory, Cherry-red Lorikeet, Caroline Lorikeet

IDENTIFICATION 24cm. Unmistakable. Plumage deep maroon with a yellow tail and olive-yellow suffusion on flight feathers. Male's bill and iris are more orange than those of the female. The birds are often seen flying swiftly at height, brief pauses in the wingbeats give the appearance of occasional banking or momentary changes in direction.

VOICE Loud and varied including a high-pitched chatter, various hissing, whistling and musical calls and some harsher notes. At dusk, soft crooning sounds are made. The birds call both in flight and when perched.

DISTRIBUTION AND STATUS Endemic to Pohnpei in the Caroline Islands, Micronesia. A report from the Truk

Islands probably involved an escaped cagebird. World population greater than 10,000. Common to abundant throughout limited range. This is the official state bird of Pohnpei; consequently no trapping or export is allowed.

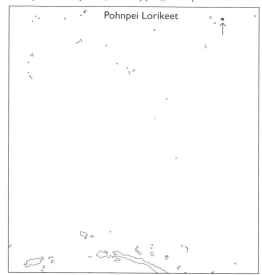
Pohnpei Lorikeet

ECOLOGY Found throughout Pohnpei island up to about 600m, occurring in a range of habitats including plantations (especially coconut palms and bananas), dense forest, secondary forest, woodland and mangrove. It is noisy (calls at roost after dark) and conspicuous, roving around in small parties of 2-12 individuals and feeding on flowering trees. The birds are sometimes seen flying high overhead, and may travel some distance over water. In larger rainforest trees they are usually found feeding in the middle storey. The diet includes nectar, pollen and fruit, and the birds have a habit of swinging upside down to feed on coconut and banana flowers. Nectar from coral trees *Erythrina fusca* and mango *Mangifera indica* fruit are especially favoured. The nest is at the top of a coconut palm or in a hollow in a large forest tree. Only one egg is laid; birds in breeding condition have been collected in Nov, but nesting generally takes place from Dec to May. A fledgling was also noted begging for food in late Sep, hissing loudly and quivering its wings.

DESCRIPTION Head and upperparts deep maroon, darkest on head. Scapulars and coverts deep maroon; flight feathers blackish on innerwebs, strongly suffused olive-yellow on outerwebs, yellowest on outermost primaries; underwing black. Underparts deep maroon edged black giving an indistinct barred appearance. Uppertail olive-yellow brighter toward tips; undertail pale olive-yellow. **Bare parts**: Bill orange; iris yellow-orange; legs dark grey.

SEX/AGE Female with more yellowish bill and greyish-white iris. Immature with more pointed tail feathers.

MEASUREMENTS Wing 136-151; tail 88-99; bill 16-20; tarsus 17-19.

GEOGRAPHICAL VARIATION None.

REFERENCES Baker (1951), Forshaw (1989), Kenning (1995), Lambert *et al.* (1993), Lodge (1991), Pratt *et al.* (1987), Pyle & Engbring (1985).

19 SCALY-BREASTED LORIKEET
Trichoglossus chlorolepidotus   Plate 4

Other names: Green-and-gold Lorikeet, Greenie, Green Lorikeet

IDENTIFICATION 22-24cm. A medium-large, mainly green lorikeet with a scalloped yellow breast and a yellow mantle-patch. The only Australian lorikeet with an unmarked green head. In flight shows an orange-red underwing flash. Swift Parrot (154) also shows this feature, as does Purple-crowned Lorikeet (37), which overlaps with feral Scaly-breasteds around Melbourne; from both these species by the barred yellow, not green, breast. The flight is swift and direct on pointed wings.

VOICE Similar to Rainbow Lorikeet (13) but higher-pitched.

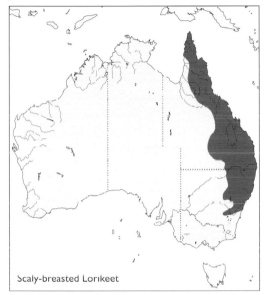

Scaly-breasted Lorikeet

DISTRIBUTION AND STATUS Occurs through the eastern seaboard of Australia and on coastal islands from the Cape York Peninsula in the north to around 35°S in New South Wales. There are occasional irruptions along watercourses west of the Great Dividing Range. For example, the species has been recorded west to around Charleville, Queensland, in the north, and to Baradine, New South Wales, in the south. Prior to 1978 the species did not regularly occur north of 15°S, but since then has colonised the Cape York Peninsula. It is generally more numerous and sedentary in the northern part of its range, where it also reaches higher altitudes (up to 600m). From 30°S the Scaly-breasted Lorikeet becomes less abundant and more nomadic in behaviour. An escaped population has become established in the eastern suburbs of Melbourne and on the Mornington and Bellarine peninsulas. Various escaped individuals may also appear further outside the regular range. World population greater than 100,000.

ECOLOGY Inhabits coastal eucalypt woodland and forests; also found in orchards and flowering street trees. Behaviour generally similar to that of Rainbow Lorikeet. Scaly-breasted Lorikeets are most noticeable in flight when large noisy flocks may be seen passing overhead. They are less conspicuous, but still noisy as they feed in the tops of flowering eucalypts, often hanging upside-down to reach the flowers. They frequently consort with Rainbow Lorikeets (the two species have interbred in the wild), and sometimes with Musk Lorikeets (35). The diet consists of pollen, nectar, fruit and insects, and as well as feeding on eucalypts, they favour banksias and *Erythrina*, and may feed on crops, sometimes causing damage. Breeding has been recorded in most months. In the south nesting begins in Aug with the season ending in Jan; in the north the season is longer with breeding beginning in May. The nest is in a high tree hollow, where two to three eggs are laid on a layer of wood dust. The adults can take up to six weeks to prepare the cavity and the whitish-downed young hatch around 25 days after the eggs are laid, fledging six to eight weeks later.

DESCRIPTION Head bright green slightly suffused turquoise-blue on rear-crown. Upperparts bright green with yellow patch in centre of mantle, formed by yellow bases to feathers, which have broad green tips producing a slightly barred effect. Upperwing green with browner innerwebs to flight feathers. Salmon-pink bar across undersides of flight feathers on innerwebs; reddish-pink underwing-coverts (redder on lesser underwing-coverts); wing-bar yellower from above. Throat bright green becoming yellow broadly tipped green on upper breast, green tips narrowing on central breast so breast appears yellow, strongly scalloped with green; sides of upper breast sometimes with slight orange-red marking, belly light green barred darker green, abdomen bright green. Uppertail bright green; undertail greyish-brown (with yellowish innerwebs); base of lateral feathers marked orange-red. **Bare parts**: Bill red; iris red; legs greyish-brown.

SEX/AGE Sexes alike. Immature with pale brown iris, brownish bill with yellow markings, and less yellow in plumage.

MEASUREMENTS Wing 120-139; tail 92-110; bill 15-17; tarsus 14-16.

GEOGRAPHICAL VARIATION None.

REFERENCES Blakers *et al.* (1984), Emison *et al.* (1987), Forshaw (1989), Lodge (1991), Pizzey & Doyle (1980), Schodde & Tidemann (1988), Slater (1989).

---

20 VARIED LORIKEET
Psitteuteles versicolor   Plate 5

Other names: Red-crowned Lorikeet, Red-capped Lorikeet, Variegated Lorikeet, Varied Lory

IDENTIFICATION 17-20cm. A distinctive species, the only Australian lorikeet with a broad white eye-ring and cere. Combination of these features, red cap and short pointed tail is diagnostic. The flight is swift and direct showing green underwing-coverts contrasting with blackish flight feathers.

VOICE A shrill rolling discordant screech, higher-pitched and less strident than that of Red-collared Lorikeet (14). The flight call has been described as thin and cricket-like. Varied Lorikeets also make sharp chattering calls while feeding and when resting utter soft twittering notes.

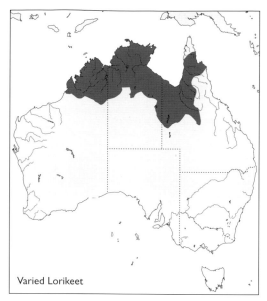

Varied Lorikeet

DISTRIBUTION AND STATUS Occurs in northern Australia and coastal islands from around Broome and the Fitzroy River, Western Australia, ranging east through the Kimberley Plateau, the northern part of Northern Territory south to the Victoria River in the east, and crossing into Queensland extending south to Mount Isa in the west and to Hughenden in the east. The species also crosses the Cape York Peninsula to the Pacific coast, occasionally occurring as far south as Townsville and Mackay. In the west it reaches north to around the Jardine River. Generally fairly common and nomadic. For example, in Darwin large numbers appear when trees are in flower, and although the birds are usually more abundant there from Apr to May and between Sep and Oct, there is insufficient data to confirm that the species is a seasonal migrant. Less common along east coast of the Cape York Peninsula, the north-east extremity of its range. World population greater than 100,000.

ECOLOGY A nomadic tropical lowland species, its movements governed by the availability of flowering trees. Varied Lorikeets are found in a range of habitats including dense eucalypt, paperbark and swamp woodlands, savanna woodland and grassland, and occasionally mangroves. They occur through the foothills, follow woodlands along water courses, and can be found in trees surrounding waterholes. They occur in pairs, small parties and large flocks (pairs remaining close together), often associating with Red-collared Lorikeets, although they are noticeably quieter. The diet includes pollen, fruits, seeds and probably insects. A number of tree species are favoured including kapok *Cochlospermum heteronemum*, bloodwoods *Eucalyptus terminalis* and paperbarks *Melaleuca leucodendron*. When feeding the birds will allow close approach and the groups spend much time clambering around to reach blossoms, allopreening and foliage-bathing. They can be aggressive towards other pollen-feeding species competing for the same blossoms. Breeding takes place throughout the year, but especially between Apr and Aug. The nest is prepared by both sexes in a limb or trunk-hollow, often near water. The cavity is lined with wood chips and chewed leaves. Two to five white eggs are laid and incubation, by

the tight-sitting female, lasts around 22 days. The young, which are fed by both parents, fledge in five to six weeks.

DESCRIPTION Top of crown and lores bright red; ear-coverts with bright yellow-green patch slightly streaked bluish-green; rear of ear-coverts and hind-crown bluish-green with yellow shaft-streaks, latter more obvious immediately below and surrounding red of hind-crown. Upperparts bright pale green suffused olive-green and shaft-streaked pale green (bright green on rump). Upperwing-coverts light green, edged and tipped paler. Flight feathers blackish on innerwebs, green on outers, with narrow bright yellow margin to leading and trailing edge of wing. Underwing-coverts green edged yellow-green. Underside of flight feathers blackish. Throat stippled yellow and bluish-green; lower throat and breast green strongly suffused pink with orange-yellow striations, belly light yellow-green with yellow striations. Uppertail green with yellow innerwebs on lateral feathers; undertail greenish-yellow, appearing darker towards tips when closed. **Bare parts**: Bill orange with a browner base to the upper mandible; large periophthalmic ring and cere white; iris yellow; legs grey.

SEX/AGE Female with darker and less extensive red on head, and less pink on breast. Immature lacks red crown and lores but shows a red forecrown. Also shows more brown on bill and a darker iris.

MEASUREMENTS Wing 108-119; tail 62-74; bill 12-13; tarsus 14-17.

GEOGRAPHICAL VARIATION None.

REFERENCES Arndt (1992), Blakers *et al.* (1984), Forshaw (1989), Lambert *et al.* (1993), Pizzey & Doyle (1983), Schodde & Tidemann (1988), Sibley & Monroe (1990), Simpson (1984), Slater (1989).

21   IRIS LORIKEET
Psitteuteles iris   Plate 5

IDENTIFICATION 20cm. A smallish, mainly green lorikeet with more yellowish underparts and a striking head-pattern. The dark smudge through the eye contrasting with a red, or red and blue, crown, green cheeks and yellow-green hind-collar are diagnostic. There are three largely similar races (see below), and females are like males but with less red in the forecrown. From Olive-headed Lorikeet (15), which also occurs on Timor, by striking head-pattern. Rainbow Lorikeets (13) in Wetar and Timor (races *capistratus* and *flavotectus*) are much larger and show a bright yellow breast contrasting with a green belly. The dissimilar Red-cheeked Parrot (95), which also occurs in Timor and Wetar, shows a scarlet face and throat and violet crown and nape (male), or largely brown head (female). The flight of Iris Lorikeet is swift and slightly undulating.

VOICE A shrill screech ending with a downward inflection.

DISTRIBUTION AND STATUS Occurs on Timor and Wetar islands, Indonesia. Formerly considered common, but not found on Wetar during a 1990 survey and only found at two localities during a nine-week survey of lowland forest in western Timor in 1993. Considered less numerous than Olive-headed or Rainbow Lorikeet on Timor. World population around 10,000. VULNERABLE.

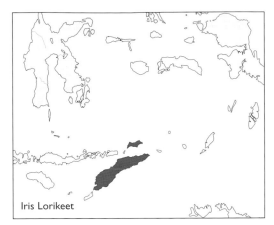
Iris Lorikeet

ECOLOGY Occurs from sea-level up to at least 1,500m (Mount Mutis in western Timor). Iris Lorikeets inhabit monsoon forest, woodland, plantations and agricultural land with flowering trees. Although they are apparently commoner at higher elevations, like most lorikeets their local abundance is based on the availability of flowering trees for feeding. Little is known of the species's breeding ecology in the wild. One record of captive breeding cited by Forshaw states that two eggs were laid, hatching in 23 days and fledging about nine weeks later.

DESCRIPTION Forehead, lores and supercilium (which extends in a narrow line around sides of rear-crown) red; lores and cheeks yellow-green; purple-blue eye-stripe extends through ear-coverts (which are centred green) and curves around rear ear-coverts; centre of crown turquoise-blue, extending to nape. Broad hind-collar yellow-green; rest of upperparts bright green. Upperwing-coverts green, flight feathers green with blackish inner-webs; underwing-coverts yellowish-green, flight feathers greyish brown below. Underparts yellow with light green suffusion; sporadic narrow green barring mainly around breast. Uppertail green with yellow innerwebs on outer feathers, undertail yellow green. **Bare parts**: Bill orange; iris orange; legs greyish-black.

SEX/AGE Adult female with forecrown green variably marked red. Cheeks more yellowish than in male. Immature like female but less red on forecrown. Bill brownish; iris brown.

MEASUREMENTS Wing 112-120; tail 65-79; bill 13-16; tarsus 14-16.

GEOGRAPHICAL VARIATION Three races.

T. i. iris (W Timor)

T. i. rubripileum (E Timor) Crown red showing little if any blue, but can show some green flecking, particularly towards rear. Hind-collar yellower. Ear-coverts bluer. Barring on breast fainter. Doubtfully distinct from nominate.

T. i. wetterensis (Wetar) Larger than both preceding races (wing 121-132; tail 67-81). Shows blue on crown, but also more red than nominate, particularly on rear-crown. Ear-coverts darker than in *rubripileum*, giving appearance of a more strongly marked face pattern. Cheeks greener than nominate. Breast-barring more extensive but narrower and more diffuse. Hind-collar yellower.

REFERENCES BirdLife (1993), Collar *et al.* (1994),

Forshaw (1989), Lambert *et al.* (1993), Mayr (1944), White & Bruce (1986).

---

22   GOLDIE'S LORIKEET
Psitteuteles goldiei   Plate 5

Other names: Red-capped Streaked Lory

IDENTIFICATION 19cm. A small, mainly dark green lorikeet with a bright red crown, light green underparts streaked darker, and a black bill. Distinctive hissing calls can often be best means of identification with flocks flying high above the forest. The other streaked lorikeets can easily be separated from Goldie's. Yellow-streaked Lory (3) is much larger, and has extensive red markings on the underparts. Varied Lorikeet (20) is confined to northern Australia, but in captivity the large white eye-ring and cere are distinctive. Striated Lorikeet (42) lacks the yellow wing-stripe of the present species and shows yellow streaking on dark green underparts, not dark green streaking on light green underparts. Goldie's Lorikeets have a distinctive flight profile with a pointed tail and swept-back wings.

VOICE A single hissing or wheezing note of level pitch; also described as a dry, high-pitched, un-musical shriek with vibrato. The call is quieter and less shrill than that of Rainbow Lorikeet (13). A soft monosyllabic hiss while feeding.

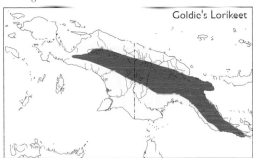
Goldie's Lorikeet

DISTRIBUTION AND STATUS Occurs patchily throughout the mountains of New Guinea from around 135°E, through the central ranges to the mountains of the Huon Peninsula and Owen Stanley range in the south-east. Generally scarce but, as with most lorikeets, can be locally plentiful when feeding trees are in flower. According to Coates, the species should be looked for in flowering trees in and around Goroka, in the eastern highlands of Papua New Guinea (one of the only reliable sites). World population above 100,000.

ECOLOGY Occurs mainly in montane primary forest and eucalyptus woodland between 1,000 and 2,200m altitude, but is nomadic and can range from sea-level to 2,800m (where found in *Nothofagus-Podocarpus* forest on Mount Hagen by Forshaw in 1970). Birds also regularly occur in flowering trees in and around highland towns and have been found in isolated groups of trees in open country. The birds are most commonly encountered in groups of 30 or more individuals which make long daily flights, often in the company of Pygmy Lorikeet (43), from their roosting sites to feed in the mid-storey and canopy of blooming trees. The diet is similar to that of most small lorikeets, and includes pollen, nectar, flowers and berries. Casuarinas and *Grevillea* feature alongside eucalypts as major food plants. Coates suggests that there may be a regular seasonal pattern in the species's movements, finding them to be locally common in lowland forest around Port Moresby between mid-Jun and early Jan. It has also been noted that the species breeds at Okapa in the eastern highlands during the rainy season. Goldie's Lorikeets often associate with *Charmosyna* lorikeets including Fairy (49), Red-flanked (45) and Pygmy (43). Little is known of the breeding ecology, but the nest is apparently built deep in dry foliage of a tall pandana where two eggs are laid.

DESCRIPTION Crown red, band around nape dull blue extending around to eye; ear-coverts and cheeks pinkish streaked dark blue. Upperparts dark green streaked black on nape and mottled yellow-green at sides of upper mantle. Upperwing-coverts dark green. Flight feathers green with blackish innerwebs and a fine yellow leading edge to outermost; fine yellow trailing edge to wing. Underwing-coverts yellowish-green marked dark green; yellow bar on underside of flight feathers on innerwebs. Underparts yellowish-green boldly striated dark green, heaviest on breast; undertail-coverts light green with dark green shafts. Uppertail dark green; undertail dull greyish-yellow. **Bare parts**: Bill black; iris brown; legs grey-black.

SEX/AGE Female with red of crown duller and less extensive. Immature with reddish crown marked dark blue; yellow streaking on upper mantle.

MEASUREMENTS Wing 98-115; tail 66-83; bill 12-16; tarsus 13-16.

GEOGRAPHICAL VARIATION None.

REFERENCES Beehler (1978b), Beehler *et al.* (1986), Coates (1985), Diamond (1972), Forshaw (1989), Sibley & Monroe (1990).

---

23 CHATTERING LORY
Lorius garrulus   Plate 7

Other names: Scarlet Lory; Yellow-backed Lory (*L. g. flavopalliatus*)

IDENTIFICATION 30cm. A mainly red lory with green wings, a blackish-tipped tail, and a yellow mantle-patch which varies according to race; in flight shows yellow underwing-coverts and a reddish bar on the underside of the primaries. Generally appears rather chubby-bodied showing broad short wings in flight silhouette. There are a number of sympatric psittacines, but none shows the combination of green wings, all-red head and underparts and yellow mantle-patch. From other *Lorius* species by the absence of a black cap. There are a number of other allopatric species with all-red heads, but they also lack the combination of green wings and yellow mantle-patch shown by the present species.

VOICE The flight call has been described as a nasal, quavering or braying note. Various loud screeching calls have also been recorded.

DISTRIBUTION AND STATUS Endemic to the northern Moluccas, Indonesia. Locally common, but around human settlements numbers have apparently been reduced

through trapping. Very popular in trade because of its imitative abilities. Milton found the species to be uncommon on Bacan in 1985 and likely to become rare because of its popularity in trade, although Smiet found Chattering Lories to be locally quite common on Halmahera, Ternate, Morotai and Bacan during observations in 1980 and 1981. Field surveys on Obi, Bacan and Halmahera, carried out by Lambert from Oct 1991 to Feb 1992, indicated that trade in the species needed to be reduced from the annual estimate of 9,600 birds to fewer than 1,000 to avoid over-exploitation. This is one of the commonest parrots in domestic trade in Indonesia. World population greater than 45,000. VULNERABLE.

Chattering Lory

ECOLOGY Although White & Bruce state that the species is common in coastal lowlands with coconut palms, recent observations seem to point to upland forested areas as the principal habitat. It is not clear whether trapping is responsible for the apparent absence from its previously preferred habitat, as seasonal movements or nomadic behaviour could also be factors. Chattering Lories are most often recorded in primary and mature secondary forest away from human settlement from the lowlands up to 1,300m. They are normally found in pairs, and are noisy and conspicuous in flight but, like many other parrots, can become difficult to detect when feeding quietly in the forest canopy. Little is known of the species's breeding ecology in the wild. A pair was seen investigating a possible nest-hole in Jun, other records include an observation of fledged young being fed during Oct and Nov, and a pair attending a presumed nest-site high in a dead tree, also during Oct. Forshaw gives details of an instance of captive breeding in which two eggs were laid with the young fledging in 76 days.

DESCRIPTION Head entirely bright scarlet. Nape and upper mantle bright scarlet; large yellow patch in centre of mantle surrounded above and below by slight dull-green suffusion; scapulars scarlet, a little darker than mantle; rump and uppertail-coverts bright scarlet. Upperwing green; coverts slightly lighter and with a vague bronze suffusion; black innerwebs to flight feathers and greater coverts; leading edge of outer primaries blackish; alula blackish-green; yellow patch at bend of wing, also slightly indicated along carpal edge. Underside of flight feathers black with broad pinkish-red band across innerwebs; coverts yellow with red bases to greaters. Underparts bright scarlet; thighs green. Basal half of uppertail red, distal half black with green suffusion; undertail basally scarlet, distal half blackish-red suffused yellow-green at tips. **Bare parts**: Bill orange; iris orange to yellowish-brown; legs greyish-black.

SEX/AGE: Sexes alike. Immature with brownish bill, and dark brown iris.

MEASUREMENTS Wing 169-189; tail 97-110; bill 24-27; tarsus 22-25 .

GEOGRAPHICAL VARIATION Three races.

> **L. g. garrulus** (Halmahera, the Widi Islands and Ternate)
> **L. g. flavopalliatus** (Bacan and Obi) From nominate by more extensive yellow mantle-patch which shows much less greenish suffusion.
> **L. g. morotaianus** (Morotai and Rau) Small yellow mantle patch suffused with green.

REFERENCES BirdLife (1993), Forshaw (1989), Lambert (1993a), Lambert *et al.* (1993), Lodge (1991), Milton (1988), Smiet (1985), S. Smith *in litt.* (1993), White & Bruce (1986).

---

24 PURPLE-NAPED LORY
Lorius domicella Plate 7

Other names: Purple-capped Lory

IDENTIFICATION 28cm. Sympatric with both Blue-eared Lory (10) and Red Lory (7) in Seram; all three share largely red underparts. This species is easily separated from both by its black cap, green wings and bright yellow underwing flash. It is quite unlike Rainbow Lorikeet (13), the other similar-sized sympatric lorikeet. Although brightly coloured, Purple-naped Lories are uncommon and can be particularly difficult to locate when silent.

VOICE A 'melodious' call is mentioned by Smiet, but the voice has not yet been fully described.

DISTRIBUTION AND STATUS Endemic to the islands of Seram and Ambon (has also been recorded on Buru: probably an escape), Indonesia. There are no recent records from Ambon or Buru, and current records come from Manusela National Park (uncommon) in central Seram and Wae Fufa (locally common) in the east. In 1987 Bowler and Taylor encountered them at a rate of 0.7 birds per hour at Kineke, in Manusela National Park; but during nearly two months of observations in 1990, only 10 individuals were seen. The species is a popular cagebird in Seram and throughout Maluku province, and expansion of external trade could pose a threat to its survival. World population was estimated at less than 20,000 in 1991, but numbers are now considered to be higher. VULNERABLE.

ECOLOGY On Seram birds are found in montane and submontane primary and secondary forest between 400 and 1,050m; also in lowland forest in the east of the island, and in cultivated areas. They occur in pairs, rarely in flocks, and may be territorial. They feed on fruits of an apparently thinly scattered *Pandanus*. The species's breeding ecology in the wild is unknown. Forshaw gives details of an instance

of breeding in aviculture in which two eggs were laid, hatching in around 25 days; the single young fledged three months later.

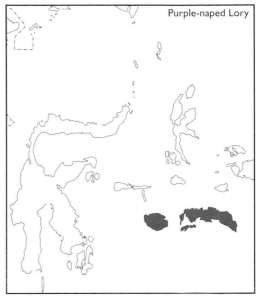

Purple-naped Lory

DESCRIPTION Forehead, crown and nape black, with variable purple patch at rear of cap; cheeks, lores and ear-coverts red. Upperparts red, darkest in centre of mantle. Upperwing green with variable white and violet patch on shoulder; bronze wash across inner greater coverts with innermost marked dull red; flight feathers blackish on innerwebs with yellow central area forming yellow underwing panel. Underwing-coverts violet-blue suffused white; greater underwing-coverts black; axillaries violet-blue suffused white. Underparts red with variable yellow band across upper breast; thighs violet-blue slightly suffused green. Tail red, broadly tipped reddish-brown. **Bare parts**: Bill orange; iris reddish-brown; legs dark grey.

SEX/AGE Sexes alike. Immature with yellow breast-band broader and more diffuse. Bill brown in very young birds.

MEASUREMENTS Wing 157-173; tail 89-105; bill 25-27; tarsus 22-25.

GEOGRAPHICAL VARIATION None.

NOTE Includes Blue-thighed Lory *Lorius tibialis* (known from a single specimen bought in a Calcutta market around 1867 and presented to London Zoo), which is now thought to be an aberrant example of *domicella*.

REFERENCES BirdLife (1993), Bishop (1992a), Bowler & Taylor (1989), Collar *et al.* (1994), Forshaw (1989), P. Jepson *in litt.* (1997), Lambert *et al.* (1993), Smiet (1985), Taylor (1990), White & Bruce (1986).

---

25 BLACK-CAPPED LORY
Lorius lory Plate 6

Other names: Western Black-capped Lory, Tricoloured Lory

IDENTIFICATION 31cm. A stout medium-sized parrot with a short rounded tail occurring through the lowlands of New Guinea and on some related islands. In flight shows obvious yellow underwing-patch, and rapid shallow wingbeats on stubby, rounded wings give a fluttering appearance. Combination of black cap, dark blue mantle band, hindneck and extensive blue markings on underparts separates this species from other members of the genus *Lorius*. The race *somu*, however, lacks the blue neck and mantle-markings and appears very similar to Purple-bellied Lory (26). It can be separated on call (Black-capped has a musical whistling call, Purple-bellied gives a distinctive coarse nasal call) and by the black, not white, cere. *L. l. somu* is also restricted to the southern central region of Papua New Guinea, whereas Purple-bellied occurs only in south-east Papua New Guinea and on offshore islands. Black-capped Lories are relatively shy and most often seen in flight when they are noisy and easily detected at or above tree-top level, particularly during the early morning and late afternoon. Two mainly highland *Charmosyna* species, Josephine's Lory (50), and Papuan Lorikeet (51), are superficially similar, but both have long, yellow-tipped tails, red foreheads and lack the purple-blue mantle of the present species.

VOICE Flight call is a loud melodious whistle described as a wader-like *wheedle wheedle*. The call is frequently repeated, sometimes with three syllables. When resting, a range of whistles and squeaks is given. The song is described as a long series of phrases each of a few notes repeated over and over. The call is more musical than that of Rainbow Lorikeet (13) or Dusky Lory (11).

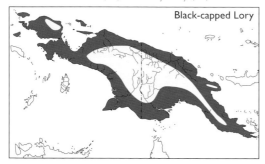

Black-capped Lory

DISTRIBUTION AND STATUS Widely distributed from western Irian Jaya, Indonesia, including Waigeo, Batanta, Salawati and Misool islands in the W Papuan group, and Yapen, Mios Num and Biak islands in Geelvink Bay, to eastern Papua New Guinea. Common to fairly common in lowlands and hills. World population greater than 100,000.

ECOLOGY Prefers primary forest and forest edges, but has also been recorded in well grown secondary forest, in some partially cleared areas and in swamp forest. Not known to occur in monsoon forest, gallery forest or coconut plantations. Black-capped Lories occur primarily in the lowlands up to 1,000m but have been recorded up to 1,750m. They are usually found in pairs, and generally in smaller groups than other sympatric psittacines, but may occur in larger groups of ten or more when gathering to feed in flowering trees. The diet includes pollen, nectar, flowers, fruit and insects. The birds prefer to feed in the canopy or middle storey where they remain quiet and inconspicuous. Unlike Rainbow Lorikeet and Dusky Lory, which generally reach similar maximum altitudes, this species has failed to adapt to secondary habitats at higher

levels in eastern New Guinea. Little is known of its breeding ecology in the wild, although there is a record of a pair excavating a nest-hole in a dead tree. Nesting apparently occurs from at least May to Oct. In captivity, two white eggs are laid and incubated for 26 days; fledging occurs in 57-70 days. The display includes body-bobbing and wing-flapping.

DESCRIPTION Black cap extends from above bill to nape where a few blue flecks appear; rest of head bright red. Black cap separated from dark purplish-blue (sometimes red-flecked) mantle by thin pinkish-red hind-collar; back, rump and uppertail-coverts bright red. Upperwing green with slight bronze sheen notably on coverts and innermost secondaries. Flight feathers with black innerwebs marked yellow forming a panel on underwing. Underwing-coverts red. Throat and upper breast red; blue of mantle extends around sides of breast to meet dark blue of belly which is slightly brighter on thighs and undertail-coverts; flanks with variable amounts of red extending up and around bend of wing. Uppertail dark blue-black, slightly suffused green centrally and with red bases to feathers (appearing dark blue only at rest); undertail dusky olive-yellow with concealed red base. **Bare parts**: Bill orange; cere and periophthalmic ring grey-black; iris yellow-orange; legs grey-black.

SEX/AGE Sexes alike. Immature with blue of underparts less extensive and with breast mainly red. Thin blue collar meets around throat. Underwing-coverts blue and yellow tipped black, not red as in adult. Bill brownish. Sexes alike.

MEASUREMENTS Wing 148-175; tail 85-103; bill 22-27; tarsus 21-26.

GEOGRAPHICAL VARIATION Seven races.
   L. l. lory (W Papuan islands and Vogelkop, Irian Jaya)
   L. l. erythrothorax (S New Guinea west to the Huon Peninsula in the north, and to the south of Geelvink Bay and on the Onin Peninsula in the south) Red on breast extends much further down than on nominate. Blue of mantle split into two bands which do not join each other or the blue of the belly.
   L. l. somu (hills of Papua New Guinea on the southern side of the central mountain ranges, from the Ok Tedi area to the Karimui area, as well as the Purari River drainage; birds to the east of the Karimui Basin belong to the previous race) Lacks blue nape and mantle of nominate and red of breast extends much further down. Resembles Purple-bellied Lory closely but shows dark grey-black not white cere.
   L. l. salvadorii (N Papua New Guinea from the Aitape area to Astrolabe Bay) From nominate and *erythrothorax* by blue and black underwing-coverts (with no red) and from nominate by red band separating blue hind-collar from blue of mantle (shared with *erythrothorax*).
   L. l. viridicrissalis (N Papua New Guinea from Humboldt Bay to the Memberamo River) Similar to *salvadorii* but with blue areas much blacker.
   L. l. jobiensis (Yapen and Mios Num islands in Geelvink Bay) Very similar to *salvadorii* but with a paler rosy tinge to red breast and lighter blue mantle and hind-neck bands.
   L. l. cyanuchen (Biak island, Geelvink Bay) Like *salvadorii* but lacking red hind-collar separating cap from mantle. Red of breast extends further down than on nominate. World population of this race is less than 5,000.

REFERENCES Arndt (1992), Beehler (1978b), Beehler *et al.* (1986), Bell (1982), Buckell (1990), T. Buckell *in litt.* (1993), Coates (1985), Diamond (1972), Forshaw (1989), Lambert *et al.* (1993), Lodge (1991), Rand & Gilliard (1967).

26   PURPLE-BELLIED LORY
Lorius hypoinochrous   Plate 6

Other names: Eastern Black-capped Lory, Louisiade Lory

IDENTIFICATION 26cm. Eastern New Guinea and surrounding islands. A stocky, medium-sized parrot with a short rounded tail; in flight stubby, rounded wings and rapid shallow wingbeats give a fluttering appearance. There is also an obvious yellow underwing-patch. Wings appear stubby and rounded. Generally similar in appearance to Black-capped Lory (25), particularly the race *somu* which is, however, allopatric. Purple-bellied can be separated at close quarters from Black-capped including *somu* by its white, not grey-black, cere. In south-east Papua New Guinea where the two species overlap on range, Black-capped, race *erythrothorax*, shows a dark purple-blue hind-collar and band across the mantle and more extensive dark blue markings on the lower underparts. Black-capped has a musical whistle whereas Purple-bellied gives a hoarse nasal call. Black-capped also shows a strong preference for forest and Purple-bellied is found in a range of habitats including coconut plantations, which Black-capped avoids. Also sympatric with White-naped Lory (27) between 500 and 750m in mountains of southern New Ireland. White-naped shows a clear white patch on nape and entirely red underparts except for some yellow markings on the sides of the upper breast. White-naped also has a weak rising whistled call, quite different from that of Purple-bellied.

VOICE Calls frequently in flight and when perched. Distinctive call is a single harsh unmusical rising and falling note, described by Coates as a loud drawn-out coarse nasal wailing or whinnying.

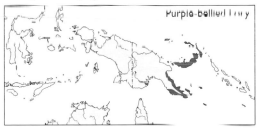

DISTRIBUTION AND STATUS Endemic to south-east Papua New Guinea and surrounding island groups. On the mainland reaches west to Lae on the Huon Gulf in the north and to Cape Rodney in the south. Occurs on islands in the D'Entrecasteaux and Louisiade archipelagos, including Goodenough, Fergusson, Normanby, Bentley, Misima, Tagula and Rossel, the Trobriands, Woodlark and islands in the Bismarck Archipelago including Long, Umboi, Sakar, New Britain, New Ireland, Witu, Lolobau, Watom, New Hanover, Tabar and Lihir. Common to locally abundant. World population greater than 50,000.

ECOLOGY Unlike Black-capped Lory, frequently found in coastal vegetation, mangroves and coconut plantations

(especially fond of coconut flowers). Also occurs in forest, along forest edge, and in secondary growth, partly cleared or inhabited areas and in gardens. Found singly, in pairs or in small parties of up to 10-20 birds. Noisy, conspicuous and active, often seen flying through tree-tops or just above canopy. On mainland, occurs in lowlands and foothills, in New Britain up to at least 450m, in New Ireland up to 750m (where sympatric with White-naped Lory), and up to 1,600m on Goodenough Island. The birds feed mainly in the canopy in noisy groups, and have been observed foraging among blossoms and fruit and feeding on flowering vines in mid-storey. Purple-bellied Lories sometimes keep company with Sulphur-crested Cockatoos (65) and Eclectus Parrots (111). Virtually nothing is known of the species's breeding ecology although an apparent display involving neck-stretching and head-bobbing has been observed.

DESCRIPTION Black cap with purple-blue gloss extending to rear of nape; rest of head red. Upperparts entirely red with a variable dusky band across mantle; upper mantle slightly more purplish than rest of upperparts. Primary coverts bluish; rest of wing green with black innerwebs to flight feathers. Underwing-coverts red tipped black, with black flight feathers showing extensive yellow patch on innerwebs. Throat and breast red becoming more purplish on upper belly; lower belly, thighs and undertail-coverts dark purplish-blue. Uppertail basally red turning green to dark blue with a green tip (appears only blue-green at rest); undertail dull olive yellow with concealed red base. **Bare parts:** Bill orange; cere white; iris orange; legs grey-black.

SEX/AGE Immature: Similar to adult but bill brownish. Sexes alike.

MEASUREMENTS Wing 163-175; tail: 83-94; bill: 23-25; tarsus 21-24.

GEOGRAPHICAL VARIATION Three races.

L. h. hypoinochrous (Misima and Tagula islands in the Louisiade Archipelago)

L. h. rosselianus (Rossel Island in the Louisiade Archipelago) Similar to nominate but lower breast marked with violet.

L. h. devittatus (SE New Guinea, the D'Entrecasteaux Archipelago, the Trobriand Islands and throughout the Bismarck Archipelago) Similar to nominate but black margins to greater underwing-coverts are absent (but usually still present in young birds).

NOTE Includes Stresemann's Lory *Lorius amabilis*, the single specimen of which, lacking the black cap, is now thought to have been an aberrant Purple-bellied Lory.

REFERENCES Arndt (1992), Beehler *et al.* (1986), Bell (1970), Bishop & Broome (1980), Coates (1985), Forshaw (1989), Hartert (1926), Lambert *et al.* (1993), LeCroy *et al.* (1984), Lodge (1991), Rand & Gilliard (1967), Sibley & Monroe (1990).

27   WHITE-NAPED LORY
Lorius albidinuchus   Plate 6

IDENTIFICATION 26cm. A distinctive but little-known species restricted to hill forests of New Ireland in the Bismarck Archipelago, Papua New Guinea. Similar to

Purple-bellied Lory (26) with which it is sympatric between 500 and 750m in southern New Ireland, but has white nape-patch, entirely red underparts except for yellow markings on sides of breast, and no obvious dark purplish suffusion on belly and undertail-coverts shown by Purple-bellied Lory. With close views, dark cere also separates this species from Purple-bellied, which has a white cere. White-naped Lory is also less stoutly built than Purple-bellied and has a whistling call, differing considerably from the distinctive hoarse nasal call of Purple-bellied.

VOICE A weak rising whistle *schweet* or *schweet-schweet*.

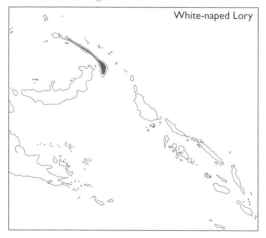

White-naped Lory

DISTRIBUTION AND STATUS Endemic to New Ireland. Fairly common throughout its limited altitudinal range. World population probably less than 10,000. NEAR-THREATENED.

ECOLOGY Known only from mountains of southern New Ireland between 500 and 2,000m, perhaps mainly around 1,000m. Normally encountered in pairs feeding on fruit or flowers of the wild 'oil palm'. Has been seen feeding in the same tree as Purple-bellied Lory without interspecific aggression.

DESCRIPTION Crown black, marked slightly violet adjacent to white nape-patch; rest of head bright red. Upperparts red. Upperwing green with bend violet marked white. Flight feathers black with green outer webs on upper surface, and broad yellow band across inner-webs. Underwing-coverts red tipped black (can show purple markings). Underparts red with yellow markings at sides of breast, and blue markings on thighs. Uppertail basally red, broadly tipped green; undertail basally red tipped dull yellow. **Bare parts:** Bill orange with dusky base to upper mandible; cere black; iris yellow to brownish red; legs grey black.

SEX/AGE Sexes alike.

MEASUREMENTS Wing 146-162; tail 86-105; bill 21-23; tarsus 20-22.

GEOGRAPHICAL VARIATION None.

REFERENCES Beehler (1978a), Coates (1985), Forshaw (1989), Lambert *et al.* (1993).

28 YELLOW-BIBBED LORY
Lorius chlorocercus Plate 7

Other names: Green-tailed Lory, Gould's Lory

IDENTIFICATION 28cm. Only member of the genus *Lorius* found in the Eastern Solomons; in flight has stout build with short tail and distinctive underwing pattern showing blue coverts and red band on underside of primaries. Adults also show a distinctive black crescent-shaped patch on side of neck. Black cap, green wings and red underparts with yellow breast-band distinguish it from other similar-sized sympatric species such as Cardinal Lory (4) and Rainbow Lorikeet (13). Duchess Lorikeet (48) is a much smaller bird, with a long thin yellow-tipped tail. It has a red, not black, forecrown, and the yellow breast-band continues around the mantle.

VOICE A shrieking *chuick-lik* or *chu-er-wee tcheeu* or *eeee-eh*, also harsher, more abrupt notes, but call is less harsh than that of Rainbow Lorikeet.

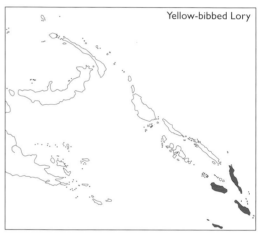

Yellow-bibbed Lory

DISTRIBUTION AND STATUS Endemic to the eastern Solomon Islands on Savo, Guadalcanal, Malaita, Ulawa, Uki, San Cristobal and Rennell. Fairly common. World population 10,000-50,000.

ECOLOGY Found in forest canopy and secondary growth at all altitudes up to 1,000m. On Guadalcanal noted to be commoner in hills than in lowlands and commonest in lower mist forest. On other islands also occasionally noted around coconut plantations. Usually occurs singly, in pairs, or in groups of up to ten birds. Ecology generally little known although presumably typical of the genus.

DESCRIPTION Cap black from above bill to nape; rest of head bright red with prominent crescent-shaped black patch at side of neck. Upperparts red; centre of mantle dusky red. Upperwing green with slight yellow-bronze sheen notably on coverts and tertials. Innerwebs of flight feathers and greater coverts black; bend of wing with a white patch and sometimes blue showing from underwing-coverts, which are blue tipped black, with a broad rose-red band on innerwebs of primaries. Axillaries purple-blue. Underparts red with a prominent yellow collar; thighs blue. Uppertail basally red, broadly tipped green; undertail basally red broadly tipped dull olive-yellow. **Bare parts:** Bill orange with dusky base to lower mandible; iris orange; legs dark grey.

SEX/AGE Immature lacks black mark at side of neck, has a restricted amount of yellow on the breast (or yellow is absent altogether). Blue of thighs carries some green markings. Bill brownish. Iris brown.

MEASUREMENTS Wing 151-175; tail 80-100; bill 21-24; tarsus 20-23.

GEOGRAPHICAL VARIATION None.

REFERENCES , BirdLife (1993), Cain & Galbraith (1956), Forshaw (1989), Lambert *et al.* (1993), Lodge (1991), Mayr (1945).

29 COLLARED LORIKEET
Phigys solitarius   Plate 8

Other names: Solitary Lory, Ruffed Lory, Fiji Lory, Collared Lory

IDENTIFICATION 20cm. A chunky, compact, mainly red and green lory with a rather short tail, restricted to islands in the Fiji group. Superficially resembles *Lorius* species showing a blackish cap, red underparts and dark belly, but morphology, particularly the long hind-crown feathers, points to a close relationship with the Pacific genus *Vini*. No members of *Lorius* occur in Fiji so there is no likelihood of confusion in the field. In captivity the bright green hind-collar, back and rump separate this distinctive species from all members of *Lorius*. In the field dark cap, green collar, and green upperparts, in combination with red underparts and dark belly, are diagnostic. Common, noisy and easily found. The flight is swift with rapid, shallow, audibly whirring wingbeats. Small noisy parties pass overhead with sudden changes in direction and occasional glides.

VOICE A penetrating mechanical screech, uttered both on the wing and while feeding, as well as various chittering calls.

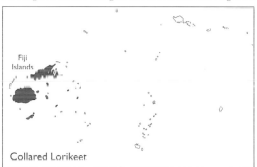

Collared Lorikeet

DISTRIBUTION AND STATUS Endemic to the Fiji Islands including the main islands of Vanua Levu and Viti Levu, plus Rabi, Taveuni, Koro, Wokaya, Ovalau, Gau, Ono, Kadavu, Matuku, Moala and some islands in the Lau Group (Naituaba, Vatu Vara, Lakeba). In the extreme south of the Fiji group it is replaced by Blue-crowned Lory (30). The species is common and the world population is estimated to fall somewhere between 10,000 and 100,000. A few are kept in captivity. The red feathers were previously used by Samoans and Tongans to edge mats, but the trade does not seem to have had any impact on the species's abundance in Fiji. Some birds are reported to have escaped on Tonga and Samoa without, however, becoming established.

ECOLOGY Conspicuous and noisy, usually encountered in pairs or small groups of five to fifteen, but flocks of up to 50 birds have been seen. Chiefly occurs in lowlands in humid forest, forest edge, plantations and second growth up to 1,200m, but may be encountered anywhere with suitable flowering trees including gardens. It is generally commoner in the wetter windward areas, being less frequent along the agricultural leeward coasts. The birds are however mobile and somewhat nomadic, being prepared to travel to flowering trees in almost any habitat. They are often seen flying above tree-tops or feeding noisily in acrobatic groups. The diet comprises a wide variety of flowers including coconut palm and drala *Erythrina indica*, also fruit including mango *Mangifera indica*. Nesting occurs in the second half of the year, especially after Aug. Two white eggs are laid in a tree-hollow and the adults aggressively defend the nest-site. Forshaw cites an instance of captive breeding in which incubation lasted 30 days and the young bird fledged almost nine weeks later.

DESCRIPTION Cap dark purple-black (with elongated feathers of hind-crown extending onto hindneck), contrasting with scarlet ear-coverts, cheeks and throat; forecrown occasionally with slight red flecking; hind-collar vivide green, extending around to sides of neck and with red tips forming band across mantle. Lower mantle, rump and uppertail coverts bright green. Upperwing green with black innerwebs to flight feathers and coverts. Underwing-coverts red and green, underside of flight feathers black. Underparts scarlet, but with lower abdomen, lower sides of rump and thighs purple-black, and undertail-coverts bright green. Uppertail light green showing variable yellow-orange spot on central feathers, outer feathers with variable pinkish orange spot at base of innerweb; undertail dull greenish-brown also showing orange spots at base. **Bare parts** Bill orange; iris yellow orange to red; legs yellowish-orange to pink.

SEX/AGE Female has more green on hindneck, less red on mantle, a pronounced green sheen on rear-crown and a brighter purple forecrown. Immature shows slight purplish flecking and some concealed greenish spots on breast; green hind-crown; red tips to elongate feathers of nape lacking or restricted up to eights months of age. Usually lacks orange tail-spots. Young also have more pointed tail feathers but lack attenuated primaries of adult. Bill browner than adult; iris brown; feet dark.

MEASUREMENTS Wing 123-140; tail: 61-69; bill 15-17; tarsus 14-19.

GEOGRAPHICAL VARIATION None.

REFERENCES Amadon (1942), Clunie (1984), duPont (1976), Forshaw (1989), Gregory-Smith (1983), Holyoak (1979), Lambert *et al.* (1993), Low (1984), Mayr (1945), Pratt *et al.* (1987), Sibley & Monroe (1990), Watling (1982a,b) Wood & Wetmore (1925).

30 BLUE-CROWNED LORIKEET
Vini australis   Plate 8

Other names: Blue-crested Lory, Samoan Lory

IDENTIFICATION 19cm. A smallish green lorikeet with a red throat, blue crown and red and purple belly-patch, occurring in southern Fiji, Tonga, Samoa and Central Polynesia. There are no sympatric confusion species, but the Red-throated Lorikeet (47) occurs through Fiji to the north and is superficially similar. Red-throated lacks the blue crown and red and purple belly-patch, and has a yellow lower border to its red throat-patch. Blue-crowned Lories fly fast, steady and direct with rapid whirring wing-beats.

VOICE A shrill, high-pitched creaky screech or whistle, delivered in flight and whilst feeding.

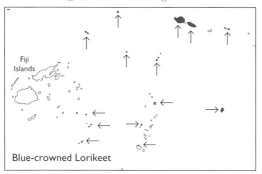

Blue-crowned Lorikeet

DISTRIBUTION AND STATUS Endemic, being restricted to some southern islands in the Fiji group, Tonga, Samoa and central Fulaga, including Vatoa, Fulaga, Moce (Lau Group, Fiji); Upolu, Savaii (Western Samoa), Ofu, Olosega and Tau (American Samoa); Niuafo'ou, Vava'u, Tofua, Uiha, Fotuha'a, Ha'afeva, Voleva, 'Eua and Tongatapu (probably now absent from both of these), Tafahi, Tungua, Niuatoputapu, (Tonga); Uvea (may now be extinct), Alofi, Futuna (Wallis & Horn Islands, to France), and further east on Niue (to New Zealand). The species's apparent historic absence from the relatively large island of Tutuila in the Samoan group is surprising, the occasional records probably relating to nomads from other islands. The only member of its genus not presently threatened with extinction. World population estimated at 50,000-100,000 individuals. Although the species is generally thought to be decreasing (probably because of predation by rats) it is still fairly common on a number of islands.

ECOLOGY Occurs in woodland, coconut palms or any habitat where there are flowering trees, from coastal areas to mountains, gardens and agricultural areas. Nomadic, sometimes travelling between islands and is often seen flying high above the canopy. Probably daily movements occur between feeding and roosting areas. Aggressive but gregarious, usually being encountered in flocks of up to 12 birds except during the breeding season when birds consort in pairs. In Samoa noted as common around villages and plantations and less common in cloud-forest and at higher elevations, in secondary growth and in rain-forest. Feeds on nectar, pollen and soft fruit. Utilises a variety of food species but particularly prefers *Erythrina*, wild hibiscus and coconut. Nests in holes in trees but has also been reported digging burrows in earth banks, although nesting in these is unconfirmed. One or two white eggs are laid. Breeding recorded in Jun and Aug. In captivity incubation has been timed at 23 days.

DESCRIPTION Forehead bright green; elongated crown feathers (as in other members of the genus) blackish-blue at base, with bright violet blue streaks extending onto nape; lores, cheeks and throat red. Upperparts bright green, tinged slightly olive on mantle and lighter green on rump and around nape. Upperwing-coverts green with blackish innerwebs to flight feathers; very fine yellow trailing and leading edges to wing. Underwing-coverts green; flight feathers greyish-black. Throat and upper breast scarlet; central breast, lower breast and flanks bright green; centre of belly with red spot and purplish-blue spot below; thighs purplish-blue with green at bases. Uppertail basally green, yellow at tips of central, slightly protruding feathers (as in all *Vini* species), lateral feathers green with yellow innerwebs; undertail yellowish-green. **Bare parts**: Bill orange; iris yellow; legs orange.

SEX/AGE Sexes alike. Immature generally duller and more olive. Throat-patch pinkish-red and much smaller; blue of crown much less pronounced; belly-patch also less pronounced with limited red suffusion and purplish-blue markings almost absent. Bill browner than in adult; iris brown.

MEASUREMENTS Wing: 101-114; tail 61-69; bill: 11-14; tarsus: 13-16.

GEOGRAPHICAL VARIATION None.

REFERENCES Amadon (1942), Banks (1982), Clunie (1984), duPont (1976), Engbring & Ramsey (1989), Evans *et al.* (1992), Forshaw (1989), Lambert *et al.* (1993), Lodge (1991), Low (1984), Rinke (1992), Sibley & Monroe (1990), Watling (1982a).

31 KUHL'S LORIKEET
Vini kuhlii   Plate 8

Other names: Kuhl's Lorikeet, Kuhl's Ruffed Lorikeet, Ruby Lorikeet, Scarlet-breasted Lorikeet, Rimatara Lorikeet

IDENTIFICATION 19cm. A small, brightly coloured lory, restricted to a few islands in the central south Pacific. This distinctive species can easily be separated from the similar, closely related Stephen's Lory (32) by its blue nape-patch and shorter red, black and green tail. Stephen's Lory, which occurs only on Henderson Island, has a long, predominantly yellow tail. The flight of Kuhl's Lory is swift and similar to that of other small lorikeets, with the wings making an audible whirring sound.

VOICE 'A shrill croak or screech'.

DISTRIBUTION AND STATUS Endemic to Rimatara in the Tubuai Islands, central-south Pacific (to France), where the population is estimated at 905 birds. It has also been introduced to Kiribati including Teraina (Washington Island) and Tabueran (Fanning Island), both prior to 1798, and to Kiritimati (Christmas Island), where six were transferred in 1957. Fossil remains indicate that the species probably also formerly occurred in the southern Cook Islands. Occasional occurrences on Tubuai Island close to Rimatara are probably escaped pets. Although the species is still relatively common on Rimatara, the recent introduction of rats gives cause for concern. The population on Tabueran (c. 200 birds) is also vulnerable to nest predation by rats. On Teraina there are around 1,000 birds and, with no confirmed threats, good *in situ* conservation potential still exists. It is possible that one or two individuals may still survive on Kiritimati. ENDANGERED.

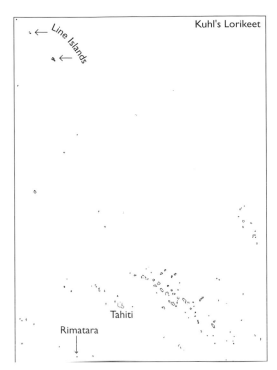

Kuhl's Lorikeet

← Line Islands

← ←

● Tahiti

Rimatara

↓

ECOLOGY On Rimatara, found in mixed horticultural woodland, forested valleys with coconuts, and around habitation; on Teraina and Tabueran it is confined to coconut plantations. Travels in pairs or small flocks and is often seen flying above the tree-tops. The diet includes nectar and pollen, and the species prefers to feed in coconut palms. Breeding is reported to be between Jan and Mar, the nest being placed in a coconut palm or a hole in a coconut still attached to the tree. Forshaw gives details of an instance of captive breeding in which a single young bird fledged about seven weeks after hatching.

DESCRIPTION Crown blackish, with elongated feathers typical of the genus, showing bright green shaft-streaking and appearing green in field, nape feathers dark purplish-blue (blacker at bases), with blue shaft-streaking; lores, throat and cheeks bright crimson. Upperparts green, more yellowish in centre of mantle, with lower back, rump and uppertail-coverts bright yellowish-green. Upperwing-coverts green, outerwebs of flight feathers green except longest primaries which are suffused blue; innerwebs black. Underwing coverts green, underside of flight feathers blackish. Breast bright crimson, becoming dark purple on belly and thighs. Under- and lateral tail-coverts light yellow-green. Uppertail has black outer- and red innerwebs, tipped green; undertail basally red, tipped olive-green. **Bare parts:** Bill yellowish-orange; iris reddish-yellow; legs orange-yellow.

SEX/AGE Sexes alike. Underparts of immature dark purple mottled with red. For up to six months the bill is brown.

MEASUREMENTS Wing 120-136; tail 64-75; bill 11-15; tarsus 14-19.

GEOGRAPHICAL VARIATION None.

REFERENCES Collar et al. (1994), Forshaw (1989),

duPont (1976), Lambert et al. (1993), Lever (1987), Lodge (1991), Long (1981), Pratt et al. (1987), Sibley & Monroe (1990), Watling (1995).

32   STEPHEN'S LORIKEET
Vini stepheni   Plate 8

Other names: Henderson Island Lorikeet, Henderson Lorikeet

IDENTIFICATION 19cm. Restricted to the extremely isolated Henderson Island in the east-central Pacific. The only similar species, Kuhl's Lory (31), does not occur on Henderson so there is no chance of confusion in the field. Should separation ever be necessary, the following characters are diagnostic: Stephen's Lory lacks the blue nape-patch of Kuhl's and shows green breast-markings absent in Kuhl's. The tail of Stephen's is longer and is yellow rather than red, green and black. Stephen's Lories are easily seen on Henderson Island in small groups flying over the tree-tops, but despite their colourful plumage they are difficult to locate once they have landed in the forest canopy.

VOICE A soft twittering while feeding; flight calls are louder.

DISTRIBUTION AND STATUS Endemic to the 30km² Henderson Island in the Pitcairn Group (to U.K.). Total population estimated to be between 720 and 1,890 individuals in 1987 (a 1992 estimate gave a population of 1,200 pairs). The population is thought to be stable, but the species is considered vulnerable because of its extremely limited range. A potentially serious threat was averted in 1983 when an American millionaire seeking to make Henderson his home had his application rejected by the UK government. Henderson is now a World Heritage Site. At present there are not known to be any Stephen's Lory's in captivity. VULNERABLE.

ECOLOGY Henderson Island is a small raised-reef island: Stephen's Lories are found in coconut palms *Cocos nucifera* along the beaches, as well as in forest away from the shore, being especially partial to forest-fringe habitats. They feed on coconut nectar, as well as on pollen and some insect larvae and small fruits. Little is known of the species's ecology, but small groups, presumably family parties, are commonly seen flying above trees in various parts of the island.

DESCRIPTION Crown green with lighter green shaft-streaks; lores, throat and cheeks crimson. Upperparts green, slightly duller than crown with yellowish cast to mantle; rump and uppertail-coverts lighter green. Upperwing-coverts and outerwebs of flight feathers green, except longest primaries which are black; innerwebs blackish. Underwing-coverts green marked red. Underparts crimson with irregular green or green and purple flecking across lower breast; belly and thighs purplish. Under- and lateral tail-coverts and flanks light green. Uppertail yellow with light green wash on outerwebs, outer feathers with indistinct orange-red spot at base of innerweb; undertail yellow with light green suffusion on outerwebs. **Bare parts:** Bill orange with darker markings at tip of upper mandible; iris pale orange; legs orange.

SEX/AGE Sexes alike. Underparts of immature green with red and purple markings on throat and belly; tail dark

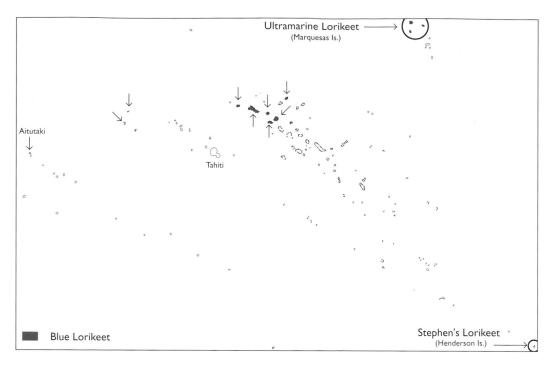

Ultramarine Lorikeet ———→
(Marquesas Is.)

Aitutaki

Tahiti

■ Blue Lorikeet

Stephen's Lorikeet
(Henderson Is.) ———→

green; bill and iris brown; legs browner than adult.

MEASUREMENTS Wing 124-133; tail 83-93; bill 11-13; tarsus 14-18.

GEOGRAPHICAL VARIATION None.

REFERENCES BirdLife (1993), Collar *et al.* (1994), duPont (1976), Forshaw (1989), Graves (1992), Rinke (1992), Sibley & Monroe (1990).

33   BLUE LORIKEET
Vini peruviana   Plate 8

Other names: Tahitian Lory, Blue Lorikeet, Tahiti Lorikeet, Indigo Lory

IDENTIFICATION 14cm. One of the most distinctive of all parrots. A small, uniformly dark glossy blue lory with a white bib and a bright orange bill and legs. Restricted to a few islands in the central South Pacific where its numbers are declining on most of its range islands. The only similar-sized mainly blue psittacine is the closely related Ultramarine Lory (34), which lacks the clearly demarcated white bib, has a longer, pale blue tail and much lighter blue upperparts showing a darker blue cap contrasting with a light blue mantle. Tahitian Lories appear black in flight with the white bib and orange bill and legs showing clearly. The flight is fast with rapid whirring beats, the birds being capable of hovering around trees while searching for food.

VOICE A high-pitched *to .. wheet* repeated over and over, and a rasping contact note. Also described as a plaintive *tsoo...tsoo* or *tee...tee* or as a three-syllable whistle.

DISTRIBUTION AND STATUS Formerly widespread in the Society Islands and the Tuamotu Archipelago, but now

gone from 15 of the 23 islands where recorded in the past (to some of which it may have been introduced), including Tahiti, Bora-Bora and Moorea, the larger islands of the Society group (date of extinction c. 1900 for Tahiti and Moorea; 1920s for Bora-Bora). Although the population decline has been linked to a number of threats including the introduction of Swamp Harriers *Circus approximans*, and the introduction of a mosquito *Culinoides* bearing avian malaria, predation by rats and cats is the most serious problem facing the species. The present range islands, including estimated populations with dates where known, are given below (but there are several more islands which have never been visited and which might yet prove to hold the species).

Society Islands: *Motu One* 250 pairs; *Manuae* 300-400 pairs in 1974 but apparent recent decline following the introduction of cats in 1975.

Tuamotu Archipelago: *Tikehau* 30 pairs in 1984; *Rangiroa* 100-200 birds before 1972, birds still present in 1991 but numbers not estimated; *Arutua* Apparently still present in 1975 but no numbers given; *Manihi* One bird seen in 1991; *Kaukura* Last visited in 1923, no population estimate; *Apataki* 1989 survey gave minimum of 300 birds.

Cook Islands: *Aitutaki* Probably introduced; up to 500 pairs present in 1991; *Hervey Island* Possibly introduced in the past but no recent information.

The population on Aitutaki seems stable and, as *Rattus rattus* is not present there, this island is probably the species's best hope for survival. There are more than 20 males in captivity, but only around ten females. The species was first bred in captivity in 1937 by Lord Tavistock but, until 1977 when a group of birds confiscated in the USA was sent to aviculturalist Rosemary Low in the UK, the birds were virtually unknown in aviculture. They have since also been bred by San Diego Zoo, whose first success with the raising of two chicks in 1979 gained international publicity when the parents, which had been confiscated from smugglers, were spared from destruction by customs officers after a public outcry. VULNERABLE.

ECOLOGY Strongly dependent on the coconut palm *Cocos nucifera* for feeding and nesting, although other species like banana and hibiscus are also frequented. They are sometimes seen around villages and in gardens. Tahitian Lories are very active, seldom staying long in one place. They are mostly seen in small groups of up to seven birds flying between flowering coconuts. They feed on nectar, but have also been recorded foraging on the ground and searching for small insects on the undersides of leaves. Breeding noted May to Jul. Nests in coconut trees, either in a hollow trunk or in a rotten coconut still attached to the tree, also recorded nesting in a decayed *Pandanus* stump. Two eggs are laid with incubation lasting 25 days and the whitish-downed young fledging in 6-8 weeks.

DESCRIPTION Crown glossy dark blue with lighter shaft-streaks; feathers of hind-crown elongated as in other members of the genus; lores and ear-coverts white. Upperparts uniformly glossy dark blue with blackish feather-bases. Upperwing glossy blue with blackish innerwebs to flight feathers (longest primary all black). Underwing-coverts dark blue, rest of underwing black. Throat and upper breast white; rest of underparts uniformly glossy dark blue with blackish feather bases. Uppertail dark blue, with slightly elongated central feathers typical of the genus; undertail blackish. **Bare parts**: Bill orange; cere orange; iris yellowish-brown; legs orange.

SEX/AGE Male slightly larger, particularly the head and bill, with a purer white bib. Feet may also be slightly darker. Immature from adult by uniformly greyish-black underparts except for slight white markings on chin. Bill black. Iris dark brown. Legs dark brown.

MEASUREMENTS Wing 107-116; tail 65-74; bill 9-11; tarsus 14-16.

GEOGRAPHICAL VARIATION None.

REFERENCES Bruner (1972), J.F. Clements *in litt.* (1991), Collar *et al.* (1994), duPont (1976), Forshaw (1989), Holyoak (1972), Jouett & Irvine (1979), King (1981), Kuehler (1990), Kuehler & Lieberman (1988), Lambert *et al.* (1993), Mitchell (1979), M.K. Poulsen *in litt.* (1985), Sibley & Monroe (1990), Wilson (1991)

---

34 ULTRAMARINE LORIKEET
Vini ultramarina   Plate 8

Other names: Goupil's Lory, Marquesas Lory

IDENTIFICATION 18cm. A small, predominantly blue lory with a darker blue cap and lighter blue rump. Adults show mainly dark blue underparts with white markings on the belly and around the throat. Immatures are entirely dark below. Along with the Tahitian Lory (33), this is the only primarily blue small parrot. There are no confusion species occurring on any of the islands where Ultramarine Lory is found. Flight is fast and direct with rapid shallow wingbeats, but may glide down slopes with wings partly closed.

VOICE A high-pitched *to-weet* given in flight and at rest. Calls also described as a strong screeching *psitt...psitt*

repeated every few seconds, or sharp piercing whistle *iiii*, or *zeeee*.

DISTRIBUTION AND STATUS Endemic to the Marquesas Islands of Nuku Hiva, Ua Pu and Ua Huka, although fossil remains show that it formerly ranged more widely. On Ua Pu the population was estimated at 250-300 pairs in 1975, but by 1988 it had crashed by around 60%, probably due to the spread of rats *Rattus rattus*, although the effect of a 1983 hurricane on the population is uncertain. On Nuku Hiva the small population of around 70 birds that still inhabited the high valleys and ridges in the north-western part of the island between 700-1,000m in 1975 may now be extinct. The only strong population now remains on Ua Huka where the species was introduced in 1940. This population had grown to 200-250 pairs by the late 1970s and was considered abundant in 1990 up to 500m with a population estimated at 1,000-1,500 birds. The main threat to the species here is the potential advent of rats, and between 1993 and 1994 14 lories were translocated to Fatu Hiva in an initial move to stay ahead of this danger (rats have apparently already gained a foothold on an island just a few hundred metres from Ua Huka); however, habitat deterioration from grazing mammals, and avian malaria, are also potential factors. CITES Appendix I. ENDANGERED.

ECOLOGY In the 1970s on Nuku Hiva these parrots were found only in pristine forest above 700m. A similar habitat preference is noted from Ua Pu, where they are mainly found in montane forest between 700 and 1,000m, but they have also been recorded in banana, coconut and mango *Mangifera indica* plantations in coastal areas. The species appears to have a broader range of habitat preferences on Ua Pu, being found at all altitudes from coasts to forested ridges. Feeds in flowering trees, particularly coconuts and *Erythrina*. The diet includes fruit and insects as well as pollen and nectar. Noisy and animated, the birds move freely between canopy and lower storeys and may allow close approach. They generally travel in pairs or groups of up to a dozen individuals. Most flights are at or below tree-top level, but for longer distances the birds may spiral up to considerable heights. Extremely active, seldom remaining long in one tree, and feeding acrobatically using the bill for support. Nesting reported to be between June and August, in a tree-hollow, in a rotten coconut, or in the old nest of another species. Two white eggs are laid and a record of captive breeding gives the fledging time as eight weeks.

DESCRIPTION Forehead iridescent bright ultramarine; crown and nape dark mauve-blue with lighter blue streaks; lores and blotches on ear-coverts white (bases of ear-coverts purplish-blue). Mantle and wing-coverts ultramarine; rump and uppertail-coverts light ultramarine. Flight feathers light blue with blackish innerwebs. Underwing-coverts dull blue. Throat dark slaty-blue with white-tipped feathers; mauve-blue breast-band with paler blue subterminal area on feathers; belly white with slaty bases to feathers giving mottled appearance; thighs dark mauve-blue; undertail-coverts light turquoise. Uppertail whitish-blue suffused light ultramarine on outer margins; undertail whitish with light ultramarine suffusion and some irregular greyish markings. **Bare parts**: Bill blackish-brown, upper mandible yellow-orange at base; iris brownish-yellow; legs orange.

SEX/AGE Sexes alike although female is slightly smaller. Immature separated from adult by absence of white on underparts, which are uniformly blackish. Also with black bill, dark brown iris and orange-brown legs.

MEASUREMENTS Wing 113-127; tail 70-80; bill 11-14; tarsus 13-17.

GEOGRAPHICAL VARIATION None.

REFERENCES BirdLife (1993), Bruner (1972), Collar *et al.* (1994), duPont (1976), Forshaw (1989), Hay (1986), Holyoak (1975), Kuehler & Lieberman (1993), Lodge (1991), Montgomery *et al.* (1980), Pratt *et al.* (1987), Sibley & Monroe (1990).

---

35   MUSK LORIKEET
Glossopsitta concinna   Plate 8

IDENTIFICATION 22cm. A small, generally green lorikeet which, like the other two members of its genus, has a pointed tail and a notched upper mandible. The crown is bright scarlet, as are the lores and ear-coverts; there is a yellow patch on the breast near the bend of the wing and brownish mantle-patch. Sympatric in coastal zone of eastern Australia with a number of potential confusion species including Little Lorikeet (36), Purple-crowned Lorikeet (37), and the less similar Scaly-breasted Lorikeet (19), and Swift Parrot (154). Musk Lorikeets often associate with Little and Purple-crowned Lorikeets and with Swift Parrots. Musk can be separated from Little by its larger size, green, not red, chin, red ear-coverts and bicoloured bill, also on voice: Little has a thinner *zit* call. From Purple-crowned Lorikeet by green, not red, underwing and scarlet, not purplish, crown. From Swift Parrot by stockier shape and green throat; Swift also has a long reddish tail and red underwing-coverts, and its call, a high-pitched *clink-clink*, is quite different. Scaly-breasted Lorikeet shows extensive yellow underparts, a yellow mantle-patch and no red facial markings. A further small, predominantly green lorikeet in Australia, Varied Lorikeet (20), is allopatric, occurring in northern Australia and showing a distinctive broad white eye-ring. The other sympatric parrot which is green with a red face is the extremely rare race *coxeni* of Double-eyed Fig Parrot (85), easily separated from Musk Lorikeet by its small size, very short tail and red throat. The flight of Musk Lorikeet is extremely rapid. Sturdy build and short pointed tail give it a 'bomb-shaped' look; the whirring sound made by the wings is clearly audible.

VOICE Very noisy. Call a rolling metallic screech, higher-pitched than Rainbow Lorikeet (13) and much fuller than Little or Purple-crowned Lorikeets. Also a sharp chattering while feeding.

DISTRIBUTION AND STATUS Restricted to Australia where it occurs widely in the south-east of the country. In the lowlands from southern Queensland (north to Rockhampton and occasionally to Bowen), where it has a mainly coastal distribution, but extends inland as far as the lower Dawson River and to about Chinchilla, ranging through New South Wales where it reaches the west slopes of the Divide, then along the Murrumbidgee and Murray Rivers to about Finley, continuing south through Victoria, where it is widely distributed, across to Tasmania (mostly the east and occasionally on King Island), and into South Australia (west to the Mount Lofty Ranges, and south to the Eyre Peninsula and Kangaroo Island). There is a small

feral population in Perth. World population judged in excess of 100,000. There are a few in captivity. The species is protected under Australian law, but some culling may be permitted in fruit-growing districts.

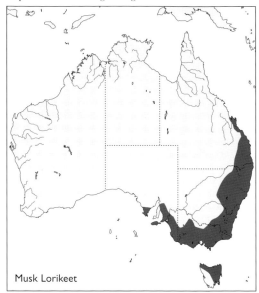

Musk Lorikeet

ECOLOGY The species's name derives from a musky smell that birds are said to be give off. Seasonally nomadic, at least in extremes of its range, relying heavily on flowering eucalyptus species; also feeds on fruit and insects. Found in many habitats from open forest to woodland, agricultural and suburban areas, including eucalyptus forest, dry forest, dense rain-forest (particularly in Tasmania) and riverine woodland. Avoids tall open forest and high-altitude areas. Often encountered in large flocks of over a hundred individuals, in which pairs, which form strong bonds, often consort together. Can be extremely confiding when feeding. Flocks are also often seen flying high overhead. Like most other lorikeets the diet consists of nectar and pollen as well as small fruits and some insects. May raid orchards, vineyards and crops, and may join with flocks of other *Glossopsitta* lorikeets and Swift Parrots. Breeding season is Aug to Jan. Nests in holes high in eucalyptus trees, the two white eggs being incubated for about 25 days and the white-downed young fledging in 6-7 weeks.

DESCRIPTION Forecrown, lores and ear-coverts scarlet; crown washed turquoise; cheeks and chin green suffused turquoise below eye. Upperparts green with an olive-brown wash across mantle extending slightly around sides of breast; rump brighter green. Upperwing green with blackish innerwebs to flight feathers and coverts; longest primary black; fine yellow trailing edge to wing. Underwing-coverts light green; flight feathers grey-black. Underparts slightly lighter and more yellowish-green than upperparts, with a slight blue-green suffusion on breast; yellow patch at sides of breast close to and sometimes obscured by bend of wing at rest. Uppertail green with more yellowish innerwebs; undertail with innerwebs yellowish-green merging into red at base. **Bare parts**: Bill black, tipped red; cere black; iris orange; legs greenish-brown.

SEX/AGE Red frontal band of female is narrower than in male, and the blue wash on crown duller. Immature generally duller, with more extensive brownish suffusion; red markings less bright and more orange; less yellow on sides of breast. Bill all dark.

MEASUREMENTS Wing 121-135; tail 86-99; bill 12-14; tarsus 13-16.

GEOGRAPHICAL VARIATION None.

REFERENCES Blakers *et al.* (1984), Emison *et al.* (1987), Forshaw (1981, 1989), Hutchins & Lovell (1985), Pizzey & Doyle (1983), Schodde & Tidemann (1988), Sibley & Monroe (1990), Simpson & Day (1984), Slater (1979), Trounson & Trounson (1987).

36   LITTLE LORIKEET
Glossopsitta pusilla   Plate 8

Other names: Green Keet

IDENTIFICATION 16cm. Very small lorikeet, predominantly green with red forecrown, lores and chin ending in a clear line, as though the front of head had been dipped in ink (no red or orange behind eye); bill black. Often associates with Musk (35) and Purple-crowned Lorikeets (37) and Swift Parrots (154). Little Lorikeet is the smallest of the four species, and can be easily separated in flight from the next smallest, Purple-crowned Lorikeet, by its yellow-green, not red underwing-coverts. Purple-crowned also shows an orange ear-covert spot (ear-coverts are green with slight yellowish-green streaking in Little), and a purple crown. Red markings on Purple-crowned are restricted to the lores. Little Lorikeet can be separated from Musk again by its green, not red, ear-coverts, smaller size, lack of bluish crown, and absence of yellow patches at sides of breast. From the slender, long-tailed Swift Parrot by its smaller size, lack of a yellow border to red facial markings, and green, not bright red shoulders; Swift Parrot also shows blue greater coverts and red undertail-coverts, absent in Little Lorikeet, and in flight Swift shows red, not green, underwing-coverts. The flight call of Little Lorikeet, a shrill *zit*, is also quite different from that of Musk Lorikeet or Swift Parrot. There is little chance of confusion with the other two small, predominantly green species in Australia: Varied Lorikeet (20) has a very obvious broad white eye-ring, and Double-eyed Fig-parrot (85) shows blue primaries, yellow flanks and blue and orange facial markings, and is also mainly encountered in rain-forest. The flight of Little Lorikeet is swift and direct, its short pointed tail giving it a 'bullet-like' appearance and its rapid wingbeats producing an audible whirring sound.

VOICE Flight call a thin, quick, slightly rolling *zit* or *zit zit*, more metallic than the call of Purple-crowned Lorikeet, repeated often. Also described as a high-pitched, short wheezing screech. Whilst feeding produces a constant twittering.

DISTRIBUTION AND STATUS Restricted to Australia where it occurs widely in the coastal south-east including mountain ranges and coastal plains. It ranges from southern Queensland (north to Cairns and inland to the Atherton Tablelands, Carnarvon National Park and Chinchilla, also on Fraser Island), through New South Wales (west to Warialda, West Wyalong and Deniliquin

and inland along the Murray River in the south), south through Victoria (widespread except north-east alpine and north-west mallee), and west to southern South Australia (extreme south-east, Yorke Peninsula and previously to the Mount Lofty Range, where last recorded in 1957). It may have declined slightly in this southern part of its range. Also reported from Tasmania (a single confirmed record) and Kangaroo Island (possibly a misidentified Purple-crowned Lorikeet). Generally common except Victoria south of the Divide and in South Australia. World population thought to be over 100,000. Protected in Australia. There are a few in captivity.

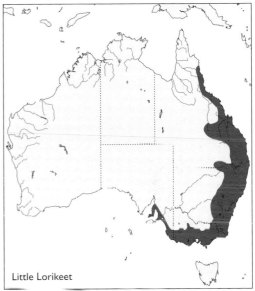

Little Lorikeet

ECOLOGY Found in a variety of habitats including tall open forests, timber along watercourses, woodlands, orchards and parks with trees in urban areas. Nomadic and similar in habits to Musk Lorikeet. Noisy and approachable when feeding. Usually encountered in flocks which congregate in flowering eucalyptus, and other blossom- and fruit-bearing trees, often in company with other lorikeets including the species mentioned above and Rainbow Lorikeets (13). When moving any distance will fly high in groups above tree tops. Feeds on pollen, nectar, fruit and berries, preferring eucalyptus species. Stays mainly in tree-tops and is inconspicuous apart from its constant calls. Breeds Jul to Jan, but as early as May in northern part of range. Nests in tree-holes high above ground, preferably in a live eucalypt near water. The three to five white eggs are incubated for about 22 days, the young fledging in 5-6 weeks.

DESCRIPTION Head green with red forecrown, lores and chin; ear-coverts with slight yellow-green streaking. Upperparts uniform mid-green with bronze-brown wash across rear of nape and mantle fading down back. Upperwing green with dark innerwebs to flight feathers and coverts; longest primary black; fine yellow trailing edge to wing and primaries with fine yellow margins to outerwebs. Underwing-coverts yellow-green; underside of flight feathers blackish-grey. Underparts green, lighter and more yellowish on belly. Uppertail green with outer feathers broadly margined orange-red at bases of yellowish innerwebs; undertail yellowish-green with lateral feathers

247

edged orange-red at bases of innerwebs. **Bare parts**: Bill black; cere black; iris orange-yellow; legs greenish-grey.

SEX/AGE Sexes alike. Immature from adult by less extensive and more orange facial markings. Bill olive-brown, iris brown.

MEASUREMENTS Wing 93-106; tail 53-65; bill 10-11; tarsus 12-13.

GEOGRAPHICAL VARIATION None.

REFERENCES Blakers *et al.* (1984), Forshaw (1981, 1989), Hutchins & Lovell (1986), Lambert *et al.* (1993), Pizzey & Doyle (1983), Schodde & Tidemann (1988), Sibley & Monroe (1990), Simpson & Day (1984), Slater (1979, 1989), Trounson & Trounson (1987).

---

37 PURPLE-CROWNED LORIKEET
Glossopsitta porphyrocephala   Plate 8

Other names: Porphyry-crowned Lorikeet

IDENTIFICATION 15-17cm. A small southern Australian lorikeet with green upperparts, bluish underparts, a purple crown, red lores, orange ear-coverts and a turquoise-blue patch at the bend of the wing. Distinguished in flight from the smaller, slighter Little Lorikeet (36) and larger Musk Lorikeet (35) by its red underwing-coverts and axillaries. The slender, longer-tailed Swift Parrot (154) also shows red on the underwing but has blue on the greater coverts on the upperwing, and reddish undertail-coverts. Purple-crowned Lorikeet is the only small lorikeet in Western Australia. In flight whirring wingbeats are clearly audible as the birds pass overhead.

VOICE A shrill *tsit-tsit-tsit*, less metallic than the call of Little Lorikeet, repeated frequently. Also a sharp chattering whilst feeding.

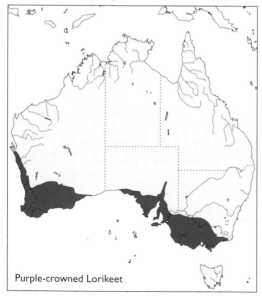

Purple-crowned Lorikeet

DISTRIBUTION AND STATUS Restricted to Australia where it is widespread in the south-east and south-west, ranging north to the mulga-eucalypt line (not in Tasmania). Range disjunct, but no racial differences are

recognised, and it is possible that birds may occasionally travel between the two populations. Nomadic flocks may also travel far inland at times. Range extends from the extreme south of New South Wales (falling short of Bega, Albury, Jerilderie and Euston, although may occur further north in mallee areas inland when blossom is abundant); throughout Victoria, especially far west, but not in north-east highland areas (sporadically south-east to Gippsland area); in South Australia to mallee areas bordering the Murray River, also Mount Lofty Range, Kangaroo Island, Eyre Peninsula, and north to the Gawler Ranges. There are no records between 133° and 128°E along the coast. In Western Australia the species occurs along the Bight Coast and to the north of the Nullarbor Plain as far as the southern part of the Great Victoria Desert; in the extreme west it reaches north to the lower Murchison River district and Shark Bay. Vagrant in north-east New South Wales and south-east Queensland. Common to abundant. Distribution varies from year to year with large numbers gathering around flowering eucalypts. The world population is thought to be in excess of 50,000. There are a few birds in captivity.

ECOLOGY Nomadic. Flowering of eucalypts is mainly responsible for their unpredictable movements, although in some areas birds may be present throughout the year. Encountered in small parties to large flocks of many hundreds of individuals, often with mixed groups of other lorikeets including Musk Lorikeets. Found in woodland and forest, but also reaching urban areas to feed on ornamental flowers. Occasional winter visitor to banksias in heath habitats. Purple-crowned Lorikeet is characteristic of drier, lightly timbered country, especially box woodland *Eucalyptus*, but also river red-gum *E. camaldulensis* and mallee (more often in mallee than Musk Lorikeet). Can be a pest in orchards. Specialises in feeding on eucalyptus pollen and nectar although will also feed on fruit. Roosts in large groups, sometimes a long way from feeding areas. Tame and unobtrusive whilst feeding, except for constant calls. More inclined to feed in lower branches and shrubs than Little Lorikeet. Crawls through leaves and flowers, often flying off and returning to feed in the same spot. Breeding Aug to Dec. Nests in a tree hole, preferably a eucalypt near water. Several pairs often occupy neighbouring hollows in the same tree and large colonies have been reported. Forshaw provides details on the breeding cycle in captivity, giving an incubation period of around 22 days with the young fledging 6-7 weeks after hatching.

DESCRIPTION Forecrown orange-yellow merging into red on lores and above and in front of eye. Crown dark purple, merging into green on nape, which can also show a few reddish-orange feathers. Spot on ear-coverts orange-yellow centred redder. Chin and throat light turquoise. Upperparts green with brownish wash on mantle and a brighter, slightly bluer-green rump. Upperwing green marked bright blue at bend and along carpal edge. Blackish innerwebs to flight feathers; fine yellow margins on primaries and fine yellow trailing edge to wing. Underwing-coverts turquoise-blue; inner coverts red with red axillaries. Throat and upper breast green washed light turquoise-blue; sides of upper breast with slight brownish wash; centre of belly washed turquoise with flanks and undertail-coverts green; yellowish patches at sides of lower breast can be obscured by folded wing. Uppertail green with yellowish innerwebs to outer feathers; warmer and more orange toward base. Undertail yellowish. **Bare parts**: Bill black; cere black; iris brown; legs grey.

SEX/AGE Sexes alike. Immature duller than adult. Purple on crown less extensive or absent.

MEASUREMENTS Wing 98-111; tail 59-65; bill 10-12; tarsus 12-14.

GEOGRAPHICAL VARIATION None.

REFERENCES Blakers *et al.* (1984), Emison *et al.* (1987), Forshaw (1981, 1989), Lambert *et al.* (1993), Pizzey & Doyle (1983), Schodde & Tidemann (1988), Simpson & Day (1984), Slater (1979), Storr & Johnstone (1979), Trounson & Trounson (1987).

38   PALM LORIKEET
Charmosyna palmarum   Plate 9

Other names: Green Palm Lorikeet, Vanuatu Lorikeet

IDENTIFICATION 15-17cm, Small, entirely green lorikeet with a long, yellow-tipped, graduated tail and a few red feathers around the chin and cheeks. Does not overlap on range with the similar Meek's Lorikeet (40) but easily separated, if ever together in captivity, by the red markings at the base of the bill; Meek's also shows a yellowish band on the underside of the secondaries. The other similar species, Red-chinned Lorikeet (39), is also allopatric, and can be separated from Palm by the red at the base of the tail and the yellow band on underwing. Red-throated Lorikeet (47), which occurs only on islands in the Fiji group, also has a yellow-tipped tail but shows more red around the face, bordered yellow on the throat, and some red markings on the thighs. The sympatric Rainbow Lorikeet (13) is 40% larger than Palm Lorikeet and unlikely to be confused in the field due to its vivid plumage, although the flight is similar: swift with rapid wingbeats clearly audible as the birds fly overhead. When moving between feeding areas flight is high and direct above tree tops, but when flushed at close range birds may weave around the canopy.

VOICE Contact call, repeated regularly in flight, is a shrill piping whistle, also described as a short high-pitched screech *tswit-tswit* or a series of quickly delivered notes *tswitswitswit*. Likened to the call of Rainbow Lorikeet but less loud and discordant. Feeding accompanied by shrill twittering and some softer notes. Flight call normally melodic but may be louder and more screeching when alarmed.

DISTRIBUTION AND STATUS South-west Polynesia in Vanuatu, the Duff Islands, Santa Cruz Islands and the Banks Islands. Range appears to expand and contract and it has been speculated that this may relate to the effect of cyclones, or sporadic colonisations as a result of population 'blooms'. For example, in Vanuatu it was recorded from Éfaté in 1879 for the first time in 30 years, and was still present there in the 1930s, but by the 1960s it had disappeared once again from this and some of the other southern islands of the group. Has also been recorded in Vanuatu from Espíritu Santo, Aoba, Maéwo, Pentecost, Malakula, Ambrym, Paama, Lopévi, Tongoa, Emaé, Nguna, Erromango, Tanna and Futuna; in the Banks group from Santa María, Uréparapara, Vanua Lava and Méré Lava; and in the Santa Cruz group from Tinakula, Utupua and Vanikoro. The world population is

thought to be less than 50,000. There are presently none in captivity. The species is protected by law in Vanuatu. NEAR-THREATENED.

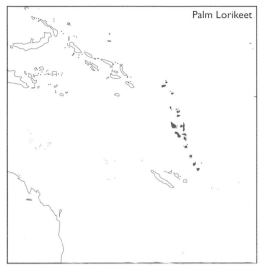
Palm Lorikeet

ECOLOGY Occurs in forests and woodlands, commoner in hills than in lowlands, and most regular in uninhabited cloud-forest above 1,000m on larger islands. Travels widely between feeding sites and is encountered in pairs or flocks in tree-tops, where its green plumage blends it in as it feeds amongst the blossoms. Pairs within flocks have been observed allopreening indicating that pair-bond is maintained when birds are in larger groups. A constant chatter betrays the presence of these lorikeets as they search for food. Feeds in palms, lianas, figs and shrubs, taking nectar, pollen, fruit and berries, and particularly fond of sago palms *Cycas circinalis*. Breeding habits are little known but a nest with two chicks on Santo, Vanuatu, in December 1961 was in a hollow tree limb, 6m above ground in cloud forest at 1,600m. Appears in lowlands sporadically, particularly when *Erythrina* and sago palms are in flower.

DESCRIPTION Head bright green showing some red markings around base of bill, lores and chin. Upperparts bright green with slight olive-brown wash across mantle. Upperwing green with blackish inner webs to flight feathers. Underwing-coverts grey-green; underside of flight feathers blackish. Underparts bright green, more yellowish on chin, throat and centre of belly (males sometimes also with a few red feathers on abdomen and thighs). Uppertail green, broadly tipped yellow on central and narrowly tipped yellow on lateral feathers; undertail yellow. **Bare parts**: Bill orange; cere orange; iris yellow; legs orange-yellow.

SEX/AGE Female with red on face reduced or absent. Immature similar to female but generally duller. Iris ochre. Bill yellow-brown.

MEASUREMENTS Wing 88-98; tail 72-91; bill 11-12; tarsus 12-14.

GEOGRAPHICAL VARIATION None.

REFERENCES Amadon (1942), BirdLife (1993), Bregulla (1992), Forshaw (1989), Lambert *et al.* (1993), Mayr (1945), Sibley & Monroe (1990).

39 RED-CHINNED LORIKEET
Charmosyna rubrigularis   Plate 9

Other names: Red-chinned Lory, Red-throated Lorikeet (also commonly used for *C. amabilis*)

IDENTIFICATION 17-20cm. A small, longish-tailed, bright green lorikeet with a red chin, orange-red bill, yellow band across underside of flight feathers and yellow tips and red bases to tail feathers. Red-flanked Lorikeet (45) is sympatric but generally occurs at lower altitudes and is slightly smaller with either red and blue ear-coverts and red flanks (male) or yellow-streaked ear-coverts (female); both sexes also show red underwing-coverts (not green as in Red-chinned Lorikeet). The other similar small but allopatric congener in New Guinea is Red-fronted Lorikeet (44), which occurs only in northern New Guinea, and shows red uppertail and underwing-coverts. Three other small green parrots show red chins: Red-throated Lorikeet (47), from the Fiji group, has a larger red throat-patch bordered below with yellow and distinctive red thighs; Palm Lorikeet (38), from south-west Polynesia, shows only a few red feathers around the base of the bill and lacks the yellow underwing-band; and Australia's much larger Swift Parrot (154) has a distinctive red shoulder-patch and underwing-coverts.

VOICE A high shrill note, less harsh than the call of Rainbow Lorikeet (13). Described as a quiet *seezp* while feeding; and the same note repeated in quick succession whilst in flight. Other calls include a harsher *see-air* and a 'strange rattle'. Red-flanked Lorikeet calls *tsss* or *seeet*, described as short, quiet, shrill and high-pitched.

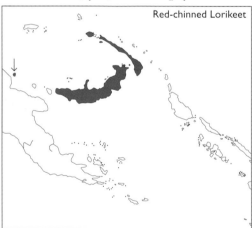
Red-chinned Lorikeet

DISTRIBUTION AND STATUS Karkar Island (off the north-east coast) and the Bismarck Archipelago (New Britain, New Hanover and New Ireland), Papua New Guinea. On Karkar it is found from sea-level to the summit but rare below 625m, and commonest between 1,150m to 1,280m. Common from about 450m upwards in New Britain, and in New Ireland from 1,500m to the summit of the Hans Meyer Range; but found as low as 70m. Tends to replace Red-flanked Lorikeet at higher altitudes, but may be sympatric with this species in some areas. The world population is thought to be less than 10,000, and although probably stable, could be threatened by habitat loss. The species is not presently thought to be in captivity.

ECOLOGY Occurs in humid forest, mainly in mountains. Usually encountered in small flocks of up to ten birds feeding in the canopy or flying overhead. May be seen in company with other nectar feeders including the much larger Rainbow Lorikeet. Can be confiding whilst feeding. Feeds on pollen and nectar and has been noted frequenting native palms in the mountains of New Ireland. Breeding habits undescribed.

DESCRIPTION Head green; ear-coverts bright emerald-green streaked pale green and appearing paler than crown; chin, upper throat and lower lores red surrounded by yellow. Upperparts darker and more olive-green than underparts. Upperwing green with black innerwebs and a fine yellow trailing edge. Underwing-coverts yellowish-green; flight feathers greyish-black with central yellow band formed by yellow spot on innerweb of each feather. Underparts yellowish-green, clearly lighter than upperparts. Uppertail green tipped yellow, lateral feathers marked black and orange-red at bases; undertail with lateral feathers red broadly tipped yellow (red more or less concealed at rest), central feathers black tipped yellow. **Bare parts**: Bill orange-red; iris orange; legs yellow-orange.

SEX/AGE Sexes alike. Immature similar to adult with less red on chin and throat.

MEASUREMENTS Wing 86-101; tail 76-97; bill 11-13; tarsus 11-13.

GEOGRAPHICAL VARIATION None. *C. r. krakari* is included here with *C. rubrigularis*.

REFERENCES Beehler (1978a), Beehler *et al.* (1986), Coates (1985), Forshaw (1989), Greensmith (1975), Lambert *et al.* (1993), Peters (1961), Rand & Gilliard (1967), Sibley & Monroe (1990).

40 MEEK'S LORIKEET
Charmosyna meeki   Plate 9

IDENTIFICATION 16cm. A small green lorikeet occurring in hill forest on the larger islands in the Solomons group. Fairly nondescript with a longish, pointed, yellow-tipped tail. Upperparts obviously darker with underparts more yellowish. Shows a distinctive bluish-green patch on forecrown (which may be difficult to see in the field). From similar Palm Lorikeet (38) and Red-chinned Lorikeet (39) on range (neither is sympatric), by absence of red around base of bill and chin, and by bluish crown-patch. Flight is swift and direct, revealing whitish-yellow bar on underside of secondaries.

VOICE A high-pitched screech similar to, but weaker than the call of Red-flanked Lorikeet (45). Also described as a high-pitched short squeak.

DISTRIBUTION AND STATUS Endemic to mountains of major islands in the Solomons group: Bougainville, New Georgia, Malaita, Kolombangara, Guadalcanal and formerly Santa Isabel. Occurs from around 300 to 1,700m but reportedly rare above 1,200m and in the lowlands. World population thought to be well under 50,000 but probably stable. No birds are known to be in captivity.

ECOLOGY Reportedly nomadic. Occurs in humid hill and mountain forest, but has also apparently been found in coconut palms in the lowlands. Usually encountered singly or in small flocks of around 10-15 birds flying through or just above the forest canopy. Larger groups may congregate in flowering trees to feed on pollen and nectar. May associate with other parrots such as Duchess Lorikeets (48), Finch's Pygmy Parrots (82), Yellow-bibbed Lories (28) and Rainbow Lorikeets (13). Breeding and nesting undescribed.

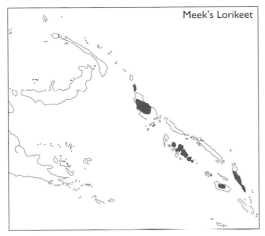

Meek's Lorikeet

DESCRIPTION Head bright green, lighter and yellower on chin and throat, darker on crown and streaked darker on ear-coverts; dark bluish-green patch above and in front of the eye. Upperparts green with strong olive-brown wash across mantle. Upperwing green with blackish innerwebs to flight feathers. Underwing-coverts yellowish green; flight feathers blackish with indistinct yellowish bar across innerwebs. Underparts yellowish-green, lighter than upperparts and becoming yellower from breast to belly. Uppertail dark green tipped yellow; undertail yellow. **Bare parts:** Bill orange; iris pale red; legs orange.

SEX/AGE Sexes alike. Immature from adult by paler bill with brownish base and shorter tail.

MEASUREMENTS Wing 74-89; tail 58-74; bill 11-13; tarsus 10-13.

GEOGRAPHICAL VARIATION None.

REFERENCES Cain & Galbraith (1956), Coates (1985), Forshaw (1989), Hadden (1981), Mayr (1945), Sibley & Monroe (1990).

---

41   BLUE-FRONTED LORIKEET
Charmosyna toxopei   Plate 9

Other names: Buru Lorikeet

IDENTIFICATION 16cm. An enigmatic species confined to the island of Buru, and known from seven specimens collected in hill forest during the 1920s. These small lorikeets are green above and yellowish-green below with a blue crown-patch, a yellow underwing bar and red bases to the lateral tail feathers. Blue-fronted and Red-flanked Lorikeets (45), although similar in size, should not be easily confused as males of the latter have red facial and flank-markings and red underwing-coverts, while females, though lacking the red markings, show prominent yellow-streaked ear-coverts, and both sexes show a blue rump. Female Red-breasted Pygmy Parrot (83) is mainly green

with a blue cap, but is tiny (9cm), short-tailed and shows distinctive black centres to the wing-coverts and pale pinkish cheeks (male is very distinctive with orange-red underparts).

VOICE A very shrill *ti...ti...ti...ti...ti.ti.ti*.

Blue-fronted Lorikeet

former distribution

DISTRIBUTION AND STATUS Endemic to Buru, Indonesia. It is evidently a rare species, but virtually nothing is known of its status. The original specimens were collected in hill forest between 850m and 1,000m. In 1980 the species was reported to be quite common in plantations, secondary and primary forest, but this record has been suggested as referring to the Red-flanked Lorikeet (but the record of this species from Buru is in fact mistaken). In 1989 two flocks of five and six birds, thought to be this species, were seen in selectively logged forest at c. 600m above Teluk Bara. There is also a 1993 report of four small unidentified lorikeets seen in the same area as the 1980 observations. The species is now considered threatened by BirdLife International, although a thorough search for it needs to be conducted before its status can be fully determined. VULNERABLE.

ECOLOGY If recent observations were indeed of Blue-fronted Lorikeets, the species may be nomadic, moving from high to low altitudes based on the availability of food (like some other small lorikeets). This could account for the paucity of records, especially for a species which is already thinly distributed. The other possibility is that the birds occur only in hill forest.

DESCRIPTION Forehead bright green, forecrown to above eye bright blue; rest of head green. Upperparts green, brighter on rump. Wing green with blackish innerwebs to flight feathers. Underwing-coverts green; flight feathers blackish with yellow band across underside of secondaries. Underparts more yellowish-green than upperparts except for mid-green undertail-coverts. Tail green, with red bases to outerwebs and dull blackish spot separating red from yellow tip (red and blackish markings broader on inner feathers). **Bare parts:** Bill orange; iris yellow-orange; legs red-orange.

SEX/AGE Female shows fainter and less extensive blue forecrown, and duller red markings at the base of the tail. Immature generally duller than adult; chin and throat greener.

MEASUREMENTS Wing 83-90; tail 65-77; bill 12-13; tarsus 11-12.

GEOGRAPHICAL VARIATION None.

REFERENCES Collar *et al.* (1994), Forshaw (1989), Jones & Banjaransari (1990), Lambert *et al.* (1993), Marsden *et al.* (1997), Sibley & Monroe (1990), Siebers (1930), Smiet (1985), White & Bruce (1986).

42   STRIATED LORIKEET
Charmosyna multistriata   Plate 9

Other names: Streaked Lorikeet, Yellow-streaked Lorikeet

IDENTIFICATION 18cm. A small, mainly green lorikeet confined to the central and western highlands of New Guinea. The underparts show bright yellow streaking; the nape is dark brown with orange-red spots at the feather-tips and the bill is distinctive, being orange with an extensive blue-grey base to the upper mandible. Three potential confusion species occur in New Guinea: Goldie's Lorikeet (22) is light yellowish-green below with dark green streaking (not dark green with yellow streaking) and has a bright red cap; Yellow-streaked Lory (3) is much larger and stockier with bright scarlet thighs and forehead and a blunt tail; Pygmy Lorikeet (43) has some yellow streaking on the breast, but is tiny with blue rear-crown, and males show a distinctive red rump and underwing-coverts. Another confusion species, the northern Australian Varied Lorikeet (20), could be encountered in captivity; this also has yellow streaking below, but shows an obvious red cap and large white eye-ring. There are also two dissimilar sympatric lorikeets: the slightly smaller nominate race of Red-flanked Lorikeet (45), which although similar in shape, shows streaked yellow ear-coverts (female), or blue ear-coverts with red face and flank-markings (male), both sexes also having an all-red bill and blue rump; and Fairy Lorikeet (49), which has red underparts and tail and a black rear-crown. The flight of Striated Lorikeet is swift and direct, the silhouette showing a longish attenuated tail. From Red-flanked Lorikeet in flight by the absence of a broad yellow band on underside of flight feathers.

VOICE Contact call, commonly given in flight, is a single drawn-out whistle, or two to three repeated notes, considered similar in quality to calls of some cuckoo-shrikes *Coracina*. There can be changes in pitch and the following variations are described by Coates: *peep; tieee; tieuw; pleeei; peee-pip; peep-ip; pi-ree;* and *pi-pi-ree.* Whistled calls may also be preceded by some chattering. Calls from flying flocks said to be reminiscent of chiming bells. The sympatric Red-flanked Lorikeet calls with a quiet, short, high-pitched *tsss* or *seeet.*

DISTRIBUTION AND STATUS Endemic to mid-montane forests of Irian Jaya and Papua New Guinea, south of the central mountains, from around 136° to 143°E. The world population is thought to be less than 10,000 but is probably stable. Small numbers in captivity. NEAR-THREATENED.

ECOLOGY Inhabits montane and hill forest and forest

edges. Chiefly found between 180m and 1,800m but has been recorded as low as 80m. Found in pairs or small groups of up to 20 birds, sometimes consorting with Red-flanked and Fairy Lorikeets (observed in mid-February in mixed flocks with these species). Prefers the tops of flowering trees where it feeds on pollen and nectar, but may also feed on epiphytes. Behaviour similar to Red-flanked Lorikeet, with which it consorts, but although flocks of Striated Lorikeets have been observed flying with Red-flanked Lorikeets, they generally form discrete single-species groups. Nesting and breeding habits unknown.

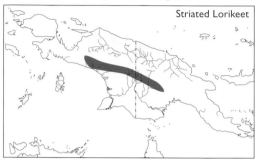
Striated Lorikeet

DESCRIPTION Crown mid-green, brown mask extending as narrow band through eye to form broad band on rear nape; ear-coverts mid-green streaked light green with brown feather-bases; chin and feathers around base of bill lightish green. Mantle mid-green showing some light green streaking, especially at sides, and a few orange-red tips to feathers where brown nape-band joins upper mantle; rump mid-green. Upperwing mid-green with blackish innerwebs to flight feathers and coverts. Under-wing-coverts green, underside of flight feathers blackish. Throat green with brown feather-bases; breast dark green boldly shaft-streaked bright yellow, this latter extending onto belly and flanks but giving way to light green streaking on thighs and undertail-coverts; vent and base of tail red. Uppertail olive, tipped lighter yellowish-brown; undertail olive-brown. **Bare parts**: Bill orange with extensive bluish-grey base to upper mandible; cere and facial skin bluish-grey; iris red; legs dark grey.

SEX/AGE Sexes alike. Immature similar to adult but shows less intense and greener streaking on underparts, less obvious orange-red nape-spots and a dark iris.

MEASUREMENTS Wing 93-102; tail 75-96; bill 14-17; tarsus 12-14.

GEOGRAPHICAL VARIATION None.

REFERENCES Arndt (1992), Beehler *et al.* (1986), BirdLife (1993), Coates (1985), Forshaw (1989), Lambert *et al.* (1993), Rand & Gilliard (1967), Sibley & Monroe (1990).

43   PYGMY LORIKEET
Charmosyna wilhelminae   Plate 9

Other names: Wilhelmina's Lorikeet, Pygmy Streaked Lorikeet

IDENTIFICATION 11-13cm. The smallest lorikeet: tiny size with a short pointed tail distinctive. Chiefly green, lighter on the underparts, with a dark cap, electric blue tips to nape feathers; yellow breast-streaks, a red rump and purple-blue uppertail-coverts (female lacks red rump). In flight male shows extensive red underwing patch extending from coverts onto flight feathers. Young birds are much less colourful (see Sex/Age). Striated Lorikeet (42) is sympatric and shows yellow-streaked underparts, but is larger, and yellow streaking is continuous from throat to belly, not restricted to breast as in Pygmy Lorikeet. There are a number of other sympatric but dissimilar species: Goldie's Lorikeet (22) is larger and shows a very obvious red cap; Fairy Lorikeet (49) is larger and shows predominantly red underparts and tail, and a black cap. Red-flanked Lorikeet (45) is also larger and shows yellow-streaked ear-coverts (female) or blue ear-coverts with red face and flank-markings (male), both sexes also showing a blue rump (although this is absent in eastern Papua New Guinea *C. p. subplacens*). Red-flanked Lorikeet also tends to occur at lower elevations than Pygmy. The three tiny pygmy parrots are potential confusion species, although only Red-breasted (83) is usually sympatric, both Yellow-capped (78) and Buff-faced (80) tending to occur at lower elevations, in flight pygmy parrots lack the pointed tail of Pygmy Lorikeet (for other differences see illustration). Other small parrots such as the smaller fig parrots and Orange-fronted Hanging Parrot (188) also lack the pointed tail of Pygmy Lorikeet and tend to be confined to lowlands.

VOICE Flight calls are high-pitched and hoarse. Pairs may make quiet contact calls described as *ts ts tsee* reminiscent of a pygmy parrot. The call is described as weaker than that of Red-flanked Lorikeet.

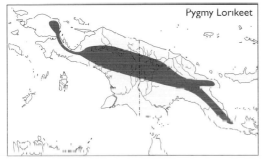
Pygmy Lorikeet

DISTRIBUTION AND STATUS Northern New Guinea in Irian Jaya (Indonesia) and Papua New Guinea. Ranges from the Arfak Mountains of Vogelkop in the west, through the central ranges, the Huon Peninsula, and south-east to the Owen Stanley Range. In the vicinity of Port Moresby (e.g. Sogeri area) it is scarce (but possibly regular between May and Nov). The world population is thought to be less than 50,000 and is considered to be stable. There are few in captivity.

ECOLOGY Chiefly inhabits humid forest and forest edge, but also adjoining savanna woodland and established secondary growth. Generally found between 1,000m and 2,200m altitude, although in the south and around Port Moresby it is occasionally encountered much closer to sea-level in lowland forest. Forages in pairs and small flocks of up to 20 birds in the canopy of flowering trees, often in the company of Goldie's and Fairy Lorikeets. Very active when feeding and often difficult to pick out because of its size and predominantly green plumage. Not uncommon but easily overlooked, and has been encountered in groups of up to 200 individuals. Often seen flying above the

canopy where it can easily be picked out in mixed flocks because of its small size. Feeds on nectar and pollen. Breeding and nesting habits unknown.

DESCRIPTION Head light grass-green; forehead yellowish-green; crown dark purple, with royal-blue suffusion at rear and bright turquoise tips to nape feathers; rear of nape with olive wash. Mantle mid-green; lower back and rump reddish-orange; uppertail-coverts dull purple-blue. Upperwing mid-green with blackish innerwebs to flight feathers and blackish primary-coverts; fine yellow trailing edge to wing. Carpal edge yellow; underwing-coverts and broad band on innerwebs of flight feathers salmon-pink; tips of flight feathers blackish. Underparts pale grass-green with prominent yellow shaft-streaks across breast. Uppertail mid-green, red at base (normally concealed in field); undertail olive-brown with yellow tips and red at base. **Bare parts**: Bill orange-red, tipped yellow; cere pinkish-red; periophthalmic ring greyish; iris yellow to orange-red; legs light grey.

SEX/AGE Female lacks red rump-patch of male, red underwing-coverts and band on flight feathers. Immature generally duller and upperparts slightly browner than adult. Lacks blue feather-tips on nape. Yellow streaks on breast less distinct or absent, and rump-markings less distinct than adult (young males do show some red on rump, red underwing-coverts and band on flight feathers). Bill and iris brownish.

MEASUREMENTS Wing 65-73; tail 44-52; bill 9-11; tarsus 9-11.

GEOGRAPHICAL VARIATION None.

REFERENCES Arndt (1992), Beehler (1978b), Beehler *et al.* (1986), Coates (1985), Forshaw (1989), Lambert *et al.* (1993), Rand & Gilliard (1967), Sibley & Monroe (1990).

44 RED-FRONTED LORIKEET
Charmosyna rubronotata   Plate 10

Other names: Red-spotted Lorikeet, Red-rumped Lorikeet, Red-fronted Blue-eared Lorikeet

IDENTIFICATION 15-18cm. Small, mainly green lorikeet with red forecrown, breast-patches, underwing-coverts and uppertail-coverts, blue ear-coverts and a pointed yellow-tipped tail (male). Female lacks red markings apart from uppertail-coverts and has blue of ear-coverts replaced by greenish-yellow streaking. Similar to the closely related Red-flanked Lorikeet (45), but male separated by the red forehead, absence of red on face and throat, red uppertail-coverts and red at side of breast not extending onto flanks; in flight, underwing shows a less distinct yellow band in the centre of the wing than in Red-flanked Lorikeet. Female Red-fronted is separated on the red uppertail-coverts and light greenish-yellow, not profuse yellow, streaking on ear-coverts; female Red-flanked also shows a prominent blue rump-patch except in the eastern New Guinea race *subplacens*. From Plum-faced Lorikeet (52), which mainly occurs only above 2,000m, by yellow, not red, underside to tail, red uppertail-coverts, orange, not black, bill, and absence of dark blue ear-coverts with white streaking.

VOICE A sharp *kss* and a quiet but harsh *queet-queet*, similar to but less harsh than that of Red-flanked Lorikeet.

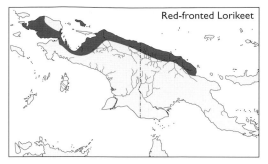

DISTRIBUTION AND STATUS New Guinea in Irian Jaya (Indonesia) and Papua New Guinea. Ranges from Vogelkop east through Maprik, the lower reaches of the Sepik and Ramu Rivers reaching Astrolabe Bay in the east. Also on Salawati in the W Papuan islands and on Biak. Red-fronted Lorikeet is patchily distributed throughout its range but may be locally common in some areas. Appears to be less common than Red-flanked Lorikeet, which it replaces at higher altitudes where the two species overlap. The world population is thought to be in excess of 100,000 individuals and stable.

ECOLOGY Inhabits humid forest, forest edges and coconut plantations, occasionally visiting trees and shrubs in open country and also reported from coconut palms. Occurs from lowlands up to 850m, usually being encountered in small flocks of up to 10 birds flying over dense forest, or feeding on flowers in the canopy, sometimes with other lorikeets. Habits are similar to those of Red-flanked Lorikeet (45). Nesting and breeding habits undescribed.

DESCRIPTION Forecrown red; rest of crown mid-green; chin, throat and ear-coverts yellowish-green with prominent purplish-blue patch in centre of ear-coverts. Upperparts mid-green; lower rump and uppertail-coverts dull red. Upperwing mid-green with blackish innerwebs and tips to flight feathers and coverts; some yellow at bend of wing. Underwing-coverts red; flight feathers blackish-brown with indistinct central yellow band. Underparts yellowish-green with prominent red patch at side of upper breast; thighs slightly greener. Uppertail blackish-brown with green edgings to central and yellow tips to outer feathers; undertail brownish with broad yellow tips (except central pair) and concealed red at base. **Bare parts**: Bill pinkish-red; cere pinkish; iris brown; legs pinkish-red.

SEX/AGE Female lacks red crown, breast-markings and underwing-coverts (which are yellowish-green) of male. Blue ear-covert patch is replaced by light greenish-yellow streaks (less profuse and greener than in female Red-flanked Lorikeet). Immature undescribed.

MEASUREMENTS Wing 80-87; tail 58-71; bill 11-13; tarsus 11-12.

GEOGRAPHICAL VARIATION Two races.
   C. r. rubronotata (Salawati Island and through northern New Guinea from Vogelkop east to the Sepik River)
   C. r. kordoana (Biak Island) Female is similar to nominate. Male has paler and more extensive crown-patch and bluer, less purple, ear-coverts.

REFERENCES Beehler *et al.* (1986), Coates (1985), Forshaw (1989), Greensmith (1975), Lambert *et al.* (1993), Lodge (1991), Rand & Gilliard (1967), Sibley & Monroe (1990).

45   RED-FLANKED LORIKEET
Charmosyna placentis   Plate 10

Other names: Beautiful Lorikeet, Blue-eared Lorikeet, Yellow-fronted Blue-eared Lorikeet, Lowland Lorikeet, Pleasing Lorikeet

IDENTIFICATION 15-18cm. Probably the most commonly encountered small green lorikeet throughout the lowlands of New Guinea and many of its surrounding islands. The male shows a red face and throat-patch, underwing-coverts, breast and flank-markings, and blue ear-coverts. The female shows yellow-streaked ear-coverts and lacks the red markings of the male. Both sexes have a red bill, yellow-tipped tail (with prominent red markings) and a blue rump (populations in eastern New Guinea, Bismarck Archipelago and North Solomons have a green rump). Flight silhouette shows moderately long tail. Similar to the closely related Red-fronted Lorikeet (44) which occurs in northern New Guinea (although tends to replace Red-flanked Lorikeet at higher altitudes); see that species for differences. Other sympatric species in New Guinea include the tiny Pygmy Lorikeet (43) and Striated Lorikeet (42), which both show yellow streaking on the underparts. Plum-faced Lorikeet (52), which generally occurs only above 2,000m, can show reddish flank-markings, but these are absent in eastern populations (*O. a. grandis*) where Red-flanked Lorikeet has been recorded at higher altitudes. Plum-faced Lorikeet also shows dark blue cheeks streaked white, an orange-red underside and tip to the tail, and the male has an obvious red cap. Both Yellow-billed (53) and Orange-billed Lorikeet (54), which occur in the central mountains of New Guinea, have entirely red (or orange) breasts, and green, not red, flanks. In the Bismarck Archipelago, Red-flanked Lorikeet is also sympatric with Red-chinned Lorikeet (39), which is all green apart from a red chin and throat, and lacks the blue ear-coverts and red markings of male Red-flanked, and the yellow ear-coverts of the female.

VOICE A short, quiet, shrill, high-pitched, staccato *tsss* or *seeet*, often repeated. Also described as a short sharp dry caustic *kssk kssk*, hoarser than other lorikeets, and as a high-pitched trilling call of three short notes. Also a shrill chattering whilst feeding.

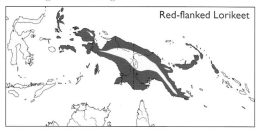

DISTRIBUTION AND STATUS Eastern Indonesia, New Guinea and the North Solomons. Occurs from the Moluccas and W Papuan islands, through the lowlands of Irian Jaya and Papua New Guinea to the Bismarck Archipelago and Bougainville. Although found mainly in the lowlands, recorded up to 1,600m at Komo in the southern highlands of Papua New Guinea; also common at higher altitudes (around 1,150m up to 1,450m) in the Karimui area to the east, but seemingly not elsewhere in the region. Reaches 300m in New Britain, above which it is replaced by Red-chinned Lorikeet. In northern New Guinea it is replaced at higher altitudes by Red-fronted Lorikeet. Widespread and common to locally abundant. The world population is thought to be in excess of 500,000 and stable. Small numbers in captivity.

ECOLOGY Chiefly a lowland species occurring in humid primary forest, forest edge, savanna, tall secondary growth, monsoon forest, sago swamps (when in flower), gallery forest, eucalyptus, coastal forest and occasionally mangrove and coconut groves. Also found in flowering trees in cultivated areas. Can be quiet and inconspicuous and, although active and noisy when feeding, may still be difficult to see amongst thick foliage. Mostly found in pairs, but occasionally in parties of 25 or more, foraging with other lorikeets in flowering trees and epiphytes or flying through or above the tree-tops in small compact noisy flocks. Feeds on pollen, nectar, flowers and seeds, mostly in the upper canopy. In New Guinea, several observations of pairs investigating arboreal termite mounds indicate that these are likely to be favoured for nesting. Fern-bases and moss-growths have also been identified as possible nest-sites. Activity at these sites has been observed between Feb and Oct. Specimens collected in eastern Papua New Guinea by Diamond in Jul and Aug 1965 were found to be in breeding condition. On Witu Island a pair with fledglings was observed by Coates in mid-Aug. Breeding probably occurs over much of the year.

DESCRIPTION Forehead and crown yellowish-green; nape green; chin, throat and lores red; ear-coverts dark blue heavily streaked light blue. Upperparts green with dull blue rump; uppertail-coverts green. Upperwing green with blackish innerwebs and tips to flight feathers. Underwing-coverts red; strong yellow band across innerwebs of blackish flight feathers. Underparts lighter yellowish green than upperparts; strong red markings at sides of breast and down flanks to sides of belly. Uppertail duller green than upperparts, tipped bright yellow, with lateral feathers red centrally on inner and slightly on outerwebs and with a subterminal black mark; undertail yellow basally, marked black and red. **Bare parts**: Bill red; iris yellow to orange, legs dull red.

SEX/AGE Female lacks yellow-green interchrown, red facial, breast, flank and underwing markings of male (underwing-coverts are yellowish-green). Blue of ear-coverts are replaced by a dark ear-patch strongly streaked yellow. Immature like female but duller green, and less extensive yellow streaking on ear-coverts (young male can show a red patch on face and greenish-yellow on forehead). Iris pale yellow, legs orange-brown.

MEASUREMENTS Wing 81-95; tail 60-71; bill 12-14; tarsus 11-14.

GEOGRAPHICAL VARIATION There are five races.

C. p. placentis (C and S Moluccas on Ambelau, Seram, Ambon, Panjang and Tayandu, through the Kai and Aru Islands, to southern New Guinea, east through the Fly and upper Purari River areas to the eastern highlands; apparently less numerous in southern Moluccas than the following race is in the northern group)

C. p. intensior (N Moluccas including Morotai, Halmahera, Ternate, Bacan, Obi, Widi and Gebe) Greener than nominate including forehead. Ear-coverts and rump-patch duller blue violet.

C. p. ornata (W Papuan islands except Gebe; Waigeo,

Batanta, Salawati and Misool, and in NW New Guinea including Vogelkop) Mantle slightly darker green than in nominate, a larger, darker blue rump-patch and a yellower forecrown. Red of throat more extensive in males.

C. p. subplacens (E New Guinea, west in south to the Bereina area near Hall Sound, and in the north through the Sepik River region to around Sarmi in the west) From nominate by green not blue rump.

C. p. pallidior (Woodlark Island and in the Bismarck Archipelago including Crown, Long, Tolokiwa, Umboi, Malai, Sakar, New Britain, Witu, Lolobau, Watom, Duke of York, New Ireland, New Hanover, Tabar, Lihir, Tanga and Feni, extending onto the Nuguria Islands, Nissan, Buka and Bougainville; also reported from Lou and Pak Islands but not elsewhere in the Admiralty Islands) Like subplacens but upperparts paler green. Ear-coverts of male lighter blue.

REFERENCES Arndt (1992), Beehler (1978b), Bell (1982), Coates (1985), Diamond (1972), Forshaw (1989), Hadden (1981), Lambert et al. (1993), Lodge (1991), Mayr (1945), Rand & Gilliard (1967), Sibley & Monroe (1990), Smiet (1985), Taylor (1990), White & Bruce (1986).

46 NEW CALEDONIAN LORIKEET
Charmosyna diadema Plate 10

Other names: Diademed Lorikeet, New Caledonian Diademed Lorikeet

IDENTIFICATION 19cm. The only small green lorikeet likely to be encountered in the forests of New Caledonia. Very rare with few definite records. The single female type specimen is mainly green with violet-blue thighs and crown-patch, a red vent, and red and black markings at the base of a green, yellow-tipped tail. The only other lorikeet occurring in New Caledonia is the much larger and very distinctive race deplanchii of Rainbow Lorikeet (18), which shows a reddish-orange breast strongly scalloped black and a bluish head. The sympatric Horned Parakeet (145), and New Caledonian Parakeet (149) are much larger, less yellowish-green and both show red markings on the head.

VOICE Not known. Possible sightings were based on a call noted as differing from that of Rainbow Lorikeet.

DISTRIBUTION AND STATUS Possibly extinct. Endemic to New Caledonia and known from two female specimens collected in 1859. The species was also reported from forests in the north of the island in the early 1900s, and was identified by islanders when shown a painting (in Delacour 1966) by Tony Stokes in December 1976. One islander claimed to have seen a single individual in the 1920s, and another had noted two on the 3 June 1976, west of Mount Panié. This latter observation was made by an experienced bushman who noticed the birds from their call, which he said was different to that of Rainbow Lorikeet. The authors agree with Collar et al. (1994) that the extent of remaining forest in New Caledonia and the size of the island indicate that this species may well still exist and that surveys should be made of suitable habitat including Mount Panié, Mount Humboldt and other highland forest areas. ENDANGERED.

New Caledonian Lorikeet

former distribution

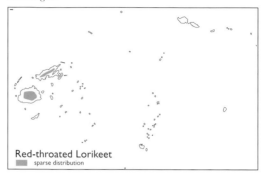

Red-throated Lorikeet
sparse distribution

is obvious in flight, which is rapid and straight on whirring wings. Inconspicuous while feeding and may be overlooked.

VOICE Brief, high-pitched squeaks uttered whilst feeding or in flight.

ECOLOGY Possible sightings only from forest. Nothing is known of the ecology of this species.

DESCRIPTION (Female only) Head green, paler on forehead and lores; crown violet-blue; cheeks and throat yellow. Upperparts green. Underparts pale green with violet-blue thighs and red vent. Upperwing green. Underwing-coverts green. Uppertail green tipped yellow, lateral feathers marked basally red and black; undertail yellow. **Bare parts**: Bill orange-red; legs orange.

SEX/AGE Male undescribed. Sexes may be alike. Immature undescribed.

MEASUREMENTS Female (from type): wing 91; tail 77; bill damaged; tarsus 16.

GEOGRAPHICAL VARIATION None.

REFERENCES Collar *et al.* (1994), Forshaw (1989), Lambert *et al.* (1993), Sibley & Monroe (1990), Stokes (1980).

47   RED-THROATED LORIKEET
Charmosyna amabilis   Plate 10

IDENTIFICATION 18cm. A small, long-tailed green lorikeet with a red throat, bordered below with yellow, red thighs and a yellow-tipped tail. Very rare and recorded on only a handful of occasions this century. Sympatric in Fiji with Collared Lory (29), which is larger and stockier with red underparts, a black cap and a bright green half-collar. Blue-crowned Lory (30) also occurs in the Fiji group, but only on islands in the southern Lau archipelago where Red-throated is absent. Blue-crowned Lory can also easily be separated from Red-throated Lorikeet by its larger size, relatively shorter tail, blue crown, red and purple belly-patch and lack of a yellow lower border to the red throat-patch. The much larger, allopatric Swift Parrot (154) only occurs in Australia, and although it has a red chin and throat bordered below by yellow, it also shows a very distinctive red shoulder-patch amongst other distinctive plumage characters (see plate). Red-chinned Lorikeet (39) occurs in the Bismarck Archipelago and lacks the red thighs and yellow border to the throat-patch of Red-throated Lorikeet. The long tail of Red-throated Lorikeet

DISTRIBUTION AND STATUS Endemic to islands in the Fiji group where it is rare and normally only occurs above 500m and below 1,000m. Occurs on Viti Levu, Ovalau (where it may now be extinct), Vanua Levu and Taveuni. In 1973 found to be not uncommon on a forested ridge at around 250m on Viti Levu by Holyoak, who also saw or heard the species on five separate days while surveying Taveuni, and believed the species to be widespread in rainforest from 550-1,000m there. The species was also recorded in rainforest between 120m and 980m by Gorman (1975) but was said to be rare. These records are among the very few documented sightings this century. The world population is thought to be less than 10,000. Despite its apparent rarity, the species may be overlooked due to its inconspicuous plumage and behaviour. Unknown in captivity. VULNERABLE.

ECOLOGY Occurs in mature montane rainforest mainly above 500m. Pairs and small restless flocks of 5-8 birds search nomadically for blossoming trees, congregating to feed on flowers, nectar and pollen. Prefers to forage in the canopy, and although reportedly driven away from feeding areas by the aggressive Collared Lory, Holyoak found the two species feeding in the same tree during observations in 1973. They feed actively, often hanging upside-down to reach flowers. Breeding and nesting habits unknown.

DESCRIPTION Head light green with lores and chin red. Upperparts light green. Wings green with blackish inner-webs and tips to flight feathers. Throat red, bordered below by narrow yellow collar; rest of underparts lighter, more yellowish-green than upperparts, particularly on centre of belly; thighs red. Uppertail slightly darker green than rump, strongly tipped yellow; undertail yellow. **Bare parts**: Bill orange; iris yellow; legs orange-red.

SEX/AGE Sexes alike. Immature generally duller. Thighs dull purple. Yellow breast-band very much fainter than in adult and red facial and throat-markings much restricted.

MEASUREMENTS Wing 94-100; tail 68-80; bill 10-11; tarsus 12-13.

GEOGRAPHICAL VARIATION None.

REFERENCES Clunie (1984), Collar *et al.* (1994), duPont (1976), Forshaw (1989), Holyoak (1979), Lambert *et al.* (1993), Mayr (1945), Pratt *et al.* (1987), Sibley & Monroe (1990), Watling (1982a).

48 DUCHESS LORIKEET
Charmosyna margarethae   Plate 11

Other names: Margaret's Lorikeet, Princess Margaret's Lorikeet

IDENTIFICATION 20cm. A strikingly patterned lorikeet with red underparts showing a strong yellow breast-band bordered above and below with black, a red head with a black rear-crown, red hind-collar bordered below by black and yellow-orange, green upperparts, an olive rump, and a red tail with a yellow tip. Males show red sides to the rump, females yellow. Immatures lack the black rear-crown and have less distinct breast-markings. The species is confined to the Solomon Islands and is extremely unlikely to be encountered in captivity. In the Solomons, the much larger Yellow-bibbed Lory (28) also shows red underparts with yellow breast-markings but has a broad green tail, red back, white shoulder-mark, black crescent-shaped neck patch, blue thighs and wing-markings, and no black border to the yellow breast-band. There are four other sympatric lories; Cardinal Lory (4), which is much larger and uniformly dull red; Rainbow Lorikeet (13), which has a mainly blue head and orange breast scalloped black; and two small green lorikeets, Meek's (40) and Red-flanked (45), of which only male Red-flanked shows a significant amount of red, but restricted to the flanks and breast. Duchess Lorikeet also superficially resembles Fairy (49), Josephine's (50) and Papuan Lorikeets (51) of Papua New Guinea, which are more frequently found in captivity. All three can, however, easily be separated from Duchess Lorikeet by the absence of a clearly defined yellow breast-band with black margins (*C. papou wahnesi* has a yellow breast-band without black margins). In its swift direct flight, Duchess Lorikeet appears small with a long pointed tail.

VOICE A rapid high metallic *chi-chi-chi-chi...* repeated frequently. Voice has a squeaky quality unlike the shrill calls of other lories. Also a repeated high *screek* whilst feeding, and a loud, high *keek-keek-keek-keek* in flight.

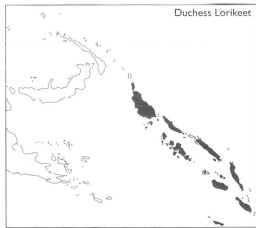

Duchess Lorikeet

DISTRIBUTION AND STATUS Endemic to the Solomon Islands including Bougainville (Papua New Guinea), Gizo, Kolombangara, Guadalcanal, Malaita and San Cristobal. Coates states that the species can often be seen in the town of Kieta, Bougainville. The world population is considered to be less than 50,000 but stable. Very rare in captivity. NEAR-THREATENED.

ECOLOGY Inhabits forest and woodland, forest edge and tall secondary growth, primarily in mountains and hills, but also in coastal coconut plantations and towns; chiefly recorded from between 100-1,350m. Often feeds in noisy groups of 10-40 birds in flowering trees and epiphytes with other lories (including Cardinal Lory). Feeds acrobatically, mainly in the forest canopy. Apart from pollen and nectar, observed feeding on fruits of *Schefflera*. Nesting and breeding habits unknown but a male was seen displaying in Jan.

DESCRIPTION Head red except for black hind-crown extending from above eye to nape. Broad red collar on hindneck bordered below by thin purple-black line with orange-red lower margin; mantle and scapulars green; rump bronze-green with red markings at sides; uppertail-coverts green. Upperwing green with black innerwebs to flight feathers. Underwing with marginal coverts green, underwing-coverts red, and underside of flight feathers black with indistinct yellow panel from central flight feathers through secondaries. Underparts red with yellow band across breast, narrowly bordered with purple-black above and a fine red margin and a broader, more diffuse purple-black border below; centre of breast sometimes with black suffusion (and red at sides of breast); undertail-coverts green. Uppertail red with black shafts and a narrow yellow tip, broadening on lateral feathers which have a black edge to innerweb and a green edge to outerweb; undertail yellow when closed, showing some red. **Bare parts**: Bill orange; iris yellow to orange-red; legs orange.

SEX/AGE Female from male by yellow, not red, sides to rump, and yellow-orange, not orange-red, lower margin to collar. Immature lacks black cap and black and orange margin to hind-collar. Also shows a very diffuse lower black border to breast-band, yellow-grey iris, orange black bill and greyish legs and feet.

MEASUREMENTS Wing 106-114; tail 84-100; bill 13-15; tarsus 13-15.

GEOGRAPHICAL VARIATION None.

REFERENCES BirdLife (1993), Cain & Galbraith (1956), Coates (1985), Forshaw (1989), Greensmith (1975), Haddon (1901), Lambert *et al.* (1993), Low (1977), Mayr (1945), Sibley & Monroe (1990).

49 FAIRY LORIKEET
Charmosyna pulchella   Plate 12

Other names: Little Red Lorikeet, Little Red Lory, Fair Lorikeet

IDENTIFICATION 17-19cm. A small, slim, mainly red lorikeet, with a long pointed tail, black hind-crown, green upperparts, tail grading from green to red to yellow, and yellow streaking on breast. In flight, shows red underwing-coverts and blackish flight feathers. The species is widespread in the mountains of New Guinea, where it is sympatric with Papuan (51) and Josephine's Lorikeets (50); although Papuan is usually encountered at higher altitudes, there may be some overlap, particularly in the Karimui area. Fairy Lorikeet can be separated from both species by its much smaller size, and (in adults) by its yellow breast-streaking. Josephine's Lorikeet, which can often be seen in association with Fairy, shows a bright red lower back in the male and bright yellow in the female, and has some lilac flecking on its (more restricted) black nape-patch; also an extensive purplish-black belly-patch (suffused green in immature). All races of Papuan Lorikeet have very obvious long tail-streamers (although sometimes broken, and lacking in immatures), and a green upper surface to the tail (colour of streamers varies with race). Eastern races of Papuan Lorikeet all show very obvious blue flecking on the nape, a red lower back in the male and yellow lower back in the female. In Vogelkop the nominate race *papou* shows some yellow markings on the underparts and less obvious blue flecking on the nape, but has a red lower back and an extensive black patch on the underparts. There is no likelihood of confusion with the mainly black melanistic forms of Papuan Lorikeet. Although the two *Neopsittacus* species, Yellow-billed (53) and Orange-billed (54) Lorikeets, tend to occur at higher altitudes, they may overlap in some areas with Fairy Lorikeet, are similar in size, so may need to be eliminated if small lories are only seen poorly in flight: both *Neopsittacus* are mainly green with orange, or orange-red, underparts, and show clear red underwing bars. Duchess Lorikeet (48) is also superficially similar, but is restricted to the Solomon Islands and shows a continuous yellow breast-band. The flight of Fairy Lorikeet is swift and direct.

VOICE Varies geographically. In western populations a nasal *ks* repeated two or three times, and a weak *ss*. In the east, a short note similar to that of Red-flanked Lorikeet (45), but sweeter, and less shrill and staccato. The call, as with those of other small lorikeets, is distinguishable only with practice.

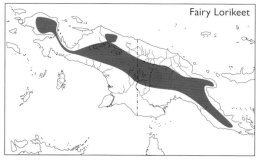
Fairy Lorikeet

DISTRIBUTION AND STATUS New Guinea in Irian Jaya (Indonesia) and Papua New Guinea, from Vogelkop east to the Huon Peninsula, Owen Stanley Mountains and the south-east ranges. World population is thought to exceed 500,000 and to be stable. Small numbers in captivity.

ECOLOGY Nomadic, occurring mainly in montane forest, forest edge and tall secondary growth. Primarily in mountains, occurring mainly between 500 and 1,800m, but also found in the lowlands down to sea-level and in the mountains as high as 2,300m. Found in pairs, or in flocks of 15 or more, congregating in the tops of flowering trees with other *Charmosyna* lorikeets, including Josephine's. Feeds on pollen and nectar. In captivity nests continuously, with incubation of 25 days shared by both parents. Usually lays two eggs in a hole in the base of an epiphyte. In the wild thought to nest between Jan and Apr (Pratt collected breeding males during Mar).

DESCRIPTION Head dark red with black rear-crown extending from above and behind eye to nape. Mantle green separated from black of rear-crown by dark red hind-

collar; lower back shows a dark violet-blue patch interspersed with a few green-tipped feathers, edged red; rump and uppertail-coverts green. Upperwing green with black innerwebs to flight feathers and black on innerwebs of coverts. Underwing-coverts red with marginal coverts green; flight feathers blackish. Underparts red showing pronounced but light yellow streaking in centre of breast, with purplish-black thighs and abdomen-patch and red undertail-coverts; faint yellow streaks on flanks and thighs. Uppertail basally green extending unevenly up sides of black shaft to about 15% of total exposed feather, remainder red narrowly tipped yellow, with outer feathers broadly tipped yellow, basally marked green and red; undertail yellow suffused red and edged green. **Bare parts**: Bill orange, tipped blackish; iris reddish-yellow; legs orange.

SEX/AGE Nominate female shows greenish-yellow, not red, sides to lower back and yellowish flank-patch extending to sides of rump. Female *rothschildi* also shows more green on underparts than male and a mottled green, not violet-blue, lower back. Immature shows a more strongly defined yellow flank-patch than female, surrounded by a strong green suffusion extending onto flanks. Lower back mainly green with little violet-blue. Upper breast mottled green (showing darker green tips and margins in younger birds), lacking clearly defined yellow streaks of adult. Crown red with black patch restricted to nape, blending into green of upper mantle and lacking the clearly defined red hind-collar of the adult (nominate). Yellow band on underside of flight feathers. Iris brown. Bill brownish-grey. Legs brownish-grey.

MEASUREMENTS Wing 86-99; tail 74-100; bill 12-15; tarsus 11-14.

GEOGRAPHICAL VARIATION Two races. A third, *C. p. bella*, described by DeVis (1900), is considered here with *C. p. pulchella*.

> *C. p. pulchella* (mountainous regions of Vogelkop, and throughout the central ranges of New Guinea to the Huon Peninsula and the Owen Stanley Ranges)
> *C. p. rothschildi* (Cyclops ranges and northern slopes of mountains above the Idenburg River, Irian Jaya) Crown-patch descends to meet eye; green suffusion behind yellow streaking on breast, and green suffusion on flanks and thighs (which can also show some yellow streaking); no obvious red collar, with more mottled black rear crown-patch meeting green mantle with a few interspersed green feathers; a much less clearly defined violet-blue patch on the lower back.

REFERENCES Bates & Busenbark (1969), Beehler (1978b), Beehler *et al.* (1986), Coates (1985), Diamond (1972), Forshaw (1989), Gyldenstolpe (1955), Lambert *et. al.* (1993), Low (1977, 1980), Pratt (1982), Rand & Gilliard (1967), Sibley & Monroe (1990), Tavistock (1929).

50 JOSEPHINE'S LORIKEET
Charmosyna josefinae   Plate 11

Other names: Josefine's Lorikeet, Josephine's Lory

IDENTIFICATION 23-25cm. A slender, medium-sized, mainly red lorikeet with green wings and a long pointed tail (less than, or equal to, body length, and although lacking the long streamers of Papuan Lorikeet, still strongly attenuated). The male has a red lower back, the female's is yellow, tending to green on the rump. Adults show a black belly-patch, suffused green in the immature. The species is widely distributed in the mountains of western and central New Guinea, where it is sympatric with two confusable species, Fairy Lorikeet (49), and Papuan Lorikeet (51). Fairy is much smaller, shows a mauve-blue or green patch on the lower back, and yellow streaking on the breast. The larger, generally higher-altitude Papuan has elongated tail streamers (except in immature birds and those in which they are broken); its three eastern races also show strong blue markings on the nape, while birds in Vogelkop have yellow markings on the breast and flanks which are absent in Josephine's Lorikeet. The upper surface of the tail in Josephine's is red with a yellow tip, while Papuan shows a green tail with yellow or orange-red streamers according to race. In flight Josephine's Lorikeet shows red underwing-coverts and blackish flight feathers, a feature shared with Papuan Lorikeet. Duchess Lorikeet (48) is also superficially similar but is restricted to the Solomon Islands and has a distinctive yellow breast-band.

VOICE Not noted to call frequently in flight, but occasionally utters a faint squeak, described as a high-pitched *kris*. When perched delivers a nasal *engg*, similar to that of Papuan Lorikeet.

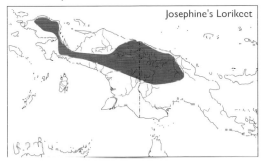
Josephine's Lorikeet

DISTRIBUTION AND STATUS New Guinea in Irian Jaya (Indonesia) and Papua New Guinea, mainly in the western and central ranges, from the Arfak Mountains and Vogelkop to the Bismarck Range in the north-east (Jimi and also Baiyer Rivers). It has been recorded from Jaya-pura on the north coast of Irian Jaya, and reaches south to Mount Bosavi, Papua New Guinea. The world population is thought to be in excess of 300,000 and stable. Small numbers in captivity.

ECOLOGY Possibly nomadic. Frequents montane forest, forest edges and partly cleared areas, mainly between 760 and 2,200m and commonest at 850-1,200m, although recorded down to sea-level. Usually seen in pairs or small parties. Despite its coloration is quite inconspicuous. Feeds in canopies of flowering trees, on flowering vines or mid-storey epiphytes, often in company with Fairy Lorikeets. Diet includes pollen, nectar, flower buds and possibly soft fruits. Nesting and breeding undescribed.

DESCRIPTION Head red with black patch extending from rear-crown to nape and down in a line to meet eye; rear-crown marked with lilac streaks; broad hind-collar red. Mantle and scapulars green; lower back red; rump with central patch of dusky blue; uppertail-coverts blue grading to red. Upperwing green with blackish innerwebs to flight feathers; marginal coverts green, remainder of underwing-coverts red; flight feathers blackish. Underparts red with a purplish-black patch in centre of belly, extending down

flanks onto thighs; undertail-coverts red. Uppertail red with yellow tip, lateral feathers with green on outerwebs; undertail yellow. **Bare parts**: Bill orange-red; iris yellow-orange; legs yellow-orange.

SEX/AGE Female shows yellow lower back, tending to green on rump. Immature with belly-patch suffused green, and thighs bluish-black. Blue rump-patch suffused with green. Lilac markings on rear-crown replaced by bluish-green. Immature female shows red lower back with a few yellow markings.

MEASUREMENTS Wing 109-130; tail 94-132; bill 16-18; tarsus 15-16.

GEOGRAPHICAL VARIATION Three races.
 C. j. josefinae (Vogelkop to the Snow Mountains)
 C. j. sepikiana (mountains of the Sepik region, Papua New Guinea, and in the western highlands east to about the Jimi River area and south to Mount Bosavi) From nominate by more extensive black patch on belly and greyer rear-crown markings. Females lack green-ish suffusion on flanks and lower back.
 C. j. cyclopum (Cyclops ranges) From nominate by lack of distinct black belly-patch and virtual absence of greyish-blue markings on rear-crown.

REFERENCES Beehler *et al.* (1986), Coates (1985), Forshaw (1989), Gyldenstolpe (1955), Lambert *et al.* (1993), Low (1977, 1980), Rand & Gilliard (1967).

51 PAPUAN LORIKEET
Charmosyna papou   Plate 11

Other names: Fairy Lorikeet/Lory; Stella's Lory (*C. p. stellae*, *C. p. goliathina*)

IDENTIFICATION 36-42cm (including tail-streamers); 16-25cm (without). One of the most beautiful of all the world's parrots. A slender, medium-sized lorikeet charac-terised by its two colour morphs and its elongated primaries and tail-streamers (which are twice as long as the lateral tail feathers, and particularly obvious in flight). The species is also sexually dimorphic in three of its four races. The nominate race, which is confined to the moun-tains of Vogelkop, Irian Jaya, has no melanistic phase and is not sexually dimorphic. It can be distinguished from all the other races by the yellow markings on the sides of the breast and flanks. It shows a black cap, lightly streaked blue, a black nape-band, green upperparts and a red head and underparts with a black belly. The two central New Guinea races are similar, are sexually dimorphic, and both have melanistic forms in which the red and yellow markings are replaced by black (melanistic males with red on back and undertail-coverts though). They lack the yellow streaking on the underparts shown by the nominate, and females show an obvious yellow patch on the lower back. The race occurring in the Huon Peninsula has a broad yellow breast-band distinguishing it from the other races. The allopatric Duchess Lorikeet (48) also has a yellow breast-band. The three red *Charmosyna* species occurring in New Guinea, Fairy (49), Josephine's (50) and Papuan, can be difficult to identify in the field, mainly because most views are brief, involving birds darting overhead. Papuan Lorikeet is noticeably larger than Fairy Lorikeet, and occurs mainly at higher altitudes (Fairy normally up to 1,800m, Papuan mainly from 1,500m upwards). Fairy lacks the long tail-streamers of Papuan and the large black patch shown by all normal morph Papuan. Josephine's, which is found mainly up to 1,200m but may occur as high as 2,000m, is more difficult to separate, but lacks the long tail-streamers of Papuan and has a red, not green, upper surface to the tail: broken-tailed or the duller immature Papuan Lorikeets may pose problems away from Vogelkop, where they show yellow-streaked underparts, but their flight profile remains distinctive, with a long neck and very slim wings showing elongated primaries. Melanistic Papuan Lorikeets are highly distinctive and unlikely to be confused with any other species, but mixed-morph birds are known to occur. The other sympatric lorikeets, Plum-faced (52), Orange-billed (54), Yellow-billed (53) and Goldie's (22), are unlikely to be confused with Papuan (see plates). The flight of Papuan Lorikeet is direct but not swift, with rapid, audible, whirring wingbeats. It has been suggested that the frequency of melanistic birds varies according to altitude and location, although there have been no systematic studies to date.

VOICE Flight call a single loud up-slurred grating *queeea*, more grating than sympatric Plum-faced and Orange-billed. Whilst feeding a quiet nasal note on one pitch that increases in volume, transcribed as *wnnaaah* or *nreeennnNGG*. Other calls include a soft *cheep...cheep* and a prolonged nasal *taa-aan* when preening, resting or moving around the tree-tops.

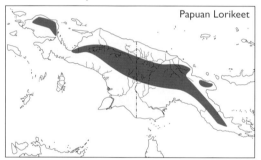

Papuan Lorikeet

DISTRIBUTION AND STATUS Central ranges of New Guinea in Irian Jaya (Indonesia) and Papua New Guinea, occurring from south-east Vogelkop to the Adelbert Range, Huon Peninsula and south-east ranges. The world population is thought to be in excess of 500,000 and stable. Exploitation in the form of hunting for plumes which are highly sought-after for tribal head-dresses, and trapping for trade are not currently thought to be factors likely to affect the population size.

ECOLOGY Encountered from about 1,200m up to the tree-line and recorded as high as 3,500m, but commonest above 2,000m and rare below 1,500m; found by Forshaw in *Nothofagus-Podocarpus* forest at 2,800m. An active and agile species usually encountered in pairs or small groups. Birds move through trees with jerky movements often flicking their tail-streamers, yet they can be quite inconspicuous amongst tree-tops. Feeds in blossom trees or flowering epiphytes attached to moss-covered branches, on nectar, pollen, possibly flowers, flower buds, fruit and small seeds. Insect larvae may also be ingested accidentally. Found in flowering trees and *Schefflera*, frequently in company of other blossom-feeding species such as Yellow-billed Lorikeet. Often seen flying low over trees or at

mid-storey level across clearings. Nesting in the wild undescribed, but Pratt observed an adult crawling over and under a large clump of epiphytes on the limb of a forest tree, perhaps searching for a nest-site. A pair in breeding condition were also collected in late August, and young have been seen in the wild during Oct and Nov. In captivity, where clutch-size has been recorded as two, incubation has lasted about three weeks with the young remaining in the nest for about two months. In display yellow thigh-patches of nominate are erected and the bird stretches to its full height, bows, hisses and makes a snapping noise with its bill.

DESCRIPTION Head red with a black patch on rear-crown and crescent-shaped mark on nape; crown-patch with some blue flecking extending back from leading edge. Lower nape and mantle uniformly red; centre of back dark emerald green; lower back bright red; rump bright light blue. Upperwing dark emerald-green with black innerwebs to flight feathers; underwing greyish-black with red coverts; marginal coverts green. Throat red, breast darker and slightly duller; lower breast lighter red with variable black patch in centre of belly, sometimes extending onto thighs; sides of breast and flanks with two obvious sets of yellow streaks; lower belly and undertail-coverts red. Uppertail green grading into orange on streamers, shaft of central feathers brownish-black; undertail yellow grading to orange on streamers. **Bare parts**: Bill orange; iris orange; legs orange.

SEX/AGE Sexes similar in nominate. See below for races. Immature duller than adult with shorter tail-streamers. A variable yellow band on underside of secondaries; rump mottled green; primary tips less elongated than in adult. Brownish-orange bill and legs; pale yellow iris.

MEASUREMENTS Wing 130-145; tail 200-252; bill 15-17; tarsus 16-18.

GEOGRAPHICAL VARIATION Four races.

C. p. papou (mountains of Vogelkop)

C. p. stellae (mountains of SE New Guinea) This race is sexually dimorphic and also has a melanistic morph. The normal morph of *stellae*, compared to the nominate, has much more extensive black nape-patch (meeting the eye) with strong violet-blue anterior streaking; this single bold patch replaces the two discrete areas of black on the crown and nape of the nominate. The tail-streamers also differ, grading from green to orange-red (rather than to orange) and then finally to yellow at the tips. Race *stellae* also lacks the bold yellow breast and flank-streaking of *papou* and its black belly-patch extends onto the flanks. Females show a conspicuous yellow patch on the lower back with green tips to longest feathers, and red uppertail-coverts (male shows red back with blue rump-patch). Red of breast appears more uniform, not darker on upper breast. In the melanistic morph the red is largely replaced by black (see *goliathina*). From *goliathina* by colour of tail-streamers (see below). Young birds with fine darker fringes to underparts.

C. p. goliathina (mountains of W, C & E New Guinea) This race is sexually dimorphic and there are two colour morphs. The normal morph is similar to *stellae*, but separated by its yellow-tipped tail-streamers (not orange-red grading to yellow). The longest uppertail-coverts are mauve-blue, not red as in *stellae*. Like *stellae*, the melanistic morph has green upperparts, and entirely blue-black underparts, head and mantle, broken only by blue streaking on the nape, and a red back and undertail-coverts in the male (blue on rump is retained by both sexes). The wings are green with black innerwebs to the flight feathers. The undertail is more greenish-yellow than in the normal morph, and the streamers are dull green grading to greenish-yellow towards the tips.

C. p. wahnesi (mountains of the Huon Peninsula) Similar to *goliathina*, but red breast is bordered below by a narrow yellow band. There is a green wash on the flanks and upper belly. The central belly and undertail-coverts are red.

REFERENCES Bates & Busenbark (1969), Beehler (1978b), Beehler *et al.* (1986), Coates (1985), Diamond (1972), Forshaw (1989), Gyldenstolpe (1955), Lambert *et al.* (1992), Low (1977, 1980), Pratt (1982), Rand & Gilliard (1967), Sibley & Monroe (1990), Tavistock (1929).

---

52   PLUM-FACED LORIKEET
Oreopsittacus arfaki   Plate 12

Other names: Whiskered Lorikeet, Plum-faced Mountain Lory

IDENTIFICATION 15-18cm. A small, slender, smallheaded and mostly green lorikeet occurring mainly above 2,000m in the montane forests of New Guinea. Unique amongst parrots in having 14, not 12, tail feathers. This is probably the commonest small lorikeet at high altitudes, and the only small green lorikeet with an all red undertail; it also shows distinctive plum cheeks and chin with white streaking, and a fine all-black bill. Quite unlike the two larger sympatric *Neopsittacus* species and Papuan Lorikeet (51) which also occurs above 2,000m (see plates). Redflanked Lorikeet (45) can sometimes range above 1,000m (particularly in the Mount Karimui area of the Eastern Highlands), and shows a similar underwing pattern with red coverts and a yellow band on the flight feathers; but it has a relatively shorter tail and hence a slightly different flight profile. With good views, the characteristic facial markings of Plum-faced Lorikeet are distinctive. Its allred undertail has a variable red or pinkish tip above (according to race). The tail of Red-flanked has yellow tips and is yellow below. The other sympatric, mainly green species, Pygmy Lorikeet (43), is only around 12cm long, has a short tail and lacks the head pattern of Plum-faced, whose flight is swift and direct with audibly whirring wingbeats.

VOICE A quiet twittering, also a short, soft, repeated *ts*, weaker than the calls of *Neopsittacus* species and Papuan Lorikeet, and described as more like a warbler (Sylviinae) than a parrot. Also described as having a squeaking call and a clucking during display. Coates notes that the call is reminiscent of a fig parrot.

DISTRIBUTION AND STATUS New Guinea in Irian Jaya (Indonesia) and Papua New Guinea, ranging from Vogelkop east to the Huon Peninsula and the south-east ranges. The world population is thought to be in excess of 300,000 and stable. Small numbers in captivity.

ECOLOGY Diamond notes that the distribution of Plumfaced Lorikeet is more or less continuous with the extent of moss forest: the species is found mainly between 2,000m

and 3,750m but may range as low as 1,000m on occasion. It is most frequently encountered in pairs or small flocks which are quite vocal, foraging acrobatically in the canopy and mid-storey, particularly on the flowers of epiphytes, and often in company with other blossom-feeders, sometimes including *Neopsittacus* lorikeets. Feeds on pollen, nectar, possibly flowers, fruits (particularly *Schefflera*) and berries. Nesting habits unknown, but birds in breeding condition have been collected in Aug and Oct. The display of underwing-markings has been noted by paired birds and may be linked to courtship, as may a head-bobbing display by the male.

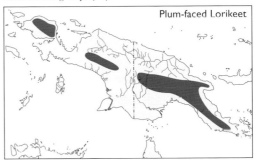
Plum-faced Lorikeet

DESCRIPTION Cap from top of bill to rear-crown scarlet; chin and cheeks plum (with bluish sheen), broken by two rows of fine white streaks. Upperparts uniformly green with slight olive suffusion on mantle. Upperwing green with blackish innerwebs to flight feathers and bluish green outerwebs to outermost primaries. Underwing-coverts and axillaries red (outer coverts marked slightly with yellow), flight feathers blackish with central yellow band. Mauve of chin extends slightly onto throat; breast green; centre of lower breast and belly suffused orange-red; lower belly green; undertail-coverts green, lightly suffused yellow at sides. Uppertail basally green, grading to blackish and ending pinkish-red, grading lighter to tip; undertail red with lateral feathers marked with black. **Bare parts**: Bill black; iris blackish-brown; legs grey.

SEX/AGE Female lacks red cap (but can show a little red on the forecrown). Immature male with red forecrown only. Young birds have a slightly 'scaly' appearance caused by the darker feather margins on the contour feathers, also duller face-markings and dull orange-yellow tip to tail.

MEASUREMENTS Wing 72-80; tail 72-88; bill 10-12; tarsus 10-11.

GEOGRAPHICAL VARIATION Three races.

O. a. arfaki (mountains of Vogelkop)

O. a. major (Snow Mountains) Larger than nominate (wing 79-93) and shows a redder tip to the tail.

O. a. grandis (mountains of central and eastern Papua New Guinea, including the south-east ranges, Huon Peninsula and Sepik region, extending west to the Victor Emanuel range) Larger than nominate (wing 81-89), and lacks reddish-orange flank- and belly-markings of other two races.

REFERENCES Arndt (1992), Beehler (1978b), Beehler *et al.* (1986), Coates (1985), Diamond (1972), Forshaw (1989), Lambert *et al.* (1993), Low (1977, 1980), Rand & Gilliard (1967), Sibley & Monroe (1990).

53 YELLOW-BILLED LORIKEET
Neopsittacus musschenbroekii Plate 12

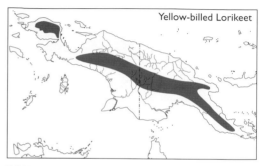

Other names: Musschenbroek's Lorikeet, Yellow-billed Mountain Lory

IDENTIFICATION 20-23cm. A medium-sized green and red lorikeet occurring mainly between 1,400m and 2,300m in the montane forests of New Guinea. Both this and the very similar, closely related Orange-billed Lorikeet (54) are somewhat reminiscent of *Trichoglossus* lorikeets. Adults of both species can be distinguished from other lorikeets by the combination of green head and red (or orange in *N. p. alpinus*) breast. The nominate race of Yellow-billed Lorikeet is the only *Neopsittacus* occurring in Vogelkop, and has no similar sympatric species. In other parts of New Guinea this species overlaps with Orange-billed Lorikeet and careful attention must be paid to the field characters of each to enable separation. Although altitudinal range can help, with Yellow-billed mainly between 1,400m and 2,300m and Orange-billed between 2,100 and 3,800m, there is considerable overlap, with the upper limit of Yellow-billed at 3,000m, and the lower extreme for Orange-billed at 1,600m (even reported as low as 800m). The main differences between the two species are: bill colour (as per name), and bill size, with that of Yellow-billed being slightly larger; Yellow-billed also shows a much stronger and more extensive brown suffusion on the nape, more obvious yellow streaking on the cheeks and yellow streaks on the crown; the undertail colour is mainly yellow (marked red) in Yellow-billed, showing orange-yellow on the closed tail, and dull olive-brown (marked red), showing olive-brown on the closed tail, in Orange-billed. Yellow-billed has a narrow yellow tip to the upper surface of the tail which is lacking in Orange-billed. Yellow-billed Lorikeet generally has less extensive red markings on the underparts, and the flank colour is also greener in Orange-billed, more yellowish-green in Yellow-billed. In the Snow Mountains, *N. m. medius* can also be separated from race *alpinus* of Orange-billed through its continuous red belly. In the easternmost populations, the size difference between the two species is most accentuated with Yellow-billed averaging around 15% larger. The two can also be separated on call. In their swift direct flight, both species show red underwing-coverts and a broad red band on the underside of the flight feathers.

VOICE Calls frequently. Voice harsh and sibilant and of typical lorikeet quality. Calls include a disyllabic screech when perched, the first note higher-pitched than the second; described as *sweet* (accent on second e) *sweew*, a shrill rolling screech in flight, also a shrill hoarse staccato *ss*, *ks* or *ts*. Another call, a repeated, trisyllabic descending and musical trill, is described as *shreedaloo*. In comparison to sympatric species, the voice is harsher, shorter and more grating, lower-pitched, more nasal and more hollow-sounding than Orange-billed Lorikeet; more staccato and stronger than Plum-faced Lorikeet (52); and weaker, shriller and less harsh than Rainbow Lorikeet (13).

DISTRIBUTION AND STATUS New Guinea in Irian Jaya (Indonesia) and Papua New Guinea. Occurs from Vogelkop east to the Huon Peninsula and south-east ranges. In Vogelkop, despite the absence of Orange-billed, the Yellow-billed population is relatively low. The world population is thought to be in excess of 300,000 and stable. Small numbers in captivity.

ECOLOGY Inhabits montane forest, forest edge, partly cleared areas and secondary growth, mainly between 1,400m and 2,500m, but recorded as low as 1,100m and as high as 3,000m. Also common in disturbed areas or in groves of *Casuarina* or *Eucalyptus* in garden areas. Appears to have adapted well to the impact of man, but is absent from places where forest has been completely eliminated over large areas. Conspicuous and noisy, encountered in pairs, small flocks, and in larger congregations of up to 50 birds in flowering trees. Over most of New Guinea, this species is replaced at higher altitudes by the smaller Orange-billed Lorikeet, but commonly found in company with latter in the upper band of its altitudinal range (except Vogelkop). Most often found in flowering trees often in company with other species including Papuan Lorikeets (51), also in fruiting *Schefflera*, and sometimes feeding at lower levels including on annual weeds at ground level. Feeds on pollen, nectar and flowers as well as small fruits and berries. Also thought to feed on seeds as a regular part of its diet, whereas Orange-billed Lorikeet is more of a nectar feeder. Like other lorikeets may ingest insects and their larvae, either deliberately or accidentally, with its other food items. Observed to run 'rodent-like' along branches. Two eggs are laid in a hole in a tall tree. Nesting period unknown but a juvenile was collected in Irian Jaya in late Aug, and a fledgling in the same area in mid-Nov. A male with worn plumage collected in Aug may have just completed a nesting cycle.

DESCRIPTION Head green, heavily suffused olive-brown, boldly streaked pale green on ear-coverts, and showing light yellow shaft-streaks on crown; darker line from above bill to lores; forehead green. Upperparts mid-green. Upperwing mid-green with blackish innerwebs to coverts and black tips to flight feathers. Underwing-coverts red. Flight feathers blackish with broad red central band. Throat greenish-yellow yielding to red from breast to above thighs. Flanks yellowish-green to sides of breast, with central area of lower breast and belly red; undertail-coverts more yellowish than rest of underparts. Uppertail green, finely tipped yellow, with brown shafts and red bases to lateral feathers; undertail orange-yellow closed, showing red bases to lateral feathers when fanned. **Bare parts**: Bill pale yellow; iris red; legs grey.

SEX/AGE Sexes alike. Immature duller than adult with less distinct head-markings, and red on underparts restricted to blotches in the centre of the belly and breast. Bill brownish-orange, iris brownish-yellow or orange. Young birds also show pointed tail feathers, which are rounded in adults.

MEASUREMENTS Wing 101-115; tail 79-92; bill 14-15.5; tarsus 14-17.

GEOGRAPHICAL VARIATION Three races.

N. m. musschenbroekii (mountains of Vogelkop)

N. m. medius (Snow Mountains and highlands of central New Guinea) Slightly larger than nominate. Ear-coverts intermediate between the greenish of nominate and the more yellowish streaking on the face of *major*. Breast scarlet.

N. m. major (Sepik region east to Huon Peninsula and the south-east ranges) Slightly larger than nominate and very slightly paler on the upperparts. Very similar to *medius* but streaking on cheeks yellower.

REFERENCES Arndt (1992), Beehler (1978b), Beehler *et al.* (1986), Coates (1985), Diamond (1972, 1985), Forshaw (1989), Gyldenstolpe (1955), Lambert *et al.* (1993), Low (1977, 1980), Rand & Gilliard (1967), Sibley & Monroe (1990).

---

54 ORANGE-BILLED LORIKEET
Neopsittacus pullicauda   Plate 12

Other names: Emerald Lorikeet, Orange-billed Mountain Lory, Alpine Lorikeet

IDENTIFICATION 18-20cm. A medium-sized green and red lorikeet occurring mainly between 2,100 and 3,800m in the montane forests of New Guinea (absent from Vogelkop). This species, along with Yellow-billed Lorikeet (53), are the only members of the Loriinae to show a green head and a red (or orange) breast. Orange-billed Lorikeet is similar to the preceding species, from which it requires careful separation: for differences see description of previous species. In the Snow Mountains, the race *N. p. alpinus* can also be separated on breast colour, which is orange in this species and red in Yellow-billed.

VOICE A gentle sibilant note, higher-pitched, more musical, quieter and less nasal than call of Yellow-billed Lorikeet. With practice the two species can be separated in the field on voice.

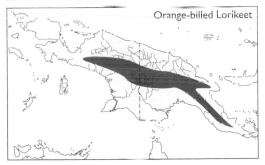

Orange-billed Lorikeet

DISTRIBUTION AND STATUS New Guinea in Irian Jaya (Indonesia) and Papua New Guinea. Ranges from Snow Mountains east as far as the Huon Peninsula and south-east ranges. The world population is thought to be in excess of 30,000 and stable. Small numbers in captivity.

ECOLOGY Inhabits moss forest and nearby partly cleared areas, mainly between 2,100 and 3,800m, with lower limit of 1,600m except for an anomalous report from as low as 800m. Normally encountered at higher altitudes than the previous species, but there is considerable overlap at altitudes below 2,500m, where the two are often found feeding in company. Quite common and often encountered in pairs, small groups or parties of up to 30 birds in flowering trees. Travels in noisy groups, and may fly high overhead to and from feeding areas. Feeds in canopy but also at mid-storey and even at lower levels close to the ground. Active and tame. Feeds on pollen, nectar, flowers, fruits and seeds, although thought to be less dependent on seeds as a regular part of its diet than the preceding species. Nesting habits are undescribed, although said to nest in holes in tall trees and lay two eggs. A male in breeding condition was collected in October.

DESCRIPTION Head green, nape slightly suffused brownish with indistinct yellowish shaft-streaks; ear-coverts dark green showing some greenish-yellow streaks; chin dark green. Upperparts green. Upperwing green with blackish innerwebs to coverts; black and red innerwebs, and black tips, to flight feathers. Underwing-coverts red; flight feathers blackish with broad red central band. Throat green; breast bright scarlet, extending down to belly and ending just above thighs; flanks green; undertail-coverts yellowish-green. Uppertail green, undertail dull olive-brown marked red on innerwebs. **Bare parts:** Bill orange-red; iris red; legs grey.

SEX/AGE Sexes alike. Immature duller than adult with far less red (or orange) on breast and a brownish bill.

MEASUREMENTS Wing 98-108; tail 82-87; bill 12-14; tarsus 14-16.

GEOGRAPHICAL VARIATION Three races.

N. p. pullicauda (Sepik region to the mountains of south-east New Guinea)

N. p. alpinus (mountains of central New Guinea including the Snow Mountains, east to the Hindenburg Range, Victor Emanuel Mountains and Fly River area) From nominate by orange breast which contrasts with red of belly and darker upperparts.

N. p. socialis (Huon Peninsula and Herzog Mountains) Similar to nominate but darker and showing less brown on nape.

REFERENCES Arndt (1992), Beehler (1978b), Beehler *et al.* (1986), Coates (1985), Diamond (1972), Forshaw (1989), Lambert *et al.* (1993), Rand & Gilliard (1967), Sibley & Monroe (1990).

---

55 PALM COCKATOO
Probosciger aterrimus   Plate 13

Other names: Cape York Cockatoo, Great Palm Cockatoo, Black Macaw, Great Black Cockatoo, Goliath Cockatoo

IDENTIFICATION 51-64cm. Unmistakable. Huge-billed all-black cockatoo with large crest and red facial skin (the heaviest cockatoo). Mandibles do not fit when closed, leaving the bicoloured (red, tipped black) tongue showing. The gape is red, the cere feathered, and the thighs bare. When alarmed the colour of the cheek-patch can darken to a deep red. This species is very unlikely to be confused with any other parrot. Red-tailed Black Cockatoo (59) is sympatric in the Cape York Peninsula, but its principal habitat is dry woodland, not rainforest. Red-tailed Black Cockatoo also shows extremely obvious red tail-patches in the male, and yellowish tail-patches in the female (which also has brownish plumage marked with yellow spots). The flight is slow, straight and level, with several slow flaps followed by a short glide, birds appearing broader-winged and shorter-tailed than the *Calyptorhynchus* species; they also have a massive head, the huge bill is tucked against the breast, and no colour shows in the tail or wings. In New Guinea, the other large dark psittacine, Pesquet's Parrot (112), can be separated by its long neck, small head and red markings on the underparts and wings.

VOICE Very vocal with a wide variety of calls. Generally higher-pitched than that of Sulphur-crested Cockatoo (65). The frequently uttered contact call, less harsh and grating than in *Calyptorhynchus* species, is a disyllabic whistle, the first note mellow and deep, the second shrill and high-pitched, prolonged and ending with an abrupt upward inflection. There are also some more raucous calls described as a very loud and far-carrying donkey-like *keeyaank!*, *eeyohn!* or *raah!*, or as a sharp guttural screech.

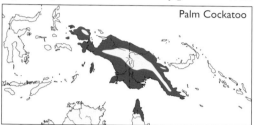

Palm Cockatoo

DISTRIBUTION AND STATUS Lowlands of New Guinea, some related islands and in the northern Cape York Peninsula, Queensland, Australia. Occurs in the Aru group, the W Papuan islands, and on islands in Geelvink Bay. Previously introduced to Kai Kecil and still present in 1981, but now possibly extinct there. In New Guinea ranges through lowlands to 1,300m, but commonest below 750m. On the Cape York Peninsula it ranges south to the Archer River in the west and to Princess Charlotte Bay in the east. The species is under pressure from habitat loss, trade and reportedly also hunting in vicinity of human habitation in New Guinea, a common method being to fire arrows smeared with sticky resin at roosting birds. The subspecies *goliath* and *stenolophus* are together thought to have a population somewhat above 20,000 and to be stable, *aterrimus* having a wild population of at least 10,000. CITES Appendix I. Small numbers (c. 350) in captivity (breeds). NEAR-THREATENED.

ECOLOGY In New Guinea found in rainforest, gallery forest and forest edge, monsoon woodland, tall secondary growth, partly cleared areas, and locally in dense savanna. In Australia found in forest, dense savanna woodland and eucalyptus and paperbark woodland adjacent to rainforest. Very conspicuous. Travels singly, in pairs, or often in parties of five or six. About an hour after sunrise birds begin calling, and gather in the tops of leafless trees above the rainforest canopy. Palm Cockatoos tend to roost singly in exposed trees at the edge of rainforest. They feed on large hard seeds of forest trees such as *Pandanus*, *Castanospermum australe*, and on palm nuts, buds and fruit. Nuts are summarily cut in half with the massive sharp-edged bill, and debris often falls from feeding trees. Palm Cockatoos commonly feed on fallen nuts on the ground, especially on seeds of *Terminalia kaernbachii* and its wild forms, and *Canarium*. In Australia nesting occurs between Aug and Feb, and has been recorded during Aug in New Guinea. In courtship displays, the male and female face

each other with erect crests, stamp and bow, and their facial skin turns a deep red. The male may strike a branch with a stick, seed or stone, whilst calling with its wings spread, as a territorial display close to the nest-site. One dull white egg is laid in a deep hole, in a high tree. The nest is lined with broken sticks and wood-chips, a feature unique to this species amongst cockatoos. The stick platform is porous and may be a metre or more deep (or sometimes only a few centimetres). It is thought that this stick platform is designed to prevent the eggs or chicks from being submerged during monsoonal rains. Chicks take between 100 and 110 days to fledge, as opposed to around 60-70 for *Calyptorhynchus* species. Incubation is by the female only and lasts for 30-35 days. After it leaves the nest the chick is fed by the parents for a further six weeks or so.

DESCRIPTION Entirely greyish-black except for forehead and lores which are almost black; head with erectile crest of elongated (up to 15cm) feathers. **Bare parts**: Bill black; facial skin red; periophthalmic ring grey; iris dark brown; legs black; bare thighs blue-grey.

SEX/AGE Upper mandible of female is less massive, particularly obvious at the base which is less deep. The bare patch of facial skin of the female is also smaller. Some immatures have the underparts and underwing-coverts narrowly scalloped yellowish-white. Bill-tip and eye-ring are white in juvenile (white in bill lost by c. 18 months). Facial skin also paler pink, particularly just below the eye.

MEASUREMENTS Wing 305-391; tail 200-253; bill 73-101; tarsus 30-41.

GEOGRAPHICAL VARIATION Three races.

> ***P. a. aterrimus*** (Aru Islands, on Misool in the W Papuan islands, and in southern New Guinea from around Merauke, east to the Gulf of Papua, and in the Cape York Peninsula, N Australia; this is probably the race introduced to the Kai Islands)
>
> ***P. a. goliath*** (W Papuan islands except Misool, and in southern New Guinea from Vogelkop east to southeast Papua New Guinea) Slightly larger than nominate but may not be separable.
>
> ***P. a. stenolophus*** (Yapen Island in Geelvink Bay, Irian Jaya, and in northern New Guinea from the Mamberamo River, Irian Jaya, east to about Collingwood Bay, eastern Papua New Guinea) Similar in size to *goliath*, but feathers of crest very much narrower.

NOTE Two other previously recognised subspecies, *P. a. intermedius* (Schlegel 1861) and *P. a. alecto* (Temminck 1835), have been included here with the nominate as they are considered inseparable.

REFERENCES Beehler *et al.* (1986), B.M Beehler *in litt.* (1997), Blakers *et al.* (1984), Coates (1985), Diamond (1972), Diefenbach (1982), Eastman & Hunt (1966), Forshaw (1989), Lambert *et al.* (1993), Low (1980), Pizzey (1980), Rand & Gilliard (1967), Schodde & Tidemann (1988), Sibley & Monroe (1990), Smiet (1985), White & Bruce (1986).

Calyptorhynchus baudinii   Plate 13

Other names: Baudin's Black Cockatoo, Baudin's Cockatoo, White-tailed Black Cockatoo (see Note)

IDENTIFICATION 55-60cm. A large blackish-brown cockatoo with white tail-patches, occurring in wetter heavily forested areas of extreme south-western Australia from Perth to Albany. This and the following species are almost identical, and are distinct from all other cockatoos except the allopatric Yellow-tailed Black Cockatoo (58). Long-billed Black Cockatoo is sexually dimorphic. Both sexes show white tail feathers, tipped black (except the central two which are all black), a white patch on the ear-coverts, a short dark erectile crest on the forecrown, fully feathered thighs and a naked cere. The female shows obvious white scalloping on the mantle and underparts, the male shows narrower brownish-white scalloping. The female also has a larger white patch on the ear-coverts, a grey, not pinkish orbital ring, and a paler bill and feet. Immatures are similar to females, but immature males may have a more restricted patch on the ear-coverts. Adult plumage is attained at the third moult. From Yellow-tailed Black Cockatoo by white, not yellow (speckled black) tail-patches; a white, not yellow, ear patch, and a greyish, not brownish, tinge to the overall plumage. Long-billed is extremely similar to White-tailed Black Cockatoo (57), but has an extended upper mandible (about 15% longer), the bill also being slightly narrower (the difference in length may be less accentuated in immature birds). Although this feature is likely to be of little use in the field, it holds the key to the separation of the two species which have very different feeding methods. Long-billed Black Cockatoo uses its longer bill to remove seeds from the marri *Eucalyptus calophylla* and related species, White-tailed uses its shorter, broader bill principally to break open cones of shrubs and pines. Close views of mixed post-breeding flocks can reveal the difference in the extension of the tip of the upper mandible from the cutting edge: this extension is roughly twice as long in *baudinii* as in *latirostris*. Although the two species are largely allopatric, post-breeding flocks may overlap (when post-breeding White-tailed Blacks move to the coast between Dec and Jun, and Long-bills forage inland in marri and jarrah *Eucalyptus marginata* woodland). Generally Long-billed is more sedentary and mainly restricted to the wetter coastal areas, whereas White-tailed is more commonly found inland in drier areas. The calls of the two species are similar; a high-pitched drawn-out whistle *whee-la*, but in Long-billed the second syllable is slightly less prolonged. In flight Long-billed Black Cockatoo looks long-winged and long-tailed, with deep, slow, buoyant wingbeats. Although Long-billed is slightly longer-winged than White-tailed, the difference averages less than 4% and is unlikely to be of much use in the field; individual Long-billed and White-tailed may show some yellow in their plumage.

VOICE Contact call in flight and sometimes when perched is a distinctive, high-pitched wailing, described as *whee-la*, *plee-erk* or *oo-lack*. The call is plaintive, lasting about half a second, with the second syllable a little longer than the first, but less prolonged than in White-tailed Black. There is also a grating or croaking whilst feeding and a harsh screech in alarm. Recently fledged young emit a constant rasping. Saunders refers to four distinct segments to the call. His research shows the mean total call length in Long-billed to be 0.47 seconds, and in White-tailed, 0.64 seconds, a difference of 0.17 seconds (36% of length). The duration of the third segment is however much different; 0.21 seconds in White-tailed and 0.06 seconds in Long-billed (a 250% difference). With experience, therefore, it is possible to identify the two species on call alone.

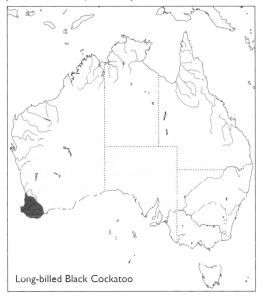

Long-billed Black Cockatoo

DISTRIBUTION AND STATUS Endemic to south-west Australia. Occurs from roughly Gingin north of Perth to east of Albany, breeding in heavily timbered hills and ranges. Its breeding distribution is mainly tied to the occurrence of karri woodland *Eucalyptus diversicolor*. The species forages north outside the breeding season (Feb-Jul) to the Darling Ranges (as far north as Gidgegannup and regularly as far as Mundaring near Perth), and east to the Stirling Ranges. Most of the breeding area is currently within state forest lands. The breeding range hardly overlaps that of White-tailed (which has however been found breeding as far south as Bunbury) and the latter species is more or less tied to the occurrence of wandoo woodland *E. wandoo*. On the whole, Long-billed is more sedentary than White-tailed, although both move to forage in marri and jarrah woodland (which occupies the area between their breeding ranges) outside the breeding season. The world population of Long-billed Black Cockatoo is thought to be below 10,000 and decreasing due to habitat loss and hunting, the principal cause for concern being the loss of nest-sites through current forestry practices. Clear-felling is removing the older trees that have the hollows suitable for nesting. Competitive interactions of breeding females further limit the number of nest-sites in areas where there are already few suitable trees. The longevity of the species may therefore be masking a low recruitment rate, and the potential for a rapid decline in the future should be countered with early action. Although legally protected, licences are granted so that growers can protect orchard crops. VULNERABLE.

ECOLOGY More sedentary than White-tailed, breeding in hills in wet sclerophyll forests where the rainfall exceeds

750mm per annum, particularly favouring karri, but may also use jarrah and marri (White-tailed mainly breeds in wandoo). The area between the ranges of the two species is mainly marri and jarrah which, in comparison to karri and wandoo, have relatively few nest-sites. Outside the breeding season, Long-billed Black Cockatoo may range to forage in other habitats, including farmland, orchards and open woodland, the noisy, conspicuous flocks keeping in contact with constant calls. When moving long distances the birds may fly at high altitudes. Outside the breeding season, occurrence is tied mainly to the distribution of marri, where typical feeding behaviour involves taking a seed capsule, cutting it off with the bill, transferring it to the left foot, and deftly removing seeds without damaging the rim of the capsule. This feeding method is quite unlike that of White-tailed, which feeds mainly by breaking open cones of various *Pinus* and shrubs. White-tailed may also feed on marri but breaks the capsule open to remove seeds with its shorter bill. Birds also feed on Proteaceae including bull banksia *Banksia grandis*, apples, pears and almonds from orchards, pomegranates, and the nectar of *Banksia* and marri flowers, sometimes taking the seeds of exotic species and those shed by trees burnt by bushfires. Long-billed also has a preference for wood-boring grubs, which form an important part of its diet. The species is wary and difficult to approach. Sentinels stand guard where flocks of 50 or more birds congregate to feed. Mainly breeds between Aug and Jan. In courtship the male raises crest, spreads tail and bows. Typically makes nest high in a eucalypt, with the site taking six or more weeks to prepare. One to two white eggs are laid, but only one young is raised; the second egg may be laid late, and not incubated after the first hatches, or one chick may fail to survive. Nestlings have creamy-white down. Incubation lasts about four weeks and, once hatched, the chick is brooded closely for about 20 days by the female. After this both parents join in feeding duty. The chick fledges about 10 weeks after hatching. There is a strong pair-bond and pairing may be permanent. The young are dependent on the adults for three to four months. Flocks in winter often seen in parties of three, with two adults and an immature bird.

DESCRIPTION Head, including short erectile crest, dusky-black, with narrow brownish-white edgings on rear-crown, lower ear-coverts and throat; obvious greyish-white patch on rear ear-coverts. Upper- and underparts dusky-black with fine brownish-white edgings. Wings blackish with very fine brownish-white edgings, outermost emarginated and with thin pale tip. Underwing brownish-black, coverts edged paler. Tail pure white except two all-black central feathers and a broad black terminal band (around 30% of tail length), black shafts, blackish speckling and black margins to outerweb of laterals (outermost with outerweb black). **Bare parts**: Bill dark grey; periophthalmic ring pinkish-red; iris dark brown; legs brown.

SEX/AGE Female shows much broader and paler greyish-white edgings to feathers of breast and mantle, giving scalloped and more greyish-white appearance overall than male. Ear-covert patch larger and whiter than in male. Bill pale grey with darker tip, not all dark grey as in male. Periophthalmic ring grey, not pink. Feet pinkish, lighter than in male. Immature slightly smaller than adult. Generally similar to female, but immature male shows smaller whitish patch on ear-coverts. In the male, the bill darkens after the second year. Adult plumage is attained in three years.

MEASUREMENTS Wing 366-394; tail 252-284; bill 49-54; tarsus 37-42. Mean culmen 53.00 against mean 44.20 in *C. latirostris*. In immatures mean for *baudinii* is 51.6, for *latirostris* 43.5.

GEOGRAPHICAL VARIATION None.

NOTE The nomenclature suggested by Schodde & Tidemann (1988) has been followed here, where *C. baudinii*, being the longest-billed of the three *C. funereus* allospecies, is called Long-billed Black Cockatoo; the other two are White-tailed Black Cockatoo (57) and Yellow-tailed Black Cockatoo (58) according to tail colour.

REFERENCES Blakers *et al.* (1984), Collar *et al.* (1994), Diefenbach (1982), Eastman & Hunt (1966), Forshaw (1981, 1989), Garnett (1992), Lambert *et al.* (1993), Lodge (1991), Low (1980), Pizzey & Doyle (1983), Saunders (1979), Sibley & Monroe (1990), Simpson & Day (1984), Storr & Johnstone (1979), Trounson & Trounson (1987).

57 WHITE-TAILED BLACK COCKATOO
Calyptorhynchus latirostris   Plate 13

Other names: White-tailed Cockatoo, Carnaby's Black Cockatoo, Slender-billed Cockatoo (see Note under previous species)

IDENTIFICATION 55-60cm. A large blackish-brown cockatoo with white tail-patches, breeding in drier areas inland from Perth and Albany, Western Australia; can commonly be seen in and around Perth itself. Between Dec and Jun, the species migrates towards the coast and overlaps with post-breeding Long-billed Blacks (56), foraging in marri and jarrah woodland. The plumage is identical to that of Long-billed (see previous species for differences).

VOICE A high-pitched drawn-out whistle *whee-la*, with the second syllable slightly longer than that of Long-billed Black Cockatoo. In alarm a harsh screech likened to the call of Sulphur-crested Cockatoo (65). Fledged young emit a constant harsh wheeze.

DISTRIBUTION AND STATUS Confined to Western Australia, mainly breeding inland from the previous species. The ranges of the two are separated by the jarrah-marri belt, which does not seem to offer sufficient nesting sites for either species. The breeding range of White-tailed is tied to the distribution of wandoo *Eucalyptus wandoo*, in the wetter areas, and salmon gum *E. salmonophloia* in the drier wheatbelt. The range begins just south of the Murchison River, extending through the coastal belt, including Perth, to about Bunbury in the south. It has also been recorded on Rottnest Island off Freemantle, and ranges inland, bordered on the east by a line running roughly through Manmanning, Wongan Hills, Kellerberring, Southern Cross, Norseman, and down to the coast at Esperance (recorded as far east as Mississippi Bay). It is absent from the extreme south-west, south of a line roughly between Busselton and Albany. Outside the breeding season, between Dec and Jun, White-tailed Blacks move into wetter areas nearer to the coast, foraging in marri *E. calophylla* and jarrah *E. marginata* woodland, and during this period they may overlap with Long-billed Blacks. Birds are rarely seen in the easternmost part of the range outside the breeding season but are generally obvious and encountered frequently in their range areas. The world population is thought to be less than 10,000, with both population and range contracting due to habitat clearance for agriculture. In some places breeding has ceased as feeding areas have become too widely separated from nesting trees: the consequent reduction in parental care, with both males and females having to forage widely during the day to find sufficient food, has resulted in increased fledgling mortality. The clearance of land, particularly sandplain areas, leading to shortages of *Banksia*, the preferred food for the species, has also played a part in the population decline. Moreover, there is more competition for nest-sites with species better able to benefit from the spread of agriculture, and older trees which provide suitable nesting hollows are not being replaced quickly enough, and regeneration is being hampered through grazing by rabbits and sheep. Finally the bird trade has in the past contributed to the problems faced by the species. One of the most obvious symptoms of the decline is the absence of the large post-breeding flocks, sometimes above 5,000, recorded in the early 1970s. Recent estimates suggest that these are no more than half this size today. Small numbers in captivity. VULNERABLE.

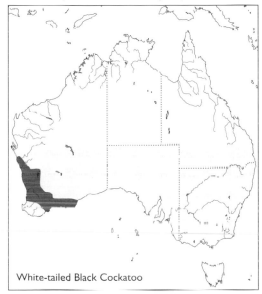

White-tailed Black Cockatoo

ECOLOGY The species breeds mainly in wandoo and salmon gum woodland. Its main food items are obtained from natural vegetation, particularly seeds from Proteaceae, and birds forage in sandplain, dry scrubland and mallee. The breeding range is in the inland belt with a rainfall between 350mm and 700mm annually. Nesting areas may be a distance from feeding areas as a result of habitat fragmentation in the wheatbelt. Where this happens, and corridors of natural vegetation are absent, breeding success has declined dramatically, or has ceased. Females are highly territorial, which also has a dispersive effect on nest sites. In combination with the limitation of sites through the activities of man, this factor is adding to the problems faced by the species. White-tailed Black Cockatoos feed mainly on seeds, favoured species including *Hakea*, *Dryandra*, *Grevillea*, marri, pines *Pinus* and sometimes *Erodium*. White-tailed Blacks use their short powerful bill to break open the hard cases of seed capsules.

Unlike Long-billed Blacks, they do not appear to favour wood-boring grubs. They may feed on the ground, particularly where seed capsules have been shed by burnt trees. Nesting is between Aug and Dec. Pairs tend to form permanent bonds, and the female selects and prepares the site, which may vary from year to year. The nest is a tree-hollow 2-20m above ground, with an entrance usually of at least 18cm in diameter. The hollow widens to around 35cm at the floor and is usually at least 15cm deep. During incubation, the female is fed by the male. Two white eggs are laid, the first being the larger. Incubation lasts about four weeks and although frequently only one young fledges two are not unusual. Fledging takes about 10-11 weeks. Once fledged, the chick is fed by both parents. Immatures stay with adults for their first year, and reach sexual maturity in four years. After the breeding season, large flocks form and birds tend to move to wetter coastal areas, where they may overlap with Long-billed Blacks. Post-breeding White-tailed Blacks are particularly fond of pine seeds and may congregate in large parties to feed in plantations. Flocks are sometimes seen in company with Red-tailed Black Cockatoos (59). Before the breeding season begins again, the large flocks begin to break up and smaller groups are regularly encountered.

DESCRIPTION Plumage as previous species.

SEX/AGE Differences as per previous species.

MEASUREMENTS Wing 355-393; tail 242-277; bill 41-46; tarsus 31-41.

GEOGRAPHICAL VARIATION None.

NOTE May be conspecific with following species.

REFERENCES Blakers *et al.* (1984), Collar *et al.* (1994), Forshaw (1981, 1989), Garnett (1992), Lambert *et al.* (1992), Lodge (1991), Pizzey & Doyle (1983), Saunders (1979), Schodde & Tidemann (1988), Sibley & Monroe (1990), Slater (1989), Storr & Johnstone (1979), Trounson & Trounson (1987).

58 YELLOW-TAILED BLACK COCKATOO
Calyptorhynchus funereus   Plate 13

Other names: Yellow-tailed Cockatoo, Funereal Cockatoo

IDENTIFICATION 55-69cm. A large dusky-brown cockatoo with obvious yellow tail and ear-covert patches and short erectile crest. Occurs throughout the coastal belt of south-eastern Australia and in Tasmania. Unlikely to be confused with any sympatric species. The only long-winged, long-tailed, all-dark cockatoo with obvious yellow tail-patches. Female Red-tailed Black (59) has orange tail-patches and lacks the yellow ear-covert patch of Yellow-tailed. Female Glossy Black Cockatoo (60) is smaller with red and yellow in the tail, and shows patchy yellow markings on the head. Some individuals of Long-billed Black (56) and White-tailed Black Cockatoo (57) can show yellow in their plumage, but they both occur only in extreme south-west Australia. The flight of Yellow-tailed Black Cockatoo appears buoyant with deep slow beats and the long tail (about half the total length) is obvious.

VOICE In flight a loud, very distinctive drawn-out whistle described as *whee-la* or *kee-ow...kee-ow*. Also a harsh alarm call. Young birds emit a constant harsh rasp.

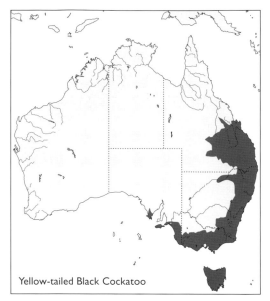

Yellow-tailed Black Cockatoo

and hold, the lower to cut. The species also feeds on wood-boring larvae, which are removed from the trunks or roots of various eucalypts and acacias. When removing larvae, birds often brace themselves 'woodpecker-fashion' with their tails, and may perch on a 'chopping platform' gouged out from the trunk. In northern New South Wales, foraging for larvae has been observed to peak in June and July, equating to the latter part of the nesting season when young birds are most demanding. This species is said to be more arboreal than the two white-tailed black cockatoos, but may feed on seeds from fallen pine-cones once flocks have removed the majority of the cones from the trees. The breeding season varies according to region. In the extreme north of its range, nesting occurs between Apr and Jul, in northern New South Wales between Jan and May, in southern New South Wales between Dec and Feb, and in South Australia and Tasmania between Nov and Jan. Some pairs may nest every year, and keep the previous year's offspring with them during much of the following nesting season. The courtship display is simple, with the male bowing, raising his crest and fanning his tail. The nest is usually in a eucalypt around 10-20m above ground, and may be used by the same pair more than once. The most usual site is a hollow in the main trunk of an old tree caused by a side branch falling. Sometimes an isolated dead or burnt tree may be chosen. Both birds prepare the nest over a period of about six weeks. During this time courtship feeding is common. To create a suitable platform for the eggs, wood chippings are ripped from around the entrance to the hollow, which is usually at least 18cm wide. The hole is normally around 1-2m deep, vertical, and around twice as wide at the base as at the entrance; one extreme example was more than 5m deep. Pairs tend to nest at least 40m apart. Normally two white eggs are laid within a period of 4-7 days. The first egg is usually larger and the first chick is frequently the only one to survive as the second is often neglected. Incubation takes around 30 days and is carried out by the female, the male feeding her around three times a day. The young bird is close-brooded by the female for around 20 days, taking around 90 days in total to fledge. From a few weeks after hatching both male and female make sorties to provide food for the growing chick.

DISTRIBUTION AND STATUS Confined to Australia, occurring in eastern coastal areas from about Gympie, Queensland, although there are records as far north as Clermont. Occurs on Fraser Island and inland in Queensland to Taroom, Chinchilla, and has also been recorded west to the Maranoa River and even as far as Cunnamulla. The range extends south through New South Wales (not uncommon around Sydney), inland to the higher western slopes of the Great Dividing Range (recorded as a vagrant to Moulamein), into Victoria where it is only absent from the extreme north and north-west. Occurs in South Australia where it ranges west to the tip of the Eyre Peninsula. It occurs on Kangaroo Island and on King, Hunter, Flinders and Cape Barren Islands in the Bass Strait, but is absent from the Yorke Peninsula. Also occurs in Tasmania. Generally common. The world population is thought to be well in excess of 20,000. Although the species may be declining in some areas through loss of habitat, the population is generally stable and the species is not presently considered threatened. There are a few in captivity.

ECOLOGY The species is tied to the higher-rainfall coastal belt, breeding in eucalyptus woodland and occurring in a variety of other habitats including pine plantations, heathland, orchards and farmland. There is much evidence of movements: birds appear to move to hills and ranges during the breeding season, and return to coastal districts (including the Sydney area) during the autumn and winter. Birds have also been seen crossing between Kangaroo Island and the mainland, and post-breeding flocks may visit King Island in the Bass Strait. The species has been recorded from around sea-level up to about 400m. Often encountered in noisy flocks, varying in size from half a dozen up to 300 or more birds. Flocks are shy and difficult to approach. When flushed they 'drop' from trees to gain velocity, and fan their tails, displaying the yellow patches and raise their crests when alighting again. Food includes the seeds of pines, eucalypts, *Hakea*, casuarinas, banksias and acacias, which are removed from their cases with the powerful bill, also fungus scraped from the inside of bark. The upper mandible is used to pierce

DESCRIPTION Head brownish-black with prominent dull yellow patch on ear-coverts. Upperparts brownish-black with narrow pale yellow margins to feathers of hindneck and back, giving scalloped appearance. Underparts slightly browner with light scalloping. Wing blackish-brown with (above) whitish margins to primary tips, and (below) yellowish margins on coverts. Central two tail feathers brownish-black, rest with blackish terminal band (about 30% of tail length) with narrow blackish outer bands on outerwebs (broader on outermost feathers) and broad yellow base forming two discrete yellow patches in fanned tail; outermost webs of outermost feathers entirely yellow; degree of brownish-black speckling and barring in tail ranges from light to heavy spotting running into distinct bars. **Bare parts**: Bill dark grey; eye-ring pinkish; iris dark brown; legs grey-brown.

SEX/AGE The female shows a light not dark grey upper mandible, a larger, brighter ear-covert patch and a dark grey, not pink, eye-ring (also some broader light edgings on underparts). The immature is slightly smaller than the adult and generally resembles the female, although the young male may show a smaller, duller cheek-patch; its bill begins to darken after the second year. Maturity is reached in 4-5 years.

MEASUREMENTS Wing 389-454; tail 311-384; bill 46.1-53.4; tarsus 34.6-41.7.

GEOGRAPHICAL VARIATION Two races.

C. f. funereus (coastal mountain forests of eastern Australia from central Queensland south through New South Wales to extreme eastern Victoria around Gippsland)

C. f. xanthonotus (between Melbourne and Gippsland through Victoria, South Australia and Tasmania, Kangaroo Island and islands in the Bass Strait, with specimens also from the Grampians; the Great Divide probably more or less bisects the ranges of the two races) Smaller than nominate (wing 345-393), with a shorter tail, claw and shorter and narrower bill. Similar in structure to *C. latirostris* but has a shorter claw and slightly longer culmen.

NOTE May be conspecific with the previous species.

REFERENCES Blakers *et al.* (1984), Eastman & Hunt (1966), Forshaw (1981, 1989), Lambert *et al.* (1993), Pizzey & Doyle (1983), Saunders (1979), Schodde & Tidemann (1988), Simpson & Day (1984), Slater (1979, 1989), Taylor & Mooney (1990), Trounson & Trounson (1987).

---

59   RED-TAILED BLACK COCKATOO
Calyptorhynchus banksii   Plate 13

Other names: Banksian Cockatoo, Red-tailed Cockatoo, Banks's Black Cockatoo (synonymous with *C. magnificus* Shaw 1790)

IDENTIFICATION 50-68cm. The only black cockatoo in much of north and central Australia, and one of the most striking of all parrots. The male shows a prominent helmet-like crest and is entirely black except for two large, bright scarlet tail-panels. The female is predominantly brownish-black, covered with yellow flecks and bars, and shows orange-yellow tail-panels barred black, and a whitish bill. The immature is similar to the female but slightly duller. There are four races, none of which is particularly distinctive. The male Glossy Black Cockatoo (60) is similar but smaller. It can be separated from male Red-tailed by its browner plumage, shorter crest and broader bill. Female Glossy can easily be separated from female Red-tailed by the irregular yellow blotches on the head, and the red tail-patches crossed with black bars (immature Glossy has an all-brownish head, but shows red tail-patches). In flight, Glossy is distinguishable by its shallow wingbeats, quite unlike the deep slow strokes of Red-tailed. Glossy is sympatric with Red-tailed only in parts of south-east Queensland. Both sexes of Yellow-tailed Black Cockatoo (58) may be confused with female Red-tailed, but have a prominent yellow patch on the ear-coverts.

VOICE A harsh metallic, rolling and far-carrying *creee creee*, *krurr* or *rur-rak*, quite unlike the soft wheezy call of Glossy Black Cockatoo. Calls frequently in flight and when perched.

DISTRIBUTION AND STATUS Confined to Australia. The species is widespread, its occurrence mainly being linked to eucalypt-lined inland river systems. Its range is still to be fully defined, owing to its nomadism and the

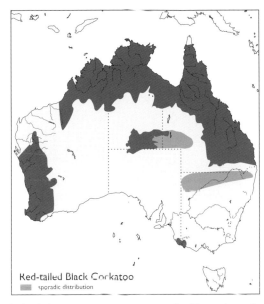

Red-tailed Black Cockatoo
■ sporadic distribution

lack of observer coverage across much of its territory. In the north there are two adjacent races, which meet at the Gulf of Carpentaria, extend from Broome, Western Australia, east into Northern Territory, south to the Gardiner Range in the west and to the upper Gregory River in the east, and north to the coast and onto a number of offshore islands, including Melville, Mornington, Groote Eylandt and the Sir Edward Pellew Group. In Queensland the species occurs widely in the north and east, including some outlying islands along the eastern seaboard, but it is absent from the tip of the Cape York Peninsula. Its range may have contracted in south-east Queensland during the last century, with a few records from northern New South Wales (Murwillumbah) as recently as 1975; today it is regularly found only south to Gayndah on the Burnett River. Inland in Queensland it is closely tied to the Cooper Creek and Diamantina River systems, while in inland New South Wales it is tied to the Darling River system, as far south as Menindee. It also ranges east on the Bogan, Macquarie and Barwon Rivers, from around Mungindi in the north to Nyngan in the south. These last two populations, separated along with central Australian birds as *C. b. samueli*, may connect with northern (nominate) birds. In central Australia the species is found throughout the Macdonnell Ranges, and from Haasts Bluff east to the western edge of the Simpson Desert, ranging north to Barrow Creek and south into northern South Australia. In south-east South Australia a small isolated population extends south of a line from Bangham through Goroke to Horsham, extreme west Victoria, and tapers south to Nelson on the coast. Of two populations in south-western Australia one is found almost exclusively in the jarrah forests of the extreme south-west, and the other (probably separated by only 50km) occurs inland in the eucalyptus woodlands of the wheatbelt, ranging north to the Minilya River; its eastern limit is not known precisely, but there are records from Cue in the north-east, Thundelarra, and from Merredin in the south, with a few others as far north as the upper Ashburton and Fortescue Rivers (although these may have been birds wandering from another apparently isolated population which is centred in the

269

upper reaches of the De Grey River system). The northern and south-western parts of the species's range appear to be the most densely populated. The world population is certainly in excess of 100,000 and thought to be stable. The species is considered to be safe and there are over 50 in public and over 100 in private collections. However, the isolated Victoria/South Australia population, separated as *C. b. graptogyne*, is endangered with perhaps only 1,000 individuals and only c. 100 breeding pairs. It depends on old or dead river red-gums *Eucalyptus camaldulensis* for nesting, and mainly on brown stringy-barks *E. baxteri* for food, both of which have been badly affected by clearance for agriculture, and by poor regeneration due to overgrazing. The fact that it was found as far east as Ballarat last century is evidence of the extent of its decline in that region. The species is fully protected by Australian law.

ECOLOGY Nomadic. Movements in northern parts of the range appear to be seasonal and predictable, with birds travelling inland during the wet season (Nov-Apr). Southern populations appear to move opportunistically in response to food availability, and in some areas large flocks may gather to exploit locally plentiful food sources. Red-tailed Black Cockatoo is the only member of its genus regularly encountered in dry agricultural areas, but it also occurs in a wide variety of other habitats from wooded coastal valleys to forest, scrub and sparsely timbered grasslands, its main habitat preference being riverine eucalypt woodland (especially river red-gums). It is absent from areas of rainforest in the Cape York Peninsula. The species's ecology varies according to race. In the wheatbelt, flocks of hundreds may be found feeding on the ground. In forested areas birds tend to form smaller groups and spend most of their time feeding in trees, coming to the ground only to drink. Food preferences also vary regionally. In the extreme south-west, the species mainly feeds on marri *E. calophylla*. Wheatbelt birds forage on she-oaks *Casuarina* and *Erodium*. They are also particularly fond of the introduced double-gee *Emex australis*, which may now be the most important component of their diet, and is probably a factor in the growth of the population in the region. Northern birds appear to have more wide-ranging tastes. The small south-eastern population feeds mainly on brown stringybarks. Birds tend to create a considerable amount of litter beneath feeding trees and are often encountered in large noisy flocks of up to 2,000 individuals, often consorting in family groups of three. Flocks are sometimes encountered in company with White-tailed and Yellow-tailed Black Cockatoos (57 and 58), but rarely mix closely. On the ground the species has an awkward waddling gait, and is wary and difficult to approach. From feeding areas, flocks may fly high and for long distances to reach their roosting trees, which are usually tall eucalypts near water, where they go to drink at dawn and dusk. When flying in to drink, birds have been observed gliding on decurved wings over several hundred metres. Roosting birds may be active and call loudly after dark, particularly on moonlit nights. Breeding has been recorded in almost every month, the pattern appearing to indicate that northern and central birds prefer to nest during the winter months, and that birds in the south-west and south-east may nest most readily during spring and autumn (*graptogyne* nests Oct-Apr). Some birds in the south-west are double-brooded, laying again just two months after the first young have fledged (*graptogyne* is also apparently double-brooded on occasion). In display, the male erects his crest and puffs out the feathers of his cheeks, almost covering his bill; the tail is fanned, and he bows and struts uttering a soft purring call. The nest is in a tree-hollow, usually around 180mm wide at the entrance and widening at the base. The nest-hole may be anything from 2-30m above ground depending on habitat, birds often choosing a dead or isolated tree. One or sometimes two white eggs are laid on a base of decaying wood, which the birds scour from the inside of the trunk. Incubation takes around 28 days. If both eggs hatch, the second chick is usually neglected and quickly dies. The chicks are covered in dense yellow down, and are close-brooded for the first two or three days by the female, and subsequently also at night. The female spends the first three weeks at the nest, and during that period is fed twice a day by the male. In total, the chick takes around 90 days to fledge, and is fed twice a day with both parents taking part in food-gathering. Red-tailed Black Cockatoos can be very long-lived, the age of 50 not being uncommon.

DESCRIPTION Entirely black except for two bright scarlet tail-panels. Prominent rounded crest, shaggy when not erect, in display protruding forward helmet-like, partially obscuring bill. Feathers on upperparts with greenish gloss and slight brownish wash. Primaries emarginated. Tail feathers basally black, marked centrally bright scarlet (with some yellow at bases of outermost laterals) and distal third black, producing bright scarlet patch either side of tail, visible above and below; outerwebs of outermost feathers black. **Bare parts:** Robust bill black; periophthalmic ring black; iris dark brown; legs greyish-brown.

SEX/AGE The female is distinctive, being generally brownish-black (blacker on mantle and wings, and browner on underparts), with fine yellow spots on head and neck, upper- and underwing-coverts, and with pale yellow-brown barring on underparts, slightly suffused orange on belly. Upperwing-coverts edged brownish; underwing-coverts blackish with pale tips. Undertail-coverts black barred brownish-grey. Tail-panels pale yellow at base, becoming progressively darker and more orange towards tip; they are crossed by blackish bars which begin as fine lines at base, broadening to tip. The pattern is brighter on upper surface of tail. Bill is whitish with a grey-brown tip. Immature resembles female but young males are less extensively spotted and quickly develop a darker bill. Young birds attain adult plumage through a series of incomplete moults, becoming progressively less speckled and less barred on tail. In the second year they begin to lose the spots on head and wing-coverts, the breast-barring diminishes and the tail reddens. In the third year most yellow spots and tail-barring disappear. Full plumage is gained in the fourth year.

MEASUREMENTS Wing 390-454; tail 272-321; bill 47-55; tarsus 32-38.

GEOGRAPHICAL VARIATION Five similar races are recognised; however, there may be considerable individual variation and also some exchange between populations of *banksii* and *samueli*.

   C. b. banksii (Gulf of Carpentaria through E Queensland)

   C. b. macrorhynchus (N Australia from around Broome, Western Australia, through Northern Territory to the Gulf of Carpentaria) Very similar to the nominate, but with a broader, more robust bill and a larger crest;

female shows yellow, not orange-yellow, tail-patches.
C. b. samueli (C Australia, SW Queensland and W New South Wales) Very similar to nominate but slightly smaller with a smaller bill.
C. b. naso (SW Australia) Smaller than nominate (wing 364-412), also has a shorter more rounded crest and a relatively more robust bill. Females brightly marked.
C. b. graptogyne (SE South Australia and SW Victoria in Edenhope area) Smaller than nominate (wing 360-375) with a smaller bill with no step in cutting edge. Females brightly marked.

REFERENCES Blakers *et al.* (1984), Cayley & Lendon (1973), Eastman & Hunt (1966), Emison *et al.* (1987, 1995), Ford (1980), Forshaw (1981, 1989), Garnett (1992), Joseph (1981a, 1982), Joseph *et al.* (1991), Lambert *et al.* (1993), Low (1980), Pizzey & Doyle (1983), Schodde (1988), Schodde & Tidemann (1988), Sibley & Monroe (1990), Simpson & Day (1984), Slater (1979, 1989), Storr & Johnstone (1979), Trounson & Trounson (1987).

---

60   GLOSSY BLACK COCKATOO
Calyptorhynchus lathami   Plate 13

Other names: Glossy Cockatoo, Latham's Cockatoo, Leach's Cockatoo

IDENTIFICATION 46-51cm. This is the smallest of the black cockatoos and is restricted to coastal eastern Australia (an isolated population also occurs on Kangaroo Island). The male is brownish-black with a short rounded crest and bright scarlet tail-patches. The female shows irregular yellow blotches on the head, the scarlet tail-patches are crossed by narrow black bars and show pale yellow edges to the innerwebs. Immatures are similar to females but lack the yellow head-markings and show indistinct yellowish feather-edgings on the breast and belly. The similar Red-tailed Black Cockatoo (59) is sympatric with Glossy in south-east Queensland, and the two are easily confused. They can be separated on call, which is soft and wheezy in Glossy and harsh and far-carrying in Red-tailed, which also has deeper wingbeats and a different flight-profile, looking longer-winged and longer-tailed. Glossy Black Cockatoos are most likely to be encountered in small unobtrusive groups feeding in casuarinas, where the females are instantly recognisable with their blotchy yellow head-markings. If a single male 'red-tailed' cockatoo is encountered alone, Glossy is distinguished by the brown head, short crest, and more bulbous bill. Although Glossy is also sympatric with Yellow-tailed Black Cockatoo (58), there is little chance of confusion, as Yellow-tailed has obvious yellow ear-coverts and tail-patches. The flight of Glossy appears buoyant with slow, rather laboured shallow wingbeats.

VOICE Contact call a soft wailing or wheezing *tarr-red*, quite unlike the harsh, loud cries of Red-tailed Black. Also a guttural alarm call, and a squeaking call made by the female and young when soliciting food from the male.

DISTRIBUTION AND STATUS Confined to Australia, where it occurs in the eastern coastal belt from around Eungella, central Queensland, ranging inland to about Augathella, and south to the west and south-west of Brisbane (also recorded from Fraser Island). The range extends into New South Wales running south from the border through the coastal ranges, being found inland about as far west as Cobar, Hillston and Griffith. The species spills over into eastern Victoria, and has been recorded from Wangaratta, Wingan Inlet, Cann River and Mallacoota. It is considered rare and local, although recorded from many locations in New South Wales. The following sites are worth trying: Warrumbungle National Park, the Nadgee Faunal Reserve, Chitchester State Forest, Bateman's Bay, Dharug National Park, the north side of Hawkesbury River between Wiseman's Ferry and Spencer, Mayall Lakes, Cocoparra National Park and even the northern suburbs of Sydney. The population on Kangaroo Island has been reduced to around 100 individuals through habitat loss (they are mostly males with probably only around 30 breeding pairs), and is considered endangered: it concentrates around American River on the west coast, along the north and east coasts of the Dudley Peninsula, and on the north coast west of Cape Cassini. Local publicity resulted in the declaration of the Lathami Conservation Park on the island in 1987. The species recently became extinct in the Mount Lofty Range on the mainland adjacent to Kangaroo Island, but birds may still occasionally cross to the mainland. The highest densities of Glossy Black Cockatoos are found in south-east Queensland and north-east New South Wales. The world population is probably greater than 5,000 and may now be stable. There are thought to be around 250 in captivity. It is thought that over the last century the species declined as a result of habitat loss, and that even now individual longevity may be masking low recruitment. The principal habitat, dense casuarina woodland, is now well represented in national parks, and the species is now probably relatively safe. It is protected under Australian law. VULNERABLE.

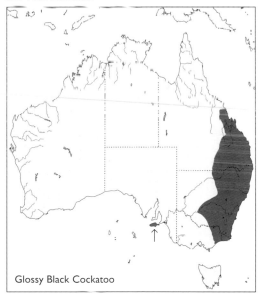

Glossy Black Cockatoo

ECOLOGY Sedentary, although there may be some local movements or post-breeding dispersal. The preferred habitat is eucalyptus woodland mixed with casuarinas or allocasuarinas, mainly in high ranges. Also found in open casuarina woodland, riverine woodland, dense forest, semi-arid woods, coastal forest, wet and dry sclerophyll forest and brigalow scrub. On Kangaroo Island, the typical

271

habitat is steep rocky hills with dense *Allocasuarina verticillata*, adjacent to semi-cleared agricultural land. The species is found in small, quiet, unobtrusive groups of up to 20 individuals, but usually in smaller parties between two and ten. Often found in family groups comprising two adults and one young. Families may roost together at regular sites (e.g. in *E. cladocalyx*), joining other birds during the day to feed. Unlike the similar Red-tailed Black Cockatoo, this species is never found in large flocks in open areas, and seldom in company with other *Calyptorhynchus*. The pair bond is strong. Birds may be seen flying together at some height when on long flights, but are tame and easily approached whilst feeding. In the early morning the birds spend time preening in the tree-tops, and may glide down to drink on decurved wings, before moving to feeding trees. The species specialises on casuarinas and allocasuarinas, including *C. torulosa*, *C. stricta* (Kangaroo Island), *C. cristata* and *Allocasuarina littoralis*, the large bill being adaptable to handle large casuarina cones. Various feeding methods are employed, and the feet are often used to hold the cones while the seeds are removed. Birds may twist the cone and rip it apart, or chunks of casing may be taken into the bill and the seeds removed with the tongue before the husk is dropped. They have also been noted feeding on fruit, wood-boring grubs, sunflower *Helianthus* seeds, acacia, banksia and eucalyptus seeds. Glossy Black Cockatoos seldom feed on the ground, but may create quite extensive litter beneath trees, where they can sometimes be detected by the tell-tale clicking of their bills as they feed. The breeding season is between Mar and Aug (southern birds are thought to be the later nesters), the nest being a hollow in a tall eucalypt. Birds are territorial around the nest. One, occasionally two, white eggs are laid on a base of decaying debris which may be more than a metre from the entrance. Incubation takes 28 days and is carried out by the female only. The chick is close brooded at first, and the male feeds the female close to the nest, having announced his arrival by calling (unlike Red-tailed Black). Later on, both parents engage in food-gathering and the chick is fed around twice a day. The chick takes 9-10 weeks to fledge but parental feeding continues for some time after the youngster leaves the nest.

DESCRIPTION Head and shaggy rounded crest dark chocolate-brown, upperparts blackish-brown with slight green gloss. Upper- and underwing blackish-brown. Underparts brownish-black, looking browner than upper-parts and lacking gloss, darker undertail-coverts. Tail with two central feathers black (glossed green), black terminal and basal bands, and black outerwebs to outermost lateral feather (also sometimes with fine black margins to other lateral feathers); red panels either side of tail as in Red-tailed Black Cockatoo. **Bare parts**: Bill greyish-black; eye-ring dark grey; iris dark brown; legs grey.

SEX/AGE Female from male by irregular and very variable yellow blotches on head and throat (sometimes appearing to form a collar or half-collar), black bars across red tail-patches (usually around eight which broaden slightly towards tip of tail), and yellow edges to innerwebs of tail feathers. Under-surface of the tail looks paler and yellower than upper. Bill a little paler than in male, but difference less pronounced than in other *Calyptorhynchus*. Young birds are similar to females but lack yellow head-patches. Young males also lack yellow tail-markings. Immatures of both sexes can show some light yellow spotting on underparts

and upperwing-coverts, although this is usually lost within the first year. Full adult plumage is thought to be attained in three years.

MEASUREMENTS Wing 317-370; tail 179-236; bill 42-51; tarsus 24-27.

GEOGRAPHICAL VARIATION Three races.

> **C. l. lathami** (coastal SE Australia except for range of *erebus*)
> **C. l. halmaturinus** (Kangaroo Island) Bill disproportionately large.
> **C. l. erebus** (outcropping ranges and adjacent lowlands in the Dawson-Mackenzie-Isaac Basin in east-central coastal Queensland) Bill disproportionately small.

REFERENCES Blakers *et al.* (1984), Cayley & Lendon (1973), Collar *et al.* (1994), Eastman & Hunt (1966), Forshaw (1989), Garnett (1992), Joseph (1981b), Lambert *et al.* (1993), Lodge (1991), Pizzey & Doyle (1983), Schodde & Tidemann (1988), Schodde *et al.* (1992), Simpson & Day (1984), Slater (1979, 1989), Trounson & Trounson (1987).

61   GANG-GANG COCKATOO
Callocephalon fimbriatum   Plate 14

Other names: Red-crowned Cockatoo, Helmeted Cockatoo

IDENTIFICATION 33-35cm. This small darkish-grey cockatoo, similar in size to a Galah (62), is confined to coastal south-eastern Australia. Both sexes show narrow whitish edgings to the feathers of both the upper and underparts, which create a barred appearance. The species is extremely distinctive and is unlikely to be confused with any other cockatoo. Because groups may continue to feed quietly even when observers are extremely close, they can sometimes be overlooked, although their distinctive creaking contact calls, the quiet 'growling' made while the birds are feeding, and the cracking of seed-pods, can help draw attention to them. The Gang-Gang Cockatoo has a distinctive laboured 'owl-like' flight, with deep sweeping wingbeats. The flight silhouette shows a short, squarish tail and rounded wings.

VOICE The contact call is a very distinctive, upwardly inflected, prolonged creaking screech. A soft 'growling' is made whilst feeding.

DISTRIBUTION AND STATUS Confined to Australia where it is found in the south-east coastal belt, extending south from the Hunter River, New South Wales (extralimital north to Dorrigo), along the coast and Great Dividing Range, reaching inland as far as Mudgee and Wagga Wagga. It occurs in central Canberra and should be looked for in the ornamental cypress trees on City Hill, particularly between Apr and Sept. It ranges through Victoria, where it occurs in the coastal ranges including the Grampians in the east, and finally in the south-west of its range it spills over into the south-east corner of South Australia mainly along the Glenelg River. The species has been recorded in northern Tasmania and on King Island in the past, and has been introduced to Kangaroo Island, South Australia. It occurs mainly in eucalyptus woodland up to an altitude of around 2,000m. Uncommon away from southern New South Wales and eastern Victoria. Introduced unsuccessfully on Kangaroo Island. The world population is probably in excess of 20,000, but may be declining slightly as a result of habitat loss. There are a few in captivity. The species is protected under Australian law.

Gang-Gang Cockatoo

ECOLOGY Nomadic at the extremities of its range. Breeds in tall open forest in the highlands and foothills, moving to winter in open woodland, riverine woodland, scrub, farmland, and suburban areas including Canberra and Melbourne. Some non-breeding birds may also summer in the lowlands. Encountered in pairs or small family groups during breeding season, and in parties of up to 60 in winter. These groups congregate where food is plentiful. Feeding birds are extremely tame and create a great deal of debris as they noisily crack open seeds. Family groups may indulge in much mutual preening, especially during the heat of the day. Small groups may erupt in playful wheeling sorties, returning to perch in the same trees. After long flights, large groups may spiral down to land in the manner of Galahs. Gang-Gang Cockatoos are mostly arboreal, usually coming to the ground only to drink. They feed on eucalyptus seed-pods, green acacia and *Pyracantha* seeds, and berries, in particular those of hawthorn *Crataegus monogyna*. Other foods include nuts, fruit and insect larvae. Flocks feed systematically, returning day after day to a productive area until the food source is depleted. During feeding, the left foot is frequently used to hold the food, particularly berry-covered twigs, while they are eaten. The breeding season falls between Oct and Jan. The nest is in a deep hollow, usually at a height of around 20m, in the trunk or main branch of a eucalypt. The chosen tree may be dead or alive and a site near water is usually preferred. Two or sometimes three white eggs are laid on a pile of decaying wood chips created as the birds chew the trunk to enlarge the nesting hollow. Both sexes take turns to incubate, the non-brooding bird remaining close to the nest. Incubation lasts around a month, with the young birds taking another six or seven weeks to fledge. The young have yellow down. Parental feeding lasts just over a month. There is an instance of wild hybridisation between a female Gang-Gang Cockatoo and a male Little Corella (71).

DESCRIPTION Head and wispy filamentary crest bright orange-red; chin and throat grey. Upperparts including scapulars, wing-coverts, rump and uppertail-coverts mid-slate, with narrow whitish feather-edgings. Flight feathers dove-grey, lacking whitish margins of rest of upperparts. Wing-coverts and flight feathers washed greenish-yellow on outerwebs; outer primaries emarginated. Underwing grey tipped paler on coverts. Underparts generally warmer grey than upperparts, with very fine yellowish-white margins becoming more pronounced on lower flanks and undertail-coverts; centre of belly has rusty suffusion. Uppertail slate-grey darkening towards tip; undertail dark grey. **Bare parts**: Bill light grey; iris dark brown; legs grey.

SEX/AGE The female can easily be separated from the male by its plain grey, not orange-red head and crest. She also appears generally paler, the feathers of the upperparts being strongly barred with yellowish-white rather than just edged whitish (including flight feathers and underwing). The barring extends to the tip of the tail in the female (the tail is plain grey in the male). The underparts of the female are also much more strongly barred than those of the male, have a pronounced greenish-yellow cast to the underparts especially from the belly downwards, and the rusty suffusion is more pronounced, extending from the breast to the undertail-coverts. Underwing-coverts also barred. The immature resembles the female but is generally duller and darker. Young males show reddish flecks on the forecrown and crest and have less extensively barred upperparts than females. The bill of the young bird is dark grey. Adult plumage is attained in around three years.

MEASUREMENTS Wing 241-267; tail 131-161; bill 28-33; tarsus 22-26.

GEOGRAPHICAL VARIATION None.

REFERENCES Cayley & Lendon (1973), Eastman & Hunt (1966), Forshaw (1981, 1989), Lambert *et al.* (1993), Lodge (1991), Long (1981), Low (1980), Pizzey & Doyle (1983), Schodde & Tidemann (1988), Sibley & Monroe (1990), Simpson & Day (1984), Slater (1979, 1989), Trounson & Trounson (1987).

---

62 GALAH
Eolophus roseicapillus   Plate 14

Other names: Roseate Cockatoo, Rose-breasted Cockatoo, Red-breasted Cockatoo

IDENTIFICATION 31-38cm. A flock of Galahs, showing first pink, then grey as the birds twist and turn in their powerful flight, is one of the most evocative sights in Australian birding. The Galah is a familiar and very distinctive species, with rose-pink underparts and underwing-coverts and dove-grey upperparts. The crest is white or pink according to race and, when not erect, creates a capped appearance. In flight the light grey rump and undertail-coverts are obvious, as is the light bar across the upperwing, and the darker tip to the tail. Galahs are frequently encountered in large flocks, and their distinctive pink and grey plumage sets them apart from all other cockatoos. The Pink Cockatoo (63) also shows pink underparts, but has white upperparts and a distinctive crest-shape and coloration (see plate). The long rounded wings, short square tail and swift powerful flight, with full wingbeats, create a distinctive jizz for the Galah, which is quite unlike that of the *Cacatua* species (which tend to have shallow erratic wingbeats and glides). Partially albinistic birds are sometimes encountered, and Galahs may also occasionally hybridise with Pink Cockatoos and Western Corellas (72).

VOICE The contact call is a thin high-pitched *chill-chill*. Some harsher notes are given in alarm. The fledgling's begging call is a wheezy whine.

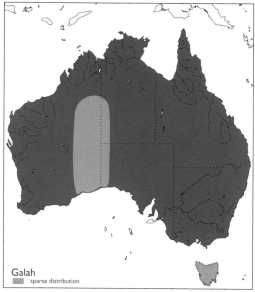

Galah
■ sparse distribution

DISTRIBUTION AND STATUS Confined to Australia where it is widespread and very abundant. Its range has increased during the last century, and particularly during the past 50 years, to encompass upland areas and even the extreme south, east and south-west regions where it was previously absent. Its spread has been attributed to a number of factors, including the proliferation of artificial drinking pools and troughs on farms, the release of captive birds (which have colonised some towns), the clearance of forest providing more open habitats, and the species's ability to cope with urban environments. It seems likely however that the primary cause has been the spread of agriculture during the present century, providing additional food in the form of both cereal crops and the seeds of grasses growing on cleared land. Today, the only area in which the species remains very thinly distributed is the Western Deserts Region, and sightings there probably relate mainly to nomadic groups. The species has occurred from time to time on King Island, and some of the other islands in the Bass Strait. It also occurs on Kangaroo Island, South Australia. In Tasmania, where it first bred in 1925, a small introduced population has gained a foothold in the south-east around Hobart, and a few birds, which may be genuine stragglers from the mainland, appear to have become established in the Launceston area. Escapes have also been recorded from Morehead in southern Papua New Guinea. The Galah is found in a variety of habitats from open country to woodland. It is common to abundant throughout most of its range, although it is still less common at altitudes above 1,250m. The world population is thought to be in excess of 5,000,000 and increasing. There are a considerable

number in captivity. Although protected in some states, the species is regarded as a pest and may be culled in others.

ECOLOGY During the breeding season pairs are sedentary, foraging mainly within 15km of the nest-site. Post- or non-breeding flocks of younger birds may wander further in search of food, and large flocks of non-breeding birds up to four years old may be encountered at any time of year; but no large-scale movements have been recorded. Although Galahs can fly at over 50km an hour, the maximum distance travelled by a ringed bird was only 473km during a two-year period. The Galah occurs in a range of habitats from woodlands to shrubland, grassland, urban areas, parks, agricultural land, paddocks and dry scrub, although it does not occur in dense forest. Outside the breeding season, large flocks of up to 1,000 birds may gather in pastures to feed. Their wheeling erratic flight, with hesitant flaps and short glides before landing, make these gatherings a spectacle to watch. These groups may consort with Little (71), Western (72) and Long-billed Corellas (73), as well as Mallee Ringnecks (126), Pink Cockatoos, and Sulphur-crested Cockatoos (65) (whose sentinel warning system they respond to). Flocks may fly a number of kilometres from their feeding areas to the roosting trees, and they may perform aerobatics as they spiral down to land. They usually take a drink before going to roost at dusk, and there may be further aerobatic displays before they settle to rest. When drinking, Galahs gulp water, standing in mud at the side of a pool or astride a twig. They may also scoop water up in flight like hirundines, or even land in the water itself to drink. Occasionally birds may be active and noisy through the night. Galahs feed almost exclusively on the ground where they walk with a waddling gait. They mainly feed on seeds, and exploit a range of species from cereals, such as oats and wheat, to grasses like button grass *Dactyloctenium radulans*, Flinders grass *Iseilema membranaceum* and Mitchell grass *Astrebla lappacea*. A wide range of other foods have been recorded, ranging from insect larvae to berries, buds, flowers and eucalyptus seeds. Although Galahs may help to control certain weed species like cape weed *Cryptostemma calendulaceum* and storksbill *Erodium cicutarium*, it is certain that they also have the potential to do considerable damage to crops. In the north, nesting takes place between Feb and Jun, elsewhere it is between Jul and Feb, but tends to be concentrated between Aug and Oct. In display, the male struts toward the female bobbing and waving his head and raising his crest, uttering soft notes and clicking his bill. He may also perform aerobatics. The nest is usually a hollow in a eucalypt that may be anything from 2 to 20m above ground. Galahs' habit of stripping bark away from the entrance to the nest-hole may sometimes be so extreme that the tree is ringbarked and dies. Cliff ledges have also been used as nest-sites. Typically, many pairs nest in close proximity, and pairs will tolerate an approach to about 3m of an intruder. These nesting groups may emit a strong odour. Both sexes take part in nest preparation, and the base of the hole is lined with green sprigs, which may also be chewed off and litter the ground around the base of the tree. Birds are thought to live for over 40 years, pair for life, and are site-faithful in choosing nest-holes. Two to six white eggs are laid, although three is a usual clutch-size. A new egg is laid every one or two days, and incubation lasts 25 days in total. Both parents take part in incubation and in caring for the young. Adults return to feed the nestlings around every three hours, interlocking bills to regurgitate food. The pink-downed young fledge in seven to eight weeks, but although the fledged young can fly strongly as soon as they leave the nest, the survival rate is low. In the first few days, the young may return to the nest at night. Thereafter they form large creches, and adults seek out their own offspring to feed. Parental feeding may last up to eight weeks before the parents break to complete their moult. In some cases, Galahs may be double-brooded. The Galah, unlike Gang-gang Cockatoo and the *Cacatua* group, appears to head-scratch over the wing.

DESCRIPTION Crown, erectile crest and nape white, with pinkish suffusion at feather-bases and thin rose-pink hind-collar. Lores pale pink; chin, throat and ear-coverts rose-pink, with vague white crescent beneath eye. Upperparts light, slightly mottled dove-grey; rump and uppertail-coverts lighter. Tertials mid-grey and flight feathers sooty-grey, outerwebs paler; primaries emarginated. Underwing-coverts rose-pink, undersides of flight feathers dull grey. Underparts uniformly rose-pink except for lower flanks and thighs, which are suffused light grey, and undertail-coverts and lateral tail-coverts, which are light grey becoming slightly darker towards tips. Uppertail light grey grading to mid-grey at tip; undertail uniform dark, very slightly brownish-grey. **Bare parts**: Bill greyish-white, prominent naked eye-ring dark greyish-red; iris dark brown to blackish; legs grey.

SEX/AGE Female like male but with a red or red-brown iris. Although birds reach adult plumage in roughly one year, young birds can be separated by the greyish suffusion on the underparts.

MEASUREMENTS Wing 248-282; tail 135-170; bill 24-30; tarsus 24-27.

GEOGRAPHICAL VARIATION Three races.

E. r. roseicapillus (N Australia)
E. r. albiceps (E Australia north to 18-20°S, west to Eyre Peninsula and C Australia) Warty red eye-ring, whitish crown contrasting with darker pink collar, large size.
E. r. assimilis (Western Australia, west of a line running roughly between Derby on King Sound to the north, and Eyre on the coast of the Great Australian Bight to the south) Separated from the nominate by the pink crown and crest, generally paler plumage and the crusty, greyish-white eye-ring.

Birds occurring in the Kimberley region may also be separable as *E. r. kuhli*, which is recognised by Forshaw on the basis of the grey-red eye-ring colour noted on the label of a single specimen.

REFERENCES Blakers *et al.* (1984), Cayley & Lendon (1973), Eastman & Hunt (1966), Forshaw (1981, 1989), Lambert *et al.* (1993), Lodge (1991), Low (1980), Pizzey & Doyle (1983), Schodde (1988), Schodde & Tidemann (1988), Sibley & Monroe (1990), Simpson & Day (1984), Slater (1979, 1989), Trounson & Trounson (1987).

---

63 PINK COCKATOO
Cacatua leadbeateri   Plate 14

Other names: Leadbeater's Cockatoo, Major Mitchell's Cockatoo

IDENTIFICATION 33-40cm. An extremely striking and familiar species. The Pink Cockatoo has a patchy distribution across the Australian interior, where it is unlikely to be mistaken for any other species. Its pink underparts, white upperparts, superb white and rose-pink crest (female with a strong yellow band), and deep rose-pink underwing and undertail make it one of the most striking of all parrots; the head appears broad and blunt in the field. There are no confusion species in Australia. The much larger Salmon-crested Cockatoo (67) also has a pinkish wash to the plumage, but the crest is a different shape and colour (see plates), and there is no contrast in colour between the upper- and underparts. The flight of Pink Cockatoo looks hesitant with quick, shallow wingbeats and regular glides. The long rounded wings and short squarish tail are typical of the *Cacatua* group. The white upperwing and pink underwing with its narrow white border make the species virtually unmistakable. It is known to have hybridised with Galah (62) in the wild.

VOICE A quavering falsetto *quee-err*, not unlike the call of Little Corella (71), but less raucous. Also a harsh alarm call. Fledglings wheeze constantly when begging for food.

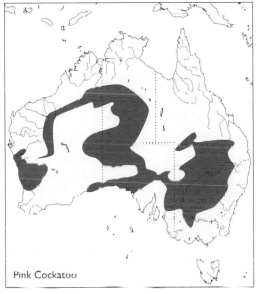

Pink Cockatoo

DISTRIBUTION AND STATUS Confined to Australia, where it ranges from south central Queensland inland of the Great Dividing Range (occasional as far east as the Darling Downs area), into New South Wales (east to Warrumbungle National Park, Parkes, Griffith and Moulamein) and north-west Victoria (Mildura and Wyperfeld National Park, where it is common, east to around Swan Hill and as a vagrant south-east to Geelong and north-east to Wangaratta). The range extends into South Australia, concentrated in the south-central region, including the Gawler and Flinders Ranges, and along the Murray River to Morgan and Renmark, but also extending west along the coast to around Eyre in Western Australia. The species is absent from the Simpson Desert, but spans the Macdonnell Ranges to the southern Kimberleys, and extends through central Northern Territory north to Hooker Creek and MacDonald Downs. In Western Australia it is centred between Geraldton, Perth and the area immediately north-east of Bullfinch, but also occurs inland in the Warburton Range, along the eastern edge of the Gibson Desert, along the northern border of the Great Sandy Desert, and in the region between the Fortescue and De Grey Rivers, with records from around Wiluna, Leonora and Kalgoorlie. There is an introduced population in Sydney. Introduced unsuccessfully in Fiji. The range has contracted slightly in South Australia, where breeding once occurred around Adelaide. Elsewhere some local declines have resulted from habitat clearance and trapping, but numbers generally appear to be stable. Competition from Galahs for nest-sites may be a potential problem in the future as the latter continue to increase. Pink Cockatoos are widespread but thinly distributed throughout their range, but may be locally common. The world population is thought to be less than 20,000. There are a small numbers in captivity. NEAR-THREATENED.

ECOLOGY Chiefly sedentary, but when food and water are short breeding adults may join wandering flocks of immature birds, and roving individuals may join flocks of other cockatoo species. Pink Cockatoos are mainly tied to the 250-400mm rainfall belt in Australia's arid interior, occurring inland of the Sulphur-crested Cockatoo (65), and favour eucalyptus woodland, particularly around watercourses, but occur in a variety of other habitats including mulga, mallee, cypress and acacia woodland, grassland and around paddocks where they join Galahs to feed on spilt grain. They are also occasionally found in she-oaks *Casuarina* and cypress pines *Callitris*. The species is wary but, when disturbed, birds do not usually move far, preferring short flights and hugging vegetation for cover. On alighting the crest is raised. Usually found in pairs or small groups up to 50 birds, sometimes in flocks of a few hundred. May be found in company with Galahs and corellas. Pink Cockatoos will feed both on the ground and in trees. They mainly feed on seeds of grasses and cereals, appearing particularly fond of the seeds of paddy melons *Cucumis myriocarpus*. Other food taken includes the fruit of native figs *Ficus*, pine cones, eucalyptus seeds, bulbs, the seeds of wild bitter melons *Citrullus lanatus*, nuts, roots and insect larvae. During and after feeding birds may bite off small twigs and sections of bark, leaving piles of debris on the ground. Pink Cockatoos tend to drink in the early morning and late afternoon, but will visit water more frequently during hot spells. The species is aggressively territorial and each breeding pair needs an area of around 500 ha. In courtship the male struts towards the female displaying his crest, bobbing and swaying his head, and lifting his wings. The female also raises her crest and bows. Courting birds make a soft chattering sound. Courtship feeding is rare but mutual preening frequent. Throughout most of the range the breeding season extends from Aug to Dec, but can commence as early as May in the north. The nest-site is a deep hollow 3-20m above ground in a eucalypt, preferably near water. The nest is lined with bark taken from around the entrance, as well as wood and sometimes even pebbles. The ground around the nesting tree is often littered with debris. The pair prepare the nest together and between two and four white eggs are laid, with incubation lasting around 26 days. The young fledge in about eight weeks and both parents brood. The male frequently takes the daylight shift with the female spending the night in the hollow. The fledged young form a family group with the adults, and parental feeding, which is carried out mainly by the male, lasts around eight weeks. The young take between three and four years to reach breeding maturity. Head-scratching is under the wing.

DESCRIPTION Spectacular crest comprising sixteen elongated, narrow, forward-curving feathers, extending beyond nape in short upward sweep when folded. Leading edge of crest white, rest of feathers with broad pinkish-red bases, usually showing narrow yellow central band, and tipped white; a few shorter, more rounded, whiter feathers above eye, giving impression of white base to crest when erect (bases of crest feathers orange-red); forehead and lores pinkish-red. Nape and upperparts white, but often with some rose-pink visible between feathers of closed wing at rest. Upperwing white with pink innerwebs to flight feathers; underwing bright rose-pink with narrow white border on both leading and trailing edges. Underparts salmon-pink (extending a little around sides of neck), grading whiter on belly and lower flanks. Uppertail white with pinkish innerwebs; undertail, apart from tips and central two feathers, rose-pink on innerwebs. **Bare parts**: Bill greyish-white; eye-ring greyish-white; iris brown; legs grey.

SEX/AGE The female shows a broader yellow band through the crest and a red, not brown, iris. Young birds show a dark iris, which lightens in females as they mature.

MEASUREMENTS Wing 248-280; tail 126-165; bill 29-32; tarsus 24-28.

GEOGRAPHICAL VARIATION Two races. Two others, *mungi* and *superflua*, are discounted due to insufficient morphological differences and geographic isolation.

   C. l. leadbeateri (E and C Australia)
   C. l. mollis (precise area of delimitation with nominate unclear; the type specimen is said to have been collected at Carnamah, Western Australia) From nominate by darker red crest with little or no yellow.

REFERENCES Arndt (1992), Blakers *et al.* (1984), Cayley & Lendon (1973), Diefenbach (1982), Eastman & Hunt (1966), Forshaw (1981, 1989), Lambert *et al.* (1993), Long (1981), Low (1980), Peters (1937), Pizzey & Doyle (1983), Schodde & Tidemann (1988), Sibley & Monroe (1990), Simpson & Day (1984), Slater (1979, 1989), Storr & Johnstone (1979).

64   YELLOW-CRESTED COCKATOO
Cacatua sulphurea   Plate 14

Other names: Lesser Sulphur-crested Cockatoo; Dwarf Sulphur-crested Cockatoo, Timor Cockatoo (*C. s. parvula*); Citron-crested Cockatoo (*C. s. citrinocristata*); Abbott's Sulphur-crested Cockatoo (*C. s. abbotti*)

IDENTIFICATION 33cm. A medium-sized cockatoo with a short squarish tail and long rounded wings. This and the following species are amongst the most easily recognised of all birds, with their long erectile yellow crests, and predominantly white plumage. Yellow-crested Cockatoo is the most westerly of the *Cacatua* group, occurring in Sulawesi and Nusa Tenggara, and as the only confusion species, Sulphur-crested (65) and Blue-eyed (66) Cockatoos, are allopatric, there is unlikely to be an identification problem in the field. Yellow-crested is the only one of the three showing a strong yellow or yellow-orange suffusion on the ear-coverts, and this feature alone should be sufficient to separate it from the two similar species if encountered in captivity. However, some individuals, particularly of the races *abbotti* and *parvula*, may have only a faint pale yellow wash on the ear-coverts (the two larger races of Sulphur-crested, *C. g. galerita* and *C. g. fitzroyi*, can also both show slight yellow suffusion on the ear-coverts). If in doubt, the maximum wing measure for *abbotti* (the larger of the two) is 273, and the minimum for the two larger races of Sulphur-crested is 295. The two smaller races of Sulphur-crested Cockatoo, like Blue-eyed Cockatoo, have prominent bright blue eye-rings and should pose no problem. Yellow-crested Cockatoo is polytypic, the distinctive Sumba race showing an orange, not yellow crest. Flight similar to Sulphur-crested Cockatoo with shallow fast wingbeats interspersed by glides.

VOICE A harsh screech *kek-kek-kek*, less raucous than Sulphur-crested Cockatoo.

Yellow crested Cockatoo

DISTRIBUTION AND STATUS Confined to Indonesia where it occurs in the lowlands of Sulawesi (actually or virtually extinct in the north), on islands in the Flores Sea, in Nusa Tenggara and on the isolated Masalembu islands in the Java Sea. It is introduced in Singapore and Hong Kong. The species is found in both forested and cultivated areas and is scarce throughout its range. The total world population is thought to be less than 40,000 and declining. Although populations of the nominate race and of *parvula* may still be close to 10,000, the Sumba race has a population estimated at between 800 and 7,200 individuals only, having declined by 80% between 1986 and 1989, while the distinctive large race *abbotti* is now represented by just nine individuals in the wild. Although habitat loss is clearly a factor in Sumba, where distribution appears tied to the extent of the original forest only around 15% of the original forest remains), trade is the main threat to the species as a whole. Trade data show that nearly 100,000 birds were exported in the years 1980-1992. The export of the Sumba race was banned in 1992 by the local authorities, and 26 birds were confiscated in the first enforcement incident in September of that year. There are probably at least 50 individuals of each subspecies in

public collections and more than 2,000 of each in private aviculture, although figures for *abbotti* are unknown. ENDANGERED.

ECOLOGY Inhabits forest edge, woodland, farmland, coconut palms, semi-arid areas and forest up to 800m (locally to 1,200m). Yellow-crested Cockatoos are usually encountered in pairs or small groups of up to ten individuals, although larger flocks may gather to feed in fruiting trees. Groups may also associate with Eclectus Parrots (111). The birds tend to be noisy and conspicuous, but can be difficult to detect when moving quietly in the canopy, and are most often seen in flight. Groups leaving their roosting sites in montane forest frequently move to foraging areas at lower altitudes which include cultivated fields. Pairs may wheel conspicuously above the forest searching for fruiting trees, and when they come to rest, may allow a reasonably close approach. The crest is usually erected when a bird lands, or when an individual is calling from a perch. Like most cockatoos they enjoy rain-bathing. Yellow-crested Cockatoos will feed in trees or on the ground. Food items include seeds, crops such as maize *Zea mays,* fruit, berries, buds, flowers and nuts (including quite large coconuts *Cocos nucifera*). Specimens have been collected on Buton in breeding condition in Sep and Oct, although in Nusa Tenggara breeding occurs in Apr and May. Up to three white eggs are laid in a tree-hollow, and incubation lasts about 28 days with both parents taking part. The young fledge in around 10 weeks and are dependent on the parents for a further two months or so.

DESCRIPTION Long, thin, forward-curving erectile crest yellow, extending beyond nape in short upward sweep when folded. Forecrown and leading feathers of crest white. Rest of plumage white, except for yellow suffusion on ear-coverts, underwing and innerwebs of undertail-coverts. Feather-bases on neck and underparts yellowish, some birds showing a slight yellow cast, particularly on breast and belly. **Bare parts**: Bill blackish; eye ring pale bluish-white; iris dark brown; legs grey.

SEX/AGE Female like male but with reddish iris and slightly smaller bill. Young birds of both sexes show a dark brownish-grey iris, but females begin to acquire the reddish coloration during the first year. The bill and feet of immatures are also lighter.

MEASUREMENTS Wing 211-245; tail 98-115; bill 29-39; tarsus 21-25.

GEOGRAPHICAL VARIATION Four races. Two previously recognised subspecies, *djampeana* and *occidentalis*, were based on bill size and are discounted, as irregular size variation is common in island cockatoos.

   C. s. sulphurea (Sulawesi patchily distributed below 500m – and on islands in the Flores Sea including Muna, Buton, Tukangbesi, Salayar, Kayuadi, Tanahjampea, Kalao, Bonerate, Kalaotoa and Madu; this race is also introduced in Singapore)

   C. s. parvula (Nusa Tenggara Islands including Sumbawa, Komodo – where still relatively common – Rinca, Flores, Pantar, Alor, Timor and adjacent Semau; records from Bali and Java probably refer to escapes, but it was at least formerly known from both Lombok and Nusa Penida off the south-east coast of Bali, so some Bali/Java records may have involved wild birds) Similar to nominate but paler yellow ear-coverts and less yellow on feathers of underparts. Bill size in this race increases clinally westward.

C. s. abbotti (Masalembu islands in the Java Sea, where rare with just 8-10 birds located during a 1993 survey) Similar to *parvula* but larger (wing 258-273).

C. s. citrinocristata (Sumba, where it is best looked for in remnant forest around Lewa, or in the east of the island where it may still be locally common; an expedition from Manchester Metropolitan University found it common in remaining forest areas in 1990, with the largest party, a group of five birds, found in primary forest near Tabundung) Slightly larger than nominate with an orange crest and yellow-orange ear-coverts. Further research may provide grounds for upgrading this race to specific status.

REFERENCES Andrew (1992), Arndt (1992), Collar & Andrew (1988), Collar *et al.* (1994), Forshaw (1989), Hoppe (1986), Inskipp *et al.* (1988), P. Jepson *in litt.* (1997), Jones & Banjaransari (1990), Lambert *et al.* (1993), Lodge (1991), Long (1981), Low (1980), MacKinnon (1988), Mason & Jarvis (1989), Peters (1961), Sibley & Monroe (1990), White & Bruce (1986).

---

65   SULPHUR-CRESTED COCKATOO
Cacatua galerita   Plate 14

Other names: Greater Sulphur-crested Cockatoo, White Cockatoo (also commonly used for *C. alba*)

IDENTIFICATION 38-51cm. A large, mainly white cockatoo with a striking erectile yellow crest, a yellow suffusion on the underside of the wings and tail, and an extremely loud screeching call; eye-ring is pale blue or white depending on race, and Australian birds show a slight yellowish wash on ear-coverts. This is the more widespread of the two 'yellow-crested' cockatoos, and is more commonly encountered in captivity. In Australia and the Trans-Fly region of New Guinea the smaller corellas can pose an identification problem at a distance, but the combination of yellow crest and blackish, not whitish, bill of Sulphur-crested Cockatoo is distinctive. Other, non-psittacine species such as egrets *Egretta* and the white phase of the Grey Goshawk *Accipiter novaehollandiae* may also be confusable at a distance. Similar to allopatric Yellow-crested Cockatoo (64), which see for separation. The two smaller subspecies of Sulphur-crested Cockatoo have blue periophthalmic rings and appear similar to Blue-eyed Cockatoo (66), which in the wild is confined to New Britain. Blue-eyed Cockatoo has a very different head-shape to Sulphur-crested, the crest being backward, not forward-curving, and the crest feathers being blunter-ended (see plate). The flight of Sulphur-crested Cockatoo looks erratic and slightly laboured, with rapid shallow wingbeats interspersed with glides on stiff wings. In flight, also note the broad rounded wings and short square tail.

VOICE A raucous, ear-splitting, creaky screech ending with a slight upward or downward inflection *ah-yai-yah* or *kai-yah!*, also a disyllabic whistling *scraw-leek*, the first note being harsher. In alarm, a series of harsh gut02ural screeches *raaa!*, and shrill squawks. Calls may be given singly or in rapid succession from a perch. Perched birds can also produce a low murmuring. Young birds produce a quiet high-pitched whine, and a grating creaky call. The call can be confused with Eclectus Parrot (111), but is unlike the high-pitched quavering calls of the corellas. The call of *triton* is said to be softer than that of the nominate race.

Sulphur-crested Cockatoo

DISTRIBUTION AND STATUS Occurs from the eastern Moluccas and W Papuan islands, through Irian Jaya and Papua New Guinea to northern and eastern Australia. In Maluku province, Indonesia, the species's wild status is uncertain: in the eastern Moluccas (Aru Islands) it occurs naturally, but other island populations may be feral. It has been recorded on Ambon (probably escapes), Bacan, Warmar, Gorong and Manawoka to the east of Seram (probably feral), the Kai Islands (introduced Kai Kecil 1980), and the Aru Islands (Pulau Kobroor, Pulau Baun). In Irian Jaya, the species is widely distributed on the mainland, and is also found in the W Papuan islands (Gebe, Waigeo, Salawati, Misool), and on islands in Geelvink Bay including Biak and Yapen. Although absent from the central mountainous belt of New Guinea above about 1,500m, the species has been recorded as high as 2,400m in the east. In Papua New Guinea found widely below about 1,000m on the mainland, and in the Trobriand, D'Entrecasteaux and Louisiade groups, including Goodenough, Normanby, Fergusson, Woodlark, Misima, Tagula and Rossel Islands. In Australia, the species is tied to the high-rainfall coastal belt, largely replacing the inland-ranging Pink Cockatoo (63). It extends from north-east Western Australia in the northern Kimberleys (Prince Regent River Reserve, Drysdale River National Park) and offshore islands, inland to the Fitzroy and Behn Rivers. It then ranges through the top end of Northern Territory north to the Cobourg Peninsula and on offshore islands including Groote Eylandt, and inland to Victoria River Downs and the upper reaches of the Roper and McArthur Rivers. It spreads into north-west Queensland around the Nicholson River region, and extends north through the Cape York Peninsula and occurs on wooded offshore islands, e.g. in the Torres Strait and Cumberland Group. In Queensland, it ranges inland as far as Mount Isa and Cloncurry, Richmond and Hughenden, Barcaldine and Blackall, Cunnamulla, Quilpie and the upper Bulloo River. The species is less common in the highlands (mainly to 1,000m, upper limit 1,500m) and more arid areas, and in the populated south-east region (Brisbane, Stanthorpe), except for the north Darling Downs area (Millmerran, and particularly around Chinchilla where it may now be increasing). In New South Wales, it occurs east of the Great

Dividing Range, and extends west to the Darling River although very thinly distributed in the central-western region (recorded from Cobar, although possibly escapes). It is also found along the Murray-Darling corridor extending up to 30 miles either side of the timber-fringe. The species is increasing as a winter visitor to urban districts of Sydney and Canberra (found on the lawns around Parliament House). In Victoria, it is widely distributed but rare around Gippsland in the extreme east (occasional to Genoa River flats), and in drier mallee areas. It also spills over into easternmost South Australia where it ranges along the Murray River from Morgan to the Victoria border, south into the Naracoorte district, and is scattered through the Mount Lofty Ranges. Its range extends west as far as the St Vincent Gulf and Kangaroo Island, and it occurs north to Wilmington and Cradock. There are no recent records from the Eyre Peninsula. The species was introduced to south-west Australia prior to 1935 and now occurs around Perth and Pinjarra. It occurs in Tasmania but is absent from the eastern forests and is found mainly in central-western and southern districts. It is now only occasional on King Island (possibly escaped birds), having become extinct around 1920 (not recorded from Flinders Island). The New Zealand population of a few hundred individuals is concentrated in the limestone country between the lower Waikato and Raglan Rivers, and in the watersheds of the Turakina and Rangitaiki Rivers. There is also a small colony in Wainuiomata Valley, Wellington. Although the populations are all thought to be introduced, the record of an exhausted bird on Kaipara Head after strong westerlies, points to the possibility that genuine vagrants may occur. Also introduced (and increasing) in the Palau Islands (Pacific) after World War II, where it is found in the 'Rock Islands' from Koror to Fil Malk (*C. g. triton*). In Indonesia, New Guinea and the Cape York Peninsula, occurs mainly in rainforest, but in eastern and north-western Australia occurs in a wide range of open habitats and riverine woodland. Generally common. In parts of Australia abundant and increasing. World population in excess of 500,000, stable and safe. May be affected by hunting for plumes in parts of New Guinea where a number of reports suggest that there may have been recent declines around inhabited areas. Despite protection it is still trapped for the pet trade in Indonesia (826 individuals confiscated in 1981 including one consignment of 500). Permits to control birds can be obtained in Australia; they are unprotected around Perth and in New South Wales. Common in captivity.

ECOLOGY Chiefly sedentary, but local movements have been recorded (between coastal Australian islands, to urban areas in winter, and during food shortages). Faithful to roosting sites. The habitat requirements of the species vary according to region. In New Guinea, it is mainly tied to the extent of forest, in Australia it occurs in a wide range of habitats from forest (including paperbark *Melaleuca*) to second growth, woodland (including swamp and riverine), mangroves, open country, agricultural land (including ricefields and palm plantations), savanna, mallee and suburban areas. It mostly occurs below 1,000m, but reaches 1,500m in some parts of Australia and 2,400m in eastern Papua New Guinea. Sulphur-crested Cockatoos will feed both in trees and on the ground. In Australia, large flocks may gather to forage on the seeds of grasses and herbs as well as on sprouting wheat, maize and bagged grain. These wary flocks employ a sentinel warning system in which one or more frequently changed lookouts raises the alarm with resounding screeches if danger looms. The crest is also raised in alarm. The species can do considerable damage to crops, but also feeds on harmful weeds such as cotton thistle *Onopordum acanthium*. Other foods include roots, rhizomes, nuts, berries including hawthorn *Crataegus monogyna*, flowers, corms, blossoms and insect larvae. Food is held in the foot and attacked with the powerful bill. The species is noisy and conspicuous at regular roosts at dusk and for a time after sunset, but is most active immediately after dawn. In the morning, birds leave roosts, drink, and move to feeding areas. They may fly at a considerable height when travelling. In Australia, large flocks of up to 2,000 individuals may gather to feed on the ground. Elsewhere smaller groups of up to a dozen are more frequently encountered. During the hottest part of the day the birds remain in trees, lazily stripping bark or breaking twigs. In Papua New Guinea, birds can be seen soaring hawk-like above the canopy, and spiralling down to gather in noisy groups in an emergent or dead tree. Sulphur-crested Cockatoos will mob raptors and have been recorded dropping leafy twigs onto a pair of Bat Hawks *Macheiramphus alcinus*. In Australia, the species associates with corellas and individuals may spread inland with corella flocks. During the breeding season, birds consort in pairs. During courtship, the male bobs and sways his head in a figure eight, utters a soft chattering and raises his crest. Mutual preening and bill touching are common. In Australia, the breeding season is between May and Aug in the north, and between Aug and Jan in the south. In New Guinea, breeding has been recorded in all months except Apr, but most records come from the period between May and Dec. The nest is in a natural tree-hollow 3-30m above ground. In Australia, a tall eucalypt near water is often chosen, although birds also nest in cavities in the limestone cliffs along the Murray River (eggs laid on sand). There is also a record from New Zealand of a nest on hay bales in a barn. Birds may nest communally. Adults usually leave the nesting area quietly at the sight of a predator. Usually, three white eggs are laid on decayed debris at the bottom of the nesting hollow, and both parents incubate for around 30 days in total. The yellow-downed young fledge in around 60 weeks, returning to roost in the nest-hollow for a further two weeks or so.

DESCRIPTION Plumage mainly white except for extensive sulphur-yellow suffusion on innerwebs of flight and tail feathers, and long, yellow, forward-curving erectile crest. Feathers of forecrown and above eye white, folded crest showing only as an upward-curving yellow protrusion from nape. Bases of feathers around cheeks and throat also yellowish; ear-coverts usually suffused yellow, **Bare parts**: Bill blackish; eye-ring white; iris dark brown, almost black; legs dark grey.

SEX/AGE Female shows a dark red, not dark brown-black, iris. Immatures are similar to adults but very young birds show faint grey markings on crown, mantle and wings. Young birds also have a browner iris.

MEASUREMENTS Wing 295-391; tail 200-236; bill 34-50; tarsus 30-35.

GEOGRAPHICAL VARIATION Four races. Size is generally variable within each population.

    C. g. gulerita (Australia east of the Nicholson River on the Gulf of Carpentaria; introduced in New Zealand)
    C. g. fitzroyi (Australia west of the Nicholson River on

the Gulf of Carpentaria, where a specimen showing characters intermediate between *fitzroyi* and *galerita* was collected) From nominate by its pale blue eye-ring and very lightly suffused yellow ear-coverts. The bill is also broader than that of the nominate.

C. g. triton (Papua New Guinea and on outlying islands, west to the W Papuan islands; also feral on some islands in the Moluccas and introduced in the Palau Islands) Smaller than nominate (wing 261-347), but larger-crested with broader, more rounded feathers. Bright pale blue eye-ring.

C. g. eleonora (Aru and Kai Islands) Smaller than the nominate (wing 261-292), and smaller-billed than *t-riton*. Bright pale blue eye-ring.

REFERENCES Andrew (1992), Beehler *et al.* (1986), Blakers *et al.* (1984), Cayley & Lendon (1973), Coates (1985), Diamond (1972), Diefenbach (1982), Eastman & Hunt (1966), Falla *et al.* (1981), Forshaw (1981, 1989), Lambert *et al.* (1993), LeCroy *et al.* (1984), Lodge (1991), Long (1981), Low (1980), Milton (1988), Peters (1961), Pizzey & Doyle (1983), Pratt *et al.* (1987), Rand & Gilliard (1967), Schodde & Tidemann (1988), Sibley & Monroe (1990), Simpson & Day (1984), Slater (1979, 1989), Smiet (1985), Storr & Johnstone (1979), Tavistock (1929), Trounson & Trounson (1987), White & Bruce (1986).

---

66 BLUE-EYED COCKATOO
Cacatua ophthalmica   Plate 14

Other names: None, but note that the name Blue-eyed Cockatoo is also sometimes applied to Little Corella (71)

IDENTIFICATION 44-50cm. A stocky white cockatoo with a rounded, backward-curving white and yellow crest, confined to New Britain and New Ireland. Superficially very similar to and once regarded as a race of Sulphur-crested Cockatoo (65), but the shape of the crest feathers and consequently the head-shape are quite different and more reminiscent of Salmon-crested Cockatoo (67) than of *galerita* (see description below). When perched the yellow in the crest is less obvious than in either of the two preceding species. There are no confusion species in the wild. Blue-eyed Cockatoo, as its name implies, has a prominent bright blue eye-ring which distinguishes it from captive Yellow-crested (64) and nominate Sulphur-crested Cockatoos. Three subspecies of Sulphur-crested Cockatoo also show blue eye-rings (*fitzroyi*, *triton* and *eleonora*), but the distinctive head-shape of Blue-eyed will separate this species easily on close examination (see plate); also, the eye-ring is brighter blue than that of *triton*. Little Corella also has a blue eye-ring but is smaller, with a whitish bill and no yellow in the crest. The flight of Blue-eyed Cockatoo is fluttering, interspersed with glides, and the yellow underwing and undertail are obvious.

VOICE When perched a series of screams ending with a downward inflection. In flight, a series of 'gull-like' notes each ending in an upslur. The call is higher-pitched, more nasal and less rasping than that of Sulphur-crested Cockatoo.

DISTRIBUTION AND STATUS Endemic to New Britain and New Ireland, Bismarck Archipelago, Papua New Guinea. Occurs in forest and partly cleared areas from the lowlands to 1,000m. Regarded as fairly common throughout most of its range but locally it may be scarce.

The world population is unknown, as is the population trend. Given the declines of other members of the genus as a result of trade, and the fragility of forest habitats in the region, it should probably be considered vulnerable until surveys have been carried out. Small numbers in captivity.

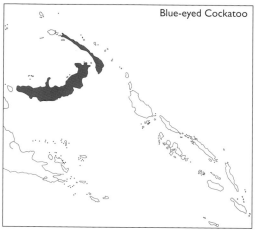
Blue-eyed Cockatoo

ECOLOGY Occurs in forest and partly cleared areas, commonest in the lowlands and rare above 900m. Encountered singly, in pairs or small parties of up to 20 birds. Conspicuous, birds often flying over the canopy screeching noisily, and may gather in groups at dusk before going to roost. Behaviour little known, but presumably similar to the closely related Sulphur-crested Cockatoo. Food is seeds, nuts, berries and fruit (particularly figs *Ficus*). The nest is in a tree-hollow, where two white eggs are laid. Incubation is shared between the sexes and lasts about 30 days.

DESCRIPTION Plumage mostly white with a backward-curving yellow crest of shorter, broader, more rounded feathers than in Sulphur-crested Cockatoo. Ear-coverts and around throat often suffused yellow; underwing and undertail suffused yellow on innerwebs. **Bare parts**: Bill greyish-black; prominent naked periophthalmic ring bright blue; iris dark brown; legs black.

SEX/AGE Female from male by reddish, not brown, iris. Immatures similar to adults.

MEASUREMENTS Wing 273-316; tail 149-179; bill 37-45; tarsus 29-33.

GEOGRAPHICAL VARIATION None.

REFERENCES BirdLife (1993), Bishop & Broome (1980), Coates (1985), Diefenbach (1982), Forshaw (1989), Hartert (1926), Lambert *et al.* (1993), Lodge (1991), Low (1980), Peters (1961), Sibley & Monroe (1990), Tavistock (1929), Wilkinson (1993).

---

67 SALMON-CRESTED COCKATOO
Cacatua moluccensis   Plate 15

Other names: Moluccan Cockatoo, Pink-crested Cockatoo, Rose-crested Cockatoo

IDENTIFICATION 40-50cm. A large-headed, large-billed, buffle-headed and generally pinkish-white cockatoo, confined to remaining forest on Seram and Ambon;

commonly encountered in captivity. The head-shape is distinctive, with its shaggy backward-curving crest. The combination of reddish-pink central crest feathers, large black bill, and yellowish underwing suffusion makes this a very distinctive species, although the plumage is variable (pink to whitish-pink) and the crests of some individuals are darker pink). Birds have a habit of ruffling up their feathers, giving them a 'cuddly' look. There are no confusion species in the wild. Although it also shows pink in the plumage, the Pink Cockatoo (63) has an entirely different crest-shape and -colour, and is suffused bright pink on the underparts and underwings. It is unlikely that any other species could be mistaken for Moluccan Cockatoo in captivity (see plate in doubt). Its flight is described as weak, fluttering and interspersed by glides; the short tail is particulary obvious when seen in flight from below.

VOICE A very loud, quavering, eerie, wailing cry *eearrsh*, which can be heard from a distance of around 1km. Also a shrill screech. Birds call most in the evening from high perches and are also vocal in flight.

Salmon-crested Cockatoo

DISTRIBUTION AND STATUS Endemic to Seram and adjacent islands, Maluku province, Indonesia, where it has been the subject of a number of recent studies, and the following list gives the areas where birds have been encountered: in the Kineke area, in Manusela National Park, central Seram (covers 1,800km², roughly 11% of the island), near Milinane, near Wahai, Loki, Wae Tana, Rumasokat, Sawai, on Gunung Binaia and Gunung Kobipoto (not located on either in 1990), Wasa, Roho, Kanekeh, Solemena, Solea Way Tualarang, Solea, the Way Mual, and also recorded in dry scrubby forest between Solea and Air Besar. Moluccan Cockatoos also occur on the islands of Haruku, Saparua and Ambon. It was still regarded as locally common in 1970, but the following decade saw a dramatic decline. Annual CITES records showed an average of more than 5,000 birds per year (recorded as definitely originating in Indonesia) entering importing countries between 1981 and 1985. These figures take no account of internal trade in Indonesia, local capture for pets, imports into non-CITES countries, or unrecorded international trade. In 1987, the Directorate General of Forest Protection and Nature Conservation (PHPA) banned exports from Seram, and in 1989 the species was included on CITES Appendix I. However, in 1990, despite the ban, Moluccan Cockatoos were still found in bird markets in both Ambon and Jakarta. The toll taken by trade in central Seram was witnessed by an Operation Raleigh team in 1987, who found the species to be rare, and absent from large tracts of suitable habitat, and in 1989, during 40 days of field-work, the same team found only 20 individual birds in prime habitat in Manusela National Park. Elsewhere on the island the situation is far better, however, and the world population is thought still to be above 8,000. VULNERABLE.

ECOLOGY The species occurs in lowland forest between 100m-1,200m (rare above 900m). Highest densities occur in undisturbed and disturbed primary lowland forest with large trees, also in open canopy forest with low vegetation, and in riverine forest. Rare in non-forested areas, less frequent in selectively logged forest, but despite trapping pressure, still occurs in mature lowland forest near settlements. Lower densities in transition and submontane forest, in second growth, degraded forest and on the edges of cultivated areas; also previously occurred in coastal areas. The birds attend regular roosts, which are easily located due to the noise they make. Trappers capture them there either with nylon fishing line snares laid out on branches or by dazzling them; they also use tame decoys to lure wild birds into traps, and trace adults to their nesting sites so the young can be taken. Once caught, trapped birds are taken to the coast, sold, and transported to Ambon on boats in packed cages. During the breeding season, birds are encountered singly or in pairs; at other times they are found in groups of up to 16 birds, although the recent population decline in Seram appears to have resulted in a dramatic reduction in the size of non-breeding flocks. The species is generally shy and flies off calling when disturbed. The birds are most active early morning and late afternoon, calling loudly when leaving and returning to roost. They can be found moving slowly but noisily through the canopy in the early morning, but are seldom seen or heard during the heat of the day. Moluccan Cockatoos feed on nuts, including young coconuts *Cocos nucifera* which they attack to get at the soft pulp, seeds and berries, as well as insects and their larvae. During display, which can last up to 20 minutes, the male and female perch in the top of an emergent or dead forest tree, raising and lowering their crests, calling loudly, breaking twigs, and making short weak fluttering flights. Breeding begins in Jul and Aug (although a pair were noted at a nesting hole in May, so season may be variable). The nest is in a high hollow in a mature tree. The cavity is lined with wood chips, two white eggs are laid, and the 28-day incubation is shared by both parents. The yellow-downed young may fledge as late as Oct; young birds take c. 4-5 years to reach maturity.

DESCRIPTION Generally pinkish-white throughout. Broad, rounded feathers of crown form long, shaggy, backward-curving erectile crest; pinkish-white on forecrown and above eye, deep rose-pink and sometimes appearing orange on rear-crown. Stronger pink tinge to breast and undertail-coverts. Primaries emarginated; secondaries unusually long; flight feathers suffused yellow on inner-webs, and greater underwing-coverts salmon-pink or orange-pink. Undertail suffused yellow and pinkish on innerwebs. **Bare parts**: Bill blackish grey; eye-ring pale bluish-white; iris virtually black; legs grey.

SEX/AGE Female has dark brown, not black iris. Immature resembles adult but very young birds have a dark grey iris.

MEASUREMENTS Wing 288-328; tail 159-189; bill 42-54; tarsus 33-35.

GEOGRAPHICAL VARIATION None.

REFERENCES Bates & Busenbark (1969), BirdLife (1993), Bowler (1988), Bowler & Taylor (1989), Collar (1989), Collar *et al.* (1994), Diefenbach (1982), Field (1992), Forshaw (1989), Gee (1993), Hoppe (1986), Lambert *et al.* (1993), Lodge (1991), Low (1980), Marsden (1992), G. Nilsson *in litt.* (1990), Peters (1961), Poulsen & Jepson (1996), Sibley & Monroe (1990), Smiet (1985), Tavistock (1929), Taylor (1990), White & Bruce (1986).

---

68   WHITE COCKATOO
Cacatua alba   Plate 15

Other names: Great White Cockatoo, White-crested Cockatoo, Umbrella Cockatoo

IDENTIFICATION 46cm. A large white cockatoo with a fan-shaped erectile crest of broad, blunt-ended feathers. Like other members of the genus, shows some yellow suffusion on the underwing and undertail. Found only on Halmahera and on a few surrounding islands in the North Moluccas, where there are no confusion species; also commonly encountered in captivity. The only large cockatoo with an entirely white crest. Head-shape when crest is relaxed closest to Salmon-crested Cockatoo (67), but White is sleeker, the crest colour, and its shape when erect, are different (see plate), and the white, not pinkish, plumage separate this species.

VOICE A loud grating screech; a hissing sound in alarm.

White Cockatoo

DISTRIBUTION AND STATUS Endemic to the North Moluccas, Maluku province, Indonesia. Occurs on Halmahera, Bacan, Ternate, Kasiruta, Tidore, Mandioli and Obi (Obi birds are probably either escapes or from the now extinct feral population on nearby Bisa). The world population is unknown but a range of 50,000-200,000 is the most recent estimate, and even this may be too low. White Cockatoo is certainly more numerous than Moluccan, but although some authorities suggest it is less popular in trade, CITES records show that similar or greater numbers have been exported from Indonesia in recent years. Birds are trapped using decoys to lure them into snares. CITES figures show that exports exceeded quotas by large amounts as early as 1984, when 12,193 were recorded in international trade (against a quota of 10,250). In addition to the birds actually recorded, 7-10% of birds die prior to export, and some are traded internally. Local people on Bacan already say that numbers have been reduced by legal trapping. Observations at Domato, Halmahera, in 1986 and 1987 indicated that there too the population may have undergone a decline, although the birds may simply have moved from the region. The longevity of the species may be masking serious problems of low recruitment. Further studies are clearly needed to understand fully its status in the wild. Field surveys from Oct 1991 to Feb 1992 suggested that the catch quota needed to be reduced to 1,710 birds from the minimum estimated take of 5,120 birds for 1991. White Cockatoos are also shot for food, and although they seem able to tolerate degraded habitats, the removal of large trees required for nesting is a further problem. Common in captivity. VULNERABLE.

ECOLOGY Occurs in lowland and hill forest up to 600m. Unlike the Moluccan Cockatoo, this species seems more able to cope with secondary growth, and in fact some observers suggest that this is its preferred habitat. Birds have been noted particularly around clearings and rivers, in degraded forest, along forest edge, in tall trees on cleared land, and even in patches of trees in agricultural land over 1km from the forest. Birds spend most of their time in the canopy, and can be seen in pairs or small parties flying above the tree-tops or perched in emergent trees. They may however forage in lower storeys where they are less conspicuous. The species is perhaps most obvious at dusk when groups of up to 50 birds may gather before roosting in large trees. The crest is raised in alarm. Feeds on seeds, fruit, nuts and berries. White Cockatoos choose a hollow in a tall tree where their two eggs are laid. The species is thought to nest in Apr. Incubation lasts 30 days and both parents brood. The young may remain in the nest for as long as 2-3 months.

DESCRIPTION Plumage entirely white except for distinct yellow suffusion on underwing and base of innerwebs on underside of tail. Backward-curving crest made up of broad, round-ended feathers and fan-shaped when fully erect. **Bare parts**: Bill greyish-black; eye-ring pale bluish-white; iris dark brown; legs grey.

SEX/AGE The female is separable from the male by its reddish, not dark brown iris. Immature birds are similar to adults.

MEASUREMENTS Wing 252-312, tail 120-168, bill 34-45, tarsus 26-33.

GEOGRAPHICAL VARIATION None.

REFERENCES BirdLife (1993), Bräutigam & Humphreys

(1992), Collar (1989), Collar & Andrew (1988), Forshaw (1989), Gee (1993), Inskipp *et al.* (1988), Lambert (1993a,b), Lambert & Yong (1989), Lambert *et al.* (1993), Lodge (1991), Milton (1988), Peters (1961), Sibley & Monroe (1990), Smiet (1985), White & Bruce (1986).

69 PHILIPPINE COCKATOO
Cacatua haematuropygia Plate 15

Other names: Red-vented Cockatoo

IDENTIFICATION 31cm. A small white cockatoo with crest, whitish bill, red undertail-coverts (tipped white), and a deep yellow suffusion beneath the tail. The species is monotypic, males and females are alike except for the eye-colour, and immatures are similar to adults. The only cockatoo native to the Philippines, but escaped cockatoos of other species may occur. Philippine Cockatoo is extremely rare and is best looked for in western districts of Palawan where there are expanses of coastal mangrove. In captivity, superficially similar to the Australian corellas and to Ducorps's Cockatoo (74), but the red undertail-coverts with whitish shafts and tips are diagnostic of this species. The flight is swift and direct with rapid wingbeats. These cockatoos are also capable of aerobatic weaving and darting to avoid capture by raptors.

VOICE A loud, harsh croaking or rasping call with two syllables.

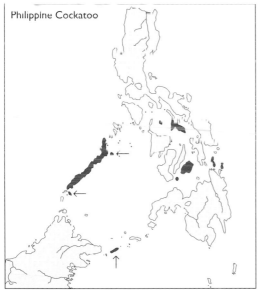

Philippine Cockatoo

DISTRIBUTION AND STATUS Confined to the Philippines, where it was once widespread and fairly common. The species has undergone a dramatic decline in recent years and must now be considered the Philippines' most threatened bird next to the Philippine Eagle *Pithecophaga jefferyi*. Although survey work is hampered by the existence of insurgent enclaves in some areas where cockatoos may still occur, recent information suggests that the species is now restricted to the following islands (where its occurrence is certain, figures are given in parentheses): Palawan, particularly St Paul's Subterranean National Park,

Napsan Road, P.C.M.C. Road, around Port Barton, Babuyan River catchment area, and including the adjacent islands of Bugsuk, Bancalan, Pandanan and south-west Dumaran (in total between 800 and 3,000 birds); Siargao (still around 50-100 birds in 1991); Mindanao, particularly the Diwata Range and Davao (100-300 birds total); Sibuyan (probably 100-300 birds); Dinagat (50-100 birds); Masbate (50-100, with birds still present in 1993); Tawitawi in the Sulu Archipelago, and probably Samar. Also possibly on Cebu (though not found in 1985 search), Leyte (not found in 1985), S Luzon (a few seen in 1988 but apparently absent from suitable habitat in the north), and Bohol (up to 12 birds); at least one pair also survives on Siquijor and a few reputedly do so on Mindoro. The population is declining through trade, habitat loss, and now possibly also because of an outbreak of psittacine beak and feather disease. The species was described as common in 1946, and was probably still widespread until the 1970s. Today this highly endangered cockatoo is absent from as much as 98% of its former range, and according to one recent report, even on Palawan, its last remaining stronghold, all the accessible nest-holes are known and regularly robbed. Roosting sites are also known, and are targets for trappers. The maximum world population estimate is presently 4,000. CITES Appendix I. There are around 20 in zoos and more than 300 in private aviculture. CRITICAL.

ECOLOGY Sedentary. The species is probably heavily dependent on coastal mangrove forest, but is also found in lowland forest, lightly degraded montane forest, open logged forest, along forest edge, and farmland when raiding ripening crops such as maize. Philippine Cockatoos are noisy and fairly conspicuous, particularly when gathering in groups to feed, or when roosting at dusk. The birds probably form larger groups outside the breeding season, and a party of 23 was recorded roosting in a coconut plantation in late Oct: the birds flew in from coastal mangroves between five and six in the evening in groups of 1-5, and at dawn they headed back in one large group. A similar observation recorded 17 roosting in a dead tree, also on the coast. Birds have been encountered flying in groups of 6-12 birds, calling constantly (which also helps to locate them even when feeding in dense vegetation). They feed on seeds, fruit (noted in isolated fruiting trees in farmland), nuts and berries. Breeding in between Feb and Jun, and a high hole in the limb of a (sometimes isolated) dead tree is a preferred site.

DESCRIPTION Mainly white throughout, with shortish, backward-curving, semi-erectile crest (base of crest feathers yellowish-pink). Ear-coverts and lores washed pinkish-yellow. Underwing suffused yellow on innerwebs of flight feathers and slightly so on greater coverts. Undertail-coverts red with white shafts and tips. Undertail strongly suffused rich yellow on innerwebs. **Bare parts**: Bill greyish-white; eye-ring greyish-white; iris black-brown; legs grey-black.

SEX/AGE Female iris tinted reddish. Immature like adult but initially with greyer and, later, browner iris.

MEASUREMENTS Wing 201-231; tail 100-110; bill 23-29; tarsus 22-24.

GEOGRAPHICAL VARIATION None.

REFERENCES M. Boussekey *in litt.* (1991), Boussekey (1993), Collar & Andrew (1988), Collar *et al.* (1994), Dickinson *et al.* (1991), duPont (1971), duPont & Rabor (1973), Forshaw (1989), Harrap (1993), Lambert (1992),

Lambert *et al.* (1993), Low (1980), Sargeant (1992), Sibley & Monroe (1990), B.R. Tabaranza *in litt.* (1991).

70   TANIMBAR COCKATOO
Cacatua goffini   Plate 15

Other names: Tanimbar Corella, Goffin's Cockatoo

IDENTIFICATION 32cm. A small white cockatoo, with a bluish-white eye-ring, a pink spot on the lores, and a yellow suffusion on the underwing and undertail. Found on islands in the Tanimbar group where there are no confusion species, but introduced in the Kai group (Tual), where Sulphur-crested Cockatoo (65) might cause a problem if either species was only seen poorly in flight. Tanimbar Cockatoo is similar to Little Corella (71), Western Corella (72) and Ducorps's Cockatoo (74), but Long-billed Corella (73) shows extensive pink markings on the breast and is unlikely to present an identification problem; if encountered in captivity, Tanimbar can be separated from Ducorps's by its pink lores, while both Little and Western have a more extensive bare patch of skin around and below the eye, which is an obvious dark blue, not bluish-white as in Tanimbar.

VOICE A noisy scream. The young make a sound like a young Cockatiel (75), and a mewing note.

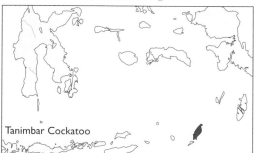

Tanimbar Cockatoo

DISTRIBUTION AND STATUS Endemic to Tanimbar and associated islands (Yamdena, Larat, Selaru), Maluku province, Indonesia. The species has also established a feral population in the Kai Islands (Tual). Although deforestation and export of the species began in the early 1970s, it was still said to be widespread on the main island of Yamdena, and also common on smaller outlying islands in the Tanimbar Group in 1981. Between 1983 and 1989, over 52,000 birds were recorded in international trade. For a species with such a limited world range, the level of trapping appeared to be unsustainable and it was added to CITES Appendix I in 1992. Nevertheless, fieldwork the following year found very high densities of birds in both forest and agricultural land, and resulted in a population estimate of over 200,000 birds. Although it is not popular as a pet within the Tanimbar group, birds may still be trapped by locals as a crop pest. Moderate numbers in captivity. NEAR-THREATENED.

ECOLOGY Occurs in coastal lowland forest, both primary and secondary, in woodland and in areas with scattered trees. Flocks also enter farmland to raid crops. Behaviour is little known. Birds have been recorded in flocks of up to 300 individuals. When alighting they tend to raise their crests, and they may be vocal at night. Other than its

preference for maize crops, food is unrecorded; breeding season is also unrecorded. In display the crest is raised and the birds strut about shrieking. Two to three eggs are laid in the nesting hollow, and incubation, which is shared by both birds, lasts about 30 days. The yellowish-downed chicks fledge about ten weeks after hatching, and parental feeding continues for a further few weeks.

DESCRIPTION White with distinct pink suffusion on lores and slight yellowish-pink tint to cheeks and ear-coverts. Bases to body-feathers pinkish, giving pinkish cast especially to breast and underparts. Underwing and undertail washed yellow on innerwebs. **Bare parts**: Bill greyish-white; periophthalmic ring bluish-white; iris brown-black; legs greyish.

SEX/AGE Female has redder iris than male. Immatures are like adults.

MEASUREMENTS Wing 210-238; tail 95-114; bill 27-33; tarsus 22-25.

GEOGRAPHICAL VARIATION None.

REFERENCES BirdLife (1993), Cahyadin (1996), Cahyadin *et al.* (1994), Collar (1989), Collar & Andrew (1988), Forshaw (1989), Inskipp *et al.* (1988), Lambert *et al.* (1993), Lodge (1991), Low (1980), Schulte (1975), Sibley & Monroe (1990), Smiet (1985), White & Bruce (1986).

71   LITTLE CORELLA
Cacatua sanguinea   Plate 15

Other names: Bare-eyed Cockatoo, Blood-stained Cockatoo, Short-billed Corella, Little Cockatoo, Blue-eyed Cockatoo (vernacular name for *C. ophthalmica*)

IDENTIFICATION 35-42cm. A medium-sized white cockatoo which occurs commonly in large flocks throughout much of northern and inland Australia. It has a short, triangular, erectile crest, pink lores, and a yellow suffusion beneath the wings and tail. In flight, it looks broad-winged and small-headed. The periophthalmic ring extends below the eye in a slight bulge, and its colour, shape and extent help separate this species from Tanimbar Cockatoo (70) (see plate). In parts of eastern South Australia and western Victoria, the ranges of Little Corella and Long-billed Corella (73) overlap slightly. Unlike Little, Long-billed shows a reddish-orange collar which is usually obvious at rest. In flight, Long-billed looks shorter-tailed and has less rounded wing-tips. The two species also differ in structure, with Little looking less stumpy and bull-headed. Little also has a considerably shorter upper mandible than both Long-billed and the other possible confusion species, Western Corella (72). Western is also larger than Little, and the two species are allopatric, their ranges being separated by the Great Sandy Desert in northern Western Australia. In flight, the larger Sulphur-crested Cockatoo (65), if seen well, can be distinguished by its heavy black bill and yellow crest (see range map). Little Corellas often form very large flocks which may travel long distances, sometimes in V-formation. In flight, the wingbeats are interspersed with periods of gliding. The species is known to have hybridised in the wild with Gang-gang Cockatoo (61) and Galah (62).

VOICE Contact call an often repeated, squeaky *wi-rup* or *wi-ri-rup*. When flocking birds are calling together, the sound has a querulous quality, a little like distant geese. There are also a variety of squeaky calls, some upwardly inflected. In alarm, a harsh *schaaair*, less raucous than the call of Sulphur-crested Cockatoo.

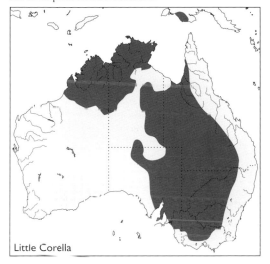

Little Corella

DISTRIBUTION AND STATUS Confined to Australia, southern Irian Jaya (Indonesia) and to southern Papua New Guinea. The species ranges from north-east Western Australia at the north-eastern limit of the Great Sandy Desert, through the Kimberley region (including Wyndham, Kununurra and the Prince Regent and Ord Rivers) and on some offshore islands (including the Buccaneer and Bonaparte archipelagos). It then spreads east into Northern Territory (south to the Gardiner Range). It is replaced in south-west Northern Territory by Pink Cockatoo (63), but ranges to Alice Springs in the south-central region (occasional). In the north it ranges through most of Arnhem Land and reaches some offshore islands (including Bathurst, Melville and Groote Eylandt). It is largely absent from the coast of the Gulf of Carpentaria, but found inland in the east through the Barkly Tableland and south to the Plenty River, with an isolated population on the western coast of the Cape York Peninsula between Normanton and Weipa, Queensland. It is widespread in south-west Queensland, ranging east to Richmond, Hughenden, Barcaldine and Charleville, but uncommon east of the Great Dividing Range, and occasional east to Townsville in the north and to the Darling Downs region (Kogan, Chinchilla, Jandowae) in the south. In New South Wales it is common in the west, ranging east to around Yanco and Rankin's Springs. In Victoria it is again concentrated in the west, ranging east to Geelong in the south (occasional) and to Koondrook on the New South Wales border in the north. It has been expanding in the Murray-Darling region since the early 1950s. In South Australia it is found mainly in the east, ranging north-west to Oodnadatta and the Lake Eyre basin. It is generally uncommon to the west of Spencer Gulf, and birds in the Gawler Ranges probably originate from escaped stock. Small populations of escapes have become established in Perth, Sydney and Melbourne. In southern New Guinea it ranges from around Kumbe (Kurik, Merauke) in extreme south-east Irian Jaya, across the Papuan border, through the Bensbach River region

and Morehead, as far as the lower Fly River The species is common to abundant through much of its range. The world population is thought to be in excess of 1,000,000 and increasing, particularly through a southward spread in South Australia and Victoria. Its increase is linked to the spread of agriculture and the availability of artificial water sources. Moderate numbers in captivity. In Australia the species is protected everywhere apart from South Australia.

ECOLOGY Sedentary, but the availability of food may concentrate post or non-breeding flocks in particular areas, or force them to move to less preferred habitats. Little Corellas breed in riverine woodland usually adjacent to perennial grasslands or agricultural areas. Outside the breeding season they may be found in a range of habitats including *Eucalyptus-Acacia* scrublands with short grass, open or lightly timbered grasslands, ricefields, sedge plains, mulga, mallee, *Callitris-Eucalyptus* woodland, semi-arid and monsoon woodland and shrubland, spinifex, saltbush *Atriplex*, mangrove, crop paddocks, roadsides, suburban areas and, particularly in New Guinea, ricefields. Outside the breeding season, huge noisy flocks of up to 70,000 birds range widely in search of food. They are strong fliers, roosting near water and taking an early-morning drink before moving to feeding grounds, often some distance away. They feed morning and afternoon, roost quietly stripping foliage from trees during the heat of the day, and at dusk return to drink and roost at established sites. Birds may indulge in 'playful' activities, rolling on their backs or hanging upside-down from wires. When feeding, flocks move along the ground in one direction with birds at the rear of the group constantly flying to the front to get at the richer pickings. They may also feed in trees and regularly use their foot to hold items which are then pulled apart with the bill, Little Corellas feed on seeds (e.g. double-gee *Emex australis*, Mitchell grass *Astrebla lappacea*, and paddy melons *Cucumis myriocarpus*), nuts, fruits, berries, flowers, roots, corms, buds, shoots, insects, wood-boring larvae and blossoms. In New Guinea, they sometimes feed alongside Sulphur-crested Cockatoos and Red-winged Parrots (120). In Australia they are most commonly found in company with Galahs. Occasionally individuals may join other flocks of cockatoos. During the breeding season, pairs break off from the non-breeding flocks of unpaired or young birds (perhaps only 20% of the flock nesting each year) and, once they have established a nest-site, remain nearby until their young have fledged. In Australia, breeding has been recorded in most months but generally appears to begin earlier in the north (May-Oct) than in the south-east (Aug-Dec). In Queensland, nesting has been recorded Dec-Apr, Jul-Oct and Feb-May. Nesting is said to be affected by climatic conditions, and to begin around three months after the end of the wet season in northern districts. Two or three broods are raised in some years. Whilst nesting, Little Corellas are quiet and secretive. Pair-bonding is strong and may be permanent. Pairs are also faithful to nest-sites, which tend to be in a high tree-hollow (3-10m above ground and c. 1m deep), often a eucalypt (e.g. *Eucalyptus camaldulensis*). Bark may be removed from the entrance to the hole and more than one site prepared. Birds have also nested in cliffs and termite mounds. Usually two to three white eggs are laid (can be from one to four) on a bed of decayed wood dust which is replaced each year, and this may lead to the hollow widening at the base and eventually being destroyed. Usually two yellow-downed chicks are raised, fledging in around nine weeks.

DESCRIPTION Head, including recumbent crest, white with concealed pinkish feather-bases; lores with pinkish wash. Upperparts and upperwing white, underwing with distinct yellow suffusion on innerwebs. Underparts and uppertail white; undertail washed yellow on innerwebs. **Bare parts**: Bill whitish-grey; periophthalmic ring greyish-blue; iris black-brown; legs grey.

SEX/AGE Sexes are alike including iris colour. Immatures show less extensive bare skin below eye, and in the nominate race it may also be whiter in young birds.

MEASUREMENTS Wing 260-313; tail 131-153; bill 30-36; tarsus 26-32.

GEOGRAPHICAL VARIATION Four races.

C. s. sanguinea (N Australia from Kimberleys to Arnhem Land, reaching east to the McArthur River, and inland to Top Springs, Wave Hill and the Pine Creek district; also found on some offshore islands)
C. s. normantoni (W Cape York Peninsula) Similar to nominate but smaller (wing 222-248). It is not certain whether birds on Mornington Island belong to this or to the nominate race.
C. s. transfreta (S New Guinea) Smaller than nominate (wing 224-255) with a brownish suffusion on underside of flight and tail feathers.
C. s. gymnopis (Widespread in much of C, E and SE Australia; may meet nominate in the north-west in the Gardiner range region) Shows more strongly marked pink lores, a slight yellow wash to the lower ear-coverts, stronger orange-pink concealed bases to the head, breast and flank feathers, and a darker blue eye-ring.

NOTE We prefer the name Little Corella to Sibley & Monroe's Little Cockatoo as it is already in wide use, and it indicates the close relationship of this to the other Australian corellas.

REFERENCES Beehler *et al.* (1986), Blakers *et al.* (1984), Cayley & Lendon (1973), Coates (1985), Eastman & Hunt (1966), Forshaw (1981, 1989), Lambert *et al.* (1993), Lodge (1991), Low (1980), Peters (1961), Pizzey & Doyle (1983), Schodde & Tidemann (1988), Sibley & Monroe (1990), Simpson & Day (1984), Slater (1989), Tavistock (1929), Trounson & Trounson (1987).

---

72 WESTERN CORELLA
Cacatua pastinator Plate 15

Other names: Western Long-billed Corella, Dampier's Cockatoo

IDENTIFICATION 39-45cm. Similar to Little Corella (71) in both plumage and structure except for its strongly elongated upper mandible and larger size. As well as lacking the orange-red breast-band, both Little and Western are longer-tailed than Long-billed Corellas (73) and have more rounded wings and the bulge on the lower part of the periophthalmic ring. Western shows more pink on the lores than the nominate race of Little, which edges into Western Australia in the Kimberley region. The two species are however separated by some 200km. The pink lore-markings of Western are similar to those shown by Little further east (*C. s. gymnopis*), but in the wild there is no real chance of confusion with either race, as the ranges

of the two do not overlap. In captivity young birds show shorter upper mandibles than adults and may look much like Little Corellas. Like the Long-billed Corella, this species spends much of its foraging time 'ploughing' the ground with its long bill, and consequently the head and underparts may carry clearly visible soil or vegetable stains.

VOICE Very similar to Little Corella. A trisyllabic chuckle, various soft quavering notes and a series of harsh shrieks in alarm.

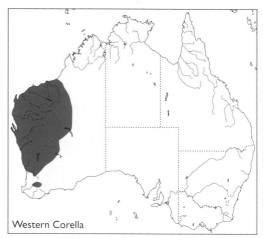
Western Corella

DISTRIBUTION AND STATUS Two disjunct populations are currently recognised, both confined to Western Australia. The nominate race (southern population), having undergone a period of serious decline which began before the turn of the century, and had all but wiped the species out by 1940, has recently begun a slow increase. Its former range extended south from the Swan and Avon Rivers (east of Perth) to Augusta in the south-west and Broomehill in the east. Today the population, which numbers around 1,500 individuals and outside the breeding season assembles in five or six flocks, is centred in the Lake Muir district (Tonebridge, Rocky Gully, McAlinden, Qualeup South, the lower Perup River, Camballup, Dinninup, Mordalup and near Mayanup). The northern subspecies has a much wider distribution and is common and increasing, particularly in the south where it has spread through the wheatbelt (since the 1950s), being recorded as far south as Northam. It now occurs throughout the wheatbelt north and east of Perth (Mukinbudin, Wongan Hills, Kalannie, Moora, Coorow, Three Springs, Morawa, Arrino, Mullewa), and along the coast to the north (Jurien Bay, Dongara, Geraldton), continuing through coastal districts north of the Murchison River, and including some offshore islands. It reaches north-east to around Port Hedland, and from there inland south-west of the Great Sandy Desert, and south to the western edge of the Gibson Desert in the extreme south-east (northern wheatbelt and the adjacent coastal region bounded by Dongara, Mullewa, Morawa, Jibberding, Kirwan, Moora, Wongan Hills, Dandaragan, and Jurien). The decline of the southern population is attributed to persecution by farmers who considered the species a crop pest. The total world population is unknown, but is thought to be expanding due to the spread of agriculture with its attendant increase in food availability. Legislation providing legal protection is also thought to have played a major role in the species's fortunes. It has recently been declared 'Rare or likely to become extinct' under the Western Australian Conservation Act. Despite protection, a few are still shot illegally each year. Few in captivity. NEAR-THREATENED.

ECOLOGY Seasonal movements have been observed in the northern wheatbelt population, with birds tagged at Kirwan and Three Springs moving 150-250km north-west to near Dongara and Geraldton after the breeding season, returning during Mar and Apr. Northern birds occur in open forest, eucalyptus woodland along watercourses, and farmland with large trees and watering holes (they often use artificial watering sites). They have also been recorded from mulga and mallee areas, and around towns and gardens. Historically, *C. p. pastinator* occurred in woodland surrounding the main forest block of south-west Western Australia. Today it is restricted to a small area of woodland and farmland. Western Corellas feed on corms and roots as well as a variety of seeds and agricultural crops. Northern birds particularly favour double-gee *Emex australis*, a weed pest. Other favoured foods include the corms of the introduced onion grass *Romulea longifolia*, which forms an important part of the species's diet, as well as rice and millet. The southern population is especially dependent on *Romulea rosea* and northern birds are partial to wheat. Western Corellas, like Long-billed, are capable of digging up to 5cm or more into the earth to reach succulent food items. Feeding flocks may be found in association with Galahs. Nesting in the northern population begins in Aug, and by the end of Nov most young have fledged. Outside the breeding season larger flocks gather in feeding and watering areas, and when the adults return to breed they are often accompanied by non-breeding immatures. Birds reach breeding maturity at three to five years of age. According to one study the youngest average estimate for nest trees is over 400 years, but this is disputed.

DESCRIPTION Head mainly white with pinkish lores and concealed orange-pink feather-bases. Rest of plumage white with concealed orange-pink bases to nape, mantle, breast and flank feathers. Upperwing white; underwing with yellow wash on inner webs of flight feathers. Uppertail white; undertail with yellow suffusion on innerwebs. **Bare parts:** Bill greyish; periophthalmic ring greyish-blue; iris dark brown; legs grey.

SEX/AGE Male and female similar. Young birds have a shorter upper mandible and the periophthalmic ring may appear greyer.

MEASUREMENTS Wing 288-330; tail 134-180; bill 39-52; tarsus 27-32.

GEOGRAPHICAL VARIATION Two races.
    C. p. pastinator (Lake Muir district of SW Western Australia)
    C. p. butleri (Western Australia, north of *C. p. pastinator*) Smaller with a shorter upper mandible.

REFERENCES BirdLife (1993), Blakers *et al.* (1984), Cayley & Lendon (1973), Ford (1987), Forshaw (1981, 1989), Garnett (1992), Lambert *et al.* (1993), Lodge (1991), Mawson & Long (1994), Pizzey & Doyle (1983), Schodde & Tidemann (1988), Sibley & Monroe (1990), Simpson & Day (1984), Smith & Moore (1991, 1992b), Trounson & Trounson (1987).

73 LONG-BILLED CORELLA
Cacatua tenuirostris Plate 15

Other names: Eastern Long-billed Corella, Slender-billed Corella, Long-billed Cockatoo

IDENTIFICATION 35-41cm. A bull-necked, stumpy-looking, mainly white cockatoo, occurring in a small area of south-eastern Australia. This species has the shortest crest of the corellas, and can appear very round-headed. The reddish-orange gorget is diagnostic (although not very obvious from a distance), and in combination with the strongly marked pinkish forehead and lores (extending above and below the eye in a 'mask'), and the extremely long upper mandible (almost appearing deformed), makes this species particularly distinctive. Its range overlaps slightly with that of the Little Corella (71), and it is most easily separated by the reddish collar. Young Long-bills may have a less distinct breast-band, however, as well as a shorter upper mandible; the more elliptical, paler blue periophthalmic ring (see plate for precise shape) should confirm identification. This species can be separated from Western Corella (72) on range, and again by its obvious breast-band. Like Western, feeding flocks may soil their underparts and heads whilst foraging for corms and roots. The flight profile is different from the other two corellas, the birds appearing larger-headed and shorter-tailed, with more pointed wings. It is sometimes also considered more pigeon-like. The tail is square-ended (Little has a more rounded tail). In normal flight the wingbeats are interspersed by short glides. Long-bills show only a slight yellow suffusion on the underwing, but a strong suffusion below the tail.

VOICE A distinctive, quavering, chuckling contact call *ri-rip* or *wirup*, higher-pitched and softer than Little Corella. Also some squeaky conversational notes and a harsh alarm screech, higher-pitched than Sulphur-crested Cockatoo (65).

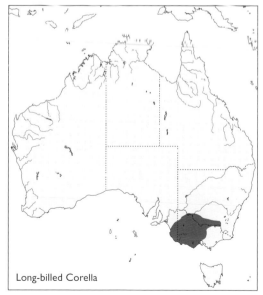

Long-billed Corella

DISTRIBUTION AND STATUS Endemic to the Murray-Darling region and adjoining coast. The species favours higher-rainfall districts, and occurs in a zone of intense agricultural development (both pasture and crops). It ranges from extreme south-east South Australia (Naracoorte, Penola, Glencoe, Lucindale, Frances, Wolseley) through south-central Victoria (Edenhope, Hamilton, the Grampians, Horsham, Dimboola), east through Ararat, Creswick and Lake Corangamite to the western edge of Port Phillip Bay. It also occurs around Nagambie, Barmah Forest, Goulburn River and Echuca to the north. In New South Wales it has a limited range along the Victoria border and in the south Riverina region, from around Euston through Moulamein, Deniliquin, Koondrook and Mathoura east to around Finley. Records also come from further north near Hay, Griffith and the Lachlan River. The species has also bred west to Lake Gol Gol. It is commonest in Victoria around Hamilton, Edenhope and the Grampians. In New South Wales it is more thinly distributed, and birds may be more inclined to sporadic movements. In 1976, 25-30 birds escaped in the McLaren Flats region near Adelaide and may still be found in the area. Records from Sydney also relate to escapes. At the time of European settlement, the Long-billed Corella was much more widely distributed than it is today, formerly occurring along the Darling and Murrumbidgee Rivers, and also reaching as far east as the Mornington Peninsula on the southern Victoria coast. Its decline has been attributed to a number of factors, including climatic changes in the north of its range, the spread of pastoral farming, land-use changes, reduction in available nest-sites through woodland clearance (particularly of river red-gums Eucalyptus camaldulensis), trapping for the pet trade and persecution by farmers. In the last 30 years it has been given legal protection from persecution, and has begun to increase again, apparently as a direct consequence. It is generally sparsely distributed but common to abundant in parts of western Victoria. The world population is in excess of 250,000 and increasing. Small numbers in captivity. The species may be trapped under permit in some areas.

ECOLOGY Sedentary, but local movements of post- and non-breeding flocks have been recorded, particularly in south-west New South Wales. Long-billed Corellas favour tree-lined watercourses running through farmland, particularly with river red-gums and bull-oaks *Allocasuarina*, and are commoner than Sulphur-crested Cockatoo, Galah (62) and Little Corella in this habitat. They also occur in open forest, savanna woodland, farm pastures, paddocks and stubble-fields. They are rarely found far from water and will make use of man-made tanks to drink. Long-billed Corellas are frequently encountered in large flocks, but during the breeding season pairs separate from the bigger roaming groups of immature and non-breeding birds, and can be found in small parties close to their nesting trees. In western Victoria where the species has its main stronghold, flocks of up to 2,000 birds may gather during the summer to exploit abundant food sources, and are regarded as crop pests. Flocks are noisy and conspicuous, roosting in favourite sites close to water and rising early to drink before moving out to their feeding areas. They feed on the ground, often moving across fields in a wave, with the rear-most birds constantly flying to the front to get to the richer pickings. Long-billed Corellas are known to use the 'sentinel warning system' commonly employed by Sulphur-crested Cockatoos, with which the species sometimes associates (alert birds warning feeding flocks of approaching danger). Birds may spend time resting in the tree-tops, where they are particularly conspicuous, and they sometimes associate with Galahs when feeding. During the heat of the day groups gather in trees, feeding again in the afternoon before returning to drink and roost. At dusk, they sometimes indulge in noisy sorties around the roosting sites before settling. During feeding, the bill is used as a plough to dig a furrow and expose any edible material. The birds commonly become stained on the head and underparts through contact with soil and vegetable matter. The corms of onion grass *Romulea longifolia* are favoured as a food item, but the diet is varied and includes seeds, nuts, fruits, berries, roots and bulbs as well as insects and their larvae. They will also take newly sown grain and ripening crops, including sunflower *Helianthus* seeds. Flocks have also been observed feeding on recently burnt areas. The upper mandible grows quickly and is worn down through feeding. Most nesting occurs between Sep and Oct, although the breeding season runs from Jul to Dec. The nest-site is usually a high hollow in a living eucalypt near water (river red-gums are often favoured). Birds are also known to nest in cliff cavities at Tower Hill State Game Reserve and near Mortlake. From two to four white eggs are laid on a bed of decaying wood dust, the yellow-downed chicks hatching in 24-29 days. Usually only one chick is reared to maturity, leaving the nest in around seven weeks. Parental feeding lasts around three weeks after the fledgling leaves the nest.

DESCRIPTION Head and vestigial crest white; lores and forehead reddish-orange (extending backwards to just above and below eye), with reddish markings sometimes on sides of chin and throat; bases of head feathers reddish-orange (may show slightly when feathers ruffled). Mantle white with reddish feather-bases; rest of upperparts white. Wings white with yellowish wash on underside of flight feathers. Narrow reddish-orange band across upper breast (breast feathers with orange-pink bases); lower edge irregular; rest of underparts white (with less obvious reddish bases to feathers), but sometimes with very slight pinkish cast. Tail white, undertail with yellowish wash. **Bare parts**: Bill greyish white; large periophthalmic ring pale blue (lacks obvious bulge shown by Little and Western Corellas); iris dark brown; legs grey.

SEX/AGE Sexes similar (including iris colour). Young birds have less reddish-orange on the breast and a shorter upper mandible.

MEASUREMENTS Wing 272-290; tail 112-132; bill 40-52; tarsus 25-32.

GEOGRAPHICAL VARIATION None.

REFERENCES BirdLife (1993), Blakers *et al.* (1984), Cayley & Lendon (1973), Eastman & Hunt (1966), Emison *et al.* (1987), Forshaw (1981, 1989), Lambert *et al.* (1993), Lodge (1991), Low (1980), Peters (1961), Pizzey & Doyle (1983), Schodde & Tidemann (1988), Sibley & Monroe (1990), Simpson & Day (1984), Slater (1979, 1989), Sparks & Soper (1990), Tavistock (1929), Trounson & Trounson (1987).

74 DUCORPS'S COCKATOO
Cacatua ducorpsii Plate 15

Other names: Solomon Islands Cockatoo, Ducrops's Cockatoo, Solomons Corella, White Cockatoo (but this is also the common name for *C. alba* and is sometimes also applied to Sulphur-crested Cockatoo)

IDENTIFICATION 30-35cm. A small cockatoo with a neat, triangular, erectile crest. The species is entirely white except for a yellow wash on the underwing and undertail. This is the only cockatoo in the Solomon Islands and is unlikely to be confused with any other species in the field. It is most similar to Tanimbar Cockatoo (70), which can be separated in captivity by its pink lore-spot and whitish-blue, not blue, eye-ring. Little Corella (71) is also similar, but has a much larger, darker blue eye-ring, and shows a little pink suffusion on the lores (limited in nominate which is in any case separable on shape and colour of the facial skin-patch). This is also true of the much longer-billed Western Corella (72). Long-billed Corella (73) shows extensive pink suffusion on the face and breast and is unlikely to present an identification problem. The flight of Ducorps's Cockatoo (which is sometimes described as butterfly-like) is buoyant and erratic, with shallow jerky wingbeats interspersed with glides on down-curved wings.

VOICE Two harsh questioning notes, *érrk-errk...érrk-errk*, often extended to *érrk-érrk-érrk-érrk*. Also a variable, loud, harsh and nasal *hounk kerrk hounk hunk*, with the emphasis on the first note of each pair, the second being lower and downwardly inflected. Other calls include a harsh up-and-down *aak-ack-aak* which may be expanded into a rolling screech.

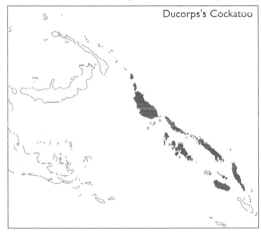

Ducorps's Cockatoo

DISTRIBUTION AND STATUS Endemic to the Solomon Islands. The species's range extends from Buka and Bougainville (Papua New Guinea) in the west, into the Solomons, where it ranges through the Shortland Islands, and east to Guadalcanal and Malaita. In the Solomons group the species has been recorded from Choiseul, Santa Isabel, Malaita, Vella Lavella, Kolombangara, Ranongga, Gizo, Mbava, New Georgia, Rendova, Tetepare, Vangunu, Nggatokae, the Russell Islands, Nggela Sule and Guadalcanal, but is absent from the San Cristobal group. Considered common in a variety of habitats with its upper altitudinal limit at around 1,800m. The world population is thought to be over 100,000 and stable. Trade is a possible future threat, as is habitat loss, particularly given the rate

of clearance of lowland forest in the region. The species is kept as a pet in villages, but the low numbers involved indicate that at present this is not an issue of real conservation concern. Small numbers elsewhere in captivity.

ECOLOGY Widespread from coast to mountains in a range of habitats including, forest, forest margins, secondary growth, gardens, woodland and towns. It is scarcer at high altitudes and on Guadalcanal it is generally absent above the lower border of the mist-forest. It is most frequently encountered up to 700m, but has been recorded as high as 1,800m. The species is noisy and conspicuous, usually being encountered in pairs or small flocks, flying high above the tree-tops, or perching in the top of an exposed tree. Quite wary and flies off screeching loudly when disturbed. The species also raises its crest when excited. Ducorps's Cockatoo feeds on seeds, berries, fruit, buds, blossoms and insects and their larvae. The fleshy part of an epiphyte was also found in the stomach of one specimen. Groups may raid gardens for pawpaws *Carica papaya* and yams *Dioscorea*. Nesting habits are unknown.

DESCRIPTION White cockatoo with yellow suffusion on innerwebs of underwing- and undertail coverts. Bases of crest, cheek, mantle and breast feathers pinkish. **Bare parts**: Bill greyish; periophthalmic ring pale blue; iris black-brown; legs grey.

SEX/AGE Female with redder iris.

MEASUREMENTS Wing 232-274; tail 107-121; bill 27-34; tarsus 24-27.

GEOGRAPHICAL VARIATION None.

REFERENCES BirdLife (1993), Cain & Galbraith (1956), Coates (1985), Collar (1989), Forshaw (1989), Greensmith (1975), Hadden (1981), Lambert *et al.* (1993), Lees (1991), Lodge (1991), Low (1980), Mayr (1945), Peters (1961), Sibley & Monroe (1990).

---

75 COCKATIEL
Nymphicus hollandicus Plate 38

Other names: Quarrion

IDENTIFICATION 29-33cm. Along with the Budgerigar (155) this is one of the most familiar parrots and is a common cagebird all around the world. Largely grey with a prominent white wing-flash, upward-curving crest and yellow face with an orange patch on the ear-coverts. Commonly found in large flocks throughout mainland Australia. In flight the long tail, pointed wings and white wing-patch are obvious.

VOICE A plaintive *queel, queel-queel* or *weero*.

DISTRIBUTION AND STATUS Common and widespread through most of Australia, mainly in arid and semi-arid areas, and absent from wetter coastal districts (birds in Tasmania more likely to be escapes than vagrants, as are birds around Sydney). Also absent from northern Cape York Peninsula and from extreme southern areas in winter, and from extreme northern districts in summer. Following rains large numbers may appear in the interior where birds are generally absent (the species as a whole may have benefited from the provision of artificial watering sites through the spread of farming). Occasional escapes (e.g. in New York, U.S.A.) have failed to become established. World population above 1,000,000 and safe.

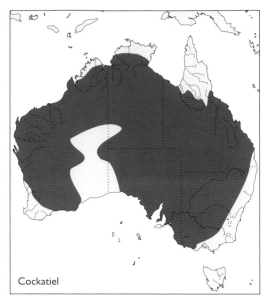

Cockatiel

ECOLOGY Nomadic in north (although apparent regular movements north to around Darwin in winter), seasonal migrant in south (arriving in the extreme south in spring and leaving late autumn). Found in a variety of habitats including open woodland, acacia scrub, riverine forest, spinifex, farmland, orchards, plains and roadsides. Generally found in drier areas in pairs or flocks up to 100 birds, but over 1,000 have been seen gathered at dumps of rice-husks. They often associate with Budgerigars in large flocks at watering places. Cockatiels have the habitat of perching along limbs when alighting in trees. They feed mainly on seeds, especially acacias and wheat, and can be an agricultural pest in some areas. In the north, nesting takes place between Apr and Jul, in the south from Aug to Dec. The nest is in a tree-hollow lined with wood dust, the site normally being located near water as the birds drink every day. Between one and seven eggs are laid, although four is more normal. The young birds are mainly fed early and late in the day, and fledge in three to four weeks, remaining in family groups with the parents for around one month.

DESCRIPTION Head and base of upward-curving crest pale yellow; central ear-coverts orange fringed paler at rear margin; lores, nape and longer crest feathers grey. Upperparts dark dove-grey. Wings grey with white coverts and secondaries. Underparts lighter grey. Tail mid- to dark grey, base of central uppertail lighter. **Bare parts**: Bill grey; iris dark brown; legs grey-brown.

SEX/AGE Female and immature male with duller facial markings and pronounced fine lighter barring on rump, flanks and tail. Outermost tail feathers yellowish barred grey. Underside of flight feathers lightly barred.

MEASUREMENTS Wing 161-179; tail 155-178; bill 14-15; tarsus 15-17.

GEOGRAPHICAL VARIATION None.

REFERENCES Blakers *et al.* (1984), Lambert *et al.* (1993), Lodge (1991), Long (1981), Schodde & Tidemann (1988), Sibley & Monroe (1990), Slater (1989), Smith & Moore (1992a), Storr & Johnstone (1979), Taylor (1987).

76   KEA
Nestor notabilis   Plate 16

Other names: Mountain Parrot

IDENTIFICATION 46cm. Only in the mountains of South Island, New Zealand. A large, stocky, olive-brown parrot with an elongated upper mandible. The underwing-coverts and rump are orange-red, there is a turquoise-blue suffusion on the upperwing, and the short squarish tail has a greenish suffusion on the upper surface and a dark subterminal band. The only likely confusion species is the Kaka (77), which is warmer brown, shows a distinctive pale cap, an orange suffusion on the ear-coverts, and a crimson hindneck and belly; it is also almost exclusively found in lower-altitude forests. Both species show reddish underwings in flight, but Kea is distinguished by its blue primaries and bluish-green tail. One of the best places to see Keas is Arthur's Pass, north-central South Island. They are attracted to cars, and will remove windscreen-wiper blades. The parking area near the picnic site just before the crest of the pass is a favourite location.

VOICE A descending, drawn-out *keaaaa*, ending with a quaver. Also some softer conversational calls, and a subsong at the nest. Lacks the musical notes of Kaka.

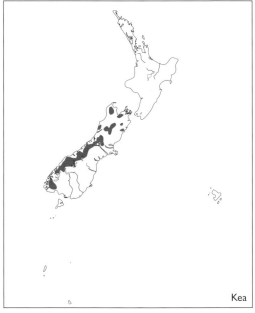

Kea

DISTRIBUTION AND STATUS Endemic to the South Island of New Zealand (although vagrants have been recorded on North Island, e.g. in the Tararua Range), and found mainly between 950m and 1,400m in high-level forests and subalpine shrublands. The range extends from south-west Southland (e.g. Wilmot Pass), north through the Fiordland National Park (e.g. near Te Anau, Homer Tunnel), Westland and the Southern Alps (e.g. Westland National Park, Fox and Franz Josef Glaciers, Mount Cook National Park), Arthur's Pass National Park and Craigieburn Forest Park, Nelson Lakes National Park and Big Bush State Forest, the Seaward Kaikoura Range (e.g. Mount Manakau), the Marlborough region, the Richmond Range, finally reaching the highlands around Mount

Cobb, at its north-west extreme. The world population has been estimated at between 1,000 and 5,000 birds; concentrations around tourist sites give the false impression that the species is commoner. Keas were once thought to be sheep killers, and between 1860 and 1970 thousands were killed by farmers. As a result, the population has almost certainly declined and fragmented. The species has been fully protected since 1986. There are a few in captivity. NEAR-THREATENED.

ECOLOGY Keas have been recorded from just above sea-level up to 2,400m, and are commonly found close to human habitation and tourist sites. Despite this, their principal habitat is around the tree-line between 950m and 1,400m. They tend to favour steep-sided valleys with beech *Nothofagus cliffortioides* forest, replaced by subalpine scrub at higher altitudes. They are strong fliers, and their noisy, conspicuous flocks may be seen wheeling high above the valley floor. They are tame, playful and inquisitive. Groups of predominantly male Keas are known to forage around camp-sites and carparks, and sometimes do damage to cars and tents. During the summer they can be active at night. During the winter they tend to move to lower altitudes beneath the snow line, but some groups remain to scavenge around ski lodges. They will feed on carrion including dead sheep but, despite rumours, there is no evidence that Keas attack and kill healthy sheep. They feed both in trees and on the ground, being mainly vegetarian, and their diet includes leaves, buds, roots, seeds, berries, blossoms and nectar (which the fringe-tipped tongue helps extract), as well as some insects. They are probably a vector for the seeds of berry-bearing plants, e.g. snow totara *Podocarpus nivalis*. Keas are highly social, and have overlapping ranges that vary in size, although 'core areas' including the nest and roosting site remain discrete. Breeding birds remain within a kilometre or so of their nests, but non-breeders are much more mobile and movements of up to 60km have been recorded in ringed birds. The pair is the basic social unit, but Keas are non-territorial and groups are highly fluid. As few as 10% of the total adult male population may breed in any one year, and non-pair nest-visits and matings sometimes take place. Pair-bond and nest site fidelity are both strong, with the nest often taking a number of seasons to complete. Nesting occurs between Jul and Jan. Two to four white eggs are laid, in a burrow or hollow log lined with twigs, leaves and lichens. The nest-site is often at the base of a rock outcrop within the forest, but an exposed boulder above the tree-line may also be chosen. The eggs are laid over a number of days, and incubation, which is carried out only by the female, lasts around 21-28 days. During this time the male roosts nearby and gathers food to feed his mate. Initially the male provisions the female with all the food to be fed to the chicks, but after a few weeks she also leaves the nest to help in foraging. The white-downed chicks fledge in 13-14 weeks, and continue to be fed by both adults, who accompany them for a month to six weeks. In Jan or Feb, after the breeding season, Keas tend to gather in larger flocks which may number 50 or so individuals.

DESCRIPTION Head olive-brown; narrow crown feathers finely shaft-streaked black; ear-coverts and lores more uniform dark brown; feathers of nape slightly more yellowish, with brownish-black edgings and shafts. Mantle and uppertail-coverts bronze-green with black shafts and crescent-shaped edgings; back and rump red-orange, with blackish shafts and tips. Flight feathers, primary and greater coverts strongly suffused turquoise-blue on outer-webs (greener on secondaries); innerwebs of primaries barred lemon-yellow. Underwing-coverts and axillaries reddish-orange; underside of flight feathers brown, barred yellow on innerwebs of primaries, barred orange on innerwebs of inner secondaries. Feathers of underparts light olive-brown edged dark brown. Uppertail suffused bluish-green, with innerwebs barred orange-yellow and a blackish subterminal band with paler tips; undertail olive-yellow with dark subterminal band and barring showing basally; pointed shafts of tail feathers extend a little beyond webs. **Bare parts**: Bill brownish-black; cere dark brown, with some short hair-like feathers; iris dark brown; legs blackish-grey.

SEX/AGE Males are larger, and have longer upper mandibles than females (averaging 12-14% longer). Young birds have greener rumps, yellow ceres, yellow periophthalmic rings, a pale base to the lower mandible, and paler more yellowish legs. The yellow bare parts are lost after about two years in the female, three in the male.

MEASUREMENTS Wing 302-330; tail 146-175; bill 43-53; tarsus 45-49.

GEOGRAPHICAL VARIATION None.

REFERENCES Bond & Diamond (1992), Bond *et al.* (1991), Ellis (1987), Falla *et al.* (1981), Forshaw (1989), Gardner (1988), Gooders (1969-1971), Holdaway & Worthy (1993), Jackson (1960, 1963), Kirk *et al.* (1993), Lambert *et al.* (1993), Lodge (1991), Mallet (1972), McPherson (1990), Robertson (1985), Sibley & Monroe (1990), Wakelin (1991), Wilson (1990), Wilson & Brejaart (1992).

77   KAKA
Nestor meridionalis   Plate 16

Other names: New Zealand Kaka, Common Kaka

IDENTIFICATION 45cm. A thinly distributed resident of the native forests of New Zealand, locally common and conspicuous on some offshore islands and in parts of southern South Island. The Kaka is a stout, dark brown parrot with a large bill, pale cap, orange ear-coverts, and a red underwing, hind-collar and belly. The only likely confusion species is the Kea (76), which generally occurs at higher altitudes and is restricted to South Island (except for occasional vagrants). Kaka can be separated by its pale cap, darker and generally warmer brown plumage, red hind-collar and belly, and by call. Some individuals may show colour variation, with the upperparts shading from brown to cream. In flight, Kakas look large and dark, and show a heavy head and bill. Groups of birds are often heard before they are seen flying through the canopy.

VOICE In flight, a grating *krraaa*, and a warbling, liquid, almost chuckling whistle *weedle-weedle*. There is also a *choock, choock* call. A subsong is sometimes given at the nest by the female.

DISTRIBUTION AND STATUS New Zealand and offshore islands. The species is scattered through South Island, from Stewart Island (especially around Halfmoon Bay) in the south, north through the western ranges, from around Lake Hauroko through Fiordland (e.g. Eglington

Valley, where it is relatively common, and around Mount Aspiring), Westland and the Paparoa Range. It also occurs in the upper Hope River valley, Nelson Lakes National Park, the Richmond Range and the Abel Tasman National Park region. In North Island, it is mainly restricted to large forest blocks. It is also present in small numbers in the Tararua Range in the south, and there are a few isolated populations in other areas, including the Raukumara Range, and possibly still the Coromandel Peninsula. In central North Island, moderate numbers of Kaka are found in the tracts of native bush to the south and north-west of Lake Taupo, including the Ruahine Range (few), Tongariro National Park, the Kaimanawa Mountains, Pureora Forest Park, and Urewera National Park to the east. Kakas are also occasionally encountered in North-land. Stable populations occur on some offshore islands too, particularly Kapiti and Little Barrier. Other islands that support Kaka include Hen & Chickens Islands, Great Barrier Island, Fanal and Mayor. The world population is estimated at less than 5,000 and declining and fragmenting as a result of predation, particularly of nesting females and chicks (e.g. by mustelids and rats), competition for food from introduced wasps *Vespula* (particularly in autumn), and habitat loss and degradation (e.g. by Brush-tailed Possums *Trichosurus vulpecula*). Few in captivity. VULNERABLE.

Kaka

ECOLOGY Restricted to unbroken tracts of low- to mid-altitude *Nothofagus* and *Podocarpus* forest, although occasional visits to gardens or orchards have been recorded, particularly in winter. Kakas are normally found between 450m and 850m in summer, and from just above sea-level up to 550m in winter, although they have been recorded as high as 1,500m. They are frequently seen in pairs, but larger groups can be encountered after the breeding season. They are powerful fliers and noisy flocks may be heard travelling above the forest. Long-distance movements are sometimes undertaken. Kakas are active from at least half an hour before dawn until after dusk, when they may perform long and noisy pre-roosting flights. They are also often active at night. During the day they feed quietly in the canopy. Studies in South Island beech *Nothofagus* forests show that in spring Kakas spend about 30% of their time feeding on honeydew, which is secreted by the scale insect *Ultracoelostoma assimile*. Honeydew is less important in winter, and during the summer and autumn competition from wasps reduces this still further. The larvae of the Kanuka longhorn beetles *Ochrocydus huttoni* are also an important food, and birds may spend considerable amounts of time using their strong bills to chisel away bark to reach the grubs. Where possums are scarce, and sufficient mistletoe (Loranthaceae) is available, Kakas may spend as much as 60% of their foraging time feeding on its flowers and berries. Elsewhere a variety of food items has been recorded including fruit (e.g. miro *Podocarpus ferrugineus*, buds, seeds (e.g. kauri *Agathis australis*), nectar (including rata *Metrosideros excelsa*) which it gathers with the help of its fringed tongue, and sap. During the day, the only indication of a Kaka's presence may be the sound of bark being whittled and falling from the trunk. Food items are held up to the bill in the foot. On some offshore islands Kakas have become very tame, and can be hand-fed. Research in Big Bush State Park, South Island, has shown that Kaka do not breed every year. This could be a recent response to competition for food from introduced wasps, rather than a feature of the species's ecology. Nesting takes place between Nov and Jan. A tree-hollow, usually 3-9m above ground is the usual site, and the opening may be widened by the birds. Four to five white eggs are laid on a base of wood dust. Incubation lasts around 24 days, and is carried out by the female, which leaves the nest at dawn and dusk to be fed by the male. A non-pair helper may also feed the incubating bird. North Island fledglings have white down, those in South Island are grey. Chicks fledge in around ten weeks, having been fed by both parents. The Kaka's lifespan is thought to be around 20 years.

DESCRIPTION Crown grey-white, nape appearing grey-brown owing to broad brownish feather-margins; bluish-grey cast below eye and at sides of nape; lores grey-brown; ear-coverts strongly marked with orange; sides of chin suffused reddish-brown. Upperparts greenish-brown with darker brown fringes and shafts; hindneck crimson with yellow and brown feather-tips and browner bases; mantle sometimes with a few red markings; rump and uppertail-coverts red with brown feather-margins and shafts. Upperwing with innerwebs of flight feathers notched with pink. Underwing-coverts and axillaries scarlet tipped darker and with yellowish tips to marginal underwing-coverts; underside of flight feathers with four pinkish-orange notches appearing densely barred in flight. Breast olive-brown, feathers showing subterminal russet margin with darker brown tips and bases. Belly to undertail-coverts red, with brown shafts and margins. Tail brown, tipped paler with shafts projecting slightly beyond webs and showing slight barring on innerwebs. **Bare parts**: Bill brownish-grey, heavier than that of Kea; cere brown with a few bristle-like feathers; iris dark brown; legs dark grey.

SEX/AGE Male larger with a longer bill. Immatures have yellow base to lower mandible.

MEASUREMENTS Wing 265-306; tail 151-190; bill 42-54; tarsus 35-44.

GEOGRAPHICAL VARIATION Two races.
 N. m. meridionalis (South Island)
 N. m. septentrionalis (North Island) Smaller than

nominate and much duller. Darker olive-brown above and on breast, with darker-tipped feathers. Crown duller. Crimson of collar more mottled and less obvious.

REFERENCES Beggs & Wilson (1988, 1991), Collar *et al.* (1994), Ellis (1987), Falla *et al.* (1981), Forshaw (1989), Gardner (1988), Holdaway & Worthy (1993), Kirk *et al.* (1993), Lambert *et al.* (1993), Lodge (1991), McPherson (1990), Robertson (1985), Wakelin (1991).

78 YELLOW-CAPPED PYGMY PARROT
Micropsitta keiensis Plate 17

Other names: Kai Islands Pygmy Parrot

IDENTIFICATION 9-9.5cm. Like other members of the genus this is a diminutive stub-tailed parrot which specialises in climbing trees like a nuthatch *Sitta*, and gleaning lichen from the surface of the bark. It braces the elongated spines at the tips of its tail feathers (unique to this genus among parrots) against the trunk for support, and has long claws to help gain purchase. The pygmy parrots are the smallest of the psittacines, and in flight are easily mistaken for passerines. Their high-pitched calls, unique feeding habits and blunt-headed flight-profile should all aid in locating and identifying members of the genus. The Yellow-capped Pygmy Parrot is predominantly green with a yellow-ochre crown, brown face, yellow undertail-coverts, and blue tail at rest. There are three populations, all of which occur in lowland forest, but no sympatric pygmy parrots. Although the dissimilar Red-breasted (83) also occurs in Vogelkop it is altitudinally allopatric, not usually being found below 500m (see plate for plumage differences). The flight of Yellow-capped Pygmy Parrot is swift and direct with audible wingbeats.

VOICE A faint, high-pitched squeak *tsii* or *psii*, very similar to that of Buff-faced Pygmy Parrot (80) of northern New Guinea.

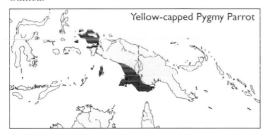
Yellow-capped Pygmy Parrot

DISTRIBUTION AND STATUS Yellow-capped Pygmy Parrots occur in the W Papuan islands, including Waigeo, Gebe, Kafiau, Salawati and Misool; through Vogelkop and the Onin Peninsula, Irian Jaya; in the Kai and Aru Islands; and in southern New Guinea between the Mimika and Fly Rivers. The species is locally common; the world population is in excess of 100,000 and stable.

ECOLOGY Occurs in lowland forest, secondary growth and sometimes around habitation and in coconuts. The species's ecology is similar to that of the Buff-faced Pygmy Parrot. Birds are found singly, in pairs or small groups, and can range from the understorey to about 20m above ground. They clamber about trunks and limbs, and may descend head-first on occasions. They feed on lichen,

fungus, seeds, fruit and insects. Most lichen is gathered directly from the bark-surface. They nest and roost in cavities in arboreal termite nests, excavating the cavity themselves; the tunnel slopes upwards and may kink before reaching the nest-chamber. Two white eggs are laid in the unlined cavity (dimensions around 20cm x 15cm), which may be occupied by additional roosting adults (up to four) during the breeding season. The exact role of these birds is unknown but they may be nest 'helpers'. Nesting has been recorded from Oct to Mar.

DESCRIPTION Crown ochre-yellow, warmer and browner on forehead; lores, chin and area below eye brown; ear-coverts dark green tending to lighter green on cheeks and throat. Upperparts dark green with black centres to wing-coverts, feathers usually very narrowly margined with black; flight feathers black with green outerwebs; underwing-coverts green. Underparts lighter, more yellowish green, usually with fine dark fringes; undertail-coverts yellow and green. Uppertail iridescent slightly greenish-blue centrally, outer feathers blackish with yellow spot at tip; undertail dark blue and yellow. **Bare parts**. Bill dark grey, iris brown, legs dark grey.

SEX/AGE Sexes similar. Immature like female but with a dark-tipped, pale yellowish bill.

MEASUREMENTS Wing 59-66, tail 25-31, bill 7-8; tarsus 8-9.

GEOGRAPHICAL VARIATION Three races.
> *M. k. keiensis* (Kai and Aru Islands)
> *M. k. viridipectus* (S New Guinea) Similar to nominate but darker.
> *M. k. chloroxantha* (W Papuan islands, Vogelkop and the Onin Peninsula) Crown duller. Underparts with red markings in male, tinged yellowish in female.

REFERENCES Beehler *et al.* (1986), Coates (1985), Forshaw (1989), Gyldenstolpe (1955), Hornbuckle (1991), Lodge (1991), Peters (1961), Rand & Gilliard (1967), Sibley & Monroe (1990), Smith (1992), White & Bruce (1986).

79 GEELVINK PYGMY PARROT
Micropsitta geelvinkiana Plate 17

IDENTIFICATION 9cm. The only pygmy parrot on Numfor and Biak islands in Geelvink Bay, Irian Jaya. A distinctive species. The birds are mainly green with grey-brown heads and black centres to the wing-coverts. The undertail-coverts are yellow and the central tail feathers blue. Similar Buff-faced Pygmy Parrot *M. pusio* has a buff, not grey-brown, face.

VOICE A quick *tseet* or *tsit tsit tsit* given in flight, and a drawn out *tsee tsee*.

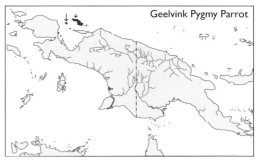
Geelvink Pygmy Parrot

DISTRIBUTION AND STATUS Occurs only on Numfor and Biak islands, Indonesia, up to about 300m. In 1991 the world population was thought to be around 10,000 and stable, but in 1997 searches for the species over a 12-day period suggested it is either now rare or easily overlooked, with observations on only a single day and aural contact on one other. NEAR-THREATENED.

ECOLOGY Occurs in lowland rainforest, secondary growth, open cultivated areas with isolated trees, and around native gardens, up to 300m or higher. Birds are found in parties of 4-5, and have been seen associating with other birds in low berry-bearing trees in forest. Very shy. They excavate cavities in arboreal termite nests in which they lay their eggs (cavities also used for roosting overnight), often close to the ground. Nesting at least mid-Jun to Aug. Arndt found two young in one nest which were visited by the female every two hours. The chamber was lined with dust from the termite mound and contained some broken eggshell and feathers.

DESCRIPTION Ear-coverts brown merging to greenish-blue at rear, crown purplish-blue; upperparts green, median coverts with blackish centres. Flight feathers black with narrow green edgings on outerwebs. Underparts green with centre of breast and belly ochre-yellow, warmer towards breast. Undertail-coverts yellow. Central tail feathers blue, outer black and green tipped with yellow spots. **Bare parts**: Bill grey; iris red or orange-brown; legs grey.

SEX/AGE Female with less blue in crown and underparts greenish-yellow. Young with bill mostly yellow tipped grey.

MEASUREMENTS Wing 54-61; tail 23-30; bill 7-8; tarsus 8-10.

GEOGRAPHICAL VARIATION Two races.

M. g. geelvinkiana (Numfor) Blue in crown (stronger in male), with more green mottling around the head.
M. g. misoriensis (Biak) Male has a brown head with yellow and orange belly-markings, female a blue crown and greenish underparts.

REFERENCES Arndt (1992), Beehler *et al.* (1986), B.M. Beehler *in litt.* (1997), BirdLife (1993), Forshaw (1989), Lambert *et al.* (1993), Rand & Gilliard (1967).

---

80 BUFF-FACED PYGMY PARROT
Micropsitta pusio   Plate 17

Other names: Blue-crowned Pygmy Parrot, Little Pygmy Parrot

IDENTIFICATION 8.5cm. Widespread in lowland forest in northern and south-eastern New Guinea and on some outlying island groups. The plumage is predominantly green, the species being distinguished by the combination of blue crown and buffy face and supercilium. Female Red-breasted Pygmy Parrots (83) are very similar, but lack the buff supercilium (their blue cap extending down to the eye), and have paler and pinker cheeks than in female Red-breasted. Where the two overlap on range, Buff-faced also occurs at lower altitudes, but some stragglers may be encountered outside the normal altitudinal limits of both. Some races of Finsch's Pygmy Parrot (82) also show blue crowns, but lack the buff face. Geelvink Pygmy Parrot (79) can also show a blue crown but is restricted to Numfor and Biak islands. Pygmy Lorikeet (43) occurs at higher altitudes, has a pointed, not rounded tail, different feeding habits and a yellow-streaked breast. The sympatric Orange-fronted Hanging Parrot (188) is a similar size, but has a bright red lower back and rump, yellow forecrown, red breast-markings and different habits (see that species). Buff-faced Pygmy Parrots can be difficult to locate when feeding in the canopy and, although fairly common, may be difficult to see and usually best located by call. The flight is swift and direct (can be slightly undulating) with audible wingbeats.

VOICE An almost inaudible high-pitched tinkling *ssii ssii*, or a wheezing *tzip* or *szeeei szeeei szeeei* frequently repeated. In alarm a shrill *tseet*. Feeding birds are normally silent.

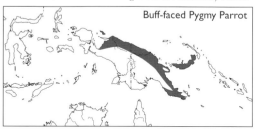
Buff-faced Pygmy Parrot

DISTRIBUTION AND STATUS Lowlands of northern New Guinea from the west coast of Geelvink Bay, Irian Jaya, to extreme south-east Papua New Guinea; absent from the highlands of the Huon Peninsula and from the Owen Stanley Ranges above about 500m, but found on some of northern New Guinea's offshore islands including Kairiru, the Schouten Islands, Manam, Karkar and Bagabag. The species occurs in the lowlands of the southern coastal region west to about the Purari River. It is found in the Bismarck Archipelago, including Umboi, Tolokiwa, Sakar, the Witu Islands, Lolobau, New Britain, Watom and Duke of York. It also occurs in the D'Entrecasteaux Archipelago on Fergusson and in the Louisiade Archipelago on Misima and Tagula. The world population is well in excess of 100,000 and stable.

ECOLOGY Found in lowland forest, hill forest, gallery forest and secondary growth from sea-level up to 500m, rarely to 830m. It is also found locally in heavy savanna and coconut *Cocos nucifera*. The species is common and confiding but can be hard to locate because of its small size. Birds can also sometimes be glimpsed flying in small groups above the canopy, and have a finch-like flight-profile. They tend to consort in pairs or groups of up to 30, moving rapidly along lianas and across the trunks or limbs of trees (or down head-first) using their long claws to grip and their tails as props, gleaning lichen and fungi from bark, but also sometimes taking seeds, fruit and insects (which may be ingested accidentally). They frequently pause while feeding and turn their heads right round, possibly to search for predators. They excavate nesting cavities in active arboreal termitaria e.g. of *Microcerotermes biroi*, and a nest has also been found in a terrestrial termitarium, the entrance only a metre from the ground. There is a ledge either side of the entrance-hole (which is excavated first) and this distinguishes their holes from those of other species which tunnel into termite nests such as Common Paradise Kingfishers *Tanysiptera galatea*. Up to three white eggs are laid, and nesting has been recorded almost year-round. Adults roost communally and up to eight birds have been recorded from one cavity.

DESCRIPTION Forehead, face and chin buff-brown mottled darker, sometimes with paler, more yellowish supercilium; centre of crown dull blue merging to green at nape. Upperparts green with wing-coverts centred black. Flight feathers black finely edged green; underwing-coverts yellow-green; underside of primaries greyish-black, slightly suffused yellow. Underparts yellowish-green, paler on centre of breast and belly; undertail-coverts yellow. Tail dull blue centrally with black shaft and suffusion near tip, outer feathers black with yellow spots near tips on innerwebs (some green suffusion on outerwebs). **Bare parts**: Bill dark grey; iris brown; legs grey or pinkish.

SEX/AGE Female slightly duller than male around face. Young with greenish-blue crown and less buff on face.

MEASUREMENTS Wing 59-69; tail 24-27; bill 7-8; tarsus 8-10.

GEOGRAPHICAL VARIATION Four races.

>*M. p. pusio* (SE New Guinea west to about Astrolabe Bay on the north coast, and to the Purari River in the south; also in the Bismarck Archipelago)
>
>*M. p. harterti* (Fergusson Island in the D'Entre-casteaux Archipelago) Head-markings duller than nominate, throat washed blue. Less yellow below than *M. p. stresemanni*.
>
>*M. p. stresemanni* (Misima and Tagula in the Louisiade Archipelago) Like *M. p. harterti* but slightly larger and with more yellow below.
>
>*M. p. beccarii* (N New Guinea and on offshore islands, from around Astrolabe Bay in the east to the west coast of Geelvink Bay) Generally darker than the nominate race particularly on the face, including supercilium.

REFERENCES Arndt (1992), Beehler (1978b), Beehler *et al.* (1986), B.M. Beehler *in litt.* (1997), Bell (1982), Bishop & Broome (1980), Coates (1985), Forshaw (1989), Gyldenstolpe (1955), Hartert (1926), Hornbuckle (1991), Lambert *et al.* (1993), Lodge (1991), Peters (1961), Rand & Gilliard (1967), Sibley & Monroe (1990).

---

81 MEEK'S PYGMY PARROT
Micropsitta meeki   Plate 17

IDENTIFICATION 10cm. A tiny green parrot with a dull, scaly yellow breast and brown and yellow scalloped head. It occurs only in the Admiralty and St Matthias island groups of the Bismarck Archipelago, where it is the only representative of the genus.

VOICE A high-pitched *sweet, tseet, zeeee* or *zeeeep*, and a high *see-seet see-sit* with second pair thinner and closer together.

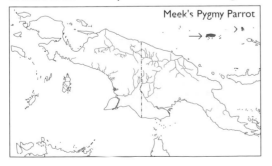

Meek's Pygmy Parrot

DISTRIBUTION AND STATUS Endemic to lowland forest up to 700m on islands in the north-west Bismarck Archipelago including Manus, Lou and Rambutyo in the Admiralty group and Mussau and Emira in the St Matthias group. The species is locally common; the world population is thought to be in excess of 10,000 and stable.

ECOLOGY Not well known. Occurs in forest, tall secondary growth, and even in trees around habitation. Birds are found in small groups feeding on lichen and fungi gleaned from tree-trunks. The habits are like those of Buff-faced Pygmy Parrot (80). The nest, which is in an arboreal termite mound, may sometimes be very close to the ground.

DESCRIPTION Head feathers dark brown basally, strongly scalloped yellow on ear-coverts and sides of throat, and usually with vague yellow supercilium; crown feathers with fine greyish-yellow tips. Upperparts dark green finely margined darker with black centres to median coverts. Primaries black with fine green edgings; secondaries mainly green. Underwing-coverts yellow tipped darker, underside of flight feathers blackish. Breast and centre of belly dull yellow, mottled slightly with brown at feather-tips; flanks and vent dark green; undertail-coverts yellow. Tail light greenish-blue centrally, lateral feathers blackish with yellow spots at tips or with dull blue and yellow tips. **Bare parts**: Bill pale yellowish-pink; iris brownish-yellow; legs pink.

SEX/AGE Females like males. Immature undescribed

MEASUREMENTS Wing 58-65; tail 24-30; bill 7-10; tarsus 9-11.

GEOGRAPHICAL VARIATION Two races.

>*M. m. meeki* (Admiralty Islands)
>
>*M. m. proxima* (St Matthias group) The face is a paler and more yellowish grey than that of the nominate; slight greenish suffusion against yellow markings, and a yellow frontal band meeting the supercilia.

REFERENCES BirdLife (1993), Coates (1985), Forshaw (1989), Greensmith (1975), Lambert *et al.* (1993), Peters (1961), Sibley (1951), Sibley & Monroe (1990).

---

82 FINSCH'S PYGMY PARROT
Micropsitta finschii   Plate 18

Other names: Emerald Pygmy Parrot

IDENTIFICATION 9.5cm. A tiny green stub-tailed parrot confined to lowland forest on islands in the Bismarck Archipelago and the Solomon Islands. It is sympatric with Red-breasted Pygmy Parrot (83) on New Ireland, Bougainville and Guadalcanal. Red-breasted is encountered mainly at higher altitudes, and although females also possess blue crowns Finsch's has a green, not pale pinkish-buff, face. The flight of Finsch's is direct and swift with rapid beats interspersed with withdrawn wings.

VOICE A flat harsh *tzit* and a babble of squeaks while feeding. A soft whispering *chuiwehwi*, a high thin *seeetz*, a *sit-sit-sit-sit-sheeett* in flight, and a shrill *chilp*. Similar to but louder than Buff-faced Pygmy Parrot. Will respond to an imitation of its calls.

DISTRIBUTION AND STATUS Occurs in the Bismarck Archipelago including New Hanover, Tabar, Lihir and New

Ireland, through Bougainville into the Solomons on Choiseul, Santa Isabel, Malaita, Vella Lavella, Gizo, Kolombangara, New Georgia, Rendova, the Russell Islands, the Florida Islands, Nggela Sule, Guadalcanal, Uki and San Cristobal. World population in excess of 100,000 and stable. Not kept in captivity.

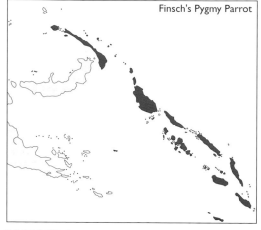

Finsch's Pygmy Parrot

ECOLOGY Commonest in lowland to mid-altitude primary forest, occurring up to 900m (lower limit of mist-forest where they are replaced by Red-breasted), but occurs in a range of habitats including overgrown gardens, casuarinas, secondary growth, open scrubby areas and occasionally coconuts *Cocos nucifera*. This is a vociferous and active species but is still easy to overlook. Birds are encountered alone, in pairs or in groups of 3-6 birds feeding acrobatically, sometimes climbing downwards head-first and using their tails as props against the bark. They work the trunks and limbs of the canopy and mid-storey to glean lichen and fungi, and have also been recorded taking casuarina seeds. One to two eggs are laid in a cavity which the birds excavate over a period of several weeks in an active arboreal termite nest (which is also used for roosting). The entrance tunnel slopes upwards and at dusk several birds may enter to roost inside. As the young grow larger one of the adults will roost in the tunnel rather than the cavity. Adults with recently fledged young were observed in Jan 1995 in southern New Ireland. Main breeding period speculated to be from Mar to May.

DESCRIPTION Head bright green, slightly paler and yellower on chin and throat, which are flecked pale blue. Upperparts bright green, with fine darker fringes and black centres to median-coverts. Flight feathers black with fine green margins; underwing-coverts greenish-yellow. Underparts pale yellowish-green with fine darker fringes and feathers in centre of belly orange-red; undertail-coverts yellow, longest tipped bluish-green. Uppertail centrally dull blue, laterally black tipped blue and yellow; undertail black tipped yellow but mostly obscured by long yellow undertail-coverts at rest. **Bare parts**: Bill blackish; cere pink; iris orange-red; legs grey.

SEX/AGE Cere pink in male, greyish in female. Females lack red markings on underparts and have pink, not blue, feathers on the chin. Immature with light greyish bill and reddish brown, not orange-red, iris. In juvenile birds the cere is greyish in both sexes. Immature males of the nominate race lack the blue chin and red markings on the abdomen.

MEASUREMENTS Wing 61-67; tail 26-34; bill 7-8; tarsus 9-10.

GEOGRAPHICAL VARIATION Five races.

> *M. f. finschii* (S Solomons including San Cristobal, Uki and Rennell) The crown is green and the male shows reddish markings on the centre of its abdomen.
> *M. f. aolae* (SC Solomons including Russell and Florida, Guadalcanal and Malaita) There is a light blue spot on the rear crown and no red on the underparts of the male.
> *M. f. tristrami* (W Solomons including Vella Lavella, Gizo, Kolombangara, Rubiana, New Georgia and Rendova) Green crown, but males lack orange-red on underparts.
> *M. f. nanina* (N Solomons including Bougainville and Choiseul) Blue tinge to crown (but less than *M. f. aolae*). Male lacks red on underparts.
> *M. f. viridifrons* (Bismarck Archipelago including New Hanover, New Ireland, Tabar and Lihi) The crown, cheeks and chin are blue, and some males show red on the underparts.

REFERENCES Arndt (1992), B.M. Beehler *in litt.* (1997), BirdLife (1993), Cain & Galbraith (1956), Coates (1985), Forshaw (1989), Greensmith (1975), Hadden (1981), ICBP (1992), Lambert *et al.* (1993), Lees (1991), Mayr (1945), Peters (1961), Sibley (1951).

83   RED-BREASTED PYGMY PARROT
Micropsitta bruijnii   Plate 18

Other names: Mountain Pygmy Parrot, Bruijn's Pygmy Parrot, Bruijn's Red-headed Pygmy Parrot

IDENTIFICATION 8-10cm. The only pygmy parrot in montane forest over 1,000m (but ranges lower), occurring on Buru, Seram, the highlands of Papua New Guinea, the Bismarck Archipelago and some of the Solomon Islands. Males are distinctive, green above with a blue collar and eye streak, pink throat and orange-red underparts with green flanks. The Buff-faced Pygmy Parrot (80) is similar to female Red-breasted, but occurs at lower elevations and shows a buffy supercilium and a buffier face. In New Ireland and on the larger Solomon Islands, Red-breasted is sympatric with Finsch's Pygmy Parrot (82) which, like female Red-breasted, also shows a blue cap. Finsch's lacks the pale face, however, and is generally at lower altitudes. The flight of Red-breasted is swift with slight undulation and audible wingbeats.

VOICE A very high-pitched, tinkling, insect-like *ks*, or series of *ks* notes. There is also a shrill penetrating *tseet* or *tsee tsee*. The call is louder, harsher and more often disyllabic than that of Buff-faced.

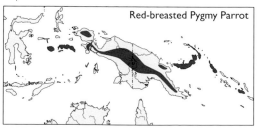

Red-breasted Pygmy Parrot

DISTRIBUTION AND STATUS Occurs on the islands of Buru and Seram, and in mountain forests throughout New Guinea, the Bismarck Archipelago, and three of the Solomon Islands. In New Guinea, it occurs in the Tamrau and Arfak mountains of Vogelkop, along the Onin Peninsula, and through the central mountain belt, including the Kubor Mountains, and reaches the Adelbert, Saruwaged and Owen Stanley ranges in the north and south east. It also occurs in New Britain and New Ireland (Hans Meyer Range) and on Bougainville, Kolombangara and Guadalcanal in the Solomons. The species is considered fairly common but local, and is probably under-recorded due to its small size and preference for the forest canopy. The world population is in excess of 100,000 and stable.

ECOLOGY Red-breasted Pygmy Parrots occur in primary and secondary montane forest, along forest margins, and have also been recorded in *Albizia* shade trees in coffee plantations. They are usually found from 500 to 3,000m, but may range lower, with a record of a vagrant at sea-level. The species is usually found in pairs or parties of up to 20, moving quickly in tight groups through the mid- to upper canopy. They are most often located by their weak high-pitched calls. The birds favour dead trees and may 'jump' from one branch to another as they search nuthatch-fashion for fungi and lichens to feed on. They also take fruit and flowers. Unlike other pygmy parrots, they bore their nest cavities into the sides of dead trees, not termitaria. The entrance tunnel leads upward to the cavity and enters at the rear. One cavity was measured at 100 x 55mm, and had a lining of wood chips. Breeding has been recorded from Dec to Mar.

DESCRIPTION Crown variably rose-pink tinged brown towards nape; cheeks, chin and ear-coverts pale buffy-pink tinged rose; line from eye to nape iridescent blue. Broad band on rear of nape iridescent blue, rest of upperparts green with fine dark margins. Flight feathers black finely fringed green; wing coverts green with black centres. Underwing-coverts greyish-black. Underparts rose-pink, darker towards vent, with narrow collar of iridescent blue on upper breast, merging to green of flanks below and reaching round to meet blue hind collar above; sides of breast blue, vent green, undertail-coverts dark rose-pink. Central tail feathers dull blue above with black spot at tips, outer black with yellow-orange tips. **Bare parts**: Bill grey; cere pink; iris brown; legs grey.

SEX/AGE Female mainly green and lacking rose-pink underparts and blue collar of male. Pink crown is also replaced by blue (except for forehead which is buff-pink), and the undertail-coverts are yellow-green not pink. The underwing-coverts show some greenish markings and the throat is greyish-white. Young males are like females but show orange on the underparts, and have white foreheads and lores.

MEASUREMENTS Wing 61-70; tail 22-27; bill 5-7; tarsus 8-9.

GEOGRAPHICAL VARIATION Four races.
  M. b. bruijnii (mountains of New Guinea)
  M. b. pileata (Buru and Seram) Male has a darker buffy-red crown which extends further down to the blue hind-collar.
  M. b. necopinata (Bismarck Archipelago) The male's crown is brown with a yellowish centre. The cheeks, throat and middle of breast and abdomen are red-

dish-orange. The undertail-coverts are yellow. The female is like the nominate female but the crown is a more purplish-blue.
  M. b. rosea (Solomons) The red of the underparts is richer but restricted to the centre of the lower breast and abdomen. The red of the cheeks and crown are also richer. Female like nominate female.

REFERENCES Arndt (1992), Beehler (1978b), Beehler *et al.* (1986), Bowler & Taylor (1990), Cain & Galbraith (1956), Coates (1985), Diamond (1972), Forshaw (1989), Gee (1993), Greensmith (1975), Hadden (1981), Hornbuckle (1991), Jones & Banjaransari (1990), Lambert *et al.* (1993), Lodge (1991), Mayr (1945), Peters (1961), Pratt (1982), Rand & Gilliard (1967), Sibley & Monroe (1990), Smith (1992), Taylor (1990), White & Bruce (1986).

84   ORANGE-BREASTED FIG PARROT
Cyclopsitta gulielmitertii   Plate 19

Other names: William's Fig Parrot, King of Holland's Fig Parrot

IDENTIFICATION 13cm. A small green parrot with striking facial markings and a short pointed tail, widespread in the lowlands of New Guinea and also present in the W Papuan and Aru Islands. All forms show mainly green upperparts and belly, blue flight feathers, a distinctive facial pattern and (except nominate female) at least some orange or yellow on the breast. This is the smallest of the fig parrots, but still about one-third larger than the largest pygmy parrot. Red-breasted Pygmy Parrots (83) occur at higher altitudes, have red, not orange, breasts, generally pale buffy faces, and no blue in the wing. Buff-faced Pygmy Parrot (80) is sympatric through much of northern New Guinea but, apart from its much smaller size, has an entirely buff face with no darker markings, and again no blue in the wing. Double-eyed Fig Parrot (85) occurs throughout the New Guinea lowlands and is of similar size to Orange-breasted, but has a light green breast, yellow flanks, and the males of the three sympatric races have distinctive scarlet facial markings. Occurring in the lowlands of northern Irian Jaya east of Geelvink Bay is the larger Salvadori's Fig Parrot (88), in which the male shows a red breast and a very different facial pattern (see plate). In northern Papua New Guinea, Salvadori's is replace by Edwards's Fig Parrot (87) in which the male again has an obvious fiery orange-red breast, but this is separated by a dull bluish band, while the elongated yellow ear-coverts bordered above by a black eye-stripe are diagnostic. Both of the preceding species also lack the blue wing-flash in flight. Pairs or small groups of Orange-breasted Fig Parrots fly swiftly overhead, showing their short pointed tails. The similar-sized small lorikeets *Charmosyna* all have longer tails.

VOICE Flight call, a shrill, frequently repeated *tseet*, similar to that of Double-eyed Fig Parrot but higher-pitched. Another call has been described as a chirping *chip-chip-chip*, like small coins clinked together. Whilst feeding a subdued chattering, as well as various wheezing calls, and a high-pitched staccato *kss*. There is also a short *ts* call, said to be less sharp, shrill or grating than that of Red-flanked Lorikeet (45).

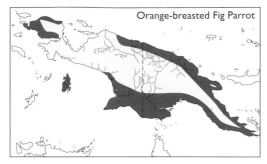

Orange-breasted Fig Parrot

DISTRIBUTION AND STATUS Widely distributed, abundant and easily observed in lowland rainforest throughout much of New Guinea. The westernmost race is isolated, occurring only on Salawati in the W Papuan islands, and in the lowlands of Vogelkop, western Irian Jaya. Elsewhere in New Guinea the range is continuous through the northern lowlands from the eastern rim of Geelvink Bay around the Memberamo River, through the Sepik River region and the lowlands of the Huon Peninsula, to Milne Bay in the extreme east. The range continues west through the lowlands of southern New Guinea through the Purari and Fly River regions to the lowlands of south-east Irian Jaya at around 138°E; also on the Aru Islands. Orange-breasted Fig Parrots appear to be commoner in southern New Guinea than in the north. The world population is thought to be in excess of 100,000 and stable.

ECOLOGY Occurs in rainforest, swamp forest, *Melaleuca* woodland, dense savanna and partly cleared areas from sea-level to around 300m, rarely recorded higher than 800m, the highest known altitude being 1,100m. They are usually encountered in small active groups of 6-10, either flying above the forest calling, or congregating where they can forage for figs or other fruits in the canopy or lower storeys. Whilst feeding the birds can be difficult to detect as they clamber around quietly, although they may swing upside-down to feed, sometimes dropping debris as they do so. The diet includes the seeds of figs and other fruit, as well as whole small fruits, nectar taken from flowers and occasional insects. Orange-breasted Fig Parrot nests are located in globular arboreal termitaria, high in forest trees. Up to three holes may be excavated, and nesting may be communal. Nests have also been found in the base of a complex of epiphytes. Little information is available on breeding season, activity having been reported at apparent nest-sites from Sep through to Jun. These sites may however also be used for roosting, and a record of a male regurgitating food near an entrance hole in Jan probably indicates breeding during that month at least.

DESCRIPTION Forehead and forecrown dark blue, cheeks and ear-coverts buff-yellow with variable dull black bar across face; rear-crown and entire upperparts dark green. Flight feathers black with dark blue outerwebs, blue at bend of wing; yellow edgings on innerwebs of inner wing-coverts and flight feathers except outermost primaries. Underwing grey with green coverts tending to blue at leading edge. Chin yellow; breast orange; rest of underparts yellowish-green, lighter around vent. Uppertail green; undertail dull grey-green. **Bare parts:** Bill black; iris brown; legs grey.

SEX/AGE The female has a green breast, darker face with a blue forehead and forecrown (blue extends slightly through eye), and a black patch beneath the eye; the ear-coverts are orange, and the yellow lores are bordered below by green which runs into blue at the rear. Young are similar to females.

MEASUREMENTS Wing 91-97; tail 34-42; bill 14-16; tarsus 12-15.

GEOGRAPHICAL VARIATION Seven races. The variations in pattern are fairly complex and the most distinctive races are illustrated on Plate 19.

> *C. g. gulielmitertii* (Salawati and in the W part of Vogelkop)
>
> *C. g. nigrifrons* (N New Guinea east to the lower Sepik River) Similar to the nominate, but the forecrown is black, not blue (both sexes).
>
> *C. g. ramuensis* (N New Guinea in the Ramu River area) Smaller than nominate (male wing 82.5). Very similar to *amabilis*, but forecrown variably suffused with blue and black.
>
> *C. g. amabilis* (N coast of E New Guinea from the Huon Peninsula to Milne Bay) Smaller than nominate (male wing 83.6). Male distinctive with sides of head, throat, breast and upper abdomen pale yellow, lacking orange and black marks on ear-coverts. Female with black crown and cheek-spot pale whitish-yellow face, and pale orange breast with lighter feather fringes giving a slightly scalloped appearance at close range.
>
> *C. g. suavissima* (SE coast of New Guinea to around the Purari River in the west) Smaller than nominate (male wing 77.3). Male with orange breast, large black patch below eye, whitish rear ear-coverts and lores, blue forecrown and yellow wing-bar. Female with blue face, white mark at base of bill and behind eye, orange ear-coverts and an orange suffusion against a green breast.
>
> *C. g. fuscifrons* (Fly River west to around 138°E) Smaller than nominate (male wing 80.2). Similar to *C. g. suavissima* but male has blackish forecrown, less orange on the breast, a smaller black cheek-patch, and a whitish throat. The female is like *suavissima*, but the blue of the face is replaced by black (except at sides of throat).
>
> *C. g. melanogenia* (Aru Islands) Very similar to *fuscifrons* but female with less orange below.

REFERENCES Arndt (1992), Beehler *et al.* (1986), Bell (1982), Bell & Coates (1979), Coates (1985), Diamond (1972), Forshaw (1989), Hornbuckle (1991), Lambert *et al.* (1993), Lodge (1991), Peters (1961), Rand & Gilliard (1967).

---

85 DOUBLE-EYED FIG PARROT
Cyclopsitta diophthalma Plate 20

Other names: Two-eyed Fig Parrot, Double-eyed Dwarf Parrot, Dwarf Fig Parrot, Lorilet; Coxen's Fig Parrot, Coxen's Double-eyed Fig Parrot, Coxen's Two-eyed Fig Parrot, Coxen's Blue-browed Fig Parrot, Blue-browed Fig Parrot, Red-faced Lorilet, Coxen's Lorilet, Southern Fig Parrot (*C. d. coxeni*); Red-browed Fig Parrot, Blue-faced Fig Parrot, Macleay's Lorilet, Northern Fig Parrot (*C. d. macleayana*); Marshall's Fig Parrot, Cape York Fig Parrot (*C. d. marshalli*)

IDENTIFICATION 13-16cm. A tiny green parrot which

ranges through the lowland forests of New Guinea, and also occurs in three isolated populations in north-eastern and eastern Australia. All races share mainly green plumage with bright yellow flanks and blue primaries, most also showing distinctive red and blue facial markings. Double-eyed Fig Parrots are small, chunky and relatively large-headed and billed, with a short pointed tail. They are reminiscent of small lorikeets in behaviour, and are often first noticed as they dart through the canopy giving their thin high-pitched calls. This is the smallest Australian parrot and is sympatric with the similar-sized Little Lorikeet (36), which also has red facial markings but which also has green, not blue, primaries, and lacks yellow flank-markings. In New Guinea, the common and widespread Red-flanked Lorikeet (45) is a possible confusion species, but is much slimmer and longer-tailed: the red flanked males should present no difficulty in the field, and both sexes show a bright red, not greyish-black, bill. Orange-breasted Fig Parrot (84) is also sympatric in parts of New Guinea, but all races show at least some orange or yellow on the breast, have blackish forecrowns, and lack bright red or turquoise facial markings. The three other fig parrots, Edwards's (87), Large (86) and Salvadori's (88), are all larger with distinctive plumage features depicted on plates 19 and 21. In flight, Double-eyed Fig Parrots move fast and direct with very rapid wingbeats, the under-wing showing a pale bar; brief pauses as the wings are drawn to the body cause no undulation.

VOICE A thin, high pitched *seet-seet* given frequently in flight, and immediately before taking off and after alighting. Other calls include a chattering twitter and a high-pitched rolling screech, given in alarm or when going to roost. A similar call is given by one bird of a pair while the other repeats a *chink* note. The flight call is more disyllabic, staccato and harsh than that of Little Lorikeet, and is slightly reminiscent of the call of a Budgerigar (155). The larger fig parrots have stronger calls, and the call of Orange-breasted is higher-pitched. Double-eyed Fig Parrots will respond to an imitation of their call note.

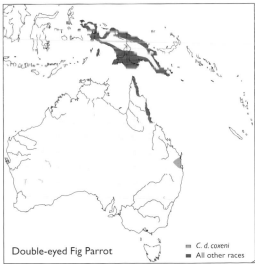

Double-eyed Fig Parrot
- ■ *C. d. coxeni*
- ■ All other races

DISTRIBUTION AND STATUS Occurs throughout much of New Guinea and parts of north-east Australia. In the far west it is found on Waigeo, Salawati, Misool and Kafiau in the W Papuan islands, Indonesia. It is widespread but patchily distributed through the New Guinea mainland, being absent only from central Vogelkop and the central mountain belt above 1,600m, although it has been recorded above 1,800m locally. It occurs in the Aru Islands, and on Fergusson and Goodenough Islands in the D'Entrecasteaux group, and on Tagula in the Louisiade group. In Australia, the most northerly of three isolated populations occupies the tip of the Cape York Peninsula from the Jardine River in the north-west, south to around Lockhart River in the east, sometimes as far south as the northern edge of Princess Charlotte Bay; the central population occupies the coastal district from around Cooktown in the north through Cairns and the Atherton district to about Townsville in the south; the southernmost population, now very reduced with fewer than 50 records in the past century, formerly extended from Gympie, Queensland, south to around the Richmond River, New South Wales, reaching inland to the Bunya Mountains (in 1976 two birds were recorded near Koreelan Creek in Feb and two near Lamington National Park in Dec). The world population estimate is in excess of 100,000 and stable, but the status of two subspecies is less assured: *C. d. macleayana* has a world population in the region of 5,000 individuals and may be in decline, although it does breed in parks and gardens around Cairns; *C. d. coxeni* may total as few as 200 birds, having suffered as a result of lowland rainforest destruction throughout its limited range, where it was probably never common. The third Australian subspecies, *C. d. marshalli* is still quite common. In New Guinea, the species is scattered, and considered rare in Vogelkop and absent from many parts of the southern lowlands, occurring mainly at higher altitudes in the southern watershed. Orange-breasted probably replaces this species in much of this area. It is probable that the species is under-recorded because of its small size and unobtrusive habits. Protected by law in Australia. *C. d. coxeni* is listed on CITES Appendix I.

ECOLOGY Sedentary with some post-breeding dispersal. Found in a range of low- to mid-altitude habitats including rainforest, secondary growth, forest edge, riverine forest, and occasionally dry forest and open eucalypt woodland. In Australia birds are also found in parks, gardens, scrub, cultivated areas and mangrove; *C. d. coxeni* was probably concentrated in alluvial forest, but also occurs in dry lowland forest and lowland and hill rainforest. The species is heavily dependent on figs *Ficus* in all habitats. Birds are usually encountered in pairs or small groups, drawing attention to themselves with their constant high-pitched calls as they fly through or above the canopy. They feed quietly, creeping unobtrusively through the foliage, often betraying their presence only by the stream of debris falling as they break into fruits to reach the seeds. Outside the breeding season, groups of up to 200 birds may roost together, disbanding into smaller parties to feed during the morning and afternoon. When alarmed, the wings are flicked and the birds call in an agitated fashion. During rains, bathing takes place in wet foliage, and allopreening is common. Fig seeds are the principal food item, birds often returning to the same ripe fruit until all the seeds are gone. The diet also comprises small whole fruits, nectar, insect larvae, and fungus or lichen gleaned from bark. Birds may feed in groups with other fig parrots and, in Australia, with rosellas *Platycercus* and lorikeets. Breeding probably begins in New Guinea during Mar, and in Australia the main season runs from Aug to Nov. When breeding the birds split into pairs which are territorial around their feeding trees. The nest is an enlarged cavity in a tree-trunk or limb, 8-20m above ground. Most nest preparation is carried out by the female, who roosts in the hollow and spends much of the day there during excavation. She may experiment with more than one nest-hole. Courtship feeding is common. The entrance hole is about 4cm in diameter, and the two white eggs are laid at 48-hour intervals on decayed wood-dust at the base of the chamber, about 20cm or so below the opening. Incubation lasts 18 days and the white-downed young fledge in 7-8 weeks, having been fed by the female alone for the first 3-4 weeks. They return to roost in the hollow for a short while after fledging.

DESCRIPTION Front half of crown, lores, cheeks and ear-coverts bright scarlet with some slightly elongated feathers; bright turquoise mark above and in front of eye, extending back slightly above and below eye; green line above and behind eye; light violet-blue mark below red at rear of ear-coverts extending towards throat; narrow orange-yellow band behind red of crown merging to green of rear-crown. Upperparts bright green with indistinct light olive suffusion on mantle. Wing-coverts bright green; primary coverts blue; primaries with dull turquoise-blue outerwebs and blackish innerwebs; flight feathers (except outermost primaries) with yellowish-white band visible from below; innermost wing-coverts marked red, underwing-coverts green edged yellow. Underparts paler, slightly more yellow green than upperparts, with strong yellow flash along flank from near bend of wing. Uppertail green; undertail greyish. **Bare parts:** Robust, strongly notched bill, lead-grey with a blackish tip; cere dark grey; iris dark brown; legs greyish-green.

SEX/AGE Female has cheeks buff, not red. Immature like female. Young males acquire adult plumage in 14 months.

MEASUREMENTS Wing 81-92; tail 34-46; bill 14-15; tarsus 13-15.

GEOGRAPHICAL VARIATION Eight races, one of which, *C. d. coxeni*, may merit specific status.

C. d. diophthalma (W Papuan islands and in NW New Guinea, reaching east to around Astrolabe Bay in the north and 138°E in the south, being absent from the Central Highlands where it is replaced by the following race)

C. d. coccineifrons (SE New Guinea from around Astrolabe Bay in the north to the Fly River in the south, extending west through the Central Highlands to around 139°E) Generally darker than nominate. Broader yellow-orange band on crown.

C. d. aruensis (S New Guinea ranging from around 138°E east to the Fly River and onto the Aru Islands) Male lacks yellow-orange crown-band (very slight on mainland birds), and mark in front of the eye is greener. The chin is light blue, and the area below the ear-coverts more mauve. The upperparts are also a yellower green. Female has no red on face, showing a turquoise-blue crown, lores and upper ear-coverts, and mauve-blue sides to the throat. The cheeks are a light greyish-buff.

C. d. virago (Fergusson and Goodenough Islands in the D'Entrecasteaux group) Male shows less, and paler, red on head than preceding race, and lacks blue patch in front of eye. The violet-blue band below the ear-coverts is almost absent, and the upperparts are

paler than in nominate. Female has a red spot on forecrown, and the face is mainly green with a blue tint to the crown, with no mauve band below the ear-coverts.

C. d. inseparabilis (Tagula Island in the Louisiade Archipelago) Sexes alike, with head entirely green except for a red spot on the forecrown, bordered with blue at the rear (slightly duller in female). Underparts yellower green.

C. d. marshalli (northern tip of the Cape York Peninsula, Queensland, Australia) Very similar to *aruensis*, but male with mark in front of eye deeper blue. Red of face paler than *aruensis*, blue of primaries darker and yellow crown-band more prominent.

C. d. macleayana (NE Queensland around Cooktown south to Townsville; breeds in and around Cairns) Male with bold scarlet band from base of lower mandible across cheeks and ear-coverts. Forecrown bright scarlet. Lores and area above and in front of eye bright turquoise. Area immediately below eye bright turquoise-green. Green stripe above and behind eye. Mauve band below ear-coverts. Female lacks red facial band and has buff cheeks strongly marked turquoise-blue.

C. d. coxeni (formerly extreme SE Queensland and NE New South Wales; range now very limited, probably occurring only in the Lamington National Park area) Sexes similar, somewhat larger and more yellowish green than the nominate. Cheeks and ear-coverts orange-red bordered below by blue, with some orange-red on lores. Lacks blue mark in front of eye, instead showing a light blue spot on the green fore-crown. Orange-red more restricted (mainly absent from the lores) in female.

REFERENCES Beehler (1978b), Beehler *et al.* (1986), Blakers *et al.* (1984), Coates (1985), Diamond (1972), Eastman & Hunt (1966), Forshaw (1967, 1981, 1989), Garnett (1992), Gyldenstolpe (1955), Hornbuckle (1991), Iredale (1956), Joseph (1988b), Lambert *et al.* (1993), Lodge (1991), Martindale (1986), Peters (1961), Pizzey & Doyle (1983), Rand & Gilliard (1967), Schodde (1978), Schodde & Tidemann (1988), Sibley & Monroe (1990), Slater (1979, 1989).

86   LARGE FIG PARROT
Psittaculirostris desmarestii   Plate 21

Other names: Desmarest's Fig Parrot, Desmarest's Dwarf Parrot, Golden-headed Fig Parrot, Golden-headed Dwarf Parrot

IDENTIFICATION 18-20cm. A small but stocky parrot with a large head and short tail, ranging through the forested lowlands of western and southern New Guinea. The species is mainly green with a blue breast-band, fiery red forecrown, black bill, and cheeks and ear-coverts which vary from greenish through yellow to orange-red according to race. The male of the much larger Red-cheeked Parrot (95) is superficially similar in pattern to the south-east New Guinea race of this species, but can be easily separated by its bright red upper mandible (see plate 24 for further obvious differences).

VOICE A distinctive high, thin, down-slurred call as well as some chattering and quiet clinking notes. The calls are louder than those of smaller lorikeets and fig parrots, but less strident than those of Red-cheeked Parrot or Rainbow Lorikeet (13). At the nest a continually repeated *chet chet*.

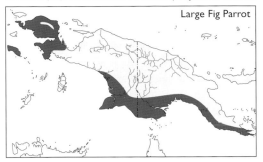

Large Fig Parrot

DISTRIBUTION AND STATUS Western and southern Irian Jaya, Indonesian New Guinea, ranging from the W Papuan islands (Batanta, Salawati and Misool), through Vogelkop to the Bomberai and Onin Peninsulas in the south, and the Wandamen Peninsula in the north, into the southern and south-eastern lowlands and foothills (to Karimui area) from around 137°E, reaching to about Popondetta on the north coast of the south-eastern peninsula. The species is only locally common, with a stable world population estimated at greater than 150,000. The western subspecies are probably declining due to habitat loss and trade.

ECOLOGY Found in lowland and hill forest, riverine forest, forest edge and occasionally savanna generally below 1,100m, locally up to 1,650m. The birds gather in small groups to feed high in fruiting fig trees, cutting into the fruit with their sharp bills to expose the seeds. The birds will jump from branch to branch as they move around, and in flight dart rapidly through the canopy in small flocks of 2-6 birds, calling constantly. They have been recorded in breeding condition at various times of the year, with breeding behaviour noted in Jul and Sep. Little is known of their breeding habits but birds are known to nest communally in groups of up to three pairs, and have been observed in noisy groups in the vicinity of presumed nest-holes high in forest trees. During courtship allopreening is common, and during copulation the male places one foot on the female's back and one on its perch. Head-scratching is over the wing.

DESCRIPTION Forecrown fiery orange, paler towards nape; lores red-orange; area before and below eye bright light turquoise and violet-blue; cheeks and slightly elongated lower ear-coverts bright pale green, suffused light orange in centre. Narrow hind-collar blue. Upperparts green with indistinct light olive wash on lower back and rump; wing-coverts green with orange spots on tips of innermost greater coverts, outerwebs of flight feathers bluer-green than coverts and margined yellow at tips; innerwebs blackish-brown; bend of wing light blue. Underwing-coverts turquoise-green (longest yellow); underwing with yellow band on innerwebs except for outermost primaries. Underparts lighter green, broken by a continuous narrow pale blue band on upper breast bordered below by a dull broken reddish band. Uppertail green; undertail greyish-green. **Bare parts**: Bill black; iris dark brown; legs grey-green.

SEX/AGE Females like males, except in the southern lowlands where they lack the yellow hind-collar present in males (in this race young birds are like females). Immatures have a dingy yellowish crown in most races, although south-eastern immatures have a green crown. In Misool, young have a blue eye-spot which is lost in adult plumage.

MEASUREMENTS Wing 106-118; tail 49-62; bill 18-20; tarsus 17-18.

GEOGRAPHICAL VARIATION Six races.

P. d. desmarestii (W and N Vogelkop)

P. d. intermedia (Onin Peninsula) Crown more orange, cheeks and ear-coverts with some orange feathers; blue hind-collar indistinct or absent.

P. d. occidentalis (Salawati and Batanta and the opposite coast of Vogelkop, from at least Sorong to Teminabuan, and south on the Bomberai Peninsula) Cheeks and ear-coverts orange-yellow, upper ear-coverts somewhat elongated and bright golden yellow. Lacks blue hind-collar. Blue mark below eye paler than in nominate race. Rear of crown more yellowish.

P. d. blythii (Misool) Similar to preceding, but lacks blue mark below eye and has brighter orange cheeks.

P. d. godmani (SW New Guinea intergrading with the following race in the Fly River region) No blue below eye. Brilliant golden yellow elongated ear-coverts and more extensive blue breast-band, with lower reddish band indistinct or absent. Brighter scarlet forecrown. Male with yellow hind-collar.

P. d. cervicalis (SE New Guinea from east of the Fly River in the south to Popondetta in the north) Entire head appears orange-red interspersed with some yellow on the throat and rear ear-coverts. No blue below eye. There is a broad blue hind-collar and the blue breast-band is darker than in other races, owing to dull reddish-brown suffusion of entire band, but with some slight orange suffusion below. Intermediate birds occur in the zone of intergradation. Young with green crown.

REFERENCES Arndt (1992), Beehler *et al.* (1986), Coates (1985), Diamond (1972), Forshaw (1989), Gee (1993), Gyldenstolpe (1955), Hornbuckle (1991), Iredale (1956), Lambert *et al.* (1993), Lodge (1991), Peters (1961), Rand & Gilliard (1967), Schodde (1978), Sibley & Monroe (1990), Smith (1991, 1994).

87 EDWARDS'S FIG PARROT
Psittaculirostris edwardsii   Plate 19

IDENTIFICATION 18cm. A small, stocky parrot with large head and short pointed tail, found only in lowland forests of north-eastern New Guinea. In common with the other two members of the genus, the ear-coverts are elongated and brightly coloured. Males are extremely distinctive, with bright yellowish green forecrowns, and brilliant yellow ear-coverts, mixed with red, and with pale blue towards the tips. A greyish-black band extends back from the eye to the nape; the throat and most of the underparts are reddish, separated by a purplish-blue band on the upper breast, and the innermost wing-coverts are also marked red. There are no sympatric confusion species. The range of Salvadori's Fig Parrot (88) comes close to the western extreme of this species to the west of the Irian Jaya–New Guinea border at around 140°E. Both male and female Salvadori's have yellow, not red, throats, and the red on the upper breast of male Salvadori's does not extend to the belly. In southern New Guinea, the closely related Large Fig Parrot (86) can be separated on range, and by its red, not green, crown and blue breast. For differences from the smaller, dissimilar Orange-breasted Fig Parrot (84) see Plate 19 and notes for that species.

VOICE A short sharp metallic *ks* 'like the sound of coins falling on concrete'. The call is louder and harsher than that of Double-eyed Fig Parrot (85). Other calls are described by Greensmith as *screet-screet* or *screet-a-lut*, reminiscent of the flight call of Rainbow Lorikeet (13) but softer.

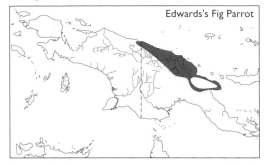

DISTRIBUTION AND STATUS Endemic to the northern New Guinea lowlands in Irian Jaya and Papua New Guinea. Occurs commonly in the north-east from around Jayapura along the coastal lowlands, and reaching inland to around Pagwi, Chambri Lake and the Jimi River. It is found in the Sepik River region, and extends east to the lowlands of the Huon Peninsula and Markham River. The world population is thought to be in excess of 100,000.

ECOLOGY Occurs in humid lowland forest, partly cleared areas, forest edge as well as near human habitation, up to about 800m. The birds are usually found in pairs or small noisy flocks, although groups of as many as 400 birds have been found gathering in the tops of fruiting trees. They are quick-moving, and will hang upside-down to reach food items. The diet comprises fruit, including figs *Ficus* and casuarinas, nectar and probably insects. They have been seen in mixed flocks with Double-eyed Fig Parrots. Nesting behaviour has been noted from Jan to May, and a display, which involved the male rubbing bills with the female and fluttering above its perch, was noted in Oct. The nest is in a hole, high in a forest tree.

DESCRIPTION Forehead and crown bright yellowish-green, with greener fringe to rear; nape with band of greyish-brown above band of blackish-grey extending towards eye; area before and just behind eye green. Elongated lower ear-coverts and throat fiery red-orange, interspersed with some dull green basal feathers, and upper rear ear-coverts (also elongated) golden-yellow interspersed with orange, the longest being light turquoise-blue with paler shafts. Upperparts darkish green: bend of wing with light blue mark. Flight feathers black marked green on outerwebs and (except outermost primaries) with yellow innerwebs forming a bar on under-wing; innermost wing-coverts marked orange-red. Underwing-coverts bluish-green, longest tipped yellow. Purplish-blue gorget with a few lighter green feathers; centre of breast and upper belly rich orange-red; flanks, thighs and undertail-coverts yellowish-green. Uppertail green; undertail dull olive-yellow. **Bare parts**: Bill black; iris brown to red-brown; legs light grey.

SEX/AGE The female lacks the red centre to the breast and upper belly, and has a more extensive purple-blue breast-band tending to pale violet interspersed with red below. Immatures are like females but with greenish-yellow ear-coverts.

MEASUREMENTS Wing 103-118; tail 47-63; bill 17-20; tarsus 16-18.

GEOGRAPHICAL VARIATION None.

REFERENCES Arndt (1992), Beehler *et al.* (1986), BirdLife (1993), Coates (1985), Diamond (1972), Forshaw (1989), Greensmith (1975), ICBP (1992), Lambert *et al.* (1993), Peters (1961), Rand & Gilliard (1967).

---

88 SALVADORI'S FIG PARROT
Psittaculirostris salvadorii   Plate 19

Other names: Whiskered Fig Parrot

IDENTIFICATION 19cm. Replaces Edwards's Fig Parrot (87) in north-west New Guinea, and the two are struc-turally very similar with their stocky profiles and elongated ear-coverts. Salvadori's has a relatively restricted range and is considered globally threatened, but may still be locally common in some areas. Males have red breasts and yellow ear-coverts, lacking the scarlet throat and belly, blackish nape and purple-blue breast-band of Edwards's; both sexes also have a blue mark behind the eye. Large Fig Parrots (86) show distinctive fiery-orange crowns. Like congeners, these fig parrots fly rapidly through or below the canopy in search of fruiting trees.

VOICE Similar to congeners. Either a staccato trill with a shrill, harsh quality in flight, or a weaker high-pitched call when perched.

DISTRIBUTION AND STATUS Endemic to northern Irian Jaya, Indonesia, occurring in lowland forests from the eastern edge of Geelvink Bay to Humboldt Bay (roughly from 137° to 141°E), reaching inland through the northern slopes of the Van Rees Mountains to 700m. Not rare within its small range, but heavy trapping for the local bird trade is considered a serious threat to its survival, as is forest clearance. World population estimated at around 10,000. VULNERABLE.

ECOLOGY Salvadori's Fig Parrot occurs in forest, along forest edge, in partly cleared areas and near human settlement. The birds subsist mainly on the seeds of figs *Ficus*, and groups forage in the canopy of fruiting trees, sometimes mixing with other species. They also take fruit, nectar and flowers. They will hang upside-down to feed, and may make brief sorties above the canopy. The species is most frequently encountered in pairs or small groups, and nests colonially. Little is known of its ecology.

DESCRIPTION Forehead and crown bright green with some blue suffusion; cheeks and elongated ear-coverts golden yellow; spot behind eye pale blue; nape yellow. Upperparts green; innermost wing-coverts tipped orange-red. Underwing-coverts dull green. Upper breast with bright red band, rest of underparts bright yellowish-green, brighter and lighter than upperparts. Uppertail green; undertail yellow. **Bare parts:** Bill black; iris red-brown; legs grey.

SEX/AGE Female lacks obvious scarlet breast-band of male, which is replaced by a green band showing few dull red feathers at the sides. Young male has red showing through blue breast-band, dark iris.

MEASUREMENTS Wing 109-118; tail 58-79; bill 18-20; tarsus 16-18.

GEOGRAPHICAL VARIATION None.

REFERENCES Arndt (1991), Beehler (1982), Beehler *et al.* (1986), BirdLife (1993), Collar & Andrew (1988), Collar *et al.* (1994), Diamond (1985), Forshaw (1989), D. Gibbs verbally (1991), Hornbuckle (1991), Iredale (1956), Lambert *et al.* (1993), Peters (1961), Rand & Gilliard (1967), Schodde (1978), Sibley & Monroe (1990).

---

89   GUIABERO
Bolbopsittacus lunulatus   Plate 21

IDENTIFICATION 15cm. A small, stocky, bright green parrot restricted to the Philippines. The only species in its genus, but strongly resembling one of the *Psittaculirostris* fig parrots in structure. The very short rounded tail is distinctive. Male Guiaberos are superficially similar to the sympatric Blue-crowned Racquet-tail (102), but have green crowns and napes terminating in a narrow blue hind-collar lacking in *P. discurus*; they also lack the elongated tail-racquets obvious in both male and female *P. discurus*. Female Montane Racquet-tails (98) are also generally similar to male Guiaberos, but show obvious tail racquets, lack the contrasting pale green rump, blue facial markings and hind-collar, and are generally found at higher altitudes. The Guiabero has swift, direct flight.

VOICE Undescribed.

DISTRIBUTION AND STATUS Restricted to the lowlands of islands in the Philippines including Luzon, Mindanao, Samar, Leyte and Panaon. Fairly common with a world population estimated at more than 50,000.

ECOLOGY Inhabits open woodland, forest, forest edge, secondary growth, savanna, farmland, orchards and mangroves, in the lowlands up to about 600m. The birds gather in fruiting trees sometimes in groups of up to 50, but most easily detected in flight. While feeding they move quietly and can be difficult to locate. The diet includes fruit, especially guavas *Psidium guajava*, but the species's ecology is little known. A female in breeding condition was collected in Mar.

DESCRIPTION Head mainly green, strongly suffused light blue around eye, on lores, chin and (vaguely) throat. Mantle slightly darker green than crown, bordered above with narrow pale blue collar; rump and uppertail-coverts

pale yellowish-green. Primary coverts blue; other wing-coverts mid-green; flight feathers with bluish outerwebs, alula mid-blue. Underwing-coverts bright green, greater underwing-coverts edged yellow; rest of underwing greyish with pale yellow bar across innerwebs of flight feathers (except outermost primaries). Underparts uniform green, slightly paler than upperparts. Closed tail bright green above, pale blue below. **Bare parts:** Bill greyish black; iris dark brown; legs greyish.

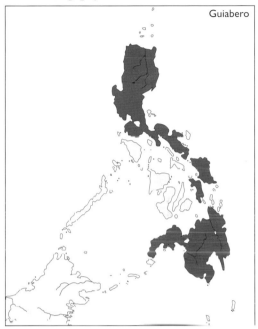

Guiabero

SEX/AGE Females show much less blue on the face, and have yellowish hind-collars and rumps, both showing darker scalloping. Immatures are like females, but with pale bills.

MEASUREMENTS Wing 94-100, tail 30-35, bill 15-19; tarsus 14-15.

GEOGRAPHICAL VARIATION Four races.
> *B. l. lunulatus* (Luzon)
> *B. l. intermedius* (Leyte) Male with more blue on the face and forecrown. Darker blue hind-collar.
> *B. l. callainipictus* (Samar) Poorly distinguished subspecies with generally more yellow-green plumage.
> *B. l. mindanensis* (Mindanao and Panaon) Male with darker blue hind-collar; paler green head contrasts with darker green back.

REFERENCES C. Brewster *in litt.* (1991), Dickinson *et al.* (1991), duPont (1971), Forshaw (1989), Lambert *et al.* (1993), Sibley & Monroe (1990).

---

90   BLUE-RUMPED PARROT
Psittinus cyanurus   Plate 22

IDENTIFICATION 18cm. A wide-ranging species, occurring through the lowland forests of Thailand, Malaysia, Borneo and Sumatra. Males are distinctive with red bills, blue heads and rumps, black backs and green wings with yellowish edgings to the upperwing-coverts and bright red underwing-coverts. The underparts are greyish. Blue-rumped Parrots are unlikely to be confused with any other species in the wild. They are sympatric only with two members of the larger, extremely long-tailed *Psittacula* group, and with the tiny Blue-crowned Hanging Parrot (184), none of which presents identification problems. The red underwing-coverts of this species are diagnostic. In flight, Blue-rumped Parrots have a distinctive silhouette with a very short blunt tail. The flight is swift and the birds are vocal on the wing.

VOICE The flight call is a shrill, sharp, chittering *chi, chi, chi* or *chew-ee*. There are also some more musical whistling notes, most often uttered while perched.

Blue-rumped Parrot

DISTRIBUTION AND STATUS Ranges from around 11°N in Peninsular Thailand and southern Tenasserim, Burma, through Peninsular Malaysia, Singapore, Sumatra and Borneo (Kalimantan, Sarawak, Sabah and Brunei). It is found in the Riau (including Bintan) and Lingga island groups north of southern Sumatra, on Bangka, and, to the west of Sumatra, on Simeuluë and the Mentawai group including Siberut, Sipura, Pagai Utara and Pagai Selatan. It is only locally common, and less abundant than the sympatric *Psittacula* species throughout most of its range. The world population is thought to be greater than 100,000, but probably declining everywhere and already sparsely distributed in the north of its range through massive habitat loss compounded by trapping. The world population of the Simeulue race may be less than 5,000. NEAR-THREATENED.

ECOLOGY There is some evidence of possible regular movements in north of its range, with birds seen passing over Fraser's Hill, Malaysia, at 1,300m. The species is also said to be a seasonal visitor to parts of southern Burma. It occurs in lowland forest (generally below 700m) and related habitats, including open woodland, secondary growth, orchards, mangroves, dry forest, swamp forest, cultivated areas, including oil palm *Elaeis guineensis* plantations near forest (where post-breeding concentrations are regarded as pests in some areas), dense scrub

and coconut *Cocos nucifera* groves. They are not shy, and can be found in groups of up to 20 birds, either foraging quietly and slowly at canopy level, flying swiftly above the forest, or wheeling around above the tree-tops calling continuously. The diet consists of seeds, fruit and blossoms. The breeding season runs from Feb to May in Malaysia, and from Jun to Sep in Borneo, but birds have been seen inspecting possible nest-holes at other times of the year. During courtship allopreening is common; the male jumps in display and places both feet on the female's back during mating. Up to three eggs are laid in a high tree hollow, but little is known of the breeding cycle.

DESCRIPTION Crown to nape greyish-blue, brightest on forecrown; lower cheeks and chin greyish-brown; nape sharply demarcated from black mantle, which is lightly mottled grey; lower back and rump light violet-blue, brighter than blue of head. Shoulder-patch maroon-red; upperwing-coverts mid-green, edged yellowish-green, particularly on inner median and greater coverts; primary coverts blue; flight feathers green, with primaries finely edged yellow along inner edges; carpal edge blue and yellow. Underwing dark, with bright red underwing-coverts and axillaries. Underparts greyish-brown becoming dull blue-green, marked yellow, on vent. Uppertail blue-green centrally, outer feathers light yellow with greener outer-webs; undertail yellow. **Bare parts:** Large bill with notched upper mandible red, lower mandible duller; iris yellowish-white; legs blue-grey.

SEX/AGE Female has a brownish head and upper mandible; lacks black back and shows only a little blue on the rump; the underparts are light green, not grey-brown as in the male. Young are like females but with green heads.

MEASUREMENTS Wing 111-126; tail 39-46; bill 18-21; tarsus 13-15.

GEOGRAPHICAL VARIATION Three races.
P. c. cyanurus (Peninsular Burma, Thailand, Malaysia, Singapore, throughout Borneo, and on Sumatra and related northerly islands)
P. c. pontius (the Mentawai group S from Siberut) Like nominate but larger (male wing 134.4).
P. c. abbottii (Simeulue) Male with green suffusion on forecrown, black hind-collar, green mantle and green rump (marked turquoise), and greenish underparts. Female with green head. Larger again than *P. c. pontius* (male wing 144.2).

REFERENCES Arndt (1992), Forshaw (1989), Gore (1968), Holmes & Nash (1990b), Jalan & Galdikas (1987), King & Dickinson (1975), Lambert *et al.* (1993), Lekagul & Cronin (1974), Lekagul & Round (1991), MacKinnon & Phillipps (1993), van Marle & Voous (1988), Medway & Wells (1976), Nash & Nash (1985, 1988), Peters (1961), Sibley & Monroe (1990), Silvius & Verheugt (1986), Smith (1981), Smythies (1981, 1986), Vuthipong (1992).

91   BREHM'S TIGER PARROT
Psittacella brehmii   Plate 23

Other names: Brehm's Ground Parrot

IDENTIFICATION 19-24cm. All tiger parrots are green with brown heads, red undertail-coverts and barred plumage. They are all somewhat alike, and care is required to separate the individual species. The genus comprises two larger species, Brehm's and Painted (92), and two smaller species, Modest (93) and Madarasz's (94). Brehm's is the large lower-altitude (mainly 1,500-2,600m) tiger parrot, and males can be separated from the two smaller sympatric species by the yellow crescent at the side of the neck. The dense narrow barring above and below separate the female. The species can generally be separated from the higher-altitude Painted Tiger Parrot (92) by its dull olive-brown, not rusty or bright olive-brown, crown. Two of the three races of Painted Tiger Parrot also have the rump and uppertail-coverts barred black and red, not black and yellowish-green as in this species, while the third (western) race, although lacking the red rump, shows green cheeks and ear-coverts, which are brown in Brehm's. In the east, male Painted Tiger Parrots also have a complete yellow hind-collar, rather than just a yellow crescent at the side of the neck, while females show bluish cheeks (brownish in Brehm's).

VOICE Mainly quiet, but one call, typical of members of the genus, is a plaintive, nasal *ee-yur*.

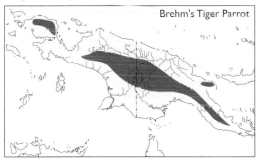

Brehm's Tiger Parrot

DISTRIBUTION AND STATUS New Guinea in three isolated populations, one in Vogelkop, Irian Jaya, the second throughout the central and south eastern highlands of New Guinea, and the third in the highlands of the Huon Peninsula (*P. picta* is absent here and Brehm's occurs at higher altitudes than usual). The species is widespread, but generally uncommon; the world population is thought to be in excess of 100,000.

ECOLOGY Occurs in montane forest, including podocarp and beech *Nothofagus* forest, and forest edge, mainly from 1,500 to 2,600m, with the extremes at 1,100m and 3,800m. Brehm's Tiger Parrots occur mostly below Painted Tiger Parrots, but there is a zone in which they are altitudinally sympatric between 2,500m and 3,000m. The birds are often found singly, or in small groups, and allow a close approach. They spend much time feeding in the sub-canopy or even near ground-level on seeds and berries (including conifers and podocarps), although they are found at higher levels in the forest too. They move around sluggishly, often using their bill to balance, and may remain motionless at times. They only make short flights, never flying above the canopy. They have been flushed from the grass in forest breaks. Little is know of the nesting behaviour, but two nestlings were taken from a nest in Jun.

DESCRIPTION Head olive-brown, merging to narrow hind-collar of fine black and green barring; yellow crescent at side of neck. Mantle tightly barred black and green; greenest in centre of back, merging to black barred yellowish-green on lower back and rump; uppertail-coverts

barred black and greenish-yellow. Wings dark green with dark fringes on median coverts; flight feathers blackish edged green on outers with a yellowish margin; bend of wing bluish. Underwing-coverts green. Underparts generally dull uniform green; undertail-coverts red. Uppertail green; undertail greyish-black. **Bare parts**: Bill greyish-blue, white at tip; iris reddish-orange; legs grey-green.

SEX/AGE Female lacks yellow crescent on neck; breast and flanks are densely barred yellow and black. Young birds have green and yellow barring on the breast. Young with orange-red undertail-coverts tipped yellowish, and pale bill.

MEASUREMENTS Wing 118-124; tail 76-90; bill 17-20; tarsus 17-21.

GEOGRAPHICAL VARIATION Four races.
> *P. b. brehmii* (Vogelkop)
> *P. b. intermixta* (C New Guinea) Underparts and barring on back more yellowish-green. Slightly larger.
> *P. b. harterti* (Huon Peninsula) Paler head and less yellowish-green in plumage. Smaller.
> *P. b. pallida* (SE New Guinea) Not strongly differentiated from nominate. Bill narrower.

REFERENCES Beehler (1978b), Beehler *et al.* (1986), Coates (1985), Diamond (1972), Forshaw (1989), Gyldenstolpe (1955), Iredale (1956), Lambert *et al.* (1993), Lodge (1991), Pallister & Hurrell (1989), Peters (1961), Rand & Gilliard (1967), Schodde (1978), Sibley & Monroe (1990), Smith (1992).

---

92   PAINTED TIGER PARROT
Psittacella picta   Plate 22

Other names: Painted Ground Parrot, Mountain Victoria Ground Parrot, Timberline Parrot

IDENTIFICATION 19cm. Barred, mainly green plumage, red undertail-coverts and brown crown, as in other tiger parrots, but crown is brighter than in the other species. This is the only tiger parrot to show either blue cheeks or a blue breast-patch, the western race has a yellow and black rump, the two eastern races barred red rumps, in either case obvious in flight. This is the larger of the two high-altitude (2,500-4,000m) tiger parrots, Modest Tiger Parrot (93) being the smaller but also reported considerably lower. Males have either a yellow hind-collar, or yellow crescent at the side of the neck, and unbarred green underparts, marked blue in the centre of the upper breast. Females of the western race are most likely to be confused with the lower-altitude Brehm's Tiger Parrot (91), but that species shows olive-brown, not green-blue, cheeks and ear-coverts, a more greenish rump and a greyer-brown mantle (Painted lacks contrast between greyer mantle and greener back). The two smaller tiger parrots are less similar in plumage, with males lacking yellow collars or neck-marks, and females lacking the dense barring on both upper- and underparts: female Modest (93) has a barred breast, but the upperparts, though faintly barred, appear almost uniform green.

VOICE Various calls, similar to those of Brehm's Tiger Parrot, have been reported. The most typical allegedly differs between populations, with birds in the east producing a musical, slightly nasal *nhrr-a-rehn*, those in the west calling *err-ee*. A harsh but subdued *chee-zeeddd* or *tschi-ziddd* has also been reported.

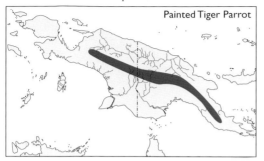
Painted Tiger Parrot

DISTRIBUTION AND STATUS Endemic to the central mountain belt of New Guinea. Restricted to high montane forests, from the W Pegunungan Maoke through the central mountains, including the Tari region, around Kandep, Mount Hagen, Mount Kubor as far as the Owen Stanley Range in the south-east. The world population is thought to be more than 100,000.

ECOLOGY The species inhabits montane forest, glades and edge, stunted moss forest, secondary growth, alpine and subalpine shrubs, reportedly as low as 1,370m (it may generally occur lower in the south-east than elsewhere), but normally between 2,400 and 4,000m, above Brehm's Tiger Parrot. The birds are generally quiet and rather sluggish, but are not shy, occurring singly, in pairs or in groups of up to six; they have also been seen feeding in mixed groups with Madarasz's Tiger Parrot (94). They often feed in low bushes or on the ground, and will fly up to higher vegetation when flushed. The diet includes seeds, berries, and the fruit of conifers *Dacrydium*. Little is known of the species's ecology and the only information on breeding behaviour is that birds in breeding condition have been collected in Jun and Aug.

DESCRIPTION Head mainly warm chestnut-brown, brighter on crown and duller and greyer on cheeks, with narrow yellow hind-collar reaching around sides of neck. Mantle green, barred black; rump and uppertail-coverts dull red, barred black. Wings green with outerwebs of flight feathers edged yellow. Underwing-coverts yellow-green. Chin brown, upper breast with central blue mark and undertail-coverts red; otherwise underparts uniform mid-green (slightly lighter than upperparts). Uppertail dark green; undertail grey-black. **Bare parts:** Bill pale bluish-grey tipped whitish; iris orange-red; legs dark grey.

SEX/AGE Female lacks yellow hind-collar, has bluish cheeks, a yellow and black barred breast, and more densely barred upperparts. Young birds are similar to females.

MEASUREMENTS Wing 105-114; tail 68-73; bill 12-15; tarsus 17-20.

GEOGRAPHICAL VARIATION Three races.

P. p. picta (SE Papua New Guinea including the Owen Stanley Range)

P. p. excelsa (central mountains of New Guinea) The crown is more olive-brown than in the nominate.

P. p. lorentzi (highlands of W New Guinea) Crown olive-brown, male with yellow mark at side of neck (instead of full collar). Both sexes with blue-green cheeks and ear-coverts, and black and yellow barred rump, lacking any red. Area around vent more yellow-green than in nominate.

REFERENCES Arndt (1991), Beehler (1978b), Beehler *et al.* (1986), BirdLife (1993), Coates (1985), Diamond (1972), Forshaw (1989), Greensmith (1975), Iredale (1956), Lambert *et al.* (1993), Lodge (1991), Pallister & Hurrell (1989), Peters (1961), Rand & Gilliard (1967), Sibley & Monroe (1990), Smith (1992).

93 MODEST TIGER PARROT
Psittacella modesta　　　　　　Plate 23

Other names: Modest Ground Parrot, Barred Little Parrot

IDENTIFICATION 14-15cm. A small, short-tailed parrot occurring in the montane forests of New Guinea. Males are green with brown head, greyish-brown breast, green belly, dark barring on the rump, red undertail-coverts and, away from Vogelkop, a yellow hind-collar. The species is very similar to Madarasz's Tiger Parrot (94), which usually occurs at lower altitudes where the two are sympatric. The males are easily confused, but Madarasz's generally has much stronger yellow mottling against the brown of the head, and lacks the yellow hind-collar. Female Madarasz's lacks the barring on the underparts and has a green, not brown, head, with black and pinkish barring on the nape. The two larger tiger parrots, Brehm's (91) and Painted (92), both have far more extensive barring on the upperparts in both sexes; in males the brown is restricted to the throat, and does not extend down the breast as it does in Modest; and there are various other specific plumage differences (see Plates 22 and 23). Of the two smaller tiger parrots only this species occurs in Vogelkop.

VOICE A quiet plaintive *peep*.

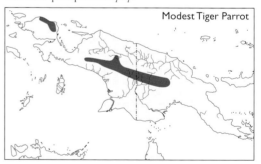
Modest Tiger Parrot

DISTRIBUTION AND STATUS New Guinea in Irian Jaya, Indonesia, and Papua New Guinea. Scattered through the highlands, occurring in the mountains of Vogelkop (isolated population), then from around 136°E through the central mountain belt into the central ranges, including the Tari area, the Victor Emanuel range and Mount Hagen district, reaching to around 145°E. The range overlaps with that of Madarasz's for 1,200 km along the central ranges, and where the two overlap Modest is usually found at slightly higher altitudes than Madarasz's. The world population is thought to be greater than 50,000. The species is locally common.

ECOLOGY Found in montane rainforest, moss forest, forest edge and secondary growth, from 1,200 to 4,000m (mostly 1,700-2,800m). The Modest Tiger Parrot is a quiet, unobtrusive bird which is quite tame and easily over-looked, tending to prefer mid- or lower storey forest, and foraging by creeping or hopping sluggishly, often remaining still for periods. The birds are found singly or in pairs, and feed on seeds and small fruits. There is no information on breeding ecology, but a male in breeding condition was collected in Jun.

DESCRIPTION Head olive-brown with indistinct yellow centres to feathers of crown and nape. Mantle dark green, with faint darker margins to feathers; rump indistinctly barred greenish-yellow and blackish. Uppertail-coverts green fringed darker. Wings dark green marked blue at bend. Underwing-coverts yellow. Outer flight feathers blackish edged green at bases and with fine yellow margins to inner- and outerwebs. Breast greyish-olive to below bend of wing, belly paler, coloured dull green; undertail-coverts red. Uppertail dark green; undertail blackish. **Bare parts**: Bill blue-grey, whitish at tip; iris orange; legs blue-grey.

SEX/AGE Female with breast barred dark brown and pink, flanks barred green and yellowish-green. Young birds like females.

MEASUREMENTS Wing 91-97; tail 47-59; bill 13-14; tarsus 15-17.

GEOGRAPHICAL VARIATION Three races.

P. m. modesta (mountains of Vogelkop)

P. m. collaris (mountains of C Irian Jaya) Similar to nominate but with irregular yellow hind-collar. More rusty on sides of head and neck. Female also with variable yellow tint to nape.

P. m. subcollaris (C Irian Jaya to around 145°E) Like previous race, but narrower and brighter yellow collar, and a darker head and back. Female also with variable yellow on nape.

REFERENCES Arndt (1992), Beehler *et al.* (1986), BirdLife (1993), Coates (1985), Diamond (1972), Forshaw (1989), Greensmith (1975), Hornbuckle (1991), Lambert *et al.* (1993), Lodge (1991), Pallister & Hurrell (1989), Peters (1961), Rand & Gilliard (1967), Schodde (1978), Sibley & Monroe (1990), Smith (1992).

---

94 MADARASZ'S TIGER PARROT
Psittacella madaraszi Plate 23

Other names: Madarasz's Ground Parrot, Plain-breasted Little Parrot

IDENTIFICATION 14-15cm. A small, squat, mainly green parrot occurring in the montane forests of New Guinea. Males are very similar to male Modest Tiger Parrots (93), but never show the yellow hind-collar (only the allopatric Vogelkop race of Modest lacks a distinctive yellow hind-collar). Madarasz's also shows more prominent yellow scaling against the brown of the head in the male. Females can easily be separated from female Modest Tiger-parrots by their unbarred underparts. The forecrown is bluish, and the nape is barred black with pinkish tips to the feathers. The rump is also faintly barred. The two larger tiger parrots both show more scaling on the mantle, and have other specific plumage differences (see Plates 22 and 23). Neither sex in this species shows barred underparts. Of the two smaller tiger parrots only this species occurs in the mountains of the Huon Peninsula and in south-east New Guinea.

VOICE A plaintive, high-pitched, soft *huwee-hee* or *whreen*, clearly distinct from yet reminiscent of the calls of congeners.

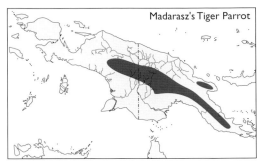
Madarasz's Tiger Parrot

DISTRIBUTION AND STATUS New Guinea from the mountains of central Irian Jaya, Indonesia, through the central highlands of Papua New Guinea to the south-east ranges, with an isolated population in the uplands of the Huon Peninsula. The world population is considered to be in excess of 50,000.

ECOLOGY Madarasz's Tiger Parrot generally occurs below Modest where the two are sympatric, and generally between 1,200 and 2,500m, but has been reported much lower. It inhabits forest, secondary growth and occasionally partly cleared areas, being especially fond of beech *Nothofagus* forest. It is a quiet, sluggish and inconspicuous species, roosting in pairs in the lower storeys of the forest and calling at dusk. It feeds on seeds, fruit, hard berries and leaf pulp, foraging alone or in pairs at various levels within the forest. They have been observed in company with Painted Parrots (92). Little is known of their breeding ecology, but they have been collected in breeding condition in Jun and reported laying in mid-Sep.

DESCRIPTION Head brown, slightly paler on cheeks and ear-coverts owing to light shaft-streaks; crown strongly mottled yellow, throat also showing some light yellow mottling. Mantle and back green, with fine dark margins to feathers; rump barred greenish-yellow and black. Wings green, marked blue at bend and along leading edge; flight feathers blackish with green outerwebs showing a fine yellow margin. Underwing-coverts light green, underside of flight feathers with yellow suffusion on innerwebs. Throat and upper breast light greyish-brown; rest of underparts slightly yellowish green, paler than upperparts, except for red undertail-coverts. Uppertail green, undertail blackish. **Bare parts**: Bill blue-grey, white at tip; iris brownish-red; legs grey.

SEX/AGE The female has a green head with forecrown bluish and nape densely barred black and pinkish-orange. The rest of the upperparts are slightly more strongly barred than in the male, and the underparts are uniform green, lacking the brownish throat and upper breast, but sometimes with some obscure breast-barring. Young birds are similar to females.

MEASUREMENTS Wing 83-95; tail 47-55; bill 12-15; tarsus 14-18.

GEOGRAPHICAL VARIATION Four races.

P. m. madaraszi (SE New Guinea)

P. m. huonensis (mountains of the Huon Peninsula) Male with brown of crown more yellowish, and female lacking pinkish tips to nape feathers.

P. m. hallstromi (mountains of C and EC Papua New Guinea) Male with slightly darker brown head and throat, with narrower yellow streaks, back also darker green. Female with brighter nape-markings.

REFERENCES Beehler (1978b), Beehler *et al.* (1986), Coates (1985), Diamond (1972), Forshaw (1989), Lambert *et al.* (1993), Lodge (1991), Peters (1961), Rand & Gilliard (1967), Schodde (1978), Sibley & Monroe (1990).

---

95 RED-CHEEKED PARROT
Geoffroyus geoffroyi　　　Plate 24

Other names: Red-cheeked Geoffroy's Parrot, Geoffroy's Parrot, Geoffroy's Song Parrot

IDENTIFICATION 21 cm. This is a medium-sized bright green parrot with a square-ended tail, widespread and common throughout the Moluccas, New Guinea and associated islands, and within a very small range in the north of the Cape York Peninsula, Australia. The male Red-cheeked Parrot is reminiscent of the allopatric Blossom-headed Parakeet (200) which has a black collar and a very long tail. Female Blue-rumped Parrot (90) is somewhat similar to the female of this species, but is allopatric, and has diagnostic red underwing-coverts (as well as other plumage differences). Red-cheeked Parrots are rare in captivity. Their fast jinking flight with short rapid beats has been compared to that of the European Starling *Sturnus vulgaris*. The birds may fly high above the trees, do not glide, and their blue underwing-coverts are obvious from below.

VOICE Various different calls have been noted across the species's range. In the eastern highlands of New Guinea the birds produce a series of identical notes *kee! kee! kee! kee!* repeated at a rate of two or three per second for five to ten seconds, each note being upslurred (virtually identical to the call of Spangled Drongo *Dicrurus hottentottus*, and could also be confused with Blue-collared Parrot – see 96 – from a distance). A weak three-note call has been described from birds in southern New Guinea, and various other calls have been noted elsewhere including a metallic *hang*, and a loud screeching *kreek-kreek*, *aank* or *aank-aank*.

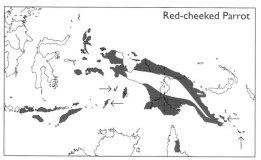

Red-cheeked Parrot

DISTRIBUTION AND STATUS Widespread from Lombok in the west ranging through the Moluccas, the lowlands of New Guinea, and occurring in associated island groups east to Rossel in the Louisiade Archipelago. The species occurs in the north-east of the Cape York Peninsula, Australia, at its southerly extreme, and ranges north to Morotai in the northern Moluccas. In many areas throughout its range it is the most abundant parrot (rarer above 800m), even around habitation. Despite this, it may

be extinct on Ambon, and may be affected by trapping in various parts of its range. World population above 1,000,000 and considered safe.

ECOLOGY Recorded from primary and secondary forest, savanna with trees, plantations, open woodland, mangrove and farmland, to an altitude of 1,400m. Generally replaced by the closely related Blue-collared Parrot at higher altitudes. Exclusive to rainforest in northern Australia. The birds are usually seen wheeling high above the trees, calling loudly. In northern Australia groups of birds, many still in family units, have been seen leaving their roosting trees in riverine forest early in the day, and on their way to feed in denser rainforest some stopped and perched in the exposed upper branches of tall trees, calling loudly for a few minutes and quivering their wings before moving on. The reason for this behaviour is unknown but it may be a form of food-begging by maturing young. During the day the birds are less conspicuous, but may draw attention to themselves by the discarded food items falling from their feeding trees as they forage. They are normally found in pairs or small parties, gathering in larger groups only in fruiting trees. The diet includes seeds, fruit and blossoms, and the birds may hang acrobatically to reach their food. The nest is a hollow which the birds excavate high in a rotten limb of a forest tree, sometimes also a knot-hole; probably only the female excavates. The entrance to the nest is 80-90mm across, and the tunnel, which may twist so as to hide the two to four eggs, can be as much as 42cm long. The female incubates alone, and is fed by the male during this time. In the west breeding takes place between Apr and at least Sep, when an active nest was found in Seram. In New Guinea nesting has been recorded in most months including Feb in the north, and between Apr to Dec elsewhere. In Australia the season appears to extend from Aug to Dec. Little information on the breeding cycle is available as the species has never successfully been bred in captivity.

DESCRIPTION Face rose-red to just above eye, pinker on ear-coverts; forecrown rose-red, mid-crown to nape mauve-blue. Upperparts mid-green, wing with reddish patch on inner lesser-coverts; flight feathers with green outerwebs and dusky innerwebs; narrow yellow margin to innerweb of greater coverts and secondaries. Underwing-coverts and axillaries bright blue; rest of underwing dusky blackish. Underparts green, more yellowish on lower flanks. Uppertail green, lateral feathers suffused yellow; undertail yellowish-green. **Bare parts:** Bill with upper mandible orange-red, lower mandible blackish; iris yellow; legs grey.

SEX/AGE Female with brown head and black upper mandible. Young with greenish head, dark iris and pale bill. Young males move through a 'female-stage' plumage before they begin to acquire male characters (birds take more than a year to mature). Young birds also lack the red mark on the lesser coverts.

MEASUREMENTS Wing 136-154, tail 68-75; bill 17-19; tarsus 16-18.

GEOGRAPHICAL VARIATION Fifteen races.

　　G. g. geoffroyi (Timor and Wetar)
　　G. g. floresianus (Lombok, Sumbawa, Flores and Sumba) Larger (male wing 158-178) and darker than nominate, with darker reddish patch on lesser-coverts.
　　G. g. cyanicollis (Morotai, Halmahera and Bacan) Males are darker generally with a prominent light blue

collar behind the mauve of the rear-crown, which extends to the sides of the neck and borders the red throat. Mantle washed bronze-brown, no reddish-brown on wing-coverts. Underparts tinged bluish. Female with blue collar like male, dark brown head and mauve on crown.

G. g. obiensis (Obi) Like previous race but showing a reddish patch on the lower back and a broader light blue collar.

G. g. rhodops (Buru, Boano, Ambon, Haruku, Saparua, Seram, Gorong and Manawoka) Darker than *floresianus* and larger again (male wing 175-195).

G. g. keyensis (Kai Islands) Paler than *floresianus* and more yellowish-green. Larger again than *rhodops* (male wing 182-201). Concealed red bases to crown feathers. Female with lighter head.

G. g. timorlaoensis (Tanimbar) Like previous race but smaller (male wing 172-181), less blue on crown and lighter rump and tail. Female also with paler head.

G. g. aruensis (Aru Islands, southern and south-eastern New Guinea, Fergusson Island and N Australia from around the Pascoe River to the McIlwraith Range; has been recorded in the Karimui area and around Lake Kutubu where the species probably reaches its highest regular altitude) Similar to *floresianus* but male paler, female with paler head and green on crown.

G. g. orientalis (S Huon Peninsula area) Like following race but with red-brown in lesser coverts. Female with pale head (doubtfully distinct from *aruensis*).

G. g. sudestiensis (Misima and Tagula Islands) No red in lesser coverts, bend of wing green, paler than the following race and *aruensis*. Female with green on crown.

G. g. cyanicarpus (Rossel Island) No red in lesser coverts. Bend of wing blue in both sexes. Cheeks washed with mauve in male.

G. g. minor (N New Guinea reaching the north coast of the Huon Peninsula in the east) Like *jobiensis* but red of rump duller, more red in lesser coverts and slightly smaller. Bronze wash on mantle.

G. g. jobiensis (Yapen and Mios Num in Geelvink Bay) Like minor but red rump brighter, red lesser coverts paler, more red on forehead.

G. g. mysoriensis (Biak and Numfor) Like *minor* but underwing-coverts darker blue, blue of hindneck and red of throat more extensive at rear, red on lesser coverts more obvious, no bronze on mantle, and rump darker red.

G. g. pucherani (Waigeo, Batanta, Salawati, Misool, and in Vogelkop, W New Guinea) Dark red rump, dark blue underwing-coverts, reddish patch in lesser coverts small or absent, little brown on mantle.

REFERENCES Arndt (1992), Beehler *et al.* (1986), Bell (1970), Bishop (1992a), Blakers *et al.* (1984), Coates (1985), Diamond (1972), Forshaw (1966, 1981, 1989), Gyldenstolpe (1955), Lambert *et al.* (1993), Lodge (1991), Milton (1988), Peters (1961), Pizzey & Doyle (1983), Rand & Gilliard (1967), Schodde & Tidemann (1988), Sibley & Monroe (1990), Slater (1989), S. Smith *in litt.* (1993), Taylor (1990), White & Bruce (1986).

96   BLUE-COLLARED PARROT
Geoffroyus simplex   Plate 24

Other names: Simple Parrot; Lilac-collared Song Parrot, Lilac-collared Geoffroy's Parrot (*G. s. buergersi*)

IDENTIFICATION 23-25cm. A stocky, medium-sized, nondescript green parrot occurring in submontane and montane forests through most of the New Guinea mainland. The most distinctive fieldmark is the bright blue flash of the underwing-coverts visible in flight; only males show a blue collar. This species is similar in structure to other two members of its genus, Red-cheeked (95), and Singing Parrots (97), but is the only one at higher altitudes in New Guinea, and the only one in which both sexes show an all green head. The altitudinally sympatric tiger parrots *Psittacella* all show some degree of barring in their plumage. Male Eclectus Parrots (111) also show an all-green head, but have bright red flanks and underwing-coverts and a pale orange upper mandible. Blue-collared Parrots commonly make long flights above the canopy of montane forest, one of the only parrot species to do so. Although the birds are almost invisible when perched, and less often seen than heard, they can be identified during high flights by their distinctive silhouette with more pointed, swept back wings than Red-cheeked Parrots. The flight is twisting, and the short blunt tail is obvious.

VOICE A wide variety of calls including a rolling repetitious *kri kro* call, and a series of other musical whistles, shorter creaky calls and sharp cries. The call sounds harsh from nearby, more musical or chime-like from a distance, and can be confused with that of Red-cheeked Parrot.

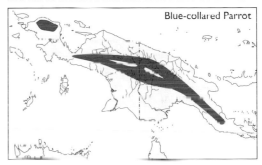
Blue-collared Parrot

DISTRIBUTION AND STATUS New Guinea in Irian Jaya, Indonesia, and Papua New Guinea, with an isolated population in Vogelkop from the Tamrau to Arfak Mountains. The main population is spread through the central highlands, being absent from the higher central areas but reaching the Owen Stanley Range in the extreme east. Generally common, but difficulty of detection makes birds seem less abundant. The world population has been estimated at more than 50,000.

ECOLOGY The species occurs mainly in humid hill and mid-montane forest, along forest edge and in secondary growth between 500 and 2,300m, being commonest between 800 and 1,900m. Variations in food supply can bring birds to lower elevations than normal (even to near sea-level). The birds are shy and difficult to detect when perched, flying at the sight of a human intruder. Large flocks of up to 200 birds may be seen and heard flying overhead. The species tends to form larger parties than Red-cheeked Parrot, although single birds, pairs or small groups are sometimes encountered. The birds feed quietly in the canopy on seeds, fruits, berries and perhaps nectar. They are particularly fond of the seeds of *Castanopis* and *Lithocarpus* oaks. Little is known of the breeding ecology. One excavated nest with three young was found in mid-Jan, nine metres high, close to the top of a stump. The entrance was 80mm in diameter, and the hollow itself was 200mm across and 400mm deep. Nesting has also been recorded in Oct.

DESCRIPTION Head green, paler and more yellowish on chin and lower cheeks, with a faint but clearly marked blue collar across upper breast and hindneck. Upperparts darkish green. Bend of wing yellow; brownish patch on inner median coverts; greater coverts with yellowish-green edging; flight feathers black with green outerwebs; pale line along inner edge of tip of closed wing formed by yellowish tips to innerwebs of flight feathers. Underwing-coverts and axillaries blue. Underparts paler, more yellowish-green than upperparts. Uppertail green; undertail yellowish. **Bare parts**: Bill greyish-black; iris pale yellowish-white; legs greenish-grey.

SEX/AGE Females lack the blue collar of the males but have a little blue on the rear-crown. Young birds have no blue on the head or collar at all, a greyish-white, not yellowish-white, iris, and a paler bill than adults.

MEASUREMENTS Wing 148-157; tail 67-75; bill 20-21; tarsus 17-18.

GEOGRAPHICAL VARIATION Two races.
  G. s. simplex (Vogelkop)
  G. s. buergersi (remainder of range) The collar of the male is duller but more extensive at rear. Also slightly larger.

REFERENCES Beehler (1978b), Beehler *et al.* (1986), Coates (1985), Diamond (1972), Forshaw (1989), Gyldenstolpe (1955), Hornbuckle (1991), Iredale (1956), Lambert *et al.* (1993), Lodge (1991), Peters (1961), Pratt (1982), Rand & Gilliard (1967), Schodde (1978), Sibley & Monroe (1990).

---

97 SINGING PARROT
Geoffroyus heteroclitus   Plate 24

Other names: Yellow-headed Song Parrot, Yellow-headed Geoffroy's Parrot, New Britain Yellow-headed Parrot, New Ireland Yellow-headed Parrot, Song Parrot

IDENTIFICATION 23-25cm. Lowland and hill forest in Bismarcks and Solomons. Medium-sized pale green parrot with a short blunt tail. Both sexes are largely green, but males have distinctive pale yellow heads, broad pale grey collars, and yellow upper mandibles. Singing Parrots are structurally similar to the other two members of the genus, Red-cheeked (95) and Blue-collared Parrot (96), but are the only representative in the Bismarcks or Solomons, and the only one to show an obvious yellow head in the male (no other parrot in the region is green with a bright yellow head). The drab females are similar to female Red-cheeked, but show a greyish head and hind-crown merging into a green nape, not a clear demarcation between a brown crown and green nape. Young Red-cheeked Parrots have greenish, not greyish, crowns. Blue-collared Parrots have all-green heads. Olive-headed Lorikeets (15), which

occur in Nusa Tenggara (Timor and nearby islands), have a yellowish head, but are structurally dissimilar and have a small orange-red bill. The flight of Singing Parrot is rapid and direct, showing bright blue underwing-coverts from below.

VOICE A variety of musical and harsher calls, similar to other members of the genus. The species produces a wavering song described as a soft whistle rising deliberately in double beats *wuwu wowo wewe wiwi*, various short sharp calls including a shrill *chee* or *chiark-chiark*, and a rapid raucous *kyeer-kyeer-kyeer*, also described as a musical *kee-owl-owl* or *kreel-kreel-kreel* with emphasis on the last note. The call is closer to Blue-collared Parrot than Red-cheeked.

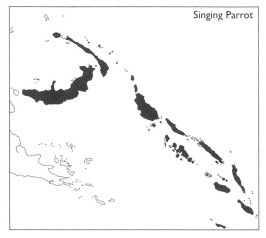

Singing Parrot

DISTRIBUTION AND STATUS Endemic to islands in the Bismarck and Solomon groups. The species ranges through the following islands and island groups: Umboi, New Britain, Lolobau, Duke of York, New Ireland, New Hanover, Tabar, Lihir, Buka, Bougainville (all Papua New Guinea), Choiseul, Santa Isabel, San Jorge, Malaita, Maramasike, Vella Lavella, Kolombangara, New Georgia, Rendova, the Florida Islands, Guadalcanal, Ulawa, San Cristobal and Rennell (Solomons). Generally scattered through suitable habitat and locally common. The world population is considered to be below 100,000, with the Rennell Island race contributing 5,000-20,000. The species is probably suffering due to the loss of habitat throughout its range, but is not considered threatened.

ECOLOGY Occurs in damp, undisturbed lowland and hill forest generally below 600m but to a maximum of 1,760m in southern New Ireland. Also found in partly cleared areas, forest edge, second growth and gardens. The birds are often first heard calling from the tops of exposed or isolated trees, or seen flying swiftly above the canopy. They are found alone, in pairs, or consorting in small groups. They have been recorded alongside Cardinal Lories (4) and Duchess Lorikeets (48) on Bougainville. They are often quiet and difficult to detect when perched in dense foliage; when disturbed, they fly off rapidly, landing in other thick vegetation seemingly without slowing. The diet includes seeds, fruit, blossoms and buds. The nest is a hollow excavated by the female in a dead stump or rotten tree, but nothing else is know of the species's breeding ecology.

DESCRIPTION Head bright pale yellow; broad band across nape blending into mantle pale bluish-grey; throat similar. Upperparts light green. Median coverts marked reddish-brown; pale yellow margins to innerwebs of inner flight feathers. Underwing-coverts bright blue. Upper breast greyish-blue; rest of underparts pale, slightly yellowish-green, lighter than upperparts. Uppertail mid-green; undertail greyish with yellow outerwebs to lateral feathers. **Bare parts:** Bill with upper mandible pale yellow, lower dark grey; iris pale yellow; legs greyish-green.

SEX/AGE Females have all-dark bills, and lack the yellow head and greyish collar; instead the crown is greyish and the cheeks are brownish-green. Immatures have greener heads than females, a pale bill and dark iris.

MEASUREMENTS Wing 149-170; tail 73-86; bill 19-22; tarsus 18-20.

GEOGRAPHICAL VARIATION Two races.
> *G. h. heteroclitus* (everywhere except for Rennell Island in the extreme southern Solomons)
> *G. h. hyacinthinus* (Rennell Island) Greyish-blue collar of male more extensive, especially below. Both sexes with blue on primary coverts and bend of wing.

REFERENCES BirdLife (1993), Bishop & Broome (1980), Cain & Galbraith (1956), Coates (1985), Forshaw (1989), Greensmith (1975), Hadden (1981), Hartert (1926), Lambert *et al.* (1993), Loes (1991), Lodge (1991), Peters (1961), Schodde (1978), Sibley (1951), Sibley & Monroe (1990)

---

98   MONTANE RACQUET-TAIL
Prioniturus montanus   Plate 25

Other names: Luzon Montane Racquet-tail, Red-crowned Racquet Parrot

IDENTIFICATION 30cm. A medium-sized, mostly green parrot which shares elongated shafts to its central tail feathers, and tail spatules, with the other members of the genus. The species occurs only in forests of Luzon, Philippines, above 700m. Males have a blue face and red crown spot, females only a little blue on the face. The species is sympatric in Luzon with both Blue-crowned Racquet-tail (102) and Green Racquet-tail (101). Blue-crowned has a blue crown in both sexes but males lack the red crown-spot; Green, now rare and probably confined to remoter forests of the Sierra Madre at 300-700m, is uniform light yellow-green, yellower around the face, with a blue uppertail.

VOICE 'A shrill screech'.

DISTRIBUTION AND STATUS Endemic to Luzon. Still common in Cordillera Central (e.g. Mount Pulog area) and Sierra Madre but threatened by trapping and loss of habitat elsewhere. World population less than 10,000. VULNERABLE.

ECOLOGY Little known. Occurs in humid montane forest from 850m to around 2,900m. The birds feed on seeds, fruit, berries and nuts, and have also been recorded raiding fields in company with Green Racquet-tails. Breeding takes place in Aug and Sep. One nest was in a tall oak *Quercus* stump with the entrance 3-4m above ground.

DESCRIPTION Head green with strong turquoise-blue suffusion on face; red spot on centre of crown. Upperparts dull green. Wings green, outerwebs of flight feathers

green, innerwebs dull greyish, with narrow yellow margin; innerwebs of inner secondaries marked pale yellow. Underwing-coverts green, underside of flight feathers bluish; paler innerwebs to inner secondaries. Underparts more yellowish-green than back. Uppertail green in centre, blue tipped black laterally; undertail dusky with bluish margin to innerwebs; spatules blackish. **Bare parts:** Bill bluish; iris dark brown; legs blue-black.

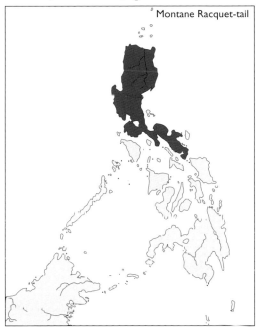

Montane Racquet-tail

SEX/AGE Female lacks red crown-spot and has less blue on crown; also shorter racquets. Young have central tail with narrow feathered extensions. Feathers eventually lose barbs to leave spatules.

MEASUREMENTS Wing 152-172; tail 98-147; bill 18-21; tarsus 16-19.

GEOGRAPHICAL VARIATION None.

REFERENCES Arndt (1992), BirdLife (1993), Collar *et al.* (1994), Dickinson *et al.* (1991), duPont (1971), Forshaw (1989), Lambert *et al.* (1993), Sargeant (1992), Sibley & Monroe (1990).

---

99   MINDANAO RACQUET-TAIL
Prioniturus waterstradti   Plate 25

Other names: Mindanao Montane Racquet-tail

IDENTIFICATION 30cm. Confined to a handful of forested mountains in Mindanao, Philippines. Generally green, with bluish-green suffusion on the face and an olive wash on the rump; males and females are similar. The species is sympatric in Mindanao with one congener, Blue-crowned Racquet-tail (102), distinguished by its obvious blue crown. Female Mindanao Racquet-tail is similar to allopatric Montane Racquet-tail (98), but has less blue on face and green outer tail feathers.

VOICE A 'screeching' call.

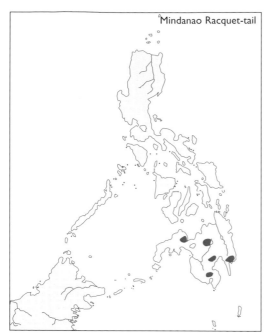
Mindanao Racquet-tail

al. (1994), Dickinson et al. (1991), Forshaw (1989), Lambert et al. (1993), Peters (1961), Sargeant (1992), Sibley & Monroe (1990).

100 BLUE-HEADED RACQUET-TAIL
Prioniturus platenae   Plate 25

Other names: Palawan Racquet-tail

IDENTIFICATION 27cm. Restricted to Palawan and a few nearby islands, western Philippines, where it is the only representative of its genus. Males are very distinctive, showing an all-blue head and a strong blue suffusion on the underparts; females have less blue. The species is similar to, and was previously considered conspecific with, the widespread Blue-crowned Racquet-tail (102). The two species are allopatric and all races of Blue-crowned lack the clearly defined all-blue head and blue suffusion on the underparts of Blue-headed.

VOICE Not recorded.

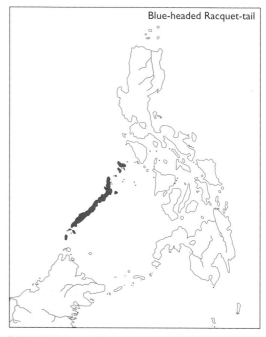
Blue-headed Racquet-tail

DISTRIBUTION AND STATUS Endemic to the highlands of Mindanao, Philippines. Records come from Mount Apo, Mount Malindang, Mount Katanglad, Mount Mayo, Mount Matutum, Mount Lebo, Anakan, Civolig, Mount McKinley, Lake Faggamb, and Baracatan, but the total population, estimated at just 5,000, may now be confined to as few as five mountains. The species has almost certainly declined due to habitat loss, and trapping may also be a factor. VULNERABLE.

ECOLOGY Occurs in humid montane forest chiefly between 850m and 2000m, but has been recorded as low as 450m. Little is known about the habits of this species, which until recently was considered conspecific with Montane Racquet-tail (98). Most observations concern small flocks of two to ten birds. Apparently occurs in lower densities than other members of its genus and undertakes altitudinal movements on a daily basis.

DESCRIPTION Head bright green, with slightly bluer-green suffusion on cheeks, lores and forecrown. Mantle duller green; rump with distinct olive hue. Wing green, with dusky innerwebs to flight feathers, narrowly margined yellow on inner edge; carpal edge yellow. Underwing-coverts green; underside of primaries with bluish tinge. Underparts yellowish-green, yellowest on undertail-coverts. Uppertail green with lateral feathers tipped blackish; undertail bluish; spatules blackish. **Bare parts**: Bill light grey; iris brown; legs blackish-grey.

SEX/AGE Adults similar, female with shorter tail extensions. Juvenile undescribed.

MEASUREMENTS Wing 149-164; tail 98-147; bill 17-20; tarsus 14-18.

GEOGRAPHICAL VARIATION The race *P. w. malindangensis* has been proposed for birds in mountains of northern Mindanao, but any differences appear slight.

NOTE This species may be conspecific with *P. montanus*.

REFERENCES Arndt (1992), BirdLife (1993), Collar et

DISTRIBUTION AND STATUS Endemic to Palawan and associated islands, western Philippines. Recorded from Balabac, Dumaran and islands in the Calamian group (Culion, Calawit, Busuanga). Uncommon and declining due to rapid habitat clearance and trapping. The world population is estimated as 10,000 but declining. The species is uncommon but regular in the St Paul's Sub-terranean National Park. VULNERABLE.

ECOLOGY Little known. The species occurs in humid lowland forest and nearby cultivation. Birds are most often recorded in small groups and their habits are presumably similar to those of other racquet-tails.

DESCRIPTION Head bright light blue. Mantle and back light mid-green; rump slightly brighter green. Wings green, flight feathers with blackish innerwebs. Underwing-coverts turquoise-green, strongly suffused blue. Breast and upper belly green, strongly suffused blue; vent and undertail-coverts yellowish-green, undertail-coverts bright. Uppertail green, lateral feathers blue-green with black tips; undertail dusky, suffused blue; spatules blackish. **Bare parts**: Bill bluish-white; iris yellowish; legs black.

SEX/AGE Female without blue on underparts (or just a slight blue wash) and a slight turquoise-blue wash on the head, lacking the obvious blue cap of the male; also with shorter tail extensions. Juvenile undescribed.

MEASUREMENTS Wing 152-164; tail 105-156; bill 17-21; tarsus 16-19.

GEOGRAPHICAL VARIATION None.

REFERENCES Arndt (1992), BirdLife (1993), Collar *et al.* (1994), Dickinson *et al.* (1991), duPont (1971), Forshaw (1989), Lambert *et al.* (1993), Sargeant (1992), Sibley & Monroe (1990).

---

101 GREEN RACQUET-TAIL
Prioniturus luconensis   Plate 25

Other names: Green-headed Racquet-tail

IDENTIFICATION 29cm. A rare species confined to Luzon and Marinduque, northern Philippines. This is the most uniformly yellow-green of the genus and apart from a yellowish face, bluish primaries and uppertail it is relatively nondescript. The sexes are similar. It is sympatric in Luzon with Blue-crowned Racquet-tail (102) which, as its name implies, can be distinguished by the blue crown shown by both sexes. The other racquet-tail in Luzon is Montane (98), which shows a distinctive blue face and red crown in the male. Both sexes of Green Racquet-tail also have more blue in the uppertail than Montane Racquet-tail.

VOICE Not recorded.

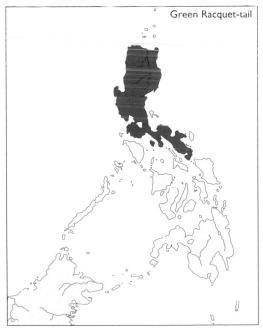
Green Racquet-tail

DISTRIBUTION AND STATUS Endemic to Luzon and Marinduque, northern Philippines. Although the species was regarded as fairly common late last century in central Luzon, it appears to have undergone a rapid decline in recent years. It has not been recorded from the Cordillera Central this century, and may now have its stronghold in the Sierra Madre, where it was reported to be generally rare or uncommon in the early 1990s. It is now considered to be rare throughout Luzon except perhaps in the Subic Bay Naval Forest Reserve (Bataan, east of Manila). There are no recent records from Marinduque. The population, estimated at no more than 10,000, is threatened by habitat loss and degradation, and by trapping. ENDANGERED.

ECOLOGY Previously recorded from mid-storey lowland primary forest, and nearby maize fields, mostly below 700m. Recent records are of small groups of up to seven birds flying over degraded or selectively logged forest away from settlements. The diet includes fruit, young corn, rice, seeds and flowers. Young have been observed in Luzon during May. The nest is apparently a tree hollow. Little else is known about the habits of this rare parrot.

DESCRIPTION Head light green suffused yellow-green around lores and base of bill. Mantle light green, slightly yellowish. Wings mid-green; outerwebs of first three primaries green suffused blue; innerwebs dusky, innermost with pale inner margin. Underwing-coverts yellow-green, underside of flight feathers dusky suffused blue. Underparts yellowish-green, yellowest on undertail-coverts. Uppertail green, lateral feathers strongly suffused dark bluish-green and tipped darker; undertail bluish. **Bare parts**: Bill pale bluish-grey; iris dark brown, legs grey.

SEX/AGE Female has shorter tail racquets. Young has typical tail lacking racquets but showing attenuated feathered tips to central feathers.

MEASUREMENTS Wing 142-158; tail 114-155; bill 16-18; tarsus 16-18.

GEOGRAPHICAL VARIATION None.

REFERENCES Arndt (1992), BirdLife (1993), Collar & Andrew (1988), Collar *et al.* (1994), Dickinson *et al.* (1991), duPont (1971), Forshaw (1989), Lambert *et al.* (1993), Poulsen (1995), Sargeant (1992).

---

102 BLUE-CROWNED RACQUET-TAIL
Prioniturus discurus   Plate 26

IDENTIFICATION 27cm. The most widespread of its genus, being found throughout most of the Philippines. Males and females are not strongly dimorphic. All birds are generally green with a blue crown, lacking the red crown-spot of male Blue-winged Racquet-tail (103), which in any case is allopatric occurring only in islands in the Sulu Group, south-west Philippines (Blue-crowned extends south-west only to Jolo where Blue-winged does not occur, despite reports to the contrary). Blue-crowned is sympatric with three other racquet-tails, Mindanao (99), Montane (98), and Green (101), none of which shows the unmarked blue crown of this species. Flight fast with rapid wingbeats but appears laboured.

VOICE A 'shrill screech'.

DISTRIBUTION AND STATUS Resident and not uncommon through most islands in the Philippines including Luzon, Catanduanes, Masbate, Mindoro, Guimaras, Negros, Tablas, Sibuyan, Cebu, Samar, Leyte, Bohol, Mindanao, Olutanga, Basilan and Jolo. Seems unlikely to be under immediate threat unless trapping pressure is substantially accelerated. The world population is estimated at least 10,000 but probably declining due to trapping and habitat loss. NEAR-THREATENED.

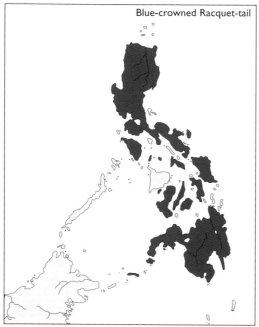

Blue-crowned Racquet-tail

ECOLOGY Humid forest, mangroves, plantations and cultivation in lowlands and mountains to 1,750m. Seen flying overhead in small noisy groups of five to a dozen birds outside the breeding season. Groups gather to feed in fruiting trees including bananas. The diet includes fruit, berries, nuts, and seeds. Nesting Apr to May in Negros, during May in Leyte and during Apr in Mindanao. A record from 1945 indicates that post-breeding dispersal may occur as birds began to appear on Calicoan off southern Leyte in mid-summer, becoming increasingly common through to Oct.

DESCRIPTION Head bright green strongly suffused bright blue on crown and brighter green on cheeks and lores. Upperparts mid-green. Wings green, darker on innerwebs of flight feathers, with narrow pale margin along innermost edge; outer primaries blue-green. Underwing-coverts green, underside of flight feathers greenish-blue. Underparts light yellowish-green. Uppertail green, lateral feathers basally blue with black tips; undertail strongly suffused blue; spatules blackish. **Bare parts:** Bill whitish; iris dark brown; legs grey.

SEX/AGE Female like male with shorter tail racquets. Young with less blue on crown and lacking racquets.

MEASUREMENTS Wing 148-166; tail 102-137; bill 20-21; tarsus 15-19.

GEOGRAPHICAL VARIATION Four races.
> *P. d. discurus* (Jolo and Mindanao, Olutanga, Basilan, Guimaras and Luzon)
> *P. d. whiteheadi* (Negros, Bohol, Samar, Leyte, Masbate and Cebu) Less blue on crown.

P. d. nesophilus (Tablas, Sibuyan and Catanduanes) Blue on crown further reduced.
P. d. mindorensis (Mindoro) Green forehead and violet-blue patch on centre of crown.

REFERENCES Arndt (1992), Brooks *et al.* (1992), Dickinson *et al.* (1991), duPont (1971), Dutson *et al.* (1992), Forshaw (1989), Lambert *et al.* (1993), Parkes (1971), Peters (1961), Potter (1953), Sargeant (1992), Sibley & Monroe (1990).

103 BLUE-WINGED RACQUET-TAIL
Prioniturus verticalis   Plate 25

Other names: Sulu Racquet-tail

IDENTIFICATION 30cm. Confined to islands in the south-western Sulu Archipelago, Philippines, the only member of its genus to occur there. Males can easily be distinguished from females by the red spot in the centre of the blue crown. Previously considered conspecific with Montane Racquet-tail (98) but this species occupies a lowland habitat niche and, although superficially similar to Montane, shares more plumage characters with Yellow-breasted Racquet-tail (104) of northern Sulawesi. From Montane Racquet-tail by the lack of blue facial markings, instead showing an obvious blue crown, and blue suffusion on the outer primaries; also has a pale yellow-green mantle and underparts, which are more uniform green in Montane (especially the mantle). Yellow-breasted Racquet-tail shows a more clearly demarcated yellowish-green mantle (yellow-green markings more accentuated in males of both species).

VOICE Not recorded.

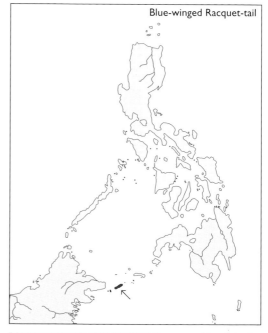

Blue-winged Racquet-tail

DISTRIBUTION AND STATUS Occurs on islands in the south-west Sulu Archipelago, including Tawitawi, Bongao, Manuk Manka, Sanga Sanga, Tumindao and Sibutu.

Although reportedly common in mangroves in Tawitawi last century the species appears to have undergone a serious decline. Today the world population is estimated at less than 5,000 and the species is being affected by trapping and the rapid clearance of the last forests on its range islands. The birds are also apparently used for target practice by the islanders, many of whom own rifles. In 1991 small numbers were observed near undisturbed forest. In 1994 Tawitawi was rapidly being cleared of its remaining forest and only six birds were seen. ENDANGERED.

ECOLOGY A lowland species of humid forest, forest edge, mangroves, dense remnant forest patches and associated agricultural areas. The birds are most often seen in pairs in high fast flight over dense vegetation. They feed in fruiting trees, and are then quiet and difficult to detect. A nest was discovered in Sep 1991 attended by a female bird: the nest-hole was in a large palm with a broken top in a grove close to forest.

DESCRIPTION Head bright green, brightest around lores and base of bill; forecrown bright blue with central red spot. Mantle light yellowish-green; back and rump mid-green. Wings green, with dark blue wash on both webs of all primaries. Underwing-coverts green. Underparts light yellowish-green, greener on belly, vent, and undertail-coverts. Uppertail green, outer feathers with black tips; undertail dusky, suffused blue on edges of innerwebs; tail spatules blackish. **Bare parts:** Bill whitish-grey; iris dark brown; legs grey.

SEX/AGE Female has slight blue in crown but no red crown-spot; yellow-green areas duller. Young without racquets.

MEASUREMENTS Wing 163-185; tail 98-147; bill 21-24; tarsus 16-19.

GEOGRAPHICAL VARIATION None.

REFERENCES Arndt (1992), BirdLife (1993), Collar et al. (1994), Dickinson et al. (1991), duPont (1971), duPont & Rabor (1973), Forshaw (1989), Lambert (1993c), Lambert et al. (1993), Sargeant (1992), Sibley & Monroe (1990).

104 YELLOW-BREASTED RACQUET-TAIL
Prioniturus flavicans   Plate 26

Other names: Red-spotted Racquet-tail, Yellowish-breasted Racquet-tail

IDENTIFICATION 37cm. Occurs in northern Sulawesi where it is sympatric with Golden-mantled Racquet-tail (105). This species has a blue crown and light yellow mantle in both sexes, although the male has a brighter mantle and a red crown-spot. It is similar to Golden-mantled Racquet-tail, but lacks the orange hind-collar of the male, and the greyish suffusion to the mantle and wings shown by both sexes of that species; it is also noticeably heavier in flight and has a call less harsh than that of Golden-mantled. It is also similar to the allopatric Blue-winged Racquet-tail (103) which has a less strongly defined yellowish mantle. This species does not occur in Sulawesi south of about 1°N.

VOICE A drawn-out screech with an alternating pitch, and a *chang-chang*, presumably in alarm.

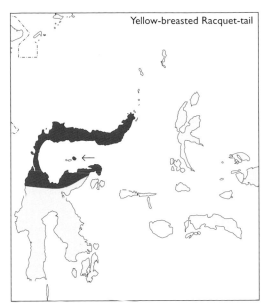
Yellow-breasted Racquet-tail

DISTRIBUTION AND STATUS Occurs in northern Sulawesi, Indonesia, and on related islands including Bangka, Lembeh and Togian. The species also possibly occurs on islands in the Sangir and Banggai groups. Although it may be declining through habitat loss and some trade it is not considered threatened and is still relatively common in Dumoga-Bone reserve. Where the two overlap this species is generally less common than Golden-mantled Racquet-tail. World population estimate is below 10,000. NEAR-THREATENED.

ECOLOGY Found in primary forest generally below 1,000m, but may occasionally range as high as 1,900m. Also in trees in cultivated areas. The birds forage in mid-storey lowland and hill forest, often gathering in fruiting trees, foraging slowly amidst flocks of other frugivorous birds. Little else is known of its habits.

DESCRIPTION Head bright green, brightest around lores and base of bill. Forecrown green, rest of crown bright blue with central red spot. Mantle ochre-yellow, sharply demarcated from blue of nape and green of wings and back; back and rump mid-green. Wings green, with dusky innerwebs to flight feathers and blue in longest primary. Underwing-coverts green, underside of primaries dusky marked blue. Underparts light yellowish-green, ochre-yellow on breast. Uppertail green, outer feathers with black tips and light turquoise on outerwebs of outermost feathers; undertail dusky, suffused blue on edges of innerwebs; spatules blackish. **Bare parts:** Bill whitish-grey; iris dark brown; legs grey.

SEX/AGE Female less blue without red crown spot, underparts and mantle greener, and with shorter racquets. Young without racquets.

MEASUREMENTS Wing 176-194; tail 132-181; bill 22-25; tarsus 18-21.

GEOGRAPHICAL VARIATION None.

REFERENCES Arndt (1992), BirdLife (1993), Bishop (1992a), Forshaw (1989), Lambert et al. (1993), Rozendaal & Dekker (1989), Sibley & Monroe (1990), Watling (1983).

105 GOLDEN-MANTLED RACQUET-TAIL

Prioniturus platurus   Plate 26

Other names: Gold-mantled Racquet-tail, Gold-backed Racquet-tailed Parrot

IDENTIFICATION 28cm. Occurs throughout Sulawesi and on some associated islands. Males are probably the most distinctively marked any species in the genus, with an obvious orange hind-collar, red and blue crown and a strong grey suffusion to the green of the upperparts (red of crown lacking in Taliabu race); females also show the distinctive grey suffusion on the upperparts. The species is sympatric with Yellow-breasted Racquet-tail (104) in northern Sulawesi. Yellow-breasted is larger, appearing noticeably heavier in flight, and can be separated on call. Male Yellow-breasted lacks the orange hind-collar, and has a bright yellowish-green mantle without any grey wash to the upperparts. Female Yellow-breasted has an obvious blue crown, which is green washed greyish in the female of the present species.

VOICE Call described as a penetrating metallic *keli-keli*, or as a loud ringing screech; however, vocalisations have also been described as beautiful, melodious and varied.

Golden-mantled Racquet-tail

DISTRIBUTION AND STATUS Restricted to Sulawesi and nearby islands including Talaud, Siau, Lembeh, Togian, Banggai group, Taliabu, Muna and Buton. The species is generally common and the world population is considered to be above 10,000 and stable: numbers of the nominate race are estimated as at least 10,000 and stable, race *talautensis* is less secure with a population of around 5,000, and *sinerubris* is thought to consist of around 10,000 and probably stable.

ECOLOGY Inhabits humid forest edge, woodlands, orchards and moss-forest from the lowlands to 2,000m (commonest above 1,000m). The birds are usually seen in small noisy groups of 5-10 birds flying over forest, or during daily movements between feeding and roosting

areas. They have been seen feeding on fruiting mangos *Mangifera indica*, and the diet includes fruit, seeds and blossoms. A female in breeding condition was collected in Oct, and the nest is in a tree hollow; nothing further is known of the species's breeding behaviour.

DESCRIPTION Head light green, crown violet-grey with red spot at front edge; hind-collar ochre-orange. Mantle light grey becoming green (marked grey) on back; rump and uppertail-coverts green. Wing-coverts green, strongly suffused light grey (greener on innermost coverts); primaries green with dark innerwebs; inner secondaries green with fine yellow margins; bend of wing violet-grey, carpal edge yellow. Underwing-coverts green; underside of flight feathers marked blue. Underparts yellowish-green, greener on breast and yellowest on undertail-coverts. Uppertail green in centre, green tipped blue-black laterally; undertail pale blue; spatules blackish. **Bare parts:** Bill pale grey tipped darker and with darker lower mandible; iris dark brown; legs grey.

SEX/AGE Female lacks red and blue crown-marking and orange hind-collar; grey wash on upperparts less distinct; tail racquets shorter. Young without tail racquets.

MEASUREMENTS Wing 166-187; tail 111-183; bill 21-26; tarsus 17-21.

GEOGRAPHICAL VARIATION Three races.
> *P. p. platurus* (Sulawesi and associated islands)
> *P. p. talautensis* (Talaud group) Like nominate but with less grey above, more red and blue in crown.
> *P. p. sinerubris* (Taliabu) Lacks red in crown and has less grey on upperparts. Bend of wing suffused violet.

REFERENCES Arndt (1992), Bishop (1992b), Forshaw (1989), Lambert *et al.* (1993), Peters (1961), J. Riley *in litt.* (1995), Rozendaal & Dekker (1989), Sibley & Monroe (1990), Watling (1983), White & Bruce (1986).

106 BURU RACQUET-TAIL

Prioniturus mada   Plate 26

IDENTIFICATION 29cm. The only racquet-tail occurring on the island of Buru, where it is common. Males are distinctive, being mainly green with dark blue markings on the crown, nape and bend of wing. Female with shorter tail racquets and dark blue at bend of wing only.

VOICE A whistling call reminiscent of Red-cheeked Parrot (95) but slightly softer.

DISTRIBUTION AND STATUS Endemic to the island of Buru, Indonesia. The listing of the species as Near-Threatened was based on the assumption of a highly restricted range above 1,000m, but newly published evidence shows it to be common throughout the island with a world population estimated at 189,000-483,000 birds. NEAR-THREATENED.

ECOLOGY Found in humid primary, secondary and montane forest, also cultivated areas; previous suggestions that it is commonest above 1,000m are evidently mistaken, since fieldwork in 1989 showed it to occur at 55-620m. Most often seen in small groups of up to ten birds. Feeds on fruit, flowers, berries and seeds. Tends to replace Red-cheeked Parrot at higher elevations. Breeding Dec to Feb. Up to five young may be reared in one nest.

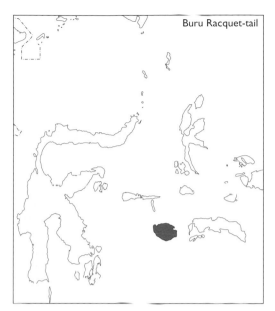

Buru Racquet-tail

DESCRIPTION Head bright green, marked dark greyish-blue on crown and nape. Upperparts mid-green, marked dark greyish-blue on upper mantle; uppertail-coverts green. Wing green with lesser coverts and bend of wing dark greyish-blue. Underwing-coverts green; underside of flight feathers bluish. Underparts yellowish-green, yellowest on undertail-coverts. Uppertail green, outer feathers tipped dark blue; undertail light blue. **Bare parts:** Bill grey; iris dark brown; legs grey.

SEX/AGE Female lacks blue on crown, nape and mantle; blue at bend of wing reduced; shorter tail racquets. Young without tail racquets, male with blue on nape.

MEASUREMENTS Wing 169-186; tail 112-151; bill 20-23; tarsus 18-20.

GEOGRAPHICAL VARIATION None.

REFERENCES Arndt (1992), BirdLife (1993), Collar & Andrew (1988), Forshaw (1989), Lambert *et al.* (1993), Marsden *et al.* (1997), Sibley & Monroe (1990), White & Bruce (1986).

107 GREAT-BILLED PARROT
Tanygnathus megalorhynchos   Plate 27

Other names: Moluccan Parrot, Island Parrot, Large-billed Parrot

IDENTIFICATION 41cm. Virtually unmistakable with its huge red bill, blue rump, variegated black and yellow wing-coverts and green head and underparts. Widespread in the Moluccas occurring in Halmahera, Buru, Seram, Tanimbar, Flores, Sumba, western Timor and islands west of New Guinea. The sexes are similar, and there are eight similar races (see below). The species is sympatric in the Talaud Islands with Blue-naped Parrot (108) and Blue-backed Parrot (109). It is easily separated from the former by its green, not blue, crown and more colourful wings, which show black and bright yellow, not black and dull orange, coverts. Blue-backed Parrot has even more uni-

form wings, a smaller bill, and in females the bill is pale yellow rather than bright red. Great-billed Parrots appear very large-headed with a relatively thin body and a longish thin tail. In flight the bright yellow underwing-coverts are obvious, as are the fast shallow wingbeats.

VOICE The contact call is a *kaw kaw* or *squawk squawk* reminiscent of Eclectus Parrot (111). It is less strident, higher-pitched and sharper than that of the other sympatric members of its genus.

Great-billed Parrot

DISTRIBUTION AND STATUS Widely but patchily distributed through Nusa Tenggara, the Moluccas and the W Papuan islands. The range includes the following islands: Sumba, Timor (extreme west) and adjacent Semau, Flores, Madu, Kalaotoa, Kalao, Tanahjampea, the Tukangbesi group of SW Sulawesi, Damar, Babar, the Tanimbar group, Seram, Haruku, Buru, Obi, Bacan, Kayoa, Halmahera, Makian, Moti, Tidore, Ternate, Morotai, Mayu, islets off N Sulawesi and the Togian group off E Sulawesi, Sangir and Talaud groups, Widi, Muor, Gebe, Waigeo, Batanta, Salawati and Misool. The nominate race appears to have been introduced to Balut off the southern tip of Mindanao, Philippines. Occasional records in Java and Bali are probably escapes, but birds on the New Guinea mainland may be genuine vagrants probably from the small islands in the W Papuan group. The species is fairly common but may be suffering some local declines through trade and habitat loss. The world population is estimated at more than 100,000 birds.

ECOLOGY Occurs chiefly in primary lowland forest, as well as secondary and coastal forest, mangrove, cultivated areas, gardens and plantations up to 1,000m. Birds regularly travel between smaller islands, and make daily flights between roosting and foraging areas, drawing attention to themselves by their loud calls both in flight and when settling to roost. They are normally found in small groups of up to a dozen individuals foraging on fruits and nuts, and commonly drop litter from their feeding trees as they discard unwanted items. Nesting has been recorded between Aug and Dec, the nest-site being a hollow around 30m high in a mature forest tree.

DESCRIPTION Head bright green. Mantle green, with narrow bluish fringes to feathers of back; rump pale blue; uppertail-coverts light green. Scapulars black edged greenish-blue; innermost lesser wing-coverts black, outermost blue-green; median-coverts black margined yellow on both webs; greater coverts blue-green margined yellow. Secondaries green with fine yellow margins; primaries strongly suffused blue on outerwebs grading through blue-green to blackish on innerwebs. Underwing-coverts and axillaries bright yellow; underside of flight feathers grey-black, innermost tinged yellow. Underparts yellow-green, tinged greener on belly, thighs and undertail-coverts. Uppertail green tipped yellow; undertail basally brown tipped light orange. **Bare parts:** Bill red; iris yellow; legs black.

SEX/AGE Males and females similar. Young with less variegated wing-coverts.

MEASUREMENTS Wing 232-251; tail 131-158; bill 41-52; tarsus 23-27.

GEOGRAPHICAL VARIATION Eight races.
> *T. m. megalorhynchos* (Halmahera, the W Papuan group and associated islands)
> *T. m. affinis* (Buru, Seram, Ambon and Haruku) Greener-blue than nominate with more greenish underwing-coverts, green scapulars, and lesser coverts mainly greenish-blue.
> *T. m. subaffinis* (Babar and Tanimbar) Blue of rump paler.
> *T. m. hellmayri* (W Timor and Semau) Light yellowish-green head, no blue margins to mantle, narrower greener edges to lesser and median wing-coverts, bend of wing green.
> *T. m. viridipennis* (Tukangbesi group, Madu and Kalaotoa) Like nominate but with almost entirely green flight feathers.
> *T. m. djampeae* (Kalao and Tanahjampea) Like *viridipennis* but slightly more blue on flight feathers and underparts slightly greener (doubtfully distinct).
> *T. m. floris* (Flores) Underparts greener than the nominate and the previous race.
> *T. m. sumbensis* (Sumba) Darker green head, darker and greener below, greenish tinge to yellow of underwing-coverts, darker blue rump.

REFERENCES Arndt (1992), Beehler *et al.* (1986), Bishop (1992a), Bowler & Taylor (1989), duPont (1971), Lambert *et al.* (1993), Lever (1987), Lodge (1991), Long (1991), MacKinnon (1988), MacKinnon & Phillipps (1993), Mayr (1944), Peters (1961), Rand & Gilliard (1967), J. Riley *in litt.* (1995), Sibley & Monroe (1990), Smiet (1985), Taylor (1990), White & Bruce (1986).

---

108 BLUE-NAPED PARROT
Tanygnathus lucionensis   Plate 27

Other names: Blue-crowned Green Parrot, Luzon Parrot, Philippine Green Parrot

IDENTIFICATION 31cm. A medium-sized, generally green parrot with a large red bill and blue crown, which occurs throughout the Philippines and on the Talaud Islands, with a few introductions elsewhere. Formerly widespread, but now considered to have dwindled to low numbers. Blue-naped Parrots are sympatric with the larger Great-billed Parrot (107) and the more uniform Blue-backed Parrot (109) in the Talaud Islands, but are smaller and more slender than Great-billed, with a less variegated wing pattern and a blue crown (also green not yellow underwing-coverts), and have a more distinctive wing pattern than Blue-backed Parrot, whose females show a pale yellowish bill and no blue crown.

VOICE Transcribed as *k..le..eeaa.* Intermediate between Great-billed which has a less strident, higher-pitched call, and Blue-backed which has a stronger, more ringing screech.

Blue-naped Parrot

DISTRIBUTION AND STATUS Occurs throughout the Philippines and in the Talaud Islands, Indonesia. Specific island records are from Balut, Bantayan, Basilan, Biliran, Bohol, Bongao, the Cagayan Islands, the Calamian Islands, Caluya, Cebu, Guimaras, Jolo, Leyte, Luzon, Maestre de Campo, Malanipa, Manuk Manka, Marinduque, Masbate, Mindanao, Mindoro, Negros, Palawan, Panay, the Polillo Islands, Romblon, Samar, Sanga Sanga, the Sarangani Islands, Samal, Sibay, Sibutu, Sibuyan, Siquijor, Tablas, Tawitawi, Ticao, Tumindao and Verde (Philippines), and Karakelong and Salibabu (Talaud). Apparently introduced to Mantanani Besar (north-west Sabah), and Si-Amil (up to 100 birds present in 1962) and Maratua off the coast of north-east Borneo; a feral population is also reported to exist around Kota Kinabalu, Sabah. Occasional escapes are occasionally reported elsewhere, including the Sangir Islands. The species was described as common on Salibabu in the Talaud group in 1978 (and more numerous there than Blue-backed Parrot) and was still seen regularly there and on nearby Karakelong during observations in 1995 (numerous on the latter in 1997). Elsewhere the species now appears to be rare and recent Philippines records come chiefly from Mindoro and Palawan, which now appears to be the species's stronghold. The birds have declined dramatically as a result of habitat loss and trapping and the world population has been thought to be below 10,000. ENDANGERED.

ECOLOGY Found in secondary forest, forest edge, plantations and in scattered trees in agricultural lands close to forest up to 1,000m, and not as strongly tied to coastal habitats as Great-billed Parrot. The birds are usually found in flocks of up to a dozen individuals, and have been found feeding in company with Golden-mantled Racquet-tails (105) in Talaud. There are regular movements between roosting and feeding areas at dusk and dawn, and the birds forage in fruiting trees and other habitats that supply their diet of seeds, berries, nuts and grain (formerly considered an agricultural pest in corn-growing areas). The breeding season is from Apr to Jun and the birds nest in a tree-hole, sometimes in a coconut palm.

DESCRIPTION Head bright green with an obvious bright pale blue suffusion across rear-crown and nape. Upperparts light yellowish-green with pale blue lower back and rump; uppertail-coverts light yellowish-green. Scapulars blue, edged green; shoulder black with lesser coverts black edged blue-green and greenish-orange; median coverts centred black and dull blue, broadly edged dull brownish-orange; greater coverts blue-green edged orange-yellow on inner feathers. Secondaries green with narrow yellow margins; primaries green with blackish innerwebs. Underwing-coverts green, underside of primaries blackish. Uppertail green, narrowly edged and tipped yellowish laterally, undertail dull brownish-yellow. **Bare parts:** Bill red, paler on tip and lower mandible; iris yellow; legs grey.

SEX/AGE Sexes alike. Immatures with less blue on crown and duller wing-markings.

MEASUREMENTS Wing 179-202; tail 106-131, bill 27-33; tarsus 18-25.

GEOGRAPHICAL VARIATION Three races, but others have been proposed, probably reflecting variable individual plumages.

T. l. lucionensis (Luzon and Mindoro)

T. l. hybridus (Polillo Islands) Less extensive blue on crown (blue is also tinged with violet). Wing-coverts with more green.

T. l. talautensis (through rest of range) Lacks blue on lower back, plumage less yellowish-green.

REFERENCES Arndt (1992), Collar et al. (1994), Dickinson et al. (1991), duPont (1971), duPont & Rabor (1973), Forshaw (1989), Gore (1968), Lambert (1993c), Lambert et al. (1993), Lever (1987), Long (1981), MacKinnon & Phillipps (1993), Peters (1961), J. Riley in litt. (1995), Sibley & Monroe (1990), Smythies (1981).

---

109 BLUE-BACKED PARROT
Tanygnathus sumatranus   Plate 28

Other names: Müller's Parrot, Mueller's Parrot, Azure-rumped Parrot

IDENTIFICATION 32cm. The only member of its genus occurring throughout Sulawesi. The species is sympatric with Great-billed Parrot (107) in the Sangir and Talaud Islands, and with Blue-naped Parrot (108) in Talaud and throughout the Philippines. This is the least well-marked of the three, especially on the wing-coverts, which are mainly green edged yellowish-green, and it shares with them a blue rump (although Blue-naped in Panay, Negros, Samar, Leyte and Mindanao has a green rump), but there is no blue on the head as in Blue-naped; bill red in male. Some Blue-backed Parrots can show a rufescent wash around the throat, a feature supposedly unique in this genus to the previously recognised Rufous-tailed Parrot (see below).

VOICE A harsh screech *kea* or *ki-ek...ki-ek...ki-ek* frequently given in flight and at night; also a strange series of squeaks, gratings and clear bell-like notes. The voice has been described as loud, raucous and ringing, being deeper and throatier than the previous two *Tanygnathus* species (and quite different from that of Blue-naped Parrot).

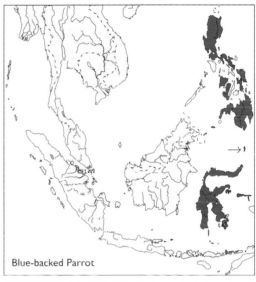

Blue-backed Parrot

DISTRIBUTION AND STATUS Occurs in Sulawesi, and on related islands including Buton and Tobea in the south-east, the Togian and Banggai groups to the east, and Talisei, Bangka and Manadotua in the north, extending north through the Sangir group onto at least Karakelong in the Talaud group. In the Philippines the species ranges from the Sulu Archipelago in the south-west including at least Bongao, Sanga Sanga, Sibutu, Tawitawi, Jolo, Loran and Basbas. It also occurs on the main Philippines islands of Luzon, Samar, Leyte, Panay, Negros, and Mindanao, as well as the Polillo Islands, but is extremely rare in the country. Elsewhere generally widespread and locally common, although trapping and habitat loss have led to declines in some areas. Apparently less common than Blue-naped Parrot where the two co-occur, but not currently considered threatened. World population estimated at around 50,000.

ECOLOGY Occurs chiefly in lowland and lower montane forest, along forest edge, and occasionally in plantations or paddyfields up to 800m (less common in coastal habitats). The birds are generally found in pairs or small groups and can be quite approachable. They have been known to damage crops, including corn, and are often active at night. The diet includes fruit, seeds, nuts and berries. Little is known of the species's breeding cycle, but a female in breeding condition was collected in Apr, and birds have been seen investigating possible nestholes in Sep, with nestlings being found in Sulawesi during Nov.

DESCRIPTION Head and mantle light yellowish-green (mantle slightly more yellowish). Lower back, rump and uppertail-coverts strongly suffused light blue. Wings darker green than mantle with fine yellowish-green margins to coverts; primary coverts marked blue; bend of wing marked turquoise-blue; primaries green on outer and blackish on innerwebs. Underwing-coverts greenish-yellow; underside of flight feathers blackish. Underparts light yellowish-green. Uppertail green, marked yellow on innerwebs of lateral feathers; undertail variable from yellow to dusky brown. **Bare parts**: Bill red; iris yellow; legs grey.

SEX/AGE Female like male but with pale yellow bill, less yellow-green mantle and less blue in the wing-coverts. Young male gains red bill after ten to twelve months.

MEASUREMENTS Wing 201-221; tail 114-128; bill 29-35; tarsus 21-23.

GEOGRAPHICAL VARIATION Six races.

T. s. sumatranus (Sulawesi and related islands)

T. s. sangirensis (Sangir Islands and Karakelong) More blue at bend of wing and on lesser coverts. Head slightly darker green than body. Iris yellow.

T. s. burbidgii (Sulu Archipelago) Darker green with a lighter collar. Iris yellow.

T. s. everetti (Panay, Negros, Leyte, Samar and Mindanao) Mantle and back dark green, rump darker blue. Head light green contrasting with mantle. Slight blue suffusion on mantle. Iris red.

T. s. duponti (Luzon) Generally dark green with a pronounced yellow collar and yellowish underwing-coverts. Iris red.

T. s. freeri (Polillo Islands) More uniform plumage with less contrast between upperparts and wing. More yellowish green, especially on nape. Iris red.

NOTE Includes Rufous-tailed Parrot *T. heterurus* based on a single specimen which was probably an aberrant *T. sumatranus*.

REFERENCES Arndt (1992), Bishop (1992b), Dickinson *et al.* (1991), duPont (1971), duPont & Rabor (1973), Forshaw (1989), Lambert *et al.* (1993), Peters (1961), Rozendaal & Dekker (1989), Sargeant (1992), Sibley & Monroe (1990), Watling (1983), White & Bruce (1986).

---

110 BLACK-LORED PARROT
Tanygnathus gramineus   Plate 28

Other names: Buru Green Parrot

IDENTIFICATION 40cm. Restricted to hill forests on the island of Buru, Indonesia. This species is at least partially nocturnal and there is no good information on its habits and status. It is a large, almost entirely green parrot, with a black line from the bill to the eye and a turquoise-green crown. Males have a red bill. The allopatric congeners, Great-billed (107) and Blue-naped Parrots (108), both have strongly variegated wing-coverts and other plumage differences. The other congener, Blue-backed Parrot (109), also allopatric, has a blue lower back and lacks the

black lores of this species. In Buru, there are three other medium-sized, mostly green parrots, but all are smaller than Black-lored. Female Red-cheeked (95) has a brown head and blue underwing-coverts obvious in flight. Male Eclectus (111) has red underwing-coverts and flanks and dark blue primaries. Buru Racquet-tail (106) is altitudinally sympatric, and females are confusingly nondescript, but show green lores, yellow undertail-coverts and a pale blue underside to the tail, while males have a grey-blue nape, mantle and shoulder; the tail racquets are diagnostic, but may be difficult to see, or broken, and are extremely short in the female.

VOICE Like that of Great-billed Parrot, but more drawn-out and higher-pitched.

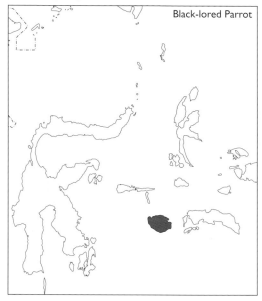

Black-lored Parrot

DISTRIBUTION AND STATUS Endemic to Buru, Indonesia. It is thought to occupy areas in the north-west of the island, but its present status is difficult to assess owing to its nocturnal habits and precipitous habitat. There is a recent record of birds heard as they were flying long distances downhill just after dusk at around 1,100m. The current world population estimate is 5,000 birds. VULNERABLE.

ECOLOGY Very little is known of this species. It occurs in mountain forest above 600-700m and has also been reported from lowland, hill and coastal areas. It is at least partially nocturnal, although sightings of birds perched in tree-tops during the day show that, like Blue-backed Parrot, it may also be active during the day.

DESCRIPTION Head green, with black line from top of bill to eye; crown suffused turquoise-blue. Upperparts grass-green. Wing-coverts mid-green; flight feathers slightly darker green with dull blackish margins to innerwebs. Underwing blackish with pale yellow-green coverts. Underparts lighter, more yellowish-green, especially on lower cheeks and breast. Uppertail mid-green faintly tipped yellow; undertail warm olive-brown. **Bare parts**: Bill red; iris yellow; legs greyish.

SEX/AGE Female with grey-brown, not red, bill. Immature undescribed.

MEASUREMENTS Wing 255-263; tail 149-161; bill 33-35; tarsus 25-26.

GEOGRAPHICAL VARIATION None.

REFERENCES BirdLife (1993), Collar *et al.* (1994), Forshaw (1989), Jones & Banjaransari (1990), Lambert *et al.* (1993), Lodge (1991), White & Bruce (1986).

---

111 ECLECTUS PARROT
Eclectus roratus   Plate 28

Other names: Kalanga, Grand Eclectus Parrot, King Parrot; Red-sided Eclectus Parrot (*E. r. polychloros*)

IDENTIFICATION 35cm. A stocky, broad-winged, short-tailed parrot occurring from Sumba and the Moluccas through New Guinea to the Solomons and extreme northern Australia. Males are predominantly green with blue flight feathers, red flanks and underwing-coverts, and red and yellow bills. Females are predominantly red with black bills, mauve-blue flight feathers, and most races also show purplish-blue bellies and mantles. Females are generally more racially dimorphic than males (see below) and the species varies in size according to population. The species is large and colourful and unlikely to be confused with any other parrot. The flight silhouette is unique with the short tail, broad wings and extended neck (the birds can look black in flight, especially in poor light). The rapid shallow wingbeats on wings held below the body axis, interspersed with short glides, are distinctive. Common and easily detected, even around habitation through much of its range. This is the only large New Guinea parrot that is either mostly green or mostly red. Papuan King Parrot (118) is slimmer and longer-tailed, Red-cheeked (95) much smaller.

VOICE In flight a loud, hoarse, screech repeated continuously or in short bursts described as *krraach-krraak*, likened to that of Sulphur-crested Cockatoo (65) but quieter and more croaking. In addition to various other alarm screeches, there is a mellow, horn like *tuwee tuwee*, a bell like *chee-ong* (perhaps as a prelude to copulation) and a metallic chuckling sound, apparently made by the female only.

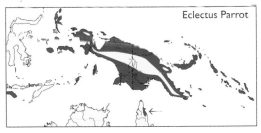

Eclectus Parrot

DISTRIBUTION AND STATUS Sumba in Nusa Tenggara, Indonesia, and the Moluccas including Buru, Seram, Ambon, Haruku, Saparua, the Gorong Islands (apparently introduced), Obi, Damar, Bacan, Halmahera, Mare, Ternate and Morotai, into the W Papuan islands including Waigeo, Batanta, Salawati and Misool; thence through the lowlands of New Guinea, and in the Tanimbar, Kai and Aru Islands to the south and on islands in Geelvink Bay (Numfor, Biak, Yapen, Mios Num). In the east, Eclectus Parrots occur in the D'Entrecasteaux and Louisiade

groups, Papua New Guinea, including Goodenough and Normanby, and in the Trobriand Islands and extending through the Bismarck Archipelago including Umboi, New Britain, the Witu Islands, Lolobau, Watom, Duke of York, New Ireland, New Hanover, Tabar, Lihir, Tanga and Feni, reaching Manus and Rambutyo in the Admiralty group and Nissan in the south. The species is also found through the Solomons, including Buka and Bougainville (to Papua New Guinea) east to San Cristobal and its satellites. There is a population isolated in the northern Cape York Peninsula, Australia, which ranges from the Iron Range and Pascoe River region, south to the MacIlwraith Range, and birds regularly visit smaller islands in the Torres Strait from the New Guinea mainland. There is an introduced population of the race *polychloros* on Koror and some smaller islands in the Palau group in the Pacific, but occasional escapees in Hawaii have apparently failed to become established. This is one of the commonest and most familiar parrots throughout much of its range. World population above 300,000. Local trapping on Ambon, Saparua and Haruku has apparently rendered the species extinct in these three islands. The distinctive Sumba population is endangered.

ECOLOGY Occurs in a broad range of habitats from forest to second growth, savanna, mangrove, coconut plantations and eucalyptus woodland, up to 1,900m. The species is commonest in lowland forest, coastal habitats and around cultivation. The birds are found singly, in pairs or in small groups often comprised of just male birds (presumably during breeding). They sometimes soar hawk-like above the forest and draw attention by their raucous calls as they fly over the canopy, or perch on an exposed branch. They are wary, foraging groups usually remaining in the tree-tops, although birds have been recorded feeding close to or even on the ground. They are most active at dawn and dusk as they travel to and from their roosting areas where noisy groups of up to 80 birds wheel above the trees before they settle for the night. They have been recorded roosting with Yellow-crested Cockatoos (64) in Sumba. The species is considered an agricultural pest in parts of New Guinea. The diet includes fruit, seeds, blossoms, buds, nuts and nectar; they are especially fond of *Pandanus*, banana, maize, figs and papaya. Breeding can apparently occur at any time of year in Papua New Guinea, while the Australian population nests between Jul and Feb; it has been recorded during Nov in Buru, during Aug in Seram, and between Jun and Sep in the Solomons. Up to eight birds have been recorded attending one nest. It is not clear whether these are nest-helpers, young from a previous brood still attached to the family group, or additional laying females. In display the birds engage in mutual preening and head bobbing. The nest-site is a hollow up to 30m high in a tall, sometimes exposed tree; the cavity may be as much as 6m deep. The two eggs are laid on a bed of wood-dust and the grey-downed young hatch in about 26 days, taking 12 weeks to fledge. During incubation the female alone broods, leaving the nest twice a day to be fed by the male; she is also fed by the male when the chicks first hatch, but later begins to feed herself.

DESCRIPTION Head and upperparts bright green. Wing-coverts green; bend of wing and carpal edge blue; primary coverts dark blue. Flight feathers with outerwebs very dark blue, innerwebs black on inner edge. Underwing-coverts bright red; underside of flight feathers black. Underparts green with red flanks and axillaries. Uppertail green narrowly tipped pale yellow, lateral feathers suffused blue distally and tipped yellow (outermost with most blue); undertail black with yellow tips. **Bare parts**: Bill red tipped yellow, lower mandible black; iris orange; legs grey-brown.

SEX/AGE Female very distinctive, being bright red with a purple collar across the upper mantle, with blue-black flight feathers, purple-blue underwing-coverts, light purplish suffusion on the breast, dull purple-blue lower breast and belly, red undertail-coverts tipped yellowish, and a red tail tipped yellowish (feather-bases darker). The bill is black and the iris is usually yellow (variable). Young birds moult straight into adult plumage but have brownish bills.

MEASUREMENTS Wing 228-247; tail 105-133; bill 34-40; tarsus 22-24.

GEOGRAPHICAL VARIATION Ten races.

E. r. roratus (Moluccas including Buru, Seram, Ambon, Saparua and Haruku)

E. r. vosmaeri (N Moluccas) Larger than nominate (male wing 265-282). Male with lighter green plumage, more red on flanks, yellow tip to tail broader. Female lighter red, broader yellow tip to tail and yellow on undertail-coverts.

E. r. westermani (known only from a few specimens from captive stock with no recorded place of origin) Smaller than nominate (male wing 210-231). Male lacks visible red flanks when wings are closed and shows green outer margins to flight feathers. Female darker red with broader yellow tip to tail. The possibility that the few specimens are aberrant individuals of *E. r. roratus* has not been ruled out.

E. r. cornelia (Sumba) Larger than nominate (male wing 262-272). Male with more blue in tail, upperparts lighter green. Female entirely red except for carpal edge, underwing-coverts and flight feathers, which are blue. Narrow yellow tip to tail.

E. r. riedeli (Tanimbar Islands) Smaller than nominate (male wing 209-224). Male with broad yellow tip to tail (25mm). Female like previous, but shows bright yellow undertail-coverts.

E. r. polychloros (W Papuan islands, throughout New Guinea and on associated islands including the D'Entrecasteaux and Louisiade Archipelagos) Larger than nominate (male wing 240-279). Male more yellowish-green, yellow tip to tail approximately 10mm. Female with red breast and less purplish blue of underparts restricted to belly, green on outerweb of primaries. Narrow blue periophthalmic ring. Undertail-coverts red.

E. r. biaki (Biak) Like former but smaller (male wing 229-242). Like previous but female with hindneck and underparts brighter red (dubiously distinct race).

E. r. aruensis (Aru Islands) Like previous, male with slightly broader yellow tip to tail. Female lighter red, especially tail.

E. r. macgillivrayi (N Australia) Like *polychloros* but larger (male wing 276-296).

E. r. solomonensis (Bismarck Archipelago and the Solomon Islands) Smaller than *polychloros* (male wing 215-255) and green of male more yellowish, female lighter red. Size reduces clinally west to east.

REFERENCES Arndt (1992), Beehler (1978b), Beehler *et al.* (1986), Bishop (1992a), Bishop & Broome (1980), Blakers *et al.* (1984), Bowler & Taylor (1989), Cain *et al.*

(1963), Coates (1985), Diamond (1972), Draffan *et al.* (1983), Forshaw (1981, 1989), Gyldenstolpe (1955), Hartert (1926), Lambert *et al.* (1993), Lever (1987), Long (1981), Milton (1988), Peters (1961), Pizzey & Doyle (1983), Rand & Gilliard (1967), Schodde & Tideman (1988), Sibley & Monroe (1990), Simpson & Day (1984), Slater (1989), Taylor (1990).

112 PESQUET'S PARROT
Psittrichas fulgidus   Plate 16

Other names: Vulturine Parrot

IDENTIFICATION 46cm. Restricted to the hill forests of New Guinea. One of the most distinctive of all parrots with its long hooked bill and exposed facial skin, literally giving it a 'vulture-like' profile. The plumage too is striking, with black upperparts, a scalloped breast, red belly, uppertail-coverts and wing-patches. These large, stout parrots are unlikely to be confused with any other psittacine species. The partially sympatric Palm Cockatoo (55) is the closest in terms of size and general coloration, but has a massive crest and bill, lacks the red underparts, has a longer tail, and is found chiefly at lower altitudes. It is in fact more likely that, with poor views through the canopy, a flying Pesquet's Parrot could be written off as a crow *Corvus* or Blyth's Hornbill *Rhyticeros plicatus* than confused with another parrot. The species has a distinctive flight profile with its long, slender neck and bill, broad wings, robust body and short tail. The wingbeats are rapid, shallow, and interspersed with short glides.

VOICE A harsh, rasping or growling, drawn-out scream, *aaar* or *caar*, 'like heavy cloth being torn', given frequently in flight, similar to but higher-pitched, weaker and less rasping than that of Sulphur-crested Cockatoo (65), and audible from some distance; may be uttered singly, in pairs or continuously. A double-call has also been described, in which the first note is at a constant pitch and hoarse, the second up-slurred, nasal and squeaky.

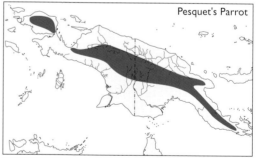

Pesquet's Parrot

DISTRIBUTION AND STATUS Confined to Irian Jaya, Indonesia, and Papua New Guinea. It ranges from the Tamrau Mountains, Vogelkop, western Irian, east through the Snow Mountains and Central Ranges (including the upper Fly River, Lake Kutubu and Karimui districts), to the Owen Stanley Ranges and Huon Peninsula, in eastern Papua New Guinea. The species is patchily distributed in montane forest, and is considered rare in most areas. The world population is thought to be above 10,000 but declining, mainly through hunting for food and feathers (which are more prized even than bird-of-paradise

Paradisaeidae plumes). The introduction of the gun has significantly increased pressure on the species in more densely inhabited areas. Habitat loss and trade in live birds are also thought to pose potential threats. Small numbers in captivity. VULNERABLE.

ECOLOGY Pesquet's Parrots are found chiefly in primary and tall secondary montane rainforest from 600 to 1,200m. They do however occur up to 2,000m, and are occasional as low as 50m. The species is thought generally to have a low population density, with the highest concentrations found in tracts of relatively undisturbed forest where birds are free from persecution. These large, conspicuous parrots are commonly encountered in pairs or in groups of up to 20 individuals, perched at the top of exposed trees, or flying noisily through or above the canopy. They hop jerkily around the branches with much wing-flicking, and may remain in the tops of emergent trees during rain. They have been observed flying to roost in a solitary tree at dusk. Pesquet's Parrots feed mainly on the soft pulp of fruits like figs *Ficus*, mangos *Mangifera indica* and climbing pandanus; they have also been seen feeding on the large flowers of *Freycinetia mangospandans*. During feeding, the base of the bill may become coated with fruit pulp, and it is likely that the extent of exposed facial skin has evolved to prevent feather-matting. Reproductive habits in the wild are unknown, but birds in breeding condition have been collected from Feb to May. In captivity a pair was observed courtship feeding; these birds laid two eggs, which were incubated by the female for 31 days, and the single yellow-white downed chick was fed by both parents.

DESCRIPTION Head black, forepart unfeathered, rest covered in small bristly black feathers with patch of stiff red feathers above ear-coverts. Nape, mantle, back and rump blackish-brown with fine pale edgings. Uppertail-coverts red with black bases. Upperwing black with outer median and greater coverts (except for innermost) and outerwebs of central flight feathers red; primary coverts black. Underwing black with red lesser and median coverts. Breast browner than upperparts with a scalloped effect produced by pale margins to feathers; belly, flanks and undertail-coverts red. Tail black. **Bare parts:** Bill black; facial skin black; iris dark brown; legs blackish-grey.

SEX/AGE The female lacks the red patch at the side of the head and is slightly smaller on average. In immature birds the red markings are duller.

MEASUREMENTS Wing 285-318; tail 154-198; bill 36-44; tarsus 28-34.

GEOGRAPHICAL VARIATION No races are recognised but there appears to be considerable size variation.

REFERENCES Arndt (1993), Beehler (1978b), Beehler *et al.* (1986), Coates (1985), Collar *et al.* (1994), Diamond (1972), Forshaw (1989), Gyldenstolpe (1955), Lambert *et al.* (1993), Rand & Gilliard (1967), Schodde (1978), Sibley & Monroe (1990).

---

113   CRIMSON SHINING PARROT
Prosopeia splendens   Plate 29

IDENTIFICATION 42cm. A large, slim, long-tailed parrot occurring on the islands of Kadavu, Ono and Viti Levu in the Fiji group. The upperparts are mainly green except for a broad blue collar. The head and underparts are red,

and there is a prominent blue wing-flash. The species is structurally reminiscent of a king parrot *Alisterus* or Red-winged Parrot (120), but with a black rather than red bill. Masked Shining Parrot (114), which also occurs on Viti Levu, is of similar size and structure, but lacks the bright red underparts, instead showing a yellow central patch and green flanks. The combination of black bill, green rump and blue collar is sufficient to separate this species from members of structurally similar genera. The similar Red Shining Parrot (115) has a narrower blue collar, and maroon rather than red underparts. In flight Crimson Shining Parrots have shortish, rounded wings and look large-headed because of their heavy bills.

VOICE Similar to but reportedly higher-pitched than that of Red Shining Parrot.

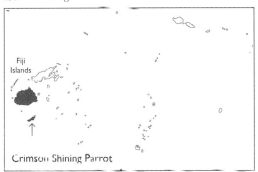

Crimson Shining Parrot

DISTRIBUTION AND STATUS Endemic to Fiji where it occurs naturally on the islands on Kadavu (including around Vunisea) and Ono. It has also been introduced to Viti Levu and probably to the Yasawa Group and Ovalau in the past (no recent records). The species may be declining on Viti Levu due to trade, although the possible negative effects of competition with the native Masked Shining Parrot are currently unknown. The world population is thought to be between 5,000 and 10,000. NEAR-THREATENED.

ECOLOGY Found in forest, farmlands and towns both in the lowlands and hills. Food, habits and breeding behaviour presumably similar to those of Red Shining Parrot with which it was, until recently, considered conspecific.

DESCRIPTION Head and underparts bright rich red, slightly darker on lores; broad hind-collar violet-blue, becoming turquoise toward rear edge. Rest of upperparts bright pale green with fine darker margins and a glossy sheen on back and wings. Median coverts green, greater coverts blue-green; primaries and primary coverts deep violet-blue with black on innerwebs; secondaries grade from blue to green on innermost feathers. Underwing-coverts marked blue-green and red; axillaries pale green. Uppertail green tipped blue, lateral feathers violet-blue with blackish innerwebs; undertail black. **Bare parts:** Bill black; iris red-orange; legs black.

SEX/AGE The male has a larger bill and head, features which are noticeable in the field with good views of a pair.

MEASUREMENTS Wing 213-245; tail 193-228; bill 24-32; tarsus 25-27.

GEOGRAPHICAL VARIATION None.

REFERENCES Arndt (1993), BirdLife (1993), Clunie (1984), Forshaw (1989), Lambert *et al.* (1993), Lever

(1987), Lodge (1991), Long (1981), Pratt *et al.* (1987), Sibley & Monroe (1990), Watling (1982a), Wood & Wetmore (1925).

114 MASKED SHINING PARROT
Prosopeia personata   Plate 29

Other names: Masked Musk Parakeet, Masked Parakeet, Yellow-breasted Musk Parrot

IDENTIFICATION 47cm. A large, long-tailed, forest-dwelling parrot which occurs only on the island of Viti Levu in the Fiji group. This distinctive species is mainly green with a black face, staring red eye, yellow stripe down the centre of the underparts, and a light blue wing flash. No other parrot combines black face, red eye and yellow stripe on underparts. The similar-sized Crimson Shining Parrot (113), which also occurs on Viti Levu, has bright red underparts and a blue collar. The flight profile of Masked Shining Parrot is distinctive with a large head, long tail and short rounded wings. The flight itself is heavy and slightly undulating, punctuated by regular glides on spread wings.

VOICE A raucous, penetrating, repetitious screech *raaa* or *kreee*, given in flight or when perched. In alarm, the call is louder, higher-pitched and more quickly repeated. There is also a dry-sounding bill-rattle, and cackling notes are sometimes uttered. The calls are lower-pitched than those of Red Shining Parrot (115) and somewhat reminiscent of an Eclectus Parrot (111).

Masked Shining Parrot

DISTRIBUTION AND STATUS Endemic to Fiji, occurring only on the island of Viti Levu (although the species has also been recorded from the nearby island of Ovalau in the past). On Viti Levu, it is not uncommon in the forested interior including around Nadarivatu and Tomanivi in the north, Nadrau in the centre and the Vunidawa district to the east. The world population is considered to be greater than 5,000, but declining due to habitat loss. The large trees required for nesting are being felled, and tracts of mature forest are now fragmented in many areas. The possibly damaging effect of inter-specific competition from introduced Crimson Shining Parrots remains unstudied. NEAR-THREATENED.

ECOLOGY Occurs from sea-level to at least 1,200m in mature forest and secondary growth of windward and intermediate vegetation zones, straying into village gardens, farmland and mangroves; also found along forest edges near agricultural land and in trees bordering forest watercourses. Masked Shining Parrots are generally

sociable and are found either singly, in pairs, or outside the breeding season in flocks of up to 40 birds. Birds are sometimes glimpsed flying swiftly through the forest or travelling above the canopy. They are noisy and are often heard before they are seen; their raucous calls being one of the natural alarm calls of the forest; like Red Shining Parrots they often call at the first sign of a human intruder, and are generally timid and difficult to approach when perched. They perch high in trees but descend to lower storeys to feed on berries, and gather in loose, noisy groups in fruiting trees; they may also raid cropfields. The diet comprises mostly fruit, e.g. mango *Mangifera indica*, guava *Psidium guajava*, figs *Ficus* and bananas, but also flowers, insects, seeds and berries, as well as cultivated grain. When feeding the birds manipulate food items with their foot and can move deftly around using their bill to grip small branches. They are powerful and have been seen flying off carrying a mango when disturbed. Breeding takes place between Jul and Sep. The nest is a hole or crack in a large forest tree, or a cavity in the top of a stump. Two or more white eggs are laid in a hollow enlarged using the powerful bill. The birds emit a strong odour.

DESCRIPTION Forecrown, lores, cheeks and chin black. Upperparts bright pale green (brighter and with a glossier sheen on crown and nape). Outer greater coverts, primary coverts and primaries blue with dark innerwebs. Underwing-coverts green. Throat, upper breast, flanks, vent and undertail-coverts green; centre of breast and belly bright yellow, a few feathers tipped green, yellow shading into variable orange patch on lower belly. Uppertail green; undertail black. **Bare parts**: Bill black; iris orange-red; legs grey-black.

SEX/AGE The male has a heavier head and bill than the female. Young birds have blotchy, paler bills, less black on the face and a brown iris.

MEASUREMENTS Wing 225-250; tail 200-259; bill 25-34; tarsus 23-29.

GEOGRAPHICAL VARIATION None.

REFERENCES Arndt (1993), BirdLife (1993), Clunie (1984), Davis & Fisher (1993), duPont (1976), Forshaw (1989), Gorman (1975), Gregory-Smith (1983), Holyoak (1979), Lambert *et al.* (1993), Lodge (1991), Mayr (1945), Peters (1961), Pratt *et al.* (1987), Sargeant (1990), Sibley & Monroe (1990), Watling (1982a), Wood & Wetmore (1925).

115 RED SHINING PARROT
Prosopeia tabuensis   Plate 29

Other names: Red-breasted Musk Parakeet, Tabuan Parakeet, Maroon Musk Parakeet, Maroon Parakeet

IDENTIFICATION 45cm. A large, long-tailed parrot with green upperparts, blue wing-flash and maroon head and underparts, occurring in forest and associated habitats on islands in the Fiji and Tongan groups. The type specimen was collected in Tonga, where the species is introduced, and may be racially hybrid; the nominate subspecies now occurs only on Gau in the Fiji group, where birds may also have descended from introduced or hybrid stock, and on 'Eua in Tonga, showing variable characters usually with some maroon feathers on the rump and a distinct blue hind-collar. Like the Crimson Shining Parrot, this species is reminiscent of a king parrot *Alisterus*, but has a black, not red, bill; female Australian King Parrot (116) has a black bill but also has a green head and breast. The allopatric Crimson Shining Parrot (113) is similar but with red, not maroon, underparts and a broad blue hind-collar. The heavy flight of the Red Shining Parrot is slightly undulating and interspersed with glides, the long tail and blunt head giving a distinctive profile.

VOICE A harsh, loud *nea nea* and a grating *arrr* repeated in bursts. Also a softer *ra-ra-ra-ra*, a dry bill rattle, various other hoots, squawks and screeches and a distinctive *tok* when it approaches the nest. Calls during the night. Notes are softer and higher-pitched than those of Masked Shining Parrot (114).

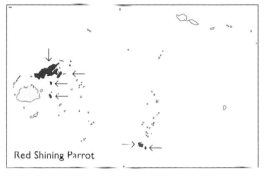

Red Shining Parrot

DISTRIBUTION AND STATUS Occurs naturally on islands in the Fiji group including Vanua Levu, Kioa, Taveuni, Qamea, Laucala, Koro and Gau (probably introduced) In Tonga, the species was introduced on Tongatapu before European contact, where it has since become extinct due to habitat loss, and on 'Eua where it is still fairly common especially in eastern, northern and south-western forests (estimated population between 700-1,000 birds in 1988). The species benefits in part from agriculture, but is heavily dependent for nesting on mature forest trees, which are being cleared across most of its range. The species is also threatened by trade, and is hunted for food and plumes Many young birds are taken to be reared locally as pets because they learn to talk easily. The total world population is thought to be in excess of 20,000, but the Taveuni race has probably less than 5,000 birds and its population status gives cause for concern There has been a sharp decline in numbers in some areas owing to habitat loss, although the species remains locally common at low elevations on most of its range islands.

ECOLOGY Occurs in mature forest and through a range of associated habitats including secondary growth, forested gullies (for nesting), coconut plantations, village gardens, farmland, mangroves and scrub. It has been recorded from 100m up to 1,750m, but is commonest between about 400 and 1,000m. Red Shining Parrots are alert, inquisitive birds and are encountered singly, in pairs, or in flocks of up to 40 individuals outside the breeding season. They are not shy, and noisy groups are easily located gathering in favoured feeding locations. The birds also sit conspicuously in tree-tops, or fly calling above the canopy. They feed on the fruits and seeds of a wide range of forest trees, e.g. *Myristica hypargyraea*, which is of particular importance on 'Eua. They also feed on mango *Mangifera indica*, pawpaw *Carica papaya*, guava *Psidium guajava* and bananas. They are agile climbers, and move about in search of food using their bill to grasp small branches.

They hold food items in their foot as they bite with their powerful bill, and chew into wood to extract insect larvae. They feed mostly in the upper canopy, but will sometimes also raid cornfields. Birds commonly perch almost vertically upright and swing their head rhythmically back and forward, presumably in a form of display. Breeding in Fiji takes place from Jun to Jan, and on 'Eua from May to Oct. Two or three dull white eggs are laid in a cavity in a forest, or occasionally a plantation tree. Favourite species include *Rhus taitensis* and *Laportea harveyi*. The entrance is usually high up, often at 12m or more, with an entrance of around 15cm in diameter. The hollow is enlarged by use of the powerful bill so as to extend from around 0.5m to 5m down, and is lined with chips of rotten wood. Nesting pairs are usually no closer than 120m apart. Eggs are laid at two-day intervals, and the female incubates for 24 days, brooding and feeding the young alone about three times a day, with food gathered by the male. The young have whitish down which turns dark grey after about 12 days. The young are brooded for the first 15-18 days, and fledge in seven weeks.

DESCRIPTION Variable. Head dark brownish-red, darker, almost blackish on forehead, lores and chin (can show blue flecking around base of lower mandible) Upperparts green with narrow blue hind-collar and some maroon tips to rump feathers. Greater coverts blue-green; primary coverts violet-blue. Flight feathers with blackish innerwebs; outerwebs greenish on inner secondaries, shading through greenish-blue to deep violet-blue on outer primaries. Underwing-coverts blue-green; underside of flight feathers black. Underparts maroon (lighter than head) flecked lightly with green in parts. Uppertail green suffused blue towards tips of central feathers and on outerwebs of lateral feathers, undertail blackish, **Bare parts**: Bill black; iris bright orange to orange-red, legs grey-black.

SEX/AGE Females are smaller billed with smaller, rounder heads than males. Young birds up to about 100 days old have a brown iris and a blotchy yellowish bill.

MEASUREMENTS Wing 230-258; tail 204-236; bill 26-35; tarsus 20-27.

GEOGRAPHICAL VARIATION Four races.
> *P. t. tabuensis* (Gau in the Fiji group and 'Eua in Tonga)
> *P. t. atrogularis* (Vanua Levu and Kioa) Shows a broad blue collar and green rump.
> *P. t. koroensis* (Koro) The blue collar is lacking, broken or very narrow. The rump is maroon and some feathers of the lower back are also tipped maroon. Underparts darker maroon.
> *P. t. taviunensis* (Taveuni, Qamea and Laucala) Smaller than nominate (male wing 217.9). Lacks blue collar and has very little maroon edging on the rump; lores and forehead less blackish.

REFERENCES Arndt (1993), BirdLife (1993), Clunie (1984), Davis & Fisher (1993), duPont (1976), Forshaw (1989), Holyoak (1979), Lambert *et al.* (1993), Lever (1987), Lodge (1991), Long (1981), Mayr (1945), Peters (1961), Rinke (1987, 1988, 1989, 1992), Sargeant (1990), Sibley & Monroe (1990), Watling (1982a).

116 AUSTRALIAN KING PARROT
Alisterus scapularis   Plate 29

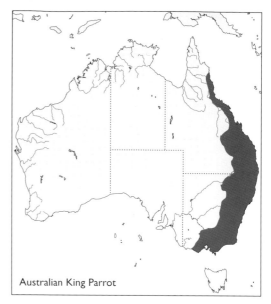

Australian King Parrot

Other names: Scarlet-and-green Parrot, King Lory, King Parrot (also used for Eclectus Parrot and Red-capped Parrot)

IDENTIFICATION 38-44cm. Common in forest and modified habitats along the east coast of Australia. A distinctive largish parrot with a broad, long, rounded tail and cuckoo-like flight profile, somewhat reminiscent of a Red-winged Parrot (120). Males are distinctive with a red head and bill, red underparts, dark blue hind-collar and rump, and pale green scapulars, but females and young have green heads, and most groups comprise mainly green-headed birds. No other Australian Parrot shows an entirely red head and underparts and green upperparts. All members of this genus are structurally reminiscent of shining parrots *Prosopeia*. The Crimson Shining Parrot (113) has similar coloration to the male Australian King Parrot, but has an all-dark bill, blue wing-flash and green rump. It also lacks pale scapulars. Unlike this species, shining parrots are not sexually dimorphic in plumage. The Moluccan King Parrot (117), which is not sexually dimorphic, has a number of races similar to male Australian King Parrots. All show a bluer upper surface to the tail, variable amounts of blue on the back, lack the clearly defined pale green scapulars, and conceal the dark centres to the undertail-coverts. Male Papuan King Parrots (118) are distinctive with an obvious pale green patch on the wing-coverts. Females of the two species are very similar (except *A. c. moszkowskii*, which does not exhibit strong dimorphism), but Australian can be separated from Papuan by the more obvious green bases to the red-tipped undertail-coverts (those of Papuan have mauve bases); Papuan lacks the pink tips to the tail feathers shown by Australian, and has darker head and underparts (the green breast shows more dark reddish suffusion). The somewhat erratic, twisting and turning flight of Australian King Parrot is heavy, strong and direct, with rhythmic, leisurely wingbeats. The tail is fanned slightly on landing. In winter large flocks can be seen flying to roost over parts of Canberra. This species has been known to hybridise with Red-winged Parrot (120) in the wild.

VOICE The flight call is a loud *carrack-carrack* or *crassak-crassak*, repeated frequently. There are also a variety of other calls including a piping *sweeeee* given by the male, a raucous metallic alarm call, a quiet guttural cackling whilst feeding, and a metallic *chack*.

DISTRIBUTION AND STATUS Occurs throughout coastal eastern Australia, inland to western slopes of the Great Dividing Range, extending from Cooktown in northern Queensland, south through the Atherton district, then through Eungella, Blackall, Moonie and into New South Wales where it reaches inland roughly to Bingara, Mudgee and Albury. In Victoria it is confined to the south-east, Portland being its south-western limit. It is common in Canberra, particularly during the autumn and winter, and occasional escapes are seen in Adelaide, along the Murray River and in western Victoria. Otherwise there are no records west of 143°E. The species also occurs on Fraser, Stradbroke and Broughton Islands. The world population is considered to be well in excess of 50,000 and stable, although it may have been affected by trade and habitat loss to some degree.

ECOLOGY Australian King Parrots undertake regular post-breeding dispersal from higher forested areas – occurring as high as 1,625m, but rare above 1,200m – to lower more open habitats; other apparently weather-related movements have been noted. Moderate distances may be involved, and one banded bird was recovered 270km from its ringing site. During the breeding season birds are found in dense forest (wet sclerophyll forest), forested gullies and associated habitats, including more open eucalyptus woodland and savanna woodland bordering riverine forest. Outside the breeding season, they are found in a broader variety of habitats including cultivated areas, parks, orchards and occasionally suburban gardens. They are usually encountered in pairs or small groups, but post-breeding flocks of immatures may build up to 50 or more birds. Individuals often perch conspicuously on high exposed branches. When feeding, however, birds remain wary and fairly quiet. They gather to feed in the early morning, sometimes in mixed groups with rosellas *Platycercus* and other parrots, then sit quietly through the hottest part of the day, becoming active again during the late afternoon. Noisy high-flying flocks can often be seen returning to roost in the evening. The diet consists of fruit, berries, nuts, seeds, insect larvae, flowers, buds and other vegetable matter. The species is partial to mistletoe *Viscum album*, eucalyptus and acacias, and may do damage in orchards and cropfields, coming to ground and waddling round awkwardly as they forage on potatoes, maize and other crops. When feeding, they will hold a food item in their foot as they prise it open with their bill. If disturbed, these parrots fly quickly to cover but may become tame in some farm areas. During courtship, males head-bob, wing-flick and puff up their feathers; the female responds by head-bobbing in return, and by soliciting food. The breeding season lasts from Sep to Feb. The nest is a hollow in a live or dead tree (often an older eucalypt with hollow limbs). The nest entrance is usually at some height, and between three and six (usually four) eggs are laid in a deep hollow on a bed of wood-dust. The female incubates alone for 20 days with the male remaining in the vicinity to feed her. The white-downed young fledge in around five weeks and are fed by both parents at the nest after they are about half-grown. After fledging, family parties are formed. Head-scratching is over the wing.

DESCRIPTION Head and underparts bright scarlet, except for black, broadly red-tipped undertail-coverts. Narrow hind-collar dark blue blending into dark green of mantle (mantle feathers fringed darker still); lower back and rump dark blue. Scapulars pale, slightly bluish-green, forming distinctive 'braces'; wing-coverts green, and flight feathers green with blackish innerwebs. Underwing-coverts dark green suffused blue. Uppertail black with slight blue suffusion on outerwebs of lateral feathers; undertail black. **Bare parts**: Bill bright coral-red, tipped black; iris yellow; legs grey.

SEX/AGE Female strongly dimorphic, with crown and upperparts green (including uppertail-coverts and tail, but not rump which is lighter blue than in male). The face and breast are a dull green with a warm reddish suffusion Females may occasionally show some pale scapulars. The undertail-coverts are green, strongly tipped red. The central tail feathers are green, the lateral blackish narrowly tipped pink. The bill is a dark blackish-brown. Immature birds are like females but with a paler bill and dark iris. Younger females show less red below. Males gain adult plumage during a slow moult beginning at about 16 months, and continuing for another 14-15 months. Birds breed in immature plumage.

MEASUREMENTS Wing 206-233; tail 176-223; bill 22-23; tarsus 24-26.

GEOGRAPHICAL VARIATION Two races.

   A. s. scapularis (E Australia, south of about Rockhampton and Blackall, Queensland)
   A. s. minor (Cooktown N Queensland, to around Townsville, with an isolated population in the Eungella district) Like nominate but smaller (male wing 185-202).

REFERENCES Arndt (1993), Blakers *et al.* (1984), Campbell (1974), Emison *et al.* (1987), Forshaw (1981, 1989), Lambert *et al.* (1993), Lodge (1991), Peters (1961), Pizzey & Doyle (1983), Schodde & Tidemann (1988), Sibley & Monroe (1990), Simpson & Day (1984), Slater (1979, 1989).

---

117 MOLUCCAN KING PARROT
Alisterus amboinensis   Plate 30

Other names: Island King Parrot, Amboina Red Parakeet, Ambon King Parrot

IDENTIFICATION 35-40cm. A large, long-tailed parrot with red underparts, green wings and blue back, rump and tail (wings also blue in Halmahera race). Found in dense forest through the Moluccas into western New Guinea, where it abuts the western extreme of the Papuan King Parrot (118). This is the only king parrot with all-red underparts and without pale green or greenish-yellow markings on the scapulars or wing-coverts. The allopatric Crimson Shining Parrot (113) is superficially similar but has a green mantle, rump and base of tail; it also has an all-dark bill which is only shown in the Buru race of the present species. The flight is buoyant and direct with strong rhythmic beats.

VOICE A shrill screech *kree..kree*, similar to that of Papuan King Parrot.

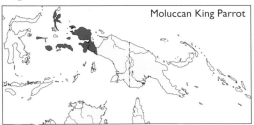

Moluccan King Parrot

DISTRIBUTION AND STATUS Occurs from Peleng and the Sula Islands eastward through the Moluccas, including Halmahera, Buru, Ambon and Seram. It is also found in the W Papuan islands, including Waigeo, Batanta and Salawati. On the New Guinea mainland it is found from Vogelkop and the Bomberai Peninsula east to about 135°E. Generally uncommon owing to trade and habitat loss through most of its range. The world population is considered to be in the region of 60,000 birds. Populations of the subspecies occurring on Peleng and in the Sula group are both much reduced. NEAR-THREATENED.

ECOLOGY Occurs in dense humid primary and secondary forest, and occasionally in adjacent plantations, farmland and gardens, from the lowlands to around 2,100m. The birds are usually found in pairs or small groups, and are very quiet when feeding and shy at all times, remaining in thick foliage and flying to cover calling loudly at the first sign of an intruder. The diet includes *Lithocarpus* acorns, as well as the hard fruits, buds and berries of other forest trees. Nothing is known of the breeding cycle in the wild, but nesting is reported to take place between Feb and Apr. Nests containing two young have been found on two occasions in tree-hollows. An instance of breeding in captivity gave incubation at 19 days, with the young fledging in nine weeks. Courtship feeding was noted, and two eggs were laid.

DESCRIPTION Head, neck, nape and upper mantle bright red, with sharp demarcation to dark violet-blue lower mantle, back, rump and uppertail-coverts. Wings green except for blue inner lesser coverts and carpal edge. Underwing black with violet-blue coverts. Underparts bright red, with mauve bases to undertail-coverts sometimes visible; flanks with a little blue. Uppertail very dark blue; undertail grey-black with broad pink margins to lateral feathers. **Bare parts**: Bill with base of upper mandible orange-red, lower blackish; iris orange; legs grey-black.

SEX/AGE Female like male. Immature with more green on back; brownish-black bill; paler eye-ring and darker iris than adult. Pink tips to outer tail feathers. Matures in one year.

MEASUREMENTS Wing 200-214; tail 208-235; bill 21-24; tarsus 21-25.

GEOGRAPHICAL VARIATION Six races.

   A. a. amboinensis (Ambon and Seram)
   A. a. sulaensis (Sula Islands) Lacks pink webs on lateral tail feathers and upper mantle is green not blue.
   A. a. versicolor (Peleng Island) Similar to Sula race but with no green on back. Smaller than nominate (male wing 175-183).
   A. a. buruensis (Buru) Bill completely black. Green

suffusion on back. Less pink on webs of second and third lateral tail feathers than nominate, but first with broad edging.

A. a. hypophonius (Halmahera) Upperparts including wings entirely dark purplish-blue, lacking green. Lesser coverts brighter than rest of wing. Lacks pink webs to lateral tail feathers.

A. a. dorsalis (W Papuan islands and on the W New Guinea mainland) Like nominate but lacking pink webs to lateral tail feathers. Smaller than nominate (male wing 175-193).

REFERENCES Arndt (1991), Beehler *et al.* (1986), van Bemmel (1948), Forshaw (1989), Gee (1993), Gyldenstolpe (1955), Hornbuckle (1991), Jones & Banjaransari (1990), Lambert *et al.* (1993), Lambert & Yong (1989), Lodge (1991), Peters (1961), Rand & Gilliard (1967), Sibley & Monroe (1990), Smiet (1985), Taylor (1990), White & Bruce (1986).

118 PAPUAN KING PARROT
Alisterus chloropterus **Plate 30**

Other names: Green-winged King Parrot

IDENTIFICATION 36-38cm. A large, long-tailed parrot occurring in forest throughout much of northern and south-eastern New Guinea. The male is distinctive, showing red head and underparts, blue collar, black mantle, blue rump and tail, and green wings with a pale yellowish-green patch across the coverts. Although birds in northern New Guinea show little sexual dimorphism, throughout the rest of the range, females are relatively drab, and closely resemble female Australian King Parrots (116). The two species are allopatric but there may be confusion over captive birds: Female Papuan lacks the pink tips to the tail feathers shown by female Australian, and the breast is a darker green and more blotchy (Australian has a paler, more uniform warm olive-green breast); the tail of Papuan is blackish, not green above; the undertail-coverts of Australian also have more obvious dark green bases. This species meets the westernmost extreme of the Moluccan King Parrot (117) at around 135°E in western New Guinea, but the two are easily separated, with the pale wing-coverts of Papuan being diagnostic for northern birds (to the south the dimorphic females can easily be separated by their green breasts). Strong, deep, rhythmic wingbeats and a long dark tail are obvious in the slightly erratic flight (birds usually fly below the canopy).

VOICE A sharp *shhk* or *keek* in flight, and when perched a series of mournful notes on descending pitch *eree-eree-eree*, either downslurred or upslurred. Call said to be softer and higher-pitched than that of Australian King Parrot.

DISTRIBUTION AND STATUS The northern race ranges from Geelvink Bay, east to around Aitape on the north coast. The eastern race is confined to the south-east including the Huon Peninsula in the north and to around Hall Sound in the south. The third race is spread through the central highlands, ranging north to the Sepik River and abutting the Huon Peninsula, south to the upper Fly River and west to around 135°E. Although locally common, the species is probably suffering from trade to some degree. The world population is estimated at around 70,000 birds.

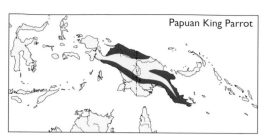

Papuan King Parrot

ECOLOGY Occurs in dense forest from near sea-level to 2,800m. Birds are also sometimes found in cultivated areas at higher altitudes, in more open habitats with casuarinas, and in secondary growth. They are heard more often than seen, and are most frequently glimpsed flying between trees through breaks in the forest. Single birds, pairs or groups of up to ten feed quietly and inconspicuously in the lower and mid-forest storeys, and can be approached quite closely as they forage deliberately for fruit, seeds, berries and nuts; when disturbed, they usually only fly a short distance. Little in known of the breeding cycle, but nesting is reported to start in Mar with two to three eggs being laid. The incubation period is 21 days, and fledging takes 35 days. Young reach independence in 50 days.

DESCRIPTION Head bright red, hind-collar broad blue extending up nape to rear-crown and sides of upper breast. Mantle blackish-green, appearing black in field; lower back, rump and uppertail-coverts dark violet. Wing dark green with broad yellowish-green patch across lesser, inner median and innermost greater coverts; flight feathers green, with dusky innerwebs. Underwing-coverts violet-blue. Underparts bright red, with hidden darker bases to undertail-coverts. Uppertail blue-black; undertail black. **Bare parts**: Bill black with red base to upper mandible; iris orange; legs dark grey-black.

SEX/AGE Female mostly green above, lacking pale wing-patch, with a dark blue rump and blackish tail. Head and breast green (mottled reddish), and remainder of underparts red. Underwing-coverts green. Undertail-coverts with darker centres, but this is less obvious than in female Australian. Base of upper mandible browner than in male. Young like female but with pink tips to tail feathers, a greener breast, and a darker bill and iris.

MEASUREMENTS Wing 183-194; tail 200-229; bill 20-23; tarsus 20-22.

GEOGRAPHICAL VARIATION Three races.

A. c. chloropterus (SE New Guinea)

A. c. callopterus (C New Guinea) Male with narrower blue band across mantle, not extending towards rear-crown. More green in mantle.

A. c. moszkowskii (N New Guinea) Sexes generally similar. Female lacks or shows only a slight blue nape-band, and has green mantle and markings at sides of breast. Male with violet extending further down back than nominate. Both sexes can show pink tips to tail feathers. Immature with narrower, duller wing-patch and green markings on breast.

REFERENCES Arndt (1991), Beehler (1978b), Beehler *et al.* (1986), Bell (1982), Coates (1985), Cooke (1992), Diamond (1972), Forshaw (1989), Iredale (1956), Lodge (1991), Rand & Gilliard (1967), Sibley & Monroe (1990).

119 OLIVE-SHOULDERED PARROT
Aprosmictus jonquillaceus **Plate 31**

Other names: Timor Red-winged Parrot, Timor Crimson-winged Parrot, Timor Parrot

IDENTIFICATION 35cm. A medium-sized, longish-tailed parrot, relatively common in a variety of habitats on the islands on Timor, Wetar and Roti in Nusa Tenggara, green with a blue rump, yellow-tipped tail, and yellow-green and red wing-coverts. Structurally, *Aprosmictus* parrots are reminiscent of king parrots *Alisterus* and shining parrots *Prosopeia* but are smaller than both, with shorter, squarer tails. There are few sympatric species that could cause confusion, but in western Timor race *hellmayri* of Great-billed Parrot (107) also has a green head, blue rump and yellow-tipped tail; but it also has an enormous red bill, and lacks the red wing-patch of this species, instead showing yellow scaling across blackish wing-coverts. In captivity, male Red-winged Parrots (120) can be separated easily by their black mantles and secondaries and huge red wing-patch. Female Red-winged Parrots have black, not green, outerwebs to the outer secondaries; pinkish, not yellow, webs to the lateral tail feathers; greenish-blue, not blue, outerwebs to the outermost primaries; paler yellowish margins to the inner wing-coverts, and red tips to the greater coverts.

VOICE Similar to but less raucous than Red-winged Parrot.

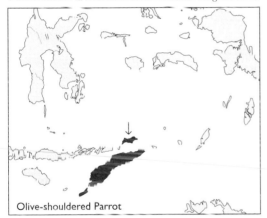

Olive-shouldered Parrot

DISTRIBUTION AND STATUS Endemic to and fairly common on Timor (e.g. around Camplong, Kupang, Lelogama, Mutis and Dili), Wetar and Roti. The world population is estimated at around 10,000, and is probably stable, although like most Indonesian parrots the species is vulnerable to trapping and habitat loss. Moderate numbers in captivity. NEAR THREATENED.

ECOLOGY On Timor the species is found in woodland, acacia savanna, primary and secondary forest from sea-level to 2,200m (extreme 2,600m). On Wetar, observed in recently logged forest near the coast in 1990. The species's ecology is probably similar to that of Red-winged Parrot, but is little known; observations of flying birds involve pairs and small flocks, and a pair allowed a close approach as they sat quietly three metres up in a large tree.

DESCRIPTION Head bright pale green. Mantle and back distinctly darker green than head and underparts, showing blue suffusion; rump bright pale turquoise-blue. Uppertail-coverts light yellowish-green. Upperwing with lesser coverts light yellow-green merging to darker blue-green at bend of wing; outer median coverts bright scarlet, inner feathers light yellow-green with some tipped red. Outer greater coverts scarlet, inner feathers light green, some showing red tips; a few turquoise-green feathers at carpal edge; primary coverts green with blue suffusion at tips of outerwebs; secondaries mid-green, primaries mid-green with blue suffusion on outerwebs of outermost feathers. Underwing-coverts yellowish-green; underside of flight feathers black. Underparts light green, more yellowish on thighs and undertail-coverts. Uppertail darkish green tipped yellow, with yellowish outerwebs to lateral feathers; undertail blackish-brown tipped yellow, with yellowish suffusion on outerwebs of lateral feathers. **Bare parts:** Bill orange-red, tipped yellow; iris orange; legs blackish-grey.

SEX/AGE Female lacks blue suffusion on mantle, shows less contrast between the head and mantle, has yellowish tips to the red greater coverts, and has a browner iris. Immature has green, not yellow-green, wing-coverts and a pale brown iris.

MEASUREMENTS Wing 173-191; tail 145-175; bill 17-21; tarsus 19-21.

GEOGRAPHICAL VARIATION Two races.

> *A. j. jonquillaceus* (Timor and Roti)
> *A. j. wetterensis* (Wetar) Smaller than nominate (male wing 172-180). Yellow-green of wing-coverts duller, red reduced, less blue on lighter green mantle.

REFERENCES BirdLife (1993), Bishop (1992a), Forshaw (1989), ICBP (1992), Lambert *et al.* (1993), Lodge (1991), Mayr (1944), Mees (1975), Sibley & Monroe (1990), S. Smith *in litt.* (1993), White & Bruce (1986).

120 RED-WINGED PARROT
Aprosmictus erythropterus **Plate 31**

Other names: Red-shouldered Parrot, Blood-winged Parrot, Crimson-winged Parrot

IDENTIFICATION 30-33cm. A noisy, medium-sized parrot with a long squarish tail, found in southern New Guinea and in northern and east-central Australia. It occupies a range of habitats, but is particularly fond of riverine woodland. Males are striking with a green head and underparts, large red wing-patch, blue rump and black mantle, females and immatures being mainly green. The similar-shaped Australian King Parrot (116) lacks the red wing-patch, shows red below in both sexes, is larger and longer-tailed, and mainly occurs along the coast, east of the Great Dividing Range, where Red-winged is less common. In New Guinea, Red-winged is perhaps only likely to be confused with male Eclectus Parrot (111), which, however, has red on its flanks not wing-coverts, a shorter tail, and a dark lower mandible. Female Mulga Parrots (136), the allopatric south-western race *narethae* of Bluebonnet (134) and Turquoise Parrot (152) also show red in the wing, but all three are smaller, with long thin tails and major plumage differences (see plates). Female Superb Parrot (121) is superficially similar to female Red-winged, but lacks the red wing-patch. Female Red-winged Parrot closely resembles Olive-shouldered Parrot (119); see that species for differences. The flight of Red-winged Parrot is distinctive, being erratic with deep buoyant beats.

VOICE A chirping *chillip* or *chiweep*, a harsher *chit-chit* call, and various chirpy twittering notes. Young birds produce a crowing note when begging for food.

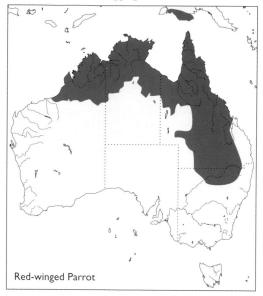

Red-winged Parrot

DISTRIBUTION AND STATUS Confined to Australia, and to the south coastal districts of eastern Irian Jaya, Indonesia, and Western Province, Papua New Guinea. In New Guinea, the species is confined to the region between the Digul and Fly Rivers. In Australia it extends from around Broome in Western Australia (recorded west to Anna Plains, and south-west to the Edgar Range) through the Kimberley region including some offshore islands (Buccaneer and Bonaparte Archipelagos, Osborne and Sir Graham Moore Islands, Admiralty Gulf islands) into Northern Territory around Nicholson. It ranges north to the Cobourg Peninsula and south to around the Camfield Range and Dunmarra Roadhouse, reaching some offshore islands including Melville and Groote Eylandt. It spreads east into Queensland at the Nicholson River, occurs on the Cape York Peninsula with records down the coast to around Rockhampton (occasional further south), and reaching inland to around Dajarra, south of Mount Isa and south-east through the lower Diamantina River system, Windorah, Quilpie, Mitchell and St George. In inland New South Wales the extreme points of its range lie at Inverell in the east, Gunnedah, Dubbo and Mudgee in the south and Hay, Menindee and Broken Hill near the South Australia border. It also occurs north into the Darling River basin, and has been recorded in north-east South Australia around northern Lake Eyre and Cooper Creek. Wandering individuals have been recorded at Renmark and Victory Downs, the latter possibly an escape. Escapes also occur in Sydney and Melbourne. The species is common in suitable habitat except at its range limits. World population well above 100,000 and the species is considered safe. Moderate numbers in captivity. Protected by law.

ECOLOGY Resident but nomadic at edges of range. Occupies subtropical and semi-arid eucalypt and casuarina woodland, forest edge, riverine woodland, acacia scrub, mangrove, farmland, cypress pine *Callitris* scrub, and lowland savanna; in inland Australia it is chiefly tied to the extent of wooded river systems. Usually found in small groups of up to fifteen birds, numbers rarely building up to over 50 in any one flock. The largest groups are likely to form at the end of the breeding season when family parties gather at feeding sites. The species is common and conspicuous, but not particularly approachable; when disturbed, birds may fly for some distance, often calling loudly. They sometimes associate with Pale-headed Rosellas (131) and Mallee Ring-necks (126), and will feed beneath trees although more usually seen coming to ground to drink. The diet includes seeds, fruit, flowers and insects; in mangroves, mistletoe *Loranthus* is particularly favoured. Nesting may begin as early as Apr or May in the north, but Aug-Feb is the main breeding period further south. During courtship, the male perches close to the female, exposing his blue rump, and chatters quietly. The nest is usually located in a eucalypt, and the eggs are laid in a deep hole lined with wood debris. Three to six white eggs are incubated for around 20 days by the female, who is fed by the male until the white-downed chicks hatch. The young are cared for by both parents and fledge in about five weeks. Head-scratching is under the wing.

DESCRIPTION Head bright green with blue-green sheen on crown and nape. Mantle, back and scapulars black. Lower back and rump bright blue, lighter towards tail; uppertail-coverts yellowish-green with yellowish suffusion at base. Bend of wing light yellow-green. Carpal edge blackish. Upperwing-coverts bright scarlet. Tertials and primaries marked blackish on innerwebs, green on outerwebs; secondaries also suffused black on outerwebs; primary coverts dark green suffused black. Underwing black with green coverts. Underparts bright, pale, slightly yellowish-green. Uppertail darkish green tipped yellow with lateral feathers blackish on innerwebs tipped yellow; undertail blackish with pale tips. **Bare parts**: Bill coral-red; iris red-brown; legs grey-black.

SEX/AGE Female is predominantly green with a smaller red wing-patch (only an apical spot on inner greater coverts, but increasing on outers; restricted to outer feathers of median coverts) than the male, and has no black on the mantle; outerwebs of outer secondaries black. The green is also duller, and slightly yellower on the underparts. The rump is duller blue, and the blue sheen on the crown and nape of the male is absent. The undertail has yellowish tips and pinkish edgings. Immatures are similar to females, but with a browner iris and yellow bill early on. Young males attain adult plumage at the third annual moult, but may show black mantle feathers earlier than this.

MEASUREMENTS Wing 183-208; tail 139-152; bill 16-20; tarsus 21-23.

GEOGRAPHICAL VARIATION Two races.

A. e. erythropterus (Australia south of about Cooktown on the north-east coast, merging into *coccineopterus* to the west)

A. e. coccineopterus (S New Guinea and from Western Australia, east through Northern Territory to the Cape York Peninsula, Queensland) Male with more blue on crown and nape. Both sexes slightly paler, and female also duller green than nominate.

REFERENCES Andrew (1992), Arndt (1992), Beehler *et al.* (1986), Blakers *et al.* (1984), Buckingham & Jackson (1988), Coates (1985), Ford (1988), Forshaw (1981, 1989), Lambert *et al.* (1993), Lodge (1991), Peters (1961), Pizzey & Doyle (1983), Rand & Gilliard (1967), Schodde &

Tidemann (1988), Sibley & Monroe (1990), Simpson & Day (1984), Slater (1979, 1989), Storr & Johnstone (1979).

121 SUPERB PARROT
Polytelis swainsonii　　　　Plate 31

Other names: Barraband Parrakeet, Barraband's Parrot, Green Leek

IDENTIFICATION 36-42cm. A distinctive bright green parrot, restricted to south east Australia. The species is strongly dimorphic, the male being extremely striking with a yellow throat, scarlet breast-band and yellow forecrown, the female mainly green with a bluish suffusion on the head, reddish-orange thighs and pink innerwebs to the lateral tail feathers. Both sexes have a distinctive flight profile with a long tail and narrow swept-back primaries. There are no likely confusion species. The female is somewhat nondescript, but while all male flocks may be encountered during the breeding season, females are always likely to be in company with the striking males.

VOICE A low-pitched, slightly scratchy *terwip* or *wi-ri-rip*, sometimes starting on a tremulous note. A clear whistle, *whee*, and various quavering trills and harsher calls. In comparison to Cockatiel (75), the call is deeper and harsher, lacking upward inflection at the end.

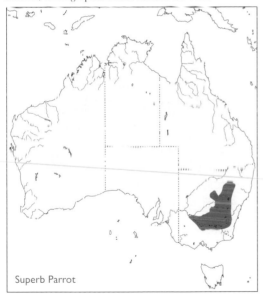

Superb Parrot

DISTRIBUTION AND STATUS Confined to Australia, where it occurs only in New South Wales and extreme northern Victoria. The species is concentrated in two main areas: on the south-west slopes of the Great Dividing Range (Cowra, Boorowa, Cootamundra and Yass regions), and in the New South Wales Riverina zone. In the latter the range extends along the Murrumbidgee River from around Hay to Darlington Point, Narrandera and Wagga Wagga. It is also found north to Goolgowi and the Lachlan River, and south to the Edward and Murray Rivers (Barham, Deniliquin, Tocumwal, Cobram, Yarrawonga and Albury). In northern Victoria, it concentrates along the Goulburn and Ovens Rivers, and in the Barmah Forest

area. Vagrants occasionally appear further west along the Victoria–New South Wales border. Superb Parrots do not normally breed above 33°S, but at least part of the population disperses north to around 30°S at the end of the breeding season. These birds are found from Apr to Aug in north-east New South Wales from Gunnedah to Narrabri, Gilgandra and Coonamble, and amongst the river systems to the west (Barwon, Namoi, Macquarie, Castlereagh, Marthaguy Creek). Occasionally presumed passage migrants turn up further west around Tottenham and Hermidale. Escapes have been recorded around Sydney and Melbourne. The species is locally common but with a world population estimated at only around 5,000 and declining due to habitat clearance; it has probably also suffered from trapping. Moderate numbers in captivity. Protected by law. VULNERABLE.

ECOLOGY Part of the population is migratory, wintering north of the main breeding range. Habitat preferences of breeding populations vary slightly from east to west, with birds on the slopes of the Great Dividing Range nesting and foraging in open box woodland *Eucalyptus*, which is the dominant vegetation type. Here the species is found nesting away from watercourses, and utilises a range of tree species. In the Riverina region to the west, birds almost exclusively breed in riparian river red-gum *E. camaldulensis* woodland, foraging in nearby box woodland (key species include black box *E. bicolor*, yellow box *E. melliodora* and white cypress pine *Callitris columellaris*). They are also sometimes found in farmland and towns. Flock size is usually small, but groups of up to 100 have been recorded after the breeding season. Superb Parrots feed in trees, in the understorey, and will also come to ground, where they can be fairly approachable, taking spilt grain at roadsides and keeping company with Yellow Rosellas (129) and Cockatiels (75). The diet includes fruit and blossoms of acacias and eucalypts, fruit of shrubs (e.g. *Exocarpus*); seeds of crops, grasses, weeds and herbs. The breeding season runs from Sep to Dec. In display the male bows to the female with fluffed-up head, and the pair indulge in courtship feeding. During the breeding season males will remain in flocks and forage away from the nest, returning to feed the sitting females. This continues until around a week after the young hatch, when the female also joins in foraging activities. Although lone pairs are common, Superb Parrots will nest in colonies of up to six pairs. The nest itself is a hollow, lined with wood debris, high in a live or dead tree. Individual sites tend to be re-used. Four to six white eggs are laid, hatching in about 20 days. The young fledge in around 5-6 weeks, after which the birds vacate the breeding area.

DESCRIPTION Forehead, crown, chin and throat bright yellow; rear-crown bright green washed turquoise-blue; ear-coverts and lores green. Upperparts bright green. Upperwing bright green with dark suffusion on inner margins of innerwebs and blue suffusion on outerwebs (fine yellow rear margin to flight feathers); carpal edge bluish; primary coverts light blue; primaries elongated. Underwing-coverts bright green; underside of flight feathers blackish-brown. Underparts bright pale green, with thin, bright red gorget between yellow of throat and green of breast. Uppertail bright green, with elongated central feathers darker at slightly bulbous tip, outer feathers edged bluish on outerwebs; undertail blackish with poorly defined pale tips to lateral feathers. **Bare parts**: Bill coral-red; iris orange-yellow; legs blackish.

Female is mostly green, suffused pinkish-brown on the throat and bluish-grey on ear-coverts and crown. The mantle is a duller, browner green, contrasting with the green rump and darker flight feathers. The underparts are paler, the thighs orange-red. She also has distinctive pink edgings and pinkish-yellow tips to the innerwebs of the undertail. Iris yellow. Immature like female but with brown iris. Male attains adult plumage in around 12 months.

MEASUREMENTS Wing 173-192; tail 196-261; bill 14-17; tarsus 19-22.

GEOGRAPHICAL VARIATION None.

REFERENCES Blakers *et al.* (1984), Buckingham & Jackson (1988), Collar *et al.* (1994), Emison *et al.* (1987), Forshaw (1981), Garnett (1992), Joseph (1988b), Lambert *et al.* (1993), Lodge (1991), Pizzey & Doyle (1983), Schodde & Tidemann (1988), Sibley & Monroe (1990), Slater (1989), Storr & Johnstone (1979), Webster (1989, 1992).

---

122 REGENT PARROT
Polytelis anthopeplus   Plate 31

Other names: Rock Peplar Parakeet, Rock Pebbler Parakeet, Black-tailed Parakeet, Mountain Parakeet, Smoker, Marlock Parakeet

IDENTIFICATION 37-41cm. A striking parrot found in riverine woodland, scrub and farmland in south-east and south-west Australia. Although appearing largely olive on the ground, the blue-black and yellow male is striking in flight; the duller female shows the same distinctive yellow and red wing-markings and basic plumage pattern. The long tapering tail is obvious. No other Australian parrot combines all-yellow underparts with a large yellow wing-patch. Yellow Rosella (129), which is sympatric with the eastern population of Regent Parrot, has yellow underparts but a blue throat and blue upperwing-coverts. Regent Parrots have swift and graceful flight, and when migrating may fly at considerable heights.

VOICE A low-pitched, liquid *ulrick-ulrick*, said to be harsher than the call of Superb Parrot (121). Also a soft twittering, and a harsh call made by young birds when begging for food.

DISTRIBUTION AND STATUS Confined to Australia where it is found in two widely separated populations. In Western Australia it occurs mainly in the wheatbelt, extending north to Ajana, inland to Laverton and Karonie, and down to Israelite Bay on the south coast; it is found south of Perth, but has not fully colonised the forested south-west corner. In south-east Australia the range has contracted in recent years. In South Australia the species occurs along the Murray River from around Morgan to the New South Wales– Victoria border (seven colonies). In Victoria it occurs in Wyperfeld National Park and along the Wimmera River south to Lake Hindmarsh, but breeding probably ceased at Lake Albacutya as recently as 1988. In New South Wales it is found in isolated pockets along the Murray River, and around the mouth of the Murrumbidgee River. Along the New South Wales– Victoria border it is now clustered in four areas, and is absent 100km either side of Mildura; there are a few pairs

along the Darling River north to Pooncarie, and along the Wakool River to the east. There is some post-breeding dispersal, but birds are unlikely to be found north-east of Balranald or south of Dimboola, except perhaps during periods of drought. Locally common in riverine forest and mallee *Eucalyptus gracilis* areas. The world population is thought to be in excess of 15,000, but the eastern race is by far the smaller of the two. Clearance of mallee, road kills, the take-over of nesting hollows by honeybees *Apis mellifera*, and human persecution are all considered threats. Despite some early expansion in the south-west with the spread of agriculture, the species is now declining there too. Clearance of salmon gums *E. salmonophloia*, which are used for nesting, and changes in cereal handling methods resulting in less grain spillage for birds to feed on, are contributory factors. Fully protected by law in all but a few south-west regions. Moderate numbers in captivity.

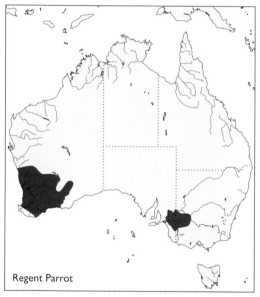

Regent Parrot

ECOLOGY Mainly resident in the east, although birds are dispersive after the breeding season. More regular movements have been recorded in the western population, with southerly dispersal during summer, and a concentration below 32°S in the autumn. Birds then move north-east in winter. Movements of up to 320km have been recorded. Eastern birds are tied to open riparian river red-gum *E. camaldulensis* woodland with associated mallee *E. gracilis* scrub. They also occur in box woodland *Eucalyptus*, areas with slender cypress pine *Callitris preissi*, orchards and vineyards. In the west, the species is less mallee-dependent and is found in acacia and eucalyptus woodland (e.g. *E. wandoo*, *E. salmonophloia*) and in farmland. Regent Parrots are not found in the forests of the south-west corner, but have been recorded in forest clearings there. Outside the breeding season, birds may be found in noisy flocks of a hundred or more, but are generally wary. They mainly feed on the ground. The diet generally comprises seeds of grasses, herbs, fruit, berries, buds and blossoms. Cereal crops and nuts from orchards are also taken, as well as spilt grain from roadsides. In the east, males tend to feed in mallee scrub (e.g. white mallee *E. dumosa* and red mallee *E. socialis*) during the breeding season. Nesting takes place between Aug and Jan, and birds nest either in isolated pairs or form colonies of up to (rarely) 18 pairs. Courtship feeding occurs, and males also feed the sitting females at the nest, having moved away from the nesting trees to forage in single-sex flocks. The nest-site is a deep hollow in a broken limb, around 20m high in a large, old, dead or dying river red-gum, close to permanent water. Often these nest-holes are re-used. Three to six (usually four) white eggs are laid on decayed wood debris, and the female incubates for around 21 days. The white-downed young fledge in around 5-6 weeks and remain with the parents for a few weeks more.

DESCRIPTION Head yellow, tending to olive-yellow on crown and nape. Mantle olive-green; scapulars dark olive-brown; lower back and rump rich yellow, tending to yellow-olive on uppertail-coverts. Lesser and median coverts yellow; greater coverts bluish-black on outer feathers, red with yellow tips on innermost feathers; tertials greyish-black on innerwebs, pinkish-red, tipped yellow on outers; primary coverts blue-black; primaries and secondaries bluish-black with black innerwebs. Underwing-coverts yellow; underside of flight feathers brownish-black. Underparts yellow, duller olive-yellow on undertail-coverts with some indistinct orange markings around the vent. Tail black, with a dark blue suffusion on central feathers and outerwebs of lateral feathers on upperside, and very slight pale suffusion at tips on underside. **Bare parts** Bill pinkish-red; iris orange-brown; legs grey.

SEX/AGE Female much greyer below and greener above, also showing greener ear-coverts and lores. The dull blue at the bend of the wing extends onto the wing-coverts, which are more greenish-yellow than in the male. Rump dull olive-green; duller and less red in wing than male. Tail bluish-green above, tipped and edged pink on lateral feathers below (margins of three outer feathers). Young males usually show more yellow on the head. Adult plumage acquired in 14 months after an eight-month moult.

MEASUREMENTS Wing 170-203; tail 185-229; bill 16-20; tarsus 18-23.

GEOGRAPHICAL VARIATION Two races.
P. a. anthopeplus (SW Australia)
P. a. monarchoides (SE Australia) Male much brighter than nominate, particularly yellow of underparts.

REFERENCES Arndt (1992), Beardsell (1985), Blakers *et al.* (1984), Buckingham & Jackson (1990), Emison *et al.* (1987), Forshaw (1981, 1989), Garnett (1992), Joseph (1988b), Lambert *et al.* (1993), Lodge (1991), Pizzey & Doyle (1983), Schodde (1993), Schodde & Tidemann (1988), Sedgewick (1988), Sibley & Monroe (1990), Simpson & Day (1984), Slater (1979, 1989), Storr & Johnstone (1979).

123   ALEXANDRA'S PARROT
Polytelis alexandrae   Plate 31

Other names: Princess of Wales Parakeet, Queen Alexandra's Parakeet, Alexandra Parakeet, Alexandra's Parrot, Rose-throated Parakeet, Spinifex Parrot (also used for Night Parrot *Geopsittacus occidentalis*), Alexandrine Parakeet (also the common vernacular name for *Psittacula eupatria*)

IDENTIFICATION 46cm (including elongated tail). An attractive, rare and nomadic species confined to the arid interior of west-central Australia. Generally light olive-brown tinged with pastel hues. Pale pink throat and pale yellowish-green wing-coverts are obvious. Extremely long tail of male is also distinctive. Alexandra's Parrots are confined to sparsely populated areas, and their movements are unpredictable. They are probably best searched for in the Great Sandy Desert of northern Western Australia, in sandy areas with scattered casuarinas, or where river red-gums *E. camaldulensis* provide breeding sites near water. The only possible confusion species is the Regent Parrot (122), which also shows yellowish upperwing-coverts, but lacks the pinkish throat and blue back and rump. Although they are allopatric, extralimital occurrences of both species could conceivably overlap in south-west Western Australia; see plate for further plumage differences. In flight, which is slightly undulating with irregular wingbeats, Alexandra's Parrots show a distinctive silhouette with narrow pointed wings and an extremely long tail; the contrasting dark blue primary coverts form a dark mark on the forewing. The male's tail is especially obvious when the birds first take flight, and when landing birds 'drop' to the ground suddenly. When landing in trees they may perch along, rather than across a branch. They make high flights during movements.

VOICE Generally quiet. A single clear whistle, *queet* or *wheet*, similar in quality to the call of Cockatiel (75), but not as thin, and shorter, lacking upward inflection at the end. Also a rapid chuckling and some soft twittering notes.

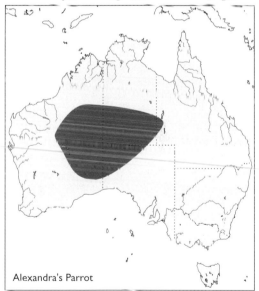

Alexandra's Parrot

DISTRIBUTION AND STATUS Confined to the interior of Australia where generally very rare and little recorded. The species may not appear in parts of its range for two decades or more before returning and breeding. In Western Australia it ranges from the Great Sandy Desert north to the Fitzroy River west to around Wiluna, Sandstone, Menzies and Coolgardie and east through the Gibson and Great Victoria Deserts. In Northern Territory it occurs north to the Newcastle Waters and Stuart Plains area, and south to around Alice Springs. In Queensland it is very rare in the extreme south-west but there is a recent breeding record from around Cloncurry. In South Australia it ranges east to around Oodnadatta, and there is a 1986 record from the Great Victoria Desert about 25km north of the Nurrari Lakes. There is disagreement over its conservation status. The recent lack of records of large breeding groups, as once reported, is cited as a possible indication of population decline, but little real information exists, and the world population is estimated to lie between 1,000 and 20,000 birds. Recent study suggests that the species could be irruptive rather than nomadic, and that a core population may be resident in the area around Lake Tobin, Western Australia. Trade, fires, changing land-use regimes and predation have all been cited as possible threats. Protected by law. Large numbers in captivity. VULNERABLE.

ECOLOGY Highly nomadic and little known in the wild. Occurs in the sandy deserts of arid central Australia, often far from water. Birds may arrive in an area where they have been absent for many years, nest, and quickly leave again. They are found in hummock grassland, dry riverine eucalyptus woodland, acacia scrub, mulga *Acacia aneura* and sandy areas with scattered desert oaks *Allocasuarina decaisneana*. Birds are encountered singly, in pairs or small groups of up to 15. There are also some older records of larger breeding colonies. The birds feed on the ground and can then be quite tame. The diet includes the seeds of spinifex *Triodia mitchelli* and mulga grass *Danthonia bipartita*. Other food items such as nectar have also been reported. Breeding has been recorded from Sep to Jan, although nesting is probably prompted by rain, may be irregular, and is also sometimes colonial. During lively, noisy display, the male raises a few feathers on its crown, spreads its wings and tail. The preferred nest-site is a high hollow in a river red-gum *E. camaldulensis* lined with wood debris (desert oaks have also been used). Four to six white eggs are laid and incubated by the female for around 21 days. Whilst sitting she is fed by the male. The white-downed young fledge in 5-6 weeks and all birds quickly vacate the nesting area.

DESCRIPTION Head light olive-brown, strongly washed pastel-blue on crown and nape, and slightly below eye; chin and throat pale pink. Mantle and scapulars olive-brown tinged greenish with fine dark shaft-streaks; back and rump pastel-blue; uppertail-coverts grey-green. Upperwing-coverts bright yellowish-green with a few greener feathers around bend of wing; primary coverts dark blue-green; primaries blue-green with yellowish-brown leading edge and darker brown margins to innerwebs (third longest primary has a spatulate tip); secondaries pale greenish-blue with yellowish margin (more pronounced on outerweb); tertials grey-green with darker innerwebs. Underwing-coverts bright green, yellower towards leading edge; underwing greyish-brown with broad pale yellow inner margin to innerwebs. Underparts generally pale olive-grey, with pink of throat extending onto upper breast; belly and flanks washed light bluish-green; thighs and lower flanks rose-pink; undertail-coverts olive-yellow. Uppertail olive-brown washed green close to shaft and blue towards tips, lateral feathers blue-grey edged and tipped pink; undertail black with broad pink tips and margins. **Bare parts**: Bill red; iris orange-yellow; legs grey.

SEX/AGE Female has a shorter tail (average over 6cm less than male) and lacks spatulate tip to third primary. Wing-coverts are duller and greener, and mantle shows

less green suffusion. Crown, back and rump show little blue. Immatures similar to females; males acquire adult plumage in around 14-18 months.

MEASUREMENTS Wing 163-198; tail 203-292; bill 14-17; tarsus 19-23.

GEOGRAPHICAL VARIATION None.

REFERENCES Allen (1987), Blakers *et al.* (1984), Buckingham & Jackson (1990), Collar & Andrew (1988), Collar *at al.* (1994), Forshaw (1981), Garnett (1992), Lambert *et al.* (1993), Lodge (1991), Pizzey & Doyle (1983), Sedgewick (1988), Sibley & Monroe (1990), Simpson & Day (1984), Slater (1979, 1989), Storr & Johnstone (1979).

124 RED-CAPPED PARROT
Purpureicephalus spurius Plate 31

Other names: Hookbill, Pileated Parakeet, Australian Red-capped Parakeet, King Parrot (also commonly used for Eclectus Parrot and Australian King Parrot)

IDENTIFICATION 35-38cm. A very striking species, the male with dark red cap and light green face, blue underparts (apart from bright red thighs and undertail-coverts), blue-green upperparts and a yellow rump; female duller. Most often encountered in conspicuous flocks made up of mainly immature birds. Adults tend to be sedentary and are difficult to locate as they feed quietly in the canopy. The birds have a characteristic upright stance when perched. The sympatric western race *semitorquatus* of Port Lincoln Ringneck (125) has a blackish head with a red frontal band (not a complete red cap) and a bright yellow hind-collar; it also lacks the yellow rump, a feature which is very obvious in Red-capped Parrot when the birds are in flight. The flight pattern of this species is very distinctive with rapid fluttering wingbeats followed by an undulating glide on closed wings.

VOICE A low, slightly grating *check* or *chep* and a multi-syllabic *che-re-rek*, *chi-ri-rip* or *chi-ri-ri-rip*. Calls regularly in flight, but usually remains quiet while feeding. The alarm call is a sharp shriek repeated several times, and the young have a squeaky begging call.

DISTRIBUTION AND STATUS Confined to the south-western corner of Western Australia. The species ranges from around the Moore River north of Perth (occasionally to Dandaragan), through the forested south-west corner, usually within 100km of the coast, reaching inland to Lake Grace in the east and to Esperance on the south coast. Red-capped Parrots are regular in the suburbs of Perth, and breed in King's Park in the city centre. The species is common, especially in marri *Eucalyptus calophylla* forests. The world population is thought to be above 20,000. Moderate numbers in captivity. Can be shot as a pest in a small number of areas.

ECOLOGY Paired adults are sedentary, but noisy, conspicuous bands of up to 20 young birds rove in search of food. Red-capped Parrots favour eucalyptus forest and are specialised for feeding on marri, the elongated upper mandible being adapted for dislodging the plant's large seeds, which are removed as the fruit is held and rotated. Marri fruits are available throughout the year and provide the staple food source. Red-capped Parrots also occur in orchards (sometimes doing damage), towns, wooded paddocks and mallee *Eucalyptus gracilis* forest, and may also feed on roadsides where they forage for grass seeds. Pairs remain inconspicuous for large parts of the day while they feed quietly in the canopy, but sometimes come to ground in clearings to feed on fallen fruit. Apart from marri, the birds will also feed on other eucalypts, e.g. jarrah *E. marginata*, and on casuarinas, *Grevillea*, *Hakea*, and have also been recorded taking blossoms and insects. Nesting takes place between Aug and Dec. In display the male raises his crown feathers and tail, droops his wings and calls noisily. Courtship feeding is regular, and the male also feeds the incubating female. The usual clutch size is five, but may vary from four to nine. The eggs are white and are laid on a bed of wood-dust at the bottom of a tree-hollow, usually high in a marri. Incubation lasts 20 days, and the male does not begin feeding the white-downed chicks until two weeks after they hatch. Fledging occurs in around five weeks; young remain with the parents for a short while after leaving the nest.

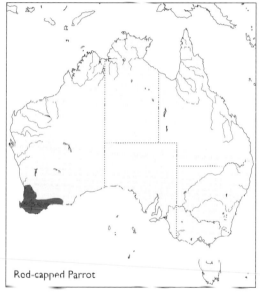

Red-capped Parrot

DESCRIPTION Crown and nape dark carmine red; throat and cheeks bright yellowish-green, becoming slightly yellower at sides of neck. Mantle light sea-green; rump yellow; uppertail-coverts green. Upperwing with greater coverts green tending to blue on outermost feathers; emarginated primaries, and primary coverts, blackish edged dark blue on outerwebs. Underwing coverts blue; underside of flight feathers blackish. Throat light yellowish-green; breast and belly mauve-blue, becoming paler towards vent; thighs and undertail-coverts red, with some green feathers on lower flanks. Broad-based tail with green central feathers, bluer towards tips; lateral feathers basally dark grading through blue to white at the tip; undertail pale blue, tipped white. **Bare parts**: Bill with elongated upper mandible, light bluish-grey; iris dark brown; legs brown.

SEX/AGE Female duller, with green in crown and more brownish breast; both she and immature show pale bar across underside of flight feathers. Immature has dark green upperparts, a duller, more greenish-yellow rump (can show some rusty marks), green markings on the

undertail-coverts, duller red thighs, a browner breast, only a little mauve below and a duller green tail; male has a rusty forehead, gaining the red crown-feathers in scattered patches, the first showing at about five months. Most adult features are acquired during the first spring moult, and the transition is completed the following summer.

MEASUREMENTS Wing 152-166; tail 187-217; bill 21-25; tarsus 20-24.

GEOGRAPHICAL VARIATION None.

REFERENCES Blakers *et al.* (1984), Buckingham & Jackson (1990), Forshaw (1989), Lambert *et al.* (1993), Lodge (1991), Mawson & Massam (1996), Peters (1961), Pizzey & Doyle (1983), Schodde & Tidemann (1988), Sibley & Monroe (1990), Simpson & Day (1984) Slater (1979, 1989), Storr & Johnstone (1979).

125 PORT LINCOLN RINGNECK
Barnardius zonarius   Plate 32

Other names: Yellow-collared Parrot, Zoned Parrot, Western Ringneck, Bauer's Parrot, Yellow-naped Parakeet, Ring-necked Parrot, Twenty-eight Parrot (*B. z. semitorquatus*)

IDENTIFICATION 35-44cm. A widespread and familiar bird across much of the west of Australia. Bold and conspicuous, chiefly dark green with a contrasting black head and yellow hind-collar; the blue cheeks, yellow belly and very pale bill are also distinctive, as is the long tail. In extreme south-west Australia birds show a red frontal band (sometimes lacking in females) and a light green, not yellow, belly. There are no real confusion species, as no other green Australian parrot shows a mainly black head (Rainbow Lorikeet – see 13 – has a yellowish green hind-collar and a dark head but a bright reddish-orange breast). The closely related Mallee Ringneck (126) is similar in appearance, but apart from a small zone of hybridisation in South Australia the two species are allopatric. All races of Mallee Ringneck have much paler heads than Port Lincoln, and (except the northern race) red frontal bands. The sharp contrast between blackish crown and nape and bright yellow collar is diagnostic of Port Lincoln which has an undulating flight, the deep wingbeats interspersed with glides on folded wings.

VOICE The species tends to be more vocal than the Mallee Ringneck, with a variety of calls including a disyllabic *whee-eck*, a short alarm call *vatch*, a strident *put-kleepit-kleepit* or *kling kling-kling-kling*, and various chattering notes. The south-western race has a distinctive call which is often rendered *twenty-eight*, although *tooweet-terweet* is closer to the true sound. The immature has a two-note *ter-lp*.

DISTRIBUTION AND STATUS Widespread in western, central and southern Australia. The species is distributed from Port Augusta, the Eyre Peninsula and Gawler Ranges, north through central South Australia into Northern Territory, where it spreads through the Macdonnell Ranges and is found north to Newcastle Waters and Winnecke Creek. Birds may also range further east towards the Queensland border at times, and an extralimital eastern record comes from Pine Creek in New South Wales. In Western Australia, the species is increasing in the south-west where it is concentrated from around King George Sound in the south to the Murchison River in the north, reaching inland to Kalgoorlie and Wiluna to the east.

Further north, it is scattered through the north-west corner, and extends east to the upper reaches of the de Grey River system. There is a small, probably isolated population in the extreme east of Western Australia in the Gardiner Range region. Escapes have been recorded in the Port Wakefield district, around Melbourne, Canberra, Sydney, Darwin, and Hobart in Tasmania. A population of probable escapes in the Mount Lofty Ranges was destroyed to prevent interbreeding with Mallee Ringnecks, but there is a zone of hybridisation with the Mallee Ringneck in the Flinders Range, and the two species meet and may hybridise elsewhere too. The world population is probably well above the present estimate of 100,000 given by Lambert *et al.* (1993), the species having generally adapted well to land-use changes. Moderate numbers in captivity. Birds may be shot under permit in some districts to prevent damage to orchards.

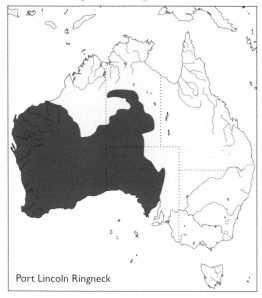

Port Lincoln Ringneck

ECOLOGY Mainly sedentary, with occasional movements during climatic extremes. The species occupies a broad range of habitats including river red-gums *E. camaldulensis* along watercourses, acacia and mallee *E. gracilis* scrub, open eucalyptus woodland, farmland, desert scrub and suburban areas. In general it has adapted better to the impact of settlement than Mallee Ringneck, and has been particularly successful in the south-west wheatbelt where birds are commonly seen on roadside verges feeding beneath tall shrubs. The race *semitorquatus* has a more specific habitat requirement, preferring tall coastal eucalypt forests, particularly marri *E. calophylla*. Port Lincoln Ringnecks form strong pair-bonds and are normally encountered in small family parties or groups of up to eight birds. They are generally conspicuous, noisy and inquisitive, being most active morning and evening. They tend to remain quiet whilst feeding on the ground, but will chatter noisily as they forage in the canopy above. Groups gather to roost after drinking, but may remain active after sunset. The diet comprises nectar, blossoms, seeds, fruit and insects and their larvae (which are sometimes reached by stripping bark). Cereal crops and orchards are often raided, and birds have been recorded digging up the corms of onion grass *Romulea longifolia*.

The more arboreal south-western race has a preference for ripening eucalyptus fruits, especially those of marri. Nesting is from Jun to Feb, and starts earliest in the north. The birds are territorial around the nest-site, and there is much squabbling at the start of the breeding season. In display, the male droops his wings, wags his tail, chatters loudly and bobs his head. Courtship feeding is also common. The birds nest at varying heights, usually in a prepared natural tree-hollow lined with decaying wood debris. Between four and seven (usually five) white eggs are laid, and there are sometimes two broods. The female incubates for c. 19 days and leaves the nest only to feed herself or be fed by the male. At first she feeds the chicks alone, but a week after hatching the male joins in, the young leaving the nest about four weeks later. Family parties remain together for a period after the young fledge.

DESCRIPTION Head blackish-brown with cheeks, sides of throat and lower ear-coverts densely flecked dark blue (may show a few red flecks on forecrown); hind-collar bright yellow. Mantle dark mid-green with very fine dark fringes; rump slightly brighter and glossier green; uppertail-coverts very slightly duller than rump. Outer median coverts bright, slightly greenish-yellow, inner greener; greater coverts green with greenish-blue inner margins and pale green outer margins on outermost feathers; bend of wing turquoise, extending slightly onto lesser coverts; primary coverts dark brown with dark blue outerwebs; flight feathers blackish, strongly emarginated on outer feathers, showing blue outerwebs grading to greyish-blue toward tips. Underwing blackish with turquoise-blue coverts. Breast dark green with fine dark fringes; upper belly bright yellow, lower belly green lightly suffused with yellow; undertail-coverts yellow-green. Central tail feathers dark green grading to dark blue, outer pale blue with dark bases and white tips; undertail pale blue. **Bare parts:** Bill greyish-white; iris brown; legs grey.

SEX/AGE The female has a slightly smaller bill and head, slightly browner head, and may show an underwing-bar. Immatures, which tend to show a pale wing-bar (disappearing earlier in males than females), are duller with a brownish head and greyish-brown suffusion on mantle and breast; the tail is mostly green above. Adult plumage is attained in 12-15 months.

MEASUREMENTS Wing 168-185; tail 157-218; bill 17-22; tarsus 20-24.

GEOGRAPHICAL VARIATION Three races.

B. z. zonarius (E of about 120°E)

B. z. semitorquatus (forested SW corner roughly between Perth and Albany, with broad zones of intergradation with nominate, intermediates being found in Perth for example, and with *occidentalis*) Larger than nominate, males showing a striking red forehead which may be subdued or occasionally absent in females; the belly is pale green, not yellow, with very fine dark fringes. The call is also distinctive (see above). Most birds of both sexes show wing-bars.

B. z. occidentalis (NW Western Australia from about 20°S, south to Geraldton and south-east to Wiluna) Smaller and paler than nominate, with more turquoise in the greens. The yellow belly-patch is larger and paler, and the head is greyer, lacking the red frontal band of *semitorquatus*.

REFERENCES Arndt (1992), Blakers *et al.* (1984), Buckingham & Jackson (1990), Cain (1955), Emison *et al.*

(1987), Forshaw (1981, 1989), Lambert *et al.* (1993), Lodge (1991), Peters (1961), Pizzey & Doyle (1983), Schodde & Tidemann (1988), Sibley & Monroe (1990), Simpson & Day (1984), Slater (1979, 1989), Storr & Johnstone (1979), Taylor (1987).

126 MALLEE RINGNECK
Barnardius barnardi   Plate 32

Other names: Mallee Parakeet, Barnard's Parakeet, Buln Buln, Bubba-bulla, Ring-neck Parakeet (also the common vernacular name for *Psittacula krameri*); Cloncurry Parrot (*B. b. macgillivrayi*).

IDENTIFICATION 32-35cm. This is the eastern counterpart of the Port Lincoln Parrot (125), and although it is less striking its subtly shaded plumage makes it a very attractive species. From a distance it appears green with a yellow nape and lower breast band (or belly). In flight the light green rump contrasts strongly with the darker back. The nominate race has a red forehead, pale green crown, darker band from the eye meeting at the nape, a dark blue-green mantle and a narrow orange-yellow lower breast-band; the "Cloncurry Parrot" of north-central Queensland is a washed-out version of this. There are no likely confusion species. The Port Lincoln Ringneck has a black, not pale greenish-blue, head and is largely allopatric, although in the Flinders Range, where the two species meet, a hybrid population shows variable plumage characters (see below). The flight of the Mallee Ringneck is undulating and reminiscent of a rosella *Platycercus*. When landing in trees, birds tend to swoop upwards onto a branch and fan their tails.

VOICE Generally less noisy than the Port Lincoln Ringneck. Calls include a harsh metallic alarm call, a ringing, high-pitched *kling-kling-kling* or *put-kleep put-kleep* (less strident than the similar calls of Port Lincoln Ringneck), a *kwink kwink* or *chuk chuk chuk* and a chattering whilst feeding in trees (tends to be quiet whilst feeding on the ground).

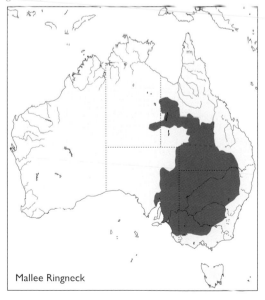

Mallee Ringneck

DISTRIBUTION AND STATUS The interior of eastern Australia west of the Great Dividing Range, with a virtually isolated population in north-west Queensland extending across the Northern Territory border along the upper Nicholson River in the north, and reaching Glenormiston, western Queensland, in the south; its eastern limit is around Kynuna. The northern race meets the nominate in the Forsythe Range region, and the species then extends south with its eastern limit running close to Barcaldine, Mitchell and Goondiwindi and into New South Wales. To the south it extends east through Moree, Dubbo and Wagga Wagga to reach Kerang in Victoria. In the west, the species is scattered through western Queensland as far as the Cooper Creek region of South Australia around Innamincka. In New South Wales, it is found west to the Darling basin around Broken Hill. It occurs along the Murray River, and in Victoria it extends through the north-west corner south to around Edenhope. In south-east South Australia it ranges through Naracoorte and the Mount Lofty Ranges to Port Augusta and the Flinders Ranges, where it meets and intergrades with the Port Lincoln Ringneck (125); the two species also meet further north. Escaped birds have been recorded in Brisbane, Melbourne and Sydney. The species is generally common in suitable habitat throughout its range, with a world population above 500,000 and probably stable; nevertheless, it has been less able to adapt to land-use changes than the Port Lincoln Ringneck. Moderately common in captivity in Australia.

ECOLOGY Mainly sedentary, but there may be some small-scale movements in response to climatic changes. The species occupies the arid mallee *Eucalyptus gracilis* belt, and adjacent *Callitris* and *Acacia* scrubland. It is also found in a range of related habitats. The northern race prefers river red-gums *E. camaldulensis* along seasonal watercourses, and is more arboreal. The species is generally less common in settled areas and in wetter regions. Large flocks are rare, with pairs or small parties being the usual social units. Less bold and inquisitive than the Port Lincoln Ringneck, but the two species share similar habits, diet and displays. The Mallee Ringneck has been recorded feeding in company with Yellow Rosellas (129), Pale-headed Rosellas (131), Red-rumped Parrots (135) and Bluebonnets (134). The nest is in a tree-hollow, and usually four to five eggs are laid on decaying wood debris. In the north the breeding season tends to be governed by climate, and nesting coincides with post wet-season seeding. In the south, breeding begins in Jul or Aug and the season may be extended through to Jan with a second brood. Incubation lasts around 20 days and is carried out by the female. The young fledge in about five weeks and remain in family parties with the parents for a short time.

DESCRIPTION Forehead and lores bright red; forecrown yellow; rest of crown light green, streaked with turquoise and slightly suffused with yellow towards nape; rear ear-coverts light green, cheeks and throat light blue; dull grey-green band around rear of nape extending forward to eye; narrow hind-collar slightly greenish-yellow. Mantle dark greyish-blue; rump pale, slightly bluish-green; uppertail-coverts bright green. Bend of wing and lesser coverts deep turquoise; outer median coverts yellowish-green, inner suffused blue and tipped greener; inner greater coverts yellow-green, outer light sky-blue; emarginated flight feathers and primary coverts blackish with dark blue outerwebs; inner secondaries green on outerwebs. Underwing blackish with light blue coverts. Underparts pale yellowish-green with yellow band across lower breast, which is suffused with deep orange. Uppertail dark green grading to blue, outer feathers blue tipped paler with darker bases; undertail light blue. **Bare parts**: Bill greyish-white; iris dark brown; legs grey.

SEX/AGE The female is generally less contrasting and vivid, with a dull greyish-green mantle and usually a pale wing-bar. The immature is generally much browner, especially on the crown, mantle and underparts; the breast-band is broader and more orange, and there is normally a pale wing-bar. Adult plumage is attained at 12-15 months.

MEASUREMENTS Wing 153-170; tail 169-186; bill 17-19; tarsus 20-22.

GEOGRAPHICAL VARIATION Two races and one hybrid population often referred to as *B. b. whitei*.

   B. b. barnardi (Forsythe Range in WC Queensland through New South Wales, Victoria and SE South Australia)

   B. b. macgillivrayii (interior of NW Queensland and nearby Northern Territory) A small washed-out and more uniform version (generally more yellowish-green) of the nominate, lacking red frontal band, darker nape-band, line to the eye and patch of deep turquoise at the bend of the wing. The mantle is light green and the entire belly is yellow rather than just a lower breast-band; the uppertail is a lighter green. In flight this race looks more uniform, and there is less contrast between the mantle and rump. The duller young show a rusty frontal band during the first few months.

   B. z. zonarius x *B. b. barnardi* ("*B. b. whitei*"). This hybrid population occurs in the Flinders Range where the ranges of Mallee and Port Lincoln Ringnecks meet. The plumage is variable, but generally shows a larger yellow patch on the belly than nominate, a dark greyish-brown crown (lacking the dark nape-band), a lighter mantle contrasting less with the rump (which is also darker than that of nominate *B. barnardi*), less yellow in the wing-coverts, and also sometimes a bluer-green breast and a blue line at the junction between crown and yellow nape-band. Some birds with variable intermediate characters have been reported from further north, and further surveys are needed to ascertain the full extent of hybridisation between the two species.

REFERENCES Arndt (1992), Blakers *et al.* (1984), Buckingham & Jackson (1990), Cain (1955), Ford (1988), Forshaw (1981, 1989), Lambert *et al.* (1993), Lodge (1991), Peters (1961), Schodde & Tidemann (1988), Sibley & Monroe (1990), Simpson & Day (1984), Slater (1979, 1989), Taylor (1987).

---

127 GREEN ROSELLA
Platycercus caledonicus   Plate 33

Other names: Tasmanian Rosella, Yellow-bellied Rosella, Yellow-breasted Parakeet, Tussock Parrot, Mountain Parrot (also used for Crimson Rosella), Tasman Parrot

IDENTIFICATION 32-37cm. Restricted to Tasmania and the Bass Strait islands, where it is common in a range of habitats. It has uniform, dark brownish-olive upperparts

which contrast with its yellow crown, rich yellow underparts and blue cheeks. The forehead is red, often with a reddish wash on the breast although generally more pronounced in females. Apart from the dissimilar Eastern Rosella (132), all other closely related species are allopatric. Of these, the Yellow Rosella (129) is similar but has a paler, yellower mantle with obvious dark feather-centres producing a scaled effect; it is also paler yellow below, and adults have light greenish-blue central tail feathers, those of Green Rosella being dark olive-green. Western Rosella (133) also shows green on the upperparts, but both sexes are strongly marked with red below and have yellow cheeks (immatures lack yellow cheeks but still show extensive red markings on the underparts). Immature Crimson Rosellas (128) have uniform green upperparts, but paler than in Green; there are also large areas of red on the head and underparts. The flight of Green Rosella is strong, direct and less undulating than congeners, with only brief glides.

VOICE The species has a characteristic *kushuck* or *cussick* call note, with a variety of similar notes including *chwee*, *tweek* or *kwick-kweek*. There is also a piping whistle repeated several times in quick succession, and a clinking alarm call. Flocks create a musical chatter whilst feeding.

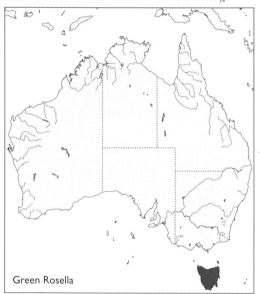

Green Rosella

DISTRIBUTION AND STATUS Endemic to Tasmania and to islands in the Bass Strait including King and Flinders Islands, the Kent Group and the Hunter Islands. It has also been recorded from Maatsuyker Island off southern Tasmania. Escaped birds may be found around Sydney. The species is common and widespread within its range, with a stable world population in excess of 50,000. Small numbers in captivity. The Green Rosella is protected but may be killed under permit when damaging crops.

ECOLOGY Sedentary, occurring in a range of habitats from lowlands to around 1,500m in alpine country. Breeds in eucalypt forests, and occurs in rainforest, montane forest, riverine forest, scrub, roadside hawthorns *Crataegus*, orchards, gardens and cleared country. It is less common in farmland and heathland. Adults are usually found in small groups of 4-5 birds, but larger post-breeding flocks, mainly comprising immatures, are encountered in autumn and winter. The species is sometimes found in association with Eastern Rosella. Although Green Rosellas are not shy they may be inconspicuous when feeding on the ground, where they take the seeds of grasses and shrubs. Much foraging also takes place amongst foliage, and the berries of hawthorn and subalpine shrubs like *Coprosma* are favoured; the diet also comprises nectar, insects and the fruits of orchard trees. Like other members of the genus, Green Rosellas have a strong pair-bond. Their display too is similar to that of the other rosellas. The nest-site is usually a tree-hollow where 4-5 white eggs are laid (as many as eight have been recorded). During the nesting season, which runs from Sep to Feb, pairs disperse and can be very secretive. The female incubates for 20-22 days, leaving the nest only to feed herself or be fed by the male. The young fledge in around five weeks and stay with their parents for about another month.

DESCRIPTION Forehead and lores bright red, crown rich yellow marked red, mottled with dark olive-brown towards rear; lower cheeks and throat powder blue; ear-coverts rich yellow edged darker. Strong contrast between yellow of crown and dark, uniform olive-brown of mantle, whose feathers have fine sea-green fringes; feathers of rump and uppertail coverts also have a distal orange-yellow suffusion, producing a distinct orange-yellow cast. Bend of wing blue; lesser coverts black; inner median coverts black edged dark green, outer light blue, greater coverts mid-blue with inner feathers black edged green; secondaries blackish with blue outerwebs (innermost edged green); primaries blackish-brown with dark blue outerwebs and margins; tertials blackish-brown with indistinct green fringes. Underwing blackish, with blue coverts and axillaries. Underparts rich yellow, variably marked red-orange on upper breast and undertail-coverts (which also show a slight subterminal blue suffusion). Uppertail dull olive-green tipped dull blue, lateral feathers pale blue tipped white (darker on innerweb at base); undertail pale blue tipped white. **Bare parts**: Bill greyish-white; iris dark brown; legs grey.

SEX/AGE The female is smaller than the male (female wing 165-176, male 180-193) and has a smaller bill; also more often shows an orange-red wash on the upper breast and occasionally a wing bar. Immatures are duller than adults, show greener wing-coverts and have olive-grey upperparts and olive yellow underparts; there is also a pale underwing bar. Adult plumage is attained after first complete moult at around 15 months.

MEASUREMENTS Wing 165-193; tail 170-199; bill 15-19; tarsus 21-26.

GEOGRAPHICAL VARIATION None.

REFERENCES Arndt (1992), BirdLife (1993), Blakers *et al.* (1984), Buckingham & Jackson (1990), Cain (1955), Forshaw (1981, 1989), Lambert *et al.* (1993), Lodge (1991), Peters (1961), Pizzey & Doyle (1983), Schodde & Tidemann (1988), Sibley & Monroe (1990), Slater (1979, 1989).

128 CRIMSON ROSELLA
Platycercus elegans   Plate 33

Other names: Pennant's Parakeet, Mountain Lowry, Mountain Parrot (also used for Green Rosella), Red Parrot (Norfolk Island only)

IDENTIFICATION 32-37cm. A distinctive, mainly dark red rosella with blue cheeks and tail, two-tone wing-flashes, and black centres to the mantle feathers. It prefers the forested uplands of eastern Australia, and extends from southern Queensland to south-east South Australia. There are also isolated populations on Kangaroo Island in the south and in the Atherton Tableland region in northern Queensland. The species has been introduced to Norfolk Island where it is common, and to New Zealand. Sexes are alike, but immatures are distinctive, with light olive-green upperparts, a mixture of red and green feathers on the head and underparts and a wing-bar. Northern birds show more red in their juvenile plumage. Some Norfolk Island birds may show aberrant yellow markings. This species is extremely distinctive and there are no sympatric confusion species. The other mainly red rosella is Western (133), which shows yellow not blue cheeks. The hybrid Adelaide Rosella (*P. elegans* x *P. flaveolus*) is generally more orange-yellow, with pale margins to the mantle feathers, and is allopatric (small region of South Australia in the Flinders Range region). Crimson Rosellas have an undulating flap-and-glide flight, and the tail is spread on landing.

VOICE Very vocal with a range of calls which are generally quieter and deeper than those of Eastern Rosella. The main notes are a harsh *ten-week*, a piping whistle *per-pi-chi-chuck*, a three-note *kwick-kweek-kwick*, a fluting liquid *wheedoo-cheedle*. There is also a range of chattering calls when perched.

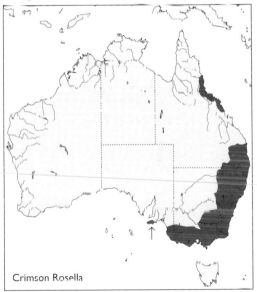

Crimson Rosella

DISTRIBUTION AND STATUS Confined to coastal eastern Australia where it is widely distributed in forested areas along and east of the Great Dividing Range. There is an isolated northern population which ranges from around Atherton, north-east Queensland, south to the Clarke Range and Eungella (the Eungella population may also be isolated). The main population ranges from around Gympie, south-east Queensland in the north, across the border into New South Wales, reaching Warrumbungle National Park, Bathurst and Wagga Wagga, where it comes close to the eastern extreme of the Yellow Rosella (129). In Victoria it ranges east to the Grampians and the Edenhope district, where it spills into extreme south-east South Australia, reaching Kingston at its western extreme. There is also an isolated population on Kangaroo Island. The species occurs wild around Sydney, Brisbane and Melbourne, and escapes have been seen around Perth. Records from northern Tasmania and the Bass Strait islands probably also relate to escapes. It is common on Norfolk Island where it was introduced in the 19th century, but is absent from nearby Nepean and Philip Islands and an attempt to introduce the species to Lord Howe Island failed. It is also introduced in New Zealand where it occurs in the western suburbs of Wellington, and a few birds may also linger in the Dunedin district of South Island where they may hybridise with introduced Eastern Rosellas. The world population is above 200,000. Moderate numbers in captivity. Birds may be eradicated under permit in states where crop destruction occurs.

ECOLOGY Dispersive in winter along fringes of range. The species is common in forests where annual rainfall exceeds 500mm. In the north it tends to prefer forested hills at about 450m-1,900m, mainly 600-1,500m; further south it is common at all altitudes. It is predominantly a forest-breeding species but may be encountered in a range of other habitats both during and after nesting, including farmland, heath and towns. Large parties of adults are rare but young birds gather in flocks and are commoner in more open habitats. Crimson Rosellas are not shy and can be approached closely while they sit stripping twigs for insect larvae in the heat of the day, or feed in parks or gardens. Their varied diet includes blossoms, nectar and the seeds of grasses and trees (sometimes in orchards). Birds are vocal while feeding in foliage and may be found in the company of Eastern Rosellas (132). The display is similar to that of congeners, the male drooping his wings, fanning and wagging his tail, bobbing his head and chattering. Courtship feeding is common and there is a strong pair-bond. Nesting takes place between Aug and Feb, and the 3-8 white eggs are laid in a forest tree-hole on a base of wood debris. The hole may be enlarged by the birds in preparation. On Norfolk Island, the rotten trunks of dead Norfolk Island pines *Araucaria heterophylla* are favoured. Holes in buildings have also been used elsewhere. During the 21-day incubation, and for a short time after hatching, the male feeds the female twice a day. After this the male also feeds the young, which fledge in five weeks and may remain with both parents for a month or so after leaving the nest.

DESCRIPTION Head bright crimson with powder-blue lower cheeks and throat. Mantle feather black with broad crimson margins (intensity slightly variable); rump and uppertail-coverts crimson. Inner lesser and inner median wing-coverts black; bend of wing, outer lesser and median coverts light lavender-blue; outer greater-coverts light lavender-blue, inner black with red margins; primary-coverts violet-blue; flight feathers blackish with fine white outer margin on outermost and violet-blue outerwebs (outermost emarginated); secondaries black with violet-blue outerwebs; tertials black with red margins. Underwing blackish with blue coverts. Underparts rich crimson. Uppertail blue washed green centrally, outer feathers with blackish innerwebs and violet-blue outerwebs, and a pale tip on both webs; undertail pale blue tipped blackish when closed. **Bare parts**: Bill greyish-white; iris dark brown; legs grey-brown.

SEX/AGE Female smaller with narrower bill, sometimes with a wing-bar. Immature very different, with olive-green upperparts (including uppertail), and greyish-green underparts. The centres to the mantle feathers are dark brown, and the black wing-markings of the adult are replaced by green. The rump of very young birds is greenish-orange. There is a pale underwing-bar (made up of pale spots on innerwebs). Red feathers first show on the head, breast, rump and undertail-coverts and are moulted in through the first autumn. Adult plumage is attained in around 15 months. In the northern population immatures are mainly red, and there are fewer green immatures on Norfolk Island than in mainland populations.

MEASUREMENTS Wing 164-188; tail 170-201; bill 16-20; tarsus 21-24.

GEOGRAPHICAL VARIATION Three races.
> *P. e. elegans* (SE Queensland north to the Clarke Range, through E New South Wales and Victoria to extreme SE South Australia; introduced to Norfolk Island and New Zealand))
> *P. e. nigrescens* (Atherton Tableland district, Bellenden Ker Range and nearby coastal districts of north-east Queensland) Smaller than nominate (wing 147-168) and darker red, with narrower red margins to the mantle feathers. Juveniles fledge mainly red.
> *P. e. melanoptera* (Kangaroo Island, South Australia) Darker red with narrower red edgings to mantle feathers, but doubtfully distinct as some mainland birds appear equally dark.

REFERENCES Arndt (1992), Blakers *et al.* (1984), Buckingham & Jackson (1990), Cain (1955), Campbell (1974), Ellis (1987), Emison *et al.* (1987), Falla *et al.* (1981), Forshaw (1981, 1989), Hermes (1985), Lambert *et al.* (1993), Lever (1987), Lodge (1991), Long (1981), Peters (1961), Pizzey & Doyle (1983), Robertson (1985), Schodde *et al.* (1983), Schodde & Tidemann (1988), Sibley & Monroe (1990), Simpson & Day (1984), Slater (1979, 1989).

129 YELLOW ROSELLA
Platycercus flaveolus   Plate 33

Other names: Yellow-rumped Rosella, Yellow-breasted Parakeet

IDENTIFICATION 30-34cm. A generally pale yellow rosella with a red forehead and blue cheeks, found only along wooded river systems in south-east Australia. The superficially similar Green Rosella (127) is allopatric, being restricted to Tasmania, and is uniformly dark olive-green above, lacking the scalloped mantle of Yellow. Paler Adelaide Rosellas (*P. elegans* x *P. flaveolus*) could also be confused with this species, but the yellow areas of *flaveolus* are replaced by orange-yellow in Adelaide. Immature Yellow Rosellas are paler and yellower than young Adelaide hybrids and lack any traces of orange-red in their plumage (except on the forehead). The flight of the Yellow Rosella is undulating with short periods of gliding on closed wings.

VOICE Similar to but slightly higher-pitched than Crimson Rosella; birds are generally less vocal.

DISTRIBUTION AND STATUS Endemic to south-east Australia where it occurs along timbered watercourses in south-west and south-central New South Wales, northern Victoria and extreme south-eastern South Australia. In the extreme east of its range the species is probably limited by the extent of river red-gums *E. camaldulensis*, which are used for nesting. Yellow Rosellas occur on the main river systems in the region, extending east along the Murray from around Mannum, South Australia, to Albury, New South Wales. They also occur north along the Darling River to about Tilpa, the Lachlan River to Hillston, the Murrumbidgee River to Yass, and south into northern Victoria along the Goulburn River to Shepparton and the Ovens River to Wangaratta. The species meets the hybrid population of Adelaide Rosellas in the Mannum district, and further interbreeding may occasionally occur. There is little range overlap with the Crimson Rosella (128), but the two coexist in different habitats along the Ovens River. Occasional vagrants have been recorded (e.g. north to Peak Hill), so the two may occasionally also meet elsewhere. Escapes occur in the suburbs of Melbourne. The Yellow Rosella is common in suitable habitat within its range, but may have declined slightly owing to irrigation schemes removing riverine forest in some districts. The world population is above 50,000. Small numbers in captivity. The species is fully protected.

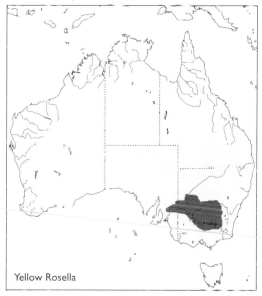

Yellow Rosella

ECOLOGY No regular long-distance movements have been recorded, but some vagrancy occurs. The Yellow Rosella is restricted to riverine forest, chiefly comprising river red-gums used for breeding. It may also be found in adjacent habitats, including box *Eucalyptus* woodland, floodplain forest, dry woodland, mallee *E. gracilis*, farmland and towns. The species mixes with Superb Parrots (121), and Mallee Ringnecks (126). Where it coexists with the Crimson Rosella near Wangaratta, the two occupy different habitats, with Crimson preferring *Eucalyptus* forests of box-ironbark or peppermint. Yellow Rosellas are usually found in pairs or small flocks, and although their behaviour resembles that of Crimsons, they are more arboreal, less vocal, and occur almost exclusively in riverine, not forest, ecosystems. They are most easily detected by the twittering calls made by groups feeding in trees. On the ground they can be harder to detect. The diet includes the seeds of eucalypts and acacias, fruits, blossoms, berries and insects. Although they are less

confiding than other rosellas they will readily drink at man made irrigation sites. The display is similar to that of Crimson Rosella, and the breeding season lasts from Aug to Jan. The typical nest-site is a tree-hollow in a river red-gum close to water. The four to five white eggs are laid on a base of wood debris, and the female incubates for around 19 days, leaving the nest twice a day to feed herself or be fed by the male. The young fledge in about five weeks and continue to depend on the adults for a short time after leaving the nest.

DESCRIPTION Forehead bright red; cheeks and throat mid-blue; lores reddish-orange; forecrown orange-yellow; rear-crown and ear-coverts pale yellow, mottled slightly with blackish-brown, particularly on rear ear-coverts and sides of neck. Mantle black with broad yellow feather-edgings; rump and uppertail-coverts yellow. Bend of wing blue; lesser and inner median coverts black, outer medians light blue; greater coverts light blue, with innermost black edged yellow; flight feathers blackish edged blue on outerwebs, lightest on secondaries; tertials centred black edged yellow. Underwing blackish with blue coverts. Underparts uniform yellow, with fine dark feather fringes and with variable slight orange-red markings around throat and on upper breast (both sexes). Uppertail with central feathers light blue washed greenish and tipped darker, outer feathers blue (darker on innerwebs) grading to white on tips; undertail pale blue tipped white. **Bare parts**. Bill greyish-white; iris brown; legs grey.

SEX/AGE The smaller, narrower-billed female usually shows a pale underwing-bar. Immatures show a similar wing-bar and are generally a dull, pale greenish-yellow, with a duller, more restricted red frontal band, grey-green mantle with a only few dark feather-centres, appearing less scalloped; the rump is more orange, the tail greener above, the underparts a pale yellow-green. Some birds assume adult-like plumage on fledging, most take 15 months.

MEASUREMENTS Wing 159-178; tail 162-199; bill 15-19; tarsus 20-25.

GEOGRAPHICAL VARIATION None.

REFERENCES Arndt (1993), BirdLife (1993), Blakers *et al.* (1984), Buckingham & Jackson (1990), Cain (1955), Emison *et al.* (1987), Forshaw (1981, 1989), Lambert *et al.* (1993), Lodge (1991), Peters (1961), Pizzey & Doyle (1983), Schodde & Tidemann (1988), Simpson & Day (1984), Slater (1979).

129X ADELAIDE ROSELLA
Platycercus elegans x *P. flaveolus*

Other names: Blue-cheeked Rosella, Pennant's Rosella

IDENTIFICATION 36cm. Restricted to the Mount Lofty and southern Flinders Ranges of south-east South Australia. Like Crimson Rosella (128) but orange-red not crimson, with yellow fringes to the mantle feathers and a yellow suffusion around the nape. There is considerable variation between individuals and populations. Juveniles are mostly green in appearance, with orange-red head and vent-markings. There are two effectively isolated populations, with northern birds being paler. From Crimson Rosella by orange-red not crimson plumage, and pale yellowish margins to the mantle feathers. From Yellow Rosella (129) by warmer, redder plumage. Neither species overlaps with the range of this hybrid to any large extent, although Adelaide and Yellow Rosellas meet near Mannum and may occasionally interbreed. Adelaide Rosellas are common in parks and gardens of suburban Adelaide.

VOICE Like Crimson.

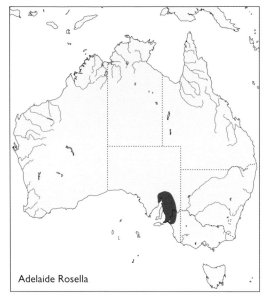

Adelaide Rosella

DISTRIBUTION AND STATUS Occurs in the Mount Lofty and southern Flinders Ranges of South Australia, from Willunga in the south, to Mannum in the east, Peterborough in the north and Port Augusta and Quorn in the west. Sometimes found in Adelaide suburbs. Escapes occur around Sydney. The two breeding populations are separated between 33° and 33°40'S. The world population is in excess of 50,000. Moderate numbers in captivity. The birds are protected by law but permits can be issued to prevent crop damage.

ECOLOGY Sedentary in a range of habitats including timbered valleys and watercourses, open forests and woodlands, tall dry mallee *Eucalyptus gracilis*, wooded farmlands and roadsides. Tends to be found mainly along watercourses in the drier parts of its range. The Adelaide Rosella has adapted to cleared habitats, and feeds on the seeds of eucalypts like river red-gums *E. camaldulensis*, on fruit, insects, nectar and spilt grain. The birds feed on the ground and in trees. They are not timid, and have done damage in orchards. As adults they are found in small groups, but young birds gather in larger, wandering flocks after the breeding season. Nesting takes place between Sep and Dec, and the display and nesting habits are similar to those of Crimson and Yellow Rosellas. Five eggs are laid, incubation is by the female lasting 19 days, and the young fledge in five weeks.

DESCRIPTION Variable. Like *P. elegans* but paler red and suffused with orange-yellow on rear ear-coverts, nape and rump. Mantle feathers greyer black than in *elegans*, and edged pale yellow-orange near nape, reddish-orange on scapulars, and greyish-orange lower down back; rump olive-yellow with variable reddish-orange markings. Inner median and greater coverts black edged orange and grey. Underparts show a few all-orange feathers (which are shaft-streaked and margined yellow-orange). Wing and tail-

markings lighter blue than in *elegans*. Central tail blue washed green. **Bare parts:** Bill greyish; iris brown; legs grey-brown.

SEX/AGE Female is like male but sometimes with a wing-bar. Immatures show a wing-bar and are olive-green above, duller below with a greyish abdomen. The crown, forehead, throat, thighs and undertail-coverts are orange-red, the rump yellowish-olive and the uppertail dull green. First-autumn birds develop warmer underparts and a more clearly scalloped mantle (feathers with a green subterminal margin and orange-red edging). Adult plumage is attained in around 15 months, but colours continue to become stronger with age.

MEASUREMENTS Wing 159-182; tail 173-196; bill 16-18; tarsus 20-21.

GEOGRAPHICAL VARIATION There are two populations, often referred to as *P. adelaidae* (southern) and *P. subadelaidae* (northern), separated by about 60km.

> *P. adelaidae* (in south from around Willunga to S Mount Lofty Ranges) Darker than northern birds, but with some yellower individuals present.
> *P. subadelaidae* (around Port Augusta, the southern Flinders Ranges and Adelaide) Dull orange-yellow underparts and little orange on rump.

There may also be intermediate forms with characters between *flaveolus* and *P. adelaidae* in the Mannum region.

REFERENCES Arndt (1993), Blakers *et al.* (1984), Buckingham & Jackson (1990), Cain (1955), Christidis & Boles (1994), Forshaw (1981, 1989), Lambert *et al.* (1993), Peters (1961), Pizzey & Doyle (1983), Schodde & Tidemann (1988), Sibley & Monroe (1990), Slater (1989), Taylor (1987).

130 NORTHERN ROSELLA
Platycercus venustus   Plate 33

Other names: Brown's Parakeet, Brown's Rosella, Smutty Parrot

IDENTIFICATION 28-30cm. A distinctive creamy-yellow rosella with a very obvious black cap, blue and white cheeks and a red vent and undertail-coverts. The mantle is boldly scalloped black and cream, and the pale breast is marked with fine blackish fringes. The creamy scapulars create a pair of 'braces' either side of the mantle. There are no sympatric confusion species. The male Hooded Parrot (137) is sympatric and has a black cap, but it is bright turquoise-blue below with a large yellow wing-patch. The flight of the Northern Rosella is undulating, and the tail is fanned on landing.

VOICE Similar to Eastern Rosella (132). The variety of notes include a piping repetitive whistle *pi-pi-pi-pi-pi*, a resounding *click-a-du*, a short *cuick-quick*, and various harsh calls and chattering notes.

DISTRIBUTION AND STATUS Scattered through coastal areas of the Kimberley region, Western Australia, the northern sections of Northern Territory, and just spilling over the Queensland border at its eastern extreme. The species extends from around the Napier Ranges in the west Kimberley region, east through the Kimberley Plateau, reaching inland to Springvale. It then crosses the Northern Territory border, extending east with its southern limit along the Victoria River, inland to around Katherine, and along the McArthur River. It is also found along the Nicholson River at the Queensland border, and occurs on a number of offshore islands including Koolan, Augustus, Coronation, Bathurst and Melville. It is occasionally found in the suburbs of Darwin. The species is generally uncommon throughout its range. The world population is less than 50,000, and may be declining. Small numbers in captivity. Protected fully by law.

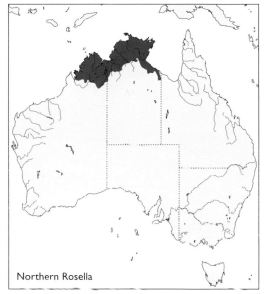

Northern Rosella

ECOLOGY Sedentary. Found in a range of habitats up to 560m, from savanna and monsoon woodland characterised by *Callitris*, paperbark *Melaleuca* ecosystems, riverine woodland, scrub, clearings, roadsides, farmland, urban areas, creeks in hill country and mangroves. The Northern Rosella is shy and is usually found in small unobtrusive groups, but is noisier and more conspicuous at the start of breeding, which normally takes place between May and Sep, although reported at other times of year. Tends to be more arboreal than other rosellas but will feed on the ground. The diet comprises fruit, buds, blossoms, nectar, and the seeds of acacias, eucalypts, grasses and paperbark. The nest-site, chosen by the male, is normally a tree-hollow in a eucalypt close to water. Mating takes place throughout the breeding season. The two to four white eggs are laid on wood debris and incubation lasts 19 days, the young fledging in about seven weeks. Family parties form after fledging.

DESCRIPTION Crown to below eye black; lower cheeks and throat white merging to violet-blue at rear and below. Mantle black boldly edged creamy yellow; scapulars with very broad pale margins forming pale braces; lower back and rump pale cream-yellow, finely fringed black. Bend of wing blue; inner lesser coverts black, outer lesser and median coverts light blue with very fine darker fringes; greater coverts blue. Flight feathers blackish with blue outerwebs (secondaries with pale leading edge fringes); tertials black with cream edgings. Underwing blackish with blue coverts. Underparts cream with fine black fringes, broader on upper breast, which also shows fine reddish shafts; thighs marked red; undertail-coverts and vent bright red. Uppertail dark blue with slight greenish wash,

outer feathers pale blue tipped white with darker bases; undertail pale blue tipped white. **Bare parts:** Bill greyish-white; iris brown; legs grey.

SEX/AGE Female smaller with narrower bill, most showing a wing-bar. Immatures also mostly show a wing-bar, plus red flecks on a duller head early on and greener, shorter tail feathers. Adult plumage attained in 12 months.

MEASUREMENTS Wing 138-154; tail 141-165; bill 14-17; tarsus 18-20.

GEOGRAPHICAL VARIATION The amount of blue and white on the cheeks varies between western and northern populations, but no races are recognised.

REFERENCES Arndt (1993), Blakers *et al.* (1984), Buckingham & Jackson (1990), Cain (1955), Forshaw (1981, 1989), Lambert *et al.* (1993), Lodge (1991), Peters (1961), Pizzey & Doyle (1983), Schodde & Tidemann (1988), Simpson & Day (1984), Slater (1979, 1989).

131 PALE-HEADED ROSELLA
Platycercus adscitus Plate 33

Other names: Mealy Rosella, Blue Rosella, White-headed Rosella

IDENTIFICATION 28-32cm. A bright yellow and blue rosella with red undertail-coverts, and a light-coloured head lacking any red markings in the adult male. The species occurs in eastern Queensland and extreme northeastern New South Wales, varying from north to south. The species is superficially similar to the allopatric Yellow Rosella (129), but lacks the red forehead and blue chin; moreover, Yellow also has entirely yellow underparts, lacking the blue markings and red undertail-coverts of this species. The flight of the Pale-headed Rosella is strongly undulating with short glides on closed wings. The subspecies *P. a. palliceps* hybridises with Eastern Rosella in the wild.

VOICE Like Eastern Rosella. As both species have a rich variety of variable calls it is difficult to pick out any constant differences, but the *crik-onk* flight call of this species is said to be deeper and harsher than the equivalent call of Eastern.

DISTRIBUTION AND STATUS Confined to eastern Australia where it is scattered through the Cape York Peninsula, reaching south to the Gilbert River in the west, and extending south through coastal eastern Queensland to northern New South Wales. In Queensland its inland limit runs roughly through Croydon, Richmond, Longreach, Charleville and Bingara. It also occurs on Fraser Island and around Brisbane, as well as in other coastal districts. In New South Wales the range is limited to the north-east, extending inland to Bourke and south to around Coffs Harbour on the coast. Escapes have been recorded in Sydney and Melbourne, and there was an unsuccessful introduction to Hawaii earlier this century. The species is altitudinally parapatric with Eastern Rosella (132) in south-east Queensland. Common in suitable habitat within its range. The world population is above 100,000. Moderate numbers in captivity. Fully protected.

ECOLOGY Sedentary except for some local movements on the edges of its range associated with climatic extremes. Found mainly in the lowlands in a wide variety of habitats including open woodland, scrub, riverine woodland, grasslands, roadsides, *Lantana* thickets, farmland, orchards and coastal heath. The species does not readily spread into dry areas even along watercourses, and is normally found only where annual rainfall exceeds 200mm. Usually encountered in pairs or flocks feeding quietly on the ground or chattering in the foliage. The birds are noisy and conspicuous early and late in the day but unless flushed may be difficult to see along roadsides as they feed on the ground. Groups associate with Mallee Ringnecks (126) and Red-winged Parrots (120). The species has benefited from cultivation and the provision of artificial watering sites. The diet consists of fruit, flowers, seeds (e.g. of scotch thistle *Carduus nutans*), nectar, insects and nuts. Occasional damage to orchards has been recorded. Breeding runs from Sep to Jan in the south but is rain-dependent in the north, usually occurring from Feb to Jul following the wet season, but sometimes in other months of the year. The three to five white eggs are laid on wood debris in a tree-hollow near water (nests have also been found in fenceposts). The female incubates for 19 days and the young fledge in around five weeks, when they join the adults to form roving family groups.

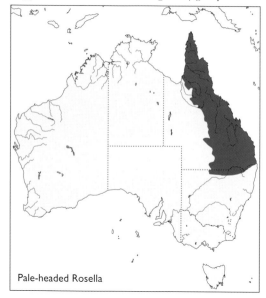

Pale-headed Rosella

DESCRIPTION Head pale yellow with white cheeks and blue sides to lower throat; sides of nape brighter yellow showing some fine darker scaling. Mantle black with bold pale yellow fringes, most pronounced on scapulars forming braces; rump and uppertail-coverts yellowish or greyish, fringed darker. Bend of wing blue; inner lesser and median coverts black, some with blue fringes; outer lesser and median coverts light blue; greater coverts slightly darker blue than medians on outerwebs, blackish on inners. Flight feathers (including primary coverts) blackish with dark blue outerwebs; tertials with light yellow and bluish fringes. Underparts show extremely fine darker fringes, with pale yellow breast and pale blue belly becoming greenish-blue on flanks and vent; undertail-coverts bright red. Uppertail dark green merging to blue, lighter on outer feathers which are tipped white with darker bases; undertail light blue tipped white. **Bare parts**: Bill grey; iris dark brown; legs grey.

SEX/AGE Female has a variable pale wing-bar. Immature duller than adult with less blue below, some reddish feathers showing on the forecrown, and a wing-bar. Red feathers are lost in around three months and adult plumage is acquired in about 16 months.

MEASUREMENTS Wing 140-160; tail 142-164; bill 15-18; tarsus 19-21.

GEOGRAPHICAL VARIATION The species varies clinally from north to south and is divided into two subspecies which overlap in the Atherton district of north-east Queensland.

    P. a. adscitus (Cape York Peninsula south to around Atherton) The extent and intensity of the blue cheeks reduces southwards, and the yellow intensifies.

    P. a. palliceps (around Atherton, NE Queensland south to N New South Wales) Variable. Underparts generally a uniform pale blue (breast may be patchy), very pale head lacking blue throat. Upperparts richer yellow than nominate. Rump washed with blue.

REFERENCES Arndt (1993), Blakers *et al.* (1984), Buckingham & Jackson (1990), Cain (1955), Ford (1988), Forshaw (1981, 1989), Lambert *et al.* (1993), Lodge (1991), Peters (1961), Pizzey & Doyle (1983), Schodde & Tidemann (1988), Sibley & Monroe (1990), Slater (1989).

132 EASTERN ROSELLA
Platycercus eximius Plate 33

Other names: Common Rosella, Rosehill Parakeet, Red Rosella, Rosella Parakeet, Red-headed Rosella, Nonpareil Parrot, White-cheeked Rosella; Golden-mantled Rosella, Yellow-mantled Rosella, Splendid Rosella (*P. e. elecica*)

IDENTIFICATION 29-34cm. A flashy, unmistakable species which occurs in south-eastern Australia and Tasmania; introduced to New Zealand. The combination of a red head, white cheeks, blue wing-flash and yellow body makes this an extremely distinctive species. It has a loud, penetrating call, swift undulating flight, and the pale green rump is noticeable as the birds take flight. There is a rare red morph which can be separated from *P. eximius* x Crimson Rosella *P. elegans* hybrids by its pure white cheeks (not blue, or white and blue). Occasionally other aberrant individuals as well as hybrids with Pale-headed Rosellas (131) may be encountered.

VOICE The calls are generally higher-pitched than those of the Crimson Rosella, with a rich variety of different notes, most being similar to the calls of Pale-headed and Northern Rosellas (130). The flight call is a sharp *kwink-kwink*, there is an alarm screech, various chattering notes given while feeding, a piping *pi-pi-pi-pi-pi* and a liquid *weedle-cheedle*, *week-wi-deek* or *click-a-du*.

DISTRIBUTION AND STATUS Confined to south-east Australia where it ranges from around Gympie, Bribie Island and the Darling Downs district in extreme south-east Queensland, south through New South Wales, reaching inland to Moree, Parkes, Griffith and Hay, and spilling into Victoria where it is absent only from the north-west region, reaching west as far as Edenhope. In south-east South Australia the species is largely confined to the area between Bordertown and Salt Creek, but a population also occurs in the southern Mount Lofty Range which originated from captive stock. In Tasmania it is widely but sparsely distributed, and has been recorded from King Island in the Bass Strait. There are small introduced populations in New Zealand's South Island concentrated around Dunedin (includes some Crimson x Eastern hybrids) and on the Banks Peninsula, and a larger population in North Island which ranges from the extreme north of the island, down the west coast through Raglan, New Plymouth and inland to Pirongia and Taupo; birds are also found in the Wellington and Lower Hutt districts, the Tararua Range, around Gisborne and along the Coromandel Peninsula, but are rare south of Auckland. The world population is in excess of 500,000, and stable or increasing. There is some nest-site competition with European Starlings *Sturnus vulgaris* in Tasmania. Moderate numbers in captivity. The species has benefited from the spread of agriculture, and although protected by law, can be destroyed under licence.

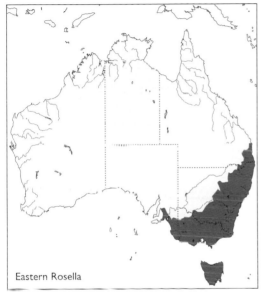

Eastern Rosella

ECOLOGY Sedentary, but there is some local post-breeding movement, mainly of immatures. Eastern Rosellas occur in a range of habitats including open forest, woodland, riverine forest, eucalypt copses, forest margins, grassland, paddocks, farmlands and suburbs. In New Zealand, pine forests and native bush are utilised. The species is found in areas where the annual rainfall exceeds 400mm, and at elevations up to 1,250m. It is not partial to mallee *Eucalyptus gracilis* and in drier areas tends to occur only along wooded watercourses. It is confiding, usually being encountered in pairs or small groups, and although it is brightly coloured it may be quite inconspicuous on the ground. It associates with Crimson and Pale-headed Rosellas and Red-rumped Parrots (135). Large flocks are sometimes found from the end of the breeding season to early spring. Birds drink early in the day, feed, rest during the hottest hours and strip twigs, then feed and drink again before roosting. The diet includes seeds, berries, grain, fruit, blossoms, nectar and insects. They feed both in trees and on the ground, have a liking for banksias, scotch thistle *Carduus nutans*, and may do damage in orchards. Nesting takes place between Jul and Mar, and at the start of the breeding season birds begin to squabble. Courtship feeding between pairs is common, and in display the male droops his wings, erects his breast and rump feathers, and fans and wags his tail while bowing his head. The nest is often in a tree-hollow, but other sites have been used including excavated burrows of the Rainbow Bee-eater *Merops ornatus*, telegraph poles and stump holes. The site is prepared and cleared and males will defend it against intruders. The four to six (maximum nine) eggs are laid on decayed wood-dust, and incubated by the female for around 18 days. At first she is fed by the male only; 10 days after hatching both parents join in until the young fledge in around 33 days. They will then remain with the parents for over a month, unless there is a second brood. Head-scratching is over the wing. Birds can live at least nine years.

DESCRIPTION Head bright scarlet with white cheeks and throat. Upperparts with black feather-centres, narrowly margined with yellow and some green on outer fringes; rump and uppertail-coverts light yellowish-green with fine dark fringing. Bend of wing blue; lesser coverts black; median and greater coverts light blue, with more greenish-blue edgings on inner coverts. Flight feathers black, edged blue on outers and with fine yellow margins; inner secondaries with greener edgings, and tertials with fine yellow and green margins; primaries emarginated. Underwing blackish with blue coverts. Upper breast bright scarlet, lower breast yellow with very fine, slightly darker margins; vent greenish-yellow; undertail-coverts scarlet. Uppertail green merging to blue at the tips, with outers feathers light blue tipped white with darker bases; undertail light blue tipped white. **Bare parts**: Bill grey-white; iris dark brown; legs grey brown.

SEX/AGE The slightly smaller female has a duller red head and greener upperparts, particularly the back of the nape; many also show a pale wing-bar. Young birds are like females but show even more green on the nape, less red on the head, greener margins to the mantle feathers, and males show a wing-bar up to their first moult. Young birds begin to show more red feathers on the rear-crown during the autumn, full adult plumage being attained in 12-18 months.

MEASUREMENTS Wing 138-161; tail 146-178; bill 15-17; tarsus 19-22.

GEOGRAPHICAL VARIATION Three races.

P. e. eximius (around the Hunter River, New South Wales, to SE South Australia; north of the Hunter River found west of the Great Dividing Range. This is the race introduced in New Zealand)

P. e. elecica (S Queensland to around the Hunter River in New South Wales, meeting the nominate at around at 32°S; north of the Hunter River found east of the Great Dividing Range) The head and breast are darker red, the rump is blue- or turquoise-green, and there are broad, brighter yellow edgings (slightly greener in female) to the mantle feathers.

P. e. diemenensis (Tasmania) Larger white cheek-patches and more extensive and darker red on head and breast.

REFERENCES Arndt (1992), Blakers *et al.* (1984), Buckingham & Jackson (1990), Cain (1955), Ellis (1987), Emison *et al.* (1987), Falla *et al.* (1981), Forshaw (1981, 1989), Lambert *et al.* (1993), Lever (1987), Lodge (1991), Long (1981), Peters (1961), Pizzey & Doyle (1983), Robertson (1985), Schodde (1988), Schodde & Tidemann (1988), Sibley & Monroe (1990), Slater (1989), Tzaros (1992), Wyndham *et al.* (1983).

133 WESTERN ROSELLA
Platycercus icterotis   **Plate 32**

Other names: Yellow-cheeked Rosella, Stanley Parakeet

IDENTIFICATION 25-30 cm. The smallest rosella and un-like any other parrot in Western Australia. The com-bination of yellow cheeks, red underparts and largely green upperparts makes this a very distinctive species. It is confined to a small area of Western Australia, within which no other rosella occurs. The flight is buoyant and fluttering with slight undulations, recalling a *Psephotus* parrot. Flights are mainly short with only brief glides.

VOICE Calls are reminiscent of Mulga Parrot (136) but more frequently uttered. The soft, quiet notes include a *tink-tink*, or *chink chink*, and a soft melodious whistle *wee-wee*. There are also some harsher calls.

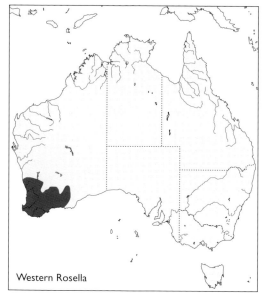

Western Rosella

DISTRIBUTION AND STATUS Endemic to Western Australia where it ranges from around Dongara in the north to Israelite Bay on the south coast, reaching inland to a line running roughly through Lake Dundas, Southern Cross and Moora. Sometimes found in parks in Perth. The species is common and appears to have benefited from forest clearance and agriculture. The world population in excess of 100,000. Small numbers in captivity. Birds can be persecuted under permit.

ECOLOGY Mainly sedentary although in the north post-breeding dispersal takes some birds coastwards; in general long flights are uncommon. Western Rosellas occur in open and partly cleared eucalypt woodland and forest, riverine forest, farmland, orchards, towns, clearings, roadsides, gardens, pastures, wooded savanna and shrub-land, but generally avoid heathland areas. They are found in pairs and small parties, which are quiet and often tame, particularly when feeding unobtrusively on spilt grain close to farm buildings; they may form larger flocks where food is plentiful. The diet consists of the seeds of grasses and herbs, insects, fruits, berries, flowers, nectar and buds. Pair-bonding is strong and pairs indulge in allo-feeding all year. The breeding season lasts from Aug to Dec, with egg-laying

at its height during Sep. The nest-site is usually a tree-hollow with the cavity lined with decaying wood debris. The female incubates the three to seven (usually five) white eggs for 20 days, being fed by the male during this time. The young fledge in 30 days.

DESCRIPTION Head scarlet with pale yellow cheeks and throat. Mantle black, fringed red on upper (in older birds), yellow-green and red in centre, green on lower; rump dark green with rusty suffusion (more evident in females). Bend of wing blue; lesser-coverts black with some green fringes; outer median and greater coverts dark blue; innermost greater coverts green centred darker; inner median coverts black tipped blue-green. Primaries blackish edged dark blue on outerwebs; secondaries black mar-gined blue-green on outerweb; tertials and innermost secondaries fringed green. Some males show a pale wing-bar. Underparts bright scarlet. Uppertail dark green tinged blue towards tip, outer feathers blue tipped white, darker basally; undertail pale blue tipped white. **Bare parts**: Bill grey; iris dark brown; legs brownish-grey.

SEX/AGE Female with slightly duller cheek-patch, and greenish-yellow mottling on the head, around sides of throat, breast and flanks (may be extensive in some birds). Lacks red edging to mantle feathers which have duller black centres, looking more uniform with greyish-green edgings. There is an underwing-bar and more green on the generally duller wing-coverts. Immature lacks cheek-patch, and is a dull uniform green with a orange-brown suffusion to the face, less blue in the wing, and a wing-bar. During the first autumn a little red appears on the head and breast and yellow in the cheek. Adult plumage is attained after a rapid complete moult at 14 months. Young males show more red than females and birds may breed while still in juvenile plumage.

MEASUREMENTS Wing 130-150; tail 212-149; bill 12-15; tarsus 17-20.

GEOGRAPHICAL VARIATION Two races.
> *P. icterotis* (extreme SW Western Australia)
> *P. xanthogenys* (drier areas inland of jarrah *Eucalyptus marginata* belt, but with a zone of intergradation with the nominate) Generally paler than the nominate, male showing more extensive red edgings on mantle. The green areas of the back are paler and greyer (suf-fused light sky-blue). Tail blue without traces of green.

REFERENCES Arndt (1992), BirdLife (1993), Blakers *et al.* (1984), Buckingham & Jackson (1990), Cain (1955), Forshaw (1981, 1989), Lambert *et al.* (1993), Lodge (1991), Peters (1961), Pizzey & Doyle (1983), Schodde & Tidemann (1988), Sibley & Monroe (1990), Simpson & Day (1984), Slater (1989), Storr & Johnstone (1979).

134 BLUEBONNET
Northiella haematogaster   **Plate 34**

Other names: Bulloke Parrot, Crimson-bellied Parrot; Yellow-vented Bluebonnet (*N. h. haematogaster*); Red-vented Bluebonnet (*N. h. haematorrhous*); Little Blue Bonnet, Naretha Parakeet (*N. h. narethae*)

IDENTIFICATION 26-30cm. A medium-sized, pale olive-brown parrot which may appear somewhat nondescript from a distance except for its dark (blue) face. Occurs in a variety of habitats with the main populations concentrated in south-east Australia. This is the only Australian parrot showing an olive mantle and breast, red on the underparts and a blue face. The rosella-like flight is fast, erratic and slightly undulating, with distinctive rapid shallow beats and short glides.

VOICE A distinctive harsh *chack... chack-a-chack-a-chack*, and a reedy whistle *peeoo*. The western race also has a soft *cloot-cloot* and a loud *ack-ack-ack*.

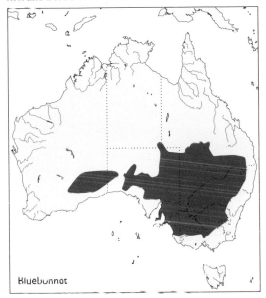

Bluebonnet

DISTRIBUTION AND STATUS Confined to Australia where there are four populations, one of which is isolated in south-east Western Australia from the Nullarbor Plain west to around Kalgoorlie. Birds belonging to this western race are also found in western South Australia around Ooldea and Colona, but are probably escapes. Further east the species ranges through eastern South Australia from Bordertown west through Salt Creek, Adelaide, northern parts of the Yorke and Eyre Peninsulas, and north through the Lake Eyre basin to the Simpson Desert to around Commonwealth Hill Station (but largely absent from the Flinders Range). From northern South Australia it extends into southern Queensland west of the Great Dividing Range, reaching east to around Windorah, Charleville, Mitchell and Goondiwindi. In New South Wales it is again found west of the Divide, and reaches east to a line roughly running through Warialda, Orange and Wagga Wagga (extralimital record east to Gunning). In Victoria it occasionally reaches as far east as Rochester and south-east to Bendigo and Beaufort. The species is common in suitable habitat. The world population is probably in excess of 100,000, although the western race *narethae* may have fewer than 5,000 individuals and has suffered from trapping in the past. Small numbers in captivity. Fully protected by law.

ECOLOGY Sedentary, but *narethae* is dependent on rains and subject to local seasonal movements. There is a difference in habitat preference with range and race. Eastern birds occupy a range of habitats including open woodland, riverine woodland, remnant mallee *Eucalyptus gracilis* and farmland. In the Lake Eyre region, the species

is found in open country with scattered trees, and the western race *narethae* typically prefers arid areas with desert she-oak *Casuarina cristata* and mulga *Acacia aneura*. Bluebonnets are usually found in pairs or small parties of up to 20 birds. When disturbed they scatter noisily, remaining close to the ground as they fly to nearby trees. In alarm, the feathers on the forehead are raised. The species is extremely active, and boisterous groups assemble to drink early in the day before going to feed. They feed both in trees and on the ground, are capable of running quickly, and have a distinctive upright stance. They are less active during the heat of the day, and whilst on the ground tend to remain quiet. Western birds may congregate in larger groups than is typical in the east, and are more sociable and confiding than the other races. Up to 100 birds have been recorded feeding with Mulga Parrots (136) and Port Lincoln Ringnecks (195) in homestead gardens. In Queensland, Bluebonnets may congregate with Mallee Ringnecks (126) and Pale-headed Rosellas (131). The diet includes berries, blossoms, insect larvae and nectar; spilt wheat is also taken. Western birds commonly feed on the seeds of acacias, and all races feed on the seeds and fruit of a range of arid-zone shrubs, grasses and trees. In display the male performs head-bobbing, tail-wagging and courtship-feeding; there is also a slow flapping display-flight. Nesting takes place between Jul and Dec in eastern populations, but western birds are dependent on rains and may nest at other times of the year. The nest-chamber is in a deep tree hollow, usually with a relatively small entrance hole high above the ground. Between four and seven (usually five) white eggs are laid on decaying wood debris, and two to four white-downed chicks are raised. Incubation lasts 20 days and is carried out by the female. The male feeds her until the chicks are about two weeks old, and the young fledge in four to five weeks, staying with the parents for a short while.

DESCRIPTION Forehead and face mid-blue, lighter on brow; rest of head olive grey, ear coverts shaft-streaked pale olive. Upperparts olive-grey, brighter and yellower on rump. Bend of wing bright pale blue; inner median coverts bright olive suffused reddish, outer olive-grey suffused light blue; inner greater coverts olive-yellow, outer violet-blue; primary coverts dark blue. Flight feathers black edged blue; tertials olive-brown marked yellowish-olive on outerweb. Underwing-coverts blue, underside of flight feathers black. Upper breast pale olive-brown sometimes mottled yellowish; lower breast and belly pale yellow marked red; thighs red with narrow yellow margins; vent and undertail-coverts yellow. Central tail feathers olive-brown washed blue, outer feathers blue tipped white with dark bases to innerwebs; closed tail appears whitish below, with dark subterminal mark sometimes evident. **Bare parts**: Bill greyish-white; iris pale grey; legs grey.

SEX/AGE Sexes alike but both female and immature show a pale wing-bar. Both are also duller, with females showing less blue in the face, and immatures with less red below. Immature plumage is lost after just a few months. Fledglings have a yellow bill.

MEASUREMENTS Wing 118-140; tail 147-187; bill 14-18; tarsus 19-21.

GEOGRAPHICAL VARIATION Four races with some intergradation.

    N. h. haematogaster (South Australia, Victoria, southern New South Wales and SW Queensland; there is a zone of intergradation where this meets the following race in C New South Wales and S Queensland at around 146°E, from around Barellan in the south to the Warrego River drainage)

N. h. haematorrhous (EC New South Wales and SC Queensland) From nominate by its reddish-chestnut wing-patch (inner median and greater coverts, tertials and secondaries), greener tint to blue shoulder-patch, and red undertail-coverts; plumage slightly brighter in north of range.

N. h. pallescens (Lake Eyre Basin, South Australia, and along watercourses flowing into the lake including Cooper Creek; intergrades with nominate, e.g. in Lake Frome area of South Australia, and its range may extend into New South Wales and Queensland; northernmost confirmed records come from Cowarie, and the racial identity of birds further north than this, including those from Lake Muncoonie, is presently uncertain) Paler than nominate with a smaller red belly-patch and more yellowish upperwing-coverts.

N. h. narethae (fringes of Nullarbor Plain, Western Australia, mainly north-west, ranging from around Kalgoorlie in the west to the north-east of Eucla, at its eastern limit; birds showing characters of this race have also been recorded across the South Australia border around Ooldea and Colona, but these probably originated from escaped stock; rare south of transcontinental railway, but recently extended south to the Eyre Highway, possibly because of artificial watering sites) Forehead greenish-blue, more obvious pale ear-coverts than nominate, more pale mottling on breast, shoulder greenish-blue, outer lesser and median coverts red-orange, inner lesser and median coverts olive-yellow, belly and thighs yellow, flanks greyish, undertail-coverts and vent red. More pronounced sexual dimorphism than in other races, with stronger light blue on forehead of male, and duller, more rusty, lesser coverts in female.

REFERENCES Blakers *et al.* (1984), Buckingham & Jackson (1990), Emison (1982), Emison *et al.* (1984), Forshaw (1981, 1989), Lambert *et al.* (1993), Lodge (1991), Odekerken (1991), Peters (1961), Pizzey & Doyle (1983), Schodde & Tidemann (1988), Sibley & Monroe (1990), Simpson & Day (1984), Slater (1979, 1989), Storr & Johnstone (1979), Taylor (1987), Trounson & Trounson (1987).

135   RED-RUMPED PARROT
Psephotus haematonotus   Plate 34

Other names: Redrump, Red-backed Parrot, Scarlet-rumped Parrot

IDENTIFICATION 25-28cm. A small, long-tailed parrot, common in drier parts of south-east Australia. The male is blue and green, with a distinctive red rump, yellow shoulder-patch and yellow underparts, the female dull olive with a green rump contrasting with the olive-grey of the mantle in flight. The male is similar to the closely related Mulga Parrot (136), which however shows a red nape and yellow forehead, red (not yellow) on lower belly and only a little red on the uppertail-coverts. Female Mulga is brighter than the nondescript female Red-rumped, showing a rusty nape, yellowish forehead and a red shoulder-patch; female and immature Mulgas also have a

distinctive pale blue rump-patch. The smaller *Neophema* parrots lack the red rump and have a distinctive hesitant flight pattern and higher-pitched tinkling calls. The flight of Red-rumped Parrot is swift with slight undulations and brief glides; the tail is fanned on landing.

VOICE The main call is disyllabic *tswee-chilip*, the first note thin and explosive, the second fuller and more truncated. There is also an unusual warbling trill and some harsher squabbling calls.

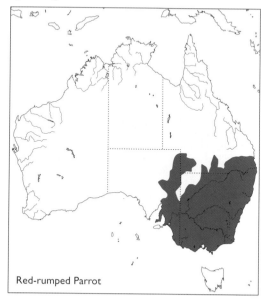

Red-rumped Parrot

DISTRIBUTION AND STATUS Confined to south-eastern Australia, ranging north from the Eyre and Yorke Peninsulas, South Australia, through the Flinders Range to the Lake Eyre basin and Innamincka in the north-east. The species is spreading eastwards through Victoria, and reached Melbourne in the mid-1970s, but is still scarce in the extreme east of the state. However, in New South Wales it can be found around Sydney and along the coast to the north, and extends inland through most of New South Wales (largely absent north-west of the Darling River). In Queensland it reaches Windorah in the west and around Charleville, Chinchilla and Brisbane in the east. It is common and increasing in the north and towards the coast from southern Queensland to southern New South Wales, and has benefited from the spread of agriculture. The world population is over 200,000, and the species is protected by law.

ECOLOGY Sedentary, but some local movements of post-breeding flocks have been recorded at the edges of its range. Red-rumped Parrots favour open and riverine woodland, grassland and farmland up to 1,000m, where the annual rainfall is less than 800mm. They are also found in suburban areas, favouring golf-courses, roadsides and parks, and locally in mangroves. Generally they replace Bluebonnets (134) and Mulga Parrots in wetter areas. They are usually encountered in pairs or small groups, but post-breeding flocks numbering 100 or more are not uncommon. In these groups the pair-bond is maintained and allopreening is common. Red-rumped Parrots are sociable, and when returning to roost the high flying flocks call constantly. The birds spend most of their feeding time on the ground where they scurry around in active groups, but they will also forage in trees and shrubs. The diet comprises a mixture of grass and herb seeds, also shoots, leaves, blossoms and spilt grain. In order to reach the seedhead, birds will perch on the stem of a small plant until it gives way under their weight and bends to the ground. They rest during the heat of the day and can remain fairly inconspicuous unless disturbed. The breeding season runs from Jul to Jan, but may be more dependent on rains in the north than elsewhere. The display involves tail-wagging, head-bobbing and wing-drooping by the male, as well as courtship-feeding. Nesting can be in small colonies, with a few pairs in one tree, but pairs defend the limb in which their nest is situated and some squabbling often occurs at the start of the breeding season. The nest is a tree-hollow at varying heights, often in a eucalypt, but a tree-stump or even the eaves of a building may provide a suitable site. Between two and eight (usually four to five) white eggs are laid on a base of wood-dust. The female incubates alone for around 20 days, fed regularly by the male. At first, males remain in small feeding parties, but as the chicks grow older these groups begin to disperse and the males join in feeding the young directly. The white-downed young fledge in four to six weeks.

DESCRIPTION Head bright pale green, slightly iridescent, and with a pale blue forecrown and suffusion on throat. Mantle greyish-green with fine dark fringes; lower back and rump dull scarlet; uppertail-coverts bright green. Bend of wing bright violet-blue; carpal edge dark blue; lesser coverts blue-green, outer median coverts yellow, inner pale blue-green; greater coverts blue-green, inner lighter; primary coverts dark blue. Flight feathers blackish with dark blue outerwebs and yellowish leading margin; tertials grey-green with dark innerwebs. Underwing-coverts dark blue. Breast light green with a slight yellow suffusion, belly bright yellow, breast and belly feathers with very fine darker fringes; thighs, vent and undertail-coverts whitish, sometimes suffused yellow green. Uppertail greenish brown with lateral feathers greenish-blue tipped white; undertail seemingly whitish when closed. **Bare parts:** Bill black; iris brown; legs grey.

SEX/AGE The female is much duller than the male, being generally greyish-green. There is some light mottling on the ear-coverts, the breast is light greyish-olive with slightly darker fringes, and the belly is whitish with a slight blue-green suffusion. The wing-coverts are a more uniform greyish-olive than the male's (median coverts pale blue). The outerwebs of the flight feathers are duller and greener, and the rump is green. The bill and iris are paler, and there is a pale wing-bar. Immatures have the pale wing-bar, and males are darker and more olive than females with a narrow red rump; blue-green feathers begin to show on head, breast and wing-coverts first. Immature females show a pale bill and eye. Adult plumage is acquired in two to three months, but young males retain the wing-bar and have a duller rump for another year.

MEASUREMENTS Wing 120-141; tail 129-158; bill 11-13; tarsus 14-18.

GEOGRAPHICAL VARIATION Two races.
 P. h. haematonotus (most of the range)
 P. h. caeruleus (probably isolated in the Lake Eyre region of South Australia at Etadunna and Innamincka, but may spill into far NW New South Wales and SW Queensland) Paler than nominate, the male also be-

ing bluer, showing a less extensive yellow belly, a paler red rump and central tail-feathers washed blue. The female is pale grey with an extensive yellowish-white belly.

REFERENCES Blakers *et al.* (1984), Buckingham & Jackson (1990), Emison *et al.* (1987), Forshaw (1981, 1989), Kloot (1988), Lambert *et al.* (1993), Lodge (1991), Peters (1961), Pizzey & Doyle (1983), Schodde & Tidemann (1988), Sibley & Monroe (1990), Simpson & Day (1984), Slater (1979, 1989), Taylor (1987).

136 MULGA PARROT
Psephotus varius   Plate 35

Other names: Varied Parakeet, Many-coloured Parakeet

IDENTIFICATION 26-31cm. The male Mulga is a slender emerald-green parrot, with a yellow frontal band and shoulder-patch and a russet hind-crown. The abdomen is yellow marked red, and the rump pale blue-green with a red spot on the uppertail-coverts; females and immatures are duller with a pale wing-bar in flight. The pale blue-green rump-band and yellow forehead distinguish this from any other parrot. The species appears more slender than the closely related Red-rumped Parrot (135) due to its longer tail, and the pale blue-green, not red or green, rump is obvious in flight. The flight of Mulga Parrot is swift and buoyant with rapid fluttering beats interspersed by glides, producing a slight undulation. When disturbed the birds fly off close to the ground, spreading their tail when landing.

VOICE The flight call is a distinctive, frequently repeated *chweet-chweet chweet-chweet*. Also a rapid musical twittering when perched.

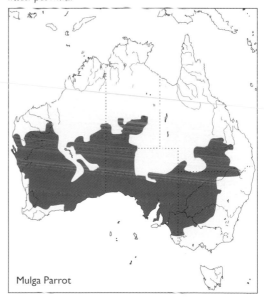
Mulga Parrot

DISTRIBUTION AND STATUS Confined to southern Australia where it is widespread and fairly common in suitable habitat, ranging east from the wheatbelt of Western Australia to the west of the Great Dividing Range. In Western Australia, the species extends south to Lake

Grace in the far west, then north through Northam and Moora to around Carnarvon and east to the south-west of the Great Sandy Desert, south through Kathleen Valley, and Leonora to the west of the Great Victoria Desert. It is scattered through the Nullarbor Plain in the south, and also occurs north of the Great Victoria Desert, spilling across into the McDonnell Ranges in Northern Territory at its northern extreme. It occurs throughout western and southern South Australia, ranging east to around Oodnadatta in the northern part of the state, and along the southern coastal belt through the Eyre and Yorke Peninsulas. It reaches north-western Victoria in the Big Desert and Lake Hindmarsh regions, and spreads north-east through the Murray-Darling Basin and central New South Wales as far as Grenfell, Dubbo and Moree, and north into south-central Queensland east to the Darling Downs, north through Mungindi and Charleville and west to the Grey Range and Windorah. The Mulga Parrot has spread into the wheatbelt from drier areas to the north-east since European settlement. The world population is above 100,000 and safe, although there may have been a decline in the south due to mallee *Eucalyptus gracilis* clearance. The species is fully protected.

ECOLOGY Mainly sedentary except for some seasonal movements in response to the availability of water. The species prefers dry open woodlands and plains with a variety of vegetation types including mallee, mulga *Acacia aneura*, casuarina, saltbush *Atriplex vesicaria* and sea samphire *Crithmum maritimum*. It also occurs in mallee scrub with nearby croplands, and in the driest parts of its range in riverine woodland. Mulga Parrots are rarely found in large flocks and tend to consort in pairs or small groups, and are less active than Red-rumped Parrots. They feed on the ground beneath trees, along roadsides, amongst foliage, or on spilt grain in open paddocks. When feeding they can be confiding, and fly up to perch in a nearby tree if disturbed. They rest quietly in foliage during the heat of the day, and feed and drink morning and evening. They feed on grass and herb seeds, the seeds of acacias, berries such as mistletoe *Viscum album*, fruits and insects. Nesting takes place from Jul to Dec, but also at other times of year, especially after good rains. The display is similar to that of Red-rumped Parrot and includes mutual preening. The nest is usually in a tree-hollow, although some man-made and other natural holes, like sand-bank tunnels, have been used. Much of the Mulga Parrot's habitat includes small, stunted trees where the nest entrance may be close to the ground, although riverine woods do provide higher nest-hollows. The female incubates for 19 days and the male remains nearby to feed her and warn of danger. The white-downed young fledge in four weeks and join the adults to form family groups on leaving the nest.

DESCRIPTION Head bright emerald-green, forehead orange-yellow, nape dull red. Mantle dark green with fine dark edgings; lower back with a pale blue-green band bordered above and below by a dark blue-green line; uppertail-coverts bright green marked red-orange centrally. Bend of wing turquoise-blue; lesser coverts orange-yellow; median coverts light blue-green; outer greater coverts mid-blue, inner green edged lighter blue; primary coverts dark blue. Flight feathers black with dark blue outerwebs (inner secondaries edged greener); tertials green with innerwebs marked black. Underwing-coverts blue. Breast bright green with fine dark fringes, shading to yellow, with orange fringes, on undertail-coverts; belly and thighs strongly marked red. Uppertail bronze-green at base becoming blue-green, and grading to dull blue towards tip, outer feathers basally green and blue tipped white; undertail basally light blue grading to white and tipped black. **Bare parts**: Bill dark grey; iris brown; legs grey.

SEX/AGE Female much duller with forehead dull orange-yellow, cheeks and forecrown pale green, nape suffused reddish-brown, upperparts mainly greyish-olive, light turquoise rump with paler band. Breast olive-brown, belly and undertail-coverts pale green. Shoulder-patch russet, wing-coverts generally light brownish-green tipped light blue, with lighter blue bend of wing and greater coverts. Off-white wing-bar. Bill brownish-grey. Immature like female, but young male with orange-yellow abdomen and shoulder-patch with a wing-bar, young female duller than adult. Adult plumage is attained in two to three months; males lose wing-bar in 12 months.

MEASUREMENTS Wing 125-145; tail 155-174; bill 12-14; tarsus 15-17.

GEOGRAPHICAL VARIATION None.

REFERENCES Blakers *et al.* (1984), Buckingham & Jackson (1990), Emison *et al.* (1987), Forshaw (1981, 1989), Lambert *et al.* (1993), Lodge (1991), Peters (1961), Pizzey & Doyle (1983), Saunders (1989), Schodde & Tidemann (1988), Sibley & Monroe (1990), Simpson & Day (1984), Slater (1979, 1989), Storr & Johnstone (1979), Taylor (1987).

137 HOODED PARROT
Psephotus dissimilis   Plate 35

Other names: Black-hooded Parakeet, Anthill Parrot

IDENTIFICATION 25.5-28cm. An extremely striking species restricted to dry woodlands of northernmost Australia. The male has a black cap, turquoise underparts and a golden-yellow shoulder-patch. Females are light green with a pale turquoise suffusion on the cheeks, belly and rump. The closely related Golden-shouldered Parrot (138) is very similar in appearance, but occurs only in the Cape York Peninsula of northern Queensland, and the male differs from male Hooded in its yellow forehead and lores, smaller yellow shoulder-patch and reddish belly-patch. Females are very similar, but Golden-shouldered shows faint red markings against a white lower belly, with bluish undertail-coverts, not a bluish belly with pinkish vent and undertail-coverts; it also has a brownish suffusion on the crown, a yellowish forehead and greener cheeks. Northern Rosella (130) is sympatric with Hooded Parrot and also has a black cap, but lacks the turquoise underparts and yellow wing-patch. Hooded Parrots have a slender flight profile, and males are extremely striking with a brilliant yellow flash showing on the wing. The flight is swift and slightly undulating. Birds sometimes perch conspicuously on telephone wires, and may undertake longer flights at height.

VOICE Contact call a *chiwee* and a harsher *tchick*, higher-pitched than the call of Golden-shouldered Parrot. Also, various high chattering calls and some harsher notes, similar to those of Red-rumped Parrot (135).

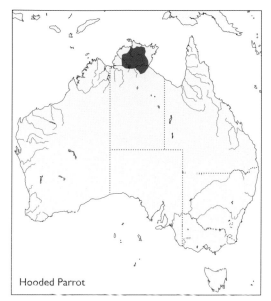

Hooded Parrot

DISTRIBUTION AND STATUS Endemic to northern Australia where it occurs in the western part of Arnhem Land, Northern Territory, ranging from the South Alligator River, south-west to Pine Creek and south-east to Mataranka. Birds are also scattered further east and west as far as the Roper and upper Daly Rivers. The species formerly extended east to the MacArthur River, but its range, which embraces Kakadu National Park, has contracted in recent times. It is generally uncommon. Although now fully protected, trapping is thought to have been a problem in the past, along with burning and grazing regimes which may limit the availability of dry season grass seed. Mining also threatens habitat in part of the species's range. The world population is probably in excess of 15,000. Moderate numbers in captivity. CITES Appendix I. NEAR-THREATENED.

ECOLOGY Sedentary, although some early records from Melville Island probably relate to post-breeding dispersal. Scattered sparsely through dry open woodland, especially *Melaleuca*-dominated flood-plains and spinifex *Triodia* grassland with terrestrial termite mounds, also in eucalypts along watercourses and rocky ridges. They are generally encountered in pairs or small parties, but after the breeding season, from Sep onwards (late dry season), they may congregate in groups of up to 100 to feed. The diet is primarily the seeds of seasonal grasses during the dry season and perennials during the wet. Variation in the ability to master feeding techniques for the various seed types may explain the apparent dispersal of immatures in the early wet season. Birds feed quietly on the ground, resting in foliage near water during the heat of the day. When drinking, they often walk out into the water along sandy spits. They are sometimes seen feeding on roadside verges, often in association with Black-faced Woodswallows *Artamus cinereus*. The eggs are laid from late Jan to mid Apr, at the end of the wet season, and the nest is tunnelled into a terrestrial termitarium. The direction and height of the nest entrance is variable, but nest-chamber temperatures are more stable within the larger mounds. A recent study of nesting ecology in the Northern Territory showed a density of 0.45 to 0.70 nests per km², with 50%

of the eggs producing fledglings. Between two and six white eggs are laid, and the white-downed young are incubated for around 20 days by the female, fledging in about five weeks. Females will sometimes roost together away from their nests during the heat of the day.

DESCRIPTION Cap, lores and area below and in front of eye black, merging into grey-brown of mantle (upperparts darker than in Golden-shouldered). Rump turquoise-blue, uppertail-coverts greener. Wing-coverts golden-yellow (greaters dark grey on innerweb). Flight feathers blackish with turquoise-green suffusion on leading edge of outerwebs (fine yellow outer margin on outermost). Underwing-coverts and bend of wing bluish-green; underside of flight feathers blackish-brown. Cheeks, neck and breast turquoise-blue suffused slightly with emerald-green; rest of underparts turquoise except for undertail-coverts which are orange-red tipped yellow. Uppertail-coverts with dark bars. Central tail feathers bronze-green above tipped black, lateral blue-green tipped white, with blackish central bar; undertail seemingly light blue tipped black when closed. **Bare parts**: Bill pale grey; iris dark brown; legs mid-brown.

SEX/AGE Female generally pale, slightly yellowish-green, with brighter yellow-green wing-coverts, blackish flight feathers, and a turquoise suffusion on the rump, from the lower breast to the belly, and vaguely on the cheeks. Vent and undertail-coverts suffused salmon-pink (latter with paler margins); pale wing-bar. Immature birds are like females, but males have darker heads and brighter cheeks. Adult plumage is gained at the second annual moult. Very young birds have yellow bills.

MEASUREMENTS Wing 115-127; tail 148-162; bill 12-14; tarsus 14-18.

GEOGRAPHICAL VARIATION None.

REFERENCES BirdLife (1993), Blakers *et al.* (1984), Brouwer & Garnett (1990), Buckingham & Jackson (1990), Collar & Andrew (1988), Forshaw (1981, 1989, 1990a), Garnett & Crowley (1995), Hutchins (1985), King (1981), Lambert *et al.* (1993), Peters (1961), Pizzey & Doyle (1983), Reed & Tidemann (1994), Schodde & Tidemann (1988), Sibley & Monroe (1990), Simpson & Day (1984), Slater (1979, 1989).

138 GOLDEN-SHOULDERED PARROT
Psephotus chrysopterygius   Plate 35

Other names: Golden-winged Parrot, Ant-bed Parrot

IDENTIFICATION 24-27cm Extremely rare and restricted to a tiny area of northern Queensland centred around Musgrave. The entire world range may be as little as 800 km². Male and female are similar in appearance to the respective sex of Hooded Parrot, but males show a yellow forehead, red belly marked with white, and a duller and more restricted yellow shoulder-patch, while females show some red markings on the lower belly and lack the latter's salmon suffusion on the vent and undertail-coverts; they also show a brownish crown, yellowish forehead and greener cheeks. Like the Hooded Parrot, this species has a slender, long-tailed profile, and a characteristic upright posture when perched. The flight is swift and slightly undulating.

Two-syllable contact call *tchweep* or *tchirrup*, not as high-pitched as that of Hooded Parrot. Also described as a whistle-like *fweep-fweep* or *few-weep...few-weep*.

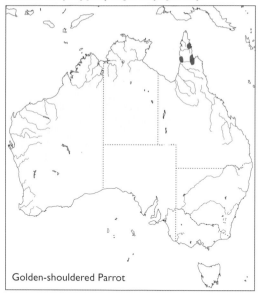

Golden-shouldered Parrot

DISTRIBUTION AND STATUS Endemic to north-east Australia where it occurs only in a small area north of the Morehead River and south from Musgrave, northern Queensland. There are presently at least four populations, each with between 30 and 100 birds, so that the world population may be no more than 500 individuals, or 150 breeding pairs. A record from 1980 extended its known range north to the Pascoe River, but in general it has contracted markedly in the last 100 years, previously ranging south to around Normanton. It was trapped heavily in the past, especially from the mid-1960s to the early 1970s. However, grazing and burning regimes, the spread of tea trees *Leptospermum*, cat predation and nest disturbance by tourists may all have played a further part in the species's decline. Although it is now protected, some trapping probably still goes on. CITES Appendix I. Small numbers in captivity. ENDANGERED.

ECOLOGY Sedentary except for some post-breeding dispersal, which may take birds into mangroves. The birds breed along the edges of partly inundated drainage depressions with scattered terrestrial termite mounds in mixed open woodland and grass understorey, common trees in such habitat including melaleucas and eucalypts (e.g. *Eucalyptus polycarpa*). Golden-shouldered Parrots are usually found singly, in pairs or in family parties, sometimes gathering in flocks of up to 30 birds. The birds feed and drink in the morning and late afternoon, resting in foliage during the hottest part of the day. They feed on the ground where they can be quite confiding, flying to nearby trees when disturbed; they will walk into water holes to drink. They subsist primarily on the seeds of grasses (e.g. *Panicum*, *Setaria* and *Eragrostis*), either fallen or plucked from the seedhead. During the wet season, food may be scarcer and, like Hooded Parrots, they probably then rely heavily on perennial species. Breeding takes place between Apr and Aug. The male makes short flights around the female during courtship, whilst raising his frontal feathers in a short crest and sidling towards her with breast feathers

puffed out. The nest-hollow is excavated in a terrestrial termite mound still damp from the wet season. The birds utilise two types of mound, conical ones made by *Amitermes scopulus* and meridian ones made by *A. laurensis*; conical mounds are preferred because the temperature remains more constant, while in meridian mounds the entrance is usually north-facing. Mounds may contain a number of partially completed chambers, although birds may also re-use hollows from previous years. The entrance hole, some 45-125cm above ground, is around 4cm in diameter and leads through a 15-60cm tunnel to a rounded chamber about 25cm long. The chamber itself remains free of litter owing to the larvae of a moth *Trisyntopa scatophaga* which lays its eggs at the same time as the parrots; the larvae pupate when the chicks fledge. The five to six or even seven white eggs are incubated by the female for around 20 days; the chicks take about five weeks to fledge, and are brooded for around a week at first. The male joins in with feeding the chicks and stands guard atop the nesting mound for periods during the day. The birds are capable of flying straight into the tunnel without alighting, but generally use their tail to gain purchase against the mound. The male joins in feeding the chicks, and calls to the female when arriving at the nest, the two often leaving to feed away from the nest together. Pairs are territorial and tend to nest around a kilometre apart. Once the young leave the nest they are fed by the parents for a further two weeks or so, but remain in small family parties for some time. They may breed before attaining adult plumage.

DESCRIPTION Crown black, with forehead, lores and area below eye yellow, tinged slightly greenish-blue; black of cap merges into grey-brown of mantle, with some slight blue suffusion at rear of nape. Rump bright turquoise, uppertail-coverts greener. Median wing-coverts bright yellow; greater coverts blackish-brown marked light turquoise-blue. Flight feathers blackish edged turquoise-blue on outerwebs. Underwing-coverts blue. Underparts turquoise-blue (greener on cheeks), except for lower abdomen and undertail-coverts which are red marked white at bases and tips of feathers. Central tail feathers basally bronze, tipped blue-black, lateral feathers greenish-blue tipped white, with blackish central bar; undertail bluish-white tipped black. **Bare parts**: Bill pale grey; iris dark brown; legs brownish-grey.

SEX/AGE Female generally dull yellowish-green with a brownish wash on crown and a yellowish forehead. Flanks, lower breast and rump are washed pale blue; the belly is whitish-green marked red, and there is a pale wing-bar. Immature birds are similar to females, but males have darker crowns and more turquoise cheeks. There is a body moult at four months, and full adult plumage is attained in around 16 months. Very young birds show yellow bills.

MEASUREMENTS Wing 106-113; tail 133-157; bill 11-13; tarsus 14-15.

GEOGRAPHICAL VARIATION None.

REFERENCES BirdLife (1993), Blakers *et al.* (1984), Brouwer & Garnett (1990), Buckingham & Jackson (1990), Chapman (1990), Collar & Andrew (1988), Collar *et al.* (1994), Forshaw (1981, 1989, 1990a), Garnett (1992), Garnett & Crowley (1995), Hutchins (1985), Joseph (1988b), King (1981), Lambert *et al.* (1993), Peters (1961), Pizzey & Doyle (1983), Schodde & Tidemann (1988), Sibley & Monroe (1990), Simpson & Day (1984), Slater (1979, 1989), Weaver (1982, 1987).

139 PARADISE PARROT
Psephotus pulcherrimus   **Plate 35**

Other names: Beautiful Parrot, Scarlet-shouldered Parrot, Soldier Parrot

IDENTIFICATION 27-30cm. It is extremely unlikely that any individuals of this species still exist, but it is included here to help prevent confusion with similar species which could lead to erroneous reports. The male Paradise Parrot was the only Australian species to show a combination of a black cap, red shoulder and belly, turquoise-green underparts and turquoise rump, the female having a smaller red shoulder-patch, pale orange suffusion on the breast and a pale blue belly. The sympatric red-shouldered form *haematorrhous* of the Bluebonnet (134) lacks blue or green on the underparts, the red forehead and black crown; it is also stockier, generally appears greyish-brown with a darker blue face, and has a different call. Some early reports of Paradise Parrot from the Archer River may have referred to Golden-shouldered Parrots (138), which can show very worn plumage at the end of the breeding season; even then, however, the yellow wing-coverts and frontal band of male Golden-shouldered are diagnostic at close range. Like its congeners, this species appeared slim and long-tailed and perched in a characteristic upright position.

VOICE Alarm call a short metallic *queek*. Also a plaintive *tit-sweet* and various soft musical whistles.

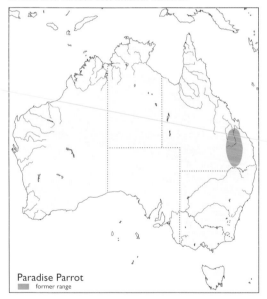

Paradise Parrot
former range

DISTRIBUTION AND STATUS Almost certainly now extinct with no confirmed records since 1927. Previously ranged through south-east Queensland and north-east New South Wales north to around Rockhampton, with a few records further north still, inland to Mantuan Downs, and to Moree and Inverell in the south. The species was also recorded from near Casino and Brisbane. It was locally common before widespread overgrazing and artificial fire regimes began reducing its food supply. A severe drought in 1902 has also been cited as a contributing factor, along with excessive trapping and the spread of the exotic prickly

pear. From the 1880s to the 1920s the species underwent a rapid decline, the last breeding record coming from the Burnett River area of south-east Queensland in 1922. CITES Appendix I. EXTINCT.

ECOLOGY Paradise Parrots inhabited open grassy eucalypt woodland with scattered terrestrial termite mounds. They were also found in scrubby grassland and along wooded watercourses. The birds fed quietly on the ground in pairs or family parties on the seeds of grasses and herbs. They would take fallen seeds, remove them from the seedhead with the bill, or clamber onto the stem to bend it to the ground where it was more easily reached. They nested in termite mounds or earth banks and occasionally other locations. The breeding season lasted from Apr to Aug, the breeding behaviour being similar to that of the two preceding species.

DESCRIPTION Centre of crown black, forehead and lores bright red, ear-coverts and cheeks turquoise-green, with some yellow around the eye. Crown grades into dark grey-brown of mantle; rump turquoise-blue, uppertail-coverts slightly greener. Bend of wing red; lesser, median and inner greater coverts bright red; outer greater coverts and tertials dark grey-brown; primary coverts black. Primaries blackish with fine dull turquoise margins to outerwebs; secondaries dark brown. Underwing-coverts and axillaries blue. Throat and upper breast bright green tipped slightly darker; lower breast and upper abdomen turquoise, again tipped darker; lower abdomen and vent red tipped white; undertail-coverts red. Central tail feathers bronze-green basally, grading darker and bluer towards tips; lateral feathers greenish-blue tipped bluish-white; undertail appears bluish-white when closed. **Bare parts**: Bill greyish; iris brown; legs greyish-brown.

SEX/AGE Female lacks the pronounced red markings of the male, with underparts paler, suffused buff, slightly scalloped orange-brown on the face and breast, and washed palest turquoise on the belly and undertail-coverts; rump pale turquoise. The crown is brownish-black, sometimes with red on the forehead, and the red shoulder-patch is limited to the lesser and inner median coverts. There is a whitish wing-bar. Immatures are duller than females and also show a wing-bar; young males show some green feathers on the face and have a blacker crown and more obvious red shoulder-patch.

MEASUREMENTS Wing 121-135; tail 143-182; bill 12-14; tarsus 16-19.

GEOGRAPHICAL VARIATION None.

REFERENCES Blakers *et al.* (1984), Collar & Andrew (1988), Forshaw (1981, 1989), Garnett (1992), Joseph (1988b), King (1981), Lodge (1991), Peters (1961), Pizzey & Doyle (1983), Schodde & Tidemann (1988), Sibley & Monroe (1990), Simpson & Day (1984), Slater (1979, 1989).

140 ANTIPODES PARAKEET
Cyanoramphus unicolor   **Plate 36**

Other names: Antipodes Green Parakeet, Antipodes Island Parakeet, Antipodes Unicolour Parakeet, Uniform Parakeet

IDENTIFICATION 29-31.5cm. The largest *Cyanoramphus*

parrot. Only found on Antipodes Island and its satellites, where it can be separated from the sympatric Red-fronted Parakeet (142) by its larger size, bright emerald-green (not red) crown, and broad, blunt, pale-based bill. When disturbed it usually makes for cover quietly, while Red-fronted normally flies off calling. Despite their highly terrestrial habits, Antipodes Parakeets are strong flyers and can be seen swooping around the slopes or above the main plateau in good weather.

VOICE Similar to Red-fronted but has some deeper and softer conversational notes. Calls transcribed as *pretty-dick* and *twenty-eight*. Also a deep, resonant *kok-kok-kok-kok-kok* with a bubbling quality in common with other *Cyanoramphus* species. Alarm call varies from a soft clucking to a loud high-pitched chatter. Young beg with a rapid high *aw-dit-dit aw-dit-dit-dit*.

Antipodes Parakeet

Antipodes Islands

DISTRIBUTION AND STATUS Endemic to the main Antipodes Island, plus Bollans, Leeward, Inner Windward and Archway Islands. World population 2,000-3,000. Although common and stable within its range, the species is permanently at risk from the accidental introduction of predators, which could wipe it out in a short time. A few birds are kept in captivity in New Zealand. VULNERABLE.

ECOLOGY Occurs in dense tall *Poa littorosa* tussocks, open scrub and *Carex* sedge. Habitat on the island also comprises areas of prickly fern *Polystichum vestitum* and *Coprosma antipoda* scrub. The birds are commonest on steeper slopes and near watercourses, but are found singly or in small groups; they walk and climb when feeding, which is undertaken mainly in the morning and before dusk. The main diet is leaves, which are chewed; piles of crushed chewings still attached to the plant are a distinctive sign of feeding. They also consume leaves, seeds, berries, the remains of dead penguins and petrels, and the eggs of seabirds, and freely enter colonies of Rockhopper *Eudyptes crestatus* and Erect-crested Penguins *E. sclateri* between Oct and May to investigate food sources. (The sympatric Red-fronted Parakeet avoids interspecific competition by

exploiting a niche provided by seeds, flowers, berries and invertebrates.) Birds are very tame and inquisitive, and may peck at tent seams. When alarmed they disappear into dense vegetation, keeping silent or giving a short alarm call. Over the middle of the day they bask and preen in sheltered areas. They bathe in pools and roost in burrows. Nesting is from Oct to Jan. During breeding, females have overlapping ranges and males remain well spaced, keeping territorial disputes to a minimum. Nests are placed in well-drained burrows up to a metre deep, beneath tall tussocks. Five white eggs are incubated for around 28 days, and one to three grey-downed young are raised. The male will feed the female and young, and continues for at least a week after the chicks leave the nest, by which time they can fly strongly. The young of Red-fronted Parakeets fledge a little later, further ameliorating any competition between the two species. Adults moult after breeding. The young reach breeding maturity in one year.

DESCRIPTION Generally yellowish-green, yellower below, and sometimes with irregular yellow markings on upperparts. Crown and face bright emerald-green with slight bluish sheen. Alula, primary coverts and outerwebs of outer primaries blue; greater coverts with yellow edgings; tertials also with yellowish fringes. Underwing-coverts green. Underside of flight feathers blackish-brown. Pointed tail dark green above with yellow edges to outerwebs; undertail yellowish with paler outerwebs. **Bare parts**: Bill tipped black, basally pale blue-grey; iris variable, from yellow to reddish-brown; legs stout, greyish-brown.

SEX/AGE Sexes alike, but female slightly smaller. Young birds are shorter-tailed than adults with a pinkish base to the bill when newly fledged.

MEASUREMENTS Wing 141-157; tail 116-150; bill 19-24; tarsus 25-28.

GEOGRAPHICAL VARIATION None.

REFERENCES BirdLife (1993), Collar & Andrew (1988), Collar *et al.* (1994), Falla *et al.* (1981), Forshaw (1989), Lodge (1991), Phipps (1983), Robertson (1985), Sibley & Monroe (1990), Taylor (1985).

141 NORFOLK ISLAND PARAKEET
Cyanoramphus cookii   Plate 36

Other names: Norfolk Parakeet, Green Parrot, Norfolk Island Green Parrot

IDENTIFICATION 30cm. Restricted to the forests of the Mount Pitt Reserve on Norfolk Island. Mainly green with a blue wing-flash and red head-markings. Only two parrot species occur on the island, the other being the introduced Crimson Rosella (128), whose adults are mainly bright red and pose no identification problem, while juveniles, though mostly green, are usually found in company with adults and show blue cheeks and red markings on the lower abdomen. The Norfolk Island Parakeet has only recently been separated from Red-fronted (142) and New Caledonian Parakeet (143): it is similar to both but larger and heavier-billed, the red of the crown extending farther back and the red on the ear-coverts forming a discrete patch rather than extending the stripe from the lores through the eye (a feature shared by the other two species). The flight is swift, with rapid shallow beats punctuated by glides on outstretched wings, and is less undulating than that of the rosellas.

VOICE Loud *kakakaka*, *kek-kek-kek-kek-kek* or *kek-kik-kek*.

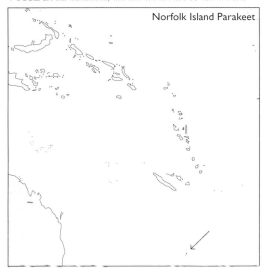

Norfolk Island Parakeet

DISTRIBUTION AND STATUS Endemic to Norfolk Island, where the world population was 40 (plus 13 in captivity) in 1991, but slowly increasing. The species is largely confined to the 465 ha Mount Pitt National Park, declared in 1986, occasionally entering surrounding forest. It was formerly more numerous, but a sharp decline occurred when European settlers began clearing the island's forests. Nesting trees were lost, and birds were also killed to protect crops. The problem was compounded by introduced predators, particularly black rats *Rattus rattus*, and the introduced nest-competitors in the form of rosellas and European Starlings *Sturnus vulgaris*. The species survived a disease outbreak that wiped out many rosellas in 1976, and only one affected bird was seen. In 1983 the Australian National Parks and Wildlife Service began a captive-breeding programme which has had some success. The Mount Pitt National Park is now managed for the parakeets, and rosellas, cats, rats and honeybees *Apis mellifera*, which also compete for tree-hollows, are carefully controlled. Potential nest-sites have also been improved, particularly in an attempt to exclude rats. As the parakeets rarely raise a full clutch to maturity, some eggs have been pulled for hand-rearing. The establishment of a second population on Philip Island has been suggested as a potential next step for the species's recovery. CITES Appendix I. Fully protected. CRITICAL.

ECOLOGY Sedentary. The species occurs in rainforest and very occasionally in gardens (previously in groups in orchards). Large groups are no longer seen and pairs or small parties are most frequently encountered. Birds are most easily located by call, and are active early morning when they can be seen twisting and turning through the trees on darting flights, or perched at the top of an exposed Norfolk Island pine *Araucaria heterophylla* calling loudly. They also rest to preen in sunny locations, but during the day they spend much of their time feeding unobtrusively in forest trees, particularly on the cones of Norfolk Island pines. Because of their tameness they can easily be overlooked as they feed, and the clicking of their bills and falling debris are often the only sign of their presence. They also feed on the ground, sweeping litter aside with their feet in search of seeds. The diet includes a variety of fruits, shoots, blossoms and the seeds of shrubs and trees like bloodwoods *Baloghia lucida* and introduced wild olives *Olea africana*. The main nesting period falls between Oct and Dec, but can be more extended and sometimes occurs more than once a year. The nest-site is usually a hollow in a living tree, ironwoods *Nestegis apetala*, bloodwoods or Norfolk Island pines being favoured, although tree-ferns have also been used. The entrance is normally within two metres of the ground, and leads to a metre-long tunnel ending in a chamber 20-40cm in diameter. One to eight, usually six, white eggs are laid and incubated by the female for 21 days. The three to four young fledge in about 44 days, and while they are in the nest the male feeds the hen when she leaves the hollow, and she in turn feeds the chicks (courtship feeding is also common). The fledglings are dependent on the adults for another two to three weeks. In some cases, males may complete the rearing of the brood while the female begins a new clutch at an alternative site.

DESCRIPTION Generally bright green with slightly yellower underparts. Forehead, crown, lores and discrete patch behind eye red. Upperwing-coverts green; primary coverts and outerwebs of primaries violet-blue; fine yellowish outer margin to outer primaries. Underwing-coverts yellowish-green; red patch either side of rump. Uppertail dark green with yellower edges to outerwebs; undertail dusky grey. **Bare parts**: Bill blue-grey on upper mandible grading to black at tip, lower mandible greyish-black; iris red; legs grey-brown.

SEX/AGE Female slightly smaller with smaller narrower bill and less red behind eye; females and some males show a wing-bar. Immatures show a brown iris, shorter tail and less obvious red head-markings.

MEASUREMENTS Wing 128-150; tail 136-183; bill 17-23; tarsus 21-25.

GEOGRAPHICAL VARIATION None.

REFERENCES BirdLife (1993), Collar *et al.* (1994), Forshaw (1981, 1989), Garnett (1992), Hay (1986), Hermes (1985), Hicks (1992), Hicks & Greenwood (1989), King (1981), Lambert *et al.* (1993), Phipps (1983), Schodde *et al.* (1983), Sibley & Monroe (1990, 1993), Taylor (1985).

142 RED-FRONTED PARAKEET
Cyanoramphus novaezelandiae Plate 36

Other names: Kakariki, New Zealand Parakeet, Red-crowned Parakeet, Red-fronted New Zealand Parakeet, Red-fronted Kakariki, Red-crowned Parrot (also used for Jardine's Parrot and Green-cheeked Amazon); Reischek's Parakeet (*C. n. hochstetteri*); Kermadec Parakeet (*C. n. cyanurus*); Chatham Island Red-crowned Parakeet (*C. n. chathamensis*)

IDENTIFICATION 23-28cm. A medium-sized stocky parakeet with a long graduated tail and longish legs, occurring in New Zealand and on some outlying islands. The species is mainly green with red head-markings, a red patch either side of the rump and a blue wing-flash. It closely resembles the recently separated allopatric Norfolk Island Parakeet (141), and New Caledonian Parakeet (143) (see descriptions under these species for differences). It also resembles the closely related sympatric Yellow-fronted Parakeet (144), from which it can be separated by its red, not yellow, crown and red eye-stripe; their calls are similar but distinguishable. The two species occasionally hybridise in the wild, particularly in the Chatham Islands, although control measures to prevent genetic swamping of the indigenous Yellow-fronted Parakeets there is proving effective (see *C. a. forbesi* below); hybrids show yellow or orange feathers in the red of the crown, especially at the hind margin. The flight is swift, direct and slightly undulating, with brief glides on outstretched wings. The tail is usually spread on landing.

VOICE A rapid *ki-ki-ki-ki-ki* or *kek-kik-kek* given as the bird takes off and also in flight. There are also a variety of soft chattering calls, a soft musical *tu-tu-tu-tu*, as well as a trisyllabic call rendered as *pretty-dick* or *do be quick*. All calls are stronger and lower-pitched than those of Yellow-fronted.

Kermadec Island ⟶

Chatham Islands

Antipodes Islands

Auckland Islands

Red-fronted Parakeet

DISTRIBUTION AND STATUS Occurs in New Zealand and on a number of adjacent and outlying island groups. Before European settlement, the species was widespread on the mainland, but in the 1890s the population began to crash as a result of habitat clearance and predation by introduced mustelids and cats. Today the species is scarce on the mainland and occurs only in the larger forest blocks, from Northland to the Coromandel Peninsula, Pirongia, Pureora and Hauhungaroa in central North Island, to Urewera, Raukumara and Huiarau in the east, and south to the Ruahine and Tararua Ranges. In South Island the species occurs around Nelson, in the Arthur's Pass area, in the Dunedin district and in Fiordland National Park. It is also found on a number of New

Zealand's offshore islands, where it is generally more numerous than on the mainland, including: Three Kings, Poor Knights (no Yellow-fronted here), Hen and Chickens, Tiritiri Matangi (introduced), Little Barrier (common), Great Barrier (scarce), Mercury, Aldermen, Kapiti, Stewart (and surrounding islets) and the Auckland Islands (Enderby, Rose, Ewing and Adams). Races are also found in the Kermadec group (Macauley, Meyer, Napier, Dayrell and Chanters, with stragglers to Curtis and Raoul), Chatham Islands (uncommon on Chatham and Pitt, abundant on South East Island, and controlled on Mangere and Little Mangere to prevent interbreeding with *C. a. forbesi*), and in the Antipodes Islands (Antipodes, Bollans, Leeward, Archway and Windward Islands). The world population is certainly in excess of 15,000 but still decreasing owing to habitat loss and predation. Hybridisation with Yellow-fronted Parakeets is also a problem in some populations. The Chatham Island race is threatened, with a population of less than 1,000. The Kermadec race is still relatively common with around 10,000 individuals on Macauley. There are at least 4,000-5,000 birds in the Antipodes group. Captive birds have been liberated in the Wairarapa and Waitakere Ranges. CITES Appendix I.

ECOLOGY Habitat includes native forest on mainland New Zealand to open scrub on some outlying islands and tussock grassland on Antipodes Island. The species is generally more partial to forest edge and open areas than Yellow-fronted, and in regions where the two are sympatric it generally occurs at lower altitudes. The birds are often first located by call as they shoot over or through the forest canopy, and are most frequently encountered in pairs, which remain together through the year. However, groups gather at food sources in any month, and where fresh water is scarce birds may also congregate to drink at springs or seepages. In the Kermadec Islands, flocks form to bathe in intertidal pools and roost communally (probably elsewhere also). The birds feed actively in the early morning, resting and preening during much of the day, and feeding again in the afternoon. They forage both in the canopy and on the ground for a wide range of vegetable material including fruits, seeds, leaves, buds, berries, flowers, nectar and shoots; fallen seed is especially favoured in autumn and winter. The species also feeds on invertebrates, honeydew and, in the Kermadecs, even seaweed and small limpets *Scutellastra kermadecensis*. Nesting takes place between Oct and Mar, with most laying in Oct-Dec. Between two and ten (usually five to nine) white eggs are laid in a tree-hollow lined with powdered wood, although other sites, including rock crevices, ground burrows and tussock *Poa litorosa* burrows have also been used, as have a variety of linings including feathers, moss and grass. The birds are territorial in the vicinity of the nest and may use a favoured site repeatedly. Incubation is carried out by the female and lasts 18-20 days, starting with the second egg (laying at one- to two-day intervals). The grey-downed chicks fledge in five to six weeks and the male will assist feeding either via the female or directly for a week or so after fledging. In large fledged broods some less-developed young may sometimes be seen. The adults undergo a post-breeding moult. Birds 'ant' using substitute vegetable matter.

DESCRIPTION Generally bright mid-green (occasionally with some variable yellow markings), with a crimson frontal band, lores and line through eye extending onto ear-coverts; centre of crown crimson extending back to above eye, with a green superciliary area. Upperparts uniform bright green with a red patch either side of rump. Alula, primary coverts and outerwebs of primaries violet-blue. Primaries emarginated with fine yellow outer margins; outerwebs of secondaries greener. Underwing-coverts green; pale spot on each innerweb of secondaries forms a wing-bar in some males. Underparts generally a more yellowish, paler green. Uppertail green; undertail dark grey. **Bare parts**: Bill basally pale bluish-grey, tipped black; iris red; legs greyish-brown.

SEX/AGE Female slightly smaller, although this may be less obvious in worn plumage when males may have a shorter tail. The male's larger head and bill should still be obvious given close comparative views. Females have an obvious wing-bar. Young birds have shorter tails, a pale reddish-brown iris, less distinct head-markings and, when recently fledged, a pinkish base to the bill.

MEASUREMENTS Wing 125-139; tail 115-158; bill 14-17; tarsus 19-22.

GEOGRAPHICAL VARIATION Four extant races; two others, formerly on Lord Howe and Macquarie Islands, are now extinct.

C. n. novaezelandiae (New Zealand and its offshore islands, as well as the Auckland Islands)
C. n. cyanurus (Kermadec Islands) More blue on flight feathers than nominate and shows a bluish-green tail. The underparts are also slightly greener.
C. n. chathamensis (Chatham Islands) Larger than nominate with a more emerald-green facial area and slightly yellower underparts.
C. n. hochstetteri (Antipodes Island and its surrounding islets) Slightly larger than nominate and generally much more yellowish-green, with more obvious yellow leading edge to the outer primaries. The blue wing-flash is less distinct, the red head-markings and rump-patches are more orange-red, and the iris is orange.

REFERENCES Ellis (1987), Falla *et al.* (1981), Forshaw (1989), Gardner (1988), Garnett (1992), Heatherbell (1992), Lambert *et al.* (1993), Lodge (1991), Peters (1961), Phipps (1983), Riley (1982), Robertson (1985), Sibley & Monroe (1990), Taylor (1985).

---

143 NEW CALEDONIAN PARAKEET
Cyanoramphus saisseti   Plate 36

IDENTIFICATION 26cm. The only medium-sized green parrot on New Caledonia with red patches either side of the rump. Superficially similar to the slightly larger sympatric Horned Parakeet (145), but lacks the crest, black face-patch and strong blue suffusion on the uppertail of that species. The species has recently been separated from Red-fronted Parakeet (142), and is distinguished by its bright yellow throat, yellower underparts, yellowish-green superciliary area and paler red head-markings. It is also similar to Norfolk Island Parakeet (141), but is much brighter yellow below. All three are, in any case, allopatric.

VOICE Undescribed but probably similar to Red-fronted.

DISTRIBUTION AND STATUS Endemic to the main island of New Caledonia where records come from the

Rivière-Bleue Forest Reserve and montane forest areas in the north and north-west, as well as from near Nouméa at 150m. There are few reports and poor observer coverage of the island, and although considered generally uncommon the species may still be fairly widespread and perhaps also reasonably common in some undisturbed areas.

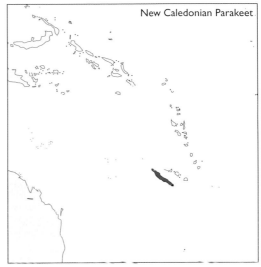

New Caledonian Parakeet

ECOLOGY Occupies indigenous montane forests. The New Caledonian Parakeet is usually found singly or in pairs feeding quietly and unobtrusively in the lower or middle storey, or scratching for seeds on the ground. Although they are not shy, they can be very quiet and hard to observe, flying swiftly through the upper canopy, sometimes perching and resting high in trees. They feed on the fruits and seeds of plants including casuarinas and pawpaws *Carica papaya*. Nesting takes place between Nov and Jun and two to four eggs are laid on a bed of leaves in a tree-hollow.

DESCRIPTION Generally bright mid-green, with frontal band, lores and line through eye red, extending in a narrow line onto ear-coverts; centre of crown red extending back to above eye, with a yellow-green superciliary area. Upperparts uniform bright green with red patch either side of rump. Alula, primary coverts and outerwebs of primaries violet-blue; fine yellow outer margin to outer primaries. Wing-bar present in some males. Throat bright yellow, rest of underparts yellow-green. Uppertail green slightly washed blue; undertail dark grey. **Bare parts**: Bill basally bluish-grey, tipped black; iris dark red; legs dark grey.

SEX/AGE Female and immature show a wing-bar.

MEASUREMENTS Wing 114-135; tail 130-170; bill 13-18; tarsus 17-21.

GEOGRAPHICAL VARIATION None.

REFERENCES Arndt (1992), Forshaw (1989), Mayr (1945), Phipps (1983), Sibley & Monroe (1990, 1993), Stokes (1980), Taylor (1985).

144 YELLOW-FRONTED PARAKEET
Cyanoramphus auriceps   Plate 36

Other names: Kakariki (also used for Red-fronted Parakeet), Yellow-fronted New Zealand Parakeet, Yellow-crowned Parakeet, Yellow-fronted Kakariki; Forbes's Parakeet (*C. a. forbesi*); Orange-fronted Parakeet (orange-fronted morph, sometimes given the specific or subspecific name *C. a. malherbi*)

IDENTIFICATION 23-25.5cm. A smallish, mainly green parakeet with a conspicuous red forehead and red patches either side of the rump, a yellow crown and a blue wing-flash, occurring in larger native forests of mainland New Zealand and on some surrounding islands. Red-fronted Parakeet (142) is sympatric and can best be separated by its red, not yellow, crown and its red ear-coverts and eye-stripe; but both species show red foreheads. Yellow-fronted Parakeet has a rare orange-fronted morph which is sometimes considered a full species. Orange-fronted birds are only found in some populations and can be difficult to separate in poor light or without good views. This form shows an orange, not red, forehead, and orange patches either side of the rump. There were only a handful of records this century until a few individuals were recently found mixed with Yellow-fronted birds at Lake Sumner Forest Park in the Hope River area, and in the Hawden River Valley, both on South Island. Yellow-fronted and Red-fronted Parakeets hybridise occasionally in the wild, and hybrids between *C. a. forbesi* and *C. n. chathamensis* threaten the genetic purity of the former in the Chatham Islands. Hybrids show some orange and yellow feathers in the crown, particularly towards the rear margin, as well as an orange patch behind the eye. The flight of this species is swift, buoyant and interspersed with glides on outstretched wings. On South Island, Yellow-fronted Parakeets are often found in the company of Yellowheads *Mohoua ochrocephala*.

VOICE Very similar to Red-fronted but higher-pitched and weaker, especially the flight call *ki-ki-ki-ki-ki* or *keek-keek-keek-keek*.

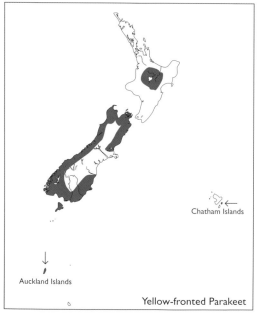
Chatham Islands

Auckland Islands

Yellow-fronted Parakeet

DISTRIBUTION AND STATUS Confined to New Zealand and some offshore islands. The species's range and numbers were badly affected by habitat clearance and introduced predators with the advent of European settlement, but may now be increasing; it is probably commoner than Red-fronted on the mainland. The world population is thought to be less than 5,000. Yellow-fronted Parakeets are largely absent north of Auckland, but are moderately common in some of the larger forest blocks including Urewera, Raukumara, the Motu River area, Pirongia, Pureora, Ruahine, Tararua, and on South Island in the Abel Tasman National Park, the Nelson District, the Paparoa Range, Arthur's Pass area, the Hope River and Canterbury Districts, and in Fiordland around Te Anau and Cascade Creek. The possibility of further habitat clearance continues to be a threat to the species. Yellow-fronted Parakeets also occur on the following offshore islands: Three Kings, Hen, Big Chicken, Little Barrier, Great Barrier (rare), Kapiti (rare), the Chetwode Islands (no Red-fronted here), Stewart Island and satellite islets, Codfish, Solander, Ruapuke and the Auckland Islands, including Adams Island. The species also occurs in the Chatham Islands where the race *C. a. forbesi* has suffered through loss of habitat, as well as competition and hybridisation with Red-fronted Parakeets: both hybrids and Red-fronted Parakeets survive better in opened-up areas, and habitat improvement and control of hybrids is helping a slow recovery, with just 16 *forbesi* on Little Mangere and 40 on Mangere (Mangere is now a reserve, but the status of Little Mangere is still in dispute). *C. a. forbesi* is listed on CITES Appendix I. NEAR-THREATENED.

ECOLOGY On the mainland, chiefly in lush montane native forest favouring *Nothofagus* and *Podocarpus* ecosystems from around 600m. Although birds are found at much lower altitudes than this, the species tends to be found higher than Red-fronted, especially where their ranges overlap. Yellow-fronted is also more closely tied to continuous bush, and is less common in open habitats tolerated by Red-fronted. It is commoner on offshore islands where predation by introduced mammals is reduced. Birds are most frequently found in pairs or small groups feeding in the middle or upper storey of the forest or in larger shrubs. Although generally more arboreal than Red-fronted, they tend to feed on the ground more boldly on offshore islands. The diet consists of vegetable matter including shoots, buds, berries, flowers and seeds, plus invertebrates such as caterpillars, e.g. *Heliostibes vibratrix* and scale insects *Ultracoelostoma assimile*. Insects appear to be more important in the diet of Yellow-fronted than in that of Red-fronted. Breeding habits are similar to Red-fronted but birds seem more territorial around the nest. Most eggs are laid from Oct to Dec but nesting has occurred in almost all months, presumably in response to food availability. Five to nine white eggs are laid and incubated for 18-20 days. The young, tended by the female who in turn is fed by the male, fledge in five to six weeks.

DESCRIPTION Generally bright mid-green; frontal band and lores scarlet; ear-coverts green; centre of crown bright yellow to above eye. Upperparts green with a red patch either side of rump. Alula, primary coverts and outerwebs of primaries violet-blue. Underwing-coverts green with blue at leading edge; underwing-bar sometimes present. Underparts more yellowish-green, sometimes with yellow markings. Tail green above, dark grey below. **Bare parts**: Bill pale blue-grey at base, blackish at tip; iris orange-red; legs grey-brown.

SEX/AGE Females are slightly smaller than males. Young birds have paler bills, shorter tails and a pale brown iris. Female and young show an underwing-bar.

MEASUREMENTS Wing 106-112; tail 107-120; bill 11-15; tarsus 17-22.

GEOGRAPHICAL VARIATION Two races.

C. a. auriceps (New Zealand, on nearby offshore islands and in the Auckland Islands)

C. a. forbesi (Mangere and Little Mangere in the Chatham Islands) Larger than nominate (wing 121-131), heavier-billed, brighter green above, more yellowish below, with greener sides to the face, and a more limited red frontal band (does not reach the eye).

NOTE Genetic analysis of *C. a. forbesi* shows it to be strongly differentiated and possibly of specific status. The same work suggests that the orange-fronted morph should be reinstated as a separate species, *C. malherbi*.

REFERENCES Arndt (1992), Ellis (1987), Falla *et al.* (1981), Flack (1976), Forshaw (1989), Gardner (1988), Harrison (1970), King (1981), Lambert *et al* (1993), Lodge (1991), Nixon (1981), Peters (1961), Phipps (1983), Sibley & Monroe (1990), Robertson (1985), Taylor (1985), Triggs & Daugherty (1988, 1996).

---

145 HORNED PARAKEET
Eunymphicus cornutus Plate 36

Other names: Crested Parakeet

IDENTIFICATION 32cm. Found only in the hill forests of New Caledonia. This striking species resembles New Caledonian Parakeet when seen from a distance, but has much more yellow on the face, breast and particularly the hind-crown, and lacks red patches either side of the rump. The black area surrounding the bright orange eye, with no red mark on the ear-coverts, are diagnostic, as are the two red-tipped black crest feathers which can be seen from close range. The closely related Uvea Parakeet (146) is restricted to the nearby island of Uvea, has much less black, yellow and red in the face (face generally appearing green), and shows a crest of six upward-curving greenish-black feathers with no red tips. The flight of the Horned Parakeet is swift and slightly undulating.

VOICE The species shrieks harshly in alarm and has a range of chuckling notes when perched or feeding; at dawn, probably for contact, *ca-ca*; also a raucous *ko-kot... ko-kot.*

DISTRIBUTION AND STATUS Endemic to the main island of New Caledonia, where owing to the lack of observer coverage opinions over the species's status vary. It is probably stable but may be threatened by trade to some degree. Recent records from Rivière Bleue Forest Reserve indicate it is relatively common there; it has also been found at Mois de Mai. It almost certainly commonest in less accessible areas above 470m.

ECOLOGY Inhabits humid indigenous forests, second growth and savanna woodland. The species's stronghold is in the tall kauri *Agathis australis* forests of northern New Caledonia. It also occurs in mixed *Araucaria* forest. The birds are at times wary, but some will allow a close approach. They are most frequently heard before they are

seen (flying above the tree-tops), but remain silent and hence difficult to detect much of the time. They occur in pairs and small parties of up to ten birds, which will fly 100m or more when disturbed to land in the tree-tops, departing silently if pursued further. They feed on flowers, nuts, fruits, berries, seeds of trees and shrubs, and are also fond of ripe pawpaw *Carica papaya* (a snare placed in a pawpaw is a common trapping method). Horned Parakeets roost in the tree-tops or in tree-hollows, becoming active around an hour before dawn. In display they bow several times, ruffle their feathers, shake their crests and call intermittently. Breeding takes place from Oct to Dec, with the nest being in a hollow limb or cavity in a living tree e.g. *Metrosideros demonstrans*. Two to four eggs are laid and two young are usually raised to fledging.

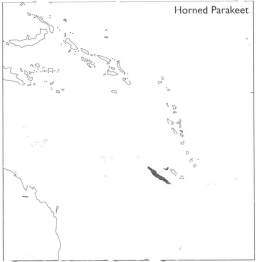

Horned Parakeet

DESCRIPTION Head with bright red, slightly ruffled feathers on centre of forecrown (basally black), two elongated black feathers with red tips rising from mid-crown; ear-coverts yellow-orange, lores and sides of cheeks black, and lower cheeks greenish-black (exposed skin around eye black); hind-crown and nape bright yellow-orange grading through yellow to bright yellow-green on upper mantle. Upperparts green, with greenish-orange rump. Wing-coverts green. Primaries violet-blue on outer-webs, blackish on innerwebs; secondaries greener on outerwebs. Underwing-coverts green. Underparts light yellowish-green with slight bluish tinge to tips of undertail coverts. Uppertail green basally, strongly suffused blue towards tip; undertail dark grey. **Bare parts:** Bill blue-grey tipped black; iris orange, eye black.

SEX/AGE Sexes alike. Young have greyer, less extensive facial markings, the ear-coverts are pale green, the hindneck is olive green, the bill horn-coloured and the iris brown.

MEASUREMENTS Wing 151-171; tail 139-175; bill 17-21; tarsus 19-22.

GEOGRAPHICAL VARIATION None.

REFERENCES BirdLife (1993), Forshaw (1989), King (1981), Lambert *et al.* (1993), Lodge (1991), Mayr (1945), Sibley & Monroe (1990), Stokes (1980).

146 UVEA PARAKEET
Eunymphicus uvaeensis   Plate 36

IDENTIFICATION 32cm. Only in mature forests on the island of Uvea north of New Caledonia. Similar to the allopatric Horned Parakeet (145) but with a green, not yellow, face and nape and an upward-curving crest of six greenish-black feathers; the red of the crown is restricted to the centre of the forehead.

VOICE Unrecorded.

DISTRIBUTION AND STATUS Confined to the 110 km² island of Uvea in the Loyalty Islands. Introduced unsuccessfully to nearby Lifu. The species occurs in isolated forest patches now restricted to the coast, mainly in the St Joseph district between Cape Rossel and Cap Escarpé. Only 15-25 km² of suitable habitat was judged to remain on the island in 1993 with around 70-90 birds were present, although a fuller survey has suggested a total population of 617. The past decline was caused through extensive conversion of forest to agriculture, hunting and trade; birds are still caught using a noose inside a pawpaw *Carica papaya* fruit, and because the island is a flat, easily accessible atoll exports are difficult to control. Birds bought from trappers for A$50 can be sold on by dealers for as much as Aus $1,000. The delicate political situation on Uvea, as the Kanak Liberation Front struggles for independence from France, has made conservation work for the species difficult. Trust is being placed in a captive breeding programme based at Parc Forestier near Nouméa on New Caledonia. Island-to-island transfers may also still be considered feasible.

ECOLOGY Little known; chiefly dependent on mature native forests with kauri *Agathis australis* pines.

DESCRIPTION Generally bright mid-green. Head green, lighter on ear-coverts with some light shaft-streaks; centre of forecrown red with six wispy blackish-green upcurving feathers forming a small crest; rear-crown darker green; lores and lower cheeks dark green. Upperparts light green, paler on rump. Wing-coverts green; outerwebs of primaries greenish-blue with black innerwebs. Underwing-coverts green. Underparts light yellowish-green. Uppertail green with a slight blue suffusion distally, and blue edges to lateral feathers; undertail greyish. **Bare parts**: Bill blue-grey at base, blackish towards tip; iris orange; legs grey.

SEX/AGE Sexes similar.

MEASUREMENTS Wing 149-169; tail 127-158; bill 18-22; tarsus 18-22.

GEOGRAPHICAL VARIATION None.

REFERENCES Collar *et al.* (1994), Forshaw (1989), Hay (1984, 1986), King (1981), Lambert *et al.* (1993), Mayr (1945), Peters (1961), Rinke (1992), Robinet *et al.* (1996), Sibley & Monroe (1990).

---

147 BOURKE'S PARROT
Neopsephotus bourkii   Plate 35

Other names: Bourke Parrot, Bourke's Parakeet, Blue-vented Parakeet, Pink-bellied Parakeet

IDENTIFICATION 19cm. A small, slender parrot locally common in drier areas of inland Australia. Mainly brownish with a pink belly and blue wing-flash. Pale edgings on wing-coverts and mottled breast make the plumage somewhat cryptic against the ground in dry areas. The male shows a blue forehead, which is generally absent in the female. There are no other small, mainly pinkish-brown parrots, the only possible confusion species being the Bluebonnet (134), which appears mainly olive-brown from a distance but has a dark blue face. In flight Bourke's Parrots are more likely to be confused with doves (e.g. Peaceful Dove *Geopelia placida*) than other psittacines, but the blue wing-flashes and pink belly are diagnostic. Bourke's Parrots sometimes drink from roadside pools after dark, and observers should be wary of mistaking them for Night Parrots (157). The flight is swift and darting, the downswept wings briefly left open between beats, giving a hesitant, irregular, wader-like pattern recalling *Neophema* parrots, but white tips to the outer tail feathers separate this species.

VOICE A mellow *chu-wee*, various chirrupy twitters, softer and higher-pitched than the calls of Budgerigar (155). There is a shrill metallic alarm call *kleet-kleet* or *kik-kik*, and a plaintive warbling call.

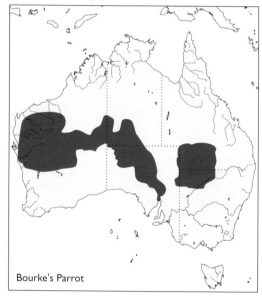

Bourke's Parrot

DISTRIBUTION AND STATUS Scattered through the interior of Australia where it is nomadic but locally common. The species ranges from the west coast of Western Australia around Geraldton inland to the Ashburton River and south through Leonora, through the Gibson and Great Victoria Deserts into southern Northern Territory to around 20°S. It spreads from north-west South Australia south-east through Woomera to Port Augusta, also extending north through Oodnadatta and the Lake Eyre and Lake Frome regions. Birds to the east of the Flinders Range may be isolated, since there are no records between 139° and 140°E. The species has apparently declined in central New South Wales owing to overgrazing by livestock and rabbits, and is now found mainly in the west from around Broken Hill to the Paroo River; nomads have, however, been recorded further east to around Narrandera in the south and Lightning Ridge in the north. In southern Queensland birds occur east to around Dirranbandi and Cunnamulla, and north to Winton.

Escapes have been recorded around Brisbane. The world population is considered to be greater than 50,000. The species is probably increasing in the west owing to agricultural expansion including the provision of man-made watering sites.

ECOLOGY Nomadic and slightly crepuscular. The birds may arrive in an area and remain there for a number of years before disappearing completely again. Found in drier inland areas favouring open mulga *Acacia aneura* and eucalyptus woodland. Also found in riverine woodland and *Callitris* scrub. During dry spells up to a thousand birds may gather at waterholes which they will visit morning and evening during summer months, and all day in the winter (large numbers drink alongside Common Bronze-winged Pigeons *Phaps chalcoptera*). Large groups can be seen heading rapidly to these drinking places, uttering quiet calls on whistling wings, and flying low through the scrub. Bourke's Parrots are easily overlooked as they forage or rest quietly in pairs or flocks on the ground and in vegetation. They are apt to remain still when approached, allowing close observation, or dart quickly for cover, sometimes using the wood of a dead tree as camouflage. The species is active after dark. The diet is mainly made up of grass seeds and fresh shoots. These parrots breed from Aug to Dec according to rains. The display is similar to that of a *Neophema* parrot, the male standing erect with spread wings and tail. The nest is a hollow in a mulga or casuarina, usually 1-3m above ground. Three to six white eggs are laid, and the birds may be double-brooded. During incubation the female sits tightly, leaving nest only once a day to be fed by the male, who flies noisily around the nesting tree at the approach of an intruder. The white-downed young hatch in around 18 days, fledge in about four weeks, and are fed by the parents for another week after leaving the nest.

DESCRIPTION Frontal area blue, chin, lores and area around eye whitish, appearing as an eye-ring from a distance; ear-coverts and upper cheeks brown, stippled with paler and darker spotting and suffused pinkish; crown and hindneck grey-brown margined darker. Upperparts grey brown, edged paler on scapulars, rump and uppertail-coverts darker, with some pale blue showing at sides. Bend of wing mid-blue; lesser-coverts powder-blue; median coverts dark edged paler, with outer coverts edged blue; greater coverts dark with yellowish-white edgings and slightly suffused blue; primary coverts blue, tipped darker. Primaries blackish marked blue on outerwebs and finely edged yellowish-white; inner secondaries grey blue on outerwebs and brown on innerwebs, edged pale greenish-yellow. Underwing-coverts blue. Breast brown with pink suffusion at feather tips, appearing generally pinkish-brown; belly bright pink; thighs, lower flanks, sides of rump, vent and undertail-coverts bright pale blue. Uppertail brown lightly suffused greyish-blue, lateral feathers with blackish innerwebs and white tips with pale blue outerwebs; undertail pale blue-white (central and second two sets of tail feathers of equal length). **Bare parts:** Bill greyish-black (no notch in upper mandible); iris brown; legs grey-brown.

SEX/AGE Female generally lacks the blue forehead, shows less blue in the wing, and has a pale underwing-bar (also sometimes present in young males). Young birds are duller with less pink below. Adult plumage is attained in around five months.

MEASUREMENTS Wing 106-120; tail 88-110; bill 9-12; tarsus 13-15.

GEOGRAPHICAL VARIATION None.

REFERENCES Blakers *et al.* (1984), Forshaw (1981, 1989), Lambert *et al.* (1993), Lodge (1991), Peters (1961), Pizzey & Doyle (1983), Schodde & Tidemann (1988), Sibley & Monroe (1990), Simpson & Day (1984), Slater (1979, 1989).

---

148 BLUE-WINGED PARROT
Neophema chrysostoma　　　　　Plate 37

Other names: Blue-banded Parakeet (all members of genus alternatively know as "parakeet" or "grass-parakeet")

IDENTIFICATION 20cm. A small, longish-tailed, olive, yellow and blue parrot which breeds in south-east Australia and Tasmania and has a broad winter distribution across south-east Australia. It occupies a variety of habitats and feeds mainly on the ground on grass seeds. This species is generally similar in appearance to congeners, and is especially difficult to separate from Elegant Parrot (149) with which it is sympatric in parts of its mainland range. Mixed flocks of the two species can be encountered outside the breeding season. Blue-winged is generally a duller olive-green in appearance, with more extensive mid-blue median and greater coverts, with only a little paler blue on the innermost greater coverts; Elegant is overall more olive-yellow than olive-green, appearing brighter on face, undersides and rump (this last noticeable in flight), and has distinctively marked turquoise-blue median-coverts giving the wing a two-tone appearance. With close views it is possible to separate the two on facial markings, as the blue frontal band of Blue-winged stops at the eye (and appears less two-tone) whereas in Elegant it continues above and slightly behind the eye. Male Blue-winged has a distinct yellow suffusion on the rump. The rare Orange-bellied Parrot (151) is also partly sympatric, and all three may be encountered together. Blue-winged Parrots can sometimes show orange bellies, but have blue, not green, central tail feathers, and yellow, not green, lores. Orange-bellied Parrots also appear sturdier than Blue-winged, are greener above, and have less blue in the upperwing-coverts. When disturbed, groups of Blue-winged Parrots either fly high in small groups, or zig-zag ahead to land on the ground or in trees. *Neophema* parrots have a swift darting flight in which the wings are briefly left open between beats, the pattern recalling a small wader.

VOICE A high-pitched *zzt-zzt, sit sit* or *brrrt brrrt* in alarm, or when flushed an extended *chappy-chappy-brrt-chippy-chippy-brrt*. There is also a soft warbling tinkle or subdued twittering while feeding. The call has been compared to that of Yellow-rumped Thornbill *Acanthiza chrysorrhoa*.

DISTRIBUTION AND STATUS During the breeding season (Sep to Jan) the birds are found below 36°S, being concentrated in wetter parts of south-east South Australia and southern Victoria, and in Tasmania. In winter they are largely absent from Tasmania and range much further north in south-east Australia, reaching southern Queensland (to about 26°S, e.g. Thargomindah, Cunnamulla, Chinchilla), and spread west to eastern South Australia, reaching the Eyre Peninsula in the south and ranging north to around the Queensland border; they also range east to western parts of New South Wales (also occasional to southern coastal districts there in summer). It is not known whether the southern mainland population is resident and the Tasmanian birds are migrants, overflying the mainland breeders to winter further north, or if the entire population moves north in winter. There are relatively few records from King and Flinders Islands which suggests that, unlike Orange-bellied Parrots, most birds overfly the Bass Strait direct to the mainland. Blue-winged Parrots are generally common in most types of open country and are probably the commonest parrot in Tasmania, where they breed south to Macquarie Harbour on the west coast and are found throughout the midlands in suitable habitat. Flocks of up to 2,000 juvenile birds may form in north-west Tasmania prior to autumn migration. World population above 20,000.

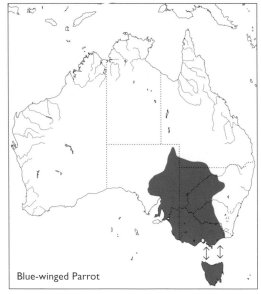

Blue-winged Parrot

ECOLOGY Nocturnal migrant. The least specialised of its genus, being recorded from a wide range of habitats from sea-level to around 1,200m. Blue-winged Parrots are found in savanna woodland, grasslands, orchards, forest clearings, farmland, coastal saltmarshes and dune systems, heath, saltbush *Atriplex* areas, mallee *Eucalyptus gracilis*, mulga *Acacia aneura* and a range of other open habitats. The birds are found in pairs or small parties, and outside the breeding season will form larger groups, sometimes consorting with Elegant Parrots and occasionally with the rare Orange-bellied Parrot in southern coastal areas. Blue-winged Parrots forage on the ground for seeds (e.g. sunflower *Helianthus*), as well as taking fruit, blossoms and insects. They are quite approachable, usually flying up to a nearby tree when disturbed. In display the male droops his wings, bobs his head and regurgitates food for the female. The nest-site is a hollow which may be in a eucalypt, stump, fence post or even a fallen log. The female selects the site, and several pairs may nest in a single tree; sites are sometimes re-used in successive years. The breeding season runs from Sep to Jan, or early Feb. During incubation the male feeds the female close to the nest-site and mating occurs while the clutch is still being laid. Shortly after the four to six white eggs hatch, the female joins in with food collection. The white-downed young

hatch in 20 days, fledge 30 days later, and remain with the parents for a short while after leaving the nest.

DESCRIPTION Crown olive-green suffused yellow on forecrown; frontal band blue (lighter on rear edge), reaching from forehead to eye (but not beyond); lores bright yellow; ear-coverts and face greyish-olive. Upperparts dull olive-green. Wing-coverts mid-blue, lighter on a few feathers of inner greater coverts. Primaries black, edged deep violet-blue on outerwebs and with fine yellow margins; inner secondaries with green outerwebs, middle secondaries with blue on outerwebs; tertials olive-green. Underwing-coverts blue. Breast light green shading to yellow on belly and undertail-coverts. Uppertail bluish-grey tipped darker, lateral feathers yellow with darker bases. **Bare parts**: Bill greyish-black with pinkish lower mandible and cutting edge to upper mandible; iris dark brown; legs pinkish-grey.

SEX/AGE Female duller than male with a smaller frontal band and often a wing-bar. Young birds lack the frontal band and most show a wing-bar; bill orange in very young birds.

MEASUREMENTS Wing 105-155; tail 100-124; bill 9-12; tarsus 14-16.

GEOGRAPHICAL VARIATION None.

REFERENCES Blakers *et al.* (1984), Eckert (1990), Forshaw (1981, 1989), Lambert *et al.* (1993), Lodge (1991), Pizzey & Doyle (1983), Schodde & Tidemann (1988), Sibley & Monroe (1990), Simpson & Day (1984), Slater (1979, 1989).

149 ELEGANT PARROT
Neophema elegans   Plate 37

IDENTIFICATION 21-24cm. A small, typical *Neophema* parrot with two disjunct populations in south-east and south-west Australia. The species is very similar to the sympatric Blue-winged Parrot (148) but can be separated with careful observation (see that species); the two only overlap in south-east Australia (excluding Tasmania). Elegant can show an orange patch on the underparts like Orange-bellied Parrot (151), but latter is extremely restricted in range and is stockier, darker, more grass-green, and has green, not yellow, lores, and green, not blue, central tail feathers. Rock Parrot (150) also has the blue frontal band passing through the eye, but is much duller, has blue lores, and is restricted to coastal habitats. These birds feed mainly on the ground and when flushed their flight is reminiscent of a small wader (e.g. snipe *Gallinago*).

VOICE A grating *zit*, *tsit-tsit* or *tsit-tsit-tsit*, and a soft twittering while feeding.

DISTRIBUTION AND STATUS There are two morphologically identical but well separated populations, although the species is nomadic so that birds may appear outside of the normal range on occasion. In the south-west the species occurs west of a line from around Esperance on the south coast of Western Australia north through Merredin to Moora on the north-west coast. It has spread through the wheatbelt from drier areas to the north-east and is now found in the vicinity of Perth, as well as occasionally reaching north to Point Cloates and the Fortescue River. In the south-east it occurs in southern

South Australia on the Eyre Peninsula, on Kangaroo Island (present in summer), and in southern districts around Port Augusta, Port Wakefield and near Adelaide, in the Mount Lofty Range, reaching north to the northernmost part of the Flinders Range. The species is irregular east of 140°E, with few records from the New South Wales Riverina north to the Paroo River; it is also irregular in north-west Victoria. The south-west population is growing, while that in the south-east is believed stable although the species is generally less common and its historical range there is difficult to determine owing to possible confusion with Blue-winged Parrots. World population above 30,000.

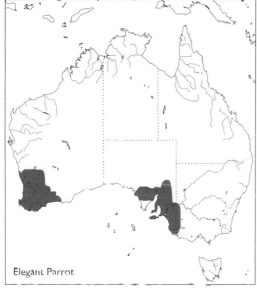

Elegant Parrot

ECOLOGY Partially nomadic in open woodland, agricultural areas, lightly wooded savanna, mallee *Eucalyptus gracilis*, acacia scrub, saltbush *Atriplex* plains, saltmarshes and, in the south-west, forest clearings. Outside the breeding season large flocks (sometimes mixed with Blue-winged Parrots in the south-east) gather to feed on the seeds of native and introduced grasses and shrubs; sunflower seeds *Helianthus* are also commonly taken. The birds blend in well while feeding in low shrubbery and can be difficult to detect, waiting until an observer is very close before flushing. The breeding biology is similar to that of Blue-winged Parrot, the nest being placed in a hollow in a tree-trunk or limb and lined with wood-dust. Breeding takes place between Aug and Dec and the four to five white eggs are incubated by the female for 18 days, with the young fledging 30 days later.

DESCRIPTION Crown olive-green with obvious dark blue frontal band with a thin but distinct lighter blue rear margin; lores bright yellow; face yellowish-olive. Mantle and back greenish-olive tinged yellower on rump. Bend of wing blue; innermost wing-coverts olive-green; median-coverts tipped light blue, greater coverts edged mauve-blue; primary coverts blackish with violet-blue margins. Primaries black edged dark violet-blue; secondaries yellow-olive with blue outer margins on outermost. Underwing-coverts violet-blue. Throat and breast yellowish-green becoming bright yellow on belly and undertail-coverts, sometimes with orange patch between legs. Uppertail greyish-blue, darker towards the tips, lateral feathers yellow

with darker bases. **Bare parts**: Bill black, with lower mandible and cutting edge to upper mandible pinkish; iris dark brown; legs grey.

SEX/AGE Female slightly duller and may show a slight wing-bar. Young birds lack the frontal band, and females especially may show a wing-bar. Adult plumage is gained in three to four months.

MEASUREMENTS Wing 104-115; tail 106-120; bill 9-11; tarsus 14-16.

GEOGRAPHICAL VARIATION None.

REFERENCES Blakers *et al.* (1984), Eckert (1990), Forshaw (1981, 1989), Lambert *et al.* (1993), Pizzey & Doyle (1983), Saunders (1989), Schodde & Tidemann (1988), Sibley & Monroe (1990), Simpson & Day (1984), Slater (1979, 1989), Storr & Johnstone (1979), Taylor (1987).

150 ROCK PARROT
Neophema petrophila Plate 37

IDENTIFICATION 21-24cm. The dullest of the *Neophema* parrots and also the most specialised. Rock Parrots are not uncommon on small offshore islands in southern and south-west Australia during the breeding season, and on the adjacent mainland during the winter. They are similar to Blue-winged (148) and Elegant (149) Parrots, but show much less blue on the wing-coverts, have more uniform olive-brown plumage, and the blue frontal band extends through the eye and onto the lores (the lores are yellow in the other two species). The birds often nest close to the surf, and in high winds remain close to the ground when flushed, preferring low bushes and rock crevices for shelter. On calmer days, they will make off in high zig-zagging flights. Like congeners, they can show orange bellies, but unlike the darker Orange-bellied Parrot (151) they have blue lores and tails and lack the bright green upperparts of that species. The bright yellow vent and undertail-coverts contrast with the generally dull plumage from a distance; the birds tend to stand with an upright posture.

VOICE A metallic disyllabic *zit-zit, zit tee* or *tsit-tseet* repeated rapidly when flushed, reminiscent of Purple-crowned Lorikeet (37). Also a subdued *titter-titter* when feeding.

DISTRIBUTION AND STATUS There are two populations separated by the Great Australian Bight, which offers no offshore islands for nesting. The eastern population reaches from around Robe, South Australia, in the east, to the Nuyts Archipelago at about 133°E in the west (although recorded from Kangaroo Island, breeding has not been confirmed there). The western population extends from Israelite Bay and the Recherche Archipelago, Western Australia, west around Cape Leeuwin and north to Shark Bay. North of Perth the species nests on the mainland, but elsewhere birds occupy coastal islands at least for breeding, also sometimes travelling from the mainland to roost on offshore islands. The population on Rottnest Island off the coast of Perth suffered in the past from illegal trapping, but has grown rapidly in recent years. The species is regarded as a common resident and partial nomad throughout its range; to date, coastal islands have not been subject to the same development pressures as mainland areas. The world population is greater than 20,000.

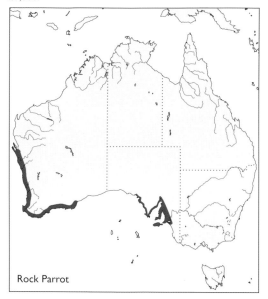

Rock Parrot

ECOLOGY Rock Parrots breed on small rocky offshore islets where their nests are less vulnerable to predation, and there is a marked post-breeding dispersal to the nearby mainland. The birds can be found in scrubby areas near the coast, in coastal grasslands, along estuarine waterways, in mangroves and in sandy areas near the shore. They are rarely encountered far from the sea at any time of year. On islands they can be found along the shore itself, or in nearby vegetation including saltbush *Atriplex*, casuarinas, and in particular pigface *Carpobrotus*. They feed mainly on the seeds and fruit of halophytic shrubs and succulents, and have also been recorded taking spilt grain. Large groups sometimes gather on the ground at an abundant food source, but like congeners they can be difficult to see until they are flushed. Their plumage is not very water-repellant and on wet days they can appear waterlogged and consequently very dark. The nest is usually in a crevice between seashore boulders, often with the entrance obscured by vegetation. Sometimes seabird burrows are used, including those of the Wedge-tailed Shearwater *Puffinus pacificus*. The birds breed from Aug to Dec or as late as Feb (possibility of double-brooding). Display, incubation and other details of breeding biology similar to previous two species.

DESCRIPTION Head dull olive-green except for broad mid-blue frontal band (lighter blue on rear edge) extending through eye onto lores. Upperparts dull olive-green. Inner wing-coverts olive-green, outer mauve-blue, central lighter blue; primary coverts blue-black. Primaries black with grey-blue outerwebs and fine yellow margins. Underwing-coverts dark blue, sometimes with slight wing-bar. Throat and breast dull olive-green becoming olive-yellow to bright yellow on undertail-coverts; sometimes with some orange on belly. Uppertail dull blue tipped brownish, lateral feathers yellow with darker bases. **Bare parts**: Bill greyish with a pink base and lower mandible; iris dark brown; legs pinkish-grey.

SEX/AGE Females are like males but duller with less blue

in the face. Young birds lack the frontal band; some females with wing-bar.

MEASUREMENTS Wing 104-115; tail 102-117; bill 10-12; tarsus 14-18.

GEOGRAPHICAL VARIATION Birds in the east are said to be generally darker but no races are currently recognised.

REFERENCES Blakers *et al.* (1984), Eckert (1990), Forshaw (1981, 1989), Joseph (1988b), Lambert *et al.* (1993), Peters (1961), Pizzey & Doyle (1983), Schodde & Tidemann (1988), Sibley & Monroe (1990), Simpson & Day (1984), Slater (1979, 1989), Storr & Johnstone (1979).

151 ORANGE-BELLIED PARROT
Neophema chrysogaster   Plate 37

IDENTIFICATION 21cm. One of Australia's rarest birds with a maximum population of around 200 individuals confined to a small breeding range in south-western Tasmania and a larger wintering range along the coast of southern Australia (although most birds concentrate around Port Phillip Bay near Melbourne). Orange-bellied Parrots are similar to Blue-winged (148) and Elegant (149) Parrots, but are stockier and darker, and their upperparts are grass-green without olive tones; the lores are green, not yellow, and the central tail feathers are green, not blue. The duller Rock Parrot (150) has blue lores and uppertail, and the blue frontal band extends back past the eye. The orange belly of the present species is helpful but not diagnostic, as congeners also sometimes show orange underparts.

VOICE A characteristic buzzing, created by the repetition of a sharp *chitter-chitter* call. Also some softer tinkling notes.

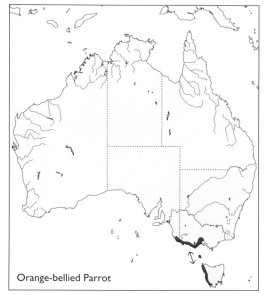

Orange-bellied Parrot

DISTRIBUTION AND STATUS Birds nest along the forested margin of the coastal plain and feeds in the sedge-lands of the World Heritage Area of south-western Tasmania, Australia, between Macquarie Harbour and Port

Davey. They migrate across islands in the west of the Bass Strait (mainly King Island) to the southern coast of Australia, to winter from around Mar to Jul mainly along the shores of Port Phillip Bay, Victoria (largest numbers at Point Wilson and Swan Island, including Queenscliffe Golf Course). They are also winter in small numbers from Gippsland, Victoria, west to the Coorong, South Australia. They occasionally turn up in winter or on passage elsewhere in Tasmania and surrounding islands, and individuals have spent the summer on the mainland. Each summer around 40 pairs breed, and an analysis of nine nests showed an average offspring of 1.7 young. The post-breeding population generally increases by about 50 individuals to around 170 birds, but the smaller returning population suggests relatively high annual mortality. Adults start leaving the breeding area in Feb and progress gradually up the coast of Tasmania, crossing the Bass Strait mainly via King Island (also recorded in the Hunter Group) to the coast of south-east Australia (young birds usually leave a month or so later). The birds tend to move around on the mainland, and are found in South Australia later in the winter. They return to breed in Sep and Oct, usually travelling directly back to their breeding grounds. From 1979 to 1990 the wintering population remained relatively stable, with counts from 67 to 126 individuals recorded each year (with up to 50% of the known world population being present at Point Wilson). Last century the species apparently occurred in flocks of thousands (and bred as far east as Sydney up to about 1907). The loss of wintering habitat and capture for the bird trade are cited as factors in its decline. The potential loss of wintering habitat continues to be a threat, as does competition from introduced herbivores, disturbance, and the possibility of mineral exploration and development. A detailed recovery plan includes the management of wintering habitat by the exclusion of grazing animals, the diversion of economic activity, and the development of Murtcaim Wildlife Management Area close to Point Wilson. Captive-bred birds have been released and paired with wild individuals. CITES Appendix I. ENDANGERED.

ECOLOGY Mainly a nocturnal migrant, but evidence of predation by Peregrines *Falco peregrinus* along migration routes shows that some diurnal movement must also occur. Birds also move around in winter apparently in response to food availability, foraging in coastal saltmarsh and related habitats characterised by halophytic vegetation such as *Salicornia*, *Arthrocnemum*, *Juncus*, *Suaeda* and the introduced sea rocket *Cakile maritima*. They are also found in paddocks and other open habitats, but seldom more than 10km from the coast. They feed mainly on seeds, and have been recorded feeding with Blue-winged and Elegant Parrots on sunflower *Helianthus* seeds. The flocks sometimes employ a 'sentry' system to warn them of predators. When the birds first arrive back on the breeding grounds they tend to roost communally in dense *Melaleuca* stands. They breed in mature trees, often in timbered creeks, adjacent to sedge- and heathlands that have been burned within the last 7-12 years (less frequent in more mature heaths), buttongrass *Mesomelaena sphaerocephala* being an important food source there. The breeding season runs from Oct to Mar or Apr and the nest-site tends to be a hollow in a tall eucalypt (often a west coast peppermint *Eucalyptus nitida*), sometimes used in successive years. The birds can breed in their first summer and remain paired for life. Four to six white eggs are laid

and incubated by the female, who is fed by the male until shortly after the chicks hatch. Incubation lasts around 21 days and the chicks fledge around 30 days later. Non-pair nest visits have been recorded.

DESCRIPTION Crown, nape and mantle bright green, with a dark blue frontal band with a lighter blue rear edge, not extending beyond eye; face and lores yellowish-green. Bend of wing blue and green; inner wing-coverts green, outer mid-blue; primary coverts dark blue. Primaries black with blue outerwebs and fine yellow margins; inner secondaries edged green grading to blue on outermost. Underwing-coverts blue. Breast green, grading through yellowish-green to yellow on undertail-coverts; belly strongly marked orange. Uppertail green (bluer at tip), lateral feathers yellow with darker greenish-blue bases. Bare parts: Bill black; iris dark brown; legs grey.

SEX/AGE Female with duller, one-tone frontal band, smaller orange belly-patch, and often a wing-bar. Young birds with a faint frontal band, prominent wing-bar and pale bill.

MEASUREMENTS Wing 106-113; tail 95-110; bill 10-12; tarsus 15-17.

GEOGRAPHICAL VARIATION None.

REFERENCES Blakers *et al.* (1984), Brouwer & Garnett (1990), Brown (1984), Brown & Wilson (1984), Collar & Andrew (1988), Collar *et al.* (1994), Eckert (1990), Forshaw (1981, 1989), Garnett (1992), Joseph (1988b), Lambert *et al.* (1993), Loyn & Chandler (1978), Loyn *et al.* (1986), Menkhorst (1992), Pizzey & Doyle (1983), Schodde & Tidemann (1988), Sibley & Monroe (1990), Simpson & Day (1984), Slater (1979, 1989), Starks (1991a, 1991b), Starks *et al.* (1992), Tasmania Department of Parks Wildlife & Heritage (1991), Watts (1986).

152 TURQUOISE PARROT
Neophema pulchella   Plate 37

IDENTIFICATION 20cm. A small, brightly coloured *Neophema* occurring along and to the east of Australia's Great Dividing Range. Males are easily identified by their bright blue faces, yellow underparts, reddish shoulder-patches and extensive two-tone blue wing-flashes. The less distinctive females still have more blue in the face than any other *Neophema* except the allopatric Scarlet-chested Parrot (153). In captivity, female Turquoise can be separated by its more whitish lores, less blue on the face and darker blue wing-coverts. Turquoise Parrots can show an orange suffusion on the underparts. They have a fast erratic flight and the tail is spread on take-off and landing.

VOICE A soft yet penetrating disyllabic whistle and a high-pitched twittering while feeding.

DISTRIBUTION AND STATUS A century ago the species ranged from eastern Queensland to south-central Victoria, but underwent a major population crash attributed to the spread of pastoralism, a major drought in 1902 and possibly also trapping. It began to increase again in the 1940s and, although it has not recovered in central Queensland, today ranges patchily from south-east Queensland (north to around Chinchilla and Mary-borough) through eastern New South Wales (reaching the coast near Sydney, extending south to Nowra) into Victoria west to Bendigo. There is also an isolated population in eastern Victoria. The increase probably continues in Victoria and New South Wales (the presence of strong populations in some national parks indicates that cessation of grazing abets the species's recovery). Because birds often nest close to the ground, they are vulnerable to predation by foxes, and the provision of artificial nest-sites sometimes appears to be effective. Other threats include habitat loss and degradation (including loss of nesting sites), but it is no longer considered threatened, and is now relatively common in some areas. World population estimated at around 20,000. There are around 8,000 in captivity in Australia. NEAR-THREATENED.

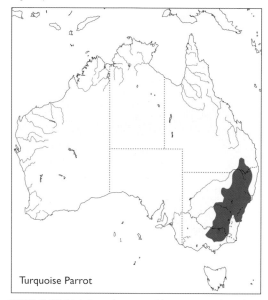

Turquoise Parrot

ECOLOGY Mainly sedentary with some post-breeding dispersal from woodland to pasture. The species occurs in a range of lowland habitats including grassland, heathland, scrub, orchards, tree-lined creeks through farmland, and woodland margins; it also ranges along the slopes of the Great Divide and associated wooded ridges to the west. It is most often found in flocks or small parties foraging on the ground for the seeds of native and introduced grasses and herbs; communal roosts are not uncommon. Breeding mainly takes place between Aug and Dec, but in some areas birds breed twice annually, some nesting also occurring from Apr to May. The nest is a hollow in a eucalypt or sometimes a stump close to the ground (often with a long entrance tunnel and an underground chamber). The four to five white eggs are incubated for around 18 days, with the chicks fledging in a further 30 days. Nests sometimes contain some green leaves and it is probable that these are gathered by the female and carried to the nest tucked into the rump feathers.

DESCRIPTION Head bright turquoise-blue, darker on forecrown, and with a yellowish chin and green rear-crown. Upperparts green. Inner lesser and median wing-coverts reddish-chestnut; median coverts light blue; greater and primary coverts violet-blue (innermost greater coverts green). Primaries black with mid-blue outerwebs and very fine pale yellowish outer margins; secondaries black with yellow-green outerwebs tending to blue on outer feathers.

Underwing-coverts violet-blue. Underparts bright yellow with slight orange tinge on throat and breast; orange abdomen-patch present in some birds. Central two pairs of tail feathers bright green, lateral feathers yellow with green bases. **Bare parts:** Bill black; iris dark brown; legs pinkish-brown.

SEX/AGE Female much duller than male and lacks chestnut shoulder-patch. The underparts are also much greener, especially on the breast. The lores are whitish, and the amount of blue on the face is substantially reduced. There is a wing-bar. Young birds are like females, but young males have a little chestnut showing in the wing and darker blue faces.

MEASUREMENTS Wing 100-113; tail 93-110; 10-12; tarsus 14-16.

GEOGRAPHICAL VARIATION None.

REFERENCES Blakers *et al.* (1984), Forshaw (1981, 1989), Hutchins (1985), Joseph (1988b), Lambert *et al.* (1993), Pizzey & Doyle (1983), Quin (1991), Sibley & Monroe (1990), Simpson & Day (1984), Slater (1979, 1989).

153 SCARLET-CHESTED PARROT
Neophema splendida   Plate 37

Other names: Scarlet-breasted Parrot, Splendid Parakeet, Scarlet-chested Parakeet

IDENTIFICATION 19-22cm. A small, brightly marked parrot now considered globally threatened, although large parts of its range are difficult to survey and seldom visited by birdwatchers. The male is perhaps the most distinctive in its genus with its bright scarlet breast. Females are very similar to female Turquoise Parrots (152), but have more blue on the face and lighter blue wing-coverts. Scarlet-chested Parrots are thinly distributed throughout the more arid inland parts of southern and south-western Australia, but are irruptive and have occurred much further east, even occasionally reaching north-western Victoria. When taking off and landing the tail is spread showing the bright yellow lateral feathers.

VOICE A soft twittering, less penetrating than the calls of congeners.

DISTRIBUTION AND STATUS This rare nomad has a wide historical range, but is probably now concentrated in better-vegetated parts of the Great Victoria Desert, with records from around Kalgoorlie, Western Australia, east through the northern Nullarbor Plain into South Australia on the northern Eyre Peninsula, around Port Augusta and in mallee areas north of the Murray River, as far as north-west Victoria, western New South Wales, south-west Queensland and the Macdonnell Ranges of Northern Territory. A flock of 240 birds was recently recorded in the Great Victoria Desert, but the world population is considered to be only 5,000-10,000 and there is insufficient information to verify its stability. There are, however, around 10,000 in captivity in Australia. VULNERABLE.

ECOLOGY The species is irruptive and birds frequently arrive in an area, nest for a number of years, then disappear again. They are capable of nesting shortly after arriving in a new region, although the length of incubation and time to fledging are the same as for other members of the genus. Generally confined to arid areas in the interior of southern Australia, notably mallee *Eucalyptus gracilis*, mulga *Acacia aneura*, open eucalyptus (e.g. marble gum *E. gongylocarpa*) and casuarina-dominated woodland, usually preferring a ground cover of spinifex *Triodia*. The species feeds mainly on grass seeds, and although it has been suggested that it gets most of its moisture from chewing succulent plants, birds will drink water directly. They feed on the ground and form fairly large flocks outside the breeding season. Nesting is semi-colonial, often with several pairs in neighbouring trees. The preferred site is a tree-hollow where three to six white eggs are laid. Like Turquoise Parrots, the females will carry green leaves to the nest tucked into their rump feathers. Breeding generally takes place between Aug and Jan, but may occur at other times of year under suitable conditions. Incubation lasts about 18 days and the young fledge in a further 30 days.

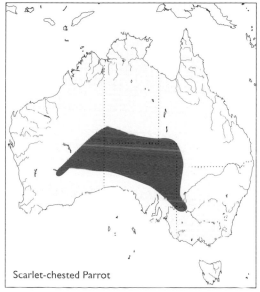

Scarlet-chested Parrot

DESCRIPTION Face and forecrown bright light turquoise, darker on chin and throat. Upperparts green. Bend of wing dark blue; wing-coverts bright light turquoise; primary coverts deep violet-blue. Primaries black with slight blue wash on outerwebs; outer secondaries with greenish-blue on outerwebs shading to green on outerwebs of inner secondaries and tertials. Underwing-coverts dark blue. Breast bright scarlet; sides of breast and flanks green; rest of underparts bright yellow. Uppertail green, outer feathers tipped yellow. **Bare parts**: Bill black; iris dark brown; legs grey-brown.

SEX/AGE Female much duller than male, with green breast and belly and restricted blue on face. Females and young birds usually show wing-bars. Young males take four months to reach near-adult plumage but brighten for a further two years.

MEASUREMENTS Wing 108-123; tail 88-102; bill 9-10; tarsus 14-16.

GEOGRAPHICAL VARIATION None.

REFERENCES Blakers *et al.* (1984), Brouwer & Garnett (1990), Collar & Andrew (1988), Collar *et al.* (1994), Emison *et al.* (1987), Forshaw (1981, 1989), Garnett (1992), Hutchins (1985), Joseph (1988b), Lambert *et al.*

(1993), Lodge (1991), Peters (1961), Pizzey (1993), Robinson *et al.* (1990), Sibley & Monroe (1990), Simpson & Day (1984), Slater (1979, 1989), Storr & Johnstone (1979).

154 SWIFT PARROT
Lathamus discolor   Plate 38

Other names: Clink, Red-faced Parrot, Red-shouldered Parrot, Swift Lorikeet

IDENTIFICATION 23-25.5cm. A slim, lorikeet-like parrot breeding in Tasmania and wintering on the Australian mainland. Swift Parrots are mainly bright green with a blue crown, red frontal area, yellow lores, red chin, dark russet shoulder-patch, blue wing-flash, red spot on the tertials and red underwing-flash, tail and undertail-coverts. The colour of tail and its coverts plus their distinctive calls distinguish them when they occur in mixed flocks with lorikeets, but three sympatric lorikeets, Rainbow (13), Scaly-breasted (19) and Purple-crowned (37), also show red underwing-coverts, although these and other *Glossopsitta* are otherwise dissimilar, all (e.g.) lacking red undertail-coverts (see plates). Male Mulga Parrots (136) have reddish vents and bellies, but they have mainly yellow undertail-coverts, broad blue tails with white lateral feathers and a prominent yellow shoulder-patch; they are also largely allopatric. Swift Parrots have long thin wings and tails, and their fast, direct, but erratic flight produces an audible whirring; they weave quickly through the trees, or fly high with seemingly random direction changes.

VOICE A metallic *clink-clink* call given in rapid succession to produce a tinkling chatter; also a piping *pee-pit pee-pit*. Both calls quite unlike the screeching of most lorikeets. While feeding the birds produce a subdued rosella-like chatter.

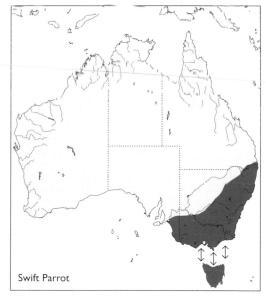

Swift Parrot

DISTRIBUTION AND STATUS Endemic breeder on Tasmania (mainly central and eastern) and islands of the Furneaux Group in the Bass Strait. After some post-breeding dispersal to western Tasmania from Jan, the birds migrate for the winter to the south-east Australian mainland, autumn passage occupying Feb–May, spring passage Aug– Oct. Although some birds stay to winter in Tasmania, breeding has never been confirmed on the mainland. In winter the species is nomadic, being concentrated in central and southern Victoria, but extending from the Mount Lofty Range, eastern South Australia, along and mainly to the south of the Murray River into New South Wales, where it is found west to Griffith, Ivanhoe and Warialda, and has occurred in large numbers around Canberra and Sydney in the east; it also ranges into Queensland inland to Chinchilla and the lower Dawson River and north to around Duaringa, with records of vagrants as far as Bowen. A 1988/1989 survey estimated the breeding population at 1,320 pairs with a post-breeding population of around 5,000. The forests in which the birds breed have been extensively cleared throughout its range, and birds continue to be trapped for trade. Large flocks making up significant percentages of the world population are sometimes encountered on the mainland, including some reports of up to 1,000 birds passing over Sydney in winter. Protected by law but birds can still be killed under permit in Tasmania if damaging orchards. VULNERABLE.

ECOLOGY A mainly nocturnal migrant, while birds wintering on the mainland are nomadic in response to food availability, although flocks may stay in the same area for weeks and roost in the same tree. Swift Parrots occur in forest, eucalyptus woodland, towns, grassland, open country with flowering trees, with a breeding habitat preference for dry sclerophyll forest. They are usually found foraging in small flocks, frequently darting between trees before settling to feed again and allowing a close approach. They are noisy and active, and almost exclusively arboreal, staying near the tops of trees and coming to ground usually only to drink. They call whilst feeding and may hang upside-down to reach blossoms. Like lorikeets, with which they commonly associate, Swift Parrots have brush-like tongues to enable them to extract nectar from tree blossoms. The diet also comprises sugary lerps (insect secretions e.g. of *Spondyliaspis*), larvae of other insects, fruit, berries and the seeds of a variety of plants. In western Tasmania the dominant eucalypt, the blue gum *E. globulus*, provides a key food source from around Jan when it begins flowering. Birds are very vocal when gathering to roost and swoop and circle as they find a place to perch. Breeding runs from late Sep to early Jan, with egg-laying in Oct–Nov. In display the male bows and rises, with courtship feeding being common. The nest is a tree-hollow, usually high in a eucalypt and commonly a mature or senescent blue gum, and pairs sometimes breed in close proximity to each other. Three to five white eggs are laid on decayed debris and brooded by the female alone. She leaves the nest morning and afternoon to be fed by her mate. Incubation lasts about 20 days and the young fledge in around six weeks, with a partial moult at a few months being reported in captive birds, which acquired adult plumage the following autumn. Polygamy has been noted in captivity.

DESCRIPTION Head bright emerald-green, with a bright red forehead, bright yellow lores and red chin and centre to throat (surrounded by yellow); centre of crown mid-blue. Upperparts bright green; shoulder and lesser coverts deep crimson; inner median and greater coverts mid-green, outer coverts light turquoise; primary coverts, alula and leading edge of wing dark blue. Primaries black and slightly emarginated, with a dark blue suffusion and narrow yellow outer margin and a pale yellow inner margin; tertials with red spots on innerwebs. Underwing-coverts and axillaries dark red, some birds with a pale underwing-bar. Underparts paler, more yellowish-green than upperparts; undertail-coverts red (with pale shafts and yellow tips). Uppertail dull brownish-red tipped dark blue, lateral feathers dull blue edged brownish-red; undertail greyish-brown. **Bare parts**: Bill yellowish-brown; iris yellow; legs pale brown.

SEX/AGE Female like male but with duller and less red on face and always with a wing-stripe. Immature duller, showing a pale wing-stripe and less red on the throat and undertail-coverts. Iris brown.

MEASUREMENTS Wing 116-124; tail 105-125; bill 12-14; tarsus 14-17.

GEOGRAPHICAL VARIATION None.

REFERENCES Arndt (1992), BirdLife (1993), Collar *et al.* (1994), Forshaw (1981, 1989), Lambert *et al.* (1993), Peters (1961), Pizzey & Doyle (1983), Schodde & Tidemann (1988), Sibley & Monroe (1990), Simpson & Day (1984), Slater (1979, 1989), Trounson & Trounson (1987), Tzaros & Price (1996).

155 BUDGERIGAR
Melopsittacus undulatus   Plate 38

Other names: Shell Parakeet, Budgerygah

IDENTIFICATION 18-20cm. Perhaps the world's best known parrot. A very popular cagebird in a variety of colours (commonly blue), but wild Budgerigars are predominantly green and yellow. These small parrots are often encountered in large noisy flocks in the interior of Australia. In flight the flocks twist and turn in unison like some waders, and the birds will glide on downcurved wings (reminiscent of a quail *Coturnix*). Budgerigars are unlikely to be mistaken for any other parrot with their small size, pointed wings and tails, bright yellow wing-bars, and distinctive plumage pattern.

VOICE A continuous pleasant warbling *chirrup*, a sharp chattering and a subdued disyllabic screech.

DISTRIBUTION AND STATUS Widely distributed throughout the interior of Australia, but rare in eastern coastal districts and the extreme south-west (absent from Tasmania, Arnhem Land and Cape York Peninsula). The species can be common to extremely abundant, but is nomadic and may shift areas from year to year. Birds frequently irrupt from the arid zone into wetter areas and there is a seasonal shift towards the south during the summer, but this may be affected by annual rainfall patterns. They have been introduced unsuccessfully to a number of places around the world (or have escaped from captivity and failed to become established) including South Africa, UK, Japan, Hong Kong, Puerto Rico, Brazil, Switzerland, Colombia, the Society Islands, New Zealand and Oman. In the USA the species has failed to colonise Hawaii and California (escapes also regular in New York City), but in Florida a population which was originally introduced in the St Petersburg area in the early 1950s now numbers more than 3,000 birds; these birds are mobile and have been recorded along the east coast from around Jacksonville south to Miami, and in the west from around Hudson south to Fort Myers, occasionally ranging north to Gainsville. Escaped birds may occasionally show up in Tasmania. World population estimated at around 5,000,000.

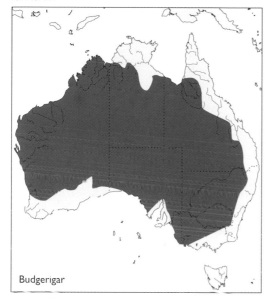

Budgerigar

ECOLOGY Occupies a range of habitats in the arid interior of Australia, frequently irrupting into semiarid and subhumid areas. Some apparently seasonal movements occur in parts of the species's range, with a general northward shift during winter; movements into western New South Wales and Victoria, arriving late spring or early summer and departing in winter, have also been noted. The species is found in grasslands with spinifex *Triodia*, dry mallee *Eucalyptus gracilis* and mulga *Acacia aneura* scrub, riverine woodland and farmland. Despite claims that birds can survive without water, they are frequently found close to it, and gather in large numbers (up to 15,000) at watering holes to drink (large numbers also reportedly die during drought periods). They tend to be most active early in the day, sitting quietly through the hottest hours. They are ground-feeders, primarily taking grass seeds, e.g. spinifex and Mitchell grass *Astraleba*, also the seeds of crop plants (in Florida they visit bird tables). Although breeding can take place at any time of year and is frequently stimulated by an abundance of food (the birds being capable of more than one brood), nesting frequently coincides with the main period of grass seeding, which tends to be during the winter in the north, and during the spring and summer in the south. The birds nest in a small tree-hollow, hole in a stump or log on the ground (also nest-boxes in Florida), where four to eight white eggs are laid. They nest communally, and hollows may be shared. The male feeds the female during incubation which lasts around 18 days, the chicks taking a further five weeks to fledge.

DESCRIPTION Forecrown bright yellow; rear-crown and ear-coverts yellow finely barred black. Mantle feathers centred black and margined yellow to produce a scalloped appearance; lower back and uppertail-coverts bright

green. Lesser and median wing-coverts centred black and margined yellow; greater coverts centred black and green, fringed yellow. Flight feathers black fringed yellow and suffused green, with prominent central yellow bar. Underwing-coverts green. Chin and throat yellow; sides of chin with prominent purple mark and row of black spots either side; rest of underparts light green. Tail bright blue-green with prominent yellow band close to base on lateral feathers. **Bare parts**: Bill brownish tipped yellow; iris white; legs grey.

SEX/AGE Female with brownish (not blue) cere during breeding. Young birds duller with a darker iris and barred forehead. Adult plumage is attained in 3-4 months and males can produce sperm within 60 days of leaving the nest.

MEASUREMENTS Wing 93-104; tail 88-103; 9-11; tarsus 13-15.

GEOGRAPHICAL VARIATION None.

REFERENCES Blakers *et al.* (1984), Forshaw (1981, 1989), Lambert *et al.* (1993), Lever (1987), Long (1981), Pizzey & Doyle (1983), Sibley & Monroe (1990), Simpson & Day (1984), Slater (1979, 1989), Storr & Johnstone (1979), Taylor (1987).

156 GROUND PARROT
Pezoporus wallicus   Plate 38

Other names: Swamp Parrot, Buttongrass Parrot

IDENTIFICATION 28-33cm (tail 16cm 20cm). A medium-sized, slender, long-tailed parrot, bright green with black and yellow camouflage patterning, confined to isolated pockets of heath and scrub in coastal south-west and south-east Australia. It is terrestrial and (contrary to common belief) diurnal, but shy and skulking, so is rarely seen unless flushed on audibly whirring wings before diving back into cover after 30m or so. Its zig-zag flight, recalling Common Sandpiper *Actitis hypoleucos* or snipe *Gallinago*, is interspersed with glides on downcurved wings; once a bird has gone to ground it will bolt into thick vegetation and can be hard to relocate. No sympatric parrot shows similar behaviour; identification clinched by short rounded wings with yellow wing-bar on both surfaces. The graduated tail is long and pointed with green central feathers barred yellow, and obvious yellow outer feathers with black bars (tail held slightly up in flight). There are no likely confusion species. The Night Parrot (157) is superficially similar, but has an unbarred yellow abdomen and is confined to Australia's arid interior (for other plumage differences see plate). Some *Neophema* parrots are found in heath and scrub habitats, but all are smaller than Ground Parrot, have characteristic tinkling or zizzing flight calls, and show blue wing-flashes.

VOICE To see Ground Parrots in the wild, knowledge of call types and calling periods is essential. Birds call 30 minutes before sunrise and 20 minutes (shorter period but more frequently) after sunset throughout the year. They may call in flight, also occasionally during early morning and late afternoon on overcast days. Several whistling calls (thin, high-pitched, resonant, chiming and almost insect-like) are used throughout the year: a single rising whistle; a 'double' or 'stutter' rising scale, e.g. *tee-ti* *tee-ti tee-ti tee-ti* or *tee-titi tee-titi tee-titi tee-titi*; and a level *tee-tee-tee*, the call most frequently given in flight. During the breeding season, males make a frog-like croaking (followed by a distinct click) when approaching the nest. Chicks produce a harsh *carr*, and juveniles have quavering or trilling begging call.

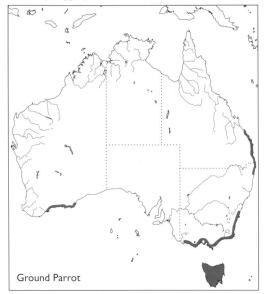

Ground Parrot

DISTRIBUTION AND STATUS Confined to Australia. The range has contracted in recent times and the species is now found only in isolated pockets of coastal heath and sedgelands, extending south from southern Queensland, where a population of around 3,000 birds is scattered through Fraser Island and the nearby mainland including Cooloola National Park, Wide Bay Military Reserve, Fraser State Forest and Great Sandy National Park. It is locally common through New South Wales, occurring at a number of coastal sites including Evans Head, the Broadwater National Park, Byron Bay, Morton National Park, around Cape Howe, and at Barren Grounds and Nadgee Nature Reserves. It enters Victoria at Croaj-ingolong National Park, and occurs in suitable habitat along the coast at a number of sites including Wilson's Promontory National Park and the Discovery Bay Coastal Park in the west. Post-breeding dispersal takes some birds to the Gippsland and Ninety Mile Beach areas, but they may also travel further afield including upland areas inland. The species is now extinct in South Australia and on the Bass Strait islands. In Tasmania it is fairly common in the south-west, but small pockets in the central and south-east regions are probably now in decline. The eastern subspecies is considered nationally vulnerable (outside Tasmania), but the western subspecies, which has a total population of around 450 birds confined to Fitzgerald River and Cape Arid National Parks, is endangered. Populations have declined as a result of extensive habitat clearance, drainage for development, agriculture and forestry, and badly timed fire regimes (which affect heath but not sedgeland). Despite protection, the western population is still extremely vulnerable to naturally occurring fires which can decimate large tracts of heathland habitat in hours. The spread of soil fungi *Phytophthora*, which affect the composition of plant communities, is also considered a potential threat. Predation by introduced cats and foxes appears to have only minor impact on most Ground Parrot populations, but damage to scrub cover by grazing cattle probably renders areas unsuitable for nesting. World population (both races) around 100,000. Protected by law. None is known to be in captivity. CITES Appendix I.

ECOLOGY Ground Parrots occur in both heathland and sedgeland, and although their specific habitat preference varies between populations, they are generally less common in the latter. In coastal eastern Australia, birds favour temperate and subtropical shrubby heath, with thick cover dominated by grass-tree *Xanthorrhoea resinosa* and associated with *Banksia* woodland. In Tasmania, a mosaic of low heath and sedge, lacking larger shrubs, and dominated by buttongrass *Gymnoschoenus sphaerocephalus*, supports the highest population density. In Western Australia, the species tolerates older, more open heath, but is present at very low densities. Although Ground Parrots normally occur in relatively large tracts of habitat, they have been found in areas as small as 20 ha. In heathland ecosystems, the response of different plant communities to fire, which affects the level of ground cover and seeding, determines habitat suitability. Although there is variation between habitats and populations, Ground Parrots tend to colonise heathland around one year after fire, begin nesting after four years, are at peak densities at between eight and ten years, and then begin to decline, with total abandonment after about 20 years. In Western Australia the density peak is later, and in Tasmania birds may persist in heaths unburnt for up to 35 years. Birds also occasionally turn up in pastures. Individual home ranges average around nine hectares, but do overlap. The species is mainly sedentary and birds live in territorial pairs. Between Feb and May there is wide post-breeding dispersal (begins Dec in the west) into more marginal habitats, with records away from the usual range (seen up to 120km from nearest breeding area in the Australian Alps, Victoria). Ground Parrots are active through the day with peak periods at dawn, during mid-morning and in late afternoon; they seem to make unforced flights only during calling periods. Birds feed on the ground on a wide variety of seeds (up to 40 species including sedges and rushes), also leaves, shoots and small invertebrates. In Tasmania 25 species of food plant are anticipated, with the bulk of the diet comprising species from the Restionaceae. During mid-autumn and late spring birds tend to forage in drier areas, moving to wetter habitats during summer and early autumn. Night roosts are in dry areas irrespective of season. Nesting begins during Jul in the north-east, Aug in the West, and is delayed until Oct in Tasmania. Usually three to four (extremes two to six) white eggs are laid in a cup made of chewed grass stems and buried in dense vegetation with access only by a small tunnel-like entrance. The eggs are incubated only by the female, who is fed by the male. The black-downed chicks hatch in about 21 days and fledge after 20-28 days, sheltering in vegetation close to the nest at first. Although Ground Parrots are single-brooded, successful nesting following failure of the first clutch has been recorded. Usually only two chicks are raised giving a rather high rate of egg failure for the species.

DESCRIPTION Forehead orange-red, crown and nape green streaked black; ear-coverts and throat green with fine dark shaft-streaks. Feathers of upperparts centred black with narrow yellow bars and bright green fringes, producing a cryptic pattern. Carpal edge pale blue. Flight feathers green on outer- and blackish on innerwebs, with a pronounced yellow wing-bar visible on upper- and under-wing. Underwing-coverts greenish-blue grading to brownish; underside of flight feathers greyish. Breast green, lightly streaked black; abdomen, thighs and undertail-coverts greenish-yellow barred black. Uppertail green barred yellow, lateral feathers green on outer- and yellow on innerwebs, both barred black; undertail yellow barred blackish-brown. **Bare parts**: Bill brownish-grey; iris dull yellow; long slender legs brown (with long dark claws).

SEX/AGE Sexes alike. Immatures are duller, lack the orange-red forehead, and have a brown iris and shorter tail.

MEASUREMENTS Wing 118-139; tail 158-200; bill 12-15; tarsus 24-27.

GEOGRAPHICAL VARIATION Two races. A third, *P. w. leachi*, used for Tasmanian birds, may require reinstatement, since a series we examined showed consistently darker plumage.

P. w. wallicus (coastal districts of E Australia and Tasmania)

P. w. flaviventris (coastal SW Australia) From nominate by brighter yellow belly with less black barring.

REFERENCES Baker & Whelan (1994), Blakers *et al.* (1984), Bryant (1992, 1994), Buckingham & Jackson (1990), Collar & Andrew (1988), Emison *et al.* (1987), Forshaw (1981, 1989), Garnett (1992), King (1981), Lambert *et al.* (1993), Lodge (1991), McFarland (1991a,b,c, 1992), Meredith (1984), Ovington (1978), Peters (1961), Pizzey & Doyle (1983), RAOU (1991), Schodde & Tidemann (1988), Sibley & Monroe (1990), Simpson & Day (1984), Slater (1979, 1989), Storr & Johnstone (1979), Trounson & Trounson (1987), Wade (1975), Watkins (1985), Watkins & Burbidge (1992).

157 NIGHT PARROT
Geopsittacus occidentalis   Plate 38

Other names: Spinifex Parrot

IDENTIFICATION 22-26cm. Extremely rare, thinly spread, nocturnal, skulking and probably nomadic, this is one of the world's most difficult birds to see. It has been recorded from all Australian states, but there are very few recent records. Night Parrots have flat bills, reminiscent of Kakapo (158) with no notch in upper mandible, and there are a few hair-like feathers around the cere. The plumage generally appears yellowish-green and is cryptically marked with dark streaks and bars. The tail is short and wedge-shaped and the legs are long with short claws. The species is superficially similar to the Ground Parrot (156), but is allopatric, being restricted to the dry interior, whereas Ground Parrots are found only in the swampy heaths and pastures of coastal south-west and south-east Australia. Night Parrots are also smaller, dumpier, shorter-tailed, generally yellower (with an unbarred yellow belly), and lack the Ground Parrot's orange-red frontal band (but young Ground Parrots lack the frontal band); the much longer central tail feathers of Ground Parrot are green with a brown shaft and narrow yellow bars. When landing after being flushed, Night Parrots are said to glide down again before bolting off at an angle, whereas Ground Parrots drop almost vertically. Night Parrots are probably best searched for in seeding spinifex *Triodia* during wet seasons, or on marsh samphire *Salicornia* flats around inland lakes during drier periods. The most likely sighting would be of a medium-sized, long-winged green parrot with a slightly indicated yellow wing-bar, flushed from beneath a spinifex bush, flying swiftly for a short distance, before disappearing into dense cover. It is worth noting that although Night Parrots have been reported on roads, groups of Bourke's Parrots (147) may also gather to drink at pools on roads after dark.

VOICE A sweet, low, mournful, two-tone whistle. A 'frog-like' croak in alarm, and a few sharp notes sometimes uttered in flight after flushing.

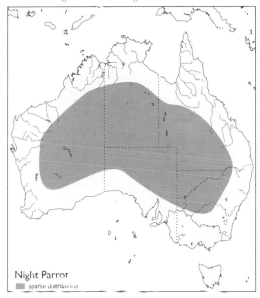

Night Parrot
■ sparse distribution

DISTRIBUTION AND STATUS Confined to the arid interior of Australia. Specimens or reports come from all Australian states, particularly central and northern Western Australia (Mount Farmer, Nichol Spring, north of Glenayle, southern Kimberleys, and west to the Cue district), South Australia (Lake Eyre, south of Oodnadatta, Gawler Ranges, the Eyre Peninsula and Cooper's Creek), south-central and north-western Northern Territory (MacDonnell Ranges, Tanami Desert), and far south-west Queensland (Lake Muncoonie and around Boulia). There is a 1913 report from around Murrayville and Cowangie, Victoria, and another from around Ross Springs (regularly flushing up to five birds) between 1954 and 1959. There is also an 1897 record from the Oxley district, New South Wales. The species has never been common, but was recorded more frequently towards the end of last century (e.g. 16 collected in the Lake Eyre region of South Australia in the 1870s). Because of its skulking habits, many sightings remain unconfirmed, and this makes it difficult to assess its true status. Even so, as observer coverage has increased, reporting frequency has declined, and it seems certain that the population is decreasing. The cause of this is unknown but it may relate to the introduction of predators such as cats, rats, dogs or foxes. Changes in fire regimes, and the introduction of camels, which deplete water sources, have also been cited as possible causes.

There have been reports in every decade since its discovery, and from all states in recent years except Victoria (last recorded in 1950s). The most notable recent sighting was of four birds on the eastern side of Cooper's Creek, 8km due east of Lake Perigundi, north-east South Australia, in June 1979. The birds were flushed from tangled poverty-bush *Sclerolaena intricata* and flew a short distance before pitching into dense lignum *Muehlenbeckia cunninghamii*. In 1990 a long-dead individual, the first museum specimen since the 1880s, was picked up in south-west Queensland, 36km north of Boulia. A sequence of more recent records of single birds and pairs (Mar 1992 to Jun 1993) south of Cloncurry, around 150 km north of the area in which the dead bird was found, confirm the local persistence of the species. The world population is unknown, but may be very small and is likely to be declining. There are none in captivity. The Night Parrot has been afforded legal protection in Australia since 1937. CITES Appendix I. CRITICAL.

ECOLOGY The ecology of the Night Parrot is little known, but it is almost certainly nomadic, depending on a combination of samphire flats with associated lake systems, and spinifex sandplains, to which birds move to when rain causes the spinifex to seed. Other habitats include areas of mulga *Acacia aneura* and saltbush *Atriplex*, with large freshwater pools, rocky areas with spinifex (particularly limestone), margins of salt lakes, and grassy areas. Night Parrots are thought to roost singly during the day, probably in concealed tunnels in dense scrub. After dark they may fly some distance to freshwater pools to drink before moving to feeding areas. Most sightings have involved single birds, pairs or groups up to four, but parties of eight have been reported at drinking places. Breeding has been recorded in Jul and Aug. Four or five white eggs are laid in a stick-lined cavity inside a spinifex tussock entered through a narrow tunnel.

DESCRIPTION Head generally greenish-brown; crown densely streaked blackish-brown, showing more yellow towards nape; cheeks and ear-coverts finely barred and stippled brown and yellowish-green. Upperparts yellowish-green, cryptically marked brown and yellow; mantle feathers yellow centrally ringed brown and edged green; back and rump with brown separated into three bars against yellow-green background, middle bar tending to show as blotches either side of shaft; uppertail-coverts with several brown bars separated by yellow and narrowly fringed green. Upperwing-coverts marked yellow and brown, edged green. Flight feathers brown with olive-green margins and a narrow yellow wing-bar on inner feathers of both surfaces. Underwing-coverts pale green stippled brown. Throat yellowish-green marked brown, breast yellow barred brown (each feather with two brown bars) with a slight green suffusion, particularly at sides, resulting from narrow green feather-fringes; flanks yellow, barred brown; belly and undertail-coverts yellow. Tail narrow and pointed; uppertail yellow barred brown, recalling gamebird (yellow appears as a series of narrow wedges along feather-edge); undertail yellow barred brown. **Bare parts:** Bill yellow brown; iris orange-brown; legs brown.

SEX/AGE Sexes alike. Immatures are duller than adults.

MEASUREMENTS Wing 132-153; tail 88-115; bill 10-14; tarsus 20-24.

GEOGRAPHICAL VARIATION None.

REFERENCES Blakers *et al.* (1984), Boles *et al.* (1994),

Collar & Andrew (1988), Collar *et al.* (1994), Emison *et al.* (1987), Forshaw (1981, 1989, 1991b), Garnett (1992), Garnett *et al.* (1993), King (1981), Lambert *et al.* (1993), Menkhorst & Isles (1981), Pizzey & Doyle (1983), Schodde & Tidemann (1988), Sibley & Monroe (1990), Simpson & Day (1984), Slater (1989), Storr & Johnstone (1979), Wade (1975).

158 KAKAPO
Strigops habroptilus   Plate 16

Other names: Owl Parrot

IDENTIFICATION 50-63cm. Now found only on a few of New Zealand's offshore islands, the Kakapo is the world's heaviest (males up to 3.6 kg) and, despite its large rounded wings, only flightless parrot. It is secretive and nocturnal, skulking in vegetation during the day, and its cryptically patterned green and brown upperparts blend in with its surroundings, making it virtually impossible to find without tracker-dogs or radio telemetry. As the Kakapo is also now restricted to areas that cannot be visited by casual observers, it probably ranks as the most difficult bird species in the world to see in the wild. Kakapo home ranges are usually around 35-50 ha in size. The following signs can indicate their presence: distinctive cryptically marked feathers; compact cylindrical droppings with coils of finely ground plant material and white traces of uric acid (these have a herb-like smell when fresh); tightly compressed 'chews' hanging from or close to fibrous vegetation (often crescent-shaped, bleached in the sun and with bill impressions); neatly clipped vegetation; bill impressions in grubbed earth; and extensive, well-worn 'track and bowl' systems created by males for display (see below). In some years, the male's nocturnal booming display call can be heard from distances of 1km or more (mainly during Dec to Mar, but occasionally also in Nov and Apr). As a rule, booming takes place away from a bird's normal home range (up to 7km). There are no confusion species.

VOICE A dull, short, quickly repeated booming made by the male during display (like the sound made by blowing across a bottle-top); a strangled shriek sometimes described as a *skrark*, with a donkey-like braying quality, and a repetitious 'chinging' sound, with a slight echo after each 'ching'.

DISTRIBUTION AND STATUS Previously found in both North and South Islands of New Zealand. The species has undergone a steep decline since European settlement, and is now one of the world's rarest birds with a known population of less than 60 individuals. All the birds have been translocated from their former ranges to three offshore islands: Maud (five birds); Codfish (c. 29 birds) and Little Barrier (16-19 birds). It is still possible that there may be one or more birds on Stewart Island, but it is extremely unlikely that any remain in Fiordland (last birds in Milford Sound area) or north-west Nelson (despite a 1985 report). The population decline is mainly attributed to predation by introduced species such as cats and stoats. The Kakapo has a strong odour, and its main defence, remaining motionless and invisible, is of no use against these species, which hunt by smell. Habitat clearance and degradation by introduced grazing mammals are also thought to be factors in the Kakapo's range contraction. If it were not for the substantial efforts of the New Zealand

Department of Conservation, the Kakapo would almost certainly now be extinct. In 1977 a previously unknown population was discovered in southern Stewart Island. These birds were at risk from feral cats whose population could not be controlled effectively, and were relocated to smaller islands, where in some cases they are now being given supplementary food to encourage breeding. In 1991 two chicks were raised on Little Barrier, and in 1992 three eggs hatched on Codfish. In March 1994 the total population was 47 birds (but nine missing individuals) including only eight females which were proven breeders. The 1997 breeding season was the most successful since 1981 with four chicks hatching on Codfish, bringing the total population to 54 (first chicks since 1992). There are two birds presently held in captivity as part of the recovery programme. CITES Appendix I. EXTINCT IN THE WILD.

Kakapo

ECOLOGY Formerly occurred from sea-level to around 1,200m (optimum about 1,000m in high-rainfall areas), favouring climax beech *Nothofagus* and podocarpus forests, regenerating subalpine scrub and snow tussock *Danthonia* grassland. Although flightless, Kakapos are strong climbers and walkers, sometimes covering many kilometres in one night. They are opportunistic feeders, so the diet is varied seasonally and annually and includes leaves, roots, fruits, ferns, mosses, fungi and seeds. Food species include pink pine *Halocarpus biformis*, stinkwood *Coprosma foetidissima*, rimu *Dacrydium cupressinum*, Hall's totara *Podocarpus halli* and mountain flax *Phormium cookianum*. The species is a lek breeder. Males clear 'track and bowl' systems in which several small circular display arenas are linked by pathways (up to 60m long), often on ridges or other prominent places from which the booming resonates. Kakapo are normally solitary, but prior to breeding a number of males may converge to within earshot to lek vocally and attempt to attract females, which visit briefly to mate. During display the body is inflated and the bird produces a series of loud booming calls, accompanied by a series of wing-flaps. These displays may last all night at the height of the booming season. Males may boom in years when females

do not nest, but there is no nesting in non-booming years. It has been suggested that booming is stimulated by a super-abundance of pollen early in the summer, indicating that sufficient food will be available for the nestlings later on, or by weight fluctuations resulting from changes in food availability in the preceding months. Breeding success is dependent on the female being able to gather all the food required for the young within walking distance of the nest, but even when food is plentiful not all the females will breed. Kakapo nest in thick vegetation, rotten trees or ready-made holes. Two to four (occasionally five) eggs are laid on a bed of wood-dust and feathers. Eggs are laid in Jan or Feb with incubation taking around 25 days. The white-downed young are brooded for two weeks and fledge in 10-12. Parental care is by the female only. Kakapo moult is protracted, may not take place every year, and begins after booming (male) or after the young fledge (female).

DESCRIPTION Forehead yellowish-brown; crown feathers black with broad green margins; supercilium yellowish-green; facial disc yellow-brown and covered in long hair-like feathers; ear-coverts darker (with pale streaks), chin lighter. Upperparts subtly marked olive yellow and brown with light moss-green tips and yellow shafts (upperparts with slight bluish sheen); uppertail-coverts with more yellow close to shaft. Primaries and secondaries marked brown and cream on outerweb, innerweb with cream barring along inner margin. Underwing-coverts yellowish marked brown, underside of primaries and secondaries brown barred cream. Underparts pale greenish-yellow, each feather showing a pale yellow shaft-streak with warm brown and greenish-yellow transverse blotches or bars; undertail-coverts greener. Tail with wispy, often hanging and abraded tips; uppertail dark greyish-brown, patterned with light olive-brown; undertail greyish-black with dull olive-brown bars. **Bare parts:** Flattish bill pearly-grey with ivory tip and bristle-like feathers around base; prominent cere blue-grey; iris dark brown; legs and large feet grey-brown.

SEX/AGE The male is larger (around 25% heavier) with a broader bill and head, and is generally brighter and yellower than the female. The tips of the innerweb of the five outer primaries show faint yellow markings in male, absent in the female. Immature generally duller with browner facial disc and paler bill. In birds up to two years old the five outer primaries are pointed (rounded in adult), with the outerweb showing light and dark bars of similar widths (only thin dark bars in adults). Young birds also have more extensive light bars on the innerwebs.

MEASUREMENTS Wing 252-285; tail 203-250; bill 34-43; tarsus 45-57.

GEOGRAPHICAL VARIATION None, but Stewart Island birds are said to be more olive than those from Fiordland.

REFERENCES Best (1984), Best & Powlesland (1985), Cemmick & Veitch (1987), Falla *et al.* (1981), Forshaw (1989, 1990b, 1991a), Gardner (1988), King (1981), Lambert *et al.* (1993), Lloyd (1992ab), Long (1981), McPherson (1990), D.V. Merton *in litt.* (1992), Merton & Empson (1989), Merton *et al.* (1991), Morris & Atkinson (1984), Poulton (1982), Powlesland (1989), Powlesland *et al.* (1992), Robertson (1985), Rosewarne (1997), Sibley & Monroe (1990).

159 VASA PARROT
Coracopsis vasa   Plate 39

Other names: Greater Vasa Parrot (*C. v. vasa*); Western Vasa Parrot (*C. v. drouhardi*); Comoro Vasa Parrot (*C. v. comorensis*)

IDENTIFICATION 50cm. A largish, rather sombre-looking brownish-black parrot with rounded tail and stout pale pinkish bill (dark grey outside breeding season). Slow flapping wingbeats suggest a short-headed but otherwise elongated ragged crow. Upperparts (particularly wings) show greyish-blue tinge, especially *C. v. drouhardi* and *C. v. comorensis*. Birds can be hard to locate when dark plumage blends with shadows below forest canopy. Largely sympatric Black Parrot (160) very similar, but all races of Vasa are larger and somewhat paler, with grey-brown, not dark brown, legs and the periophthalmic skin extending to the bill; moreover, Vasas are less graceful in flight, some breeding birds lose most of head feathers to reveal yellow or orange skin, and (in western Madagascar) their greyer undertail-coverts and faint black subterminal band on the relatively pale tail contrast with the uniform dark brownish-grey tail of Black Parrot. May fly at great height when travelling to or from communal roosting sites. May be very tame and approachable when feeding below forest canopy.

VOICE Varied repertoire. Voice generally (but not always) harsher and less melodious than Black Parrot. Range of whistling calls includes pleasant-sounding *weee-ooo*, also delivered in higher-pitched, penetrating and sometimes grating and discordant form, and a *cho-cho-chi-chi-chi* song possibly related to breeding. Some whistling calls are short and sharp; others are followed by a short puppy-like yapping. Also a loud throaty *greee-yarr*, harsh squawks, raucous *kraar*, rather nasal and vibrating *scurureah*, and *pee-aw* or *fee-eu* on a descending scale.

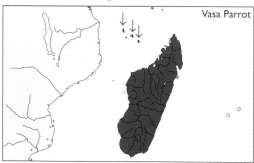
Vasa Parrot

DISTRIBUTION AND STATUS Madagascar and Comoro Islands (Grand Comoro, Mohéli, Anjouan). Mostly common to abundant but range in Madagascar has possibly contracted due to large-scale deforestation in centre of island. Officially treated as a harmful species, birds being heavily persecuted because of crop predation (especially rice) and captured for domestic and international live bird trade. Also hunted for food. Occurs in several protected areas and, although persecution and trapping intense in some areas, apparently not yet at risk.

ECOLOGY Variety of habitats from moist dense forest to open subdesert woodland and savanna, including *Medemia* palm savanna. Frequents habitats modified by human activity; sometimes visits cultivated lands. Primarily lowlands from sea-level to 1,000m. On Comoros, birds generally associated with moist evergreen forest above 300m but visit more open country to feed. Within forest habitat, usually seen in the tops of trees although birds will descend to ground-level for feeding. Generally encountered in small noisy parties but congregates in larger flocks when feeding or roosting. Birds roost in tops of tall trees with at least one individual awake to warn of danger; said to be active on moonlit nights. Seeds, nuts, berries and fruits are consumed, with damage claimed to crops such as rice, millet and maize; apparently less frugivorous than Black Parrot. Breeding season probably Oct–Dec. Nest in a hollow tree-trunk or limb. In western Madagascar, baobabs *Adansonia* are often used, sometimes with several nests in the same tree. Birds (especially males) may show cloacal protrusions whilst breeding.

DESCRIPTION Plumage generally brownish-black with a faint paler greyish tinge on upperparts, especially wings and uppertail. Primaries narrowly margined grey on outerwebs. Underside of flight feathers pale grey. Under-tail-coverts grey with variable black streaking on feather-shafts. Tail with faint dark subterminal band; undertail pale grey. **Bare parts**: Bill usually pale pinkish-horn but grey following moult; iris brown; bare patch of periophthalmic skin (extending to bill) light grey; legs pale grey-brown.

SEX/AGE No sexual dimorphism on plumage. Breeding females may become bald on the head, around eyes and throat with exposed skin becoming mustard-yellow or orange. Immatures from adults on paler grey-brown plumage and paler skin around eyes. Patch of bare skin around eyes smaller than adult or absent.

MEASUREMENTS Wing 299-322; tail 185-209; bill 34-40; tarsus 31-34.

GEOGRAPHICAL VARIATION Three races.
> *C. v. vasa* (E Madagascar; in SW and NW Madagascar, intermediates with *drouhardi* are found)
> *C. v. drouhardi* (W Madagascar) Smaller (length 450; wing 275-295) and paler than nominate. Underparts are more grey with undertail coverts appearing whitish, upperparts show a distinct grey-blue tinge. Dark subterminal band on tail.
> *C. v. comorensis* (Grand Comoro, Mohéli and Anjouan in the Comoro Islands) Smaller (length 450; wing 256-295) and paler than nominate, differing from *drouhardi* in having underparts tinged chocolate-brown rather than grey, and brown undertail coverts rather than grey or whitish.

REFERENCES Benson (1960), Dee (1986), Forshaw (1989), Langrand (1990), McBride (1996), Moreau (1966), Nicoll & Langrand (1989), Wilkinson (1994).

160 BLACK PARROT
Coracopsis nigra   Plate 39

Other names: Lesser Vasa Parrot; Bangs's Black Parrot (*C. n. libs*); Seychelles Black Parrot (*C. n. barklyi*)

IDENTIFICATION 35cm. Almost uniform dark blackish-brown with stout pale bill (darker outside breeding season). Most easily confused with larger sympatric Vasa Parrot (159), which see for differences. Graceful in flight with strong rhythmic wingbeats interspersed with gliding phases, contrasting with the flat laborious crow-like flapping of Vasa.

VOICE Varied repertoire, generally more pleasant-sounding than Vasa Parrot. Melodious fluting whistles, often delivered in groups of about 4-6 different notes. Some calls more shrieking and discordant. Other whistling calls include disyllabic *too-it*, short *wit wit wit* notes, quite eerie sounds, and series of clear and tuneful trisyllabic *cheee-chooo-cheee* whistles followed by a fourth similar but lower-pitched component. This last call is quite distinct from any of Vasa Parrot. Also a *caark*, softer than the squawk of Vasa.

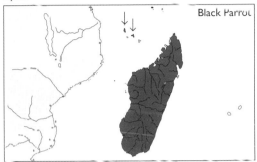

Black Parrot

DISTRIBUTION AND STATUS Madagascar, Comoro Islands (Grand Comoro and Anjouan) and Praslin Island (Seychelles), where possibly introduced. Races found in Madagascar and the Comoros are generally described as common. Officially treated as pest species in Madagascar where birds are persecuted because of crop damage; also hunted for food and pets. Despite sometimes intense persecution, apparently not yet at risk and occurs in many protected areas in Madagascar. The Praslin race, occurring in the Vallée de Mai Reserve, is severely depleted (probably fewer than 100 birds remain) and is considered critically endangered; competition for nest-sites with Indian Mynas *Acridotheres tristis* may be among the threats to remaining birds.

ECOLOGY Resident with some diurnal foraging movements. Inhabits variety of forest and savanna habitats including man-modified ecosystems, wooded surroundings of towns and villages as well as remaining primary forests from sea-level to 2,050m. Occurs more in denser forest, marshy forest (including mangroves) and brush than Vasa Parrot, which is said to avoid larger areas of humid forest. Usually seen in small noisy groups, either flying or in the bare branches of tree-tops; active on moonlit nights. On Seychelles, however, birds rarely form flocks and are generally seen singly or in pairs except where favoured foods are locally abundant. Not known to form mixed species flocks with Vasa Parrot. Food consists of a variety of seeds, berries, fruits and nuts; more frugivorous than Vasa Parrot. Specific reported food items include fruits of *Afzelia bijuga* and *Chassalia*, seeds of *Cinnamosma fragrans*, blossoms of *Symphonia* and some leaves. On Madagascar, consumption of insect galls also reported. Attacks crops and on Comoros reported as pest in cacao plantations where birds feed on unripe pods. Main foods of Praslin population include *Verschaffeltia splendida*, *Averrhoa bilimbi*, *Phoenicophorium borsigionum*, *Deckenia nobilis*, *Chrysobalanus icaco* and *Ficus rubra*. Nest in hollow tree-trunk or limb usually above 15m. Breeding probably Nov–Feb. Clutch 2-3.

DESCRIPTION General plumage blackish-brown (iridescent green sheen during breeding season) with inconspicuous greyish markings on undertail-coverts and grey outerwebs to primaries. Underside of flight feathers pale grey. Uppertail brownish-black; undertail pale grey; dark sub-terminal band. **Bare parts**: Bill horn-coloured, appearing greyer after moult; iris dark brown; narrow grey peri-ophthalmic ring (does not reach bill); legs dark brown.

SEX/AGE No sexual dimorphism. Immatures paler than adults with pale undertail-coverts and yellowish tinge on bill and pale grey tips to tail feathers. Buff edges to wing-coverts are thought to distinguish at least some immature birds.

MEASUREMENTS Wing 216-252; tail 135-164; bill 21-24; tarsus 22-26.

GEOGRAPHICAL VARIATION Four races, but some authors consider *C. n. sibilans* and *C. n. barklyi* as indistinguishable.

   C. n. nigra (E Madagascar; intermediates with *libs* found in north-west and south-west)
   C. n. libs (W Madagascar) Paler than nominate, underparts browner, upperparts tinted blue-grey. No dark subterminal band on tail.
   C. n. sibilans (Grand Comoro and Anjouan in the Comoro Islands) Smaller (length 300, wing 188-193) and paler than nominate, and chocolate rather than blackish brown. No grey in outerwebs of primaries.
   C. n. barklyi (Praslin in the Seychelles where small remaining population is centred on the Vallée de Mai) Very similar to *C. n. sibilans* but shows greyish-blue reflections in outerwebs of primaries. Some *barklyi* specimens show paler undertail coverts than body plumage, while they are the same colour in *sibilans*.

REFERENCES Arndt (1992), Benson (1960), Dee (1986), Forshaw (1989), Gaymer *et al.* (1969), Goodman & Putnam (1996), Langrand (1990), Louette (1988), Merritt *et al.* (1986), Milon *et al.* (1973), Nicoll & Langrand (1989), Penny (1974).

---

161 GREY PARROT
Psittacus erithacus   Plate 39

Other names: African Grey Parrot

IDENTIFICATION 33cm. Unmistakable large grey parrot (largest in Africa) with striking short scarlet tail. Silvery belly, underwing-coverts and rump. Breast, mantle and upperwing-coverts slate-grey with primaries very dark grey. Facial area whitish. Bright scarlet tail and undertail-coverts distinguish it from all other parrots. In many localities this species is especially noticeable at dawn and dusk when noisy flocks pass high overhead in fast direct flight on rapid shallow wingbeats between roosting and feeding areas.

VOICE Very vocal with wide repertoire of squawks, whistles, shrieks and screams given both in flight and when perched, and including mimicry of other birds and mammals. Calls include harsh grating *scraark scraark scraark*, noisy *scree-at*, short sharp *scrat scrat scrat* and *creee-ar creee-ar creee-ar* calls with a honking nasal quality that recalls geese. Harsher calls sometimes interspersed with range of whistling sounds, sometimes ascending or descending in pitch, including a pure-toned *weee-ooo weee-ooo* and *teee-ooo*. Some whistles are long and rolling with a rather eerie quality, others suggest a bubbling sound; some are short and rapidly repeated, others are very high-pitched and penetrating. Voice sometimes suggests air blown across top of a bottle, and a descending *dooo-o-ooo* followed by a loud harsh *screeek* is often heard. A harsh loud screech signals alarm. Flocks often very noisy. Extraordinary mimic of human and other sounds in captivity.

Grey Parrot

DISTRIBUTION AND STATUS W and C Africa, from Guinea-Bissau and Sierra Leone east through southern Mali, Côte d'Ivoire, Ghana and Nigeria to southern Cameroon, extending onto Bioko and Príncipe islands in the Gulf of Guinea; from Gabon and Congo through northern Zaïre, Uganda and western Kenya, south-western and east-central Zaïre and north-western Tanzania. Mainly sedentary. Common where large tracts of forest persist and still abundant in some localities, especially in the Congo basin rainforests. However, due to extensive forest loss in some parts of range (e.g. from Nigeria to Sierra Leone) and trapping on massive scale (second most heavily traded parrot in world in 1980s) there have been drastic declines in some places (e.g. in Liberia, Ghana, Kenya and around Kinshasa, Zaïre, and other Congo basin cities).

ECOLOGY Inhabits primary and secondary rain-forest, forest edges and clearings, gallery forest and mangroves; wooded savanna, cultivated land and even gardens are also frequented. Mostly confined to lowland areas, although in east of range recorded to 2,200m. Reaches highest densities in lowland primary forest, intermediate in montane primary forest and lowest in coconut plantations. Gregarious, forming large communal roosts of up to 10,000 individuals, often at some distance from feeding areas. Preferred roost-sites are trees or palms over water or on islands in rivers. Disperses in smaller groups (up to 30) for feeding. Diet consists of a variety of seeds, nuts, fruits and berries. Food is generally gathered by climbing among top branches of trees. Reported food items include fruits and seeds of *Ficus, Heisteria, Dacryodes, Petersianthus, Combretum, Macaranga, Raphia, Harungana, Ceiba, Blighia, Bombax, Celtis, Caccia, Parkia, Terminalia* and *Prunus*. The flesh of oil-palm *Elaeis guineensis* fruit is highly favoured food in some areas with fruits often carried long distance before being consumed. In Bioko, fruits of *Cola tragacantha*

are preferred. Can be a pest and for instance causes considerable damage to maize crops in some areas. Nest in tree-cavity (e.g. *Terminalia, Ceiba* or *Distemonathus*) 10-30m above ground. Sometimes breeds in loose colonies of up to several hundred pairs (in Príncipe for example) but in most places nesting is solitary. Breeding season varies with locality. In East Africa, breeding recorded Jan–Feb and Jun–Jul, both dry periods. Young fledglings reported for sale from Mar onwards in Ghana. Other records suggest as a rule dry-season breeder. Clutch 2-3, sometimes 4.

DESCRIPTION Feathers of lores, cheeks, forehead and crown silver-grey with paler grey tips. Those of mantle and lower back darker slate-grey with pale margins giving scalloped appearance; lower back and rump silver-grey. Upperwing-coverts, secondaries and scapulars slate-grey. Primaries darker grey (almost black), paler below than above. Underwing-coverts pale grey, except for dark grey greater coverts. Breast feathers slate-grey with pale grey margins merging into much paler silvery feathers of belly; flanks and thighs pale silvery-grey. Tail and tail-coverts bright scarlet. Older birds may show scarlet feathers scattered among grey of body plumage, especially on thighs and belly becoming quite extensive in some individuals. **Bare parts**: Bill black; iris yellow; bare facial area white with some fine white hairs; legs dark grey.

SEX/AGE No sexual dimorphism on plumage. Immatures have tails darker red towards tip, grey tinge on undertail-coverts and grey iris.

MEASUREMENTS Wing 232-259; tail 79-95; bill 32-39; tarsus 25-28.

GEOGRAPHICAL VARIATION Two races. A third, *P. e. princeps*, restricted to the islands of Príncipe and Bioko, is said to be larger and darker than *P. e. erithacus* but appears doubtfully valid. On the other hand, some authors regard the two races below as separate species.
    P. e. erithacus (Equatorial Africa from south-eastern Côte d'Ivoire to W Kenya, NW Tanzania, S Zaïre and N Angola)
    P. e. timneh (W parts of the moist Upper Guinea forests and bordering savannas of West Africa from Guinea-Bissau, Sierra Leone and S Mali to Côte d'Ivoire east to at least 70km east of the Bandama River. Feral population occurs with nominate at Abidjan, Côte d'Ivoire) Darker than nominate and red of tail feathers duller, darker and generally maroon (not scarlet). Uppertail-coverts grey tinged red (not scarlet). Upper mandible reddish tipped black. Smaller than nominate (wing 203-225).

REFERENCES Alick *et al.* (1993), Demey & Fishpool (1991), Forshaw (1989), Fry *et al.* (1988), Gautier *et al.* (1993), Gore (1994), Grimes (1987), Helsens (1996), Juste (1996), Louette (1981), Mackworth-Praed & Grant (1952), Serle *et al.* (1977), Zimmerman *et al.* (1996).

162 BROWN-NECKED PARROT
Poicephalus robustus   Plate 40

Other names: Levaillant's Parrot; Cape Parrot (nominate)

IDENTIFICATION 33cm. Bulky short-tailed parrot with top-heavy appearance owing to large head and bill, latter with long fine tip. Combination of dull olive-brown head and neck (greyer in *P. r. suahelicus* and *P. r. fuscicollis*), dull green wing-coverts contrasting with grass-green underparts and rump (latter clearly visible in flight) and orange-red on bend of wing and thighs distinguishes this species from related, but considerably smaller, Meyer's (166), Senegal (164) and Brown-headed Parrots (169), with which it is partly sympatric (see relevant accounts for range overlaps). Similar-sized and partly sympatric Jardine's Parrot (163) does not show contrast between head and neck colour and remainder of body plumage. Head of nominate may appear golden in field. Very shy and generally not approachable.

VOICE Series of piercing *screeet screeet screeet* shrieks emitted in flight. Softer more contented sounds heard whilst birds at rest. Voice similar to Meyer's Parrot but more resonating and grating. Although repertoire appears relatively limited in wild, captive birds mimic human and other sounds.

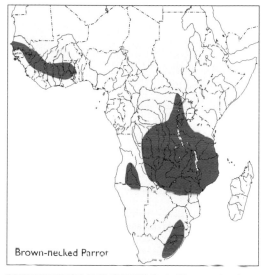

Brown-necked Parrot

DISTRIBUTION AND STATUS Probably occupies three separate ranges, in West, south central and southern Africa. In West Africa, found from Gambia and southern Senegal east to Ghana and Togo. In south-central Africa, from south-western Congo, southern and eastern Zaïre, south-western Uganda, Rwanda and from central Tanzania to northern Namibia, northern Botswana, Zambia and Zimbabwe. Occurs in South Africa from north-eastern Transvaal to eastern Cape Province. Foraging parties wander unpredictably and may roost away from traditional sites for weeks. Sometimes makes seasonal movements in relation to food availability, e.g. in the northern savannas of Ghana. Local and mostly uncommon throughout range, although more numerous and frequent in Ghana. Southern subspecies considered vulnerable in South Africa where, although erratic movements give impression of fluctuating population, it has suffered a decline because of trapping for live bird markets, habitat destruction and persecution by pecan nut farmers; only fragmented patches of native vegetation now remain.

ECOLOGY Inhabits variety of woodland types including *Rhizophora* mangroves (e.g. Gambia), riverine woodlands (e.g. Ghana, Zimbabwe), savanna woodland (e.g. Nigeria, Côte d'Ivoire), montane forests at 3,750m (e.g. eastern Zaïre) to lowland forest (e.g. southern Zaïre). Southern

African birds particularly favour *Acacia mearnsii* and *Podocarpus* forest at 1,000-1,700m, separating altitudinally and ecologically from race *suahelicus*, which occurs in lowland forest. Southern African birds (also perhaps other races) form communal roosts before dispersing to remote feeding areas (up to 90km) in small parties. Sometimes seen singly but more usually encountered in groups of up to 20 (sometimes 50). Forms mixed flocks with congeners. In Zimbabwe, apart from daily foraging trips, longer seasonal movements in search of *Uapaca* and *Syzygium* fruits are undertaken. Fruits of *Ficus*, *Olea capensis*, *Mimusops caffra*, *Acacia molissima*, *Melia azedarach*, *Terminalia*, *Calodendron capense* and *Commiphora*, seeds of *Acacia mearnsii* and *Monotes glaber* and nuts of parinari palms are also recorded. However, seeds may be preferred since fruit pulp is sometimes discarded in favour of pips and kernels. Recorded taking millet in Zimbabwe and Malawi, piles of harvested peanuts in Gambia and occasionally in apple orchards, but nowhere sufficiently numerous to be serious pest. Southern African birds feed almost exclusively on *Podocarpus* fruits when available. Uses bill to climb among branches when feeding in trees, also feeds on ground. Birds make rather secretive daily trips to take water. Nest in existing tree-hollows (including in *Brachystegia*, *Adansonia* or *Podocarpus*) 6-12m above ground. Breeding season varies with locality. In Gambia, egg-laying reported Feb and Apr whilst in Zimbabwe estimated or recorded Mar-Jun, Oct and Nov. In South Africa, breeding recorded Jun and Aug-Oct. Clutch 2-4.

DESCRIPTION Head, neck and throat olive-brown to olive-yellow with darker (almost black in some birds) flecks, especially on crown; lores and cheeks blackish; dull red frontal band occasionally present in male (generally obvious in female). Mantle feathers and scapulars dull dark green edged brighter green; rump bright grass-green. Coverts at leading edge of wing from carpal joint to base of primaries bright orange-red; upperwing-coverts dark green to black with lighter green margins; underwing-coverts blackish and green. Primaries and secondaries black above, dark brown below. Breast, belly and vent bright grass-green; thighs bright orange-red. Uppertail black; undertail dark brown. Some birds (about 10%) have scattered yellow feathers in plumage. **Bare parts**: Bill whitish-brown or horn; iris dark brown to reddish-brown; legs blue-grey.

SEX/AGE Females generally (but not invariably) possess well-defined orange-red frontal band. Immature birds lack orange-red markings on wing-coverts and thighs but are thought always to show some red on forehead.

MEASUREMENTS Wing 201-223; tail 81-97; bill 31-37; tarsus 21-25.

GEOGRAPHICAL VARIATION Three races; some authors treat the nominate as a separate species.

> **P. r. robustus** (Confined to extreme SE Africa, mainly Cape Province, Natal and Transvaal, South Africa)
> **P. r. suahelicus** (Mozambique and Zimbabwe through Malawi and Zambia north to S Tanzania and SE Zaïre and west to N Namibia and Angola; also Transvaal, South Africa, east of the Drakensberg) Head and neck silvery. Female shows faint reddish wash in place of clear red frontal band of nominate. Blue tinge on rump.
> **P. r. fuscicollis** (Gambia and S Senegal to N Ghana and Togo) Similar to *suahelicus* but green of body plumage

slightly more bluish beneath and on rump (some overlap in this regard with nominate). Broader edges to coverts and scapulars giving greener appearance above. Female has extensive red cap.

REFERENCES Boshoff (1989), Collar (1997), Elgood *et al.* (1994), Forshaw (1989), Fry *et al.* (1988), Gore (1990), Grimes (1987), Mackworth-Praed & Grant (1962), Newman (1988), Penry (1994), Roberts (1984), Rowan (1983), Tarboton *et al.* (1987), Wirminghaus (1994, 1996).

---

163 JARDINE'S PARROT
Poicephalus gulielmi   Plate 40

Other names: Red-headed Parrot, Red-crowned Parrot, Congo Red-crowned Parrot

IDENTIFICATION 28cm. Large green parrot with red markings on forehead, leading edge of wing and thighs (orange in West African race). Distinguished from similar-sized and partly sympatric (in Rwanda, possibly Uganda and near mouth of Congo) Brown-necked Parrot (162) by green (not olive-brown) head and neck, darker green body plumage and proportionally smaller, darker bill. Rump is yellow-green compared to grass-green in Brown-headed Parrot. Only other large parrot found in Africa's rain-forests is the very different Grey Parrot (161).

VOICE Generally noisy. High-pitched harsh chattering *scureeat tchareek scurureeat scurureeat* screams. Call repeated in short phrases followed by pause. Some more bubbling and melodious notes may accompany shrieking sounds including a rather drawn-out whistling *teee-oooo*. Quieter whistling notes whilst feeding. Flocks can produce noisy, grating and sometimes constant cacophony. High-pitched screech when alarmed.

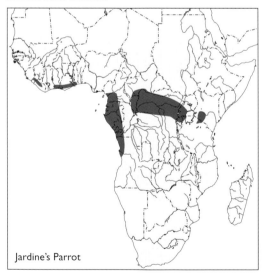

Jardine's Parrot

DISTRIBUTION AND STATUS Several apparently disjunct distributions. In West Africa in Liberia east to Côte d'Ivoire and southern Ghana. In western-central Africa from southern Cameroon south to north-western Angola. An apparently separate population ranges through northern Zaïre and southern Central African Republic east to south-western Uganda and Rwanda. Also found in

highlands of Kenya and Northern Tanzania. Sedentary with local movements. Locally common to abundant in many localities in eastern part of range, apparently declining in others (possibly as result of deforestation). Perhaps at risk around Kilimanjaro because of trapping for trade. Scarce in west of range. Occurs in several protected areas including Korup National Park in Cameroon and Bia National Park in Ghana.

ECOLOGY Inhabits montane *Juniperus* and *Podocarpus* forest in Kenya and Tanzania between 1,800 and 3,250m where it may rely on primary vegetation. Confined to lowland rain-forest in remainder of range (below 700m in West Africa) but not restricted to primary formations, with records from tall shade-trees in coffee plantations in Angola and secondary forests in Ghana. Usually stays in tree-tops whilst feeding or resting. Generally in groups of up to 10 birds but forms larger flocks where food abundant. Substantial congregations sometimes occur at roosting sites. In Kenya, birds make lengthy diurnal foraging trips (60km) following gallery forests whilst crossing otherwise *Acacia*-dominated savanna woodland. Diet thought to be comprised of a variety of seeds, fruits, flowers and insects. *Spathodea* seeds, oil-palm *Elaeis guineensis* nuts, *Podocarpus* fruits and flowers and seeds of *Grevillea robusta* are among recorded food items. Probably takes some insects. Sometimes associates with Rameron Pigeons *Columba arquatrix* and Sharpe's Starlings *Pholia sharpii* when feeding on *Olea capensis*. Solitary breeder. During mating, male reported to sway rhythmically, without flapping wings, while perched on female's back. Nest located in cavity 3-12m above ground. On Mount Meru (Tanzania), nests recorded in live *Hagenia*, *Podocarpus* and *Juniperus* trees. Egg-laying recorded Nov and Jan (Tanzania), Sep (Zaïre) and Mar, Jun and Sep-Nov (Kenya). Clutch of 2-4 glossy white eggs.

DESCRIPTION Forehead and forecrown bright red; lores and chin blackish; cheeks, hind-crown and nape dark grass-green with scattered feathers showing blackish centres. Mantle feathers and scapulars black with broad green margins giving scalloped appearance; rump and uppertail-coverts bright yellowish-green. Wing-coverts black with dark green margin; leading edge of wings from carpal joint to base of primaries bright red. Primaries and secondaries black. Underwing-coverts dark green and blackish. Underparts dark green with scattered feathers showing black central band; thighs bright red. Tail black. **Bare parts**: Upper mandible grey, blackish towards tip with paler patches at base, lower mandible blackish; iris orange; legs dark grey to black.

SEX/AGE Sexes similar. Immature birds lack red on forehead, leading edge of wings and thighs; green in plumage slightly paler than adult. Young birds sometimes show red in underwing-coverts. Feathers in forehead buffish tipped green.

MEASUREMENTS Wing 194-214; tail 72-85; bill 33-35; tarsus 21-23.

GEOGRAPHICAL VARIATION Three races.

P. g. gulielmi (S Cameroon through Rio Muni, Gabon, Congo, Cabinda to NW Angola and east through Zaïre to S Uganda and Rwanda)

P. g. fantiensis (Upper Guinea rain-forests of West Africa in Liberia, Côte d'Ivoire and S Ghana) Smaller than nominate (mean wing 186). Forehead, leading edge of wings and thighs orange or orange-red (but not red) and more extensive, in at least some birds. Underparts paler green with fewer black markings.

P. g. massaicus (Both sides of the Great Rift Valley from Mount Elgon in Kenya south to Mount Meru and Kilimanjaro in N Tanzania) Red restricted to forehead. Paler than nominate with few if any black markings below.

REFERENCES Cordeiro (1994), Demey & Fishpool (1991), Forshaw (1989), Fry *et al.* (1988), Green & Carroll (1991), Grimes (1990), Helsens (1996), Lewis & Pomeroy (1989), Mackworth-Praed & Grant (1952, 1970), Rodewald *et al.* (1994), White (1965), Williams & Arlott (1980), Zimmerman *et al.* (1996).

164 SENEGAL PARROT
Poicephalus senegalus   Plate 40

Other names: Yellow-bellied Senegal Parrot (*P. s senegalus*); Yellow-vented Senegal Parrot (*P. s. mesotypus*); Orange-breasted Senegal Parrot, Orange-bellied Senegal Parrot, Red-vented Senegal Parrot, Scarlet-bellied Senegal Parrot (*P. s. versteri*)

IDENTIFICATION 23cm. Combination of rather small size, short tail, grey head and yellow, orange or red abdomen easily distinguishes this species from Ring-necked Parakeet (194), the only other common parrot inhabiting the forest mosaic and savanna woodlands of West Africa. Overlaps marginally with smaller Meyer's Parrot (166) in extreme south-western Chad and north-eastern Cameroon, and with slightly larger Niam-Niam Parrot (165) in extreme south-western Chad; both latter lack distinctive orange-yellow belly. Allopatric Red-bellied Parrot (168) has grey, not green, upperparts. Direct flight with deliberate deep wingbeats not as fast as congeners. All-yellow morphs recorded from Gambia.

VOICE Noisy with repertoire comprised of wide (but characteristic) range of mainly harsh and high-pitched screeches, squawks and whistles. Calls include high *screeat screeat screeo screee* and jangling metallic *screelelelee screelele steee ow steee-ow* cries; also abrupt jangling *steeet steeet* and *sst-eeet sst-eeet*. Whistling calls include rhythmically repeated *peweeo peweeo peweeo* sound. More raucous when agitated.

DISTRIBUTION AND STATUS West Africa. From Guinea (including Iles de Los), Senegal, Gambia southern Mauritania and southern Mali through the forest-savanna mosaic of Côte d'Ivoire, Burkina Faso, southern Niger, Ghana (also at coast), Benin and Togo to Nigeria, Cameroon and south-western Chad. Mostly sedentary but seasonal visitor in some (especially more northern), e.g. birds move south along River Niger in Mali with onset of drier periods. Rainy-season visitor to southern Mauritania and movements occur in Nigeria with drier north vacated outside wet season. Generally frequent to very common but may be scarce in drier, more marginal habitats. Popular pet both locally and outside range but apparently not seriously affected by trade.

ECOLOGY Found in wide variety of wooded habitats ranging from open farmland with scattered palms and trees to closed-canopy forests. Optimum habitat appears to be relatively open savanna woodland with numerous *Adansonia digitata* or *Parkia filicoides*. In Ghana reported from riverine woodlands and marshes. Probably only

found below 1,000m. Gregarious, at least outside breeding period. Usually seen in pairs or parties up to 20 but larger flocks may gather to exploit locally abundant food. Undertakes both diurnal and longer-term movements in relation to food supply; consequently, numbers fluctuate widely in some areas. Diet comprised of variety of fruits, seeds and leaf buds. Recorded food items include fruit and seeds of *Kaya senegalensis, Pterocarpus erinaceus, Ficus, Parkia, Sclerocarya birrea, Butyrospermum parkii, Vitex cienkowskii, Adansonia, Ximenia americana* and *Acacia albida*. Also takes crop plants including millet and peanuts. Nest in tree-cavity at 10m or higher. Breeding period appears to vary with locality. In moister areas season may be prolonged. Nest-hole commonly in cavity in larger branch of *Adansonia* or *Parkia*. In region of Gambia and Senegal Rivers eggs recorded Apr, May, Aug and Sep and from Nov to Feb. In drier areas (such as Mali) breeding probably limited to wet season (May-Oct). Clutch 2-4.

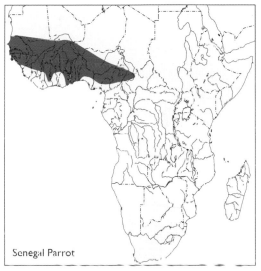

Senegal Parrot

DESCRIPTION Forehead, crown, lores and nape dark slate-grey; paler chin and cheeks; ear-coverts silvery. Mantle, scapulars and back bright green; rump and uppertail coverts paler with yellowish tinge. Upperwing-coverts bright green; secondaries and primaries dark brown with green margins to outerwebs. Underwing coverts yellow. Throat grey, merging into grass-green breast (paler than green on upperparts); lower breast and belly bright yellow with orange central tinge; thighs green, undertail-coverts bright yellow. Tail brownish-green. **Bare parts**: Bill grey; iris yellow with black orbital ring; cere blackish; legs dark brown.

SEX/AGE Sexes similar on plumage. Immature generally duller than adult with dull brown head, no silvery ear-coverts; sometimes extensive green on underparts with yellow confined to patches on flanks. Iris dark brown.

MEASUREMENTS Wing 151-160; tail 64-70; bill 20-26; tarsus 17-21.

GEOGRAPHICAL VARIATION Three races; however, *P. s. mesotypus* may represent a clinal variant of the nominate.

P. s. senegalus (Senegal, Gambia, Guinea, S Mauritania and S Mali to Burkina Faso and N Nigeria, where it intergrades with *P. s. versteri*)

P. s. versteri (Ivory Coast and Ghana east through Togo and Benin to W Nigeria north to Ilorin, Ibi and Zaria) Upperparts darker green than nominate. Orange-red lower breast and abdomen.

P. s. mesotypus (E and NE Nigeria, S Niger, N Cameroon, extreme SW Chad and possibly extreme NW Central African Republic) Generally paler than nominate with orange belly.

REFERENCES Claffey (1995), Elgood *et al.* (1994), Forshaw (1989), Fry *et al.* (1988), Gore (1990), Green (1990), White (1965), Wilkinson & Beecroft (1985).

---

165 NIAM-NIAM PARROT
Poicephalus crassus   Plate 42

IDENTIFICATION 25cm. Predominantly grass-green short-tailed parrot with olive-brown head, nape and upper breast. Larger than Meyer's Parrot (166), with which it overlaps throughout much of range, and Senegal Parrot (164), which occurs sympatrically in extreme southwestern Chad and (possibly) western Central African Republic. Distinguished from allopatric Brown-headed Parrot (169) by extension of olive-brown on head to chest, green (not yellow) underwing-coverts and larger size. Shy and difficult to approach, either flying off calling loudly or remaining still relying on foliage for cover when disturbed.

VOICE Sharp, rather clear and penetrating *scree-ooot scree-ooot*. Call less jangling and harsh than Senegal and Meyer's Parrots. Flocks create excited cacophony of sound. Tone alters when alarmed.

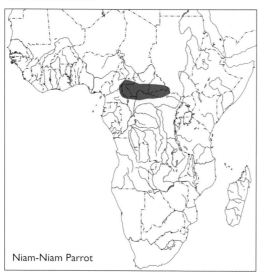

Niam-Niam Parrot

DISTRIBUTION AND STATUS Northern Central Africa south of Sahara. Thought to occur in eastern Cameroon (where status unclear) through central and southern Central African Republic, extreme south-western Chad and extreme north Haut-Zaïre to south-western Sudan (Bahr-el-ghazal). Sedentary with local movements. Status poorly known but thought to be generally common, although scarcer in south-west Sudan.

ECOLOGY Frequents wooded savanna country, forest

savanna mosaic, moist savannas and *Syzygium-Adina* riparian woodland in savanna up to 1,000m. Commonly near water. Recorded in pairs or small parties. Regular daily movements take place including to mountainous areas where birds visit tall trees for feeding. Diet poorly known but certainly includes a variety of seeds; reported food items include millet and grain. Few details on reproductive biology but thought to nest Aug-Sep during rains. Nest and eggs undescribed.

DESCRIPTION Whole head, except for silvery ear-coverts, dull olive-brown; nape olive brown. Mantle feathers and tertials brown margined dark green; back, rump and uppertail-coverts bright grass-green. Upperwing-coverts dark green; innermost secondaries dark green; margined of flight feathers brown with dark green outerwebs. Throat and upper breast dull olive-brown; lower breast, belly, thighs and undertail-coverts grass-green. Tail feathers dark brown tipped and margined dark green. **Bare parts:** Bill yellowish-horn, upper mandible darker with black tip; iris yellow; legs blackish.

SEX/AGE Sexes similar. Grey-brown hood of immatures shows strong olive-yellow markings; mantle is more green. Underparts paler and more yellowish than adult. Innermost secondaries edged with yellow. Upper mandible paler than adult and tipped grey.

MEASUREMENTS Wing 164-168; tail 64-75; bill 24-25; tarsus 18-20.

GEOGRAPHICAL VARIATION None.

NOTE Previously treated as race of morphologically similar Brown-headed Parrot.

REFERENCES Carroll (1988), Forshaw (1989), Fry *et al.* (1988), Lippens & Wille (1976), Louette (1981), Mackworth-Praed & Grant (1970).

---

166 MEYER'S PARROT
Poicephalus meyeri   Plate 41

Other names: Brown Parrot, Sudan Brown Parrot

IDENTIFICATION 21cm. Only African parrot showing combination of extensive blue or blue-green on underparts and blue or blue-green rump on otherwise ashy-brown upperparts, yellow on carpal joint and (except for races *damarensis* and most *reichenowi*) striking yellow crown. One of the smallest *Poicephalus* parrots but considerably larger than any of the lovebirds *Agapornis*. Occurs together with Rüppell's Parrot (170) in south-western Angola and possibly northern Namibia, and with Brown-headed Parrot (169) in a narrow overlap zone between north-eastern Transvaal and south-eastern Zimbabwe. Race *damarensis* distinguished from Rüppell's by blue-green (not mostly brown) underparts, and *transvaalensis* from Brown-headed (with which it may sometimes hybridise) by bluer underparts, extensive yellow markings around carpal joint on upper surface of wing, and yellow crown (absent in some individuals). Orange belly easily distinguishes Senegal Parrot (164) which overlaps with Meyer's in extreme south-western Chad. The scarcer Brown-necked Parrot (162, race *suahelicus*), which occurs sympatrically over much of central southern Africa, is easily separated by considerably larger size and lack of yellow markings. Red-bellied Parrot (168) overlaps with Meyer's in Tanzania and Kenya where it is separated by orange underparts and underwing-coverts (male) or green underparts and grey head (female). Meyer's often perches conspicuously in dead tree. Flight is swift, strong, direct and usually near to ground. When flushed from trees, birds drop to just above ground before making off at high speed. Characteristic two-note call given in flight.

VOICE In common with other *Poicephalus* species, utters series of harsh screeches including abrupt *screeak scree-eak scree-ah screeat* calls interspersed with brief pauses. A characteristic synchronised *klink-kleep* duet call given by birds in flight. Distinctive snoring or growling *kraw-her* sound sometimes rising to a shricking cry when alarmed. Flocks can create chorus of very loud excited calls. Captive-reared birds can learn to mimic a variety of sounds.

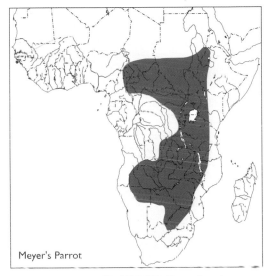

Meyer's Parrot

DISTRIBUTION AND STATUS Central and eastern Africa. From north-eastern Cameroon and southern Chad through northern Central African Republic to central and southern Sudan and western Ethiopia, south through Uganda, western Kenya, eastern Zaïre and Tanzania to Malawi, Zambia, Angola, north-eastern Botswana, Zimbabwe, extreme western Mozambique, Namibia and Transvaal (South Africa). A feral population in eastern Cape Province, South Africa, is thought to have died out. Nomadic in some areas during drought periods, when may occur outside normal range; otherwise resident with local movements. Generally common to very common and is most abundant parrot in some parts of range (e.g. Zimbabwe and Angola) although scarce in other areas and absent from some apparently suitable habitats. Decline reported from some parts (e.g. Transvaal) thought to be result of habitat destruction. Also persecuted in some localities owing to damage to crops (e.g. in middle Zambesi because of damage inflicted on ripening *Ziziphus* berries).

ECOLOGY Found in a wide variety of woodland habitats from dry savanna through gallery and riparian woodlands to secondary growth around cultivation. Reported from woodland dominated by *Terminalia laxiflora* and *Isoberlinia doka*, *Combretum* bushlands and *Acacia* grasslands; also *Brachystegia* and *Syzygium-Adina* riparian woodlands. Avoids lowland rain-forests of the Congo basin and other humid forests including parts of the eastern highlands of Zimbabwe and Nkhata Bay district of Malawi. Shows preference for taller trees in drier savanna habitats - particularly *Adansonia* specimens. May be confined to gallery woods in drier parts of range and is generally found in vicinity of water. Where sympatric with Red-bellied Parrot Meyer's is confined to riverine woodland. In Kenya, found largely in areas with annual rainfall in excess of 500mm. Recorded occasionally from suburban areas. Generally in lowlands but reported to 1,250m in Ethiopia, 2,200m in East Africa and to 1,500m in eastern highlands of Zimbabwe. Occurs in pairs or small parties of 3-5 birds (possibly family groups); up to 50 may congregate at food source outside breeding season. Roosts in tree cavities. Generally shy and wary. Diet consists of fruits, nuts and seeds, including *Ficus*, *Ziziphus abyssinica*, *Uapaca nitidula*, *Monotes glaber*, *Combretum*, *Grewia*, *Sclerocarya*, *Pseudo-lachnostylis*, fruits of large riparian growth trees such as *Afzelia quanzensis* and *Melia volkensii*, cultivated oranges and flowers of *Schotia brachypetala*. Fruit pulp less important than hard seeds and in miombo woodland Meyer's Parrot is one of very few species to consume seeds of *Brachystegia* and other leguminous trees. Also takes grain and regarded as crop pest in some areas. Consumes some insects, including caterpillars. May range widely in search of food during droughts. Nests solitarily in tree-cavity 3-10m above ground, during dry season (e.g. Mar-Jun in Zimbabwe, May to Sep in Zambia and Malawi, Jul in Angola and Dec or Jan in Sudan). Clutch 2-4.

DESCRIPTION Forehead, lores, cheeks, ear coverts and nape ash-brown; crown bright yellow. Mantle feathers ash-brown edged blue or blue-green tinge in some birds; scapulars ash-brown, some individuals showing blue or blue-green tips; rump bright turquoise-blue or blue-green; uppertail-coverts greener. Outermost lesser and median upperwing-coverts bright yellow, remainder showing variable green tinge, especially towards tips. Primaries and secondaries ash-brown with narrow paler margins to outerwebs. Underwing-coverts bright yellow in some birds but greyish-brown feathers in greater underwing-coverts in others. Chin, throat and upper breast ash-brown; remainder of breast and belly turquoise-blue or blue-green; thighs yellow; undertail-coverts turquoise-blue or blue-green; Tail ash-brown. **Bare parts**. Bill dark grey or black; cere black; iris orange-red; bare periophthalmic skin blackish; legs blackish.

SEX/AGE Sexes similar. Juvenile generally more greenish-brown. No yellow on crown or thighs and yellow area on upperwing surfaces is smaller. Underwing-coverts green and brown with little or no yellow. Underparts more greenish. Iris dark brown.

MEASUREMENTS Wing 141-149; tail 55-68; bill 20-25; tarsus 16-19.

GEOGRAPHICAL VARIATION Six races.

> *P. m. meyeri* (Extreme NE Cameroon through S Chad, N Central African Republic and S Sudan eastwards to W Ethiopia north to Eritrea)
>
> *P. m. saturatus* (Extreme E Zaïre, through Burundi, Rwanda and Uganda eastwards into W and C Kenya east to Meru and locally in interior Tanzania south to Ruaha National Park) Darker than nominate (especially brown parts), rump less pure blue than nominate showing some green feathers. Dark centres to feathers on underside give mottled appearance.

Intergrades with *matschiei* in Tanzania.

P. m. matschiei (SE Kenya through E and C Tanzania to SE Zaïre, N Malawi, N Zambia and E Angola) Paler brown than *saturatus* and blue-green tinge to margins of scapulars less pronounced than nominate. Green colours bluer (especially beneath). Female shows patch of yellow feathers at base of lower mandible.

P. m. transvaalensis (Parts of N and C Mozambique north of Save River through S Zambia and C and S Zimbabwe to NE Botswana – see *P. m. damarensis* – and W Transvaal) Paler brown than *matschiei*, bluer still on rump and below. Yellow areas on crown often reduced and sometimes lacking altogether (especially in males). Thought to hybridise with *P. cryptoxanthus*.

P. m. reichenowi (N and C Angola from Malange and central highlands to Huila, possibly also adjacent parts of Zaïre) Similar to *matschiei* but yellow crown usually absent. Rump paler blue. Average size larger than *matschiei* (wing 153-176).

P. m. damarensis (S Angola, NE Namibia and N Botswana) Always lacks yellow crown. Said to be paler than *reichenowi*. Intergrades with *transvaalensis* in region of Okavango delta, Botswana, and with *reichenowi* in Angola.

REFERENCES Bretagnolle (1993), Britton (1980), Carroll (1988), Forshaw (1989), Fry *et al.* (1988), Irwin (1981), Lewis & Pomeroy (1989), Mackworth-Praed & Grant (1952, 1962, 1970), Newman (1989), Roberts (1984), Rowan (1983), Stubblefield (1994), Tarboton *et al.* (1987), Traylor (1965), White (1970), Wilson & Wilson (1994).

167 YELLOW-FACED PARROT
Poicephalus flavifrons   Plate 41

Other names: Yellow-fronted Parrot, Shoa Parrot

IDENTIFICATION 28cm. Only medium-sized parrot regularly found within most of its restricted highland range. Overlaps with Red-bellied Parrot (168) in south of range (Rift Valley) and with Meyer's Parrot (166) in north and possibly south-west, but at least partly separated from both on elevation. Easily told from these and other African parrots by combination of bright yellow mask and green body plumage. Belly and rump paler than nape, mantle and upperwing-coverts. Usually in small parties that call in fast dashing flight. Birds spend much time noisily feeding in tree-tops but fall silent if approached, before suddenly flying off calling loudly.

VOICE Loud, shrill unmusical whistles and screeches.

DISTRIBUTION AND STATUS Endemic to the highlands of western Ethiopia, but exact range unclear. Frequent to common in forested areas; considered commonest in the higher, more northern parts of range. Probably sedentary although some periodic movements into Addis Ababa.

ECOLOGY Generally inhabits *Juniperus* and *Podocarpus* forests from 1,800-2,900m, mainly in *Hagenia* above 2,900m. Also found in light woodlands interspersed with *Ficus* trees in the cultivated plateau country and in gallery forests in *Acacia* savanna. Also in *Acacia-Ficus* riverine forest from about 300m. Occasional visitor to urban areas, e.g. gardens and parks in Addis Ababa. Generally in pairs, small family parties or flocks up to 20; often in mixed flocks with Black-winged Lovebirds (173). Birds probably use

same roosting trees each night. Diet thought to comprise grain, seeds and fruits, with ripe fruits of *Dovyalis abyssinica* reported, Nov. Considered a minor crop pest in some areas. Breeding habits largely unknown but suspected that nest generally in tree-cavity.

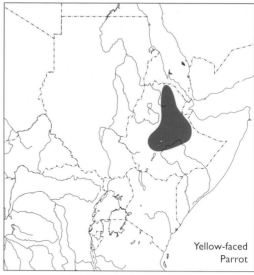

Yellow-faced
Parrot

DESCRIPTION Forehead, crown, lores, cheeks and ear-coverts bright yellow, often with orange wash; small area bordering yellow feathers around cheek often with brownish-grey tinge. Feathers of nape, mantle and scapulars dark green with paler, brighter green margins; rump and uppertail-coverts paler and brighter green than rest of upperparts. Upperwing-coverts dark green with paler green margins, sometimes with yellow on leading edge of wing and base of primary-coverts. Primaries and secondaries brown with narrow paler margins to outer-webs. Chin and thighs sometimes flecked yellow but otherwise underparts uniform bright green. Tail dark blackish-brown. **Bare parts:** Upper mandible blackish-grey, lower whitish; iris orange-red; legs dark brownish-grey.

SEX/AGE Mask lacks orange wash and sometimes less extensive in female. Immatures like adult but mask dull yellowish olive-green, not yellow.

MEASUREMENTS Wing 161-180; tail 71-92; bill 22-27; tarsus 18-20.

GEOGRAPHICAL VARIATION Two races, but *aurantiiceps* doubtfully valid.

    P. f. flavifrons (Thought to occur in C and N regions of Ethiopia's western highlands)

    P. f. aurantiiceps (Known only from the Masango or Maschango area and the Upper Gila River in SW Ethiopia) Facial markings orange.

REFERENCES Abdu *et al.* (1992), Ash & Gullick (1989), Forshaw (1989), Fry *et al.* (1988), Mackworth-Praed & Grant (1952), Succow (1990), Urban & Brown (1971), White (1970).

168 RED-BELLIED PARROT
Poicephalus rufiventris **Plate 41**

Other names: Orange-bellied Parrot, African Orange-bellied Parrot, Red-breasted Parrot, Abyssinian Parrot

IDENTIFICATION 25cm. Medium-sized parrot of dry bush and wooded country. Male distinguished from other African parrots by combination of deep orange belly, ash-brown upperparts and bright pale bluish rump. Females and juveniles told from Meyer's (166) and Brown-headed (169) Parrots by absence of yellow on head and/or wings. Allopatric Senegal Parrot (164) has green (not brown) upperparts and dark head, and all subspecies show at least some yellow (as well as orange) on belly. Since Red-bellied Parrots are generally encountered in pairs or family parties, orange belly of adult male is generally a reliable guide to identity of flock. Particularly swift bullet-like flight just below tree-top level accompanied with shrill screech is characteristic. Marginally sympatric or parapatric with larger Yellow-faced Parrot (167) in Ethiopia, Brown-headed in parts of Kenya, Meyer's in west of range and possibly Jardine's (163) in Kenya and Tanzania.

VOICE Harsh, rather abrupt and high-pitched *screeeak screeek sceeeareat* calls interrupted by brief pauses. Also lower-pitched and more guttural *creerrat* call recorded. Flocks can create loud excited chorus.

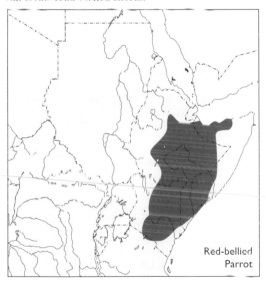

Red-bellied Parrot

DISTRIBUTION AND STATUS East Africa. From north-eastern Tanzania, eastern and northern Kenya into the Horn of Africa in southern and eastern Ethiopia (including Rift Valley) and western and northern Somalia. Widespread within range and generally frequent to common. Absent in coastal lowlands. Largely sedentary with seasonal movements in some areas.

ECOLOGY Usually associated with semi-arid vegetation including dry bush areas and *Acacia-Commiphora* steppe woodlands. Tends to avoid dense foliage and often perches on bare dead branch. In south of range, prefers *Adansonia*-studded savanna. Where sympatric with Meyer's Parrot (west of range) birds avoid riverine woodlands and inhabit more open savanna. In Ethiopia encountered in *Acacia-Chrysopogon* savanna up to 2,000m. Seasonal altitudinal

movements in relation to food supply reported from Somalia, where birds move to about 2,000m from Jul-Sep in search of wild figs *Ficus*. Otherwise, generally below 1,400m. Usually in pairs or family parties of 3-4 birds; seldom in larger flocks. Apart from figs, seeds (including *Acacia*), fruits of *Balanites aegyptiaca*, *Cordia ovalis* and *Dalbergia melanoxylon*, and maize are among reported food items. Drinks frequently and often found near water. Nests in cavity 2-3m above ground in terrestrial termite mound or 10m or more in dead tree. Female recorded in breeding condition in Mar (Tanzania) and feeding young in Jul and Oct. Recorded laying dates May and Jun, Ethiopia; Jan-May, Somalia, where half-grown chicks also recorded in Jan. Sometimes loosely colonial, Somalia, with single pairs in baobabs c. 100-200m apart. Clutch 1-2 ivory-white eggs.

DESCRIPTION Crown, nape and lores ashy-brown, cheeks the same but sometimes tipped orange; ear-coverts slightly paler. Mantle and scapulars ashy-brown; back deep bluish-black; rump iridescent pale blue or bluish-green. Upperwing slightly darker than head and back; primaries brown. Underwing-coverts orange; underside of flight feathers pale brown. Throat and chest ashy-brown with orange tinge; breast orange; belly to undertail-coverts pale green sometimes showing orange-tinged feathers. Tail dark ashy-brown. **Bare parts.** Bill, cere and orbital skin black; iris orange-red; legs black.

SEX/AGE Female has upper breast grey, lower breast pale green sometimes tinged orange. Head paler and greyer than male. Underwing-coverts greyish. Immatures generally similar to female but young males have orange underwing coverts and may show brown markings on breast.

MEASUREMENTS Wing 148-158, tail 69-76; bill 21-26; tarsus 17-20.

GEOGRAPHICAL VARIATION Two races, but *pallidus* may not be valid.
> *P. r. rufiventris* (C Ethiopia, Kenya and NE Tanzania)
> *P. r. pallidus* (Somalia and E Ethiopia) Brown head and throat paler than nominate.

REFERENCES Archer & Godman (1937-1961), Britton (1980), Forshaw (1989), Fry *et al.* (1988), Lewis & Pomeroy (1989), Mackworth-Praed & Grant (1952), Massa (1995), Safford *et al.* (1993), Williams & Arlott (1980), Zimmerman *et al.* (1996)

169 BROWN-HEADED PARROT
Poicephalus cryptoxanthus **Plate 42**

Other names: Concealed-yellow Parrot

IDENTIFICATION 22cm. Smallish plain green parrot with brown head. In flight shows bright yellow underwing-coverts. Distinguished from sympatric Brown-necked Parrot (162, race *suahelicus*) by much smaller size, absence of red thighs and carpal patches and by greenish, not bluish, rump; from Meyer's Parrot (166) – with which it may hybridise – by dull green underparts, green upperwing-coverts and back; from allopatric Orange-bellied Parrot (168) by green upperparts; and from allopatric Niam-Niam Parrot (165) by yellow underwing-coverts and more limited extension of brown hood onto upper breast. Birds with yellow feathers scattered throughout head and body plumage are occasionally encountered. Has fast dashing flight on slightly decurved wings in conspicuous and noisy small flocks. More cryptic at rest as birds hide behind branches, even in bare trees.

VOICE Usual call in flight an ear-splitting strident disyllabic *chree-oo... chree-oo* rising in pitch on the second note. Also a sharp *kreek* and a high-pitched staccato *tchaa tchaa tchaa tchaa*. Feeding often accompanied by softer chattering sounds. Nestlings make continuous rasping sound when alarmed.

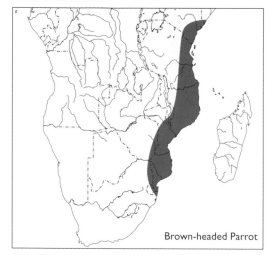

Brown-headed Parrot

DISTRIBUTION AND STATUS South-eastern Africa. From north-eastern South Africa (Swaziland, Zululand and Transvaal) through south-eastern Zimbabwe, Mozambique and southern Malawi to eastern Tanzania (including Pemba and extreme southern Zanzibar) and extreme south-eastern Kenya. Occurs Wasiri Island. Apparently sedentary. In places common, especially near coast and in south of range, but in some other areas scarce or rather local; possibly even extinct Zanzibar. Increasingly vulnerable to habitat loss and fragmentation and probably undergoing general decline. Largely confined to protected areas in Zululand and eastern Transvaal.

ECOLOGY Found in almost any woodland and riparian forest within the forest-savanna and dry woodlands of south-eastern Africa, but appears to avoid miombo woodland and prefer areas with baobabs. Recorded from coconut plantations, riparian forest, edges of smallholdings and mangroves. Confined to lowlands (below 1,200m in Tanzania and 1,000m in Malawi). Gregarious; usually in small flocks of c. 12 birds but up to 50 may gather at food source. Sometimes associates with Brown-necked Parrot and recorded feeding with Green Pigeon *Treron australis*. Diet includes figs, berries of cultivated cassava *Manihot esculenta*, seeds of *Adansonia*, coconut palm flowers, new tree shoots, fruits of *Pseudocadia zambesica*, pods of *Acacia nigrescens* and *Albizia gummifera*, unripe seeds of *Erythrina* and nectar from *Aloe* and *Kigalia* flowers; also takes millet and maize and in some areas regarded as a pest. Forages with slow, deliberate, clambering movements and often holds food item with foot. Drinks daily around midday. Nest in tree-cavity, often old woodpecker nest in an *Adansonia* 5-10m above ground. Breeding Apr-Oct depending on locality. Clutch 2-3 shiny white rounded eggs.

DESCRIPTION Entire head, including nape, chin and throat chocolate brown; ear-coverts paler. Mantle brown but greener towards tail; scapulars brown with dark green margins; rump and uppertail-coverts bright grass-green. Upperwing-coverts green, sometimes with small yellow patch on bend of folded wing; underwing-coverts yellow. Primaries brown with blue-green outerwebs; secondaries brown. Feathers of upper breast brown narrowly edged green towards lower breast; rest of underparts grass-green but darker feather-bases may give mottled appearance. Tail dark brown with greenish wash, narrowly margined and tipped dark green. **Bare parts:** Upper mandible and cere greyish-black (darker towards tip), lower pale, almost white; iris pale greenish-yellow; periophthalmic ring and legs dark grey to black.

SEX/AGE Sexes similar. Immatures generally duller than adults and with brown iris.

MEASUREMENTS Wing 145-164; tail 58-72; bill 19-22; tarsus 15-18.

GEOGRAPHICAL VARIATION Two races. A third, *zanzibaricus*, from Pemba and extreme south of Zanzibar (where possibly extinct) is reportedly like *P. c. tanganyikae* but slightly larger, and probably not distinct.

    P. c. cryptoxanthus (E southern Africa from E Zululand, E Swaziland and E Transvaal to S Mozambique and SE Zimbabwe. May perhaps hybridise with *P. meyeri tranvaalensis* in narrow overlap zone in NE Transvaal and SE Zimbabwe)

    P. c. tanganyikae (Mozambique north of the Save River through S Malawi and E Tanzania to coastal Kenya) Generally paler than nominate. Mantle greener and underparts brighter and 'cleaner' than nominate. Bib of brown feathers on throat and upper breast much smaller than nominate and head more olive-brown.

REFERENCES Britton (1980), Forshaw (1989), Fry *et al.* (1988), Irwin (1981), Lewis & Pomeroy (1989), Roberts (1984), Rowan (1983), Ryall (1991, 1994), Tarboton *et al.* (1987), Taylor (1996), Wirminghaus (1995).

170 RÜPPELL'S PARROT
Poicephalus rueppelli   Plate 42

Other names: Brown Parrot, Damara Parrot

IDENTIFICATION 22cm. Medium-sized dull brownish parrot with bright blue (brown with bluish tinge in male) rump, lower belly and tail-coverts. Combination of blue lower belly, yellow underwing-coverts and thighs, and absence of green in plumage distinguishes this from all other African parrots, including the allopatric Red-bellied Parrot (168); from marginally sympatric Meyer's Parrot (166, race *damarensis*) also by latter's much paler and greener blue on underparts that extends to throat (also usually in different habitats); from the larger Brown-headed Parrot (162, race *suahelicus*), which overlaps widely in northern Namibia and Angola, also by lemon-yellow patch on carpal joint. Flight swift and direct. Often perches in tops of tall trees where it may sit motionless and be hard to see. When disturbed, adopts upright posture and calls loudly before making off at high speed.

VOICE Monotonous short sharp *quaw*. Shrill shrieks increasing in pitch and volume uttered in alarm before taking flight. Said to be more muted than congeners.

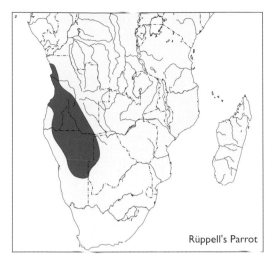

Rüppell's Parrot

DISTRIBUTION AND STATUS South-western Africa, from south-western Angola (Luanda) to Damaraland, western Ovamboland and northern Namaqualand (region of Rehoboth), northern Namibia. Some local nomadic movements in relation to food supply, otherwise resident. Generally reported as locally common although fluctuations may occur with nomadic shifts and numbers depleted by trapping with Namibia (most of species's range) now estimated to hold only 9,000 birds. Although not reported as at risk, small population, restricted range and illegal trapping pressure are perhaps leading to decline with recent shrinkage in observed flock sizes.

ECOLOGY Inhabits woodlands along dry watercourses, dry woodlands (including *Euphorbia* forests), dry steppe and thornveld, showing a preference for areas with *Adansonia* or other tall trees, also in *Commiphora/Acacia* formations on the Namibian escarpment. Not recorded above 1,250m in Angola. Generally found close to water, in small flocks (up to 20 birds); sometimes in greater numbers where food plentiful. Feeds on various parts (buds, shoots, nectar, flowers, seeds, pods, etc.; fruit endocarp believed most important) of *Acacia karoo*, *A. albida*, *A. erubescens*, *Prosopis juliflora*, *Faidherbia albida*, *Terminalia prunoides*, *Combretum imberbe*, *Grewia*, *Elephantorisa*, *Tapinanthus*, *Ficus* and melons; insect larvae are also recorded. Birds thought to drink morning and evening. Nest in old woodpecker hole up to 5m above ground. Thought to breed from Feb-May although juvenile birds reported Sep; breeding may be more closely linked to rainfall than season. Usual clutch 3-5 white rounded eggs.

DESCRIPTION Head generally dusky earth-brown but paler on sides of face with silvery ear-coverts. Nape, mantle and scapulars earth-brown with slightly paler and rather indistinct silvery tips to most feathers (especially on nape); rump brown with blue wash, occasionally with odd bright blue feathers. Upperwing-coverts earth-brown. Leading edge of wing from carpal joint to base of primaries bright yellow. Primaries and secondaries otherwise earth-brown above, paler below. Underwing-coverts bright yellow. Underparts mostly uniform brown, distinctly paler than upperparts; thighs bright yellow; undertail-coverts and posterior of flanks with blue wash, some feathers sometimes tipped bright blue. Tail darker earth-brown than rest of plumage. **Bare parts**: Bill greyish-black; cere

black; iris orange-red; periophthalmic ring black; legs black.

SEX/AGE Lower back, rump, uppertail-coverts, lower belly, undertail-coverts and posterior portion of flanks bright blue in female. Immature like female but blue areas duller and less extensive, body paler brown, thighs brown. Underwing-coverts and carpal joint brown or brownish-yellow; pale margins on wing-coverts.

MEASUREMENTS Wing 138-157; tail 62-77; bill 20-25; tarsus 17-19.

GEOGRAPHICAL VARIATION None.

REFERENCES Brickell (1985), Dean *et al.* (1988), Fry *et al.* (1988), Mackworth-Praed & Grant (1962), Newman (1988), Roberts (1984), Rowan (1983), Selman & Hunter (1996).

171 GREY-HEADED LOVEBIRD
Agapornis canus Plate 43

Other names: Lavender-headed Lovebird, Madagascar Lovebird

IDENTIFICATION 15cm. Only lovebird found in Madagascar, Comoro Islands, Réunion, Rodrigues and localities in the Seychelles. Male generally green with grey head, nape, throat and upper breast; more yellowish below and brighter on rump; black underwing-coverts and dark subterminal band on green tail. Generally encountered in noisy flocks of 5-30 (sometimes more) in swift twisting flight or feeding on ground in compact groups. When disturbed, birds retire to vantage point on grass stems or bushes, returning to food quickly when danger passed. Sometimes associates with various finches.

VOICE Variety of whistles and squawks reported from feeding flocks including a metallic *plee plee*. Subdued chatter recalling Budgerigar (155) also reported, especially during courtship display. Series of high-pitched calls signal alarm.

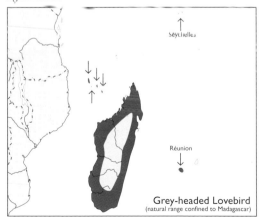

Grey-headed Lovebird
(natural range confined to Madagascar)

DISTRIBUTION AND STATUS Natural range Madagascar where generally common, especially in more open country in coastal regions, but now rare in east and absent or scarce on central plateau. Introduced to Comoros, Seychelles, Rodrigues, Réunion, Mauritius, Zanzibar and Mafia; apparently died out on last three and in only small numbers in Rodrigues and Réunion, but widespread and generally common in Comoros. In Seychelles, initially established widely in Mahé but now confined to suburbs around Victoria and a few west coast localities; small population reported on Silhouette. Attempted introductions to other islands and the African mainland have failed. Trapped for live bird trade and widely held in captivity outside range.

ECOLOGY In Madagascar favours sparsely wooded country, palm savanna, forest edge, degraded forest, scrub and cultivated land such as ricefields up to about 1,500m. Uses clearings into dense forest on mountain slopes but apparently not recorded from evergreen closed-canopy forest. Reported from vicinity of towns and villages and often seen by roads. Introduced populations show similar habitat preferences. Gregarious, usually in flocks of up to 30 birds but may concentrate in larger numbers where food abundant, sometimes associating with Madagascar Red Fody *Foudia madagascariensis*, Sakalava Weaver *Ploceus sakalava* or Madagascar Mannikin *Lonchura nana*. Often roosts communally on bare branches. Sedentary. Diet comprised principally of grass seeds. In Seychelles commercially grown elephant grass *Panicum maximum* preferred; in Comoros unopened flowering shoots of *Stenotaphrum* grass taken. Birds also take rice spread out to dry around villages and farms. Nest located in tree-cavity; chamber lined with chewed leaf fragments or wood shavings from interior of hollow and with grass stems carried by female between body feathers. Nesting recorded Nov-Dec in Madagascar: probably breeds during rains (Nov-Apr) in Comoros. Usual clutch 3-4 but up to eight recorded in captivity. Incubation probably by female alone.

DESCRIPTION Head and neck pale grey. Mantle and scapulars green; rump much brighter grass-green than rest of upperparts. Upperwing-coverts green, alula darker. Flight feathers green above, darker towards tips and on margin of outerwebs; brownish-grey below. Underwing-coverts black. Throat to upper breast pale grey; lower breast to undertail-coverts pale yellowish-green. Uppertail grass-green, brighter laterally, with broad black subterminal band; undertail greyish-green subterminally barred black. **Bare parts:** Upper mandible bluish-white, lower pinkish-white; iris dark brown; legs pale grey.

SEX/AGE Head, neck and breast of female green; upperparts sometimes browner than male. Underwing-coverts green. Immature resembles adults but grey hood of male suffused with green, especially on nape; bill yellowish with black at base of upper mandible.

MEASUREMENTS Wing 88-101; tail 41-50; bill 11-12; tarsus 12-14.

GEOGRAPHICAL VARIATION Two races.
> *A. c. canus* (Lowland Madagascar, except for arid SW. Populations introduced elsewhere appear to be this race)
> *A. c. ablectanea* (Arid SW lowlands of Madagascar, intergrading with nominate around Bekopata and Ankavandra) Greener (less yellowish) beneath, grey hood of male darker and bluer.

REFERENCES Dee (1986), Forshaw (1989), Goodman & Putnam (1996), Langrand (1990), Louette (1988), Nicoll & Langrand (1989), Penny (1974), Rutgers & Norris (1979), Turner (1991).

172 RED-FACED LOVEBIRD
Agapornis pullarius   Plate 43

Other names: Red-headed Lovebird

IDENTIFICATION 15cm. Plumage generally green, more yellowish below with electric-blue rump. Bright red forecrown, forehead, cheeks, lores and throat (orange in female) distinctive. Black underwing-coverts of male sometimes helpful in identification. Broadly sympatric (in much of Central Africa) with Black-collared Lovebird (174), overlaps with Fischer's Lovebird (176) in area around southern Lake Victoria and Black-winged Lovebird (173) in south-western Ethiopia, and approaches range of Peach-faced Lovebird (175) in Cuanza River region, Angola. Distinguished from these and other lovebirds by combination of green upper breast with red (or orange) crown, face and throat.

VOICE Generally rather weak, with a high-pitched chirruping *si si si si si si*, delivered in short bursts both in flight and whilst perched, and a pleasant trilling, a less melodious *screeteet screeteet* and a shorter whistling *tchiri tchiri*.

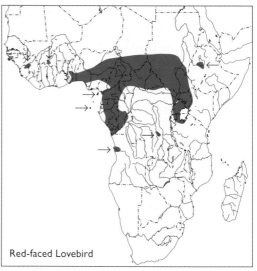

Red-faced Lovebird

DISTRIBUTION AND STATUS Occurs widely but patchily across West and Central Africa. Reported Guinea, northern Sierra Leone and northern Côte d'Ivoire in the region of Boundiali and Tingrela; in Ghana, found in north and east of country south and west to around Accra. Occurs in southern Togo and Benin and into central and southern parts of Nigeria, although apparently absent from coastal regions. On Gulf of Guinea islands (extinct Príncipe). Irregularly distributed through Cameroon south to Cabinda and north-western Angola (possibly south to Cuanza River) and from Central African Republic and extreme south of Chad to southern Sudan and northern Zäire; throughout Uganda and reported from extreme west Kenya, north-west Tanzania, Burundi and Rwanda. An apparently isolated population exists in southwest Ethiopia. Generally sedentary but some local migrations and nomadism reported (e.g. Nigeria, Uganda and Tanzania). Abundance varies widely: common in some areas (e.g. Niger floodplain, Nigeria and Brazzaville, Congo) but abundant only locally (e.g. Ethiopia):

uncommon in many other areas (e.g. Angola, southern Ghana – where apparently nearly extinct – and western Kenya). Abundance also varies owing to nomadic habits, but a genuine overall decline appears to have occurred in many areas this century. Trapped for live bird trade with large numbers in captivity outside range.

ECOLOGY Inhabits moist lowland savanna, isolated patches of heavier forest within savanna, riverine woodland and scrub, and more open habitats, including abandoned plantations, cultivated land and pasture. Prefers secondary forests and penetrates primary formations only in the vicinity of grassy clearings. Generally below 1,500m but up to 2,000m in Uganda. Forms fast-flying flocks of as many as 30 but usually fewer birds, breaking into pairs whilst breeding. Flocks roam widely in search of food but return to preferred communal roost. In captivity often sleeps hanging upside-down. Diet composed principally of grass seeds including cultivated varieties (millet and sorghum), often eaten before ripe. Fruit (*Psidium* and *Ficus*) occasionally eaten and birds in captivity take insect larvae. Regarded as serious crop pest in some areas. Breeds solitarily. Nest-cavity located in tree (generally excavated by woodpecker), in hole dug in side of arboreal ant or termite nest or occasionally in terrestrial termitaria. Nest composed of pad of seed husks, shredded grass leaves and perhaps hardened excrement; apparently constructed by female only. Breeds during rains when grasses seeding. Clutch 3-6 (sometimes more in captivity) with eggs evidently laid at intervals.

DESCRIPTION Forehead, forecrown and lores bright orange-red; hindcrown, nape, mantle and scapulars bright green; rump bright pale blue; uppertail-coverts bright green but paler than back. Upperwing-coverts bright green; small area of bright pale blue on carpal joint. Primaries and secondaries green on outerweb, blackish on inner. Underwing-coverts black; underside of flight feathers blackish. Chin and throat bright orange-red; rest of underparts bright grass-green (paler than upperparts). Central tail feathers green, lateral ones green marked red with black subterminal band and yellow (or yellowish-green) tip. **Bare parts**: Bill coral red, cere whitish; iris dark brown; legs grey or greyish green.

SEX/AGE Head, chin and throat of female orange bordered yellowish behind. Underwing-coverts green. Immature like adult female but orange on head and throat less bright or yellowish. Young male shows black underwing-coverts. Bill reddish brown.

MEASUREMENTS Wing 84-98; tail 35-41; bill 13-14; tarsus 12-14.

GEOGRAPHICAL VARIATION Two races.
  A. p. pullarius (Guinea and Sierra Leone to Sudan, south to Zäire and Angola, with southern limits of distribution poorly documented)
  A. p. ugandae (Ethiopia, Uganda, E Zäire, Rwanda, W Kenya and Tanzania) Rump possibly on average paler than nominate.

REFERENCES Britton (1980), Carroll (1988), Claffey (1995), Elgood *et al.* (1994), Evans & Balmford (1992), Forshaw (1989), Fry *et al.* (1988), Green & Carroll (1991), Grimes (1987), Lewis & Pomeroy (1989), Louette (1981), Mackworth-Praed & Grant (1952, 1970), Sargeant (1994), Turner (1991), Urban & Brown (1971), White (1970), Williams & Arlott (1980).

173 BLACK-WINGED LOVEBIRD
Agapornis taranta   Plate 43

Other names: Abyssinian Lovebird

IDENTIFICATION 16-17cm. Mostly green with red face and forehead (green in female), black flight feathers, black underwing-coverts (green in female) and green tail with black subterminal band. Partially sympatric, and broadly similar, Red-faced Lovebird (172) distinguished by red or orange (not green) throat and blue (not green) rump. Distinguished from all other lovebirds by combination of green rump and throat with blackish flight feathers. Only lovebird to manipulate food with foot. Usually encountered in small flocks in tops of tall trees where plumage blends well with foliage. Flight swift and direct.

VOICE Shrill *kseek* whistle during flight. Also shrill twittering.

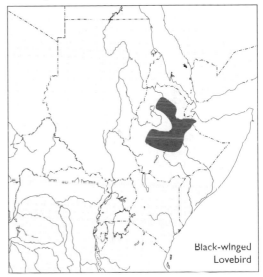

Black-winged Lovebird

DISTRIBUTION AND STATUS Endemic to highlands of Ethiopia from Eritrea south through to Harer and Addis Ababa to Bale including Rift Valley. Frequent to common in montane forest; relatively uncommon in lower-altitude savanna. Trapped for local markets and traded internationally; large numbers in captivity outside range. Regarded as minor crop pest and may become target of chemical spraying used against birds.

ECOLOGY At higher altitudes (1,800-3,800m) typically associated with montane forest dominated by *Podocarpus*, *Juniperus*, *Hagenia* and *Hypericum*; lower down (to 1,400m) found in grassy savanna and woodland characterised by *Acacia*, *Combretum* and *Euphorbia*, also frequenting cultivated areas and reported from the fringe of urban Addis Ababa. Gregarious, at least outside breeding season, when birds are usually found in small flocks (8-20) in tops of taller trees, gathering in larger numbers where food locally abundant. Roosts communally in tree-cavity (often old woodpecker or barbet nest). Sometimes associates with Yellow-fronted Parrots (167). Occasionally rests upside-down in captivity. Diet consists largely of tree fruits including figs *Ficus* and berries of *Juniperus*. Undertakes seasonal movements in relation to food availability. Nests in tree-cavity but also reported in hole in wall and perhaps even weaver's nest. In captivity, female carries nesting material (small fragments of twigs, leaves and grass) tucked into almost any part of plumage. Only lovebird that uses own feathers for nest. Eggs reported Mar-Nov. Unclear if laying linked to timing of rains. Usual clutch five but 3-8 reported in captivity.

DESCRIPTION Forehead, lores and feathered periophthalmic ring red; rest of head and nape green tinged brown. Mantle and scapulars green, rump and uppertail-coverts brighter green. Upperwing-coverts green except for black outer primary coverts. Primaries blackish-brown with narrow green margin to outerweb; secondaries black. Underwing-coverts black. Chin and throat pale green tinged brown; rest of underparts pale green. Central tail feathers green broadly tipped with black, lateral ones green with yellow innerweb, subterminally barred black with green tip. **Bare parts**: Bill coral red; iris dark brown; legs grey.

SEX/AGE Female lacks red on head, and underwing-coverts sometimes marked green. Immature like female with yellowish bill. Young males show black underwing-coverts with scattered red feathers on forehead.

MEASUREMENTS Wing 95-106; tail 41-53; bill 17-18; tarsus 14-15.

GEOGRAPHICAL VARIATION No races generally recognised but *A. t. nana* (from SW Ethiopia) has been proposed on basis of shorter wing and smaller bill.

REFERENCES Abdu *et al.* (1992), Arndt (1996), Ash & Gullick (1989), Forshaw (1989), Fry *et al.* (1988), Mackworth-Praed & Grant (1952), Rutgers & Norris (1979), Succow (1990).

---

174 BLACK-COLLARED LOVEBIRD
Agapornis swindernianus Plate 43

Other names: Swinderen's Lovebird, Liberian Lovebird

IDENTIFICATION 13cm. Predominantly green with striking bright-blue rump and uppertail-coverts. Aside from female Grey-headed Lovebird (171), only member of genus with wholly green head. Adult further distinguished from congeners by black nuchal collar bordered posteriorly with yellow (brick-red in *A. s. zenkeri* and *A. s. emini*). Partially sympatric Red-faced Lovebird (172) has red, not blackish, bill and no collar. Generally encountered in small flocks flying swiftly over forest canopy. Birds generally remain in tree-tops where their plumage blends well with foliage. Quite shy and unapproachable. Only rarely near to ground level when (e.g.) visiting fields.

VOICE Various subdued twittering and creaking calls including a shrill rattling metallic *chinga chinga chinga*, rapidly repeated. Also noisy screeching sounds. Flocks generate considerable chattering noise.

DISTRIBUTION AND STATUS West and Central Africa in at least two (possibly three or four) disjunct populations. In West Africa the species ranges from Liberia, Côte d'Ivoire (Taï Forest) to southern Ghana where recently recorded from Bia National Park. In western Central Africa it extends from southern Cameroon south into Gabon and east into northern Congo and extreme south-western

Central African Republic and Zaïre. It also occurs from Congo basin into western Uganda. Status poorly known. Scarce in West Africa, possibly declining owing to continuing habitat loss; in Ghana considered rare and probably confined to forest reserves. Described as frequent in Gabon and Zaïre and as reasonably common in Bwamba lowlands of Uganda.

Black-collared Lovebird

ECOLOGY Inhabits lowland evergreen rain-forest, both primary and secondary, usually below 700m but reported to 1,800m in Uganda. Occasionally visits cultivated land. Generally in small flocks (up to 20 birds) but larger gatherings reported in dry season. Largely arboreal, mainly in tree-tops where birds may be very difficult to detect and only noticed when calling. Forms communal roosts at habitual sites. Principal food item apparently fig *Ficus* seeds taken from fruit in mature forest, vicinity of forest clearings and trees growing around villages; also millet, maize and other seeds, insects and their larvae. Birds in Ituri district, Zaïre, observed feeding in rice and sesame crops. Breeding biology largely unknown but nest reported from arboreal termitaria and suspected breeding, northern Congo basin, Jul.

DESCRIPTION Forehead, lores and crown emerald-green. Narrow black band across nape bordered yellow behind. Mantle and scapulars green; rump and uppertail-coverts bright blue. Upperwing-coverts green. Flight feathers blackish with green outerweb on upper surface. Underwing-coverts emerald green. Underparts rather dull pale green, especially on breast; flanks brighter. Central tail feathers largely black tipped green; remainder red at base, tipped green with broad black subterminal band. **Bare parts**: Bill greyish-black; iris yellow; legs dusky greenish-yellow (perhaps some seasonal variation in iris and leg colour).

SEX/AGE Sexes similar. Immature like adult but nuchal collar and lower margin absent. Green of head, blue of rump and red in tail duller than adult. Iris brown. Bill pale grey with black spot at base.

MEASUREMENTS Wing 90-100; tail 30-36; bill 13-15; tarsus 12-13.

GEOGRAPHICAL VARIATION Three races, one doubtful.

A. s. swindernianus (Upper Guinea rain-forests of West

Africa in Liberia, Côte d'Ivoire and Ghana. Birds in east apparently intermediate with *zenkeri*)

A. s. zenkeri (S Cameroon, Gabon and SW Central African Republic) Neck posterior to black nuchal collar bordered with brick-red suffusion extending to band on breast.

A. s. emini (W Zaïre at Bolobo and Gamangui to Ituri through to W Uganda at Baraka. Range in relation to last race unknown and may not be distinct from it) Brick-red on neck and breast less extensive or intense than *zenkeri*.

REFERENCES Arndt (1996), Britton (1980), Demey & Fishpool (1991, 1994), Forshaw (1989), Fry *et al.* (1988), Green & Carroll (1991), Grimes (1987), Louette (1981), Mackworth-Praed & Grant (1970), Turner (1991), White (1970), Williams & Arlott (1980).

175 PEACH-FACED LOVEBIRD
Agapornis roseicollis   Plate 44

Other names: Rosy-faced Lovebird, Rosy-headed Lovebird, Rose-ringed Lovebird

IDENTIFICATION 16cm. Plumage predominantly green; pale below, darker above. Bright blue rump and uppertail-coverts. Red frontal band. Face and upper breast of adult male is bright rose-pink or red in Angolan race (duller in female and immature). Combination of green nape, blue rump and pink on face and upper breast distinguishes this from other lovebirds. Often encountered in small, noisy, fast-flying flocks; flight with sudden turns.

VOICE Short, high-pitched and sharp *shreek* uttered once or repeated, especially when agitated. Most vocal in flight. Individual calls merge into trill-like sound in flock. Captive birds duet.

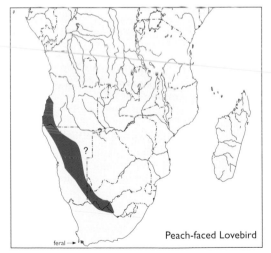

Peach-faced Lovebird

feral →

DISTRIBUTION AND STATUS South-western Africa. In Angola, where range poorly known, the species occurs in the region of Sumba (perhaps further north) southwards parallel to coast through Namibia to northern Cape Province, South Africa. May extend east through northern Namibia to Lake Ngami, Botswana, although there are no recent records from there. A 1992 sighting at Victoria Falls, Zimbabwe, suggests eastern limits poorly understood or

nomadic behaviour. Main range lies within c.400 km of Atlantic coast. Records from Transvaal considered escapes. A feral population exists in the Fish Hoek sector of Cape Peninsula, South Africa. Locally common or even abundant near water, evidently scarcer in east. Strong nomadic tendencies dictated at least partly by water availability. Heavy trapping for trade has caused substantial declines in southern Angola and possibly elsewhere. Large numbers in captivity outside range.

ECOLOGY Frequents dry wooded country to 1,500m. Reported from subdesert steppe, savanna woodland with sparse tree cover, woodland belts along rivers, and cultivated land; often near standing water. Generally in parties of 5-20 birds but up to several hundred may gather where grass seeds ripening or at water source. Roosts in nest of Social Weaver *Philetairus socius* and White-browed Sparrow-weaver *Plocepasser mahali*. Birds huddle in small groups on branches in cooler weather. Diet mainly seeds, sometimes taken from ground, including grasses, *Albizia* and *Acacia*; visits gardens for sunflower seeds and cultivated land for millet and maize, but not considered serious pest owing to sparse agriculture in regions inhabited. Also feeds on flowers of *Albizia* and takes foliage of other plants, e.g. *Euphorbia*. May drink several times a day. Nests in rock crevice, masonry or communal nests of Social Weaver or White-browed Sparrow-weaver. Nest a deep cup of bark strips or grass leaves cut by female and carried to nest in rump feathers. In weaver nest, no additional material added. Nests communally. Usual clutch 4-6 (3-8 in captivity). Incubation by female only. Breeding recorded Feb-Mar, Apr and Oct; most egg-laying apparently Feb-May.

DESCRIPTION Bright red frontal band shading to delicate rose-pink extending over lores, ear-coverts and cheeks onto throat; feathered periophthalmic ring white. Crown, nape, scapulars and mantle grass-green; rump and uppertail-coverts bright blue. Upperwing-coverts and alula green. Primaries and secondaries blackish-brown with green outerwebs on upper surface. Underwing-coverts green with bluish tinge. Throat and upper breast rose-pink; remainder of underparts green, paler than upperparts. Upper tail dark bluish-green centrally, sometimes with rather ill-defined dark subterminal band; outer feathers black at base, bordered red with black subterminal band tipped dark green; undertail dark bluish-green. **Bare parts:** Bill whitish with grey-green tinge; cere white; iris brown; legs grey.

SEX/AGE Sexes similar, although pink on head, throat and breast of female duller. Immature has restricted red frontal band and duller pink face to breast. Base of upper mandible black.

MEASUREMENTS Wing 98-110; tail 44-50; bill 17-19; tarsus 14-16.

GEOGRAPHICAL VARIATION Two races.

A. r. roseicollis (Namibia and N Cape Province, South Africa. It is not known if feral population in Cape Peninsula is this or next race)

A. r. catumbella (SW Angola. Range in relation to nominate unclear) Green, red and pink plumage brighter, especially on face and upper breast which are red rather than pink.

REFERENCES Brooke (1984), Cocker *in litt.* (1992), Forshaw (1989), Fry *et al.* (1988), Mackworth-Praed & Grant (1962), Roberts (1984), Rowan (1983), Tarboton *et al.* (1987), White (1970).

176 FISCHER'S LOVEBIRD
Agapornis fischeri   Plate 44

IDENTIFICATION 15cm. Largely green, darker above, paler and more yellowish beneath, with orange-red face, red bill, white periophthalmic ring, blue rump, brown crown and nape bordered with golden-brown collar extending to broad golden patch on upper breast. Distinguished from Red-faced Lovebird (172), sympatric on islands in south of Lake Victoria, by golden-brown collar, golden breast and white eye-ring, and from Yellow-collared Lovebird (177), which overlaps narrowly at the south-east margins of its range, by orange, not yellow, breast. Hybrid Fischer's x Yellow-collared Lovebirds may occur among feral populations, but are not known in natural areas of sympatry. Combination of brown crown and nape, orange-red face and blue rump distinguishes Fischer's from congeners in captivity. Generally in small flocks, often near water. Usually quite tame and approachable.

VOICE High-pitched twittering and whistling including a short, sharp, grating *chirick chirick* interspersed with more melodious *chireek* sounds. Melodious chirruping notes recall Budgerigar (155) whilst harsher noises sound like rapid grating of comb teeth over edge of table. Grating sounds sometimes interspersed with high-pitched *tingk tingk* sounds. Flocks often detected first by sound of calling birds.

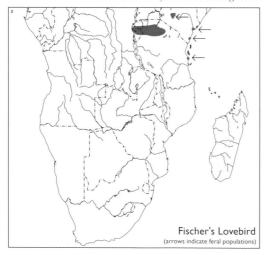

Fischer's Lovebird
(arrows indicate feral populations)

DISTRIBUTION AND STATUS Northern and north-western Tanzania from Kondoa in south-east, Serengeti National Park in north and Lake Manyara in east; possibly closer to Kenyan border in some areas. In Rwanda and Burundi the species is either a recent natural colonist, or feral since c.1970, or an irruptive visitor in response to drought. Reported from Ukerewe and Kome islands in southern Lake Victoria. Feral populations established in region of Dar es Salaam and Tanga, Tanzania, and around Mombasa, Nairobi, Naivasha and Isiolo, Kenya. Probably some local dry-season movements with drought-year irruptions. Within restricted range often common, even abundant, but in some areas scarce and apparently declining, especially outside protected areas where low density attributed to trapping for trade. May now be endangered by live bird trade. Large numbers in captivity outside range. NEAR-THREATENED.

ECOLOGY Found in wooded grasslands characterised by *Acacia, Commiphora*; especially in west also in more open grasslands with *Adansonia* and cultivated country. Commonest in *Acacia tortilis* savanna with other *Acacia* and *Balanites aegyptiaca* trees and ground flora including *Penisetum, Digitaria, Themeda* and *Eustachys* grasses. In south of range present in woodland with *Borassus aethiopum* palms. Riverine woodland with *Ficus, Ziziphus, Tamarindus, Aphania, Garcinia* and *Eckbergia* is important dry-season habitat. Avoids miombo woodland. Generally at 1,100-2,000m. Often near water, especially in hot weather. Gregarious, at least outside breeding season, and generally in small flocks. Sometimes forms more substantial gatherings, e.g. where food abundant. Roosts in nest of Rufous-tailed Weaver *Histurgops ruficauda*, a Tanzanian endemic. Diet consists mainly of grass seeds such as *Penisetum mezianum*, millet and maize, but the species is not judged a serious pest; also takes seeds of *Acacia*, the weed *Achyranthes asper*, fallen berries, and fruits of *Ficus, Rhus villosa* and *Commiphora*. Drinks every day. Breeds colonially. Nests in base of fronds on palm tree head, in abandoned cavity-nest of other bird species or, where birds have established feral populations, in crevices in buildings; also occasionally in nest of Rufous-tailed Weaver. Nest composed of pad of grass stems and bark strips carried by female in bill. Egg-laying mainly in dry season from Jan-Jul; precise timing dependent on locality. Clutch generally 5-6 but ranges from 3-8.

DESCRIPTION Frontal band, lores and cheeks bright red shading to orange-red on chin and throat and golden-orange on upper breast; crown and nape brown. Broad golden-brown collar contiguous with golden-orange breast-band. Mantle, scapulars and anterior portion of rump green; posterior rump and uppertail-coverts dark blue. Upperwing-coverts green; primaries and secondaries blackish-brown with green margins to outerwebs. Underwing-coverts green; underside of flight feathers dark greyish-black. Lower breast to undertail-coverts pale yellowish-green. Tail bluish-green with all but central feathers basally marked orange; indistinct dark subterminal band. **Bare parts**: Bill coral red, whitish towards base of upper mandible; cere white; iris brown; periophthalmic ring white, c.2mm wide; legs pale grey.

SEX/AGE Sexes similar. Immatures have reduced blue on uppertail-coverts and are duller than adults, particularly on collar, head and breast; black markings sometimes on base of upper mandible.

MEASUREMENTS Wing 88-98; tail 38-44; bill 16-18; tarsus 14-16.

GEOGRAPHICAL VARIATION None.

NOTE See Note under Yellow-collared Lovebird.

REFERENCES Arndt (1996), Beesley (1973), Bhatia *et al.* (1992), Britton (1980), Forshaw (1989), Fry *et al.* (1988), Fuggles-Couchman (1984), Lewis & Pomeroy (1989), Mackworth-Praed & Grant (1952), Rowan (1983), Turner (1991), Williams & Arlott (1980).

177 YELLOW-COLLARED LOVEBIRD
Agapornis personatus   Plate 44

Other names: Masked Lovebird, Black-masked Lovebird, Black-faced Lovebird, Black-headed Lovebird

IDENTIFICATION 15cm. Easily distinguished from other lovebirds by blackish-brown mask and bold lemon-yellow breast extending round sides of neck and nape forming striking yellow collar. Remainder of plumage predominantly green; darker above, paler below. Coral red bill. Natural range marginally overlaps Fischer's Lovebird (176) in region of Babati to Lake Manyara and Ngare Nanyuki, Tanzania; feral populations also occur with Fischer's in Kenya and Tanzania. Latter distinguished by golden-brown (not yellow) breast, red frontal band, lores and cheeks, and paler crown and nape. Hybrids occur where feral birds sympatric, but are not known from natural area of sympatry. Generally in small flocks in savanna country.

VOICE Sustained high-pitched twittering delivered from perch or in flight.

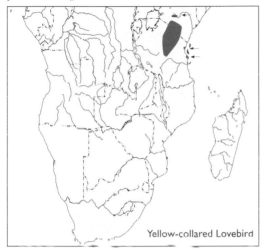

Yellow-collared Lovebird

DISTRIBUTION AND STATUS Except for one south-west Kenyan record (at Taveta), the species appears confined to the plateau in east and south Tanzania from north of Mount Meru south to Morogoro and west to Rukwa and Mbeya. In Kenya, sizeable feral populations exist at Naivasha (c. 6,000 birds in 1986), Nairobi and Mombasa, smaller ones at several highland and coastal localities; in Tanzania, at Dar-es-Salaam and Tanga. Sedentary, generally common and sometimes abundant. Wild population probably declining owing to large-scale trapping for bird trade. Large numbers in captivity outside range.

ECOLOGY Occurs in well-wooded grasslands, including cultivated areas, with *Acacia*, *Commiphora* and, especially, *Adansonia*, at 1,100-1,800m. Avoids miombo woodland. Generally in small flocks of 4-5 but sometimes up to 100. Diet consists of grass seeds, millet and sorghum, feral birds taking *Cassia* seeds and reportedly weed seeds from lawns. Requires regular access to water and may drink several times a day. Breeds colonially. Nest usually located in tree-cavity with strong preference for *Adansonia*. May also use vacant domed nest of another species. In Dar-es-Salaam, nest sometimes in building cavity or vacant nest of Little Swift *Apus affinis*. Nest is complex domed structure built from long stalks and strips of bark carried to nest by female in bill. Eggs laid in dry season (Mar-Apr and Jun-Jul). Clutch 3-8 in captivity.

DESCRIPTION Entire head, throat and upper nape dark blackish-brown merging to yellow on lower nape and upper mantle, forming distinct collar. Remainder of mantle, scapulars and rump green; uppertail-coverts blue. Upperwing-coverts green; primaries green, darker and dusky on innerweb; outerwebs of secondaries green, innerwebs black. Underwing-coverts green; underside of flight feathers dark greyish-black. Breast bright lemon-yellow; belly and undertail-coverts pale green. Tail mostly green but all feathers, except for central pair, marked with dull orange; blackish subterminal band. **Bare parts**: Bill coral-red, whitish at base of upper mandible; cere white; iris brown; periophthalmic ring white (c.2mm wide); legs pale greyish.

SEX/AGE Sexes similar. Immature like adult but head less dark and glossy; yellow collar duller; black markings sometimes on base of upper mandible.

MEASUREMENTS Wing 90-98; tail 39-45; bill 16-19; tarsus 12-16.

GEOGRAPHICAL VARIATION None.

NOTE The Yellow-collared Lovebird is sometimes treated as the nominate race of single species in which it is united with Fischer's, Nyasa (178) and Black-cheeked (179) Lovebirds. All have a broad bare white periophthalmic ring and show behavioural similarities. Pending further analysis they are treated here as separate species.

REFERENCES Bhatia *et al.* (1992), Britton (1980), Fry *et al.* (1988), Lewis & Pomeroy (1989), Mackworth-Praed & Grant (1952), Turner (1991), White (1970), Williams & Arlott (1980), Zimmerman *et al.* (1996).

178 NYASA LOVEBIRD
Agapornis lilianae   Plate 44

Other names: Lilian's Lovebird

IDENTIFICATION 15-16cm. Predominantly green, darker above, paler and more yellowish below with yellow patch on nape. Distinguished from all other lovebirds, including superficially similar Peach-faced (175) and Fischer's (176), by combination of orange-red face and throat and green rump and uppertail-coverts. Only other lovebird occurring naturally in vicinity (c. 150km to west), and which may occur with feral Nyasa Lovebirds at Choma, southern Zambia, is Black-cheeked (179), which has dark hood. Flight fast and direct in flocks.

VOICE Shrill, high-pitched call in flight and at rest. Also chattering cry like rattling metal chain, but shriller.

DISTRIBUTION AND STATUS Several disjunct populations in restricted area in south-eastern Africa. Occurs in middle Zambezi valley from upper Lake Kariba around Binga east to Tete Mozambique, in belt north and south of Zambezi below 1,000m including Angwa and Hunyani valleys, Zimbabwe, and Lunsemfwa and Lukusashi valleys, Zambia. In north-eastern Zambia, also found in Luangwa valley north of 14°20'S to Lundazi, apparently isolated from Zambezi valley birds and possibly introduced. In Malawi, isolated population located in mopane woodland in region of Lake Malombe south of Lake Malawi. Also in scattered populations in southern Tanzania. Feral birds thought to occur (at least in past) in Choma district and Mazabuka, southern Zambia. Birds in southern Namibia are escapes. Generally common, in places abundant, although probably declining overall due to loss of habitat, e.g. in the Kariba basin. May be vulnerable owing to restricted range and evident ecological sensitivity. Apparently sedentary but may make local movements in response to food supply. Trapped for live bird trade. Large numbers in captivity outside range.

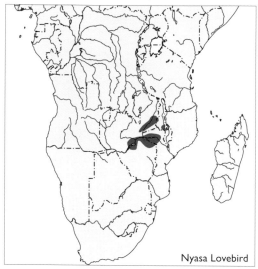

Nyasa Lovebird

ECOLOGY Found in mopane *Colophospermum mopane* and *Acacia* woodland on alluvium and in riparian forest in river valleys generally below 1,000m, preferring areas with fig trees. Avoids miombo woodland. Highly gregarious and usually in noisy flocks of 20-100 birds, sometimes many more, especially where food plentiful. Non-breeders form communal roosts in tree-hollows where 4-20 birds sleep clinging to walls of chamber. Before settling at roost-site, birds engage in much squabbling and chasing. Food is mainly grass seeds, including *Oryza perennis* and cultivated varieties such as millet (especially unripe) and sorghum, also seeds of annual herbs and *Acacia*, flowers of *A. albida*, *Erythrophloeum africana*, *Vitex duamiana* and *Cordyla africana*, berries and leaf buds. Food is gathered direct from plants and on the ground. Visits water often. Breeds colonially. Nest is a bulky domed structure with entrance tube built from bark strips, twigs and stalks carried to nest-site by female in bill. Nest-site in mopane tree-cavity or possibly in nest of Buffalo Weaver *Bubalornis albirostris*. Feral birds at Lundazi nest in eaves of buildings. Breeding reported Jan and Feb (possibly introduced birds) and Sep in Zimbabwe and Jan-Jul in Zambia. Clutch 3-8 in captivity.

DESCRIPTION Forehead, forecrown, lores and cheeks brick-red merging to orange washed yellowish-green on hindcrown, ear-coverts, sides of neck and nape, but occasionally (including specimen collected from Malawi and unlikely to be hybrid with Black-cheeked Lovebird) brick-red replaced by dark crimson and orange by dark brown. Mantle and scapulars bright green, rump and uppertail-coverts likewise but paler. Upperwing-coverts bright green; sometimes yellow on alula; outerwebs of primaries and secondaries green; innerwebs blackish. Underwing-coverts green with some blue feathers; underside of flight feathers blackish. Throat and upper breast orange-red to salmon-pink; lower breast to undertail-coverts pale green. Tail green, all except central feathers with orange-red base and indistinct dark subterminal band. **Bare parts:**

Bill coral red; cere white; iris brown; bare periophthalmic ring white (c.2mm wide); legs pale grey.

SEX/AGE Sexes similar. Immatures like adult but black suffusion on ear-coverts and black markings at base of upper mandible.

MEASUREMENTS Wing 89-95; tail 35-41; bill 14-16; tarsus 13-15.

GEOGRAPHICAL VARIATION None.

NOTE See Note under Yellow-collared Lovebird.

REFERENCES Baker (1991), Benson *et al.* (1971), Forshaw (1989), Fry *et al.* (1988), Irwin (1981), Mackworth-Praed & Grant (1962), Medland (1995), Roberts (1984), Turner (1991), White (1970).

179 BLACK-CHEEKED LOVEBIRD
Agapornis nigrigenis   Plate 44

Other names: Black-faced Lovebird

IDENTIFICATION 13-14cm. Small, predominantly green (darker above, paler beneath) with conspicuous blackish-brown hood and rusty-orange patch on upper breast. Combination of dark head, green nape and rump distinguishes this from all other lovebirds. Not naturally sympatric with any congeners, being separated from natural range of Nyasa Lovebird (178), which shows similar habitat preferences but has greenish-orange head and orange throat, by about 150km of miombo woodland in the Zambesi valley downstream from Victoria Falls; these two forms may, however, co-occur ferally.

VOICE Shrill high-pitched chatter.

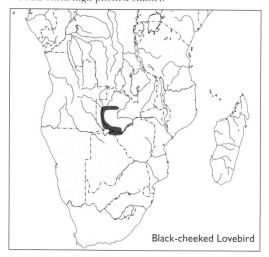

Black-cheeked Lovebird

DISTRIBUTION AND STATUS Highly restricted range (perhaps only 6,000km²) from southern Kafue National Park, south-western Zambia (very small numbers only), along Zambesi valley to Victoria Falls, Zimbabwe. Birds possibly also occur in the Caprivi region of adjacent extreme north-eastern Namibia at, e.g., Impalia Island at the confluence of the Zambesi and Chobe Rivers; possibly also in northernmost tip of Botswana. Dry-season core areas of mopane woodland total only about 2,500km² but birds spread into fields when crops ripening (causing some damage). Some local seasonal movements. Formerly common within restricted range but now local, uncommon and under serious threat. Appears susceptible to trapping for bird trade (which although banned reportedly continues at least for local markets) and possible hybridisation with feral Nyasa Lovebirds. Drought conditions (perhaps reflecting long-term climate change) have already led to disappearance from some localities and may seriously affect status and distribution. Changing agricultural practices (from sorghum and millet to maize) is another possible contributory cause of decline. However, the poor agricultural potential of land within its range means that large-scale habitat loss to expansion of cultivation is not imminent. Estimated total wild population about 10,000. Held in captivity, many in South Africa. ENDANGERED.

ECOLOGY Found in mopane *Colophospermum mopane* and *Acacia* woodland in river valleys at 600-1,000m adjacent to woodland with *Baikiaea plurijuga* upon which birds are reliant during wet season. Also occurs in riparian forests and attracted to fig trees. Avoids miombo *Brachystegia*. Generally found within easy reach of reliable water source, in small flocks of up to a few dozen birds. May roost communally like Nyasa Lovebird. Diet consists of seeds (those of annual herbs important), grain, flowers, buds and berries. Known food items include seeds of *Amaranthus*, *Rottboellia exaltata*, *Rhus quartiniana*, *Albizia anthelmintica*, *Combretum mussambicense*, *Syzygium guineense* and the grasses *Hyparrhenia* and *Eragrostis*; also young leaves of *Pterocarpus antunesiana*. Breeding only known from captivity but thought to resemble Nyasa Lovebird. Breeding Nov-Dec, perhaps Sep at Victoria Falls.

DESCRIPTION Forehead, lores and ear-coverts dark blackish-brown fading to dark brown on crown, sides of neck and nape, and forming dark mask. Mantle, scapulars, rump and uppertail-coverts green. Upperwing-coverts green with bluish suffusion on outer feathers, including alula; outerwebs of primaries and secondaries green with bluish suffusion, darker and greener at tips; innerwebs greyish, black at tips. Underwing-coverts yellowish-green and green. Chin and anterior portion of throat blackish fading to rusty-orange patch on lower throat and upper breast (orange brighter during breeding); rest of underparts mostly pale, slightly yellowish, green, brighter emerald on flanks and around thighs. Tail green except for four outer feathers which show patch of red; dark green subterminal spot on all except central feathers. **Bare parts**: Bill coral red, white at base; iris brown; bare periophthalmic ring white (c.2mm wide); legs grey brown.

SEX/AGE Sexes similar. Immature has underparts washed dark green; feathers on breast and belly with dark margins. Blackish base to bill.

MEASUREMENTS Wing 90-98; tail 40-45; bill 14-16; tarsus 13-14.

GEOGRAPHICAL VARIATION None.

NOTE See Note under Yellow-collared Lovebird.

REFERENCES Arndt (1996), Collar *et al.* (1994), Collar & Stuart (1985), Dodman (1995), Forshaw (1989), Fry *et al.* (1988), Irwin (1981), Kemp & Kemp (1987), Kilmer (1994), Mackworth-Praed & Grant (1962), Roberts (1984), Rowan (1983), Tarboton *et al.* (1987), Them (1989).

180 VERNAL HANGING PARROT
Loriculus vernalis   Plate 45

Other names: Green Hanging Parrot (also common vernacular for *L. exilis*), Indian Lorikeet, Indian Hanging Parrot

IDENTIFICATION 13cm. The most widespread of its genus, the Vernal Hanging Parrot is common through much of its range, which extends from around central-west India to Thailand and Indochina, being replaced by Blue-crowned Hanging Parrot (184) in the south but also occurring on the Andaman and Nicobar Islands. The species shows a coral bill, red rump and blue underwing and undertail. It is the smallest parrot throughout its range, and its size and stub-tailed appearance are distinctive. The head and breast appear largely green with a light blue suffusion on the lower throat, distinguishing this from other members of the genus, which all show distinctively coloured crown or breast-markings. In common with other hanging parrots this species roosts hanging upside-down from a leafy branch. Some other parrot species have also been recorded sleeping or resting upside-down e.g. Barred Parakeet (272), some *Agapornis* species particularly Red-faced Lovebird (172), and Green-rumped Parrotlet (276). The flight of Vernal Hanging Parrot consists of rapid beats followed by a brief pause and dip, reminiscent of a finch *Fringilla*. The species can also hover.

VOICE Two main calls have been recorded, a repetitious whistled *chee-chee-chee* or *pe-zeez-eet*, and a sharp *tsit-tsit* or *tsee-sip*. There is also a rasping sound made after feeding, as well as various twittering and warbling sounds.

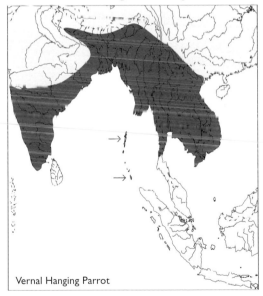

Vernal Hanging Parrot

DISTRIBUTION AND STATUS Widespread, occurring from the west coast of India at about 19°N through at least Maharashtra, Madhya Pradesh, Karnataka, Kerala, Tamil Nadu, Andhra Pradesh, Orissa, West Bengal, Assam, Nagaland, Manipur and Tripura, and also occurring on the Andaman and Nicobar Islands. In Nepal small numbers occur in the lowland terai, and the species has been recorded from the Chitwan area. It occurs in Bhutan;

south-west Szechwan through Yunnan, and possibly east to Kwangtung, in China; Sylhet, Comilla and Chittagong in Bangladesh; Myanmar including the Mergui Archipelago; Thailand south to around 10°N (also recorded further south on Phuket Island); Laos; Cambodia; and Vietnam. The species has not been recorded in Sikkim, Hong Kong or Malaysia. It is common through much of its range and the world population is thought to be above one million and stable.

ECOLOGY Some movements, possibly related to seasonal rains, have been noted but require further study. The species occurs in a range of habitats including evergreen and deciduous forest, forest edge, clearings, secondary growth, brush, bamboo thickets, orchards and overgrown cultivation, up to about 2,000m. Birds are found in pairs, family parties, loose flocks of up to 50 individuals or mixed flocks with other birds. Their size and coloration make them unobtrusive, but they are not shy and can be found foraging in the canopy, sometimes drawing an observer's attention by short circular flights around the tree-tops. They feed acrobatically in flowering trees on nectar (e.g. of coral trees *Erythrina*) and in fruiting trees especially figs *Ficus* or guava *Psidium guajava* as well as various berry-bearing and seeding species like bamboo and casuarina. They will also take palm wine collected in pots, and can then become intoxicated, and may do some damage in orchards. They hop between branches and climb nimbly using both bill and feet, sometimes appearing to 'spiral' as they ascend. They rest, preen and sleep hanging upside-down from one or both feet, although young birds may remain upright; head-scratching is over the wing. Like *Agapornis*, they cut small strips of bark, leaf and other vegetable matter, tuck them into the contour feathers and carry them to the nest as lining. Breeding takes place between Jan and Apr. Two and four white, often brown-stained eggs are laid in a cavity in a rotten stump. The narrow entrance is sometimes enlarged by the birds, and the metre-deep hole may extend below ground-level in exceptional cases, although an entrance 2-10m above ground is more normal. Incubation, which lasts around 22 days, is undertaken by the female, who sits very tightly when brooding. The male helps feed the chicks as they mature over a five-week period.

DESCRIPTION Head bright green, lighter and more yellowish on chin. Rest of upperparts green with lower back, rump and uppertail-coverts bright crimson. Wing-coverts slightly darker green than mantle. Primaries bright green with blackish innerwebs and a slight blue-green suffusion on outerwebs of outermost feathers; secondaries black with green outerwebs and some green on innerwebs. Underwing bright turquoise-blue (innerwebs of feathers), except coverts and axillaries which are pale green. Underparts yellower-green than upperparts, with a light blue patch on the throat. Uppertail green; undertail turquoise-blue. **Bare parts**: Bill coral-red with yellow tip; iris brown to whitish-yellow; legs pale brown to yellowish-orange.

SEX/AGE Females are slightly duller than males and have a less extensive blue throat-patch. Young birds lack the blue throat-patch altogether and have a lighter bill, some green showing on the rump, narrower tail feathers, and brownish legs. Young birds take at least a year to mature.

MEASUREMENTS Wing 86-94; tail 33-38; bill 10-13; tarsus: 11-13.

GEOGRAPHICAL VARIATION None.

REFERENCES Ali & Ripley (1981), Arndt (1992) Baker (1927), Buckley (1968), Forshaw (1989), Hough (1989), Inskipp & Inskipp (1985), King & Dickinson (1975), Lambert *et al.* (1993), Lekagul & Cronin (1974), Lekagul & Round (1991), Medway & Wells (1976), Meyer de Schauensee (1984), Peters (1961), Ripley *et al.* (1987), Robson (1991), Sibley & Monroe (1990), Smythies (1986), Wildash (1968).

181 CEYLON HANGING PARROT
Loriculus beryllinus   Plate 45

Other names: Ceylon Lorikeet

IDENTIFICATION 13-14cm. Restricted to Sri Lanka where it is the only member of its genus and the only non-*Psittacula* parrot. The species differs from Vernal Hanging Parrot (180) in its red crown, orange nape and reddish mantle-markings. The combination of an entirely red crown blending into an orange nape and upper mantle distinguishes this from other hanging parrots, except two races of Colasisi, *L. p. apicalis* and *L. p. dohertyi* (182), and the closely allied Black-billed Hanging Parrot (183), but the males of all three have a red bib, while the females have blue on the face and brown, not whitish, irides. Colasisis also have an extremely long upper mandible, while Black-billed has a black bill in both sexes. The flight of Ceylon Hanging Parrot is similar to that of the preceding species.

VOICE The call is a sharp trisyllabic *twitwitwit*. Various squeaky warblings have also been recorded.

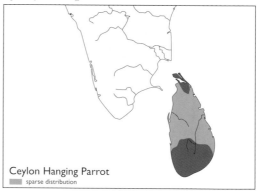

Ceylon Hanging Parrot
▨ sparse distribution

DISTRIBUTION AND STATUS Endemic to Sri Lanka, where most records come from the south, although it has been recorded north to Trincomalee and should be expected in suitable habitat throughout the country. It is not regarded as an uncommon species, with the world population estimated at 10,000, and stable; however, the bird trade is judged a potential threat. Records include from near Colombo, around Kandy, Yala and Gal Oya National Parks, the Welimada district, and south to Galle and Hambantota on the coast.

ECOLOGY Found in a range of habitats from sea-level to 1,600m, reaching the higher altitudes with seasonal conditions. The species is found in coconut groves, evergreen and deciduous forest, semi-cultivated areas, open woodland and around habitation. Birds are not shy, and are usually encountered in pairs or family groups, although outside the breeding season larger flocks congregate high in flowering trees. They are active and acrobatic when feeding, and forage on fruits including figs *Ficus* and guava *Psidium guajava*; berries; blossoms including *Erythrina*, *Salmalia* and *Eucalyptus*; seeds, including *Casuarina*; and they have been recorded becoming intoxicated after drinking palm wine collected in pots attached to the tree-trunks. In display, the male approaches his mate in upright stance, with bill raised, throat-patch puffed up, tail spread and rump-feathers erect, while producing a squeaky warble. Head-bobbing and courtship-feeding also take place. Breeding begins in Jan and although the main nesting period is between Mar and May a second brood is sometimes raised through to Sep. The nest is in a hollow branch and lined with fragments of vegetation which the female carefully cuts with the bill and carries to the nest-site tucked into her rump feathers. She alone incubates the two to four white eggs, sitting tightly, screeching and creating a 'thumping' sound if disturbed. At fledging the young have the face bare, presumably to avoid soiling with liquid food.

DESCRIPTION Crown red, merging into an orange-yellow nape; supercilium, lores and area in front of eye light green (slightly suffused pale blue); sides of forecrown red. Mantle green, suffused orange yellow and slightly reddish centrally; back green; rump and uppertail-coverts red. Upperwing green except for blackish innerwebs of flight feathers; underwing bright turquoise except for green coverts and axillaries. Underparts bright green, paler and more yellowish than upperparts and marked light blue on the throat. Uppertail green; undertail turquoise. **Bare parts**: Bill light orange-red, paler at tip, iris whitish; legs dusky yellow.

SEX/AGE Female like male but duller and with only a trace of blue on the throat. Young birds are duller still, the crown tinged reddish, the blue throat-patch absent or poorly marked, the rump with some green feathers, the bill paler and the iris and feet brown; the face is naked at fledging.

MEASUREMENTS Wing 87-95; tail 38-42; bill 12-13; tarsus 11-12.

GEOGRAPHICAL VARIATION None.

REFERENCES Ali & Ripley (1981), Arndt (1992), Baker (1927), BirdLife (1993), Forshaw (1989), Henry (1955), Lambert *et al.* (1993), Lodge (1990), Sibley & Monroe (1990).

---

182 COLASISI
Loriculus philippensis   Plate 45

Other names: Philippine Hanging Parrot, Luzon Hanging Parrot

IDENTIFICATION 14cm. One of only two members of its genus occurring in the Philippines. A typical hanging parrot, being mainly green with a red rump, blue underwing and undertail. Unlike other hanging parrots this, and the following species, show a distinct blue suffusion at the sides of the rump. Both sexes show a varying amount of red, orange or yellow on the crown according to race. Females show some blue on the face, and males have a red bib, which is yellowish-green in females (extent varying

according to race). Races of Colasisi vary according to the crown and breast pattern. Some subspecies also show a reddish-orange hind-collar (see plate). Birds in the Sulu Archipelago were previously included in this species but are now separated as Black-billed Hanging Parrot (183), differing in crown pattern (see plate 45) and colour of bill. Two races of Colasisi, *L. p. apicalis* and *L. p. dohertyi*, are similar to Ceylon Hanging Parrot (181; see that entry for differences). These small parrots have a characteristic undulating flight in common with other members of the genus.

VOICE Flight call a high-pitched whistle reminiscent of a Goldeneye *Bucephala clangula*.

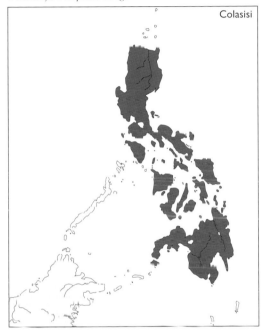

Colasisi

DISTRIBUTION AND STATUS Restricted to the Philippines (less the Sulu Archipelago) where resident and widespread except on Palawan. Its abundance varies according to race. In general, the species is locally common up to 1,000m, but has been recorded as high as 2,500m (Mount Apo, Mindanao). The world population is considered to be greater than 20,000 but declining due to habitat loss. The Mindoro race is near-threatened, and both the Cebu and Siquijor races are almost extinct through habitat loss (as birds are commonly caged and traded between islands, contemporary records of birds from Siquijor require confirmation on plumage characters to establish if they relate to the native races). The combined populations of Mindoro, Sibuyan, Negros, Panay, Tablas, Romblon, Masbate, Ticao, Guimaras and Basilan (races *L. p. mindorensis*, *L. p. bournsi*, *L. p. regulus* and *L. p. dohertyi*) probably total no more than 5,000 birds.

ECOLOGY The species occurs in forest, along forest edge, in secondary growth, bamboo, woodland, cultivated areas near villages, orchards and coconut groves. Birds are found singly, in pairs or family groups, occasionally in small flocks, sometimes with other birds. They forage in the upper levels of flowering or fruiting trees, but sometimes in lower storeys, feeding on blossoms, nectar, fruits (including figs) and seeds, and occasionally becoming intoxicated on fermenting coconut *Cocos nucifera* nectar. In display the male turns round and round on his perch, and courtship-feeding has been recorded; other displays are similar to Blue-crowned Hanging Parrot (184). The female tucks nesting material into her contour feathers, and breeding-condition birds have been recorded from Apr to Aug. Three eggs are laid and incubated by the female for 20 days, the chicks fledging in five weeks.

DESCRIPTION Head bright green with scarlet forecrown-patch narrowly bordered orange-red at rear-edge; chin yellowish-green; narrow hind-collar orange and red, with a slight yellowish wash on nape. Upperparts bright green with dark crimson rump and uppertail-coverts (sides of lower back washed light blue). Wings bright green with darker innerwebs to flight feathers. Underwing light turquoise-blue except for green outermost coverts. Centre of throat bright red, grading to red-orange on centre of breast (which has yellow feather-bases); rest of underparts bright green, lighter and yellower than upperparts. Uppertail green; undertail blue. **Bare parts:** Bill coral red; iris dark brown; legs dark orange.

SEX/AGE The female has the face marked blue and lacks the red bib, which is replaced by a yellow-green wash. The crown of the female is washed yellowish-orange (stronger than in the male). Young birds have a duller crown and a paler bill.

MEASUREMENTS Wing 89-100; tail 40-44; bill 13-14; tarsus 11-13.

GEOGRAPHICAL VARIATION Nine races.

L. p. philippensis (Luzon, Polillo, Banton, Catanduanes and Marinduque)

L. p. mindorensis (Mindoro) Yellow-orange nape-line only faintly indicated (not forming hind-collar as in nominate). Crown greener. More extensive turquoise patch either side of rump.

L. p. bournsi (Sibuyan) Male with red only on frontal area and obvious yellow onto centre of crown (female with much less yellow on crown), but male's crown shows less yellow than the following race. Orange nape-line of male is less distinct in female. Female with less blue in face than nominate.

L. p. regulus (Negros, Panay, Tablas, Romblon, Masbate, Ticao and Guimaras; recorded on Siquijor) Similar to previous race but male with far more yellow in crown (female shows a fainter yellow suffusion but still more than previous race). Nape-line fainter than in *bournsi*. Male with more scarlet breast-patch.

L. p. chrysonotus (Cebu) Frontal area red and rest of crown bright golden-yellow extending onto mantle, and showing a fine reddish hind-collar. Male with more orange on lower part of throat-patch. Female crown similar but less well-marked.

L. p. worcesteri (Samar, Leyte, Calicoan, Buad, Biliran, Maripipi and Bohol; birds on Bohol may be separable) Male with smaller, more scarlet throat-patch than previous race. Both sexes show a more extensive red crown tending to orange-red at rear margin. There is a small orange hind-collar patch and a slight reddish-orange suffusion on the mantle.

L. p. siquijorensis (Siquijor but possibly extinct; locals reported bird there in 1992 but not necessarily this subspecies) Male with smaller red bib and larger red crown-patch than nominate, and a green hind-crown. Lacks nape-mark. Female with more blue in face.

L. p. apicalis (Mindanao, Balut, Siargao, Camiguin,

and Dinagat) Two aberrant specimens previously attributed to *L. salvadorii* are larger, with less red on the crown, more blue on the tail, and darker green coloration. Entire crown of this race scarlet grading into an orange nape and orange- to reddish-washed mantle in both sexes (duller in female). Red of rump brighter and more orange at top.

L. p. dohertyi (Basilan) Perhaps more orange on mantle but doubtfully distinct from previous race.

REFERENCES Arndt (1992), Dickinson *et al.* (1991), duPont (1971), duPont & Rabor (1973), Dutson *et al.* (1992), Forshaw (1989), Lambert *et al.* (1993), Lodge (1990), Parkes & Dickinson (1991), Potter (1953), Sargeant (1992), Sibley & Monroe (1990), M.P. Walters *in litt.* (1992).

183 BLACK-BILLED HANGING PARROT
Loriculus bonapartei   Plate 45

IDENTIFICATION 14cm. Previously included in Colasisi (182), which it replaces, as the sole member of the genus, in the Sulu Archipelago. The combination of red forecrown, grading to golden-orange at the nape, and black bill are diagnostic for both sexes. Apart from lacking these features, the most similar races of Colasisi, *L. p. apicalis* and *L. p. dohertyi*, have much redder-orange napes and a strong orange suffusion on the mantle. Female Ceylon Hanging Parrot (181) has a redder crown, reddish suffusion on the mantle, red bill and a whitish iris (males lack the red bib of Sulu birds).

VOICE 'A musical note' is the only published reference to the species's call.

DISTRIBUTION AND STATUS Restricted to islands in the Sulu Archipelago, Philippines, including: Sibutu, Bongao, Sanga Sanga, Manuk Manka, Tawitawi, Siasi and Jolo.

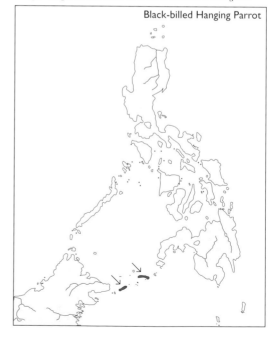

Black-billed Hanging Parrot

ECOLOGY The species is little known, but its habits and ecology are presumably similar to that of Colasisi. Found commonly from coastal coconut groves into the interior, where it has been recorded in dense forest as well as in partially cleared areas. Noted feeding on palm flowers and flying between tree-tops. No data on breeding.

DESCRIPTION Forecrown red, shading backwards through orange on crown to golden-yellow on hind-crown, with a clear line of demarcation from green mantle; lores and cheeks bright green. Mantle faintly washed orange centrally; rump and uppertail-coverts bright crimson (blue suffusion at sides of rump). Wings bright green with blackish innerwebs to flight feathers. Underwing-coverts turquoise green; rest of underwing blue (underside of innerwebs). Chin and throat bright scarlet; rest of underparts bright green. Uppertail green; undertail blue. **Bare parts**: Bill black; iris brown; legs from orange to greyish.

SEX/AGE The female has a more uniform reddish-orange crown grading to a richer mid-orange on the nape. The lores and cheeks are pale blue, and the red bib is replaced by green.

MEASUREMENTS Wing 91-99; tail 42-51; bill 12-14; tarsus 12-14.

GEOGRAPHICAL VARIATION None.

REFERENCES Arndt (1992), Dickinson *et al.* (1991), duPont (1971), duPont & Rabor (1973), Forshaw (1989), Sibley & Monroe (1990).

184 BLUE-CROWNED HANGING PARROT
Loriculus galgulus   Plate 46

Other names: Sapphire-crowned Hanging Parrot, Malay Hanging Parrot, Malay Loriquet

IDENTIFICATION 12cm. A widespread species found from southern Thailand through Malaysia, Borneo, Sumatra (only member of its genus present in these last three) into extreme west Java and around Jakarta. Males are distinctive with their dark blue crown-patches, red bibs, orange mantle-markings and black bills, with a clearly marked yellow band across the back above the red rump. The species's northern limit comes very close to the southern extreme of Vernal Hanging Parrot (180) in peninsular Thailand at around 10°N. Although the males are easily separated on breast colour, females are rather similar; adult female Blue-crowns have black, not coral red, bills and an orange suffusion on the mantle. Blue-crowned always has a dark iris, which is sometimes whitish in Vernal. It may be recorded as an escape in other parts of South-East Asia. The only other species which overlaps on natural range is Java's Yellow-throated Hanging Parrot (194), which has a bright yellow chin and throat in the male and a yellowish chin in the female. Flight is direct on whirring wings.

VOICE A shrill, buzzy, far-carrying *z-z-z-z-eeee*, *dzeeet* or *dzii*, higher-pitched than the call of Vernal Hanging Parrot, and usually monosyllabic. The is also a squeaky alarm call rendered as *zrie-ie*, and a rasping sound made after feeding.

DISTRIBUTION AND STATUS Ranges south from around 10°N in peninsular Thailand, through Malaysia and Singapore, occurring on some surrounding islands including the Anambas Islands, the Riau Archipelago and Batam. The species is widespread through Sumatra and occurs on offshore islands including Tuangku, Nias, Pini, Batu, Siberut, Sipura, Enggano, and to the north on Bangka, Mendanau and Belitung. It is present in suitable habitat throughout Borneo, and on Labuan and Maratua islands off the coast. Its presence in extreme western Java, in the Labuhan area, may be the result of escapes; the population around Jakarta is certainly feral. It is generally a common resident throughout its range. The world population is thought to be above 100,000 but may be subject to effect from the cagebird trade.

Blue-crowned Hanging Parrot

ECOLOGY Birds netted at night passing over Fraser's Hill, Malaysia, indicate that there is some nocturnal dispersion. Extralimital records have also come from offshore islands. The species occurs from the lowlands through to around 1,300m, being found in forest, edges, riverine growth, mangrove, secondary growth, lightly wooded areas, bamboo clumps, orchards, inhabited areas and coconut groves. The birds frequent the canopy and middle storey, travelling alone, in pairs or, outside the breeding season, in groups of up to 150 which invade fruit orchards. The birds take swinging strides through the vegetation with a comical air, using the bill to help climb, and the tail as support. Food is sometimes held in the foot and brought to the bill, which is itself constantly wiped against the vegetation. Like other hanging parrots, this species roosts upside down and may also rain-bathe in the same position. It feeds on flowers, buds, fruit, nuts, and various seeds. Breeding behaviour has been recorded between Jan and Aug. Courtship-feeding takes place, the male displaying with head-bobbing, red feathers fluffed, tail spread, body upright, and calling with a soft *jeet-jeet* and a twitter. The nest is placed 5-12m above ground in a natural tree-cavity enlarged by the birds. One entrance was 8cm across with the cavity 45cm deep and 30cm wide. Nesting material is cut and carried to the hollow in the contour feathers. Three to four often brown-stained white eggs are laid. The young are white-downed. In captivity fledging has been reported occurring in five weeks, and non-pair birds have been recorded assisting at the nest.

Head bright green with dark blue patch on centre to rear-crown. Upperparts green with clearly marked orange-brown patch on centre of mantle, yellow band across lower back and scarlet rump and uppertail-coverts. Wings green with darker innerwebs to coverts and flight feathers. Underwing-coverts green, with underside of flight feathers blue. Throat and upper breast with bright scarlet patch, remainder of underparts slightly paler green than upperparts (and more yellowish on flanks). Uppertail green; undertail blue. **Bare parts**: Bill black; iris dark brown, appearing black; legs yellowish-brown.

SEX/AGE Females lack the red bib, having generally dull yellowish-green underparts. The blue crown-patch is much duller, and the orange mantle is less well-marked than in the male. Young birds lack the blue crown, have only an indistinct orange wash on the mantle and a yellowish bill. Maturation takes from two to four years with young males showing the red throat as the first sign of adult plumage.

MEASUREMENTS Wing 79-89; tail 29-36; bill 10-12; tarsus 10-12.

GEOGRAPHICAL VARIATION None.

REFERENCES van Balen & Lewis (1991), Buckley (1968), Dickinson *et al.* (1991), Forshaw (1989), Gore (1968), Holmes & Burton (1987), Holmes & Nash (1990b), King & Dickinson (1975), Lambert *et al.* (1993), Lekagul & Cronin (1974), Lekagul & Round (1991), Lodge (1990), MacKinnon & Phillipps (1993), van Marle & Voous (1988), Medway & Wells (1976), Nash & Nash (1985, 1988), Peters (1961), Sibley & Monroe (1990), Silvius & Verheugt (1986), Smythies (1981), Strange & Jeyarajasingam (1993).

---

185 SULAWESI HANGING PARROT
Loriculus stigmatus   Plate 46

Other names: Celebes Hanging Parrot, Celebes Spotted Hanging Parrot, Red-capped Hanging Parrot, Red-crowned Hanging Parrot

IDENTIFICATION 15cm. The largest hanging parrot, occurring commonly through most of Sulawesi. It is sympatric with the much smaller Red-billed Hanging Parrot (193), and the two are very difficult to separate in flight, which is how they are most frequently seen. Male Sulawesi Hanging Parrots are easily separated from Red-billed Hanging Parrots by their bright red crowns; both sexes show a small red carpal-mark lacking in Red-billed, and a black, not coral-coloured, bill (but young birds have a yellowish bill), and birds lack the blue around the red of the throat in male Red-billed. Female Red-billed lacks a red bib, or has a much smaller one, unlike the present species. The only other hanging parrots to show a black bill and red crown are the allopatric Black-billed (183), which has an orange hind-crown and nape, and the nominate race of Moluccan (186), which has a shorter tail with the red uppertail-coverts extending almost to its tip, a whitish iris and a brighter red rump (Sulawesi has a very dark red rump).

VOICE A soft, high-pitched, di- or trisyllabic squeak *tsu-tsee* or *tsu-tsee-tsee* reminiscent of Common Kingfisher *Alcedo atthis*, given constantly in flight. An alarm squeal has also been noted. The limited information available suggests the call is similar to that of Red-billed but lower-pitched.

DISTRIBUTION AND STATUS Reportedly common throughout Sulawesi, from the Minahassa Peninsula in the north, including Bangka and Lembeh Islands, through to the south, where it is also found on Muna and Buton offshore. It also occurs on the Togian Islands. The world population is considered to be in excess of 100,000.

ECOLOGY Little is known of the species's ecology. Possible seasonal movements have been noted. It is reportedly not found deep in primary forest and is commoner along forest edge, in open country, and sometimes around habitation, up to 1,000m. Birds are normally encountered singly or in pairs, either flying overhead or feeding in flowering trees. The diet comprises fruit and nectar from blossoms. Breeding activity has been reported in Feb, from Apr to Jun, and in Aug and Oct. Nest-holes in thick bamboo have been recorded.

DESCRIPTION Head bright green with bright red crown ending in clear line across rear-crown and not extending onto nape. Upperparts green, lightly suffused orange-yellow on mantle; rump and uppertail-coverts dark crimson. Wings green with darker innerwebs to flight feathers; carpal edge with small red mark. Underside of wing turquoise-blue with green lesser coverts. Underparts bright green with red stripe down centre of chin and throat. Uppertail green (fine paler green tips to feathers); undertail light blue. **Bare parts**: Bill black; iris pale yellow; legs pinkish-orange.

SEX/AGE Females lack the red crown and have a narrower red bib; iris may be darker. Young birds lack the red crown, have a less distinct and more yellowish bib, a yellow, not red, carpal-mark, and are generally duller green.

MEASUREMENTS Wing 89-97; tail 35-44; bill 10-12; tarsus 11-13.

GEOGRAPHICAL VARIATION Slight differences in the extent of orange-yellow in the mantle of some island populations are not considered sufficient to differentiate them.

REFERENCES Forshaw (1989), Holmes & Wood (1979), Lambert *et al.* (1993), Lodge (1990), Rozendaal & Dekker (1989), Sibley & Monroe (1990) Watling (1983), White & Bruce (1986).

186 MOLUCCAN HANGING PARROT
Loriculus amabilis   Plate 46

Other names: Wallace's Hanging Parrot (also common vernacular for *L. flosculus*), Halmahera Hanging Parrot

IDENTIFICATION 11cm. Confined to a few islands in the Moluccas where it is the only representative of the genus. Crown red (in males) and mantle green on Halmahera and Bacan; crown green and mantle orange or red in Sula, Banggai and Peleng.

VOICE A rapid, weak, high-pitched, buzzy or staccato, two- or three-note call or a series of notes given in flight.

Moluccan Hanging Parrot

DISTRIBUTION AND STATUS Endemic to C Indonesia, where it occurs on islands off north-east Sulawesi including the Banggai (Peleng, Labobo) and Sula (Scho, Taliabu, Mangole, Sulabesi) archipelagos, and in the N Moluccas on Kasiruta, Bacan, Halmahera and Morotai. The world population is considered to be greater than 20,000 and probably stable although slightly affected by trade. The Sula Islands race is probably down to around 5,000 birds due to habitat loss. The status of the race occurring on Banggai and Peleng is insufficiently known.

ECOLOGY Occurs in primary and secondary forests in the lowlands up to 800m, along forest edge, in mangroves and coastal casuarinas, at the edge of agricultural land, around villages and sometimes in coconut groves. The species is most frequently found singly, in pairs or small groups in the vicinity of flowering trees. Like other hanging parrots, nesting material is tucked into the contour feathers to be carried to the nest. Little is known of the nesting habits, but courtship-feeding has been recorded.

DESCRIPTION Head green with red forecrown. Mantle tinged slightly with orange; rump and uppertail-coverts dark red, latter extending almost to tip of tail. Wings green with blackish innerwebs to flight feathers; carpal-mark red and yellow. Underwing blue with greenish-blue coverts, Chin red; rest of underparts more yellowish green than

upperparts, especially undertail-coverts. Uppertail green; undertail bluish with fine yellowish tips. **Bare parts:** Bill black; iris yellowish-white; legs orange.

SEX/AGE Female with green crown, red spots on forehead and throat. Brown iris. Young birds with yellowish markings around bib, and at carpal edge. Pale brown iris.

MEASUREMENTS Wing 71-84; tail 31-33; bill 9-10; tarsus 9-11.

GEOGRAPHICAL VARIATION Three races. The latter two should perhaps be regarded as a separate species, Sula Hanging Parrot *L. sclateri* (Wallace 1862).
  L. a. amabilis (Halmahera and Bacan)
  L. a. sclateri (Sula Islands) Larger than nominate (male wing 89-102) and with a longer tail. Crown green with reddish-brown bases to frontal feathers. Mantle orange marked with red.
  L. a. ruber (Banggai and Peleng Islands) Like previous race, but mantle red, suffused yellow-orange below, and separated from green of nape by a yellow line.

REFERENCES van Bemmel (1948), BirdLife (1993), Coates & Bishop (1997), Forshaw (1989), Gee (1993), Lambert & Yong (1989), Lambert *et al.* (1993), Lodge (1990), Sibley & Monroe (1990), Smiet (1985), White & Bruce (1986).

187 SANGIR HANGING PARROT
Loriculus catamene   Plate 46

IDENTIFICATION 12cm. Only on Sangir Island to the north of Sulawesi, and the only representative of the genus there. Similar to the nominate race of Moluccan Hanging Parrot (186), but the undertail-coverts are reddish-orange edged green, the tail feathers are tipped red, and there is a yellow-green carpal-mark.

VOICE Distinctive high, trilling *tsw...tswee... tsssweeee.,, eee,* the first note being hard. Single notes are also given in flight.

Sangir Hanging Parrot

DISTRIBUTION AND STATUS Endemic to Sangir Island. Almost all the original vegetation on Sangir has now been replaced by coconut and nutmeg plantations, and the secondary vegetation of abandoned gardens. Observations during the mid-1980s found it to be not uncommon in coconut groves, and two pairs were observed on steep tree-cropped volcanic slopes in 1986. In 1995 the species was recorded from all wooded habitats on the island from sea-level to around 900m (also found around Tahuna). The birds were most often seen in mixed plantations but also in forest patches and coconut groves. **ENDANGERED.**

ECOLOGY Found in pairs or small groups around coconut flowers and flowering shrubs, with parties of up to four birds being most frequently encountered in mixed plantations. The species has adapted to secondary habitats and the main food source appears to be coconut nectar. A roost of 17 birds is the largest reported group. One nest containing two eggs was collected in 1985.

DESCRIPTION Head green with red forecrown and bib. Upperparts green with slight orange wash on mantle; rump and elongated uppertail-coverts red. Wing slightly darker green with blackish innerwebs to flight feathers; carpal edge yellowish-green. Underwing blue with greenish-blue coverts. Underparts green with yellowish belly and red undertail-coverts marked green. Uppertail green with red tips; undertail blue. **Bare parts:** Bill black; iris brown; legs orange.

SEX/AGE Female has no red in crown, red of bib reduced to a few spots, and green undertail-coverts. Young male with yellow carpal edge, lacks red crown but shows red bib.

MEASUREMENTS Wing 82; tail 34-38; bill 10; tarsus 10-11.

GEOGRAPHICAL VARIATION None.

REFERENCES Arndt (1992), Collar & Andrew (1988), Collar *et al.* (1994), Forshaw (1989), Lambert *et al.* (1993), J. Riley *in litt.* (1995), Sibley & Monroe (1990), White & Bruce (1986).

---

188 ORANGE-FRONTED HANGING PARROT
Loriculus aurantiifrons   Plate 47

Other names: Golden-fronted Hanging Parrot, Misool Hanging Parrot, Bat Lorikeet, Papuan Hanging Parrot

IDENTIFICATION 9-10cm. An extremely small hanging parrot, occurring through much of New Guinea and on a number of offshore islands where there are no sympatric congeners. The male is the only hanging parrot with a pure yellow forecrown (it also has a red bib); all other species with yellow on the crown have a red frontal area. The female is the only black-billed hanging parrot with a green crown, red uppertail-coverts, red bib and no red carpal-mark, differentiated chiefly by size and from female Sulawesi Hanging Parrot (185) and female Moluccan Hanging Parrot (186) by lack of red carpal-mark, from female Wallace's (192) and both sexes of Red-billed (190) by black bill, and from male and female Green-fronted Hanging Parrot (189) by red, not greenish-yellow, rump. The sympatric pygmy parrots *Micropsitta* lack the red rump and are most often found creeping around on the bark of

trees, not foraging on flowers. The similar-sized Pygmy Lorikeet (43) shows a longer, pointed tail in flight (as well as other plumage differences), the present species a blue underwing. The flight is rapid and fluttering.

VOICE A harsh, sibilant, high-pitched, rapidly delivered *tseo tseo tseo*, sometimes made into a warbling song, which has also been described as a series of buzzing *chzeee* notes recalling a thornbill *Acanthiza.* The flight call is described as a descending series of two, three or four buzzy notes, like that of Yellow-streaked Lory (3) in miniature.

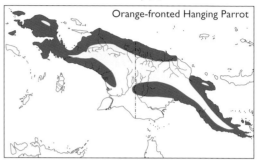
Orange-fronted Hanging Parrot

DISTRIBUTION AND STATUS Widely distributed, but not particularly common, through much of lowland New Guinea in both Irian Jaya, Indonesia, and Papua New Guinea, but may be absent from much of the south-central mainland. As the species's size, habits and coloration make it fairly inconspicuous, further fieldwork may show that it is continuous in the north and south of New Guinea with clinal variation in size. The range includes the following offshore islands: Misool, Waigeo, Karkar, Fergusson and Goodenough. The world population is greater than 100,000 and is considered stable.

ECOLOGY Occurs in lowland rainforest to around 1,200m (occasionally to 1,600m), along forest edge, in palm plantations, secondary growth, casuarinas, pines, gardens and partly cleared areas. The species is inconspicuous and generally difficult to detect except when calling as it flies over the canopy. It is generally found in groups of two to four, foraging at various levels in the forest. Birds sometimes perch and sing from an exposed branch (possibly part of their courtship behaviour). They have been recorded running their bill along casuarina needles, probably searching for lerp insects. The diet also includes buds, fruit and flowers. Nesting has been recorded from Jul to Oct, and on one occasion a bird was reportedly found incubating four eggs in a hollow 12m above ground. Birds have also been recorded visiting holes in arboreal termitaria, perhaps to roost.

DESCRIPTION Head green with forecrown a rich yellow (sharp demarcation from green of rear-crown). Upperparts green with bright red rump and uppertail-coverts extending nearly to end of tail; sides of rump with yellow markings. Wings green with blackish innerwebs to flight feathers. Underwing blue with green coverts. Chin red, rest of underparts slightly more yellowish than upperparts (especially undertail-coverts). Uppertail green tipped yellow; undertail bluish. **Bare parts:** Bill black; iris whitish; legs brownish-black.

SEX/AGE Female has forecrown and face green with reddish feather-bases and tinged pale blue. Smaller red bib. Brown iris. Young birds lack the red crown and throat and have a brownish bill.

MEASUREMENTS Wing 65-69; tail 26-27; bill 7; tarsus 9-11.

GEOGRAPHICAL VARIATION Three races.

L. a. aurantiifrons (Misool)

L. a. batavorum (Waigeo and in NW New Guinea east to the Sepik River in the north, and to about 137°E in the south) Male with less yellow in forehead. Female similar to nominate.

L. a. meeki (SE New Guinea, west in the north to the Madang area, west of the Huon Peninsula, and in the south to the Fly River and through the foothills inland to beyond the Irian Jaya border, also on Fergusson and Goodenough Islands; birds on Karkar Island are apparently intermediate, suggesting clinal variation) Male like male *batavorum* but slightly larger. Female also similar to nominate but larger again, and bases of forecrown feathers yellow-brown.

REFERENCES Arndt (1992), Beehler *et al.* (1986), Bell (1970), Coates (1985), Diamond (1972), Forshaw (1989), Iredale (1956), Lambert *et al.* (1993), Lodge (1990), Peters (1961), Rand & Gilliard (1967), Schodde (1978), Sibley & Monroe (1990).

---

189 GREEN-FRONTED HANGING PARROT
Loriculus tener   Plate 47

Other names: Bismarck Hanging Parrot

IDENTIFICATION 10cm. Restricted to islands in the Bismarck Archipelago. Generally green with an orange bib, and the only hanging parrot with a yellowish-green rump.

VOICE Not documented.

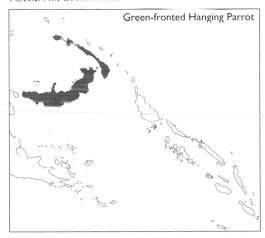

Green-fronted Hanging Parrot

DISTRIBUTION AND STATUS Endemic to islands in the Bismarck Archipelago, recorded from New Britain, New Ireland, Duke of York and New Hanover, but the only information on its status is that it is allegedly uncommon. NEAR-THREATENED.

ECOLOGY An extremely poorly known species. It has been recorded in forest, along forest edge and in partly cleared areas from the lowlands to the low hills.

DESCRIPTION Head green. Upperparts green except for obvious yellowish-green rump and uppertail-coverts. Upperwing green with darker innerwebs to flight feathers.

Underwing blue with green coverts. Chin orange-red; rest of underparts green. Uppertail green; undertail blue. **Bare parts**: Bill black; iris yellowish-white; legs brownish-yellow.

SEX/AGE The female has the forecrown and face tinged bluish. Young birds lack the orange throat-spot and have a pale brown bill.

MEASUREMENTS Wing 64-70; tail 25-30; bill 6-7; tarsus 8-10.

GEOGRAPHICAL VARIATION None.

REFERENCES Arndt (1992), BirdLife (1993), Coates (1985), Forshaw (1989), Lambert *et al.* (1993), Sibley & Monroe (1990).

---

190 RED-BILLED HANGING PARROT
Loriculus exilis   Plate 47

Other names: Lilliput Hanging Parrot, Celebes Lilliput Hanging Parrot, Tulabula Hanging Parrot, Green Hanging Parrot

IDENTIFICATION 10.5cm. The smaller and less common of the two members of its genus occurring in Sulawesi. When seen perched, it is distinguished by its green crown and coral-red bill; male Sulawesi Hanging Parrot (185) has a red crown and both sexes have black bills. Females lack or possess a much-reduced red bib (red bib well-defined in female Sulawesi). Males have the red bib surrounded by blue, lacking in male Sulawesi. The two species are difficult to separate in flight and the calls are reportedly similar. Within the genus as a whole, the combination of a green crown, red bib and red bill is only repeated in Wallace's Hanging Parrot (192), which also has an orange wash on the nape and the bib is larger.

VOICE A *tseet-tseet*, reportedly similar to the call of Sulawesi Hanging Parrot, but higher-pitched.

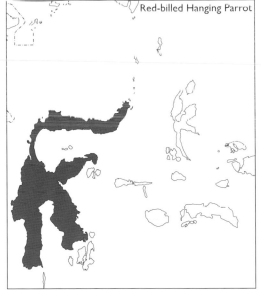

Red-billed Hanging Parrot

DISTRIBUTION AND STATUS Endemic to Sulawesi where it is found from the Minahassa Peninsula in the north through to the south. The world population is estimated to be in excess of 10,000. The species is generally uncommon.

ECOLOGY Generally little known. Occurs in forest, woodland, coastal mangrove, around villages and in open country from the lowlands to hill forest at about 1,000m, being found at similar altitudes and in similar habitats to the Sulawesi Hanging Parrot. The birds are found in groups of up to five or so, foraging in the canopy on fruiting figs or the nectar of flowering trees; their foraging movements have been likened to the crawling movements of pygmy parrots *Micropsitta*. Larger flocks have been encountered in mangroves during May, although the species may breed twice a year, in Feb and Aug; it is not known if these represent post-breeding concentrations or nomadic groups. A hole in a dead palm is the only known record of a nesting location.

DESCRIPTION Head green, brightest around base of bill and suffused bluish-green on chin, throat, forecrown and lower cheeks. Upperparts mid-green with darkish red rump and uppertail-coverts (extending well down tail); sides and base of rump greenish-yellow. Wings green with dark innerwebs to flight feathers; carpal-mark light green. Underwing turquoise with green coverts. Throat red edged pale blue extending onto upper breast; rest of underparts bright green, slightly lighter than upperparts. Uppertail green with pale yellowish tips; undertail pale bluish-green. **Bare parts**: Bill coral red; iris yellow; legs orange.

SEX/AGE Female lacks red bib (or has bib much reduced). Also has a reduced blue suffusion on the breast and a brown iris. Young birds have a smaller red bib, a more yellowish-brown bill, and a pale brown iris.

MEASUREMENTS Wing 64-69; tail 24-32; bill 7-8; tarsus 8-10.

GEOGRAPHICAL VARIATION None.

REFERENCES Forshaw (1989), Lambert *et al.* (1993), Lodge (1990), Rozendaal & Dekker (1988), Sibley & Monroe (1990), Watling (1983), White & Bruce (1986).

---

191 YELLOW-THROATED HANGING PARROT
Loriculus pusillus Plate 47

Other names: Javan Hanging Parrot, Little Hanging Parrot

IDENTIFICATION 12cm. Occurs only in Java and Bali. The combination of green crown and (in male) bright yellow throat or (in female) paler yellow-green throat is diagnostic, although the yellow throat-patch can be difficult to see. The flight is whirring on short stumpy wings.

VOICE Described as a thin, high-pitched *zri-ie* or a shrill ringing *sree-ee* given in flight. A squeaky chattering has also been recorded.

DISTRIBUTION AND STATUS Endemic to Java and Bali where it is generally uncommon. The world population is thought to be greater than 10,000, but may have declined owing to forest clearance. NEAR-THREATENED.

ECOLOGY Recorded from forest, along forest edge, and in swamp forest from the lowlands to 1,850m. Possibly nomadic in response to local plant phenology. The species

is active, clambering acrobatically about in the canopy when foraging, and resting and sleeping upside-down like other members of the genus. The birds are found singly, in pairs or in groups of up to eight feeding on nectar, fruit (including figs *Ficus*), leaf buds, and flowers such as *Cassia* and *Erythrina*. Larger groups sometimes gather in a feeding tree. Although inconspicuous, the birds draw attention as they fly between trees at canopy level on whirring wings, giving their shrill calls. Two buffish eggs are laid in a tree-hole, palm or tree-fern, occasionally in old barbet or woodpecker nest, lined with cut pieces of leaf. Nesting in western Java has been recorded from Mar to May. The female sits tightly and can be lifted from the nest.

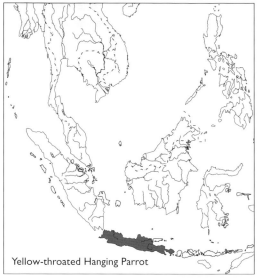

Yellow-throated Hanging Parrot

DESCRIPTION Head bright green. Upperparts green with a faint orange-yellow wash on mantle; rump and elongated uppertail-coverts bright red. Wings green with dark innerwebs to flight feathers. Underwing turquoise with green coverts. Throat bright yellow, rest of underparts bright green. Uppertail green, lateral tail-coverts yellowish; undertail pale blue. **Bare parts**: Bill orange; iris yellowish-white; legs orange.

SEX/AGE Female and immature have much reduced yellow on throat.

MEASUREMENTS Wing 82-90; tail 31-37; bill 9-10; tarsus 10-11.

GEOGRAPHICAL VARIATION None.

REFERENCES Arndt (1992), Forshaw (1989), Holmes & Nash (1990a), Lambert *et al.* (1993), Lodge (1990), MacKinnon (1988), MacKinnon & Phillipps (1993), Mason (1989), Richards & Richards (1988), Sibley & Monroe (1990).

---

192 WALLACE'S HANGING PARROT
Loriculus flosculus Plate 47

Other names: Flores Hanging Parrot

IDENTIFICATION 12cm. A little-known species that until recently was thought possibly to be extinct. It is restricted to the island of Flores where it is the only hanging parrot. The combination of green crown, large red bib (reduced or lacking in females), orange nape and red bill is diagnostic.

VOICE Flight call is a sharp screeching *strrt strrt*, louder and lower-pitched than the call given when perched (which is more reminiscent of a flowerpecker *Dicaeum*). A call given during what appeared to be a display flight is described as *chi-chi-chi-chi-chi-chi*.

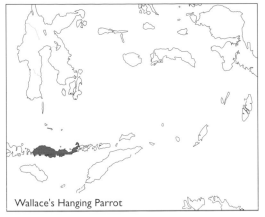

Wallace's Hanging Parrot

DISTRIBUTION AND STATUS Endemic to Flores where it is historically known from a single locality, but was found to be locally common in primary semi-evergreen rainforest at 400-980m (most from 850-980m in fruiting figs *Ficus*) during a 1993 survey. These birds were recorded in the Tanjung Kerita Mese proposed protected area near Paku, western Flores. A 1987 record from eastern Flores comes from Gunung Egon at 1,000m. **VULNERABLE.**

ECOLOGY Appears to require semi-evergreen montane rainforest. Birds have been seen in fruiting trees, and outside the breeding season gather in small flocks of up to 20 birds. Their altitudinal distribution seems to be closely tied to the distribution of fruiting figs. The diet includes nectar, fruits, buds, flowers and seeds. They are easily overlooked owing to their small size and mainly green plumage, and are most often seen in flight when they can be identified on size, shrill calls and rapid whirring wingbeats. They are most frequently seen either in or flying above the canopy. Apparent displays involving wing-shivering, -drooping and -flicking to reveal the red rump have been observed.

DESCRIPTION Head green. Upperparts green with faint orange hind-collar; rump and uppertail-coverts red. Wings green above with blackish innerwebs to flight feathers, bluish-green below. Chin red; rest of underparts green, lightest on undertail-coverts. Uppertail green, tipped lighter; orange-red tips to lateral feathers; undertail greenish-blue. **Bare parts:** Bill coral red; iris orange; legs orange-yellow.

SEX/AGE Female with red bib reduced or lacking. Young with smaller red bib, duller bill and legs.

MEASUREMENTS Wing 79; tail 33; bill 11; tarsus 12.

GEOGRAPHICAL VARIATION None.

REFERENCES Arndt (1992), BirdLife (1993), Butchart *et al.* (1993), Collar *et al.* (1994), Forshaw (1989), Lambert *et al.* (1993), Lodge (1990), Sibley & Monroe (1990).

193 ALEXANDRINE PARAKEET
Psittacula eupatria   Plate 48

Other names: Alexandrine Ring-necked Parakeet, Greater Rose-ringed Parakeet, Great-billed Parakeet, Large Parakeet; Large Indian Parakeet (*P. e. nipalensis*); Large Ceylonese Parakeet (*P. e. eupatria*); Large Burmese Parakeet (*P. e. avensis*); Large Andaman Parakeet (*P. e. magnirostris*); Thai Rose-ringed Parakeet (*P. e. siamensis*)

IDENTIFICATION 58cm. Large, predominantly green with very long graduated tail and conspicuous red bill. Black moustachial stripe and rose-pink collar of male distinctive. Range partially or wholly overlaps with most congeners. However, prominent maroon shoulder-patch, massive bill and considerably larger size generally distinguish this from congeners. Overlapping Plum-headed Parakeet (199), Slaty-headed Parakeet (196) and Finsch's Parakeet (197) show maroon at bend of wings but are smaller, with deep red or bluish-grey hoods. Deliberate rhythmic wingbeats propel Alexandrine Parakeets in graceful, direct and fast flight.

VOICE Calls generally harsh and loud, and include ringing *trrrieuw*, loud *kee-arr* and *keeak*, deep *klak-klak-klak-klak*, harsh scolding *scree* and resonant *g-raaak g-raaak*. Shrieking cries accompany mobbing of predators and voice harsher and more grating when alarmed. Flocks sometimes indulge in excited chorusing. Mimics human and other sounds in captivity. Calls deeper, more raucous and resonant than Ring-necked Parakeet (194) but some shrieking notes are similar.

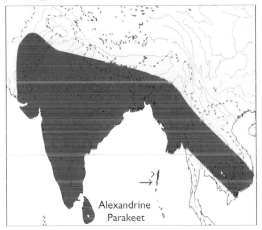

Alexandrine Parakeet

DISTRIBUTION AND STATUS Status in Afghanistan unclear but possibly in extreme north-east around Jalalabad. In Pakistan, isolated colonies in Sind and Peshawar but more widespread and frequent in irrigated lowlands of Punjab; occurs from Indian Punjab, Himalayan foothills and southern Nepal south through all of India and Sri Lanka and east through Bangladesh, Bhutan and Assam into central and southern Burma (not known from north), extending through northern Thailand and central and northern Kampuchea and Laos into central and South Vietnam. Present in Andaman Islands (not south of the Ten Degree Channel) and on Narcondam Island (India) and in the Cocos Islands (Bangladesh), Bay of Bengal. Seasonal movements in some areas and locally nomadic in others. Generally common, but much scarcer in east and sporadically distributed through southern India. Declined Sri Lanka where now rare and mainly in north. Collection of young from nests leading to steep declines in Thailand and probably in other parts of Indochina. Occurrence around some urban areas could be due to escaped cage birds.

ECOLOGY Occurs in a variety of moist and dry forests and woodlands but also cultivated areas, mangroves (e.g. *Rhizophora mucronata* in Bay of Bengal islands) and coconut plantations, chiefly in lowlands up to 900m; in Pakistan Punjab extends to subtropical pine *Pinus roxburghii* zone and penetrates irrigated plantations in desert areas; ascends Himalayan foothills in sal *Shorea* and riverine forests rarely to 1,600m. In Bandhavgarh National Park, birds were found to prefer denser forest than Plum-headed and Ring-necked Parakeets. Generally encountered in small parties, but forms substantial gatherings where food abundant and at communal roosts where birds from considerable area may gather in a single large tree. Diet comprises variety of wild and cultivated seeds, flowers and flower buds, nectar, grain, fruit and vegetables. Considered serious pest in some places: 70% of food taken in farmed areas of Pakistan is crop produce. Feeds mainly in early morning and late afternoon. Known foods include guava *Psidium guajava*, nectar of *Salmalia*, *Butea* and *Erythrina*, fleshy petals of *Bassia latifolia* and young leaves of vegetables. Nest located in tree-cavity (e.g. *Dalbergia*, *Shorea* or *Salmalia*), palm or, very rarely, building, but generally away from human settlement. Nest-chamber lined with wood shavings produced during excavation or enlargement of barbet or woodpecker hole; entrance usually neat and round. Breeding season from Nov/Dec to Mar/Apr depending on location (e.g. Feb-Mar in Punjab and Andaman Islands and Dec-Feb in central Burma).

DESCRIPTION Forehead, lores and crown bright green merging to lavender-blue on cheeks, ear-coverts and hindcrown; faint dark line from posterior cere to eye-ring; bold narrow black stripe from base of bill laterally across base of cheeks, joining with broad rose-pink collar encircling hindneck. Nape, mantle, scapulars, rump and uppertail-coverts greyish-green. Lesser upperwing-coverts maroon; remainder of upperwing-coverts green (brighter and more emerald than body plumage). Primaries and secondaries greyish-green with dark tips to innerwebs above, blackish below. Underwing-coverts grey-green. Underparts yellowish green, breast with greyish tinge. Uppertail pale green tipped yellow; undertail golden-yellow. **Bare parts**: Bill red with paler tip; cere whitish; iris pale yellow; legs greyish-pink.

SEX/AGE Female lacks black and pink collar markings and is generally duller. Immature resembles female (young male sometimes distinguishable by larger size).

MEASUREMENTS Wing 189-215; tail 255-355; bill 29-36; tarsus 19-22. Males generally larger but considerable overlap with females.

GEOGRAPHICAL VARIATION Five races.

  P. e. eupatria (Peninsular India south from about 18°N, and Sri Lanka)

  P. e. nipalensis (Pakistan through India from Punjab to Assam, Bangladesh, Nagaland and Manipur, including Himalayan foothills and Nepal, south to about 18°N; contact zone with *avensis* unknown) Larger and greyer than nominate, with less lavender in head and broader black moustachial stripe.

  P. e. magnirostris (Bay of Bengal islands: Andamans, Cocos and Narcondam) From *nipalensis* by narrow blue band anteriorly bordering rose-pink collar and by brighter red shoulder-patch; from other races by more massive bill.

  P. e. avensis (C and S Burma to about 16°N; possibly in E Assam but contact zone with *nipalensis* and *siamensis* unknown) Similar to *magnirostris* but neck yellower, bill smaller and narrow blue band on collar reduced or absent. More yellow beneath than *P. e. nipalensis*.

  P. e. siamensis (W and N Thailand, Laos, Kampuchea and Vietnam) Face and neck yellowish, nape bluish. Slightly smaller than *P. e. avensis*.

REFERENCES Ali & Ripley (1981), Arndt (1996), Deignan (1945), Forshaw (1989), Inskipp & Inskipp (1985), Luft (1994), Ripley (1982), Roberts (1991), Rutgers & Norris (1979), Smythies (1986), Thewlis *et al.* (1995), Tyabji (1994), Wildash (1968).

194 RING-NECKED PARAKEET
Psittacula krameri   Plate 48

Other names: Rose-ringed Parakeet, Green Parakeet, Long-tailed Parakeet, Senegal Long-tailed Parakeet; Northern Rose-ringed Parakeet (*P. k. borealis*)

IDENTIFICATION 40cm. Predominantly green with large red bill and very long graduated tail. Only member of genus in Africa but wholly or partially overlaps with most other *Psittacula* parakeets in south Asia. Distinguished from all congeners, including very rare Mauritius Parakeet (195), which see for details, by combination of green or bluish-green head, pale grass-green (not emerald- or dark green) body plumage, absence of maroon shoulder-patches and (in adult male) black and pink collar markings.

VOICE Very noisy, especially at communal roosts, with wide range of shrieks, whistles and other sounds in vocal repertoire. Characteristic calls, often delivered in batches of 3-6 followed by a pause, include shrill, rather harsh *kee-ak kee-ak kee-ak*, either loud or softer and more musical, higher-pitched on first note; rasping *kreh kreh kreh kreh* from flocks; chattering *chee chee* in flight, especially when approaching nest; *ak ak ak* issued as warning; quiet trilling and whistling notes when feeding and in courtship. Some calls have a toy trumpet or piping quality.

DISTRIBUTION AND STATUS Old World's most widely distributed psittacine, occurring in tropical Africa north of the moist forest zone and much of southern Asia. Ranges from westernmost Africa (Mauritania, Senegambia, Guinea-Bissau) east through Mali, southern Niger, northern Ivory Coast, northern Ghana, Burkina Faso, Togo and Benin to northern Nigeria and Cameroon, southern Chad, northern Central African Republic, southern Sudan to northern Uganda and Ethiopia, Djibouti and northwestern Somalia. In Asia, from western Pakistan, southern Nepal through India, Bangladesh and Sri Lanka to central Burma. Many introduced populations including in the USA, England, Germany, Netherlands, northern Egypt, Kenya, coastal Ivory Coast (possibly wild relict), South Africa (Natal and Zululand), Mauritius, Arabian Peninsula, Singapore, Macao and China in and around Hong Kong. Mainly sedentary but apparently some movements in more

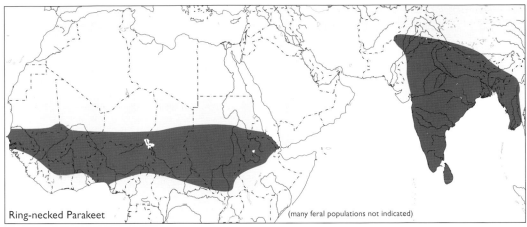

Ring-necked Parakeet   (many feral populations not indicated)

seasonal parts of African range (e.g. rainy season visitor to parts of southern Mauritania). Frequent to abundant in Africa and most of Asia; fairly common in Burma. Abundance increased 20th century in relation to expansion of agriculture. Resident and mostly sedentary. Widely bred in captivity.

ECOLOGY Very adaptable. Found in variety of woodland types from light secondary moist forest, riparian woodland, mangroves through savanna grassland, open farmland with scattered trees to parks and gardens in urban areas, ranging as high as 1,600m in Asia, 2,000m in Africa. Highly gregarious, especially outside breeding season, forming large noisy flocks sometimes of several thousand birds. Roosts communally, often with crows, mynas or other parrots. Diet comprises a variety of cereals, weed and tree seeds, fruit, nuts, flowers and nectar, wild and cultivated; composition varies seasonally with birds in (e.g.) Indian Punjab exploiting weed seeds in Apr-Jun and sorghum in Aug-Jan. Inflicts damage on crops, especially citrus fruit, sunflower and maize. In Africa takes fruits of e.g. *Ziziphus*, *Tamarindus*, *Adansonia*, *Psidium*, *Acacia albida* and *Slassus*. Food in Asia includes seeds of *A. arabica*, *Prosopis spicigera*, *Casuarina equisetifolia* and *Crotolaria medicaginea* and fruits of *Morus alba*, *Bridelia retusa*, *Dalbergia*, *Ficus*, *Xanthium*, *Melia* and *Albizia*. Non-territorial and sometimes loosely colonial whilst breeding. Nests in natural tree-cavity or enlarged hole of other species, rock crevice or building; in Africa, always high in tree. Season chiefly Jan-Apr but recorded breeding to Jul. Typical clutch 3-4 but up to six eggs recorded.

DESCRIPTION Forehead, forecrown, cheeks and lores bright yellowish-green; narrow dark line between cere and eye-ring; hindcrown, nape and sides of neck pale lavender-grey broken on sides of neck by narrow black stripes; black neck markings contiguous with broad black stripes on lower cheeks merging to solid black chin. Rose pink collar on hindneck, mantle and back pale green with olive tinge; rump and uppertail-coverts slightly brighter. Lesser and median upperwing-coverts bright green (darker than body); greater coverts dark green; primaries and secondaries dark green with darker (almost black) margin to innerwebs. Underside of flight feathers grey; underwing-coverts yellowish-green. Underparts yellowish-green. Uppertail centrally blue with yellowish tips, green laterally; undertail centrally blackish, yellowish-olive laterally. **Bare parts**: Upper mandible deep crimson tipped black, lower

blackish-red; cere whitish; iris yellowish-white; legs pinkish.

SEX/AGE Female lacks black neck, cheek and chin markings, pink collar and bluish suffusion on neck; has shorter central tail feathers. Immature similar to female but bill slightly paler, iris greyish; male acquires collar in third year.

MEASUREMENTS Wing 143-157; tail 177-278; bill 18-21; tarsus 15-17.

GEOGRAPHICAL VARIATION Four races.

P. k. krameri (Senegambia through West and Central Africa to W Uganda and S Sudan)

P. k. parvirostris (Sennar district in E Sudan through N Ethiopia to Djibouti and N Somalia) Head and cheeks less yellowish than nominate. Bill smaller and upper mandible brighter red, less blackish towards tip. Birds in eastern Sudan intermediate between *parvirostris* and nominate.

P. k. borealis (Pakistan through N India to about 20°N, Nepal and Bangladesh to Burma. Birds in parts of the Middle East, Mauritius, Macao, and parts of SE China are thought to be this race) Larger than nominate with wholly red upper mandible and black markings on lower mandible. Bluish suffusion on neck behind ear-coverts; underparts more greyish than nominate.

P. k. manillensis (Peninsular India south of about 20°N and Sri Lanka. Feral populations in England, other parts of Europe, USA and Singapore appear to be of this race) Larger than other races (male wing 162-180), slightly paler and yellower than *borealis*. Facial markings more distinct than nominate. Lower mandible black.

REFERENCES Ali & Ripley (1981), Arndt, (1996), Cramp (1985), Erritzoe (1993), Forshaw (1989), Fry *et al.* (1988), Inskipp & Inskipp (1985), Meyer de Schauensee (1984), Ripley (1982), Roberts (1991), Saini *et al.* (1994), Smythies (1986), Tyabji (1994).

---

195 MAURITIUS PARAKEET
Psittacula echo   Plate 48

Other names: Echo Parakeet

IDENTIFICATION 42cm. Bright emerald-green, darker above, more yellowish beneath, male with broad black moustachial stripe extending on side of neck where bordered pink behind, crown and sides of neck adjacent to neck-stripe tinged bright blue. Only surviving native parrot on Mauritius, now very rare within very limited range, but danger of confusion with the introduced Ring-necked Parakeet (194). Mauritius Parakeet is darker, larger and heavier with broader, shorter tail than Ring-necked; in field, most reliably separated by voice and by slower wingbeats and shorter tail; black bill of female reliable guide in good light. Quite tame and approachable.

VOICE Normal contact call a low nasal *chaa-chaa....chaa-chaa* at a rate of two notes per second, sometimes interspersed with harsher, more scolding notes. When excited, a higher-pitched *chee-chee-chee-chee-chee-chee*, at 3-4 notes per second and often delivered in flight accompanied by rapid shallow wingbeats. *Ark* in alarm. Melodious whistling heard in perched birds and quiet purring reported from newly alighted females; buzzing and wheezing sounds also reported. Generally more nasal and resonant than Ring-necked Parakeet with distinct trumpet-like qualities; excited calls are clearer and less harsh than Ring-necked.

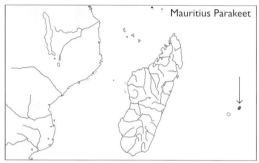

Mauritius Parakeet

DISTRIBUTION AND STATUS Endemic to Mauritius, Indian Ocean, although formerly also on Réunion. Remaining birds confined to last fragments of native forest vegetation. Once widely (but apparently thinly) distributed but now reduced to tiny relict population in south-western plateau around Black River Gorges and Mount Cocotte. Mainly sedentary but some slight seasonal shifts with food availability. Principal cause for (apparently) long-term decline is habitat loss (most natural vegetation cleared for agriculture and forestry), nest predation by introduced species such as crab-eating macaque *Macaca fascicularis* and rats *Rattus*, competition with Ring-necked Parakeets (introduced about 1886) and the effects of disease and storms. Total area of available habitat about 50km². Population c. 7-11 birds in 1984 increasing to c. 30 birds in wild and 8 in captivity in 1995 with 40-50 birds in wild by 1996. Intensive conservation programme includes captive breeding in Mauritius (first successful breeding 1993-1994), predator control and veterinary assistance for wild birds, ecological research and habitat protection. National park now protects last natural woodlands but encroachment by exotic flora poses continuing serious long-term threat. CITES Appendix I. CRITICAL.

ECOLOGY Closely linked to native vegetation. Remaining population centred on an area of upland forest containing some of largest specimens of (e.g.) *Canarium paniculatum*, *Syzygium contractum*, *Mimusops maxima* and *Labourdonnaisia* left on Mauritius. Lower-level scrub forests are also important, especially for feeding. Generally solitary, in pairs or small parties (especially after breeding), but extreme scarcity must limit normal social behaviour. Thought to favour communal roosting. Takes wide range of parts and products of native plants including buds, young shoots, leaves, flowers, fruits, seeds, twigs, sap and bark. Introduced plants are rarely eaten. Recorded food plants include *Calophyllum* (an especially favoured genus), *Canarium paniculatum*, *Tabernaemontana mauritiana*, *Diospyros*, *Erythrospermum monticolum*, *Eugenia*, *Labourdonnaisia*, *Mimusops maxima*, *M. petiolaris*, *Nuxia verticillata* and *Protium obtusifolium*. Favoured foraging areas vary with season. Nests in cavity in large living emergent native tree (often *Mimusops* but also *Calophyllum* or *Canarium*) usually at 6-10m. Entrance hole 10-15cm diameter. Peak egg-laying late Sep into early Oct but may take place Aug-Nov. Clutch 2-4.

DESCRIPTION Lores and cheeks grass-green deepening to emerald-green on upper cheeks, forehead and crown; broad moustachial stripes on lower cheeks and chin attenuating on sides of neck; narrow black neck-stripes bordered above by blue-tinged patches with ear-coverts and sides of neck, and below by pink lines extending to hindneck without forming complete collar. Upperparts, including upperwing, emerald-green. Underparts paler and more yellowish. Uppertail green; undertail dull brownish. **Bare parts**: Upper mandible red, lower blackish; iris pale yellow to greenish-yellow; legs blackish.

SEX/AGE Female lacks black moustachial stripes and black, pink and bluish markings on sides of neck; dark green on cheeks shades to yellowish-green collar on hindneck; dark (almost black) upper mandible. Immature like female but at fledging bill is red in both sexes, turning darker later in females.

MEASUREMENTS Wing 175-190; tail 162-200; bill 21-24; tarsus 19-22.

GEOGRAPHICAL VARIATION None.

NOTE Mauritius Parakeet is sometimes considered conspecific with *P. eques* (formerly Réunion, now extinct) or Ring-necked Parakeet. Lack of authenticated specimens (and disappearance) of former, and morphological and behavioural differences with latter, render allospecies treatment appropriate.

REFERENCES Collar & Stuart (1985), Collar *et al.* (1994), Erritzoe (1993), Forshaw (1989), Jones (1985), Jones & Duffy (1992, 1993), Lovegrove (1995), Lovegrove & Wadum (1994), Wadum (1994).

196 SLATY-HEADED PARAKEET
Psittacula himalayana   Plate 49

Other names: Himalayan Slaty-headed Parakeet, Grey-headed Parakeet, Hodgson's Parakeet

IDENTIFICATION 40cm. Predominantly green with grey head, black on lower cheeks, orange-red bill and long yellow-tipped central tail feathers conspicuous in flight. Very similar to closely related Finsch's Parakeet (197) and likely to be confused where the two abut or overlap (see Finsch's Parakeet). Confusion possible with several other sympatric *Psittacula* parakeets: from Alexandrine (193) by smaller size, grey head and tendency to higher altitude; from Ring-necked (194) by grey head; from Blossom-headed (200) and Plum-headed (199) by grey (not mauve-pink and bluish) head and from latter by yellow (not white) tip to tail; from Red-breasted (204) by green (not pinkish) breast and by darker grey head. Adults distinguished from remaining congeners in captivity by combination of grey head, black cheeks and yellow-tipped central tail feathers. Flight fast and direct, accompanied by high-pitched two-note cries. Generally in small flocks or family parties.

VOICE High-pitched *too-i...too-i* given in flight, harsher than homologous call of Blossom-headed and higher-pitched than that of Ring-necked. Harsher cries include single shrill *screee-eet* at rest, and harsh grating *tchree-ee-eet*. Also utters more melodious notes whilst perched, especially in company. One call combines harsh *scree-eet* with melodious *tee-o-i*. Excited flocks produce far-carrying chorus of calls.

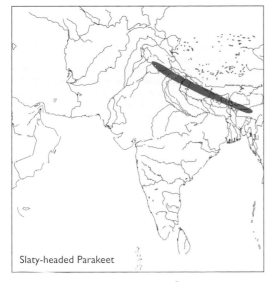

Slaty-headed Parakeet

DISTRIBUTION AND STATUS Occurs in western Himalayas where it is only parrot commonly found above 1,350m, from east in Afghanistan through northern Pakistan, northern India and Nepal to Bhutan, western Arunachal Pradesh and Assam (to about 92°E) north of the Brahmaputra. Generally common although scarce in some parts of range. Small captive population. Apparently not caught or traded in significant numbers.

ECOLOGY Highland forest to c. 2,500m in summer; lower in winter, rarely to 250m. Otherwise resident, but numbers subject to local fluctuations governed by food supply. Occupies denser forest than most congeners, but preferably tracts close to orchards or farms with tall trees. Recorded from a variety of hillside and steep valley woodlands including oak, cedar, oak-*Rhododendron* and pine. Generally in small flocks or family parties, not usually in large aggregations although flocks of 50 recorded at end of monsoon. Mixed flocks with Ring-necked, Blossom-headed and Plum-headed Parakeets recorded. Report of single-sex flock of 15 males, Nov, Nepal. Feeds on variety of cultivated and wild fruits, nuts and seeds depending on season. Recorded food items include berries of *Cornus*, *Viburnum* and *Duranta*, seeds of *Terminalia myriocarpa*, pine *Pinus* seeds, acorns *Quercus dilatata* and *Dalbergia* seed pods, flowers of *Bauhinia purpurea*, nectar from *Woodfordia*

fruticosa. Although overall economic impact probably slight, regarded locally as pest owing to attacks on crops such as maize, apples (blossom and fruit), pears and walnuts *Juglans regia*. Nest located high (6-20m) in natural tree-hollow; cavity excavated in rotten branch or old modified nest-hole of other species. In eastern Afghanistan, nest usually in old hole of Scaly-bellied Woodpecker *Picus squamatus*. Several nests often close together. Breeding season in west of range Mar-May (perhaps later at higher altitude); departs breeding area Jul. Clutch 3-5.

DESCRIPTION Forehead, crown, lores and ear-coverts slaty-grey; chin and lower cheeks black, extending laterally as continuous narrow black collar producing sharp boundary between dark head and bright green hindneck and nape, whose colour fades to duller green on rest of upperparts. Outer lesser wing-coverts green, maroon inner coverts with distinct patch on shoulder; remaining upperwing-coverts green. Primaries green with narrow yellow margins to outerwebs; secondaries green. Underwing-coverts bluish-green. Underparts bright pale green. Uppertail bright blue-green tipped chrome-yellow centrally, outer feathers green with yellowish tips; undertail bright yellow. **Bare parts**: Upper mandible orange-red tipped yellowish, lower paler and yellower; cere whitish; iris creamy-white; legs greenish-yellow.

SEX/AGE Female smaller, duller on nape, generally shorter-tailed and almost always lacking maroon shoulder-patch. Immature dull brownish-green on head, apparently acquiring slaty-grey after first winter. Young birds with dark iris.

MEASUREMENTS Wing 158-177; tail 199-243; bill 20-23; tarsus 15-17.

GEOGRAPHICAL VARIATION None.

NOTE See note under Finsch's Parakeet.

REFERENCES Ali (1979), Ali & Ripley (1981), Arndt (1996), Biswas (1959), Forshaw (1989), Green (1986), Hendricks (1982), Husain (1959), Inskipp & Inskipp (1985), Roberts (1991), Rutgers & Norris (1979) Sibley & Alquist (1990).

---

197 FINSCH'S PARAKEET
Psittacula finschii   Plate 49

Other names: Slaty-headed Parakeet, Eastern Slaty-headed Parakeet, Grey-headed Parakeet, Burmese Slaty-headed Parakeet

IDENTIFICATION 36cm. Predominantly green with grey head, black lower cheeks and collar, red bill and long pale yellow-tipped central tail feathers. Very similar to Slaty-headed Parakeet (196), which may overlap or abut in Bhutan and western Arunachal Pradesh, India (to about 92°E). Finsch's is most easily told by bright blue-green ring forming lower border to black collar and by longer, narrower central tail feathers with duller yellow tips; also generally smaller and paler, back more yellowish, head bluer, underwing-coverts darker, but perhaps not distinguishable in field. Of several other partially or widely sympatric *Psittacula* parakeets, told from Alexandrine (193) by smaller size, grey head and tendency to higher altitude; Ring-necked (194) by grey head; Blossom-headed (200) and Plum-headed (199) by grey (not mauve-pink and bluish) head and from latter by yellow (not white) tip to tail; from Red-breasted (204) by green (not pinkish) breast and darker grey head; from Lord Derby's (203) by smaller size and green (not lavender-blue) underparts. Adults distinguished from other, captive congeners by combination of grey head, black cheeks and yellow-tipped central tail feathers. Flight fast, direct and accompanied by high-pitched two-note cries. Generally in small flocks or family parties.

VOICE As Slaty-headed Parakeet.

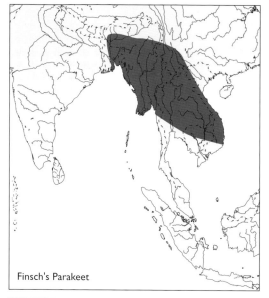

Finsch's Parakeet

DISTRIBUTION AND STATUS Eastern Himalayas to Indochina. Ranges from Bhutan east into Arunachal Pradesh and south through Nagaland, Assam (south of the Brahmaputra River), Manipur, Mizoram and eastern Bangladesh (Sylhet and Chittagong area). Through Burma (south to Tenasserim), south-western China (central Szechwan and northern Yunnan), hilly districts of northern and south-west Thailand, southern Laos, Kampuchea and Vietnam, especially the western slopes of the central mountains. Generally common (in some places very common) resident, but scarce in some areas and subject to local fluctuations in numbers and irregular occurrence. Recent decline in Thailand suspected since now uncommon in more accessible areas. Uncommon in China. Some seasonal altitudinal movements in some parts of range. Very popular cage bird in parts of native territory.

ECOLOGY Similar to Slaty-headed Parakeet. Frequents oak, teak, cedar and pine forest, open wooded hillsides and cultivated land with tall trees between 650 and 3,800m (in Yunnan, China), rarely down to 250m, generally in or not far from hilly terrain. Mainly in forest, Vietnam, but reported both as rare near cultivation and as tolerant of lower and more open habitats. Generally in small flocks or family parties, but larger groups reported, including birds feeding on grit in a streambed in Burma. Diet thought to resemble Slaty-headed; items reported include leaf buds, seeds of *Dendrocalamus longispathus*, fruit of wild cherries *Prunus* and flowers. Breeds in central and southern Burma Jan-Mar. One nest with four eggs at 12m in *Xylia dolabiformis* tree.

DESCRIPTION Forehead, crown, lores and ear-coverts bluish slaty-grey; chin and lower cheeks black, forming a continuous narrow collar producing a sharp boundary between dark head and bright blue-green ring on hind-neck. Nape yellowish-green fading to duller green on rest of upperparts. Upperwing-coverts green except for maroon inner coverts forming distinct patch on shoulder; primaries green with narrow yellow margin to outerweb; secondaries green. Underwing-coverts dark bluish-green. Underparts bright pale green. Uppertail centrally lilac-blue tipped dull pale yellow, outer feathers green with yellow innerwebs and tips; undertail ochre. **Bare parts:** Upper mandible coral-red to vermilion tipped yellow, lower mandible yellow; cere whitish; iris creamy-white to yellow; legs greenish.

SEX/AGE As Slaty-headed Parakeet.

MEASUREMENTS Wing 141-152; tail 187-276; bill 20-22; tarsus 15-16.

GEOGRAPHICAL VARIATION None.

NOTE Sometimes regarded as conspecific with Slaty-headed Parakeet, but lack of intergradation in possible area of overlap in Bhutan and north-eastern India (Arunachal Pradesh) suggests allospecies treatment appropriate.

REFERENCES Ali & Ripley (1981), Deignan (1945), Forshaw (1989), Husain (1959), Meyer de Schauensee (1984), Sibley & Alquist (1990), Smythies (1986), Wildash (1968).

198 INTERMEDIATE PARAKEET
Psittacula intermedia   Plate 49

Other names: Rothschild's Parakeet

IDENTIFICATION 36cm. Predominantly green parakeet with very long blue central tail feathers tipped yellow. Plumage exactly intermediate between Plum-headed (199) and Slaty-headed (196) Parakeets and the evidence is now strong that this form is a hybrid between those two species (see Note below).

VOICE Unknown.

DISTRIBUTION AND STATUS Known from a handful of skins (collected in late 19th century) of unknown provenance but commonly said to be from the western Himalayas (India). More recently described (1986) from a small number of live birds appearing in markets reportedly from the plains of Uttar Pradesh, India, although some or all have subsequently been found to be *cyanocephala* x *krameri* hybrids. Were it a full species, the rarity of specimens and absence of field observations would indicate its range must be restricted and its numbers very small. VULNERABLE.

ECOLOGY Unknown.

DESCRIPTION Forehead, lores and periophthalmic area purplish-maroon; crown, ear-coverts and most of cheeks bluish slaty-grey; chin, broad stripe on lower cheeks and stripe extending around part of hindneck black; hindneck otherwise emerald-green. Mantle and upper back duller green with olive tinge; lower back, rump and uppertail-coverts brighter emerald-green. Lesser upperwing-coverts with small maroon patch; rest of upperwing-coverts bluish-green. Flight feathers green. Underwing-coverts bluish-green. Underparts green but paler and more yellowish than above. Central tail blue, green at base and tipped pale to bright yellow; outer feathers greenish-blue on outerwebs, greenish-yellow on innerwebs with bright yellow tips. **Bare parts:** Bill mainly orange-straw with red at base of maxilla.

SEX/AGE Some authors suggest that the maroon wing-patch identifies male birds but this is not proven. However, female and immature undescribed.

MEASUREMENTS Wing 151-160; tail 167-206; bill 18-21; tarsus 14-16.

GEOGRAPHICAL VARIATION None.

NOTE Pending publication of a full review concluding that the Intermediate Parakeet is of hybrid origin, we tentatively retain it here as a species.

REFERENCES Biswas (1959, 1989), Collar *et al.* (1994), Forshaw (1989), Husain (1959), Rasmussen & Collar (in prep.), Sane *et al.* (1987), Walters (1983).

---

199 PLUM-HEADED PARAKEET
Psittacula cyanocephala   Plate 49

Other names: Blossom-headed Parakeet; Northern Blossom-headed Parakeet (*P. c. bengalensis*); Southern Blossom-headed Parakeet (*P. c. cyanocephala*)

IDENTIFICATION 33cm. Delicately built, mainly green parakeet with elongated blue central tail feathers conspicuously tipped white in flight. Male has small maroon shoulder-patch, bluish-green rump, red face and blue hindneck. Broad black moustachial stripes form narrow black collar bordered below by bright pale green band on nape and sides of neck. Very similar Blossom-headed Parakeet (900) sympatric in Bhutan and West Bengal (see Blossom-headed Parakeet). Distributed in ranges of Ring-necked (194), Alexandrine (193), Slaty-headed, (196), Finsch's (197), Malabar (201), Red-breasted (201) and Emerald-collared (202) Parakeets, but male distinguished by red face and blue hindneck, while absence of maroon shoulder-patch separates female from superficially similar Slaty-headed and Finsch's, and green (not grey) nape separates it from Malabar and green (not grey) mantle and back from Emerald-collared. Blue-green (not green) underwing-coverts distinguish immature Plum-headed from immature Ring-necked Parakeet. Perches with upright stance in tops of trees. Flight swift and arrow-like.

VOICE Flight call a distinctive *toowinck-toowinck*, more musical than Ring-necked. Complicated male song consists of long sequence of rising and falling *queah-quah, kwik-kwink-queeah* notes. Shrill *kooy*, rapid *pe-pe-pe-pe pe-pe* and chattering *twee-eet* also reported. Flocks sometimes use wide range of notes creating cacophony of different-pitched cries with some calls quite melodious and others discordant. Chattering scolding alarm cries at approach of predators.

DISTRIBUTION AND STATUS Lower Himalayan hills from north-east Pakistan across to Nepal, Bhutan and West Bengal and through virtually all India and Sri Lanka plus Rameswaram Island. Generally frequent although evidently declined in Sri Lanka owing to habitat loss so that birds now largely absent in lowlands. Also declined Kathmandu valley, Nepal. Resident, but wanders locally nomadic outside breeding season in response to food supply; more predictable seasonal movements in some areas. Large captive population.

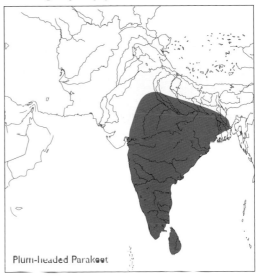
Plum-headed Parakeet

ECOLOGY Favours mosaic of woodland and farmland in plains and foothills including moist deciduous forest, sal *Shorea* forest and subtropical stands of pine *Pinus roxburghii*, generally below 500m in north of range but locally to 1,500m. Occurs in small flocks but larger congregations form at abundant food, particularly ripening crops, and at noisy communal roosts in bamboo thickets or other dense vegetation. Forages in mixed flocks with Slaty-headed and Malabar Parakeets. Recorded food items include flowers of shrub *Adhatoda vasica* and wild pomegranate *Punica granatum*, nectar from *Salmulia, Butea* and *Bassia* flowers, grain including sorghum and maize, fruits of fig and apricot, red peppers and thistle seeds (*Echinops* and *Cnicus*). Strong preference for bamboo seeds noted, Bandhavgarh National Park, but sometimes destructive of cultivated crops. Possibly more frugivorous than congeners and preferring smaller seeds. Nests in hollow in trunk or bough, sometimes an enlarged old nest of woodpecker or barbet. In Pakistan, tall dead or dying *Pinus roxburghii* favoured for nest-site. Neat round entrance hole. Nest-chamber unlined except for construction debris. Often breeds in loose colonies. Male defends nest-site from competing species (such as Ring-necked Parakeet) for some weeks before breeding. Female incubates alone. Season chiefly Dec/Jan-Apr; occasionally also Jul-Aug in Sri Lanka. Clutch 4-5, rarely 6.

DESCRIPTION Forehead, lores, cheeks and ear-coverts bright mauve-red fading to blue on lower cheeks, crown and hindneck, with black moustachial stripe forming narrow black collar bordered posteriorly by broad pale green band. Mantle, back and scapulars dark green; rump and uppertail-coverts bright pale bluish-green. Lesser and median upperwing-coverts bright green with maroon patch on lessers; greater coverts and alula darker and duller. Primaries and secondaries dark green. Underwing-coverts bluish-green. Underparts yellowish-green. Upper-tail centrally bright blue with white, slightly spatulate, tips, outer feathers yellowish-green. **Bare parts**: Upper mandible orange-yellow, lower blackish but pale flesh at chin; iris yellowish-white; legs greenish-grey.

SEX/AGE Female head dull bluish-grey, yellowish on throat and sides of neck, without black markings or maroon on wing-coverts; mandibles paler, tail somewhat shorter. Immature head greenish sometimes tinged grey; central tail feathers shorter.

MEASUREMENTS Wing 126-146; tail 152-225; bill 16-19; tarsus 13-15.

GEOGRAPHICAL VARIATION Three races sometimes recognised but *P. c. bengalensis* is a weak clinal variant of nominate and is not accepted here. *P. c. rosa* is a synonym of *P. roseata juneae* (see Plum-headed Parakeet).

    P. c. cyanocephala (Sri Lanka, Rameswaram Island and India north to about 20°N where it intergrades with next race)

    P. c. bengalensis (Lower Himalayas from Pakistan to Bhutan and India south to about 20°N) Underwing-coverts green, tail paler blue, no bluish tinge on rump and uppertail-coverts.

REFERENCES Ali & Ripley (1981), Arndt (1996), Fleming *et al.* (1976), Forshaw (1989), Inskipp & Inskipp (1985), Luft (1994), Ripley (1982), Roberts (1991), Tyabji (1994).

---

200 BLOSSOM-HEADED PARAKEET
Psittacula roseata   **Plate 49**

Other names: Rose-headed Parakeet, Rosy-headed Parakeet; Eastern (Assam) Blossom-headed Parakeet (*P. r. roseata*); Arakan Blossom-headed Parakeet (*P. r. juneae*)

IDENTIFICATION 33cm. More delicate that most congeners. Predominantly green with long blue, white-tipped central tail feathers (conspicuous in flight). Small maroon shoulder-patches. Face of male mauve-pink, crown and hindneck powder-blue; broad black moustachial stripes form black collar. Upper mandible yellowish-orange, lower blackish. Sympatric with very similar Plum-headed Parakeet (199, race *bengalensis*) in Bhutan and West Bengal, and often indistinguishable in field; good views show Blossom-headed has pinkish (not red) forecrown, lores, cheeks and ear-coverts, and no bright green collar. Female Plum-headed lacks maroon shoulder-patches. Male distinguished from overlapping Alexandrine (193), Ring-necked (194), Slaty-headed (196), Finsch's (197), Red-breasted (204) and Lord Derby's (203) Parakeets by pink and blue head. Female separated from super-ficially similar Slaty-headed and Finsch's Parakeets by paler head, dark grey (not yellowish) lower mandible, absence of black collar, yellowish patch around neck and whitish (not bright yellow) tip to central tail feathers. Flight fast and direct in small parties. Voice relatively tuneful.

VOICE Softer and more musical voice than other *Psittacula* parakeets with characteristic *tweetoo twee twee too too tweetoo* calls. Sharper *tooi* uttered in flight. Softer, musical and conversational notes at rest.

DISTRIBUTION AND STATUS Foothills of eastern Himalayas to Indochina. From Sikkim (India) and Bhutan south through Assam to Bengal and Bangladesh and eastwards through northern and central Burma, southern

China (Yunnan, Guangxi and Guangdong provinces), Thailand, Laos, Kampuchea and Vietnam. Mainly sedentary with seasonal movements in south-western Burma where birds are common Mar-Apr but otherwise scarce. Generally common although decline evident in some areas (e.g. Thailand and Burma) owing mainly to large-scale deforestation, trapping and perhaps persecution. Scarce in Vietnam. Resident but some local movements in relation to food supply. Kept in captivity and apparently subject to heavy trapping in some parts.

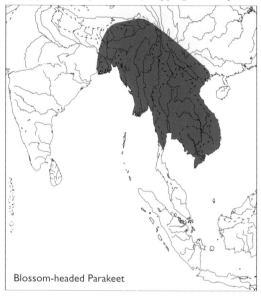

Blossom-headed Parakeet

ECOLOGY Inhabits light forest, including savanna, secondary growth, forest edge, clearings and cultivated land. Persists in partially deforested areas and appears to prefer forest edge adjoining cultivation. Mainly in lowlands to about 1,500m. Usually in small parties, forming larger congregations where food abundant. Joins mixed flocks with Ring-necked, Plum-headed and Red-breasted Parakeets and roosts communally in dense vegetation. Diet similar to Plum-headed Parakeet. Nest located in tree-cavity, usually at moderate height. Birds either excavate the hollow themselves or modify old nests of other species (e.g. woodpecker or barbet). Nests generally in loose colony of several pairs. Clutch 4-5 (rarely six); eggs more spherical than congeners. Breeding Jan-Apr (sometimes May).

DESCRIPTION Forehead, lores, cheeks and ear-coverts mauve-pink fading to powder-blue on lower cheeks, sides of neck, crown and hindneck, with broad black moustachial stripes forming narrow black collar between blue of head and green of body; nape bright grass-green fading to duller green on upperparts. Upperwing-coverts mostly green with maroon patch on inner lesser and median coverts; outer greater coverts and alula darker green. Pri-maries dark green (darker on innerweb) with narrow yellowish margin to outerweb. Underwing-coverts green. Underparts pale green. Uppertail centrally bright blue, tipped creamy-white, outer feathers green on outerweb, yellowish-green on inner, tipped yellow; undertail dull yellowish. **Bare parts**: Upper mandible yellowish-orange, lower black; cere whitish; iris yellowish-white; legs grey-green.

SEX/AGE Female has head pale bluish-grey, with no black

moustache and collar replaced by dull olive-yellow ring extending from nape around sides of neck; tail slightly shorter. Upper mandible yellow, lower dark grey. Immature has greenish head, grey tinge to chin and yellowish mandibles until 15 months, when both sexes develop plumage similar to adult female; male acquires adult plumage at about 30 months.

MEASUREMENTS Wing 128-148; tail 141-179; bill 17-20; tarsus 14-16.

GEOGRAPHICAL VARIATION Two races.

> *P. r. roseata* (Foothills of Himalayas in Bhutan and N Bengal through Assam and E Bangladesh, intergrading with *juneae* in the south-east near border of Tripura at 91-92°E)
>
> *P. r. juneae* (E Bangladesh to Burma north and east through S China, Thailand, Laos, Kampuchea and Vietnam) Generally more yellowish, maroon wing-patch more extensive and wing, on average, shorter. Uppertail paler blue centrally.

REFERENCES Ali & Ripley (1981), Harvey (1990), Meyer de Schauensee (1984), Ripley (1982), Round (1988), Smythies (1986), Wildash (1968).

---

201 MALABAR PARAKEET
Psittacula columboides — Plate 50

Other names: Blue-winged Parakeet, Bababudan Parrot

IDENTIFICATION 38cm. Dove-grey underparts and mantle contrast with blue (male) or blue-green (female) rump. Male's grey underparts unique for genus, and this plus mainly grey head distinguish it from partially sympatric Alexandrine (193), Ring-necked (194) and Plum-headed (199) Parakeets. Long central tail feathers blue tipped yellow above, bright golden-yellow below. Primaries blue. Black moustachial stripes forming narrow black collar in both sexes, male with collar bordered below by bright blue-green band extending around throat. Immatures greyer than young Ring-necked or Plum-headed Parakeets and show bluish rump. Generally in small groups first noticed by loud calling. Flight swift and direct. Plumage blends well with foliage.

VOICE Harsh, high-pitched and sometimes rather grating *screeek*, rapidly repeated on wing. Sharp *cheet cheet cheet* sometimes in repeated short bursts. Flocks very noisy. Voice quite different from that of Plum-headed Parakeet.

DISTRIBUTION AND STATUS Western Ghats, India, in narrow strip parallel to west coast from Pune (19°N), Maharashtra, through Karnataka to Kerala and Tamil Nadu at 8°27'N in the south. Mainly resident but some nomadic movements occur in response to food availability. Variously reported as common, generally common to uncommon, but bird trade and habitat loss evidently causing a decline, not yet sufficient to place the species at risk.

ECOLOGY Largely confined to upland evergreen rain-forest (primary and secondary) but reported from other formations including adjacent deciduous forest with bamboo and particularly in abandoned coffee and rubber plantations, and often near light cultivation. Mostly occurs between 450-1,000m but exceptionally above 1,600m and down to about 60m. Usually in family parties or small flocks. At lower altitudes associates with Plum-headed Parakeet, completely replacing it higher up and in wetter forest. Diet comprises seeds and fruits, especially wild figs; buds, flowers and nectar of *Erythrina* and *Grevillea* (shade-plants in tea and coffee plantations) regularly eaten. May be highly destructive of sorghum and fruit crops. Nest-cavity excavated in branch or trunk at 6-30m or located in enlarged woodpecker or barbet hole. Ironwood trees *Mesua ferrea* especially favoured. Usual clutch 4. Season Jan-Mar.

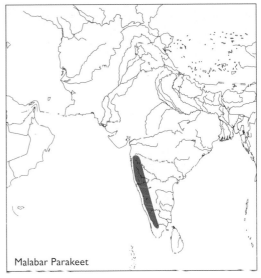

Malabar Parakeet

DESCRIPTION Lores and upper cheeks grass-green, with blue tinge at edges of green fading to dark dove-grey on crown, lower cheeks, sides of neck and hindneck; broad black moustachial stripes attenuate to form black collar in turn fringed below with bright blue-green band extending around throat. Mantle dove-grey fading to greyish-green on back and scapulars; rump and uppertail-coverts pale bluish green, sides of rump yellowish. Lesser coverts dark green subterminally tipped dark grey edged buffish; inner median coverts green with pale buffish margins; alula and greater coverts blue. Primaries and secondaries blue, darker on innerwebs. Underwing-coverts bluish-green. Throat bright pale bluish-green; breast dove-grey fading to bluish-yellow on rest of underparts; blue tinge on thighs. Uppertail centrally bright blue tipped yellow, lateral feathers greenish-blue on outerweb, bright yellow on inner; undertail bright golden-yellow centrally, otherwise brown with yellow tip. **Bare parts:** Upper mandible bright red tipped yellow, lower brown becoming orange at chin; iris pale to bright yellow; legs greenish-grey.

SEX/AGE Female smaller, with little or no green on face and both mandibles brownish. Underparts greyish-yellow, more yellowish towards vent. Less grey on mantle and tail shorter. Immature shows greyish-green in place of grey plumage of adult. Black collar and green neck band absent.

MEASUREMENTS Wing 135-160; tail 171-266; bill 22-25; tarsus 15-17.

GEOGRAPHICAL VARIATION None.

REFERENCES Ali & Ripley (1981), BirdLife International (1993), Forshaw (1989).

202 EMERALD-COLLARED PARAKEET
Psittacula calthrapae   Plate 50

Other names: Layard's Parakeet, Calthorp's Parakeet

IDENTIFICATION 29cm. Grey mantle and back, emerald-green collar, blue rump, blue-grey head and green face. Adults distinguished from sympatric Ring-necked (194), Alexandrine (193) and Plum-headed (199) Parakeets by grey back, blue rump and relatively short tail, and from last species by more direct flight. Immature differs from Ring-necked by blue-grey rump and darker green plumage. Superficially similar to Malabar Parakeet (201) of Western Ghats, India, but male has green (not blue) wings and both sexes show green (not grey or yellowish-grey) underparts. Flight swift, dashing and direct. In pairs or small noisy parties. Sometimes quite approachable whilst feeding.

VOICE Distinctive loud harsh chattering screams, *greek greek greek greek greek*, generally given on wing. Usually quiet whilst feeding. Flocks of excitedly birds generate very loud noise.

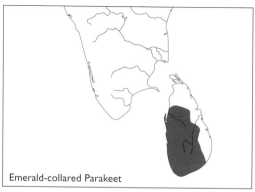

Emerald-collared Parakeet

DISTRIBUTION AND STATUS Central-southern and south-western Sri Lanka. In Central Province north of Matale through highlands around Kandy south and west into Western and Sabaragamuwa Provinces to northern Southern Province. Occurs east to around Galoya National Park and south in Uva Province to Haputale. One pre-1880 record from Eastern Province. Unconfirmed sight record from the Maldives thought to be escaped bird. Reportedly abundant in 19th century and apparently still numerous in some areas, but declining owing to habitat loss arising from (e.g.) conversion of natural and semi-natural forest to plantation and capture for trade. Scarce in captivity outside range.

ECOLOGY Well-wooded country to 1,600m but recorded to 2,000m, using a variety of vegetation types including natural and semi-natural moist forest, tea plantation and botanic gardens; often at forest edge, generally in small parties or pairs. Sedentary, mostly in Hill Zone, but ranges over lowlands, especially in wet forest near sea-level. After feeding, birds congregate in trees chattering loudly and persistently. Before roosting, they wander about calling loudly. Diet thought to be similar to Ring-necked and Plum-headed Parakeets although arboreal habits render it more frugivorous and less destructive of crops. Recorded in company of Brahminy Mynas *Sturnus pagodarum* feeding on kanda *Macaranga tomentosa* fruit. Favoured foods include figs and fruit of wild cinnamon *Cinnamomum*

verum. Nests in tree-hollow, usually at considerable height. Competition for nest-cavities often intense, especially with Plum-headed Parakeet. Cavity lined with decayed wood and dust. Clutch 2-4. Season Jan-May and sometimes Jul-Sep.

DESCRIPTION Forehead, lores, upper cheeks and periophthalmic region grass-green; crown, hindneck and sides of neck blue-grey, with poorly defined black moustachial stripes ending on side of neck around eye-level; nape bright emerald green. Mantle and upper back pale grey; scapulars green to yellowish-green; lower back, rump and uppertail-coverts bright blue to blue-grey. Upper lesser wing-coverts pale yellowish-green; median-coverts grass-green; greater-coverts darker green. Primaries and secondaries dark green with bluish tinge on outerwebs. Underwing-coverts green. Underparts pale green, more yellowish around thighs. Uppertail centrally bright blue tipped yellow, lateral feathers green with yellowish inner-webs; undertail rich golden-yellow. **Bare parts**: Upper mandible bright coral red, lower blackish with red tinge; iris white through yellowish to greenish-yellow; legs greenish-grey.

SEX/AGE Female duller than male with blackish mandibles. Immature lacks grey plumage of adult and rump is bluish-grey. Recently fledged birds have pink bills which turn black after first moult then red again later in males.

MEASUREMENTS Wing 135-145; tail 117-135; bill 20-23; tarsus 16-17.

GEOGRAPHICAL VARIATION None.

REFERENCES Ali & Ripley (1981), BirdLife International (1993), Forshaw (1989), Henry (1955), Legge, (1880), Luft (1994), Phillips (1978), Ripley (1982), Rutgers & Norris (1979).

---

203 LORD DERBY'S PARAKEET
Psittacula derbiana   Plate 50

Other names: Derbyan Parakeet, Derby's Parakeet, Chinese Parakeet, Upper Yangtze Parakeet

IDENTIFICATION 50cm. Largest parrot in range and only member of genus with lavender-blue underparts, easily distinguishing it from the partially sympatric Finsch's (197) and Blossom-headed (200) Parakeets, which are pale green beneath. Similar to (altitudinally allopatric) western race *fasciata* of Red-breasted Parakeet (204) but latter has paler, rosier underparts. Black throat and stripes extending from periophthalmic region to join at top of bill are striking; no collar markings. Upper mandible of male bright red, female blackish. Forms noisy flocks.

VOICE High-pitched, pure-sounding *creeo creeo creeo* call. Also *graaa graaa* recalling a rather high-pitched crow.

DISTRIBUTION AND STATUS Himalayas and southern Tibetan Plateau east of about 93°E. From Arunachal Pradesh and Assam, India, to south-eastern Tibet and south-western China in western Szechwan to about 32°N and western Yunnan south to about Tengchong at 25°N. Summer visitor to north-eastern India (May-Sep). Apparently resident elsewhere with some seasonal altitudinal movements. Generally common. Live birds traded in small numbers and modest captive population outside range. NEAR-THREATENED.

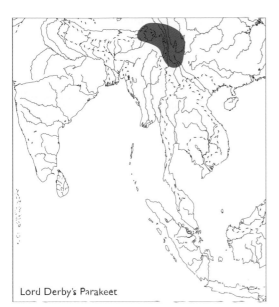

Lord Derby's Parakeet

ECOLOGY Highland forest from 1,250 to 4,000m. Thought to make seasonal vertical migrations but seen in Tibet at 3,300m even in mid winter. Reported mainly from coniferous or mixed *Pinus* and *Quercus* forest, also from alpine *Rhododendron* growth. Visits cultivated valleys, especially at harvest. Gregarious, generally in noisy flocks of up to several dozen birds. Only rarely encountered in pairs or singly. Recorded food items include barley, maize, catkins of *Populus ciliata*, cones of *Pinus tabulaeformis* and cultivated fruits according to availability, including peaches; can be highly destructive of crops. Believed to take some invertebrates, leaf buds and berries. Nest-hole located in tree-hollow, usually at some height, commonly in *Populus ciliata*. Breeds Jun. Clutch in captivity 2-3.

DESCRIPTION Crown and lower cheeks lavender-blue shading through pale iridescent blue on forehead to bright pale green on upper cheeks and periophthalmic region; narrow black stripe extends horizontally from eyes to above bill; broad black moustachial stripes merge below chin to create large patch. Nape to uppertail-coverts green, brightest on mantle. Upperwings green with yellow or yellow-margined feathers in median and greater coverts, creating distinct pale patch. Primaries and secondaries emerald-green. Underparts to belly lavender-blue; thighs, vent and undertail-coverts grass-green. Uppertail centrally blue, outer feathers blue on outerweb, green on inner; undertail brownish. **Bare parts**: Upper mandible red tipped yellowish, lower black; cere blue-grey; iris straw-coloured; legs dark grey.

SEX/AGE Female has bill black. Immature has green head and much paler underparts. Very young birds have pink bills turning black later and then red again in males.

MEASUREMENTS Wing 208-228; tail 207-266; bill 29-35; tarsus 19-23.

GEOGRAPHICAL VARIATION None.

REFERENCES Ali & Ripley (1981), Arndt (1996), Cheng (1987), Forshaw (1989), Meyer de Schauensee (1984), Perry (1990), Rutgers & Norris (1979), Vaurie (1972).

204 RED-BREASTED PARAKEET
Psittacula alexandri Plate 51

Other names: Moustached Parakeet, Banded Parakeet, Bearded Parakeet, Rose-breasted Parakeet, Pink-breasted Parakeet; Indian Red-breasted Parakeet (*P. a. fasciata*); Javan Parakeet (*P. a. alexandri*); Kangean Moustached Parakeet (*P. a. kangeanensis*); Andaman Moustached Parakeet (*P. a. abbotti*); Simeulean Moustached Parakeet (*P. a. cala*); Babi Moustached Parakeet (*P. a. major*); Nias Moustached Parakeet (*P. a. perionca*).

IDENTIFICATION 33cm. Only rosy-breasted *Psittacula*, hence easily distinguished from sympatric congeners. Head blue grey with heavy black patches on lower cheeks and chin, and narrow black stripes running from eyes to join above cere. Lower belly and upperparts green with yellowish patches on upperwing-coverts. Long graduated tail with blue central feathers. Typically seen in noisy flocks travelling low in relatively slow flight through open country, rising to perch in tall tree top; quieter whilst feeding.

VOICE Wide variety of calls, varyingly raucous, nasal, high-pitched and plaintive. Voice quite different to Alexandrine (193) and Ring-necked (194) Parakeets. Raucous, loud trumpeting scream, shrill whistles and rather nasal honking *cheent cheent* interspersed with more grating notes. Shrill *ek ek* and short, sharp *kuink* repeated rapidly by several birds in disturbed flock. *Kak-kak-kak-kak-kak* heard in Nepal, and piercing *kekekekeke* from young birds. Flocks produce noisy sounds or call on single raucous note. Calling birds conspicuous on morning and evening roost-flights.

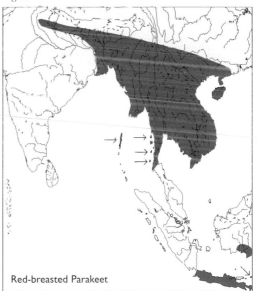

Red-breasted Parakeet

DISTRIBUTION AND STATUS Central Himalayas to Indochina, China and western Indonesia. From the lower Himalayas in northern India at about Dehra Dun east through Nepal, Sikkim and Bhutan north into south-western Yunnan, China; south through Assam, Manipur and Nagaland, India, to Bangladesh and east through Burma (including Mergui Archipelago), Indochina, Malay Peninsula to about 9°N (a 1889 record from Kelantan

413

River at about 5°N suggests range contraction) to Guangxi and Guangdong provinces and Hainan Island, southern China. Occurs Andaman Islands and in Indonesia on Java, Bali, Karimunjawa, Kangean, southern Borneo (where probably introduced from Java) and Simeuluë, Nias and Banyak off western Sumatra. Eggs of escaped captive birds found Singapore and a single record (presumably an escape) from Hong Kong. Resident but some local movements dictated by food supply. Commonest parrot in some parts of range but with a substantial decline in Thailand and Laos in recent years and local extinctions (e.g. Java and Bali) owing to the live bird trade; the nominate race may be at risk as a result. Small numbers in captivity outside range (principally nominate and *fasciata*).

ECOLOGY Usually below 2,000m (rarely above 345m in Nepal) in all types of forest and wooded areas including dry forest, moist-deciduous secondary jungle, mangroves, coconut and mango groves, cultivated areas with trees (including shifting hill cultivation), parks and urban areas. In Himalayan region avoids dense evergreen forest. Gregarious, usually in flocks of 6-10 birds, less frequently to 50 and very exceptionally in thousands, larger flocks gathering when favoured food (e.g. mango or rice) available, sometimes mixing with Slaty-headed (196) or Finsch's Parakeets (197). Forms communal roosts in tall trees, bamboo thickets or sugarcane. Diet includes wild figs'and other wild and orchard fruit, flowers and nectar (especially e.g. *Parkia speciosa* and *Erythrina variegata*), nuts (e.g. chestnuts *Castanea*), fruit (e.g. mango), berries, seeds (e.g. *Albizia*), leaves and cereals such as rice and maize, so causes serious crop damage especially to rice. Nests in natural tree-cavity or often old woodpecker or barbet hole, generally at 3-10m and often in loose colony. Hollow lined with wood shavings. Clutch 2-4. Breeding mostly from Dec-Apr depending on locality and altitude; in Java, recorded all months except Apr.

DESCRIPTION (*P. a. fasciata*) Crown, forehead, upper cheeks and ear-coverts pale lavender-grey suffused blue and pink, with pale green tinge around eyes and thin black stripes from eyes to above cere; lower cheeks and sides of chin black bordered lavender-grey below. Nape bright green; upperparts duller green. Median coverts ochre (forming distinct patch), greater coverts green with ochre margins to outerwebs; other upperwing-coverts green. Primaries and secondaries green. Underwing-coverts pale green. Throat to upper belly salmon-pink; lower belly to undertail-coverts grass-green, with sporadic yellow feathers on inner thighs. Uppertail mostly blue with green tips centrally, outer feathers green; undertail brownish. **Bare parts**: Upper mandible coral-red with yellowish tip, lower blackish; cere pale grey; iris straw-yellow to bright pale yellow; legs pale grey.

SEX/AGE Breast of female redder than male, iris whitish-yellow and tail on average shorter. Bill all black. Immature birds have all-green underparts and crown but may show some pinkish feathers on head. Cheek-patches initially dull brownish-black turning black after first moult. Reddish bill of juvenile turns blackish (and then red again in mature male). Wing-patch only suggested by ochre margins to outerwebs of median-coverts.

MEASUREMENTS (*P. a. fasciata*) Wing 153-171; tail 140-198; bill 22-26; tarsus 16-19.

GEOGRAPHICAL VARIATION Seven races. All but the first two are endemic to small island groups or single islands. *P. a. fasciata* (described above) is the most widespread. A further race, *P. a. major* (of Babi and Lasia, W Sumatra, Indonesia), has been proposed but is probably synonymous with *perionca*.

P. a. alexandri (Java and Bali; birds of this race in S Borneo are thought to have been introduced from Java) Head bluer than *fasciata* with blue-grey band between black cheek/ chin patches and pink of throat. Both mandibles of both sexes red; no green tinge around eyes.

P. a. fasciata (Continental Asia from N India through lower Himalayas, Burma including Mergui Archipelago, Thailand and Indochina to S China including Hainan)

P. a. kangeanensis (Kangean Islands, Java Sea, Indonesia) Head greyer (less blue). Bill heavier than nominate and both mandibles red in both sexes.

P. a. dammermani (Karimunjawa Islands, Java Sea, Indonesia) Perhaps on average larger than *P. a fasciata* (wing 172-180). Pink on breast darker than nominate. Pink extends from throat to sides of neck in female. Heavier bill than nominate. Both mandibles red in both sexes.

P. a. perionca (Nias Island, W Sumatra) As *fasciata* (including sexually dimorphic bill coloration) but paler and larger (length 370, wing 171-194) with no green tinge around eyes.

P. a. cala (Simeuluë Island, W Sumatra) As *fasciata* but belly blue (especially male), breast darker pink and lores, forehead and lower belly strongly suffused pale blue.

P. a. abbotti (Andaman Islands) Similar to *fasciata* (including sexually dimorphic bill coloration) but larger (length 360, wing 163-181) and paler.

REFERENCES Ali (1979), Ali & Ripley (1981), Arndt (1996), Cheng (1987), Deignan (1945), Dymond (1994), Fleming *et al.* (1976), Forshaw (1989), Harvey (1990), Inskipp & Inskipp (1985), MacKinnon (1988), van Marle & Voous (1988), Medway & Wells (1976), Meyer de Schauensee (1984), Ripley (1982), Round (1988, 1991), Smythies (1981, 1986), Cheng (1987), Wildash (1968).

205 NICOBAR PARAKEET
Psittacula caniceps   Plate 50

Other names: Blyth's Parakeet, Blyth's Nicobar Parakeet, Grey-headed Parakeet

IDENTIFICATION 33cm. Large, grey-headed and rather dull green parakeet with long graduated tail and heavy black chin-patch. Upper mandible bright coral-red in male, black in female. Sympatric race *nicobarica* of Long-tailed Parakeet (206) easily distinguished by red cheeks, dark-green crown, blue rump, blue elongated central tail feathers and distinctive call (see Voice). Difficult to locate visually in dense foliage but presence revealed by distinctive call. Flight swift and direct. Usually in pairs or parties of four or five with birds maintaining continuous loud shrieking.

VOICE A wild screeching note may be repeatedly uttered both at rest and in flight, although birds are often silent. Raucous and loud crow-like *kraan kraan* separates Nicobar from screeching calls of Long-tailed Parakeet.

Nicobar Parakeet

DISTRIBUTION AND STATUS Endemic to Nicobar Islands, Indian Ocean, India. Recorded from Great Nicobar, Montschall and Kondul. Resident. Conservation status unknown but potentially at risk from habitat loss to expanding rice cultivation; also from bird trade, although there is little local use as pets and no known international traffic. Recently designated national parks should protect large areas of remaining habitat. Numbers probably stable. NEAR-THREATENED.

ECOLOGY Inhabits high rain-forest. Generally remains in dense foliage of canopy, especially when not feeding. Usually in pairs or small parties. Diet unknown except that fruits of *Pandanus*, abundant on inhabited islands of the Nicobar group, are used extensively. Breeding unknown.

DESCRIPTION Crown, upper cheeks and ear-coverts pale grey; black stripe from periophthalmic region through lores to forehead; lower cheeks and chin black. Nape and upper mantle pale grey suffused blue; rest of upperparts dull grass-green. Upper-wing-coverts green; primaries and secondaries green with dark tips. Underwing-coverts green. Underparts green, slightly paler than upperparts. Elongated central tail feathers green with grey fringe, outer green. **Bare parts**: Upper mandible coral-red, lower black; cere dark grey; iris orange-red; legs dark grey.

SEX/AGE Female has both mandibles black, grey of head and nape more strongly suffused blue, and slightly shorter tail. Immature similar to female.

MEASUREMENTS Wing 202-222; tail 241-378; bill 28-33; tarsus 21-23.

GEOGRAPHICAL VARIATION None.

REFERENCES Ali & Ripley (1981), Forshaw (1989), Ripley (1982), Rutgers & Norris (1979).

---

206 LONG-TAILED PARAKEET
Psittacula longicauda   Plate 51

Other names: Malayan Red-cheeked Parakeet, Malaccan Red-cheeked Parakeet (nominate); Andaman Long-tailed Parakeet, Andaman Red-cheeked Parakeet, Tytler's Parakeet (*P. l. tytleri*); Nicobar Long-tailed Parakeet (*P. l. nicobarica*)

IDENTIFICATION 42cm. Long-tailed green parakeet generally located by raucous cries from canopy. Combination of red cheeks, green crown, pale greyish-green nape and mantle and elongated blue central tail feathers distinguishes it from congeners such as sympatric Blyth's Parakeet (205) in Nicobar Islands, Red-breasted (204) and Alexandrine (193) Parakeets in Andaman Islands and feral Ring-necked Parakeet in Singapore. Usually in small restless noisy flocks flying fast with great agility.

VOICE Loud and not unlike Ring-necked Parakeet (194). Wide variety of screeches and other cries including high-pitched, rather melodious *pee-yo pee-yo pee-yo* and more raucous shrieks. Nasal, quavering, somewhat goose-like *graaak graaak graaak* from feeding birds. Scolding *cheet cheet cheet cheet* given in bursts.

Long-tailed Parakeet

DISTRIBUTION AND STATUS Bay of Bengal islands to Borneo. Ranges from Coco (Bangladesh) and the Andaman and Nicobar (India) Islands through Sumatra (including Enggano, Nias, Bangka and Belitung Islands), Malay Peninsula south from Sungei Patani (about 6°N) to Singapore, Riau Archipelago and Bintan, east through Anambas Islands to Borneo including Natuna and Karimata Islands. Common resident in Andaman and Coco Islands. In Nicobars described in late 19th century as 'excessively abundant' but few recent details. Resident in Malay Peninsula but possibly passage migrant in Singapore. May show migratory movements in Sumatra where probably declining owing to loss of primary lowland rain-forest. Unevenly distributed in Borneo, and in Kalimantan numbers fluctuate through poorly understood seasonal movements. Local resident in Sabah. Commoner in coastal districts in Sumatra and Borneo. Occurrence generally unpredictable, being abundant in a locality for a period then absent for years.

ECOLOGY All kinds of lowland (below 300m in Sumatra) evergreen forest from mangroves, swamp-forest, rain-forest to oil-palm (*Elaeis*) plantations and coconut groves. Prefers edge of high forest, especially with large dead trees, including near cultivated areas. Visits parks and gardens in Nicobars. Gregarious. Flocks of thousands reported from Andamans and Borneo but smaller groups (under

20) more usual, especially during breeding. Mixed flocks with Blue-rumped Parrots (90) reported from Kalimantan. Food of nominate race includes camphor *Dryobalanops* and *Dillenia* fruit; Nicobar race feeds largely on fruit with papaya *Carica papaya* and *Pandanus* especially favoured; outer covering of betel nuts *Areca catechu* occasionally taken. Elsewhere feeds on orchard and plantation fruit (e.g. oil-palm *Elaeis*), grain and seeds, and can have impact on ripening rice (e.g. Andaman Islands) and oil-palm fruit (e.g. Malay Peninsula). Nest in cavity of usually dead tree, often at considerable height (e.g. possible nest in *Koompassia* tree on Sumatra at 45m); on Andamans commonly in *Pterocarpus marsupium*; on Nicobars once in *Pandanus* at c.4m and in large forest tree at 10m. Breeds in colonies. Clutch 2-3 laid on decaying wood dust or bark strips etc. Eggs Dec-Feb and nestlings Jul, Malay Peninsula; Feb-Mar on Nicobars and Andamans. Eggs reported Jul in Sumatra.

DESCRIPTION Lores blackish-green fading to dark green on crown; cheeks, ear-coverts and hindneck bright salmon-pink; lower cheeks and chin black. Nape and mantle pale greenish-grey fading to bright blue on back; rump and uppertail-coverts green. Lesser and median coverts green strongly tinged ochre; primary coverts, outer greater coverts and outer secondaries blue; remaining flight feathers mainly green. Underwing-coverts yellowish. Underparts yellowish-green (greener on breast). Elongated central tail feathers blue with yellow tips; outer green. **Bare parts:** Upper mandible red, lower brownish; cere pale grey; iris yellowish; legs grey.

SEX/AGE Tail of female shorter, bill brownish, cheek-patches dark green (not black), paler pink on face, crown darker green. Immature largely green with brownish pink upper cheeks and dark patches on lower cheeks and chin. Young males show bluish patch on lower back and sometimes reddish on upper mandible.

MEASUREMENTS Wing 143-155; tail 154-270; bill 20-24; tarsus 15-17.

GEOGRAPHICAL VARIATION Five races. All except the nominate form are endemic to island groups or single islands; *modesta* perhaps warrants full species status.

P. l. longicauda (Malay Peninsula to Singapore and Sumatra including Nias and Bangka, Borneo and the Anambas Islands)

P. l. defontainei (Riau Archipelago and Bintan, Natuna, Karimata and Belitung Islands, Indonesia) Similar to nominate but cheeks redder in both sexes with orange streaks. Crown slightly more yellowish.

P. l. modesta (Enggano Island, W Sumatra) Considerably larger than nominate (wing 190-208). Cheeks deep crimson fading to dull pink on neck; crown browner. Primaries and secondaries green, underparts greener. Pale greenish-blue on back. Bill notch also distinct from nominate.

P. l. tytleri (Coco Islands through Andamans south to Ten Degree Channel) Crown pale green with no pink on neck. Hindneck and mantle pale grey fading to pale blue on back.

P. l. nicobarica (Nicobar Islands) Close to *tytleri* but nape and mantle more strongly suffused green. Larger than both *tytleri* and nominate (wing 190-206). Upperparts more yellowish-green than nominate and washed pale blue. Ear-coverts and cheeks deeper red than nominate. Crown, nape and mantle tinged olive in female.

REFERENCES Ali & Ripley (1981), Arndt (1996), Forshaw (1989), Gore (1968), Holmes & Nash (1990b), van Marle & Voous (1988), Medway & Holmes (1976), Ripley (1982), Rutgers & Norris (1979), Smythies (1981).

207 HYACINTH MACAW
Anodorhynchus hyacinthinus   Plate 52

Other names: Hyacinthine Macaw, Black Macaw, Blue Macaw

IDENTIFICATION 90-100cm. Very large macaw, almost entirely violet-blue with black undersides to wings and tail in flight. Very long tail, long rather pointed wings, massive bill and disproportionately large head. Bright yellow bare eye-ring and crescent-shaped lappets bordering lower mandible (latter may be hidden by feathers whilst birds resting). Only possible confusion species are the (allopatric) Lear's and Glaucous Macaws (209), which are both more greenish-blue (latter greyer-headed), smaller and with smaller, half-moon-shaped pale yellow lappets at base of lower mandible. Generally in pairs or small flocks in wooded country with palm groves. Flies with slow deliberate wingbeats with birds sometimes travelling at great height but usually low (lower than other large macaws). Very tame in some areas. Active on bright moon-lit nights.

VOICE Very loud croaking and screeching sounds including *kraaaa* and screeching *trara* warning cry. Call sometimes comprises two rapidly repeated bursts with brief pause before repeat. Whilst (e.g.) settling at communal roost, birds also produce scolding, yapping and growling sounds that recall small dog. Other reported calls include *trarrree-arree*, a deep purring and a *kru* copulation call that can last for many minutes. Flocks can produce considerable noise. Many calls, especially deeper, more guttural sounds, possess vibrating quality.

DISTRIBUTION AND STATUS Interior of central South America, perhaps in several broad separate areas. In Amazonia in Pará from the Rio Tapajós east to catchment of the Rio Tocantins extending south possibly to north-westernmost Tocantins. At least formerly present north of Amazon river (in Amapá, Amazonas and Roraima, Brazil) and perhaps may still be so although there are no known recent records. Distributed through interior north-eastern Brazil roughly centred on the Chapada das Mangabeiras at the junction between Maranhão, Piauí, Goiás and Bahia, Brazil (the Gerais region). A third major population is based around the pantanal habitats of the upper Rio Paraguay basin in south-western Mato Grosso, Mato Grosso do Sul, Brazil, and extending into adjacent eastern Bolivia and extreme northern Paraguay. Generally resident but perhaps seasonal movements in Amazon distribution in relation to food plant ecology. Territory between three current main distributions may still be occupied although given recent trends this seems unlikely. Range linked to distribution of favoured food plants (palms). Formerly common, in some areas (e.g. Mato Grosso) improbably described as 'abundant'. Now occurs rather patchily with recent and probably continuing declines owing principally to illegal domestic and smaller, but significant, international trade in live birds. Also hunted for plumes (especially Pará) and food. Declining in some areas (e.g. eastern Amazonia) owing to habitat alteration or loss. Total wild population estimated at 3,000 (1992). CITES Appendix I. VULNERABLE.

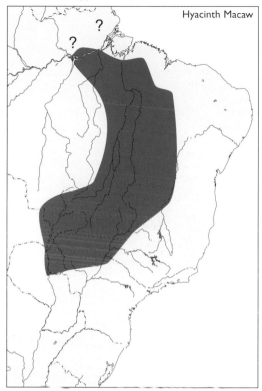

Hyacinth Macaw

ECOLOGY Exploits wide range of habitats rich in various nut-bearing palm species. In Amazonian Brazil avoids continuous humid forest, preferring palm-rich várzea and seasonally moist formations with clearings. In drier parts of north-eastern Brazil inhabits plateau country dissected by rocky, steep-sided valleys with deciduous cerrado woodland, gallery forest and *Mauritia* palm swamp. In the pantanal region birds frequent gallery forest with palm groves in wet grassy areas. Generally in pairs, family parties or small flocks (usually up to 10); much larger flocks reported before decline. Diet principally consists of locally available nuts of various palms, including (in Amazonia) *Maximiliana regia*, *Orbignya martiana* and *Astrocaryum*; in north-eastern Brazil *Syagrus coronata* and *Orbignya eicherii*; in pantanals mostly *Scheelea phalerata* and *Acrocomia*. Palm nuts taken from plant or on ground (latter especially after fire or when available as undigested remains in cattle droppings). Other fruits (e.g. *Ficus* sp.) reported, as well as aquatic molluscs *Pomacea*. Birds drink fluid from unripe palm fruits. Nests in tree-cavity or (in north-eastern Brazil) rock crevice. Favoured nest-trees in Mato Grosso, Brazil, include *Enterolobium* and *Sterculia striata*. In north-east Brazil, nesting occurs in dead *Mauritia* palm when not in cliff. Clutch generally two (rarely one or three) laid Aug-Dec, perhaps slightly later in pantanal.

DESCRIPTION Entire plumage glossy deep violet-blue, slightly paler on head. Underside of flight and tail feathers black. **Bare parts**: Bill black, crescent-shaped lappets at base of lower mandible rich bright yellow, yellow

longitudinal band on black tongue; iris chestnut; bare periophthalmic ring rich bright yellow; legs black.

SEX/AGE Sexes similar. Immature with shorter tail and eye-ring and lappets paler yellow. Older adults show lighter grey or whitish legs.

MEASUREMENTS Wing 388-426; tail 433-562; bill 83-94; tarsus 38-46.

GEOGRAPHICAL VARIATION None.

REFERENCES Abramson *et al.* (1996), Clark (1991), Collar in press (1997), Collar *et al.* (1992, 1994), Dubs (1992), Forshaw (1989), Juniper (1994), Munn *et al.* (1989), Ridgely (1981, 1989), Ridgely *in litt.* (1997), Roth (1988), Sick (1993), Yamashita *in litt.* (1995), Yamashita & Valle (1993).

208 LEAR'S MACAW
Anodorhynchus leari   Plate 52

Other names: Indigo Macaw

IDENTIFICATION 70-75cm. Large blue macaw with very long tail and massive bill, more greenish on large head and neck. Half-moon-shaped pale yellow lappets border lower mandible. Bare eye-ring yellow. No other macaws found in restricted range. Only possible confusion species, both allopatric, are the nearly or actually extinct Glaucous Macaw (209), with a greyer head and greener overall wash, and Hyacinth Macaw (207), which has bright yellow lappets along entire base of bill, is larger and bulkier, darker with more uniform deep violet-blue plumage. Flight steady and level on strong deliberate wingbeats.

VOICE Croaking and screeching sounds including *preee ah* and *ara-ara-trahra* cries. Voice noticeably weaker, less vibrating and higher-pitched than Hyacinth Macaw

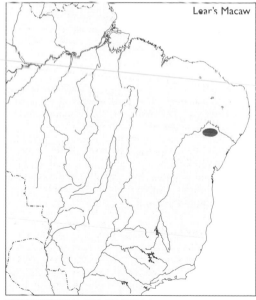

Lear's Macaw

DISTRIBUTION AND STATUS Confined to the Raso da Catarina plateau, north-eastern Bahia, Brazil. Mainly occupies an area of c. 8,000km² in the middle Rio Vasa

Barris in the south of the plateau. Two main colonies are known, one either side of the Vasa Barris. Birds make diurnal movements south to Santo and Euclides da Cunha and possibly north to north-western edge of the plateau to feed. A smaller outlying population exists several hundred kilometres from the Vasa Barris birds and there are unconfirmed reports of other small groups in the remote dry interior of northern Bahia. Resident, birds remaining within reach of preferred nesting and roosting cliffs. Population estimated at 139 birds (117 plus 22) with evidence of decline during last 100 years. Pressures derived from the bird trade, hunting, loss of food plants to livestock grazing, disturbance and possibly inbreeding depression could quickly lead to extinction. Part of range falls within the Estação Ecológica do Raso da Catarina, a federal reserve, and the species is protected under Brazilian law. Practical measures for wild birds, including artificial regeneration of *Syagrus* palms, underway. Several specimens held in captivity (at least 13 in 1992) but breeding is sporadic and uncoordinated. CITES Appendix I. CRITICAL.

ECOLOGY Inhabits dry, rugged caatinga (thorn scrub), especially in areas with *Syagrus coronata* palms. Requires sandstone cliffs for roosting and nesting. Gregarious and generally in flocks but very low numbers limit flock size. Forms communal roosts in weathered crevices near top of 30-50m walls of steep-sided sandstone ravines. Several birds roost in larger holes whilst others cling to rockface or rest on ledges. Birds leave roost in parties for foraging areas before dawn and return at dusk. Staple food item is *Syagrus* palm nuts (one bird may take 350 nuts in a day). Seeds of *Melanoxylon* are also taken, especially when *Syagrus* nuts scarce (Jul-Sep). Other reported foods include fruits of *Jatropha pohliana*, *Dioclea* and *Spondias tuberosa*, *Agave* flowers and maize. Fluid from unripe palm fruit is perhaps major source of moisture. Birds forage in trees and on ground. Nest located in cliff-face crevice. Clutch (in captivity) three. Breeds Feb-Apr (wet season) possibly to coincide with maximum availability of palm nuts.

DESCRIPTION Head and nape greenish-blue. Mantle feathers darker greenish-blue with narrow paler margins. Remaining upperparts, upperwing-coverts and flight feathers violet-blue. Underside of flight feathers dark charcoal grey. Throat and upper breast dull greenish-blue; lower breast and belly pale blue with paler tips to some feathers. Uppertail violet-blue; undertail charcoal grey.
Bare parts: Bill black with half-moon-shaped lappets bordering lower mandible pale yellow, base of tongue yellow appearing as extension of lappets when mouth open; iris chestnut; bare periophthalmic ring pale yellow; legs dark grey.

SEX/AGE Sexes similar. Immature with shorter tail and paler yellow lappets and eye-ring.

MEASUREMENTS Wing 374-406; tail 354-481; bill 65-71; tarsus 34-41.

GEOGRAPHICAL VARIATION None.

REFERENCES Collar *et al.* (1992, 1994), Forshaw (1989), King (1981), Munn (1995), Ridgely (1981), Sick (1993), Yamashita (1987), Yamashita *in litt.* (1995).

209 GLAUCOUS MACAW
Anodorhynchus glaucus   Plate 52

IDENTIFICATION 68-72cm. Large rather pale turquoise-blue macaw with large greyish head, massive bill and very long tail. Half-moon-shaped pale yellow lappets border lower mandible. Bare eye-ring yellow. Only possible confusion species are the allopatric Lear's (208) and Hyacinth (207) Macaws. Hyacinth is larger, bulkier and a richer violet-blue, with bright yellow lappets the length of the base of the bill, whilst Lear's is slightly darker with a bluer head. Probably now extinct.

VOICE No information.

Glaucous Macaw

DISTRIBUTION AND STATUS South-eastern South America where apparently occurred in middle reaches of major rivers including the Río Paraná, Río Uruguay and Río Paraguay, with most evidence of former distribution from Corrientes province, northern Argentina; also occurred in western Uruguay and far south-east Brazil (Rio Grande do Sul and Paraná), and evidently in southern and eastern Paraguay. Claims for Bolivia appear mistaken. Almost certainly now extinct following precipitous decline in early to mid-19th century. Very few reliable records from 20th century. Extinction probably linked to extensive clearance of main food plants and hunting. CITES Appendix I. EXTINCT.

ECOLOGY Probably occupied subtropical gallery forests with cliffs, but also used lightly wooded palm-rich savannas. The few contemporary records by naturalists suggest that it was gregarious. Dietary staple likely to have been nuts of *Butia yatay* palms (closest size-equivalents in range to *Syagrus* nuts used by Lear's Macaw, which has same bill dimensions). Reported nesting in steep bank or cliff, or less usually in tree-cavity.

DESCRIPTION General plumage pale powder-blue, almost turquoise above, with heavy grey tinge to head and underparts. Uppertail greenish-blue; undertail greyish.

Bare parts: Bill dark blackish-grey, bare lappets at base of lower mandible yellow but paler than periophthalmic skin; iris dark brown, bare periophthalmic skin yellow; legs dark grey.

SEX/AGE No information.

MEASUREMENTS Wing 352-373; tail 340-381; bill 63-68; tarsus 34-40.

GEOGRAPHICAL VARIATION None.

REFERENCES Belton (1984), Collar *et al.* (1992, 1994), Forshaw (1989), Yamashita & Valle (1990).

---

210 SPIX'S MACAW
Cyanopsitta spixii   Plate 52

Other names: Little Blue Macaw

IDENTIFICATION 55-57cm. Mainly blue macaw, lighter beneath. Head greyish and paler than body, sometimes appearing almost white at distance. Disproportionately long (even for macaw) graduated tail and long narrow wings striking. Iris appears bright at close quarters. Only 'blue' macaw in tiny area of distribution; however, largely green Red-bellied Macaw (219) has been confused with Spix's in past leading to mistaken conclusions about latter's range and habitat. In captivity Spix's distinguished from Hyacinth (207) and Lear's (208) by smaller size, grey head, dark grey naked loral patch, and absence of yellow lappets and eye-ring. Birds formerly along seasonally moist creeks, now virtually extinct.

VOICE A resonant *kraaa*, weaker and more wavering than Hyacinth Macaw. Also some screeching sounds. Although less powerful than some other macaws, call is audible at some distance.

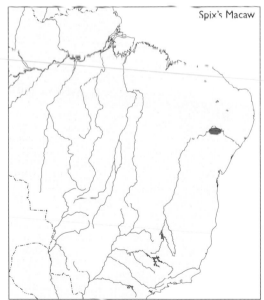

Spix's Macaw

DISTRIBUTION AND STATUS Endemic to tiny area of lower Rio São Francisco valley, northern Bahia, Brazil. Known with certainty only from south bank of Rio São Francisco between riacho Curaçá and riacho Vargem in extreme northern Bahia. Formerly possibly ranged over far larger area of north-east Brazil embracing much of the 'Gerais' region including southern Maranhão, north-east Goiás, south-west Piauí and northern Bahia, but reports from some of these areas apparently based on misidentification and even misinformation supplied by bird trappers. Virtually extinct; known wild population consists of single bird (male). A captive female released in 1994 as a putative mate disappeared. Sporadic sightings elsewhere in north-east Brazil remain unconfirmed. Scarcity ultimately due to diminution of remaining habitat (now less than 30km²) owing to chronic grazing pressure, with poor regeneration of caraiba *Tabebuia caraiba* trees; however, proximate cause of rarity has been trapping for the live bird trade. About 30 specimens in captivity (1994) but systematic breeding for release beset by legal and logistic difficulties involving 'owners'. Captive birds are mainly related to one another posing probable future genetic threats; ability of captive-bred released birds to survive in absence of wild bird open to question. Protected by Brazilian legislation. CITES Appendix I. CRITICAL.

ECOLOGY Strongly associated with *Tabebuia*-dominated gallery woodland growing along seasonal creeks (riachos) in the caatinga (semi-arid thorn scrub) zone. Reports of birds from cerrado savannas or more usual caatinga habitat (i.e. lacking *Tabebuia caraiba* woodland), and the view that the species is ecologically linked to *Mauritia flexuosa* palms remain uncorroborated and, in view of the wide availability of these habitats, wholly improbable. When last few birds were discovered in 1980s they showed strong gregarious behaviour. These and remaining bird show(ed) strong habitual traits, using e.g. favoured perches on bare branches high up in tall trees, daily flight paths, and particular nest-sites (one reportedly used continuously for 50 years). Last wild bird associates strongly with Blue-winged Macaws (221). Reported to sometimes roost on top of cacti, e.g. *Cereus squamosus*. Food items include seeds of *Cnidoscolus phyllacanthus* and *Jatropha pohliana*, seeds and fruits of *Melanoxylon*, fruits of *Maytenus rigida* and *Ziziphus joazeiro*, and possibly nuts of *Syagrus coronata* palms, although latter probably too hard and large for bird's relatively delicate bill. Nests in tree-hollow, most often in mature *Tabebuia caraiba*, at least several metres above ground. Normal clutch 2-3 (four in captivity). Breeding generally Nov-Mar, perhaps varying in relation to timing and intensity of rains.

DESCRIPTION Forehead, cheeks and crown pale bluish-grey shading to blue-grey on nape to violet-blue on mantle, back and rump. Upperwing-coverts and flight feathers violet-blue. Underside of flight feathers dark grey. Throat pale grey; feathers of upper breast bluish-grey with paler blue margins creating (rather obscure) scalloped effect; lower breast and belly show similar pattern but brighter. Uppertail violet-blue; undertail dark grey. **Bare parts**: Bill black; cere, naked lores and periophthalmic ring dark grey; iris mustard yellow; legs dark brownish-grey.

SEX/AGE Sexes similar. Immature darker above with bare lores and eye-ring whitish. Iris dark brown. Maxilla with central vertical horn-coloured marking. Tail shorter.

MEASUREMENTS Wing 247-299; tail 265-378; bill 31-35; tarsus 22-27.

GEOGRAPHICAL VARIATION None.

REFERENCES Collar *et al.* (1992, 1994), Forshaw (1989),

Griffiths & Tiwari (1995), Juniper (1990, 1990a, 1991), Juniper & Yamashita (1990, 1991), Ridgely (1981), Roth (1988), Sick (1993).

211 BLUE-AND-YELLOW MACAW
Ara ararauna   Plate 53

Other names: Blue-and-gold Macaw, Yellow-breasted Macaw, Blue Macaw

IDENTIFICATION 75-83cm. Large macaw, ultramarine blue above, mostly golden-yellow below, with long tail, large black bill and bare white facial patch with narrow lines of black feathers. Only possible confusion species in wild or in captivity is the sympatric (in parts of Amazonian Bolivia) and much rarer Blue-throated Macaw (212), with which Blue-and-yellow may sometimes form mixed flocks and roosts; see under Blue-throated for distinguishing features. Generally in pairs, family parties (3-4) or flocks up to c. 25 in wooded country. Flying birds often give loud raucous calls. Flight strong and leisurely, often at some height.

VOICE Loud raucous cries including harsh *raaa, kewaaaaa, scureeeak* and *scaaark*. Most calls rather guttural with many sounds conveying rather wavering delivery. Voice similar to other larger members of genus but Scarlet Macaw (215) is less shrieking.

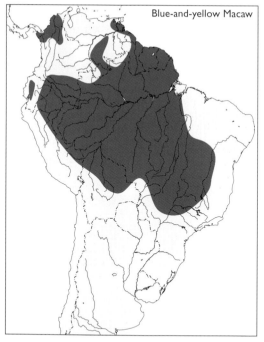

Blue-and-yellow Macaw

DISTRIBUTION AND STATUS Eastern Panama and tropical lowlands of South America to south-east Brazil, Bolivia and Paraguay. In Panama from upper Río Bayano (perhaps only formerly) to eastern Darién mainly in drainage of Río Tuira and Río Chucunaque. Throughout lower tropical zone (to 500m) in Colombia; apparently absent Cauca Valley, Nariño, and wet pluvial forests of central Chocó. In eastern lowlands of Ecuador, and perhaps formerly in Guayas on Pacific slope. Tropical zone of Venezuela mostly south of Orinoco, only in Monagas on north bank (e.g. Río Amana drainage). Extinct Trinidad c1970; escaped captives reported since. Widespread in savannas and coastal river systems of Guianas and Surinam. Widespread in Brazil but extinct from southern Bahia to Rio de Janeiro and in Santa Catarina during 1950s or 1960s; remains in south-east Brazil only in western São Paulo state and there as a wanderer from populations further west in pantanal region and lowlands of Bolivia and Peru. Current status in Paraguay (probably north-east, perhaps also formerly in south) unclear. Records for Argentina remain uncorroborated. Generally resident but some seasonal foraging movements. Locally common but evidently declining in Panama. Fairly common in less disturbed parts of Colombia. Scarce, patchy and declining west of Andes in Colombia and Ecuador. Local in Venezuela. Most numerous large macaw in coastal Surinam and apparently very common in north-western Guyana, much less numerous in south; local in French Guiana because of persecution. Commonest large macaw in parts of Brazil (especially Amazonia) but rarest in pantanals. Locally common in Amazonian Peru but drastic decline around major trapping centres (e.g. Iquitos and Pucallpa). Apparently uncommon north-western Bolivia but common (at least locally) in east. Recent range contraction and decline in accessible areas (mostly at periphery of range) owing to (often illegal) trapping for trade, hunting and habitat loss. Occurs in many protected areas. Widespread in captivity.

ECOLOGY Wooded country, often near water, including edge of lowland humid forest (mostly varzeá, avoiding lowland terra firme forest), gallery forest in savanna, savanna with scattered trees and palms, swamp forest and buriti *Mauritia* palm swamp. Also deciduous forest away from water in Colombia and Panama. Sometimes forages in more open country, coming to ground for e.g. palm fruits. Gregarious. Usually in pairs, family parties or flocks of up to 25 (sometimes many more, especially near roost). Birds most often seen morning and evening en route between roost and feeding areas. Regular communal roosting sites in trees. Diet consists of a variety of locally available fruits (especially of various palms), nuts, leaf-buds, etc., recorded items including fruits of *Astrocarium, Mauritia* and *Acrocomia* palms, seeds of *Platypodium grandiflorum, Sloanea, Brosimum, Sorocea, Spondias, Inga, Parkia, Hura crepitans* and *Enterolobium*, nectar of *Combretum laxum* and aril of *Hymenaea courbaril*. Birds feed quietly high in canopy, often near clearing. Large numbers may congregate at favoured riverbank locations, often with other parrot species, to take the mineral-rich clay soils that are exposed there. Nests in high hole in dead palm (e.g. *Mauritia flexuosa*). Breeding Feb-Mar, Surinam (eggs/nestlings); Jan-May, Trinidad (formerly); Dec-Feb, Colombia (birds in breeding condition). Eggs reported Feb in Guyana and Nov-Jan in Peru. Clutch two.

DESCRIPTION Forehead and sides of head to behind eye bright green fading to bright ultramarine blue on crown and nape. Upperparts bright ultramarine. Upperwing-coverts bright ultramarine; flight feathers deep violet-blue above, golden-yellow to olive-brown below, depending on light; underwing-coverts yellow. Broad yellow patch on sides of neck and ear-coverts bordered anteriorly by black stripe broadening to form black throat-patch. Underparts bright yellow with slight orange suffusion; undertail-coverts blue. Uppertail deep violet with ultramarine suffusion; undertail golden-yellow to olive-brown depending on light; tips of new tail feathers with broad webs (soon ragged and worn, especially when breeding). **Bare parts**: Bill dark grey; naked cere and facial patch (including lores and cheeks to behind eyes) white traversed by narrow lines of black feathers on lores and upper cheeks (facial skin flushing pink in excitement); iris pale yellow; legs dark grey.

SEX/AGE Sexes similar. Immature with brown iris.

MEASUREMENTS Wing 360-392; tail 490-524; bill 61-69; tarsus 33-39.

GEOGRAPHICAL VARIATION None.

REFERENCES Brown (1974), Collar in press (1997), Dubs (1992), Evans (1988), Forshaw (1989), Friedmann & Smith (1950), ffrench (1985, 1992), Haffer (1975), Haverschmidt (1968), Hilty & Brown (1986), Meyer de Schauensee (1949, 1966), Meyer de Schauensee & Phelps (1978), Parker (1991), Ridgely (1981), Ridgely in litt. (1997), Ridgely & Gwynne (1989), Robbins et al. (1985), Roth (1988), Short (1975), Sick (1993), Snyder (1966), Tostain et al. (1992), Wetmore (1968), Willis & Oniki (1992), Yamashita in litt. (1995).

---

212 BLUE-THROATED MACAW
Ara glaucogularis   Plate 53

Other names: Wagler's Macaw, Caninde Macaw

IDENTIFICATION 85cm. Large macaw, turquoise-blue above, largely bright yellow beneath with broad blue throat-patch and narrow yellow stripe on side of neck. Large bill, long tail. Bare pale facial skin traversed with narrow lines of blue feathers. Similar to sympatric, much commoner (by factor of 20 at least) and widespread Blue-and-yellow Macaw (211) with which it may roost and form mixed flocks; distinguished by broad blue throat-patch (which may appear black, as in Blue-and-yellow, in dim light), narrow yellow stripe on sides of neck (not broad yellow patches), wholly blue head, duller blue upperparts, and flesh-coloured (not white) bare skin at base of bill. In poor light or at distance Blue-throated is slimmer, with proportionately longer tail and smaller upper mandible. Generally in pairs, less often small flocks. Flight fairly swift and direct on powerful wingbeats.

VOICE Loud raucous calls when alarmed, but higher-pitched and rather softer than those of Blue-and-yellow Macaw, so that the two can be told apart at hundreds of metres.

DISTRIBUTION AND STATUS Endemic to small area of western Amazon basin in north-east Bolivia. Exact range and status unclear as discovery of wild birds only made in 1990s. Available details suggest birds concentrated in three main areas in Beni (and possibly northern Santa Cruz) Department, mostly in the catchment of the Río Mamoré and its tributaries about 300km west to east and 200km north to south, roughly centred on the town of Trinidad. Reports of birds in Tarija and Chiquisaca are unproven. Occurrence in Paraguay and northern Argentina remains uncorroborated and appears unlikely. Apparently resident. Scarce and highly dispersed. Total wild population probably between 100 to 1,000 birds. Threatened by illegal

trade and possibly by competition with other large macaw species for (e.g.) nest-sites. Protected by domestic legislation. Several hundred birds in captivity. CITES Appendix I. ENDANGERED.

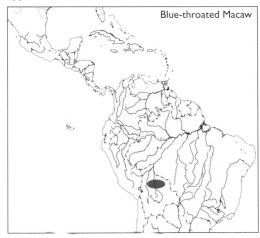
Blue-throated Macaw

ECOLOGY Inhabits seasonally flooded (Oct-Apr) mosaic of savannas, *Attalea* palm groves and low-stature species-poor tropical forest in humid lowlands (200-300m). Habitat characterised by scattered meandering ribbons and 'islands' of woodland with *Tabebuia avellanedae/T. impetiginosa*, with considerable pressure from cattle-ranching including seasonal burning to promote grass regrowth. Local presence probably depends on availability of palm fruits, especially those of *Attalea phalerata*, *Acrocomia totai* and *Scheelea princeps*. Generally in pairs; apparently less gregarious than close congeners. Young believed to stay with parents for only brief period, perhaps explaining infrequency of reports of small flocks or family parties. Probably roosts communally, sometimes with Blue-and-yellow and Green-winged (210) Macaws. Birds use habitual perches in tall trees, especially *Tabebuia*. Diet probably largely comprises palm fruits including *Attalea phalerata* and *Acrocomia totai*, supplemented by seeds and leaves of *Huia orbitans*, inflorescences of *Syagrus botryophora* and *Astrocarium vulgare* palms. Birds consume ripe and nearly ripe fruit and take liquid from immature *Attalea* palm fruits. Nest-cavity in *Acrocomia* palm or tall *Tabebuia* tree. May use hole previously occupied by other species, e.g. woodpeckers. Breeding probably Aug-Nov; young fledge Nov-Dec.

DESCRIPTION Forehead, crown and nape turquoise-blue. Nape, mantle, scapulars and back turquoise-blue, slightly duller than on head, slightly paler and brighter on rump and uppertail-coverts. Upperwing-coverts and flight feathers turquoise-blue above, primaries darker. Underwing-coverts yellow, flight feathers yellowish below. Throat with broad turquoise patch extending to lower ear-coverts and separated from crown by narrow yellow stripe; breast and belly bright yellow; vent and undertail-coverts pale blue. Uppertail dull blue; undertail yellowish-brown. **Bare parts**: Bill greyish-black; cere and skin adjacent to mandibles flesh-pink; bare skin on lores and cheeks white, traversed by five to eight narrow lines of blue feathers; iris yellow; legs dark grey.

SEX/AGE Sexes similar but males possibly with darker blue throat-patch. Immature from adult by brown iris;

undertail-coverts possibly paler turquoise and broadly edged yellow.

MEASUREMENTS Wing 330-363; tail 422-480; bill 47-56; tarsus 31-32.

GEOGRAPHICAL VARIATION None.

NOTE This bird has been problematic for taxonomists. It was once treated as a race or morph of Blue-and-yellow Macaw; moreover, there is a difference of opinion over whether one early description refers to this form, a hybrid or Blue-and-yellow Macaw, and thus some authors still refer to it as *Ara caninde*.

REFERENCES Brace *et al.* (1995), Collar *et al.* (1992, 1994), Forshaw (1989), Hesse (1993), Ingels *et al.* (1981), Jordan & Munn (1993, 1994), Lanning (1982), Morvan (1994), Yamashita *in litt.* (1995).

---

213 MILITARY MACAW
Ara militaris   Plate 54

Other names: Green Macaw, Blue-green Macaw

IDENTIFICATION 85cm. Large, mostly green macaw with bright red frontal patch, blue flight feathers and bright pale blue rump. Very large bill. Bare pinkish face traversed by narrow lines of blackish feathers. In flight appears vivid turquoise and green from above and green with metallic yellow underwings from below. Distinguished from very similar (probably allopatric) Great Green Macaw (214) by more prominent bluish tinge on hindneck, slightly smaller size, wholly black and smaller bill (pale tip to upper mandible in Great Green), darker, more olive-green plumage, and dull red (not orange) on base of central tail feathers. Sympatric (in northern South America) Chestnut-fronted Macaw (218) distinguished by much smaller size and red underwing-coverts. Overlapping (in northern Mexico) Thick-billed Parrot (225) smaller with proportionately much shorter tail. Smaller Red-fronted Macaw (217) of Bolivia told in captivity by orange-red forehead and crown and orange lesser upperwing-coverts. Usually in pairs or small groups, either perched at top of tree or in flight on slow graceful wingbeats, often calling loudly.

VOICE Loud and strident. Calls include loud harsh *wa-a-ahk*, raucous drawn-out *cr-a-a-a-k*, shrieking *dree-eee-ah* and *arrh-eee-arh*. Calls audible at considerable distance.

DISTRIBUTION AND STATUS Mexico plus several disjunct populations in South America south to north-west Argentina. Widely distributed in Mexico from Sonora (where recorded to 28°45'N) and Chihuahua in the north through to Chiapas in the south and east, where birds may be geographically isolated. Absent from Caribbean lowlands; former occurrence in Guatemala unconfirmed. In Colombia west of Andes south to Dagua Valley, Magdalena Valley, and on west slope of east Andes from Santa Marta mountains in north through eastern Andes of Ecuador to Huánuco in Peruvian Andes. Northern Venezuela in Sierra de Perijá and from north-western Zulia to Distríto Federal. In Peru mostly in eastern Andes, especially Marañón region, but at least formerly a regular migrant to Pacific slope Sep-Oct (reported on west slope at e.g. 6°50'S) to exploit seasonally available fruit. On east slope of Bolivian Andes in Santa Cruz, Chuquisaca and Tarija and extreme north-west Argentina in Salta and possibly Jujuy. Seasonal movements in many areas, e.g. visitor to western Caquetá, Colombia, from western slope of east Andes. Rare southern Mexico (possibly extinct Chiapas), more numerous east and north-west where flocks of several hundred reported late 1970s. Very local in Andes and at risk in Venezuela owing to habitat loss and trade. Fairly common in northern Santa Marta region but sporadic elsewhere in Colombia. Flocks up to 60 reported in Manu National Park, Peru, and up to 60 observed in Amboró National Park, Bolivia. Very rare in Argentina with only sporadic reports in recent years. Recent declines owing to habitat loss and bird trade. Large numbers in captivity. CITES Appendix I. VULNERABLE.

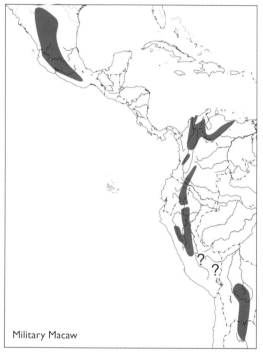

Military Macaw

ECOLOGY Mainly in foothills of mountainous terrain in wooded country with canyons mostly from 500 to 1,500m, locally to 2,000m, (recorded 3,100m in Peru, 2,400m in Bolivia) but regularly also to sea-level in Pacific Mexico and Santa Marta region, Colombia. In Mexico, mostly in secluded uplands in semi-arid and arid woodland and *Quercus* and *Pinus* forest; occasionally in lowland humid and riparian formations, with altitudinal movements to lower-lying dense thorn-forest in Nov-Jan. Humid forest in Colombian Andes. In Venezuela in rain-forest in hilly areas to about 600m, sometimes also in drier, more open forest. Generally in pairs or small flocks (up to 10) but far larger aggregations reported in roosting flights. Communal roosts on cliff-faces or large trees. Diet consists of variety of fruits and nuts, etc., including fruits of *Melia azedarach* and *Ficus* and seeds of *Hura crepitans*. Nest usually in cliff crevice; sometimes in large tree (e.g. *Acer*, *Pinus* or *Enterolobium*) where (Mexico) birds have been observed using former nest-chamber of Imperial Woodpecker *Campephilus imperialis* in dead pine. Eggs Jun, Mexico. Clutch 2-3.

DESCRIPTION Forehead and anterior lores bright red;

crown bright grass-green. Nape pale turquoise-blue fading to grass-green tinged olive on mantle and back, some mantle feathers with pale blue tips; rump and uppertail-coverts bright pale blue. Upperwing-coverts grass-green tinged olive with some ochre flecking; greater coverts with blue tips. Primaries green with blue outerwebs and tips; secondaries green. Underwing-coverts green, underside of flight feathers yellowish olive-green. Throat brown tinged olive; breast and belly green; undertail-coverts pale blue. Uppertail orange-red broadly tipped blue; undertail uniform yellowish olive-green. **Bare parts**: Bill greyish black; bare skin of posterior lores and cheeks white with flesh pink tinge, traversed by narrow lines of blackish feathers on cheeks, red ones on posterior lores; iris pale yellow; legs dark grey.

SEX/AGE Sexes similar. Immature undescribed but like large congeners iris probably brown and tail shorter (see Great Green Macaw).

MEASUREMENTS Wing 345-374; tail 330-419; bill 50-59; tarsus 30-34.

GEOGRAPHICAL VARIATION Four races have been proposed. *A. m. sheffleri* (of SE Sonora, NE Sinaloa and SW Chihuahua, Mexico) was split solely on basis of tail length, but data equivocal with much overlap; apparent clinal intergrade with *mexicana* indicates that *sheffleri* is invalid. Validity of *mexicana* (Mexico) and *boliviana* (Bolivia and NW Argentina) also questioned on basis of close biometric and plumage similarities with 'nominate' (Colombia, Venezuela, Ecuador and Peru), although Bolivian birds tend to show some reddish-brown on throat and feathered parts of cheeks. Migratory tendencies could suppress emergence of racial differences (in South America at least) by placing apparently isolated populations in contact. Great similarities between birds throughout large range suggests that no consistent visible racial differences exist. Great Green Macaw possibly conspecific with Military thereby further confusing situation (see Great Green Macaw).

REFERENCES Abramson (1996), Baker (1958), Binford (1989), Bond & Meyer de Schauensee (1942), Clinton-Eitniear (1984), Collar *et al.* (1994), Edwards (1972), Fernández-Badillo *et al.* (1994), Fjeldså & Krabbe (1990), Forshaw (1989), Friedmann *et al.* (1950), Hilty & Brown (1986), Howell & Webb (1995), Koepcke (1961), Meyer de Schauensee & Phelps (1978), Nores & Yzurieta (1994), Peterson & Chalif (1973), Ridgely (1981), van Rossem (1945), Rowley (1984), Schaldach (1963), Short (1974), Yamashita *in litt.* (1995).

---

214 GREAT GREEN MACAW
Ara ambigua   Plate 54

Other names: Buffon's Macaw, Green Macaw, Grand Military Macaw, Grand Green Macaw; Guayaquil Green Macaw (*A. a. guayaquilensis*)

IDENTIFICATION 77-85cm. Large, mostly green macaw with bright red frontal patch, blue flight feathers and very large bill. Bare face traversed by narrow lines of blackish feathers. Features separating this from very similar (probably allopatric) Military Macaw (213) are given under that species. Widely sympatric Chestnut-fronted Macaw (218) distinguished by much smaller size and red

underwing-coverts. Smaller Red-fronted Macaw (217) of Bolivia distinguished in captivity by orange-red forehead and crown and orange on shoulder. Great Green usually in pairs or small flocks in or near humid forest. Flight on strong slow wingbeats often with loud raucous calls.

VOICE Loud squawks and growls including *aaaahrk* and *aowrk*. Also creaking or groaning *aaa* sound. Voice deeper, more resonant and far-carrying than Scarlet Macaw (215).

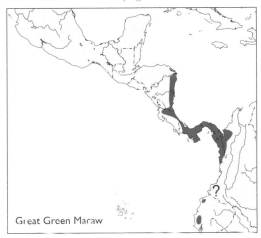

Great Green Macaw

DISTRIBUTION AND STATUS Eastern Honduras to western Colombia and western Ecuador. Caribbean lowlands of eastern Honduras through eastern Nicaragua to lowlands of Costa Rica mostly on Caribbean slope, including Cordillera Guanacaste. In Panama mostly on Caribbean slope but also locally on Pacific. From eastern Panama to tropical zone of Colombia west of western Cordillera of Andes south to upper Río Atrato and Baudó mountains (possibly as far as Buenaventura) and east to northernmost end of western Andes in upper Sinú Valley. In western Ecuador known mostly from Chongon Hills north-west of Guayaquil; also from further north in Esmeraldas, possibly into extreme south-western Colombia although forests here are perhaps too wet (see Geographical Variation). Numbers fluctuate locally owing to seasonal foraging movements. Local occurrence in Costa Rica often coincides with fruiting of *Dipteryx* trees. Local but still commonest large macaw, Panama. However, generally uncommon, with recent large-scale decline owing to deforestation apparent throughout range. Extirpated from much of Ecuador where population (as few as 100 birds) is threatened by habitat loss to urbanisation and agriculture. Exploitation of *Dipteryx* trees poses serious threat in Costa Rica. Occurs in several protected areas including Darién Biosphere Reserve, Panama, Rio Plátano Biosphere Reserve, Honduras, and Cotacachi-Cayapas Ecological Reserve, Ecuador, but seasonal wanderings suggest these areas are insufficient alone to preserve populations. Less common than Military in captivity and rarely bred. CITES Appendix I. VULNERABLE (included as subspecies of Military Macaw by Collar *et al.* 1994).

ECOLOGY Mainly in lowland humid forest but also in strongly deciduous formations in (e.g.) Chongon region of south-west Ecuador. In Costa Rica in lowland primary forest and clearings with tall trees, occasionally in lower montane forests. Crosses open country between forest fragments and visits remnant *Dipteryx* in pastures. Remote forests in Panama. In Ecuador inhabits humid lowlands, deciduous forest and lower montane forest but ranges into more open areas to feed. Reaches 600m in Cordillera Guanacaste, Costa Rica; 1,000m, more rarely 1,500m, in Darién, Panama. Less gregarious than other large macaws but usually in pairs, groups of 3-4, more rarely up to about dozen. Diet includes fruits of *Lecythis costaricensis*, *Dipteryx panamensis*, *Sloanea*, *Dalium guianesis* and *Ficus*, and flowers of *Symphonia globulifera*. Forages in canopy. One nest in Guayas, Ecuador, in cavity in *Cavanillesia plantifolia* tree. Nesting reported Aug-Oct in Ecuador. Breeds dry season (Dec-Apr) Costa Rica.

DESCRIPTION Forehead and anterior lores dark red; crown bright green, suffused bluish on nape. Mantle and back greenish olive-brown; scapulars the same but some with blue tips; rump and uppertail-coverts bright pale blue. Lesser and median coverts greenish olive-brown; greater coverts greenish-blue. Primaries and secondaries blue, darker on margin of innerweb. Underwing-coverts yellowish-olive; rest of underwing golden-olive. Dull black feathers on upper throat bordering lower mandible; rest of throat, breast and belly yellowish-green, feathers of lower belly with concealed red bases; undertail-coverts pale blue. Uppertail centrally orange-red with blue tips, outer feathers progressively more blue, outermost entirely blue; undertail golden-olive. **Bare parts**: Upper mandible blackish at base, horn towards tip and bordering cutting edge, lower mandible blackish; bare skin of posterior lores and cheeks pinkish traversed by narrow lines of dark red feathers on lores and black on cheeks; iris dull yellow; legs dusky grey.

SEX/AGE Sexes similar. Immature tail tipped dull yellow, green plumage duller than adults (especially beneath), iris brown. Older adult birds sometimes show flecks of turquoise in plumage, especially on hindneck and breast.

MEASUREMENTS Wing 356-422; tail 330-468; bill 65-81; tarsus 34-41.

GEOGRAPHICAL VARIATION None.

NOTE An Ecuadorian specimen intermediate between Great Green and Military suggests hybridisation, thereby raising possibility that the two forms are conspecific. Although separated ecologically, Military and Great Green Macaws could be in contact in lower Cauca Valley, Colombia, and in north-west Ecuador and western Colombia. Great Green Macaws (mainly in lowland humid forest) use deciduous forests whilst Military Macaws (principally upland dry forest birds) are recorded from lowland humid forest. Both make seasonal movements and, in the case of the Military at least, long-distance displacements between preferred habitats. Wing and tail length for Mexican Military Macaw and nominate Great Green show considerable overlap. Pending collection of further details, Great Green and Military are here treated as separate species.

GEOGRAPHICAL VARIATION Two races, but further details are required to establish validity of *guayaquilensis*.

    A. a. ambigua (Honduras to SW Colombia and perhaps NW Ecuador. Distribution in relation to next race poorly documented)

    A. a. guayaquilensis (Possibly confined to SW Ecuador although range sometimes given as all W Ecuador and possibly SW Colombia) Bill smaller, with more greenish underside of flight and tail feathers.

REFERENCES Abramson (1986), Berg & Horstman (1996), Bjork & Powell (1995), Evans (1986), Fjeldså *et al.* (1987), Forshaw (1989), Haffer (1975), Hilty & Brown (1986), King (1981), Meyer de Schauensee (1949, 1966), Monroe (1968), Ridgely (1981), Ridgely *in litt.* (1997), Ridgely & Gwynne (1989), Slud (1964), Stiles *et al.* (1989), Waugh (1995), Wetmore (1968).

---

215 SCARLET MACAW
Ara macao   Plate 53

Other names: Red-blue-and-yellow Macaw, Red-and-yellow Macaw, Red-breasted Macaw

IDENTIFICATION 80-96cm. Large, mostly red macaw with long pointed tail and usually conspicuous bright yellow upperwing-coverts. Flight feathers, back, rump and short outer tail feathers blue. Large bare white facial patch. Widely sympatric Green-winged Macaw (216) is darker red, with green upperwing-coverts and narrow lines of red feathers on otherwise bare facial patch. Tail of Scarlet is longer than Green-winged (although this feature varies with wear) and tip appears red whereas in Green-winged it is dark like rest of tail. Often in pairs flying at some height or perched in tops of tall trees. Flight direct on strong shallow wingbeats with tail-tip wiggling up and down. Noisy.

VOICE Harsh strident screeching calls including *rrraaaaa*, loud rasping *reck*, *raak* and *rowwwka*. Call more drawn-out than Blue-and-yellow Macaw (211) but difficult to separate. Sounds include a variety of screeches, harsh guttural squawks and harsh drawn-out growling *scree-e-e-e-t*. Relaxed birds make quieter noises including sound similar to creaking door. Said to be generally coarser and more grating than Blue-and-yellow and Green-winged Macaws.

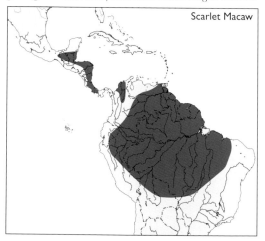

Scarlet Macaw

DISTRIBUTION AND STATUS Middle America from southern Mexico to Panama and (apparently disjunctly) in tropical South America south to eastern Bolivia. In Mexico formerly in southern Tamaulipas, southern Veracruz, Oaxaca, Tabasco, Chiapas and Campeche and through lowlands of Guatemala to remoter parts of Belize, where most recent records are from the Guacamayo River. Formerly widespread Honduras, El Salvador and Nicaragua; Costa Rica mostly on Pacific slope. In Panama confined to Coiba Island, south-western Azuero Peninsula and Chiriquí, where birds may formerly have wandered from Costa Rica. In tropical zone of Colombia including Magdalena Valley, Caribbean coast and Amazonian region with one recent record from Nariño. In Venezuela in Apure, north-eastern Monagas, south-western Sucre, and widely across llanos in Bolívar and Amazonas. Occurs widely in Guianas and throughout Amazon basin of Brazil, eastern Ecuador and eastern Peru. In northern and eastern Bolivia in Santa Cruz, Beni and possibly Pando. Absent west of Andes. Makes seasonal movements in search of fruit and is regular seasonal visitor to some areas. Locally common but evidently declining throughout range, especially around developing centres, owing to habitat loss, trade and hunting for food and plumes; total Middle American population probably no more than 4,000. Extirpated from most of former range in Mexico (not recorded Tamaulipas since 19th century) and persists in fair numbers only in Selva Lacandona, Chiapas. Generally rare Guatemala but commoner in remoter areas, at least formerly (e.g. western Petén). Extinct El Salvador. Widespread but uncommon on Caribbean slope of Honduras; extinct on Pacific slope. Nearly extinct on Pacific slope of Nicaragua but persists in remote north-east. Formerly widespread on the Caribbean slope of Costa Rica, now only in north-east; few localities on Pacific slope (e.g. Península de Osa). Fairly common on Coiba, Panama. Local Venezuela. Fairly common in the Amazon basin and the Guianas, especially in remoter areas. Less numerous than Green-winged in Guyana and Venezuela. Widespread in captivity but rarely bred. CITES Appendix I.

ECOLOGY Lowland tropical forest and savanna. In Mexico in remote portions of humid forest. On arid Pacific slope in Honduras birds forage in open (including cultivated) country; marginally in pine forest above rain-forest in Mosquita region. In Costa Rica in deciduous and humid forest and more open areas and edges with scattered stands of tall trees. Inhabits intact and partially cleared lowland rain-forest as well as gallery forest in Colombia. In rain-forest, savanna and llanos in Venezuela. Prefers terra firme rain-forest in Surinam and rain-forest and savanna in Guyana. Often near rivers throughout range. Below 240m Oaxaca, Mexico, but reported to 1,100m in Honduras, 1,500m in Costa Rica, 500m in Colombia and 450m in Venezuela. Generally in pairs, parties of 3-4 or flocks of up to about 30, with up to 50 roosting communally in tall trees (including mangroves). Often perches in tops of tall trees. Diet includes fruits of *Inga, Micropholis, Sterculia, Bursera, Dipteryx, Ficus, Spondias mombin, Hura, Eschweilera* and *Terminalia* and fruits and nuts of various palms; seeds of *Jacaranda, Dialium, Caryocar, Hevea, Euterpe, Cedrela* and *Sapium*, flowers and nectar of (e.g.) *Virola* and *Erythrina*. Feeds in canopy, usually silently. May associate with other parrot species where food abundant. Nests in large cavity of dead tree. Prefers soft-wooded species so that hollow can be modified. Breeding mostly Feb-Apr in Mexico and northern Central America but earlier in Costa Rica and Panama; Oct-Mar, Mato Grosso, Brazil; Nov-Apr, Peru.

DESCRIPTION All of head (except for bare lores and cheeks), neck, nape and anterior mantle bright red. Feathers of lower mantle red tipped yellow; scapulars yellow with green tips, back to uppertail-coverts bright blue. Lesser upperwing-coverts bright red; most of median and greater coverts bright yellow tipped variably with green; primary coverts and alula blue. Flight feathers blue above, below olive-green on innerwebs, red on outer; underwing-coverts red. Throat to belly bright red; undertail-coverts light blue. Uppertail centrally red with blue tips, outer feathers blue; undertail centrally red. **Bare parts**: Upper mandible horn with black at tip and base, lower mandible blackish; bare skin of lores and cheeks white, pinkish in excitement; iris yellow, olive close to pupil; legs charcoal.

SEX/AGE Sexes similar. Immature with shorter tail and brown iris.

MEASUREMENTS Wing 368-426; tail 454-649; bill 59-71; tarsus 35-37.

GEOGRAPHICAL VARIATION Two races.
  A. m. macao (Costa Rica south through South America)
  A. m. cyanoptera (SE Mexico to Nicaragua) Larger than nominate with blue tips to yellow wing-coverts.

REFERENCES Binford (1989), Clinton-Eitniear (1981), Dickey & van Rossem (1938), Edwards (1972), Friedmann *et al.* (1950), Haverschmidt (1968), Hilty & Brown (1986), Howell (1957, 1972), Land (1970), Lowery & Dalquest (1951), Meyer de Schauensee (1949), Meyer de Schauensee & Phelps (1978), Monroe (1968), Paynter (1955), Peterson & Chalif (1973), Ridgely (1981), Ridgely *in litt.* (1997), Ridgely & Gwynne (1989), Russell (1964), Sick (1993), Slud (1964), Smith (1991), Smithe (1966), Snyder (1966), Stiles *et al.* (1989), Traylor (1941), Vaughan (1983), Weidenfeld (1994), Wetmore (1968), Whitney (1996).

216 GREEN-WINGED MACAW
Ara chloroptera   Plate 53

Other names. Red-and-green Macaw, Red-and-blue Macaw, Red-blue-and-green Macaw

IDENTIFICATION 73-95cm. Large, mostly red macaw with long tail, conspicuous green upperwing-coverts and very large bill. Bare white facial patch traversed by narrow lines of red feathers. Told from widely sympatric Scarlet Macaw (215) by green (not bright yellow) upperwing-coverts, darker red plumage and slightly larger size, but immature Green-winged may show some yellowish-green on upperwing-coverts. Generally in pairs, small flocks of several pairs or (less often) family parties. Sometimes associates with Scarlet or Blue-and-yellow Macaws.

VOICE Powerful but often less harsh than Scarlet Macaw. Calls include very low strident *raw*, a prolonged *ahhra* in flight, a very harsh loud *screeee-ah* and a yelping *dreeeat*. Loud, dry *graaah* suggests amplified Carrion Crow *Corvus corone* to European ears. Also gives higher-pitched shrieking *scree-er* and *scururee-er* calls.

DISTRIBUTION AND STATUS Eastern Panama and South America south to northern Argentina. In Panama formerly west to Caribbean slope of former Canal Zone (although these records may have involved escapes), now only remoter parts of east (e.g. upper Bayano Valley). Tropical zone of Colombia in Magdalena Valley, Caribbean coast, Amazonian region and west of Andes south to upper Río Atrato and Baudó mountains. Lowland Venezuela but absent in north from Portuguesa to Monagas. Mostly interior of Guianas. Throughout Amazon basin of Brazil, eastern Ecuador, Peru and north-east Bolivia in Beni, Cochabamba and Santa Cruz. In Brazil formerly to Espírito Santo, Rio de Janeiro and interior Paraná; now apparently absent; still occurs in Mato Grosso and relict population remains in Morro do Diablo State Forest, western São Paulo. Persists in northern and eastern chaco of Paraguay but now vanished from Misiones, Chaco, Formosa (possibly a few birds remaining) and Salta, Argentina, where last reliable record was in 1917. Resident. Generally uncommon following decline caused by capture for trade and habitat loss. Locally distributed Panama, Venezuela, Bolivia. Widespread Amazon basin but usually less common than Scarlet and Blue-and-yellow Macaws (quite rare in eastern Ecuador) although this situation reversed in Venezuela and Guianas (and perhaps elsewhere). Mostly absent near population centres and declining or already disappeared at peripheries of range owing to habitat loss, trade and hunting. Widespread in captivity.

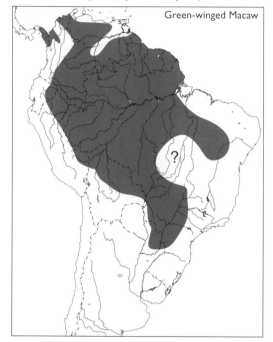

Green-winged Macaw

ECOLOGY Occupies terra firme rain-forest in north of range, apparently avoiding swampy areas; in south and east of range often in more open drier formations including floodplain forest, upland forest and dry woodland (Bolivia), entering savanna in Paraguay. Requires large trees for nesting. Reported to 1,000m in Panama, 500m in Colombia, 1,400m in Venezuela. Generally in pairs or small flocks; less inclined to larger aggregations than Scarlet Macaw, but sometimes associates with this and Blue-and-yellow Macaw. Birds roost in rock crevices where such sites are used for nesting. Diet includes fruits of *Acrocomia* and *Caryocar* (south-west Brazil) and fruits and seeds of *Copaifera langsdorfii* and *Hymenaea courbaril* (north-east Brazil). Forages in canopy. Nests chiefly in cavity of large tree but commonly also in crevices in rockfaces, especially in Gerais region of Brazil. Breeding Nov-Apr, Peru; Jan, central Brazil; nesting or prospecting, Dec, Surinam. Clutch 2-3.

DESCRIPTION Forehead, crown, sides of neck, nape and

mantle red; back to uppertail-coverts light blue, scapulars green. Lesser coverts red with concealed green bases; median coverts green; primary coverts, outer secondaries and primaries blue, latter with black margin to innerwebs; inner secondaries and inner greater coverts wholly or partially green. Underwing red. Underparts red except for pale blue undertail-coverts. Uppertail centrally red broadly tipped blue, with shorter outer feathers blue; undertail dark red. **Bare parts**: Upper mandible mostly ivory-white with cutting edge blackish, lower blackish; bare white skin on lores and cheeks traversed by narrow lines of red feathers, skin flushing pink in excitement; iris light yellow; legs black.

SEX/AGE Sexes similar. Immature with shorter tail and brown iris, sometimes also with yellow on upperwing-coverts.

MEASUREMENTS Wing 380-421; tail 440-531; bill 71-84; tarsus 36-44.

GEOGRAPHICAL VARIATION None.

REFERENCES Contreras *et al.* (1991), Dubs (1992), Forshaw (1989), Haverschmidt (1968), Hayes (1995), Hilty & Brown (1986), Meyer de Schauensee (1949, 1966), Meyer de Schauensee & Phelps (1978), Narosky & Yzurieta (1989), Naumburg (1930), Nores & Yzurieta (1994), Olmos (1993), Parker (1991, 1993, 1993a), de la Peña (1988), Ridgely (1981), Ridgely *in litt.* (1997), Ridgely & Gwynne (1989), Roth (1988), Sick (1993), Short (1975), Snyder (1966), Tostain *et al.* (1992), Wetmore (1968).

217 RED-FRONTED MACAW
Ara rubrogenys   Plate 54

Other names: Red-cheeked Macaw

IDENTIFICATION 60cm. Medium-sized olive-green macaw with orange-red forehead, crown and ear-coverts and orange-red lesser upperwing-coverts forming conspicuous shoulder-patch. Flight feathers mostly blue; tail olive, tipped blue. No sympatric congeners but from all other *Ara* in captivity by combination of orange-red forehead, crown and ear-coverts, olive rump and rather small bare facial patch; adult from sympatric Mitred Conure (232) by much larger size and more extensive orange-red plumage on head and wings. Commutes morning and evening between roosting and foraging areas, often at some height in pairs, families or flocks. Noisy, and rather tame where unmolested.

VOICE Short, shrill ringing call, similar to Chestnut-fronted Macaw and reminiscent of *Aratinga*; frequently given in flight, when foraging or at rest. Call of immature less powerful and higher-pitched. Calling frequency increases with heightened social excitement. More raucous *raaah*, closer to larger *Ara*, given in alarm. Pairs also emit more melodious calls in duet. Harsh squealing and shrieking recalls sounds of excited domestic pigs.

DISTRIBUTION AND STATUS Endemic to small area on east Andean slope of central-southern Bolivia, from southern Cochabamba and western Santa Cruz through Chuquisaca to eastern Potosí, principally in valleys of Ríos Grande, Mizque and Pilcomayo. Total range estimated at 20,000km², with 18,000km² in Grande/Mizque system and 2,000km² in the Pilcomayo valley, between 1,100 and

2,500m (locally post-breeding to 3,000m). Very local movements occur in response to food availability. Locally common but declining and threatened with global extinction; world population estimates range from less than 1,000 to 5,000 birds with recent census inclining to former figure. Threatened mainly by habitat destruction. Estimated 40% of natural vegetation in range lost to agriculture (1991) with other areas degraded by excessive grazing. Several important food trees are harvested for fuel, and birds are persecuted as a crop pest. Former heavy trade in live birds reduced by Bolivian live bird export ban but illegal trapping continues. Protected nationally. Several hundred in captivity but breeding programmes uncoordinated and offer no management tool. CITES Appendix 1. ENDANGERED

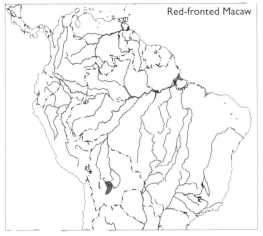

Red-fronted Macaw

ECOLOGY Inhabits subtropical xerophilous thorny scrub with many cacti (including *Cereus, Neocardenasia, Cleistocactus, Echinopsis, Opuntia, Quiabentia pereziensis* and endemic *Lobivia caineana*) and scattered trees and shrubs (especially leguminaceous species including *Prosopis kuntzei, Acacia aroma, Cnidoscolus* and *Schinus molle*). A further critical habitat feature is steep-sided, undisturbed riverside cliffs for nesting and roosting. Birds often occur in cultivated areas. Gregarious, larger flocks forming in pre-roosting flights and after breeding (Mar-Jun), but pairs remain discernible in flocks. Diet includes various seeds and fruits including *Cenchrus, Tribulus, Cnidoscolus, Prosopis kuntzei, P. juliflora, P. chilensis, Aspidosperma, Schinus molle, Ziziphus mistol* and *Jatropha risinifolia*; however, natural food often scarce and birds feed extensively on crop plants, especially groundnuts *Arachis hypogea* and unripe maize. Nests singly or in loose colonies in cliff-face crevice, in wet season with egg-laying reported Nov-Apr. Clutch 1-3, usually two. Most pairs fledge one offspring annually.

DESCRIPTION Forehead, anterior lores, crown and some ear-coverts bright orange-red. Hindcrown, nape and mantle olive-green with orange tips to some feathers; scapulars brownish-olive; rump and uppertail-coverts olive, paler than on mantle. Lesser coverts, bend of wing and carpal edge orange-red; median coverts olive-green, some tipped pale orange, outermost suffused blue; greater coverts mostly blue becoming more olive towards body; outerwebs of primaries blue, inner olive. Lesser underwing-coverts orange-red, remaining underwing-coverts olive-yellow. Underparts olive green with red thighs.

Uppertail olive with blue suffusion and blue tip; undertail yellowish-olive. **Bare parts:** Bill dark grey; bare posterior lores and upper cheeks white traversed with narrow lines of dark brown feathers; iris orange; bare periophthalmic skin white; legs dark grey.

SEX/AGE Sexes similar. Immature duller, with less extensive orange-red on head and ear-coverts and without orange-red on wing.

MEASUREMENTS Wing 295-314; tail 275-351; bill 46-52; tarsus 24-30.

GEOGRAPHICAL VARIATION None.

REFERENCES Boussekey *et al.* (1991), Clark & Patiño (1991), Collar *et al.* (1992, 1994), Fjeldså & Krabbe (1990), Forshaw (1989), Lanning (1982, 1991a), Pitter & Christiansen (1995), Ridgely (1981).

218 CHESTNUT-FRONTED MACAW
Ara severa   Plate 54

Other names: Severe Macaw, Brazilian Green Macaw

IDENTIFICATION 40-49cm. Small green macaw with long pointed tail, with bluish-green crown, inconspicuous chestnut forehead and large bare white patch on lores and cheeks. Red underwing-coverts and blue flight feathers, brownish-red on undersides. Range overlaps with Red-shouldered (223), Blue-winged (221), Red-bellied (219), Yellow-collared (222) and Blue-headed (220) Macaws but is distinguished from them by combination of red underwing-coverts, large white facial patch, chestnut forehead and (except for some red feathers on thighs) wholly green underparts. Generally in pairs or small flocks, sometimes with Red-bellied Macaw or Orange-winged Amazons (342); larger gatherings at roosts. Flight fast and direct on wingbeats faster than larger macaws with loud raucous calls.

VOICE Loud voice. Calls include harsh grinding screeches that sometimes sound like braying donkey. An *ahhaarra* call when perched is similar to Blue-and-yellow Macaw (211). Higher-pitched *ghehh* in flight. At times birds have quieter, less harsh calls.

DISTRIBUTION AND STATUS Eastern Panama and South America south to central Bolivia. The species occurs in eastern Panama in the tropical zone (records west to northern Canal Zone probably referring to escapes) and on the Pacific slope of Andes south to southern Ecuador (Guayas to Pichincha) and in northern lowlands of Colombia south to upper Río Sinú Valley, extending down the Andean foothills of Colombia in the Cauca and Magdalena valleys to Antioquia. East of the Andes it occupies the Amazonian lowlands of Colombia, Ecuador, Peru and Bolivia in La Paz, Beni, Cochabamba and Santa Cruz, ranging east from the Andean foothills through western and southern Amazon Basin (although not known in much of Brazil north of Amazon, e.g. at Manaus or along the Rios Negro and Branco). It is spread through the tropical zone of Venezuela in Zulia and from western Apure to Aragua, north-western Bolívar and Amazonas along the Orinoco, reaching the Guianas and Amapá, Brazil. South of Amazon it extends into Mato Grosso, Brazil, but a record from southern Bahia is unconfirmed. Resident with seasonal altitudinal movements in some

427

areas (e.g. western Ecuador and northern Venezuela). Fairly common to common over much of range, and while severe habitat has caused local declines (e.g. Cauca Valley, Colombia; western Ecuador), moderate deforestation has led to increases in some areas. Although not reported in Guyana since the early 19th century it remains common in Surinam, especially in some coastal areas. The species is held in captivity but demand is not great.

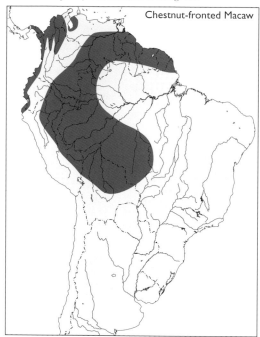

Chestnut-fronted Macaw

ECOLOGY Forest (including partly cleared and secondary formations), forest edge and more open country with trees including humid lowland forest with clearings, varzeá, swamp-forest with dead trees, palm groves, gallery forest and savanna with pastures. Generally avoids continuous terra firme forest but transient birds may stop off to feed. Birds occur to 1,000m in Colombia (but may ascend to c. 1,500m in lower limits of subtropical zone), 1,500m (perhaps seasonally) in eastern Ecuador, 350m in Venezuela. Usually in pairs or small flocks with larger aggregations in roosting flights. Roosts communally, often between fronds of palm trees. Diet includes seeds of *Hura crepitans*, *Sapium aereum*, *Cedrela odorata* and *Cupania cinerea*, pulp and seeds of *Inga laterifolia*, *Micropholus melinoneana*, *Euterpe precatoria* and *Gulielma*, and fruit of *Ficus*, *Cecropia feulla*, *Caraniana* and various palms (especially species with smaller fruits); also flowers of (e.g.) *Virola* and *Erythrina*. Birds feed quietly in canopy where they may be hard to detect. Nests in cavity in dead palm or tree, often over water, and unusually in rock crevices. Probably breeds Mar-May, Colombia; Feb-Mar, Panama; Sep-Dec, Surinam. Clutch 2-3.

DESCRIPTION Forehead dark chestnut; crown and nape green with strong blue suffusion. Mantle, scapulars and back green with strong olive tone brightening to grass-green on rump and uppertail-coverts. Most wing-coverts green tinged olive with alula and primary coverts blue; flight feathers blue above, with blackish margins to innerwebs and tips, dull red below. Lesser underwing-

coverts and some feathers at bend of wing bright red; greater underwing-coverts greyish-red. Lower cheeks and chin dark chestnut; underparts otherwise grass-green, less olivaceous than upperparts; feathers on thighs red basally. Uppertail centrally brick-red at base, greenish in centre and tipped blue; outer feathers bluish with dull red on innerwebs; undertail dull red. **Bare parts**: Bill black; large bare skin on lores and cheeks pale ivory white traversed by narrow lines of dark chestnut feathers; iris pale orange; legs blackish.

SEX/AGE Sexes similar although some females might show paler, less prominent chestnut band on forehead. Immature undescribed but may have darker iris.

MEASUREMENTS Wing 232-253; tail 200-244; bill 35-41; tarsus 22-25.

GEOGRAPHICAL VARIATION Birds in the western part of the range have been distinguished under the name *castaneifrons* on the basis of average size differences, but the degree of variation and overlap is too great to be convincing.

REFERENCES Arndt (1996), Blake (1961), Bond (1955), Chapman (1917), Desenne & Strahl (1994), Dubs (1992), Fernández-Badillo (1994), Forshaw (1989), Friedmann (1948), Gyldenstolpe (1945a), Haverschmidt (1968), Hilty & Brown (1986), Meyer de Schauensee (1949, 1966), Meyer de Schauensee & Phelps (1978), Naumburg (1930), Ridgely (1981), Ridgely *in litt.* (1997), Ridgely & Gwynne (1989), Rutgers & Norris (1979), Sick (1993), Snyder (1966), Tostain *et al.* (1992), Wetmore (1968).

219 RED-BELLIED MACAW
Orthopsittaca manilata   Plate 55

IDENTIFICATION 44-48cm. Small, mostly green macaw with long pointed tail and swept-back pointed wings, giving birds streamlined appearance in their fast flight; small bill, flat back to head and rounded chest tapering sharply back to tail-tip all increase distinctiveness of flight silhouette. Told from other small green macaws by combination of yellowish underwings, large yellow facial patch, reddish belly (not always easy to see) and blue forehead. Birds may appear rather blue in evening light, perhaps explaining apparent confusion with Spix's Macaw (210). Rather similar (but ecologically distinct) Blue-winged Macaw (221) has conspicuous red patch on forehead, red on rump and white facial skin. Some superficially similar *Aratinga* conures have relatively shorter wings and no bare yellow facial skin. Unobtrusive when feeding in *Mauritia* palms; otherwise generally seen in flight. Gregarious.

VOICE Rather high-pitched, sometimes higher than smaller Red-shouldered Macaw (223). Plaintive wailing *choiiaaa* in flight. Loud *wrrrake* and loud rhythmical *sreeet screet* also reported. Purring noises when feeding. Loud excited chorus sometimes given by flocks. Some calls possess rather vibrating quality.

DISTRIBUTION AND STATUS Northern South America east of the Andes. In Colombia ranges from Meta and western Vaupés to Putumayo and Amazonas, extending across north-eastern Venezuela to Trinidad and the Guianas, where apparently restricted to coastal areas. Occurs eastern Ecuador, north-eastern Peru and northern Bolivia and through much of Amazonian Brazil east to

Pará and from western Bahia and Goiás to Mato Grosso. Apparently absent from most of Venezuela and the northern Amazon basin of Brazil in catchment of Rio Negro. Small numbers are reported from northern São Paulo, Brazil. Probably resident in some areas but at least partially migratory elsewhere (e.g. north-western Bolivia where birds were reported common Sep-Nov but were absent Nov-Jan of another year). Locally common; distribution closely linked to *Mauritia* palms. Population probably stable. However, in north-eastern Brazil *Mauritia* fruit used in confectionary manufacture and trunks of palms for some construction purposes. Rare in captivity.

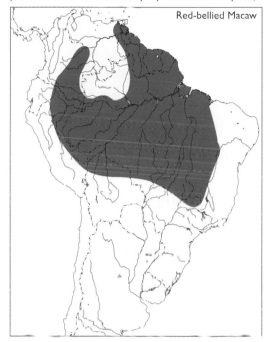

Red-bellied Macaw

ECOLOGY Dependent on *Mauritia* palms, stands of which occur locally in swampy or seasonally flooded terrain in a range of habitats from dense moist forest to gallery forest and more open savannas and grasslands. Birds occasionally wander into cultivated country and have been reported from mangroves. Generally below 500m. Gregarious with flocks of over 100 reported. Usually roosts in *Mauritia* palms where birds cling to inside of frond clusters. Feeds mostly on palm *Mauritia flexuosa* fruits but berries and the fruits of *Roystonea oleracea* and *Euterpe* are also taken. Nests in dead palm (usually *Mauritia*), often over water, or in tree-cavity, often in nest-site previously used by Orange-winged Amazon (342), Trinidad. Nesting reported Feb and Sep, Trinidad; Feb-May, Colombia; Feb-Jun, Guyana. Clutch two (four reported in captivity).

DESCRIPTION Forehead and crown bright blue fading to greenish-blue on nape and sides of neck. Mantle and scapular grass-green suffused olive and indistinctly edged yellowish, giving scaly effect; back and rump grass-green, some feathers with pale bluish tips; uppertail-coverts grass-green. Lesser and median coverts grass-green suffused olive with yellowish margins; alula and primary coverts green with blue outer webs; inner greater coverts green. Flight feathers blue narrowly edged and tipped green. Underwing with yellowish-green coverts and flight feathers

yellowish. Feathers of throat and upper breast with pale bluish-grey centres and yellowish-green margins; those on lower breast and upper belly without pale centres but some with dull dark red margins; belly dull dark red; undertail-coverts bluish-green. Uppertail centrally green with yellowish margins; undertail yellowish. **Bare parts**: Bill black; bare lores and cheeks yellowish-white; iris dark brown; legs dark grey.

SEX/AGE Sexes similar, males possibly on average larger. Immature with pale tip to bill and smaller dark red patch on belly.

MEASUREMENTS Wing 230-255; tail 200-251; bill 27-30; tarsus 21-24.

GEOGRAPHICAL VARIATION None.

NOTE Red-bellied Macaw is usually included in the genus *Ara*. However, Pinto and others (e.g. Sick 1993, Whitney 1996) regard the small green macaws (known in Brazil as 'maracanãs') as generically distinct from the larger species ('araras') and closer to *Aratinga*. Recognising the need to split the small macaws from the behaviourally and morphologically distinct *Ara*, we restore the Red-bellied and Red-shouldered Macaws respectively to the monotypic genera of *Orthopsittaca* and *Diopsittaca*, with the closely related Blue-headed, Blue-winged and Yellow-collared in *Propyrrhura*.

REFERENCES Brown (1974), Chapman (1926), Dubs (1992), ffrench (1992), Forshaw (1989), Friedmann (1955), Gilliard (1941), Gyldenstolpe (1945a), Haverschmidt (1968), Hilty & Brown (1986), Meyer de Schauensee (1949, 1966), Meyer de Schauensee & Phelps (1978), Naumburg (1930), Parker (1991), Parker *et al.* (1993), Ridgely (1981), Ridgely *in litt.* (1997), Sick (1993), Snyder (1966), Tostain *et al.* (1992), Traylor (1958), Whitney (1996), Willis & Oniki (1993).

---

220 BLUE-HEADED MACAW
Propyrrhura couloni   Plate 55

Other names: Coulon's Macaw

IDENTIFICATION 40cm. Small, mostly green macaw with blue head, the contrast of these colours sometimes making a good fieldmark. Distinguished from sympatric Chestnut-fronted (218) and Red-bellied (219) Macaws by dark bare skin on face, more extensive and obvious blue feathers on head, pale bill and voice (see below). Generally seen in flight and probably frequently overlooked.

VOICE Flight call is a rather quiet purring, or regular soft, nasal, slightly rasping *raah* sounds. Shrieks and squawks are higher-pitched and less rasping than closely related (allopatric) Blue-winged Macaw (221). Sympatric Red-bellied Macaws have squeakier calls often delivered in chorus.

DISTRIBUTION AND STATUS Western Amazon basin in extreme western Brazil (only from Acre, sporadically), eastern Peru in the and extreme north-western Bolivia. In Peru it is known from the upper Río Huallaga Valley in Loreto, San Martín and Huánuco (including the outskirts of Tingo María), from one locality on the eastern slope of Serra de Divisor in the Río Ucayali catchment, on the Río Curanja, Río Purús catchment, Río Apurímac in Cuzco and in Madre de Dios west of Puerto Maldonado, around

Puerto Maldonado and on Río Tambopata 50km from the Bolivian border; occurs in Manu National Park. In Bolivia it has been found in La Paz and perhaps south to Beni with indications that birds regularly occur south on the eastern Andean foothills in Bolivia south to 14°30'S. Local and erratic in occurrence, but apparently fairly common in places. Perhaps expanding its rather limited range in south-western Amazonia owing to forest degradation. Rare in captivity.

ECOLOGY In upper tropical forests between 150 and 1,550m. Prefers disturbed or partly open habitats with birds mostly occurring at forest edge along rivers, in clearings and around partly forested settlements; also reported from swampy areas with *Mauritia* palms in forest. This species possibly prefers foothill to lowland forest. Not very gregarious; generally in pairs or groups of three, apparently not associating with Chestnut-fronted Macaw. Diet and breeding undescribed. Young birds seen with adults Apr.

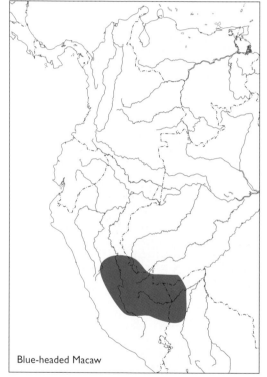

Blue-headed Macaw

DESCRIPTION Forehead with narrow black band fading to blue on crown; ear-coverts and sides of neck blue fading to green on nape. Upperparts green with slight olive tinge on rump and uppertail-coverts. Lesser, median and inner greater coverts green; outer greater coverts blue. Flight feathers blue above (some green on secondaries), olive-yellow beneath. Underparts green, slightly more yellowish than above. Uppertail mostly blue but central feathers green distally, dull red in middle and tipped blue; under-tail dull olive-yellow. **Bare parts**: Bill mostly horn, black at base; bare skin on lores and upper cheeks rather grey with bluish tinge and traversed anteriorly by lines of very small black feathers; iris yellow; legs greyish-pink.

SEX/AGE Sexes similar; male possibly larger on average. Immature with dark iris.

MEASUREMENTS Wing 218-233; tail 188-243; bill 37-42; tarsus 21-25.

GEOGRAPHICAL VARIATION None.

NOTE Sometimes regarded as conspecific with Blue-winged Macaw. They are treated here as allospecies on a precautionary basis because of the worsening conservation status of the Blue-winged Macaw. See also Note in Red-bellied Macaw (219).

REFERENCES Arndt (1996), Forshaw (1989), Machado de Barros (1995), O'Neill (1969, 1974), Parker *et al.* (1990), Parker & Remsen (1987), Ridgely (1981), Rutgers & Norris (1979), Short (1975), Sick (1993), Traylor (1958).

221 BLUE-WINGED MACAW
Propyrrhura maracana   Plate 55

Other names: Illiger's Macaw

IDENTIFICATION 39cm. Small, mostly green macaw with pointed tail, prominent red forehead and bare yellowish-white face in otherwise bluish head, and indistinct red patch on belly. Distinguished from partly sympatric, rather similar Chestnut-fronted Macaw (218) by red forehead, yellowish (not red) underside of wings and tail and red abdominal patch, and from similar (but ecologically distinct) Red-bellied Macaw (219) by red on forehead and rump and paler facial skin. Narrowly overlapping Yellow-collared Macaw (222) has yellow band on nape. Flight jerkier than other small macaws. Combination of bare white face, red forehead and red on belly separates this from other long-tailed mainly green parrots in captivity. Generally in pairs or small flocks flying fast at tree-top height, calling loudly.

VOICE Screeching *kreh* and raucous *aaugh*.

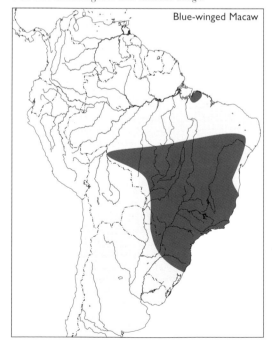

Blue-winged Macaw

DISTRIBUTION AND STATUS Eastern South America from south of Amazon. In Brazil it ranges from southern Pará and Maranhão (including one record from the coast) south and west through Piauí, Pernambuco, Bahia, Tocantins, Goiás and Minas Gerais to Mato Grosso, with a recent recolonisation of Rio de Janeiro state and records from Rio Grande do Sul up to 1930; into eastern Paraguay and formerly north-east Argentina in Misiones and northern Corrientes. Apparently resident. Major decline in recent decades, probably owing to large-scale deforestation, yet also lost from localities where apparently suitable habitat remains. Now mostly uncommon and local, remaining common only in the Serra Negra, Pernambuco, and Serra do Cachimbo, Pará, Brazil. Scarce in Paraguay, where it appears to persist in small fragmented populations; previously common in Argentina, now apparently extinct. Small numbers in captivity. Occurs in several protected areas, at least in small numbers. Legally protected in all range states. CITES Appendix I. VULNERABLE.

ECOLOGY Inhabits tropical and subtropical evergreen and deciduous forest (including Atlantic rain-forest and cerrado savanna) with apparent preference for forest edge or forest close to water. In extreme northern Bahia, Brazil, inhabits *Tabebuia caraiba* gallery woodland in caatinga zone alongside Spix's Macaw (210) where birds avoid flying over open country, preferring to remain among trees. Reported to 1,000m. Generally in small flocks except when breeding. Birds observed taking seeds of introduced *Melia azedarach* in north-eastern Brazil; no other details on diet. Evidence of breeding in Dec (Brazil) and Feb (Argentina). Nest in tree-cavity. Clutch four.

DESCRIPTION Forehead bright red; crown, ear-coverts and sides of neck blue fading to grass-green on nape and mantle; lower back reddish, rump and uppertail-coverts green. Upperwing-coverts grass-green; upper surface of flight feathers blue with greyish margins to innerwebs and black tips. Underwing coverts green, underside of flight feathers dull yellow. Throat bluish-olive green; breast and upper belly green with strong olive suffusion; lower belly with dull reddish patch; vent and undertail-coverts green with olive suffusion. Uppertail basally olive shading to reddish-brown with blue tip; undertail dull yellow. **Bare parts:** Bill black; bare lores and cheeks yellowish-white; iris orange-yellow; pale yellow on periophthalmic ring and yellow at base of mandible; legs grey with yellow feet.

SEX/AGE Sexes similar but female may have smaller area of red on forehead. Immature paler blue on head, pale tip to upper mandible and less red beneath.

MEASUREMENTS Wing 204-227; tail 181-217; bill 31-37; tarsus 20-24.

GEOGRAPHICAL VARIATION None.

NOTE Blue-winged Macaw is sometimes included in *Ara*. See Note in Red-bellied Macaw (219).

REFERENCES Belton (1984), Collar *et al.* (1994), Dubs (1992), Forshaw (1989), Juniper (1991), Lowen *et al.* (1996), Meyer de Schauensee (1966), Naumburg (1930), Nores & Yzurieta (1994), Olmos (1993), Ridgely (1981), Rutgers & Norris (1979), Sick (1993), Short (1975).

222 YELLOW-COLLARED MACAW
Propyrrhura auricollis   Plate 55

Other names: Golden-collared Macaw, Yellow-naped Macaw, Golden-naped Macaw, Cassin's Macaw

IDENTIFICATION 40cm. Small, mostly green, macaw with mostly blue flight feathers, blackish forehead, long tail and conspicuous bare white facial skin, plus unique bright yellow collar-patch (reddish in immature). Rather similar to (and, in Paraguay, Mato Grosso and perhaps Goiás, marginally overlapping) Blue-winged Macaw (221) but distinguished from this and all other congeners by bright yellow collar-patch. From all *Aratinga* conures by yellow collar and bare cheeks and lores. Flight swift and direct in pairs or small groups.

VOICE Loud shrieking *screee-at screee-at* sounds to European ears like Black-headed Gull *Larus ridibundus*. Loud and harsh alarm call said to resemble voice of Blue-crowned Conure (228).

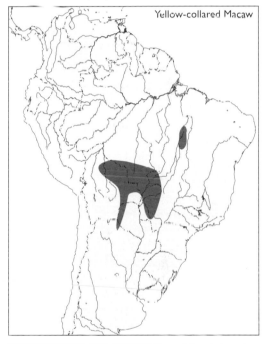

Yellow-collared Macaw

DISTRIBUTION AND STATUS Central South America. The species ranges from north-west Argentina in eastern Jujuy and northern Salta (reports from Misiones and Formosa appear incorrect) north through eastern and northern Bolivia in Santa Cruz, Beni and Tarija, occurring in northern Paraguay mainly west of the Río Paraguay but largely absent in the drier areas of chaco. It extends into south-western Mato Grosso and Mato Grosso do Sul, Brazil, where its northern and eastern limits are unclear; it also occurs (possibly disjunctly) in western Goiás, north-eastern Mato Grosso and extreme south-eastern Pará, where birds are reported in and around Ilha do Bananal. Mostly resident but apparently seasonal movements in some areas. Generally common and persists in areas where substantial habitat modification taken place. Scarcer at edge of range in Paraguay. Formerly traded internationally, but status apparently unaffected by trapping.

ECOLOGY Occurs in a variety of forest, forest edge, woodland and savanna habitats: moist upper tropical and subtropical forest in Argentina, dry forest in Bolivia, chaco in Paraguay and pantanal, open cerrado and gallery forest in Brazil. Tolerates considerable habitat modification and remains common in some areas with extensive agricultural development (e.g. around Santa Cruz, Bolivia). Mainly below 600m but occurs to 1,700m in north-west Argentina. Generally in pairs or small flocks (mostly outside breeding season). Larger flocks form at roosts and where food abundant, birds then appearing less obviously paired than do other macaws in similar aggregations. Diet includes *Byrsonima* fruits, *Erythrina* flowers, *Ficus*, maize and seeds of *Guazuma tomentosa*, *Spondias lutea*, *Adelia mesembinifolia*, *Astronium fraxinifolium* and *A. urundeuva*. Occasionally feeds on ground. Nest in tree-cavity. Breeds from Dec (Argentina). Clutch 2-4.

DESCRIPTION Forehead, feathered part of cheeks and forecrown black fading to bluish-green on hindcrown and sides of neck; nape with broad golden-yellow collar. Upperparts green with blue bases to some feathers. Lesser and median coverts green; alula and primary coverts blue. Primaries blue; secondaries green, strongly tinged blue on outerwebs. Underwing-coverts olive-yellow; underside of flight feathers dull yellowish. Underparts green. Central uppertail reddish-brown at base, green in centre, blue distally with black tips; outer feathers mostly blue; undertail dull yellowish. **Bare parts**: Bill blackish with slaty tip; bare skin on lores and cheeks white with straw tint; iris orange; legs flesh pink.

SEX/AGE Sexes similar. Immature has nuchal collar reddish.

MEASUREMENTS Wing 198-224; tail 175-204; bill 33-37; tarsus 19-22.

GEOGRAPHICAL VARIATION None.

NOTE Yellow-collared Macaw is sometimes included in *Ara*. See Note in Red-bellied Macaw (219).

REFERENCES Arndt (1996), Dubs (1992), Forshaw (1989), Meyer de Schauensee (1966), Narosky & Yzurieta (1989), Naumburg (1930), Nores & Yzurieta (1994), Parker (1993), de la Peña (1988), Ridgely (1981), Short (1975), Sick (1993), Stone & Roberts (1934), Yamashita *in litt.* (1995).

---

223 RED-SHOULDERED MACAW
Diopsittaca nobilis   Plate 55

Other names: Hahn's Macaw; Noble Macaw (*A. n. cumanensis*)

IDENTIFICATION 30cm. Smallest macaw. Mostly grass-green with bluish forehead, red greater underwing-coverts and red at bend of wing. Underside of flight feathers and tail golden-olive. Most easily distinguished from other small macaws by absence of blue in flight feathers. From similar *Aratinga* conures, especially White-eyed Conure (235), by rather conspicuous bare white skin on lores and upper cheeks. Outside breeding season often in large noisy flocks; flight fast on rapid jerky wingbeats. Sometimes associates with Red-bellied Macaw (219) but latter is larger with blue in flight feathers.

VOICE Noisy and especially vocal in flight. High-pitched

kreeek-kreeek and more throaty *ahk-ahk-ahk-ahk-ahk-ahk*, with calls often delivered in two or three bursts followed by brief pause: thus birds sometimes give loud and rather honking *yaark yaark... yaark yaark...*, etc. Some calls have a vibrating quality and faltering delivery, suggesting larger macaw species, although at other times the voice is reminiscent of some *Aratinga*. Other sounds suggest calls of Red-bellied Macaw. Flocks can create loud excited chorus.

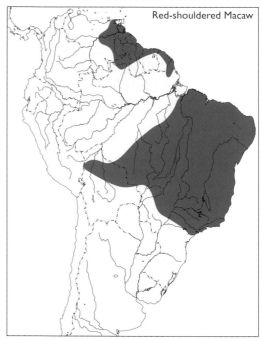

Red-shouldered Macaw

DISTRIBUTION AND STATUS Northern South America east of the Andes south to central Brazil. In eastern Venezuela it occurs mostly south of the Orinoco (Delta Amacuro and parts of Bolívar) but also in extreme eastern Monagas. The few records from Trinidad are probably of escaped captive birds. It occurs through the Guianas in areas of seasonal forest (mainly near the coast) and in Brazil north of the Amazon in Roraima, Amapá and northern Pará. It reappears disjunctly in interior Brazil south of the Amazon from south-eastern Pará and Maranhão to the pantanals of Mato Grosso and south through the dry north-east in Piauí, Bahia and reportedly Alagoas south to Espírito Santo, Rio de Janeiro and north-western São Paulo (with an introduced population in São Paulo city). It occupies central and eastern Bolivia and south-east Peru, where reported from the Pampas de Heath. Generally resident, but seasonal movements in some areas (e.g. coastal Guianas) and distribution patchy, especially north of Amazon where suitable habitat scattered. Generally common, especially in central and north-eastern Brazil, but uncommon in the Guianas. Few in captivity but some international trade in live birds.

ECOLOGY Occurs in a variety of rather open wooded habitats, including savannas with scattered bushes and palm (e.g. *Mauritia* sp.) groves (Surinam), sand-belt forests, forest-fringed savannas and coastal plantations (Guyana), cerrado with especially *Mauritia* palm groves (interior Brazil) and fringes of the caatinga (north-eastern Brazil) with *Mauritia* palm. Persistent feature of preferred habitat is presence of palms, especially *M. flexuosa*, *Orbignya martiana* and *Maximiliana maripa* (latter especially in southern Amazon region); also known from marshy areas with palms, gallery woodlands and cultivated areas. Avoids large tracts of closed-canopy forest, but occurs around human habitation and is common in Georgetown City, Guyana. Reaches 1,400m in Venezuela south of the Orinoco. Gregarious, often in large flocks outside breeding season; otherwise in pairs. Diet probably similar to close relatives including locally available nuts, seeds, fruits and flowers, but some indication that seeds favoured; known items include flowers of *Terminalia argentea* and *Erythrina glauca*, and *Cordia* berries, with *Euterpe* fruits also reported. Takes cereal and fruit crops and regarded as a pest in some areas. Nests in tree-cavity, arboreal termitarium or hole in living palm. Copulations reported Oct, south-western Brazil; probably breeds Feb-Jun, Guyana. Clutch four in captivity.

DESCRIPTION Forehead, forecrown and area above eyes blue; remainder of head and upperparts, including wings and upper surface of tail, grass-green. Red at carpal joint and on leading edge of wing. Lesser and median underwing-coverts red; greater underwing-coverts brownish; underside of flight feathers golden-olive. Underparts green but more yellowish than above. Underside of tail golden-olive. **Bare parts.** Bill blackish; bare skin on lores and upper cheeks white; iris orange-brown; legs black.

SEX/AGE Sexes similar; females perhaps a little smaller. Immature head all green; lacks red at carpal joint.

MEASUREMENTS Wing 163-177; tail 122-152; bill 25-27; tarsus 16-18.

GEOGRAPHICAL VARIATION None.

NOTE Red-shouldered Macaw frequently included in *Ara*. See Note in Red-bellied Macaw (219).

GEOGRAPHICAL VARIATION Three races. Size increases from north to south and all differences may simply be clinal.

 D. n. nobilis (North of Amazon in S Venezuela, N Brazil and the Guianas)

 D. n. cumanensis (N and E Brazil to south of Amazon. Intergrades with *longipennis* in interior C Brazil) Similar to nominate but larger (c. 33cm), maxilla whitish-horn, forehead bluer.

 D. n. longipennis (Mato Grosso, Goiás and W Minas Gerais, Brazil. Birds from NE Bolivia and SE Peru are probably of this race) Similar to *cumanensis* but larger (c. 35cm) with more yellowish and olive underparts.

REFERENCES Brown (1974), Dubs (1992), ffrench (1992), Forshaw (1989), Gilliard (1941), Haverschmidt (1968), Meyer de Schauensee (1966), Meyer de Schauensee & Phelps (1978), Naumburg (1930), O'Neill (1981), Remsen & Ridgely (1980), Ridgely (1981), Sick (1993), Snyder (1966), Teixeira *et al.* (1986), Tostain *et al.* (1992), Yamashita *in litt.* (1995), Young (1929).

---

224 YELLOW-EARED PARROT
Ognorhynchus icterotis   Plate 61

Other names: Yellow-eared Parakeet/Conure

IDENTIFICATION 42cm. Similar build to small macaw. Yellowish beneath, green above with broad, bright yellow

ear-patches and yellow frontal band. Dark green patches on sides of neck converge on throat to contrast with otherwise yellowish underparts. Large dark bill. Distinguished from possibly overlapping (in Colombia) Red-fronted Conure (231) by larger size and broad yellow patches on sides of head. Possibly confusable with the Golden-plumed Conure (248) in wild but Yellow-eared larger with more extensive yellow markings on head and darker, heavier bill. In pairs or small flocks. Very rare indeed.

VOICE Disyllabic nasal goose-like calls which at a distance may sound like a musical babbling.

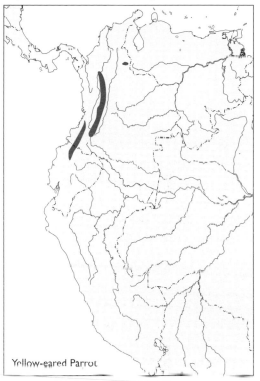

Yellow-eared Parrot

DISTRIBUTION AND STATUS Restricted to northern Andes in northern Ecuador and western Colombia between 1,200 and 3,400m (mostly 2,500-3,000m). Occurs (or occurred) in all three Andean chains in Colombia: records in the West Andes are from the southern portion north to Cauca and possibly Valle; in the Central Andes from the west slope in Antioquia, Caldas and Cauca and on east slope in Tolima and Huila; in the East Andes from the west slope and eastern watershed in Norte de Santander, the east slope in Cundinamarca and at the head of the Magdalena Valley in Huila. Reported northern Ecuador from Carchi, Imbabura and Pichincha. Probably wanders seasonally with evidence that it is present, Ecuador, Nov-Feb and in Colombia for rest of year. Formerly considered common and in some places even abundant but now very scarce and local. Drastic decline in 20th century owing to large-scale deforestation over much of range and perhaps decline of favoured *Ceroxylon* palm species, several of which are themselves threatened owing to cattle-grazing and invasive plants. Recent records sporadic and the species may now be confined to a few localities in Colombia, including Cerro Munchique region (western Andes in Cauca) where some still undisturbed forest remains, at head of Magdalena Valley, and in the north-west Andes in Ecuador. Recorded (sporadically) in several protected areas including Parque Nacionale Cueva de los Guácharos, Colombia, and Cotocachi-Cayapas reserve in Pichincha, Ecuador. Total population very small and on verge of extinction. Very rare in captivity and remaining birds could be at threat from trapping. CITES Appendix I. CRITICAL.

ECOLOGY Wet montane forest in the upper subtropical and lower temperate zones, sometimes frequenting areas with partial forest clearance. Association with *Ceroxylon* palms exists but dependence on these species uncertain since birds absent from areas where such palms abundant. Birds generally reported in small flocks or in pairs. Known to feed on *C. quindiuense* and *C. alpinum* but probably takes fruit of all other species in this genus; other recorded foods include *Saurania tomentosa* and *Sapium* fruits. Birds sometimes forage in more open country, returning to forest to roost. Reported nesting in loose colony about 25m high in *Ceroxylon* palms. Breeding May (northern Tolima), birds in breeding condition Mar (Huila). Breeds Jul-Oct Ecuador. Clutch four.

DESCRIPTION Crown grass-green with emerald suffusion; forehead with broad yellow band extending to lores, upper cheeks and below eyes to ear-coverts, where feathers elongated and form wide yellow fan; lower cheeks and sides of neck green. Upperparts, upperwing-coverts and flight feathers grass-green. Underwing yellowish-green on coverts, dull yellowish on flight feathers. Underparts yellowish with green tinge becoming darker on belly, thighs and vent. Uppertail green; undertail dull red. **Bare parts**: Upper mandible blackish, lower mandible grey; bare periophthalmic skin pale grey; iris orange; legs grey.

SEX/AGE Sexes similar. Immatures undescribed.

MEASUREMENTS Wing 216-233; tail 161-220; bill 33-37; tarsus 20-23.

GEOGRAPHICAL VARIATION None.

REFERENCES Arndt (1996), Chapman (1917), Collar *et al.* (1992, 1994), Fjeldså & Krabbe (1990), Forshaw (1989), Hilty & Brown (1986), Krabbe & Sornoza Molina (1996), Meyer de Schauensee (1949), Moore (1977), Ridgely (1981).

---

225 THICK-BILLED PARROT
Rhynchopsitta pachyrhyncha   **Plate 62**

Other names: Thick-billed Macawlet

IDENTIFICATION 38cm. Rather like small green macaw with long wings and long wedge-shaped tail, scarlet forehead and stripe over eye, heavy black bill and bright yellow on underwing-coverts conspicuous in flight. Overlaps with Military Macaw (213), which is much larger with proportionately much longer tail, blue rump and blue in flight feathers, while Lilac-crowned Amazon (330) has considerably shorter tail (although long for an amazon), lacks yellow on underwings and has more raucous voice. Wandering Thick-bills possibly seen in Coahuila, Mexico, alongside very similar Maroon-fronted Parrot (226), which however lacks yellow on underwing, is darker and larger, and has maroon (not scarlet) on forehead. From small

green macaws in captivity by feathered cheeks and lores. Birds sometimes in pairs or singly but more often in flocks with birds moving quietly through treetops. Flocks sometimes pass over at considerable height in V-formation. Flight powerful and direct with long glides.

VOICE Various screeches, screams, shrieks and squawks. Harsh, rolling and extended *cra-ak* and *graa-ah* calls often heard. Laughing *kah ha* and *kah-ha-ha-ha-ha-ha*, etc., also reported. Voice similar to macaw but higher-pitched. Loud calls can be heard at 3km, but echos off rockfaces and around canyons sometimes make it difficult to locate birds.

Thick-billed Parrot

DISTRIBUTION AND STATUS Core range lies in western and central Mexico with sporadic movements north and south. Occurs Sierra Madre Occidental in southern Chihuahua, southern and western Durango, adjacent parts of eastern Sonora and Sinaloa; confirmed breeding only first two states. Like other avian pine seed specialists, birds wander widely after breeding, chiefly but sporadically to south-western Mexico in Jalisco, Colima and Michoacán, formerly east to Veracruz (although records possibly involved Maroon-fronted Parrot) and possibly Coahuila. Formerly sporadic visitor to (and possibly breeding resident in) Arizona (especially in Chiricahua Mountains in south) and New Mexico, USA, but no large-scale invasions since early 20th century and last known natural occurrence in 1938. Presence is determined by pine seed availability; core breeding range appears to be the most constantly occupied area. Major decline in 20th century has resulted primarily from habitat loss and degradation, with birds absent where large pines removed, mainly by forestry operations. Loss from USA attributable to hunting, but presence there probably only short-term, either when feeding conditions unusually favourable (or else very unfavourable in Mexico). Recent threats in Mexico are the live bird trade and continuing habitat loss to ranching, drug-growing and logging (loss of old trees for nesting is a major problem placing this species at higher risk than the smaller-ranged but cliff-nesting Maroon-fronted Parrot). Confiscated and captive-bred birds were released in Arizona in the late 1980s with first proven USA breeding soon after, but birds have now largely disappeared. No protected areas in Sierra Madre Occidental. CITES Appendix I. ENDANGERED.

ECOLOGY Inhabits mature upland *Pinus* forests or *Pinus* with *Pseudotsuga*, *Populus* and/or *Quercus* in secluded and often rugged country, occasionally also in lowland localities. Mostly occurs at 1,500-3,000m with breeding usually at 2,000-3,000m. Preference (in Mexico) for stands with *Pinus arizonica* and *P. ayacahuite*; potential (former) US range perhaps determined by northern extent of *P. leiophylla*. Generally in flocks. Communal roosting on inaccessible cliffs or trees with dense foliage. Diurnal movements up to 40km between roost and foraging areas. Diet comprised largely of pine seeds (including *P. teocote* and *P. leiophylla*) extracted from cones with powerful bill; seeds and buds of *Pseudotsuga*, fruits of *Prunus capuli* and acorns also reported. Nests in tree-cavity, usually in pine but also reported in *Populus tremuloides* and *Pseudotsuga taxifolia*; generally in dead or partly dead tree with chamber excavated from smaller hollow initiated by (e.g.) woodpecker such as Northern Flicker *Colaptes auratus* or caused by fungal decay of heartwood; sometimes close together (in same tree) when sites available, but more usually scattered. Breeding coincides with pine seed ripening; birds usually arrive in the breeding area Apr-May, with eggs laid mid-Jun to late Jul. Young leave nest from early Sep to late Oct. Clutch 2-4, usually three, perhaps variable with size of *Pinus* seed crop.

DESCRIPTION Forehead, lores and broad stripe over and to behind eye bright scarlet; small patch of brownish feathers on lores directly in front of eye; crown, cheeks and sides of neck green with yellowish tinge. Upperparts green with indistinct olive tinge on scapulars. Upperwing-coverts green with red feathers at carpal joint. Flight feathers green above with blackish tips and margins to innerwebs, grey below. Greater underwing coverts yellow, other coverts green. Underparts green with red on thighs. Uppertail green; undertail greyish. **Bare parts**: Bill black; bare periophthalmic skin yellowish-white; iris yellowish-orange; legs grey.

SEX/AGE Sexes similar. Immature with horn-coloured bill, greyish bare periophthalmic skin, and no scarlet feathers behind eye or red on carpal joint.

MEASUREMENTS Wing 254-276; tail 160-178; bill 36-41; tarsus 22-24.

GEOGRAPHICAL VARIATION None.

NOTE Thick-billed frequently treated as conspecific with Maroon-fronted Parrot. Although evidently sharing recent common ancestor, allospecies treatment considered appropriate owing to size, plumage and behavioural differences.

REFERENCES Arndt (1996), Collar *et al.* (1992, 1994), Davis & Bennett (1972), Edwards (1972), Forshaw (1989), Friedmann (1950), Howell & Webb (1995), King (1981), Lanning & Shiflett (1981, 1983), Peterson & Chalif (1973), Risser (1980), van Rossem (1945), Snyder *et al.* (1989, 1994).

---

226 MAROON-FRONTED PARROT
Rhynchopsitta terrisi   Plate 62

Other names: Maroon-fronted Macawlet

IDENTIFICATION 40-45cm. Resembles small green macaw with wedge-shaped tail, heavy black bill, red on bend of wing and maroon forehead and stripe over eye (maroon may appear black in field); endemic to Mexico. In Coahuila its range may possibly sometimes be overlapped by the similar Thick-billed Parrot (225), which see for differences. It also sometimes overlaps with Military Macaw (213), which is much larger with proportionately much longer tail, blue rump and blue in flight feathers. Maroon-fronts overhead appear bright green with contrasting dark tail. From small green macaws in captivity

by feathered lores and cheeks. Generally in flocks moving about quietly in crowns of trees or passing at some height.

VOICE High-pitched rolling *cra-ak*. At a distance birds reportedly sound exactly like a noisy group of Acorn Woodpeckers *Melanerpes formicivorus*, a common breeding resident in their range. Echos can make calls difficult to trace.

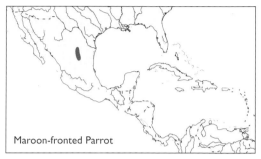

Maroon-fronted Parrot

DISTRIBUTION AND STATUS Restricted distribution in north-eastern Mexico. Confined to Sierra Madre Oriental in south-eastern Coahuila near Saltillo, central-western Nuevo León, including mountains to south-west of Monterrey, and mountains of western Tamaulipas. Total range about 300km north to south, averaging 60km west to east with breeding possibly only in northern third. Like Thick-billed Parrot makes seasonal (but probably less wide-ranging) movements in response to pine seed availability, apparently occurring in south of range in Oct-Apr only (old reports of Thick-billed Parrots in Veracruz may pertain to this species). Rare, very local and extirpated many areas. Now confined to relatively restricted (compared to Sierra Madre Occidental) areas of remaining pine forest (probably about 7,000 km² of suitable forest remaining in 18,000 km² range). Decline is principally due to habitat loss to logging, agriculture, burning and grazing, but cliff-nesting habit obviates need for old or dead trees. Selective logging may reduce pine diversity and therefore food availability. Total population not known to exceed 2,000 birds. Occurs Cumbres de Monterrey National Park and El Taray Sanctuary, near Monterrey. CITES Appendix 1. VULNERABLE.

ECOLOGY Upland mixed *Pinus, Abies* and *Quercus* woodland, usually at 2,000-3,000m, exceptionally to 1,300m and 3,700m. Generally in flocks. Birds roost in nest whilst breeding but otherwise communally in trees or on cliffs. One roost observed in late 1970s held 1,600 birds. Diet comprises mostly pine seeds extracted from cone with powerful bill, including *Pinus arizonica, P. gregii, P. teocote, P. montezumae, P. cembroides* and *Abies*. Also eats acorns and takes nectar from *Agave macroculnis* flowers. Nests in holes in limestone cliffs in or near mixed conifer forest, sometimes colonially. Reports of tree-nesting appear mistaken with very few trees in range large enough to accommodate nests. Chick rearing synchronised with ripening of pine seeds, usually in late summer and autumn, although one male was in breeding condition in May.

DESCRIPTION Forehead, most of lores and stripe over eye to above ear-coverts dark brownish-maroon; small patch in front of eye on lores dark brown; cheeks, sides of neck and crown bright green. Nape and rest of upperparts green with brownish-olive suffusion. Red patch on carpal area; upperwing-coverts greenish-olive. Flight feathers greenish olive above with darker tips and innerwebs. Underwing dark brownish-grey. Underparts green with brownish-olive suffusion on throat and breast; thighs flecked maroon. Uppertail green; undertail dark brownish-grey. **Bare parts**: Bill black; bare periophthalmic skin yellowish-white; iris yellowish-orange; legs grey.

SEX/AGE Sexes similar. Immature with brown eyes and paler bill.

MEASUREMENTS Wing 283-290; tail 185-204; bill 40-42; tarsus 23-24.

GEOGRAPHICAL VARIATION None.

NOTE Frequently treated as conspecific with Thick-billed Parrot (see Note in Thick-billed Parrot).

REFERENCES Collar *et al.* (1992, 1994), Davis & Bennett (1972), Edwards (1972), Forshaw (1989), Friedmann *et al.* (1950), Howell & Webb (1995), King (1981), Lawson & Lanning (1981), Peterson & Chalif (1973), Robins & Heed (1951), Wege & Long (1995).

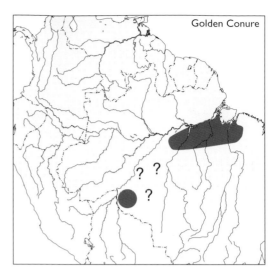

Golden Conure

---

227 GOLDEN CONURE
Guaruba guarouba Plate 56

Other names: Queen of Bavaria's Conure, Golden Parakeet

IDENTIFICATION 34cm. Clear bright yellow plumage of adult unmistakable. Flight feathers green above and dusky-yellow on underside. Greater upperwing-coverts green. Immature (primarily identifiable by keeping company with adults) dull olive-brown with bright green flight feathers and greater upperwing-coverts. No lookalike species in wild but in captivity possibly confused with Sun Conure (238), which has orange-red lores and ocular region, orange-yellow breast and belly, brown and blue (not yellow) uppertail and blue flight feathers; immature dull orange beneath. Golden Conure occurs in small flocks in terra firme rain-forest usually travelling just above canopy.

VOICE High-pitched vibrant *kray* given singly or as series of 3-4 notes per second, repeated after brief pause. Prolonged strident *kewo* reported in courtship. Captive birds have a rapidly repeated *keek-keek-keek*. Voice generally softer than *Aratinga* conures.

DISTRIBUTION AND STATUS Amazonia, south of Amazon in Brazil, from west bank of Rio Tapajós east through the catchments of the Xingu and Tocantins north of 5°N, Pará, to the east bank of Rio Turiaçu in western Maranhão. Not known from Ilha de Marajó and avoids várzea forest (e.g. immediately south of the Amazon). Recent records from Rondônia and Mato Grosso (far outside previously known range) suggests distribution poorly understood. Apparently ranges over large areas but not known if movements predictable or related to (e.g.) seasonal availability of food. Rare throughout range (already lost from some eastern parts) and no doubt declining owing to very extensive, rapid and continuing deforestation and forest fragmentation in both western and eastern Amazonia. Illegal capture for domestic and international live bird markets and hunting for food and sport pose serious additional pressures. Protected areas in range inadequate and regularly violated by (e.g.) illegal cutting of timber such as mahogany *Swietenia macrophylla*. CITES Appendix I. ENDANGERED.

ECOLOGY Inhabits terra firme tropical rain-forest, avoiding várzea (seasonally inundated) forest although in post-breeding period birds may wander into this habitat from directly adjacent dryland forest. When breeding, birds occupy forest next to clearings (e.g. new fields). Gregarious at all times of year. In flocks of 3-30 birds (mostly 6-10). Roosts communally in tree-cavities in non-breeding season with several hollows in area used alternately on successive nights. Habitual and regular use of roosting and feeding areas suspected owing to predictable diurnal routines. Sometimes seen feeding with other parrot species. Birds generally forage in tall forest but will take some cultivated plants; recorded items (all fruits or pseudofruits) include *Euterpe*, which is especially favoured, *Anarcardium spruceanum*, *A. occidentale*, *Protium* and *Tetragastris*, *Visnia gujanensis*, *Inga*, *Byrsonima crassifolia*, *Carapa guianensis*, *Cecropia* and *Oenocarpus bacaba*; also flowers and buds (e.g. *Symphonia*), and crops including maize and mango in some areas. Nests in high tree-hollow (15-30m) in trunk or main branch of living or dead tree. Nest tree usually isolated but close to intact forest. Old nest of other species may be used with birds enlarging cavity where necessary. Usually breeds communally with several females contributing to clutch although single pairs also reported. Young of different stages of development sometimes in same nest. Normal clutch per hen 2-4 (perhaps up to six); 14 chicks reported in single captive nest where all six adults helped rear young. Breeding generally wet season (Dec-Apr).

DESCRIPTION Entire head, upperparts, underparts and tail bright yellow. Greater coverts, primaries and secondaries dark green (one or two yellow flight feathers in some birds). Underwing-coverts yellow, underside of flight feathers dusky-yellow. Shafts of tail feathers white. **Bare parts**: Bill pale pinkish, browner at base of upper mandible; bare orbital ring whitish; iris orange to brownish-orange; legs pinkish.

SEX/AGE Sexes similar. Immature dull olive-brown streaked dark green above. In transition to maturity, head, uppertail and back are last to acquire bright yellow of adult plumage.

MEASUREMENTS Wing 200-218; tail 141-165; bill 35-37; tarsus 19-23.

GEOGRAPHICAL VARIATION None.

NOTE This species is sometimes included in *Aratinga*, but behavioural, ecological and morphological factors indicate its greater appropriateness in a monotypic genus.

REFERENCES Collar *et al.* (1992, 1994), Forshaw (1989), King (1981), Lo (1995), Meyer de Schauensee (1966), Oren & Novaes (1986), Oren & Willis (1981), Ridgely (1981), Schoenwald & Schoenwald (1992), Sick (1993), Walters (1974).

---

228 BLUE-CROWNED CONURE
Aratinga acuticaudata　　　　　Plate 56

Other names: Blue-crowned Parakeet, Sharp-tailed Conure

IDENTIFICATION 37cm. The only *Aratinga* conure with blue forehead and crown, although blue sometimes difficult to discern in field, present in mainly lowland areas of dry forest in several major parts of South America. Long pointed tail reddish beneath (conspicuous as bird alights). Pink upper mandible noticeable and pale feet often visible in flight. Congeners smaller except Mitred Conure (232), with head wholly green or green with red markings. From small macaws by feathered cheeks and lores. Often seen in small noisy flocks in swift direct flight.

VOICE Loud, rapidly repeated *cheeah-cheeah*. Very different to partly sympatric Brown-throated Conure (245).

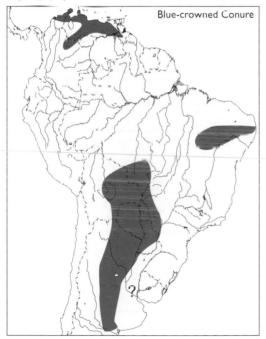

Blue-crowned Conure

DISTRIBUTION AND STATUS South America in several disjunct populations from Venezuela to Argentina. One major area extends from north-east Colombia (east of Andes south to Meta) including the Guajira Peninsula and the Santa Marta Mountains into north-west Venezuela east to Monagas (including Margarita Island) and south to northern Bolívar. A second lies in north-east Brazil in

eastern Piauí, northern Bahia, Pernambuco and Alagoas. A third occurs in southern South America from eastern Bolivia and western Mato Grosso, Brazil, south through Paraguay and Argentina south to La Pampa and south-western Buenos Aires, perhaps also western Uruguay. Fairly common, Colombia. Frequent, Venezuela, but abundance varies with season. Rare to fairly common in Bolivia. In north-east Brazil it is the most abundant parrot in some localities. Common to fairly common (but possibly declining) in northern Argentina. At best rare in western Uruguay. Margarita race very rare (100-200 birds remaining) owing to habitat loss to tourism, taking of young for pets and predation by rats. Large numbers held in captivity (over 94,000 birds exported from Argentina in 1985-1990).

ECOLOGY Inhabits dry deciduous forest and associated open habitats including semi-desert. Recorded from caatinga and cerrado with stands of *Mauritia* and *Buriti* palms in north-east Brazil, from gallery forest in Venezuela and Colombia, virtual desert in Bolivia, and pampas in Argentina, also cultivated areas and pasturelands in dry forest zones. Generally in lowlands (to 400m Colombia, 600m Venezuela) but ascends to 2,650m in Bolivia where birds inhabit leguminous woodland with columnar cacti. Usually in pairs or small flocks but in larger aggregations outside breeding season, especially where food abundant, resulting in considerable local movements and consequent fluctuations in local numbers. In some places birds roost in crevices in rocky cliffs. Observed in association with Mitred and White-eyed (235) Conures. Feeds in trees and bushes and on ground, recorded food items including *Sorghum* and *Bambusa* seeds, berries of *Condalia lineata* and fruit of cacti and crops such as mango *Mangifera*; insects possibly also taken. Nests in tree-cavity, often high up, including cultivated species such as mango or guava, or in cavities in sandstone cliffs. Eggs Dec, Paraguay and Argentina; breeding probably Mar-Jul, Venezuela. Recorded clutch two.

DESCRIPTION Forecrown, forehead, lores and cheeks bright pale blue. Sides of neck, nape, mantle, scapulars and back bright green; rump and uppertail-coverts paler green. Upperwing-coverts bright green; alula with bluish tinge. Primaries and secondaries green above with pinkish tinge on innerwebs, golden-olive below. Underwing-coverts green. Underparts mostly dull green with olive tinge; some breast feathers suffused blue. Uppertail green on outerwebs, brick-red on innerwebs, merging to dull green at tip; undertail brick-red fading distally to dull brown. **Bare parts:** Upper mandible pinkish, lower greyish, bare periophthalmic region creamy-white; iris orange-yellow; legs pale pink.

SEX/AGE Sexes similar on plumage. Immature has blue on head restricted to forehead and crown, no blue tinge on breast. Young of nominate have pale bill.

MEASUREMENTS Wing 181-200; tail 165-189; bill 25-29; tarsus 18-21.

GEOGRAPHICAL VARIATION Five races.

　　A. a. acuticaudata (S South America from E Bolivian lowlands to Mato Grosso in Brazil, Paraguay, N Argentina and possibly W Uruguay) Larger than other races with bluer head and duller underparts.

　　A. a. neumanni (At 1,500 to 2,650m, above nominate on eastern slopes of Bolivian Andes in Cochabamba, Santa Cruz, Chuquisaca and probably Tarija provinces) Only forehead, lores and forecrown blue, rest of head green.

A. a. haemorrhous (NE Brazil in caatinga of Piauí and Bahia) Both mandibles pale pinkish, underparts brighter green and blue on head more restricted than in nominate.

A. a. koenigi (N Venezuela and NE Colombia) Similar to last race but innerwebs of undersides of tail feathers less brownish-red. This and next race smaller than others (34cm).

A. a. neoxena (Margarita Island, Venezuela) Similar to *haemorrhous* but bluish-green on breast and belly; smaller than other races except *koenigi* (34cm).

REFERENCES Arndt (1996), Dubs (1992), Fjeldså & Krabbe (1990), Forshaw (1989), Friedmann & Smith (1950), Hilty *et al.* (1986), Meyer de Schauensee (1948-1952, 1966), Narosky & Yzurieta (1989), Nores & Yzurieta (1994), Parker (1993), Rutgers & Norris (1979), Short (1975), Sick (1993), Teixeira *et al.* (1989), Yamashita *in litt.* (1996).

---

229 GREEN CONURE
Aratinga holochlora   Plate 58

Other names: Green Parakeet, Mexican Green Conure (Parakeet); Orange-throated Conure (*A. h. rubritorquis*); Pacific Parakeet, Nicaraguan Green Conure (*A. h. strenua*)

IDENTIFICATION 32cm. Fairly large, wholly green conure (except race *rubritorquis*), darker above, more yellowish beneath, with a long pointed tail. Sympatric conures are smaller with shorter tails and more erratic flight. Olive-throated Conure (242), which overlaps in the Gulf lowlands of Mexico, Honduras and Nicaragua, also separated by brown underparts and blue in wing, while Orange-fronted Conure (243), sympatric on the Pacific slope from Mexico to Honduras, identified by brown throat, orange frontal patch and blue in wings. In captivity Green Conure distinguished from adults of other green *Aratinga* conures by green underwing-coverts and crown, and lack of red on forehead. In large noisy flocks in non-breeding season. Rather deep wingbeats are rapid but less so than smaller sympatric conures.

VOICE Sharp squeaky notes and loud harsh calls including a high-pitched *screek... screek* in flight. Some calls with trilling quality. Also shrill noisy chatter.

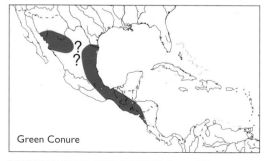

Green Conure

DISTRIBUTION AND STATUS From Nicaragua to extreme southern Texas, USA (making it the most northerly occurring *Aratinga*). Main range extends from northern and western Mexico in southern Sonora, north-

east Sinaloa and southern Chihuahua (perhaps disjunctly) through central and eastern Mexico, including Nuevo León, San Luis Potosí, Tamaulipas and Veracruz to southern Oaxaca and Chiapas, then east through southern and central Guatemala to El Salvador, Honduras and southern Nicaragua. Apparently mainly resident but at least local movements in some areas in relation to food supply. Annual visitor north to extreme southern Texas, USA. Status in northern and western Mexico uncertain but thought stable though not numerous. Fairly common in southern Mexico, Guatemala and the Honduran highlands, less so (and seasonal) in lowlands (to 300m). Common in El Salvador. However, an overall decline has occurred owing to conversion of forest to intensive agriculture. Traded in small numbers locally and internationally.

ECOLOGY All kinds of wooded habitats except tropical rain-forest. In eastern Mexico, mostly in upland forest with some movement to dry deciduous woods at lower elevations during non-breeding season; in both moist and scrubby open woodland and farmland in Guatemala and in upland forest above 900m in Honduras, including cloud-forest and *Pinus* forest with some movement to 300m in non-breeding season. In Nicaragua from 1,060 to 1,500m in *Pinus* forest. Recorded to 2,100m in Mexico (race *brewsteri* mostly at 1,250-2,000m) and 2,600m Guatemala. In flocks whilst not breeding, sometimes of more than 100 birds. Larger aggregations where food plentiful. Diet consists of seeds, nuts, berries and fruits, recorded items including fruits of *Myrica mexicana*, *Mimosa* seeds and maize (can be destructive of crops). Nest located in tree-cavity (e.g. old woodpecker hole), rock crevice, hole in building or termite mound. Colonial nesting reported in cave in eastern Mexico. Breeding reported Jan, eastern Mexico (young in nest); Apr, Tamaulipas, southern Mexico; Feb-Mar, El Salvador; male in breeding condition Aug, Guatemala. Usual clutch probably four.

DESCRIPTION Crown, forehead and lores green tinged olive, cheeks brighter green; sometimes scattered orange-red feathers on throat, cheeks, neck and nape. Upperparts grass-green tinged olive with slightly brighter green on rump. Upperwing-coverts grass-green with bluish tinge to primary-coverts. Primaries and secondaries green above with bluish tinge on outerwebs, metallic olive-yellow below. Underwing-coverts yellowish-green. Underparts yellowish-green. Uppertail grass-green; undertail yellowish-olive. **Bare parts**: Bill horn; bare periophthalmic region pale greyish; iris yellowish-orange or orange; legs yellowish-brown.

SEX/AGE Sexes similar. Immature with brown iris.

MEASUREMENTS Wing 160-175; tail 107-141; bill 23-26; tarsus 15-19.

GEOGRAPHICAL VARIATION Four races.

A. h. holochlora (E and S Mexico from Nuevo León and San Luis Potosí in the north through Tamaulipas to Veracruz, Oaxaca and Chiapas in the south)

A. h. brewsteri (Mountains of NW Mexico in S Sonora, NE Sinaloa and S Chihuahua) Darker green than *holochlora* with bluish suffusion on crown.

A. h. strenua (Apparently principally in Pacific lowlands of Central America from Oaxaca and Chiapas in Mexico to S Nicaragua, but recorded to 1,350m in El Salvador and to 2,100m in Guatemala) On average larger (wing 173-185, bill and legs stouter), slightly duller and less yellowish below than nominate.

A. h. rubritorquis (Gulf slope of Central America from E Guatemala, where it may be confined to arid sections of the Río Mocagua valley, to N Nicaragua; irregular in El Salvador. Mostly in drier highland forest) Like nominate but slightly smaller (wing 152-163), with darker ocular ring, olive-tinged underparts and with variable-sized patch of orange-red or red on throat of most adult birds (birds in south with more orange throat). Immatures and some adults with green throat.

NOTES (1) *A. h. strenua* is often treated as allospecific Pacific Parakeet but biometric data questioned and literature confusing; morphological differences between nominate and *strenua* are certainly very slight. Regular sympatry with other races in southern Mexico (and possibly Pacific slope of Guatemala), Honduras, Nicaragua and El Salvador remains unproven, but completely green individuals of '*rubritorquis*' reported from Honduras could be *strenua*, and a recent report of communal roosting between these two races could prove significant (see below) if in the breeding period.

(2) The red throat of *A. h. rubritorquis* and its rather different habitat have recently been adduced as evidence for full species status. This tends to be supported by observations of behavioural differences in a communal roost with *strenua* in El Salvador. We retain it as a race of *holochlora* only tentatively.

(3) *A. (h.) brevipes* was formerly classed as race of Green Conure but now often treated as a species (see Socorro Conure).

REFERENCES Binford (1989), Clinton-Eitniear (1980, 1984), Dearborn (1907), Dickey & van Rossem (1938), Forshaw (1989), Friedmann *et al.* (1950), Howell & Webb (1995), Griscom (1932), Land (1970), Lowery & Dalquest (1951), Monroe (1968), Noegel (1986), Peterson & Chalif (1973), Sibley & Monroe (1990).

230 SOCORRO CONURE
Aratinga brevipes   Plate 58

Other names: Socorro Parakeet, Socorro Green Parakeet

IDENTIFICATION 32cm. Wholly green long-tailed conure. Very similar indeed to most races of Green Conure (229) but darker beneath and vocally discernible. Only parrot found on Socorro, off west coast of Mexico. Unknown in captivity. Usually in pairs or small noisy flocks. Tame and quite easily approached.

VOICE High-pitched screeching or piping *krree kree* calls are notably different from Green Conure. Flocks give shrill chirping sounds; also persistent short *kee kee kee* screams when perched.

DISTRIBUTION AND STATUS Endemic to Socorro in the Revillagigedo Islands 650km off the west coast of Mexico. Population estimated at 400-500 birds in 1992 (roughly nine birds per km² of suitable habitat). Considered common, but recent decline possible owing to loss of preferred native habitat (still present on about 22% of the island) and erosion arising from excessive sheep grazing. Predation by feral cats may also be a threat. VULNERABLE.

ECOLOGY Most commonly in *Bumelia*, *Ilex* and *Guettarda* forest with trees at least 8m tall. Usually above 500m (especially on south side of Socorro) owing to loss of preferred vegetation to sheep at lower elevations in most parts of range. Recorded to 4m where native forest persists (in canyons) near sea-level especially on tall specimens of *Croton masonii*, *Conocarpus erecta* and *Ficus*. Usually in flocks up to about 40 birds, rarely up to 100. Larger flock formation not obviously linked to roosting, but generally in smaller flocks (up to 6) or just pairs whilst breeding. Recorded foods include *Bumelia*, *Guettarda*, *Ilex* and *Psidium* seeds and fruit pulp, with *Opuntia* and *Ficus* fruits notably in the dry season. Nests in tree-cavity, especially *Bumelia socorrensis*. Clutch unknown but breeding thought to commence Nov.

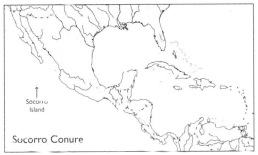

Socorro Conure

DESCRIPTION Crown, forehead and lores grass-green, sides of neck slightly brighter; head and neck sometimes with one or more scattered orange-red feathers. Upperparts grass-green, slightly brighter on rump. Upperwing-coverts grass-green with bluish tinge to outer greater coverts. Primaries and secondaries green above with bluish tinge on outerwebs, olive-yellow below. Underwing-coverts green. Underparts grass-green. Uppertail dark green, undertail yellowish-olive. **Bare parts** Bill horn coloured; bare periophthalmic region greyish; iris yellowish orange or orange; legs yellowish-brown.

SEX/AGE Age- and gender-related differences unknown although immature may differ, like Green Conure, on iris colour.

MEASUREMENTS Wing 169-174; tail 136-155; bill 26-29; tarsus 17-10.

GEOGRAPHICAL VARIATION None.

NOTE The Socorro Conure is frequently considered a race of Green Conure. However, plumage differences (principally green instead of yellowish-green underparts and absence of olive suffusion above) and structural distinctions (tenth primary shorter than the seventh, instead of vice versa as in *holochlora*) suggest that allospecific treatment may be appropriate.

REFERENCES Brattstrom & Howell (1956), Howell & Webb (1995), Rodríguez-Estrella *et al.* (1992), Wetmore (1941).

231 RED-FRONTED CONURE
Aratinga wagleri   Plate 57

Other names: Wagler's Conure, Scarlet-fronted Parakeet; Cordilleras Conure, Cordilleran Parakeet (*A. w. frontata*)

IDENTIFICATION 36cm. Mainly green, long-tailed

conure, darker above and paler, more yellowish below. Red crown, forehead and lores, some birds with scattered red feathers on throat. In Colombia and Venezuela told from Blue-crowned Conure (228) by red, not blue, on crown. In western Ecuador and north-west Peru *A. w. frontata* (which has red bend of wing and thighs) distinguished from Red-masked Conure (233) by lack of red underwing-coverts and red cheeks (some of latter also have red throat). On eastern slope of Andes in southern Peru sympatric Mitred Conure (232) distinguished by brownish-red forehead, red cheeks, fewer or no red feathers at bend of wing and harsher call. Combination of red crown, green cheeks and green underwing-coverts distinguishes Red-fronted from all other green conures in captivity. From all small macaws by feathered lores and cheeks. Flight swift and direct on rapid shallow wingbeats.

VOICE Loud and strident *steak* or *chee-ey* cry, sometimes repeated. Some calls with squeaking quality suggestive of domestic donkey. Flocks maintain loud screeching chatter. Mitred Conure has very much deeper and harsher voice.

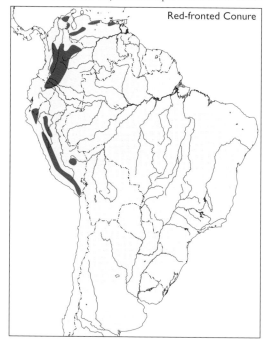

Red-fronted Conure

DISTRIBUTION AND STATUS North-western and western South America in Andes from Venezuela to Peru. In Venezuela it ranges from the Paria Peninsula west on the lower Andean slopes (500-2,000m, higher further south) to the Sierra de Perijá and into northern Colombia, including the Santa Marta region, then on west and central Andean ranges although apparently absent in extreme south-west Colombia. Status on eastern Andean slope in Colombia uncertain (some records). Found through lower slopes of Andes in southern Ecuador into Peru south to Tacna at c. 18°S. Apparently mainly on the western Andean slope in Peru but also reported from the Marañón Valley south to Ayacucho and Apurímac in the central Andes. Generally resident but seasonal visitor to some areas. Patchily common, even abundant, but scarce or absent in many areas; scarcer in south. Range contraction in some parts (e.g. Colombia) owing to habitat loss. Trapped for

live bird trade with 16,644 exported from Peru in 1982 alone.

ECOLOGY Inhabits moist and humid forest (including cloud-forest and second growth with *Acacia*, *Prosopis* and *Ochroma*) mostly in the upper tropical and lower subtropical zones but also penetrating the subtemperate zone. In Peru, reported from semi-arid cloud-forest. Reported at lower elevations in humid plantations, cornfields and cactus scrub. Key habitat requirement is cliffs for breeding and roosting. Generally to 2,000m but ranges above 3,000m in Peru. Gregarious, generally in flocks of c. 20, sometimes up to 300. Roosts communally on cliffs with diurnal movements to feeding areas. Diet comprises a variety of fruits, nuts and seeds; can include grain crops and fruit plantations. Generally feeds in canopy. Nests colonially on rocky cliffs. Breeding reported late Dec-Jun in northern Colombia and Apr-Jun in Venezuela. Clutch undescribed.

DESCRIPTION Forehead and crown bright red; lores and cheeks dark grass-green with scattered red feathers in some birds. Nape to uppertail-coverts dark grass-green. Upperwing-coverts dark grass-green; flight feathers green tinged emerald above, olive-yellow below and on greater underwing-coverts, remaining underwing-coverts green. Underparts yellowish-green, sometimes with scattered red feathers on throat and thighs. Uppertail dark green; undertail olive-green. **Bare parts**: Bill pale horn; bare periophthalmic ring grey; iris yellow; legs brownish.

SEX/AGE Sexes similar. Immature with reduced (or even absent) red feathers on head.

MEASUREMENTS Wing 171-191; tail 134-158; bill 26-29; tarsus 17-20.

GEOGRAPHICAL VARIATION Four races.
  A. w. wagleri (NW Venezuela and W Colombia from west side of E Andean cordillera south to N Nariño)
  A. w. transilis (Coastal mountains of N Venezuela east to Paria Peninsula, Sucre. Possibly recorded from Belén, Caquetá, on the eastern slope of the E Andean Cordillera in Colombia. Occurrence in relation to nominate unclear) Darker than nominate with red less extensive posteriorly on crown. Smaller than *wagleri* (c. 34cm).
  A. w. frontata (W Ecuador and Peru south to about 18°S) Red on head more extensive than in nominate, extending to posterior of eye. Red thighs and bend of wing in most birds. Larger than nominate (c. 40cm).
  A. w. minor (Marañón Valley south to Ayacucho and Apurímac in C Andes of Peru) Like *frontata* but smaller (c. 38cm) and greener with paler red feathers. Some specimens with yellow at bend of wing.

REFERENCES Arndt (1996), Bond (1955), Chapman (1917), Fjeldså & Krabbe (1990), Forshaw (1989), Hilty & Brown (1986), Koepcke (1961, 1983), Meyer de Schauensee (1949), Meyer de Schauensee & Phelps (1978), Morrison (1947), Parker *et al.* (1982), Ridgely (1982), Ridgely *in litt.* (1997), Todd & Carriker (1922), Wetmore (1939).

232 MITRED CONURE
Aratinga mitrata   **Plate 57**

IDENTIFICATION 38cm. Mainly green, duller and paler beneath with olive suffusion. Forehead brownish-red merging to bright red on crown, lores and cheeks. Scattered red feathers throughout but especially on neck and bend of wing. Underwing-coverts green. Sympatric race *minor* of Red-fronted Conure (231) has green cheeks, red (not brownish-red) forehead and red feathers at bend of wing. White-eyed Conure (235), sympatric in Peru, northern Argentina and Bolivia, has red and yellow underwing-coverts. Blue-crowned Conure (228), sympatric in eastern Bolivia and extreme north-western Argentina, has blue (not red) crown. Nominate Mitred separable from all other green conures in captivity by combination of red cheeks and olive-green underwing-coverts. Small macaws have bare lores and cheeks.

VOICE Strident *weee weee queiiee queiiee weee weee* and loud, rather abrupt *cheeah cheeah* call that has faint toy trumpet quality. Deeper and harsher than Red-fronted Conure.

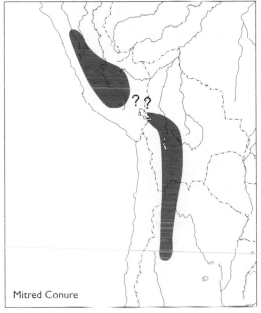

Mitred Conure

DISTRIBUTION AND STATUS South-western South America from southern Peru through western central Bolivia to northern Argentina. In large valleys of central Peru from Huánuco (10°S) to Cuzco. Appears to occur disjunctly in valleys of eastern Andes of western-central Bolivia, where reported from La Paz, Santa Cruz, Cochabamba, Oruro, Padilla and Sucre south to north-west Argentina in Jujuy, Salta, Tucumán and Catamarca south (doubtfully) to La Rioja and Córdoba. Generally resident but some seasonal movements are reported in northern Argentina and Bolivia. Locally distributed within overall range although more widespread south of Cochabamba, Bolivia. In Argentina generally common, abundant in some localities (apparently most numerous in Catamarca and Salta), but perhaps in overall decline. Held in captivity and traded in large numbers internationally (mainly from Bolivia) in late 1980s. Race *alticola* apparently rare.

ECOLOGY Generally in dry subtropical vegetation but also recorded from temperate zone: montane deciduous forest, drier cloud-forest, cultivated areas, grassy hills with tall herbs, bushy areas with fields and scattered trees and leguminaceous savanna with dry fields and patches of *Prosopis* woodland. Often near tall, steep rockfaces. Usually from 1,000 to 2,500m in Argentina but recorded to 4,000m (possibly *A. m. alticola*) in Peru. Rarely, if ever, descends to lowlands. Commonly in groups of 2-3 but up to 100 outside breeding season. Generally feeds in areas of natural forest but also takes grain. This and other parrots migrate to Lerma valley in north-western Argentina to feed on ripening berries, Oct. Nests in cliff or in tree-hollow. Eggs reported Dec at Orán, Argentina. Clutch probably 2-3.

DESCRIPTION Forehead brownish-red merging to bright red on forecrown; lores and cheeks to behind eyes bright red; sides of neck dark green with scattered red feathers. Upperparts from hindcrown to uppertail-coverts dark green sometimes with a few scattered red feathers (especially on nape). Upperwing-coverts and flight feathers (above) dark green sometimes with one or two red feathers at bend of wing; flight feathers brownish-olive below. Underwing-coverts dull green. Underparts dull, paler green with olive tinge, usually with scattered red markings, especially on thighs. Uppertail dark green with brownish tips; undertail brownish. **Bare parts**: Bill whitish; bare periophthalmic ring creamy-white; iris orange-yellow; legs brownish.

SEX/AGE Sexes similar. Immature with reduced red feathers on head, especially cheeks, and brown (not orange) iris.

MEASUREMENTS Wing 192-207; tail 156-182; bill 29-32; tarsus 19-21.

GEOGRAPHICAL VARIATION Two races.
> *A. m. mitrata* (C and S Peru through C Bolivia south to NW Argentina)
> *A. m. alticola* (Temperate zone of C Peru in Cuzco region) Darker than nominate with red on head restricted to forehead with scattered red feathers on lores, neck and sides of head. No red on thighs.

NOTE The high-altitude race *alticola* possibly merits specific status; the nominate form closely approaches its type locality.

REFERENCES Cabot & Serrano (1988), Fjeldså & Krabbe (1990), Forshaw (1989), Hoy (1968), Morrison (1947), Narosky & Yzurieta (1989), Nores & Yzurieta (1994), Parker *et al.* (1982), de la Peña (1988), Ridgely (1981).

233 RED-MASKED CONURE
Aratinga erythrogenys   **Plate 57**

Other names: Red-headed Conure

IDENTIFICATION 33cm. Mainly green conure with striking red head and red underwing-coverts. Paler and more yellowish beneath. Partly sympatric (but ecologically separated) race *frontata* of Red-fronted Conure (231) distinguished by green underwing-coverts and cheeks. Red-masked separated from other mainly green conures in captivity by red extending to behind eyes and over cheeks (joining at chin in most birds), large red patch at bend of wing with red underwing-coverts. Small macaws have bare lores and cheeks.

VOICE Trilling *screee-ah* or *squeee-ee-at* and louder, more excited *screet* calls with distinct nasal quality. Rasping call with second note more drawn-out and buzzing sounds also reported. Flocks create loud chorus of calls.

Red-masked Conure

DISTRIBUTION AND STATUS Western Ecuador and extreme north-west Peru. In Ecuador the species has been recorded from Manabí close to the Equator south through Pichincha, Los Ríos, Guayas, Azuay, El Oro and Loja to Tumbes, Piura, Lambayeque and Cajamarca in northern Peru as far as the Chachapoyas region, Amazonas (6°10'S). In Ecuador it is confined to the Pacific lowlands, western slope of the Andes and inter-Andean valleys but is apparently absent from eastern slope; similar pattern in Peru bit most easterly record in Amazon catchment (Río Utcubamba valley) at 77°54'W. Seasonal movements to and from more arid areas, otherwise resident. Usually considered common (described as commonest parrot at several localities in El Oro province, Ecuador), but numbers fluctuate widely in some localities owing to irregular seasonal movements; moreover, genuine and in some areas quite drastic decline has occurred, reflecting combined effects of habitat loss and collection for live bird trade, e.g. in Guayas, Ecuador. Reported from at least eight protected areas, seven of which are in Ecuador. Kept in captivity locally (where it is most frequent captive parrot) and traded in large numbers internationally, especially from Peru. NEAR-THREATENED.

ECOLOGY This conure occupies a range of arid to humid vegetation types from sea-level to 2,500m but more usually below c. 1,000m: humid evergreen forest, deciduous forest, dry thorny scrub to open desert with cacti; also degraded

forests, farmed areas with scattered trees, and around urban areas. It tends to prefer arid and semi-arid habitats but former view that moist forest habitats are avoided seems mistaken. Gregarious, especially outside breeding season; generally in pairs or groups up to 12 birds, with aggregations of c. 200 at communal roosts. Flocks of several thousand previously reported from Guayaquil, Ecuador, no longer occur. Often associates in mixed flocks with Grey-cheeked Parakeets (284) and has been noted in mixed flocks with Bronze-winged Parrots (318). Few details exist on feeding preferences but seasonal movements from more arid areas are probably related to food supply. Reported foods include fruits of *Hyeronima*, Anacardiaceae, Oleaceae and Boraginaceae, flowers of *Erythrina*. Nests in hole in mature (e.g.) *Ceiba trichistandra* or *Cochlospermum vitifolium* or in termite nest, with one report of cliff-nesting. Breeds south-west Ecuador in the rainy season (Jan-Mar). Clutch 2-4.

DESCRIPTION Forehead, crown, lores, cheeks and area around eyes bright red, usually forming complete mask joining at chin (sometimes extending to red throat-patch). Nape to uppertail-coverts dark grass-green, sometimes with scattered red feathers. Lesser upperwing-coverts with some red feathers and bend of wing red; remaining upperwing dark grass-green, with emerald tinge to outerwebs of primaries. Flight feathers golden-brown below; lesser underwing-coverts bright red, greater yellowish-brown. Underparts yellowish-green sometimes with red flecking and almost always with red thighs. Uppertail dark grass-green; undertail greyish-brown. **Bare parts:** Bill pale horn; bare periophthalmic ring whitish; iris yellow; legs brownish.

SEX/AGE Sexes similar. Immature with green head and thighs.

MEASUREMENTS Wing 171-186; tail 138-150; bill 26-29; tarsus 18-20.

GEOGRAPHICAL VARIATION None.

REFERENCES Best & Clarke (1991), Best *et al.* (1993, 1995), Forshaw (1989), Kiff (1989), Marchant (1958), Parker *et al.* (1982), Ridgely (1981), Rutgers & Norris (1979), Williams & Tobias (1994).

234 FINSCH'S CONURE
Aratinga finschi   Plate 58

Other names: Crimson-fronted Parakeet

IDENTIFICATION 25-28cm. Mainly green conure (paler beneath) with conspicuous red and yellow underwing-coverts and red forehead and front of lores. For separation from partly sympatric Olive-throated Conure (242) see under that species. Adult Finsch's separable from other green *Aratinga* in captivity by combination of red forehead and red and yellow underwing-coverts. From all small macaws by feathered lores and cheeks. In tight, twisting, fast-flying flocks on rapid shallow wingbeats, birds may resemble waders over mudflats.

VOICE Varied repertoire. Most frequent call a dry strident *kih-kih-kih-keh-keh*, with high-pitched, sometimes trilling *cheee-at cheee-at* in flight. Also has shrill chattering sounds, whistled chirps and squawks, a scolding *scree-ah*, some squeaky calls and (at communal roost) a rattling frog-like noise. Some calls have vibrating quality recalling a small macaw, others are a mixture of harsh and melodious sounds. Chorusing flock sometimes creates jangling metallic cacophony.

Finsch's Conure

DISTRIBUTION AND STATUS Southern Central America from Nicaragua to Panama. The species occurs in south-eastern Nicaragua south of the Río Grande, and in Costa Rica mostly on the Caribbean slope although on the Pacific side resident on Península de Osa in the far south-west and a seasonal visitor to the Cordillera Guanacaste in the north and on the central plateau around San José. In Panama it reaches east to about 82°W but is probably only seasonal in the lower highlands of Chiriquí. Flocks range over wide areas and the species evidently occurs in many areas only as a post-breeding visitor. Mostly common or locally common with numbers increasing in Costa Rica and Panama, probably owing to deforestation. Kept in captivity and traded internationally in small numbers.

ECOLOGY Inhabits tropical and subtropical zones to 1,400m in Costa Rica and 1,600m in western Panama, in lightly wooded or open country with scattered trees, secondary growth, woodland edge, coffee plantations and cultivated land; only irregular or seasonal in extensively forested areas. Gregarious, generally in flocks of up to 30, but up to several hundred, drawn from wide catchment area, gather at communal roosts in tops of trees or palms. Roost-sites (sometimes near towns) are traditional but disturbance causes abandonment. Recorded foods include flowers and fruits of *Erythrina* and *Inga*, fruits of *Croton*, *Zanthoxylum* and *Ficus* and grain such as sorghum and maize. Marked declines in roost sizes, Jul, Panama, suggests birds are then breeding, perhaps in more wooded country; but no nest has been recorded.

DESCRIPTION Forehead and anterior lores bright red; head and neck otherwise green except for scattered red feathers. Upperparts and upperwing-coverts grass-green, with red feathers at bend of wing. Flight feathers green above, darker towards tips with faint bluish tinge on innerwebs, golden-brown below. Lesser and median underwing-coverts red, greater yellow, other coverts pale green. Underparts pale green, sometimes with red on lower tibia. Uppertail grass-green; undertail golden-brown. **Bare parts** Bill pinkish-horn with tip and cutting edge of upper mandible greyish; bare periophthalmic ring whitish; iris orange; legs grey.

SEX/AGE Sexes similar. Immature lacks red on forehead, anterior lores, tibia and scattered markings of adult; underwing-coverts more orange.

MEASUREMENTS Wing 162-176; tail 132-139; bill 25-27; tarsus 17-20.

GEOGRAPHICAL VARIATION None.

NOTE Some authors treat this species as a race of White-eyed Conure (235; see under that species).

REFERENCES Forshaw (1989), Howell (1957), Ridgely & Gwynne (1989), Rutgers & Norris (1979), Slud (1964), Stiles *et al.* (1989), Wetmore (1968).

235 WHITE-EYED CONURE
Aratinga leucophthalmus　　　Plate 57

Other names: All-green Conure, Green Conure, White-eyed Parakeet

IDENTIFICATION 32cm. Mainly green conure with conspicuous yellow and red underwing-coverts and bright red on bend of wing. From sympatric Blue-crowned Conure (228) by yellow and red underwing-coverts and voice. From Mitred Conure (232), marginally sympatric in Bolivia and Argentina, by green forehead and coloured underwing-coverts. Combination of green crown and forehead with yellow and red underwing-coverts and red at bend of wing separates White-eyed from other mainly green conures in captivity. Rather similar (allopatric) adult Cuban Conure (236) separated by olive tinge to yellowish greater underwing-coverts. From all small macaws, notably Red-shouldered (223), by feathered lores and cheeks. Often seen in small parties in swift straight flight at some height over trees or rivers.

VOICE Varied repertoire. Calls include a loud penetrating *neeep neeep*, shrieking *scree-ah screet scree* and scolding, grating *scraaah scraaah*. More melodious chirruping notes sometimes accompany or replace harsher cries, e.g. flight calls are sometimes completed with distinctive melodious trill, and flocks sometimes produce chorus of chirrups and trills that lack any grating quality. Voice higher-pitched than Red-shouldered Macaw.

DISTRIBUTION AND STATUS Most widespread *Aratinga* conure, found throughout South America east of the Andes south to northern Argentina. It occurs from the Guianas (not Guyana) west disjunctly through Venezuela (from Anzoátegui and Monagas through Delta Amacuro to Bolívar and Amazonas) to Amazonian Colombia (north to northern Meta), Ecuador and Peru. It ranges through all inland Brazil and possibly reaches the coast in São Paulo and Rio Grande do Sul (but absent in the arid north-east, mountainous areas of the northern Amazon basin in Brazil and Venezuela, and the Rio Negro catchment in Brazil and Colombia). It occurs in eastern Bolivia through Paraguay to Argentina south to Santa Fe and Entre Ríos (possibly northern Buenos Aires) including Tucumán and Catamarca (no recent reports from Catamarca or Santa Fe while reports from Santiago del Estero, Córdoba and San Luis are probably erroneous). It is also found in higher parts of Uruguay. Generally resident but some seasonal movements seem to occur in some areas. Most numerous in centre of range, less so at edges. Locally abundant in central Amazonia and Mato Grosso, Brazil, and in eastern

Peru. Common in Colombia. Fairly common in coastal Surinam and gallery forests of Santa Cruz, Bolivia. Patchily distributed in northern Bolivia where variously described as common to uncommon. Common in Argentina, especially in north. Large captive population with high volume of international trade (particularly from Argentina where the species is perhaps at some threat from trapping).

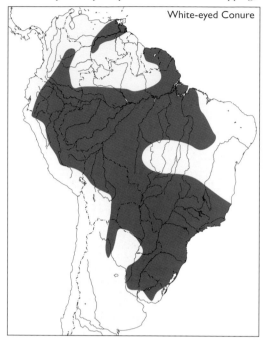

White-eyed Conure

ECOLOGY This species occurs in a range of mainly lowland forest and woodland habitats, but reaches 1,700m in Ecuador and 2,500m in Bolivia. In Amazonia, it is found in tropical rain-forest mostly adjacent to rivers (including várzea forest), scattered woodland and cultivated land in the pantanals, mangroves, savanna and palms in the Guianas, chaco-type woodland in the south of its range, gallery and floodplain forests in Bolivia. Highly gregarious, commonly forming flocks of several hundred birds (more usually up to 30) which range widely between roosts and feeding areas. In Amazonia, birds generally travel along banks of rivers but also cross large tracts of forest to reach hidden oxbows and marshes. Roosts in large communal gatherings in trees, canefields and caves. Associates with Blue-crowned Conure, Blue-headed Parrot (313), Chestnut-fronted Macaw (218) and Crimson-bellied Conure (252) in mixed flocks, mostly whilst foraging. Diet depends on habitat but includes wide variety of nuts, seeds, fruits, berries, flowers and insects. Generally forages in canopy but grass seeds also taken. Reported foods include fruits of palms and *Goupia glabra, Tetragastris altissima* and *Allantoma lineata,* and *Erythrina* and *Ficus* flowers. Nest usually in high tree-cavity (often a palm) but also in limestone caverns in Mato Grosso, Brazil. Breeding reported Nov-Dec, Argentina; Jul-Aug, eastern Peru; Jan-Apr, Mato Grosso; Feb, Guianas. Clutch 2-4.

DESCRIPTION Head dark grass-green with scattered red feathers, especially on lores, cheeks, sides of neck and throat, the head and nape of some birds showing almost entirely green, others solid red blotches on cheeks with numerous scattered red feathers elsewhere. Upperparts dark grass-green with one or two scattered red feathers. Upperwing dark grass-green with some red at bend of wing; underwing with golden-brown flight feathers, red outer and green inner lesser coverts, yellow outer and green inner greater coverts. Underparts grass-green with scattered red feathers on throat and breast, sometimes forming distinct patches. Uppertail dark green; undertail brownish. **Bare parts**: Bill pinkish-yellow; bare peri-ophthalmic ring greyish-white; iris yellowish-orange; legs grey.

SEX/AGE Sexes similar. Immature has few red feathers on head, no red at bend of wing, olive outermost greater underwing-coverts.

MEASUREMENTS Wing 166-188; tail 134-162; bill 24-28; tarsus 17-20.

GEOGRAPHICAL VARIATION Two races. The name *propinquus* has been applied to supposedly larger birds from SE Brazil, but this population is apparently continuous with nominate and it appears at best a clinal variant. A single specimen taken in the north of Meta, Colombia, bears the name *nicefori* and is argued to be intermediate between White-eyed and Finsch's Conure (234), causing these two to be treated as conspecific. However, in the absence of further information, this specimen is regarded here as an aberrant *callogenys* (which it resembles). Further confusion arises from apparent tendency for White-eyed Conures to show wide size variation over relatively small areas.

　　A. l. leucophthalmus (Guianas south to Argentina and west to Amazon basin)
　　A. l. callogenys (W Amazon basin from SE Colombia and extreme NW Brazil south into Amazonian Ecuador and Peru. Evidently intergrades with nominate in central Amazon basin where birds pass for either race) On average larger than nominate with more robust bill. Birds in west darker green.

REFERENCES Arndt (1996), Belton (1984), Bond (1955), Bond & Meyer de Schauensee (1942), Chapman (1926), Contreras *et al.* (1991), Cuello & Gerzenstein (1962), Dubs (1992), Forshaw (1989), Gyldenstolpe (1945a,b), Haffer & Fitzpatrick (1985), Haverschmidt & Barruel (1968), Hilty & Brown (1986), Meyer de Schauensee (1966), Narosky & Yzurieta (1989), Naumburg (1930), Nores & Yzurieta (1994), Parker (1991, 1993), de la Peña (1988), Short (1975), Sick (1993), Snyder (1966).

236 CUBAN CONURE
Aratinga euops　　　　　　　　Plate 58

Other names: Red-speckled Conure, Cuban Parakeet

IDENTIFICATION 26cm. Mainly green, with rather delicate build for genus. Paler and more yellowish beneath with scattered red markings on head, neck, nape and underside, red at carpal area and leading edge of wing, with red and olive-yellow underwing-coverts. Confined to Cuba where no confusion species exist. From other largely green adult *Aratinga* in captivity by combination of green forehead and red and olive-yellow underwing-coverts. Similar adult White-eyed Conure (235) is larger and bulkier with brighter yellow greater underwing-coverts. In small groups or family parties generally in treetops or in fast direct flight. Usually detected in foliage by chattering call. Quite tame.

VOICE Almost continuous shrill screeching given in flight. Chattering or squawking sounds whilst at rest. Also high-pitched piping trills.

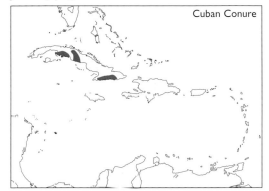
Cuban Conure

DISTRIBUTION AND STATUS Formerly one of the commonest endemic birds of Cuba and the Isle of Pines but now limited to several strongholds in remoter parts of Cuba including Península de Zapata, the district around Cienfuegos and the Trinidad Mountains in the west-central part of island, and Sierra Maestra in the extreme east. Resident but some seasonal (perhaps altitudinal) movement suggested by birds descending from Trinidad Mountains, Sep Oct. Extinct Isle of Pines by 1913, owing principally to heavy trapping for live export, and now generally rare in Cuba, the decline attributed to habitat loss, trade and persecution as pest. The present population, although comparatively tiny, is perhaps stable. The species occurs in very few protected areas; most important is Ciénaga de Zapata National Park. Small numbers in captivity outside Cuba, especially eastern Europe. International trade currently small. VULNERABLE.

ECOLOGY Inhabits savanna mostly where *Copernica* and *Thrinax* palms occur, woodland edge and cultivated land with trees. Although reported from heavily modified habitats, such as eucalyptus groves in open country and degraded evergreen forest fragments in palm savanna, the species survives only near large tracts of primary forest. Generally in family parties or small flocks but sometimes larger gatherings of several hundred are reported, birds will mix with the commoner endemic White-headed Amazon (320). Diet consists of fruits of mango, papaya, guava, *Roystonea* palms, *Melicoccus bijugatus* and *Spondias luteus*, and seeds of *Inga vera* and, on Isle of Pines, *Pinus caribbea*; shoots, millet, berries and grass seeds also taken. Previously persecuted for extensive damage of orange, coffee and maize crops. Nests, sometimes semi-colonially, in hollow palm (e.g. *Sabal florida*), tree-cavity or active arboreal termite nests, with woodpecker holes, particularly of Cuban Green Woodpecker *Xiphidiopicus percussus*, favoured. Egg-laying May-Jul. Clutch 2-5, usually three.

DESCRIPTION Head, sides of neck and nape grass-green with scattered red feathers sometimes forming blotches. Upperparts and upperwing grass-green, primaries and secondaries with dark green tips and margins to innerwebs; carpal edge with scattered red feathers and leading edge of wing red. Underwing with golden-brown flight feathers, red lesser and median coverts and olive-yellow greater coverts. Underparts yellowish-green with

olive suffusion, sometimes with scattered red feathers, especially on throat and/or thighs. Uppertail dark green with olive tinge; undertail yellowish-brown. **Bare parts**: Bill horn; conspicuous periophthalmic skin bluish-white; iris yellow; legs brownish.

SEX/AGE Female has more orange underwing-coverts. Immature has green and red underwing-coverts, yellowish (not red) carpal edge, grey iris and no scattered red feathers.

MEASUREMENTS Wing 132-147; tail 119-132; bill 18-19; tarsus 13-16.

GEOGRAPHICAL VARIATION None.

REFERENCES Barbour (1923), Bond (1958), Collar *et al.* (1992, 1994), Forshaw (1989), Silva (1981), Todd (1916).

---

237 HISPANIOLAN CONURE
Aratinga chloroptera   Plate 58

Other names: San Domingo Conure, Hispaniolan Parakeet

IDENTIFICATION 32cm. Mainly green conure, paler beneath, with conspicuous red underwing-coverts and red leading edge to wing. Scattered red feathers on head, neck or underparts. No confusion species in natural range. Difficult to detect in foliage where birds remain hidden and silent if disturbed. Often encountered in noisy flocks travelling in fast and direct flight. In captivity, adult separated from other largely green *Aratinga* conures by combination of red underwing-coverts and green head, similar White-eyed (235) and Green (229) Conures separated by yellow and red and yellowish-green underwing-coverts respectively. Introduced Olive-throated Conure (242) has prominent blue band on length of wing, no red in plumage.

VOICE Shrill screeching cries in flight. No other details

Hispaniolan Conure

DISTRIBUTION AND STATUS Confined to Haiti and Dominican Republic, Hispaniola, Greater Antilles. Formerly on Mona Island (*A. h. maugei*), extinct between 1892 and 1901, probably as result of hunting pressure and possibly disturbance from blasting at guano mine; possibly also once on Puerto Rico, where if ever present probably extinct by end of 19th century, most likely to habitat loss and hunting. On Hispaniola major and continuing decline owing to habitat destruction, trade and persecution, especially in Haiti where possibly now extinct. In Dominican Republic still apparently occurs in a few upland areas, e.g. Cordillera Central. Possibly small feral populations in Puerto Rico and Florida. Small numbers in captivity outside range and small volume international trade probably continues. VULNERABLE.

ECOLOGY This species occupies all kinds of natural habitat from arid lowland forest to palm savanna, but evidently prefers upland (including *Pinus*-dominated) forest to 3,000m, ranging sparsely (perhaps owing to persecution) into adjacent cultivated areas. Generally in pairs or small flocks but sometimes (at least in past when more abundant) in gatherings of over a hundred. Pairs discernible within even large flocks. Few details exist on diet but apparently similar to congeners and comprised of locally available fruits, seeds, nuts, buds, flowers and grain, specific recorded items including figs *Ficus* and maize. Nests in tree-cavity (including old woodpecker hole) or arboreal termitaria. Clutch 3-5 (exceptionally seven).

DESCRIPTION Entire head and sides of neck grass-green with a few scattered red feathers. Upperparts and upper-wing-coverts grass-green with extreme outer median-coverts red. Primaries and secondaries green with dark bluish-green tips and margins to innerwebs. Underwing with yellowish-brown flight feathers, more greyish towards tips, green coverts except red outer lesser and median coverts and green and red primary-coverts. Underparts yellowish-green usually with scattered red feathers. Upper-tail dark green; undertail brownish-grey. **Bare parts**: Bill horn; bare periophthalmic ring whitish; iris yellowish; legs brownish-grey.

SEX/AGE Sexes similar. Immature has less red and more green on underwing-coverts, no red on upper surface of leading edge of wing and grey at base of bill and on cutting edge.

MEASUREMENTS Wing 167-185; tail 120-151; bill 26-27; tarsus 16-20.

GEOGRAPHICAL VARIATION Two races have been described, but the now extinct *maugei* from Mona (and possibly Puerto Rico), duller beneath with more red on underwing-coverts, may not be valid.

REFERENCES Bond (1956, 1974), Collar *et al.* (1994), Dod (1992), Forshaw (1989), Terborgh & Faaborg (1973), Silva (1991), Wetmore & Swales (1931), Wiley (1991).

---

238 SUN CONURE
Aratinga solstitialis   Plate 59

Other names: Yellow Conure

IDENTIFICATION 30cm. Mainly bright yellow with blue and green flight feathers. No confusion species in wild but told from allopatric Golden Conure (227) in captivity by lighter build, orange tinge to breast and belly, black bill, reddish lores and ocular region, partly blue (not entirely green) flight feathers and brownish and blue uppertail. Small noisy flocks travel in swift direct flight. Birds surprisingly inconspicuous when perched quietly in foliage.

VOICE A high, shrill, grating, two-note *screeek screeek*, repeated 3-6 times in rapid succession between pauses. Also wheezy notes and chuckling sounds.

DISTRIBUTION AND STATUS North-eastern South America. The species ranges from Mount Roraima in extreme northern Brazil (a single 1848 record previously attributed to Venezuela), adjacent Pacaraima Mountains, Venezuela, and Guyana north to Pomeroon River, east through Surinam (apparently unknown in north) and French Guiana to Brazil in Amapá, Pará and eastern Amazonas (western limits around Rio Branco catchment, and locally south of the Amazon from around Santarém to region of Rio Canumá). Although generally regarded as common, sporadic records suggest local occurrence within large range. Kept for pets locally and trapped for live bird trade.

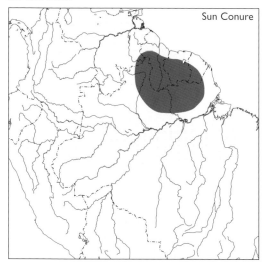

Sun Conure

ECOLOGY Generally in savanna or dry forest with palm groves but also locally in seasonally flooded (várzea) scrub on both banks of Amazon, below 1,200m. Generally in flocks of up to c. 30 birds, with larger aggregations at fruiting trees. Diet is poorly documented but expected to consist of locally available fruit, berries, nuts, buds and flowers, etc., known items including legume pods, small melastomataceous fruits, red cacti fruits and possibly *Malpighia* berries. Nests in tree or palm cavity (e.g. *Mauritia*). Nest with single chick Feb, Surinam. Clutch around four.

DESCRIPTION Lores, ocular region and ear-coverts variably rich yellow to bright orange-red; forehead, crown and nape rich bright yellow with orange tinge shading to bright yellow on mantle, back and rump; uppertail-coverts yellow with odd blue feather. Scapulars green with blue tips and innerwebs; lesser and median coverts yellow with variable green markings; greater coverts green tipped yellow, primary coverts blue. Flight feathers green above, primaries with blue tips and innerwebs; grey-brown below. Underwing-coverts yellow (or orange and yellow). Throat orange shading to yellow on upper breast; lower breast and belly orange; flanks, vent and undertail-coverts yellow. Uppertail mainly yellowish-green with blue tips; undertail grey with yellowish tinge. **Bare parts**: Bill dark brownish-black; iris dark brown to black; legs brownish.

SEX/AGE Sexes similar. Immature generally duller than adult with yellow on head and body replaced with dull greenish-orange. Lesser and median upperwing-coverts green.

MEASUREMENTS Wing 146-162; tail 121-146; bill 19-25; tarsus 16-18.

GEOGRAPHICAL VARIATION None.

NOTE The Sun Conure is frequently treated as conspecific with Jandaya Conure (239) and Golden-capped Conure (240). However, given (a) that these three are morphologically and behaviourally different, (b) that intermediate forms are unknown and hybrids uncommon, even in the narrow contact zone between Golden-capped and Jandaya Conures in Goiás, Brazil, and (c) that apparent Sun/Jandaya intergradation in the lower Amazon may actually reflect age-related differences and individual variation, they are here treated as three allospecies.

REFERENCES Brown (1974), Forshaw (1989), Haverschmidt (1968), Joseph (1992), Meyer de Schauensee (1966), Meyer de Schauensee & Phelps (1978), Ridgely (1981), Sick (1993), Snyder (1966).

239 JANDAYA CONURE
Aratinga jandaya   Plate 59

Other names: Jenday Conure, Jendaya Conure, Yellow-headed Conure (Parakeet), Flaming Parakeet

IDENTIFICATION 30cm. Very distinctive, with underparts deep orange-red becoming slightly paler and yellower towards head; crown yellowish-orange. Upperparts green with blue in wing and tail. Distinguished from partly sympatric Blue-crowned (228), White-eyed (235), Peach-fronted (244) and Cactus (246) Conures by orange underparts and yellow crown. Rather similar (but much scarcer) Golden-capped Conure (240) distinguished in marginal contact zone in Goiás by green upper breast and throat. From Sun Conure (238) in captivity by green back and upperwing coverts. Generally in small noisy flocks in caatinga woodland or scrub, sometimes in taller humid forest. Shy and difficult to detect in vegetation. Flight swift, often quite close to ground with sudden changes of direction.

VOICE In captivity shrill screeching *kink-kink-kank* with last note higher in pitch. Noisy shrill calls in flight.

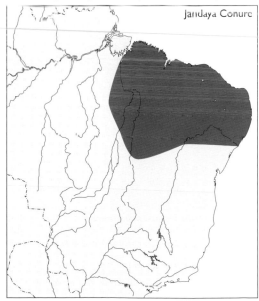
Jandaya Conure

DISTRIBUTION AND STATUS North-eastern Brazil. The species extends from around Belém, north-eastern Pará, and São Luís, Maranhão, south to northern and eastern Goiás and east through Piauí, Ceará, Rio Grande do Norte, Paraíba, Pernambuco, Alagoas and probably extreme northern Bahia. Locally common and, although perhaps declining in some areas, it may generally be extending its range through colonisation of areas cleared of moist high forest, especially in Pará and Maranhão. Status in east of range unknown. Held in captivity with perhaps serious consequences arising from undocumented illegal internal Brazilian trade and possibly smuggling to South-East Asia.

ECOLOGY Transitional deciduous woodland, cerrado, scrub and areas cleared of moist forest. Sporadically at edge of humid forest and caatinga. In coconut palms in coastal Pernambuco; also frequents farmland and pasture. Generally in flocks of c. 12 birds but sometimes in pairs or singly. Reported foods include seeds, berries and fruits of certain Melastomataceae, *Mangifera*, *Mauritia* palms and *Cecropia*; birds may damage maize crops. Nests in tree-cavity at least 15m from ground. Young in nest Dec, Maranhão; breeds Aug-Dec, Belém area. Clutch probably three.

DESCRIPTION Sides of neck, cheeks, lores, ear-coverts and forehead orange, deeper on ear-coverts, around eyes and lores; crown and nape yellowish-orange (some birds with paler, more yellowish head). Mantle and scapulars olive-green; back and upper rump green with horizontal orange-red barring from red tipped green feathers; lower rump and uppertail-coverts olive-green. Primary-coverts blue, other coverts green (brighter than mantle). Flight feathers above blue on outerwebs, blackish towards tips; below grey. Underwing-coverts orange-red. Underparts deep orange-red, slightly paler on upper breast and throat; undertail-coverts green. Uppertail olive with blue tips; undertail charcoal-grey. **Bare parts**: Bill greyish-black, bare periophthalmic skin pale grey; iris brown; legs grey.

SEX/AGE Sexes similar. Immature has yellow head and neck with green markings; paler orange beneath.

MEASUREMENTS Wing 153-165; tail 129-146; bill 22-25; tarsus 15-18.

GEOGRAPHICAL VARIATION None.

NOTE Jandaya Conure is frequently treated as conspecific with Sun and Golden-capped Conures (see Note under Sun Conure).

REFERENCES Forshaw (1989), Meyer de Schauensee (1966), Ridgely (1981), Rutgers & Norris (1979), Sick (1993).

240 GOLDEN-CAPPED CONURE
Aratinga auricapilla   Plate 59

Other names: Golden-headed Conure, Flame-capped Parakeet, Golden-capped Parakeet, Gold-capped Conure

IDENTIFICATION 30cm. Red-bellied conure with green upper breast and throat, bright red forehead and yellow crown. Upperparts mostly green. Distinguished from overlapping Blue-crowned (228), White-eyed (235), Peach-fronted (244) and Cactus (246) Conures by dull red belly. The smaller, and partially sympatric, Maroon-bellied Conure (251) is separated by its barred pale breast and throat and red tip to tail. Similar Jandaya Conure (239), marginally sympatric in Goiás, lacks green upper breast and throat and is wholly orange-red beneath. Usually in pairs or flocks of 4-10 birds. Quite tame and approachable but birds difficult to locate in foliage.

VOICE Undescribed.

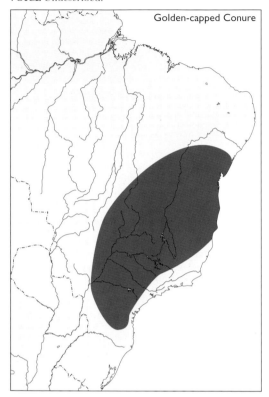

Golden-capped Conure

DISTRIBUTION AND STATUS South-eastern Brazil. The species ranges from northern Bahia, eastern Goiás and Minas Gerais east and south into coastal eastern Brazil (Espírito Santo, Rio de Janeiro, São Paulo, Paraná and possibly Santa Catarina). Listing of Rio Grande do Sul apparently mistaken, but the species may yet be found in extreme eastern Mato Grosso do Sul. Single 1918 record from Paraguay close to Paraná border may be of escaped birds. Generally uncommon and patchily distributed resident, extirpated in many places with present range defined by remaining forest. Most current strongholds are evidently in Minas Gerais, where the species was considered common in 1987 in remaining habitat fragments. It is very rare or extinct in Santa Catarina, Paraná, São Paulo, Rio de Janeiro and Espírito Santo, and scarce in Goiás and Bahia. The decline is due to continuing forest clearance and trapping for trade. Several protected areas including Monte Pascual National Park (Bahia) and Rio Doce State Park (Minas Gerais) hold populations. Rare in captivity, especially outside Brazil. VULNERABLE.

ECOLOGY Forest, forest edge and clearings in forest, including coastal moist evergreen Atlantic forest and natural deciduous and cerrado-type woodlands of interior. Apparently prefers primary formations. Scarce or absent from pastureland with trees or second growth, even in vicinity of remaining original forest. Reported to 2,180m (Serra do Caparaó, southern Espírito Santo). Gregarious,

generally in flocks of 12-20, more rarely 40. Diet comprises seeds and fruits, recorded foods including maize, okra and unspecified sweet soft fruits; the species was a crop pest in some areas before its precipitous decline to comparative rarity. There are few details on breeding ecology but nesting probably occurs Nov-Dec.

DESCRIPTION Lores, frontal band and ocular region bright red; crown bright golden-yellow; ear-coverts, cheeks and sides of neck green. Nape and mantle rather dull green; back and upper rump green variably tipped red or orange; lower rump and uppertail-coverts green. Lesser and median upperwing-coverts green; greater and primary-coverts, secondaries and outerwebs and tips of primaries blue. Underwing-coverts orange-red; underside of flight feathers grey. Chin and throat yellowish-green fading to greenish-orange on upper breast and dull deep red on belly; vent, thighs and undertail-coverts green. Uppertail brownish tipped blue, sometimes with outer-webs of outer feathers blue; undertail grey. **Bare parts**: Bill greyish-black; bare periophthalmic skin grey; iris yellowish; legs grey.

SEX/AGE Sexes similar. Immature has little or no red on rump, duller yellow crown, greener breast and less extensive red on belly.

MEASUREMENTS Wing 160-169; tail 128-152; bill 22-25; tarsus 16-18.

NOTE Golden-capped frequently treated as conspecific with Sun (238) and Jandaya Conures (see Note under Sun Conure).

GEOGRAPHICAL VARIATION Two races.
> *A. a. auricapilla* (N and C Bahia, Brazil)
> *A. a. aurifrons* (S Goiás, Minas Gerais and from Espírito Santo to Santa Catarina, Brazil. Birds in S Bahia intermediate between this race and nominate) Upperparts wholly green (no red margins to feathers on back and upper rump). Breast greener, lacking orange tinge of nominate.

REFERENCES Collar *et al.* (1992, 1994), Forshaw (1989), Ridgely (1981) Sick (1993).

---

241 DUSKY-HEADED CONURE
Aratinga weddellii   Plate 60

Other names: Dusky-headed Parakeet, Weddell's Conure, Dusky Conure

IDENTIFICATION 28cm. Only *Aratinga* conure with grey head; otherwise mainly green, darker above, more yellowish beneath. Blue in flight feathers and upperwing-coverts. Conspicuous large bare white ocular patch. Dull blue fringes to brownish-grey feathers gives head scaly appearance. Green underwing-coverts. Breast sometimes shows turquoise tinge. Widely sympatric White-eyed Conure (235) distinguished by red on head, greener underparts and conspicuous red and yellow underwing-coverts (see Voice). Grey head separates Dusky-headed from other congeners. In small flocks at forest edge (e.g. along rivers).

VOICE Mostly calls in flight, including nasal *je-eek*; usually quiet at rest. Call much less rasping and grating than sometimes similar-sounding White-eyed Conure.

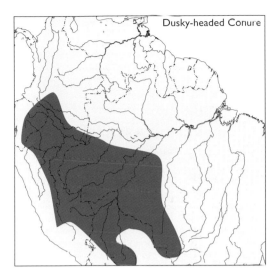

Dusky-headed Conure

DISTRIBUTION AND STATUS Western Amazon basin. The species occupies the tropical zone of south-east Colombia east of the Andes from Vaupés through Caquetá to eastern Oriente of Ecuador and south through northern and eastern Peru, penetrating western Amazonas, Acre, Rondônia and extreme north-western Mato Grosso, Brazil, and Bolivia south to Cochabamba. Apparently nomadic in some parts of range. Generally common, even in areas partially deforested and settled, and perhaps increasing owing to clearance and fragmentation of dense forest. Not common in captivity but formerly some international trade.

ECOLOGY Lowland, mainly water-associated forest, reported to 500m in Colombia and exceptionally at 750m in Bolivia. Evidently favours várzea and floodplain forest and tall growth in swamps. Also in forest remnants in humid savanna and cleared areas with remnant woodland patches. Also known from coffee and cane plantations; apparently seldom flies over dense forest. Usually in pairs or small parties but flocks of 75 reported where food abundant. Forages in canopy for wide range of seeds, fruits (e.g. of palms), flowers (e.g. of *Erythrina* and *Dioclea*) and berries, and on rotting branches for insects and their larvae. Visits exposed clay banks. Nests in cavity in tree (such as old woodpecker nest) or arboreal termite nest (four nests at Leticia, Colombia, 4-13m). Incubating bird Feb, Colombia. Bird in breeding condition Aug, Bolivia. Breeding Jun-Sep, Loreto, eastern Peru; Apr-Jul, Mato Grosso. Clutch 3-4.

DESCRIPTION Head brownish-grey, with dull blue fringes giving scaly appearance. Upperparts grass-green, feathers of nape with paler yellowish margins and some on mantle, back and rump with ginger or brownish centres, giving brownish appearance. Scapulars variably edged brown and green; lesser, median and inner greater coverts grass-green with paler green margins; outer greater and primary coverts dark blue. Primaries and secondaries mostly blue with green outerwebs or green margin to outerweb on primaries; very dark (almost black) tips. Underwing-coverts green; underside of flight feathers dull grey. Breast pale green with turquoise suffusion; belly and undertail-coverts pale yellowish-green, greener on flanks. Uppertail green, blue towards tips; undertail dull grey. **Bare parts**: Bill shiny black; cere pinkish-grey; broad bare peri-ophthalmic patch white; iris yellowish-white; legs dark grey.

SEX/AGE Sexes similar. Immature like adult but iris dark.

MEASUREMENTS Wing 136-152; tail 97-119; bill 20-22; tarsus 15-18.

GEOGRAPHICAL VARIATION None.

REFERENCES Arndt (1996), Bond & Meyer de Schauensee (1942), Dubs (1992), Forshaw (1989), Gyldenstolpe (1945a,b), Hilty & Brown (1986), Meyer de Schauensee (1949, 1966), Naumburg (1930), Parker (1991), Ridgely (1981), Sick (1993).

---

242 OLIVE-THROATED CONURE
Aratinga nana   Plate 56

Other names: Aztec Parakeet (*A. n. astec*)

IDENTIFICATION 23cm. Mainly green conure, brownish and olive beneath with prominent blue band along length of wing. From sympatric (in Mexican Gulf lowlands to Nicaragua) Green Conure (229) by brownish (not green) underparts and blue flight feathers, and (on Caribbean slope from Nicaragua to Panama) Finsch's Conure (234) by green (not red) forehead, blue on flight feathers, tendency to smaller flock size and habit of remaining below forest canopy or in tops of small trees. Orange-fronted Conure (243), overlapping in Comayagua valley and other localities in Honduras (and perhaps marginally in Tehuantepec isthmus, Mexico, and in eastern central Guatemala) distinguished by voice and orange patch on forehead. Combination of brownish and olive underparts with dark blue outerwebs to flight feathers separates Olive-throated from congeners in captivity.

VOICE Noisy shrieking chatter rising in pitch at end. High-pitched *screek* similar to White-crowned Parrot (317). Also melodious trilling interspersed with harsher grating chatter, and chirps and cry recalling Boat-billed Flycatcher *Megarhynchus pitangua* also reported. Voice generally less strident than Green Conure. Flocks create loud excited chorus.

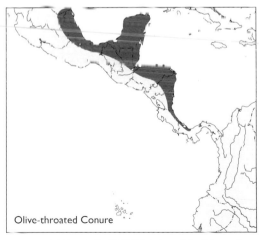

Olive-throated Conure

DISTRIBUTION AND STATUS Gulf and Caribbean slope of Middle America, and Jamaica. In Mexico the species ranges from eastern San Luis Potosí and southern Tamaulipas south through Veracruz to Oaxaca, northern Chiapas and Yucatán; then through humid northern

449

Guatemala and the Caribbean slope of Honduras, Nicaragua and Costa Rica to western Panama. It occurs throughout Jamaica except high mountains and the wet John Crow range in the east. Resident and locally common to abundant (commonest parrot in some localities) although it has probably declined in some areas (e.g. Jamaica and Costa Rica) owing to habitat loss. Less common in southern Costa Rica and uncommon in Panama where possibly seasonal visitor from south of Limón. Introduced Hispaniola. Trapped for live bird market but uncommon in international trade.

ECOLOGY Mostly inhabits forest and forest edge (especially adjacent to rivers) in humid lowland zones (to 1,100m in Honduras, 700m in Costa Rica and 300m in southern Mexico), but less frequent in larger tracts of rainforest and reported in arid areas (Veracruz) and pine forest (Honduras), open country with scattered trees (including cultivated areas) and plantations. Commonest in Jamaica in mid-level wet limestone forests. Generally remains below canopy. Larger groups (c. 30) may form after breeding or where food abundant. Mixed flocks with Finsch's Conure reported in Costa Rica. Recorded foods include figs *Ficus*, *Psidium*, *Inga*, *Hura* and *Hyeronima* fruits and unripe tamarind pods. Attacks crops, especially maize, and regarded as highly destructive in some areas. Preferred nest-site in arboreal termitarium where birds excavate cavity; tree-hollows also used. Nests often by river or forest edge. Breeds Mar, Jamaica; Apr-May, Belize and Guatemala. Clutch 3-4.

DESCRIPTION Head and upperparts dark green; feathered area of cere yellow to orange-red. Upperwing-coverts dark green, outer more emerald. Outer secondaries and inner primaries deep dark blue tipped black above; outer primaries blue only towards tips. Greater underwing-coverts and underside of flight feathers dull slate or brownish-grey; remaining coverts light green. Chin, throat and sides of neck chocolate-brown merging to brownish-olive on upper breast turning yellowish on lower breast and belly; undertail-coverts light green. Uppertail dark green with blue suffusion, especially towards tip; undertail metallic yellowish-olive. **Bare parts**: Bill brownish-horn with tips of mandibles paler; iris yellow to orange; legs blackish-grey.

SEX/AGE All plumages similar but immature has brown iris.

MEASUREMENTS Wing 132-147; tail 92-118; bill 17-19; tarsus 13-15.

GEOGRAPHICAL VARIATION Three races. Panamanian and Honduran birds previously bore the respective names *extima* and *melloni*, but the slight regional variations in Central America (e.g. birds in the south are paler and those from Tabasco, Mexico, and Honduras are darker) warrant no further separations than those below.

    A. n. nana (Jamaica, apparently in most areas except for high mountains and the wet John Crow range)
    A. n. astec (Veracruz, Mexico, to Panama) Similar to nominate but throat and (especially lower) underparts paler brown, bill perhaps on average smaller.
    A. n. vicinalis (E Mexico south to Veracruz. Contact zone with last race not known) Slightly larger than *astec*, brighter above and greener below.

NOTE The mainland population is sometimes treated as a full species under the name *A. astec*, but the differences from Jamaican birds are minimal.

REFERENCES Bennett & Davis (1972), Binford (1989), Carriker (1910), Edwards (1972), Forshaw (1989), Griscom & Moore (1950), Howell & Webb (1995), Land (1970), Lowery & Dalquest (1951), Monroe (1968), Peters (1931), Peterson & Chalif (1973), Ridgely & Gwynne (1989), Russell (1964), Slud (1964), Smithe (1966), Stiles *et al.* (1989), Wetmore (1943, 1968).

243 ORANGE-FRONTED CONURE
Aratinga canicularis   Plate 60

Other names: Petz's Conure, Orange-fronted Parakeet

IDENTIFICATION 24cm. Mainly green conure, more yellowish-olive beneath, with orange-red frontal band extending to lores, blue crown and blue in flight feathers. Pale eye-ring. Green Conure (229), sympatric on Pacific slope from Mexico to Nicaragua, lacks orange band, blue on crown and blue in wings (this last separates immature Orange-fronts). For separation from partly sympatric Olive-throated Conure (242) see that species. Finsch's Conure (234), possibly sympatric in Guanacaste region of Costa Rica, lacks blue in flight feathers. For separation from allopatric Peach-fronted Conure (244) see that species. Flight in small flocks swift and darting on strong deep wingbeats with brief glides.

VOICE Calls range from pure piping whistles to harsh grating screeches. High-pitched *scree scree* (higher than Green Conure) and *can can can*, like partially sympatric White-fronted Amazon (323). Chirruping and chattering sounds from perched birds.

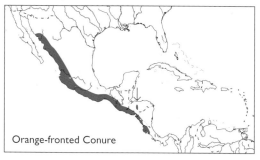
Orange-fronted Conure

DISTRIBUTION AND STATUS Pacific slope of Middle America from north-west Mexico to north-west Costa Rica. The species extends from Sinaloa and western Durango south along the Mexican Pacific lowlands to Chiapas and through Guatemala, El Salvador, Honduras and Nicaragua into Costa Rica, formerly to San José, but recent range contraction north-west. Caribbean range is restricted to Comayagua valley of the central Honduran highlands. Very common resident; partially nomadic after breeding when birds may move to higher altitudes. Trapping for live bird trade apparently led to decline in numbers and range contraction in Costa Rica and possibly elsewhere, but volume of international trade small.

ECOLOGY Lightly wooded country or open areas with scattered trees in arid and semi-arid lowlands, including thorn-forest and tropical deciduous woodland; the species is most abundant below 600m, but reaches 1,500m in arid central highlands of Honduras after breeding, when flocks of c. 50 birds, sometimes many more, form, although established pairs remain identifiable within them. Birds adapt well to partly cleared habitats, roosting in palm and mango plantations, often near towns; communal roosts with White-fronted Amazons have been noted in riparian woodland in Guatemala. Largely arboreal. Diet includes seeds of *Ceiba* and *Inga*, fruits of *Ficus*, *Bursera* and *Brosimum*, and flowers of *Gliricidia* and *Combretum*, with damage sometimes done to ripening maize and banana. An active termitarium, usually of *Nasutitermes nigriceps*, is the preferred nest-site, several pairs sometimes excavating holes in close proximity; otherwise a tree-cavity (e.g. old woodpecker hole) is used. Breeding Mar-May, Oaxaca, Mexico; Jan-May, El Salvador; dry season, Costa Rica.

DESCRIPTION Forehead with broad orange-red band extending onto lores and anterior forecrown; crown blue crown fading on nape to grass-green upperparts. Upper wing-coverts green. Flight feathers (above) blue on outerwebs, green with black tips and edges on innerwebs; (below) grey. Underwing-coverts yellowish-green. Throat, sides of neck and breast pale olive-brown shading to pale yellowish-olive on belly and undertail-coverts. Uppertail green tipped blue; undertail dull olive-yellow. **Bare parts**: Bill pale horn; cere whitish; bare periophthalmic region whitish; iris pale yellow; legs greyish brown.

SEX/AGE Sexes similar. Immature has much smaller orange frontal patch and brown iris.

MEASUREMENTS Wing 129-142; tail 95-112; bill 17-19; tarsus 13-15.

GEOGRAPHICAL VARIATION Three races.
  A. c. canicularis (Pacific slope of SW Mexico from Tehuantepec isthmus and Chiapas through Pacific Central America to NW Costa Rica)
  A. c. eburnirostrum (Pacific lowlands of S Mexico from E. Michoacán to Oaxaca. Range in relation to last race uncertain) Similar to nominate but sides of lower mandible grey and belly yellower.
  A. c. clarae (Sinaloa and W Durango south to Michoacán, Mexico) Similar to nominate but smaller orange frontal band, lores blue, sides of lower mandible dark grey.

REFERENCES Arndt (1996) Binford (1989), Carriker (1910), Dickey & van Rossem (1938), Davis & Bennett (1972), Edwards (1972), Forshaw (1989), Friedmann *et al.* (1950), Land (1970), Monroe (1968), Peterson & Chalif (1973), Rowley (1966), Schaldach (1963), Slud (1964), Stiles *et al.* (1989), Wetmore (1941, 1944).

---

244 PEACH-FRONTED CONURE
Aratinga aurea   Plate 59

Other names: Golden-crowned Conure, Half moon Conure, Brown-chested Conure, Peach-fronted Parakeet

IDENTIFICATION 26cm. Largely green conure with orange frontal band, brownish throat and breast, pale olive underparts and blue flight feathers. Smaller that most other *Aratinga*. Large range overlaps with several congeners, including Cactus (246), Brown-throated (245), Blue-crowned (228), White-eyed (235), Golden-capped (240) and Jandaya (239) Conures. Peach-fronted told from these and most other close relatives by combination of green head with orange frontal band and pale olive underparts. Very similar (allopatric) Orange-fronted

Conure (243) of Pacific Middle America distinguished in captivity by orange frontal band extending to lores and bare ocular patch (feathered orange in Peach-fronted). Generally in pairs or small noisy flocks. Flight swift and buoyant.

VOICE Shrill screeching in flight. No other information.

Peach-fronted Conure

DISTRIBUTION AND STATUS Central and eastern South America. North of the Amazon the species occurs in Pará and Amapá plus Caviana Island (mouth of Amazon), Brazil, and possibly southern Surinam. South of the Amazon the range extends through Pará, eastern Amazonas, Rondônia and Mato Grosso, Brazil, to northeast Bolivia and eastern Peru where reported from (e.g.) the Pampas de Heath region, then eastwards through most of interior Brazil to Bahia, Minas Gerais, Mato Grosso do Sul and north-west Paraná into Paraguay (in west and north-east) and northern Argentina (northern Salta, eastern Formosa Corrientes and possibly Chaco). Reports from Rio Grande do Sul, Brazil, appear mistaken. Common in central portion of range and commonest member of genus in much of interior Brazil. Evidently more local and scarce towards the northern and southern extremities of distribution with very few recent reports from Argentina (Formosa in 1987, Corrientes in 1983), where historical abundance suggests large-scale decline in 20th century. The species is possibly increasing in some areas, however, owing to agricultural expansion into humid forest. Large-scale exports to international markets, late 1980s, included major consignments from Argentina undoubtedly involving smuggled birds from Brazil.

ECOLOGY The species favours open wooded habitats including all kinds of deciduous forest, gallery woodland (especially in south of range), *Mauritia* palm swamp and savanna, also cultivated areas, below 600m. In Brazilian Amazonia, it occurs in low scrubby vegetation on sandy soils, avoiding dense evergreen forest. In interior eastern Brazil it occupies caatinga and cerrado formations with natural grassland. Generally in flocks, but in isolated pairs whilst breeding. Reported feeding with Blue-crowned Conure on fruiting tree and in pre-roosting flock with Blue-fronted Amazon (338) and Scaly-headed Parrot (315) in Piauí, Brazil. Diet includes seeds (but not pulp) of *Ilex*, *Banisteriopsis*, *Campomanesia*, *Eucalyptus* and *Symplocos*, fruits and blossoms of *Erythrina* and *Terminalia*, flowers of *Qualea* and *Caryocar* and insects including termites and larvae of flies, beetles and moths. Crop damage occurs in some areas. When feeding on ground (e.g. on grain after harvest) body plumage may become soiled. Nests in arboreal termitaria or hollow trunk or limb. Birds observed at nest-hole Jun-Jul, Peru. Flocks breaking up into breeding pairs Jan, Mato Grosso. Clutch 2-3 (Argentina).

DESCRIPTION Forehead bright orange; crown deep blue; feathered periophthalmic patch orange bordered anteriorly with blue; anterior lores orange, otherwise brown; cheeks olive-brown; ear-coverts green. Nape, mantle and back dark green; rump and uppertail-coverts green with some ginger tips. Scapulars brownish-green; lesser and median coverts dark green; greater and primary coverts rich dark blue. Primaries blue on innerwebs and tips, otherwise green; secondaries blue. Flight feathers below brownish-grey; underwing-coverts pale yellowish-olive. Throat and upper breast brownish-olive; underparts otherwise pale olive. Uppertail dark green with brownish tinge on innerwebs and blue tips; undertail brownish-grey. **Bare parts**: Bill grey-black; narrow bare periophthalmic ring grey; iris yellowish-brown; legs grey.

SEX/AGE Sexes similar. Immature has broad bare periophthalmic patch, narrower frontal band, paler bill and grey iris.

MEASUREMENTS Wing 133-151; tail 109-130; bill 16-19; tarsus 14-16.

GEOGRAPHICAL VARIATION Two races.
    A. a. aurea (North of Amazon to Bolivia and Peru south through Paraguay to extreme NW Argentina in Salta)
    A. a. major (Range poorly understood but possibly centred on chaco in Paraguay, Bolivia and N Argentina in Formosa) Larger than nominate (wing to 164) but apparently intergrades. Darker green with yellower frontal band.

REFERENCES Antas & Cavalcanti (1988), Belton (1984), Contreras *et al.* (1991), Dubs (1992), Forshaw (1989), Graham *et al.* (1980), Gyldenstolpe (1945a), Narosky & Yzurieta (1989), Naumburg (1930), Nores & Yzurieta (1994), Parker (1993), de la Peña (1988), Ridgely (1981), Short (1975), Sick (1993), Stone & Roberts (1934).

---

245 BROWN-THROATED CONURE
Aratinga pertinax   Plate 60

Other names: Brown-throated Parakeet, Yellow-cheeked Parakeet, Caribbean Parakeet; St Thomas's or Curaçao Conure (*A. p. pertinax*), Brown-eared Conure, Veragua Parakeet (*A. p. ocularis*), Orange-cheeked or Guiana Brown-throated Conure (*A. p. chrysophrys*)

IDENTIFICATION 25cm. A small green and dull brown conure which shows considerable racial diversity, especially in presence and/or extent of orange or yellow on head (see Geographical Variation). The widespread north-west

South American form *aeruginosa* is olive-green above with a greenish-blue crown extending to nape, dark brown frontal band and most of head, orange-yellow ocular region, dull brown throat and upper breast, orange centre of belly orange in otherwise pale green underparts, and blue in flight feathers. Partly sympatric Blue-crowned Conure (228) has green cheeks, throat and flight feathers, and reddish undertail. Overlapping Finsch's (234) and Red-fronted (231) Conures have mainly bright green plumage and (respectively) conspicuous red and yellow underwing-coverts and red frontal band. Peach-fronted Conure (244), occurring in range of Brown-throated in Brazil and Guianas, has green head with orange frontal band. Similar but allopatric Cactus Conure (246) shows mainly orange underparts with green confined to vent, thighs and under-tail coverts. In small fast-flying noisy flocks or pairs. Often quite tame.

VOICE Very vocal. Flight calls include constant high-pitched metallic screeching, and harsh grating *scraart scraart* cries, rapidly repeated. Disyllabic *tchrit tchrit* and *cherr-cheedit*; second note sustained then abruptly terminated. Quieter chattering sounds at rest.

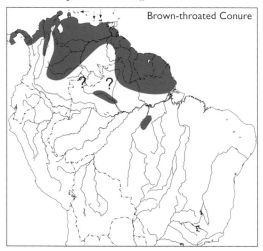

Brown-throated Conure

DISTRIBUTION AND STATUS Northern South America, Panama and islands of southern Caribbean. In Panama it is present on the Pacific slope, rarely on the Caribbean side, even in the Canal Zone. However, it occupies the Caribbean lowlands of northern and north-east Colombia from Río Sinú east to the Guajira Peninsula including the lower and middle Magdalena Valley, and occurs at low elevations in the eastern Andes and the upper Orinoco lowlands south to northern Vaupés. It probably occurs throughout Venezuela and extends onto the islands of Margarita, Tortuga (Venezuela), Curaçao, Aruba and Bonaire (Dutch Antilles); introduced to St Thomas, Virgin Islands, 19th century. It ranges through the Guianas and northern Brazil from Roraima to Amapá, and is distributed (possibly disjunctly) in upper Rio Tapajos catchment, Pará, and in Rio Negro catchment, Amazonas. Although patchily distributed it is generally common to abundant, in places the commonest parrot (e.g. localities in Guyana). Locally common in Panama and reportedly very common on Rios Negro and Branco, Brazil. Range possibly expanding owing to deforestation. Generally resident with local seasonal movements (e.g. Santa Marta region, Colombia) related to food availability and dispersal to breeding areas.

Trapped for trade but no apparent impact except for the small-island race *tortugensis*.

ECOLOGY The species occupies all kinds of open wooded country from savanna, gallery formations, deciduous edges, cactus scrub, mangroves, cultivated land with scattered trees, plantations and gardens, usually below 1,200m. Generally in flocks or pairs, larger aggregations where food abundant and at communal roosts. Takes wide variety of foods, including (north-west Venezuela) seeds of *Cassia*, *Peltophorum*, *Lagerstroemia* and *Cedrela*, fruits of *Muntingia*, *Swietenia*, *Psidium* and *Solanum* and flowers of *Tabebuia*, *Delonix*, *Erythrina* and *Gliricidia*. Causes damage to crops (e.g. millet, mango) but not widely persecuted. Reported feeding with macaws and amazon parrots. Noisy squabbling may accompany feeding. Nest-cavity usually excavated in arboreal termitarium; tree-hollow used less often, and rock crevices and excavated earth bank also reported. Often breeds in small colonies. Clutch 3-7. Breeding Feb-Apr Meta, Colombia; Feb-Apr, Venezuela; any time of year (usually after rain), Surinam, Curaçao, Aruba and Bonaire.

DESCRIPTION (*A. p. aeruginosa*) Anterior lores, frontal area, lower cheeks, sides of neck and ear-coverts dark brown, dark shaft-streaks visible on cheeks; feathered periophthalmic region orange-yellow; crown greenish-blue. Upperparts olive-green. Lesser and median coverts green; primary and greater coverts bluish-green. Primaries and secondaries (above) green, dark blue on tips, blue outerwebs on secondaries; (below) dark grey. Underwing-coverts yellowish-green. Throat and upper breast dark brown; underparts otherwise dull yellowish-green with orange patch on central belly. Uppertail bluish-green, bluer towards tip; undertail greyish-yellow. **Bare parts**: Bill brownish-grey; bare orbital ring yellowish-white; iris yellow; legs grey.

SEX/AGE Sexes similar. Immature greener on head, lacking orange-yellow around eye and with less orange on belly.

MEASUREMENTS (*A. p. aeruginosa*) Wing 127-141; tail 98-108; bill 18-20; tarsus 14-15.

GEOGRAPHICAL VARIATION Fourteen races. However, several may prove to be clinal intermediates. The form *ocularis* of Panama has been treated as the allospecific Veragua Parakeet.

A. p. pertinax (Curaçao and introduced to St Thomas) Extensive but variable amount of yellow on forehead, cheeks, lores and throat. May be duller or more orange below and behind eyes. Crown green with only slight indication of blue.

A. p. xanthogenia (Bonaire) Brighter (almost citrine) head than nominate, yellow extending variably onto forecrown/nape.

A. p. arubensis (Aruba) Face and throat dull brownish-olive. Narrow line over eye yellow. Crown greenish-blue.

A. p. aeruginosa (N Colombia, NW Venezuela and upper Rio Branco catchment, NW Brazil) See Description.

A. p. griseipecta (Río Sinú valley, N Colombia. Range in relation to *aeruginosa* unclear) Similar to last race, with cheeks, throat and upper breast olive-grey, shaft-streaks on cheeks absent, olive-grey of breast more restricted and merging with green of breast rather than sharply defined. Very little blue on green crown.

A. p. lehmanni (E Colombia and possibly Venezuela) Resembles *aeruginosa* but feathered yellowish ring around eye more extensive, blue on head confined to forecrown and less blue in flight feathers.

A. p. tortugensis (Tortuga Island, Venezuela) Similar to *aeruginosa* but larger (wing 140-148), orange-yellow on sides of head and underwing-coverts more yellowish.

A. p. margaritensis (Margarita and Los Frailes Islands, Venezuela. Birds from Paria Peninsula on mainland N Venezuela may be of this race; see next race) Whitish forehead, cheeks and ear-coverts olive-brown with greenish-blue forecrown.

A. p. venezuelae (N and C Venezuela. Contact zones with other Venezuelan races poorly understood: see *aeruginosa*, *surinama* and *chrysophrys*) Similar to last race but paler and more yellowish above.

A. p. chrysophrys (SE Venezuela, interior Guyana and N Roraima, Brazil) Similar to *margaritensis* and *venezuelae* but forehead pale brownish-yellow.

A. p. surinama (French Guiana and Surinam through coastal Guyana to Delta Amacuro, NE Venezuela) Similar to *margaritensis* but with narrow orange-yellow frontal band, orange-yellow around eyes extending onto cheeks and yellowish-green (not brown) throat.

A. p. chrysogenys (Rio Negro region and possibly Rio Solimões, N Brazil; no other details on range) Similar to *aeruginosa*, but darker.

A. p. paraensis (Upper Rio Tapajós and Rio Cururu, Pará, Brazil) Similar to *aeruginosa* but iris red and outerwebs of primaries and secondaries blue.

A. p. ocularis (Pacific slope of Panama) Distinctive yellow patch below and behind eye (absent in immatures). Forehead and crown green with bluish tinge in some birds. Throat, upper breast, cheeks and lores warm brown; ear-coverts slightly darker.

NOTE See Note under Cactus Conure.

REFERENCES Albornoz & Fernández-Badillo (1994), Aldrich & Bole (1937), Brown (1974), Darlington (1931), Forshaw (1989), Friedmann (1948), Friedmann & Smith (1950), Haverschmidt (1968), Holland (1922), Meyer de Schauensee (1949, 1950, 1966a), Meyer de Schauensee & Phelps (1978), Parker *et al* (1993), Ridgely (1981), Ridgely & Gwynne (1989), Rutgers & Norris (1979), Sick (1993), Snyder (1966), Sturgis (1928), Voous (1963 1983), Wetmore (1939, 1968).

---

246 CACTUS CONURE
Aratinga cactorum   Plate 60

IDENTIFICATION 26cm. Orange-yellow or yellow belly, brown throat and breast, blue flight feathers with green upperparts. Range broadly overlaps with that of several congeners. Peach-fronted Conure (244), locally allopatric, distinguished by orange frontal band and feathered ocular region; Golden-capped (240) and Jandaya (239) by yellow crown and red belly; Blue-crowned (228) by blue head and green underparts; and White-eyed (235) by green underparts and red and yellow underwing-coverts. In captivity Cactus told from Brown-throated (245) by absence of yellow on head, brownish forehead and sharp delineation of brown upper breast, orange-yellow belly and green vent and thighs. Difficult to detect in foliage and most often located at rest by call. In pairs or small groups. Swift flight appears laboured as wings remain below horizontal.

VOICE Very vocal with calls often emitted constantly for long periods. Typical sounds include a *cri cri cri* and a strident *screeet screeet* rapidly repeated 3-6 times between pauses. Softer screeching whilst feeding.

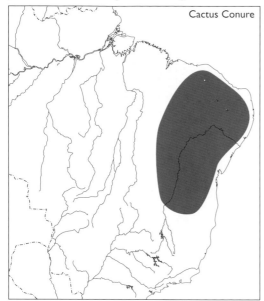

Cactus Conure

DISTRIBUTION AND STATUS Interior north-east Brazil. Birds range from the drier parts of Bahia and adjacent north-eastern Minas Gerais north to Piauí and south-eastern Maranhão, through western Pernambuco to Paraíba and north to Rio Grande do Norte and Ceará. Absent from coastal areas: a record from Belém at the mouth of the Amazon in Pará appears mistaken or possibly refers to an escape. Generally common (commonest parrot in some localities) with stable population, although decline inevitable in some areas owing to large-scale loss of habitat to agriculture and exotic tree plantations. Continuing degradation and conversion of caatinga by grazing and cultivation respectively pose long-term threat. Occurs in Serra do Capivara National Park. Some local persecution owing to crop predation. Trapped for trade with small numbers in captivity.

ECOLOGY Range closely matches dry, thorny caatinga vegetation of north-east Brazil, but embraces drier semi-desert areas created by over-grazing and taller dry forest (caatinga arborea) and lusher seasonal savanna (cerrado) woodlands. Generally in pairs or (mainly outside breeding season) flocks of up to c. 20 birds, more where food (such as rice crops) abundant. Diet comprises seeds, fruits (including cactus), berries, nuts, flowers and buds, taken both in trees and bushes and on ground. Sometimes raids crops (e.g. rice, grapes and maize). Breeding undocumented in wild. Clutch of six reported in captivity.

DESCRIPTION Forehead, lores and lower cheeks dull brown; crown with slaty tinge; sides of neck, nape and upperparts to rump grass-green. Primary coverts bluish-green on outerwebs, remaining coverts grass-green. Flight feathers (above) green on innerwebs, bluish-green on outerwebs, blue-black at tips; (below) greyish. Underwing-coverts greenish-yellow. Throat and upper breast dull brown; lower breast and belly fairly bright orange-yellow; thighs and vent greenish-yellow. Uppertail green, four central feathers distally blue; undertail greyish. **Bare parts**: Upper mandible horn, greyish at base and on lower mandible; bare periophthalmic patch white; iris brownish-orange; legs slaty-grey.

SEX/AGE Sexes similar. Immature paler than adult, with green crown, more olive upper breast and throat, and darker iris.

MEASUREMENTS Wing 136-140; tail 94-125; bill 18-20; tarsus 13-15.

GEOGRAPHICAL VARIATION Two races.
> *A. c. cactorum* (Bahia south of Rio São Francisco and adjacent portions of NE Minas Gerais in NE Brazil)
> *A. c. caixana* (Caatinga zone on left side of Rio São Francisco from NW Bahia through Piauí and W Pernambuco to Ceará and Maranhão) Generally paler than nominate, with yellow rather than orange belly.

NOTE Cactus Conure has been treated as a race of Brown-throated, but whilst captive hybrids have been reported these two forms are clearly distinct and regarded as allospecific.

REFERENCES Arndt (1996), Forshaw (1989), Olmos (1993), Ridgely (1981), Rutgers & Norris (1979), Sick (1993), Yamashita *in litt.* (1996).

---

247 BLACK-HOODED CONURE
Nandayus nenday   Plate 61

Other names: Nanday Conure, Black-masked Conure, Black-hooded Parakeet

IDENTIFICATION 30cm. Mainly green conure, more yellowish beneath, with dark head and bill, long tail, blue in flight feathers and blue breast. Dull brownish-black undersides of flight feathers visible in flight and red thighs may be noticeable. Similar build to closely related *Aratinga* conures, including overlapping Blue-crowned (228) and White-eyed (235), but combination of black head with green ear-coverts and sides of neck distinctive. In flocks in swift direct flight on strong rapid wingbeats calling noisily. Generally in open country with birds sometimes walking on ground. Associates with Monk Parakeets (269) in mixed flocks. Usually quite tame and approachable but rather unobtrusive in foliage.

VOICE Calls include *kree-ah kree-ah* and *krehh* and *chriie chriie chriie*, latter similar to voice of White-eyed Conure. Powerful voice also resembles that of several similar-sized species including Sun (238), Jandaya (239) and Golden-capped (240) Conures. Birds are especially vocal in flight.

DISTRIBUTION AND STATUS Central-southern South America. The species occurs in a band approximately 200km east to west centred on the pantanals of the upper Río Paraguay basin, in eastern Santa Cruz, south-east Bolivia, south-west Mato Grosso and western Mato Grosso do Sul, Brazil, south through central Paraguay to Formosa and Chaco and northern Santa Fe, Argentina (occasional in Misiones and Corrientes). A report from Santiago del Estero is probably erroneous. Several feral populations exist in (e.g.) Buenos Aires and California. May wander outside breeding season into central chaco. Generally common and locally abundant, especially where food plants concentrated. In Argentina most numerous in Formosa, and commonest parrot in parts of Mato Grosso. Trapped for trade, with over 114,000 exported from Argentina, 1985-1990, although many of these birds probably originated in Paraguay. Habitat is often modified by grazing and an overall decline in numbers has probably occurred.

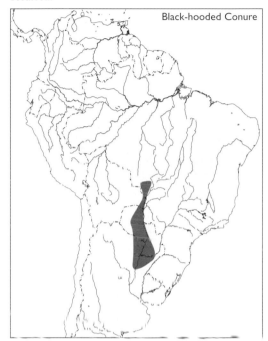

Black-hooded Conure

ECOLOGY Birds inhabit open lowlands to about 800m including moister parts of the eastern chaco (one report from the dry chaco in Bolivia), pantanals and cattle rangelands with palms. In the eastern chaco and lower Río Paraguay basin they favour areas with *Copernicia* palms growing in seasonal floodplains with drought-related xerophytic vegetation, and are reported from palm swamps in Santa Cruz, Bolivia. Gregarious, with up to a dozen birds whilst breeding; often several hundred birds gather when roosting. Diet includes *Copernicia* fruits, sometimes taken from the ground; may cause damage to cultivated crops, e.g. maize. Often seen drinking at waterholes. Nests in cavity in tree, palm or large fence-post, e.g. in cattle corral. Breeding Nov, Mato Grosso. Clutch four.

DESCRIPTION Forehead, crown, anterior lores and most of cheeks sooty-black; sides of neck and ear-coverts pale yellowish-green; some brown or reddish feathers at margin of black hood and grass-green nape. Mantle and back grass-green fading to pale yellowish-green on rump and uppertail-coverts. Scapulars mostly green but some median feathers with dark blue innerwebs; wing-coverts mostly green but primary coverts blue. Flight feathers dark blue above with paler outerwebs on some primaries; below dull brownish-black. Most underwing-coverts pale yellowish-green. Throat pale yellowish-green shading to pale powder-blue on upper breast; remaining underparts pale yellowish-green except red thighs and some powder-blue feathers in undertail-coverts. Uppertail reddish brown,

blue distally; undertail dull brown. **Bare parts:** Bill sooty black; bare periophthalmic skin pale grey; iris reddish-brown; legs pinkish-flesh.

SEX/AGE Sexes similar. Immature has less blue on throat and upper breast.

MEASUREMENTS Wing 170-190; tail 139-178; bill 22-26; tarsus 17-20.

GEOGRAPHICAL VARIATION The name *campicola* has been given to specimens taken 265km west of Puerto Casado, Paraguay, based on shorter tail and wing and alleged plumage differences. However, the associated description appears inaccurate or based on aberrant specimens.

NOTE Some authors include Black-hooded Conure in *Aratinga*. Although clearly very close, morphological distinctiveness warrants treatment in separate genus.

REFERENCES Brodkorb (1938), Contreras *et al.* (1991), Dubs (1992), Forshaw (1989), Kratter *et al.* (1993), Lopez (1992), Naumburg (1930), Nores & Yzurieta (1994), Parker (1993), Ridgely (1981), Sick (1993), Short (1975), Wetmore (1926a), Yamashita *in litt.* (1996).

248 GOLDEN-PLUMED PARROT
Leptosittaca branickii   Plate 61

Other names: Golden-plumed Parakeet/Conure

IDENTIFICATION 34cm. Mainly green parrot with elongated yellow feathers forming tuft behind eye, distinctive orange and yellow patch on lower breast, dull reddish underside to tail and with narrow orange frontal band and orange and yellow lores. Possibly overlaps with Mitred Conure (232) in catchments of upper Río Marañón and upper Río Apurímac, Peru, and Red-fronted Conure (231) in parts of Colombia, southern Ecuador and northern Peru, although former may be ecologically separated; told from both by yellow tufts behind eyes and yellow and orange breast-band. Distinguished from Yellow-eared Conure (224) in central Andes of southern Colombia and northern Ecuador by smaller size, less extensive yellow on sides of head and paler bill. Restless, seldom remaining in one tree for more than 5-10 minutes. Flight usually low over canopy unless crossing valley. Generally in flocks of 3-20.

VOICE Voice resembles small macaw (quieter) or Red-fronted Conure (more nasal). Calls include vibrant *chree ah* shrieks, and those from flocks can be loud and far-carrying. Harsh *scraart* from perched bird. Birds frequently call to one another whilst feeding and utter characteristic soft continuous chatter which often locates feeding flocks before they are seen.

DISTRIBUTION AND STATUS Northern Andes from Colombia to southern Peru. The species is known from all three ranges of Colombian Andes: in the west on Cerro Munchique and at borders of Tolima, Risaralda, Quindío and Caldas; in the centre from northern Caldas to Cauca, including Volcán Puracé; in the east in eastern Nariño. It is reported from six or seven areas in Ecuador, including Imbabura in the north and the Chilla mountains in El Oro, high mountains in Azuay and Morona Santiago, and several localities in Loja in the south. In Peru it ranges from Amazonas and Cajamarca departments south through San Martín, La Libertad, Huánuco and Junín to Cuzco. Seasonal and nomadic, uncommon and very local, especially in Colombia where a drastic decline is due to deforestation; in Ecuador it is scarce, possibly commoner in south-east, but absent from apparently suitable habitat on the eastern Andes. In Peru, where deforestation is less severe, it may be more widespread. Local occurrence unpredictable and perhaps linked to fruiting of preferred food plants. Occurs (but perhaps not resident) in many protected areas including Parque Nacional (PN) Puracé in central Andes of Colombia, PN Podocarpus in southern Ecuador and PN Manu, Peru. VULNERABLE.

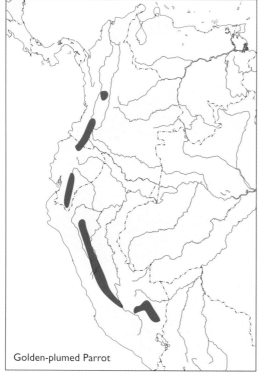

Golden-plumed Parrot

ECOLOGY Birds occur in high-altitude formations, chiefly at 2,400-3,400 m but down to 1,400m at times, including temperate forest, elfin woodland, cloud-forest and treeline shrubbery, birds sometimes crossing cleared areas to visit remnant patches. Distribution possibly linked to *Podocarpus* trees, at least in Azuay province and parts of Colombia, but study is needed to confirm this. Birds make diurnal altitudinal movements to the páramo, returning to lower forests to roost, but in PN Puracé this pattern is reversed, with birds roosting communally in the páramo zone (above 3,000m) and descending to feed during the day. Generally in flocks (at least outside breeding season) of up to c. 20 birds (sometimes more). Reported diet includes *Podocarpus* cone seeds, *Prumnopitys montanus*, *Croton* seeds, *Styrax subargentea*, *Gynoxis nitida*, *Ficus* and maize; generally forages in canopy (birds frequently moving between trees), sometimes in shrub layer and fields. Nests probably in tree-cavity. Birds in breeding condition Feb, Colombia, and mating birds Aug, Ecuador.

DESCRIPTION Crown, most of forehead, cheeks, sides of neck and ear-coverts grass-green; narrow frontal band

on lower forehead orange extending onto upper lores; lower lores yellow extending in stripe below ocular ring to join elongated yellow tuft behind eye. Upperparts grass-green. Upperwing green. Underwing-coverts greenish yellow; underside of flight feathers dull yellow. Underparts green, slightly more yellowish than above, with large indistinct yellow and orange patch on lower breast. Uppertail green with dull red on innerwebs; undertail dull red. **Bare parts**: Bill horn; cere grey; bare periophthalmic skin pale whitish-grey; iris orange; legs grey.

SEX/AGE Sexes similar. Immatures undescribed.

MEASUREMENTS Wing 178-194; tail 165-201; bill 23-27; tarsus 18-21.

GEOGRAPHICAL VARIATION None.

NOTE Some authors include this species in *Aratinga*. However, facial plumes are distinctive and monotypic genus *Leptosittaca* appears justified.

REFERENCES Arndt (1996), Bloch *et al.* (1991), Bond (1955), Chapman (1926), Collar *et al.* (1992, 1994), Fjeldså & Krabbe (1990), Forshaw (1989), Hilty & Brown (1986), King (1989), Rasmussen *et al.* (1996), Ridgely (1981), Toyne *in litt.* (1996), Whitney (1996), Williams & Tobias (1994).

---

249 PATAGONIAN CONURE
Cyanoliseus patagonus   Plate 62

Other names: Burrowing Parrot, Patagonian Parrot

IDENTIFICATION 42-46cm. Rather like small macaw. Upperparts and long tail dull olive-brown with bright yellow rump and (except in Chile) bright yellow belly with orange patch in centre; blue flight feathers. Range overlaps with several other long-tailed parrots: Slender-billed Conure (268) in parts of Chile, Austral Conure (267) in southern Argentina and parts of Chile, Blue-crowned Conure (228) in northern Argentina, and Monk Parakeet (269) over much of Argentine range north from Río Negro. Patagonian Conure easily distinguished from these mainly green parrots by larger size, yellow rump and brown upperparts. Commonly in large noisy flocks, sometimes crowding onto posts and telephone wires in open country. Flight often close to ground on swift rhythmic wingbeats.

VOICE Very noisy. Disyllabic shrieking *scree-ah scree-ah*. Loud *gyeee gyeee gyeee* when alarmed. Noisy flock at nesting burrows can sound to European ears like group of shrieking Black-headed Gulls *Larus ridibundus*.

DISTRIBUTION AND STATUS Southern South America. The species ranges from northern Santa Cruz and Chubut in Argentina north through Río Negro and La Pampa to Buenos Aires, San Luís, Córdoba, San Juan, La Rioja, Catamarca, Tucumán and Salta, then west through southern Uruguay. It was recorded in the 1920s from central Formosa, Argentina, well outside normal range, and formerly in central Chile from northern Los Lagos north to Atacama but is now confined to a few localities in the Andean foothills in (e.g.) Bío Bío. Some seasonal movements occur, including northward migration of southern birds in the Argentine winter and downslope displacements in Chile. Abundance variable in Argentina where still locally common or abundant but elsewhere (e.g.

Córdoba and eastern Buenos Aires) rare or occasional. Scarce and sporadic, Uruguay. Drastic decline during 20th century in Chile so that *C. p. bloxami* considered at risk, with population estimated at under 3,000 in late 1980s. Decline there and in parts of Argentina attributable to trapping for trade, hunting for food, conversion of grasslands to croplands and persecution as a crop pest. Probably still declining overall.

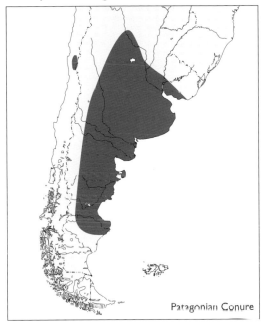

Patagonian Conure

ECOLOGY The species generally inhabits open grassy country but is also reported from savanna, wooded valleys with cliffs, and farmland to about 2,000m. Generally in quite arid country but often occurs near rivers or streams. Gregarious, forming large flocks, sometimes in excess of 1,000 birds, with communal roosts in trees, on wires (sometimes in towns) and in tunnels excavated for nesting. Diet chiefly comprises seeds and fruit with fruit predominating during the summer months (Nov-Feb), reported foods including berries of *Lycium salsum* and *Discaria*, fruits of *Geoffroea decorticans*, *Prosopis caldenia*, *P. chilensis* and *P. flexuosa* and seeds of *Carduus mariana*. Sometimes damages grain crops; often feeds on or near the ground. Breeds colonially in burrows excavated in cliffs (usually limestone or sandstone in Chile) often with commanding view. In San Luís, Argentina, breeding reported in wet season (Nov-Apr), birds returning to nesting cliffs in Sep. Egg-laying Nov-Dec, San Luís, with birds dispersing from breeding sites Apr; apparently earlier in Chile. Clutch 2-4.

DESCRIPTION Forehead, crown, lores, cheeks and nape olive-brown with slight yellowish tinge; sides of neck, mantle and back olive-brown; rump and uppertail-coverts bright canary yellow. Scapulars brown, some slightly suffused blue; primary coverts blue, other coverts brownish olive-yellow. Primaries and outer secondaries blue with dark margins to distal innerwebs; inner secondaries brownish suffused blue. Underwing-coverts olive-yellow; underside of flight feathers brown. Breast olive-brown with creamy-white area on side of upper breast; rest of under-

parts canary yellow with orange-red patch across central belly. Uppertail brown tinged blue, especially next to shafts; undertail brown. **Bare parts**: Bill sooty greyish-black; bare periophthalmic skin whitish; iris pale yellow; legs pale yellowish-brown.

SEX/AGE Sexes similar. Immature has horn upper mandible and brown iris.

MEASUREMENTS Wing 232-252; tail 215-263; bill 27-31; tarsus 23-25.

GEOGRAPHICAL VARIATION Four races.
    C. p. patagonus (S Argentina from N Santa Cruz north through Río Negro and La Pampa approximately to latitude of Buenos Aires and S Uruguay in east and Lake Nahuel Huapi in S Neuquén in west. It may penetrate to west slope of Andes in remote regions of Los Lagos and Aisen in E Chile)
    C. p. andinus (NW Argentina in Catamarca, Tucumán, Salta, La Rioja, San Juan and Mendoza. Range in relation to nominate unclear but apparent area of intergradation in C Argentina) Similar to nominate but lacks bright yellow on belly and pale areas on sides of breast and has duller olive-tinged rump. This and next race have browner upper wing-coverts than nominate.
    C. p. conlara (San Luis and Córdoba, Argentina) Darker breast than other Argentine races
    C. p. bloxami, previously *C. p. byroni* (formerly in central provinces of Chile, now very restricted) From nominate by larger size (wing 250-263), darker brown upperparts, throat and lower breast, larger, heavier bill and more extensive creamy patches on sides of breast (in some birds merging to form pale breast-band).

REFERENCES Araya *et al.* (1993), Bucher *et al.* (1987), Cuello & Gerzenstein (1962), Fjeldså & Krabbe (1990), Forshaw (1989), Hellmayr (1932), Johnson (1967), Narosky & Yzurieta (1989), Nores & Yzurieta (1994), de la Peña (1988), Weimann (1926a,b).

250 BLUE-THROATED CONURE
Pyrrhura cruentata   **Plate 63**

Other names: Blue-chested, Ochre-marked, Red-rumped Conure or Red-eared Conure/Parakeet

IDENTIFICATION 30cm. Mainly green long-tailed conure with yellow patches on sides of neck, red on ear-coverts and around eyes, blue throat and upper breast and crimson on rump and belly. Well-defined dark cap. Plumage rather variable, some birds lacking crimson patch on belly. Range overlaps with same-sized Maroon-bellied (251) and nominate form of (smaller) White-eared (256) Conures although former has a higher-altitude distribution. Separated from these, all other *Pyrrhura* in captivity and several partly sympatric *Aratinga* (e.g. White-eyed, 235) conures by combination of yellow patches on sides of neck, blue throat and well-defined dark cap backed by blue band on nape. Often in fast flight (with shallow undulations) in noisy flocks just above canopy. Difficult to detect whilst foraging quietly in foliage.

VOICE Noisy. High-pitched rapid chattering calls in flight. Some sounds with slight grating quality but generally less harsh than most *Aratinga* conures.

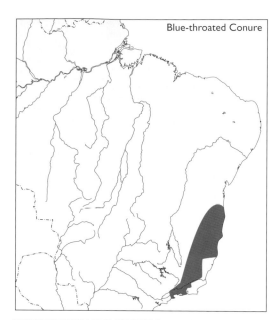

Blue-throated Conure

DISTRIBUTION AND STATUS Eastern Brazil from Bahia to Rio de Janeiro. It was formerly known from Jequié and Ilhéus, Bahia, but most northerly recent reports are from Rio Jequitinhonha, south of which reports stem from remnant patches of forest (including in Monte Pascoal National Park) to border with Espírito Santo. Birds persist in the few forested parts of eastern Minas Gerais such as Rio Doce State Park, Caratinga Reserve (near Raúl Soares) and near Mantena, and in several localities in northern Espírito Santo including Córrego Grande and Sooretama Biological Reserves and Sooretama's neighbouring Linhares Reserve. It is apparently absent from the south of the state but survives near Desengano State Park in Rio de Janeiro state, the southernmost site at which it is certainly known. Resident. Common and widespread in late 19th century but declined dramatically with massive deforestation within range for agriculture, logging, mining, roads and urban development. Final stronghold (the only place where birds remain common) is the Sooretama/Linhares reserve complex; much smaller numbers exist in other (mostly protected but widely separated) forest remnants. Habitat loss continues in Bahia with some sites (e.g. Monte Pascoal) under intense pressure. Rare in captivity but trapping for illegal trade is an additional threat. Listed in CITES Appendix I and protected under domestic Brazilian law. VULNERABLE.

ECOLOGY Mainly in primary Atlantic rain-forest or forest edge and sometimes in slightly modified natural forest, penetrating agricultural areas where tall forest trees shade cacao crops. Not known from seasonal or dry forests. Generally in lowlands below c. 400m but to 960m in Minas Gerais. Gregarious, generally in flocks of 6-20 (mainly 8-12), at least where locally common. Food plants include *Talisia esculenta, Alchornea iricurana, Mabea fistulifera, Trema micrantha* and *Cecropia*. Fruits of *Miconia hypoleuca* may be important in periods of scarcity. Birds feed in canopy and in lower edge vegetation, never outside forest; once observed feeding with Golden-capped Conure (240). Nests in hollow tree. Evidence suggests breeding Jun-Oct. Clutch 2-4.

DESCRIPTION Forehead, crown and hindneck dark brown with pale orange sides to some feathers (especially posteriorly) giving speckled appearance; lores, upper cheeks, superciliary area and ear-coverts dull red merging on sides of neck with yellowish patch bordered behind by blue band running across nape; lower cheeks green. Mantle, back and scapulars green; broad dull crimson patch on lower back and rump; uppertail-coverts green. Bend of wing bright red; upperwing-coverts green. Outerwebs of primaries blue, green on innerwebs; secondaries green on outerwebs, grey on inners; flight feathers tipped dark. Lesser underwing-coverts olive green, greater grey; underside of flight feathers grey washed olive. Chin green; throat and upper breast blue with some dark tips; underparts otherwise green with variable-sized crimson patch on belly. Uppertail gold with green tinge; undertail maroon. **Bare parts**: Bill grey; bare periophthalmic skin grey; iris yellowish-orange; legs grey.

SEX/AGE Sexes similar, but iris perhaps brighter in male. Immature duller with less red at bend of wing.

MEASUREMENTS Wing 144-152; tail 124-136; bill 18-20; tarsus 15-17.

GEOGRAPHICAL VARIATION None.

REFERENCES Collar *et al.* (1992, 1994), Forshaw (1989), Galetti & Stotz (1996), Ridgely (1981), Sick (1993), Whitney (1996).

251 MAROON-BELLIED CONURE
Pyrrhura frontalis   Plate 63

Other names: Reddish-bellied, Maroon, Brown-eared, Scaly-breasted Conure/Parakeet; Azara's Conure/Parakeet (*P. f. chiripepe*); Blaze- or Bronze-winged Conure/Parakeet (*P. f. devillei*); Krieg's Conure/Parakeet (*P. f. kriegi*)

IDENTIFICATION 25-28cm. Mainly green long-tailed conure with rather dark face, maroon patch on belly and brown ear-coverts. Tail mainly bronze above with dull red tip, dull maroon beneath. Light subterminal edges to dark-tipped olive-brown breast and throat feathers gives scaly appearance. Range overlaps with similar-sized Blue-throated (250) and White-eared (256) Conures although Maroon-bellied is at higher altitudes in the north of its range (Rio de Janeiro to Bahia). White-eared separated by green and maroon uppertail, maroon rump and red at bend of wing, Blue-throated by yellow patches on sides of neck and blue on throat and breast. Overlaps with similar Green-cheeked Conure (254) but race *devillei* has bright red at bend of wing and bright red and yellow underwing-coverts whilst race *chiripepe* has green rather than dull red uppertail. Monk Parakeet (269), which overlaps in northern Argentina, Paraguay and southern Brazil), told by pale grey breast and head. Maroon-bellied is distinguished from similar congeners in captivity by combination of green rump (but note some reddish-brown feathers on lower back), bronze uppertail, brown ear-coverts and absence of blue on neck and breast. It occurs in small, tight, noisy flocks but is generally silent when perched. Swift darting flight recalls small pigeon. Most conspicuous small parrot over much of range.

VOICE Noisy in airborne flocks with rapid harsh screeches mixed with longer, higher-pitched, more penetrating calls;

described as *kree-ah kree kree uh* and *yiiec yiiec*. A *yaak yaak yaak* when alarmed. Generally silent when perched.

DISTRIBUTION AND STATUS South-eastern South America from south-east Brazil to northern Argentina. The species occurs in Brazil from southern Bahia through coastal states to Rio Grande do Sul, and west into south-eastern Minas Gerais and southern Mato Grosso, through Paraguay (spread of records suggests presence throughout except far west), northern Uruguay and northern Argentina in Misiones, Corrientes, eastern Formosa, Chaco and, sporadically in past, northern Santa Fe (a population in Buenos Aires probably descends from escapes), and into south-east Bolivia. Resident. Locally common to very common (e.g. Misiones) but rarer elsewhere (e.g. Corrientes) and extirpated in places owing to conversion of forests to agriculture. Traded in large numbers with substantial exports in late 1980s involving average of over 5,000 birds per year. Large captive population.

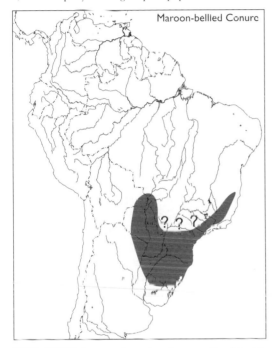

Maroon-bellied Conure

ECOLOGY Birds range through various woodland, forest, edge and pantanal habitats, including remaining patches of *Araucaria* (e.g. Rio Grande do Sul). In northern Paraguayan chaco they seem almost confined to riparian growth along the Río Paraguay and its major tributaries. In south-east Brazil they occur mainly in highlands to 1,400m; elsewhere in lowlands up to c. 1,000m, where generally tolerant of disturbance, even visiting urban parks in, e.g., Asunción, Rio de Janeiro and São Paulo, and feeding in gardens (Rio Grande do Sul). Gregarious, usually in flocks of 6-12 (up to c. 40) birds. In south-east Brazil food includes pulp of *Euterpe edulis*, seeds of *Schinus, Xylopia, Cecropia, Croton, Miconia, Ficus, Psidium* and *Pinus*, flowers of *Ambrosia* and *Vernonia* and arils of *Proteum*; elsewhere *Araucaria* (very important food source in southern Brazil) nuts and fruits of *Campomanesia xanthocarpa* and *Podocarpus lambertii*, homopteran galls on *Persea pyrifolia* leaves, and fly larvae. Orange and maize crops visited, but depredations light compared to cereal damage by Monk Parakeet. Nests in tree-cavity. Breeds Oct-Dec. Clutch 5-6.

DESCRIPTION Narrow frontal band dull red with a few brighter red feathers behind cere; lores blackish; feathers on cheeks and crown greyish-green with blackish tips; ear-coverts olive-brown. Upperparts grass-green with a small area of reddish-brown on lower back. Primary coverts bluish-green, wing-coverts otherwise grass-green, some feathers sometimes with olive tinge. Primaries blue on outerwebs, green on innerwebs, with dark tips; secondaries mainly green. Sides of neck, throat and breast olive-brown, feathers subterminally pale fawn and tipped blackish, producing scaly effect; lower breast green with maroon patch in centre of belly; flanks, thighs and undertail-coverts green. Uppertail green on basal half, shading through bronze to reddish tips; undertail dull maroon. **Bare parts**: Bill grey, sometimes paler at base of mandible; cere yellowish-white; bare periophthalmic skin pale whitish-grey; iris dark brown; legs dark grey.

SEX/AGE Sexes similar. Fledgling lacks maroon on belly. Immature also reportedly duller than adult with darker iris. Immature of race *devillei* has no red at bend of wing.

MEASUREMENTS Wing 127-141; tail 120-131; bill 16-18; tarsus 14-16.

GEOGRAPHICAL VARIATION Three races. A fourth, *kriegi*, from Minas Gerais to Rio Grande do Sul, Brazil, has been proposed on the basis of a very narrow brownish-red tip to tail. It is probably not valid.

   P. f. frontalis (SE Brazil from S Bahia to Rio Grande do Sul including SE Minas Gerais and S and SE Mato Grosso)

   P. f. devillei (SW Brazil, SE Bolivia and N Paraguay; see Note) Bend of wing and lesser underwing-coverts bright red, greater underwing-coverts yellow. Forehead and crown pale brown. Perhaps smaller than nominate.

   P. f. chiripepe (C and S Paraguay, N Uruguay and N Argentina. Overlaps and breeds with *devillei* in N Paraguay and SW Brazil) As nominate but upper surface of tail wholly olive-green. Some orange red markings at bend of wing in some birds.

NOTE Blaze-winged Conure *P. f. devillei* widely treated as full species, but hybridation with the western race *chiripepe* of Maroon-bellied Conure reliably reported from the narrow zone of sympatry in northern Paraguay and southern Brazil, suggesting conspecificity. Chromosome analysis of Maroon-bellied and Green-cheeked Conures suggests that there is continuing gene flow between these two rather similar forms, suggesting they are also conspecific, but their traditional status as separate species is accepted here pending further study.

REFERENCES Belton (1984), Contreras *et al.* (1991), Dubs (1992), Narosky & Yzurieta (1989), Nores & Yzurieta (1994), de la Peña (1988), Ridgely (1981), Short (1975), Sick (1993), Valentine (1987), Wetmore (1926a), Yamashita *in litt.* (1996).

252 CRIMSON-BELLIED CONURE
Pyrrhura perlata   Plate 64

Other names: See Note

IDENTIFICATION 25cm. Long-tailed green and bluish-green conure with red underwing-coverts and striking crimson belly. Flight feathers blue with maroon tail. Distinguished from the slightly smaller sympatric Painted Conure (255) by red underwing-coverts and bright red underparts. Erratic flight in tight flocks on rapid wingbeats interrupted with glides. Birds become silent and still when disturbed and may be difficult to detect in foliage.

VOICE Noisy, with constant chattering whilst fluttering about in tree-tops. Call written *tieww kritieww*.

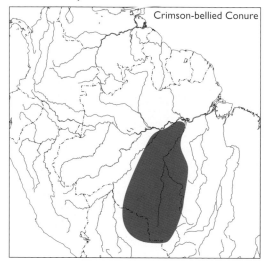
Crimson-bellied Conure

DISTRIBUTION AND STATUS Central southern Amazon basin of Brazil. The species occurs in western Pará and eastern Amazonas in the drainages of the Rios Madeira and Tapajós south to northernmost Mato Grosso on e.g. Rios Roosevelt and Aripuanã. It is reported from adjacent parts of Bolivia and probably occurs widely east of Río Mamoré in Beni and Santa Cruz. Generally common but perhaps declining owing to forest loss in parts of range (e.g. along Rio Jiparaná in Rondônia, Brazil). Rare in captivity.

ECOLOGY Generally in lowland terra firme tropical rainforest. Birds occupy drier lowland forests in northern Mato Grosso and are reported from forest edge, clearings and second growth, also fig-dominated forests in eastern Bolivia. Generally in small flocks and sometimes in mixed parties with Painted Conures and Golden-winged Parakeets (287). Larger gatherings formerly reported. Often descends to rivers and streams to bathe and drink and takes soil at clay licks. Reported food items include *Cecropia* catkins, small fruits of *Trema micrantha*, fruits of *Ficus*, *Eugenia* and *Zanthoxylum*, and flowers of *Bertholletia excelsa* and *Dioclea glabra*. Breeds Aug-Nov, probably also Apr-Jun. Clutch in captivity 3-9 with mean of five. No other information on breeding but presumably similar to congeners with nest in tree-cavity.

DESCRIPTION Lores and cheeks yellowish-olive with brownish tinge; forehead, crown and hindneck dark slaty tipped buff, giving speckled appearance especially

posteriorly where increasing blue in bases of feathers. Upper mantle blue; lower mantle to uppertail-coverts green. Scapulars green at base, blue towards tips; lesser wing-coverts olive-green; median and greater coverts mainly blue. Flight feathers blue above, secondaries with green on outerwebs; dark slaty-grey below. Underwing-coverts bright red. Sides of neck, throat and upper breast mainly brown with some blue markings and buff tips, giving scaly appearance; lower breast and most of belly bright crimson; flanks, thighs and undertail-coverts blue with greenish tinge. Uppertail mainly maroon, green basally and narrowly tipped blue; undertail dark slaty-grey.
Bare parts: Bill brownish-black; bare periophthalmic skin greyish-white; iris dark brown; legs slate-black.

SEX/AGE Sexes similar. Immature lacks bright crimson on underparts; sometimes with dark margins to scapulars.

MEASUREMENTS Wing 125-140; tail 96-109; bill 16-18; tarsus 15-17.

GEOGRAPHICAL VARIATION None.

NOTE *P. perlata* was previously widely known as *P. rhodogaster*.

REFERENCES Arndt (1996), Arndt & Roth (1986), Dubs (1992), Forshaw (1989), Meyer de Schauensee (1966), Naumburg (1930), Parker *et al.* (1991), Ridgely (1981), Sick (1993).

253 PEARLY CONURE
Pyrrhura lepida   Plate 64

Other names: Miritiba Pearly Conure (*P. l. coerulescens*); Neumann's Pearly Conure (*P. l. anerythra*)

IDENTIFICATION 24cm. Long-tailed green and bluish-green conure with red underwing-coverts. All races of Pearly Conure, with exception of *P. l. anerythra* (which has green underwing-coverts), distinguished from other *Pyrrhura* in captivity by combination of red underwing-coverts and blue on thighs, flanks and undertail-coverts. For separation from Painted Conure (255) see under that species. Habits very like Crimson-bellied Conure (252).

VOICE Noisy chattering notes.

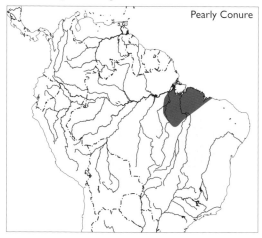
Pearly Conure

DISTRIBUTION AND STATUS North-east Brazil south

of the Amazon. The species is known from the catchment of the Xingu and its tributaries, from the Rio Pracuí and left bank of the Rio Tocantins, and occurs from Belém and Rio Capim, Pará, east to around São Luis, Maranhão, and from northern Maranhão east of Rosário, but is apparently no longer found in some coastal areas where previously reported. Generally uncommon and locally extinct (e.g. northern Maranhão) owing to large-scale deforestation, although is apparently tolerant of some habitat disturbance. The race *coerulescens* of northern Maranhão east of Rosário is perhaps close to extinction owing to almost total habitat loss. The species occurs in protected areas but their integrity is compromised by illegal logging.

ECOLOGY Generally in lowland terra firme tropical rainforest. Birds have been reported from forest edge, clearings and second growth. There is no information on diet or breeding, but presumably similar to congeners.

DESCRIPTION Head dark blackish-brown with slight buffy mottlings on nape; ear-coverts creamy white; cheeks dull bluish-green. Upper mantle blue; lower mantle to uppertail-coverts green. Scapulars green at base, blue towards tips; lesser wing-coverts green slightly tinged olive; median and greater coverts mainly blue; some red on leading edge of wing. Flight feathers blue above, secondaries with green on outerwebs; dark slaty-grey below. Underwing-coverts bright red. Sides of neck, throat and upper breast mainly brown with some blue markings and buff tips giving scaly appearance; remaining underparts green with blue suffusion on flanks and thighs. Uppertail mainly maroon, green basally and narrowly tipped blue. **Bare parts**: Bill brownish-black; bare periophthalmic skin greyish-white; iris dark brown; legs slate-black.

SEX/AGE All plumages apparently similar.

MEASUREMENTS Wing 125-131; tail 104-116; bill 15-16; tarsus 13-16.

GEOGRAPHICAL VARIATION Three races.

P. l. lepida (Belém and Río Capim, Pará, east to São Luis, Maranhão)

P. l. coerulescens (N Maranhão east of Rosário) As *lepida* but greyer on throat and upper breast, with green on upper cheeks, black on lower breast.

P. l. anerythra (Tributaries of the upper Xingu, from the Rio Pracuí and the left bank of the Río Tocantins) Similar to nominate but leading edge of wing and underwing-coverts green, not red.

NOTE *Pyrrhura lepida* is the new name for the taxonomic entity *P. perlata*, whose name has been shown to have been first applied to an immature Crimson-bellied Conure.

REFERENCES Arndt & Roth (1986), Collar (1997), Forshaw (1989).

---

254 GREEN-CHEEKED CONURE
Pyrrhura molinae   Plate 63

Other names: Argentine Conure (*P. m. australis*); Crimson-tailed Conure (*P. m. phoenicura*); Santa Cruz Conure (*P. m. restricta*); Yellow-sided Conure ('*P. hypoxantha*')

IDENTIFICATION 25cm. Mainly green long-tailed conure with scaly breast, brown head, maroon tail and maroon patch on belly. Light grey patch on ear-coverts. Blue in flight feathers with upper- and underwing-coverts

mainly green. Sympatric with Black-capped Conure (261) in yungas of Bolivia and possibly southern Peru; latter separated by red outer primary coverts. Rather similar to Maroon-bellied Conure (251) whose partly sympatric race *devillei* (see Note in Maroon-bellied Conure) is separated by bright red on bend of wing and lesser underwing-coverts and yellow on greater underwing-coverts. Other races of Maroon-bellied can be separated with care in captivity by more extensive green on basal half of uppertail. Combination of mainly green upper- and underwing-coverts, maroon on belly and green rump and cheeks separates Green-cheeked from other similar congeners in captivity. Most often seen in fast, low, rather erratic and slightly undulating flight. Difficult to detect whilst feeding quietly in tree-tops.

VOICE Calls with incessant shrill screeching *kree-ayt*, second note lower than first. Sharp *kreet* or *quee* also reported. More melodious notes sometimes accompany harsh cries. Quiet whilst feeding.

Green-cheeked Conure

DISTRIBUTION AND STATUS Central interior of South America. The species occurs in Mato Grosso and Mato Grosso do Sul, south-west Brazil, and in Beni, La Paz, Cochabamba, Chuquisaca, Tarija and Santa Cruz, eastern Bolivia, through to the fringes of the chaco. It may occur through northern Bolivia to extreme southern Peru where a hybrid with Black-capped Conure was taken (see Note under Black-capped Conure). Apparently absent from pantanal lowlands and restricted in the Río Paraguay basin to isolated patches of chaco woodland on higher ground on the river's right bank. In north-west Argentina it occurs in Salta, Jujuy and, less frequently, Tucumán (a record from Catamarca is probably erroneous). It may occur on the north-west fringes of Paraguay but not proven. Some local seasonal movements may occur, birds at higher elevations descending lower in winter (Mar-Aug). Generally common (very common in Salta and Jujuy); highest densities in deciduous woodland; commonest

461

parrot in forested valleys of eastern Bolivia but probably declining there owing to rapid clearance. Traded in some numbers during 1980s and widespread in captivity outside range.

ECOLOGY The species inhabits dense, often low forests and woodlands with glades, primary and secondary in condition, including fringes of chaco, savanna, deciduous and gallery woodland in pantanal, and moist mossy cloud-forest on eastern Andes where reported to 2,900m, possibly to treeline. In Brazil race *sordida* is found mainly in deciduous forest above 500m. Gregarious (at least outside breeding season), generally in flocks of 10-20, sometimes many more. No information on diet but probably similar to close congeners; forages in tree-tops. Nests in hollow in tree. Eggs Feb, north-west Argentina. Clutch 3-4.

DESCRIPTION Narrow frontal band and lores reddish-brown to blackish; crown brown or greyish-brown laterally marked bluish and green, hindcrown and nape tipped blue; cheeks and sometimes superciliary area green with olive tinge; ear-coverts light grey to pale buff. Upperparts green. Primary coverts bluish-green with remaining coverts mainly green except for some scattered blue, yellow or orange feathers on leading edge of wing. Primaries blue, secondaries green with some blue near shafts; both greyish below. Underwing-coverts green. Feathers on breast, throat and sides of neck brown at base with pale buff, light grey or dull yellowish tips, giving scaly effect; central belly with variable-sized maroon patch (just scattered feathers in some birds); sides of belly, thighs and lower breast green; undertail-coverts bluish-green. Uppertail maroon with green to base of central tail feathers (concealed beneath coverts); undertail maroon. **Bare parts:** Bill grey; cere white; bare periophthalmic skin whitish; iris brown; legs grey.

SEX/AGE Sexes similar. Immature duller with darker iris and less distinct maroon patch on belly.

MEASUREMENTS Wing 129-140; tail 119-142; bill 16-19; tarsus 14-17.

GEOGRAPHICAL VARIATION Five races. A further form possibly exists in La Paz, Bolivia, where birds resembling this species but lacking a maroon belly-patch were observed in dry forests in the Machariapo Valley in 1993 (but these may have been immatures, which are known to roam in flocks in the early months of their independence).

P. m. molinae (Highlands of E Bolivia. Distribution in relation to next race unclear)

P. m. phoenicura (Yungas of NE Bolivia to WC Mato Grosso, Brazil) From nominate and *australis* in having basal half of central tail feathers green. Some birds show yellow on leading edge of wing.

P. m. australis (Salta, Jujuy, Catamarca and Tucumán, NW Argentina, and Tarija, SE Bolivia) Slightly smaller than nominate (wing 125-132), pale margins to throat and breast feathers narrower, maroon area on breast more extensive with less blue on undertail-coverts.

P. m. sordida (S Mato Grosso and Mato Grosso do Sul) Cheeks paler than nominate, red on belly less prominent and edging to feathers on throat and breast less distinct. Yellow-bellied morphs occur (see Note).

P. m. restricta (A few localities in Bolivia) Bluer than other races, with bluish patch on lower cheeks and strong blue suffusion on undertail-coverts. Blue tips to feathers on nape and hindneck form more distinct collar than in nominate.

NOTE A conure with largely yellow underparts from south-west Brazil was formerly treated as a separate species, Yellow-sided Conure *P. hypoxantha*. It is now judged to be a mutation of the race *P. molinae sordida*. See also Note under Maroon-bellied Conure regarding possible con-specificity with Green-cheeked Conure.

REFERENCES Arndt (1996), Bond & Meyer de Schauensee (1942), Dubs (1992), Fjeldså & Krabbe (1990), Forshaw (1989), Gyldenstolpe (1945b), Meyer de Schauensee (1966), Narosky & Yzurieta (1989), Naumburg (1930), Nores & Yzurieta (1994), Pearman (1992), de la Peña (1988), Ridgely (1981), Short (1975), Sick (1993), Yamashita *in litt.* (1996).

---

255 PAINTED CONURE
Pyrrhura picta   Plate 64

Other names: Blue-winged Conure, Santarém Conure (*P. p. amazonum*); Bonaparte's Conure (*P. p. lucianii*)

IDENTIFICATION 22cm. Rather small, mainly green, long-tailed conure with striking pale rounded scales or half-diamond-shaped markings on breast. Forehead, lores, area under eyes, bend of wing dull red. In the race *rosiefrons* forehead and crown are also red and much brighter. Red on carpal area visible in flight. Nominate has blue forehead and forecrown whilst all races have brown hindcrown and hindneck, maroon patch on belly and rump and light ear-coverts. Similar Black-tailed Conure (259), which overlaps in parts of Amazonia, distinguished by red underwing-coverts, green rump and virtual absence of maroon feathers on underparts. Fiery-shouldered Conure (258), sympatric in upper tropical zone of the pantepuí region of north-east South America, distinguished by extensive yellow and orange on leading edge of wing and less distinct scaling on breast and throat. Race *anerythra* of Pearly Conure (253), which widely overlaps with Painted in Amazonia, has green edge of wing, less obvious scaling on breast and mainly green belly. Crimson-bellied Conure (252) is striking deep red on belly. Black-capped Conure (261) distinguished in western Amazon basin by darker crown, less striking breast-scaling and red outer primary coverts. Combination of distinctive breast-scaling, maroon on rump and belly, green underwing-coverts and dull red on lores and cheeks identifies Painted Conure in captivity. In fast tight flocks in twisting, slightly undulating flight.

VOICE Harsh, forceful calls include a descending *ee-ee-m* flight call and single *eeek* contact call. Solitary birds call *peea* to relocate flock. Alarm is an excited yelping *yiarrup*. A *kleek* and some chirruping sounds (often quite loud) given when perched. Easily separated vocally from Black-capped Conure in area of sympatry.

DISTRIBUTION AND STATUS Panama and northern South America in several disjunct populations from Venezuela and the Guianas to eastern Peru. The species is known in Central America only from the south-western portion of the Azuero Peninsula in southern Panama; in Colombia in the lower Río Sinú valley, on the western slope of the eastern Andes in Magdalena and possibly in the intervening lowlands; in Venezuela in the Perijá mountains of Zulia, Bolívar and southern Delta Amacuro; in Guyana from the Courantyne and Essequibo Rivers and from Annai and the Amuku Mountains; in Surinam on coastal sand-ridges and in the interior; and in French Guiana. It extends from northern Brazil south to Goiás and northern Mato Grosso, and penetrates south-east Ecuador (Río Macuma) and eastern Peru from (e.g.) Río Pampas; probably also northern Bolivia. It may make some local seasonal (altitudinal) movements but remains poorly known and apparently rather patchy in distribution and abundance. Declining in some areas owing to deforestation, and conservation status of the restricted-range races *pantchenkoi*, *eisenmanni* and *subandida* perhaps deteriorating. Traded during 1980s and widely held in captivity outside range.

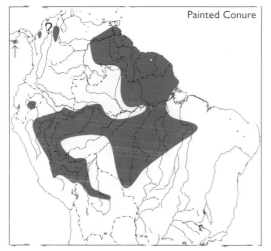

Painted Conure

ECOLOGY The species generally occupies wooded habitats including riverine formations, mature evergreen forest and cloud-forest. It occurs at forest edge and occasionally in cleared areas, inhabiting both terra firme and várzea forest in lowlands, and ranging from sea-level to 1,800m in Venezuela and to upper tropical zone (1,200m) in Peru and south-east Ecuador. Generally in pairs, trios or flocks of up to c. 20. Reported foods include fruits of *Goupia glabra*, *Bassagu guianensis*, *Trema micrantha*, *Heisteria spruceana*, *Zanthoxylum rhoifolium*, *Cordia*, *Protium*, *Alchornea*, *Drypetes*, *Mimosa*, *Byrsonima*, *Dicella*, *Heteropterys*, *Cecropia*, *Ficus*, *Psidium*, *Pourouma*, *Eugenia* and *Euterpe*, flowers and fruit of *Cochlospermum orinocense* and *Symphonia globulifera*, *Allantoma lineata*, *Bertholletia excelsa* and *Dioclea glabra*, flowers of *Erythrina*, seeds of *Cecropia* and algae from ponds; reported eating Diptera larvae in Amazonia. Nests probably in tree-hollow: seen investigating cavity in *Anacardium excelsum*. Birds in breeding condition Jan-Feb, Panama, with fledged young reported late Mar and Apr. Breeds Dec-Feb, Guyana, and Jul-Sep, south of range. Clutch 4-5 in captivity.

DESCRIPTION Narrow frontal band, lores, upper cheeks and area around eye dull red; lower cheeks dull red with blue tips on some feathers; forecrown blue, hindcrown and hindneck dull reddish-brown with a few blue flecks; ear-coverts buff. Nape bluish-green merging to green on mantle, scapulars and upper back; lower back maroon; rump and uppertail-coverts green. Upperwing-coverts green except for blue outer primary coverts and some red feathers in carpal area. Primaries blue above, greyish beneath. Underwing-coverts green. Feathers on throat, breast and sides of neck dull brown with broad buff

margins, resulting in striking scaling in shape of half-diamonds or half-circles; lower breast and sides of belly green, centre of belly maroon; undertail-coverts green. Tail green basally, maroon distally. **Bare parts**: Bill brownish-grey; bare periophthalmic skin greyish; iris brown; legs grey.

SEX/AGE Sexes similar. Immature *roseifrons* has less red on head than adult.

MEASUREMENTS Wing 115-130; tail 90-108; bill 14-17; tarsus 13-16.

GEOGRAPHICAL VARIATION Eight races. Three further names, *microtera*, *orinocensis* and *cuchivera*, do not appear to warrant perpetuation.

P. p. picta (Guianas into Bolívar and the S Delta Amacuro, Venezuela)

P. p. amazonum (Both banks of lower Amazon including lower Rio Tapajós and Rio Tocantins) Similar to nominate but blue on forecrown restricted to band in front of eyes; periophthalmic skin blackish; and on average less green on base of tail.

P. p. lucianii (W Amazon basin of Brazil where known from upper Rio Madeira, Rio Solimões and Porto Velho, Rondônia. Birds from south of Leticia, Colombia, resemble this race) Little or no blue on forehead and forecrown; little or no red on bend of wing.

P. p. roseifrons (W Amazon basin on upper Rio Juruá, Brazil. Possibly also in E Peru) Crown and facial area bright red (less extensive in immature). Red on bend of wing reduced or absent in some birds.

P. p. subandina (Lower Río Sinú valley, Colombia) Similar to nominate but narrow band on forehead and lores extending to below eyes is brownish-red; cheeks bluish-green, crown dark brown, bend of wing without red and ear-coverts yellowish brown rather than buff.

P. p. caeruliceps (Western slope of E Andes in Magdalena, Colombia) Similar to nominate but with reddish band from forehead and lores to below eye becoming brownish-red on upper cheeks. Extensive blue on head and absence of blue on cheeks separates from *subandina*. Larger than nominate and *eisenmanni* (wing 121-123).

P. p. pantchenkoi (Perijá Mountains, Venezuela/Colombia border) Similar to nominate but with red area on forehead, lores and over ocular area (including above eyes), becoming brownish on upper cheeks. Greyish brown crown and absence of blue on cheeks separates this race from *caeruliceps* and *subandina*.

P. p. eisenmanni (South-western Azuero Peninsula, Panama) Similar to nominate but with narrow red frontal band, red lores and red below eyes becoming reddish-brown on upper cheeks. Bend of wing green or with only scattered red feathers and scaling on breast less striking than nominate. From *subandina* by absence of blue on cheeks and more extensive red on face.

NOTE It has been suggested that Painted is conspecific with White-eared Conure (256) and that the newly discovered Panamanian race *eisenmanni* of Painted Conure provides the link (but it has also been mooted that *eisenmanni* itself might better be given species status, as might several other isolated forms of *picta* as here constituted). Painted and White-eared Conures are here treated as separate species pending further investigations.

REFERENCES Arndt (1996), Bond (1955), Delgado (1985), Desenne (1994), Desenne & Strahl (1994), Gyldenstolpe (1945a), Haverschmidt (1968), Hilty & Brown (1986), Meyer de Schauensee (1949, 1966), Meyer de Schauensee & Phelps (1978), Naumburg (1930), Pearson (1974), Ridgely (1981), Sick (1993), Snyder (1966), Tostain *et al.* (1992), Whitney (1996).

---

256 WHITE-EARED CONURE
Pyrrhura leucotis   Plate 64

Other names: Blue-naped Conure, Emma's Conure, Salvadori's Conure (*P. l. emma*); Maroon-faced Parakeet, (Brazilian) Grey-breasted Conure (*P. l. griseipectus*); Monagas White-eared Conure (*P. l auricularis*); Pfrimer's Conure (*P. l. pfrimeri*)

IDENTIFICATION 22-23cm. Rather small, delicate, long-tailed conure with dark head, contrasting white or pale brownish patch on ear-coverts and blue or bluish-green on nape. Pale central band and dark tips to feathers on breast gives scaly pattern. Maroon patch on back and rump and on belly. Bright red patch at bend of wing. Nominate race sympatric with Maroon-bellied (251) and Blue-throated (250) Conures: former occurs at higher altitude and distinguished by mainly bronze uppertail and mainly green rump, latter by yellow patches on sides of neck and blue on throat and breast. Red-eared Conure (264), partly sympatric in northern Venezuela, generally occurs at higher altitude (usually at about 1,000-1,700m) and has green rump, red ear-coverts and no blue on nape. White-eared is only scaly-breasted long-tailed small parrot in the central and north-east Brazilian parts of its range. Separated from other scaly-breasted *Pyrrhura* in captivity by combination of dark head, pale ear-coverts, maroon cheeks, rump and belly, and blue on throat, neck and nape; but some races of (allopatric) Painted Conure (255) are very similar to some races of White-eared and should be separated with caution. Restless; in small flocks in fast, slightly undulating flight.

VOICE Calls include high-pitched, yelping, rather staccato *chee cheet chee* and *ki ki* sounds, and a *teet* whilst perched. Quieter and purer-sounding than most *Pyrrhura*.

White-eared Conure

DISTRIBUTION AND STATUS Several disjunct populations in northern and eastern South America. In northern Venezuela the species occurs in tropical and lower subtropical zones in mountains from Yaracuy to Miranda and disjunctly from Anzoátegui to Sucre and Monagas. In north-eastern Brazil it reappears in Ceará and perhaps disjunctly in Alagoas and Pernambuco, with an outlying population in central-eastern Brazil in Goiás. In south-eastern Brazil it extends from southern Bahia through coastal states and south-east Minas Gerais to São Paulo. Some seasonal dispersal may occur to and from deciduous habitats. Locally fairly common in northern Venezuela with a substantial population in Guatopo National Park, Miranda. In serious trouble in north-east Brazil as locally preferred (higher-elevation) forest continues to be cleared, and likewise in lowland south-east Brazil where it now mainly persists in protected but widely scattered relict populations such as the Sooretama/Linhares reserve complex in Espírito Santo and the Rio Doce State Park in Minas Gerais. The single known locality in Goiás holds *Astronium faccinifolium* trees used extensively for fence-posts, and the future there is uncertain. Formerly traded internationally but export restrictions in range states have rendered it rare in captivity.

ECOLOGY The species inhabits forest, edge and adjacent clearings with scattered trees including naturally shaded cacao plantations (Bahia), sometimes entering parks and villages; mostly in lowlands (e.g. to 600m in south-eastern Brazil) but reported to 1,700m in cloud-forest in northern Venezuela, and in higher elevation forest in north-east Brazil. Gregarious, usually in flocks of c. 15-20. Takes similar food to congeners in captivity and probably has comparable diet to close relatives in wild, where recorded feeding on *Miconia hypoleuca* and said to attack grain. No information on breeding in wild except that it occurs May-Jul, Venezuela. Clutch 5-9 in captivity.

DESCRIPTION Most of cheeks and forehead brownish-maroon with blue before and above eye and on lower cheeks; crown and nape dark brown flecked brownish-orange from pale-tipped feathers; ear-coverts white to pale brownish; nape greenish-blue. Mantle and upper back green with indistinct dark margins to some feathers; lower back, rump and uppertail-coverts maroon. Wing-coverts green except blue primary coverts and red patch at bend of wing. Primaries blue. Underwing with lesser coverts green, greater coverts dark greyish, flight feathers grey. Feathers on throat and sides of neck blue at base with buff subterminal band and blackish tips; breast feathers with less or no blue and instead with brown bases; underparts otherwise green with large maroon patch on centre of belly. Uppertail maroon with green edges to base of outerwebs of lateral feathers; undertail dull reddish-brown. **Bare parts**: Bill black; cere blackish; bare peri-ophthalmic skin greyish-white; iris dark orange-brown; legs dark grey.

SEX/AGE All plumages similar.

MEASUREMENTS Wing 115-125; tail 97-115; bill 13-15; tarsus 13-14.

GEOGRAPHICAL VARIATION Five widely disjunct races.
> *P. l. leucotis* (S Bahia to São Paulo including SE Minas Gerais in SE Brazil)
> *P. l. griseipectus* (Ceará, Alagoas and the Serra Negra in Pernambuco, NE Brazil) Patch on ear-coverts whiter and more extensive than nominate. No blue above

eyes but blue band on nape more pronounced. Ocular skin blackish. Basal half of uppertail green.

P. l. pfrimeri (One locality in Goiás, CE Brazil) Similar to nominate but has dull blue crown, nape and back of head. Breast and throat greenish-blue or blue with pale edges.

P. l. emma (Mountains from Yaracuy to Miranda, N Venezuela) Similar to nominate but forehead to nape blue. Striking white cere and dull white ocular skin. Dull yellow subterminal band to feathers on lower breast.

P. l. auricularis (Mountains from Anzoátegui to Sucre and Monagas, N Venezuela). Similar to *emma* but darker green with dark grey cere and ocular skin.

REFERENCES Arndt (1996), Collar (1997), Desenne & Strahl (1994), Forshaw (1989), Galetti & Stotz (1996), Meyer de Schauensee (1966), Meyer de Schauensee & Phelps (1978), Ridgely (1981), Sick (1993), Teixeira *et al.* (1988), Yamashita *in litt.* (1996).

---

257 SANTA MARTA CONURE
Pyrrhura viridicata   Plate 65

Other names: Santa Marta Parakeet

IDENTIFICATION 25cm. Mainly green long tailed conure with orange and red on leading edge and bend of wing and underwing-coverts. Narrow red frontal band. Red patch on belly often forms distinct broad transverse bar. Blue in primaries with dull red undertail. Only *Pyrrhura* conure within restricted range and only sympatric confusion species is Red-fronted Conure (231), distinguished by its larger size, more extensive red on head and wholly green tail, flight feathers, upperwing-coverts and belly. Not known in captivity (at least not outside Colombia) but combination of green cheeks, absence of scaling on breast and neck, bluish-green primary coverts, green rump and red and yellow on bend of wing and on underwing-coverts separates this from congeners. Forms noisy fast-flying twisting flocks. Birds alight suddenly in tree crown, clamber along branches and utter softer notes. Timid, refusing close approach.

VOICE Screeching calls similar to Painted Conure. Softer chattering notes whilst climbing in branches.

Santa Marta Conure

DISTRIBUTION AND STATUS Endemic to the Santa Marta massif, north-east Colombia. Recorded localities include La Cumbre, east of Taquina at the foot of the Páramo Mamarongo, and Cerro Quemado in the San Lorenzo Mountains. Some seasonal altitudinal movements occur. Nearly all the subtropical forest habitat is either designated as forest reserve or national park, but forest clearance for marijuana plantations has been extensive, as has been the use of herbicides to combat it, so that only 15% of original forest remains (mostly on northern slopes), including a mere 200 km² at the species's preferred altitude. Fairly common within this very restricted range but population probably below 5,000 birds. VULNERABLE.

ECOLOGY The species inhabits cooler humid mountain forest and forest edge mainly in subtropical zone, sometimes also grass- and bracken-covered slopes with montane shrubs; chiefly at 1,800-2,800m. Generally in small flocks; one report of 16 birds. No information on diet and little on breeding. Birds reported in nest Jun, and juvenile and breeding-condition adults reported Sep.

DESCRIPTION Forehead bright red; lores, crown, cheeks and sides of neck green with brownish suffusion, with some maroon tips; ear-coverts brownish-maroon. Nape dull green brightening on upperparts. Primary coverts bluish-green; leading edge of wing and carpal area marked bright red and orange; other coverts bright green. Primaries blue on outerwebs with narrow bluish-green outer margin; secondaries green. Underwing with lesser coverts mottled bright orange and red, greater dull olive-brown with yellow margins, flight feathers dull olive-brown. Underparts bright green with scattered red and orange feathers on lower breast sometimes forming distinct broad band; base of belly feathers maroon. Uppertail green tinged dull maroon, especially on innerwebs; undertail dull red. **Bare parts**: Bill flesh at base, otherwise ivory with olive tinge; bare periophthalmic skin white; iris brown; legs dull black.

SEX/AGE Sexes similar. Immature undescribed.

MEASUREMENTS Wing 137-146; tail 104-123; bill 15-17; tarsus 14-16.

GEOGRAPHICAL VARIATION None.

REFERENCES Collar *et al.* (1994), Fjeldså & Krabbe (1990), Forshaw (1989), Hilty & Brown (1986), Meyer de Schauensee (1949), Ridgely (1981), Todd & Carriker (1922).

---

258 FIERY-SHOULDERED CONURE
Pyrrhura egregia   Plate 65

Other names: Fiery-shouldered Parakeet

IDENTIFICATION 25cm. Mainly green long-tailed conure with bright orange marked yellow on carpal area, leading edge of wing and underwing-coverts. Primary coverts blue (bright yellow in some birds). Narrow maroon frontal band. Brownish crown with broad bare whitish eye-ring. Pale edges to feathers on throat, upper breast and sides of neck give scaled appearance. Characteristic species of the pantepui region, replaced in adjacent lowlands by Painted Conure (255), although the two may overlap in the upper tropical zone: Painted distinguished by maroon on rump, more obvious scaling on breast and relatively small red patch on carpal area (not extensive yellow and orange extending along leading edge of wing). No other geographically close relatives. From congeners in captivity by orange and yellow on wing and underwing-coverts. Inhabits mountainous forest regions, generally in pairs or small noisy flocks. Flight with shallow undulations.

VOICE Noisy. No specific information.

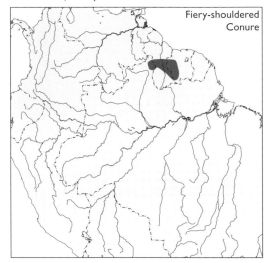

Fiery-shouldered Conure

DISTRIBUTION AND STATUS Restricted distribution in the pantepui region of interior north-eastern South America. The species is known from Venezuela in the Gran Sabana of south-eastern Bolívar at Mount Roraima and Arabopó and from Mount Auyan-tepui and Mount Ptari-tepui. It occurs in adjacent western Guyana at (e.g.) Kamarang River and upper Mazaruni River, Merumé Mountains and Pakaraima Mountains south to Annai. Reports from Surinam remain unconfirmed. It probably occurs in north-eastern Roraima, Brazil. Range inaccessible and few details on status but apparently fairly common. Large part of Venezuelan range included in Gran Sabana National Park. Small numbers exported from Guyana in late 1980s and subsequently bred in captivity.

ECOLOGY The species inhabits forests, edge and woodlands in upper tropical and subtropical zones in precipitous uplands at 700-1,800m. Generally in flocks of c. 7-25 birds. No information on diet except that birds visit Amerindian villages Jul-Aug to feed on fruits of (e.g.) ripe guavas. Little information on breeding; occurs Mar-Apr with young fledging May-Jun.

DESCRIPTION Narrow maroon frontal band; crown, lores, hindneck and upper cheeks brownish; ear-coverts reddish-brown; feathers on sides of neck basally green with buff subterminal band and narrow dark tip giving scaly appearance. Upperparts green with faint narrow dark margins to some feathers. Carpal area and leading edge of wing orange marked yellow; primary coverts usually blue but sometimes bright yellow; upperwing-coverts otherwise green. Outerwebs of flight feathers blue. Underwing-coverts orange marked with yellow; underside of flight feathers greyish. Feathers on throat and breast basally green with buff subterminal band and dark tip giving scaly appearance; underparts otherwise green but most feathers on belly maroon at base and tipped green, sometimes forming maroon patch. Uppertail very dark maroon, green

at base; undertail greyish. **Bare parts**: Bill horn; bare periophthalmic skin white; iris brown; legs brownish-black.

SEX/AGE Sexes similar. Immature has much less yellow and orange on upperwing and underwing-coverts; crown green and scaling on breast and sides of neck less pronounced.

MEASUREMENTS Wing 125-139; tail 99-117; bill 15-17; tarsus 13-14.

GEOGRAPHICAL VARIATION Two races.
> *P. e. egregia* (Extreme SE Venezuela in SE Bolívar at Mount Roraima and Arabopó and highlands of W Guyana)
> *P. e. obscura* (Subtropical zone of Mount Auyan-tepui and on Mount Ptari-tepui in E Bolívar, Venezuela) Similar to nominate but upperparts darker green and underparts slightly so. Maroon patch on belly less frequent and less prominent.

REFERENCES Chapman (1931), Clubb & Clubb (1990), Desenne & Strahl (1994), Forshaw (1989), Gilliard (1941), Meyer de Schauensee (1966), Meyer de Schauensee & Phelps (1978), Ridgely (1981), Snyder (1966), Zimmer & Phelps (1946).

259 BLACK-TAILED CONURE
Pyrrhura melanura   Plate 65

Other names: Maroon-tailed Conure/Parakeet; Souancé's Conure/Parakeet (*P. melanura souancei*); Pacific Black-tailed Conure/Parakeet (*P. melanura pacifica*)

IDENTIFICATION 24-25cm. Mainly green long-tailed conure. Leading edge of wing and primary coverts red. Cheeks and ear-coverts green. Underside of tail blackish. White ocular skin (grey in race *pacifica*). Breast feathers green or greyish-green on bases with buff tips giving scaly appearance (see Geographical Variation). Painted Conure (255) overlaps in western Amazonia but shows more obvious scaling on breast and sides of neck, maroon cheeks and green primary coverts. The probably allopatric Brown-breasted Parakeet (263) has mainly bright yellow primary coverts and leading edge to wing, maroon ear-coverts and more faintly patterned, browner breast. Distinguished from similar Fiery-shouldered Conure (258) in captivity by green underwing-coverts and absence of maroon patch on belly. The race *berlepschi* mixes (at least seasonally) in Cordillera du Cutucú, Ecuador, with the rare White-breasted Conure (262), which has paler breast, bright orange ear-coverts and more red on upperwing. Black-tailed is told from other *Pyrrhura* in captivity by combination of red primary coverts, scaly breast and sides of neck, and glossy blackish undertail. Travels in noisy flocks in shallowly undulating flight, crossing open terrain very close to ground. Becomes silent and still at approach of danger. Sometimes perches in isolated trees.

VOICE Loud raucous shrieking *screeet screeet screeet* in flight or when flushed. Call similar to Painted Conure.

DISTRIBUTION AND STATUS North-western South America in western Amazon basin, southern portion of Orinoco catchment and Pacific slope of Andes in south-western Colombia and western Ecuador. In Venezuela the species is found in central southern Bolívar along upper Río Paragua and in Amazonas south of Río Ventauri; in western Amazon basin of Brazil between Rios Negro and Solimões. It occurs in the central Andes of Colombia in the upper Magdalena Valley from southern Tolima to Huila and disjunctly east of Andes (in lowlands and to c. 500m in foothills) from the Macarena Mountains south through eastern lowland Ecuador and north-east and eastern Peru. A separate population occurs west of the Andes in north-west Ecuador south to northern Los Ríos, with a single record in Nariño, south-west Colombia. Mainly resident but apparent seasonal absence in some parts of Colombia suggests regular movements. Patchily distributed but mainly common and most numerous parrot in some parts of range such as upper Magdalena Valley and perhaps parts of Esmeraldas in north-west Ecuador. Presumed decline in some areas (e.g. Pacific slope of Ecuador) owing to habitat loss. Poorly known eastern Peru. Not a popular local cagebird but traded internationally in significant numbers in late 1980s and fairly well known in captivity outside range.

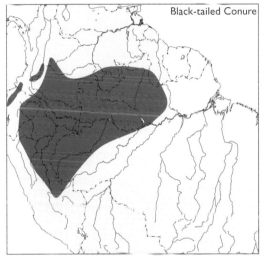

Black-tailed Conure

ECOLOGY The species occupies tropical to temperate zone formations including várzea, lowland and pre-montane rain-forest and cloud forest, often in partly cleared areas and edges and tolerant of secondary forest; at 150-300m in Venezuela (nominate), to 3,200m on eastern Andean slopes (*souancei*), 1,600-2,800m on east slope of central Andes (*chapmani*), to 1,700m in Nariño (*pacifica*), to 1,500m (*berlepschi*). Generally in flocks of 6-12, remaining in tree-tops when resting but moving to lower branches to forage. Few details on diet, with known foods including fruits of *Miconia theaezans* (upper Magdalena Valley), *Fagara tachnelo* and tree bark (Amazonia). Little information on breeding, which occurs Apr-Jun, Río Napo headwaters, Ecuador. Copulation observed Jan (Colombia). Clutch four in captivity.

DESCRIPTION Lores, forehead, crown and hindneck brownish, tipped paler reddish-brown on crown forming speckled pattern; cheeks, ear-coverts and area behind eyes green; brown on hindcrown shades to green on nape. Upperparts green with olive tinge on some feathers. Primary coverts red with yellow tips; leading edge of wing red; upperwing-coverts otherwise green with olive tinge. Primaries dark greenish-blue with dark tips. Underwing coverts green; underside of flight feathers blackish. Throat and breast feathers green or greyish-green with pale buff margins giving striking scaly effect, pale edges becoming less distinct on sides of neck; belly and undertail-coverts green with dark olive tinge. Uppertail dark maroon with outer feathers basally green; undertail glossy black. **Bare parts**: Bill pale greyish; bare periophthalmic skin whitish; iris dark brown; legs grey.

SEX/AGE Sexes similar. Immature has less red (more green) on primary coverts.

MEASUREMENTS Wing 125-136; tail 98-119; bill 15-16; tarsus 13-15.

GEOGRAPHICAL VARIATION Five races. Two, *berlepschi* and *chapmani*, were formerly considered separate species. Morphological (and apparently structural) distinctiveness of the Pacific slope isolate *pacifica* could, however, be used to argue full species status, and further investigation is warranted.

P. m. melanura (Western Amazon basin in NE Peru, W Brazil, E Ecuador, E Colombia except below, and S Venezuela)

P. m. souancei (E Colombia from Macarena Mountains south-west to Putumayo through E Ecuador possibly to extreme N Peru. Probably confined to slopes of E Andes and mostly replaced by nominate in lowlands) Similar to nominate but with little or no yellow on tips of primary coverts. Wider pale margins to feathers on breast and sides of neck and broader green margins to tail feathers. Sometimes with brownish patch on belly.

P. m. berlepschi (Huallaga Valley, E Peru, and SE Ecuador at Cordillera Cutucú. One specimen with characteristics of this race reported from head of Magdalena Valley suggesting occurrence in Colombia) Similar to last race but with even broader pale margins to breast feathers (some Ecuador birds reported with almost entirely white breasts), less red on leading edge of wing and more pronounced brownish patch on belly. Distribution in relation to *souancei* inadequately documented and they may not be distinct. See Note under White-breasted Conure.

P. m. pacifica (NW Ecuador and SW Colombia) Darker and less olive than other races with grey rather than white ocular skin. Bill blackish and more delicate than other races. No yellow tips to primary coverts. Pale edges to breast feathers darker and narrower than other races. Forecrown green with very narrow reddish-brown frontal band. Tail relatively shorter than nominate.

P. m. chapmani (Eastern slope of upper Magdalena Valley in C Andes from S Tolima to Huila at about 1,600-2,800m) Very broad pale (buff) edges to feathers on breast extending further onto sides of neck than nominate. Sometimes with brownish patch on belly. Larger than nominate (wing 133-142, tail 118-133).

REFERENCES Arndt (1996), Bond (1955), Chapman (1926), Desenne & Strahl (1994), Evans (1988), Fjeldså & Krabbe (1990), Forshaw (1989), Friedmann (1948), Hilty & Brown (1986), Meyer de Schauensee (1949), Meyer de Schauensee & Phelps (1978), Ridgely (1981), Ridgely & Gaulin (1980), Ridgely & Robbins (1988), Sick (1993), Whitney (1996).

260 EL ORO CONURE
Pyrrhura orcesi   Plate 65

Other names: El Oro Parakeet

IDENTIFICATION 22cm. Rather small, mainly green long-tailed conure with red on forehead and forecrown (green in immature), virtually no scaling on breast and blue in primaries. Red on outer primary and median coverts. Only *Pyrrhura* within limited range in western Ecuador. Superficially similar to allopatric Rose-crowned Conure (265), which has more red on head and white primary coverts. Geographically (and taxonomically) closest relative is Black-tailed Conure (259), which occurs (race *pacifica*) on west slope of Andes over 200km north of northernmost site for El Oro Conure, and shows black undertail, bold breast-scaling and no red on forecrown. Red on outer upperwing, red forecrown and virtual absence of breast-scaling separate El Oro from other congeners, and smaller size and dull maroon tip to upper surface of tail distinguish it from superficially similar *Aratinga* conures. Small flocks in moist Pacific slope forest.

VOICE Rather trilling but quite harsh and metallic *tchreeet tchreeet* flight call. Quieter chirruping from perched birds sometimes sounds like Budgerigar (155). Calls considerably higher-pitched than Black-tailed Conure.

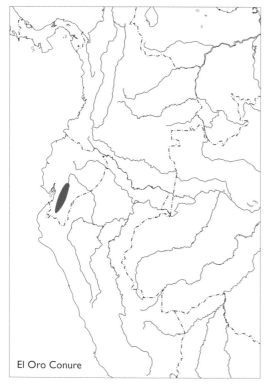

El Oro Conure

DISTRIBUTION AND STATUS Pacific slope of Andean foothills in Ecuador. This parrot was first recognised west of Piñas in El Oro province in Ecuador in 1980; subsequent reports suggest its range is confined to an area only 100km from north to south and between 5-10km wide. Piñas appears to represent the southern limit with the northernmost record from north-east of Naranjal in Azuay.

Fluctuations in numbers at Piñas suggest some seasonal movements or decline owing to further habitat loss. Apparently quite numerous in areas where suitable habitat remains but evidently greatly reduced in numbers owing to extensive forest conversion to (e.g.) pasture and plantations. Fairly extensive, apparently suitable habitat remains within tiny suspected range with 1987 satellite images suggesting 50-80% forest cover intact, and an estimated 2,000-20,000 birds in 1992. No known protected areas in range. VULNERABLE.

ECOLOGY This species inhabits moist epiphyte-laden (cloud-) forest, generally in cloud from before dawn to about midday, in the upper tropical zone between 600 and 1,300m, although a 1939 specimen collected at *c.* 300m suggests it ranged lower when habitat was available. Although primary formations appear to be favoured, birds can evidently exist (at least for the short term) in rather fragmented forest: a population discovered in 1991 about 40km north of Piñas at Buenaventura lives in orchards and gardens with only tiny patches of remaining wet forest. Generally in flocks of about 4-12 birds but one gathering of 60 birds reported. Specific food items include fruits of *Ficus*, *Heliocarpus popayanensis*, *Hyeronima* and (probably fruit) of *Cecropia*, with drinking observed from small bromeliad. Begging behaviour of recently fledged young in Jun and Aug suggests nesting Mar-Jul.

DESCRIPTION Forehead, forecrown and lores bright red, sometimes with scattered red feathers on crown or breast; cheeks and ear-coverts green; crown green with faint greyish suffusion, nape green; sides of neck green but with rather indistinct pale buff or grey margins on some feathers, giving faint scaling. Upperparts green. Alula, outer median coverts and outer primary coverts bright red; other coverts green. Outerwebs of primaries and outer secondaries blue with very narrow green outer margins. Underparts green, slightly more olive than upperparts with very faint scaling on breast (from indistinct pale edges) and variable reddish patch on belly. Uppertail green with maroon tips; undertail dull greyish-green strongly suffused dark maroon. **Bare parts**: Bill horn; bare periophthalmic skin pinkish-white; iris dark brown; legs black.

SEX/AGE Female thought to have green lores. Immature has mostly green forecrown and outermost upperwing-coverts.

MEASUREMENTS Wing 117-132; tail 89-103; bill 16-17; tarsus 13-15.

GEOGRAPHICAL VARIATION None.

REFERENCES Best *et al.* (1993), Collar *et al.* (1992, 1994), Forshaw (1989), Ridgely and Robbins (1988).

261 BLACK-CAPPED CONURE
Pyrrhura rupicola   Plate 66

Other names: Rock Conure; Sandia Conure (*P. rupicola sandiae*)

IDENTIFICATION 25cm. Mainly green long-tailed conure with black cap and red outer primary coverts and leading edge of wing. Olive cheeks contrast with dark crown; striking scaly breast; green uppertail. Sympatric with Green-cheeked Conure (254) in northern Bolivia (wild hybrids may occur: see Note) and possibly extreme southern Peru, and with Painted Conure (255) in western Amazonia, but distinguished by darker crown and red outer primary coverts, and from latter also by less scaly breast. From other congeners in captivity by these features and mainly green uppertail. Usually remains in tops of tall trees, rarely descending below c. 30m. Gregarious, in flocks in fast, shallowly undulating flight generally at canopy height.

VOICE Reputedly distinct from partly sympatric Painted Conure but no details available.

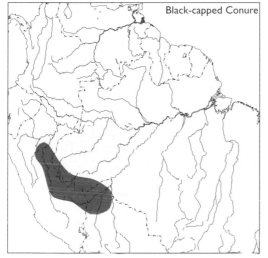

Black-capped Conure

DISTRIBUTION AND STATUS Western Amazon basin. It has been recorded in eastern Peru from southern Loreto to Madre de Dios and Puno, and in northern Bolivia in Pando, La Paz and Yungas and lowlands of northern Beni east to the border with Rondônia, Brazil, with one record to date in extreme western Brazil (Rio Branco, Acre). Generally common (perhaps scarcer at edges of range) but may be declining locally owing to habitat disturbance. Status is unlikely to alter in near future as large areas of habitat remain intact, and present in several protected areas including Manú National Park, Peru. Apparently rarely persecuted. Scarce in captivity.

ECOLOGY Humid lowland tropical forest, including both várzea and terra firme formations, is the preferred habitat, with less frequent occurrence in the east Andean foothills, generally below c. 300m. Gregarious, usually in flocks of up to c. 30; smaller groups in breeding season. Generally feeds in canopy but no specific information on diet or breeding. Believed to nest Feb-Mar, but copulation observed Sep. Clutch up to seven in captivity.

DESCRIPTION Lores, forehead and crown dark blackish-brown; cheeks, ear-coverts and superciliary area yellowish-olive; hindneck dark brown with narrow pale edges. Upperparts green. Outer primary coverts, alula and leading edge of wings bright red; other coverts mainly green. Flight feathers mainly bluish-green above with narrow black tips; dark grey below. Underwing-coverts green. Feathers on throat, sides of neck and upper breast black at base with broad whitish margins, becoming yellowish-white on lower breast and almost there forming unbroken pale band; belly and undertail-coverts green with maroon tinge in centre of belly. Uppertail mainly green. **Bare parts**: Bill slaty-grey; cere pale grey; bare periophthalmic skin whitish; iris brown; legs blackish.

SEX/AGE Sexes similar. Immature has nearly all-green primary coverts and leading edge to wings.

MEASUREMENTS Wing 124-135; tail 105-120; bill 16-17; tarsus 13-16.

GEOGRAPHICAL VARIATION Two races, possibly not distinct.

P. r. rupicola (C Peru. Range in relation to next race poorly documented)

P. r. sandiae (SE Peru, extreme W Brazil and N Bolivia) Narrower pale edges to feathers on breast, throat and sides of neck, with edges absent on hindneck.

NOTE An apparent hybrid with Green-cheeked Conure has been taken in Puno, southern Peru, raising the possibility that these forms are conspecific.

REFERENCES Arndt (1996), Bond (1955), Bond & Meyer de Schauensee (1942), Gyldenstolpe (1945b), O'Neill (1981), Ridgely (1981), Sick (1993), Whitney (1996).

262 WHITE-BREASTED CONURE
Pyrrhura albipectus   Plate 65

Other names: White-breasted Parakeet, White-necked Parakeet/Conure

IDENTIFICATION 24cm. Long-tailed, mostly green conure with very pale breast. Red primary coverts, blue primaries and brownish-grey cap. Only *Pyrrhura* with buffy white throat and breast but may be confused with race *berlepschi* of Black-tailed Conure (259) which co-occurs (at least seasonally) in the Cordillera du Cutucú in south-eastern Ecuador (see Note). White-breasted separated by paler breast, bright orange ear-coverts and more red on upperwing. Combination of white breast and hindneck, orange ear-coverts and red primary coverts safely separates this from other small conures in captivity. Generally in small flocks of 5-8 and up to c. 20 birds in rapid slightly undulating flight just above tree canopy.

VOICE Constant rapid *screet screet* calls in flight. Single *skee* or *week* chirps whilst feeding, repeated more rapidly and erratically to create noisy clamour from flock prior to taking flight. Juveniles beg with persistent noisy high pitched note.

DISTRIBUTION AND STATUS This species is confined to south-east Ecuador in three separate areas: Parque Nacional (PN) Podocarpus in Zamora-Chinchipe province on east slope of Andes and further south at Panguri; Cordillera de Cutucú (where known for certain only in western part) in Morona-Santiago; and in the Ecuadorian portion of the central Cordillera del Condor (not recorded on Peruvian side but may occur there). Probably resident. Apparent absence from some localities at certain times of year (e.g. Cordillera de Cutucú) possibly only reflects less conspicuous behaviour of breeding birds. Whilst overall population small (low density and limited range suggest a few thousand), birds are common in parts of PN Podocarpus, but may be vulnerable to rapid deforestation in upper tropical zone on east slope of Andes. Moreover, although much intact habitat remains in the subtropical zone, mining, logging and small-scale farming could also destroy forest at higher altitudes (including PN Podocarpus). Trade in live birds exists within Ecuador and may exert an additional pressure.

Apart from PN Podocarpus, the species occurs in Shuar Indian reserves in Cordillera de Cutucú and the Río Nangaritza valley (adjacent to PN Podocarpus). VULNERABLE.

White-breasted Conure

ECOLOGY The species inhabits humid forest in the upper tropical and subtropical zones, perhaps preferring upland forest along rivers; recorded between about 900 and 2,000m, mostly at 1,400-1,800m (600m for one specimen appears mistaken). It occurs in primary forest but tolerates some habitat disturbance and is known from partly cleared areas. Generally in flocks of a dozen or less, sometimes up to 50. Recorded food items include flowers of the vine *Piptocarpha poeppigiana*, seeds of *Mollia gracilis*, fruits of *Ficus*, *Miconia punctata* and *Alchornea glandulosa*, berries of *Tetrorchidium macrophyllum* and flowers of the liana *Mikania leiostachya*, with suggestion that the first two are highly favoured at least seasonally. Generally feeds in higher branches but descends within metres of ground to exploit favoured food plants. No information on nesting except that one specimen taken Apr appeared to have just finished breeding whilst juvenile being fed by adults in Sep suggested breeding May-Jul.

DESCRIPTION Narrow frontal band brownish-red; lores and crown to hindneck greyish-brown with paler tips to some feathers, giving mottled appearance; upper cheeks green marked yellow; ear-coverts orange with some bright yellow marks; lower cheeks and sides of neck white with dusky margins to some feathers, giving hint of scaling; hindneck white marked brown and green. Upperparts bright green. Leading edge of wing and primary coverts bright red; other coverts green. Primaries blue with narrow ultramarine borders to outerwebs. Underwing with coverts mainly green but some red on greater coverts, flight feathers greyish. Throat white merging to creamy yellow

on breast and upper belly; remaining underparts green with some maroon markings in centre of belly. Uppertail basally green, maroon distally; undertail greyish-black. **Bare parts**: Upper mandible blackish horn-grey, lower pale horn-grey with blackish-grey on sides; bare periophthalmic skin ivory-white; iris blackish; legs black.

SEX/AGE Sexes similar. Immature reported to have virtually all of leading edge of wing and primary coverts green and paler orange ear-coverts with fawn (not reddish-brown) frontal band.

MEASUREMENTS Wing 135-141; tail 100-107; bill 16-17; tarsus 14-16.

GEOGRAPHICAL VARIATION None.

NOTE Mixed flocks of White-breasted and Black-tailed Conures in the Cordillera de Cutucú at 1,000-1,200m has led to speculation that these forms may be conspecific. Individual White-breasted Conures in these flocks showed morphological differences to those at higher altitude (1,200-1,700m), but whether these differences were related to age, hybridisation or simply random variation is unclear. However, this observation remains insufficient alone to justify reducing White-breasted to a race of Black-tailed; further field investigation is required.

REFERENCES Bloch *et al.* (1991), Collar *et al.* (1992, 1994), Krabbe & Sornoza (1994), Rasmussen *et al.* (1996), Ridgely (1981), Ridgely & Robbins (1988), Toyne *in litt.* (1996), Toyne (1994), Toyne *et al.* (1992).

263 BROWN-BREASTED CONURE
Pyrrhura calliptera   Plate 66

Other names: Flame-winged Conure, Beautiful Conure

IDENTIFICATION 23cm. Rather small, mainly green conure with brown breast and bright yellow (sometimes orange) on wing, conspicuous in flight. Tail proportionately shorter than many congeners. Pale yellowish bill. Only *Pyrrhura* in limited range and easily told by yellow on wings. Not known in captivity but distinguished from other *Pyrrhura* by combination of brown breast, yellow on wings and yellowish bill. Flight slightly undulating in tight, fast-flying flocks.

VOICE Noisy. Harsh far-carrying *screeyr screeyr*.

DISTRIBUTION AND STATUS Eastern Cordillera of the Colombian Andes. It has been reported on both slopes of the eastern Andes in Colombia, mainly in Cundinamarca and Boyacá but now apparently absent on west slope (all reports were before 1914 in Cundinamarca). Known range extends from Fusagasugá (4°21'N) in the south to extreme north-eastern Boyacá (7°25'N) in the north, very close to the Venezuela border (may yet be found just inside Venezuela, and perhaps occurs, or occurred, further south in extreme western Meta). Some seasonal altitudinal movements are possible. Reportedly common in early 20th century in Cundinamarca but deforestation has caused apparent extirpation with recent negative searches. Much habitat remains in Boyacá where birds are at least locally common but continuing deforestation has resulted in highly fragmented populations that are considered at long-term risk. Present in Chingaza National Park and adjacent Carpanta Biological Reserve. Not known in captivity. VULNERABLE.

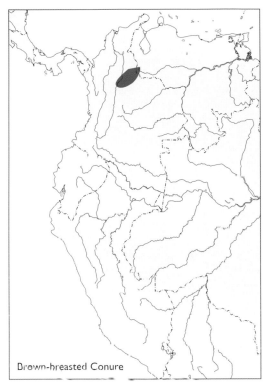

Brown-breasted Conure

GEOGRAPHICAL VARIATION None.

REFERENCES Collar *et al.* (1992), Fjeldså & Krabbe (1990), Forshaw (1989), Hilty & Brown (1986), Ridgely (1981).

264 RED-EARED CONURE
Pyrrhura hoematotis   Plate 66

Other names: Blood-eared Conure

IDENTIFICATION 25cm. Small, mainly green long-tailed conure with red ear-coverts, brown forehead and maroon tail conspicuous in flight. Blue in primaries and primary coverts. Rather indistinct maroon patch on belly. Pale tips to brown feathers gives scaled pattern on sides of neck and breast (less distinct on latter). Pale bill. Although often at higher elevations than partly sympatric race *emma* of White-eared Conure (256), overlap zone is broad, at 1,000-1,700m; distinguished by green rump, red ear-coverts and absence of blue on nape. No other sympatric *Pyrrhura* occur within restricted range. Similar, allopatric Sulphur-winged Conure (266) has yellow on wings and all-green belly. Birds often quite tame. Generally in flocks; flight fast and slightly undulating. Birds sometimes hang upside down whilst feeding

VOICE Rapidly repeated *ca ca ca ca ra ca.*

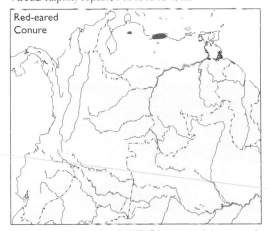

Red-eared Conure

ECOLOGY This conure frequents upper subtropical and temperate zone cloud- and other humid forests with e.g. *Weinmannia tormentosa* and *Quercus humboldtii*, mainly between 1,800 and 3,000m but once perhaps regularly down to 1500m on west slope and reportedly to 3,400m on east slope, where habitat is elfin woodland and páramo with bushes or scattered patches of forest with *Clusia*, *Weinmannia* and *Brunellia colombiana*; also in shrubbery and second growth with interspersed areas of subpáramo, peatbog páramo and man-made clearings. Birds cross clearings and may feed in stubble in treeless areas. Gregarious, generally in flocks of 6-14 although 40 once reported. Recorded foods include fruits of *Cecropia*, *Clusia* and *Brunellia colombiana* and seeds of *Rubus*, *Espeletia uribeii* and cultivated maize. Virtually no information on nesting; breeding-condition birds collected Aug and Oct.

DESCRIPTION Green or greenish-brown on cheeks and superciliary area; lores, forehead and crown brown, sometimes with some green tips on crown and especially hindcrown; ear-coverts maroon. Nape to uppertail-coverts green. Alula, leading edge of wing (including carpal area) and primary coverts variably yellow to fiery-orange; other coverts green. Primaries bluish-green (birds showing more orange on upperwing have more blue in primaries). Underwing-coverts green; underside of flight feathers dull grey. Throat, sides of neck and breast feathers reddish-brown with rather indistinct pale margins, giving scaly effect; belly and undertail-coverts green with maroon patch in centre of belly. Tail green tipped maroon, brighter above, duller beneath. **Bare parts**: Bill yellowish-horn; iris brownish-yellow; legs brownish.

SEX/AGE Sexes similar. Immature has upperwing-coverts wholly or nearly all green.

DISTRIBUTION AND STATUS The species is known only from coastal mountains of northern Venezuela, with westernmost record at Cubrio (69°35'W) in Lara, easternmost in Miranda (66°38'W). However, most records are from Aragua to Miranda; Cubrio is in fact the only known site in Lara and the population there is apparently disjunct (race *immarginata*). Diurnal movements from upland roosts to lower feeding areas occur; also apparently some local seasonal movements governed by food availability. Fairly common over much of rather restricted range and especially numerous in Henri Pittier National Park; status in Lara unknown. Much suitable habitat remains within range outside protected areas, and there is a relatively low deforestation rate, albeit with steady habitat loss around Cubrio. Absent or very rare in captivity.

ECOLOGY Birds inhabit montane and cloud-forest with open areas and low scattered trees, often at edge or in clearings, mainly at 1,000-2,000m but reported between 600 and 2,400m. Gregarious, mainly in groups of 3-12 outside breeding season but rarely up to 100. Diet and breeding poorly documented: known foods include guava *Psidium* and petioles of some broadleaved trees, possibly to extract insect larvae; probably breeds Aug (wet season).

DESCRIPTION Forehead brown with bluish edges to feathers; cheeks green; crown and nape feathers green with paler, more yellowish tips. Upperparts green. Primary coverts and perhaps some feathers in carpal area blue; other coverts green. Primaries blue with black tips. Underwing with lesser coverts green, other coverts black. Throat and breast olive-brown with dark margins to some feathers creating scaly pattern; sides of neck also scaly but dark-tipped feathers paler greyish-buff; belly and undertail-coverts green green with ill-defined maroon patch in centre of belly. Uppertail maroon narrowly tipped olive; undertail coppery-red. **Bare parts**: Bill pinkish-horn; iris and legs brownish.

SEX/AGE Sexes similar. Immature not described.

MEASUREMENTS Wing 121-133; tail 98-121; bill 15-18; tarsus 13-15.

GEOGRAPHICAL VARIATION Two races.
> *P. h. hoematotis* (Aragua to Miranda including Distrito Federal)
> *P. h. immarginata* (Cubrio, Lara) Like nominate but breast and sides of neck greener and with less obvious scaling. No yellowish tips to crown and nape feathers.

REFERENCES Arndt (1996), Fernández-Badillo *et al.* (1994), Forshaw (1989), Meyer de Schauensee & Phelps (1978), Ridgely (1981), Whitney (1996).

---

265 ROSE-CROWNED CONURE
Pyrrhura rhodocephala   Plate 66

Other names: Rose-headed Parakeet

IDENTIFICATION 24cm. Small, mainly green long-tailed conure with rose-red cap sometimes joining darker red patch on ear-coverts. White primary coverts. Tail rather light red beneath and dull red above. Blue primaries. No other *Pyrrhura* occurs within its very restricted range. Allopatric race *roseifrons* of Painted Conure (255) shows red on head but is easily distinguished by strong scaling on breast and throat. Bold red cap and white primary coverts distinguish adult Rose-crowned from all other small long-tailed South American parrots. Flight swift and direct. Gregarious in wooded country with clearings.

VOICE Apparently quieter than other *Pyrrhura* conures.

DISTRIBUTION AND STATUS This parrot is endemic to the Andes of extreme north-west Venezuela on both slopes of the Cordillera de Mérida from Táchira to Trujillo. The easternmost record is from 70°20'W and the northermost at 9°28'N, both in Trujillo, with records throughout the mountains of Mérida and northern Barinas, the western- and southernmost site being in Táchira at 8°01'N 71°46W. It is probably resident but daily movements occur over considerable distances. Fairly common and reported decline owing to deforestation not yet considered problematic. Occurs in several apparently effective protected areas, but continuing deforestation in

its small range must pose a long-term threat. Absent in captivity, at least outside Venezuela. NEAR-THREATENED.

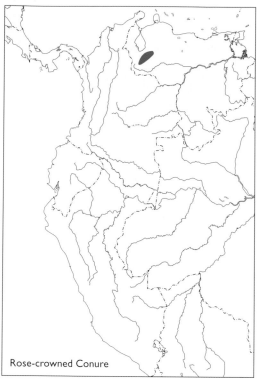

Rose-crowned Conure

ECOLOGY The species mainly occupies the subtropical zone (locally higher and lower) in montane humid forest and elfin woodland (including secondary growth and partly cleared areas, forest edge and páramos), mainly at 1,500-2,500m, but with extremes of 800-3,400m. Gregarious, generally in flocks of 10-30 outside breeding season; larger gatherings in roosting trees. No information on diet or breeding; said to breed May-Jun.

DESCRIPTION Forehead, lores and crown rose-red, forming red cap that sometimes extends to join darker red patch on ear-coverts; cheeks green. Nape to uppertail-coverts green. Primary coverts white, other coverts green except sometimes for scattered orange red feathers on bend of wing. Outerwebs of flight feathers blue with black tips. Underwing-coverts green. Feathers on throat, breast and sides of neck olive-green with brownish tips giving only very faint scaling effect; belly slightly more olive than upperparts with dull red patch in centre; undertail-coverts green. Uppertail brownish-red; undertail lighter red. **Bare parts**: Bill pale horn; bare periophthalmic skin white; iris brown; legs dark slaty-grey.

SEX/AGE Sexes similar. Immature shows bluish-green crown with scattered red feathers, blue primary coverts and greenish base to tail.

MEASUREMENTS Wing 130-142; tail 97-115; bill 16-18; tarsus 14-16.

GEOGRAPHICAL VARIATION None.

REFERENCES Desenne & Strahl (1991), Fjeldså & Krabbe (1990), Meyer de Schauensee & Phelps (1978), Ridgely (1981).

266 SULPHUR-WINGED CONURE
Pyrrhura hoffmanni　　　　　Plate 66

Other names: Hoffmann's Conure (Parakeet)

IDENTIFICATION 23cm. Small, mainly green conure with long rounded tail and red ear-coverts. Yellow on upperwing largely concealed at rest but conspicuous in flight and may appear as translucent bar when birds pass overhead. Green on uppertail, dull red beneath. Sometimes occurs (and most likely confused in field) with Finsch's Conure (234), which is larger, with red on forehead (not ear-coverts) and no yellow on wings. Range also overlaps with shorter-tailed Tovi Parakeet (285), which has green wings and ear-coverts and occurs chiefly in lowlands (thus mostly separated altitudinally). Sulphur-winged is only *Pyrrhura* in its range and is reliably separable from congeners in captivity on combination of red ear-coverts, yellow in wing and green breast. May be hard to locate and approach in woodland and often shy, but tamer whilst feeding; more obvious in fast, slightly undulating flight, when birds call noisily.

VOICE High-pitched, piercing and grating *toweet-deet-deet toweet* in flight may sound more like flock of noisy songbirds than parrots. Penetrating *zeewheet* whilst perched.

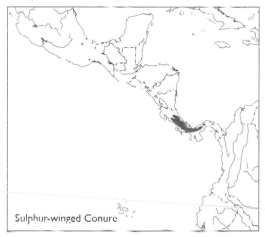

Sulphur-winged Conure

DISTRIBUTION AND STATUS Confined to southern Costa Rica and western Panama. The species occurs in highlands over the southern half of Costa Rica including the Caribbean slope foothills, mountains of the southern central plateau and both slopes of Cordillera de Talamanca, sometimes also the Cartago and Paraíso region and Volcán Irazú. In western Panama it occurs mainly in western and central Chiriquí and adjacent Bocas del Toro in higher mountains (including Volcán Chiriquí and the high ridges above Boquette) and at lower elevations around (e.g.) Laguna de Chiriquí and Almirante Bay. The easternmost Panamanian record is from east of Central Cordillera in 1868 at 80°11'W, but birds are now only occasionally reported east of 82°W and those east of Laguna de Chiriquí may be wanderers. Some altitudinal movements (higher in dry season) may occur; birds are perhaps only sporadic at extremities of range. Reportedly common in middle to upper elevations of Cordillera de Talamanca and its outliers, and judged fairly numerous throughout core range. Habitat now greatly fragmented but birds are still apparently numerous, including in areas where forest partially cleared. Rare in captivity.

ECOLOGY Birds are found mainly in mountainous country, preferring montane forests in the subtropical zone, mainly from 1,000 to 2,400m, but reported at 550m (Almirante Bay region, Panama) and 3,000m (Costa Rica). They seem to tolerate considerable habitat disturbance, including logged forest, second growth and partly cleared areas, shrubbery and treed pastures. Usually in pairs or more often small flocks of 5-15. May make daily altitudinal movements to exploit food plants, returning to mountains to roost. Foraging occurs in canopy or in smaller trees and shrubs near the forest edge. Food includes fruits of *Ficus*, *Croton*, *Leandra*, *Myrtis* and *Miconia*. Nests in tree-hollow, including e.g. old woodpecker hole, 8-20m from ground. Breeds dry season (Jan-Jun). One clutch of six in captivity.

DESCRIPTION Some individual variation in plumage. Feathers on forehead, crown, cheeks and nape green with yellow centres (proportion of yellow greatest on forehead, least on hindcrown); ear-coverts deep crimson. Upperparts green. Leading edge of wing sometimes green, sometimes yellow; lesser and median coverts mainly green sometimes with some yellow on outer median coverts and alula; yellow on base of outerwebs of greater-coverts. Outerwebs of primaries largely blue; inner primaries and secondaries with bright yellow patch mainly on base of innerwebs; flight feathers tipped black. Underwing with lesser coverts green, greater coverts greenish-yellow, central portion of flight feathers yellowish, tips greyish. Chin reddish; throat, sides of neck and upper breast green with yellowish tips to feathers giving faint barred effect; belly, flanks and undertail-coverts green. Uppertail green; undertail reddish. **Bare parts**: Bill and cere pale pinkish-horn; bare periophthalmic skin white to yellowish white; iris brown; legs dull grey.

SEX/AGE Breeding male has yellow streaks on crown feathers which are additionally red tipped in mature *gaudens*; sexes otherwise similar. Immature has less yellow on head and chest and less yellow in wing.

MEASUREMENTS Wing 126-140; tail 102-111; bill 16-18; tarsus 13-15.

GEOGRAPHICAL VARIATION Two races.
> *P. h. hoffmanni* (S Costa Rica)
> *P. h. gaudens* (W Panama) Very similar to nominate but feathers on crown and nape with more yellow and variably tipped red or orange-red (in some individuals red-tipped feathers may extend onto back, throat and breast). Underparts slightly darker.

REFERENCES Blake (1958), Forshaw (1989), Peters (1931), Ridgely (1981), Ridgely & Gwynne (1989), Slud (1964), Stiles *et al.* (1989), Wetmore (1968).

267 AUSTRAL CONURE
Enicognathus ferrugineus　　　　　Plate 61

Other names: Austral Parakeet, Emerald Parakeet

IDENTIFICATION 35cm. Mainly green long-tailed conure, darker above and paler beneath with metallic blue sheen on wings. Dull red on forehead and lores, centre of belly and uppertail. Dark edges to body feathers and upperwing-coverts give barred effect. Slender-billed Conure (268), sympatric (sometimes in mixed flocks) in parts of central-southern Chile from Chiloé island to O'Higgins, is larger, generally brighter and less barred, with bright crimson lores and forehead and elongated upper mandible. Patagonian Conure (249), overlapping (in Bío Bío, and possibly elsewhere in central Chile and parts of southern Argentina), is larger and browner with a conspicuous yellow belly and rump. Gregarious, generally in flocks. Flight swift, noisy and direct, sometimes close to ground. Birds sometimes perch next to larger branches and boughs in tops of tall trees and are then difficult to locate. Often quite tame.

VOICE Very vocal. Contact call *grie grie*. Alarm call a more strident *grieee grieee grieee*. Harsher grating sounds are sometimes mixed with more melodious chirruping cries. Calls slightly weaker than Slender-billed Conure, but some more resonating.

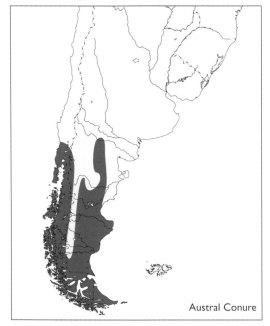

Austral Conure

DISTRIBUTION AND STATUS Extreme southern South America and the most southerly distributed New World parrot. It occurs throughout Tierra del Fuego north through Chile to O'Higgins province. East of the Andes in Argentina it ranges through Santa Cruz, Chubut, western Río Negro and western Neuquén. Generally resident, even in far south, but birds move to foothills to breed (at least in Tierra del Fuego) and some less predictable local movements may occur in the north. Generally common; reportedly very common to abundant in forested coastal Tierra del Fuego. Large areas of intact habitat remain and birds occur in several extensive protected areas. Very scarce in captivity.

ECOLOGY This conure occurs mostly in wooded country including *Nothofagus*, *Araucaria* and *Quercus* forest but also in more open habitat with *Berberis darwinii* and *Drimys winteri* shrubs, also cultivated areas, mainly at sea-level in southern part of range but up to 1,200m and even 2,000m further north. It is chiefly reported in flocks of 10-15 but larger aggregations (over 100) known; flock of 10 or so

reported mobbing Red-backed Hawk *Buteo polyosoma* in Tierra del Fuego. Predominantly seed-eating (can cause damage to grain crops) with reported food items including seeds of grasses and bamboo, *Drimys winteri*, acorns and *Araucaria* nuts, plus fruits, berries and leaf-buds of e.g. *Nothofagus* and bulbous roots. Nests in tree-cavity, filling very deep hollows with twigs and reported building twig-nests where no cavities available. Breeding Nov-Dec. Clutch 4-8.

DESCRIPTION Lores and forehead rather dull brick-red; forecrown with yellow-centred green feathers shading to dark-edged olive-green feathers on mid-crown. Feathers of upperparts olive-green with darker margins, giving barred effect. Upperwing-coverts with dark margins. Flight feathers green with metallic blue suffusion. Underwing-coverts green with dark tips; underside of flight feathers pale grey. Underparts chiefly pale olive-green with (except on thighs) darker margins, and broad dull red patch on central belly. Uppertail dull dark red; undertail dull greyish-red. **Bare parts**: Upper mandible black tipped dusky horn, lower mandible dusky horn; iris russet-brown; legs dark grey.

SEX/AGE Sexes similar. Immature has duller red on head and duller, less extensive red belly-patch.

MEASUREMENTS Wing 187-204; tail 148-178; bill 19-21; tarsus 17-19.

GEOGRAPHICAL VARIATION Two races.
> *E. f. ferrugineus* (Aisén in extreme S Chile and S Chubut in extreme S Argentina to Tierra del Fuego)
> *E. f. minor* (Aisén north to O'Higgins, Chile, and Chubut north to Neuquén, Argentina) Smaller (wing 175-193) and darker with less extensive (sometimes absent) red belly-patch.

REFERENCES Araya *et al.* (1993), Arndt (1996), Forshaw (1989), Housse (1949), Humphrey *et al.* (1970), Johnson (1967), Narosky & Yzurieta (1989), Nores & Yzurieta (1994), de la Peña (1988), Ridgely (1981).

268 SLENDER-BILLED CONURE
Enicognathus leptorhynchus   Plate 61

Other names: Chilean Conure/Parakeet, Slender-billed Parakeet, Slight-billed Parakeet

IDENTIFICATION 40-43cm. Green conure with dull red tail, bright crimson lores and forehead, blue-green flight feathers and very narrow, elongated upper mandible. Sympatric (sometimes mixing) with Austral Conure (267), which see for differences. Possibly overlapping (in Bío Bío, and perhaps elsewhere in central Chile) with endangered Chilean race *bloxami* of Patagonian Conure (249), which is larger and browner with conspicuous yellow belly and rump. Gregarious; flight swift and direct, sometimes at some height in large noisy formations (straggling lines), especially on migrations between breeding and wintering quarters.

VOICE Very vocal; often an almost permanent chattering and screeching. Loud, rather harsh *scraart scraart* when perched.

DISTRIBUTION AND STATUS This species is confined to central Chile from Santiago south through coastal lowlands and foothill valleys on the Pacific slope south to

Chiloé island and perhaps Río Palena in northern Aisén; also on Mocha Island off the south-west coast of Bío Bío. Some seasonal altitudinal movements occur, with birds moving from coastal lowlands to foothills between spring and autumn (Sep-May). Fairly common but has apparently suffered a decline in recent decades owing to deforestation, shooting and Newcastle disease. Less common and perhaps only sporadic at northern and southern extremities of range. Taken locally for pets but quite rare in captivity outside Chile. NEAR-THREATENED.

Slender-billed Conure

ECOLOGY The Slender-billed Conure inhabits forested country, mainly with *Nothofagus* and *Araucaria*, but may occur in more open cultivated land or pasture, especially in winter, ranging down to sea-level in winter and up to 2,000m in summer. Generally in flocks, from a few individuals to several hundred even in breeding season; large communal roosts sometimes consist of several thousand birds. Diet is composed of seeds of both wild and cultivated plants (sometimes considered a pest), including thistles and grain, seeds of *Araucaria* cones (Mar-Apr) opened with elongated bill, acorns, *Nothofagus* seeds and bulbous roots. Guard birds usually watch over feeding flock. Nests usually in unlined tree-hollow, often at some height and with several pairs using same tree; very deep hollows are filled with twigs to raise level of base. Occasionally nests in rock crevices and may build twig-nest (in e.g. *Chusquea* bamboo thicket) if no tree-cavities available. Breeding Nov-Dec. Clutch 5-6.

DESCRIPTION Lores, forehead and narrow ring of feathers around eyes bright crimson; cheeks and sides of neck green; feathers of crown, nape, mantle and back green with dark margins giving barred effect (heaviest on crown, where feathers brighter and more emerald). Scapulars, rump and uppertail-coverts green. Primary coverts green with blue suffusion; other coverts green. Flight feathers bluish-green above with dark margins on innerwebs near tips; pale grey below. Underwing-coverts yellowish-green. Underparts yellowish green with faint dull red patch in centre of belly. Uppertail dull red, greenish towards tip; undertail dull red suffused greyish. **Bare parts**: Upper mandible dark grey tipped horn, lower mandible horn; narrow bare periophthalmic ring grey; iris orange-red; legs grey.

SEX/AGE Sexes similar. Immature darker, with shorter upper mandible, less red on face and little or no red on belly.

MEASUREMENTS Wing 206-226; tail 150-197; bill 27-37 (female's perhaps averages shorter than male's); tarsus 22-25.

GEOGRAPHICAL VARIATION None.

REFERENCES Araya *et al.* (1993), Fjeldså & Krabbe (1990), Forshaw (1989), Hellmayr (1932), Housse (1949), Johnson (1967), Ridgely (1981).

269 MONK PARAKEET
Myiopsitta monachus   Plate 62

Other names: Quaker Parrot, Quaker Parakeet, Grey-breasted Parakeet; Cliff Parakeet (*M. m. luchsi*)

IDENTIFICATION 33cm. Mostly green parakeet with long pointed tail, conspicuous grey breast with pale barring, grey throat and head, and dark underside to wings. Diffuse yellowish band (bright yellow in highland Bolivian race *luchsi*) on lower breast with blue in flight feathers. Presence sometimes indicated by large untidy communal twig-nests. Range overlaps with several other mainly green small- to medium-sized long-tailed parrots, but combination of grey breast and head with dark underwings (pale in *luchsi*) distinctive. Generally in large noisy flocks. Sometimes associates with Black-hooded Conure (247). Usually in flocks of up to about 20, sometimes many more. Flight fast and direct on rapid wingbeats.

VOICE Very vocal with wide vocabulary. Usual note at rest or in flight is a rasping metallic *chape* sometimes ended with shriller *yee*. Other vocalisations include a piping chatter – *quak quaki quak wi quarr* – plus penetrating screeches, rapidly repeated squawks in courtship and conversational chatter whilst feeding. Calls almost continually around communal nests.

DISTRIBUTION AND STATUS The Monk Parakeet occurs in the lowlands of southern South America east of the Andes from Bolivia to Patagonia. It is reported from eastern and northern Bolivia in south-eastern La Paz, southern Cochabamba, western Santa Cruz, and northern Chuquisaca and possibly other areas (e.g. Tarija). It occurs Paraguay and southern Brazil in south and western Mato Grosso, Mato Grosso do Sul and the south-western two-thirds of Rio Grande do Sul (not known beyond Porto Alegre), throughout Uruguay and in Argentina south to Río Negro and probably northern Chubut. The species is generally common and reportedly abundant in Uruguay and Rio Grande do Sul (but may not breed there). Commonest parrot over much of range and greatly expanding locally owing to plantations of *Eucalyptus* in otherwise treeless areas, partial deforestation in other areas, elimination of predators and expansion of food crops. Persecuted in places but overall effect on population apparently slight (but the endemic Bolivian race *luchsi* is local and possibly quite rare). Feral populations established at number of localities outside range, including Puerto Rico, Florida and New York (USA) (where there are fears it could become a major agricultural pest), Rio de Janeiro (Brazil), Berlin (Germany), Austria and various Mediterranean locations. In live bird trade locally and internationally with large numbers in captivity.

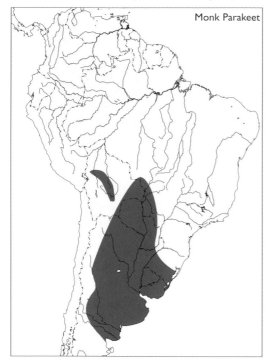

Monk Parakeet

ECOLOGY Monk Parakeets are mostly found in dry wooded country or open country with trees including gallery forest, isolated clumps, palm groves, woodlots, savanna and thorn scrub with cacti, also cultivated and urban areas with planted trees, chiefly below 1,000m (race *luchsi* reaching 3,000m). Birds generally occur in pairs or flocks of 30-50, with much larger gatherings outside breeding season. They roost communally, sometimes in nest whilst not breeding. Diet includes wide range of wild and cultivated seeds, fruits and vegetable matter including grass seeds and grain, cactus stems, root vegetables and tree fruits, sometimes also insects and their larvae. Feeds in trees and on ground, sometimes with other species including pigeons and cowbirds. Unique among parrots in habitually constructing nest of twigs (commonly from *Celtis* bushes) in tree branches (sometimes on telephone poles, etc.). Sometimes builds single nests (especially in drier areas) but often communally with individual nests (perhaps 100, more usually about 10) combined to form large untidy structures several metres across, with entrances from the side or below. Each nest is lined with chewed twig debris. Those of *luchsi* are always built on cliffs (only rarely in other races). Nests are sometimes used by Spot-winged Falconet *Spiziapteryx circumcinctus* and other birds for nesting and roosting. Breeding Oct-Dec. Clutch generally 4-6 but 1-11 reported.

DESCRIPTION Forehead to mid-crown, lores and cheeks pale ashy-grey; hindcrown and nape grass-green fading to slightly duller green on mantle, back and scapulars; rump grass-green. Primary coverts blue; other coverts green. Flight feathers blue above. Underwing has lesser coverts green, greater coverts and innerwebs of flight feathers blue. Throat and upper breast ashy-grey (darker on breast) with pale margins to feathers giving barred effect; lower breast pale yellow; abdomen, thighs and vent pale green. Uppertail green with blue in centre parallel to shafts; undertail pale bluish-green. **Bare parts:** Bill horn; iris brown; legs grey.

SEX/AGE Sexes similar. Immature has forehead tinged green.

MEASUREMENTS Wing 146-161; tail 122-145; bill 18-22; tarsus 17-20.

GEOGRAPHICAL VARIATION Four races. Two, *calita* and *cotorra*, are very similar and there is confusion over their respective ranges; they may not be distinct.

    M. m. monachus (Argentina in SE Santiago del Estero, E Córdoba, S Santa Fé, Entre Ríos and Buenos Aires; Uruguay)

    M. m. calita (Santa Cruz and Tarija, Bolivia, Paraguay where range unclear, and Argentina from C Formosa, Salta and Jujuy south to Río Negro and possibly Chubut) Smaller than nominate (c. 27cm) with bluer wings, head darker grey.

    M. m. cotorra (S Brazil in W Mato Grosso and Mato Grosso do Sul and probably Rio Grande do Sul, Argentina in E Formosa, Chaco, N Santa Fé, Corrientes and Misiones, the Bolivian and Paraguayan chaco and south along Río Paraguay and Paraná. Range in Bolivia and Paraguay in respect of reported range of *calita* unclear) Very like *calita* but supposedly brighter, belly less yellow.

    M. m. luchsi (Intermontane valleys of E Andes of Bolivia from SE La Paz, S Cochabamba and W Santa Cruz to N Chuquisaca and possibly other areas. Apparently isolated altitudinally from *M. m. cotorra* and/ or *M. m. calita*) Smaller than nominate and generally brighter than other races, with bright yellow lower breast, paler underwings, dark area at base of upper mandible and breast entirely pale grey with barred effect absent.

NOTE The race *luchsi* is quite distinct both morphologically and behaviourally and may warrant allospecies treatment. Pending further information regarding the delineation of its range with that of *M. m. cotorra* it is included here as a subspecies.

REFERENCES Aramburú (1995), Belton (1984), Contreras *et al.* (1991), Cuello & Gerzenstein (1962), Harrison (1973), Hayes (1995), Lanning (1991b), Martella & Bucher (1984), Meyer de Schauensee (1966), Naumburg (1930), Navarro *et al.* (1992), Nores & Yzurieta (1994), Parker (1993), de la Peña (1988), Short (1975, 1976), Sick (1993), Stone & Roberts (1934), Wetmore (1926a).

270 SIERRA PARAKEET
Psilopsiagon aymara   Plate 67

Other names: Grey-hooded Parakeet, Aymara Parakeet

IDENTIFICATION 19-20cm. Small, rather elegant and mainly green parakeet with long narrow pointed tail, dark crown and pale grey throat and breast. Flanks and underwing-coverts greenish-yellow. Belly greenish. Mountain Parakeet (271), widely sympatric but generally at higher altitudes and more terrestrial, is similar in size but with shorter tail, blue in flight feathers and yellow or green (not grey) breast. Generally ranges over hills in small tight flocks of up to 20 birds, sometimes more, in rapid, undulating, usually low (not often above 30m) flight. Often observed perched atop or inside low bushes and trees.

VOICE Rather weak. Excited twittering, warbling and chattering *cheer psi psi cheer psi* calls are high-pitched and reminiscent of songbird, e.g. Barn Swallow *Hirundo rustica*.

Sierra Parakeet

DISTRIBUTION AND STATUS Andes from southern Bolivia to northern Argentina and perhaps Chile. In western Bolivia it is known from La Paz and Cochabamba south to Tarija and Potosí, and in north western Argentina on Andean slopes from Jujuy south to Mendoza and east to hills of western Córdoba. In northern Chile (e.g. Tarapacá) it is variously reported as resident, visitor or absent. Some seasonal altitudinal movements occur, birds moving higher in summer. Generally common and apparently under no pressure; small numbers are trapped and exported as cagebirds.

ECOLOGY Prefers shrubby or wooded arid habitats in hills and ravines (one report from an *Alnus*-clad ravine with *Polylepis* along stream at base), dense scrub and trees around settlements and in agricultural areas, occurring in high Andean steppes sometimes to the altiplano, generally from about 1,800 to 3,400m, sometimes lower (to 1,200m in winter) and reportedly up to 4,000m in Tucumán, Argentina. Gregarious, generally in small flocks at least outside breeding season; larger gatherings at water. Berries and other fruits are consumed, plus grass seeds and those of several composite herbs (e.g. *Viguera*), birds often descending to ground to pick up fallen fruit and seeds from among grass. Nests in burrow excavated in earth banks, holes in cacti or crevice in deserted building;

sometimes in loose colonies. Eggs Nov, Tucumán. Clutch 4-5, up to seven in captivity.

DESCRIPTION Forehead and lores to hindneck (including ear-coverts) brownish-grey, forming cap level with line running just below eye. Mantle green faintly tinged olive; back and scapulars green; rump and upper-tail-coverts slightly brighter green. Upperwing-coverts green. Flight feathers green with black tips. Underwing-coverts greenish-yellow. Chin and throat pale whitish-grey; breast pale silvery-grey, sometimes with bluish tinge to feathers on sides of breast; flanks pale greenish-yellow; belly and undertail-coverts green with faint bluish tinge. Uppertail green; undertail greyish. **Bare parts**: Bill pale flesh; iris dark brown; legs brownish-grey.

SEX/AGE Sexes similar but male may have brighter grey on breast. Immature has shorter tail.

MEASUREMENTS Wing 92-101; tail 80-106; bill 10-12; tarsus 12-14.

GEOGRAPHICAL VARIATION None.

NOTE This species is usually included in *Bolborhynchus*.

REFERENCES Arndt (1996), Bond & Meyer de Schauensee (1942), Canevari *et al.* (1991), Fjeldså & Krabbe (1990), Forshaw (1989), Hellmayr (1932), Johnson (1967), Narosky & Yzurieta (1989), Nores & Yzurieta (1994), de la Peña (1988), Ridgely (1981), Rutgers & Norris (1979), Stotz *et al.* (1996), Wetmore (1926a), Whitney (1996).

271 MOUNTAIN PARAKEET
Psilopsiagon aurifrons   Plate 67

Other names: Golden-fronted Parakeet; Robert's Parakeet (*B. a. robertsi*); Margarita's Parakeet (*B. a. margaritae*)

IDENTIFICATION 17-19cm. Small parakeet with long slender tail and pale pinkish or horn-coloured bill. Distinct blue panel on closed wing. Males in western Peru have bright yellow breast and/or face but females, juveniles and birds in south of range are mainly green. Only native parakeet in coastal Peru. Widely sympatric with similar-sized Sierra Parakeet (270), and partly sympatric with Andean Parakeet (273), see under these species for differences. Calls loudly and is usually quite conspicuous. Gregarious outside breeding season and often seen in scattered flocks of 10-30 birds, sometimes many more. Flight swift, direct and slightly undulating (unlike Andean Parakeet).

VOICE Rather weak, piping *tchee-tchee tchee-tchee* recalls (for Europeans) Pied Wagtail *Motacilla alba*. Other high-pitched unmusical twitterings reported as *treet*, *tzirr-zirr* or *zrit*.

DISTRIBUTION AND STATUS In several disjunct populations in central and southern Andes from Peru to Argentina and Chile. Occurs in western Peru in La Libertad and disjunctly from Ancash and Lima to Arequipa. Reappears in Puno region of south-east Peru and south through west Bolivia highlands from La Paz, Cochabamba and Potosí into northern Chile in Tarapacá and Antofagasta. Occurs Argentina (possibly disjunctly from Bolivian and Chilean range) from Jujuy, Salta and western Tucumán through Catamarca, La Rioja, Córdoba and San Juan to Mendoza, with range extending west of

Andes to central Chile in mountains of Santiago. Occurrence in San Luis, Argentina, requires confirmation. Local seasonal movements include birds arriving in mountains of Santiago, Sep, and departing at end of summer. Perhaps nomadic in some parts of range in non-breeding season. Uncommon to fairly common Argentina, and apparently generally common where scrubby vegetation remains at high altitude. Scarcer in Chile. Race *robertsi* remains virtually unknown. Rare in captivity.

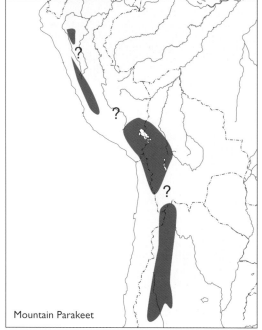

Mountain Parakeet

ECOLOGY Shrubby and wooded habitats including riparian thickets and thorny scrub, fog vegetation in coastal western Peru and open grasslands with scattered bushes and cacti on puna, entering cultivated areas, plantations and urban gardens and parks; generally at 1,000-2,900m in western Peru but sometimes to sea-level. In southern Peru (Puno) through Bolivia to northern Argentina and Chile, birds are mainly found on altiplano at 3,000-4,500m; chiefly at c. 2,500m in Argentina south from Catamarca. Gregarious. Forages in bushes and on ground for fallen berries and seeds, etc.; in desert puna reported feeding on buds and seeds of *Lepidophyllum, Fabiana densa, Adesmia* and other leguminous shrubs. Nests in crevice or hole in inaccessible rocky outcrops or high banks; sometimes colonially. Eggs reported Oct-Dec, northern Chile; breeds Feb-Mar, Argentina. Clutch 3-6 in captivity.

DESCRIPTION Forehead, lores, lower cheeks and chin bright lemon-yellow; upper cheeks, ear-coverts, crown and sides of neck green. Upperparts green. Primary coverts greenish-blue, other coverts green. Outerwebs of primaries violet-blue, of secondaries bluish-green. Underwing with coverts grey, flight feathers bluish-green. Throat to belly bright lemon-yellow with some greenish-yellow on sides of breast; thighs to undertail-coverts green. Uppertail green; undertail greyish-green. **Bare parts:** Bill pale pinkish-horn; iris brown; legs flesh.

SEX/AGE Female has yellowish-green where male bright lemon-yellow. Immature generally as female but with shorter tail. Young captive males show pronounced yellow face-markings.

MEASUREMENTS Wing 89-99; tail 75-90; bill 11-12; tarsus 13-14.

GEOGRAPHICAL VARIATION Four races. Males of two northern races (both confined to W Peru) show yellow in plumage. Southern two races (from S Peru to Argentina and Chile) are all green.

> *P. a. aurifrons* (W Peru from Ancash and Lima to Arequipa)
>
> *P. a. robertsi* (One locality in the Marañón Valley, La Libertad, NW Peru) Similar to nominate but slightly darker green; yellow on male restricted to forehead, lores and chin. Yellow patches on chin and head separated by green cheeks. Bill horn.
>
> *P. a. margaritae* (Puno, Peru, south through Bolivia to N Chile in Tarapacá and Antofagasta, and Argentina in Jujuy, Salta, W Tucumán and N Catamarca) Duller and darker than nominate with no yellow in plumage. Horn-coloured bill. Female slightly darker than male. This and next race are more compact and shorter-tailed than nominate.
>
> *R. a. rubrirostris* (Argentina in mountains of Catamarca, La Rioja, Córdoba, San Luis, San Juan and Mendoza, and C Chile in mountains of Santiago) All-green plumage is greyer and bluer than last race, cere pink; otherwise similar.

NOTE Mountain Parakeet is often included in *Bolborhynchus* and the race *margaritae* was formerly called *orbygnesius*. See Note under Andean Parakeet.

REFERENCES Araya *et al.* (1993), Bond (1955), Bond & Meyer de Schauensee (1942), Fjeldså & Krabbe (1990), Forshaw (1989), Hellmayr (1932), Johnson (1967), Koepcke (1983), Meyer de Schauensee (1966), Narosky & Yzurieta (1989), Nores & Yzurieta (1994), de la Peña (1988), Ridgely (1981), Rutgers & Norris (1979), Whitney (1996).

272 BARRED PARAKEET
Bolborhynchus lineola   Plate 67

Other names: Banded Parakeet, Lineolated Parakeet

IDENTIFICATION 16-17cm. Sparrow-sized, mainly green parakeet, paler and more yellowish beneath with short wedge-shaped tail and pointed wings. Black patch on shoulders can be useful fieldmark at distance. Fairly bold black bars on median and greater coverts with fainter narrow bars on upperparts and flanks make this the only parrot in range to show barred plumage, but this is very difficult to see in field. Partly sympatric Andean Parakeet (273) has all green plumage; *Touit* parrotlets have square-ended tails; *Forpus* parrotlets are smaller and mostly at lower elevations. Similarly proportioned (and much commoner) Tovi Parakeet (285) is mainly confined to lowlands and shows bright yellow underwing-coverts. Barred often located when calling in high flight (sometimes several hundred metres up) but can be hidden in cloud. Flight rapid, direct (not undulating) and rather buzzy on powerful deep wingbeats with birds often in tight wheeling flocks rather like shorebirds. Usually silent when perched and often overlooked when feeding quietly in preferred tree-top habitat.

VOICE Melodious chirping and cheeping notes. Highly vocal in flight, flock creating loud musical chatter like small songbirds. Distinctive *cheeoo-it cheeoo-it*. Prior to flight, alarmed birds may give harsh nasal chattering *jur jur jur jur*.

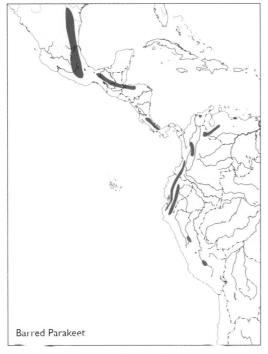

Barred Parakeet

DISTRIBUTION AND STATUS Southern Mexico to western Panama and disjunctly in Andes from Venezuela to Peru. In Mexico on Atlantic slope in uplands of Veracruz, Oaxaca, Chiapas and possibly (a single questioned record) Guerrero, then in southern Guatemala (recorded sporadically) and uplands of Honduras, with one report from Nicaragua at Santa María de Ostuma; mountainous parts of Costa Rica (not known from north-west, e.g. Cordillera de Guanacaste) and western Panama (apparently absent from centre and east). Distributed through Andes of north west Venezuela in Distrito Federal, Táchira and Mérida; scattered localities in Colombia in subtropical zone of western, central and eastern Andes and the Santa Marta massif; Andes of Ecuador, with recent records from south; Andes in Peru in Huánuco, Ayacucho and Cuzco, with birds seen in the north possibly this species. Scattered records (occurs erratically) and strong nomadic tendency (movements perhaps related to seeding bamboo) suggest occurrence may be continuous. Apparently rather rare and local over much of range but reportedly common in Honduras and even locally abundant in the Talamanca range, Costa Rica. Deforestation rife in parts of range but birds travel widely over cleared land and occur (at least sporadically) in protected areas, suggesting low risk at present. There are specimens in captivity outside range states.

ECOLOGY Mainly in montane forests in subtropical zone, less often in upper tropical vegetation. Reported from humid evergreen forest, pine forest, drier open woodland, clearings and pastures with tall trees. Occurs where landslides have opened forest to bamboo proliferation.

Sometimes at lower elevations in winter and at times frequents lowland rain-forest in central America. Reported from 900 to 2,400m, Mexico; mainly above 1,500m, Honduras, but down to c. 600m after breeding; mainly above 1,500m in western Panama but recorded there and in Costa Rica down to 600m; 900-1,500m, Venezuela, mainly 1,600-2,600m, Colombia, and to 2,900m, southern Ecuador. Gregarious, sometimes in gatherings of several hundreds, and forms large communal roosts in tops of tall trees. In smaller groups or pairs during Central American dry season. Reported food genera include *Myrtis*, *Heliocarpus* and *Miconia*, *Cecropia* catkins and bamboo seeds; occasionally forages in cultivated areas where reported taking maize. Nests in tree-cavity. Probably breeds dry season, Costa Rica; possibly Dec, Panama; Jul-Aug, Colombia.

DESCRIPTION Lores, cheeks and ear-coverts green; forehead bluish-grey; crown and upperparts green with narrow blackish feather-tips forming narrow transverse bars. Lesser coverts mainly black forming patch on shoulder; median and greater coverts green with black tips forming bold wing-bars; leading edge of wing yellowish. Outermost primary black, rest green on outerwebs. Underwing with coverts green indistinctly barred and spotted blackish, flight feathers green. Underparts yellowish-green with some indistinct barring on flanks and sides of breast and black spots on tips of some undertail-coverts. Uppertail green tipped black; undertail yellowish-green. **Bare parts:** bill and cere pale pinkish-flesh; bare periophthalmic skin grey; iris brown; legs pale pinkish-flesh.

SEX/AGE Female has less heavy black markings. Immature paler with less distinct barring.

MEASUREMENTS Wing 102-107; tail 53-58; bill 11-13; tarsus 12-14.

GEOGRAPHICAL VARIATION Two races.
  B. l. lineola (S Mexico to W Panama)
  B. l. tigrinus (N Venezuela to Peru) Darker and more heavily barred than nominate.

REFERENCES Fjeldså & Krabbe (1990), Forshaw (1989), Hilty & Brown (1986), Howell & Webb (1994, 1995), Land (1970), Martínez-Sánchez (1989), Meyer de Schauensee (1949), Meyer de Schauensee & Phelps (1978), Monroe (1968), Rasmussen *et al.* (1996), Ridgely (1981), Ridgely & Gwynne (1989), Slud (1964), Stiles *et al.* (1989), Wetmore (1968).

273 ANDEAN PARAKEET
Bolborhynchus orbygnesius   Plate 67

IDENTIFICATION 16cm. Small, uniformly bright green parakeet with blue in flight feathers, pale bill and medium-length, broad-based but pointed tail. Southern races of Mountain Parakeet (271) are rather similar (and partly sympatric) but Andean is stockier, with broader, less graceful tail, richer, darker green plumage and tends to fly higher. Mountain Parakeet also tends to prefer denser taller forest, and males of northern races are separated by extensive yellow in plumage. Partly sympatric Barred Parakeet (272) distinguished by black patch on shoulders and rather bold black wing-bars. *Touit* parrotlets are smaller with square-ended tails whilst *Forpus* are smaller still and occur at lower altitudes. Rather quiet and often overlooked when perched. When flushed, birds usually fly only a short distance before settling again. Flight is swift and direct (not undulating) on powerful, rapid, deep wingbeats. Tight flocks recall wheeling shorebirds.

VOICE Chattering *dydydy gy, dydydy gy* or series of *gurk* calls in flight. Also *chi-teet chi-teet*, often repeated rapidly and sometimes extended to *chi-tee-teet chi-tee-teet*. Rolling *rrueet e rrueet e rrueet e* from flushed birds. Weaker calls whilst perched. Voice richer than Mountain Parakeet.

DISTRIBUTION AND STATUS Occurs in north-west Peru from Cajamarca and La Libertad through the valleys of the central and eastern Andes to northern Cochabamba and Santa Cruz, Bolivia; also on west slope of Peruvian Andes at least in Lima department and perhaps elsewhere. Some seasonal altitudinal movements with birds descending to montane valleys after breeding. Range and abundance poorly known but reportedly common in temperate woods in southern Peru. Probably less abundant than Mountain Parakeet, but only sparse human settlement in range so little or no persecution and numbers probably stable.

Andean Parakeet

ECOLOGY Mainly in semi-arid upland woods in the subtropical and temperate zones including drier cloud-forests with *Tillandsia*-clad *Polylepis*, bushy habitats in ravines in more open country, elfin woodland at edge of páramo and grassy slopes with bromeliads and scattered woodland patches. Apparently prefers woodland with diverse range of tree species and seemingly avoids dense tall forest. Reported near human habitation and frequents farmland. Occurs above 1,500m in Lima, Peru, but usually considerably higher at 3,000-4,000m or more, with birds above the treeline at some localities (recorded over 6,000m). Wintering birds occur lower in montane valleys. Gregarious; in pairs, small parties and sometimes large flocks of over 300 birds. Diet comprises seeds, buds and berries, with birds reported feeding in bamboo, brambles and leguminaceous trees. Takes food directly from vegetation or on ground. Breeds in burrows in steep banks.

DESCRIPTION Head green, yellowish-green on face. Mantle, back and scapulars a slightly olive-tinged green; rump and uppertail-coverts green. Upperwing-coverts green. Outerwebs of primaries rather dull blue with narrow pale margins; innerwebs sooty. Underwing bluish-

green. Underparts yellowish-green. Uppertail green; undertail metallic bluish-green. **Bare parts**: Bill pale greyish-horn; narrow bare periophthalmic ring grey; iris dull yellowish; legs brownish.

SEX/AGE Sexes similar, although male has been claimed to have yellower lores, forehead and chin. Immature has shorter tail.

MEASUREMENTS Wing 101-115; tail 56-68; bill 11-13; tarsus 14-16.

GEOGRAPHICAL VARIATION None.

NOTE Previously used name *B. andicolus* is synonymous with modern treatment as *B. orbygnesius*. See Note under Mountain Parakeet to avoid confusion with former trinomial classification of *Psilopsiagon aurifrons margaritae*, formerly *Bolborhynchus a. orbygnesius*.

REFERENCES Bond (1955), Bond & Meyer de Schauensee (1942), Fjeldså & Krabbe (1990), Forshaw (1989), Meyer de Schauensee (1966), Koepcke (1983), Morrison (1939, 1947), Ridgely (1981), Roe & Rees (1979), Whitney (1996), Whitney *et al.* (1994).

274 RUFOUS-FRONTED PARAKEET
Bolborhynchus ferrugineifrons Plate 67

IDENTIFICATION 18cm. Small, stocky, dull green parakeet with rather short pointed tail. Narrow rufous band on forehead, lores and around base of rather bulbous bill. Paler on uppertail-coverts and yellowish on throat, cheeks and breast. Bluish-green in wings. Only small parrot regularly found in its restricted high-altitude range. Barred Parakeet (272) occurs in central Andes of Colombia, but lower than Rufous-fronted (mainly 1,600-2,600m) and distinguished by smaller size, paler bill, black shoulder-patch and wing-bars, and faint barring on upperparts and flanks. Mainly in pairs or small noisy flocks up to c. 15 birds, easily approached. Most obvious in swift direct flight on rapid strong wingbeats. Flushed birds fly short distance before settling again.

VOICE Reportedly similar to Andean Parakeet (273).

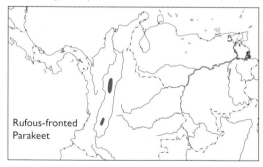
Rufous-fronted Parakeet

DISTRIBUTION AND STATUS Endemic to high slopes of central Andes of Colombia, where reported from two general areas. The more northerly cluster of records involves the Nevado del Ruiz and Nevado del Tolima volcanic complex where the departments of Tolima, Quindío, Risaralda and Caldas meet. The southern area is on the slopes of Volcán de Puracé in Cauca. Uninterrupted high mountains lie between these two areas so distribution may be continuous at low density throughout the central Andean chain from Caldas to Cauca. Most woodland and páramo habitat in range has been cut over for firewood or is heavily grazed and burned and remains in only scattered patches. Birds occur in several protected areas including Alto Quindío Acaime Reserve and Los Nevados National Park, latter considered the species's last stronghold: it is common there with over 100 birds observed during eight hours in 1993. However, overgrazing may pose long-term threat to this site. Generally at low density (perhaps only one bird per km²) and scarce. Total population perhaps 1,000-2,000 birds, probably fewer. Occasionally kept as pets locally but not known in captivity outside range. ENDANGERED.

ECOLOGY Occupies upper temperate and lower páramo zone of high mountains in shrubland, sparsely wooded slopes near treeline, and more open habitats including potato fields; records are from 2,800 to 4,000m, most above 3,200m. Probably wanders outside breeding season. Gregarious and roosts communally on cliffs Feeds mainly on ground on grass seeds, e.g. *Calamagrostis effusa*, and on herbs, e.g. flowers and achenes of *Espeletia hartwegiana*. Reported to nest in cliffs. Breeding-condition male taken mid Jan.

DESCRIPTION Narrow band on forehead and lores and at base of bill brownish-red; cheeks and throat yellowish-green; crown, hindneck, mantle, scapulars, wing-coverts and rump green, uppertail-coverts a slightly paler green. Outerwebs of primaries bluish-green. Underwing bluish-green. Throat and breast yellowish green tinged olive; rest of underparts yellowish-green. Uppertail green; undertail green tinged bluish. **Bare parts:** Bill yellowish-horn with grey base to upper mandible; narrow periophthalmic ring grey; iris dark brown; legs grey.

SEX/AGE Sexes similar. Immature undescribed.

MEASUREMENTS Wing 121-125; tail 68-75; bill 13-15; tarsus 15-17.

GEOGRAPHICAL VARIATION None.

REFERENCES Arndt (1996), Collar *et al.* (1992, 1994), Forshaw (1989), Graves & Giraldo (1987), Hilty & Brown (1986), Salaman & Gandy (1993).

---

275 MEXICAN PARROTLET
Forpus cyanopygius   Plate 68

Other names: Blue-rumped Parrotlet, Turquoise-rumped Parrotlet; Sonora Parrotlet (*F. c. pallidus*); Tres Marias or Grayson's Parrotlet (*F. c. insularis*)

IDENTIFICATION 13cm. Very small, mainly green parrotlet with short tapered tail. Male shows turquoise blue in wings and on rump, but his turquoise underwing-coverts difficult to see in flight. Generally in pairs or small flocks. Distinctive inhabitant of Mexican Pacific lowlands and foothills with no similar species in range. Male distinguished from other *Forpus* in captivity by combination of rather uniform green body and turquoise (rather than deeper blue or green) on wings and rump, but care needed in separating race *spengeli* of Blue-winged Parrotlet (277). Green plumage blends with foliage and perched birds are hard to locate. Mostly first found by voice but callers often not seen until in flight, which is rather fast,

deeply undulating and generally at canopy-height on rapid buzzing wings, in tight, compact flocks twisting and turning in unison.

VOICE Call is high-pitched, thin, tinkling *cree*. Although not especially powerful, voice is penetrating and audible at some distance. Birds constantly chatter in flight and can generate chorus that suggests more birds than actually present. Quieter while perched.

Mexican Parrotlet

DISTRIBUTION AND STATUS Endemic to western Mexico from around Alamos in southern Sonora south through Sinaloa, Nayarit (including the Tres Marías Islands) and Jalisco to Colima, with most southerly known record from Manzanillo Bay (19°03'N). Range extends east into Durango and Zacatecas. Occurrence irregular with local abundance fluctuating widely, perhaps related to local food availability. Large-scale modification of habitats has occurred within range but species remains common (at least locally). Race *insularis* perhaps at risk in the Tres Marías where 20th century observers have either found very few birds or failed to locate any at all. Fairly frequent in captivity.

ECOLOGY Gallery and deciduous woodland, plantations, scrub, semi-arid open country and cultivated areas with trees, mainly in lowlands and foothills with most records from southern Sonora at 360-455m, locally higher in western Durango and Zacatecas with upper limit of c. 1,320m. Breeding-condition birds have been collected above 900m indicating possible breeding at higher altitudes. Gregarious, forming flocks of 4-30 or more, sometimes with Orange-fronted Conure (218). Little information on diet or breeding: birds observed taking *Ficus* fruits, berries and grass seeds from ground; breeds May-Jul. Clutch three in captivity.

DESCRIPTION Lores, cheeks, forehead and ear-coverts yellowish-green. Mid-crown to upper back green; lower back, rump and uppertail-coverts turquoise-blue. Greater coverts turquoise-blue, other coverts green. Primaries green, secondaries dark bluish narrowly edged turquoise on outerwebs. Underwing with coverts turquoise-blue and green, flight feathers dark bluish-green. Underparts green tinged yellowish. Uppertail green; undertail duller. **Bare parts:** Bill and cere pale greyish-flesh; narrow periophthalmic ring grey; iris dark brown; legs pinkish.

SEX/AGE Female all green. Immature as female, with some blue feathers in rump and wing-coverts of young male.

MEASUREMENTS Wing 88-91; tail 38-42; bill 12-13; tarsus 11-13.

GEOGRAPHICAL VARIATION Three races. However, some authorities consider birds from north of range (*pallidus*) doubtfully distinct from nominate. See also Note under Blue-winged Parrotlet.

> *F. c. cyanopygius* (Pacific slope of Mexico from Sinaloa to Colima)
>
> *F. c. insularis* (Tres Marías Islands) Larger, with darker, greyer green upperparts. Male has darker turquoise markings, glaucous suffusion to underparts, darker bill.
>
> *F. c. pallidus* (SE Sonora and extreme N Sinaloa) Similar to nominate but green paler and greyer. Some males show blue feathers at bend of wing.

REFERENCES Arndt (1996), Forshaw (1989), Friedmann *et al.* (1950), Howell & Webb (1995), Grant (1965), McLellan (1927), Peterson & Chalif (1973), Ridgely (1981), van Rossem (1945), Shaldach (1973), Short (1974), Stager (1957), Stotz *et al.* (1996).

---

276 GREEN-RUMPED PARROTLET
Forpus passerinus   Plate 69

Other names: Blue-winged Parrotlet (see Note), Common Parrotlet; Guiana Parrotlet (nominate)

IDENTIFICATION 13cm. Very small stocky parrotlet with short tapered tail. Plumage mainly green with male showing turquoise-blue on upperwing and ultramarine on underwing-coverts. Male rump brighter green than rest of plumage (only male *Forpus* to show green rump, a key feature when comparing captive birds). Blue-winged Parrotlet (277), possibly sympatric on south bank of Amazon, has male with cobalt-blue on rump, female with less yellowish forehead. The scarcer Dusky-billed Parrotlet (279), overlapping in the Guianas and eastern Amazonia, has grey upper mandible and (male) blue rump. *Touit* parrotlets are larger without undulations in flight. Flight is deeply undulating and generally at canopy level. Tight groups in flight twist and turn in unison. Noisy flocks may be conspicuous moving between shrubs, but birds can be difficult to locate when settled in foliage.

VOICE Rather rattling, metallic, finchlike *chitit chitititit*. Flight call is *phil-ip phil-ip phil-ip*. Flocks can create loud chattering sound. Pairs prospecting for nest-sites emit rapid chattering recalling Budgerigar (155). A penetrating *tsup tsup* may accompany aggression.

Green-rumped Parrotlet

DISTRIBUTION AND STATUS Northern South America from the Guianas to Colombia. Occurs throughout Guyana and Surinam to Amapá, Brazil, then westwards north of Amazon in Pará to eastern Amazonas with an isolated population in Roraima, and south of Amazon from the Rio Tapajós to the Rio Anapú. In Venezuela birds occur north of the Orinoco from Zulia and Táchira to Sucre and Monagas and south of it in northern Bolívar and Delta Amacuro. Range extends into north-east Colombia at the base of the Santa Marta massif, eastern Norte de Santander and perhaps Arauca and Vichada. Introduced Jamaica, Tobago (numbers increasing), Barbados and Martinique but extinct on last. Occurs Trinidad and Curaçao where possibly also introduced. Perhaps locally nomadic in response to food availability. Generally widespread and common and perhaps increasing with clearance of dense forest. Fairly common in captivity.

ECOLOGY Frequents all kinds of wooded habitats except rain-forest and other dense cover, hence found in forest edge, rather open agricultural habitats and suburban areas. Mainly in tropical zone but also penetrates subtropical vegetation in e.g. Venezuela where reported to 1,800m. Gregarious, at least outside breeding season, forming flocks of up to 100 birds and noisy communal roosts. Diet comprised mainly of small seeds, notably grasses, but also flowers, buds, berries and fruits, with favoured food-plants including *Croton hirtus*, *Hypsis suaveolens*, *Wissadula*, *Cyperus*, *Scoparia dulcis*, *Melochia parviflora*, *Lagerstroemia indica*, *Anona*, *Hibiscus sabdariffa* and *Psidium guava*. Birds settle on grass stems to bend seed head to ground where seeds eaten. Nests usually in unlined tree-cavity, including old nest-hole of woodpecker; also reported from eaves of houses (Jamaica), excavated arboreal termitaria and cavities in fence-posts. Eggs laid Jul-Nov, sometimes into Dec, Venezuela; Feb-Aug, Trinidad; breeds May-Oct, Colombia. Clutch 4-10 with seven apparently average for wild birds. About half of wild females attempt second brood.

DESCRIPTION Crown, sides of neck and hindneck green; forehead, cheeks and ocular areas slightly paler, brighter green. Mantle, upper back and scapulars green; lower back, rump and uppertail-coverts bright emerald green, sometimes bluish-green. Greater coverts ultramarine-blue, other coverts green. Flight feathers green above with dark tips, rather pale bluish-green below. Underwing-coverts ultramarine-blue. Underparts green tinged yellowish. Tail bright green with some yellow on outer feathers. **Bare parts**: Bill and cere pale pink; narrow periophthalmic ring greyish-pink; iris dark brown; legs pale pink.

SEX/AGE Female lacks blue markings on wings and shows yellowish forehead. Immature similar to adult.

MEASUREMENTS Wing 77-86; tail 31-41; bill 11-13; tarsus 11-12.

GEOGRAPHICAL VARIATION Five races.

> *F. p. passerinus* (Guyana, French Guiana and Surinam. Also in Jamaica and possibly Barbados)
>
> *F. p. viridissimus* (N Bolívar and Delta Amacuro, Venezuela, and Trinidad) Plumage darker green than nominate (darker from west to east) with darker and duller blue on wings of male. Underwing-coverts greener than in nominate. Female not readily separable from nominate female.
>
> *F. p. cyanophanes* (Río Césare valley in the Santa Marta region of NE Colombia eastwards through Guajira)

As last race but with more extensive blue on wing forming distinct patch when folded, more extensive blue on underwing-coverts.

F. p. cyanochlorus (Upper Rio Branco, Roraima, N Brazil) Similar to nominate but darker violet-blue on underwing-coverts. Female variously considered more yellowish than and inseparable from nominate female.

F. p. deliciosus (Both banks of Amazon from Amapá west to the lower Rio Madeira) Male has rump emerald with bluish tinge, blue in secondaries. Female has more extensive yellow on head than nominate with more yellowish undertail-coverts.

NOTE This species has been previously treated as conspecific with *Forpus crassirostris* (previously *xanthopterygius*) and known as Blue-winged Parrotlet. Most modern authors treat them as allospecific and reserve the name Blue-winged Parrotlet for *F. crassirostris*. They appear to occur together in the central Amazon with no signs of interbreeding.

REFERENCES Arndt (1996), Beissinger & Waltman (1991), Bond (1968), Buckley & Buckley (1968), Desenne & Strahl (1991, 1994), ffrench (1992), Forshaw (1989), Friedmann (1948), Haverschmidt (1968), Hilty & Brown (1989), Holland (1922), Meyer de Schauensee (1966), Meyer de Schauensee & Phelps (1978), Ridgely (1981), Snyder (1966), Stotz *et al.* (1996), Voous (1965), Waltman & Beissinger (1992), Wetmore (1939)

---

277 BLUE-WINGED PARROTLET
Forpus crassirostris   Plate 69

IDENTIFICATION 12cm. Very small, stocky, mainly green parrot with short tapered tail, male with blue on upper and underwing-coverts and rump. Range may marginally overlap in Amazon basin of Brazil with that of Green-rumped Parrotlet (276), which see for differences, and more widely in western Amazonia with that of Dusky-billed Parrotlet (279), which is most readily told by its dusky grey upper mandible and thin squeaky voice. Amazonian Parrotlet (290) of western Amazonia is all green with powdery blue forehead, lores and crown. Tui Parakeet (288), widespread in Amazonia, is best separated by larger size, yellow on head and no blue rump. Cobalt-winged Parakeet (286) of western Amazonia is again larger with no blue rump. Blue-winged is told from other *Forpus* in captivity by very small size, blue rump and wing-coverts in male, pinkish bill and absence of blue around eyes; male from very similar Mexican Parrotlet (275) in captivity by darker blue spots on turquoise underwing-coverts. Females difficult to separate from other female *Forpus* although generally more yellowish beneath. Blue and yellow mutations naturally occur. Flight swift and deeply undulating, generally at canopy level, on fast buzzy wingbeats. Gregarious.

VOICE High-pitched chattering *zit zit zit zit* in flight. Constant sparrowlike twittering from flocks.

DISTRIBUTION AND STATUS South America from Amazon basin to northern Argentina with separate population in northern Colombia. This latter occurs in arid Caribbean lowlands from Cartagena across lower Magdalena Valley south to northern Bolívar and east to base of Santa Marta massif. The species reappears in extreme south Colombia around Leticia and possibly in Putumayo, and is recorded from adjacent north-east Ecuador and through eastern Peru to eastern Bolivia in Beni and Santa Cruz; it extends through western Amazon basin of Brazil east to eastern Amazonas and into much of interior eastern Brazil south-east possibly as far as Rio Grande do Sul. Apparently absent from eastern and north-eastern parts of Brazilian Amazon with its north-eastern limits in Maranhão and Ceará. Occurs in north-east Argentina in Misiones, north-eastern Corrientes, eastern Chaco and eastern Formosa. Found in eastern Paraguay and may occur further west in chaco. Apparently introduced Jamaica but current status unknown. Mainly resident but altitudinal migrant in south-east Brazil, with seasonal movements in Argentina in relation to food supply. Common in east of range, sometimes locally abundant (e.g. parts of northern Bahia). Less abundant in west, being uncommon and local (perhaps declined) in northwest Colombia and sparse through eastern Peru and Bolivia. Perhaps increasing in parts of western Amazon with clearance of dense forest but probably declining in Paraguay where previously common and now rare. Trapped for trade with captive birds outside range countries. Trade unlikely to have affected abundance in wild.

Blue-winged Parrotlet

ECOLOGY Frequents drier wooded habitats such as open and riparian woodland, cerrado and caatinga; at edge of range found in savanna, palm groves, semi-arid scrub and pastures. In western Amazon appears to be mainly distributed along rivers in lighter riparian growth. Mainly in lowlands but reported to 1,200m in mountains of southeast Brazil. Gregarious, in flocks up to 50. Food includes fruits of *Cecropia*, seeds of *Mikania* and *Trema micrantha* and flowers of *Ambrosia* and *Marcgravia*; forages in open, sometimes on ground. Nests chiefly in tree-cavity but also arboreal termitarium, fence-post, nest of Rufous Hornero *Furnarius rufus*, which may be seized by force and lined with grass stems, or even nest of Red-rumped Cacique *Cacicus haemorrhous*. Clutch 3-7.

DESCRIPTION (*F. c. vividus*) Forehead, crown, hindneck and ear-coverts green; cheeks, ocular area and lores emerald-green. Upperparts and wings green except for cobalt-blue lower back, rump, primary and greater coverts, and blue towards base of secondaries. Underwing with coverts rich cobalt-blue, flight feathers dark dull metallic blue. Underparts green tinged yellowish with emerald feathers around thighs and vent. Uppertail green; undertail duller. **Bare parts**: Bill and cere dull pinkish with grey base to upper mandible; bare periophthalmic skin pale grey; iris dark brown; legs dull pinkish-grey.

SEX/AGE Female all green. Immature similar to respective adult but blue of young male intermixed with green.

MEASUREMENTS (*F. c. vividus*) Wing 80-89; tail 34-44; bill 11-13; tarsus 11-13.

GEOGRAPHICAL VARIATION Six races.

F. c. vividus (N Argentina, Paraguay and E Brazil north to Bahia where it intergrades with next race) See Description above.

F. c. flavissimus (Maranhão, Piauí, Ceará and NE Brazil south to N Bahia) Generally paler and more yellowish than nominate. Male forehead, throat and cheeks yellow.

F. c. olallae (North bank of middle Amazon where known from north of Itacoatiará and north side of lower Rio Solimões around Codajáz) Weakly differentiated from next race but blue on upperwings and rump darker, blue on underwing-coverts paler. Also darker green above, emerald green forehead. This and next race also perhaps on average smaller than nominate (wing 76-79, tail 32-34).

F. c. crassirostris (W Amazon in S Colombia, E Ecuador and Peru east to C Amazonas, Brazil) Like nominate but blue paler with emerald-green forehead. Primary coverts pale greyish-violet contrasting with darker cobalt-blue greater coverts. Upper mandible compressed laterally in centre.

F. c. spengeli (N Colombia from Cartagena across lower Magdalena Valley south to N Bolívar and east to base of Santa Marta Mountains and west slope of Sierra de Perijá. One doubtful record from C Panama) Male rump and wing markings turquoise-blue; much paler than nominate. Birds from around El Carmen de Bolívar in N Bolívar are darker and perhaps represent an undescribed race. See Note above.

F. c. flavescens (Bolivia and SE Peru) Similar to nominate but paler blue rump in male, underparts and facial area more yellowish, undertail more bluish.

NOTES (1) This species, previously regarded as conspecific with *Forpus passerinus* (see Note under Green-rumped Parrotlet), is widely known under the unavailable name *xanthopterygius*; the previously nominate race *xanthopterygius* takes the name *vividus*.

(2) The isolated northern Colombian race *spengeli* of Blue-winged Parrotlet resembles the Mexican Parrotlet (275) and may better be classified as a race of the latter or even, as some recent authors have concluded, a full species in its own right. Further investigation is warranted.

REFERENCES Arndt (1996), Belton (1984), Bond (1968), Bond & Meyer de Schauensee (1942), Canevari *et al.* (1991), Collar (1997), Contreras *et al.* (1991), Darlington (1931), Forshaw (1989), Galetti (1996), Gyldenstolpe (1945a,b), Hilty & Brown (1989), Meyer de Schauensee

(1966), Nores & Yzurieta (1994), de la Peña (1988), Ridgely (1981), Short (1975), Sick (1993), Traylor (1958), Wetmore (1968).

278 SPECTACLED PARROTLET
Forpus conspicillatus Plate 68

IDENTIFICATION 13cm. Very small, stocky, mainly green parrotlet of north-west South America, with short tapered tail and pale pinkish bill. Male shows blue around eyes (often not very obvious), on upperwing-coverts, at bend of wing and on rump. Only *Forpus* species in range but approaches north Colombian race *spengeli* of Blue-winged Parrotlet (277) in the lower Magdalena Valley, and Santa Marta race *cyanophanes* of Green-rumped Parrotlet (276) in extreme north-east Colombia. Male told from former by blue at bend of wing and around eyes and from latter by blue rump. All-green females difficult to separate although rump of Spectacled is more emerald. Range of Dusky-billed Parrotlet (279) approaches Spectacled in eastern Colombian lowlands; separated by darker upper mandible and absence of blue around eyes (latter feature separates male Spectacled from other *Forpus* in captivity). Flight undulating and generally at canopy level. Deliberate movements of feeding birds recall crossbills *Loxia*. When flushed, birds drop out of trees before making off and swooping up to alight some 50-100m distant. Twittering of flocks draws attention but birds perched in foliage difficult to locate. Generally in small flocks or pairs.

VOICE Twittering sound comprised of short finchlike notes.

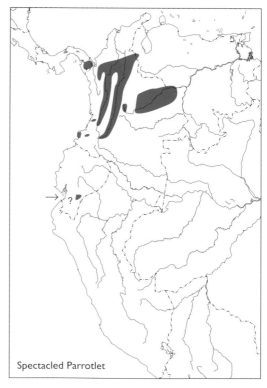

Spectacled Parrotlet

DISTRIBUTION AND STATUS Panama, Colombia and western Venezuela. In eastern Panama birds occur in lower Río Tiura Valley at (e.g.) El Real, wandering west almost to Canal Zone. Present in Colombia in several disjunct populations: west of Andes in south-western Nariño near Tumaco and in drier upper reaches of the Ríos Patía and Dagua, in the Sinú, Cauca and Magdalena (south to Huila) Valleys and across the southern Caribbean lowlands east to the west slope of Sierra de Perijá. Reports from Bogotá plateau probably of escaped captives. Distributed through lowland llanos of eastern Colombia from Meta to Casanare and Vichada including adjacent western Venezuela on the Meta in Apure. A parrotlet in temperate zone forests (to about 3,000m) in Loja, Ecuador, may be this species. Mainly resident but apparently some local seasonal movements. Uncommon and local in eastern Panama but perhaps increasing and expanding westwards with clearance of dense forest. Commonest *Forpus* in Colombia where range recently expanded (e.g. upper Magdalena Valley) owing to forest clearance; reportedly abundant to 2,200m in Cundinamarca. Popular in captivity locally but rare outside range. Numbers apparently not seriously affected by trade although possibly declined through trapping in Venezuela.

ECOLOGY Prefers lightly wooded habitats such as edge of lowland evergreen forest, thorn scrub, llanos, gallery woodland and cultivated areas with scattered trees, penetrating denser forests where there are clearings with scattered trees, generally at 200-1,800m but to 2,600m at Sabana de Bogotá (where perhaps escaped from captivity). Gregarious outside breeding season; forms communal roosts. Diet includes grass and weed seeds, fruit, berries, blossoms and buds. Feeds on ground and in vegetation. Nests in cavity in tree, fence-post or palm frond at almost any height (often only 1-2m from ground). Eggs reported Jan-Mar, Colombia. Clutch 4-5.

DESCRIPTION Lores, cheeks, forehead and crown bright emerald-green; area around and behind eyes to ear-coverts cobalt-blue; hind- and sides of neck green faintly tinged brownish. Mantle, upper back and scapulars green with olive suffusion; lower back and rump bright cobalt-blue; uppertail-coverts green. Lesser coverts at bend of wing, outer median coverts and primary and greater coverts bright cobalt-blue; other coverts and primaries green. Underwing with coverts cobalt-blue, flight feathers pale bluish-grey. Underparts paler green than above with distinct bluish tinge. Uppertail green; undertail paler and duller. **Bare parts:** Bill and cere pink; narrow periophthalmic ring grey; iris dark brown; legs pink.

SEX/AGE Female all green, paler above than male, with more yellowish forehead and more yellowish beneath.

MEASUREMENTS Wing 75-84; tail 36-41; bill 11-12; tarsus 9-11.

GEOGRAPHICAL VARIATION Three races. A further race ('*pallescens*'), reportedly paler than *caucae*, might exist in the Río Patía area of SW Colombia.

> **F. c. conspicillatus** (E Panama and N Colombia)
> **F. c. metae** (Amazonian lowlands of Colombia into W Venezuela) Like nominate but blue around eye in male reduced to line above and behind eye. Female more yellowish.
> **F. c. caucae** (W Colombia) Like nominate but more yellowish and blue on wings and rump less deep.

REFERENCES Arndt (1996), Desenne & Strahl (1991),

Fjeldså & Krabbe (1990), Forshaw (1989), Hilty & Brown (1989), Meyer de Schauensee & Phelps (1978), Miller (1947), Munves (1975), Ridgely (1981), Ridgely & Gwynne (1989), Stotz *et al.* (1996), Wetmore (1968).

279 DUSKY-BILLED PARROTLET
Forpus sclateri   Plate 69

Other names: Sclater's Parrotlet; Schomburgh's Parrotlet (*F. s. eidos*)

IDENTIFICATION 12cm. Very small, stocky, rather dull green parrotlet with dark grey maxilla. Male shows dark blue on rump and upper- and underwing-coverts. Overlaps with Green-rumped Parrotlet (276) in north-east Amazonia and with Blue-winged Parrotlet (277) in central and western Amazonia. Male of former has green (not blue) rump; latter a pale bill. Possibly occurs with Spectacled Parrotlet (278) in llanos of eastern Colombia where male Dusky-billed separated by absence of blue around eyes. Female from other female *Forpus* by dark bill. Both sexes are also darker than other *Forpus*. Amazonian Parrotlet (290) of western Amazonia is all green with powdery blue forehead, lores and crown. Tui Parakeet (288), widespread in Amazonia, is best separated by larger size, yellow on head and no blue rump. Cobalt-winged Parakeet (286) of western Amazonia is again larger with no blue rump. Flight is swift, undulating and generally at canopy level, with fast buzzy wingbeats. Quite conspicuous whilst calling and moving restlessly in fruiting tree, but difficult to detect when quietly perched in foliage.

VOICE Twittering and chattering calls. Thin whistling notes.

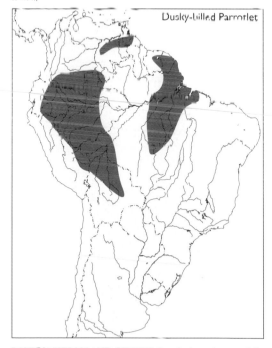

Dusky-billed Parrotlet

DISTRIBUTION AND STATUS South America patchily from the Guianas to northern Bolivia. Although reported from Guyana and French Guiana there are no records (at least not recently) from Surinam. It occurs in the eastern Amazon basin of Brazil in Amapá, Maranhão and Pará, and in the western Amazon basin from the upper Río Negro to northern Mato Grosso; in Venezuela south of the Orinoco on lower Río Caura and Río Cuyuni (a record from Carabobo in the north is apparently mistaken); in eastern Colombia south from extreme south-eastern Guainía (on Río Negro) to Caquetá through eastern Ecuador and eastern Peru south to northern Bolivia to at least Beni. Reasonably frequent in west of range (commonest *Forpus* in range in Ecuador and Colombia) but scarcer eastwards, with few records in Venezuela and Guianas. Evidence for decline in eastern Amazonia (around Belém) and for possible increase in Colombia, perhaps linked to reduction of dense forest. Rare in captivity.

ECOLOGY Lowland tropical rain-forest in clearings, edge, riparian growth, várzea, secondary habitats and savannas, mainly in lowlands (150-250m, Venezuela; to 500m, Colombia), but extending into subtropical forests at 1,500-1,800m in eastern Andes of Ecuador. Gregarious; outside breeding season sometimes in flocks of 100 or more. Diet comprises seeds (e.g. *Cecropia miparia*), berries, buds, etc. Takes mineral soil from river banks alongside other parrots. Nests in tree-cavity. Breeding reported Jul, Peru.

DESCRIPTION Forehead, lores, cheeks and crown emerald-green, sometimes forming distinct mask; sides of neck, hindneck, mantle, upper back and scapulars rather dark, dull green with slight olive tinge; lower back and rump dark cobalt-blue; uppertail-coverts dull dark green. Primary and greater coverts dark blue. Primaries with green outerwebs; secondaries dark blue with green tips. Under-wing with coverts dark cobalt-blue, flight feathers bluish-grey. Underparts dull dark green with slight olive tinge. Uppertail dark green; undertail paler. **Bare parts:** Upper mandible and cere dark blackish-grey, lower mandible lighter; narrow periophthalmic ring dark grey; iris dark brown; legs grey.

SEX/AGE Female all green except yellowish on forehead and forecrown, contrasting with darker green on hind-crown. Immature like respective adult but duller.

MEASUREMENTS Wing 78-86; tail 32-40; bill 10-12; tarsus 10-12.

GEOGRAPHICAL VARIATION Two races.
  F. s. sclateri (W Amazonia from S Colombia to N Bolivia)
  F. s. eidos (Guainía, Colombia, east to lower Rio Madeira, Brazil, and north-east through N Amazonia and S Venezuela to the Guianas) Similar to nominate but paler green, more yellowish beneath, male with paler blue on rump and wings amd rather bright emerald-green face.

REFERENCES Arndt (1996), Chapman (1926), Desenne & Strahl (1994), Forshaw (1989), Gyldenstolpe (1945a), Hilty & Brown (1989), Meyer de Schauensee (1966), Meyer de Schauensee & Phelps (1978), Ridgely (1981), Sick (1993), Snyder (1966), Tostain *et al.* (1992).

280 PACIFIC PARROTLET
Forpus coelestis   Plate 68

Other names: Celestial Parrotlet, Lesson's Parrotlet

IDENTIFICATION 12-13cm. Very small stocky parrotlet with short tapered tail. Mainly yellowish-green beneath and pale olive-brown (male) or green (female) above. Male shows blue on wings and rump. Bright green plumage conspicuous in flight with contrasting brown and blue on upperparts of flying male distinctive. Range approaches Yellow-faced Parrotlet (281) in Marañón Valley, north-west Peru, with possible occasional contact in the Bagua area: Pacific has green (not yellow) underparts and crown. Male from other *Forpus* in captivity in being brown above, green below; female from other female *Forpus* by bluish-green streak behind eye. Widely sympatric Grey-cheeked Parakeet (284) is larger and green above without blue on wings and rump. Flight undulating and generally at canopy level. Usually in small noisy groups of 4-10, sometimes many more. Birds well camouflaged in foliage.

VOICE Short high-pitched twittering and chirruping *chitit chitit* sounds with a metallic tinkling quality.

Pacific Parrotlet

DISTRIBUTION AND STATUS The species occurs in western Ecuador in Manabí from latitude of Río Chone valley south through southern Pichincha, Los Ríos and Guayas (including Puna Island) to El Oro and Loja, entering north-western Peru in Tumbes, Piura, Lambayeque, Cajamarca south to La Libertad as far as latitude of Trujillo (c. 8°S). Apparently patchily common, sometimes abundant; most numerous in arid areas. Population apparently not yet seriously affected by trade in live birds or conversion of natural and semi-natural habitats to agriculture. Probably most numerous *Forpus* in captivity.

ECOLOGY Frequents range of mostly dry wooded habitats such as thorny scrub, deciduous forest, dense cactus scrub with balsa trees, banana and mango plantations, riparian vegetation, irrigated fields in savanna and gardens, but also recorded from tropical humid vegetation such as coastal mangroves. Most records are from sea-level to below 1,000m but found at 2,150m on west slope of Andes at Huancabamba, eastern Piura, Peru, and at 1,570-1,650m in southern Loja, Ecuador. Generally gregarious, forming large flocks where food abundant. Diet includes grass seeds, berries, fruits (of e.g. *Tamarindus, Amaranthus spinosus*) and cactus fruits. Forages in vegetation and on ground. Nest in cavity in tree, cactus, fence-post, pipe or nest of Pale-legged Ovenbird *Furnarius leucopus*, Necklaced Spinetail *Synallaxis stictothorax* or Fasciated Wren *Campylorhynchus fasciatus*. Breeds Jan-May. Sometimes rears second brood. Clutch 4-6.

DESCRIPTION Cheeks, lores, forehead and crown bright apple-green; area behind eyes and faint band on hindneck blue. Mantle, upper back and scapulars pale olive-brown; lower back and rump rich dark cobalt blue; uppertail-coverts bright bluish-green. Primary and greater coverts deep cobalt-blue with some blue at bend of wing; other coverts pale olive-brown. Base of inner primaries and outer secondaries cobalt-blue, flight feathers otherwise green on outerwebs and bluish-green below. Underwing-coverts and axillaries deep cobalt-blue. Underparts apple-green, slightly duller than on face and head; bluish tinge to feathers on vent and undertail-coverts. Uppertail bright bluish-green; undertail slightly duller and more yellowish. **Bare parts:** Bill and cere pale pink; periophthalmic ring grey; iris dark brown; legs pale pink.

SEX/AGE Female is green (not pale brown) above and lacks blue on wings, rump and hindneck; blue markings behind eyes are paler. Immature similar to respective adult but male colour (especially brown) paler.

MEASUREMENTS Wing 79-88; tail 37-44; bill 12-13; tarsus 11-13.

GEOGRAPHICAL VARIATION None.

REFERENCES Arndt (1996), BirdLife International (1992), Brockner (1991), Chapman (1926), Forshaw (1989), Lantermann (1996), Marchant (1960), Meyer de Schauensee (1966), Ridgely (1981), Williams & Tobias (1994).

---

281 YELLOW-FACED PARROTLET
Forpus xanthops   Plate 68

IDENTIFICATION 11cm. Very small stocky parrotlet with short tapered tail, greyish-brown upperparts, blue rump and yellow beneath and on cheeks and crown. For separation from Pacific Parrotlet (280), which may be locally sympatric, see under that species. Combination of yellow crown and underparts and blue rump in both male and female separates from other *Forpus* in captivity. Flight undulating and generally at canopy level. In small flocks.

VOICE Unknown.

DISTRIBUTION AND STATUS Endemic to upper Río Marañón Valley, northern Peru, in relatively small area running roughly north-south through just over two degrees latitude: northernmost record is at 5°37'S in western Amazonas, southernmost from around Huamachuco at 7°57'S in northern La Libertad. Probably locally numerous but poorly known, and overgrazing by goats may be degrading habitat; main cause of concern is trapping for trade, with great wastage through high post-capture mortality (40-100%). Trade ban perhaps leading

to recovery in wild population. In captivity outside range countries. VULNERABLE.

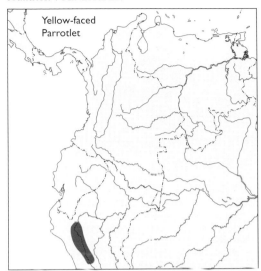

Yellow-faced
Parrotlet

ECOLOGY Occupies rather usually arid, lightly wooded habitats in the upper tropical and subtropical zones, including scrub, riparian vegetation, open balsa woodland, cactus *Prosopis* montane desert and open country with scattered trees and cacti. In one survey area, birds kept mainly above riverine growth in plant community dominated by mixture of cacti (*Cereus, Cepholocereus, Opuntia, Melocactus, Loxanthocereus*), shrubs and bromeliads (*Pitcairnia, Deuterocohnia, Capparis*) and trees (*Sapindus, Cassia, Cordia*). Most records from 1,000-1,600m but known at 600m and observed up to 2,440-2,745m. Gregarious; one communal roost observed in *Gynerium* canebrake and another in orange orchard. Diet consists of cactus and tree fruits, seeds and flowers, including seeds or fruit of *Cercidium*, flowers of *Bombax discolor*, grass and wheat seeds with possible reliance on latter as natural seed availability declines in Jun-Jul with onset of dry season. Breeds Mar-Apr. Nest in cavity in bank, wall or tree (including in former woodpecker hole) with up to 70 pairs in communal nesting area. Clutch 3-6.

DESCRIPTION Forehead, lores, crown, cheeks and ear-coverts bright lemon yellow; streak behind eye grey tinged blue merging with greyish-brown on hindneck. Mantle, scapulars and upper back greyish-brown; lower back, rump and uppertail-coverts, primary and greater coverts cobalt-blue, other coverts greyish-brown. Inner secondaries and base of inner primaries bluish; other flight feathers green on outerwebs, bluish-green below. Underwing-coverts cobalt-blue. Underparts mainly lemon yellow, tinged green around thighs and vent and to lesser extent on sides of breast. Uppertail green; undertail paler. **Bare parts:** Bill pinkish-horn, grey on centre of upper mandible; cere pink; periophthalmic ring grey; iris dark brown; legs pink.

SEX/AGE Female has smaller, paler blue patch on rump, no blue on upperwing-coverts, fainter blue in flight feathers, less bright underparts. Immature unknown but probably similar to respective adult as in other young *Forpus*.

MEASUREMENTS Wing 89-94; tail 40-48; bill 14-15; tarsus 12-15.

NOTE Yellow-faced was formerly regarded as race of Pacific Parrotlet but it appears they could be in contact where their ranges approach in the upper Marañón Valley around Bagua. Whilst they clearly have a recent common ancestor they may better be treated as separate species.

REFERENCES Arndt (1996), Begazo (1996), BirdLife International (1993), Bond (1955), Collar *et al.* (1992, 1994), Forshaw (1989), O'Neill (1981), Ridgely (1981), Stotz *et al.* (1996).

---

282 PLAIN PARAKEET
Brotogeris tirica   Plate 70

Other names: All-green Parakeet, Tirica Parakeet

IDENTIFICATION 23cm. Small long-tailed green parakeet with blue in flight feathers, greenish-yellow underwing-coverts and pale bill. Canary-winged Parakeet (283), which overlaps in interior south-eastern Brazil, has conspicuous patch of yellow on upperwing surface. Plain Parakeet distinguished from several *Pyrrhura* in range by all-green plumage and absence of scaling on breast, from overlapping *Touit* parrotlets by long pointed (not short square) tail and from sympatric *Aratinga* conures by smaller size and absence of red and yellow in plumage. Less active than Maroon-bellied Conure (251) whilst feeding in trees and climbs rather than flutters around branches. All-blue mutants have been reported from Serra do Cubatão, São Paulo, and have been bred in captivity. Plumage blends well with foliage and resting birds are hard to locate. Generally in pairs or small parties in swift direct flight on rapid wingbeats.

VOICE Noisy, especially in flight. Usual flight call is a shrill penetrating disyllabic screech. Harsher notes while resting or feeding in trees.

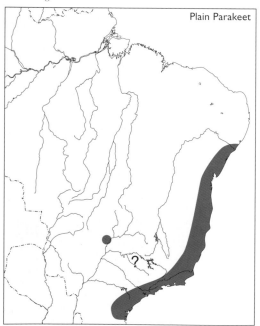

Plain Parakeet

DISTRIBUTION AND STATUS The species occurs in south-east Brazil from Alagoas south through eastern and southern Bahia, Espírito Santo, southern Minas Gerais, Rio de Janeiro, eastern São Paulo and Paraná to Santa Catarina. Single records from Rio Grande do Sul and Goiás are considered doubtful. Some seasonal movements. Uncommon to fairly common depending on locality but apparently only reported very common in São Paulo city. Declined since European settlement of eastern Brazil but less so than other regionally endemic parrots. Occurs in several protected areas (e.g. Itatiaia National Park). Rare in captivity.

ECOLOGY Found in wider range of habitats than any other parrot endemic to Brazil's Atlantic forest: in lowlands and uplands, forest canopy and forest edge, parks and gardens (in e.g. Rio de Janeiro and São Paulo), even city plazas with mature trees, farmland with trees, scattered woodlots and patches of secondary growth. Apparently most numerous in forest edge habitats. Generally in lowlands but reported to 1,200m in Itatiaia Massif on the Rio/São Paulo state border. Gregarious. Generally in pairs or small flocks, sometimes several hundred together. Diet items include pulp of *Posoqueria latifolia*, seeds of *Ficus*, *Trema micrantha*, *Xylopia brasiliensis*, *Vriesea*, *Rhipsalis*, *Cecropia glazioui*, *Hyeronima alchorneoides* and *Merostachis*, seeds and flowers of *Tibouchina mutabilis* and *Psitticanthus*, flowers of *Norantea brasiliensis* and *Eucalyptus* and nectar of *Pseudobombax*. Takes insects and their larvae. Nests in arboreal termitarium, palm crown or natural tree-hollow, in São Paulo city in crevice in building. Termitarium sites are generally shaded, requiring birds in open country to have access to gallery forest for breeding. Breeding reported Sep and young birds Jan. Usual clutch in captivity four.

DESCRIPTION Forehead, lores, crown and cheeks rather pale green with yellowish tinge. Sides of neck and nape green, bluer than on head. Upperparts green but slightly darker than rest of plumage. Most wing-coverts green, some feathers tinged brownish-olive especially on lesser and median coverts. Primary coverts, primaries and outer secondaries violet-blue with narrow green margins to outerwebs. Underwing with coverts greenish-yellow, flight feathers bluish-green. Underparts pale yellowish-green tinged bluish on sides of breast, thighs and undertail-coverts; flanks yellowish. Uppertail green with blue tinge to central feathers; undertail greyish blue-green. **Bare parts**: Bill pale horn; iris brown; legs pinkish.

SEX/AGE Sexes similar. Immature with little or no blue on primary coverts.

MEASUREMENTS Wing 116-128; tail 106-131; bill 16-18; tarsus 13-15.

GEOGRAPHICAL VARIATION None.

REFERENCES Belton (1984), Forshaw (1989), Ridgely (1981), Rutgers & Norris (1976), Sick (1993), Stotz *et al.* (1996), Teixeira *et al.* (1985), Willis & Oniki, (1991), Yamashita *in litt.* (1995), Yamashita *in litt.* (1996).

283 CANARY-WINGED PARAKEET
Brotogeris versicolurus   Plate 70

Other names: Yellow-chevroned, Yellow-winged or Orange-winged Parakeet (*B. versicolurus chiriri* and *behni*); White-winged Parakeet (nominate); Behn's Parakeet (*behni*)

IDENTIFICATION 25cm. Small, mainly green parakeet with longish pointed tail and yellow (in southern races) or yellow and white (in northern race) on upperwings. White flight feathers of nominate appear transparent in flight. Range overlaps with several congeners. Plain Parakeet (282), sympatric in interior south-east Brazil, is separated by all-green upperwing. Cobalt-winged Parakeet (286), overlapping in western Amazonia, is told by orange on chin, blue (not bluish-green) underwing, and lack of yellow and white on wing. Golden-winged (287) and Tui Parakeets (288), also present in much of Amazon basin, show (former) orange on primary coverts (not extensive yellow and white on upperwing surface), and (latter) green upperwing and yellow on head. Both Cobalt- and Golden-winged Parakeets favour forest canopy. Sierra (270) and Mountain (271) Parakeets distinguished from Canary-winged (on eastern Andes in Bolivia and Argentina) by (former) dark head and grey breast and (latter) yellowish underparts. Separated from *Pyrrhura* conures by yellow and/or white on wings. Rather noisy and in large flocks outside breeding season. Flight swift and direct. Birds may be difficult to detect in foliage.

VOICE Shrill metallic notes in flight described as *chiri.. chiri.. ri* (Argentina), *te ele tee* (Peru).

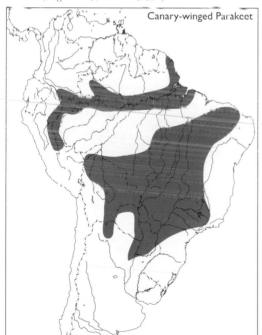

Canary-winged Parakeet

DISTRIBUTION AND STATUS South America east of Andes. Occurs through central Amazon basin from extreme south-east Colombia (mainly around Leticia), eastern Ecuador and north-east Peru (south to Río Ucayali in Loreto) east to French Guiana (no recent records),

Amapá and Mexiana island in the Amazon delta, Brazil. Reported south of Amazon from e.g. lower reaches of Rio Tapajós (race *chiriri*) and from Belém (race *versicolurus*). Apparently occurs disjunctly further south in South America from northern and eastern Bolivia (from Beni to Tarija) east across interior Brazil from Mato Grosso to Ceará in north and to São Paulo in south. Apparently absent in coastal forests of eastern Brazil. Occurs in Paraguay in eastern moist chaco south into extreme northern Argentina in Formosa, Chaco, Misiones, Salta and Corrientes. Introduced to or feral in several areas outside range, including Puerto Rico, where apparently locally numerous, Lima (Peru), California, Costa Rica and Buenos Aires (Argentina). Generally resident, migratory in (e.g.) Rio de Janeiro and southern Pará. Abundance varies over large range; fairly common in eastern Bolivia, common to abundant in Mato Grosso, rather local over much of Amazonia although most abundant parrot in parts (e.g. Amazon delta), rare to uncommon in Argentina (perhaps extinct in Corrientes and Chaco). Common in captivity following large-scale exports from several countries in 1970s and 1980s.

ECOLOGY Frequents wide range of habitat types, including moist, seasonal and riparian forests, pantanal, savanna and city parks. Chiefly in lowlands but *behni* reported to 2,700m in arid zones with scattered *Prosopis* and *Schinus* trees in Bolivia, whilst *chiriri* inhabits central Brazilian plateau at c. 1,000m. Gregarious, forming large flocks and communal roosts outside breeding season, sometimes with several hundred birds; large flocks observed Mato Grosso, Nov, before breaking to pairs in Jan. Diet items include flowers of *Erythrina*, seeds of *Bambusa* and fruits of cultivated *Inga*. Nests in arboreal termitarium (e.g. *Nasutitermes*) in shaded location (thus requiring access to gallery forest) or in tree-hollow. Probably breeds Jan, Mato Grosso.

DESCRIPTION Head green, lores sparsely feathered. Nape, mantle, scapulars and back green slightly tinged olive; rump and uppertail-coverts green. Lesser coverts green suffused brownish-olive; median coverts green; primary coverts blue; greater coverts yellow. Outer primaries green with blue bases; inner primaries and secondaries white with yellowish tinge. Underwing with coverts pale green, flight feathers bluish-green. Underparts slightly yellowish-green. Uppertail green; undertail bluish-green. **Bare parts:** Bill yellowish-horn; bare periophthalmic skin pale greyish-white; iris brown; legs pale pinkish.

SEX/AGE Sexes similar. Immature may show yellow edges to green greater coverts and less or no white on primaries and secondaries (nominate).

MEASUREMENTS Wing 116-125; tail 80-94; bill 14-17; tarsus 13-15.

GEOGRAPHICAL VARIATION Three races. However, *B. chiriri* may warrant species status if it proves to be sympatric with *versicolurus* in the Amazon basin (it has been reported from southern Pará). Pending further details, Ridgely (1981) and Forshaw (1989) are followed with *chiriri* and *versicolurus* considered as races of a single species.

    B. v. versicolurus (N South America mainly north of Amazon from French Guiana and Pará, Brazil, to Colombia, Ecuador and Peru south to Loreto)

    B. v. chiriri (N Bolivia south to Santa Cruz east through S Amazon basin to NE Brazil and through Paraguay to N Argentina. Approaches range of next race in Paraguay) Similar to nominate but lacks white on upperwing with primaries and secondaries green. Lores more densely feathered.

B. v. behni (Central Bolivia south to north of Salta, Argentina) Very like *chiriri* but larger (wing 127-137) and undertail more bluish.

REFERENCES Arrowood (1991), Contreras *et al.* (1991), Dubs (1992), Fjeldså & Krabbe (1990), Forshaw (1989), Gyldenstolpe (1945b), Hilty & Brown (1986), Koepcke (1983), Meyer de Schauensee (1949), Narosky & Yzurieta (1989), Naumburg (1930), Navas & Bó (1996), Nores & Yzurieta (1994), de la Peña (1988), Ridgely (1981), Short (1975), Sick (1993), Tostain *et al.* (1992), Yamashita *in litt.* (1995, 1996).

284 GREY-CHEEKED PARAKEET
Brotogeris pyrrhopterus Plate 70

Other names: Orange-winged Parakeet, Orange-flanked Parakeet

IDENTIFICATION 20cm. Small, mainly green parakeet with pointed tail, grey cheeks and ear-coverts, blue crown and reddish-orange at bend of wing (not always visible in perched birds) and on underwing-coverts. Generally conspicuous in flocks of 6-10. May just enter the restricted range of El Oro Conure (260), which has green cheeks, red on forehead and upper surface of wings and green underwing-coverts. Grey-cheeked Parakeet distinguished (in western Ecuador) from Red-winged Parrotlet (294) by pointed (not square-ended) tail and reddish-orange (not yellow) on underwing-coverts. No other *Brotogeris* in restricted range but combination of grey cheeks, blue crown and reddish underwing-coverts separates this from congeners in captivity. Forms flocks which may be conspicuous when calling but difficult to detect whilst quietly perched. Flight swift and direct and climbs in lively manner in branches.

VOICE Unmelodious grating *stteeet stteeet stteeet*, repeated rapidly. Flight call more pleasant trilling *stleeet stleeet*. Voice similar to Tovi (285) and Cobalt-winged Parakeet (286).

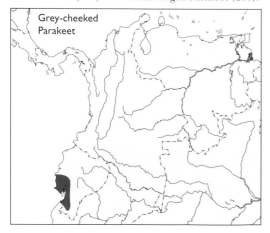
Grey-cheeked Parakeet

DISTRIBUTION AND STATUS The species is known from the Pacific slope of south-west Ecuador from the Río

Chone Valley, Manabí, in the north (0°41'S) mainly through the lowlands to Loja in the south with records from Los Ríos, Guayas, Azuay and El Oro, extending into adjacent extreme north-west Peru in Tumbes and reaching its southernmost point at Ayabaca, Piura, at 4°38'S. Two main populations appear to exist, one in coastal Ecuador in Manabí and Guayas, the other athwart the border of Ecuador and Peru, this latter being the greater stronghold from Tumbes to Amaluza, Loja. Generally rather scarce but remains locally common where native woodland remains; mainly uncommon in Peru. Decline in 20th century is due to habitat loss and international and local trade (more than 97,000 traded internationally 1982-1990). Locally extirpated by habitat loss (e.g. Babahojo valley, Guayas) while absence in some apparently suitable areas may reflect seasonal movements. Trapping, although illegal, appears to continue, at least to satisfy local demand; international trade banned in both range states. Shortage of nest-sites may limit overall breeding effort. Although it is not yet considered at threat of extinction, its occurrence in protected areas (e.g. Cerro Blanco Reserve, Ecuador, and Tumbes National Forest, Peru) is insufficient to assure survival on present trends. Wild population estimated at 15,000 birds (1995). NEAR-THREATENED.

ECOLOGY The species is found in a variety of wooded habitats, preferably thick primary deciduous woodland with *Ceiba trichistandra*, where most abundant, but also degraded and secondary formations, premontane dry forest, arid *Acacia* scrublands and farmland with large trees adjacent to forest; also reported from banana plantations, Tumbes, and from degraded humid forest, Loja, but is probably only sporadic visitor to heavily degraded areas. Usually in lowlands but reported up to 1,400m, Ecuador, and 700m, Peru. Generally in pairs or flocks of up to a dozen but gatherings of hundreds reported (large groups rare in recent years); sometimes associates with other parrots including Red-masked Conure (233) and Bronze-winged Parrot (318). Birds in north-west Peru fed on flowers and seeds of large trees including *Erythrina*, *Chorisia* and *Cavanillesia plantifolia*, *Cecropia* catkins, *Ceiba* fruits and figs *Ficus*. Sometimes feeds on crops such as banana. Nests in cavity in large tree such as *Erythrina* or *Bombax* or in arboreal termitarium. Birds seen investigating nest-holes Feb, and copulation noted Aug. Main breeding period likely to coincide with wet season (Jan-Mar). Clutch 4-7, usually five.

DESCRIPTION Crown and nape pale blue; rest of head pale grey. Upperparts green. Orange patch on bend of wing. Lesser and median coverts brownish olive-green; primary coverts dark blue; greater coverts green. Primaries dark green with slight bluish tinge; secondaries green. Underwing with coverts reddish-orange, flight feathers bluish-green. Underparts mainly yellowish-green (considerably paler than upperparts) with bluish tinge to thighs. Uppertail green; undertail bluish-green. **Bare parts**: Bill pale horn; bare periophthalmic skin whitish; iris brown; legs pinkish.

SEX/AGE Sexes similar. Immature duller than adult with green crown, blackish upper and dark brown lower mandible.

MEASUREMENTS Wing 112-125; tail 63-75; bill 16-18; tarsus 13-15.

GEOGRAPHICAL VARIATION None.

REFERENCES Arndt (1996), Best & Clarke (1991), Best

et al. (1993, 1995), Bloch *et al.* (1991), Forshaw (1989), Parker *et al.* (1995), Ridgely (1981), Williams & Tobias (1994), Yamashita *in litt.* (1995).

285 TOVI PARAKEET
Brotogeris jugularis   Plate 71

Other names: Orange-chinned Parakeet, Brown-shouldered Parakeet, Beebee Parakeet

IDENTIFICATION 16-18cm. Small, mainly green parakeet with tapered tail, large bronze-brown shoulder-patch, bright yellow on underwing-coverts and orange chin (latter a weak fieldmark). Only small sharp-tailed parrot with brownish wing-patch and orange chin. Most conspicuous small parrot in much of range, often flying high calling loudly. Sympatric with several *Aratinga* conures, including Orange-fronted (243) and Brown-throated (245), but these are larger with longer tails. *Forpus* parrotlets are even smaller than Tovi Parakeet, lack yellow underwing-coverts and (like *Touit* parrotlets) have square-ended tails. Barred Parakeet (272), which may occur with Tovi in subtropical montane areas from Mexico to Venezuela, is separated by close dark barring on upperparts, flanks and upperwing-coverts. Also occurs with several *Pyrrhura* conures which are, however, more slender, longer-tailed and scaly-breasted. Gregarious. Birds chatter noisily and continuously whilst feeding in trees and are especially vocal when taking wing in swift, twisting, distinctive bounding flight. Plumage blends well with foliage and birds may be difficult to detect visually in tree canopy. Aberrant blue individuals reported. Often perches on high bare branches.

VOICE Shrill and noisy chattering in flight. Other calls include a scratchy *ru-u-a a a* or *ack uck ack*, more musical *week week kweekkee roo kke roo kee too*, harsh, scolding *cuhiueet* rapidly repeated, sometimes interspersed with more melodious (sometimes trilling) sounds, and clipped *chi chi chi* and *chee chi-chit*. Birds especially noisy whilst foraging in flocks during morning and evening. Paired birds may duet when showing aggression towards (e.g.) nest competitor or predator.

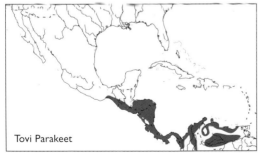

Tovi Parakeet

DISTRIBUTION AND STATUS This parakeet occupies the arid Pacific lowlands of Mexico in Oaxaca and Chiapas (reports from Guerrero doubtful) and adjacent Guatemala and El Salvador, Pacific lowlands of Honduras but both Pacific and Caribbean slopes of Nicaragua. In Costa Rica it is mainly a Pacific-slope bird but enters Caribbean lowlands adjacent southern Lake Nicaragua, ranging throughout Pacific and Caribbean lowlands of Panama, including Coiba and Cébaco islands. It occurs west of the Andes in Colombia south to the Río Atrato and in the Caribbean lowlands to the Santa Marta region and Sierra de Perijá and south to the upper Magdalena Valley and lowland Norte de Santander and Arauca. In Venezuela it extends from north of the Orinoco in Zulia, northern Táchira, western Mérida, the coastal mountains Yaracuy and Carabobo and in lowland Portuguesa, Cojedes, Barinas, Apure and Guárico. Mainly resident but wanders locally in some areas (e.g. some post-breeding dispersal noted El Salvador). Generally common to abundant but apparently uncommon locally (e.g. Oaxaca). Captured for trade and common in captivity in range countries.

ECOLOGY Generally in wooded or partly wooded country including scrub, deciduous, dry and humid forests, plantations, edge of clearings and cultivated or grassy areas with large trees. Tolerates human habitation and frequents town parks and gardens. Most numerous in partly deforested areas. Mainly in tropical zone but ascends to subtropical vegetation in (e.g.) Guanacaste mountains, Costa Rica; reported to 500m (Guatemala), 900m (Honduras), 1,360m (El Salvador), 1,200m (Costa Rica), 1,000m (Venezuela). Usually in pairs or small flocks with larger gatherings where food abundant. More gregarious outside breeding season. Roosts communally in (e.g.) palm trees and forms pre roosting assemblages. Diet items include seeds and fruits of *Bombax* trees, *Ficus*, *Muntingia*, *Byrsonima*, *Cecropia*, *Ceiba* and flowers and nectar of *Erythrina*, balsa and guava. Chiefly feeds in canopy but can be destructive of crops (e.g. mango). Nests usually in tree-hollow (including old woodpecker nests) but also arboreal termitarium. At times colonial. Breeding reported Mar, Mexico; Jan, El Salvador; Feb-Apr, Panama; Jan-Mar, Colombia. Clutch 4-8.

DESCRIPTION Forehead, crown, hindneck and upper cheeks bright green with bluish tinge; lores and lower cheeks duller green with olive tinge. Feathers on mantle and upper back olive green with greener tips; scapulars green with bronze-brown tips; lower back and rump bluish-green. Lesser and median coverts bronze-brown forming large shoulder-patch; primary coverts blue; greater coverts green. Flight feathers greenish-blue above, bluish-green below with lesser underwing-coverts yellow. Bright orange spot on throat; underparts otherwise yellowish-green, bluer from belly to undertail-coverts. Uppertail bluish-green; undertail paler and more yellowish. **Bare parts** Bill pale horn; bare periophthalmic skin whitish; iris dark brown (reported as straw, Guatemala); legs pinkish.

SEX/AGE All plumages similar.

MEASUREMENTS Wing 105-112; tail 55-68; bill 15-17; tarsus 13-14.

GEOGRAPHICAL VARIATION Two races. The name *chrysopogon* has been proposed for birds from Mexico to NW Costa Rica on doubtful basis of more yellowish-green plumage and paler wing-coverts. See also Note in Cobalt-winged Parakeet (286).

B. j. jugularis (Mexico to N Colombia north and west of Andes)

B. j. exsul (Venezuela and Colombia in Arauca and Norte de Santander) Underparts wholly green lacking bluish tinge on undertail-coverts. Orange chin spot is small and pale and mantle and upper back is brown rather than olive.

REFERENCES Binford (1989), Dickey & van Rossem (1938), Edwards (1972), Forshaw (1989), Hilty & Brown

(1986), Howell (1957), Howell & Webb (1994, 1995), Land (1970), Meyer de Schauensee (1949), Meyer de Schauensee & Phelps (1978), Miller (1947), Monroe (1968), Peterson & Chalif (1973), Ridgely & Gwynne (1989), Slud (1964), Stiles *et al.* (1989), Stotz *et al.* (1996), Wetmore (1966), Yamashita *in litt.* (1995).

286 COBALT-WINGED PARAKEET
Brotogeris cyanoptera   Plate 71

Other names: Deville's Parakeet; Gustave's Parakeet (*B. c. gustavi*); Beni Cobalt-winged Parakeet (*B. c. beniensis*)

IDENTIFICATION 18cm. Small, mainly green parakeet with fairly short pointed tail and yellowish forehead (greenish in upper Huallaga Valley, Peru). Flashing blue wings conspicuous in flight but orange spot on chin indistinct. Tui Parakeet (288), sympatric in much of western Amazonia, lacks orange on chin but shows prominent yellow patch on forehead. Sympatric Canary-winged (283) is told by yellow or yellow and white on upperwings. Golden-winged (287), recorded in upper Rio Negro, Brazil, is separated by orange feathers on upperwing. Male *Forpus* parrotlets show blue on wing but are smaller, while *Touit* parrotlets are slightly smaller with short square tails. Cobalt-winged is less often seen at clearings and forest edge than congeners and most often in small flocks in canopy of tall forest (where plumage blends well with foliage). Often encountered calling noisily in swift direct flight over clearings.

VOICE Call quite scratchy but less than Golden-winged Parakeet with apparently more melodious chirruping calls in repertoire, including clear *splink splink* calls. Some phrases combine harsh and melodious notes. Voice said to be similar to Tui Parakeet.

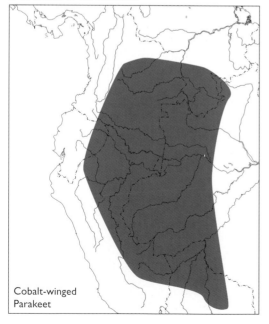

Cobalt-winged Parakeet

DISTRIBUTION AND STATUS This parakeet occurs in southern Venezuela in the upper Orinoco catchment,

Amazonas; north-west Brazil from the Rio Negro west through catchments of Rios Purús and Juruá; tropical zone of Colombia south and east from western Meta; eastern Ecuador where reported from (e.g.) Río Napo; eastern Peru where known in (e.g.) catchments of Ríos Ucayali, Huallaga and Heath; and north-east Bolivia where reported from (e.g.) lowlands of Cochabamba and Beni. Common to abundant over most of range (16 pairs per km² in Manu National Park, Peru) and huge areas of habitat remain in range; however, race *gustavi* may be less numerous or underrecorded and nominate heavily traded in eastern Peru where it is one of the commonest pet birds and locally reduced in numbers (e.g. around Iquitos). Rare in captivity outside range.

ECOLOGY Occurs mainly in lowland tropical rain-forest, in both seasonally flooded and terra firme formations but probably more numerous in latter, but using most well-wooded habitats in moist tropical zone including semi-open savanna of Guainía, south-eastern Colombia. Crosses clearings but rarely perches or feeds outside forest. Recorded to 100-180m in Venezuela and 600m at base of Colombian Andes; fairly common to 1,050m (exceptionally to 1,350m), San Martín, Peru. Gregarious, generally in flocks of up to about 30 outside breeding season. No details on food or breeding. Diet probably similar to congeners. Forages in canopy. Breeding-condition birds Jun, Colombia. Clutch five in captivity.

DESCRIPTION Forehead and lores yellow; crown, sides of neck and nape bluish-green; cheeks paler and more yellowish green than crown. Mantle, back and scapulars brownish-olive; rump and uppertail-coverts green. Lesser and median coverts brownish-olive; greater coverts green; primary coverts violet-blue. Flight feathers violet-blue above with outer primaries showing narrow green margins to outerwebs, blue below. Underwing with lesser coverts green, greater coverts blue. Bright orange spot on chin; underparts otherwise yellowish-green with faint bluish tinge on sides of breast. Uppertail blue centrally, lateral feathers green with yellowish-green on innerwebs; undertail yellowish-green. **Bare parts**: Bill pinkish-horn; cere white; bare periophthalmic skin pinkish-white; iris dark brown; legs pink.

SEX/AGE Sexes similar but female has less extensive yellow on forehead. Immature has duller yellow forehead and darker bill.

MEASUREMENTS Wing 113-123; tail 49-64; bill 15-18; tarsus 13-15.

GEOGRAPHICAL VARIATION Three races, but details on range and consistent plumage differences are few. Race *gustavi* has been regarded as a full species.

    B. c. cyanoptera (Upper Orinoco and W Amazon basin south to northernmost Bolivia)
    B. c. gustavi (Upper Huallaga Valley, Peru) As nominate but with greenish forehead and lores, fainter bluish tinge on crown and green outer primary coverts. Bend and edge of wing yellow. Birds in lower Huallaga Valley are intermediate with nominate.
    B. c. beniensis (N Bolivia) As nominate but paler green, green outer primary coverts and yellow on bend and leading edge of wings. Birds intermediate with nominate at base of eastern slope of Andes in region of Río Beni.

NOTE Cobalt-winged has been treated as race of allopatric Tovi Parakeet (285), to which it is evidently closely related.

Their morphological differences suggest that they are separate and we follow most recent authors in regarding them as two species.

REFERENCES Arndt (1996), Bond (1955), Bond & Meyer de Schauensee (1942), Davis (1986), Desenne & Strahl (1991, 1994), Forshaw (1989), Friedmann (1948), Gyldenstolpe (1945a,b), Hilty & Brown (1986), Meyer de Schauensee (1949), Meyer de Schauensee & Phelps (1978), O'Neill (1981), Ridgely (1981), Sick (1993), Yamashita *in litt.* (1995).

287 GOLDEN-WINGED PARAKEET
Brotogeris chrysopterus   Plate 71

Other names: Rio Negro Parakeet (*B. c. tenuifrons*); Golden-fronted Parakeet (*B. c. tuipara*)

IDENTIFICATION 17-18cm. Small, stocky, mainly green parakeet with rather short pointed tail, orange (yellow in Rio Madeira catchment) primary coverts, blue primaries and pale bill. Forehead and chin-spot brown (north of Amazon) or orange (south bank of lower Amazon) but a weak fieldmark. Canary-winged (283) and Tui (288) Parakeets overlap with Golden-winged; former split by yellow and white on wing, latter by green primary coverts and prominent yellow spot on head. Golden-winged also overlaps with Cobalt-winged Parakeet (286) in Brazil's upper Rio Negro; told by orange (not blue) primary coverts. *Touit* parrotlets are slightly smaller with square-ended tails. *Pyrrhura* conures have scaly breasts and longer tails. Tends to remain in forest canopy where its plumage blends well with foliage. Most often seen in flight or detected as noisy flocks in tree-tops.

VOICE Flight call quite harsh and scratchy *tchr tchr tchr*, rapidly repeated 9-6 times between pauses. Also a *chil chil chil* or *chii chiit* and softer babbling notes. Noisy screeching whilst mobbing predator.

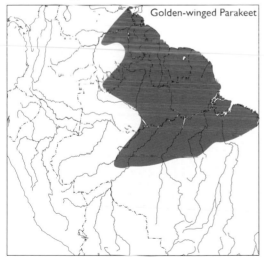

Golden-winged Parakeet

DISTRIBUTION AND STATUS The species has been recorded north of the Amazon from the Rio Negro drainage, Brazil, in eastern Venezuela (Sucre, Monagas and north and eastern Bolívar) and the Guianas to Amapá, Brazil. In Guyana reported from (e.g.) Demerara, Kanuku

Mountains, Mazaruni, Potaro, Rupununi and lower Essequibo Rivers; in Surinam from the coastal sand-ridges to the interior; widespread in French Guiana. Known from Manaus and Cojadás area on the Amazon and occurs south of the river on the Rio Madeira into northern Mato Grosso and probably northernmost Bolivia; also extends east through Pará to the Amazon delta, northern Maranhão and perhaps south to northern Piauí. Mainly resident although birds may wander locally (irregular wanderings reported, Surinam). Generally common but declining locally owing to deforestation (e.g. eastern Amazonia). Small numbers exported but uncommon in captivity.

ECOLOGY Mainly inhabits lowland rain-forest but reported at 1,200m in cloud-forest north of Orinoco in Venezuela and on the Surinam savannas; ranges into clearings to feed and occasionally appears in urban areas with large trees (e.g. Paramaribo, Surinam). Gregarious, usually in small flocks of 8-16 outside breeding period; sometimes up to 100 on fruiting trees. Birds roost communally in tree-cavity or arboreal termitarium. Diet includes nectar from flowers (also in some cases fruit) of *Norantea*, *Inga lateriflora*, *Erythrina amazonica*, *Virola surinamensis*, *Tabebuia serratifolia*, *Pithecellobium pedicellare*, *Bertholletia excelsa*, *Allantonia lineata* and perhaps *Micropholis melinoneana*, fruits of fig *Ficus* and *Astrocaryum* palm, berries of *Trema micrantha*, small woolly seeds of Bombacaceae trees, and (in mixed flocks with *Pyrrhura* conures) seeds from *Alibutia edulis* and *Cecropia miparia*. Birds generally forage in canopy but also observed taking algae and thiarid snails from freshwater whilst levels low in dry season. Nests in tree-hollow or arboreal termitarium. Occupied nests reported Nov, Feb and Apr, Surinam. Up to six birds reported at one active nest suggesting some kind of cooperative breeding or use of nest-chamber as roost. Clutch 3-4.

DESCRIPTION Forehead brown; head otherwise rather bright green with bluish tinge. Mantle, back and scapulars green with olive suffusion; rump and uppertail-coverts green. Lesser, median and greater coverts green with olive suffusion; primary coverts bright orange. Primaries blue with green tips and margins to outerwebs; secondaries green. Underwing with coverts green, primaries blue. Brown spot on chin; underparts otherwise green. Uppertail green with outer feathers olive on innerwebs; undertail more yellowish. **Bare parts**: Bill pale pinkish-horn; bare periophthalmic skin whitish; iris dark blackish-brown; legs pale bluish-green.

SEX/AGE Sexes similar. Juvenile has green (not orange) primary coverts.

MEASUREMENTS Wing 103-111; tail 50-66; bill 15-18; tarsus 13-14.

GEOGRAPHICAL VARIATION Four races. A fifth, *solimoensis*, has been described from Manaus and Cojadás districts, Amazonas, Brazil, on weak basis of paler frontal band and chin spot to nominate.

    B. c. chrysopterus (Brazil north of Amazon, E Venezuela and the Guianas)

    B. c. tuipara (South bank of lower Amazon) Brown chin spot and frontal band of nominate replaced with orange. Paler and more yellowish-green and perhaps on average larger (c. 18cm).

    B. c. chrysosema (Catchment of Rio Madeira and tributaries) Yellow primary coverts, yellowish forehead and lores, yellow margins to outer tail feathers; c. 19cm

B. c. tenuifrons (Confluence of Rios Cauaburi and Negro, Amazonas, Brazil) Like nominate but has only narrow, barely discernible brownish frontal band.

REFERENCES Arndt (1996), Desenne (1994), Desenne & Strahl (1991, 1994), Forshaw (1989), Friedmann (1948), Friedmann & Smith (1955), Haverschmidt (1968), Meyer de Schauensee (1966), Meyer de Schauensee & Phelps (1978), Parker *et al.* (1993), Sick (1993), Snyder (1966), Tostain *et al.* (1992), Yamashita *in litt.* (1995).

---

288 TUI PARAKEET
Brotogeris sanctithomae   Plate 71

Other names: St Thomas's Parakeet

IDENTIFICATION 17cm. Small, mainly green parakeet with rather short pointed tail, pronounced yellow patch on forehead and forecrown (with yellow also extending in streak behind eyes in birds from eastern Amazon basin) and quite dark orange-brown bill. Distribution of Canary-winged (283), Cobalt-winged (286) and Golden-winged (287) Parakeets overlap with that of Tui Parakeet: Golden- and Canary-winged are respectively told by orange or yellow (or yellow and white) on upperwing surface; Cobalt-winged shows flashing blue wings in flight and less prominent and less extensive yellow on head. Tui is less often in forest canopy than Golden and Cobalt-winged Parakeets, instead frequenting second growth with clearings. Only slightly larger than *Forpus* parrotlets but none of latter occurring in range of Tui Parakeet has yellow on head; *Touit* parrotlets have square-ended tails; *Pyrrhura* conures are larger and longer-tailed. Flight buzzy and rather undulating. Noisy chattering flocks may be encountered along rivers.

VOICE High-pitched dry *screek* repeated constantly in flight. Calling birds create incessant shrill chattering.

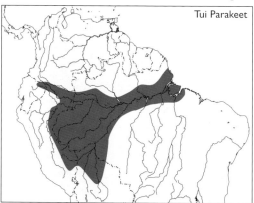

Tui Parakeet

DISTRIBUTION AND STATUS The species is confined to the Amazon basin from south-east Colombia (Leticia area), north-east and south-east Peru and western Brazil possibly to right bank of Rio Negro and in catchments of Rios Purús, Solimões (east to about Cojadás) and Juruá south to northern Bolivia in Pando and Beni, occurring in the eastern Amazon possibly disjunctly from around mouths of Rios Negro and Madeira east to Amapá and eastern Pará possibly as far as Belém area. Apparently sedentary. Local (e.g. Loreto, Peru) but common or

abundant in many places (e.g. near Leticia). Kept as pet locally but uncommon in captivity outside range. Perhaps locally reduced owing to trade (e.g. Peru) but effect of habitat loss within range still minor. Present in many protected areas (e.g. Manu National Park, Peru).

ECOLOGY Mainly in second growth in moist lowland tropical rain-forest areas, várzea on banks of larger rivers and river islands, clearings near watercourses; to 100m in Colombia and 300m in Peru. Gregarious, generally in small flocks; sometimes in larger gatherings. Few details on food but birds seen taking *Erythrina* blossoms, Colombia. Nests in arboreal termitarium or tree-hollow. Seen at nest in May and Jul with begging young Jun, Colombia.

DESCRIPTION Forehead and forecrown bright yellow; rest of head and nape bluish-green. Mantle, back, and scapulars rather dark green, paler and brighter on rump and uppertail-coverts. Alula blue on innerweb, green on outerweb; primary coverts greenish-blue; coverts otherwise green, lesser and median faintly suffused olive. Flight feathers greenish-blue on outerwebs, dark green on innerwebs, and dull blue below; lesser underwing-coverts green, greater blue. Underparts yellowish-green. Uppertail green; undertail more yellowish. **Bare parts:** Bill fairly dark orange-brown; cere pale pinkish; iris brown; legs greyish-horn colour.

SEX/AGE All plumages similar.

MEASUREMENTS Wing 101-115; tail 52-62; bill 12-15; tarsus 12-14.

GEOGRAPHICAL VARIATION Two races are recognised. Birds from Rio Juruá region reported to have longer culmen (14-16) than those from Rios Purús and Solimões.
   B. s. sanctithomae (W Amazon basin from SE Colombia to N Bolivia)
   B. s. takatsukasae (Both banks of lower Amazon east from junction of Rio Negro to E Pará) Yellow streak behind (and sometimes below) eye extends onto ear-coverts. Yellow patch on forehead sometimes larger.

REFERENCES Arndt (1996), Forshaw (1989), Gyldenstolpe (1945a,b), Hilty & Brown (1986), Meyer de Schauensee (1949, 1966), Ridgely (1981), Sick (1993), Yamashita *in litt.* (1995).

---

289 TEPUI PARROTLET
Nannopsittaca panychlora   Plate 72

Other names: Roraima Parrotlet

IDENTIFICATION 14cm. Very small, almost wholly green parrotlet with short square-ended tail, rather pointed wings and yellowish area around eyes. Paler green beneath with yellowish-green undertail-coverts. Similar proportions to *Forpus* parrotlets but with all-green plumage, with yellow area around eyes and more protruding bill: altitudinally overlapping Green-rumped Parrotlet (276) shows blue greater upper- and underwing-coverts and bright emerald-green rump; male Dusky-billed Parrotlet (279) has blue flight feathers and rump. Sapphire-rumped (295) and Seven-coloured (291) Parrotlets are slightly larger with red on tail, latter also with pale green head and yellow on upperwing-coverts *Brotogeris* parakeets are larger, with pointed tails and yellow or orange on upperwing surface.

Mostly seen morning and evening in noisy flocks flying fast and high over tree-tops. Flies lower during frequent fogs that characterise preferred montane habitat. Feeds silently in trees where plumage blends well with foliage.

VOICE Lively twittering sounds from flocks.

DISTRIBUTION AND STATUS This chiefly montane parrotlet occurs in several disjunct populations in eastern Venezuela and adjacent western Guyana, focused on the Gran Sabana of eastern Bolívar, Venezuela (e.g. Mounts Roraima and Auyan Tepui); it is also present around Mount Duida and the Río Ventauri lowlands, Amazonas, and in western Guyana from Kamarang River area; a more distant population occupies the Paria Peninsula (e.g. Mount Papelón), Sucre, north-eastern Venezuela. Probably occurs in extreme northern Roraima, Brazil. Apparently locally common and stable but perhaps declined on the Paria Peninsula owing to large-scale deforestation. Much of range included in Gran Sabana National Park. Scarce in captivity.

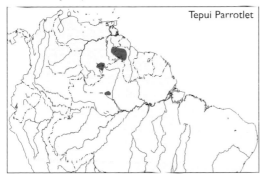

Tepui Parrotlet

ECOLOGY Birds inhabit moist montane forest in upper tropical and subtropical zones, and at least at times lowland rain-forest around the tepuis, generally at 750-1,850m (Gran Sabana) but observed at summit of Auyan Tepui at 2,200m and near summit of Mount Roraima at 2,200m; at 750-950m in Sucre. May breed in subtropical zone and descend to tropical zone to feed. Recent sight records of birds in lowlands suggest at least seasonal occurrence at lower altitude. Gregarious, commonly in flocks of 100 or more although usually up to 20. No information on feeding and breeding except birds have been seen taking fruits of figs *Ficus* near Auyan-tepui.

DESCRIPTION Head green with yellowish-olive tinge; ocular area yellow extending further below and behind eye than above. Upperparts green (brighter and less olive than on head). Upperwing-coverts green with narrow yellowish leading edge to wing. Flight feathers green with tips of primaries blackish; dull brownish below, underwing-coverts green. Underparts yellowish-green becoming greenish-yellow on undertail-coverts. Uppertail green; undertail more yellowish. **Bare parts**: Bill greyish-horn; cere grey; narrow periophthalmic ring dark grey; iris brown; legs pinkish.

SEX/AGE Sexes similar. Immature undescribed.

MEASUREMENTS Wing 88-98; tail 37-43; bill 11-13; tarsus 12-14.

GEOGRAPHICAL VARIATION None.

REFERENCES Chapman (1931), Desenne & Strahl (1991, 1994), Forshaw (1989), Gilliard (1941), Meyer de

Schauensee & Phelps (1978), O'Neill *et al.* (1991), Ridgely (1981), Snyder (1966), Stotz (1996), Whitney (1996).

290 AMAZONIAN PARROTLET
Nannopsittaca dachilleae Plate 72

IDENTIFICATION 12cm. Very small green parrotlet with short square-ended tail, rather pointed wings, powdery-blue lores, forehead and crown, greenish-yellow chin and pale pinkish bill. Birds show pale bare area around eyes. Like *Forpus* in size and proportions but has more protruding, slender bill and males of overlapping Sclater's (279) and Blue-winged (277) Parrotlets have blue on wings and rump while their all-green females lack blue on head. Much smaller than *Brotogeris* parakeets and smaller than *Touit* parrotlets. Seen in tight flocks low over rivers or perched in small groups in trees, quietly clambering about in foliage like arboreal mice whilst feeding. Slight vocalisation from one bird stimulates whole flock to call before taking flight.

VOICE High-pitched piping calls recall poultry chicks. Chirping, squeaking and chattering sounds of flock are similar to Blue-winged Parrotlet but differ from the harsher, grating and more gravelly notes of Sclater's.

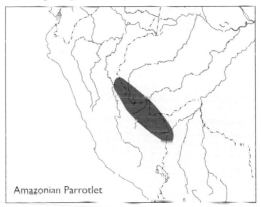

Amazonian Parrotlet

DISTRIBUTION AND STATUS A recently described species known from the western Amazon basin in south-east and southern Peru on the Río Sheshea (Ucayali), and in the Tambopata Reserve on the Río Manu and from the Río Heath (Madre de Dios); also reported from Bolivian bank of Río Heath in La Paz. It remains to be established if distribution continuous between Bolivia and Ucayali. Possible association with bamboo suggests nomadic tendencies. Apparently distributed rather locally but common to very common some areas, although initial observations indicate that it is rare in north-west Bolivia. NEAR-THREATENED.

ECOLOGY Lowland forest near watercourses; observed in small *Calocophyllum spruceanum* and *Cecropia membranacea* trees next to river and in bamboo groves; to 300m. Gregarious and generally in small flocks of 3-12 birds. Diet includes seeds of bushes, trees and bamboo, foods including fruits of *Rhipsalis* (an arboreal epiphytic cactus) and a *Coussapoa* vine, *Cecropia* catkins and seeds of *Vernonia* and bamboo *Guadua*; visits mineral-rich river banks alongside other small parrots such as Sclater's Parrotlet or Tui (288) and Cobalt-winged (286) Parakeets. Nests in hole in base of large arboreal bromeliad or other epiphyte; one suspected nest 25m from ground. Adults noted alloppreening and passing food Jul-Sep.

DESCRIPTION Lores, forehead and crown powdery-blue; cheeks and chin paler yellowish-green; nape and sides of neck green. Upperparts and wing-coverts green, with olive tinge on mantle and wing-coverts. Flight feathers green with blackish tips and margins to innerwebs. Underparts yellowish-green. **Bare parts**: Bill and cere pale pink; narrow peri-ophthalmic ring white; iris brown; legs rich reddish-pink.

SEX/AGE Sexes apparently similar. Female on average slightly smaller than male. Immature possibly duller than adult.

MEASUREMENTS Wing 80-90; tail 40-50; bill 10-12; tarsus 9-13.

GEOGRAPHICAL VARIATION None.

REFERENCES Arndt (1996), O'Neill *et al.* (1991), Parker (1991), Parker *et al.* (1991), Whitney (1996).

---

291 LILAC-TAILED PARROTLET
Touit batavica   Plate 73

Other names: Seven-coloured Parrotlet, Black-winged Parrotlet, Scopoli's Parrotlet

IDENTIFICATION 14cm. Very distinctive small parrot with short lilac tail, green head, dark upperparts and pale powdery-blue breast. Forehead and lores yellow; greater wing-coverts yellow tipped bright blue so that, at distance, birds appear black and green with pale wing-band. Range overlaps with similar-sized Scarlet-shouldered Parrotlet (292) in northern Venezuela and Guyana, and with Sapphire-rumped Parrotlet (295) in Guyana and Surinam: both show green underparts and former lacks lilac tail and shows red underwing-coverts whilst latter has blue rump and brown on head. Green-rumped Parrotlet (276), sympatric in east of Lilac-tailed's range, told by almost all-green plumage and slightly smaller size. Caica Parrot (306) occurs in Venezuela and the Guyanas but is much larger with black head. Inconspicuous when perched and usually noted in small loose noisy flying flocks. Flight swift and direct on rapid shallow wingbeats with no undulation. Wings appear rather broad. Generally stays in tree-tops.

VOICE High-pitched *screee-eeet*, rising in pitch on second part of call, given continuously in flight. Flocks utter confused chorus of nasal squealing calls *ee-eeth* (perhaps same as preceding) quite unlike Green-rumped Parrotlet. Birds also have a short trilling and soft chattering. Generally silent whilst feeding.

DISTRIBUTION AND STATUS The species occurs in north-east South America, in Guyana from around Mazaruni and Essequibo Rivers and Bartica, mainly in coastal Surinam, apparently widespread in French Guiana and possibly present in adjacent Amapá, Brazil; in eastern Venezuela in eastern Bolívar (e.g. on Río Cuyuni) and Delta Amacuro and north of the Orinoco in Sucre, Distrito Federal, Aragua and Mérida. Presence on Trinidad (apparently not Tobago) may involve feral escapes. Some declines owing to deforestation but large areas of suitable habitat remain and the species occurs in several protected areas. Birds reported Surinam as irregular wanderers.

Locally distributed but probably fairly common. Rare in captivity but only member of genus known to be traded internationally.

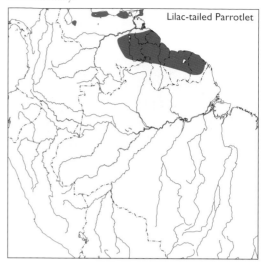
Lilac-tailed Parrotlet

ECOLOGY Occurs in the canopy of primary forest or taller secondary growth in tropical and subtropical zones but may be seen lower down at forest edge and at clearings, in both dry deciduous and humid forest, reportedly also cloud-forest in subtropical Venezuela and in trees close to human habitation on Trinidad. Mainly in lowlands but in Venezuela to 1,700m. Generally in flocks of 10-30 or more outside breeding season and highly gregarious both whilst feeding and at roost. Diet consists of range of flowers, fruits and seeds, including mango seeds. Nests in hole in tree (e.g. old woodpecker nest) or cavity in arboreal termitarium. Breeding Jan-Mar, Trinidad. Clutch 5-6.

DESCRIPTION Forehead, lores and chin golden-yellow; cheeks and crown shiny apple-green; hindneck and nape yellow with dark margins giving scaly appearance. Upperparts black. Lesser and median coverts black; primary coverts black; greater coverts yellow with vivid blue on tips and innerwebs forming distinctive bar; pinkish-red on leading edge of wing. Flight feathers black with narrow green margins to outerwebs of primaries; inner secondaries yellow with greenish on innerwebs and tips. Underwing with coverts blue marked yellow and red, flight feathers bluish. Throat, breast and anterior portion of belly pale powdery-blue; underparts otherwise pale green. Uppertail bluish-lilac in centre, laterally more reddish-lilac with black subterminal bar; undertail paler. **Bare parts**: Bill yellowish-horn; iris yellow; legs yellowish-brown.

SEX/AGE Sexes similar. Immature with pale green edges to mantle, powdery turquoise breast, no shiny green on cheeks, pale grey iris and greyer bill.

MEASUREMENTS Wing 101-119; tail 43-48; bill 15-16; tarsus 12-14.

GEOGRAPHICAL VARIATION None.

REFERENCES Arndt (1996), Desenne & Strahl (1991, 1994), Fernández-Badillo *et al.* (1994), ffrench (1992), Forshaw (1989), Haverschmidt (1968), Meyer de Schauensee (1966), Meyer de Schauensee & Phelps (1978), Ridgely (1981), Snyder (1966), Tostain *et al.* (1992), Whitney (1996).

292 SCARLET-SHOULDERED PARROTLET
Touit huetii
Plate 73

Other names: Red-winged Parrotlet, Huet's Parrotlet

IDENTIFICATION 16cm. Small, mainly green parrot with striking red underwing-coverts and short square tail. Blue on upperwing, cheeks and forehead, conspicuous white skin around eyes and pale yellowish bill further separate this from other small parrots. Red underwing-coverts distinguish it from Lilac-tailed Parrotlet (291), which overlaps in northern Guyana and eastern Venezuela, and from Sapphire-rumped (295) and Spot-winged Parrotlets (298), which occur from Meta, Colombia, to northern Peru. Red underwing-coverts also safely separate it from slightly smaller *Forpus* parrotlets. Orange-cheeked Parrot (304), sympatric in western Amazon and perhaps marginally in Colombia east of the Andes, shows red blaze on underwings but is larger with distinctive orange cheeks and black head. Birds may be almost undetectable whilst perched or climbing silently in foliage and are most often seen in flight. Deep steady strokes on rather broad wings propel birds in level (not undulating) flight. Distinctive flight calls from compact flocks; seldom alone or in pairs.

VOICE Soft disyllabic *touit* (Peru), *witch witch* (Guyana), strident *kloot* (Brazil) and rasping *juwee* (Bolivia) calls reported from birds in flight. Occasional harsh *juvii* sound. Voice quite distinct from Lilac-tailed Parrotlet.

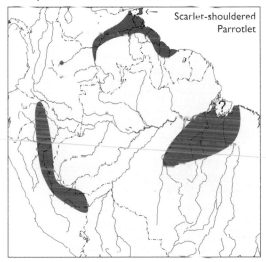

Scarlet-shouldered Parrotlet

DISTRIBUTION AND STATUS Northern South America where reported from several widely disjunct areas; known with certainty in Colombia only from base of Cordillera Macarena, Meta (e.g. Río Güejar) but probably also in eastern Guainía at mouth of Río Guaviare given a record from San Fernando de Atabapo in adjacent Venezuela. Sporadic Venezuelan records suggest range extends from western Amazonas and through lowland northern and eastern Bolívar to Monagas and perhaps Delta Amacuro. Reported Trinidad where rare resident or perhaps seasonal visitor. Occurs northern Guyana in (e.g.) Berbice and Mabaruma. Reported Brazil south of Amazon in Pará from Serra do Cachimbo and Rio Cururu in south and west respectively and probably occurs east to lower Rio

Tocantins (e.g. Marabá) and Belém. Record from northern Goiás at Araguatins. Birds at the Rio Aripuanã, Mato Grosso, Brazil, were possibly wanderers. Occurs western Amazon basin in eastern Ecuador (e.g. Napo) and eastern Peru. Peruvian records from 35km north-east of Tingo María (Huánuco), Pucallpa (Ucayali) and Santa Elena on the Río Tapiche (Loreto). Also reported from northern-most Bolivia (Pando) but status there uncertain. Paucity of records and apparently disjunct distribution perhaps reflect inconspicuous and retiring habits as much as apparent local distribution and rarity. Sporadic records from outside previously known range may indicate continuous occurrence across central and southern Amazon basin. Apparently nomadic in western Amazonia and perhaps elsewhere. Probably declining locally with deforestation (e.g. Pará) but much intact habitat remains. Some local but no known international trade.

ECOLOGY Prefers edge and canopy of lowland humid forest but may also frequent understorey. Chiefly in terra firme forest but also várzea. Reported to 1,200m in Peru where considered commonest in upper tropical forest; 400m, Colombia; 100-200m, Venezuela, where usually near rivers. Generally gregarious, sometimes in large flocks; communal roosts in (e.g.) dense foliage of tree crown. No information on diet and little on reproduction. Male in breeding condition at Fernando de Atabapo, Venezuela, Apr; possible nesting Mato Grosso, Brazil, Sep-Dec.

DESCRIPTION Anterior cheeks blue; forehead and lores darker blackish-blue; sides of neck green with olive tinge to ear-coverts; crown and nape dull green tinged olive. Back, mantle and scapulars green; rump and uppertail-coverts slightly brighter emerald-green. Lesser, median and outer greater coverts blue; primary coverts black. Primaries and outer secondaries (above) black with narrow green margin to outerwebs; (below) bluish. Bend of wing and underwing-coverts scarlet. Underparts yellowish-green becoming yellow on undertail coverts yellow. Tail green centrally, lateral feathers red with broad black subterminal band. **Bare parts:** Bill pale yellowish-horn, broad bare periophthalmic ring white; iris brown; legs brown.

SEX/AGE Female shows green lateral tail feathers with yellowish on innerwebs. Immature as female but lacks blackish-blue on lores and forehead.

MEASUREMENTS Wing 107-126; tail 40-45; bill 13-15, tarsus 11-13.

GEOGRAPHICAL VARIATION None.

REFERENCES Arndt (1996), Blake (1962), Desenne & Strahl (1991, 1994), ffrench (1992), Forshaw (1989), Hilty & Brown (1986), Junge & Mees (1958), Meyer de Schauensee (1966), Meyer de Schauensee & Phelps (1978), O'Neill (1969), Parker *et al.* (1991), Parker & Remsen (1987), Ridgely (1981), Sick (1957, 1993), Snyder (1966), Stotz *et al.* (1996), Whitney (1996).

293 RED-FRONTED PARROTLET
Touit costaricensis
Plate 73

Other names: Red-winged Parrotlet (see Note)

IDENTIFICATION 15cm. Small, mainly green parrot with short square tail, confined to Costa Rica and Panama. Red on bend of wing (reduced or absent in female) very prominent in flight from above, with yellow inner underwing-coverts conspicuous from below. Red on forehead, crown and lores, with narrow red streak below eyes. Similar (but allopatric) Red-winged Parrotlet (294) extends to eastern Panama but is told by blue forehead and much more limited red on head. Sympatric Tovi Parakeet (285) lacks red/yellow on wings and red on head, and has brown shoulders and wedge-shaped tail. Broadly sympatric Barred Parakeet (272) shows close dark barring on upper surface (visible in good light), lacks red/yellow on wings and has wedge-shaped tail. Generally in humid forest where most often seen in pairs or small flocks flying to feeding areas. Deep steady strokes on rather broad wings propel birds in level flight.

VOICE Scratchy *dree dree deeah dree durr* notes alternately slurred up or down in pitch. Soft rolling *chrrik* whilst feeding.

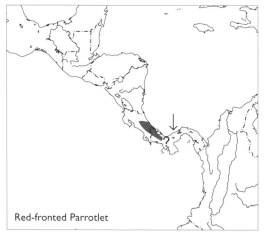

Red-fronted Parrotlet

DISTRIBUTION AND STATUS The few records from Costa Rica come mainly from central-southern highlands on the Caribbean slope where the range appears to extend south from around Monteverde, Volcán Turrialba and Limón. Although no records from much of eastern Costa Rica, its occurrence may be continuous along the Talamanca Cordillera (perhaps only on the Caribbean slope) to western Panama. The handful of Panamanian specimens and sight records are mainly from the western highlands with an outlying easterly report near Coclèo. Evidently uncommon to rare and presumably in decline owing to continuing deforestation (at least in lowland areas) in limited range. Occurs in several protected areas. No known reports of captive birds. NEAR-THREATENED.

ECOLOGY Generally in canopy of cool wet forest in middle altitudes. Moves to understorey at least at forest edge and flies over clearings. Reported on occasion in lowlands (sometimes to sea-level, especially in south-eastern Costa Rica) where perhaps a seasonal visitor. Tolerates some habitat disturbance. Observed in association with Red-headed Barbet *Eubucco bourcierii* and Blue-and-gold Tanager *Buthraupis arcaei*, both species associated with very wet cool forests in the upper tropical and subtropical zones. Observed to 3,000m in Costa Rica in early dry season and regularly reported at 500-1,000m during wet season. Generally in pairs or small family flocks. Reported food items are fruits of trees and epiphytes such as *Cavendishia* and *Clusia* but probably also includes

blossoms and seeds. Family group size generally 4-5 suggesting usual clutch 2-3. Probably breeds during dry season.

DESCRIPTION Forehead, anterior crown, lores and streak below eyes red; sides of neck, cheeks and upperparts green with hindcrown and nape slightly duller and more yellowish. Inner wing-coverts green; outer lesser and median coverts and leading edge of wing red; primary coverts black. Primaries and outer secondaries black with green margin to outerwebs of primaries. Inner underwing-coverts yellow, outer underwing-coverts red. Feathers at base of bill, on chin and throat yellowish-green; breast, belly and undertail-coverts green tinged yellowish. Tail light greenish-yellow tipped black (except on outermost feathers) and subterminally dark green. **Bare parts:** Bill pale yellowish-horn; cere and bare periophthalmic skin grey; iris greyish-brown; legs slaty.

SEX/AGE Female has less red on upperwing-coverts but perhaps more yellow on underwing-coverts; probably averages smaller than male. Immature has little or no red on head.

MEASUREMENTS Wing 111-121; tail 37-45; bill 15-17; tarsus 12-13.

GEOGRAPHICAL VARIATION None.

NOTE Red-fronted Parrotlet is sometimes treated as conspecific with Red-winged Parrotlet (294) of northern South America and Panama. Whilst these taxa are clearly allied and share a recent common ancestor, most authors now treat them as separate on the basis of their clear and consistent plumage differences. Structural divergence may also exist in that *costaricensis* seems to show longer uppertail-coverts (extending nearly to the end of the tail) than its southern counterpart, whilst (although sample small) sexual dimorphism is suggested on wing and tail length in *costaricensis* but not *dilectissima*.

REFERENCES Forshaw (1989), Ridgely (1981), Ridgely & Gwynne (1989), Slud (1964), Stiles *et al.* (1989), Wetmore (1968), Whitney (1996).

294 RED-WINGED PARROTLET
Touit dilectissima   **Plate 73**

Other names: Blue-fronted Parrotlet

IDENTIFICATION 15cm. Small, mainly green, short-tailed parrot with blue forehead, spot at base of bill and ear-coverts. Red upperwing-coverts (reduced or absent in females) and red and yellow underwing-coverts flash conspicuously in flight. Black primary coverts sometimes visible in flight and red markings on head may be seen at close range. Only small, short-tailed parrot in range to show red and/or yellow on wings. Distinguished from rather similar (but allopatric) Red-fronted Parrotlet (293) by blue forehead and much more limited red on head. Sympatric Tovi Parakeet (285) lacks red/yellow on wings and blue on head, has brown shoulders and wedge-shaped tail. Sympatric Barred Parakeet (272) shows (in good light) close dark barring on upperparts, lacks red/yellow on wings and has wedge-shaped tail. Generally in pairs or small compact flocks calling softly in level twisting flight with deep steady beats of rather broad wings low over tree-tops or through forest.

VOICE Flight call is a rather weak, high-pitched, whining, nasal *tuu-eet*. Silent whilst feeding or perched in foliage.

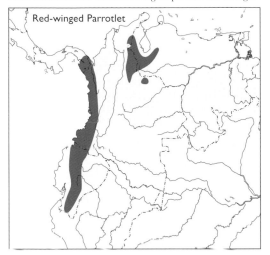

Red-winged Parrotlet

DISTRIBUTION AND STATUS The species occurs in north-west South America into eastern upland Panama where reported from (e.g.) Cerro Pirre, Darién. In Colombia and Ecuador it is found west of Andes south to at least to northern Los Ríos and probably to near Peruvian border. Also in northern Andes above Ocaña (border of Norte de Santander and César), Colombia, and north-west Venezuela in Sierra de Perijá, Zulia, and eastern Andean cordillera in Mérida and south-western Trujillo. No evidence of continuous occurrence between Panamanian, western Andean and northern Andean distributions but, given unobtrusive habits and small total number of records, it cannot be assumed that three isolated populations exist. Some seasonal altitudinal movements occur. Infrequently observed and probably uncommon to rare. Presumably declining locally from deforestation (especially in Colombia) but present in several protected areas and under no immediate threat. Not known in captivity.

ECOLOGY Inhabits humid and wet forest, including tall secondary growth and cloud-forest, mainly in upland areas but also reported from lowlands perhaps as seasonal visitor, 100-1,700m, Colombia (most numerous 800-1,400m); 1,300-1,600m, Venezuela. Gregarious; birds roost communally in forest canopy. Diet includes small seeds and probably also fruits and blossoms. Breeding-condition males taken Jun, Colombia; adult leaving arboreal termitarium Jan, and juveniles with parents Jul, Panama.

DESCRIPTION Narrow red frontal band; forehead and forecrown blue; lores and narrow band beneath eyes red (sometimes bordered blue) extending from lores to ear-coverts; upper cheeks and sides of neck green; lower cheeks and chin yellowish; hindcrown to nape dull green tinged olive. Mantle, back and scapulars green; rump and uppertail-coverts slightly brighter green. Inner coverts green; outer lesser and median coverts and central primary coverts red; outer primary coverts black. Primaries and outer secondaries black with green margin to outerwebs of primaries. Underwing with outer coverts red, inner coverts yellow, flight feathers dull dark greenish-blue. Underparts green, slightly yellowish, with yellow flanks. Black-tipped tail green centrally, yellow laterally. **Bare parts**: Bill greyish, tipped dull horn on upper mandible; cere blackish-grey; bare periophthalmic skin whitish; iris brownish-yellow; legs blackish-brown.

SEX/AGE Female shows less (or no) red on upperwing surface. Immature like female but little or no blue on forehead; red on frontal band and lores reduced or absent.

MEASUREMENTS Wing 110-120; tail 41-49; bill 15-18; tarsus 12-14.

GEOGRAPHICAL VARIATION None.

NOTE See Note under Red-fronted Parrotlet.

REFERENCES Desenne & Strahl (1991, 1994), Forshaw (1989), Hilty & Brown (1986), Meyer de Schauensee (1949, 1966), Meyer de Schauensee & Phelps (1978), Ridgely (1981), Ridgely & Gwynne (1989), Stotz *et al.* (1996), Wetmore (1968), Whitney (1996).

---

295 SAPPHIRE-RUMPED PARROTLET
Touit purpurata   Plate 74

Other names. Purple Guiana Parrotlet

IDENTIFICATION 17cm. Small, mainly green, parrot with short square tail, blue rump (sometimes hard to see) and brown scapulars and tertials forming distinctive stripes on back. Dark crimson outer tail feathers. From smaller *Forpus* parrotlets by square-ended (not wedge-shaped) tail and direct (not undulating) flight. Cobalt-winged Parakeet (286) overlaps in western Amazonia where it is told by its larger size, wedge-shaped tail and blue primaries. Tui Parakeet (288), occurring widely in Amazon basin, is separated by pointed tail and yellow forehead. Deep steady strokes on rather broad wings propel birds in level flight. Generally in pairs or small flocks flying at or below canopy level; most often seen only fleetingly whilst crossing streams or rivers. Easily overlooked whilst perched quietly in foliage.

VOICE Rather quiet. Calls include nasal, hornlike *hoya* or *keree-ke-ke* in flight. Voice sometimes suggests larger parrot.

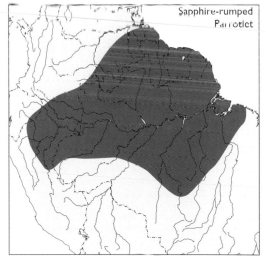

Sapphire-rumped Parrotlet

DISTRIBUTION AND STATUS This species is endemic to northern South America, mainly in the Amazon basin, from extreme northern Peru, eastern Ecuador (Pastaza) and Colombia east of Andes in western Caquetá (e.g. Tres Esquinas) and extreme south-eastern Guainía (along Río Negro) east south of the Brazilian Amazon to Pará and northern Maranhão, north of the Amazon along the Uaupés ad Içana through the Rio Negro catchment to Manaus; then through southern Venezuela from Amazonas along the Orinoco south from the Río Ventauri, at Cerro Yapacana, and Cerro Duida and from southern Bolívar in the tepuis of the Gran Sabana and upper Río Caura, into Guyana, along (e.g.) Barima, Mazaruni and Kamarang Rivers and south to Bartica, becoming local in Surinam and French Guiana. Unobtrusive so possibly often overlooked, but apparently nowhere in large numbers and may be genuinely uncommon, even rare. Perhaps more numerous in lower reaches of Amazon basin. Recent and continuing deforestation in some parts of range but much suitable habitat remains and occurs in several protected areas. Rare in captivity.

ECOLOGY Mainly inhabits canopy of lowland humid terra firme and várzea forest (possibly preferring latter) but also known from savanna in Surinam. In lower, more open woodland at higher altitude in Venezuela and in isolated woodlots in otherwise cleared areas. Reported to 400m, Colombia, and 1,200m on Cerro Duida, Venezuela. Gregarious, generally in groups of 12-40 birds. Observed eating fruits of *Clusia grandiflora*, *Pouroma guianensis* and figs *Ficus* and feeding in trees of Sapotaceae and Myrtaceae. Forages chiefly in canopy but observed in low bushes and occasionally on ground. Female excavating hole in tree in várzea tree Nov, Colombia; birds at nest in arboreal termitarium Apr, Surinam, and breeding-condition male Mar, Venezuela. Clutch 3-5.

DESCRIPTION Forehead, crown, ear-coverts and sides of neck brownish-olive; lores and cheeks green; hindneck dull green with brownish suffusion. Mantle and upper back green; scapulars and tertials dark brown; rump blue; uppertail-coverts green. Blue feathers at bend of wing; primary coverts blackish-brown, coverts otherwise green. Flight feathers brown above on innerwebs and tips, otherwise green; dull bluish-green below. Underwing-coverts green. Underparts pale slightly yellowish emerald-green with ochre suffusion on sides of belly. Black-tipped tail green centrally, dark crimson laterlly with black margins to outerwebs. **Bare parts**: Bill greyish with pale horn tip to upper mandible; iris black; legs grey.

SEX/AGE Female has tail (except central feathers) with green subterminal band. Immature more yellowish beneath, black on tail confined to tips; greenish-olive from forehead to nape and on lower ear-coverts.

MEASUREMENTS Wing 110-123; tail 42-50; bill 13-16; tarsus 12-15.

GEOGRAPHICAL VARIATION Two races.
> *T. p. purpurata* (SE Amazonas, Venezuela, to the Guianas and E Amazon basin of Brazil)
> *T. p. viridiceps* (Rio Negro catchment of NW Brazil, Venezuela west from Cerro Duida to Colombia, Ecuador and Peru) Like nominate but with forehead, crown and hindneck green, flanks less yellowish-green, and outer tail feathers showing purplish sheen to broad black edging.

REFERENCES Arndt (1996), Desenne & Strahl (1991, 1994), Forshaw (1989), Gilliard (1941), Haverschmidt (1968), Hilty & Brown (1986), Meyer de Schauensee

(1949), Meyer de Schauensee & Phelps (1978), Ridgely (1981), Snyder (1966), Tostain *et al.* (1992).

296 BROWN-BACKED PARROTLET
Touit melanonotus   Plate 74

Other names: Black-backed Parrotlet, Black-eared Parrotlet, Wied's Parrotlet

IDENTIFICATION 15cm. Small, mainly green parrotlet with extensive blackish-brown patch on back and short square tail, outer feathers red with broad black tips. Golden-tailed Parrotlet (297), although more a bird of lowland forest, may co-occur (at least for part of the year), when separated by golden tail, green back with brown scapulars (forming contrasting dark longitudinal stripes) and paler, slightly brighter green plumage. Blue-winged Parrotlet (277) is smaller, frequents more open country, is much commoner and more conspicuous, males showing violet-blue on wings and rump; females are all green. Plain Parakeet (282) occurs in range but has longer pointed tail and blue in flight feathers. Most likely to be seen at or below canopy level in swift level flight. Otherwise constantly hidden in foliage creeping along larger branches and avoid perching in open. Birds always land on inside branches of tree crown. Best guide may be characteristic call.

VOICE Characteristic rattling *tewrew-tewrew*. In flight, call may resemble that of Boat-billed Flycatcher *Megarhynchus pitangua*.

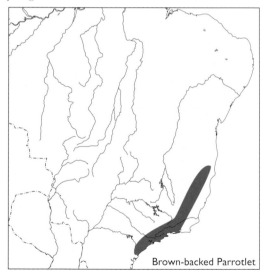

Brown-backed Parrotlet

DISTRIBUTION AND STATUS This parrotlet has a restricted range in south-east Brazil, from Bahia (three 19th century records) to southern São Paulo, leapfrogging Espírito Santo (but presumably extinct or overlooked there). Sporadically but widely reported in Rio de Janeiro state, including Serra Cantagalo, Serra dos Orgãos National Park and from around Teresópolis, including near Desengano State Park. Also reported from the Itatiaia massif (including Itatiaia National Park) where distribution may include adjacent parts of Minas Gerais. Observed in other unspecified localities in the Serra do Mar in Rio de Janeiro state and has been observed in Rio de Janeiro city in (e.g.) the Tijuca National Park and Corcovado mountain forest. Reported at several localities in São Paulo state south to Ilha do Cardoso near the border with Paraná. Some seasonal movements or dispersal (perhaps mainly altitudinal and over relatively short distances) may occur as in some other *Touit* parrotlets, and, also like other *Touit*, Brown-backed appears to occur at low density and its unobtrusive habits must cause it to be frequently overlooked. Nevertheless, it is at considerable risk from widespread forest loss and fragmentation, particularly if it visits lowland areas (where clearance worst) on seasonal or occasional basis. Recorded in several protected areas such as Serra do Mar State Park and Itatiaia National Park. Not known in captivity. ENDANGERED.

ECOLOGY Mainly reported from humid forest on lower montane slopes. Most records are from 500-1,000m (1,400m in Itatiaia National Park) but some are from lowlands to near sea-level (e.g. Ilha do Cardoso). Gregarious and generally in small flocks of 3-20 birds. Virtually no information on feeding or breeding; known food items include seeds of large leguminous forest trees and fruits of *Rapanea acuminata*.

DESCRIPTION Forehead, lower cheeks, sides of neck, crown and hindneck dull grass-green; lores and upper cheeks paler and more yellowish green; ear-coverts brownish. Mantle, back and centre of rump dull blackish-brown; scapulars, sides of rump and uppertail-coverts green. Inner lesser and median coverts, alula and primary coverts blackish-brown (latter with narrow green margins to outerwebs); other coverts dull grass-green. Tertials brown, flight feathers otherwise green on outerwebs with dull blackish-brown on tips and innerwebs. Underwing with coverts dull green, flight feathers dull greyish-green. Chin yellowish, underparts otherwise dull pale green with bluish-grey cast on sides of breast. Uppertail centrally green with black spot at tips of outerwebs, outer feathers bright red at base with broad black subterminal bands and small patch of green at tips; undertail paler and duller green with greyish spot at tip, pale red on outer feathers. **Bare parts**: Bill yellowish-horn distally, greyer towards base; iris grey; legs grey.

SEX/AGE Females may show duller bluish grey on underparts. Immature undescribed.

MEASUREMENTS Wing 107-116; tail 41-46, bill 14-15; tarsus 11-13.

GEOGRAPHICAL VARIATION None.

REFERENCES Collar *et al.* (1992, 1994), Forshaw (1989), Ridgely (1981), Sick (1993), Stotz *et al.* (1996).

---

297 GOLDEN-TAILED PARROTLET
Touit surda   Plate 74

IDENTIFICATION 16cm. Small, mainly green with short square golden-yellow tail. Dark scapulars form longitudinal stripes on back. Yellowish on cheeks, lores and forehead. For separation from Brown-backed Parrotlet (296), probably sympatric at least seasonally, see that species. Blue-winged Parrotlet (277) is smaller, frequents more open country, is much commoner and more conspicuous, males showing violet-blue on wings and rump, females being all green. Overlapping Plain Parakeet (282)

has longer pointed tail and blue in flight feathers. Habitually keeps inside forest canopy where it is very inconspicuous and easily overlooked. Mostly seen in flight in small groups. Deep steady strokes on rather broad wings propel birds in level flight.

VOICE No details.

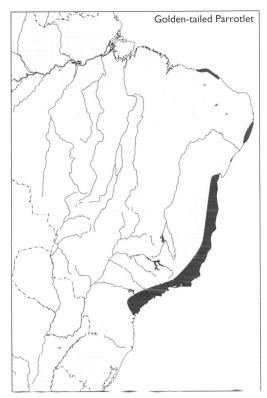

Golden-tailed Parrotlet

DISTRIBUTION AND STATUS This parrotlet extends through the Atlantic forests of eastern Brazil, including coastal areas of the north-eastern states of Paraíba, Pernambuco and Alagoas with an outlying record from Camocim in northern Ceará where fragments of humid forest exist in coastal areas. There are sporadic but widespread records (mainly) from coastal Bahia and Espírito Santo, and in Rio de Janeiro from (e.g.) Teresópolis, around Itatiaia National Park, Nova Friburgo and Cabo Frio, with a few reports from São Paulo south-west to Ilha do Cardoso near border with Paraná. Reports from Pará and Goiás are unsubstantiated and probably mistaken. Apparent seasonal occurrence in some areas suggests migratory tendencies. Appears to occur at low densities and (excepting one report from lower Rio Tietê, São Paulo) it was considered rare in 19th century. Like other members of genus is undoubtedly often overlooked. However, many former localities no longer inhabited, with lowland forest completely removed or heavily degraded, especially in north of range, where it may be nearly extinct. Occurs in several protected areas including Pedra Talhada Biological Reserve (Alagoas), the highly problematic Monte Pascoal National Park (Bahia), Linhares and Sooretama Reserves (Espírito Santo), Desengano State Park (Rio de Janeiro) and Ilha do Cardoso State Park (São Paulo). Unknown in captivity. ENDANGERED.

ECOLOGY Mainly in humid lowland forest but occasionally extending up adjacent lower montane slopes. One observation is of birds in canopy of a secondary forest fragment surrounded by open country and other reports suggest birds visit fruiting trees in otherwise deforested areas to feed. May occur in cacao plantations where forest trees shade crop plants (see Blue-throated Conure, 250), but this has not been proven. Found at 700m in Alagoas and to 800m Espírito Santo, Rio de Janeiro and São Paulo. Birds appear to live in flocks (mainly 6-12), perhaps comprised of family groups. Feeding and breeding virtually unrecorded; fruits of *Spondius lutea* and *Rapanea schwackeana* are among reported foods. A female taken Sep, Alagoas, was not in breeding condition.

DESCRIPTION Forehead, lores, superciliary area and cheeks yellowish; crown, hindneck, ear-coverts and sides of neck green with narrow dark margins, giving a vauge scaled appearance. Mantle and back green with rump and uppertail-coverts slightly brighter, more emerald. Scapulars and inner tertials warm brown; primary coverts dark brown, coverts otherwise green. Flight feathers brown above with narrow green margins to outerwebs; dull brown below. Blue on feathers at carpal edge of wing. Underwing-coverts green. Chin yellowish; breast rather yellowish-green, brighter on belly and undertail-coverts. Tail centrally green with faint black markings at tips, laterally golden-yellow with narrow black tips on upper surface. **Bare parts**: Bill yellowish-horn; iris grey; legs grey.

SEX/AGE Female perhaps duller beneath, with greener lateral tail feathers with green tips and margins. Immature undescribed.

MEASUREMENTS Wing 115-130; tail 46-53; bill 14-16; tarsus 12-14.

GEOGRAPHICAL VARIATION The name *ruficauda* has been proposed for birds from north-east of range (in Pernambuco) on the doubtful basis of more brownish lateral tail feathers and smaller size.

REFERENCES Collar *et al.* (1992, 1994), Forshaw (1989), Ridgely (1981), Sick (1993), Stotz *et al.* (1996), Whitney (1996).

---

298 SPOT-WINGED PARROTLET
Touit stictoptera   Plate 74

Other names: Brown-shouldered Parrotlet

IDENTIFICATION 18cm. Small with short square tail. Plumage mainly green with pale spots on dark upperwing surface and dull orange on outer median coverts. Commoner Scarlet-shouldered Parrotlet (292) perhaps overlaps Spot-winged (at least at lower altitude) but shows conspicuous red or red and yellow on wings. Cobalt-winged Parakeet (286) occurs to elevations usually occupied by Spot-winged Parrotlet but is separated by pointed tail and flashing blue wings in flight. Spot-winged creeps quietly around canopy and are then very difficult to see. Flight usually above canopy, less often at or below it. Deep steady strokes on rather broad wings propel birds in level (not undulating) flight.

VOICE Call consists of two, sometimes three, raspy *raah-reh* or *raah-reh-reh* notes, with first slightly lower-pitched. Apparently only calls in flight.

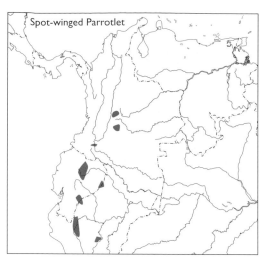

Spot-winged Parrotlet

DISTRIBUTION AND STATUS Apparently scattered occurrence from central Colombia to northern Peru, mainly in eastern Andes. in Colombia it has been recorded from the west slope of eastern Andes in Cundinamarca, from around Fusagasugá in the upper Magdalena Valley, the Cordillera Macarena, Meta, the east slope of the central Andes in Cauca and supposedly in eastern Nariño. Known in Ecuador from eastern Andean slope in Napo and Morona-Santiago (where also occurs on the west slope of Cordillera de Cutucú) and Zamora-Chinchipe; may be expected in other east Andean departments of Ecuador in suitable habitat. Range extends southwards into northern Peru in northern Cajamarca, the left bank of the lower Río Marañón in Amazonas, and northern San Martín. Seems naturally to occur at low density (in common with other *Touit* parrotlets) and is certainly overlooked owing to unobtrusive habits. It is probably genuinely rare (estimated as fairly common only in Cordillera de Cutucú and San Martín) and perhaps rather local. Deforestation more or less complete in north of range (especially in the upper Magdalena Valley) and may already be extinct (or nearly so) in Colombia. Perhaps persists in Cordillera Macarena (where there is a national park) but this area is under serious pressure from invading colonists. More secure in Ecuador and Peru where suitable habitat remains, and where recorded in at least two protected areas (Sangay National Park and Cayambe-Coca Ecological Reserve, Ecuador). Not known in captivity. VULNERABLE.

ECOLOGY Generally in tall humid subtropical forest but one report is from savanna-like woodland and another from stunted ridge-top growth (both in San Martín, Peru). Mainly at 1,000-1,700m but seen down to 500 and as high as 2,300m. Gregarious, usually in flocks of 5-12, less often to 25. Single pair reported Mar, Ecuador, with flocks seen Jun-Aug, Ecuador, and Oct-Nov, Peru. Very little information on feeding and breeding: reported feeding in fig *Ficus* and *Clusia* trees, and one specimen had eaten fruits of a loranthacean mistletoe, with a claim birds attack maize in upper Magdalena Valley; birds taken Jun, Ecuador, Jul and Oct-Nov, Peru, were not in breeding condition.

DESCRIPTION Lores and cheeks yellowish-green; forehead, crown, sides of neck and upperparts rather dull dark grass-green. Lesser and median coverts dark brown with pale buffish spots on tips, especially inner coverts; outer greater coverts dull orange, remainder dark brown with pale buff tips, innermost with green on outerwebs. Flight feathers brown above with narrow green margin to outerwebs, dull green below. Underwing-coverts green. Underparts green, slightly paler than above. Uppertail green with brown on innerwebs of lateral feathers; undertail more yellowish. **Bare parts**: Bill greyish, upper mandible tipped yellowish-horn; bare periophthalmic skin whitish, iris yellowish; legs grey.

SEX/AGE Female has green lesser and median coverts with dark brown spots, lacks orange on outer median coverts and has stronger and more extensive yellowish on face. Immature similar.

MEASUREMENTS Wing 123-134; tail 50-56; bill 16; tarsus 13-15.

GEOGRAPHICAL VARIATION None.

REFERENCES Collar *et al.* (1992, 1994), Davis (1986), Forshaw (1989), Hilty & Brown (1986), Ridgely (1981), Robbins *et al.* (1987), Stotz *et al.* (1996), Whitney (1996)

---

299 BLACK-CAPPED PARROT
Pionites melanocephula   Plate 72

Other names: Black-headed Caique, Black-headed Parrot; Pallid Caique (*P. m. pallidus*)

IDENTIFICATION 23cm Medium-sized, chunky, short-tailed parrot with white breast, black cap, yellow on throat and sides of neck and green upperparts. Looks front-heavy in flight with rather short wings. Only white-bellied parrot in range. Similar White-bellied Parrot (300) south of Amazon has apricot-orange (not black) cap. Flight direct, rapid, usually just above canopy and on fast deep wing-beats, but more often heard than seen in dense forest habitat. Wings create distinctive whirring sound, especially just after take-off. Generally in pairs or small groups of up to 10 or 30. Birds often confiding.

VOICE Highly vocal with loud, often quite melodious voice. Calls include short, resonant, high-pitched *cha-rant*, trilling and shrieking sounds, including disyllabic *screee-ah*, a whistled *toot* and another whistling call strongly resembling voice of tapir *Tapirus*. Loud *kleeek* calls with spread wings are given by birds displaying in canopy. Flocks sometimes create noisy chorus. Usually calls from cover, less often on exposed perch. Shrill *wey-ak* alarm puts flock to flight shrieking loudly.

DISTRIBUTION AND STATUS Northern South America north of Amazon from Peru and Colombia to the Guianas. The species occurs in eastern Colombia from Meta and Vichada south through eastern Ecuador and north-east and central Peru to around Pucallpa, Ucayali, also east through Venezuela, where found mainly south of the Orinoco in Bolívar, Amazonas and Delta Amacuro, but also in south-eastern Sucre, to the Guianas, and throughout northern Brazil north of the Amazon east to Amapá. A report from west of the Andes in Nariño, Colombia, has not been repeated and occurrence there uncertain. Reported as nomadic French Guiana in relation to food availability. Generally common and in places numerous. Reported as widespread and fairly common in Guyana,

common to abundant in north-east Peru, and common to quite numerous Colombia, especially in remoter parts of Amazonian lowlands. Becomes scarcer with increasing altitude. Popular pet locally (especially Venezuela) and trapped for international markets. Trade unlikely to have seriously affected numbers in wild except locally. Range has probably contracted locally in Amazonia owing to deforestation.

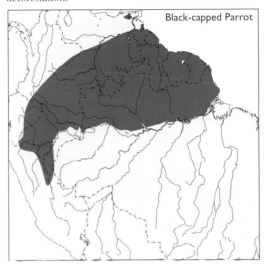
Black-capped Parrot

ECOLOGY Forest in the tropical zone including savanna and both terra firme and várzea rain-forest. Prefers forest edge and canopy and frequents tall secondary growth and clearings with large trees. Mainly in lowlands but observed at 1,100m on Auyan Tepui, Venezuela, and to about 500m, Colombia. Gregarious, usually in quite small groups but sometimes up to 30. Roosts communally, often in tree-cavities. Feeds in canopy where birds climb with great agility, but also forages at lower levels at forest edge. One or two members of feeding flock maintain watch and sound alarm at approach of danger. Observed foods include seeds of *Caraipa densiflora*, *Hevea benthamiana*, *Guarea grandiflora*, *Pourouma guianensis* and *Micropholis mensalis*, pulp of *Dialium guianensis*, *Euterpe precatoria*, *Micropholis melinoneana* and *Cynometra hostmanniana* seeds and pulp of *Clusia grandiflora*, flowers of *Eschweilera* and *Inga laterifolia* and leaves of *Sterculia excelsa*; in dry season also takes flowers of *Symphonia globulifera* and *Norantea*. Dietary preferences in captivity suggest some insects taken. Nest in high tree-cavity. Breeds Dec-Feb, French Guiana; breeding-condition birds Apr, Venezuela, and Apr-May, Colombia. Birds observed at nest Oct-Nov, Surinam. Clutch three in captivity.

DESCRIPTION Forehead, crown, upper lores and fore part of hindneck glossy black; small patch of bright bluish-emerald on lower lores and front of upper cheeks; lower cheeks, throat, sides of neck and band running over rear of hindneck pale apricot-orange. Upperparts bright green. Primary coverts violet-blue narrowly edged green on outerwebs; carpal area with yellowish feathers; coverts otherwise green. Primaries violet-blue on outerwebs. Underwing-coverts green. Breast and centre of belly whitish with creamy and/or yellowish tinge; sides of belly, thighs, vent and undertail-coverts apricot-orange. Uppertail green with narrow yellow tip; undertail duller and darker. **Bare parts**: Bill blackish-grey; cere grey; bare peri-ophthalmic skin lead-grey; iris red; legs lead-grey.

SEX/AGE Sexes similar, females possibly on average smaller. Immature has brown iris, paler orange feathers and yellowish suffusion on underparts.

MEASUREMENTS Wing 133-147; tail 66-75; bill 21-28; tarsus 17-19.

GEOGRAPHICAL VARIATION Two races.
> *P. m. melanocephala* (East and south from the Rio Negro area of N Brazil)
> *P. m. pallidus* (W Amazonia from E Colombia to C Peru) Posterior flanks, thighs, vent and undertail-coverts lemon-yellow (not orange), and throat yellower. Birds around Sarayacu, Pastaza, E Ecuador, are intermediate with nominate.

NOTE Black-capped and White-bellied Parrots are sometimes treated as a single species. This approach has been justified on the basis of hybrids from upper Amazonia (Peru/Brazil border) where the physical barrier (the Amazon) between these two taxa is narrower and the two forms are potentially less isolated. Further investigations are needed to substantiate view that (supposed) wild hybrids indicate conspecificity, since the variation within all races of both species (e.g., some older captive *P. m. melanocephala* reportedly show orange feathers on crown) may be natural and not the result of hybridisation.

REFERENCES Desenne (1994), Desenne & Strahl (1991, 1994), Forshaw (1989), Haverschmidt (1972), Hilty & Brown (1989), O'Neill (1981), Ridgely (1981), Rutgers & Norris (1979), Sick (1993), Smith (1990), Tostain *et al.* (1992), Traylor (1958), Whitney (1996).

---

300 WHITE-BELLIED PARROT
Pionites leucogaster   Plate 72

Other names: White-bellied Caique

IDENTIFICATION 23cm. Medium-sized, chunky, short-tailed parrot with apricot-orange cap, yellow on throat and sides of neck, white breast and contrasting green upperparts. Looks front-heavy in flight with rather short wings. Only white-bellied parrot in range. Similar Black-capped Parrot (299) north of Amazon has black (not apricot-orange) cap. Flight direct, rapid, usually just above canopy and on fast deep wingbeats. More often heard screeching loudly before being seen in dense forest habitat. Wings create distinctive whirring sound, especially just after take-off. Generally in small groups of up to c. 20 birds or in pairs. Birds often confiding and permit close approach before taking flight.

VOICE Wide range of calls including whistles, shrieks and chirruping sounds. Quieter twittering recalls Budgerigar (155). Whistled call similar to tapir *Tapirus*. Repertoire includes high-pitched whistling *sh-reet*, harsh noisy shrieking and soft warbling sounds. Calls often quite musical and pleasant. Loud shrill alarm call.

DISTRIBUTION AND STATUS This parrot ranges south of the Amazon in Brazil from north-western Maranhão and around Belém, Pará, west through Mato Grosso into northern Bolivia and south-east Peru to the upper Ucayali where it approaches the range of Black-capped Parrot. Reports from eastern Ecuador (well within the range of

the latter) remain unsubstantiated. Generally common but perhaps scarcer in drier forests on southern fringes of range. Not at serious risk but declining locally (e.g. eastern Amazonia) owing to deforestation, and possibly now extinct Santa Cruz, Bolivia, owing to habitat loss. Trapped for local and (at least formerly) international trade but apparently no serious impact as yet on wild populations.

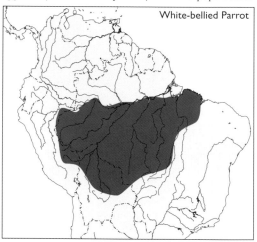
White-bellied Parrot

ECOLOGY Mainly in lowland rain-forest in both terra firme and várzea formations with probable preference for latter and for areas with clearings and edges. Also in drier forests (where less common) in south of range. Gregarious; observed in company of Blue-headed Parrots (313), eastern Amazonia. Very similar in habits to Black-capped Parrot (see relevant account) but no specific information on diet. Breeds Jan, east of range where one nest found at 30m in tree-cavity. Normal clutch probably 2-4.

DESCRIPTION Lores, cheeks and throat bright lemon-yellow; ear-coverts, forehead and crown bright reddish apricot-orange; sides of neck and hindneck apricot-orange, but paler. Upperparts green. Primary coverts blue; other coverts green. Primaries blue with green margins on outerwebs. Underwing-coverts green. Breast and centre of belly white; sides of lower belly and feathers on thighs green; undertail-coverts yellow. Uppertail green; undertail dull greyish-brown. **Bare parts**: Bill pale horn; cere pale pinkish; iris reddish-brown; legs pink.

SEX/AGE Sexes similar. Immature duller, especially yellow on face.

MEASUREMENTS Wing 133-142; tail 61-74; bill 22-25; tarsus 17-19.

GEOGRAPHICAL VARIATION Three races. Details on their ranges are scarce.
> *P. l. leucogaster* (Maranhão and Pará west to N Mato Grosso and Manaus)
> *P. l. xanthurus* (Rio Juruá to catchment of Rio Madeira in Amazonas and Rondônia, W Amazonia, Brazil. A specimen from Manaus area is intermediate with *xanthomeria* whilst birds in upper Rio Xingú show intergradation with nominate) As nominate but with yellow thighs, flanks and tail, yellow and green upper-tail-coverts.
> *P. l. xanthomeria* (W Amazon basin in SE Peru, N Bolivia and W Brazil where intergrades with last race in upper Rio Juruá) Like nominate but with bright

lemon-yellow (not green) thighs and flanks; green tail.

NOTE See Note under Black-capped Parrot.

REFERENCES Forshaw (1989), Gyldenstolpe (1945a,b), Meyer de Schauensee (1966), Parker (1991), Ridgely (1981), Smith (1990), Sick (1993), Stone (1928), Whitney (1996).

301 RED-CAPPED PARROT
Pionopsitta pileata   Plate 76

Other names: Pileated Parrot

IDENTIFICATION 22cm. Medium sized, mainly green parrot with bright red cap in male. Tail tapered and quite short. Underside of tail and underwing-coverts bluish-green. Female is mainly green on head (with blue forehead) and possible to confuse with partially sympatric (in south-east Brazil and perhaps Misiones, Argentina) female Purple-bellied Parrot (352), but is smaller, with proportionately shorter tail and paler bill. Smaller than Scaly-headed (315) and Blue-headed (313) Parrots with proportionately shorter wing and, in relation to wing, proportionately longer tail. Red-capped flies fast and direct, usually at some height. Much larger than *Touit* parrotlets with proportionately longer, more tapered tail. Birds dive steeply into tree crown when alighting and are inconspicuous as they quietly clamber among branches, although sentinels may watch from exposed perch. Permits close approach and remains momentarily still before flying off screeching loudly. In pairs or small flocks. Noisy in flight, quieter at perch.

VOICE Rapidly repeated high-pitched shrieks in flight or jumble of repeated musical squeaks and low notes. Call less staccato and more musical than sympatric Maroon-bellied Conure (251). Also trisyllabic *ch ch chee* with last note higher and more metallic. Flocks emit continuous bubbling chatter with individual notes similar to flight call.

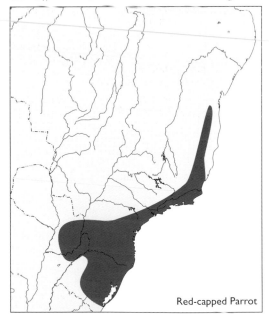

Red-capped Parrot

DISTRIBUTION AND STATUS This parrot occurs in south-east Brazil south from Bahia through the Atlantic forest belt in Espírito Santo, probably eastern Minas Gerais (no records), Rio de Janeiro, São Paulo, Paraná and Santa Catarina to Rio Grande do Sul, extending into adjacent eastern Paraguay and north-east Argentina in Misiones and possibly Corrientes (no recent records); also reported eastern Chaco, Argentina, where it may be an irregular visitor. Some seasonal movements occur in Paraná, where birds depart the interior plateau for the coast after breeding, and in Paraguay where present Amambay in Oct. Nomadic at Intervales State Park, São Paulo. Widespread but declining owing to extensive loss of forest to urban growth, agriculture and mining. Described as uncommon to fairly common in Misiones, Argentina. Apparently not yet at risk from habitat loss since birds still quite numerous where fragments of forest remain (e.g. eastern Paraguay) and will travel between them over treeless terrain. Most numerous where extensive forest remains and appears commonest in eastern Paraguay and adjacent Paraná and São Paulo, Brazil. Very rare in captivity. CITES Appendix I. NEAR-THREATENED.

ECOLOGY Inhabits forest, including moist tropical forest and *Araucaria*-dominated stands, mostly in lowlands in south of range but penetrating coastal mountains in Brazil, from about 300 to 1,500m; also in partially cleared areas. Gregarious in flocks of 10 or so; apparently infrequent in larger numbers. *Euterpe edulis* fruits found to be important winter food in eastern Paraguay; *Podocarpus* and *Solanum* fruits also recorded, and bark of *Eucalyptus*; visits orchards when fruit ripening, Rio Grande do Sul. Nest in tree-cavity. Probably breeds mainly Nov-Jan. Clutch 3-4 in captivity.

DESCRIPTION Forehead, lores, crown and anterior upper cheeks to behind eyes bright red; rufous patch on ear-coverts; lower cheeks, sides of neck and hindneck green. Upperparts green. Primary and greater coverts, alula and feathers at bend of wing violet-blue; other coverts green. Outerwebs of primaries and secondaries violet-blue edged bluish-green. Underwing bluish-green, coverts with some darker blue feathers. Underparts green with bluish tinge on breast and throat, and with yellowish tinge on belly and undertail-coverts. Uppertail centrally green, laterally violet-blue, undertail bluish green. **Bare parts**: Bill dark brown, becoming dark horn distally on both mandibles; bare periophthalmic skin light grey; iris and legs greyish-brown.

SEX/AGE Female has head mostly green but with rather pale blue on forehead. Immature as female but with green or greyish-green ear-coverts and dark patches on base of bill; young male sometimes with red restricted to forehead with orange patch behind.

MEASUREMENTS Wing 141-152, tail 64-76; bill 17-19; tarsus 14-16.

GEOGRAPHICAL VARIATION None.

REFERENCES Arndt (1996), Belton (1984), Contreras *et al.* (1991), Forshaw (1989), Galetti (1995), Ireland (1987), Lowen *et al.* (1996), Meyer de Schauensee (1966), Nores & Yzurieta (1994), Pizon *et al.* (1995), Ridgely (1981), Sick (1993), Whitney (1996), Yamashita *in litt.* (1996).

302 BROWN-HOODED PARROT
Pionopsitta haematotis   Plate 75

Other names: Red-eared Parrot

IDENTIFICATION 21-23cm. Medium-sized, rather stocky parrot with short square-ended tail and wide-eyed owlish expression. Mainly green (lighter below) with brown head and neck and light golden-brown breast. Conspicuous bright scarlet patch revealed on sides and base of underwings in flight; wings otherwise dull blue beneath. Pale bill, white lores and bare skin around eyes contrast with dark head. The similarly proportioned *Pionus* parrots are larger and their wingstrokes are much shallower; widely sympatric (from Mexico to western Panama) White-crowned Parrot (317) also lacks red axillaries and has white on head; Blue-headed Parrot (313), sympatric from Costa Rica to Colombia, has extensive red on undertail and blue on head and neck. Approaches range of Rose-faced Parrot (303) in north-west Colombia and is probably sympatric with Saffron-headed Parrot (305) in parts of north-west Colombia and eastern Panama; former has bright rose-red face, latter bright yellow head; bright red axillary-patch further separates Brown-hooded. *Touit* parrotlets are much smaller. Mostly quiet, shy and usually inconspicuous in tree-tops with presence revealed by occasional calls, falling fruit or birds taking flight. Remains quiet and still when alarmed. Birds most often seen in swift, weaving flight on fast deep wingbeats between trees.

VOICE Mostly rather quiet, especially whilst perched. Recorded sounds include brief musical *tree-lee-eeet* trill and harsher shorter *screeeah*, perhaps when alarmed. Also shrieks, resonant squawks, gurgling and squeaky notes and some warbling sounds. Voice generally mellower than most other small parrots.

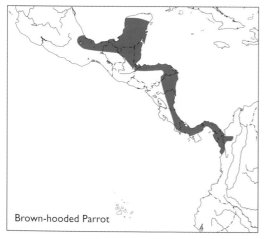

Brown-hooded Parrot

DISTRIBUTION AND STATUS This species ranges from south-east Mexico in Caribbean lowlands of southern Veracruz, Oaxaca and Chiapas, Yucatán peninsula in Campeche and Quintana Roo, possibly also Tabasco (no records), into the lowlands of northern Guatemala and the Caribbean lowlands of Honduras and Nicaragua to Costa Rica on both Pacific and Caribbean slopes and the Caribbean slope in Panama (apparently absent from savannas of the Pacific west and from the Azuero Peninsula). It extends into north-west Colombia from the western side of the Gulf of Urabá, northern Chocó and through the Río Sinú valley and Caribbean lowlands to the Magdalena in Bolívar. References to occurrence in southern Chocó and western Ecuador refer to Rose-faced Parrot (see Note in Rose-faced Parrot). Mainly resident. Some modest altitudinal movements, e.g. in Costa Rica where birds breeding at higher altitude descend to lowlands after nesting. Widely distributed (most widespread parrot in some parts of range, e.g. Costa Rica) and generally common, although abundance varies locally. Reported as fairly common in Yucatán, northern Guatemala and Costa Rica, scarcer in Panama and uncommon to fairly common in Honduras. Undoubtedly declined over much of range owing to deforestation, but small numbers can remain in partially cut-over areas. Scarce in captivity.

ECOLOGY Reported from dense primary rain-forest (including mature second growth) including low-elevation cloud-forest, forest clearings with grass and scattered trees, and plantations, to about 1,200m, Honduras; 1,600m, Oaxaca and over 3,000m, Costa Rica. Prefers forest canopy and edge. Gregarious, in small flocks of c. 6-15; never in very large numbers. Roosts in small groups in tree-hollows. Feeds on fruits and seeds of forest trees and epiphytes such as *Ficus*, *Heliocarpus*, *Croton* and *Erythrina*, and on green leaves of some mistletoes. Forages at all levels, occasionally to understorey of dense forest and even in cornfields (Guatemala); occasionally with other parrots and toucans. Nests in natural tree-cavities. Birds in breeding condition Feb, Yucatán; May-Jul, Guatemala; Aug, Panama.

DESCRIPTION Forehead, crown and hindneck dark brown, latter bordered golden-brown behind; lores whitish; cheeks and sides of neck (below and behind ear-coverts) darker than top of head (almost black in some birds) and bordered golden-brown behind, forming band over hindneck contiguous with golden-brown on breast; ear-coverts red to reddish-brown. Upperparts and wing-coverts green with slight yellowish-olive tinge, except for mainly pale-blue greater coverts and carpal area. Primaries blackish with deep purplish-blue bases; secondaries deep purplish-blue. Axillaries scarlet spreading variably onto anterior underwing-coverts; underwing otherwise dull dark blue. Lower throat and most of breast light golden-brown; lower breast and belly green. Uppertail mainly green centrally with narrow blue tips, lateral feathers more broadly tipped blue with red at base of innerwebs; undertail duller. **Bare parts**: Bill whitish-horn; cere pinkish; bare periophthalmic skin bluish-white; iris dull olive-yellow; legs yellowish-brown.

SEX/AGE Sexes similar but female perhaps duller. Immature similar to adult but paler, duller and without red ear-coverts.

MEASUREMENTS Wing 145-153; tail 57-65; bill 17-20; tarsus 16-18.

GEOGRAPHICAL VARIATION Two races.
> **P. h. haematotis** (SE Mexico to C Panama)
> **P. h. coccinicollaris** (C Panama east from Canal Zone on Caribbean slope and east from about Río Bayano on Pacific side to NW Colombia. Intergrades with nominate race in WC Panama) Lower throat and upper breast marked red.

NOTE See Note under Rose-faced Parrot.

REFERENCES Arndt (1996), Binford (1989), Blake

(1958), Forshaw (1989), Haffer (1975), Hilty & Brown (1986), Howell & Webb (1995), Land (1970), Monroe (1968), Paynter (1955), Peterson & Chalif (1973), Ridgely & Gwynne (1989), Russell (1964), Slud (1964), Smithe (1966), Smithe & Paynter (1963), Stiles *et al.* (1989), Wetmore (1968), Whitney (1996).

303 ROSE-FACED PARROT
Pionopsitta pulchra   Plate 75

Other names: Beautiful Parrot

IDENTIFICATION 23cm. Medium-sized, stocky, mainly green parrot with short square-ended tail and distinctive combination of pinkish-rose face and dark cap. Golden-brown patch on upper breast extends over sides of neck to hindneck. Approaches range of Brown-hooded Parrot (302) in north-west Colombia; blackish-brown face and red axillaries identify latter species, which see for general separation from *Pionus* parrots, whose widely overlapping representatives Blue-headed (313), Red-billed (314) and Bronze-winged (318) are further separated by extensive red on undertail and absence of red on face. *Touit* parrotlets are considerably smaller. Generally in pairs or small groups. Usually inconspicuous and quiet. More noticeable in flight.

VOICE Harsh shrieking *skreek-skreek* resembling certain calls of Blue-headed Parrot.

Rose-faced Parrot

DISTRIBUTION AND STATUS This parrot occurs from west of Andes in Colombia south from middle reaches of Río Atrato valley and the Baudó Mountains in Chocó and Antioquia to Nariño, into Ecuador to El Oro in the south-west. Mainly uncommon, but numerous locally and seasonally. Decline in population has certainly accompanied extensive deforestation on Pacific slope of Ecuador. Present status in Colombia unknown but if serious forest loss takes place west of the Andes (as it is set to) then numbers will decline further. Birds can persist in partly cleared land, but probably at lower density. Very scarce in captivity.

ECOLOGY Mature wet evergreen forest and edge, including tall secondary growth, plantations and clearings with scattered trees, mainly in tropical zone foothills (generally at 500-1,200m) but also lowlands and lower subtropical vegetation (to 2100m), especially in south of

range. Gregarious, forming groups of up to 25 or more. Forages mainly in middle storey and canopy. No details on diet; frequents banana plantations where birds sometimes cause damage. Birds in breeding condition Nov-Dec, south-western Cauca, and Jan-Mar, Chocó.

DESCRIPTION Forehead mainly pink, sometimes with some brighter red feathers; lores, superciliary area, upper cheeks and ear-coverts bright pinkish-rose forming distinctive facial disc, narrowly (broader on lower cheeks) margined with dark feathers; forecrown brown to dark blackish-brown, fading posteriorly to rich golden-brown on upper hindneck; paler golden margins to feathers on crown. Hindneck, upper mantle and sides of neck golden-brown; upperparts otherwise green. Some red and yellow at bend of wing and on lesser coverts; leading edge of wing also marked blue, primary and greater coverts violet-blue; other coverts green. Primaries blackish with paler margins to outerwebs. Underwing with greater coverts greenish-blue, lesser golden-yellowish, flight feathers dull bluish-green. Throat and breast golden-brown; belly green with faint bluish tinge, yellowish on undertail-coverts. Tail green centrally with blue tips; lateral feathers with red on base of innerweb and blue tips. **Bare parts**: Bill and cere pale pinkish-white; narrow periophthalmic ring whitish; iris grey; legs yellowish-brown.

SEX/AGE Female has golden wash on cap and around pink facial patch, reducing striking facial contrast of male. Immature has face mainly greenish-brown, red limited to line above eye and ear-coverts. Greenish on crown and hindneck.

MEASUREMENTS Wing 151-173, tail 55-67; bill 18-22; tarsus 17-20.

GEOGRAPHICAL VARIATION None.

NOTE This form has been considered a race of Brown-hooded Parrot, but while these birds are clearly close relatives and share a recent common ancestor, they are considered sufficiently distinct to warrant full species status.

REFERENCES Arndt (1996), Chapman (1926), Forshaw (1989), Haffer (1975), Hilty & Brown (1986), Parker & Carr (1992), Ridgely (1981), Whitney (1996)

304 ORANGE-CHEEKED PARROT
Pionopsitta barrabandi   Plate 76

Other names: Barraband's Parrot

IDENTIFICATION 25cm. Conspicuous orange cheek-patches on black hood and bright red underwing-coverts (obvious in flight) diagnose this medium-sized, mainly green, rather short-tailed parrot. Plumage is sufficiently distinctive to render confusion with other parrot species improbable although superficially similar Vulturine Parrot (307), probably sympatric in lower Rio Madeira, Brazil, has a yellowish stripe around head rather than patch on cheeks. Bright emerald-green body is conspicuous in flight but birds are quiet, secretive and almost invisible when feeding. For general differences from *Pionus* parrots see under Brown-hooded Parrot (302). Flight is very fast, usually at or below canopy level (not often above) and slightly twisting or rolling. Usually alone, in pairs or small groups of c. 4-6. Very shy and flushes at least hint of danger.

Flight call described as a reedy disyllabic *chewit* or *choyet*, very distinctive but sometimes similar to Blue-headed Parrot (313). Guttural *kek* or *kuk* sounds recall (to European ears) Eurasian Magpie *Pica pica*; uttered singly or in short series in flight (latter possibly as alarm notes).

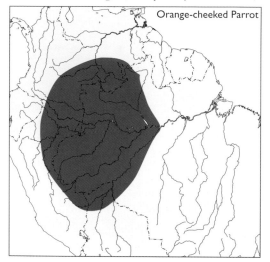

Orange-cheeked Parrot

DISTRIBUTION AND STATUS This is a bird of the Western Amazon basin and upper Orinoco. Its range extends from south-east Colombia from western Caquetá and lower Río Inirida, Guainía, to Venezuela in Amazonas and central and southern Bolívar, and in Brazil in upper Amazonia westwards from the lower Rios Negro and Madeira through the Rios Juruá and Purús and south to Mato Grosso, through eastern Ecuador and eastern Peru and to north-west Bolivia in Beni. Usually regarded as infrequent but fairly common in north-west Bolivia and numerous in the sand-belt woodlands of the lower Río Inirida, south-east Colombia; possibly more unobtrusive than genuinely scarce. Declined locally owing to deforestation but large tracts of primary forest remain in all range states. Occurs in several protected areas. Scarce in captivity.

ECOLOGY Mainly inhabits lowland terra firme forest, apparently less frequently in várzea stands. Occurs at forest edge and in partially disturbed forest, occasionally in patches of trees in otherwise deforested areas. Only reaches 150-300m in Venezuela, to 500m in south-east Colombia. Seen singly, in pairs and in small groups of up to 10 (sometimes more at e.g. mineral-rich earth bank). Active earlier in morning than other parrots and goes to roost later. Observed taking seeds or fruit from *Ficus sphenophylla*, *Pourouma*, *Pseudolmedia*, *Mimosa*, *Pithecellobium* and *Heisteria* and possibly wasp larvae from galls. Usually forages high in canopy or just below; less often lower. Regularly visits mineral-rich earth exposures in company of other parrot species. No information on nesting, but record of immature birds in Feb and Mar suggests breeding from Sep-Oct to end of year.

DESCRIPTION Head and throat black except for bright yellowish-orange area from base of bill onto lower cheek well behind eye. Upperparts green. Lesser coverts yellowish-orange; leading edge of wing red; primary coverts bluish-black; greater coverts bluish-green; other coverts green. Primaries dark blue at base and on outerwebs, otherwise

black; underwing bright red, flight feathers dull green. Upper breast golden, lower breast and belly rather bright bluish-green, thighs with yellowish-orange feathers. Tail green tipped blue, with yellow bases to innerwebs of outer feathers. **Bare parts:** Bill grey; iris brown; legs grey.

SEX/AGE Sexes similar. Immature has golden-brownish head with yellowish-brown on lower cheeks. Younger bird also has less yellow at bend of wing, some green feathers in underwing-coverts and yellow on tips of primaries.

MEASUREMENTS Wing 147-171; tail 62-71; bill 18-21; tarsus 17-19.

GEOGRAPHICAL VARIATION Two races.
> ***P. b. barrabandi*** (S Venezuela, most of Brazilian Amazon and SE Colombia, where it probably intergrades with next race)
> ***P. b. aurantiigena*** (Rio Madeira headwaters in W Brazil, NW Bolivia, E Peru and E Ecuador) Cheeks, lesser coverts, bend of wing and thighs deep orange rather than yellowish-orange.

NOTE Some authors have included *P. barrabandi*, *P. caica* and *P. vulturina* (see Note for latter species) in the genus *Eucinetus*. Whilst these taxa are evidently close and form a cluster within *Pionopsitta*, they are not sufficiently distinct to warrant a generic split.

REFERENCES Desenne & Strahl (1991, 1994), Forshaw (1989), Haffer (1975), Hilty & Brown (1986), Meyer de Schauensee & Phelps (1978), Naumburg (1930), Parker (1991), Parker & Remsen (1987), Parker *et al.* (1991), Remsen & Ridgely (1980), Ridgely (1981), Sick (1993), Whitney (1996).

305 SAFFRON-HEADED PARROT
Pionopsitta pyrilia   Plate 75

Other names: Bonaparte's Parrot

IDENTIFICATION 24cm. Medium-sized, rather stocky parrot with short square-ended tail. Combination of yellow head, neck and shoulders with red underwing-coverts (conspicuous in flight) and bright green body is diagnostic in range, although yellow head may be difficult to see in thick foliage. Similar-sized Brown-hooded Parrot (302) probably overlaps and may breed sympatrically with Saffron-headed; latter easily separated by bright yellow head and neck, but immatures are similar with Saffron-headed green on crown, dull olive-yellow on face and green on shoulders, Brown-hooded Parrot dull brown on crown. Ranges of several *Pionus* overlap Saffron-headed's but all are larger and in flight their wings (unlike *Pionopsitta*) do not go above plane of back; no *Pionus* has a bright yellow head but all show red undertail-coverts (absent in Saffron-headed). Most often noticed in small groups flying swiftly below forest canopy or at forest edge, calling loudly; inconspicuous whilst feeding quietly in canopy.

VOICE Reedy *cheweek* call similar to Orange-cheeked Parrot (304).

DISTRIBUTION AND STATUS Extreme eastern Panama in eastern Darién where reported from e.g. Pacific coast near Jaque, Río Tiura Valley, Cerro Pirre and Boca de Cupe, and in northern Colombia with most records from base of the northern Andes with closest record to Panama at Quimarí on the northern Antioquia /Córdoba border.

It is present at least temporarily on west slope of Andes where recorded from (e.g.) Sucio valley (western Antioquia), Chocó and Buenaventura, with one isolated record in northern Ecuador from the Cotocarchi-Cayapas Reserve, presumably of wanderers from further north. Absent from semi-arid regions of northern Colombia and mainly distributed through humid base of Andes from Río Sinú and lower Río Cauca to Sierra de Perijá. Occurs south in Magdalena Valley to eastern Caldas and north-western Cundinamarca and east of Andes in Norte de Santander and (perhaps as wanderer) in south-eastern Boyacá. Formerly in central Andes of Colombia to Medellín. Distributed through north-west Venezuela mainly around Maracaibo basin in Zulia (e.g. Sierra de Perijá), Táchira, Merida and western Lara. Apparently rare Panama. In northern Colombia it was numerous at several localities at base of northern Andes but is declining overall owing to deforestation, and some authors regard it as quite rare with a total population of under 10,000. Rare in captivity.

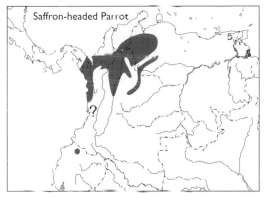

Saffron-headed Parrot

ECOLOGY Humid and wet forest including rain-forest and cloud forest; sometimes in tall secondary growth and at forest edge. In Venezuela it occurs in tropical and subtropical zones from 150-1,650m (perhaps only seasonally at higher altitudes) and to 1,000m in Colombia. Generally gregarious, in parties of up to c. 10 or in family groups. No information on diet, little on nesting. Breeding-condition birds taken Mar-Jun, Antioquia, with juveniles seen Jul, Sierra de Perijá.

DESCRIPTION Lores bare; head, hindneck and sides of neck bright yellow. Upperparts green. Lesser upperwing-coverts bright yellow with some feathers red at base; red on leading edge of wing with outer median upperwing-coverts blue, or green with blue tips. Primary coverts black with remaining upperwing-coverts green, sometimes with bluish-tips. Primaries and secondaries bluish-black with narrow greenish margin to outerwebs; tertials green. Underwing with coverts and axillaries bright red, flight feathers dull bluish. Breast olive-yellow; belly green but paler and more yellowish than above; undertail-coverts green. Uppertail green with yellow on innerwebs and blue tips; yellowish beneath. **Bare parts**: Bill pale horn; cere dull blackish; bare dark grey skin on lores extends around bare pale eye-ring; bare periophthalmic ring whitish; iris dark brown; legs grey.

SEX/AGE Sexes similar. Immature is green on crown and shoulders with brownish olive-yellow on face and throat.

MEASUREMENTS Wing 135-151; tail 60-74; bill 16-19, tarsus 15-18.

GEOGRAPHICAL VARIATION None.

REFERENCES Desenne & Strahl (1991, 1994), Forshaw (1989), Haffer (1975), Hilty & Brown (1986), Meyer de Schauensee & Phelps (1978), Ridgely (1981), Ridgely & Gwynne (1989), Wetmore (1968).

306 CAICA PARROT
Pionopsitta caica   Plate 76

Other names: Hooded Parrot

IDENTIFICATION 23cm. Medium-sized, rather stocky parrot with short square-ended tail. Black hood bordered with scaly golden-brown collar is diagnostic in range. Plumage is otherwise mainly green with some yellow on underside of tail but no red in wings. Only other black-hooded parrot in range is Orange-cheeked (304), probably sympatric in central and southern Bolívar, Venezuela, which has bright red on underside of wings and bright orange cheek patches. Vulturine Parrot (307) replaces Caica south of the Amazon and has red underwing-coverts and striking yellow stripe on sides of head. Sympatric Black-capped Parrot (299) has black confined to crown and is white beneath. Immature Caicas lack black head. For general differences from *Pionus* parrots see under Brown-hooded Parrot (302). Sympatric Dusky Parrot (319) shows red on undertail coverts. Generally in pairs or small flocks in tree tops. Flight swift below or at canopy level.

VOICE Nasal *screee-uh* (second syllable higher-pitched) followed by a short sharp *sca*. Birds in flocks recorded making scolding nasal *tchneea* and more pleasant whistled *ioou-eee-eee* calls. Also strident *ewlit* from perched birds.

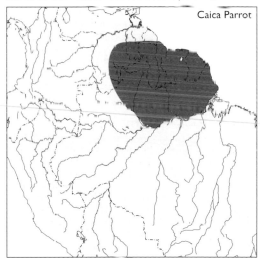

Caica Parrot

DISTRIBUTION AND STATUS North-eastern South America from south-east Venezuela in Bolívar along lower Río Caura and upper Río Cuyuni and at lower elevations in the Gran Sabana, into Guyana in lowlands west to foothills of Pakaraima Mountains and reportedly from (e.g.) Kanuku Mountains and Potaro and Mazaruni Rivers, interior Surinam, French Guiana and through north-east Brazil north of the Amazon from the Rio Branco east to Amapá. Widely but sparsely distributed and apparently mainly uncommon although fairly common some localities in Guyana. Rare in captivity. Some deforestation in range but substantial areas of undisturbed forest remain throughout.

ECOLOGY Mainly inhabits undisturbed lowland terra firme rain-forest, occasionally at forest edge but rarely if ever in várzea, ranging from 50 to 1,100m in Venezuela. Gregarious in small groups, at least outside breeding season. Birds mainly forage in tree-tops. Little information on food or breeding. Observed taking seeds of *Dracoides sagotianu*, *Protium* and *Brosimum*, and small dark red fruits of unidentified plant. Breeds Nov-Feb, French Guiana.

DESCRIPTION Lores, forehead, crown, cheeks and ear-coverts black. Feathers on hindneck and sides of neck golden-brown with darker brown margins giving scalloped effect. Upperparts green. Blue on leading edge of wing with dark cobalt-blue on primary coverts. Outer primaries dark bluish-black with narrow green margin to outerwebs. Underwing with coverts green, flight feathers dull bluish-green. Chin black; throat and breast golden olive-brown; belly green; undertail-coverts slightly more yellowish. Tail green with blue tip; innerwebs of outer feathers yellow. **Bare parts**: Bill greyish-horn; cere grey; iris yellow; legs slaty-grey.

SEX/AGE Sexes similar. Immature green on crown with yellowish olive-brown on face. Collar duller and with less striking scalloped effect. Iris darker.

MEASUREMENTS Wing 146-161; tail 60-68; bill 18-20; tarsus 16-20.

GEOGRAPHICAL VARIATION None.

REFERENCES Desenne & Strahl (1991, 1994), Forshaw (1989), Haverschmidt (1968), Meyer de Schauensee & Phelps (1978), Parker *et al.* (1993), Ridgely (1981), Sick (1993), Snyder (1966), Tostain *et al.* (1992).

---

307 VULTURINE PARROT
Pionopsitta vulturina   Plate 76

IDENTIFICATION 23cm. Medium-sized, stocky, rather short-tailed parrot, mainly green with conspicuous yellow band around head and neck and red underwing-coverts. Unmistakable with no similar species over most of range. However, it may come into contact with Orange-cheeked Parrot (304) of western Amazonia in lower Rio Madeira where latter separated by orange cheek-patches (instead of yellow stripe over head and neck). Caica Parrot (306), which replaces Vulturine on north bank of the Amazon, lacks yellow on head and neck and red on underside of wings. Immatures form separate flocks when they are identified by yellowish-orange underwing-coverts, dull orange patch on lesser upperwing-coverts and red on leading edge of wing. For general differences from *Pionus* parrots see under Brown-hooded Parrot (302). Pairs whilst breeding, otherwise groups up to eight. Swift flight at or below canopy level. Quiet and inconspicuous whilst feeding in foliage.

VOICE Flight call variously described as *iz-teret-teret tre-trayeh* and *fee chu.... fee chu*. Disyllabic call with liquid quality is quite unlike that of any other parrot.

DISTRIBUTION AND STATUS North-east Brazil south of the Amazon, from eastern Amazonas on east bank of lower Rio Madeira through Pará south to Serra do Cach-imbo, extending east to border areas with north-western Maranhão in the Rio Gurupí region. Published references to range including Venezuela (lower Río Caura) and Guyana are apparently mistaken. Generally regarded as uncommon but undoubtedly overlooked owing to retiring habits. Rapid deforestation has occurred and is continuing throughout range and there must have been a substantial decline in numbers and fragmentation of occurrence in recent decades. Occurs in protected forest in west of range but illegal logging and colonisation remain a threat even there. Rare in captivity.

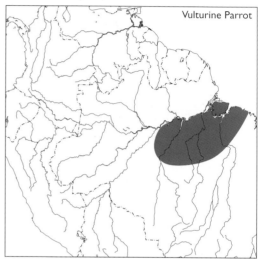

Vulturine Parrot

ECOLOGY Inhabits lowland tropical rain-forest occurring in both várzea and terra firme formations. Gregarious. Diet comprises fruits, seeds and berries taken in forest canopy. Bare head may be adaptation to highly frugivorous diet to prevent feathers becoming matted by juices. No details on reproductive biology.

DESCRIPTION Bare skin on forehead and forecrown to above eyes orange-yellow and covered with pale hairlike bristles; bare skin on lores, cheeks and centre of crown black and covered with black hairlike bristles; feathers on sides of neck and hindcrown yellow forming bright band contrasting with black of bare head; hindneck black. Upperparts green. Carpal area and lesser upperwing-coverts orange-yellow; outer median coverts with some blue; leading edge of wing red; primary coverts blue; rest of upperwing green. Primaries bluish-black with narrow bluish-green margins to outerwebs. Underwing with coverts red, flight feathers green with blackish tips. Feathers on throat and breast olive-yellow with dark tips giving scalloped effect; belly green with bluish tinge; undertail-coverts yellowish-green. Tail green with blue tips, outer feathers with yellow on base of innerwebs. **Bare parts**: Bill dark blackish-grey with paler yellowish-horn patch at base of upper mandible; cere yellowish-horn; iris brownish-orange; legs grey.

SEX/AGE Sexes similar. Immature head fully feathered (except for pale periophthalmic ring); greenish on cheeks and more olive-yellow on rest of head with no yellow collar. Bend of wing and underwing-coverts yellowish-orange. Iris darker.

MEASUREMENTS Wing 150-165; tail 60-73; bill 18-20; tarsus 16-18.

GEOGRAPHICAL VARIATION None.

NOTE This species is often placed in a monotypic genus, *Gypopsitta*. It is however very close to members of *Pionopsitta* (especially *P. barrabandi* and *P. caica*) and is best regarded as congeneric with them.

REFERENCES Arndt (1996), Forshaw (1989), Meyer de Schauensee (1966), Ridgely (1981), Sick (1993), Whitney (1996), Yamashita *in litt.* (1996).

---

308 BLACK-WINGED PARROT
Hapalopsittaca melanotis   Plate 77

Other names: Black-eared Parrot; Peruvian Black-winged Parrot (*H. m. peruviana*)

IDENTIFICATION 24cm. Mainly green with large black patches on wing and bluish on crown and hindneck. Quite small and stocky, with rather short, slightly tapered tail. There are no similar species in limited range and black wing-patches are reliable fieldmark. *Bolborhynchus* parakeets are more slender and longer-tailed whilst similarly proportioned *Pionus* parrots are larger and their wings (unlike *Hapalopsittaca*) do not go above plane of back in flight. Identified in captivity by combination of bluish forehead to hindneck (see Geographical Variation) and black on upperwing-coverts. Nominate also with black ear-coverts and ochre around eyes whilst Peruvian race shows dull brownish-orange ear-coverts. Flies with rapid deep wingbeats, often at some height. Feeds in tree-tops, sometimes conspicuously, but can be hard to detect in foliage.

VOICE Call rapid, monotonous and undistinctive, but still quite melodious. *Shrit shrit* and *ylp ylp* notes reported.

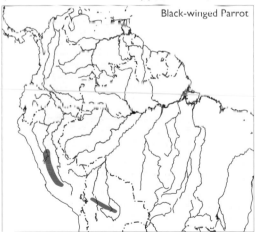

Black-winged Parrot

DISTRIBUTION AND STATUS Occurs in the eastern Andes of central Peru in Huánuco, eastern Pasco, Junín and Cuzco and (disjunctly) in the yungas of Bolivia on the eastern Andean slope in La Paz, Cochabamba and in Santa Cruz (first recorded latter state in 1992). Perhaps some seasonal elevational movements occur to temperate zones to exploit fruiting trees. Uncommon to locally fairly common; perhaps more numerous in Bolivian part of range, and at higher density in subtropical vegetation. Large tracts of undisturbed forest remain within restricted

range. Occurs in higher parts of Manu National Park, Peru. Rare in captivity.

ECOLOGY This parrot occupies humid montane forest in the upper subtropical and temperate zones, in quite tall forest and into boggy elfin growth, especially where there are fruiting trees. Sometimes at border of cultivated areas; occasionally flies over open terrain. At 2,800-3,450m in Peru and at 1,500-2,500m in Bolivia. Gregarious, generally in pairs or small groups; sometimes in quite large flocks. Apparently mainly frugivorous and perhaps favours fruits of mistletoes (e.g. *Gaiadendron*) with flocks of up to 50 apparently wandering in search of forest with an abundance of this food; may also take seeds and flowers. No information on reproductive biology.

DESCRIPTION Forehead, lores, crown, sides of neck, hindneck and upper mantle rather greyish-blue; patch of ochre feathers around eye extends onto upper cheeks; lower cheeks greyish-green; ear-coverts blackish. Lower mantle to uppertail-coverts green, but scapulars more olive. Bend of wing, lesser upperwing-coverts, most median coverts and primary coverts black. Primaries dark purplish-blue; secondaries black. Underwing with coverts bluish-green, flight feathers dull green. Chin and throat greyish-blue fading to pale grey on upper breast; lower breast and most of belly green but paler and more yellowish than above; feathers around thighs and vent brighter green; undertail-coverts green. Uppertail rather dark dull olive-green with dark purplish-blue tip; undertail dull blue. **Bare parts**: Bill pale grey; cere dark grey; narrow periophthalmic ring dark grey; iris dark brown; legs grey.

SEX/AGE Sexes similar. Immature has broad green margins to otherwise black upperwing coverts.

MEASUREMENTS Wing 148-162; tail 79-92; bill 17-19; tarsus 17-19.

GEOGRAPHICAL VARIATION Two races.
> *H. m. melanotis* (La Paz and Cochabamba, Bolivia)
> *H. m. peruviana* (Huánuco, E Pasco, Junín and Cuzco, Peru) Similar to nominate but with dull brownish-orange (not black) ear-coverts. Ochre patch around eye seems variable, with some birds showing very little, others an extensive area over forehead and onto forecrown.

REFERENCES Arndt (1996), Bond (1955), Bond & Meyer de Schauensee (1942), J. Fjeldså verbally (1993), Fjeldså & Krabbe (1990), Forshaw (1989), Peters & Griswold (1943), Ridgely (1981), Whitney *et al.* (1994), Whitney (1996).

---

309 RUSTY-FACED PARROT
Hapalopsittaca amazonina   Plate 77

IDENTIFICATION 23cm. Mainly green with red on forehead, cheeks and bend of wing, yellow lores, golden-brown breast and throat, and blue in wings and blue and red on tail. Quite small and stocky, with a rather short, slightly tapered tail and pale bill. Race *velezi* may occur (or have occurred) with Fuertes's Parrot (310) in Quindío, Colombia, where the former is separated by more extensive red on head, yellow streaks on ear-coverts and cheeks, and golden-olive hindneck (green in Fuertes's) contrasting with green mantle. The similar, but probably wholly allopatric, Red-faced Parrot (311) has brighter, less extensive, red on face and forehead with red rather than yellow lores, also greener breast and more yellow on ear-coverts and sides of neck. Similarly proportioned *Pionus* parrots are a little larger with proportionately shorter tails, and their wings do not go above plane of back in flight. Structurally similar to *Pionopsitta* parrots which however inhabit lowland forests. Generally in pairs or small flocks. Sometimes travels at height. May perch conspicuously in tree-tops or feed unobtrusively inside canopy.

VOICE *Chek chek chek* flight call reported from *Hapalopsittaca* parrots in Huila, Colombia, was probably this species.

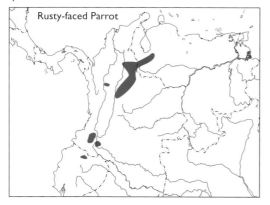

Rusty-faced Parrot

DISTRIBUTION AND STATUS This is a bird of the northern Andes. In Venezuela it has been recorded in the extreme north-west in Mérida and Táchira, with most records from within a 25km band north-west and north-east of the city of Mérida, with a further record 90km to the south-west and another 11km east, with one report in the west of Táchira near the Colombian border and another from the north (Boca de Monte). In Colombia records are from central and eastern Andes in at least seven separate areas in Norte de Santander, Santander, Cundinamarca and Caldas. Reports of *Hapalopsittaca* parrots from the head of the Magdalena Valley in Cauca and Huila may be of this species. There is an additional sighting from the high Andes of extreme northern Ecuador (Cerro Mongus) but presence in that country otherwise unknown. Locally distributed and evidently rare. Status in Venezuela critical. No recent records from northern portion of eastern Andes of Colombia and localities where previously reported as common are now wholly deforested. Although some substantial areas of suitable habitat remain, forests over most of range now cleared or very fragmented. Occurs in several protected areas, but some are very insecure (e.g. mining concession threatens El Tamá National Park, Venezuela). ENDANGERED.

ECOLOGY Mainly inhabits wet epiphyte-rich cloud-forest, sometimes quite small fragments and along edges, in temperate zone, occasionally descending to upper subtropical forests; occurs in elfin forest and in taller stands with broken canopy. Sometimes close to cultivation and seen feeding in and flying over secondary forest, with one report of birds in a reforestation plot of *Alnus acuminata* in Caldas, Colombia. Chiefly recorded between 2,200 and 3,000m (rarely lower) with most reports at about 2,500m; one report of *Hapalopsittaca* parrots at 3,750m was perhaps this species. Gregarious, generally in pairs or

flocks of up to about 25; usually fewer. Reported food items include fruits of *Clusia* and mistletoe. Birds mainly feed in canopy but sometimes forages lower down for e.g. *Phytolacca* berries. No details on breeding biology.

DESCRIPTION Forehead, forecrown, chin and cheeks from base of mandible to behind eyes dark red; lores yellow; ear-coverts, rest of cheeks, hindcrown and sides of neck greenish-olive with narrow yellow streaks; hindneck green. Upperparts including scapulars green tinged olive with rather obscure paler yellowish margins. Lesser upperwing-coverts, bend and leading edge of wing red; outer median and greater coverts dark violet-blue with primary coverts darker still. Primaries black edged with purplish-blue; secondaries mainly blue with green margins to outerwebs. Underwing greenish-blue except for red lesser coverts. Throat and breast rich golden-olive; belly, thighs and undertail-coverts green but paler and more yellowish than above. Uppertail blue with red on base of innerwebs; undertail duller. **Bare parts**: Bill horn with greyish marks at base of upper mandible; iris yellowish; legs dark grey.

SEX/AGE Sexes similar. Immature bird is duller, more olivaceous on back, with brown primaries with bluish wash and duller, brownish tail; lacks yellow streaks on cheeks and ear-coverts, and has less blue and red on head.

MEASUREMENTS Wing 144-157; tail 71-83; bill 16-18; tarsus 15-18.

GEOGRAPHICAL VARIATION Three races.

H. a. amazonina (N part of E Andes of Colombia south to Cundinamarca, with one report from extreme W Táchira, Venezuela)

H. a. theresae (Mérida and probably Táchira, extreme NW Venezuela) Similar to nominate but plumage more olive with red on face darker and more brownish.

H. a. velezi (Western flank of the high volcanic cones of the C Andes in Caldas, and possibly Quindío, Colombia; range perhaps extends south along east slope of C Andes to head of Magdalena Valley) Similar to nominate but with golden-olive hindneck contrasting sharply with green mantle; possibly longer culmen than other taxa in *H. amazonina* superspecies.

NOTE Red-faced and Fuertes's Parrot are often regarded as races of *H. amazonina*. However, the plumage differences between these taxa are sufficient (as many authors conclude) to warrant full species treatment. Furthermore, Fuertes's Parrot and race *velezi* of Rusty-faced Parrot have been found within at least 25km of one another in the central Andes of Colombia in Caldas, suggesting that they are biologically separate entities.

REFERENCES Collar *et al.* (1992, 1994), Fjeldså & Krabbe (1990), Forshaw (1989), Graves & Restrepo (1989), Hilty & Brown (1986), Meyer de Schauensee & Phelps (1978), Ridgely & Gaulin (1980).

310 FUERTES'S PARROT
Hapalopsittaca fuertesi　　　　Plate 77

Other names: Azure-winged Parrot, Rusty faced Parrot (see Note in *H. amazonina*)

IDENTIFICATION 23cm. Mainly green with red on forehead and at bend of wing, blue on crown with blue in wings and blue and red on tail. Quite small and stocky, with a rather short, slightly tapered tail and pale bill. Separation from race *velezi* of Rusty-faced Parrot (309) is treated under that species, which see also for comments on *Pionus* and *Pionopsitta*. The similar, but probably wholly allopatric, Red-faced Parrot (311) has brighter, and more extensive, red on face and forehead, with green (not red) at base of tail. Extremely rare, perhaps nearly extinct.

VOICE No details.

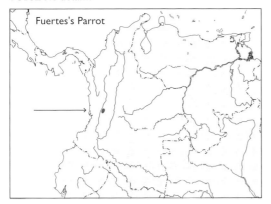

Fuertes's Parrot

DISTRIBUTION AND STATUS This parrot has a highly restricted range, being endemic to the west slope of the central Andes in Colombia, and known with certainty only from specimens taken in 1911 from sites 40km apart in Quindío and Risaralda, and from a few records since 1989 in the Alto Quindío Acaime Natural Reserve and nearby Cañon del Quindío Natural Reserve, both in Quindío. There was a possible observation from another cloud-forest locality at 3,750m in Risaralda in 1980, and possible sightings from the head of the Magdalena Valley; in both cases however (especially the latter) Rusty-faced Parrots may have been involved. Thus the only known population is in the two Quindío reserves, where only small numbers remain. Much of west slope of the central Andes in Quindío and Risaralda is now deforested; only fragments of montane forest remain. The Quindío reserves appear secure but are probably too small to ensure the parrot's effective long-term conservation. The recent discovery of the race *velezi* of Rusty-faced Parrot very close to localities known to hold (or have held) Fuertes's Parrot raised speculation that the latter is in the process of the displacement by the former. However, given that *velezi* is quite distinct from other races of Rusty-faced Parrot and is not known from elsewhere (so has no known source for its expansion) it must be assumed that the two forms have co-existed for some time, perhaps separated by altitudinal preferences. ENDANGERED.

ECOLOGY Inhabits cloud-forest (including formations with *Quercus*) rich in epiphytes and tree ferns, from 2,610 to 3,810m with most observations (mainly in the Quindío reserves) 2,900-3,150m. It is perhaps an altitudinal replacement of Rusty-faced Parrot but its apparent higher elevational preferences may be an artifact of almost total forest clearance lower down. Mainly feeds inside canopy. No information on diet or breeding but *Hapalopsittaca* parrots may be closely reliant on mistletoe berries for food.

DESCRIPTION Narrow red frontal band; lores, forecrown and area around and behind eyes olive-yellow; feathers

on crown blue; hindneck and sides of neck green. Mantle green with very faint paler margins; rest of upperparts including scapulars green. Lesser coverts, bend and leading edge of wing crimson; outer median and greater coverts dark violet-blue with primary coverts darker still and almost black. Primaries black edged with purplish-blue; secondaries mainly blue with green margins to outerwebs. Underwing greenish-blue except for crimson lesser coverts. Throat and breast green tinged golden-olive; belly, thighs and undertail-coverts yellowish-green with variable amounts of dull red on central belly. Uppertail blue with red on base of innerwebs; undertail duller. **Bare parts**: Bill horn, darker at base of upper mandible; iris yellowish; legs dark grey.

SEX/AGE Sexes similar. Immature undescribed.

MEASUREMENTS Wing 150-157; tail 77-94; bill 15-17; tarsus 16-18.

GEOGRAPHICAL VARIATION None.

REFERENCES Collar *et al.* (1992, 1994), Fjeldså & Krabbe (1990), Forshaw (1989), Graves & Restrepo (1989), Hilty & Brown (1986).

311 RED-FACED PARROT
Hapalopsittaca pyrrhops   Plate 77

Other names: Rusty-faced Parrot (see Note in *H. amazonina*)

IDENTIFICATION 23cm. Mainly green with red on forehead, face, bend of wing and underwing-coverts, with blue in wings. Some yellow on ear-coverts and cheeks. Quite small and stocky with a rather short, slightly tapered blue-tipped tail and pale bill. No similar species in limited high-altitude range but separated from allopatric Rusty-faced (309) and Fuertes's (310) Parrots of Colombia and Venezuela (and perhaps northern Ecuador in case of former) by red lores and green (not reddish) base to uppertail. For comments on *Pionus* and *Pionopsitta* parrots see under Rusty-faced Parrot. Occurs in pairs or flocks of 4-20 birds. Typically flies high (30-50m) and fast above forest canopy.

VOICE Voice generally harsh and screechy. Loud disyllabic *ch-ek che-ek* call is characteristic. First part (*ch*) is rasping with second part (*ek*) higher-pitched. Roosting birds give high-pitched *eek eek eek* followed by more throaty *thrut*; perched and foraging birds also use *eek eek eek* call. Juvenile call differs from adult typically beginning with *chur-ch-chur* followed by series of *eeks* and a chattering laugh-like *eek-ha-ha-a*. Call of Mountain Cacique *Cacicus leucoramphus* similar to perching/foraging call of Red-faced Parrot and may be confused with it.

DISTRIBUTION AND STATUS The species occurs in southern Ecuador with records from several localities on both slopes of Andes in Morona Santiago, Azuay, Loja and possibly El Oro provinces; also possibly further north in Andes of Napo. It extends across into extreme northern Peru on both slopes of high Andes in the Huancabamba region of Piura and possibly in Cajamarca. Perhaps seasonal in some areas through altitudinal displacements, but resident around Saraguro in Loja. Very scarce and locally distributed, but common in one or two localities including forest fragments in Cordillera de Chilla, northern Loja. Agricultural encroachment and felling of trees for fuel and construction materials is leading to habitat loss and fragmentation over much of limited range and the species is at serious risk as a result. It occurs in several protected areas including Sangay National Park, Morona Santiago, and Podocarpus National Park, Loja, with some of latter under threat from mining proposals. The forest patches that comprise its stronghold in the Cordillera de Chilla are unprotected and disappearing. ENDANGERED.

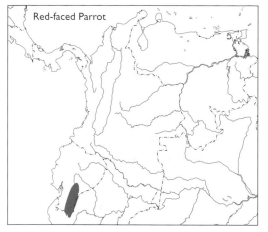

Red-faced Parrot

ECOLOGY The species inhabits wet upper montane forest in the temperate zone including rather mossy growth, open woodlands and shrubbery near the páramos. Reported from forest fragments with various degrees of degradation (e.g. understorey damage from cattle-grazing) in close proximity to pasture and there is some evidence to suggest at least tolerance of (if not preference for) secondary forest. Most records are from c. 2,800-3,000m but range is from c. 2,400 to 3,500m. Gregarious, nearly always seen in flocks of up to 20. Reported food items include fruits of *Miconia*, berries of *Viburnum*, shoots, flowers and seeds of two species of *Weinmannia*, pods of a *Clethra* and unspecified parts of two ericaceous trees, *Cavendishia bracteata* and *Disterigma alaternoides*, possibly also *Podocarpus* seeds. Birds forage from the dense canopy down into undergrowth c. 6m from ground. Only recorded nest was at 17.5m in the hollow of a lauraceous tree on the edge of a 400ha wood, part of which was degraded by cattle-grazing. Evidence for breeding in Aug-Sep, Oct-Jan and Feb-Mar. Only recorded clutch had three eggs.

DESCRIPTION Forehead, lores, forecrown, chin and front cheeks red; rear cheeks and ear-coverts with yellow streaks, in many birds forming an indistinct yellow patch; red crown bordered yellow behind, then with bluish feathers fading to green on hindneck. Upperparts including capulars green tinged olive with very faint paler yellowish margins. Lesser coverts, bend and leading edge of wing rose-red; outer median, primary and greater coverts dark violet-blue. Primaries black edged with purplish-blue; secondaries mainly blue with green margins to outerwebs. Underwing with coverts rose-red, flight feathers greenish-blue. Throat and breast green suffused golden-olive; rest of underparts yellowish-green. Tail mainly green with blue tip. **Bare parts**: Bill horn with greyish marks at base of upper mandible; iris yellowish; legs dark grey.

SEX/AGE Sexes similar. Immature has reduced red on face; nestling has light green cheek feathers.

MEASUREMENTS Wing 142-143; tail 76-93; bill 16-17; tarsus 16-17.

GEOGRAPHICAL VARIATION None.

REFERENCES Collar *et al.* (1992, 1994), Fjeldså & Krabbe (1990), Forshaw (1989), King (1989), Parker *et al.* (1985), Rasmussen *et al.* (1996), Toyne *in litt.* (1996), Toyne *et al.* (1995), Toyne & Flanagan (1996).

312 SHORT-TAILED PARROT
Graydidascalus brachyurus   Plate 75

IDENTIFICATION 24cm. Quite small, plump, mainly green parrot with very short square-ended tail. More yellowish beneath with heavy dark slaty-grey bill and distinctive pale margins to wing-coverts and scapulars. Generally near rivers where often in large numbers, especially at roost. *Pionus* parrots are proportionately shorter-tailed but with similar rapid fluttering wingbeats. Told from several potentially confusing *Amazona* species by smaller size, all-green wings and (at close range) rather frowning appearance derived from indistinct dark stripe in front of and behind eye. Festive Amazon (355) further distinguished by red on back. Generally in pairs or groups of up to c. 12. Flight usually fast and direct, often rather high. Birds approaching perch show frequent erratic rolling movements suggesting loss of control. Fairly conspicuous.

VOICE One of noisiest parrots in Amazon basin and can be detected by voice at some distance. Calls mostly loud and harsh, sometimes with characteristic gurgling quality: a strident *kia kia* and softer *kurik*, a raucous *shreek* in flight, and a slightly trilled and hornlike *fuuuuudle fuuuuudle* whilst feeding. High-pitched disyllabic calls also heard.

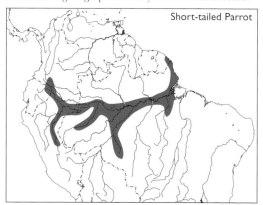

Short-tailed Parrot

DISTRIBUTION AND STATUS This is a species of the Amazon basin, occurring along rivers from eastern Pará and Amapá (Brazil) and French Guiana in the east to south-east Colombia (from Caquetá southwards), eastern Ecuador (e.g. Río Napo) and north-east Peru in west. Perhaps seasonal in some areas with presence possibly linked to flooding of riverine forests. Generally common and locally abundant, scarcer some areas (e.g. eastern Ecuador). Abundance appears to decrease as rivers become narrower upstream (perhaps related to declining extent of suitable riverine habitat). Rare in captivity.

ECOLOGY Habitat is lowland tropical rain-forest below about 400m, mainly in várzea, river-edge vegetation, forest bordering lakes or other swampy or seasonally flooded areas, especially preferring older river islands; uses secondary growth and frequents mangroves in coastal areas. Avoids terra firme forest. Sometimes in cultivated areas and one report of roost in town street. Gregarious, especially outside breeding season, forming huge roosts on river islands where birds sometimes associate with other parrot species. Birds feed mainly in canopy. Very little information on food and breeding. Specific food items include *Cecropia* catkins; cultivated fruits such as guava *Psidium* are taken when available. Breeding-condition birds Sep, eastern Brazil.

DESCRIPTION Lores, forehead, cheeks, ear-coverts and sides of neck pale apple-green; crown slightly darker with hint of grey; line of bare skin extending from cere around eyes to above ear-coverts dark grey. Mantle, back and rump grass-green with slightly paler and more yellowish uppertail-coverts. Scapulars grass-green with conspicuous broad yellow margins; primary coverts green; other coverts green with yellow margins. Primaries green, secondaries and tertials green with yellow margins. Underwing with coverts green with yellowish-green margins, flight feathers bluish-green. Underparts pale apple-green, paler than above. Central tail feathers green, slightly darker at tips; lateral tail feathers green with red at base. **Bare parts.** Bill dark slaty grey; cere dark grey; iris red; legs grey.

SEX/AGE Sexes similar. Immature lacks red on base of lateral tail feathers.

MEASUREMENTS Wing 144-160; tail 45-55; bill 23-26; tarsus 17-20.

GEOGRAPHICAL VARIATION Birds from E Amazonia have been proposed as belonging to a separate race (*insulsus*).

REFERENCES Forshaw (1989), Hilty & Brown (1986), Ridgely (1981), Sick (1993), Tostain *et al.* (1992).

---

313 BLUE-HEADED PARROT
Pionus menstruus   Plate 78

Other names: Blue-hooded Parrot, Red-vented Parrot

IDENTIFICATION 24cm. Chunky, medium-sized, short-tailed parrot, mainly green with blue on head, neck and breast. Red vent and red spot at base of bill sometimes visible in field. One of the most frequently seen and widespread of parrots in lowland South America. Flight fast and direct with typical *Pionus* flight pattern on distinctive, rather stiff wingbeats that remain well below the horizontal, primaries almost touching beneath bird on downstroke. Flocks sometimes fly high in long straggling line. Similar Dusky Parrot (319), sympatric in north-east Colombia and eastern Amazonia, is separated by blue on underside of flight feathers, quicker, shallower wingbeats and more rolling flight. Red-billed Parrot (314) can look similar to Blue-headed (especially at border of northern Colombia and northern Venezuela and in southern Venezuela) and is best separated by more extensive red on bill. Similar White-crowned Parrot (317), which overlaps in Costa Rica and western Panama, has white on head and slightly fuller wingstroke. Rather similar Scaly-headed Parrot (315) overlaps over much of south

and east of range but is more often seen in drier forests; Blue-headed otherwise distinguished by blue head and generally brighter colours. Smaller than *Amazona* with shriller, high-pitched voice, red undertail and relatively longer wings giving deeper wingbeats. *Pionopsitta* parrots are smaller and their wings rise above plane of back in flight. Mainly in pairs or, outside breeding season, pairs or small flocks. *Pionus* are seen singly more often than other similar-sized parrots. Birds sometimes perch on bare branches or palm fronds.

VOICE Strident, rather grating *tchreeet* repeated in flight. Call sometimes sounds like whipcrack. Also more pleasant whistled *cha-reet*. Single birds in flight sometimes emit rather light *wick*. Generally quiet whilst breeding but flocks create noisy chattering chorus.

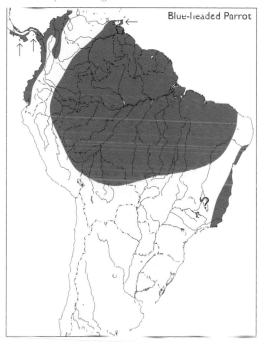

Blue-headed Parrot

DISTRIBUTION AND STATUS Blue-headed Parrots are found from Costa Rica south through South America to northern Bolivia and south-east Brazil. In Costa Rica the species occupies the coastal lowlands from north of Limón on the Caribbean slope and Golfo Dulce on the Pacific side, and extends through lowlands on both slopes in Panama, occurring on Coiba and larger islands in the Perlas Archipelago (where perhaps a visitor). It is distributed throughout the tropical zone on the west slope of the Andes and in the eastern lowlands of Colombia but is thinly spread or absent in the arid Caribbean lowlands and llanos. It occurs throughout the lowlands of Venezuela except Delta Amacuro and southern Bolívar, extending onto Trinidad and through the Guianas. West of the Andes it extends south to Manabí, Ecuador, with sporadic records from El Oro in the south-west. East of the Andes it is distributed through the western Amazon basin in eastern Ecuador and eastern Peru south to adjacent northern Bolivia in La Paz, Beni and Cochabamba (presumably present in Pando in north), and ranges widely in the Amazon basin of Brazil from Mato Grosso and the pantanal region in the south-west east to Amapá, Maranhão, Goiás and Piauí to reappear, apparently disjunctly, in eastern Brazil from Alagoas south through Bahia and coastal states, presumably also Minas Gerais, to Rio de Janeiro. Reported range sometimes includes northern Argentina but this seems mistaken. Perhaps wanders outside breeding season, at least in some parts of range, occurring in (e.g.) coastal Surinam seasonally with nomadic flocks reported in French Guiana. Common to fairly common through most of range but only patchily so in some parts. Much scarcer in eastern Brazil where perhaps at risk; declined here and in certain other parts of range (e.g. upper Cauca Valley, Colombia) related to deforestation. Frequent in captivity with some international trade.

ECOLOGY The species is found mainly in lowland tropical forest (including rain-forest, deciduous forest and savanna) but also locally in subtropical formations, cultivated areas, plantations, clearings with trees, secondary growth; it occurs (at least seasonally) in the very dry caatinga forests of interior north-east Brazil. It ranges up to c. 1,200m in Panama; 1,000m north of Orinoco in Venezuela and about 1,500m to south and in Colombia. Generally gregarious when not breeding and sometimes in quite large gatherings, especially where food is abundant or when roosting, although it is apparently normal for *Pionus* parrots to spend the night in small groups in tree-crowns. Reported food items include seeds of *Albizia, Anacardium, Caraipa, Dialium, Hevea, Clusia, Inga, Micropholis, Hura* and *Tectona*, fruits and seeds of *Goupia glabra*, various *Pseudolmedia* and *Pourouma* and flowers of *Erythrina*. Generally forages in canopy but birds sometimes take maize from fields where they can cause considerable damage. When available, they regularly visit exposed earth banks to take mineral-rich soil, often alongside other parrot species. Nests in tree-cavity, including those previously used by other bird species, sometimes in quite degraded habitat. Reported breeding Feb-Apr, Panama; Feb-Mar, Colombia; Feb, Venezuela; Mar and Oct, Trinidad; Feb-May, Ecuador. During breeding period, males conduct display flight with particular calls, slower-than-normal wingbeats and spread tail. Clutch 2-4.

DESCRIPTION Forehead, lores, crown, cheeks, sides of neck and hindneck cobalt-blue; ear-coverts blackish. Upperparts rather dull grass-green, scapulars with a brownish-olive suffusion. Lesser and median coverts somewhat variable, ranging from coppery yellowish-olive to green; other coverts green. Flight feathers green. Underwing with lesser coverts coppery yellowish-olive to green, remaining coverts green, outermost primaries blackish, remainder green. Chin and throat cobalt-blue with red bases to feathers on throat showing through as variable red patch; upper breast cobalt-blue; lower breast and belly green; undertail-coverts red. Uppertail green centrally, outer feathers blue; undertail red basally, otherwise green. **Bare parts**: Bill blackish with pinkish-red markings at base; cere dark grey; bare periophthalmic ring pale grey; iris dark brown; legs pale grey.

SEX/AGE Sexes probably similar although some authors claim male can be separated by more extensive and intense blue on breast. Immature has mainly green head and breast with scattered blue feathers.

MEASUREMENTS Wing 171-194; tail 65-78; bill 22-27; tarsus 18-22.

GEOGRAPHICAL VARIATION Three races. Despite occupation of huge range over virtually all of Amazonia, nominate form shows no consistent geographical variation and therefore no further racial splits are warranted.

> *P. m. menstruus* (East of Andes from Venezuela and E Colombia south to N Bolivia and east to mouth of Amazon)
>
> *P. m. reichenowi* (E Brazil from Alagoas to Rio de Janeiro) Blue deeper and more extensive with most feathers on underparts showing blue (many birds almost wholly blue below); no red on throat.
>
> *P. m. rubrigularis* (Costa Rica, Panama and west of Andes south to W Ecuador. Birds in N Colombia intermediate with nominate) Darker green on back and on average smaller than other races. Red on throat sometimes (not consistently) more extensive and blue on head duller than nominate.

REFERENCES Arndt (1996), Blake (1962), Bond & Meyer de Schauensee (1942), Desenne & Strahl (1991, 1994), Dubs (1992), Fernández-Badillo *et al.* (1994), ffrench (1992), Forshaw (1989), Friedmann & Smith (1955), Gyldenstolpe (1945a), Haffer (1975), Haffer & Fitzpatrick (1985), Haverschmidt (1968), Hilty & Brown (1986), Meyer de Schauensee & Phelps (1978), Naumburg (1930), Parker *et al.* (1993), Ridgely & Gwynne (1989), Sick (1993), Slud (1964), Snyder (1966), Stiles *et al.* (1989), Tostain *et al.* (1992), Toyne *in litt.* (1996), Toyne & Jeffcote (1994), Wetmore (1946, 1968), Whitney (1996).

314 RED-BILLED PARROT
Pionus sordidus   Plate 79

Other names: Sordid Parrot, Dusky Parrot (but this the common name of *P. fuscus*); Coral-billed Parrot (*P. s. corallinus*)

IDENTIFICATION 28cm. Medium-sized parrot, often quite scruffy-looking, with short square-ended tail. Plumage quite variable over large range but generally dull brownish or dark green with green flight feathers, red bill and crimson on undertail. Rather pale ocular ring. Bronze-winged Parrot (318), sympatric through much of northern Andes, is separated by blue flight feathers and tail, horn-coloured bill and brown upperwing-coverts. Blue-headed Parrot can look similar (especially to race *ponsi*, occurring at border of northern Colombia and northern Venezuela): Red-billed is best told on (higher) elevation and red bill. Dusky Parrot (319) occurs with Red-billed in the Sierra de Perijá but has blue flight feathers, paler throat and sides of neck, and rather vinaceous underparts. Northern Andean race *seniloides* of Speckle-faced Parrot (316) has white on crown and pale bill, whilst southern race *tumultuosus* (Andes from central Peru to northern Bolivia) has pale maroon head and yellowish-horn bill. Flight fast and direct, with typical *Pionus* flight pattern (see under Blue-headed Parrot, 313). Deeper wingbeats, red bill and undertail-coverts help distinguish it from *Amazona* parrots. For differences with (lowland) *Pionopsitta* see Blue-headed Parrot. Mainly in pairs or small flocks but *Pionus* species are more frequently seen singly than other similar-sized parrots. Noisy in flight and generally quite conspicuous.

VOICE Noisy, especially in flight. High-pitched, rather harsh *scree-at* repeated in flight. Flocks create loud shrieking sound.

DISTRIBUTION AND STATUS This bird has a disjunct

distribution through the highlands of northern and western South America from Venezuela to northern Bolivia. It occurs in northern Venezuela in the mountains of Anzoátegui, Sucre and northern Monagas and (apparently disjunctly) in highlands from Distrito Federal through the coastal mountains west to Lara and Falcón, then in the Sierra de Perijá, Zulia, and adjacent parts of Colombia west to the Santa Marta foothills in Magdalena, also locally in the eastern Andes in Boyacá and Huila. It ranges on the west slope of the Andes in Ecuador from Pichincha to El Oro and throughout the east slope sout into north-east Peru. Although there are no records from the east Andean slope in central and southern Peru the range includes the yungas of northern Bolivia in Santa Cruz and Cochabamba. Common locally; apparently less numerous in western Ecuador and northern Bolivia, and probably in decline locally owing to deforestation (e.g. western Ecuador, northern Venezuela and Andes of Colombia); a recent survey failed to locate race *antelius* in its largely cleared range, although the species can occur in moderately disturbed forest. Kept as pets locally but generally scarce in captivity

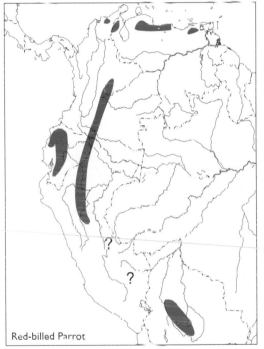

Red-billed Parrot

ECOLOGY The habitat is mainly humid forest, including montane rain-forest and cloud-forest, in the subtropical and upper tropical zones, occasionally up to lower temperate vegetation; thus elevation range 200-2,850m, but birds most frequent at 500-1,500m. Birds use secondary growth, partially deforested areas with scattered tall trees and sometimes light woodland over coffee plantations, but are less frequent in drier areas. Gregarious outside breeding season, forming flocks of up to c. 50, sometimes more where food abundant. Roosts communally but like other *Pionus* does so in small numbers. No solid information on diet. Nests in tree-cavity, sometimes in quite heavily degraded habitat. Breeding-condition birds Feb-Apr, Colombia; breeding Apr-Jun, Venezuela, Jan-May,

Ecuador; occupied nest Oct, Bolivia. Clutch three in captivity.

DESCRIPTION (*P. s. corallinus*) Feathers on forehead, lores and behind eyes green at base with broad blue edges; cheeks, ear-coverts and sides of neck mainly green with some narrow blue tips; crown and hindneck green with narrow blue edges. Mantle and back rather dull green with narrow paler greyish-blue margins; rump and uppertail-coverts green basally, more olive brown distally. Lesser and median coverts green with broad olive-brown tips; leading edge of wing, primary and greater coverts and flight feathers brighter green than upperparts and other wing-coverts. Underwing green. Chin green; throat and upper breast with broad band of violet-blue; belly green, some birds with greyish suffusion; undertail-coverts crimson. Tail green centrally, blue laterally; red at base. **Bare parts**: Bill coral-red, pale at base of upper mandible; cere dark grey; bare periophthalmic ring pale grey; iris dark brown; legs pale grey.

SEX/AGE Sexes similar. Immature shows yellowish-green undertail-coverts with some red markings; head green.

MEASUREMENTS (*P. s. corallinus*) Wing 187-206; tail 64-85; bill 22-25; tarsus 18-21

GEOGRAPHICAL VARIATION Five races. A proposed further variant, *P. s. mindoensis* from W Ecuador (claimed on basis of more yellowish-green plumage, narrower blue margins to feathers on head and absence of dark margins on wing-coverts), is probably not distinct from the most widespread form, *corallinus*.

P. s. sordidus (Lara and Falcón east to Distrito Federal, Venezuela) Much browner than *corallinus* with reduced (more turquoise) blue on throat. Feathers on upperparts with more distinctive pale margins.
P. s. antelius (Anzoátegui, Sucre and N Monagas, Venezuela) Similar to nominate but feathers lack blue edges on throat and pink centres on breast.
P. s. ponsi (Sierra de Perijá, Venezuela and Colombia, west to foothills of Santa Marta massif) Throat almost solid purplish-blue. Breast and upperparts darker and greener than nominate, lacking paler margins to feathers on back and wing-coverts
P. s. saturatus (N Santa Marta massif, Colombia) Darker and greener than nominate with feathers of upperparts lacking paler olive-brown margins. Less green on throat and cheeks.
P. s. corallinus (Colombia east of Andes, both slopes of Andes in Ecuador and on east slope in NE Peru; disjunctly in yungas of north-west Bolivia) Described above.

REFERENCES Arndt (1996), Bond & Meyer de Schauensee (1942), Chapman (1926), Desenne & Strahl (1991, 1994), Fernández-Badillo *et al.* (1994), Fjeldså & Krabbe (1990), Forshaw (1989), Hilty & Brown (1986), Holland (1922), Meyer de Schauensee & Phelps (1978), Ridgely (1981), Toyne *in litt.* (1996), Toyne & Jeffcote (1994).

315 SCALY-HEADED PARROT
Pionus maximiliani   Plate 78

Other names: Maximilian's Parrot; Tucuman Parrot (*P. m. lacerus*)

IDENTIFICATION 27cm. Medium-sized, stocky, rather dark-looking parrot, mainly brownish green with pale tip to bill, red vent and blue on sides of quite short, square-ended tail. Green wings contrast with duller body. Rather similar Blue-headed Parrot (313) occurs in much of north and east of range where Scaly-headed is distinguished by absence of blue on head, generally duller colours and preference for drier forests; immature Blue-headed is brighter and lighter than Scaly-headed with greener head. Sympatric (in south-east Brazil) Red-capped Parrot (301) is smaller than Scaly-headed, with red on head and higher-lifted wing-strokes. Mainly in pairs or small noisy flocks that travel quite high, but *Pionus* more frequently seen singly than other parrots. Flight fast and direct, with typical *Pionus* flight pattern (see under Blue-headed Parrot). Plumage blends well with foliage and birds easily overlooked whilst quietly perched. Quite tame and approachable where unmolested.

VOICE Loud voice audible at some distance, especially when travelling to and from roost. Calls include harsh squawks, low clucks and yapping *chree-ah* from birds in flight, recalling puppy-like sounds of some amazons. Softer chattering whilst perched. Rapidly repeated disyllabic call denotes alarm.

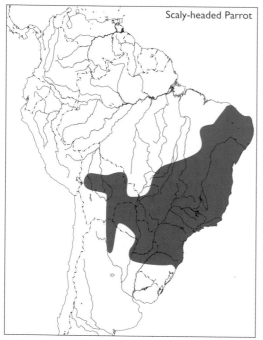

Scaly-headed Parrot

DISTRIBUTION AND STATUS The species occurs in central, southern and eastern Brazil from Maranhão and Ceará in the north-east south through Piauí, Bahia, Goiás, Minas Gerais and eastern coastal states to Rio Grande do Sul across to southern Mato Grosso (pantanal region), extending into adjacent south-east Bolivia from Santa Cruz south on the eastern Andes to northern Argentina in Salta, Tucumán and Catamarca in east and northern Santa Fe in west. Mainly resident but perhaps does not breed in drier parts of Argentine chaco. Apparently more numerous in centre of range, where abundance only exceeded by Maroon-bellied Conure (251); progressively scarcer towards periphery. Locally fairly common or common in Bolivia and locally common in northern Argentina, where most abundant in southern Salta, Tucumán and adjacent

Catamarca. Moderately common in Rio Grande do Sul and common in the pantanal; highest Brazilian densities in São Paulo. Apparent decline in some parts of range (e.g. northern Argentina) attributable to trade, but elsewhere (e.g. south-east Brazil) undoubtedly less numerous owing to forest loss.

ECOLOGY Wide range of wooded habitats but mainly in lowland dry forest ranging from very dry caatinga in interior north-east Brazil through seasonal cerrado savannas to the chaco; also in more humid forest, including gallery woodland and *Araucaria* forest, especially in south-east Brazil. Occurs in subtropical forests on east Andean slopes to about 2,000m in north-west Argentina and to about 1,500m in montane southern Brazil. Tolerant of human disturbance of forest habitats and sometimes in cultivated areas. Generally gregarious forming substantial flocks where food abundant. Probably roosts in small groups in tree-tops. Food plants include *Erythrina*, *Inga*, *Piptadenia*, *Copaifera*, *Croton*, *Pachystroma*, *Plathymenia reticulata*, *Ficus* and *Araucaria*. Nests in tree-hollow. Breeding-condition birds Oct, Paraguay, Nov São Paulo. Clutch 3-5.

DESCRIPTION Lores, forehead and ocular area rather dark dull bronze; feathers on crown, cheeks, chin and sides of neck green basally with fairly broad bronze margins giving scaled appearance; ear-coverts green with dark margins but brighter than other feathers on head. Hind-neck and mantle green becoming browner and more olive on lower upperparts, where some feathers have rather indistinct darker tips. Lesser and median coverts brownish olive-green with indistinct dark tips; alula, primary and greater coverts and flight feathers brighter green contrasting with duller, browner upperparts. Underwing dull green. Throat and upper breast dull violet-blue fading to brownish olive-green on lower breast and most of belly but becoming brighter and greener on flanks and thighs; undertail-coverts crimson. Uppertail green centrally, outer feathers mainly blue with red at base; undertail duller bluish-green. **Bare parts**: Bill black with yellow edges to upper mandible and tip of lower; bare periophthalmic skin pale grey; iris dark brown; legs grey.

SEX/AGE Sexes similar. Immature has less extensive blue on throat, feathers on head greener with less distinct margins.

MEASUREMENTS Wing 168-180; tail 69-85; bill 23-27; tarsus 18-21.

GEOGRAPHICAL VARIATION Four races. The relative distributions of *melanoblepharus* and *siy* in N Argentina and S Brazil are poorly known.

    P. m. maximiliani (NE Brazil south to S Goiás, C Minas Gerais and Espírito Santo)

    P. m. melanoblepharus (C Brazil from S Goiás and Minas Gerais south-east to Rio Grande do Sul – presumably including Santa Catarina, but see next race – and N Argentina in Misiones, Corrientes and E Chaco, where intergrades with *siy*) Darker blue on throat and darker above. Larger (wing 182-203).

    P. m. siy (Mainly extreme N Argentina in N Salta, Jujuy, Formosa and W Chaco north to Santa Cruz, Bolivia, east through Paraguayan Chaco and S Brazil reportedly to Santa Catarina and perhaps Rio Grande do Sul, possibly there making contact with *melanoblepharus*) Similar to nominate but darker beneath, purpler and less blue on breast and more yellow on back.

P. m. lacerus (S Salta, Tucumán and Catamarca, N Argentina) Similar to last race but with heavier bill, more purple breast and perhaps on average larger (wing 193-209).

REFERENCES Belton (1984), Bond & Meyer de Schauensee (1942), Contreras *et al.* (1991), Dubs (1992), Forshaw (1989), Galetti (1993), Galetti & Rodrigues (1992), Gyldenstolpe (1945b), Nores & Yzurieta (1994), Parker (1993), de la Peña (1988), Pizo *et al.* (1995), Ridgely (1981), Short (1975), Sick (1993), Willis & Oniki (1981).

---

316 SPECKLE-FACED PARROT
Pionus tumultuosus   Plate 79

Other names: Plum-crowned Parrot, Restless Parrot, Tschudi's Parrot (*P. t. tumultuosus*); White- or Grey-headed Parrot, Massena's Parrot (*P. t. seniloides*)

IDENTIFICATION 29cm. Rather scruffy-looking, short-tailed, stocky parrot with pale yellowish-horn bill, white skin around eyes and red undertail-coverts. Face, head and neck either pale vinaceous (Andes of central Peru to Bolivia) or pale grey (Andes from Venezuela to northern Peru) speckled and mottled with white. Northern birds have dull vinaceous breast; those in south are mainly green beneath. Dark eyes contrast with pale ocular skin. Sympatric Red-billed Parrot (314) has red bill. Bronze-winged Parrot (318), sympatric through much of northern Andes, is darker with blue flight feathers, brown upperwing-coverts and different voice. The rare Rusty-faced (309) and Red-faced Parrots (311) of Colombia and Ecuador respectively are readily separated by their red underwing-coverts and faces. Flight of Speckle-faced is fast, direct and often at some height, with typical *Pionus* flight pattern (see under Blue-headed Parrot, 313). Mainly in pairs or small, restless noisy flocks. Sometimes also singly or in larger groups, which might be quite tame.

VOICE A *che-reek* call (piping first note and clicking quality to second), bubbling and squealing noises, some vibrating yapping calls like some amazons, and a harsh deep *vruuuht* repeated 2-3 times. Calls sometimes dramatically change pitch

DISTRIBUTION AND STATUS This is an Andean species ranging from north-west Venezuela to Bolivia. In north-west Venezuela it occurs in Mérida and Táchira and the eastern and central Andean cordilleras in Colombia south through both Andean slopes in Ecuador to Piura in northern Peru, then on the west Andean slope and west side of Marañón Valley, Cajamarca, and on east side of the Marañón in La Libertad. It reappears apparently disjunctly on the east Andean slope in central and southern Peru south from at least Huánuco (perhaps further north) to La Paz, Cochabamba and Santa Cruz, Bolivia, although occurrence may not be continuous through southern Peru. Nomadic over much of range with wide fluctuations in abundance perhaps owing in part to altitudinal migrations. Common locally, but scarcer in northern part of range, except for Loja, southern Ecuador, where quite common. Lower density in north perhaps related to wetter forests there bearing less fruit. Probably declined in northern Andes (especially Venezuela) owing to deforestation but is probably not at immediate risk. Rare in captivity.

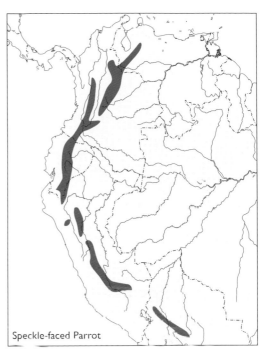

Speckle-faced Parrot

ECOLOGY In south of range the species mainly occupies humid forest in the subtropical zone but also taller cloud-forest with bamboo thickets. Further north it is mostly in the temperate zone and uses elfin woodland, wooded ravines and open areas with trees in the páramo. Birds sometimes enter agricultural land adjacent to forest, often near streams. Recorded 1,400-3,300m but mainly at 2,000-3,000m. Gregarious. Diet comprises fruits and seeds with birds seen taking fruits of *Turpinia paniculata* and a species of Clusiaceae (Huila, Colombia). Also visits maize fields and can cause damage to crop. Breeding Nov-Dec (*tumultuosus*). Usual clutch in captivity four (*tumultuosus*).

DESCRIPTION Forehead and lores vinaceous-pink, paler on chin and upper cheeks where white bases to feathers show as speckles, especially below eyes; feathers on lower cheeks and ear-coverts vinaceous-pink with white bases and bluish-grey tips, giving darker appearance; crown and hindneck paler than forehead with broad white bases to feathers giving mottled effect. Mantle, back and scapulars rather dull green; rump and uppertail-coverts slightly brighter. Upperwing-coverts green with indistinct olive tinge; outer median coverts and primary coverts slightly brighter green. Flight feathers green. Underwing green. Feathers on sides of neck, throat and upper breast mostly green at base with blue or bluish-pink tinge at tips, fading to green on lower breast; underparts otherwise green except undertail-coverts crimson. Tail green centrally, outer feathers green with narrow blue tips and red at base. **Bare parts**: Bill yellowish-horn; iris brown; legs grey.

SEX/AGE Sexes similar. Immature has green on hindneck and cheeks and mainly yellowish-green undertail-coverts.

MEASUREMENTS Wing 175-190; tail 75-86; bill 21-24; tarsus 19-22.

GEOGRAPHICAL VARIATION Two races.

    P. t. tumultuosus (C and S Peru south from at least Huá-nuco to La Paz, Cochabamba and Santa Cruz, Bolivia)

P. t. seniloides (NW Venezuela on Andean slopes south to N Peru) Head, neck and cheeks pale grey heavily speckled and mottled white with large white patch on forehead and forecrown. Breast and belly mainly rather greyish-vinaceous with bluish tips on upper breast. Immature head mainly green with some brownish marks on forehead and forecrown and white speckles on cheeks.

NOTE The two races considered here are frequently treated as separate species. We follow several recent authors in combining these taxa (albeit tentatively) in a single species on the basis of their morphological and ecological similarities.

REFERENCES Cabot & Serrano (1988), Chapman (1926), Desenne & Strahl (1991, 1994), Fjeldså & Krabbe (1990), Forshaw (1989), Hilty & Brown (1986), Koepcke (1961), Meyer de Schauensee (1966), Meyer de Schauensee & Phelps (1978), O'Neill & Parker (1977), Peters & Griswold (1943), Ridgely (1981), Ridgely & Gaulin (1982), Whitney (1996).

---

317 WHITE-CROWNED PARROT
Pionus senilis   Plate 78

Other names: White-capped Parrot

IDENTIFICATION 24cm. Medium-sized, short-tailed, stocky parrot with conspicuous white patch on (otherwise rather dark) head and throat, and speckled brown patches on upperwings. Blue in flight feathers and tail, with red undertail-coverts. Birds appear almost black at distance. Most conspicuous (at least in flight) and common parrot over much of range. Widely sympatric (from Mexico to western Panama) and similarly proportioned Brown-hooded Parrot (302) has red axillaries, no white on head and faster wingbeats, with shriller, higher and more metallic voice. Similar Blue-headed Parrot (313), overlapping in Costa Rica and western Panama, has bright blue on head (no white patch), no blue in flight feathers and slightly shallower wingstroke. Amazons are larger, lack distinctive red undertail-coverts and show red speculum in wings. Flight fast and direct, with typical *Pionus* flight pattern (see under Blue-headed Parrot), usually at some height with flock twisting in unison. Climbs deliberately among branches whilst feeding, rarely fluttering to change perch. Mainly in pairs or small flocks but also seen singly, especially whilst breeding. Fairly wary, flying off shrieking loudly at approach.

VOICE Harsh, often shrieking voice. Taped sounds include a shrieking *tchreeet*, harsh disyllabic *tchreet-er*, and *shreet*. Calls are most frequently heard in flight but birds sometimes screech continuously from tops of tall trees; at other times they remain silent and inconspicuous in tree canopy. Begging young make nasal grunting sound.

DISTRIBUTION AND STATUS Middle America from Mexico to Panama. This bird occurs in the humid tropical zone of eastern Mexico on Caribbean slope from Tamaulipas and eastern San Luis Potosí east through the southern Yucatán Peninsula in Campeche and Quintana Roo, into adjacent Belize and through the northern lowlands and eastern highlands of Guatemala. It is found throughout the Caribbean slope of Honduras mainly below 1,100m (occasionally higher) and on Roatán in the

Bay Islands, and on the Caribbean slope of Nicaragua (possibly also on the Pacific side) to Costa Rica where it stays mainly in the lowlands and foothills of the Caribbean slope, becoming progressively less numerous south from Limón; also on the Pacific slope in southern Costa Rica and on both slopes of adjacent western Panama in western Chiriquí and western Bocas del Toro. Some local migration (also apparently vertical) occurs (e.g. in parts of Oaxaca, Mexico, and parts of Costa Rica). The species is widespread but abundance varies from rather uncommon to very common depending on locality; it is perhaps most numerous in Costa Rica. Despite being frequently eaten by native peoples (at least formerly), persecuted as crop pest, taken in low numbers for live bird trade, and having parts of its range severely deforested, no serious overall decline has as yet been detected.

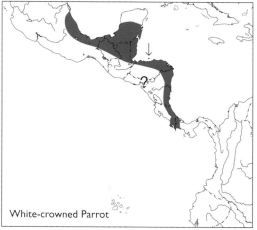

White-crowned Parrot

ECOLOGY Habitat is mainly humid forest (including heavy lowland rain-forest) and woodland but also locally pine–oak formations, savanna and moist lower montane growth. Birds have been reported from woodland and forest edge, cultivated areas and pastures with scattered trees, plantations, secondary woods with emergent trees, wooded streams and, in Costa Rica, at the edge of urban areas. Mainly in lowlands but occurs locally to 2,300m in Guatemala and to c. 1,600m in Costa Rica and 1,800m in Panama. Gregarious, mainly in pairs or (outside breeding season) small flocks; sometimes in larger gatherings of up to several hundred. Food mainly taken in canopy. Specific items include ripening seeds of *Inga* and *Erythrina* and palm fruits; sometimes growing crops of (e.g.) maize and *Sorghum*. Nests in tree-cavity or hollow palm stump. Breeds Mar, Mexico; Jan-Apr, Costa Rica; Feb-May, Honduras. Clutch four (captivity).

DESCRIPTION Forehead, crown and lores pure white. Feathers on cheeks, sides of head behind eyes and hindneck basally green with pale bluish-green or purplish-blue subterminal band and darker blue margins, giving intricate scaly appearance. Mantle and back green with coppery sheen; rump and uppertail-coverts brighter green; scapulars basally green with coppery-bronze on tips and outerwebs. Lesser and median coverts bronze with paler coppery tips giving speckled appearance; primary coverts violet-blue, greater coverts green. Primaries and outer secondaries violet-blue with green tips to outerwebs of primaries and to inner secondaries. Underwing pale bluish-green. Patch on chin and upper throat white;

feathers on breast green at base (mostly concealed) with dark blue or purplish-blue tips and paler blue subterminal band, giving scaly effect; belly generally greener (although variable amount) with less distinct blue scaling; undertail-coverts red. Tail green centrally, outer feathers blue with red at base. **Bare parts**: Bill pale yellowish with slight green tinge; iris dark brown; legs dull yellowish-grey.

SEX/AGE Sexes similar. Immature has head, hindneck and breast green, with pale yellowish margins on cheeks and crown giving pale speckled appearance.

MEASUREMENTS Wing 166-192; tail 61-78; bill 23-27; tarsus 18-21.

GEOGRAPHICAL VARIATION The form *decoloratus*, occurring from the Yucatán Peninsula to western Panama, was previously recognised on the basis of its more purplish (less blue) throat and breast and bluer wings. However, there is much non-geographical variation in *P. senilis* and the above-mentioned characters are not consistent over proposed range.

REFERENCES Binford (1989), Edwards (1972), Forshaw (1989), Griscom (1929, 1932), Howell & Webb (1995), Land (1963, 1970), Lowery & Dalquest (1951), Monroe (1968), Oliver & Austin (1929), Paynter (1955), Peterson & Chalif (1973), Ridgely (1981), Ridgely & Gwynne (1989), Russell (1964), Slud (1964), Smithe (1966), Smithe & Paynter (1963), Stiles *et al.* (1989), Tashian (1952), Wetmore (1968), Whitney (1996).

---

318 BRONZE-WINGED PARROT
Pionus chalcopterus   Plate 79

IDENTIFICATION 29cm. Medium-sized, short-tailed, stocky parrot appearing mainly very dark with contrasting pale patch on throat, further identified by red undertail-coverts, pinkish breast, pale bill and bare ocular skin. Plumage mainly dark cobalt-blue with underwing-coverts rich ultramarine. Upper- and underparts bronzy-green with brown on upperwing-coverts. Very similar Dusky Parrot (319) overlaps in Sierra de Perijá where it is distinguished by duller appearance, pale speckly collar, less coppery upperwing-coverts and browner (not bronzy-green) upper- and underparts. Red billed (314) and Speckle-faced (316) Parrots, sympatric in Andes, are generally paler, (former) with green flight feathers and red bill, (latter) green wings and pale speckling and mottling on head and neck. Flight fast and direct, with typical *Pionus* flight pattern (see under Blue-headed Parrot, 313). Often passes overhead at some height. Mainly in pairs or small flocks of 4-10 birds, sometimes singly.

VOICE Harsh screeching *chee-ee chee-ee chi-ri-ree* recorded from flock in flight. Flocks generally noisy in flight. Calls resemble those of Blue-headed Parrot.

DISTRIBUTION AND STATUS This is a northern Andean parrot present in extreme north-west Venezuela in the Sierra de Perijá, Zulia, and known in adjacent Colombia from scattered localities in all three Andean ranges (on Pacific slope south from Río Atrato area). It occurs on both slopes of the Andes in Ecuador and south into north-west Peru in at least Tumbes and Piura, possibly further south. Nomadic, undertaking some poorly documented seasonal movements. Locally distributed but can be fairly common. Declining in Colombia and western

Ecuador where clearance of subtropical forest on Andean slopes has been severe and rapid. Restricted range in north-west Peru may hold population as small as 500 birds. Extirpated from some former parts of range, e.g. Andean slopes in Cauca and Magdalena Valleys, Colombia, owing to habitat loss. Very scarce in captivity.

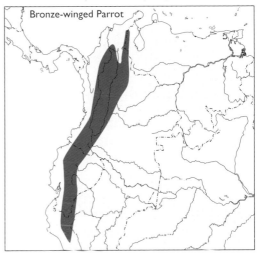
Bronze-winged Parrot

ECOLOGY The species is found mainly in humid and wet upland and montane forest but also in drier deciduous formations on the west Andean slope in Peru; it occurs at forest edge and in partly cleared areas with scattered trees, persisting in such partially cleared areas as long as patches of forest remain. It is chiefly a bird of the upper tropical and subtropical zones but sometimes wanders up to the lower margins of the temperate zone. It is most numerous in the subtropical zone but recorded from near sea-level (western Ecuador), 120m (Venezuela) and 400m (Colombia) to 2,800m (chiefly 1,400-2,400m). Gregarious, especially outside breeding season. Birds observed feeding on fruits of *Guazuma ulmifolia* and flushed from *Ficus* tree in north-west Peru. Mainly forages in canopy. Nests in tree hollow. Breeds Mar-May, Colombia. Clutch two (captivity).

DESCRIPTION Feathers on cheeks, lores, forehead and crown bluish-green basally with darker blue margins giving scaly appearance; hindneck with green bases and darker blue margins. Mantle and back bronzy-green; rump and uppertail-coverts dark cobalt-blue. Scapulars brown with green centres; lesser and median coverts green in centres with bronzy-brown subterminal bands and paler coppery-brown tips that give speckled appearance. Primary coverts, primaries and secondaries cobalt-blue; inner secondaries blue edged brown. Underwing with coverts ultramarine blue, flight feathers bluish-green. Throat with whitish patch fading into variable-sized pinkish area on upper breast (in some birds with pink spots to belly); rest of underparts with bronzy-green or bronzy-brown feathers, many showing narrow blue tips and sometimes with scattered red feathers in centre of belly; undertail-coverts red. Tail dark cobalt-blue with red at base of lateral feathers. **Bare parts**: Bill pale yellowish-horn; cere grey; bare periophthalmic skin whitish; iris dark brown; legs pinkish.

SEX/AGE Sexes similar. Immature has green head and upperparts.

MEASUREMENTS Wing 190-204; tail 74-86; bill 24-27; tarsus 19-22.

GEOGRAPHICAL VARIATION Two races.

P. c. chalcopterus (Sierra de Perijá, NW Venezuela, and Andes of Colombia, except for S part of west slope in Nariño where apparently absent)

P. c. cyanescens (SW Colombia in Nariño, Ecuador and N Peru. One report of *cyanescens* from NW Venezuela is apparently mistaken) Broader blue margins to feathers on breast, belly, mantle and back give stronger and purer blue colour than nominate.

REFERENCES Chapman (1917, 1926), Desenne & Strahl (1991, 1994), Fjeldså & Krabbe (1990), Forshaw (1989), Meyer de Schauensee & Phelps (1978), Parker (1992), Parker *et al.* (1995), Ridgely (1981).

319 DUSKY PARROT
Pionus fuscus   Plate 78

Other names: Little Dusky Parrot, Violet Parrot, Violaceous Parrot

IDENTIFICATION 26cm. Medium-sized, short-tailed, stocky parrot, mainly dull and dark with streaky pale patch on throat and sides of neck, bluish-grey head and browner body. Pale spot on base of otherwise dark upper mandible, small patch of red feathers at base of bill, blue underwing and red undertail-coverts further assist identification. In Sierra de Perijá the similar Bronze-winged Parrot (318) is distinguished by pale speckly collar, duller appearance, less coppery upperwing-coverts and browner (not bronzy-green) upperparts and underparts; in the same locality the similar-sized Red-billed Parrot (314) is told by its greener plumage and red bill. The rather dull Scaly-headed Parrot (315) overlaps in Maranhão, Brazil, but is separated by green flight feathers contrasting with duller body plumage and absence of pale patch on neck. Flight fast and direct, with typical *Pionus* flight pattern (see under Blue-headed Parrot, 313). The similarly proportioned *Pionopsitta* parrots are smaller and their wings go above plane of back in flight. Mainly in pairs or small flocks. Sometimes singly.

VOICE Loud, strident, scolding *screet* calls rapidly repeated by duetting pairs. More metallic disyllabic *street-ah* and trilling *stree-lee-tah* calls from flocks. Often quite noisy and conspicuous but at other times very quiet, even in flight.

DISTRIBUTION AND STATUS There is an isolated population in Sierra de Perijá (Colombia/Venezuela border), after which the species is found in Venezuela south of the Orinoco in Bolívar from the lower Río Caura in the north-west to the Altiplanicie de Nuria, the upper Río Cuyuni and the Sierra de Lema in the border areas with Guyana in the east, extending through the forested parts of Guyana, Surinam and presumably French Guiana (no known records) to Amapá, north-east Brazil, and ranging more widely in the Brazilian Amazon east from the Rio Negro in the north and, in the south, from the Rio Madeira to eastern Pará and Maranhão. Regular seasonal movements occur, Surinam, with birds present in the coastal region in Jul and Aug. Overall fairly common but locally distributed: reported moderately common and widespread in Guyana (although uncommon in the Kanuku Mountains of the south-west); common in the

forests of the coastal sand-ridges, savanna forests and interior of Surinam. Severe and rapid deforestation in parts of its range (e.g. Pará and Maranhão, Brazil) is presumably causing a decline. Rather scarce in captivity.

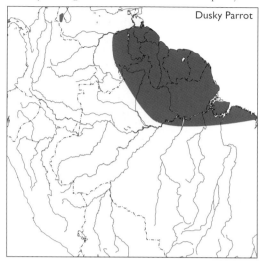

Dusky Parrot

ECOLOGY Habitat is mainly lowland rain-forest and humid forest in foothills where birds spend most time in canopy; chiefly in terra firme forest, occasionally in várzea and less often in igapó (permanently flooded forest), but also reported from savanna (Surinam), coastal gallery forest (French Guiana) and cultivated areas (albeit avoiding more open habitat and seen less often in clearings or at forest edge than some close relatives, such as Blue-headed Parrot). Occurs in Venezuela from sea-level to c. 1,000m, and at c. 1,200-1,800m on the Colombian side of the Sierra de Perijá. Gregarious, especially outside breeding season. Feeds chiefly in canopy but may drop lower to fruiting trees in clearings. Diet includes seeds of *Eschweilera* and *Micropholis*. Nests high up in tree-hollow. Appears mainly to breed Feb-May but nest reported Nov, Pará, Brazil. Clutch 3-4.

DESCRIPTION Small patch of feathers on front of lores at base of cere rose-red; otherwise lores, cheeks, forehead and crown pale lavender-blue with white bases to feathers on crown giving faint speckled appearance in some birds; ear-coverts darker and greyer forming distinct patch; feathers on throat and sides of neck white with narrow brown stripe in centre with pale lavender blue tips, forming rather streaky, incomplete collar. Feathers on mantle and back plumbeous-brown with pale margins, giving scalloped effect, especially anteriorly; scapulars, rump and uppertail-coverts darker plumbeous-brown with very faint (or absent) pale margins. Lesser and median coverts plumbeous-brown with pale margins; primary and greater coverts and flight feathers deep cobalt-blue. Underwing deep blue. Feathers on upper part of breast pale pinkish-brown with pale lavender tips; lower breast browner with less distinct lavender tinge, becoming darker and more vinaceous on belly with centre of belly in some birds rich wine colour; undertail-coverts crimson. Tail blue with red at base. **Bare parts**: Upper mandible blackish at tip with pale horn patch at base, lower mandible blackish with narrow paler base visible in some birds; bare periophthalmic skin buffy; iris dark brown; legs grey.

SEX/AGE Sexes similar. Immature has green on secondaries and on primary and greater coverts and perhaps lacks white on throat.

MEASUREMENTS Wing 160-180; tail 63-75; bill 22-26; tarsus 18-21.

GEOGRAPHICAL VARIATION None.

REFERENCES Arndt (1996), Desenne (1994), Desenne & Strahl (1991, 1994), Forshaw (1989), Haverschmidt (1968), Hilty & Brown (1986), Meyer de Schauensee (1966), Meyer de Schauensee & Phelps (1978), Parker et al. (1993), Ridgely (1981), Sick (1993), Snyder (1966), Tostain et al (1992).

---

320 CUBAN AMAZON
Amazona leucocephala   Plate 80

Other names: White-headed Amazon Parrot, Caribbean Amazon Parrot, Cuban Parrot (all races but often specifically nominate); Bahamas (Amazon) Parrot (*A. l. bahamensis*); Grand Cayman (Amazon) Parrot (*A. l. caymanensis*), Cayman Brac (Amazon) Parrot (*A. l. hesterna*); Western Cuban (Amazon) Parrot (*A. l. palmarum*)

IDENTIFICATION 32cm. Mainly green, rather large parrot with short tail, pale bill, white on head, red throat and cheeks, blue in flight feathers and vinaceous feathers on belly. Dark edges to green feathers gives distinct (sometimes heavily) barred effect, especially on nape, mantle, upperwing-coverts, sides of neck and breast. No similar species within range but distinguished from other *Amazona* in captivity by combination of red throat and cheeks and white extending from cere around eyes to crown. Adult male Yellow-lored (321), White-fronted (323), Hispaniolan (322) and Yellow-billed Amazons (321) all show white on heads, however, first distinguished by yellow lores and all by absence of red on throat (pinkish-vinaceous throat in Yellow-billed). Blunt head and fast wingbeats aid identification in poor light. Generally in noisy flocks; pairs or smaller groups whilst breeding. Birds may be quite tame in remote areas.

VOICE Variety of loud whistles, shrieks and screeches, some calls with trumpet-like qualities. Drawn-out, resonant, vibrating calls and loud scolding *yaaart yaaaa* rapidly repeated on single note. Some disyllabic calls suggest sound of braying donkey. Voice sometimes audible at considerable distance.

DISTRIBUTION AND STATUS Cuba, Isle of Pines, Bahamas and Cayman Islands. Formerly all of Cuba but now rare or extirpated in much of island. Still occurs all provinces locally but remains common in only a few strongholds including the Zapata and Guanahacabibes peninsulas and in Sierra de Najasa. Cuban population estimated at c. 5,000 (1988). Occurs Isle of Pines (Isla de la Juventud) where it severely declined in 20th century, especially during 1960s, with largest population surviving in Ciénaga de Lanier. Formerly on all major islands in the Bahamas but extirpated except for Great Inagua (patchily distributed over south, east and north) and Abaco (mostly in southern third). May visit Little Inagua from Great Inagua. Mainly in central and eastern parts of Grand Cayman where habitat loss least severe. Relict population persists on Cayman Brac but extinct on Little Cayman

around 1932. Mostly resident but some seasonal movements, e.g. in Isle of Pines where birds possibly (at least formerly) moved to coast from dry interior in non-breeding season. About 1,000 birds survive on each of Great Inagua and Abaco, Bahamas. Grand Cayman population between 674 and 1,239 birds (1985). In serious danger of being lost from Cayman Brac with 93-134 birds (1991). Decline throughout range is due to habitat destruction and trapping of live birds (for pets locally and export). Poor breeding success on Grand Cayman in 1970s was due to mosquito attacks on nestlings. Ground-nesting birds on Abaco taken by feral cats. Hurricanes may cause shortages of nest-sites and food. Probably stable Bahamas but declining overall. Cannot be considered secure in most of range. CITES Appendix I. NEAR-THREATENED.

Cuban Amazon

ECOLOGY Inhabits pine forest, broadleaved woodland (including dry evergreen formations), palm groves, mangroves and plantations, also cultivated land with trees in some areas and may visit gardens to feed on fruiting trees. Generally in small groups whilst foraging but larger groups where food abundant; pairs or family parties distinguishable in flocks. More usually in pairs whilst breeding. Roosts communally outside breeding season. Diet includes unopened leaf bud of *Roystonea* palm, cones and new tender shoots of *Pinus caribea*, *Coccoloba uvifera* and *Conocarpus erectus*, fruits and seeds of *Smilex*, *Sabal*, *Duranta*, *Exothea*, *Linodia*, *Tabebuia*, *Acacia*, *Metopium*, *Tetrazygia*, *Swietenia*, *Cupania* and *Lysiloma*. Birds are sometimes persecuted for damaging cultivated fruits and grain such as mango (*Mangifera*). Nests in palm cavity or tree-hollow created by e.g. termites or woodpecker. Breeds in vertical solution cavities in limestone on Abaco where tree nest-sites unavailable. Breeding Mar-mid summer, Cuba and Abaco. Clutch 3-4.

DESCRIPTION Plumage rather variable with body colour ranging from bright green to olive, some birds with scattered yellow feathers on wings and back. Forehead, forecrown, lores and area around eyes white; lower cheeks and throat pinkish-red; feathers of hindcrown and nape bluish-green with black margins giving heavy barred effect; similar pattern on sides of neck but bluish tinge absent; ear-coverts charcoal grey. Feathers of back and mantle green with black distal margins but barring less heavy than on nape and head; rump and uppertail-coverts green with faint dark margins to some feathers on rump. Alula, greater coverts and flight feathers blue on outerweb, grey on inner; remaining coverts green with dark margins, showing most distinct barring on lesser coverts. Underwing with coverts green with dark margins, flight feathers grey.

Breast green with dark margins to most feathers; feathers on belly with vinaceous base showing green at margins forming a variable-sized patch, barely noticeable in some birds, striking in others; thighs green or with some vinaceous feathers; undertail-coverts green. Tail feathers green with red at base. **Bare parts**: Bill yellowish-horn; iris reddish-brown; legs yellowish-brown.

SEX/AGE Sexes similar but male *caymanensis* reportedly larger and brighter than female. Immature generally shows fewer black edges to body feathers and less vinaceous on belly.

MEASUREMENTS Wing 183-204; tail 100-111; bill 23-27; tarsus 21-23.

GEOGRAPHICAL VARIATION Five races. Some authors doubt the validity of *palmarum* and *caymanensis*; the situation is confused by plumage variation within races.

A. l. leucocephala (Cuba east of Las Villas province)

A. l. palmarum (Isle of Pines and Cuba west of Las Villas province) Like nominate but with larger, darker vinaceous patch on belly and deeper red on throat. Perhaps also on average darker green.

A. l. caymanensis (Grand Cayman) From other races by turquoise tinge on breast and rump and pinkish (sometimes yellowish) suffusion in white feathers of head. Plumage more yellowish and less heavily barred than nominate (especially beneath and on upperwing-coverts), with less white on head and much less pronounced vinaceous patch on belly.

A. l. hesterna (Cayman Brac and formerly Little Cayman) Smaller and darker than nominate and *caymanensis*, most individuals with red confined to spot beneath eye and smaller white patch on crown, which lacks the pinkish tinge of *caymanensis*. Vinaceous patch on belly more extensive than last race.

A. l. bahamensis (Abaco and Great Inagua, Bahamas; previously on several other islands but now extinct) Larger than nominate with slaty-blue hindcrown and more extensive white on head. Vinaceous feathers on belly reduced or absent and red on underside of tail less extensive.

NOTE Some authors consider Cuban Amazon conspecific with Hispaniolan. However, rather pronounced morphological differences suggest they are distinct.

REFERENCES Arndt (1996), Barbour (1922), Bond (1956, 1969, 1980), Bradley & Rey-Millet (1985), Brudenell-Bruce (1975), Brykczynski (1987), Buden (1987), Forshaw (1989), King (1981), Noegel & Moss (1991), Rutgers & Norris (1979), Todd (1916), Wiley (1991).

---

321 YELLOW-BILLED AMAZON
Amazona collaria   Plate 80

Other names: Yellow-billed Parrot, Red-throated Amazon, Jamaican Amazon

IDENTIFICATION 27-30cm. Mainly vivid apple-green medium-sized parrot with short tail, blue on head and wings, narrow white forehead, pinkish throat and yellow bill sometimes conspicuous in flight. Yellowish-green tail (rosy at base) has yellow rim. Sympatric with scarcer Jamaican endemic Black-billed Amazon (325), but is slightly larger, paler and greener, with pale bill, white

forehead and pinkish throat, and more often fans its tail. Most likely confused with Cuban Amazon (320) in captivity, latter being somewhat larger with more extensive white on head (extending over forecrown around and behind eye) and deeper red on throat. Flight on shallow rapid wingbeats. Generally in small noisy flocks or pairs; sometimes in mixed flocks with Black-billed Amazon. Birds appear much darker when plumage is wet after bathing in rain. Cautious, unapproachable and easily overlooked whilst perched quietly in foliage.

VOICE Very vocal, especially in flight. Birds usually only quiet at night and during midday rest period. High-pitched screams, squawks and screeches reported including *ah-ah-eeeek* (rising on last note) and *whip-whip-waaaaark* in flight. Loud squawks at roost in early morning audible up to 3km. Quieter muttering sounds whilst preening.

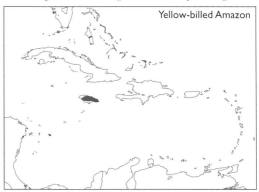
Yellow-billed Amazon

DISTRIBUTION AND STATUS Endemic to Jamaica in Greater Antilles. Chiefly in remoter (often hilly and mountainous) districts. Largest populations in centre of island from the Cockpit Country to Mount Diablo and in eastern Jamaica in the John Crow Mountains. Birds in the eastern Blue Mountains thought to be visitors from John Crow range. Also reported from the drier Hellshire Hills and Portland Ridge in south but current status there unknown. Birds in Kingston area may be escaped captives. Resident but wanders widely within rather restricted range. Still fairly common in suitable habitat but overall decline in range and population in recent decades owing principally to habitat loss and trapping for the live bird trade. Birds possibly also susceptible to loss of nest-sites and food plants caused by hurricanes. Listed as threatened by Jamaican government (1986) but not thought in immediate danger. However, continuing loss of habitat to shifting cultivation, forestry and bauxite mining, and possibly continuing illegal capture for trade, are fuelling a long-term decline. NEAR-THREATENED.

ECOLOGY Mostly in mid-level wet limestone forest (annual rainfall 1,900-4,500mm) with (e.g.) emergent *Terminalia latifolia* and *Cedrela odorata*, more arid upland forest and cultivated areas with trees, especially at the edge of forest; from sea-level to 1,200m in Cockpit Country. Generally in pairs or flocks up to c. 40; larger gatherings where food abundant (e.g. one report of 60 feeding in orange tree). Forms large communal roosts outside breeding season and sometimes seen in association with Black-billed Amazon and Olive-throated Conure (242). Birds wander widely, foraging closer to roosting site later in day. Reported food items include catkins of *Cecropia*, *Anacardium occidentale* nuts, fruits of *Pimenta dioica* and figs

Ficus, and seeds of *Melia azedarach*; birds observed feeding on oranges took only seeds, leaving fleshy fruit. Forages in middle and upper storeys. Nests in cavity high (at least 15m) in forest tree (frequently *Brosimum*) with hollow enlarged in successive years. Birds often use cavity initially excavated by Jamaican Woodpecker *Melanerpes radiolatus*. Nesting also reported in rock crevices. Courtship from Jan with eggs Mar-May. Clutch 3-4 (usually four).

DESCRIPTION Narrow band on forehead white; lores and upper cheeks with white-based blue feathers; crown blue with black tips, merging on hindcrown, sides of neck and nape into green feathers with black tips; feathers on sides of neck sometimes basally pink; ear-coverts greyish-blue with black tips. Mantle and back apple-green with black tips (latter becoming less pronounced lower down); lower back, rump and uppertail-coverts brighter yellowish green. Greater wing-coverts blue; remainder apple green. Alula and outerwebs of flight feathers blue, innerwebs dark grey. Underwing with coverts green, flight feathers bluish-green. Throat and lower cheek pinkish, sometimes tipped green; breast to belly yellowish apple-green; undertail-coverts yellowish green. Uppertail green with yellowish tips and red at base; undertail duller and more olive. **Bare parts** Bill yellowish-horn, iris brown; legs pinkish.

SEX/AGE During breeding pink throat of male becomes more brilliant and green plumage takes on metallic qualities; sexes otherwise similar. Males perhaps average slightly larger. Immature similar to adult.

MEASUREMENTS Wing 178-193; tail 88-102; bill 24-30, tarsus 18-22.

GEOGRAPHICAL VARIATION None.

REFERENCES Cruz & Gruber (1981), Downer *et al.* (1990), Fairbairn (1981), Forshaw (1989), Stebbing-Allen *in litt.* (1992), Varty (1991), Wiley (1991).

---

322 HISPANIOLAN AMAZON
Amazona ventralis   Plate 80

Other names: Sallé's Amazon Parrot, Santo Domingo Amazon, Hispaniolan Parrot

IDENTIFICATION 28cm. Mainly green, medium sized, short-tailed parrot with white forehead and eye-ring, pale bill and dark patch on ear-coverts. More yellowish on underparts with undertail-coverts and most of undertail pale greenish-yellow. Further identified by blue flight feathers (including undersides), blue crown and maroon patch on belly. Feathers of upper body (especially head and nape) have dark margins giving barred effect. Distinguished from closely related (allopatric) Cuban Amazon (320) by absence of large red throat-patch. Combination of white forehead, dark ear-coverts, blue crown and maroon belly separates Hispaniolan from other *Amazona* in captivity. Flight rather duck-like on short rapid wingbeats. Approach of flock often signalled by loud screeching. Birds pass at some height in morning and evening en route between roost and foraging areas; otherwise flies mostly over canopy.

VOICE Loud screeching and squawking in flight. Quieter growling and chattering noises at rest or whilst feeding. Shrill staccato call and clucking and whining reported during courtship in captivity.

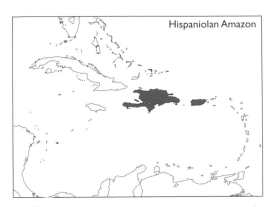

Hispaniolan Amazon

DISTRIBUTION AND STATUS Islands of Hispaniola (Dominican Republic and Haiti), Gonâve (Haiti), Saona (Dominican Republic), Puerto Rico and probably Culebra (Puerto Rico) in the West Indies. Found in moderate numbers in parts of Sierra de Baoruco, Sierra Neiba and Cordillera Central in Dominican Republic. More restricted and less numerous in Haiti with remaining population apparently largely in southern part of country. Introduced Puerto Rico where feral population derived from escaped captives and at least one consignment of illegally traded birds released after attempted import to Puerto Rico discovered. Also feral in US Virgin Islands. Formerly common Hispaniola but drastic decline during 20th century owing primarily to habitat destruction (arising from e.g. agriculture and charcoal production). Also persecuted owing to crop damage, shot for food and trapped for pets and live bird trade. By 1930s largely confined to interior mountain forests of Hispaniola. Although remains locally common, mainly uncommon to rare in natural range. Has been treated as endangered but threat of extinction probably not immediate. Population in Puerto Rico is at least several hundred and apparently increasing. Breeds readily in captivity and used as surrogate parent to rear young Puerto Rican Parrot (326) as part of recovery programme for that (highly endangered) species. NEAR-THREATENED.

ECOLOGY Wide variety of wooded habitats from arid lowland palm savannas to upland pine forest and humid montane evergreen forest. Now most commonly in mountain forest in Hispaniola owing to continuing deforestation, but birds do feed at lower altitude as well. Reported to above 1,500m (Hispaniola). In pairs whilst breeding; otherwise in small flocks usually up to about a dozen birds; much larger gatherings up to 500 birds reported in the 19th century. Pairs and pairs with young often identifiable in flock. Reported food items include seeds or fruits of *Caesalpinia*, *Psidium* and *Ficus*, seeds of wild oranges *Citrus*, maize and bananas. Nests generally in tree-cavity but also reported in rock crevice, hollow in cactus and cavity in coconut palm. Aggressively territorial whilst breeding. Breeds Feb-May. Clutch 2-3.

DESCRIPTION Forehead and lores white (extent variable); crown and upper cheeks with black-tipped blue feathers; ear-coverts and lower cheeks charcoal (extent variable); feathers on nape and sides of neck emerald-green with distinct black tips. Mantle and back grass-green with black tips, latter becoming progressively less distinct lower down; rump green, slightly yellowish; uppertail-coverts yellowish-green. Greater coverts blue, remaining coverts grass-green. Primaries and secondaries blue, darker towards tips on innerwebs. Underwing with coverts green, flight feathers bluish-green. Underparts mostly green, slightly yellowish, with most feathers showing rather indistinct black margins (especially in upper region) but sometimes with a few red feathers on chin; variably sized maroon patch in centre of belly; undertail-coverts pale greenish-yellow. Uppertail green (perhaps a little darker than rest of upperparts) with indistinct yellowish tip and outerwebs of outer feathers with blue margins; undertail yellowish with bases of outer feathers red. **Bare parts**: Bill pinkish-horn; cere pale brownish-white; bare periophthalmic skin white; iris brown; legs dull pale grey.

SEX/AGE No sexual dimorphism. Immature like adult but less blue on crown and maroon abdominal patch paler.

MEASUREMENTS Wing 171-202; tail 91-105; bill 24-29; tarsus 19-24.

GEOGRAPHICAL VARIATION None.

NOTE Some authors consider Hispaniolan Amazon conspecific with Cuban. Although closely related, they are believed distinct because of rather pronounced plumage differences.

REFERENCES Bond (1965), Dod (1992), Forshaw (1989), Schwartz (1970), Sjodahl (1985), Wetmore & Swales (1931), Wiley (1991).

---

323 WHITE-FRONTED AMAZON
Amazona albifrons   Plate 81

Other names: Spectacled Amazon (Parrot), White-browed Amazon (Parrot), White-fronted Parrot

IDENTIFICATION 23-26cm. Mainly green, medium-sized parrot with short tail, red on face, white forehead and (in male only) splash of red on upperwing conspicuous in flight. Sympatric in Yucatán Peninsula (and reported to flock) with very similar Yellow-lored Amazon (324), which see for differences. White-crowned Parrot (317), overlapping in southern Mexico and Central America, is smaller with white throat, reddish on lower belly, and deeper wingbeats. White-fronted generally occurs in pairs or small flocks, flying with shallow wingbeats that do not go above horizontal. Birds often fly close to tree-tops and show continually veering flight that uncharacteristic of genus and more like *Aratinga*.

VOICE Loud and varied. Calls include a squealing *ca-ca-ca-ca* (sounding rather like sympatric Orange-fronted Conure), barking *yack-yack-yack*, loud harsh *crack crack*, loud, harsh and trilling *graaaht*, more level but still harsh *sceeet*, disyllabic *sceee-at* and short sharp *claaat* calls. Some calls with trumpeting quality.

DISTRIBUTION AND STATUS The species ranges in Mexico from southern Sonora (north to about 28°N) throughout Sinaloa and western Durango south through the Pacific region to Oaxaca and north across Isthmus of Tehuantepec to the Atlantic coast in southern Veracruz and east through Tabasco to all of Yucatán Peninsula, including northern Guatemala and Belize. It is present in southern Chiapas and the Pacific lowlands of Guatemala and reportedly western El Salvador, extending through the Pacific lowlands, arid interior and Caribbean lowlands of Honduras to the Pacific north-west of Costa Rica and

into Nicaragua (where no details on distribution). Mostly resident but seasonal visitor in some parts of range (e.g. Yucatán, western El Salvador and mountains of eastern Guatemala). Generally common and with Orange-fronted Conure (243) is the most numerous parrot on the Pacific slope of Central America; but evidently scarce in some areas. Deforestation is possibly promoting population increases on the Caribbean slope of Central America, but birds are taken for the pet trade and hunted for food in e.g. Yucatán, where a decline may recently have occurred owing to persecution of parrots feeding on cultivated fruit after loss of wild food to effects of Hurricane Gilbert.

White-fronted Amazon

ECOLOGY This adaptable parrot uses all kinds of wooded habitats and open country with trees including moist, seasonal semi-evergreen and deciduous forest (especially at edge), pine woodlands, gallery forest, ranchland with stands of open woodland, savanna and arid tropical scrub with cacti, tending to frequent more open areas on the Caribbean slope. It generally prefers drier woodlands but where sympatric with Yellow-lored Amazon it tends to be in more humid and closed vegetation. In Yucatán it inhabits coastal coconut plantations whilst breeding. Reported to 900m (Oaxaca), 1,800m (Honduras) and 1,500m (southern Sonora: only known record outside tropical zone). In pairs when breeding but generally gregarious, occurring mostly in small flocks, with gatherings of hundreds occasionally reported and some communal roosts (e.g. in mangroves) reported to hold several thousand birds. Recorded food items include pods of *Acacia gaumeri* (Yucatán), fruits of *Lemaireocereus thurberi* and *Pachycereus* cacti and buds of *Jatropha cordata* (Sonora), *Ehretia tinifolia* and *Metopium browneii* (Campeche); also cultivated fruit such as mango and grain including maize. Birds often excited and vocal whilst feeding. Nests in tree, palm cavity or arboreal termitarium, sometimes in cavity excavated by woodpecker; *Bursera simaruba* and *Caesalpinia gaumeri* are among favoured nest-tree species in Yucatán. Breeding Jan-Jul, depending on locality.

DESCRIPTION Forehead white; lores, upper cheeks and ring of feathers around eyes red; pale blue crown merges with green of nape, which is tipped very faintly and narrowly with black and sometimes with pale blue subterminal band; sides of neck green with narrow black margins. Mantle, back and scapulars grass-green, sometimes with olive tinge; mantle with very indistinct black tips; rump green, perhaps with more emerald hue than rest of upperparts. Greater coverts and alula red, other coverts green. Outerwebs of primaries green becoming blue at tips; outerwebs of secondaries blue; innerwebs of flight feathers blackish. Underwing bluish-green. Underparts green with faint blackish edges to feathers on throat and breast. Uppertail green tipped yellow centrally, outer feathers red at base, blue on outer-webs; uppertail yellowish green. **Bare parts**: Bill dull horn, darker at tip; bare periophthalmic skin pale grey; iris pale yellow; legs pale grey.

SEX/AGE Female like male but alula and primary coverts green, although some older individuals may show some red. Immature like female but with forecrown tinged yellow. Subadult male often has some green on primary coverts.

MEASUREMENTS Wing 170-190; tail 81-101; bill 23-28; tarsus 18-22.

GEOGRAPHICAL VARIATION Three races.

A. a. albifrons (Pacific Mexico from Nayarit to Oaxaca and S Chiapas into Pacific lowlands of Guatemala. Birds in N Guatemalan lowlands and arid interior are referable to *nana*)

A. a. saltuensis (Sonora, Sinaloa and Durango, Mexico) Similar to nominate but plumage strongly suffused blue. Blue of crown extends to nape.

A. a. nana (Veracruz to Costa Rica, including entire Yucatán Peninsula) Smaller than nominate (wing 154-175, most not exceeding 170). Poorly differentiated from nominate but green of plumage perhaps paler, more yellowish. Some individuals from Pacific coast show some red on throat.

REFERENCES Binford (1989), Cano *et al* (1990), Clinton-Eitniear (1988a), Davis & Bennett (1972), Dicky & van Rossem (1933), Edwards (1972), Forshaw (1989), Friedmann *et al.* (1950), Griscom (1932), Kantak (1970), Land (1970), Levinson (1981), Monroe (1964), Paynter (1955), Peterson & Chalif (1973), Ridgely (1981), van Rossem (1945), Russell (1964), Short (1974), Slud (1964), Smithe (1966), Wetmore (1943, 1944).

---

324 YELLOW-LORED AMAZON
Amazona xantholora   Plate 81

Other names: Yucatan Amazon (Parrot)

IDENTIFICATION 26cm. Mainly green medium-sized parrot with short tail, white crown, dark ear-coverts and broad red patch around eyes, plus bright yellow lores (not easy to see at distance), blue flight feathers and red at base of tail. Male has bright red primary coverts conspicuous in flight. Sympatric with White-fronted Amazon (323) in Yucatán Peninsula where sometimes in mixed flocks and difficult to distinguish: under favourable field conditions Yellow-lored is more heavily scalloped with black, has yellow (not red) lores and dark ear-coverts; female has blue (not white) crown. Also overlaps in south of range with White-crowned Parrot (317), which is smaller with white throat, reddish on lower belly and deeper wingbeats. From other *Amazona* in captivity by yellow lores with white (blue in female) crown. In flocks in wooded country, especially at forest edge. Birds sometimes make off very close to ground when disturbed, and are inconspicuous whilst feeding quietly in foliage.

VOICE Vocalisations rather similar to those of White-fronted Amazon.

DISTRIBUTION AND STATUS The species occurs chiefly in the eastern and central parts of the Yucatán Peninsula,

Mexico, in Yucatán, Campeche and Quintana Roo; in northern parts of Belize; and on the islands of Cozumel (Mexico) and possibly Roatán (Honduras), where recent fieldwork failed to confirm its present (or former) occurrence. Common to fairly common in eastern Yucatán and on Cozumel but considered rather rare in some other parts (especially at edges) of Mexican range. Thought scarcer overall than closely related White-fronted Amazon but in some areas Yellow-lored is commoner, especially towards centre of range. Declining through deforestation (especially in north of range) and capture for trade. Occurs in several protected areas. Status in northern Belize unknown.

Yellow-lored Amazon

ECOLOGY In Yucatán birds mostly inhabit tropical deciduous forest, probably avoiding dense rain-forest. However, their exact preferences are unknown owing to the difficulty of distinguishing them from White-fronted Amazons in the field. Reported from pine *Pinus* and mixed pine and oak *Quercus* forests in northern Belize, and pine forests on high ground on Roatán. Generally in flocks, forming communal roosts of up to 1,500 birds. Birds disperse from roost in small foraging flocks. Reported food items include pods of *Acacia gaumeri*, maize and citrus fruits. Birds mostly feed in tree-tops. Nests in tree-cavity in ranchlands and around cornfields where dead trees have been left standing after felling and burning of forest. Breeding-condition birds reported Mar, Yucatán Peninsula, and young in nest Apr-May, Belize.

DESCRIPTION Lores and narrow frontal band bright yellow; most of forehead and crown white; hindcrown blue; broad band around eye including upper cheeks (but not loral area) bright red; ear-coverts dark charcoal grey. Upperparts grass-green with prominent black tips to feathers giving scalloped appearance, but uppertail-coverts yellowish-green. Primary coverts red; remaining (especially lesser and median) coverts green with black tips. Flight feathers mostly blue with green base to primaries. Underwing bluish-green. Underparts green with black tips to feathers heaviest on breast, but undertail-coverts yellowish-green. Uppertail green; undertail green with yellowish tip and outer feathers basally red. **Bare parts**: Bill yellowish-horn; iris yellow; legs grey.

SEX/AGE Female has blue (not white) crown, little or no red around eye, and green primary coverts. Immature like female but lores duller yellow and crown paler blue.

MEASUREMENTS Wing 164-177; tail 73-85; bill 24-26; tarsus 19-20.

GEOGRAPHICAL VARIATION None.

REFERENCES Cano *et al.* (1990), Davis & Bennett (1972), Edwards (1972), Forshaw (1989), Friedmann *et al.* (1950), Howell & Webb (1992), Monroe (1968), Paynter (1955), Peterson & Chalif (1973), Ridgely (1981), Russell (1964).

325 BLACK-BILLED AMAZON
Amazona agilis   Plate 81

Other names: Black-billed Parrot, All-green Amazon, Active Amazon

IDENTIFICATION 25-27cm. Mainly green, medium-sized, short-tailed parrot with blue in flight feathers and red primary coverts (partly green in female). Sympatric with commoner Jamaican endemic Yellow-billed Amazon (321), which see for differences. Differs from other *Amazona* in captivity by combination of almost entirely green head (sometimes with one or two red feathers in frontal area), green nape, rump and breast. Often overlooked whilst feeding in dense foliage; more conspicuous in flight. Birds often located by raucous calls. Generally very wary, seldom permitting close approach. If disturbed whilst feeding, birds become silent and still, thus very difficult to detect until taking flight.

VOICE Birds disperse from roost making loud pleasant calls. Soft bubbly tones audible at close quarters. Growling and whistling sounds made whilst defending nest-site from intruders. Voice higher-pitched than Yellow-billed Amazon.

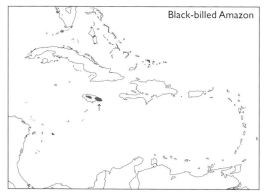
Black-billed Amazon

DISTRIBUTION AND STATUS Endemic to Jamaica, being found in the centre of the island from Cockpit Country to Mount Diablo, including the interior hills in Trelawny and St Ann and Dry Harbour Mountains, and in the eastern uplands where formerly more widespread but now only at one or two restricted localities in the John Crow Mountains. Probably resident but some seasonal movements may occur in relation to fruiting tree distribution. Formerly more widespread and common; despite evident recent decline (especially in east where now rare) still locally common. Total population thought to be less than 10,000. Continuing slow decline appears inevitable in the face of habitat loss to shifting cultivation, forestry and perhaps bauxite mining. Hurricane damage to forest habitat is persistent threat, especially when already in decline owing to other pressures. Perhaps also under pressure from continuing illegal taking of young birds for live bird trade. VULNERABLE.

ECOLOGY Primarily in mid-level wet limestone forest (annual rainfall 1,990-4,500mm) but also in agricultural plots in forest and cultivated land at forest edge. Generally in flocks of about 6-40 birds but sometimes many more (200 reported in single flock). Flocks sometimes mixed with Yellow-billed Amazon and Olive-throated Conure (242). Roosts communally, with birds dispersing to foraging areas in pairs or small flocks. Birds bathe in rain showers sometimes swinging upside-down on perch with wings held across breast so that primaries touch in middle. Feeds on seeds, fruits, berries, leaf buds and blossoms obtained mostly in middle and upper branches of forest trees, reported food items including fruits of ripe plantain *Musa*, *Cecropia*, *Ficus*, *Nectandra*, *Bryophyllum*, *Blighia sapida* and *Melia azedarach* and seeds of *Pimenta dioica*, also cultivated plants like maize and mango. Birds forage most intensively in the morning and afternoon and take water twice daily, usually drinking from a bromeliad but sometimes directly from stream. Nests in tree-cavity, including old woodpecker hole, at some height (at least 18m) in forest tree. Territorial whilst nesting but apparently little competition with Yellow-billed for nest-sites. Courtship and nest-site preparation from late Jan and Feb with breeding Mar-May. Clutch 2-3, more rarely four.

DESCRIPTION Forehead, lores, crown and cheeks emerald-green with slight blue suffusion on crown, frontal area sometimes with some red feathers; nape and sides of neck emerald-green with some showing narrow blackish margins giving slight barred effect; ear-coverts sometimes with blackish tinge. Upperparts grass-green, rump with slightly paler margins. Primary coverts red; other coverts grass-green. Primaries blue, secondaries darker blue. Underwing with coverts bluish-green, flight feathers blackish-grey. Underparts green with yellowish tinge. Uppertail grass-green; undertail yellowish; both sides with outer feathers red at base of innerwebs. **Bare parts**: Bill dark brown, paler towards tip; iris dark brown; legs blackish-grey.

SEX/AGE Female sometimes separable by fewer red primary coverts (green instead) but consistency of this difference unknown; also perhaps on average smaller on wing and tail length but clearly considerable overlap. Immature similar to adult, but primary coverts green, male showing mixture of red and green primary coverts when in moult to adult plumage; also possibly duller on head without blue suffusion and brightness of emerald in adult.

MEASUREMENTS Wing 159-176; tail 75-89; bill 23-25; tarsus 20-21.

GEOGRAPHICAL VARIATION None.

REFERENCES Collar *et al.* (1994), Cruz & Gruber (1981), Downer *et al.* (1990), Fairbairn (1981), Forshaw (1989), Stebbing-Allen *in litt.* (1992), Varty (1991), Wiley (1991).

326 PUERTO RICAN AMAZON
Amazona vittata   Plate 80

Other names: Puerto Rican Parrot, Red-fronted Amazon

IDENTIFICATION 29cm. Mainly green, medium-sized, short-tailed and extremely rare parrot, with red forehead, blue in flight feathers and more yellowish on underparts, rump and uppertail-coverts. Feathers of head, nape and throat in particular, but also generally on upper body, have black margins giving distinct barred pattern. Hispaniolan Amazon (322), introduced Puerto Rico, told by conspicuous white forehead and maroon patch on belly. Unknown in captivity outside official captive breeding programme in Puerto Rico. Last remnant population inhabits montane rain-forest in eastern Puerto Rico where birds may be encountered in pairs or small flocks.

VOICE Wide variety of whistles, squawks, bugle-like sounds and other calls combined in very complex repertoire that may be particular to each bird.

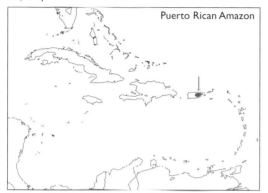

Puerto Rican Amazon

DISTRIBUTION AND STATUS Puerto Rico and formerly neighbouring islands of Mona and Culebra; reports of parrots on Vieques and St Thomas are probably of this species. Once found throughout forested regions of Puerto Rico (with possible exception of dry southern coastal strip) but since around 1960 confined to Luquillo Forest in east. Drastic decline in population and range from mid-19th century. Pre-European population probably several hundred thousand. About 2,000 (minimum) remained in 1937 and by 1950s about 200 were left; a 1968 search revealed only 24 birds. Just 16 birds existed in 1972 with 13 (all-time low) in 1975. Conservation programme, initiated in 1968, has included captive breeding, nest-site provision, detailed research on ecology and reproductive biology and control of predators and competitors. In 1992 wild population at 39-40 birds with 58 in captivity (all in Puerto Rico). Decline to near extinction caused mainly by habitat loss (by 1912 only 1% of island's virgin forests remained), hunting and taking for pets. Continuing threats to tiny remaining population include impact of hurricanes (wild population halved to 21-23 birds after passage of hurricane Hugo in 1989), competition with introduced honeybees *Apis mellifera* for tree cavities, loss of young to parasitic warble-flies *Philornis pici*, natural predation and competition for nesting cavities with Pearly-eyed Thrashers *Margarops fuscatus*. Birds on Culebra (dubiously separated as race *gracilipes*) extinct early 20th century, probably from persecution owing to crop damage and from impacts of hurricanes. Existing range protected within Caribbean National Forest. CITES Appendix I. CRITICAL.

ECOLOGY The Puerto Rican Amazon formerly frequented all major natural vegetation types (various forest habitats from mangrove to montane forest) on Puerto Rico with the possible exception of dry forests in the southern coastal regions. Its current tiny remnant population

inhabits moist montane tropical rain-forest at 200-600m. On lower montane slopes this is dominated by *Dacryodes excelsa*, with higher-elevation swamp-forest characterised by *Cyrilla racemiflora* and areas with stands of *Prestoea montana*. Birds are generally in pairs or (especially whilst feeding) small flocks, having once formed flocks of several hundred. Diet consists of a variety of fruits, seeds, flowers and leaves, including fruits of *P. montana* and *D. excelsa*, flowers of *Piptocarpha tetrantha* and bracts of *Marcgravia sintenisii*. Nests in tree-cavity; breeding in limestone hollows reported from west of island in past. Luquillo parrots generally nest in *C. racemiflora*. Birds aggressively territorial in vicinity of nest-site whilst breeding. Egg-laying Feb-Apr, possibly to coincide with fruit availability. Clutch 2-4 (generally three).

DESCRIPTION Forehead and lores red; rest of head and nape with grass-green feathers edged black giving heavy scaly appearance. Grass-green feathers of mantle, back and scapulars with less pronounced dark margins; rump and uppertail-coverts paler, more yellowish-green. Outer greater coverts blue; remaining coverts grass-green. Primaries and outerwebs of outer secondaries blue; innerwebs of outer secondaries and inner secondaries green. Underwing with coverts green, flight feathers bluish green. Underparts green tinged yellowish; feathers on throat and breast with dark edges. Uppertail green; undertail more yellowish, narrowly tipped yellow; both with blue outerwebs to outer feathers. **Bare parts**: Bill pale horn; iris brown, legs pale grey.

SEX/AGE Sexes similar. Immature apparently similar to adult.

MEASUREMENTS Wing 182-196; tail 90-104; bill 27-30; tarsus 21-24.

GEOGRAPHICAL VARIATION A very weakly differentiated race *gracilipes* inhabited the island of Culebra but apparently died out during the early 20th century (see Distribution and Status).

REFERENCES Collar *et al.* (1992, 1994), Forshaw (1989), Snyder *et al.* (1987), Wiley (1981, 1991).

---

327 TUCUMAN AMAZON
Amazona tucumana   Plate 82

Other names: Alder Parrot (Amazon)

IDENTIFICATION 31cm. Largely green, stocky, short-tailed parrot with red frontal area and red patch on upperwing. In flight, trailing edge of wings deep blue. Olive suffusion on back and wing-coverts with body heavily scalloped with black, particularly on breast, nape and back. Bill pinkish. No sympatric *Amazona* in restricted range, but rather similar allopatric Red-spectacled Amazon (328) has more extensive red on head (covering lores, forecrown and encircling eye) and red at bend of wing (green in Tucuman). Birds often wary, and well concealed by dense foliage and heavy limbs of forest trees. Generally encountered flying over tree-tops or feeding in canopy in flocks on forested slopes. Flight rather butterfly-like on stiff, rather shallow, wingbeats.

VOICE Shrieking *croeo...crieo...croe....*

DISTRIBUTION AND STATUS This is a bird of the eastern slope of the Andes of Argentina and Bolivia.

Records are from Catamarca, Tucumán, Salta (including a stronghold in Finca del Rey National Park) and Jujuy, Argentina, north into Tarija and Chiquisaca (around Padilla) in Bolivia. However, there have been no definite records from Bolivia since 1938 and the species may now be confined to Argentina in southern Salta, Catamarca and Tucumán; reports from elsewhere in Argentina (Chaco and Misiones) are apparently mistaken. Resident, with seasonal altitudinal movements and possibly some movements in relation to food supply. Conservation status poorly known owing to inaccessibility of habitat and rather retiring habits but there was evidently a serious decline in 20th century. Probably remains in reasonable numbers in large areas of undisturbed habitat (e.g. in north-west Argentina) but declining overall in response to large-scale deforestation (e.g. southern Bolivia, where possibly already lost) and until late 1980s as result of extensive international trade. CITES Appendix I.

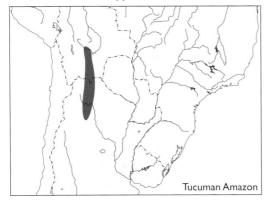

Tucuman Amazon

ECOLOGY Inhabits montane forest with alder *Alnus jorullensis*, also *Nothofagus* and *Podocarpus* forest in southern Bolivia. Reported at 1,800-2,000m above Tafi Viejo, Tucumán; 1,800m at Santa Barbara, Jujuy; 2,150-3,050 in Chuquisaca, Bolivia. Descends to about 350m during winter months and may enter city suburbs. Generally in flocks from a few to over 200 birds but usually c. 6-40. Some very large non-breeding season aggregations may contain entire regional population, e.g. 15,000 birds in Finca del Rey during non-breeding season could comprise entire Salta population. Few details on diet although *Alnus* and *Podocarpus* seeds perhaps provide a year-round staple; reported feeding on *Morus* trees at lower levels, *Erythrina* flowers and immature *Cedrela* fruits. Nests in large trunk of *Alnus* or *Podocarpus*. Breeding summer (probably Jan-Mar) in *Alnus* forest at about 2,600m. Eggs reported Jan, Chuquisaca, Bolivia. Clutch 3-4.

DESCRIPTION Forehead and upper lores red; lower lores and cheeks green; crown, nape, ear-coverts and sides of neck green with black margins giving scalloped appearance. Mantle and back green with dark margins; scapulars green with olive suffusion; rump and uppertail-coverts yellowish-green. Primary coverts red; other coverts green, median and greater showing olive tinge, median and lesser with dark tips giving scalloped appearance. Flight feathers green at base, violet-blue distally. Underwing with coverts yellowish-green with dark margins, flight feathers dull olive. Underparts slightly paler green than above with dark margins most pronounced on breast; thighs yellowish-orange; undertail-coverts yellowish-green. Tail yellowish-green, yellower towards tip; outer feathers red basally. **Bare**

parts: Bill pale pinkish-horn; cere whitish; bare periophthalmic skin white; iris orange-yellow; legs pale grey.

SEX/AGE Sexes similar. Immature has green primary coverts, lacks yellowish-orange thighs, and shows yellow flecks in (reduced) red frontal area.

MEASUREMENTS Wing 198-223; tail 90-112; bill 20-23; tarsus 20-23.

GEOGRAPHICAL VARIATION None.

NOTE This bird was formerly regarded as conspecific with Red-spectacled Amazon. They were first separated because of their supposed (in fact mistaken) sympatric occurrence in Misiones, Argentina, but their continued treatment as two species remains appropriate because of clear ecological and morphological differences, differing juvenile plumages and sexual dimorphism in Red-spectacled.

REFERENCES BirdLife International *in litt* (1993), Bond & Meyer de Schauensee (1942), Fjeldså & Krabbe (1990), Forshaw (1989), Government of Denmark *in litt.* (1989), Mosa *et al.* (1992), Narosky & Yzurieta (1989), Noegel (1989), Nores & Yzurieta (1994), de la Peña (1988), Ridgely (1981), TRAFFIC *in litt.* (1989), Wetmore (1926).

328 RED-SPECTACLED AMAZON
Amazona pretrei   Plate 82

Other names: Prêtre's Amazon (Parrot)

IDENTIFICATION 32cm. Mainly green, medium-sized, short-tailed parrot with bright red on forehead, face and edge of wings. Birds are darker above and more yellowish beneath with slightly paler underside to tail and tail-coverts and pale yellowish bill. Dark tips to many feathers (especially on back and underparts) give strong scalloped appearance. Only parrot in range with extensive red on head and wings. Immature of partly sympatric Vinaceous Amazon (346) distinguished by bluish throat and absence of red on carpal edge of wing. Allopatric Tucumán Amazon (327) has red only on forehead and no red at carpal edge. In pairs whilst breeding, with birds often moving about silently. Sometimes forms very large aggregations in winter. Flight on powerful, rapid and rather shallow wingbeats, birds sometimes tumbling and swerving erratically in flight. Separated from similarly proportioned (but smaller) *Pionus* parrots by much shallower wingbeats.

VOICE Birds en route to evening roost make loud piercing high-pitched screeches but also give lower, hoarser *caw caw keeu keeu* cries and loud repetitive *hee-o hee-o hee-o* sounds. Also some yapping cries. Very loud noise created by calling birds at large communal roosts.

DISTRIBUTION AND STATUS This species is actually or virtually confined to Rio Grande do Sul in southernmost Brazil. It has been reported from extreme north-east Argentina in Misiones, where probably now only a rare visitor following loss of all *Araucaria* forest, and very sporadically from eastern Paraguay, where breeding unlikely owing to scarcity of appropriate formations. Birds mostly occur in the centre, north and east of Rio Grande do Sul but range more widely where habitat suitable. One 19th century record from São Paulo state is considered exceptional (perhaps mistaken) and no reflection of historical distribution. Possibly in Santa Catarina, Brazil, where good tracts of *Araucaria* forest remain, but recent investigations suggest only sporadic occurrence there. Reports from Uruguay appear doubtfully valid. Principal breeding areas in Rio Grande do Sul are the south-eastern hills, the north-east and the north-central highlands. Birds breeding in the south mainly make northward post-breeding movements although a few appear to remain. Dispersal habits of northern breeders unknown but perhaps resident. Birds gather in large roosts at (e.g.) Aracuri-Esmeralda Ecological Station and at Carazinho Municipal Park in non-breeding season. Entire population possibly gathers at Esmeralda roost on occasion. Massive decline suspected in second half of 20th century owing to clearance and fragmentation of preferred (especially *Araucaria* forest) habitat, compounded by large-scale capture for live bird trade (mainly for local markets with small numbers entering illegal international trade). Birds are also hunted for food. Total population estimated (1994) at 7,500-8,500 birds. CITES Appendix I. ENDANGERED.

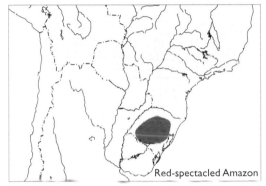
Red-spectacled Amazon

ECOLOGY This amazon is strongly associated with *Araucaria angustifolia* forest for roosting in non-breeding season. It prefers low open savanna woodland and riverine forests for breeding with e.g. *Podocarpus*, *Santia* and *Celtis* and where *A. angustifolia* is absent. Most records are at 300-1,000m but it occurs and breeds at lower elevations in southern Rio Grande do Sul. Dispersed in pairs whilst breeding but highly gregarious outside breeding season. Large communal roosts often located in plantations of exotic *Pinus* and *Eucalyptus*. Largest winter gatherings coincide with ripening of *Araucaria* seeds. Flocks of 30-50 composed of adults and recently fledged young may gather prior to dispersal from breeding areas to winter quarters. Reported food items include seeds of *A. angustifolia* (especially important May-Aug) and *Podocarpus lamberti* (important some areas Jan-Feb), fruits of *Eugenia*, *Campomanesia* and *Melia*. Diet alters with locality and season. A variety of fruit is taken in spring and summer (Oct-Feb), notably *Cupania*, *Eugenia*, *Phytolacca*, *Nectandra*, *Ocotea*, *Campomanesia*, *Cytharexylum*, *Myrcianthes*, *Blepharocalyx*, *Ficus* and *Symplocos*. Diurnal movements cover up to 100km, perhaps in relation to food availability. Nests in tree-hollow, e.g. in *Casearia*, *Quillaja brasiliensis* and *Ficus*. Breeds late Sep-Jan with young generally fledging by late Dec in south. Clutch 2-4.

DESCRIPTION Forehead, lores, forecrown and upper cheeks to ear-coverts bright red; hindcrown, nape, mantle, back and rump green with narrow black terminal band on most feathers; scapulars green; uppertail-coverts pale green. Leading edge of wing, carpal area, alula and primary coverts bright red; coverts otherwise green with narrow black tips. Flight feathers green with violet-blue

tips. Underwing green. Underparts mostly green, slightly tinged yellowish, with black tips to most feathers giving scalloped effect; thighs red; undertail-coverts pale yellowish-green. Tail green with broad pale yellowish-green tip and patches of red on base of innerwebs of three outermost feathers. **Bare parts**: Bill pale yellowish-horn with orange base to upper mandible; bare periophthalmic skin white; iris orange; legs brownish-grey.

SEX/AGE Female probably shows much less red on wing with carpal edge and primary coverts either mostly or wholly green. Immature apparently similar to adult female.

MEASUREMENTS Wing 204-220; tail 100-120; bill 22-25; tarsus 20-22.

GEOGRAPHICAL VARIATION None.

NOTE Sometimes considered conspecific with Tucumán Amazon (see Note in Tucuman Amazon).

REFERENCES Arndt (1996), Belton (1984), Collar *et al.* (1992, 1994), Forshaw (1989), Hayes (1995), Lowen *et al.* (1996), Nores & Yzurieta (1994), Sick (1993), Varty *et al.* (1994).

329 GREEN-CHEEKED AMAZON
Amazona viridigenalis Plate 81

Other names: Red-crowned Amazon (Parrot), Mexican Red-headed Parrot

IDENTIFICATION 30cm. Stocky, mostly green, medium-sized parrot with red crown, green cheeks and pale bill. Red patch on wing visible in flight. Slightly rounded tail with yellow at tip. Primaries broadly tipped blackish-blue or black. Partially sympatric Yellow-cheeked Amazon (331) has blue crown, yellow markings on face, distinct voice and slower, more laboured flight; Yellow-headed Amazon (339) has yellow on head. Adult from other *Amazona* in captivity by combination of red cap, bright green cheeks and black-tipped feathers on nape and mantle. Immature from similar adult Lilac-crowned Amazon (330) by predominantly green crown with blue largely confined to stripes over eyes and by fewer black-tipped feathers on underparts; from Brazilian race *diadema* of Yellow-cheeked Amazon by latter's crimson feathers directly in front of eye and over cere, and yellow on bend of wing. Swift flight on rapid shallow wingbeats. Generally in pairs or flocks.

VOICE Usual call includes shrill screaming note followed by three lower notes ascending in pitch as *clee-u... crack crack crack*. Screaming *kee yaw graw graw graw* and *cra cra cra* and rasping chattering *ji ji ji* also heard.

Green-cheeked Amazon
(several feral populations not shown)

DISTRIBUTION AND STATUS This species is endemic

to north-east Mexico, where records come from southern Nuevo León (south from Monterrey) through Tamaulipas (mostly in centre and south of state) and eastern San Luis Potosí to northern Veracruz south to about 21°N. It occurs as a winter visitor in Brownsville, extreme south-western Texas, USA. Current range appears confined to Tamaulipas and San Luis Potosí with no known breeding records in recent decades from either Nuevo León or Veracruz with exception of apparently feral population in suburbs of Monterrey. Feral populations in USA in California, Florida, Oahu (Hawaiian Islands) and Puerto Rico (small numbers in dry forest in south). Resident but nomadic in winter with some altitudinal movements taking birds to higher ground in winter (perhaps to exploit pine seeds and acorns) with others moving far outside breeding range to (e.g.) southern Texas. Apparently returns to breeding area in Feb. Declining throughout range but commoner near east coast, especially around Sierra de Tamaulipas, and on east slopes of Sierra Madre Oriental in Tamaulipas. Otherwise sparsely distributed and frequent only in few strongholds such as the Río Sabinas valley, Tamaulipas. Total population estimated at 3,000-6,500. Popular in captivity locally and formerly traded in large numbers internationally. Recent declines evidently result from excessive trade and continuing large-scale habitat destruction. Birds also shot in some areas owing to crop damage. No extensive protected areas in range and illegal trade continues. CITES Appendix I. ENDANGERED.

ECOLOGY Habitat is deciduous woodland, gallery forest and evergreen floodplain forest in tropical lowlands, with non-breeding birds ranging onto dry ridges as high as 1,200m in temperate zone with *Pinus* and *Quercus*. Frequents cultivated areas where large trees remain. Generally in flocks, generally larger than those of sympatric congeners (Yellow-cheeked and Yellow-headed Amazons, with which it sometimes mixes); in larger flocks in winter. Roosts communally. Reported food items include *Pinus* seeds, maize, *Ehretia* berries, *Pithecellobium* beans, acorns, and *Melia azedarach* berries; feral birds have adapted to parkland food sources including *Juglans*, *Liquidambar*, *Eucalyptus* and *Chorisia*. Nest in tree-hole including abandoned nest of Lineated Woodpecker *Dryocopus lineatus* generally 6-20m from ground. Nests reported in *Taxodium mucronatum*, *Bumelia laetivirens* and *Brosimum alicastrum* trees. Breeding Apr-May, Tamaulipas.

DESCRIPTION Lores, forehead and crown bright red with lateral margins of hindcrown and upper sides of neck showing blue feathers tipped with black; cheeks and ear-coverts bright green with no black tips to feathers; nape boldly scalloped with black-tipped green feathers. Mantle and back green with some faint black tips; rump and uppertail-coverts green. Wing-coverts green with faint black margins on some feathers. Flight feathers largely green, primaries broadly tipped dark blackish-blue or black, outer secondaries tipped blue with red on outerwebs. Underwing green. Underparts green, slightly yellowish; some feathers show indistinct dark tips. Tail green broadly tipped yellowish-green. **Bare parts**: Bill pale yellowish-horn; iris yellow; legs pale grey.

SEX/AGE Although females may on average have less red on head, there is probably no consistent sexual dimorphism. Immature has red on head much reduced, with feathers on central crown green tipped black and subterminally banded pale blue, feathers on side of crown blue forming broad band over eye.

MEASUREMENTS Wing 194-213; tail 97-116; bill 27-31; tarsus 22-25.

GEOGRAPHICAL VARIATION None.

REFERENCES Clinton-Eitniear (1986, 1988b), Collar *et al.* (1992, 1994), Edwards (1972), Forshaw (1989), Friedmann *et al.* (1950), Gehlbach *et al.* (1975), ICBP *in litt.* (1993), Lowery & Dalquest (1951), Martin *et al.* (1954), Peterson & Chalif (1973), Zimmerman (1957).

330 LILAC-CROWNED AMAZON
Amazona finschi   Plate 82

Other names: Lilac-crowned Parrot, Finsch's Parrot, Pacific Parrot; Wood's Red-fronted Parrot (*A. f. woodi*)

IDENTIFICATION 33cm. Mainly green, medium-sized parrot with longish, slightly rounded tail. Dark reddish forehead contrasts with pale bill. Red speculum in wing visible at rest and in flight. Hindneck and underparts scalloped. Combination of dull red forehead, green cheeks and lilac or powder-blue crown distinguish it from all other New World parrots. Rather similar but allopatric Yellow-cheeked Amazon (331) is rather larger, yellower, with much less distinct scalloping on underparts. Immature (allopatric) Green-cheeked Amazon (329) is similar to adult Lilac-crowned but has predominantly green crown and fewer black-tipped feathers on underparts. Often in pairs (flocks during dry season) on shallow, rather rapid wingbeats or moving quietly in tree-tops. Like other *Amazona* species may be separated from similarly proportioned *Pionus* by much shallower wingbeats. Often shy and difficult to approach.

VOICE Harsh screeching in flight. No other details.

Lilac-crowned Amazon

DISTRIBUTION AND STATUS This parrot inhabits Pacific Mexico from extreme south-eastern Sonora and south-western Chihuahua south through Sinaloa, western Durango, Nayarit, Jalisco, Colima, Michoacán and Guerrero to Oaxaca west of the Isthmus de Tehuantepec. It is mostly resident but a non-breeding visitor to (e.g. Oaxaca) lowlands in autumn. Generally common. Described as fairly common but local in south-eastern Sonora. Abundant, Colima. Very uncommon in Oaxaca highlands. Feral populations reported at various localities in USA. Popular pet bird in range and widely held in captivity internationally. Large-scale habitat loss has occurred within range but extensive areas of suitable woodland remain in rugged upland areas favoured by this parrot. NEAR-THREATENED.

ECOLOGY The species mostly inhabits wooded hills and mountains, from the tropical zone in deciduous forest at lower levels to *Quercus* and *Quercus-Pinus* woods in the uplands, with a preference for canyons with lush vegetation along streams at base; often also in arid or semi-arid scrubby vegetation, frequents forest edge or clearings, and enters cultivated areas and orchards adjacent to forest. Mainly from about 600 to over 2,000m but recorded at sea-level in Sinaloa and from sea-level to temperate forest in Colima. Reported at 360-1,700m in Sonora and 880-1,480m in Oaxaca. Generally in pairs or small flocks but larger aggregations form in dry season (300 birds reported) and at communal roosts (over 1,000 birds reported at one site in Nayarit). Food habits are very poorly documented: a particular preference for figs *Ficus* has been noted, and feeding in cultivated land reportedly causes some damage to maize and banana crops. Feral birds in Los Angeles, California, reported feeding with feral Green-cheeked Amazons. Nests in tree-hollow (e.g. *Ficus*), including former nest of woodpecker (e.g. *Phloeoceastes*) or arboreal termitarium. Parrots investigating nest-holes Feb, Colima, and nesting Mar, Nayarit.

DESCRIPTION Forehead and upper lores dull red; lower lores, cheeks and ear-coverts pale lime-green; crown, sides of neck and nape lilac or powder-blue with some feathers on crown showing narrow black margins. Mantle green with broad black edges giving distinct scalloped effect; back and scapulars green with faint black edges to some feathers; rump and uppertail coverts green, slightly brighter than back. Wing-coverts green. Primaries blue towards tip, green at base; base of outerwebs of first five secondaries red with subterminal band of yellow and blue tips, secondaries otherwise green becoming blue at tips. Underwing with coverts yellowish-green, flight feathers dull green. Throat yellowish-green with bluish tinge to some feathers; remaining underparts yellowish-green with black margins to some feathers (especially on breast) giving scalloped effect. Tail green tipped yellowish-green, lateral feathers with blue margin to base of outerwebs.
Bare parts: Bill horn; iris orange-red; legs grey.

SEX/AGE Sexes similar. Immature has iris dark brown (rather than red).

MEASUREMENTS Wing 185-208; tail 100-124; bill 27-30; tarsus 21-23.

GEOGRAPHICAL VARIATION Two races.
    A. f. finschi (S Sinaloa and W Durango through Nayarit, Jalisco, Colima, Michoacán and Guerrero to Oaxaca)
    A. f. woodi (Sonora, Chihuahua and Sinaloa) Body greener (less yellowish) than nominate, especially beneath.

REFERENCES Davis and Bennett (1972), Edwards (1972), Forshaw (1989), Friedmann *et al.* (1950), Howell & Webb (1995), Peterson & Chalif (1973), van Rossem (1945), Schaldach (1963).

331 YELLOW-CHEEKED AMAZON
Amazona autumnalis   **Plate 82**

Other names: Red-lored Amazon (Parrot), Scarlet-lored Amazon (Parrot), Red fronted Amazon (Parrot), Golden-cheeked Amazon (Parrot), Primrose-cheeked Amazon; Salvin's Parrot (*A. a. salvini*), Lilacine or Lesson's Amazon (*A. a. lilacina*)

IDENTIFICATION 31-35cm. Mainly green, short-tailed parrot with quite dark horn or grey bill, yellow cheeks (in north of range) and red frontal area (latter often difficult to detect in field). Red feathered cere in all but nominate race is unique in genus. Tail broadly tipped yellowish-green. Red patch on secondaries visible in flight. Distinguished from partially sympatric Yellow-crowned Amazon (341) in flight (silhouette) by longer tail; from Green-cheeked Amazon (329), overlapping in eastern Mexico, by lavender hindcrown and neck and by more laboured and slower flight; from widely overlapping Mealy Amazon (345) by smaller size; from Lilac-crowned (330) by yellow patch on face (except race *diadema*), somewhat larger size, yellower coloration and less distinct scalloping on underparts. Generally in pairs or loose flocks in tops of tall trees or flying on stiff shallow wingbeats. Like other *Amazona* species may be separated from similarly proportioned *Pionus* by much shallower wingbeats. Flushes noisily and flies considerable distance before alighting.

VOICE Varied repertoire. High-pitched, relatively pleasant trilling *wee ee-eee-eeet* has progressively higher pitch. Calls otherwise rather loud and strident including *keekorak keekorak* or *chikak chikak oorak oorak*, metallic *kalink kalink* and loud, scolding, disyllabic *ow-er*. Rippling *rrik* and short *chek chek* calls also heard. Calls are harsher and louder than most other amazons (including sympatric Mealy), more metallic than Yellow-headed (339).

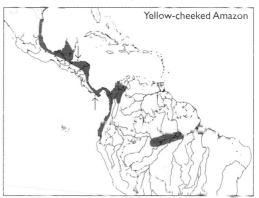
Yellow-cheeked Amazon

DISTRIBUTION AND STATUS The species ranges from Mexico south into northern South America with a disjunct population in the Amazon. It is found in the eastern humid lowlands of Mexico in southern Tamaulipas, eastern San Luis Potosí, Puebla, Oaxaca, Chiapas, Tabasco, Campeche and Quintana Roo. Records from other parts of the country (e.g. Mexico City) probably refer to escapes. It occurs in Belize and the Caribbean lowlands of Guatemala and Honduras (including Ruatán and Guanaja in Bay Islands and probably formerly on Utila) through to Nicaragua and Costa Rica, where present in humid parts of the tropical zone on both slopes (absent from dry northwest), similarly in Panama and on islands of Coiba and Escudo de Veraguas and in the Perlas Archipelago (absent from drier areas of Azuero Peninsula). In north-west Colombia it appears on the Pacific slope of the western Andes from the Panamanian border south to the Baudó Mountains and from south-western Cauca (Gaupí) south into Ecuador to the Gulf of Guayaquil. It also ranges north of Andes in Colombia to the middle Magdalena Valley and east into north-west Venezuela in Zulia (Sierra de Perijá). A disjunct population exists in the north-west Brazilian

Amazon basin between Rio Negro and Rio Solimões. Generally resident with some local seasonal habitat preferences (e.g. Yucatán Peninsula, Mexico). Generally common and most numerous parrot in some parts of range (e.g. parts of Central America) but now very rare west of Andes in Ecuador and Colombia with population of race *lilacina* estimated at 400-600. Declined drastically on Ruatán Island (Honduras) where trapped heavily for export, and perhaps extirpated Utila for same reason. Trapping combined with habitat loss has also caused declines in some other parts of its range (e.g. eastern Mexico and Ecuador). Common in captivity in some areas and traded internationally.

ECOLOGY This amazon frequents a wide range of wooded and open habitats with trees including rain-forest, tropical deciduous forest, *Pinus* woodlands, mangroves, wooded swamps, gallery forest, cultivated areas with tall trees, and plantations; also scrubby dry forest in southern Ecuador. Birds move from rain-forest (breeding season) to more open habitat in winter in the Yucatán Peninsula, Mexico. Elevations range from sea-level to 320m in Oaxaca, 1,100m Honduras, 800m on Caribbean and 1,000m on Pacific slope of Costa Rica, and 1,000m in Colombia. Birds are generally in pairs or loose flocks, and more gregarious when feeding (occasionally with macaws) and roosting: outside breeding season birds roost in tall trees in gallery forest or mangroves, with 800 birds reported at one site in Panama. Reported food items include figs *Ficus*, orange, mango, palm fruits (including those of *Cordia lutea* and *Spondias pourpurea*), coffee beans *Coffea arabica*, seeds of *Virola*, *Casearia* and *Protium*. Mainly forages in tops of tall trees. Nests in hollow of (usually dead) tree (e.g. *Tabebuia* or *Ceiba*) or in palm stub. Birds in breeding condition Apr, Oaxaca; Feb-Mar, Belize; Mar, Guatemala; Jan-Feb, Colombia. Breeds Feb-Apr, Panama; Mar-May, Belize and Jan-Mar, Ecuador. Clutch 3-4.

DESCRIPTION Forehead and lores red; cheeks to ear-coverts bright yellow; sides of neck bright green; crown and hindneck basally green broadly tipped black; nape basally green tipped black with subterminal band of lilac. Back, mantle, scapulars and rump green; upperwing-coverts green with carpal edge yellowish-green. Primaries dark bluish-black except for outer feathers which are basally green on outerwebs; outer secondaries red tipped violet-blue, inner green. Underwing with coverts yellowish-green, flight feathers green. Underparts yellowish-green, with barely perceptible darker scalloping. Tail green centrally, outermost feathers with blue margins to outerwebs. **Bare parts**: Upper mandible yellowish-horn, lower grey; narrow bare periophthalmic ring pale yellowish; iris yellowish-orange; legs greyish.

SEX/AGE Sexes similar but female may show heavier black scaling on chest (in race *salvini* at least). Immature has reduced or no yellow on face (nominate), reduced red on lores and forehead, and brownish iris. Older adults may show a little red on chin.

MEASUREMENTS Wing 195-215; tail 96-120; bill 27-32; tarsus 23-26.

GEOGRAPHICAL VARIATION Four races. *Amazona hecki* (from Colombia) is regarded as synonymous with *lilacina*. The rather poorly known *diadema* is sometimes treated as a good species.

    A. a autumnalis (Mexico to Honduras including Bay Islands)

    A. a. salvini (Honduras or Nicaragua to SW Colombia and NW Venezuela) Like nominate but cheeks green and base of tail red on innerwebs. This and nominate perhaps also with paler bill than others. Some red feathers on cere. Birds in northern Costa Rica show some yellow on cheeks (extent of yellow decreasing southwards) but referable to *salvini*. Some Panama specimens show yellow on lores. Birds from El Recreo, Nicaragua, intermediate between *autumnalis* and *salvini*.

    A. a. lilacina (W Ecuador north of Gulf of Guayaquil and possibly in Nariño, SW Colombia, where it intergrades with *salvini*) Like *salvini* but face more uniform and brighter yellowish-green, red loral patch extending over eye to form superciliary stripe. Some red feathers on cere. Perhaps with darker bill. Crown feathers with red tips.

    A. a. diadema (Amazon basin of Brazil between Rio Negro and Rio Solimões) Like *salvini* but face darker, more emerald-green and red on lores and feathered cere darker forming crimson spot in front of eye. Cheeks with slight bluish tinge. Larger than nominate and perhaps has darker bill.

REFERENCES Alrich & Bole (1937), Arndt (1996), Austin (1929), Binford (1989), Bond (1936), Chapman (1926), Desenne & Strahl (1991, 1994), Edwards (1972), Forshaw (1989), Friedmann *et al.* (1950), Hilty & Brown (1986), Howell (1957), Howell & Webb (1992, 1995), Land (1963, 1970), Lowery & Dalquest (1951), Meyer de Schauensee (1949), Meyer de Schauensee & Phelps (1978), Monroe (1968), Paynter (1955), Peterson & Chalif (1973), Ridgely (1981), Ridgely & Gwynne (1989), Russell (1964), Sick (1993), Slud (1964), Smithe (1966), Smithe & Paynter (1963), Stiles *et al.* (1989), Wetmore (1943, 1946, 1968), Yamashita *in litt.* (1996), Zimmerman (1957).

332 BLUE-CHEEKED AMAZON
Amazona dufresniana   Plate 83

Other names: Dufresne's Amazon (Parrot), Blue-cheeked Parrot

IDENTIFICATION 34cm. Large, relatively dull-coloured amazon with blue on cheeks and sides of neck, ochre lores (appearing as orange pre-ocular spot at distance) and yellowish crown. Yellow wing-patch and broad yellowish terminal band to outer tail feathers. Widely sympatric with Orange-winged (342), Yellow-crowned (341) and Mealy (345) Amazons and may also occur with Festive (335) in parts of Venezuela and north-west Guyana, but distinguished from these (and other *Amazona* in captivity) by combination of blue cheeks and yellow wing-patch. Considerably larger than similarly proportioned *Pionus* parrots. Generally in canopy; flies higher above trees than other *Amazona*. Poorly known and seemingly uncommon species, mostly found in humid forest.

VOICE Taped flight call of bird probably this species reveals trilling *cheeet cheeet cheeet* followed by whistled *dee-ooo-ar*.

DISTRIBUTION AND STATUS Range in north-eastern South America is incompletely understood owing to the small number of records from a fairly large area. Known from south and eastern Venezuela in Bolívar with isolated western record in Amazonas. Occurs in northern Guyana north of 5°N, north-east Surinam and north-east French Guiana to border with Amapá, Brazil. Probably occurs in many suitable forested areas between scattered localities for which reliable reports exist. Reported occurrence in Amapá and Pará, Brazil, may be substantiated in due course and in northern Brazil perhaps in parts of northern Roraima. Seasonal movements in some areas (e.g. from interior to coastal Surinam, Jul-Aug) may be sporadic and possibly related to availability of food. Scarcity of records from areas frequented by fieldworkers suggest that this is a low-density and rather uncommon species (in at least some parts of range). Not currently at risk but possible decline in 20th century from trapping for trade and habitat loss (particularly in the Gran Sabana region of Bolívar and parts of coastal Guianas). Occurs in several protected areas including Roraima National Park, Venezuela. Traded internationally (especially from Guyana) in small numbers during 1980s. NEAR-THREATENED.

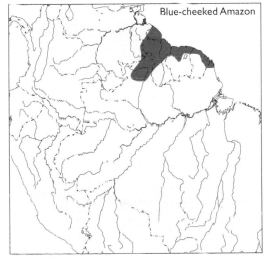

Blue-cheeked Amazon

ECOLOGY This bird is reported from rain-forest and cloud-forest in the lower subtropical zone and from savanna woodlands in Venezuela. Most birds from Guianas have been reported from gallery forest (but this is perhaps an artefact of use of river transport by observers). They occur seasonally (in cooler part of year) in the coastal sand-ridge forests of Surinam. Recorded to 1,700m, Bolívar, and 560m, Imbaimadai, Guyana. Probably occurs in small flocks for at least part of year, with larger gatherings in coastal areas. No information on diet and none on nesting except breeds Mar, Guyana. Clutch three in captivity.

DESCRIPTION Lores and feathers above cere ochre; forehead and crown yellow with broad green tips becoming progressively more extensive towards nape; cheeks, sides of neck and throat lavender-blue (paler blue at base of mandible); ear-coverts green; nape green and sides of neck blue, both with black tips giving scalloped effect. Mantle and back green, some showing indistinct black tips; scapulars, rump and uppertail-coverts green. Wing-coverts green; carpal edge yellowish-green. Primaries black with blue tips to outerwebs; outer four secondaries yellow with pale blue tips forming distinct speculum; remaining secondaries green with pale blue tips. Under wing green. Underparts green, more yellowish-green on

thighs and undertail-coverts. Tail green with (faint central, broader lateral) yellow tip. **Bare parts**: Bill grey; bare periophthalmic skin grey; iris orange; legs grey.

SEX/AGE Sexes similar. Immature has less blue on head, perhaps duller yellow on crown and more pointed outer tail feathers.

MEASUREMENTS Wing 200-226; tail 103-124; bill 32-37; tarsus 23-28.

GEOGRAPHICAL VARIATION None.

NOTE Blue-cheeked Amazon has previously been regarded as conspecific with Red-browed Amazon (333) and/or Red-tailed (334) Amazon. However, most modern authors treat all three taxa as full species and (especially considering the morphological and ecological differences that exist between them) this approach is considered appropriate here.

REFERENCES Collar (1995), Desenne & Strahl (1991, 1994), Forshaw (1989), Haverschmidt (1968), Meyer de Schauensee & Phelps (1978), Tostain *et al.* (1992), Wege & Collar (1991).

333 RED-BROWED AMAZON
Amazona rhodocorytha   Plate 83

Other names: Red-crowned Amazon (Parrot), Red-topped Amazon (Parrot), Red-capped Amazon (Parrot), Red-browed Parrot

IDENTIFICATION 35cm. Large amazon with red crown, blue cheeks and red speculum. Orange area on lores reportedly extends to (otherwise blue) throat in northern birds (see Note). Range overlaps with Orange-winged (342) and Mealy (345) Amazons but neither has red on head. Rather similar (allopatric) Red-tailed Amazon (334) has red on carpal edge of wing, no red speculum and more strikingly coloured tail. Combination of red forehead and crown, blue cheeks, orange lores, red speculum and all-green upperparts distinguish Red-browed from all other *Amazona* in captivity. Considerably larger than similarly proportioned *Pionus* parrots. In small flocks or pairs in humid forest.

VOICE Varied repertoire, sometimes incessant and raucous. Calls include *cheee-ooo* and *nee-it* sounds. *Kray-a* in flight. *Koyok-koyok*, *kow-ow* and *no-at-no at alo alo alo* also reported.

DISTRIBUTION AND STATUS This is a parrot of Brazil's Atlantic rain-forests in eastern Alagoas and further south to Rio de Janeiro. There are no records between Alagoas and sites in north-eastern Bahia, south of which the species is reported widely and from neighbouring eastern parts of Minas Gerais through Espírito Santo to Rio de Janeiro. It evidently suffered a drastic decline in range and numbers since European colonisation, with birds now confined to the last few remaining fragments of Atlantic rain-forests. Possibly extinct Alagoas, where last native lowland forests were cleared in the 1980s, but remains fairly common in at least one protected area in Espírito Santo. Current population widely scattered and susceptible to continuing deforestation (e.g. around Desengano State Park, Rio de Janeiro) and to continued illegal trade in which birds are highly valued. Occurs in several protected areas including Monte Pascoal National Park (Bahia), Rio

Doce State Park (Minas Gerais), Sooretama and Linhares Reserves in Espírito Santo and Bocaina National Park, Rio de Janeiro. CITES Appendix I. ENDANGERED.

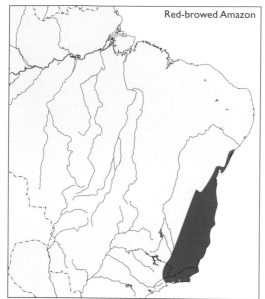

Red-browed Amazon

ECOLOGY Birds mainly inhabit humid lowland forest but also reported from highland forests (perhaps seasonally) in the interior (in e.g. Serra do Mar and eastern Minas Gerais) up to about 1,000m. Despite records from forest edge they probably do not adapt to conditions created by even partial deforestation. Roost communally in tall forest trees. No information on feeding or breeding although there is evidence to suggest young hatch Oct. Clutch up to four in captivity.

DESCRIPTION Forehead and forecrown bright red; hindcrown green broadly tipped with brownish-purple; lores orange; lower cheeks and throat pale blue (see Identification); ear-coverts and sides of neck green with blue suffusion; nape green tipped black. Upperparts green, some feathers showing faint dark tips. Wing-coverts green with yellow at carpal edge. Primaries blackish-grey; three outermost secondaries red at base, others green with violet-blue tips. Underwing-coverts green. Underparts green, paler and more yellowish than above, with some feathers showing faint pale blue tips (especially on belly and around thighs). Tail green broadly tipped yellowish, with large red subterminal patch on innerwebs of lateral feathers. **Bare parts**: Bill pale horn; iris orange; legs grey.

SEX/AGE Sexes similar. Immature has less extensive red on head and tail and red confined to only first two secondaries.

MEASUREMENTS Wing 209-229; tail 99-119; bill 29-36; tarsus 24-26.

GEOGRAPHICAL VARIATION None.

NOTE Red-browed Amazon has been widely treated as conspecific with Blue-cheeked (332) and Red-tailed (334) Amazons (see Note under *A. dufresniana*). Birds from Alagoas reportedly show orange throat, thereby suggesting racial differentiation. No subspecies has been proposed, however, and we have been unable to examine specimens.

REFERENCES Collar *et al.* (1992, 1994), Forshaw (1989), Ridgely (1981), Sick (1993), Stotz *et al.* (1996).

334 RED-TAILED AMAZON
Amazona brasiliensis   Plate 83

Other names: Purple-faced Parrot, Blue-faced Amazon (Parrot), Brazilian Green Amazon Parrot

IDENTIFICATION 35cm. Rather large, mainly green amazon with red forehead and crown and mauve-blue cheeks, ear-coverts and throat. Lacks red speculum. Yellow-tipped tail has broad red subterminal band. Apparently marginally sympatric with Vinaceous Amazon (346) in (e.g.) Jacupiranga State Park, latter told by heavy purplish suffusion on breast. May also occur with Orange-winged Amazon (342), told by yellow forehead and cheeks. Similar but allopatric Red-browed Amazon (333) has red speculum but no red at carpal edge and less strikingly marked tail. Combination of red forehead and crown, blue sides of neck, absence of red speculum, and tail pattern separates Red-browed from other *Amazona* in captivity. Generally in pairs or small flocks.

VOICE Flight call *kraaaa kraaaa*. Also *kli kli* and *krayo* similar to Blue-fronted Amazon (338).

Red-tailed Amazon

DISTRIBUTION AND STATUS This amazon is confined to a small area of coastal south-east Brazil in São Paulo and Paraná states. In coastal areas of São Paulo it extends south-west from Itanhaém, including Ilha Comprida and Ilha do Cardoso, and through virtually all coastal areas of neighbouring Paraná from Guaraqueçaba, Antonia and Paranagua to Guaratuba and on several adjacent offshore islands (e.g. Ilha do Mel). It possibly occurs in extreme north-eastern Santa Catarina adjacent to Paraná but no reliable records exist. An old record from Rio Grande do Sul appears improbable. Possibly some minor seasonal movements in winter (May-Aug). Rapid decline in 20th century has been due in part to habitat loss, with most areas densely settled and totally deforested, remaining ones threatened by housing developments (e.g. Ilha Comprida), cutting of nesting and feeding trees and palms for human use (e.g. boat construction and food) and conversion of wetlands for water buffalo and rice production (birds also face competition from domestic grazing animals for fruits of *Erythrina speciosa*). However, direct human exploitation of the species is now no less serious a problem, some related to hunting for food but most concerning illegal capture for trade. Recent study of 49 nests showed that 41 were illegally robbed of nestlings, whilst 1.27% of available habitat was lost in 1993 alone. Total wild population estimated at 3,600 birds (1995) with rapid decline to several hundred predicted. Total range probably no more than 6,000 km², with large parts of this susceptible to sea-level rise caused by climate change. Protected by domestic legislation. Occurs in several protected areas (e.g. Ilha do Cardoso, São Paulo) but only a very small proportion of birds occur in them. CITES Appendix I. ENDANGERED.

ECOLOGY The species inhabits a restricted area of lowland coastal forest and wetlands with exceptional species and structural diversity including lowland humid forest, restinga, freshwater swamps and mangroves. Its preferred coastal habitats possess complex networks of channels, swamps and wetlands. Characteristic trees of forest habitat include *Luehea* and *Andira* whilst vegetation of islands where birds roost and breed is dominated by several halophytic species and restinga formations. Some birds are apparently virtually resident in flooded forest, probably because of greater nest-site availability. Reported sympatric occurrence and association with Red-spectacled Amazon (328) in *Araucaria* forests probably mistaken. Mostly not above 300-400m but reported to 700m (Paraná). Forms communal roosts (often in mangroves) for at least part of year with over 750 reported in one gathering (1985). The fruits of *Callophyllum brasiliense* are believed to be of considerable dietary importance, with fruits of *Syagrus romanzoffianum* and *Psidium cattleyanum* also taken in quantity; other recorded foods include flowers and fruits of *Erythrina speciosa* and fruits of *Euphorbia* and *Myrcia*. Feeds in pairs or flocks of up to 20 birds. Nests in cavity of live or dead tree (e.g. *Callophyllum brasiliense*) and occasionally arboreal termite nest; usually high up, but once only 1m above flood water. Usually breeds in flooded or swampy areas, including mangroves. Breeding Sep-Feb but perhaps to Apr. Clutch 3-4.

DESCRIPTION Forehead, forecrown and lores red, hindmost red feathers on crown with purplish tips; cheeks, ear-coverts, sides of neck and throat mauve-blue; hind-crown and nape green with blackish tips. Upperparts green, some feathers on rump tipped yellow. Median and greater coverts and inner secondaries conspicuously edged yellow; leading edge of wing red and yellow. Primaries greyish-black, secondaries green becoming blue towards tips. Underwing with coverts yellowish-green, flight feathers blackish tinged bluish-green at bases of innerwebs. Underparts yellowish-green, paler on undertail-coverts. Tail green with broad greenish-yellow tips, lateral feathers marked basally with purplish-blue on outerwebs and tipped yellowish-green with broad red subterminal band. **Bare parts**: Bill pale horn with dark tip; iris orange; legs pinkish-grey.

SEX/AGE Sexes similar. Immature has less extensive red head, duller plumage generally and darker iris.

MEASUREMENTS Wing 208-215; tail 101-112; bill 27-30; tarsus 25-27.

GEOGRAPHICAL VARIATION None.

NOTE Red-tailed Amazon has been widely treated as conspecific with Blue-cheeked (332) and Red-tailed (334) Amazons (see Note in *A. dufresniana*).

REFERENCES Collar *et al.* (1992, 1994), Forshaw (1989), Martuscelli (1994, 1995), Ridgely (1981), Sick (1993).

335 FESTIVE AMAZON
Amazona festiva   **Plate 83**

Other names: Festive Parrot, Red-backed Amazon (Parrot); Bodin's Amazon (*A. f. bodini*)

IDENTIFICATION 35cm. Mainly green, rather large amazon with red rump and lower back (latter sometimes not conspicuous in flight). Feathers above and behind eyes tinged blue with blue patch on throat. Lores, frontal band and, in *bodini*, forecrown red. Range overlaps with race *diadema* of Red-lored Amazon (331) between Rios Negro and Solimões, possibly with Blue-cheeked Amazon (332) in Guyana, and widely with Yellow-crowned (341), Orange-winged (342), White-faced (344) and Mealy (345) Amazons in Orinoco and Amazon basins. Festive distinguished from these and other *Amazona* by red rump and lower back, and further separated from some close congeners by absence of red or orange wing speculum. No bare periophthalmic skin. Generally in pairs or small flocks in canopy or flying over tree-tops.

VOICE Distinctive nasal *wah-wah* in flight may sound like human laugh at distance. Wider variety of calls whilst perched including screeching *scree-ee-at* calls.

Festive Amazon

DISTRIBUTION AND STATUS Festive Amazons are found in northern South America principally as two large disjunct populations in the Amazon and Orinoco catchments. One population occupies north-west Guyana (very few records) and Venezuela in southern Apure on the Río Meta and middle Orinoco to Delta Amacuro. The second ranges from parts of lowland eastern Colombia including the lower Río Casanare, lower Río Meta and Río Vaupes south through Amazonian Ecuador (where reported from e.g. Río Napo, but few recent records) and north-east Peru, and east through western Brazil from Rio Branco, Rio Negro and lower Rio Madeira into the eastern Amazon basin in Amapá and Pará and at the mouth of the Amazon on Ilha Mexiana (where status uncertain). Probably mostly resident but sporadic occurrence at margins of range in e.g. Ecuador and Guyana suggests seasonal movements from core range. Evidently scarce in Guyana and local in Venezuela, Ecuador and Peru, but commoner in parts of western Amazonia in Brazil and locally the commonest

Amazona some areas of Colombia (e.g. near Leticia). Persecuted for live bird trade in parts of range (e.g. Peru) but swampy forest habitat not in great demand for agriculture. No apparent large-scale range contraction yet.

ECOLOGY The species frequents lowland primary and secondary rain-forest, mainly várzea, swampy forest and on river islands, also igapó (permanently flooded forest), so usually found near water and may avoid terra firme forest, although also reported from gallery forest and savannas with scattered trees. Recorded in cacao plantations in Brazil. Reported to 500m Colombia, 100m Venezuela. Generally in small flocks with larger gatherings occasionally reported. Flocks with up to 50 birds occur near Leticia May-Jun. Birds congregate in the late afternoon and evening in communal roosts. No information on food or breeding.

DESCRIPTION Cheeks and sides of neck green with strong blue suffusion; lores and narrow frontal band red; feathers above and behind eye blue; forehead rather yellowish-green, crown green but darker; feathers on nape green with faint dark terminal band. Mantle, scapulars, upper back and uppertail-coverts dark grass-green; rump and most of lower back bright red. Primary coverts violet-blue, other coverts dark grass-green. Carpal edge of wing and margin of outerwebs of primaries blue; innerwebs black; secondaries with dark blue tips, innermost secondaries green. Underwing-coverts green. Chin and throat blue; breast and belly green; undertail-coverts yellowish-green. Tail green, paler yellowish-green at tip; trace of reddish at base of some feathers. **Bare parts**: Bill horn-brown; iris yellow; legs blackish-grey.

SEX/AGE Sexes similar. Immature has mainly green rump and less blue on head.

MEASUREMENTS Wing 195-222; tail 89-110; bill 29-34; tarsus 25-28.

GEOGRAPHICAL VARIATION Two races. These are rather well differentiated, but may possibly come into contact in extensive areas of apparently suitable but poorly explored lowland habitat in the watersheds between the Orinoco and Amazon basins.

    A. f. festiva (Amazon basin)
    A. f. bodini (Orinoco and its tributaries) More yellowish-green (especially beneath) with more extensive red patch on forehead (extending to forecrown). Lores blackish and cheeks suffused lilac. Carpal edge of wing is yellowish and outerwebs of primaries green. Bill darker.

REFERENCES Arndt (1996), Desenne & Strahl (1991), Forshaw (1989), Hilty & Brown (1986), Gyldenstolpe (1945a), Meyer de Schauensee (1949, 1966), Meyer de Schauensee & Phelps (1978), Ridgely (1981), Sick (1993), Snyder (1966), Yamashita *in litt.* (1996).

---

336 YELLOW-FACED AMAZON
Amazona xanthops   Plate 84

Other names: Yellow-crowned Amazon (Parrot), Yellow-faced Parrot

IDENTIFICATION 26-27cm. Rather small, mainly green amazon with yellow on head and sometimes on underparts. Plumage rather variable with extent of yellow beneath and on head differing widely between individuals. Birds in same flock may show wholly yellow or wholly green head and be either mainly yellow or mainly green beneath. Widely sympatric Orange-winged (342) and Blue-fronted (338) Amazons distinguished by their larger size, tendency to occur in taller gallery forest and, in good light or at close range, by pale blue on forehead and red wing speculum; Yellow-faced does not apparently mix with these species. Flight faster, on deeper wingbeats, than other amazons. Similar in size and proportions to two sympatric *Pionus* but latter have rather shallow wingbeats and no yellow feathers in plumage. Reliably separated by small size from other (allopatric), mainly green *Amazona* with yellow in plumage. Characteristic species of deciduous forest areas of interior Brazil.

VOICE *Krew-e, krew-e* at rest. Flying birds heard calling *grayo-grayo-totototo*.

DISTRIBUTION AND STATUS This is a cerrado specialist confined to interior Brazil from southern Piauí south through northern and western Bahia and Minas Gerais to northern and western parts of São Paulo, extending west through Tocantins and Goiás, eastern and southern Mato Grosso and Mato Grosso do Sul and adjacent parts of eastern Bolivia. Generally nomadic, making poorly documented seasonal movements. Occurs apparently at low density over most of range. Common only locally and absent from many former parts of range. Trapped for live bird trade and range contracting owing to large-scale loss of habitat (in e.g. Minas Gerais and Bahia) due mainly to clearance for agriculture, monoculture forestry and charcoal production. An estimated 60-70% of suitable habitat was lost in 20 years up to 1994. Occurs in several protected areas but nomadic tendencies will limit their effectiveness. VULNERABLE.

Yellow-faced Amazon

ECOLOGY The Yellow-faced Amazon frequents deciduous and semi-arid deciduous woodlands and scrub, mainly seasonal cerrado woodlands with *Mauritia* palms but also drier caatinga scrub, where it may prefer forests along watercourses. It occurs in the vicinity of cultivation, and is found in pairs or flocks up to about 35. Diet consists of fruits and seeds of various cerrado trees including *Anacardium*, *Salacia crassifolia* and *Astronium fraxinifolium*. Birds reported taking unripe guava *Psidium* fruits in plantations and will visit fruiting mango trees for weeks on end. Nests generally in open area in cerrado tree such as *Vochysia*, or else a tall terrestrial termitarium (of *Armitermis*) in Emas and Brasilia National Parks. A 1920s report of breeding in rock crevices in mountain slopes remains unconfirmed.

DESCRIPTION Birds show considerable variation in plumage. Lores, forehead, forecrown, ear-coverts and upper cheeks variously marked with bright yellow and green, sometimes extending over lower cheeks and hindcrown; lower cheeks, sides of neck and hindcrown otherwise green, subterminally blue and tipped black; nape green with black tips giving scalloped pattern. Upperparts grass-green with olive tinge on some feathers. Wing-coverts green narrowly edged yellowish with lesser coverts showing olive tinge and outer primary coverts blue margins to outerwebs; carpal edge yellowish-green. Primaries and secondaries bluish-green, inner secondaries with narrow yellowish-green margins. Underwing with coverts green, flight feathers bluish-green. Throat generally green with dark tips but in some individuals bright yellow; breast and belly pale green broadly tipped dark green, giving distinct scalloped effect (some birds with scattered yellow and orange feathers or with bluish tinge, especially on flanks; others almost wholly yellow and orange with green thighs, vent and undertail-coverts; still others with green breast and yellow, orange-flecked belly). Tail yellowish green with dull red at base. **Bare parts:** Bill horn; broad bare periophthalmic ring white; iris yellow; legs pale grey.

SEX/AGE Sexes apparently similar. Immature has brown iris. Some authors suggest variability of plumage is age-related, but it appears most likely linked to genetic factors.

MEASUREMENTS Wing 188-201; tail 71-83; bill 26-28; tarsus 21-22.

GEOGRAPHICAL VARIATION None.

REFERENCES Antas & Cavalcanti (1988), Collar *et al.* (1994), Dubs (1992), Forshaw (1989), Ridgely (1981), Sick (1993), Yamashita *in litt.* (1996).

---

337 YELLOW-SHOULDERED AMAZON
Amazona barbadensis   Plate 84

Other names: Yellow-winged Amazon (Parrot), Yellow-shouldered Parrot

IDENTIFICATION 35-36cm. Large, mainly green, short-tailed parrot with yellow head (forehead very pale or white), thighs and shoulders, heavy pale bill and red speculum. Only large parrot to occur within restricted range. Yellow 'shoulders' and red speculum conspicuous in flight. Most likely to be confused in captivity with Blue-fronted (338) and Orange-winged (342) Amazons but readily separated from former by lack of blue feathers on forehead and paler bill and from latter by extensive yellow on thighs and shoulders. Generally in pairs or small flocks of up to 10 in xerophytic woodland. Birds may be overlooked whilst resting in trees and are often first detected by raucous calls.

VOICE Loud and raucous, generally with fewer musical calls than some other amazons. Calls include dry rattling *screeet* and trilling *scree-ee-ee-ak*.

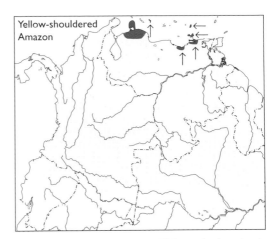

Yellow-shouldered Amazon

DISTRIBUTION AND STATUS This species is endemic to northern Venezuela and adjacent islands, in two main areas: Falcón and Lara in the west and Anzoátegui and Sucre in the east. In the west it is found in several disjunct populations from the Zulia border east to around Barquisimeto (Lara) in the south and Coro (Falcón) in the north, also on the Paraguaná Peninsula. In the east it is distributed in coastal areas of Anzoátegui state only from area of Puerto Píritu to Barcelona, with records from Sucre only on Araya Peninsula. There are populations on Isla Margarita and La Blanquilla (Venezuela), where distributed in western third of former and poorly documented in latter; also on Bonaire (Netherlands Antilles), where most records are from the hilly north-west, and formerly Aruba and possibly Curaçao (Netherlands Antilles) but extinct on the former around 1947 (1955 at latest). Probably resident with some seasonal movement within isolated ranges in response to food shortages and drought. Locally common in parts of Falcón and Anzoátegui (population on Paraguaná Peninsula very small); less well documented in Sucre and Lara. Under 1,000 birds on Isla Margarita, about 400 Bonaire. Birds are heavily collected for local trade and some enter international markets. Persecuted some areas owing to crop damage. Habitat loss is perhaps producing a steady range contraction (e.g. via tourism development on Margarita). Domestic species-specific protection is not enforced and the bird occurs only marginally in protected areas. CITES Appendix I. VULNERABLE.

ECOLOGY This is a bird of xerophytic vegetation with cacti and low thorny bushes and trees, also reported around cultivation and in mangroves; patches of denser woodland may also be an important habitat feature. Occurs to 450m on Margarita, perhaps higher on mainland. Roosts communally in taller trees or rock crevices with gathering in Falcón holding 700 birds (1989). Chiefly in pairs, family parties or small parties but larger flocks of up to 100 reported, especially at favoured food source (e.g. ripening *Malpighia* fruit). Specific foods recorded include fruits of *M. punicifolia*, *Bourreria succulenta*, *Casearia tremula*, *Terminalia catappa* and *Zizyphus spina-cristi*, seeds from the pods of *Caesalpinia coriaria* and nectar-rich blossoms of *Crescentia cujete*, tops of *Lamaireocereus griseus* cactus, and fruits of *Cereus repandus* cactus. Birds also take crop plants including avocado, mango and maize. Nests in tree-cavity or (on Bonaire) in rock crevice on limestone cliff. Reported nest-trees in

Falcón include *Bulnesia arborea* and *Prosopis juliflora*. Breeding season Mar-Sep, with nest construction mostly Apr-May and young fledging Aug (recorded breeding Oct, Bonaire). Clutch 3-4 (2-3 Bonaire).

DESCRIPTION Forehead and lores pale yellow, often white; crown bright yellow, sometimes with one or two orange feathers; upper cheeks bright yellow, lower cheeks sometimes also yellow but usually green or bluish-green sometimes with dark tips; sides of neck and hindcrown green with dark tips giving scalloped effect. Mantle, back and upper scapulars grass-green with dark tips; lower scapulars and rump grass-green; uppertail-coverts yellowish-green. Patch of feathers at carpal edge yellow, sometimes with some orange. Wing-coverts grass-green with faint dark tips. Primaries and secondaries green shading to violet-blue on distal outerwebs, but base of four outer secondaries red forming distinctive speculum. Underwing green. Throat blue in some birds, yellow in others, with remaining underparts yellowish-green with faint dark tips to most feathers giving scalloped effect, some birds (perhaps only adults) with distinct blue subterminal suffusion to feathers on breast and belly; thighs yellow; undertail-coverts bluish-green. Tail green with indistinct yellowish-green tip; lateral feathers dull orange at base. **Bare parts**: Bill pale horn; iris orange; legs grey.

SEX/AGE Sexes similar. Immature possibly lacks blue subterminal suffusion to feathers on underparts but this may not be a consistent trait. Two wild-caught immatures that died in captivity are darker green than adults with heavier black margins on mantle and a few scattered green feathers on yellow crown.

MEASUREMENTS Wing 201-205; tail 114-121; bill 26-31; tarsus 21-23.

GEOGRAPHICAL VARIATION The name *A. b. rothschildi* has been given to birds on the islands in the S Caribbean on account of less yellow on bend of wing with some red feathers mixed in, a shorter tail and less heavy bill. However, these differences are apparently age- rather than range-related.

REFERENCES Albornoz *et al.* (1994), Collar *et al.* (1992, 1994), Desenne & Strahl (1991, 1994), Forshaw (1989), Low (1981), Meyer de Schauensee & Phelps (1978), Reijns (1981), Voous (1983).

---

338 BLUE-FRONTED AMAZON
Amazona aestiva   Plate 84

Other names: Turquoise-fronted Amazon; Yellow-winged Parrot (*A. a. xanthopteryx*)

IDENTIFICATION 37cm. Fairly large, mainly green (paler beneath) amazon with extensive yellow on face and head, blue forehead and red carpal area (yellow in southern race) and speculum. Plumage somewhat variable. Distinguished from sympatric (over much of northern part of range) Orange-winged Amazon (342) by red and/or yellow feathers on carpal area and absence of pronounced green band traversing undertail. Sympatric (in interior Brazil) Yellow-faced Amazon (336) separated by smaller size and absence of blue feathers on head. Mealy Amazon (345), which overlaps in northern central-east Brazil, distinguished by absence of extensive yellow on face and head. Vinaceous Amazon (346), probably sympatric in

south-east Brazil, eastern Paraguay and northern Argentina, is readily split by absence of yellow on head and large maroon patch beneath. From similar (allopatric) Yellow-shouldered (337) and Yellow-crowned (341) Amazons in captivity by blue on face and blackish bill. Distinguished in wild from similarly proportioned *Pionus* by shallower wingbeats (wing-tips parallel at bottom of downstroke in *Pionus*). Generally in pairs or noisy flocks.

VOICE Very noisy with wide repertoire ranging from harsh squawks to more melodious sounds. Commonly heard calls include *krik-kiakrik-krik-krik-krik-krayo* and melodious *drewwo-droo-droo-droo-drewoh-drewwee-dew*. Yapping *help-help* sound recalls puppies, whilst begging *giah-giah* cry of young birds similar to call of Eurasian Magpie *Pica pica*. Excellent mimic of human and other sounds in captivity.

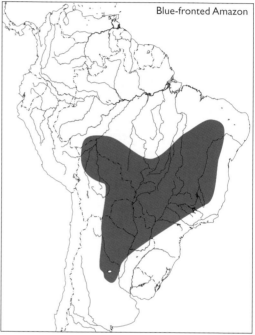

Blue-fronted Amazon

DISTRIBUTION AND STATUS A bird of interior South America, ranging from eastern Brazil in Pernambuco, Piauí, southern Maranhão and northern and western Bahia, through Goiás and Minas Gerais south to western São Paulo and formerly Rio Grande do Sul (absent from eastern coastal Brazil), and through Mato Grosso into eastern Bolivia, south throughout Paraguay and into northern Argentina in Misiones, Corrientes, Formosa, Chaco, northern Santa Fe, Jujuy, Salta, Tucumán, Catamarca and Santiago del Estero. Some seasonal movements occur, e.g. birds nesting in Argentine chaco move west to Andean foothills Mar-Sep. Generally common, in places abundant, and commonest *Amazona* over much of range and most numerous parrot in some areas. Trapped in large numbers for live bird trade with many specimens held in captivity inside and outside range. Numbers reduced in some areas owing to trapping (e.g. chaco region) with some range contraction and local extinctions owing to habitat loss (e.g. Minas Gerais), with significant problem in parts of chaco owing to selective cutting of *Schinopsis* trees. Previously reported as common in north-western Rio Grande do Sul but no recent records.

ECOLOGY The species inhabits a range of wooded habitats and open country with trees. Reported from humid forest, cerrado savannas, caatinga, gallery woodland and forest, palm groves, cultivated country with trees, and pantanal. Sometimes seen quite close to human habitation. Generally in lowlands but widely distributed over central Brazilian plateau and reported to 1,600m in arid intermontane valleys of eastern Bolivia. Commonly in pairs or flocks of several dozen birds, sometimes more. Assembles in large roosts in non-breeding season. Specific reported food items include fruits of *Enterolobium* and *Tabebuia aurea*; in Argentina birds are reported taking fruit and seeds from a wide range of plants including *Melia*, *Aspidosperma*, *Prosopis*, *Schinopsis*, *Ziziphus*, *Bulnesia* and *Cercidium*. Nests in cavity in large tree. Mainly breeds Oct-Mar. Clutch 2-3.

DESCRIPTION Forehead, upper lores and front and lower part of cheeks bright turquoise-blue; lower lores, crown, hind-cheeks, and often large patch on throat bright yellow (yellow on head variable with some birds showing green cheeks and very limited yellow on throat). Feathers on nape, sides of neck and upperparts grass-green (rather yellowish in some birds) with dark margins giving scaly appearance. Carpal edge and lesser coverts bright red, some birds showing quite extensive yellow on coverts (see Geographical Variation); other coverts green with faint yellowish border to some feathers. Primaries and inner secondaries green shading through violet-blue to black at tips; bright red bases to outer five secondaries, forming bold speculum. Underwing with coverts green, flight feathers bluish-green. Underparts yellowish-green with darker green tips to some feathers giving scalloped effect, and with blue suffusion on upper breast and belly in some birds; thighs yellow or yellowish-green. Tail green, more yellowish at tip; base of undertail red with faint green band separating more yellowish distal portion of tail. **Bare parts:** Bill blackish-grey; iris orange; legs grey.

SEX/AGE Sexes similar. Immature has iris chestnut, with green head or at least with less blue and yellow.

MEASUREMENTS Wing 199-232; tail 106-140; bill 29-34; tarsus 24-27.

GEOGRAPHICAL VARIATION Two races.
A. a. aestiva (E Brazil from Piauí and Pernambuco to São Paulo and Mato Grosso)
A. a. xanthopteryx (E Bolivia, Paraguay, N Argentina and extreme SW Brazil. Intergrades with *aestiva* in S Mato Grosso, parts of NW Paraguay and Misiones where birds with both yellow and red shoulders occur) Generally greener than nominate but some individuals very yellowish below, others with strong blue suffusion, and birds with red bases to feathers on underparts also reported. Shoulders and upper-wing-coverts yellow with yellow on head more extensive than nominate.

REFERENCES Antas & Cavalcanti (1988), Belton (1984), Contreras (1991), Dubs (1992), Forshaw (1989), Gyldenstolpe (1945b), Naumburg (1930), Nores & Yzurieta (1994), Ridgely (1981), Short (1975, 1976), Sick (1993), Stone & Roberts (1931), Wetmore (1926).

339 YELLOW-HEADED AMAZON
Amazona oratrix Plate 85

Other names: Levaillant's Amazon, Mexican Yellow-headed (-fronted) Amazon; Double Yellow-headed (-fronted) Amazon (*oratrix* and *tresmariae*); Tres Marías Amazon (*A. o. tresmariae*); Belize Yellow-headed Amazon (*A. o. belizensis*)

IDENTIFICATION 35cm. Large, mainly green amazon with bright yellow head, red speculum, and red and/or yellow on leading edge and carpal area of wing. Overlaps with Green-cheeked Amazon (329) in Tamaulipas (in e.g. Río Corona area) and eastern San Luis Potosí, with Red-lored Amazon (331) more widely on Gulf slope, Lilac-crowned Amazon (330) and White-fronted (323) over much of its Pacific range, and Yellow-lored (324) in Belize; however, safely separated from all these by yellow head, but green-headed immatures may be mistaken for sympatric congeners. From other 'yellow-headed' amazons in captivity by combination of yellow extending unbroken over entire head (Marajó race *xantholaema* of Yellow-crowned Amazon [341] has narrow yellow frontal band), green underparts and absence of blue feathers on face. Yellow-naped Amazon (340) approaches Yellow-headed in Oaxaca and Chiapas but yellow on head is confined to nape, and, sometimes, forehead and forecrown. Race confined to Sula Valley in Honduras has less yellow on head than other races (confined to forehead and crown) and sometimes shows yellow patch on nape. Moves quietly in tree-tops; flies well above canopy on shallow rapid wingbeats. Very shy some areas owing to persecution.

VOICE Variety of shrieks and whistles. Raucous but mellow screams including a rolled *kyaa-aa-uh* and *krra-aah-aa-ow*. Also loud human *wow* or *ow* sound. Often silent in flight. Excellent mimic of human and other sounds in captivity.

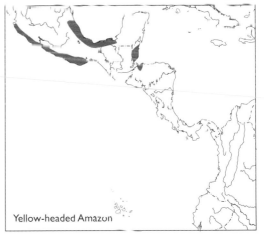

Yellow-headed Amazon

DISTRIBUTION AND STATUS The Yellow-headed Amazon is confined to Middle America in Mexico, Belize, extreme eastern Guatemala and extreme north-west Honduras. Occurs on Pacific slope of Mexico in Colima, Michoacán, Guerrero, Oaxaca (two disjunct populations on Pacific and Gulf slopes in the Isthmus region) and Chiapas; also on all four of the Islas Marías (Tres Marías) off the coast of Nayarit. Distributed on Gulf slope from central and southern Tamaulipas, easternmost San Luis

Potosí, Puebla, Veracruz, Tabasco and Campeche and into Belize and around Puerto Barios in extreme eastern Guatemala to extreme north-west Honduras in the Sula Valley. Distribution in east of range poorly documented, with occurrence in Campeche doubted and in Petén region of northern Guatemala confirmed only in 1993. Reports of birds outside normal range in Mexico (e.g. Mexico City) probably involve escapes. Feral populations in Miami (Florida) and Puerto Rico. Local, sparsely distributed and uncommon resident throughout most of range (perhaps locally common in parts of Belize) with numbers severely depleted by habitat loss and trapping for live bird markets. Sula Valley population survives as remnant. Species traded widely both within range and outside and is one of most sought-after Neotropical parrots in captivity (reputedly one of the best talkers). Most drastic declines probably in north-east Mexico where habitat loss has been most rapid and severe. Wild population probably less than 7,000 (1994). ENDANGERED.

ECOLOGY Birds frequent savanna, tropical deciduous forest (including clearings), dense thorn forest, Pacific swamp-forest, evergreen floodplain forest, dense gallery woodland, woods with *Pinus caribea* (Belize) and cultivated country with trees, mostly in lowlands below 500m. Chiefly in pairs or flocks with larger gatherings at communal roosts and favoured feeding stations. Birds roost on pine-covered ridges in Belize, moving to nearby humid forests to feed. Apparently forms flocks only rarely in Tamaulipas. Reported food items include buds, new leaves, palm fruits, *Acacia* seeds, fruits of *Macuna*, fig *Ficus*, *Zuelania guidonia*, *Bumelia laetivirens*, *Solanum* and *Pithecellobium flexicaule*; may cause damage to crops including maize, mango and unripe bananas. Nests in tree-cavity at 6-15m. In Belize, birds favour *Pinus* trees for nest-site. Breeds Feb-May in south, till June in north (e.g. Tamaulipas). Clutch usually 2-3.

DESCRIPTION Head and nape bright yellow, sides of neck sometimes with scattered green feathers. Upperparts grass-green with darker green tips to some feathers, uppertail-coverts paler. Wing-coverts green, sometimes with paler yellowish margins to some feathers; leading edge of wing and carpal area with variable red and/or yellow markings. Primaries and secondaries green at base (more emerald than coverts), blue towards tips; base of outer five secondaries bright red forming speculum. Underwing green. Chin bright yellow; throat green with variable blue suffusion and dark margins to feathers in some birds; breast and belly green with yellowish suffusion in some individuals, bluish suffusion in others; thighs with yellow feathers in some birds. Tail green with yellowish-green tips and red at base on innerwebs of lateral feathers. **Bare parts**: Bill greyish-horn; iris orange; legs grey.

SEX/AGE Sexes similar. Immature is largely green with little or no yellow on head and with no red and yellow on wing.

MEASUREMENTS Wing 206-244; tail 104-135; bill 30-37; tarsus 23-28.

GEOGRAPHICAL VARIATION Four races. A fifth, *magna*, representing Gulf slope birds, is not considered valid but reportedly shows yellow thighs and dark margins to breast feathers. Birds from around Puerto Barios in extreme E Guatemala show yellow concentrated on lores and crown. Whilst described as close to *belizensis*, birds from Puerto Barios to extreme NW Honduras perhaps represent another (not yet formally described) race of *oratrix* (or

even *A. auropalliata*) provisionally named '*guatemalensis*' (see *belizensis* below). The recently described *hondurensis* was previously widely regarded as an undescribed race of Yellow-crowned Amazon but is now treated as the southern end of a cline of diminishing yellow on the head of birds in the Yellow-headed group.

A. o. oratrix (Mainland Mexico)

A. o. tresmariae (Islas Marías, Mexico) From nominate by longer wing (male), light grass-green back, more bluish-green underparts and more extensive yellow on neck and especially on throat. Odd red feathers in head, and more frequent yellow tips to upperwing-coverts, inner secondaries and tail feathers.

A. o. belizensis (Belize) Less yellow on head than nominate, with no yellow on throat. Cheeks green, orbital ring greyish-white and probably on average smaller. Birds from Guatemala to north-west Honduras sometimes show yellow on head as broad patch on forecrown and around eyes, and perhaps represent an as yet undescribed race (referred to as '*guatemalensis*'); but some also show yellow nape feathers (see Geographical Variation in Yellow-naped Amazon).

A. o. hondurensis (Sula Valley, Honduras) Yellow on head limited to forehead and forecrown with some birds showing a yellow nape-patch. Paler bill and more extensive yellow on nape and head than *caribaea* race of Yellow-naped Amazon (340). Yellow crown-patch is also rounded or triangular versus a narrower band in *caribaea*. The *panamensis* race of Yellow-crowned Amazon (341) has a darker bill and lacks yellow nape-patch.

NOTE The taxonomic status of Yellow-headed, Yellow-naped (340) and Yellow-crowned Amazons (341) remains the subject of debate. Whilst there are distinct forms (despite the apparent absence of biological barriers) of these taxa from Mexico on the Pacific coast to South America, on the Caribbean slope of Central America (especially in Guatemala and Honduras) there are intermediate (the provisionally named '*guatemalensis*' and the *hondurensis* race of Yellow-headed) types suggesting that Yellow-headed and Yellow-naped (340) Amazons are races of a single species. The situation is evidently still confused (not least by possibly age-related plumage variations and wide individual variation within races) and there are several possible interpretations of the available evidence. Our approach tentatively treats these three taxa as recently differentiated species, but some revision may be necessary (especially in respect of the racial types occurring on the Caribbean slope of Central America) following further investigation.

REFERENCES Binford (1989), Clinton-Eitniear (1990), Collar *et al.* (1992, 1994), Edwards (1972), Forshaw (1989), Friedmann *et al.* (1950), Gehlbach *et al.* (1976), Grant (1965), Howell & Webb (1995), Lousada & Howell (1996, 1997), Lowery & Dalquest (1951), McLellan (1927), Peterson & Chalif (1973), Ridgely (1981), Russell (1964), Schaldach (1963), Stager (1957).

340 YELLOW-NAPED AMAZON
Amazona auropalliata Plate 85

Other names: Golden-naped Amazon, Honduras Yellow-naped Amazon (*A. a. parvipes*)

IDENTIFICATION 35cm. Large, mainly green amazon, paler on head and beneath, with bright golden-yellow nape and red speculum. Some individuals show variable amount of yellow on forehead. Birds on Bay Islands (*caribaea*) and Caribbean slope of Honduras and Nicaragua (*parvipes*) show red at bend of wing. Sympatric (on Ruatán) Yellow-lored Amazon (324) has white (male) or blue (female) crown. Overlaps widely with White-fronted and with Red-lored (331) Amazons in Caribbean part of range and on Bay Islands. Occurs with Mealy Amazon (345) in Honduras, Nicaragua and Costa Rica. Yellow-naped separated from all of these and other congeners in captivity by golden-yellow nape-band. Flies with rapid, shallow wingbeats. Human-sounding calls distinctive. Generally stays high in tree-tops and, except for flapping sounds when startled, usually takes off silently from perch.

VOICE Wide variety of squawks, screams and whistles. Most characteristic call described as deep, rolling *karrow* or *karra ow*, sometimes used in alarm. Many calls have human quality, suggesting a person imitating a parrot. Mostly calls in flight. Very good mimic of human sounds in captivity.

Yellow-naped Amazon

DISTRIBUTION AND STATUS The species is confined to Middle America. It occurs in the eastern Pacific lowlands of Mexico (Oaxaca and Chiapas), Guatemala (one specimen taken in Petén but status there uncertain), El Salvador (lower arid tropical zone), Honduras and Nicaragua to north west Costa Rica from southern end of Gulf of Nicoya northwards. It also occurs on the Caribbean slope of Honduras and in the Mosquitia of Honduras and neighbouring north-east Nicaragua. Found on Ruatán and Guanaja in the Bay Islands but absent Utila. Resident. Reportedly uncommon in Oaxaca and rare and declining in Costa Rica. Birds in Sula Valley, Honduras, formerly attributed to this species but now incuded in Yellow-headed Amazon. Formerly common and locally abundant but probably declining throughout range owing to conversion of habitat to agricultural uses and trapping for local and international trade. Not yet considered at overall risk of extinction but long-term status not secure if decline continues. Although reasonable numbers remain on Guanaja, the race inhabiting the Bay Islands (*caribaea*) is in serious decline owing to trapping for export (virtually 100% of chicks taken each year); also at risk from tourist development, especially on Roatán.

ECOLOGY The species inhabits semi-arid woodland, arid scrub and savannas (including those of pine *Pinus*), openings in tropical deciduous and Pacific swamp-forest, evergreen gallery forest and sometimes second growth in agricultural areas. Reported to 600m in Guatemala and 700m in Honduras. Generally in pairs or small flocks, sometimes in larger gatherings, but population decline perhaps now prevents large flocks in some areas. Forms communal roosts. Reported food items include seeds of *Cochlospermum*, *Curatella*, figs *Ficus* and ripening *Terminalia* fruits. Birds in Bay Islands observed feeding on cones of *Pinus caribaea*, with high seasonal dependence on this resource. Nests in unlined hollow of living or dead tree including pines in (e.g.) Nicaragua and Bay Islands. Breeding Feb, Oaxaca and El Salvador, Mar, Ruatán. Clutch 2-3.

DESCRIPTION Forehead and forecrown usually pale bluish-green, sometimes with narrow yellow frontal band extending to forecrown; hindcrown pale bluish-green; lores, cheeks and sides of neck green; nape with broad golden-yellow band. Upperparts green with some feathers on mantle and back faintly edged blackish; rump and uppertail-coverts slightly brighter than rest of upperparts. Wing-coverts green but more emerald than upper body; yellow feathers on leading edge of wing in some birds. Outerwebs of outer four secondaries bright red forming speculum; primaries and secondaries otherwise green with violet-blue on outerwebs and towards tips. Underwing green. Underparts pale green with a slight bluish tinge on throat. Tail green with yellowish-green terminal band, basally red and outerwebs of outer feathers edged bluish. **Bare parts:** Bill bluish, black at tip; bare periophthalmic skin greyish; iris orange; legs greyish-horn or horn.

SEX/AGE Sexes similar. Immature has green nape with yellow feathers appearing at end of first year; brown iris.

MEASUREMENTS Wing 209-234; tail 106-125; bill 34-37; tarsus 25-29.

GEOGRAPHICAL VARIATION Three races. However, birds from Bay Islands often treated as *parvipes*, not *caribaea*. Some specimens from Pacific Guatemala show yellow forehead, but apparently not as consistent racial difference.

A. o. auropalliata (Pacific slope of Middle America from Oaxaca, Mexico, to NW Costa Rica)

A. o. parvipes (Mosquitia of Honduras and NE Nicaragua) Smaller than nominate with red feathers at bend of wing, otherwise similar.

A. o. caribaea (Bay Islands, Honduras) Similar to *parvipes* but more olive beneath and paler horn bill (especially lower mandible). Adults generally with triangular patch of yellow on forecrown. Young birds show little yellow on head or nape.

NOTE Yellow-naped often considered conspecific with Yellow-headed (339) and Yellow-crowned (341) Amazons. See Note in Yellow-headed Amazon.

REFERENCES Arndt (1996), Binford (1989), Bond (1936), Davis & Bennett (1972), Dickey & van Rossem (1938), Forshaw (1989), Friedmann *et al.* (1950), Griscom (1932), Howell (1972), Howell & Webb (1992), Land (1970), Lousada (1989), Lousada & Howell (1996), Monroe (1968), Slud (1964), Stiles *et al.* (1989), Wetmore (1944).

341 YELLOW-CROWNED AMAZON
Amazona ochrocephala   Plate 85

Other names: Yellow-fronted Amazon, (Single) Yellow-headed Amazon; Panama Parrot and Panama Yellow-fronted Amazon (*A. o. panamensis*); Marajó Yellow-crowned Amazon (*A. o. xantholaema*); Natterer's Amazon (*A. o. nattereri*)

IDENTIFICATION 35-38cm. Large and mainly green, darker above and paler beneath, with yellow feathers on forehead and forecrown sometimes extending onto lores and around eyes (birds in western Amazon basin with green forehead). Further distinguished by dark margins to feathers on hindneck and nape, red speculum and red at bend of wing. Sometimes shows yellow thighs. Sympatric Orange-winged Amazon (342) has yellow cheeks and blue on lores. Yellow-naped Amazon (340), possibly sympatric in Sula valley, Honduras (see Distribution and Status), has yellow on hindneck and sometimes on forecrown. Combination of green underparts, absence of blue feathers on head, yellow crown and red at bend of wing separates Yellow-crowned from other *Amazona* in wild and captivity (see Geographical Variation). Often tame, allowing close approach. Except for flapping sounds of wings, leaves cover silently when flushed. Flies on rapid, shallow wingbeats.

VOICE Varied repertoire. Calls include rather yapping *ye-ert* and *gre-eht* sounds with tonal quality that suggests voice of immature Eurasian Magpie *Pica pica*. Harsh *screet* and louder, deeper *graaht* and vibrating *cree-ow-ee-ow* calls in flight. Loud *cacawuk* reported as commonest call in northern Venezuela, *ker-wow*, *kew-wow* on Trinidad, medium-low *aow-aow* and *ha-ha-ha* sound in Guyana. Excellent mimic of human sounds in captivity.

Yellow-crowned Amazon

DISTRIBUTION AND STATUS This parrot is found in Panama (and possibly Honduras) in Central America and in South America south to eastern Brazil and northern Bolivia. It is present in Panama mainly on Pacific slope from Chiriquí to western Darién but also on Caribbean slope (e.g. eastern San Blas); also on larger of Pearl Islands and Coiba. It is distributed in northern Colombia from northern Chocó and lower Río Atrato and along the Caribbean coast and tropical zone of Magdalena Valley to

south-east base of Santa Marta massif and western Sierra de Perijá. In eastern foothills of eastern Andes and adjacent lowlands of Colombia east through the tropical zone of Venezuela south of coastal mountains through Bolívar (where apparently not known from south) and Amazonas to Guianas and Trinidad (where status obscure owing to introduced captive birds). Present in the Amazon basin of Brazil south to north-western Mato Grosso and west into eastern lowlands of Ecuador and through Amazonian Peru to northern Bolivia. Apparently resident throughout range. Numbers much reduced in Panama but locally fairly common, especially in drier areas; commonest parrot (at least formerly) in San Blas region. Generally common (even locally abundant) in South America but numbers reduced in more accessible areas owing to trade.

ECOLOGY Birds occupy open woodland, borders of humid forest, gallery woodland, deciduous woodland, savanna, and open swampy areas in lowland rain-forest, also cultivated and suburban areas in some localities, and often near rivers. Gallery forest is preferred in Panama where birds avoid continuous moist forest, being possibly replaced there in much of South America by Orange-winged Amazon. Generally in lowlands; reported to 500m in Colombia and Venezuela and to 750m in Honduras. Generally in pairs or small flocks of 10-30 with occasional gatherings up to 300. Birds gather in communal tree-top roosts. Reported food items include ripe fruit of *Curatella americana*, *Pereskia guamacho* and other cacti. Chiefly feeds in tree-tops but reported taking maize from fields. Nest in hollow in palm stump, tree or termitarium, often low down. Breeding-condition birds Dec-Jan, Colombia; breeding Feb-May, Venezuela. Clutch 2-3.

DESCRIPTION Forehead and forecrown bright yellow; lores, cheeks and superciliary area green in most birds but sometimes with yellow extending over lores and around eyes, and some birds with concealed red bases to yellow crown feathers; sides of neck, hindneck, nape and mantle green with dark margins giving scalloped effect. Upperparts otherwise green. Upper lesser coverts red, other coverts green; leading edge of wing yellowish. Outer five secondaries green with bright red outerwebs forming speculum; flight feathers otherwise green with blue tips to secondaries and outerwebs of primaries darkening to black on tips. Underwing dull green with blackish tips. Underparts green with blue suffusion on breast, yellow feathers on thighs (often few and inconspicuous). Upper-tail green with yellowish fringes; undertail green with broad yellowish tip; both with outer feathers basally red and fringed bluish on outerwebs. **Bare parts**: Bill dark grey, reddish at base of upper mandible; iris orange; legs grey.

SEX/AGE Sexes similar. Immature has more restricted yellow patch on head, orange-red fringes to yellow crown feathers, less red at base of tail feathers, more pointed tail feathers and brown iris.

MEASUREMENTS Wing 199-220; tail 109-124; bill 31-37; tarsus 25-28.

GEOGRAPHICAL VARIATION Four races.

A. o. ochrocephala (E Colombia, Venezuela, Trinidad, Guianas and N Brazil south to lower right bank tributaries of Amazon in Amazonas and Pará)

A. o. xantholaema (Marajó Island in the mouth of the Amazon) More extensive yellow on head extending to hindcrown, around eyes and onto cheeks and ear-coverts. Often with narrow green frontal band. Bluish tinge on breast.

A. o. nattereri (S Colombia in Caquetá, E Ecuador, E Peru, W Brazil and N Bolivia. Possibly intergrades with nominate in border areas of Meta and Caquetá, Colombia) Less yellow on head than nominate with green frontal band. Cheeks, superciliary area and lores with blue tinge. Red at bend of wing often mixed with yellow feathers.

A. o. panamensis (N Colombia north and west of Andes to W Panama including Islas Perlas and Coiba. Possibly also NW Venezuela) Bill pinkish-horn, yellow feathers restricted to V-shaped patch on forehead and forecrown. Possibly on average smaller than nominate (wing 184-207).

NOTE Yellow-crowned widely regarded as conspecific with Yellow-headed (339) and Yellow-naped Amazons. See Note in Yellow-headed Amazon.

REFERENCES Arndt (1996), Blake (1962), ffrench (1992), Forshaw (1989), Friedmann (1948), Friedmann & Smith (1950, 1955), Haverschmidt (1968), Hilty & Brown (1986), Lousada & Howell (1996), Meyer de Schauensee (1949), Meyer de Schauensee & Phelps (1978), Monroe (1968), O'Neill (1981), Ridgely & Gwynne (1989), Sick (1993), Snyder (1966), Wetmore (1939, 1968).

---

342 ORANGE-WINGED AMAZON
Amazona amazonica   Plate 86

Other names: Orange-winged Parrot

IDENTIFICATION 32cm. Mostly green, medium-sized amazon with yellow and blue on head and orange speculum. Underside of tail dull orange traversed by green band. Distinguished from overlapping (in northern South America) Yellow-crowned Amazon (341) by yellow cheeks and blue above eye and on lores; from rather similar sympatric (in south of range) Blue-fronted Amazon (338) by absence of red and/or yellow feathers on carpal area and of pronounced green band across orange undertail. Combination of yellow and blue on head (no orange or red), orange speculum and green carpal area distinguish it from all other *Amazona* in field and captivity. Generally seen in flocks in flight or perched in tree-tops. Usually noisy but quieter whilst feeding. Flies on rapid shallow wingbeats, often at some height.

VOICE Very varied repertoire of harsh screeches, screams and squawks and more melodious trilling, bubbling and whistling sounds. Call notes include clear *keeeih hookik, kurik kuirk*, nasal *ahnk ahnk*, piercing shrieks, yelping *shreeep* cries, drawn-out vibrating *ch-ee-ee-ee ah* (sometimes with trumpet-like quality), short sharp *chet chet* and more melodious *plenk* calls. Loud piercing *screet* sounds sometimes uttered 3-4 times in rapid succession between pauses. Also a vibrating *gree-eee-eek* followed by a disyllabic whistling yelp. Some screeching calls sound to European ears like those of Black-headed Gull *Larus ridibundus.*

DISTRIBUTION AND STATUS This amazon has a wide range in tropical South America, mostly east of Andes from Colombia to south-east Brazil. In northern Colombia it occurs in the middle and lower Magdalena Valley and lowlands from Rio Sinú to the Santa Marta region, and throughout eastern Colombia and south through eastern

Ecuador, eastern Peru and east-central Bolivia. It is reported from all of Venezuela except Zulia and Mérida in north-west, and is widespread in the Guianas and on Trinidad and Tobago. In Brazil the species is found in most of the Amazon basin south to Mato Grosso (absent south-western pantanal) and into north-western São Paulo and Paraná. In an apparently disjunct range it reappears in eastern coastal forests of Brazil from Pernambuco in the north south to the border of Rio de Janeiro and São Paulo. Mainly resident with some minor seasonal movements in some areas. Generally common, in places abundant, and most frequently seen parrot in parts of range (e.g. mangrove forests in coastal Surinam). Numbers are perhaps depressed locally owing to hunting for food, capture for live bird trade, persecution and habitat loss; hunting is very heavy in French Guiana. However, the overall population may have increased following fragmentation and clearance of rain-forest in parts of the Amazon basin.

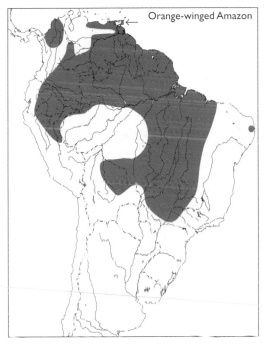

Orange-winged Amazon

ECOLOGY All kinds of lowland forest and wooded country (often near water) are used, including tropical rain-forest, savanna and other seasonal woodlands, cultivated land with trees, mangroves, várzea forest and gallery woodlands. The species frequents forest edge and second growth, tending to avoid large areas of unbroken dense forest and humid terra firme forest, where Mealy (345) is dominant amazon. It is also reported from urban areas (e.g. Belém, Brazil) and plantations, but occurs chiefly in lowlands below 500m although reported to 1,200m in Venezuela south of the Orinoco. Several pairs often combine in loose flocks, with gatherings up to about 50 birds quite common with 200 or more not unusual. Roosts communally in clump of trees, giant bamboos or palms, sometimes on forested island in river or mangroves. Roosts smaller during breeding season. Reported food items include palm fruits (e.g. *Sloanea, Richeria* and *Byrsonima*) and flowers of *Erythrina*; other food plants include *Tabebuia* serratifolia, *Curatella americana* and *Spondius monbin*. Takes crop plants in some areas including oranges and mango but perhaps only when natural food is scarce. Breeds Jan-Jun, Trinidad and Tobago; breeding-condition birds Dec-Feb, Magdalena Valley. Clutch 2-5.

DESCRIPTION Cheeks yellow; area above eye blue, sometimes extending over forehead and/or crown; forehead and crown otherwise yellow; lores generally blue; hindcrown and neck grass-green with rather faint dark margins giving scalloped appearance. Upperparts grass-green. Wing-coverts grass-green. Primaries green tipped black with broad violet-blue subterminal band; outer three secondaries bright orange-red with deep violet-blue tips, others green tipped violet-blue. Underwing with coverts green, flight feathers green with black tips. Throat yellow, sometimes with blue feathers; underparts otherwise green tinged yellowish, undertail-coverts yellowish-green. Tail with yellowish-green tip, orange-red subterminal band, central transverse green band and orange-red base; outer feathers with blue on outerwebs. **Bare parts**: Bill pale horn with darker tip; iris orange-red; legs grey.

SEX/AGE Sexes similar. Immature has brown iris.

MEASUREMENTS Wing 180-221; tail 82-112; bill 26-33; tarsus 22-26.

GEOGRAPHICAL VARIATION Two races recognised here, although difference tiny and not necessarily consistent. However, birds show considerable variation not yet linked to geography, particularly in respect of yellow and blue areas on head and orange in wings and tail. Birds from Magdalena Valley also reportedly smaller than specimens from east of Andes whilst (at least some) NE Peruvian birds show pale ashy-blue wash to plumage, more distinct black edges to feathers of hindneck and larger bills (34-35mm). *A. a. micra* (NE South America) formerly recognised as race on basis of smaller size but is generally not now recognised because (e.g.) wing length for birds from Surinam lies within range of other South American specimens (183-200mm). Valid races may, however, be isolated after additional research.

> *A. a. amazonica* (Continental South America)
> *A. a. tobagensis* (Trinidad and Tobago) Similar to nominate but speculum claimed to be larger (on outer four, not three, secondaries, but this character may not be consistent).

REFERENCES Chapman (1917), Darlington (1931), Desenne & Strahl (1991, 1994), Dubs (1992), ffrench (1992), Forshaw (1989), Friedmann (1948), Haverschmidt (1968), Hilty & Brown (1986), Junge & Mees (1958), Meyer de Schauensee (1949, 1966), Meyer de Schauensee & Phelps (1978), Ridgely (1981), Sick (1993), Snyder (1966), Stone & Roberts (1934), Tostain *et al.* (1992), Traylor (1958).

---

343 SCALY-NAPED AMAZON
Amazona mercenaria   Plate 86

Other names: Mercenary Amazon, Tschudi's Amazon, Mountain Parrot, Scaly-naped Parrot; Grey-naped or Colombian Amazon (*A. m. canipalliata*)

IDENTIFICATION 32-34cm. Mainly green amazon, dark above, paler beneath. Head and neck entirely green except

for bluish-black margins to feathers on hindcrown and sides of neck (not clear in field but giving scaly appearance at close quarters). Birds in south of range show red speculum; northern race *canipalliata* has concealed maroon spots on bases of outer secondaries. Yellow (sometimes with reddish marks) at leading edge of wing. Uppertail-coverts pale yellowish-green. Only *Amazona* in preferred high montane habitat over most of range, but at lower limits of occurrence, especially Amazon drainage of Peru and Bolivia, it possibly enters range of Yellow-crowned (341), Orange-winged (342) and Mealy (345) Amazons. Separated from congeners in field and captivity by combination of green head, 'scaly' neck and nape, and reddish-purple subterminal spots on spread lateral tail feathers; lack of red speculum in north of range is additional helpful character there. Green head and larger size separate it from several partially sympatric species of similarly proportioned *Pionus* parrots. Flight somewhat duck-like on shallow, rather stiff laboured wingbeats. Often flies at some height. In pairs or groups up to about 8. Shy.

VOICE Varied repertoire. Calls include trilling *cheeep*, a variety of whistles including pleasant *dee-lee-do-de-de-de-dor*, goose-like trumpeting calls, screeching and grating sounds and powerful harsh staccato *chark chark chark* from perch and in flight. Some sounds are quite complex and comprise a mixture of loud raucous cries interspersed with more melodious descending notes. Recalls Mealy Amazon but higher-pitched with quicker delivery.

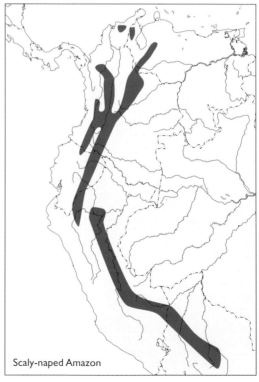

Scaly-naped Amazon

DISTRIBUTION AND STATUS An Andean amazon, ranging from north-west Venezuela to northern Bolivia. It occurs in the Andes and Mérida and Sierra de Perijá in north-west Venezuela, and in all three Andean ranges and the Santa Marta massif in Colombia, but with no records in the western Andes from Nariño in south or north of Valle in north, and unknown in the eastern Andes north of Cundinamarca, although occurrence presumably continuous through to Andes of Venezuela. It is reported throughout forested parts of the eastern Andes in Ecuador south through Peru to Bolivia in La Paz and Cochabamba, with one 19th century record from Salta in Argentina. Elevational or nomadic movements occur in some areas (e.g. Valle, Colombia), but probably mostly resident. At low density throughout range and generally uncommon, even in areas with undisturbed forest. It has undoubtedly declined owing to widespread habitat loss in Ecuador and Colombia in particular, although it remains fairly common in Santa Marta region.

ECOLOGY Birds inhabit hill and mountain forest in upper tropical, subtropical and temperate zones, including open woodland with large emergent trees, open forest on ridges and to treeline in wooded valleys and ravines in the páramo zone. Occurs in flight over deforested areas en route between fragments of suitable habitat. Reported at 800-3,200m on the east slope of eastern Andes of Peru; 1,600-3,600m in the Sierra de Perijá. Usually in pairs or small flocks with larger gatherings moving to or from communal roosts morning and afternoon. Little information on diet but observed taking figs *Ficus* and baseball-sized fruits of unidentified vine in Huila, Colombia, and apparently descends to raid fields of maize. Breeding-condition birds Mar-May, Colombia; nest-sites difficult to find and often located in inaccessible areas.

DESCRIPTION Forehead, lores, cheeks and ear-coverts green; crown to nape and sides of neck green with bluish-black tips to feathers giving scaly effect. Mantle green with some feathers showing faint dark margins; back, scapulars and rump green; uppertail-coverts paler yellowish green. Wing-coverts green with patch of yellow feathers (sometimes marked reddish-orange) on leading edge of wing. Outer three secondaries with red on base forming speculum, remainder green with bluish tips; primaries green becoming blue distally and darkening to blackish at tip. Underwing with coverts green, flight feathers green at base, blackish towards tips. Underparts lighter paler green than above with dark margins to feathers on upper breast in some birds. Uppertail green centrally with yellowish-green tips, lateral feathers basally green with large reddish-purple subterminal spots and yellowish-green tips, outerweb of outer feathers purplish; undertail innerwebs pinkish with yellowish-green tips. **Bare parts**: Bill grey with pale area at base of maxilla, iris orange; legs brownish-horn.

SEX/AGE Sexes similar. Immature thought to be similar to adults.

MEASUREMENTS Wing 195-217; tail 86-101; bill 26-31; tarsus 21-24.

GEOGRAPHICAL VARIATION Two races.

A. m. mercenaria (Peru to N Bolivia. A specimen from 'Leimebamba', Peru, has less red on speculum and in this respect approaches *canipalliata*)

A. m. canipalliata (N Peru to NW Venezuela) Red speculum absent. Bases of outer secondaries marked with maroon spots. Some individuals show scattered red feathers on crown, throat and upper breast.

REFERENCES Bond (1955), Chapman (1926), Darlington (1931), Desenne & Strahl (1991, 1994), Fjeldså &

Krabbe (1990), Forshaw (1989), Hilty & Brown (1986), Meyer de Schauensee (1949, 1966), Meyer de Schauensee & Phelps (1978), Nores & Yzurieta (1994), Ridgely & Gaulin (1980), Todd & Carriker (1922).

---

344 WHITE-FACED AMAZON
Amazona kawalli   Plate 86

Other names: Kawall's Amazon

IDENTIFICATION 36cm. Large, mainly green amazon with patch of creamy bare skin at base of bill, red speculum and yellowish-green tip to tail. Dark edges to feathers on hindneck, sides of neck, sides of upper breast and nape give scaly appearance. Range overlaps with very similar Mealy Amazon (345), although White-faced perhaps at least partially separated by stronger preference for flooded forest, and by strip of whitish skin bordering base of bill (from cere to chin), narrower greenish-yellow terminal band on slightly shorter tail, red on innerwebs of base of tail feathers, absence of red on leading edge of folded wing (yellowish-green instead), bare, fairly narrow grey ocular ring (large and creamy white in Mealy) and generally purer green plumage. The rather similar (and presumably allopatric) Scaly-naped Amazon (343) is smaller, has a darker bill, fully feathered at its base, and shows red on the leading edge of wing. Range not well documented but probably overlaps with Orange-winged (342) and Yellow-crowned (341). Combination of bare facial patch, green head, 'scaly' neck and nape and no red on carpal area may help to split from congeners at close quarters but field separation from even last two species very difficult. In captivity bare whitish skin at base of bill distinguishes this bird from all congeners.

VOICE Flight call described as *wheeou   wheeou*.

DISTRIBUTION AND STATUS The very few published records are all from the Amazon basin in Brazil: on upper Juruá (below Eirunepé), Amazonas; at the confluence of the Rio Roosevelt and Rio Aripuanã, southern Pará; and south of Santarém, Pará. There is an unpublished specimen, misidentified as Scaly-naped Amazon, labelled 'Colombia'. Possibly overlooked in field owing to morphological similarities with some of better known congeners and almost undoubtedly occurs more widely than few existing records suggest. Distribution map based on presumed occurrence between known localities. No details on population or conservation status.

ECOLOGY Inhabits tropical rain-forest with apparent preference for river edge and permanently flooded (igapó) forest. Reported food items include seeds of *Hevea brasiliensis* and *H. spruceana* trees, mesocarp of *Maximiliana maripa* palm fruits and seeds of *Eichleria* and *Joannesia*. Known nests in cavities of trees of flooded forest.

DESCRIPTION Forehead, lores, cheeks and ear-coverts green, although lores in at least some birds appear blackish. Crown, sides of neck, hindneck and nape green with broad blackish margins to feathers giving scaly appearance, with scaling more pronounced on nape and mantle. Upperwing-coverts green with median and lesser coverts showing faint dark tips; some yellowish-green feathers on leading edge of wing. Primaries green with black towards tips and some blue on outerwebs (one specimen with bright yellow outermost primary on one wing); red on outer three secondaries forms bright speculum. Underparts green with scaly effect derived from blackish tips to feathers on sides of upper breast; some dark-tipped feathers in centre of breast but less distinct; undertail-coverts more greenish-yellow. Uppertail green with broad terminal greenish-yellow terminal band, lateral feathers variably marked dull red (sometimes bordered brownish-black and edged blue) on basal half; undertail similar but slightly duller. **Bare parts**: Bill grey with creamy bare skin at base and creamy patch on upper mandible; iris reddish-orange; legs greyish.

SEX/AGE Male has grey lores and perhaps larger bill. Immature undescribed.

MEASUREMENTS Wing 241-262; tail 114-121; bill 32-40.

GEOGRAPHICAL VARIATION None.

REFERENCES Arndt (1996), Collar & Pittman (1996), Grantsau & Camargo (1989), Stotz *et al.* (1996), Yamashita *in litt.* (1996).

---

345 MEALY AMAZON
Amazona farinosa   Plate 86

Other names: Mealy Parrot; Plain-coloured Amazon (*A. f. inornata*); Blue-crowned Parrot or Guatemalan Amazon (*A. f. guatemalae*); Costa Rican or Green-headed Amazon (*A. f. virenticeps*)

IDENTIFICATION 38-40cm. Large, mainly green amazon with large white eye-ring. Tail distinctly two-toned with distal half yellowish and basal half green. Variable-sized yellow spot on crown of nominate (eastern South America). Birds from Mexico to western Panama with crown and nape blue, whilst birds in western Amazonia show green crown (see Geographical Variation). Conspicuous red speculum. Mainly green immatures of other amazons appear brighter. At close quarters, glaucous suffusion on hindneck to back suggests bird is coated with fine grey powder. Widely sympatric with Yellow-cheeked (331), Orange-winged (342) and Yellow-crowned (341) Amazons and associates with these (especially Yellow-cheeked) in mixed flocks. Large size, dull coloration,

characteristic voice and distinctly two-toned tail distinguishes Mealy from these and other *Amazona* in field (but see White-faced Amazon, 344). Often perched motionless in tree-top, moving quietly in middle branches or seen in pairs or small flocks on strong shallow wingbeats below tree-top level.

VOICE Varied repertoire including screams, whistles, babbles and squawks. Noisy, especially in flight and whilst arriving and departing from roost, with calls audible at some distance; feeding birds quieter except when with begging juveniles. Vocalisations include chattering noises followed by *chock-chock-chock-chock* and characteristic trisyllabic flight call *ta-kah-yee ta-kah-yee ta-kah-yee*. Also rolling *krrrillik krrrillik*, powerful trumpeting *ch-laaa* (sometimes rapidly repeated), raucous *chowk chowk*, conversational *crack* and *sreek* and short metallic *screee-tat*. Alighting birds make resonant *kwok* notes. Some complex phrases comprise several notes of different pitch and tone, some harsh, others quite melodious. Comical *toot toot toot* regarded as instantly recognisable; glugging sound like emptying bottle also distinctive. Voice generally deeper than other amazons.

Mealy Amazon

DISTRIBUTION AND STATUS Mealies have a wide range extending from Middle America south into the Orinoco and Amazon basins, eastern Brazil and west of Andes south to Ecuador. The species is found on the Caribbean slope of Mexico (birds reported near Mexico City are probably escapes) from Veracruz through lowland Oaxaca, Chiapas, Campeche and Quintana Roo in the southern Yucatán, into the Caribbean lowlands of Guatemala, Belize, Honduras and Nicaragua and throughout the Caribbean slope and southern Pacific region of Costa Rica and the tropical zone of Panama (including Coiba island), but is absent in more open areas of the Pacific lowlands. It has been reported in Colombia from the lower Atrato valley, Chocó and Pacific lowlands, to western Ecuador from Esmeraldas to Guayas, and occurs in the Caribbean lowlands of Colombia east through the tropical zone of the Magdalena Valley and the eastern lowlands to the Sierra de Perijá (absent from Santa Marta region and adjacent coasts). It spans Venezuela from Zulia to Amazonas and Bolívar and through the Guianas into northern and western Brazil from Amapá and Pará in the east through Roraima, Amazonas, Acre and Rondônia in the west and south in central Brazil to northern Mato

Grosso, the Amazon regions of Peru and north-west Bolivia from La Paz to Santa Cruz. There is a disjunct population in eastern Brazil from Bahia south through eastern Minas Gerais and Espírito Santo to northern São Paulo. Mainly resident with seasonal wanderings in some parts of range (e.g. Surinam where most numerous in coastal sand-ridge forests, Jul-Aug). Rather scarce in Veracruz but progressively more numerous eastwards. Common northern Guatemala where most abundant parrot after White-crowned Parrot (317), reasonably common in Belize, but uncommon Honduras. Common to abundant Costa Rica, especially in Golfo Dulce region; probably most numerous *Amazona* in Panama, especially on Caribbean slope. Fairly common in north-west Bolivia and southern Peru and reported as common, Pará, Brazil. Fairly common Guyana but less numerous than Orange-winged or Yellow-headed Amazons. Taken for food in some areas owing to large size and, although less heavily sought after than some other *Amazona*, collected for pets and international live bird trade and hunted for food (e.g. French Guiana where heavily shot). Population declines have occurred in some areas (e.g. Central America and western Ecuador) owing to deforestation.

ECOLOGY Chiefly in dense humid lowland rain-forest, especially near clearings and forest edge, but penetrates low montane rain-forest in Honduras and lower margins of subtropical zone in Panama. Frequents plantations with tall trees and occurs locally in gallery forest in savanna and more rarely deciduous forest. Generally in canopy but descends to middle level in gaps and clearings. Reported to about 290m in Oaxaca, 350m in Guatemala, 1,200m in Honduras, 500m in Costa Rica, 1,100m in Pacific Colombia. Generally in pairs or flocks of up to about 20, with larger gatherings at abundant local food sources. Forms noisy communal roosts in tall trees outside breeding season sometimes comprising several hundred birds. Reported food items include figs *Ficus*, *Brosimum*, pods of leguminous *Inga* and *Dussia*, arils of *Casearia* and *Virola*, also seen feeding on *Pithecellobium*, *Tetragastris*, *Dialium guianensis*, *Peritassa compta*, *Prionostemma aspera*, *Cochlospermum orinocense*, *Slounea grandiflora*, *Corima macrocarpa*, *Abuta grandiflora*, *Cecropia miparia*, *Heliocostylus tomentosa*, *Micropholis* and *Pouteria*. Reported attacking crops of maize in Panama. Nests in tree-cavity, often enlarged by birds before egg-laying. One record of nest in large crevice in Mayan temple. Breeding Nov-Mar, Mato Grosso; breeding-condition birds May, Guatemala; near breeding-condition birds Jan, Cauca, Colombia. Usual clutch three.

DESCRIPTION Forehead, lores and crown green, but some birds show variable amount of yellow on crown ranging from a single feather to a quite large regular or irregular patch, sometimes with a few flecks of red or concealed beneath green feathers; superciliary area, sides of neck, hindneck and hindcrown green; nape dull green with glaucous suffusion and broad dark margins giving scaly appearance. Mantle dull glaucous-green with faint dark margins; upperparts otherwise dull green. Wing-coverts dull green with glaucous suffusion and dark margins to some lesser coverts; leading edge of wing with small amount of red. Three to four outer secondaries with red patch on centre of outerweb forming bright speculum; remainder green with blue tips; primaries dark with blue on outerwebs. Underwing with coverts green, some with blackish margins, flight feathers green at base, black towards tips. Underparts green, paler than above and with

slight greyish-blue tinge. Tail basally green, distal half yellowish. Some individuals show slight red on base of outer feathers. **Bare parts**: Bill horn shading to dark greyish-brown on tip; bare periophthalmic skin creamy-white; iris reddish-orange, legs greyish.

SEX/AGE Sexes similar. Immature has brown iris.

MEASUREMENTS Wing 222-252; tail 107-143; bill 34-43; tarsus 27-31.

GEOGRAPHICAL VARIATION Five races. Three South American races show considerable internal plumage variation and to some extent overlap in defining characters. Further study may confirm that *inornata* and *chapmani* are synonymous with *farinosa*. There are also traits that appear clinal between northern and southern populations, with northern birds (*guatemalae* and *virenticeps*) showing darker bills and more blue on head (diminishing southwards) with southern populations (*farinosa*, *inornata* and *chapmani*) showing lighter, more horn-coloured bills.

A. f. farinosa (E Colombia south from Meta, lower Orinoco basin in E Venezuela and S Amazonas in south, through Amazonian Brazil from Pará to Mato Grosso to lowlands of E Peru. Disjunctly in E Brazil from Bahia to N São Paulo. Range in W Amazonia relative to *inornata* and *chapmani* is poorly documented)

A. f. inornata (Panama including Coiba island, Pacific and Caribbean lowlands of Colombia to W Ecuador and tropical zone of Magdalena Valley and on eastern base of E Andes south to Meta. Occurs in N and W Venezuela to C and N Amazonas and east in Bolivar to Río Caura) Darker, duller and more olive than other races, generally with no yellow feathers on crown. However, latter trait may not definitively split individual birds since at least one Panamanian specimen of *inornata* has yellow feathers scattered on forecrown whilst some nominate birds have almost no yellow on head. Smaller than next race (wing 240-245).

A. f. chapmani (E Ecuador and disjunctly in N Bolivia but also apparently in Peru west of E Andes. A single specimen is reported from Putumayo, S Colombia) Similar to *inornata* but larger (wing 266-269). In common with nominate and *inornata*, birds show individual variation in respect of yellow feathers on crown and frontal area.

A. f. virenticeps (Nicaragua to W Panama. Possibly intergrades with next race in E Honduras) Yellowish-green (no red) on leading edge of wing, pale blue on crown. At least one specimen shows several yellow feathers on nape.

A. f. guatemalae (Veracruz, Mexico, to Honduras) Like *virenticeps* but on average larger, and blue on crown darker and more extensive. Darker bill than nominate.

NOTE Races *guatemalae* and *virenticeps* were once both treated as full species. Whilst this approach (or more likely their separation off as two races of a single species) may ultimately prove valid, the current practice of treating these taxa as subspecies of *A. farinosa* is followed here.

REFERENCES Binford (1989), Blake (1962), Bond (1955), Bond & Meyer de Schauensee (1942), Chapman (1926), Collar & Pittman (1996), Desenne (1994), Desenne & Strahl (1991, 1994), Edwards (1972), Forshaw (1989), Friedmann (1948), Friedmann *et al.* (1950),

Griscom (1932), Gyldenstolpe (1945a), Haverschmidt (1968), Hilty & Brown (1986), Land (1970), Lowery & Dalquest (1951), Meyer de Schauensee (1949), Meyer de Schauensee & Phelps (1978), Monroe (1968), Parker (1990), Paynter (1955), Ridgely (1981), Ridgely & Gwynne (1989), Russell (1964), Slud (1964), Smithe (1966), Snyder (1966), Stiles *et al.* (1989), Stotz *et al.* (1996), Tostain *et al.* (1992), Traylor (1948, 1958), Wetmore (1968), Yamashita *in litt.* (1996).

---

346 VINACEOUS AMAZON
Amazona vinacea   Plate 84

Other names: Vinaceous-breasted Amazon (Parrot)

IDENTIFICATION 30cm. Quite large, mainly green parrot with breast strongly suffused vinous-maroon, sometimes appearing bluish. Bill red with whitish tip. Elongated feathers on nape and upper mantle with black tips and broad blue subterminal bands. Lores and forehead red. Red-spectacled Amazon (328), sympatric in Rio Grande do Sul (and possibly adjacent areas) especially where *Araucaria* stands remain, has green breast, red on forehead and crown extending to below eyes, red thighs and pale horn bill. Blue-fronted Amazon (338), overlapping in Argentina, Paraguay and parts of Brazil, has yellow on head and lacks vinous suffusion on breast. Generally in forest in pairs or flocks.

VOICE Wide variety of sounds including raucous *ki-rah* and incessant *wow-wow-wow*. Trilling flight call, *kri-ou* contact call, squeaky door sound and very loud *eeoo-de-de-eeooo* also reported. Birds make purring sounds during allopreening.

Vinaceous Amazon

DISTRIBUTION AND STATUS This parrot is endemic to south-eastern South America. In Brazil it has been found in southern Bahia, western Espírito Santo and scattered localities in Minas Gerais (an outlying record comes from the Rio São Francisco near Januária), sporadically in Rio de Janeiro (possibly a seasonal breeding visitor) but widely in São Paulo, Paraná, Santa Catarina and Rio Grande do Sul. Records in eastern Paraguay come from Amambay,

Canindeyú, Caaguazú, Alto Paraná, Itapúa and Guaíra and in northern Argentina from Misiones and possibly north-eastern Corrientes. Some seasonal movements and post breeding dispersal occur, possibly in relation to food supply (e.g. availability of coniferous tree seeds), with large-scale invasions reported in Paraguay in past. Declines in abundance take place in Rio Grande do Sul in Jan, with all gone by Mar and return in Apr for rest of year. Formerly abundant and widespread but recent dramatic contraction in range and numbers observed owing primarily to large-scale habitat destruction from expansion of agriculture and flooding from large hydroelectric dams. Trapped for live bird trade and formerly taken as game species. Occurs in several protected areas but none is large enough to hold a viable population. Former strongholds in eastern Paraguay are subject to rapid deforestation, with recent reduction in range and numbers and now probably confined to Alto Paraná and Canindeyú. Probably extinct (or very nearly so) Bahia and Espírito Santo, and few birds probably remain in Rio de Janeiro and Minas Gerais. Confined to the north and north-east of Santa Catarina and locally common only in forested parts of São Paulo and Paraná where the best remaining population is thought to survive. Persists in northern and north-eastern Rio Grande do Sul. CITES Appendix I. ENDANGERED.

ECOLOGY This amazon inhabits tropical and subtropical mixed evergreen forest; in Brazil humid coastal forest, in eastern Paraguay *Araucaria angustifolia* stands and *Euterpe edulis* woodlands. Extent of ecological dependence on coniferous trees (*Araucaria* and *Podocarpus*) is unclear but *A. angustifolia* clearly important in Misiones, Rio Grande do Sul and Santa Catarina and was possibly linked to former distribution further north in south-east Brazil. Chiefly in lowlands but reported from foothills at 1,500-2,000m in south-east Brazil where best forest remnants persist. Generally in pairs or small flocks with larger gatherings (up to about 30) in Jul-Aug. In pairs whilst breeding (usually from about Sep). Specific reported food items include flowers and fruits of *E. edulis* (which is apparently seasonally important in e.g. eastern Paraguay), seeds of *A. angustifolia*, fruits of *Achatocarpus* buds and new leaves of *Eucalyptus* and seeds of *Pilocarpus*. Birds are reported to cause damage to oranges but current low density unlikely to result in serious economic impact. Nests in hollow of large tree with evident preference for *Araucaria* where it occurs. May breed in loose colonies, including rarely in cliff crevices. Breeding Sep-Jan. Clutch 2-4.

DESCRIPTION Lores and forehead bright red; cheeks and crown green with black tips to some feathers on head; rather elongated feathers on sides of neck, nape and upper mantle green at base, broad blue subterminally and tipped black. Remainder of mantle, back and scapulars green with some feathers showing indistinct black tips; uppertail-coverts paler green. Wing-coverts green with variable red and/or yellow on leading edge of wing and carpal area. Primaries pale bluish-green; secondaries green with blue tips, base of outerwebs of outer three secondaries red, forming speculum. Underwing green. Throat and breast variable ranging from strong vinous-maroon to pale blue with strong vinous suffusion; dark subterminal band on tips of feathers gives scalloped pattern; belly green or yellowish-green sometimes with vinous suffusion; under-tail-coverts yellowish-green. Tail green with yellowish-green tip; base of lateral feathers red on innerwebs, purplish on outerwebs. **Bare parts**: Upper mandible red at base with pale tip, lower horn, reddish at base; iris orange to reddish-brown; legs grey.

SEX/AGE Sexes similar. Immature has green suffusion on breast and less extensive red on head (confined to base of upper mandible).

MEASUREMENTS Wing 203-220; tail 98-120; bill 24-29; tarsus 21-24.

GEOGRAPHICAL VARIATION No races are recognised but northern birds are reportedly larger and brighter.

REFERENCES Belton (1984), Collar *et al.* (1992, 1994), Forshaw (1989), Hayes (1995), Lowen *et al.* (1996), Meyer de Schauensee (1966), Narosky & Yzurieta (1989), Nores & Yzurieta (1994), Sick (1993).

347 ST. LUCIA AMAZON
Amazona versicolor   Plate 87

Other names: Blue masked Amazon, Versicolor Amazon (Parrot), St Lucia Parrot

IDENTIFICATION 43cm. Large, mainly yellowish-olive amazon with red speculum, bright red patch on throat and upper breast and blue head. Underparts with scattered patches of rusty brick-red. Only parrot in restricted island range but may be confused in captivity with slightly smaller Red-necked Amazon (348) from nearby Dominica, but is more olive, has heavier barring especially on underparts, brick-red suffusion on lower breast and belly, entirely red speculum and larger red area on throat and upper breast larger. Flight on shallow, powerful wingbeats sometimes quite high and at times interspersed with glides and raptor-like swoops. Birds most active early morning and evening. May be rather inconspicuous at rest during middle of day.

VOICE Loud raucous screeching. Soft purring and high-pitched cackling sounds from feeding and preening birds. Also a squeaky pig-like shrieking and goose-like honking.

DISTRIBUTION AND STATUS Confined to St Lucia in the Lesser Antilles, now in central and southern mountains but formerly more widespread occurring wherever the moist forest grew. The species has suffered a range contraction since 19th century and now occupies an area of only c. 65-70km² from Millet and Mont Lacombe in the north to Mont Beucop and Calfourc in the east, Piton Cochon, Piton St Esprit, Desrache and Grand Magasin in the south to Morne Gimie in the west and Mont Houlemon in the north-west. Survey results suggest that the south-west part of this area is the most densely populated with

parrots whilst relatively few inhabit the north-east. Abundant mid-19th century but declined rapidly to become very scarce by early 20th century. Later recovered, with 1950 population estimated at 1,000 birds. Declined again 1960s, mostly owing to shooting. 1977 survey estimated that no more than 100 birds remained. Steady increase since then with estimated 300-350 birds in 1990. Principal threats arise from habitat loss and hunting, both for food and the pet trade. Forestry practices which lead to removal of mature trees (favoured for breeding sites) could pose additional pressure. Appears less susceptible to hurricanes than congeners on Dominica but this may be due to conservation efforts rather than any intrinsic ability to withstand effects of severe storms. May compete for nest-sites with Pearly-eyed Thrasher *Margarops fuscatus*, which has increased considerably since c. 1950. A successful education campaign has effectively eliminated hunting, the core breeding areas are inside protected forest, and the species is protected by domestic legislation. CITES Appendix I. VULNERABLE.

ECOLOGY Chiefly inhabits canopy of primary montane tropical rain-forest but makes forays into secondary growth to feed. Reported in flocks of up to 20 birds. Forms communal roosts. Diet includes flowers and fruits of *Clusia*, fruits of *Talauma dodecapetala*, *Acrocomia irenensis*, *Pouteria*, *Dacryodes excelsa*, *Sloanea massoni*, *Byrsonima martinicensis*, *Miconia mirabilis*, *Pterocarpus officinalis* and *Euterpe globosa*; also bananas following passage of hurricane and presumably depletion of natural food sources. Absence from one locality late Aug-Nov possibly linked to lack of fruiting *Clusia*. Nests in tree-hollow. Nests reported from (e.g.) *Dacryodes excelsa*, *Pouteria* and *Sapium caribaeum*. Breeds Feb-Aug. Clutch generally two but usually only one young fledged per nest.

DESCRIPTION Lores, cheeks and forehead bright blue; crown, ear-coverts and lower cheeks paler blue with iridescent emerald suffusion from some angles; dark tips to feathers on head. Hindneck, nape, sides of neck and upperparts yellowish-olive, many feathers with distinct blackish tips giving strong barred effect especially in upper region. Wing-coverts yellowish olive-green, primary coverts tinged blue, rest with black tips to some feathers. Primaries blue; bases of outer secondaries red forming speculum, blue at tips; inner secondaries green at base and blue towards tips. Underwing with coverts yellowish-green with blackish tips to some feathers, flight feathers bluish-green. Chin and upper throat bright blue with blackish tips to feathers; tips of feathers on lower throat and upper breast bright red forming distinct red patch or mottled red area; breast and belly rather yellowish-green with blackish tips and brick red in the subterminal area of some feathers, giving scalloped appearance with scattered rusty patches; thighs and undertail-coverts yellowish-green. Tail bluish-green centrally, outer feathers green with broad yellowish-green tips and concealed red bases. **Bare parts**: Bill grey; iris orange; legs grey.

SEX/AGE Probably no sexual dimorphism. Immature has brown iris.

MEASUREMENTS Wing 258-288; tail 165-171; bill 31-36; tarsus 26-30.

GEOGRAPHICAL VARIATION None.

REFERENCES Collar *et al.* (1992, 1994), Forshaw (1989), Jeggo (1976), Jeggo & Anthony (1991).

Other names: Bouquet's Amazon (Parrot), Dominican Blue-faced Amazon (Parrot), Lesser Dominican Amazon (Parrot)

IDENTIFICATION 39-42cm. Large, mainly green amazon with bluish head, red and yellow speculum and bright red patch on throat and sometimes upper breast. Sympatric with Imperial Amazon (350) and, whilst there is some ecological separation, both species occur at highest densities between 500-600m. Latter is larger and bulkier with deep green back, purple head, neck and underparts; in flight lacks yellowish-green tail and has deeper wingbeats, with lower-pitched calls. For separation in captivity from St Lucia Amazon (347) see that species.

VOICE Harsh screeches and squawks. Also resonant yapping *scree-ah* which to Europeans recalls immature Eurasian Magpie *Pica pica*. Voice higher-pitched than Imperial Amazon.

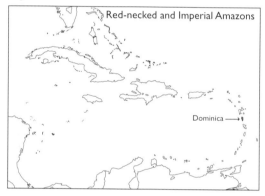
Red-necked and Imperial Amazons

Dominica →

DISTRIBUTION AND STATUS Endemic to the island of Dominica in the Lesser Antilles. Formerly widespread through the mountainous interior, including the northern peninsula. Range contraction since about 1950 with existing population centred on Morne Diablotin (1,447m, Dominica's highest mountain) which may always have been its principal stronghold but from whose southern slopes birds have been absent since a 1992 hurricane. Small numbers also reported in northern peninsula area (where apparently resident) and in central eastern part of island. Very small numbers may remain in south. Recent sporadic sightings of birds in low-lying areas of north and east and other localities in south suggest gradual recolonisation of parts of former range. Mainly resident but perhaps (at least formerly) some regular seasonal foraging movements and some nomadism from Nov-Jan. Although historical accounts of abundance conflict, drastic contraction of range and population has occurred since mid-20th century with gradual retreat into remoter forests of north and east. The decline is due to habitat loss, hunting and capture for pets. Small existing population especially vulnerable to loss of food plants and nesting sites through hurricane damage. Whilst effects of habitat loss may have been especially severe owing to birds' preference for lower-level forest (which has been under most pressure) they tolerate some disturbance and returned to former feeding areas recently after conversion to fruit-tree plantations. Hunting was probably most the

potent threat up to 1970s. Capture for local pet trade now under control owing to successful education campaign. Population in 1977 was at least 350 (probably more) but halved by effects of 1979 and 1980 hurricanes. Some recovery since then with 350 estimated in 1990 and evidence for further increases to over 500 in 1992. Remaining habitat partly protected in Northern Forest Reserve but neighbouring areas of critical conservation importance not included. Fully protected under domestic legislation. CITES Appendix I. VULNERABLE.

ECOLOGY The species inhabits the canopy of mountain rain-forest, preferring forest areas with stands of *Dacryodes excelsa*, mostly between 300-800m (highest density at 500-600m) but reported occasionally to 1,200m and formerly a regular visitor (Aug-Oct) to coastal areas. Generally in small flocks or pairs with larger loose feeding flocks formed outside breeding season. Communal roosts at traditional sites in (e.g.) large *Dacryodes* or *Sloanea berteriana*, used from year to year (but not necessarily throughout year). Diet includes fruits of *D. excelsa*, *Licania ternatensis*, *Richeria grandis*, *Amanoa caribaea*, *Simarouba amara*, *Symphonia globulifera*, *Chimarrhis cymosa*, *Pouteria pallida*, *Cordia elliptica*, *C. laevigata*, *Pithecellobium jupunba*, *Byrsonima martinicensis*, *Dussia martinicensis*, *Ormosia monosperma*, *Buchenavia capitata* and *Euterpes* palms, buds of *Anacardium occidentale* and fruits and buds of *Lonchocarpus*; also cultivated oranges, etc. Forages chiefly in canopy but also in sub-canopy and occasionally at ground level. Generally feeds morning and evening. Nests in cavity of large forest tree with most reported nests in *Dacryodes* or *Sloanea*. Breeds Feb-Jun. Productivity low with probably only one clutch every second year and usually only one young fledged per nest.

DESCRIPTION Lores, forehead, forecrown, periophthalmic area and upper cheeks bright blue; hindcrown, nape and sides of neck green with dark blue or blackish margins. Mantle, back and scapulars green with narrow faint dark margins giving subtle barred effect. Wing-coverts green; carpal edge yellowish-green. Primaries green with blue tips; outer three secondaries red at base, then yellow and tipped blue; fourth secondary yellow and tipped blue. Remaining secondaries green. Underwing with coverts green, flight feathers bluish. Chin and upper throat blue; lower throat and sometimes upper breast with variable-sized bright red patch; rest of breast and belly green; undertail-coverts yellowish-green. Tail bright green centrally, outer feathers green tipped yellowish-green with red markings at base of innerwebs. **Bare parts**: Bill horn; iris orange; legs grey.

SEX/AGE Sexes similar. Immature thought to be similar but with brown iris. Fledged young may still be noticeably smaller than adults as late as Oct of first year.

MEASUREMENTS Wing 237-260; tail 124-148; bill 29-36; tarsus 25-28.

GEOGRAPHICAL VARIATION None.

REFERENCES Collar *et al.* (1992, 1994), Evans (1988, 1991), Forshaw (1989).

349 ST. VINCENT AMAZON
Amazona guildingii   **Plate 87**

Other names: Guilding's Amazon (Parrot)

IDENTIFICATION 40cm. Large amazon with whitish or
pale yellow crown and face. Plumage highly variable with
two basic morphs, the commoner being golden-brown,
the rarer green (see Decription). Yellow tip to tail with
broad blue subterminal band. Yellow underwing-coverts
and yellow base to flight feathers in at least some birds
visible in flight. Most birds show some blue on hindneck
or sides of hindcrown. Only parrot in restricted island
range and unlikely to be confused with any other species
in captivity. Birds conspicuous during early morning and
evening with minor peak in activity shortly after midday.
Otherwise feeds and preens quietly in canopy. Rain can
render birds quiet during periods when otherwise high
activity. Flushes loudly and is noisy and conspicuous in
flight. Flight swift and direct on powerful wingbeats.

VOICE Wide repertoire including yapping cries, loud
guttural trumpeting *scree-eee-ah*, honking sounds similar
to call of domestic goose, shrieking *scree-ree-tee-leee*, bubbling
and short dog-like scolding sounds, squawks, deep grating
draaak and dry *sceeeet* sounds. Loud *quaw quaw quaw* in
flight. Some calls rather complex and comprised of trills,
resonant squawks, whistles and shrieks. Feeding birds
sometimes sound like people squabbling.

St Vincent Amazon

DISTRIBUTION AND STATUS Endemic to the island of
St Vincent in the Lesser Antilles. Distribution is closely
related to presence of native moist forest which for most
of 20th century has been confined to the east and west
sides of the island's central ridge. Presently most numerous
in the heads of the Buccament, Cumberland, Colonaire,
Congo-Jennings-Perseverance and Richmond valleys,
where much of the remaining native forest is concentrated;
elsewhere in smaller numbers. Some estimates of
abundance between 1870s and 1920s are contradictory but
the species evidently declined substantially by 1950.
Population estimates in early 1970s suggested several
hundred to 1,000 birds then remained. 1982 survey
presumed a total of 421±52 birds whilst 1988 estimate
suggested 440-500. Perhaps increased to 800 birds by 1994.
Population decline and range contraction linked to loss
of moist forest cover which once (on western side at least)
nearly reached sea-level. Deforestation appears largely to
have stopped in at least some valleys but habitat remains
at risk from forestry activities, expansion of banana
cultivation, charcoal production and loss of nest-trees to

collectors seeking young birds for trade. 1984 survey
suggested that only 16km² of primary forest survived.
Trapping for pets locally and international trade remains
a threat, but this and hunting, which was probably the
main threat from late 1950s to 1970s, have diminished in
importance following an education campaign. The
remaining population is also at risk from hurricanes which
can cause the loss of food plants and nest-sites as well as
direct mortality. In 1902 much of the parrot's favoured
habitat was destroyed by the eruption of Mount Soufrière
and these parrots are clearly vulnerable to future volcanic
eruptions. Parts of remaining forest habitat are now in
protected areas and the species is protected by domestic
legislation. CITES Appendix I. VULNERABLE.

ECOLOGY Chiefly inhabits mature moist forest from 125
to about 1,000m, but prefers low-altitude forest where it
remains. Occasionally wanders from forests to visit cultivated areas and even gardens. Gregarious and generally
in flocks of c. 20-30; otherwise in pairs. Forages in flocks
and roosts communally. Birds defend area around nest
whilst breeding but also retain flocks of about a dozen
birds whilst feeding and roosting. Reported food plants
include *Cordia sulcata, Clusia, Sloanea, Dacryodes excelsa,
Ficus, Cecropia peltata, Mangifera indica, Melisoma virescens,
Euterpe, Ixora ferrea, Micropholis chrysophylloides, Acrocomia
aculeata, Simaruba amara, Krugiodendron ferreum, Dussia
martinicensis, Andira inermis, Inga ingoides, Byrsonima
coriacea, Talauma dodecapetala, Chione verosa, Psidium guajava*
and *Aphanes erosa; Pouteria multiflora* is especially favoured.
Nests in hollow of mature forest tree such large *Dacryodes*
or *Sloanea*. Pairs begin breeding activity about Feb with
eggs laid Apr-May. In dry years, eggs may be laid as early
as Jan-Feb or as late as Jul. If conditions especially wet,
birds may not breed at all. Clutch two, rarely three. Productivity low with 50% of nests suffering natural failure
and successful nests fledging two young only in best years.

DESCRIPTION Plumage highly variable: 'golden-brown'
and 'green' morphs illustrated (see plate), former described here. Forehead, lores, superciliary area and upper
cheeks whitish; crown yellow; feathers on hindneck and
sides of neck pale blue with dark blue tips, merging with
green feathers on nape which show blackish tips. Upperparts dark brown with darker blackish tips to some
feathers. Scapulars golden-brown; outer primary coverts
with dull blue on outerwebs; wing-coverts otherwise brown
with green subterminal band and dark tips to some
feathers; carpal edge yellowish-orange with scattered green
feathers. Primaries blue with yellowish-orange bases; outer
secondaries the same with green subterminal banding,
inner secondaries green with blue tips; inner tertials dark
green tinged golden-brown on outerwebs, outer tertials
green at base becoming ultramarine towards tips.
Underwing with lesser coverts brown with green tips,
greater coverts yellow, flight feathers blackish with yellow
at base. Throat orange with blue or greenish-blue tips;
upper breast golden-brown with dark brown tips giving
barred effect; belly more yellowish golden-brown than
breast with green subterminal band and blackish tips to
some feathers; undertail-coverts greenish-yellow. Tail
orange at base with broad blue band in centre and broad
bright yellow tips. **Bare parts**: Bill pale greyish-horn; iris
orange; legs grey.

SEX/AGE Sexes similar. Immatures has more subdued
colours.

MEASUREMENTS Wing 253-275; tail 148-170; bill 32-39; tarsus 27-31.

GEOGRAPHICAL VARIATION Parrots on the eastern (windward) side of St Vincent are possibly isolated genetically from those of the western (leeward) side: the small population of eastern birds (perhaps only about 80 in 1982) reportedly show a higher proportion of 'green' individuals and have higher-pitched voices.

REFERENCES Collar *et al.* (1992, 1994), Forshaw (1989).

350 IMPERIAL AMAZON
Amazona imperialis　　　　　Plate 87

Other names: Sisserou, August Amazon (Parrot), Dominican Amazon (Parrot)

IDENTIFICATION 45cm. Largest amazon, unmistakable with deep green back and purple head, neck and underparts. Scarlet patch at bend of wing. Sympatric with Red-necked Amazon (348) and similarly most numerous between 500-600m; see that species for differences. Unobtrusive Jul-Nov but more conspicuous at other times in display on breeding territories. Flies on powerful wingbeats interspersed with glides. Large size and broad round wings sometimes suggest raptor. Generally shy and cautious. Plumage blends well with foliage in preferred mountain rain-forest and birds are difficult to see whilst quietly feeding.

VOICE Wide repertoire including range of whistles, shrieks and squawks. Voice often loud and resonating but also at times rather squeaky. Not usually very musical. Alarm, flight and some other calls resemble trumpet. If alarmed by e.g. gunshot, screeches loudly only briefly then falls silent. Also nasal *screee-at* or *screee-er*, squeaky high-pitched *screee-cooo* and quite pleasant-sounding *plink-plink-plink*. Voice generally deeper and more modulated than Red-necked Amazon. Often quiet in middle of day, calling most loudly and frequently morning and evening.

DISTRIBUTION AND STATUS (for map see Red-necked Amazon on p.552) Endemic to the island of Dominica in the Lesser Antilles. Formerly throughout the central moun-tains from around Morne Diablotin (1,447m, Dominica's highest mountain) in the north to Morne Anglais in the south. By 1950 reduced to two disjunct forested areas, around Morne Diablotin and around Morne Anglais, where last reliable sighting was in 1983. On Morne Diablotin itself, birds have been found at increasing altitudes owing to habitat loss and disturbance on the lower slopes. Now probably absent on the southern side, with the north-west side, particularly in the upper Picard River valley in the area of Morne Plaisance and Dyer Estates, being of critical importance. Early observers regarded Imperial Amazon as scarce. Later investigation (1870) revealed it to be common to abundant but numbers quickly declined owing to habitat loss, hunting and collection for pet trade. 1975 census suggested total of 150-250 birds. By 1979, only 16 on Morne Anglais, when a hurricane further reduced the population. In 1987 a survey estimated the total population at 60. A 1990 census suggested 80 parrots (possibly more, but less than 100), with 80-100 estimated in 1993. The species remains at serious risk from habitat loss (principally conversion of forest to tree-crop plantations, especially

bananas, facilitated by new infrastructure) and impacts of hurricanes (to which birds are highly vulnerable in such a restricted range) which destroy food plants and nesting sites as well as causing direct mortality. Hunting and collection for local pet markets have beenn considerably diminished by a successful conservation education programme. Foreign bird collectors remain a persistent threat but birds are extremely scarce in captivity or international commerce. Part of the habitat is protected in the Northern Forest Reserve but important neighbouring areas are excluded and remain at risk. Fully protected under domestic legislation. CITES Appendix I. VULNERABLE.

ECOLOGY The Imperial Amazon frequents the canopy of primary mountain rain-forest, sometimes in elfin forest (above 1,200m), preferring stands with mature *Dacryodes excelsa* and palms such as *Euterpe dominicana*. Principally occurs 600-1,300m but reported at 150-300m when birds descend in response to food shortages or foraging preferences. Communal roosts form at traditional sites in (e.g.) large *Dacryodes* or *Sloanea berteriana* which are used from year to year (but not necessarily throughout year). Reported food items include fruits of *Dacryodes*, *Licania ternatensis*, *Richeria grandis*, *Amanoa caribaea*, *Simarouba amara*, *Symphonia globulifera*, *Pouteria pallida*, *Tapura antillana*, flowers and fruits of *Chimarrhis cymosa*, nuts and young shoots of *Euterpe* palms. Generally feeds morning and evening. Nests in hollow in tall forest tree (e.g. *Dacryodes* or *Sloanea*). Nesting territory probably defended throughout year. Breeds Feb-Jun. Clutch two. Possibly breeds only every second year with typically only one young fledged.

DESCRIPTION Lores and forehead deep purple; cheeks and ear-coverts brownish; crown purple with dark emerald edges; sides of neck and nape deep purple with black tips, sometimes with emerald subterminal band. Mantle, back and scapulars green with bluish tips to some feathers. Wing-coverts green with scarlet at bend of wing. Primaries dark brownish-black with green at base of outerwebs; outer secondaries purple with crimson patch on outerwebs forming speculum; inner secondaries dark green tipped blue. Underwing green, coverts with blue tips. Throat, breast and belly deep purple with black tips, some feathers (especially on breast) showing pinkish-vinous or olive-green subterminal band, while others (visible from certain angles) bright blue sides and tips; thighs and sides of belly green with blue tips; undertail-coverts green with blue and vinous markings. Tail green at base with dull reddish-brown subterminal band and vinous tip. **Bare parts**: Bill dark horn, paler atbase; iris orange; legs dusky grey.

SEX/AGE Female reportedly duller. Immature has green on crown, nape and lower cheeks.

MEASUREMENTS Wing 270-299; tail 153-179; bill 36-42; tarsus 29-34.

GEOGRAPHICAL VARIATION None.

REFERENCES Collar *et al.* (1992, 1994), Evans (1988, 1991), Forshaw (1989).

351 HAWK-HEADED PARROT
Deroptyus accipitrinus   Plate 88

Other names: Red-fan Parrot, Hawk-headed Caique

IDENTIFICATION 35cm. Unmistakable when seen well. Elongated neck feathers are deep claret-red tipped bright blue, creating striking scaled effect. Neck feathers sometimes raised to create blue-edged red fan. Buffy-white cap (north of Amazon), cheeks brown with distinctive pale streaks, green upperparts and duller vinaceous and blue scaling beneath. Perched bird easily mistaken for small bird of prey. *Accipiter*-like silhouette (suggested by longish and slightly rounded tail and rounded wing-tips) is enhanced by peculiar undulating direct, rather slow, flap-and-glide flight, on stiff steady wingbeats low over canopy; tail feathers slightly spread, head lifted and wings slightly angled downward when airborne. Rising and falling display-flight resembles that of some pigeons. Fairly vocal; often first detected by distinctive voice. Generally in pairs or small groups of 3-7 birds. Sometimes perched on exposed dead tree-tops. Sometimes tame and approachable.

VOICE Several *chacks* followed by 1-5 high-pitched, almost squealing *tak tak heeya heeya* phrases in flight is distinctive. At distance, only *heeya heeya* sounds may be heard. Variety of chattering and whistling sounds at rest. Some musical whistles and bugle-like raspy *yaag* notes appear to be associated with courtship. Wailing cry reported from Surinam and Venezuela. Some calls reportedly resemble Black-headed Parrot (299).

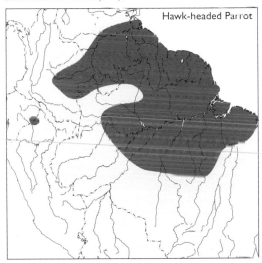

Hawk-headed Parrot

DISTRIBUTION AND STATUS This parrot occurs patchily through lowland northern South America east of the Andes. It is found in extreme eastern and south-east Colombia in Vichada south to Vaupes, ranging through south-east Venezuela south of the Orinoco to the Guyanas. It is distributed through much of the Amazon basin of Brazil, occurring north of the Solimões and along the Rio Negro east to Amapá, and south from the middle reaches of the Rio Madeira east through Pará to Belém and northern Maranhão, extending southwards to the upper reaches of Rios Tapajós and Xingu in northern Mato Grosso. May be absent from the upper Amazon although there are sporadic (few) records from the Amazonian

lowlands of Ecuador and Loreto, north-east Peru. Reported from the Rio Madeira in Rondônia at its confluence with the Rio Jaçiparaná, and the range perhaps extends into extreme northern Bolivia (c. 100km away). Some (apparently local) seasonal movements occur. Most numerous in east of range (even there apparently quite rare) becoming progressively scarcer westwards. Local in savanna and backwater region of south-east lowlands of Colombia. Collected for pets, especially in west where numbers probably reduced in wild. Some international trade occurs, with birds in captivity outside range. Rapid and severe deforestation south of Amazon in Pará and Maranhão has led to a regional decline.

ECOLOGY The Hawk-headed Parrot is a bird of lowland rain-forest, appearing to prefer terra firme formations, including gently undulating or foothill terrain (perhaps owing to greater food-plant diversity). It seemingly avoids várzea, forest edge and clearings, but there is one report of birds in flooded forest in the Río Morona drainage, Peru, and it mainly feeds in riverine forest in Venezuela. It reaches only to 400m in south-east Colombia and 200m in Venezuela. It is not very gregarious, occurring in pairs or small groups of 3-4, rarely as many as 10. Pre-breeding aggregations appear to break into pairs or trios at the onset of nesting. Roosts in tree-crowns in small groups (perhaps also singly in tree cavities). Mainly feeds in canopy. Specific reported food items include leaves and buds of *Bombacopsis*, unripe fruits of *Dialium guianense*, fruits of *Euterpe*, *Attalea fagifolia*, *Astrocaryum tucumoides* and *A. tucuma* palms. Also seen taking *Inga* and guava *Psidium guajava* in agricultural areas. Nests in tree-hollow, including that old nest of woodpecker (e.g. Red-necked Woodpecker *Campephilus rubricollis*). Rapid flapping of wings followed by gentle gliding descent give deeply undulating display flight during breeding period. Breeding Mar-Jun, Venezuela; Jan-Mar, Guyana; Feb-Apr, Surinam; Dec-Feb, Brazil. Clutch 2-3 in captivity.

DESCRIPTION Forehead and crown buffy-white, fading behind to brown with pale streaks on hindneck, this bordered posteriorly with ruff of elongated neck feathers basally rich claret-red tipped bright blue; lores brown; cheeks, throat, sides of neck and superciliary area brown heavily streaked with warm buff. Upperparts grass-green. Lesser and median wing-coverts green; primary coverts dark blackish-blue. Primaries blackish, secondaries green with dark tips. Underwing with coverts green, flight feathers blackish. Sides of breast and belly green; centre of breast and belly claret-red with blue tips, creating blue-and-red scaling effect sometimes with some green, especially on upper breast; thighs and undertail-coverts green. Uppertail green with blue tips, outer feathers with blue on outerwebs and concealed red at base of innerwebs; undertail blackish. **Bare parts**: Bill blackish, paler at tip; cere blackish; iris yellow; legs dark blackish-grey.

SEX/AGE Sexes similar. Immature has horn-coloured lower mandible and warm brown iris.

MEASUREMENTS Wing 187-201; tail 131-153; bill 28-33; tarsus 20-24.

GEOGRAPHICAL VARIATION Two races.
   D. d. accipitrinus (E Colombia, S Venezuela, Guianas and Brazil north of Amazon)
   D. d. fuscifrons (Brazil south of Amazon. Birds in Ecuador and Peru may belong here) Forehead and crown brown lacking buffy white patch of nominate.

No red bases of innerwebs of lateral tail feathers.

NOTE It has been suggested that differences in voice and plumage of northern and southern forms of Hawk-headed Parrot are sufficient to warrant their treatment as separate species. We follow the more usual approach in regarding these taxa as comprising a single species.

REFERENCES Desenne (1994), Desenne & Strahl (1991, 1994), Forshaw (1989), Haverschmidt (1968), Hilty & Brown (1986), Joseph (1988a), Meyer de Schauensee (1966), Meyer de Schauensee & Phelps (1978), Ridgely (1981), Sick (1993), Snyder (1966), Strahl *et al.* (1991), Stotz *et al.* (1996), Tostain *et al.* 1992), Whitney (1996).

352 PURPLE-BELLIED PARROT
Trichlaria malachitacea   Plate 88

Other names: Blue-bellied Parrot, Purple-breasted Parrot, Violet-bellied Parrot

IDENTIFICATION 28cm. Mainly green parrot with long, rather rounded tail and relatively short wings. Male with distinctive large purple patch on underparts, female all green, both sexes with blue tinge on underside of flight feathers and tail. No other similar parrots in Neotropical realm but possible to confuse with partially sympatric female Red-capped Parrot (301), which, however, is smaller, with proportionately shorter tail and paler bill. Flight quiet and bat-like on shallow steady wingbeats at or below (especially when crossing clearings) canopy level. Generally singly, in pairs or small (family) groups. Often quite tame and approachable. Most active at dawn and dusk, becoming very unobtrusive and difficult to locate during warmer part of day.

VOICE Usually fairly quiet. Call is a rather fast, clear whistled *soo-see-soo-soo-see-soo* and other variations on this theme, less like a parrot than a thrush. In flight birds sometimes give a rapidly repeated semi-whistled sound like a parakeet. Paired birds sometimes call in duet.

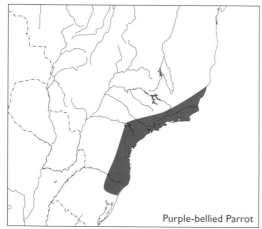

Purple-bellied Parrot

DISTRIBUTION AND STATUS This anomalous species is endemic to the Atlantic forests of south-east Brazil (a few recent records from extreme north-west Argentina in Misiones). In Bahia it has been reported with certainty only from the extreme south near Mucuri. It probably occurs in Minas Gerais, at least in the east, with one report

(perhaps erroneous) from the interior. Several records exist for Espírito Santo, with majority coming from Rio de Janeiro and São Paulo, where birds range mainly through coastal areas including Ilha do Cardoso. There are several comparatively recent reports from Paraná and a handful of mostly quite old (latest 1938) records from the north-east of Santa Catarina. In Rio Grande do Sul it is known from the band of country south of Caxias do Sul. Some seasonal movements have been thought to occur, with e.g. post-breeding dispersal to coastal lowlands from Serra do Mar, but this is now believed mistaken. Abundance poorly known owing to retiring habits, but evidently rare, with pairs well spaced and at low densities. Perhaps most numerous on east-facing slopes of the Serra do Mar in Rio de Janeiro and São Paulo. Large-scale habitat loss has certainly led to a serious decline in numbers and fragmentation of range. Although wet upland forests remain in substantial amounts on Serra do Mar, replacement of forest in valleys and on lower slopes with banana plantations could lead to further declines. Taken for local live bird markets and traded in small numbers internationally. Records exist for several protected areas but most of these may be insufficient in area to support viable populations of such a low-density species. ENDANGERED.

ECOLOGY The species inhabits wet lower montane forest, generally preferring the canopy and upper storeys of tall, bromeliad-rich forest along watercourses in valleys. It enters cultivated areas with orchards and plantations and sometimes wooded suburban areas (e.g. São Paulo). Mostly at 300-700m, perhaps to 1,000m in places, but also occurs in lowlands to sea-level. Sporadic nature of reports, with apparent absence from seemingly suitable areas, suggests some critical aspects of ecology not understood. Diet consists mainly of fruits, seeds, buds and nectar with some insects and their larvae (birds seen hawking for flying insects); specific food plants include *Pachystroma*, *Actinostemon*, *Sebastiana*, *Eugenia*, *Campomanesia* and *Euterpe edulis*, also occasionally bark, and citrus fruits from plantations. Nests in cavity in large tree or palm stump. Strongly territorial, at least whilst breeding, with nests as much as 2km apart. Breeds Sep-Jan, perhaps slightly earlier and later.

DESCRIPTION Head, neck and all of upperparts and wing-coverts grass-green. Flight feathers grass-green with narrow blue tips to primaries except outermost, which has narrow pale blue margin to outerweb. Underwing with coverts green, flight feathers bluish-green. Underparts mainly green with large purplish-blue patch on centre of lower breast and belly. Uppertail green with blue tips to central feathers; undertail bluish-green. **Bare parts**: Bill pale whitish-pink; cere pinkish; iris brown; legs grey.

SEX/AGE Female lacks purplish-blue belly-patch. Immature is like respective adult but young male has less purplish-blue on underparts.

MEASUREMENTS Wing 151-165; tail 106-115; bill 21-26; tarsus 17-19.

GEOGRAPHICAL VARIATION None.

REFERENCES Belton (1983), Collar *et al.* (1992, 1994), Forshaw (1989), Galetti (1996), Pizo *et al.* (1995), Sick (1993), Stotz *et al.* (1996), Whitney (1996).

BIBLIOGRAPHY

Abdu, H., Tesfaye, H. and Hillman, J. C. 1992. Bird conservation in Ethiopia. *Proc. VII Pan-Afr. Orn. Congr.*: 483-571.

Abramson, J. 1986. Buffon's Macaw (*Ara ambigua*). *AFA Watchbird* 13(5): 9-10.

Abramson, J., Speer, B. L. and Thomsen, J. B. 1996. *The Large Macaws: their Care, Breeding and Conservation.* Raintree, Fort Bragg, California.

Albornoz, M. and Fernández-Badillo, A. 1994. Aspectos de la biología del perico cara sucia *Aratinga pertinax venezuelae* Zimmer y Phelps (Aves: Psittacidae) en el valle del Río Guey, Aragua, Venezuela. In G. Morales, G. Novo, D. Bigio, A. Luy and F. Rojas-Suárez, eds. *Biología y Conservación de los Psitácidos de Venezuela.* Gráficas Giavimar, Caracas.

Aldrich, J. W. and Bole, B. P. 1937. The birds and mammals of the western slope of the Azuero Peninsula (Republic of Panama). *Sci. Publ. Cleveland Mus. Nat. Hist.*, 7. Cleveland, Ohio.

Ali, S. 1979. *Field Guide to the Birds of the Eastern Himalayas.* Oxford University Press, Delhi.

Ali, S. and Ripley, S. D. 1981. *Handbook of the Birds of India and Pakistan*, 3. Oxford University Press, London.

Alick, J., Gautier, J. P. and Chappuis, C. 1993. Vocal mimicry in wild African Grey Parrots. *Psittacus erithacus. Ibis* 135: 293-299.

Allen, R. J. 1987. Alexandra's Parrots in the Great Victoria Desert. *South Australian Orn.* 30: 75.

Alström, P. 1993. Understanding moult. *Birding World* 6: 198-205.

Amadon, D. 1942. Birds collected during the Whitney South Sea Expedition. *Amer. Mus. Novit.* 1176.

Andrew, P. 1992. *The Birds of Indonesia: a Checklist (Peters's Sequence)* Kukila Checklist no. 1, Indonesian Ornithological Society, Jakarta.

Antas, P. T. Z. and Cavalcanti, R. B. 1988. *Aves Comuns do Planalto Central*, Editora da Universidade de Brasília, Brasília.

Attiwill, T. 1992. A review of Australia's bird trade regulations and the problems of commercial trade in wild birds. In RAOU Report no. 83, Royal Australasian Ornithologists' Union, Moonee Ponds.

Aramburú, R. M. 1995. Ciclo anual de muda, peso corporal y gonadas en la Cotorra Comun (*Myiopsitta monachus monachus*). *Ornitología Neotropical* 6: 81-85.

Araya, B., Chester, S. and Bernal, M. 1993. *The Birds of Chile: a Field Guide.* Latour, Santiago.

Archer, G. F. and Godman, E. M. 1937-1961. *The Birds of British Somaliland and the Gulf of Aden.* Oliver and Boyd, Edinburgh and London.

Arndt, T. 1992-1996. *Lexicon of Parrots.* Verlag Arndt and Müller, Bretten.

Arndt, T. and Roth, P. 1986. Der Rotbauchsittich *Pyrrhura rhodogaster* im Vergleich mit den verschiedenen Unterarten des Blausteissittichs *Pyrrhura perlata*: Vorschlag für nomenklatorische und systematische Änderungen. *Verhandl. Orn. Ges. Bayern* 24: 313-317.

Arnold, G. W. and Weeldenburg J. R. 1990. Factors determining the number and species of birds in road verges in the wheatbelt of Western Australia. *Biol. Conserv.* 53: 295-315

Arrowood, P. C. 1991. Male-male, female-female and male-female interactions within captive Canary-winged Parakeet *Brotogeris v. versicolurus* flocks. *Acta XX Congr. Internatn. Orn.*: 666-672.

Ash, J. S. and Gullick, J. M. 1989. The present situation regarding the endemic breeding birds of Ethiopia. *Scopus* 13: 90-96.

Austin, O. L. 1929. The birds of the Cayo district, British Honduras. *Bull. Mus. Comp. Zool.* 69(11).

Baker, E. C. S. 1927. *The Fauna of British India.* Taylor & Francis, London.

Baker, J. and Whelan, R. J. 1994. Ground Parrots and fire at Barren Grounds, New South Wales: a long-term study and an assesment of management implications. *Emu* 94: 300-304.

Baker, N. E. 1991. Lilian's Lovebird in Tanzania, *Scopus* 15: 51-52.

Baker, R. H. 1951. *The Avifauna of Micronesia, Its Origin, Evolution, and Distribution.* University of Kansas Publ. Mus. Nat. Hist., 3, no. 1, Lawrence.

Baker, R. H. 1958. Nest of the Military Macaw in Durango. *Auk* 25: 98.

van Balen, S. and Lewis, A. 1991. Blue-crowned Hanging Parrot on Java, *Kukila* 5(2): 140-141.

van Balen, S., Margawati, E. T. and Sudaryanti 1988. A checklist of the birds of the Botanical Gardens of Bogor, West Java, *Kukila* 3(3-4): 82-92.

Banks, R. C. (ed.) 1982. *Wildlife and Wildlife Habitat of American Samoa. II Accounts of Flora and Fauna.* USFWS, Department of the Interior, Washington, D.C.

Barbour, T. 1923. *The Birds of Cuba.* Mem. Nuttall Ornithologists' Club 6, Cambridge, Mass.

Bartholomew, J. C., Christie, J. H., Ewington, A., Geelan, P.J.M., Lewis, H. A. G., Middleton, P. and Winkleman, B. (eds.) 1990. *Atlas of the World.* Times Books, London.

Bates, H. and Busenbark, R. 1969. *Parrots and Related Birds.* T.F.H. Publications, Neptune City.

Beardsell, C. 1985. *The Regent Parrot: A Report on the Nest Site Survey in South-eastern Australia, September 1983 to January 1984.* Australian National Parks and Wildlife Sevice, Canberra.

Beehler, B. 1978a. Notes on the mountain birds of New Ireland. *Emu* 78. 65-70.

Beehler, B. 1978b. *Upland Birds of Northeastern New Guinea.* Wau Ecology Institute, Wau, Papua New Guinea.

Beehler, B. 1985. Conservation of New Guinea Rainforest Birds. Pp.233-237 in *Conservation of Tropical Forest Birds.* ICBP Technical Publication no. 4, Cambridge, UK.

Beehler, B., Pratt, T. K. and Zimmerman, D. A. 1986. *Birds of New Guinea.* Princeton University Press, Princeton.

Begazo, A. J. 1996. Ecology and conservation of the Yellow-faced Parrotlet *Forpus xanthops. Cotinga* 6: 20-23.

Beggs, J. R. and Wilson, P. R. 1988. Kaka: a threatened species? *Forest and Bird* 250: 18-9.

Beggs, J. R. and Wilson, P. R. 1991. The Kaka *Nestor meridionalis*, a New Zealand parrot endangered by introduced wasps and mammals. *Biol. Conserv.* 56: 23-38.

Beissinger, S. R. and Waltman, J. R. 1991. Extraordinary clutch size and hatching asynchrony of a neotropical parrot. *Auk* 108: 863-871.

Bell, H. L. 1970. Additions to the avifauna of Goodenough Island, Papua. *Emu* 70: 179-180.

Bell, H. L. 1982. A bird community of New Guinean rainforest. 3 vertical distribution of the avifauna. *Emu* 82:

143-145.

Bell, H. L. and Coates, B. J. 1979. Nesting of William's Fig Parrot *Opopsitta gulielmitertii*. *Emu* 79: 230.

Belton, W. 1984. The birds of Rio Grande Do Sul, Brazil. Part 1. Rheidae through Furnariidae. *Bull. Amer. Mus. Nat. Hist.* 178(4).

van Bemmel, A. C. V. 1948. A faunal list of the birds of the Moluccan Islands. *Treubia* 19: 323-374.

Benson, C. W. 1960. The birds of the Comoro Islands: results of the British Ornithologists' Union Centenary Expedition 1958. *Ibis* 103B: 5-106.

Berg, K. S. and Horstman, E. 1996. The Great Green Macaw *Ara ambigua guayaquilensis* in Ecuador: first nest with young. *Cotinga* 5: 53-54.

Best, B. J. and Clarke, C. T. eds. 1991. *The threatened birds of the Sozoranga region, southwest Ecuador*. IBCP Study Report No. 44. International Council for Bird Preservation, Cambridge.

Best, B. J., Clarke, C. T., Checker, M., Broom, A. L., Thewlis, R.M., Duckworth, W. and McNab, A. 1993. Distributional records, natural history notes, and conservation of some poorly known birds from southwestern Ecuador and northwestern Peru. *Bull. Brit. Orn. Club.* 113: 108-119, 234-255.

Best, B. J., Krabbe, N., Clarke, C. T. and Best, A. L. 1995. Red-masked Parakeet *Aratinga erythrogenys* and Grey-cheeked Parakeet, *Brotogeris pyrrhopterus*: two threatened parrots from Tumbesian Ecuador and Peru? *Bird Conserv. Internatn.* 5: 233-250.

Best, H. 1984. The foods of Kakapo on Stewart Island as determined from their feeding sign. *New Zealand J. Ecol.* 7: 71-83.

Best, H. and Powlesland, R. 1985. *Kakapo*. John McIndoe & New Zealand Wildlife Service, Dunedin.

Bhatia, Z., Morton, K. and Peeters, H. 1992. *Aspects of the Tanzanian Wild Bird Trade with Special Reference to Fischer's Lovebird (Agapornis fischeri)*. Royal Society for the Protection of Birds, Sandy, England.

Binford, L. C. 1989. *A Distributional Survey of the Birds of the Mexican State of Oaxaca*. American Ornithologists' Union Ornithological Monographs 43.

Birchall, A. 1990. Who's A Clever Parrot Then?. *New Scientist* 125, no. 1705: 38-43.

BirdLife International 1993. Unpublished EBA Data. BirdLife, Cambridge.

Bishop, K. D. 1992a. New and interesting records of birds in Wallacea. *Kukila* 6(1): 8-34.

Bishop, K. D. 1992b. Parrots in Indonesia: a brief review of their status and conservation. In RAOU Report no. 83, Royal Australasian Ornithologists' Union, Moonee Ponds.

Biswas, B. 1959. On the parakeet *Psittacula intermedia* (Rothschild) [Aves : Psittacidae]. *J. Bombay Nat. Hist. Soc.* 56: 558-562.

Biswas, B. 1989. Taxonomic status of *Psittacula intermedia* (Rothschild). *J. Bombay Nat. Hist. Soc.* 86: 448.

Bjork, R. and Powell, G. V. N. 1995. Buffon's Macaw: some observations on the Costa Rican population, its lowland forest habitat and conservation. In J. Abramson, B. L. Speer and J. B. Thomsen, eds. *The Large Macaws: their Care, Breeding and Conservation*. Raintree, Fort Bragg, California.

Blake, E. R. 1958. Birds of Volcán de Chiriquí, Panama. *Fieldiana Zool.* 36(5): 499-577.

Blake, E. R. 1961. Notes on a collection of birds from northeastern Colombia. *Fieldiana Zool.* 44: 25-44.

Blake, E. R. 1962. Birds of the Sierra Macarena, Eastern Colombia. *Fieldiana Zool.* 44(11): 69-112.

Blakers, M., Davies, S. J. J. F. and Reilly, P. N. 1984. *The Atlas of Australian Birds*. RAOU/Melbourne University Press, Carlton.

Bloch, H., Poulsen, M. K., Rahbek, C. and Ramussen, J. F. 1991. *A Survey of the Montane Forest Avifauna of the Loja Province, Southern Ecuador*. ICBP Study Report no. 49, International Council for Bird Preservation, Cambridge, UK.

Boles, W. E. 1991. Glowing parrots. *Birds International* 3(1): 76-79.

Boles, W. E., Longmore, N. W. and Thompson, M. C. 1994. A recent specimen of the Night Parrot *Geopsittacus occidentalis*. *Emu* 94: 37-40.

Bond, A. B., Wilson, K. and Diamond, J. 1991. Sexual dimophism in the Kea *Nestor notabilis*. *Emu* 91: 12-19.

Bond, A. B. and Diamond, J. 1992. Population estimates of Kea in Arthur's Pass National Park. *Notornis* 39: 151-160.

Bond, J. 1936. Resident birds of the Bay Islands of Spanish Honduras. *Proc. Acad. Nat. Sci. Philadelphia* 88: 353-364.

Bond, J. 1955. Additional notes on Peruvian birds I. *Proc. Acad. Nat. Sci. Philadelphia* 107: 207-244.

Bond, J. 1956. *Check-list of Birds of the West Indies*. Academy of Natural Sciences, Philadelphia.

Bond, J. 1958. *Third supplement to the Check-list of Birds of the West Indies*. Academy of Natural Sciences, Philadelphia.

Bond, J. 1965. *Tenth supplement to the Check-list of the Birds of the West Indies*. Academy of Natural Sciences, Philadelphia.

Bond, J. 1968. *Thirteenth supplement to the Check-list of the Birds of the West Indies*. Academy of Natural Sciences, Philadelphia.

Bond, J. 1969. *Fourteenth supplement to the Check-list of the Birds of the West Indies*. Academy of Natural Sciences, Philadelphia.

Bond, J. 1974. *Nineteenth supplement to the Check-list of the Birds of the West Indies*. Academy of Natural Sciences, Philadelphia.

Bond, J. 1980. *Twenty-third supplement to the Check-list of the Birds of the West Indies*. Academy of Natural Sciences, Philadelphia.

Bond, J. and Meyer de Schauensee, R. M. 1943. The birds of Bolivia. Part I. *Proc. Acad. Nat. Sci. Philadelphia* 94: 307-391.

Boshoff, A. 1989. Uncertain future for the southern race of Cape Parrot. *AFA Watchbird* 16(5): 22-25.

Boussekey, M. 1993. Short activity report about the Red-vented Cockatoo in the Philippines (19 October-3 November 1992). Espace Zoologique de Saint-Martin-la-Plaine; unpublished.

Boussekey, M., Saint-Pie, J. and Morvan, O. 1991. Observations on a population of Red-fronted Macaws *Ara rubrogenys* in the Río Caine valley, central Bolivia. *Bird Conserv. Internatn.* 1: 335-350.

Bowler, J. 1988. Extinction threat to cockatoo. *Oriental Bird Club Bull.* 8: 6.

Bowler, J. and Taylor, J. 1989. An annotated list of the birds of Manusela National Park, Seram (Birds recorded on the Operation Raleigh Expedition). *Kukila* 4(1-2): 3-29.

Brace, R. C., Hesse, A. J. and White A. G. 1995. The endemic macaws of Bolivia. *Cotinga* 3: 27-30.

Bradley, P. E. and Rey-Millet, Y. J. 1985. *The Birds of the Cayman Islands*. Bradley, George Town, Grand

Cayman.

Braithwaite, L. W., Austin, M. P., Clayton, M., Turner, J. and Nicholls, A. O. 1989. On predicting the presence of birds in *Eucalyptus* forest types. *Biol. Conserv.* 50: 33-50.

Bransbury, J. 1987. *Where to Find Birds in Australia.* Waymark, Fullerton.

Brattstrom, B. H. and Howell, T. R. 1956. The birds of the Revilla Gigedo Islands, Mexico. *Condor* 58: 107-120.

Bräutigam, A. and Humphreys, T. 1992. The status of North Moluccan parrots: a summary of the findings of an IUCN field assessment. *Species* 19: 26-28.

Bregulla, H. L. 1992. *Birds of Vanuatu.* Anthony Nelson, Oswestry.

Bretagnolle, F. 1993. An annotated checklist of the birds of the north-eastern Central African Republic. *Malimbus* 15: 6-16.

Brice, A. T., Dahl, K. H. and Grau, C. R. 1989. Pollen digestibility by hummingbirds and psittacines. *Condor* 91: 681-688.

Brickell, N. 1985. The feeding and breeding of three *Poicephalus* parrots in captivity and in the wild. *Avicult. Mag.* 91: 162-165.

Britton, P. L. (ed.) 1980. *Birds of East Africa.* East Africa Natural History Society, Nairobi.

Brockner, A. 1992. A rearing project for the conservation of the Purple-naped Lory *Lorius domicellus. LoriJournal International* 3: 15-16.

Brockner, A. 1994. Der Blaugenick-Sperlingspapagei. *Papageien* 7: 150-151.

Brodkorb, P. 1938. Five new birds from the Paraguayan chaco. *Occas. Pap. Mus. Zool.* 367. University of Michigan.

Brooke, R. K. 1984. *South African Red Data Book - Birds.* South African National Scientific Programmes Report 97, Council for Scientific and Industrial Research, Pretoria.

Brooks, T. M., Evans, T. D., Dutson, G. C. L., Anderson, G. Q. A., Asane, D. C., Timmins, R. J. and Toledo, A. G. 1992. The conservation status of the birds of Negros, Philippines. *Bird Conserv. Internatn.* 2: 273-302.

Brouwer, J. and Garnett, S. 1990. *Threatened Birds of Australia: An Annotated List.* Royal Australasian Ornithologists' Union, Moonee Ponds.

Brown, P. 1974. *Ornithological Report of Guyana Expedition.* Earl of Harewood Estate, Leeds.

Brown, P. 1984. The Orange-bellied Parrot - spirit of the South West. *Wildlife in Australia* Winter 1984: 12-15.

Brown, P. 1992. The Orange-bellied Parrot recovery effort. *PsittaScene* 3(2): 5-8.

Brown, P. and Wilson, R. I. 1984. *Orange-bellied Parrot Recovery Plan.* National Parks and Wildlife Service, Tasmania.

Brown, P., Wilson, R., Loyn, R., Murray, N. and Lane, B. 1985. *The Orange-bellied Parrot - an RAOU Conservation Statement.* RAOU Report No. 14, Royal Australasian Ornithologists' Union, Melbourne.

Brown R. J. and Brown, M. N. 1980. Notes on some birds of the Upper Eloa River, Papua New Guinea. *Emu* 80: 87-89.

Bruce, M. D. 1987. Additions to the birds of Wallacea, 1. Bird records from smaller islands in the Lesser Sundas. *Kukila* 3(1-2): 38-43.

Brudenell-Bruce, P. G. C. 1975. *The Birds of New Providence and Bahama Islands.* Collins, London.

Bruner, P. L. 1972. *Field Guide to the Birds of French Polynesia.* Pacific Scientific Information Center, Bernice P. Bishop Museum, Honolulu.

Bryant, S. L. 1992. The Ground Parrot and age of vegetation in Tasmania. In RAOU Report no. 83, Royal Australasian Ornithologists' Union, Moonee Ponds.

Bryant, S. L. 1994. Habitat and potential diet of the Ground Parrot in Tasmania. *Emu* 94: 166-171.

Brykczynski, T. A. 1987. Grand Cayman parrots: an update. *AFA Watchbird* 14(4): 8-9.

Bucher, E. H., Bertin, M. A. and Santamaria, A. B. 1987. Reproduction and moult in the Burrowing Parrot. *Wilson Bull.* 99: 107-109.

Buckell, T. 1990. Consolidation of *Lorius* types *salvadorii, jobiensis, viridicrissalis.* Unpublished report, Subdepartment of Ornithology, Natural History Museum, Tring, UK.

Buckingham, R., and Jackson, L. 1988. *A Field Guide to Australian Birdsong.* Bird Observers Club of Australia, Nunawading.

Buckley, F. G. 1968. Behaviour of the Blue-crowned Hanging Parrot *Loriculus galgulus* with comparative notes on the Vernal Hanging Parrot *L. vernalis. Ibis* 110: 145-164.

Buckley, F. G. and Buckley, P. A. 1968. Upside down resting by young Green-rumped Parrotlets (*Forpus passerinus*). *Condor* 70: 89.

Buden, D. W. 1987. *The Birds of the Southern Bahamas: an Annotated Check-list.* Check-List no. 8., British Ornithologists' Union, London.

Butchart, S. H. M., Brooks, T. M., Davies, C. W. N., Dharmaputra, G., Dutson, G. C. L., Lowen, J. C. and Sahu, A. 1993. Preliminary report of the Cambridge Flores/Sumbawa Conservation Project 1993. Unpublished report.

Cabot, J. and Serrano, P. 1988. Distributional data of some non-passerine species in Bolivia. *Bull. Brit. Orn. Club* 108: 187-193.

Cahyadin, Y. 1996. The status of *Cacatua goffini* and *Eos reticulata* on the Tanimbar Islands: a preliminary analysis of field data. Pp.117-121 in D. J. Kitchener and A. Suyanto, eds. *Proc. 1st Internatn. Conf. E. Indonesian-Australian Vert. Fauna, Manado, Indonesia, November 22-26, 1994.* Indonesian Institute of Science.

Cahyadin, Y., Jepson, P. and Manoppo, B. I. 1994. Status of *Cacatua goffini* and *Eos reticulata* on the Tanimbar Islands PHPA/BirdLife Indonesia Programme, Report no.1, Bogor, Indonesia.

Cain, A. J. 1955. A revision of *Trichoglossus haematodus* and of the Australian platycercine parrots. *Ibis* 97: 432-479.

Cain, A. J. and Galbraith C. J. 1956. Field notes on birds of the eastern Solomon Islands. *Ibis* 98: 100-134.

Campbell, B. 1974. *The Dictionary of Birds in Colour.* Michael Joseph, London.

Canevari, M., Canevari, P., Carrizo, G. R., Harris, G., Mata, G. R. and Straneck, R. J. 1991. *Nueva Guia de las Aves Argentinas.* Fundación Acindar, Buenos Aires.

Cano, M. B., Ronces, R. G. and Bussio, R. C. 1990. Ecological aspects of the Yucatan parrots and perspectives for their conservation. *AFA Watchbird* 17(2): 12-21.

Carriker, M. A. 1910. An annotated list of the Birds of Costa Rica including Cocos Island. *Annals Carnegie Mus.* 6.

Carroll, R. W. 1988. Birds of the Central African Republic. *Malimbus* 10: 177-200.

Cayley, N. and Lendon, A. 1973. *Australian Parrots in Field and Aviary.* Angus & Robertson, Sydney.

Cemmick, D. and Veitch, R. 1987. *Kakapo Country.* Hodder & Stoughton, Auckland.

Chapman, F. M. 1917. The distribution of bird-life in Colombia: a contribution to a biological survey of South

America. *Bull. Amer. Mus. Nat. Hist.* 36: 1-729.

Chapman, F. M. 1926. The distribution of bird-life in Ecuador: a contribution to a study of the origin of Andean bird-life. *Bull. Amer. Mus. Nat. Hist.* 55.

Chapman, F. M. 1931. The upper zonal bird-life of Mts Roraima and Duida. *Bull. Amer. Mus. Nat. Hist.* 63.

Chapman, P. 1990. Rare Golden-shouldered Parrots observed and filmed in their habitat. *Birds International* 2(1): 23-33.

Cheng Tso-hsin 1987. *A Synopsis of the Avifauna of China.* Science Press, Beijing.

Christidis, L. and Boles, W. E. 1994. *The Taxonomy and Species of Birds of Australia and its Territories.* Monograph 2, Royal Australasian Ornithologists' Union, Hawthorn East, Victoria.

Claffey, P. M. 1995. Note on the avifauna of the Bétérou area, Borgou Province, Republic of Benin. *Malimbus* 17: 63-84.

Clark, R. O. S. and Patiño, E. D. 1991. The Red-fronted Macaw (*Ara rubrogenys*) in Bolivia: distribution, abundance, biology and conservation. Unpublished report for New York Zoological Society (WCI) and International Council for Bird Preservation.

Clark, W. D. 1991. Hyacinth Macaws: nesting habits in the wild. *AFA Watchbird* 18(3): 8-10.

Clinton-Eitniear, J. 1980. People and parrots in Mexico. *AFA Watchbird* 7(5): 39.

Clinton-Eitniear, J. 1981. Scarlet Macaw in captivity and in the wild. *AFA Watchbird* 8(6): 34.

Clinton-Eitniear, J. 1984. Notes on two *Aratinga* conures. *AFA Watchbird* 10(6): 26.

Clinton-Eitniear, J. 1986. Status of Green-cheeked Amazon in northeastern Mexico. *AFA Watchbird* 12(6): 22-24.

Clinton-Eitniear, J. 1988a. White-fronted (Spectacled) Amazon. *AFA Watchbird* 15(3): 4.

Clinton-Eitniear, J 1988b. Green-cheeked Amazon update. *AFA Watchbird* 15(4): 28-29.

Clinton-Eitniear, J. 1990. *Amazona oratrix belizensis.* *AFA Watchbird* 17(2): 26-31.

Clubb, K. J. and Clubb, S. L. 1990. First cative breeding of the Fiery-shouldered Conure (*Pyrrhura egregia*). *AFA Watchbird* 17(4): 6-7.

Clunie, F. 1984. *Birds of the Fiji Bush.* Fiji Museum, Suva.

Coates, B. J. 1985. *The Birds of Papua New Guinea,* 1. Dove Publications, Alderley, Queensland.

Coates, B. J. and Bishop, K. D. (1997) *Field Guide to the Birds of Wallacea.* Dove Publications, Alderley, Queensland.

Contreras, J. R., Berry, L. M., Contreras, A. O., Bertonatti, C. C. and Utges, E. C. 1991. *Atlas Ornitogeográfico de la Provincia del Chaco República Argentina. I. No Passeriformes.* Librería y Editorial L.O.L.A., Buenos Aires.

Collar, N. J. 1989. Red Data Birds - the cockatoos. *World Birdwatch* 11(1): 5.

Collar, N. J. 1995. On the possible occurrence of *Amazona dufresniana* in Brazil (Psittaciformes: Psittacidae). *Ararajuba* 3: 70.

Collar, N. J. 1997. Recent developments in parrot taxonomy. *Cotinga* 7: 12-13.

Collar, N. J. and Andrew, P. 1988. *Birds to Watch - The ICBP Checklist of Threatened Birds.* ICBP, Cambridge.

Collar, N. J., Crosby, M. J. and Stattersfield, A. J. 1994. *Birds to Watch 2: the World List of Threatened Birds.* BirdLife Conservation Series no. 4, BirdLife International, Cambridge, UK.

Collar, N. J., Gonzaga, L. P., Krabbe, N., Madroño Nieto, A., Naranjo, L. G., Parker III, T. A. and Wege, D. C. 1992. *Threatened Birds of the Americas: the ICBP/IUCN Red Data Book.* International Council for Bird Preservation, Cambridge, UK.

Collar, N. J. and Pittman, A. J. 1996. *Amazona kawalli* is a valid name for a valid species. *Bull. Brit. Orn. Club* 116: 256-265.

Collar, N. J and Stuart, S. N. 1985. *Threatened Birds of Africa and Related Islands.* International Council for Bird Preservation, Cambridge, UK.

Cooke, D. 1992. Moszkowski's Green-winged King Parrot. *Avic. Mag.* 98: 1-8.

Cordeiro, N. J. 1994. Forest birds on Mt Kilamanjaro, Tanzania. *Scopus* 17: 65-112.

Cramp, S., ed. 1985. *The Birds of the Western Palearctic,* 4. Oxford University Press, Oxford.

Cruz, A. and Gruber, S. 1981. The distribution, ecology and breeding biology of Jamaican Amazon parrots. In R. F. Pasquier, ed. *Conservation of New World Parrots.* International Council for Bird Preservation, Cambridge, UK.

Cuello, J. and Gerzenstein, E. 1962. Las aves del Uruguay. *Com. Zool. Mus. Hist. Nat. Montevideo* 6(93).

Darlington, P. J. 1931. Notes on the birds of Río Frío (near Santa Marta), Magdalena, Colombia. *Bull. Mus. Comp. Zool.* 71(6).

Davies, C. W. N., Barnes, R., Butchart, S. H. M., Fernandez, M. and Seddon, N. 1997. The conservation status of birds on the Cordillera de Colán, Peru. *Bird Conserv. Internatn.* 7: 181-195.

Davis, J. and Fisher, D. 1993. Fiji - December 1992. Unpublished report.

Davis, L. I. and Bennett, F. P. 1972. *A Field Guide to the Birds of Mexico and Central America.* University of Texas, Austin.

Davis, T. J. 1986. Distribution and natural history of some birds from the Departments of San Martin and Amazonas, northern Peru. *Condor* 88: 50-56.

Dean, W. R. J., Huntley, M. A., Huntley, B. J. and Vernon, C. J. 1988. Notes on some birds of Angola. *Durban Mus. Novit.* 14(4): 43-92.

Dearborn, N. 1907. A catalogue of a collection of birds from Guatemala. *Field Mus. Nat. Hist. Publ.* 125, Orn. Ser. 1(3).

Dee, T. J. 1986. *The Endemic Birds of Madagascar.* International Council for Bird Preservation, Cambridge, UK.

Deignan, H. G. 1945. *Birds of Northern Thailand.* Smithsonian Institution Bulletin 186, Smithsonian, Washington, D.C.

Delgado, F. S. 1985. A new subspecies of the Painted Parakeet (*Pyrrhura picta*) from Panama. Pp.17-20 in *Neotropical Ornithology.* Ornithological Monographs 36, American Ornithologists' Union, Washington, D.C.

Demey, R. and Fishpool, L. D. C. 1991. Additions and annotations to the avifauna of Côte d'Ivoire. *Malimbus* 12: 61-86.

Demey, R. and Fishpool, L. D. C. 1994. The birds of Yapo Forest, Ivory Coast. *Malimbus* 17: 85-89.

Desenne, P. 1994. Estudio preliminar de la dieta de 15 especies de psitácidos en un bosque siempreverde, cuenca del Río Tawadu, Reserva Forestal El Caura, Edo. Bolívar. In G. Morales, G. Novo, D. Bigio, A. Luy and F. Rojas-Suárez, eds. *Biología y Conservación de los Psitácidos de Venezuela.* Gráficas Giavimar, Caracas.

Desenne, P. and Strahl, S. D. 1991. Trade and the conservation status of the family Psittacidae in Venezuela.

Bird Conserv. Internatn. 1: 153-169.

Desenne, P. and Strahl, S. D. 1994. Situación poblacional y jerarquización de especies para la conservación de la familia Psittacidae en Venezuela. In Morales, G., Novo, G., Bigio, D., Luy, A., and Rojas-Suárez, F. eds. 1994. *Biología y Conservación de los Psitácidos de Venezuela.* Gráficas Giavimar, Caracas.

Dhondt, A. 1976. Bird observations in Western Samoa. *Notornis* 23: 29-43.

Diamond, J. M. 1972. *Avifauna of the Eastern Highlands of New Guinea.* Nuttall Ornithological Club, Cambridge, Mass.

Diamond, J. M. 1985. New distributional records and taxa from the outlying mountain ranges of New Guinea. *Emu* 85: 65-86.

Dickey, D. R. and van Rossem, A. J. 1938. The birds of El Salvador. *Field Mus. Nat. Hist.* 406, Zool. Ser. 23.

Dickinson, E. C., Kennedy, R. S. and Parkes, K. C. 1991. *The Birds of the Philippines: an Annotated Check-list.* British Ornithologists' Union, Tring.

Diefenbach, K. 1985. *Kakadus.* Horst Müller, Walsrode.

Dod, A. S. 1992. *Endangered and Endemic Birds of the Dominican Republic.* Cypress House, Fort Bragg.

Dodman, T. 1995. A survey to investigate the status and distribution of the Black-cheeked Lovebird (*Agapornis nigrigenis*) in south-west Zambia. *Bull. Afr. Bird Club* 2: 103-105.

Downer, A., Sutton, R. and Rey-Millet, J.-Y. *Birds of Jamaica: a Photographic Guide.* Cambridge University Press, Cambridge, UK.

Draffan, R. D. W., Garnett, S. T. and Malone, G. J. 1983. Birds of the Torres Strait: an annotated checklist and biogeographical analysis. *Emu* 83: 207-228.

Dubs, B. 1992. *Birds of Southwestern Brazil.* Betrona-Verlag, Switzerland.

Duckworth, W. and Kelsh, R. 1988. *A Bird Inventory of Similajau National Park.* ICBP Study Report no. 31, International Council for Bird Preservation, Cambridge.

duPont, J. E. 1971. *Philippine Birds.* Delaware Museum of Natural History, Greenville.

duPont, J. E. 1976. *South Pacific Birds.* Delaware Museum of Natural History, Greenville.

duPont, J. E. and Rabor, D. S. 1973. South Sulu Archipelago Birds. *Nemouria* 9: 35-37.

Dutson, G. C. L., Evans, T. D., Brooks, T. M., Asane, D. C., Timmins, R. J. and Toledo, A. 1992. Conservation status of birds on Mindoro, Philippines. *Bird Conserv. Internatn.* 2: 303-325.

Dymond, J. N. 1994. A survey of the birds of Nias Island, Sumatra. *Kukila* 7: 10-27.

Eames, J. C. and Robson, C. 1992. *Forest Bird Surveys in Viet Nam.* ICBP Study Report no. 51, International Council for Bird Preservation, Cambridge.

Eastman, W. R. and Hunt, A. C. 1966. *The Parrots of Australia: a Guide to Field Identification and Habits.* Angus & Robertson, Sydney.

Eckert, J. 1990. Orange-bellied Parrots feeding on a cultivated crop. *South Australian Orn.* 31: 16-7.

Edwards, E. P. 1972. *A Field Guide to the Birds of Mexico.* E. P. Edwards, Sweet Briar, Virginia.

Eisenmann, E. 1968. Behaviour of Orange-chinned Parakeets in Panamá. *Condor* 70: 86.

Elgood, J. H., Heigham, J. B., Moore, A. M., Nason, A. N., Sharland, R. E. and Skinner, N. J. 1994. *The Birds of Nigeria: an Annotated Check-list.* Second Edition. British Ornithologists' Union, Tring, UK.

Ellis, B. 1987. *The New Zealand Birdwatcher's Book.* Reed Methuen, Auckland.

Emison, W. B. 1992. The importance of remnant vegetation to the Blue Bonnet in north-western Victoria. *Australian Bird Watcher* 14: 159-164.

Emison, W. B., Beardsell, C. M., Norman, F. I., Loyn, R. H. and Bennett, S. C. 1987. *Atlas of Victorian Birds.* Department of Conservation, Forests and Lands, and the Royal Australasian Ornithologists' Union, Melbourne.

Emison, W. B., White, C. M. and Caldow, W. D. 1995. Presumptive renesting of Red-tailed Black-Cockatoos in south-eastern Australia. *Emu* 95: 141-144.

Engbring, J. and Ramsey, F. L. 1989. *A 1986 Survey of the Forest Birds of American Samoa.* USFWS, Department of the Interior.

Erftemeijer, P., Allen, G., Kosamah, Z. and Kosamah, S. 1991. Birds of the Bintuni Bay Region, Irian Jaya. *Kukila* 5(2): 85-98.

Erritzoe, J. 1993. *The Birds of CITES and How to Identify Them.* Lutterworth, Cambridge, UK.

Evans, M. and Balmford, A. 1992. The birds of the Ishasha sector of the Queen Elizabeth National Park, Uganda. *Scopus* 16: 34-49.

Evans, P. G. H. 1988. *The Conservation Status of Imperial and Red-necked Parrots on Dominica.* ICBP Study Report 21, International Council for Bird Preservation, Cambridge, UK.

Evans, P. G. H. 1991. Status and conservation of Imperial and Red-necked Parrots *Amazona imperialis* and *A. arausiaca* on Dominica. *Bird Conserv. Internatn.* 1: 11-32.

Evans, R. J. 1986. *An Ornithological Survey in the Province of Esmeraldas in North-west Ecuador, August 1986.* University of Durham.

Evans, S. M., Fletcher, F. J. C., Loader, P. J. and Rooksby, F. G. 1992. Habitat exploitation by landbirds in the changing Western Samoan environment. *Bird Conserv. Internatn.* 2: 123-129.

Fairbairn, P. 1981. Parrot conservation in Jamaica. In R. F. Pasquier, ed. *Conservation of New World Parrots.* Techn. Publ. no. 1, International Council for Bird Preservation, Cambridge, UK.

Falla, R. A., Sibson, R. B. and Turbott, E. G. 1981. *Collins Guide to the Birds of New Zealand and Outlying Islands.* Collins, Auckland.

Fernandez-Badillo, A., Fernandez-Badillo, E. and Ulloa, M. G. 1994. Psitácidos de Parque Nacional Henri Pitter, Venezuela. In G. Morales, G. Novo, D. Bigio, A. Luy and F. Rojas-Suárez, eds. *Biología y Conservación de los Psitácidos de Venezuela.* Gráficas Giavimar, Caracas.

ffrench, R. 1985. Changes in the avifauna of Trinidad. Pp.986-991 in *Neotropical Ornithology.* Ornithological Monographs 36, American Ornithologists' Union, Washington, D.C.

ffrench, R. 1992. *A Guide to the Birds of Trinidad and Tobago.* Helm, London.

Field, D. 1992. British Isles Regional Studbook No. 4: Moluccan Cockatoo. Penscynor Wildlife Park, Neath.

Fjeldså, J. and Krabbe, N. 1990. *The Birds of the High Andes.* Zoological Museum, University of Copenhagen and Apollo, Svendborg, Denmark.

Fjeldså, J., Krabbe, N. and Ridgely, R. S. 1987. The Great Green Macaw *Ara ambigua* collected in northwest Ecuador, with taxonomic comments on *Ara militaris. Bull. Brit. Orn. Club* 107: 28-32.

Flack, J. A. D. 1976. Hybrid Parakeets on the Mangere Islands, Chatham Group. *Notornis* 23: 253-255.

Fleming, R. L., Fleming, R. L. and Lain Singh Bangdel 1976. *Birds of Nepal*. Avalok, Kathmandu.

Ford, J. 1980. Morphological and ecological divergence and convergence in isolated populations of the Red-tailed Black Cockatoo. *Emu* 80: 103-119.

Ford, J. 1988. Distributional notes on North Queensland birds. *Emu* 88: 50-53.

Forshaw, J. M. 1981. *Australian Parrots*. Lansdowne Editions, Melbourne.

Forshaw, J. M. 1989. *Parrots of the World*. Lansdowne Editions, Melbourne.

Forshaw, J. M. 1990a. Antbed parrots in Danger. *Birds International* 2(1): 28-29.

Forshaw, J. M. 1990b. Recovery plan for the Kakapo. *Birds International* 2(1): 88.

Forshaw, J. M. 1991a. Kakapo chicks hatch. *Birds International* 3(1): 89.

Forshaw, J. M. 1991b. A new parrot named - a long lost one found. *Birds International* 3(1): 88.

Friedmann, H. 1948. Birds collected by the National Geographic Society's expedition to northern Brazil and southern Venezuela. *Proc. U.S. Natn. Mus.* 97: 373-570.

Friedmann, H., Griscom, L. and Moore, R. T. 1950. *Distributional Check-list of the Birds of Mexico*, 1. Cooper Ornithological Club, Berkeley.

Friedmann, H. and Smith, F. D. 1950. A contribution to the ornithology of northeastern Venezuela. *Proc. U.S. Natn. Mus.* 100: 411-538.

Friedmann, H. and Smith, F. D. 1955. A further contribution to the ornithology of northeastern Venezuela. *Proc. U.S. Natn. Mus.* 104: 463-524.

Frith, C. and Frith, D. 1992. Tari Gap - Papua New Guinea's top birding spot. *Wingspan* 6: 12-13.

Fry, C. H., Keith, S. and Urban, E. K. eds. 1988. *The Birds of Africa*, 3. Academic Press, London.

Fuggles-Couchman, N. R. 1984. The distribution of, and other notes on, some birds of Tanzania. *Scopus* 8: 1-17.

Galetti, M. 1993. Diet of the Scaly-headed Parrot (*Pionus maximiliani*) in a semi-deciduous forest in southeastern Brazil. *Biotropica* 25: 419-425.

Galetti, M. 1995. The ecology and conservation of parrots in the Brazilian Atlantic forest. *PsittaScene* 7(4): 10.

Galetti, M. 1996. Fruits and frugivores in a Brazilian Atlantic Forest. Ph.D. thesis, University of Cambridge, UK.

Galetti, M. and Rodrigues, M. 1992. Comparative seed predation on pods by parrots in Brazil. *Biotropica* 24(2a): 222-224.

Galetti, M. and Stotz, D. 1996. *Miconia hypoleuca* (Melastomataceae) como espécie-chave para aves frugívoras no sudeste do Brasil. *Revta. Brasil. Biol.* 56: 435-439.

Gardner, N. 1988. Update on bird finding in New Zealand. Unpublished report.

Garnett, S. 1992. *Threatened and Extinct Birds of Australia*. Royal Australasian Ornithologists' Union, Moonee Ponds.

Garnett, S. and Crowley, G. 1995. The Golden-shouldered Parrot. *Antbed* 6.

Garnett, S., Crowley, G., Duncan, R., Baker, N. and Doherty, P. 1993. Notes on live Night Parrot sightings in north-western Queensland. *Emu* 93: 292-296.

Garnett, S. and Crowley, G. 1995. Feeding ecology of Hooded Parrots *Psephotus dissimilis* during the early wet season. *Emu* 95: 54-61.

Gautier, J. P., Cruikshank, A. J. and Chappius, C. 1993.

Vocal mimicry in wild African Grey Parrots *Psittacus erithacus*. *Proc. VIII Pan-Afr. Orn. Congr.*: 435-439.

Gaymer, R., Blackman, R. A. A., Dawson, P. G., Penny, M. and Penny, C. M. 1969. Endemic birds of the Seychelles. *Ibis* 111: 157-176.

Gee, B. 1993. Postcard from the Spice Islands. *Birdwatch* 2(3): 48-49.

Gehlbach, F. R., Dillon, D. O., Harrell, H. L., Kennedy, S. E. and Wilson, K. R. 1976. Avifauna of the Río Corona, Tamaulipas, Mexico: northeastern limit of the tropics. *Auk* 93: 53-65.

Gilliard, E. T. 1941. The birds of Mt. Auyan-Tepui, Venezuela. *Bull. Amer. Mus. Nat. Hist.* 77: 439-508.

Gooders, J. (ed.) (1969-1971) *Birds of the World*. IPC Magazines, London.

Goodman, S. M. and Putnam, M. S. 1996. The birds of the eastern slopes of the Réscrve Naturelle Intégrale d'Andringita, Madagascar. *Fieldiana Zool.* N.S. 85: 171-189.

Gore, M. E. J. 1968. A checklist of the birds of Sabah, Borneo. *Ibis* 110: 165-196.

Gore, M. E. J. 1990. *The Birds of The Gambia: an Annotated Check-list*. 2nd edition. British Ornithologists' Union, Tring.

Gore, M. E. J. 1994. Bird records from Liberia. *Malimbus* 16: 74-87.

Gorman, M. L. 1975. Habitats of the land-birds of Viti Levu, Fiji Islands. *Ibis* 117: 152-161.

Graham, G. L., Graves, G. R., Schulenberg, T. S. and O'Neill, J. P. 1980. Seventeen bird species new to Peru from the Pampas de Heath. *Auk* 97: 366-370.

Grant, P. R. 1965. A systematic study of the terrestrial birds of the Tres Marías Islands, Mexico. *Postilla* 90.

Grantsau, R. and Camargo H. F. de A. 1989. Nova espécie de *Amazona* (Aves, Psittacidae). *Revta. Bras. Biol.* 49: 1017-1020.

Graves, G. 1992. The endemic land birds of Henderson Island, southeastern Polynesia: notes on natural history and conservation. *Wilson Bull.* 104: 32-43.

Graves, G. R. and Giraldo, J. A. 1987. Population status of the Rufous-fronted Parakeet (*Bolborhynchus ferrugineifrons*), a Colombian endemic. *Gerfaut* 77: 89-92.

Graves, G. R. and Restrepo, D. U. 1989. A new allopatric taxon in *Hapalopsittaca amazonina* (Psittacidae) superspecies from Colombia. *Wilson Bull.* 101: 369-376.

Green, A. A. 1990. The avifauna of the southern sector of the Gashaka-Gumti Game Reserve, Nigeria. *Malimbus* 12: 31-51.

Green, M. J. B. 1986. The birds of the Kedarnath Sanctuary, Chamoli District, Uttar Pradesh: status and distribution. *J. Bombay Nat. Hist. Soc.* 83: 603-617.

Green, A. A. and Carroll, R. W. 1991. The avifauna of the Dzanga-Ndoki National Park and the Dzanga-Sangha Rainforest Reserve, Central African Republic. *Malimbus* 13: 49-66.

Gregory-Smith, R. 1983. Birds of southern Viti-Levu. *Adjutant* 13: 38.

Griffiths, R. and Tiwari, B. 1995. Sex of the last wild Spix's Macaw. *Nature* 375: 454.

Grimes, L. G. 1987. *The Birds of Ghana: an Annotated Check-list*. British Ornithologists' Union, Tring.

Griscom, L. 1929. Studies from the Dwight collection of Guatemalan birds I. *Amer. Mus. Novit.* 379.

Griscom, L. 1932. The distribution of birdlife in Guatemala. *Bull. Amer. Mus. Nat. Hist.* 64.

Griscom, L. and Moore, R. T. 1950. *Distributional Checklist of the Birds of Mexico.* Cooper Ornithological Club, Berkeley.

Gyldenstolpe, N. 1945a. The bird fauna of Rio Juruá in western Brazil. *Kungl. Svenska Vetenskapsakad. Handl.* Ser. 3, 22: 1-338.

Gyldenstolpe, N. 1945b. A contribution to the ornithology of northern Bolivia. *Kungl. Svenska Vetenskapsakad. Handl.* Ser. 3, 23: 1-300.

Gyldenstolpe, N. 1955. Birds collected by Dr Sten Bergman during his expedition to Dutch New Guinea 1948-1949. *Ark. Zool.* (ser. 2) 8 (2).

Hadden, D. 1981. *Birds of the North Solomons.* Wau Ecology Institute, Wau, Papua New Guinea.

Haffer, J. 1975. Avifauna of northwestern Colombia, South America. *Bonn. Zool. Monogr.* no. 7. Museum Alexander Koenig, Bonn.

Haffer, J. and Fitzpatrick, J. W. 1985. Geographic variations in some Amazonian forest birds. Pp.147-168 in *Neotropical Ornithology.* Ornithological Monographs 36, American Ornithologists' Union, Washington, D.C.

Harrison, C. J. O. 1973. Nest-building behaviour of Quaker Parrots *Myiopsitta monachus. Ibis* 115: 124-128.

Harrison, M. 1970. The Orange-fronted Parakeet (*Cyanoramphus malherbi*). *Notornis* 17: 115-125.

Hartert, E. 1926. On the birds of the district of Talasea in New Britain. *Novit. Zool.* 33: 122-131.

Harvey, W. G. 1990. *The Birds of Bangladesh.* University Press, Dhaka.

Haverschmidt, F. and Barruel, P. 1968. *Birds of Surinam.* Oliver and Boyd, London.

Haverschmidt, F. 1972. Bird records from Surinam. *Bull. Brit. Orn. Club* 92: 49-53.

Hay, R. 1984. Pacific Islands trip report - 13 September to 6 November 1983. Unpublished Report.

Hay, R. 1986. *Bird Conservation in the Pacific Islands.* ICBP Study Report no. 7, International Council for Bird Preservation, Cambridge, UK.

Hayes, F. E. 1995. *Status, Distribution and Biogeography of the Birds of Paraguay,* Monographs in field ornithology, 1. American Birding Association.

Heatherbell, C. 1992. Anting by an Orange-fronted Parakeet. *Notornis* 39: 131-132.

Hellmayr, C. E. 1932. The birds of Chile. *Field Mus. Nat. Hist. Publ. Zool. Ser.* 19: 1-472.

Helsens, T. 1996. New information on birds in Ghana, April 1991 to October 1993. *Malimbus* 18: 1-9.

Hendricks, P. 1982. Some post-monsoon birds observed in central Nepal. *J. Bombay Nat. Hist. Soc.* 79: 247-253.

Henry, G. M. 1955. *A Guide to the Birds of Ceylon.* Geoffrey Cumberlege and Oxford University Press, Oxford.

Hermes, N. 1985. *Birds of Norfolk Island.* Wonderland Publications, Norfolk Island.

Hesse, A. J. 1993. *Ara glaucogularis* distribution study, Beni, Bolivia. Armonia, unpublished.

Hicks, J. 1992. Norfolk Island's Green Parrot. In RAOU Report no. 83, Royal Australasian Ornithologists' Union, Moonee Ponds.

Hicks, J. and Forshaw, J. M. 1989. *Cyanoramphus* parrots: successful colonisers of islands. *Birds International* 1(4): 40-47.

Hiller, C. M. 1987. Notes on Dusky Lory (*Pseudeos fuscata*) behaviours. *Loridae Newsletter* 3(1): 1-3.

Hilty, S. L. and Brown, W. L. 1986. *A Guide to the Birds of Colombia.* Princeton University Press, Princeton.

Holdaway, R. N. and Worthy, T. 1993. First North Island fossil record of Kea, and morphological and morphometric comparison of Kea and Kaka. *Notornis* 40: 95-108.

Holmes, D. and Nash, S. 1990a. *The Birds of Java and Bali.* Oxford University Press, Oxford.

Holmes, D. and Nash, S. 1990b. *The Birds of Sumatra and Kalimantan.* Oxford University Press, Oxford.

Holmes, D. and Burton, K. 1987. Recent notes on the avifauna of Kalimantan. *Kukila* 3(1-2): 2-32.

Holmes, P. and Wood, H. 1979. Report of the Ornithological Expedition to Sulawesi. Unpublished report.

Holyoak, D. T. 1970. The status of *Eos goodfellowi. Bull. Brit. Orn. Club* 90: 91.

Holyoak, D. T. 1974. Les oiseaux des îles de la Société. *Oiseau et R.F.O.* 44: 153-181.

Holyoak, D. T. 1975. Les oiseaux des îles Marquises. *Oiseau et R.F.O.* 45: 341-366.

Holyoak, D. T. 1976. Additional notes on the status of *Eos goodfellowi. Bull. Brit. Orn. Club* 96: 120-122.

Holyoak, D. T. 1979. Notes on the birds of Viti Levu and Taveuni, Fiji. *Emu* 79: 7-18.

Hoppe, D. 1986. *Kakadus: Lebensweise, Haltung und Zucht.* Ulmer, Stuttgart.

Hora, B., (ed.) 1981. *The Oxford Encyclopedia of Trees of the World.* Oxford University Press, Oxford.

Hornbuckle, J. 1991. Irian Jaya 1991. Unpublished report.

Hough, J. R. 1989. Thailand 1989. Unpublished report.

Housse, P. E. 1949. Notes sur l'avifaune du Chili. *Alauda* 17: 1-15.

Howard, R. and Moore, A. 1984. *A Complete Checklist of the Birds of the World.* Macmillan, London.

Howell, T. R. 1957. Birds of a second-growth rain forest area of Nicaragua. *Condor* 59: 73-111.

Howell, T. R. 1972. Birds of the lowland pine savanna of northeastern Nicaragua. *Condor* 74: 316-340.

Howell, S. N. G. and Webb, S. 1992. New and noteworthy bird records from Guatemala and Honduras. *Bull. Brit. Orn. Club* 112: 42-49.

Howell, S. N. G. and Webb, S. 1994. Additional information on the birds of Guerrero, Mexico. *Bull. Brit. Orn. Club* 114: 232-243.

Howell, S. N. G. and Webb, S. 1995. *A Guide to the Birds of Mexico and Northern Central America.* Oxford University Press, Oxford.

Hoy, G. 1968. Ueber Brutbiologie und Eier einiger Vögel aus nord-west Argentina. *J. Orn.* 109: 425-433.

del Hoyo, J., Elliot, A. and Sargatal, J., eds. 1992. *Handbook of Birds of the World*, 1. Lynx Edicions, Barcelona.

Humphrey, P. S., Bridge, D., Reynolds, P. W. and Peterson, R. T. 1970. *Birds of Isla Grande (Tierra del Fuego).* University of Kansas Museum of Natural History, Lawrence, Kansas.

Husain, K. Z. 1959. Taxonomic status of the Burmese Slaty-headed Parakeet. *Ibis* 101: 240-250.

Husain, K. Z. 1959. Is *Psittacula intermedia* (Rothschild) a valid species? *Bull. Brit. Orn. Club* 79: 89-92.

Hutchins, B. R. 1985. The status in captivity of four Australian parrots: *Psephotus chrysopterygius, P. dissimilis, Neophema pulchella, N. splendida. Avicult. Mag.* 91: 65-75.

Hutchins, B. R. and Lovell, R. H. 1986. *Australian Parrots: a Field and Aviary Study.* Avicultural Society of Australia, Melbourne.

Hyam, R. and Pankhurst, R. 1995. *Plants and their Names: a Concise Dictionary.* Oxford University Press, Oxford.

ICBP 1992. *Putting Biodiversity on the Map: Priority Areas for Global Conservation.* International Council for Bird Preservation, Cambridge, UK.

Ingels, J., Parkes, K. C. and Farrand, J. 1981. The status of the macaw generally but incorrectly called *Ara caninde* (Wagler). *Gerfaut* 71: 283-294.

Inskipp, C. and Inskipp, T. 1985. *A Guide to the Birds of Nepal*. Croom Helm, London.

Inskipp, T., Broad, S. and Luxmoore, R. 1988. *Significant Trade in Wildlife: a Review of Selected Species in CITES Appendix II*, 3. Birds. IUCN/CITES, Cambridge.

Iredale, T. 1956. *Birds of New Guinea*. Georgian House, Melbourne.

Ireland, T. 1987. Breeding the South American Red-capped Parrot. *AFA Watchbird* 14(5): 22-23.

Irwin, M. P. S. 1981. *The Birds of Zimbabwe*. Quest Publishing, Salisbury, Zimbabwe.

Jackson, J. R. 1960. Keas at Arthur's Pass. *Notornis* 9: 39-58.

Jackson, J. R. 1963. The nesting of Keas. *Notornis* 10: 319-326.

Jaensch, R. P. and Jaensch, L. A. 1987. Further observations in the north-west of South Australia. *South Australian Orn.* 30: 60-61.

bin Jalan, B. and Galdikas, M. F. 1987. Birds of Tanjung Puting National Park, Kalimantan Tengah: a preliminary list. *Kukila* 3(1-2): 33-35.

Janzen, D. H. 1981. *Ficus ovalis* seed predation by an Orange-chinned Parakeet (*Brotogeris jugularis*) in Costa Rica. *Auk* 98: 841-844.

Jeggo, D. 1976. A report on the field study of the St Lucia Parrot *Amazona versicolor* during 1975. *Jersey Wildlife Preservation Trust 12th Ann. Rep. 1975*: 34-41.

Jeggo, D. and Anthony, D. 1991. A report on the 1990 field survey of the St Lucia Parrot *Amazona versicolor*. *Dodo* 27: 102-107.

Johnson, A. W. 1967. *The Birds of Chile and Adjacent Regions of Argentina, Bolivia and Peru*, 2. Platt, Buenos Aires.

Johnson, T. H. and Stattersfield, A. J. 1990. A global review of island endemic birds. *Ibis* 132: 167-180.

Jones, C. G. 1985. *The biology of the critically endangered birds of Mauritius*. M.Sc. thesis: North-east London Polytechnic.

Jones, C. G. and Duffy, K. 1992. The conservation of the Echo Parakeet *Psittacula eques* of Mauritius. *PsittaScene* 4(4): 7-10.

Jones, C. G. and Duffy, K. 1993. Conservation management of the Echo Parakeet *Psittacula eques echo*. *Dodo* 29: 126-148.

Jones, M. and Banjaransari, H. 1990. Ecology and conservation of the birds of Sumba and Buru. Preliminary report, Department of Biological Sciences, Manchester Metropolitan University.

Jordan, O. C. and Munn, C. A. 1993. First observations of the Blue-throated Macaw in Bolivia. *Wilson Bull.* 105: 694-695.

Jordan, O. C. and Munn, C. A. 1994. First observations in the wild of the Blue-throated Macaw in Bolivia. *PsittaScene* 6(1): 3.

Joseph, L. 1981a. The Red-tailed Black Cockatoo in south-eastern Australia. *Emu* 82: 42-45.

Joseph, L. 1981b. The Glossy Black Cockatoo on Kangaroo Island. *Emu* 82: 46-49.

Joseph, L. 1988a. Range extension of the Red-fan Parrot *Deroptyus acciptrinus* in Amazoninan Brazil. *Bull. Brit. Orn. Club* 108: 101-103.

Joseph, L. 1988. A review of the conservation status of Australian parrots in 1987. *Biol. Conserv.* 46: 261-280.

Joseph, L. 1989. Food-holding behaviour in some Australian parrots. *Corella* 13: 143-144.

Joseph, L. 1992. Notes on the distribution and natural history of the Sun Parakeet *Aratinga solstitialis solstitialis*. *Ornitología Neotropical* 3: 17-26.

Joseph, L., Emison, W. B. and Bren, W. M. 1991. Critical assessment of the conservation status of Red-tailed Black Cockatoos in south-eastern Australia with special reference to nesting requirements. *Emu* 91: 46-50.

Jouett, J. and Irvine, G. 1979. Once-doomed Blue Lories now hatching at San Diego Zoo. News Release, San Diego Zoo.

Junge, G. C. A. and Mees, G. F. 1958. *The Avifauna of Trinidad and Tobago*. Zoologische Verhandelingen 37, E. J. Brill, Leiden.

Juniper, T. 1990. A very singular bird. *BBC Wildlife* 8(10): 674-675.

Juniper, T. 1991. Last of a kind. *Birds International* 3(1): 10-16.

Juniper, T. 1994. Hyacinth Macaw *Anodorhynchus hyacinthinus* conservation status. In C. Bath, ed. Hyacinthine Macaw *Anodorhynchus hyacinthinus* regional studbook: British Isles. Paignton Zoo, Devon (unpublished).

Juniper, T. and Yamashita, C. 1990. The conservation of Spix's macaw. *Oryx* 24: 224-228.

Juniper, A. T. and Yamashita, C. 1991. The habitat and status of Spix's Macaw *Cyanopsitta spixii*. *Bird Conserv. Internatn.* 1: 1-9.

Juste, B. J. 1996. Trade in the Grey Parrot *Psittacus erithacus* on the island of Príncipe (São Tomé and Príncipe, Central Africa): initial assessment of the activity and its impact. *Biol. Conserv.* 76: 101-104.

Kantak, G. E. 1979. Observations on some fruit-eating birds in Mexico. *Auk* 96: 183-186.

Kenning, J. M. 1995. The Ponape Lorikeet. *Caged Bird Hobbyist* 95: 42-45.

Kilmer, A. 1994. Oxford University Lovebird expedition. Unpublished report.

King, B. and Dickinson, E. C. 1975. *A Field Guide to the Birds of South-East Asia*. Collins, London.

King, J. R. 1989. Notes on the birds of the Rio Mazan Valley, Azuay Province, Ecuador, with special reference to *Leptopsittaca branickii*, *Hapalopsittaca amazonina pyrrhops* and *Metallura baroni*. *Bull. Brit. Orn. Club* 109: 140-147.

King, W. B. 1981. *Endangered Birds of the World: the ICBP Bird Red Data Book*. Smithsonian Institution Press and International Council for Bird Preservation, Washington, D.C.

Kloot, T. 1988. Red-rumped Parrots feeding on hop goodenia. *Australian Bird Watcher* 12: 242.

Koepcke, M. 1961. Birds of the western slope of the Andes of Peru. *Amer. Mus. Novit.* 2028.

Koepcke, M. 1983. *The Birds of the Department of Lima, Peru*. Harrowood, Pennsylvania.

Krabbe, N. and Sornoza, M. 1994. Avifaunistic results of a subtropical camp in the Cordillera del Condor, southeastern Ecuador. *Bull. Brit. Orn. Club* 114: 56-61.

Kratter, A. W., Sillet, T. S., Chesser, R. T., O'Neill, J. P., Parker III, T. A. and Castillo, A. 1993. Avifauna of a chaco locality in Bolivia. *Wilson Bull.* 105: 114-141.

Kuehler, C. and Lieberman, A. 1988. Zoological Society of San Diego Tahitian Lory Management Plan. Unpublished.

Kuehler, C. 1990. Saving the coconut bird: the Polynesian Lory Conservation Project. *Zoonooz* 63(8): 12-13.

Kuehler, C. and Lieberman, A. 1993. Translocation of the Ultramarine Lory. *AFA Watchbird* 19(6): 60-61.

Lambert, F. 1992. Present status of the Philippine Cockatoo in Palawan. *Species* 18: 70.

Lambert, F. 1993a. *The Status of and Trade in North Moluccan Parrots with Particular Emphasis on Cacatua alba, Lorius garrulus and Eos squamata.* International Union for Conservation of Nature and Natural Resources, Cambridge, UK.

Lambert, F. R. 1993b. Trade, status and management of three parrots in the North Moluccas, Indonesia: White Cockatoo *Cacatua alba,* Chattering Lory *Lorius garrulus* and Violet-eared Lory *Eos squamata. Bird Conserv. Internatn.* 3: 145-168.

Lambert, F. 1993c. Some key sites and significant records of birds in the Philippines and Sabah. *Bird Conserv. Internatn.* 3: 281-297.

Lambert, F., Wirth, R., Seal, U. S., Thomsen, J. B. and Ellis-Joseph, S. 1993. *Parrots: an Action Plan for their Conservation and Management.* Draft report, International Council for Bird Preservation, Cambridge, UK.

Lambert, F. and Yong, D. 1989. Some recent bird observations from Halmahera. *Kukila* 4(1-2): 30-31.

Land, H. C. 1963. A collection of birds from the Caribbean lowlands of Guatemala. *Condor* 65: 49-65.

Land, H. C. 1970. *Birds of Guatemala.* Livingston, Pennsylvania.

Lanning, D. V. 1982. Survey of the Red-fronted Macaw (*Ara rubrogenys*) and Caninde Macaw (*Ara caninde*) in Bolivia, December 1981-March 1982. Unpublished report for International Council for Bird Preservation and New York Zoological Society.

Lanning, D. V. 1991a. Distribution and breeding biology of the Red-fronted Macaw. *Wilson Bull.* 103: 357-365.

Lanning, D. V. 1991b. Distribution and nest sites of the Monk Parakeet in Bolivia. *Wilson Bull.* 103: 366-372.

Lanning, D. V. and Shiflett, J. T. 1981. Status and nesting ecology of the Thick-billed Parrot (*Rhynchopsitta pachyrhyncha*). In R. F. Pasquier, ed. *Conservation of New World Parrots.* Techn. Publ. 1, International Council for Bird Preservation, Cambridge, UK.

Lanning, D. V. and Shiflett, J. T. 1983. Nesting ecology of Thick-billed Parrots. *Condor* 85: 66-73.

Lantermann, W. 1996. Sperlingspapageien im westlichen Tiefland von Ecuador. *Gefied. Welt* 120: 339-340.

Lawson, P. W. and Lanning, D. V. 1981. Nesting and status of the Maroon-fronted Parrot (*Rhynchopsitta terrisi*). In R. F. Pasquier, ed. *Conservation of New World Parrots.* Techn. Publ. 1, International Council for Bird Preservation, Cambridge, UK.

Langrand, O. 1990. *Guide to the Birds of Madagascar.* Yale University Press, New Haven and London.

LeCroy, M., Peckover, W. S., Kulupi, A. and Manseima, J. 1984. Bird observations on Normanby and Fergusson, D'Entrecasteaux Islands, Papua New Guinea. *Wildlife in Papua New Guinea* no. 83/1, Division of Wildlife, Office of Environment & Conservation, Boroko.

LeCroy, M., Peckover, W. S. and Kisokau, K. 1992. A population of Rainbow Lorikeets *Trichoglossus haematodus flavicans* roosting and nesting on the ground. *Emu* 99: 187-190.

Lees, A. 1991. *A Representative Protected Forest System for the Solomon Islands.* Maruia Society, Nelson.

Legge, W. V. 1880. *A History of the Birds of Ceylon.* Republished 1983 by Tisara Prakasakayo, Dehiwala, Sri Lanka.

Lekagul, B. and Cronin, E. W. 1974. *Bird Guide of Thailand.* Association for the Conservation of Wildlife, Bangkok.

Lekagul, B. and Round, P. D. 1991. *A Guide to the Birds of Thailand.* Saha Karn Bhaet, Bangkok.

Lever, C. 1987. *Naturalized Birds of the World.* Longman, Harlow.

Levinson, S. T. 1981. The social behaviour of the White-fronted Amazon (*Amazona albifrons*). In R. F. Pasquier, ed. *Conservation of New World Parrots.* Techn. Publ. 1, International Council for Bird Preservation, Cambridge, UK.

Lewis, A. and Pomeroy, D. 1989. *A Bird Atlas of Kenya.* Balkema, Rotterdam.

Lippens, L. and Wille, H. 1976. *Les Oiseaux du Zaïre.* Editions Lannoo, Tielt.

Lloyd, B. D. 1992a. Ecology and conservation of Kakapo in New Zealand. In RAOU Report no. 83, Royal Australasian Ornithologists' Union, Moonee Ponds.

Lloyd, B. 1992b. New Zealand's Kakapo - the long, slow road to recovery. *Wingspan* 6: 1-2, 19.

Lo, V. K. 1995. Extensao da distribuição de *Guaruba guarouba* para o norte do Estado de Mato Grosso, Amazônia Meridional (Psittaciformes: Psittacidae). *Ararajuba* 3: 93-94.

Lodge, W. 1991. *Birds: Alternative Names.* Blandford, London.

Long, J. L. 1981. *Introduced Birds of the World.* David & Charles, Newton Abbot.

Louette, M. 1981. *The Birds of Cameroon: an Annotated Checklist.* Verhandeling Wetenschappen 43, no. 163, Brussels.

Louette, M. 1998. *Les oiseaux des Comores. Mus. Roy. Afrique Centrale Annales Ser in-8, Sci. Zool.* no. 225.

Lousada, S. 1989. *Amazona auropalliata caribaea:* a new subspecies of parrot from the Bay Islands, northern Honduras. *Bull. Brit. Orn. Club.* 109: 232-235.

Lousada, S. and Howell, S. N. G. 1996. Distribution, variation and conservation of Yellow-headed Parrots in northern Central America. *Cotinga* 5: 46-52.

Lousada, S. A. & Howell, S. N. G. 1997. *Amazona oratrix hondurensis:* a new subspecies of parrot from the Sula Valley of northern Honduras. *Bull. Brit. Orn. Club* 117: 205-209.

Lovegrove, R., Mann, I., Morgan, G. and Williams, I. 1989. Report of an expedition to ascertain the status of Red Data Book species in the Tuamoto Archipelago (French Polynesia). Unpublished report.

Lovegrove, T. 1995. Summary of Echo Parakeet conservation 1994-95 season. *PsittaScene* 7(1): 9.

Lovegrove, T. and Wadum, L. 1994. Echo Parakeet news 1993-94 season. *PsittaScene* 6(2): 10-11.

Low, R. 1977. *Lories and Lorikeets: the Brush-tongued Parrots.* Paul Elek, London.

Low, R. 1980. *Parrots, their Care and Breeding.* Blandford Press, Poole.

Low, R. 1981. The Yellow-shouldered Amazon *Amazona barbadensis.* In R. F. Pasquier, ed. *Conservation of New World Parrots.* Techn. Publ. 1, International Council for Bird Preservation, Cambridge, UK.

Low, R. 1984. *Endangered Parrots.* Blandford, Poole.

Low, R. 1985. Breeding the Tahitian Blue Lory. *Avicult. Mag.* 91: 1-14.

Low, R. 1992. The Dusky Lory - destined to become a favourite. *Loriinae Bull.* 8(4): 20-22.

Lowen, J. C., Bartrina, L., Clay, R. P. and Tobias, J. A. 1996. *Biological surveys and conservation priorities in eastern Paraguay: the final reports of Project Canopy '92 and Yacutinga '95.* CSB Conservation Publications, Cambridge.

Lowery, G. H. and Dalquest, W. W. 1951. *Birds from the State of Veracruz, Mexico.* University of Kansas, Lawrence.

Loyn, R. and Chandler, C. 1978. Avifauna Study - ICI Point Wilson Development - Progress Report - June to October. Kinnaird Hill deRohan and Young, Melbourne.

Loyn, R. H., Lane, B. A., Chandler, C. amd Carr, G. W. 1986. Ecology of Orange-bellied Parrots *Neophema chrysogaster* at their main remnant wintering site. *Emu* 86: 195-206.

Luft, S. 1994. Beobachtungen zum Fortpflanzungs-verhalten des Halsbandsittichs, *Psittacula krameri manillensis*, auf Sri Lanka. *Falke* 41: 330-338.

Machado de Barros, Y. 1995. Der Gebirgsara *Ara couloni*: Beobachtungen im Manu-Nationalpark. *Papageien* 8: 241.

MacKinnon, J. 1988. *Field Guide to the Birds of Java and Bali.* Gadjah Mada University Press, Yogyakarta.

MacKinnon, J and Phillipps, K. 1993. *The Birds of Borneo, Sumatra, Java, and Bali: the Greater Sunda Islands.* Oxford University Press, Oxford.

Mackworth-Praed, C. W. and Grant, C. H. B. 1952. *The Birds of Eastern and North-Eastern Africa*, Series I, 1. Longmans, London.

Mackworth-Praed, C. W. and Grant, C. H. B. 1962. *The Birds of the Southern Third of Africa*, Series II, 1. Longmans, London.

Mackworth-Praed, C. W. and Grant, C. H. B. 1970. *The Birds of West Central and Western Africa*, Series III, 1. Longmans, London.

Mallet, M. 1972. Keas *Nestor notabilis. Jersey Wildlife Preservation Trust 9th Ann. Rep.*: 51-53.

Marchant, S. 1958. The birds of the Santa Elena Peninsula, S.W. Ecuador. *Ibis* 100: 349-387.

Marchant, S. 1960. The breeding of some S.W. Ecuadorean birds. *Ibis* 102: 349-382.

van Marle, J. G. and Voous, K. H. 1988. *The Birds of Sumatra: an Annotated Check-List.* British Ornithologists' Union, Tring.

Marquess of Tavistock 1929. *Parrots and Parrot-like Birds in Aviculture.* F.V. White, London.

Marsden, S. J. 1992. The distribution, abundance and habitat preferences of the Salmon-crested Cockatoo *Cacatua moluccensis* on Seram, Indonesia. *Bird Conserv. Internatn.* 2: 7-14.

Marsden, S. J., Jones, M. J., Linsley, M. D., Mead, C. and Hounsome, M. V. 1997. The conservation status of the restricted-range lowland birds of Buru, Indonesia. *Bird Conserv. Internatn.* 7: 213-233.

Martella, M. B. and Bucher, E. H. 1984. Nesting of the Spot-winged Falconet in Monk Parakeet nests. *Auk* 101: 614-615.

Martin, P. S., Robins, C. R. and Heed, W. B. 1954. Birds and biogeography of the Sierra de Tamaulipas, an isolated pine-oak habitat. *Wilson Bull.* 66: 38-57.

Martindale, J. 1986. *A Review of Literature and the Results of a search for Coxen's Fig-Parrot in South-East Queensland and North-East New South Wales during 1985.* RAOU Report No. 21, Royal Australasian Ornithologists' Union, Moonee Ponds.

Martínez-Sánchez, 1989. Records of new or little known birds for Nicaragua. *Condor* 91: 468-469.

Martuscelli, P. 1994. A parrot with a tiny distribution and a big problem. *PsittaScene* 6(3): 3-7.

Martuscelli, P. 1995. Ecology and conservation of the Red-tailed Amazon. *PsittaScene* 7(3): 3-5.

Mason, V. and Jarvis, F. 1989. *Birds of Bali.* Periplus Editions, Berkeley.

Massa, R. 1995. Performance of socio-sexual activity at a communal site in the African Orange-bellied Parrot *Poicephalus rufiventris. Ostrich* 66: 141.

Mawson, P. R. and Long, J. L. 1994. Size and age parameters of nest trees used by four species of parrot and one species of cockatoo in south-west Australia. *Emu* 94: 149-155.

Mawson, P. R. and Massam, M. C. 1996. Red-capped Parrot *Purpureicephalus spurius*: moult, age and sex determination. *Emu* 96: 240-244.

Mayr, E. 1944. The birds of Timor and Sumba. *Bull. Amer. Mus. Nat. Hist.* 83: 123-194.

Mayr, E. 1945. *Birds of the Southwest Pacific.* Macmillan, New York.

McBride, P. 1996. Concern for the Greater Vasa Parrot. *PsittaScene* 8(2): 10.

McFarland, D. C. 1988. Geographical variation in the clutch size and breeding season of the Ground Parrot *Pezoporus wallicus. Australian Bird Watcher* 12: 247-250.

McFarland, D. C. 1991a. The biology of the Ground Parrot, *Pezoporus wallicus*, in Queensland. I. Microhabitat use, activity cycle and diet. *Wildl. Res.* 18: 169-184.

McFarland, D. C. 1991b. The biology of the Ground Parrot, *Pezoporus wallicus*, in Queensland. II. Spacing, calling and breeding behaviour. *Wildl. Res.* 18: 185-197.

McFarland, D. C. 1991c. The biology of the Ground Parrot, *Pezoporus wallicus*, in Queensland. III. Distribution and Abundance. *Wildl. Res.* 18: 199-213.

McFarland, D. C. 1992. Fire management and ecology of the Ground Parrot in south-eastern Queensland. In RAOU Report no. 83, Royal Australasian Ornithologists' Union, Moonee Ponds.

McLellan, M. E. 1927. Notes on birds of Sinaloa and Nayarit, Mexico, in the fall of 1925. *Proc. Calif. Acad. Sci.* 16: 1-51.

MacKinnon Vda de Montes, B. 1989. *100 Common Birds of the Yucatán Peninsula.* Amigos de Sian Ka'an, Cancún, Quintana Roo.

McNaught, R. H. and Garradd, G. 1992. On Galahs and Vortices. *Emu* 92: 248-249.

McPherson, L. B. 1990. *New Zealand Birds: a Sound Guide.* McPherson Natural History Unit, Christchurch.

Medland, B. 1995. Birdwatching in Malawi. *Bull. Afr. Bird Club* 2: 109-115.

Medway, Lord and Wells, D. R. 1976. *The Birds of the Malay Peninsula*, 5. H. F. & G. Witherby, London, in association with Penerbit Universiti Malaya.

Mees, G. F. 1975. A list of birds known from Roti and adjacent islands (Lesser Sunda Islands). *Zoologische Mededelingen* 49: 115-139.

Menkhorst, P. W. 1992. Good news for the Orange-bellied Parrot. *Bird Observer* June 1992: 3-5.

Menkhorst, P. W. and Isles, A. C. 1981. The Night Parrot *Geopsittacus occidentalis*: evidence of its occurrence in north-western Victoria during the 1950s. *Emu* 81: 239-240.

Meredith, C. W. 1984. The Ground Parrot *Pezoporus wallicus.* RAOU Conservation Statement No. 1, Royal Australasian Ornithologists' Union, Moonee Ponds.

Merritt, R. E., Bell, P. A. and Laboudallon, V. 1986. Breeding biology of the Seychelles Black Parrot (*Coracopsis nigra barklyi*). *Wilson Bull.* 98: 160-163.

Merton, D. V., and Empson, R. 1989. But it doesn't look like a Parrot! *Birds International* 1(1): 60-72.

Merton, D. V., Morris, R. B. and Atkinson, I. A. E. 1984. Lek behaviour in a parrot: the Kakapo *Strigops* habroptilus of New Zealand. *Ibis* 126: 277-283.

Meyer de Schauensee, R. 1949. The birds of the Republic of Colombia. *Caldasia* 5(23): 381-644.

Meyer de Schauensee, R. 1966. *The Species of Birds of South America and their Distribution.* Academy of Natural Sciences, Philadelphia.

Meyer de Schauensee, R. 1966. Colombian zoological survey. Part V - new birds from Colombia. *Notulae Naturae* 221.

Meyer de Schauensee, R. 1984. *The Birds of China.* Oxford University Press, Oxford.

Meyer de Schauensee, R. and Phelps, W. H. 1978. *A Guide to the Birds of Venezuela.* Princeton University Press, Princeton.

Miller, A. H. 1947. The tropical avifauna of the upper Magdalena Valley, Colombia. *Auk* 64: 351-381.

Milon, P., Petter, J. J. and Randrianasolo, G. 1973. Oiseaux. *Faune de Madagascar* 35: 1-263.

Milton, R. 1988. Investigations of parrots on Bacan and Warmar Islands, Indonesia. *Parrotletter* 1: 22-23.

Milton, R., and Marhadi, A. 1987. *An Investigation of Parrots and their Trade on Pulau Bacan (North Moluccas) and Pulau Warmar, (Aru Islands).* WWF/IUCN Conservation for Development Programme in Indonesia, Bogor.

Mitchell, J. C. 1980. First Breeding of Tahitian Blue Lories. *AFA Watchbird* 7(2): 20-24.

Monroe, B. L. 1968. *A Distributional Survey of the Birds of Honduras.* Ornithological Monograph No. 7, American Ornithologists' Union.

Montgomery, S. L., Gangné, W. C. and Gangné, B. H. 1980. Notes on birdlife and nature conservation in the Marquesas and Society Islands. *Elepaio* 40: 152-154.

Moorhouse, R. J. and Powlesland, R. G. 1991. Aspects of the ecology of kakapo *Strigops habroptilus* liberated on Little Barrier Island (Hauturu), New Zealand. *Biol. Conserv.* 56: 349-365.

Moore, H. E. 1977. Endangerment at the specific and generic levels in palms. In G. T. Prance and T. S. Elias, eds. *Extinction is Forever.* New York Botanical Garden, New York.

Moreau, R. E. 1966, *The Bird Faunas of Africa and its Islands.* Academic Press, London.

Morony, J. J., Bock, W. J. and Farrand, J. 1975. *Reference List of Birds of the World.* Department of Ornithology, American Museum of Natural History, New York.

Morrison, A. 1939. The birds of the department of Huancavelica, Peru. *Ibis* 14(3): 453-486.

Morrison, A. 1947. Notes on the birds of the Pampas River Valley, south Peru. *Ibis* 90: 119-128.

Morvan, O., Saint-Pie, J. and Boussekey, M. 1993. Preliminary observations of the Blue throated Macaw (*Ara glaucogularis*) north of Trinidad, Bolivia. Unpublished report.

Mosa, S. G., Garrido, J. L., Sauad, J. J. and Núez, V. 1992. The migration of of the Turquoize-fronted Parrot, *Amazona aestiva,* and the Alder Parrot, *Amazona tucumana,* in northwest Argentina. *Univ. Nac. Salta Fac. Cienc, Nat. Manejo de Fauna Publ. Techn.* 3(7).

Mulliken, T. A. 1995. Response to questions posed by the Royal Society for the Protection of Birds regarding the international trade in wild birds. TRAFFIC International, Cambridge.

Munn, C. A., Thomsen, J. B. and Yamashita, C. 1987. Survey and status of the Hyacinth Macaw (*Anodorhynchus hyacinthinus*) in Brazil, Bolivia and Paraguay. Unpublished.

Munn, C. A. III 1995. Lear's Macaw: a second population confirmed. *PsittaScene* 7(4): 1-3.

Narosky, T. and Yzurieta, D. 1989. *The Birds of Argentina and Uruguay: a Field Guide.* Vazquez Mazzini Editores, Buenos Aires.

Nash, S. V. 1990. *The Psittacine Trade of Irian Jaya, Indonesia.* World Wide Fund for Nature, Jayapura.

Nash, S. V. 1992. A brief overview of the parrot trade in Irian Jaya, Indonesia. In RAOU Report no. 83, Royal Australasian Ornithologists' Union, Moonee Ponds.

Nash, S. V. 1993. Concern about trade in Red-and-blue Lories. *TRAFFIC Bull.* 13: 93-96.

Nash, S. V. and Nash, A. D. 1985. A checklist of the forest and forest edge birds of the Padang - Sugihan Wildlife Reserve, South Sumatra. *Kukila* 2(3): 55-59.

Nash, S. V. and Nash A. D. 1988. An annotated checklist of the birds of the Tanjung Puting National Park, Central Kalimantan. *Kukila* 3(3-4). 93-101.

Naumburg, E. M. B. 1930. The birds of Mato Grosso, Brazil. *Bull. Amer. Mus. Nat. Hist.* 60.

Navarro, J. L., Martella, M. B. and Bucher, E. H. 1992. Breeding season and productivity of Monk Parakeets in Cordoba, Argentina. *Wilson Bull.* 104: 413-424.

Navas, J. R. and Bó, N. A. 1996. Distribución geográfica y situación actual de *Brotogeris versicolurus* en la Argentina. *Hornero* 14: 90-92.

Newman, K. 1988. *The Birds of Southern Africa.* Southern, Johannesburg.

Newman, K. 1989. *The Birds of Botswana.* Southern, Johannesburg

Nias, R. C. 1992. The Yellow-tailed Black Cockatoo on Eyre Peninsula. In RAOU Report no. 83, Royal Australasian Ornithologists' Union, Moonee Ponds.

Nicoll, M. E. and Langrand, O. 1989. *Madagascar: Revue de la Conservation et des Aires Protégées.* WWF-Fonds Mondial pour la Nature, Gland, Switzerland.

Nixon, A. J. 1981. The external morphology and taxonomic status of the Orange-fronted Parakeet. *Notornis* 28: 292-300.

Nixon, A. J. and Weeks, P. J. 1985. Parasitism of Chatham Island parakeets (*Cyanoramphus* spp.) by the nematode *Ascaridia platyceri*. *J. Royal Soc. New Zealand* 15: 123-125.

Noegel, R. 1986. First US captive breeding of the Red-throated Conure (Green Conure). *AFA Watchbird* 13(1). 4.

Noegel, R. 1989. First breeding of the Tucuman Amazon. *AFA Watchbird* CITES Issue, Fall 1989: 26-27.

Noegel, R. and Moss, G. 1991. The Cuban Amazon and its subspecies. *AFA Watchbird* 17(6): 40-45.

Nores, M. and Yzurieta, D. 1994. The status of Argentine parrots. *Bird Conserv. Internatn.* 4: 313-328.

Odekerken, P. 1991. Naretha Bluebonnets abound in a homestead garden. *Birds International* 3(1): 51-57.

Olmos, F. 1993. Birds of the Sierra da Capivara National Park in the 'caatinga' of north-eastern Brazil. *Bird Conserv. Internatn.* 3: 21-36.

O'Neill, J. 1969. Notes on Peruvian birds. *Occas. Pap. Mus. Zool. Louisiana State Univ.* 37.

O'Neill, J. 1974. The birds of Balta, a Peruvian dry tropical forest locality, with an analysis of their origins and ecological relationships. Ph.D. thesis. Louisiana State University.

O'Neill, J. 1981. Comments on the status of the parrots occurring in Peru. In R. F. Pasquier, ed. *Conservation of New World Parrots.* Techn. Publ. 1, International Council for Bird Preservation, Cambridge, UK.

O'Neill, J., Munn, C. A. and Franke, I. 1991. *Nannopsittaca dachilleae,* a new species of parrotlet from eastern Peru. *Auk* 108: 225-229.

O'Neill, J. and Parker III, T. A. 1977. Taxonomy and range of *Pionus 'seniloides'* in Peru. *Condor* 79: 274.

Oren, D. C. and Novaes, F. C. 1986. Observations on the Golden Parakeet *Aratinga guarouba* in northern Brazil. *Biol. Conserv.* 36: 329-337.

Oren, D. C. and Willis, E. O. 1981. New Brazilian records for the Golden Parakeet (*Aratinga guarouba*). *Auk* 98: 394-396.

Ovington, D. 1978. *Australian Endangered Species.* Cassell Australia, Stanmore.

Pallister, T. and Hurrell, P. 1989. Report on a birding trip to Irian Jaya, Halmahera and Batanta Island. Unpublished report.

Parkes, K. C. and Dickinson, F. C. 1991. Types, type localities, and variation in some races of the Colasisi or Philippine Hanging Parrot *Loriculus philippensis. Bull. Brit. Orn. Club* 111: 104-110.

Pearman, M. 1992. The avifauna of the Río Machariapo dry forest, northern La Paz department, Bolivia: a preliminary investigation. *Bird Conserv. Internatn.* 3: 105-118.

Penry, H. 1994. *Bird Atlas of Botswana.* University of Natal Press, Pietermaritzburg.

Parker III, T. A. 1991. *A Biological Assessment of the Alto Madidi Region and Adjacent Areas of Northwest Bolivia.* Conservation International Rapid Assessment Program.

Parker III, T. A., Castillo U., A., Gell-Mann, M. and Rocha O., O. 1991. Records of new and unusual birds from northern Bolivia. *Bull. Brit. Orn. Club* 111: 120-138.

Parker III, T. A. and Carr, J. L. 1992. *Status of Forest Remnants in the Cordillera de al Costa and Adjacent Areas of Southwestern Ecuador.* Rapid Assessment Program Working Papers 2, Conservation International, Washington, D.C.

Parker III, T. A. 1993. *The Lowland Dry Forests of Santa Cruz, Bolivia: a Global Conservation Priority.* Rapid Assessment Program Working Papers 4, Conservation International, Washington, D.C.

Parker III, T. A., Foster, R. B., Emmons, L. H., Freed, P., Forsyth, A. B., Hoffman, B. and Gill, B. D. 1993. *A Biological Assessment of the Kanuku Mountain Region of Southwestern Guyana.* Rapid Assessment Program Working Papers 5, Conservation International, Washington, D.C.

Parker III, T. A., Parker, S. A. and Plenge, M. A. 1982. *An Annotated Checklist of Peruvian Birds.* Buteo Books, Vermillion, South Dakota.

Parker III, T. A. and Remsen, J. V. 1987. Fifty-two Amazonian bird species new to Bolivia. *Bull. Brit. Orn. Club* 107: 94-107.

Parker III, T. A., Schulenberg, T. S., Graves, G. R. and Braun, M.J. 1985. The avifauna of the Huancabamba region, northern Peru. *Ornithological Monographs No. 36.* American Ornithologists' Union.

Parker III, T. A., Schulenberg, T. S., Kessler, M. and Wust, W. H. 1995. Natural history and conservation of the endemic avifauna in north-west Peru. *Bird Conserv. Internatn.* 5: 201-232.

Paynter, R. A. 1955. The ornithogeography of the Yucatán Peninsula. *Peabody Mus. Nat. Hist. Bull.* 9.

Pearson, D. L. 1974. Range extensions and new records for bird species in Ecuador, Perú, and Bolivia. *Condor* 77: 96-99.

de la Peña, M. R. 1988. *Guia de Aves Argentinas: Columbiformes a Piciformes.* Talleres Gráficos Lux, Santa Fe, Argentina.

Penny, M. 1974. *The Birds of the Seychelles and the Outlying Islands.* Collins, London.

Perry, L. 1990. The fabulous Derbyan. *AFA Watchbird* 17(2): 40-43.

Peters, J. L. 1931. Additional notes on the birds of the Almirante Bay region of Panama. *Bull. Mus. Comp. Zool.* 71: 291-345.

Peters, J. L. 1961. *Check-List of Birds of the World, 3.* Museum of Comparative Zoology, Cambridge, Mass.

Peters, J. L. and Griswold, J. A. 1943. Birds of the Harvard Peruvian expedition. *Bull. Mus. Comp. Zool.* 92: 279-327.

Peterson, R. T. and Chalif, E. L. 1973. *A Field Guide to Mexican Birds.* Houghton Mifflin, Boston.

Phillips, W. W. A. 1978. *Annotated Checklist of the Birds of Ceylon (Sri Lanka).* The Wildlife and Nature Protection Society of Sri Lanka in association with the Ceylon Bird Club.

Phipps, G. 1983. The Kakarikis. *AFA Watchbird* 10(1): 4-11.

Phipps, G. 1990. Letter. *Birds International* 2(1): 9.

Pitter, E. and Christiansen, M. B. 1995. Ecology, status and conservation of the Red-fronted Macaw *Ara rubrogenys. Bird Conserv. Internatn.* 5: 61-78.

Pizo, M. O., Simão, I. and Galetti, M. 1995. Diet and flock size of sympatric parrots in the Atlantic forests of Brazil. *Ornitología Neotropical* 6: 87-95.

Pizzey, G. and Doyle, R. 1983. *A Field Guide to the Birds of Australia.* William Collins, Sydney.

Potter, N. S. 1953. The birds of Calicoan, Philippine Islands. *Wilson Bull.* 65: 252-256.

Poulsen, M. K. 1995. The threatened and near-threatened birds of Luzon, Philippines, and the role of the Sierra Madre mountains in their conservation. *Bird Conserv. Internatn.* 5: 79-116.

Poulsen, M. and Jepson, P. 1996. Status of the Salmon-crested Cockatoo and Red Lory on Ambon Island, Maluku. *Kukila* 8: 159-160.

Poulton, S. 1982. *Kakapo: a Bibliography.* Occasional Publication No. 1, Department of Internal Affairs, New Zealand Wildlife Service.

Power, D. M. 1966. Antiphonal dueting and evidence for auditory reaction time in the Orange-chinned Parakeet. *Auk* 83: 314-319.

Powlesland, R. 1989. *Kakapo Recovery Plan 1989-1994.* Department of Conservation, Wellington.

Powlesland, R. G., Lloyd, B. D., Best, H. A. and Merton, D. V. 1992. Breeding biology of the Kakapo *Strigops habroptilus* on Stewart Island, New Zealand. *Ibis* 134: 361-373.

Pratt, T. K. 1982. Additions to the avifauna of the Adelbert Range, Papua New Guinea. *Emu* 82: 117-125.

Pratt, H. D., Bruner, P. L. and Berrett, D. G. 1987. *The Birds of Hawaii and the Tropical Pacific.* Princeton University Press, Princeton.

Pyle, P. and Engbring, J. 1985. Checklist of the birds of Micronesia. *Elepaio* 46: 57-66.

Quin, B. 1991. The quirks of turks. *Wingspan* 1991 (4): 1-2.

Rand, A. L. and Gilliard, E. T. 1967. *Handbook of New Guinea Birds.* Trinity Press, London.

RAOU 1986. Australia's smallest parrot rediscovered. Press Release, Royal Australasian Ornithologists' Union, Moonee Ponds.

RAOU 1987. Ground Parrots at Barren Grounds. *Wing-*

span 1987 (11): 9.

RAOU 1991. Ground Parrot in Tasmania. *Wingspan* 1991 (2): 2.

RAOU 1992. Help the Golden-shouldered Parrot. *Wingspan* 1992 (6): 24.

Rasmussen, J. F., Rahbek, C., Poulsen, B. O., Poulsen, M. K. and Bloch, H. 1996. Distributional records and natural history notes on threatened and little known birds of southern Ecuador. *Bull. Brit. Orn. Club* 116: 26-46.

Rasmussen, P. C. and Collar, N. J. (in prep.) *Psittacula intermedia* is a hybrid.

Reed, M. A. and Tidemann, S. C. 1994. Nesting sites of the Hooded Parrot *Psephotus dissimilis* in the Northern Territory. *Emu* 94: 225-229.

Reijns, P. J. and van der Salm, J. N. C. 1981. Some ecological aspects of the Yellow-shouldered Amazon (*Amazona barbadensis rothschildi*). In R. F. Pasquier, ed. *Conservation of New World Parrots*. Techn. Publ. 1, International Council for Bird Preservation, Cambridge, UK.

Reynolds, M. 1991. First Australian project for World Parrot Trust. *PsittaScene* 3(4): 1-3.

Richards, G. and Richards, L. 1988. Java and Bali. Unpublished Report.

Ridgely, R. S. 1981. The current distribution and status of mainland Neotropical parrots. In R. F. Pasquier, ed. *Conservation of New World Parrots*. Techn. Publ. 1, International Council for Bird Preservation, Cambridge, UK.

Ridgely, R. S. 1989. First among parrots. Hyacinth Macaws in the wild. *Birds International* 1(1): 9-17.

Ridgely, R. S. and Gaulin, S. J. C. 1980. The birds of Finca Merenberg, Hulia Department, Colombia. *Condor* 82: 379-391.

Ridgely, R. S. and Gwynne, J. A. 1989. *A Guide to the Birds of Panama*. Princeton University Press, Princeton.

Ridgely, R. S. and Robbins M. B. 1988. *Pyrrhura orcesi*, a new parakeet from southwestern Ecuador, with systematic notes on the *P. melanura* complex. *Wilson Bull.* 100: 173-182.

Riley, J. 1995. Preliminary assessment of the status and utilisation of the Red-and-blue Lory (*Eos histrio*) on the Sangihe and Talaud Islands. Technical Memorandum no. 10, PHPA/BirdLife International Indonesia Programme. Bogor, Indonesia.

Riley, M. 1982. *Know Your New Zealand Birds*. Viking Sevenseas, Wellington.

Rinke, D. 1987. The avifauna of 'Eua and its off-shore islet Kalau, Kingdom of Tonga. *Emu* 87: 26-30.

Rinke, D. 1988. On the ecology of the Red Shining Parrot (*Prosopeia tabuensis*) on the Tongan island of 'Eua, southwest Pacific. *Ecol. Birds* 10: 203-217.

Rinke, D. 1989. The reproductive biology of the Red Shining Parrot *Prosopeia tabuensis* on the island of 'Eua, Kingdom of Tonga. *Ibis* 131: 238-249.

Rinke, D. 1992. Status and conservation of parrots on tropical Pacific islands. In RAOU Report No. 83, Royal Australasian Ornithologists' Union, Moonee Ponds.

Rinke, D., Onnebrink, H. and Curio, E. 1992. Miscellaneous bird notes from the Kingdom of Tonga. *Notornis* 39: 301-315.

Ripley, S. D. 1982. *A Synopsis of the Birds of India and Pakistan*. Bombay Natural History Society, Bombay.

Ripley, S. D., Beehler, B. M. and Krishna Raju, K. S. R. 1987. Birds of the Visakhapatnam Ghats, Andhra Pradesh. *J. Bombay Nat. Hist. Soc.* 84: 540-553.

Risser A. C. 1980. Thick-billed Parrots. *AFA Watchbird* 7(1):

10-12.

Roberts, A. 1984. *Roberts Birds of South Africa* (fifth edition). John Voelcker, Cape Town.

Roberts, T. J. 1991. *The Birds of Pakistan*. Vol. I. Oxford University Press, Karachi.

Robertson, C. J. R., (ed.) 1985. *Reader's Digest Complete Book of New Zealand Birds*. Reader's Digest, Sydney.

Robbins, M. B., Parker III, T. A. and Allen, S. E. 1985. The avifauna of Cerro Pirre, Darién, eastern Panamá. Pp.198-232 in *Neotropical Ornithology*. Ornithological Monographs 36, American Ornithologists' Union, Washington, D.C.

Robbins, M. B., Ridgely, R. S., Schulenberg, T. S. and Gill, F. B. 1987. The avifauna of the Cordillera de Cutucú, Ecuador, with comparisons to other Andean localities. *Proc. Acad. Nat. Sci. Philadelphia* 139: 243-259.

Robinet, O., Barre, N. and Salas, M. 1996. Population estimate for the Ouvea Parakeet *Eunymphicus cornutus uvaeensis*: its present range and implications for conservation. *Emu* 96: 151-157.

Robins, C. R. and Heed, W. B. 1951. Birds of La Joya de Salas, Tamaulipas. *Wilson Bull.* 63: 263-270.

Robinson, A. C., Casperson, K. D. and Copely, P. B. 1990. Breeding records of Malleefowl (*Leipoa ocellata*) and Scarlet-chested Parrots (*Neophema splendida*) within the Yellabinna Wilderness Area, South Australia. *South Australian Orn.* 31: 8

Robson, C. 1991. The avifauna of Nam Cat Tien National Park, Dong Nai. *Garrulax* 8: 4-9.

Robson, C., Eames, J., Wolstencroft, J., Nguyen Cu and Truong Van La 1989. Recent records of birds from Viet Nam. *Forktail* 5: 71-97.

Rodewald, P. G., Dejaifve, P. A. and Green, A. A. 1994. The birds of Korup National Park and Korup Project Area, Southwest Province, Cameroon. *Bird Conserv. Internatn.* 4: 1-68.

Rodríguez-Estrella, R., Mata, E. and Rivera, L. 1992. Ecological notes on the Green Parakeet of Isla Socorro, Mexico. *Condor* 94: 523-525.

Roe, N. A. and Rees, W. E. 1979. Notes on the puna avifauna of Azángaro province, department of Puno, southern Peru. *Auk* 96: 475-482.

Rosewarne, K., (ed.) 1997. In brief. *World Birdwatch* 19(2): 3

van Rossem, A. J. 1945. *A Distributional Survey of the Birds of Sonora, Mexico*. Occas. Pap. Mus. Zool. Louisiana State Univ. 21.

Roth, P. 1988. Distribution, actual status and biology of Spix's Macaw *Cyanopsitta spixii*: report on 1987 activities. Unpublished.

Round, P. D. 1988. *Resident Forest Birds in Thailand: their Status and Conservation*. Monograph no. 2, International Council for Bird Preservation, Cambridge, UK.

Rowan, M. K. 1983. *The Doves, Parrots, Louries and Cuckoos of Southern Africa*. Croom Helm, London.

Rowley, I. 1990. *The Galah*. Surrey Beatty, Chipping Norton, New South Wales.

Rowley, J. S. 1966. Breeding records of birds in the Sierra Madre del Sur, Oaxaca, Mexico. *Proc. West. Foundn. Vert. Zool.* 1: 107-204.

Rowley, J. S. 1984. Breeding records of land birds in Oaxaca, Mexico. *Proc. West. Foundn. Vert. Zool.* 2: 73-221.

Rozendaal, F. G. and Dekker, R. W. R. J. 1989. Annotated checklist of the birds of the Dumoga-Bone National Park, North Sulawesi. *Kukila* 4(3-4): 85-95.

Russell, S. M. 1964. *A distributional study of the birds of Brit-*

ish Honduras. Ornithological Monographs 1, American Ornithologists' Union.

Rutgers, A. and Norris, K. A. 1979. *Encyclopaedia of Aviculture.* Blandford Press, Poole.

Ryall, C. 1991. Avifauna of Nguuni near Mombassa, Kenya, between September 1984 and October 1987. Part 1: Afrotropical species. *Scopus* 15: 1-3.

Ryall, C. 1994. Bird observations on Wasani Island, Kenya. *Scopus* 18: 34-39.

Safford, R. J., Duckworth, J. W., Evans, M. I., Telfer, M. G., Timmins, R. J. and Chemere Zewdie 1993. The birds of Nechisar National Park, Ethiopia. *Scopus* 16: 61-80.

Saini, H. K., Dhindsa, M. S. and Toor, H. S. 1994. Food of the Rose-ringed Parakeet (*Psittacula krameri*): a quantitative study. *J. Bombay Nat. Hist. Soc.* 91: 96-103.

Salaman, P. and Gandy, D. 1993. Colombia '93: Thunder Lake expedition. Preliminary report.

Sane, S. R., Kannan, P., Rajendran, C. G., Ingle, S. T. and Bhagwat, A. M. 1987. On the taxonomic status of *Psittacula intermedia* (Rothschild). *J. Bombay Nat. Hist. Soc.* 83 (suppl.): 127-134.

Sargeant, D. 1989. The Fijian Islands. Unpublished report.

Sargeant, D. E. 1992. A birder's guide to the Philippines. Unpublished report.

Sargeant, D. E. 1994. Recent ornithological observations from São Tomé and Príncipe Islands. *Bull. Afr. Bird Club* 1: 96-102.

Saunders, D. A. 1979. Distribution and taxonomy of the White-tailed and Yellow-tailed Black Cockatoos *Calyptorhynchus* spp. *Emu* 79: 215-227.

Saunders, D. A. 1989. Changes in the avifauna of a region, district and remnant as a result of fragmentation of native vegetation: the wheatbelt of Western Australia. A case study. *Biol. Conserv.* 50: 99-135.

Schaldach, W. J. 1963. The avifauna of Colima and adjacent Jalisco, Mexico. *Proc. West. Foundn. Vert. Zool.* 1(1): 1-100.

Schodde, R. 1978. *The Status of Endangered Australasian Wildlife.* Royal Zoological Society, South Australia.

Schodde, R. 1988. New subspecies of Australian birds. *Canberra Bird Notes* 13: 119-122.

Schodde, R. 1993. Geographic forms of the Regent Parrot *Polytelis anthopeplus* (Lear), and their type localities. *Bull. Brit. Orn. Club* 113: 44-47.

Schodde, R., Fullagar, P. and Hermes, N. 1983. *A Review of Norfolk Island Birds: Past and Present.* Special Publication 8, Australian National Parks and Wildlife Service, Canberra.

Schodde, R., Mason, I. J. and Wood, J. T. 1993. Geographical differentiation in the Glossy Black-Cockatoo *Calyptorhynchus lathami* (Temminck) and its history. *Emu* 93: 156-166.

Schodde, R. and Tidemann, S. C. 1988. *The Reader's Digest Complete Book of Australian Birds.* Reader's Digest, Sydney.

Schoenwald, R. and Schoenwald, J. 1992. Experiences in breeding the Golden Conure. *AFA Watchbird* 19(2): 9-11.

Schulte, E. G. B. 1975. Breeding Goffin's Cockatoo. *Avicult. Mag.* 81: 155.

Sedgwick, E. H. 1988. The status of bird species in the rural town of Harvey, Western Australia. *Australian Bird Watcher* 12: 222-231.

Seitre, R. and Seitre, J. 1992. Causes of land-bird extinctions in French Polynesia. *Oryx* 26: 215-222.

Selman, R. and Hunter, M. 1996. Rüppell's Parrot - some early results. *PsittaScene* 8(4): 5.

Serle, W., Morel, G. J. and Hartwig, W. 1977. *Field Guide to the Birds of West Africa.* Collins, London.

Serventy, D. L., and Whittell, H. M. 1948. *A Handbook of the Birds of Western Australia.* Patersons Press, Perth.

Short, L. L. 1974. Nesting of southern Sonoran birds during the summer rainy season. *Condor* 76: 21-32.

Short, L. L. 1975. A zoogeographic analysis of the South American chaco avifauna. *Bull. Amer. Mus. Nat. Hist.* 154: 163-352.

Short, L. L. 1976. Notes on a collection of birds from the Paraguayan Chaco. *Amer. Mus. Novit.* 2597.

Sibley, C. G. and Monroe, B. L. 1990. *Distribution and Taxonomy of Birds of the World.* Yale University Press, New Haven and London.

Sibley, C. G. and Ahlquist, J. E. 1990. *Phylogeny and Classification of Birds: a Study in Molecular Evolution.* Yale University Press, New Haven and London.

Sibley, C. G. and Monroe, B. L. 1993. *A Supplement to Distribution and Taxonomy of Birds of the World.* Yale University Press, New Haven and London.

Sick, H. 1957. *Touit huetii* (Temminck) from Brazil. *Auk* 74: 510-511.

Sick, H. 1993. *Birds in Brazil: a Natural History.* Princeton University Press, Princeton.

Siebers, H. C. 1930. Fauna Buruana, Aves. *Treubia* 7 (suppl.): 165-303.

Silva, T. 1981. The status of *Aratinga euops. AFA Watchbird* 8(2): 10.

Silva, T. 1991. Hispaniolan Conure in field and aviary. *AFA Watchbird* 17(6): 23-24.

Silvius, M. J. and Verheugt, W. J. M. 1986. The birds of Berbak Game Reserve, Jambi Province, Sumatra. *Kukila* 2(4): 76-83.

Simpson, K. and Day, N. 1984. *The Birds of Australia: a Book of Identification.* Lloyd O'Neil, South Yarra.

Sjodahl, S. 1985. The Hispaniolan Amazon (*Amazona ventralis*). *AFA Watchbird* 12(3): 9-10.

Slater, P., ed 1979. *A Field Guide to Australian Birds, 1: Non-passerines.* Rigby, Adelaide.

Slater, P. 1989. *The Slater Field Guide to Australian Birds.* Weldon Publishing, Willoughby.

Slud, P. 1964. The birds of Costa Rica: distribution and ecology. *Bull. Amer. Mus. Nat. Hist.* 128.

Smiet, F. 1985. Notes on the field status and trade of Moluccan parrots. *Biol. Conserv.* 34: 181-194.

Smith, G. A. 1975. Systematics of parrots. *Ibis* 117: 18-66.

Smith, G. A. 1981. The origin of Philippine parrots and the relationships of the Guaiabero *Bolbopsittacus lunulatus. Ibis* 123: 345-349.

Smith, G. A. 1990. The caique. *AFA Watchbird* 17(2): 27-32.

Smith, G. A. 1991. Geographical variation in the Scarlet Macaw. *AFA Watchbird* 18(3): 13-14.

Smith, G. T. and Moore, L. A. 1991. Foods of Corellas *Cacatua pastinator* in Western Australia. *Emu* 91: 87-92.

Smith G. T. and Moore, L. A. 1992a. Breeding of the Cockatiel *Nymphicus hollandicus* in the wheatbelt of Western Australia. *Australian Bird Watcher* 14: 155-8.

Smith, G. T. and Moore, L. A. 1992b. Patterns of movement in the Western Long-billed Corella *Cacatua pastinator* in the South-west of Western Australia. *Emu* 92: 19-27.

Smith, S. 1992. Birding in Irian Jaya. Unpublished report.

Smithe, F. B. 1966. *The Birds of Tikal.* Natural History Press, New York.

Smithe, F. B. and Paynter, R. A. 1963. Birds of Tikal, Guatemala. *Bull. Mus. Comp. Zool.* 128: 245-324.

Smythies, B. E. 1981. *The Birds of Borneo.* Sabah Society, Kota Kinabalu, and Malayan Nature Society, Kuala Lumpur.

Smythies, B. E. 1986. *The Birds of Burma.* Nimrod Press, Liss, UK, and Silvio Mattacchione, Pickering, Canada.

Snyder, D. E. 1966. *The Birds of Guyana.* Peabody Museum, Salem.

Snyder, N. F. R., Koenig, S. E., Koschmann, J., Snyder, H. A. and Johnson, T. B. 1994. Thick-billed Parrot releases in Arizona. *Condor* 96: 845-862.

Snyder, N. F. R., Snyder, H. A. and Johnson, T. B. 1989. Parrots return to the Arizona skies. *Birds International* 1(2): 41-52.

Snyder, N. F. R., Wiley, J. W. and Kepler, C. B. 1987. *The Parrots of Luquillo: Natural History and Conservation of the Puerto Rican Parrot.* Western Foundation of Vertebrate Zoology, Los Angeles.

Sparks, J. and Soper, A. 1990. *Parrots: a Natural History.* David & Charles, Newton Abbot.

Stager, K. E. 1957. Birds of the Tres Marías. *Auk* 74: 413-432.

Starks, J. 1991a. Orange-bellied Parrot Surveys in 1991. *Wingspan* 2: 13.

Starks, J. 1991b. 1991 Orange-bellied Parrot Surveys. *Wingspan* 4: 21.

Starks, J. 1992. Orange-bellied Parrot Surveys in 1992. *Wingspan* 6: 16.

Starks, J., Brown, P., Loyn, R. and Menkhorst, P. 1992. Twelve years of winter counts of Orange-bellied Parrot *Neophema chrysogaster. Australian Bird Watcher* 14: 305-312.

Steadman, D. W., Greiner, E. C. and Wood, C. 1990. Absence of blood parasites in indigenous and introduced birds from the Cook Islands, South Pacific. *Conserv. Biol.* 4: 398-404.

Stiles, F. G., Skutch, A. F. and Gardner, D. 1989. *A Guide to the Birds of Costa Rica.* Christopher Helm, London.

Stokes, A. 1980. Notes on the landbirds of New Caledonia. *Emu* 80: 81-86.

Stone, W. 1928. On a collection of birds from the Pará region, eastern Brazil. *Proc. Acad. Nat. Sci. Philadelphia* 80: 149-176.

Stone, W. and Roberts, H. R. 1934. Zoological results of the Matto Grosso expedition to Brazil in 1931. III. Birds. *Proc. Acad. Nat. Sci. Philadelphia* 96: 363-397.

Storr, G. M. and Johnstone, R. E. 1979. *Field Guide to the Birds of Western Australia.* Western Australian Museum, Perth.

Stotz, D. F., Fitzpatrick, J. W., Parker III, T. A. and Moskovitz, D. K. 1996. *Neotropical Birds: Ecology and Conservation.* University of Chicago Press, Chicago.

Strahl, S. D., Desenne, P. A., Jimenez, J. L. and Goldstein, I. R. 1991. Behavior and biology of the Hawk-headed Parrot, *Deroptyus accipitrinus,* in southern Venezuela. *Condor* 93: 177-180.

Strange, M. and Jeyarajasingam, A. 1993. *A Photographic Guide to the Birds of Peninsular Malaysia and Singapore.* Sun Tree Publishing, Singapore.

Straube, F. C. and Bornschein, M. R. 1995. New or noteworthy records of birds from northwestern Paraná and adjacent areas (Brazil). *Bull. Brit. Orn. Club* 115: 219-225.

Stubblefield, L. 1994. The birds of Ajai's Game Reserve, Uganda: a first ornithological survey. *Scopus* 18: 117-122.

Sturgis, B. B. 1928. *Field Book of the Birds of the Panama Ca-*

nal Zone. Putnam's and Sons, London and New York.

Succow, M. 1990. Zur Kenntnis der Vogelwelt des Bale-Hochlandes (Süd-Äthiopien). *Mitt. Zool. Mus. Berlin, Suppl. Ann. Orn.* 14: 3-33.

Tarboton, W. R., Kemp, M. I. and Kemp, A. C. 1987. *The Birds of the Transvaal.* Transvaal Museum, Transvaal.

Tashian, R. E. 1952. Birds from the Palenque region, Mexico. *Auk* 69: 60-67.

Tasmanian Department of Parks, Wildlife and Heritage 1991. Release of captive-bred Orange-bellied Parrots. *Wingspan* 4: 17.

Taylor, J. 1990. A status survey of Seram's Moluccan endemic avifauna. Unpublished report.

Taylor, J. 1991. Report from Indonesia. *PsittaScene* 3(1): 6.

Taylor, P. W. 1987. Birds of the Port Wakefield District, 1968-1985. *South Australian Orn.* 30: 62-69.

Taylor, R. H. 1985. Status, habits and conservation of *Cyanoramphus* parakeets in the New Zealand region. In P. J. Moors, ed. *Conservation of Island Birds.* Techn. Publ. 3, International Council for Bird Preservation, Cambridge, UK.

Taylor, R. J., and Mooney, N. J. 1990. Fungal feeding by Yellow-tailed Black-Cockatoo. *Corella* 14: 30.

Taylor, S. 1996. Brown-headed Parrot study in southern Africa. *PsittaScene* 8(4): 4.

Teixeira, D. M., Nacinovic, J. B. and Luigi, G. 1988. Notes on some birds of northeastern Brazil (3). *Bull. Brit. Orn. Club* 108: 75-79.

Teixeira, D. M., Nacinovic, J. B. and Luigi, G. 1989. Notes on some birds of northeastern Brazil (4). *Bull. Brit. Orn. Club* 109: 152-157.

Teixeira, D. M., Nacinovic, J. B. and Tavares, M. S. 1986. Notes on some birds of northeastern Brazil. *Bull. Brit. Orn. Club.* 106: 70-74.

Terborgh, J. and Faaborg, J. 1973. Turnover and ecological release in the avifauna of Mona island, Puerto Rico. *Auk* 90: 759-779.

Them, P. H. 1989. Black-cheeked Lovebirds: the parrot pearl of the dark continent. *AFA Watchbird* 16(2): 13-14.

Thewlis, R. M., Duckworth, J. W., Anderson, G. Q. A., Dvorak, M., Evans, T. D., Nemeth, E., Timmins, R. J. and Wilkinson, R. J. 1995. Ornithological records from Lao, 1992-1993. *Forktail* 11: 47-100.

Todd, W. 1990. Island cockatoos - a conservation appeal to aviculturalists. *Avicult. Mag.* 96: 54-57

Todd, W. E. C. 1916. The birds of the Isle of Pines. *Annals Carnegie Mus.* 10: 146-296.

Todd, W. E. C. and Carriker, M. A. 1922. Birds of Santa Marta region, Colombia. *Annals Carnegie Mus.* 14: 3-611.

Tostain, O., Dujardin, J. L., Érard, C. and Thiollay, J. M. 1992. *Oiseaux de Guyane.* Société d'Etudes Ornithologiques, Muséum National d'Histoire Naturelle, Brunoy, France.

Toyne, E. P. 1994. The plight of parrots in southern Ecuador. *PsittaScene* 6(3): 9-11.

Toyne, E. P. and Flanagan, J. N. M. 1996. First nest record of Red-faced Parrot *Hapalopsittaca pyrrhops. Cotinga* 5: 43-44.

Toyne, E. P., Flanagan, J. N. M. and Jeffcote, M. T. 1995. Vocalisations of the endangered Red-faced Parrot *Hapalopsittaca pyrrhops* in southern Ecuador. *Ornitología Neotropical* 6: 125-128.

Toyne, E. P. and Jeffcote M. T. 1994. Nesting records of *Pionus* species in southern Ecuador. *Bull. Brit. Orn. Club* 114: 124-127.

Toyne, E. P., Jeffcote, M. T. and Flanagan, J. N. 1992. Status, distribution and ecology of the the White-breasted Parakeet *Pyrrhura albipectus* in Podocarpus National Park, southern Ecuador. *Bird Conserv. Internatn.* 2: 237-339.

Traylor, M. A. 1941. Birds from the Yucatan Peninsula. *Field Mus. Nat. Hist. Zool. Ser.* 24: 195-225.

Traylor, M. A. 1948. New birds from Peru and Ecuador. *Fieldiana Zool.* 31: 195-200.

Traylor, M. A. 1958. Birds of north-eastern Peru. *Fieldiana Zool.* 35: 87-141.

Traylor, M. A. 1965. A collection of birds from Barotseland and Bechuanaland. *Ibis* 107: 138-172.

Triggs, S. J. and Daugherty, C. H. 1988. Preliminary genetic analysis of New Zealand parakeets. New Zealand Department of Conservation, Science and Research Internal Report no. 14 (unpublished).

Triggs S. J. and Daugherty, C. H. 1996. Conservation and genetics of New Zealand parakeets. *Bird Conserv. Internatn.* 6: 89-101.

Trounson, D. and Trounson, M. 1987. *Australia, Land of Birds.* William Collins, Sydney.

Turner, D. A. 1991. The genus *Agapornis* in East Africa. *Scopus* 15: 52-54.

Tyabji, H. N. 1994. The birds of Bandhavgarh National Park, M. P. *J. Bombay Nat. Hist. Soc.* 91: 51-77.

Tzaros, C. 1992. The red variety of the Eastern Rosella. *Australian Bird Watcher* 14: 226-229.

Tzaros, C. and Price, R. 1996. Swift Parrot Survey 1996. Royal Australasian Ornithologists' Union Website.

Urban, E. K. and Brown, L. H. 1971. *A Checklist of the Birds of Ethiopia.* Haile Sellassie I University, Addis Ababa.

Valentine, M. 1987. Chromosome analysis of Maroon-bellied and Green-cheeked Conures. *AFA Watchbird* 14(3): 19.

Varty, N. 1991. The status and conservation of Jamaica's threatened and endemic forest avifauna and their habitats following Hurricane Gilbert. *Bird Conserv. Internatn.* 1: 135-151.

Varty, N. 1994. *The Ecology and Conservation of the Red-spectacled Parrot Amazona pretrei in Southern Brazil.* Final report. Birdlife International, Cambridge.

Vaughn, C. 1983. A report on dense forest habitat for endangered species in Costa Rica. National University, Heredia. Unpublished.

Vaurie, C. 1972. *Tibet and its Birds.* H. F. & G. Witherby, London.

Voous, K. H. 1965. *Check-list of the Birds of Aruba, Curaçao, and Bonaire.* E.J. Brill, Leiden.

Voous, K. H. 1983. *The Birds of the Netherlands Antilles.* De Walberg Pers.

Vuthipong, S. 1992. Blue-rumped Parrot (*Psittinus cyanurus*): discovery of northernmost limit of its distribution. *Bangkok Bird Club Bull.* 9(2): 10-11.

Wade, P., ed. 1975. *Every Australian Bird Illustrated.* Rigby, Adelaide.

Wadum, L. 1994. Fieldwork for the Echo Parakeet. *PsittaScene* 6(4): 6-7.

Wakelin, M. D. 1991. Analysis and Review of National Kea and Kaka Databases. New Zealand Department of Conservation, Science and Research Internal Report no. 99 (unpublished).

Walters, M. P. 1974. The eggs of the Golden Conure *Aratinga guarouba.* *Bull. Brit. Orn. Club* 94: 71.

Walters, M. 1975. The status of *Eos goodfellowi.* *Bull. Brit. Orn. Club* 95: 129-131.

Walters, M. P. 1985. On the status of *Psittacula intermedia*

(Rothschild). *J. Bombay Nat. Hist. Soc.* 82: 197-199.

Waltman, J. R. and Beissinger, S. R. 1992. Breeding behaviour of the Green-rumped Parrotlet. *Wilson Bull.* 104: 65-84.

Warner, D. W. 1947. The ornithology of New Caledonia and the Loyalty Islands. Ph.D. Thesis (unpubl.), Cornell University.

Watkins, D. 1985. *Report of the RAOU Ground Parrot Survey in Western Australia.* Report no. 15, Royal Australasian Ornithologists' Union, Moonee Ponds.

Watkins, D. W. and Burbidge, A. H. 1992. Conservation of the Ground Parrot in Western Australia. In RAOU Report no. 83, Royal Australasian Ornithologists' Union, Moonee Ponds.

Watling, D. 1982a. *Birds of Fiji, Tonga and Samoa.* Milwood Press, Wellington.

Watling, D. 1982b. Notes on birds of Makogai Island, Fiji Islands. *Bull. Brit. Orn. Club* 102: 123-127.

Watling, D. 1983. Ornithological notes from Sulawesi. *Emu* 83: 247-254.

Watling, D. 1985. The distribution of Fijian land and freshwater birds, based on the collections and observations of the Whitney South Sea Expedition. *Domodomo* 3(4): 136-137.

Watling, D. 1995. Notes on the status of Kuhl's Lorikeet *Vini kuhlii* in the Northern Line Islands, Kiribati. *Bird Conserv. Internatn.* 5: 481-489.

Watts, D. 1986. An Orange-bellied Parrot at its nest. *BBC Wildlife* 4: 270-272.

Waugh, D. 1995. Buffon's Macaw in Ecuador: the urgency for conservation action. *PsittaScene* 7(1): 1-5.

WCI 1992. *The Wild Bird Trade.* WCI Policy Report No. 2, New York Zoological Society, New York.

Weaver, C. M. 1982. Breeding habitats and status of the Golden-shouldered Parrot *Psephotus chrysopterygius* in Queensland. *Emu* 82: 2-6.

Weaver, C. M. 1987. A comparison of tempratures recorded in nest chambers excavated in termite mounds by the Golden-shouldered Parrot. *Emu* 87: 57-59.

Webster, R. 1989. Superb Parrots and gum trees. *Birds International* 1(3): 52-59.

Webster, R. 1992. Ecology and management of the Superb Parrot in eastern Australia. In RAOU Report no. 83, Royal Australasian Ornithologists' Union, Moonee Ponds.

Wege, D. C. and Collar, N. J. 1991. The Blue-cheeked Amazon *Amazona dufresniana*: a review. *Bird Conserv. Internatn.* 1: 317-328.

Wetmore, A. 1926a. Observations on the birds of Argentina, Paraguay, Uruguay and Chile. *Bull. U.S. Natn. Mus.* 133: 1-448.

Wetmore, A. 1926b. Report on a collection of birds made by J. R. Pemberton in Patagonia. *Univ. California Publ. Zool.* 24: 395-474.

Wetmore, A. 1939. Observations on the birds of northern Venezuela. *Proc. U.S. Natn. Mus.* 87: 173-260.

Wetmore, A. 1941. Notes on birds of the Guatemalan highlands. *Proc. U.S. Natn. Mus.* 89: 523-581.

Wetmore, A. 1943. The birds of southern Veracruz, Mexico. *Proc. U.S. Natn. Mus.* 93: 215-340.

Wetmore, A. 1944. A collection of birds from northern Guanacaste, Costa Rica. *Proc. U.S. Natn. Mus.* 95: 25-80.

Wetmore, A. 1946. The birds of San José and Pedro González Islands, Republic of Panamá. *Smithsonian Misc. Coll.* 106: 1-60.

Wetmore, A. 1968. *The Birds of the Republic of Panamá.* Part

2: *Columbidae (Pigeons) to Picidae (Woodpeckers)*.
Smithsonian, Washington.

Wetmore, A. and Swales, B. H. 1931. The birds of Haiti
and the Dominican Republic. *U.S. Natn. Mus. Bull.*
155. Smithsonian, Washington.

White, C. M. N. 1965. *A Revised Check List of African Non-
Passerine Birds*. Government Printer, Lusaka.

White, C. M. N. and Bruce, M. D. 1986. *The Birds of Wallacea
(Sulawesi, the Moluccas and Lesser Sunda Islands, Indo-
nesia)*. Check-list no. 7, British Ornithologists' Union,
London.

Whitney, B. M., Rowlett, J. M. and Rowlett, R. A. 1994.
Distributional and other noteworthy records for some
Bolivian birds. *Bull. Brit. Orn. Club* 114: 149-162.

Whitney, B. M. 1996. Flight behaviour and other field characteristics of the genera of Neotropical parrots.
Cotinga 5: 32-42.

Wiedenfeld, D. A. 1994. A new subspecies of Scarlet Macaw and its status and conservation. *Ornitología
Neotropical* 5: 99-104.

Wildash, P. 1968. *Birds of South Vietnam* Charles E. Tuttle,
Rutland, Vermont.

Wiley, J. W. 1981. The Puerto Rican Amazon (*Amazona
vittata*): its decline and the programme for its conservation. In R. F. Pasquier, ed. *Conservation of New World
Parrots*. Techn. Publ. 1, International Council for Bird
Preservation, Cambridge, UK.

Wiley, J. W. 1991. Status and conservation of parrots and
parakeets in the Greater Antilles, Bahama Islands and
Cayman Islands. *Bird Conserv. Internatn* 1: 187-214.

Wilkinson, R. 1993. Blue-eyed Cockatoo. JSMC Working
Group, Co-ordinator's Report.

Wilkinson, R. 1994. Vasa Parrot's fascinating breeding
behaviour. *PsittaScene* 6(2): 9.

Wilkinson, R. and Beecroft, R. 1985. Birds in Falgore Game
Reserve, Nigeria. *Malimbus* 7: 63-72.

Wilkinson, R., Dutson, G. and Sheldon, B. 1991. *The
Avifauna of Barito Ulu, Central Borneo*. Study Report
no. 48, International Council for Bird Preservation,
Cambridge, UK.

Williams, G. R. and Given, D. R. 1981. *The Red Data Book of
New Zealand - Rare and Endangered Species of Endemic
Terrestrial Vertebrates and Vascular Plants*. Nature Con-
servation Council, Wellington.

Williams, J. G. and Arlott, N. 1980. *A Field Guide to the Birds
of East Africa*. Collins, London.

Williams, R. S. R. and Tobias, J. A. 1994. *The Conservation
of Southern Ecuador's Threatened Avifauna: Final Report
of the Amazula 1990-1991 Projects*. Study Report 60,
International Council for Bird Preservation, Cambridge, UK.

Willis, E. O. and Oniki, Y. 1993. New and reconfirmed
birds from the state of São Paulo, Brazil, with notes
on disappearing species. *Bull. Brit. Orn. Club* 113: 23-
34.

Willis, J. 1997. A survey of the threats to the parrots of
Seram, Maluku, Indonesia. Undergraduate thesis,
Pembroke College, Cambridge.

Wilson, K. 1990. Kea, creature of curiosity. *Forest and Bird*
21(3): 20-26.

Wilson, K. 1991. Observations of the Kuramoo (*Vini peruviana*) on Aitutaki Island, Cook Islands. *Notornis* 40:
71-75.

Wilson, K. and Brejaart, R. 1992. The Kea - a brief research
review. In RAOU Report No. 83, Royal Australasian
Ornithologists' Union, Moonee Ponds.

Wilson, N. and Wilson, V. G. 1994. Avifauna of the southern Keiro Valley with emphasis on the area around
the Kenya Florspar Mine site, August 1989-July 1993.
Scopus 18: 65-115.

Wirminghaus, O. 1994. Report on the Cape Parrot project.
PsittaScene 6(4): 12.

Wirminghaus, O. 1995. Colour variation and anomalies
in South African Parrots. *Birding in S. Africa* 47: 76-77.

Wirminghaus, O. 1996. The ecology and status of the Cape
Parrot. *PsittaScene* 8(4): 3-4.

Wirth, R. 1991. Indonesia. *PsittaScene* 3(4): 14.

Wood, G. A. 1988. Further field observations of the Palm
Cockatoo *Probosciger aterrimus* in the Cape York Peninsula, Queensland. *Corella* 12: 48-52.

Wood, C. A. and Wetmore, A. 1925. A collection of birds
from the Fiji Islands. *Ibis* 12(1): 836-837.

World Parrot Trust 1990. Australia's endangered Orange-
bellied Parrot. *PsittaScene* 2(3): 10.

WWF 1993. Sudden allure of rare parrot threatens its survival. Press release, WWF, Gland.

Wyndham, E., Brereton, J. G. and Beeton, R. J. S. 1983.
Moult and plumages of Eastern Rosellas *Platycercus
eximius*. *Emu* 83. 242-246.

Yamashita, C. 1987. Field observations and comments on
the Lear's Macaw (*Anodorhynchus leari*), a highly endangered species from north-eastern Brazil. *Wilson
Bull.* 99: 280-282.

Yamashita, C. and Valle, M. P. 1993. On the linkage between *Anodorhynchus* macaws and palm nuts, and the
extinction of the Glaucous Macaw. *Bull. Brit. Orn. Club*
113: 53-60.

Young, C. G. 1929. A contribution to the ornithology of
the coastland of British Guiana. *Ibis* (12)5: 1-38.

Zimmer, J. T. and Phelps, W. H. 1946. Twenty-three new
subspecies of birds from Venezuela and Brazil. *Amer.
Mus. Novit.* 1312.

Zimmerman, D. A. 1975. Notes on Tamaulipan birds.
Wilson Bull. 69: 273-277.

Zimmerman, D. A., Turner, D. A. and Pearson, D. J. 1996.
The Birds of Kenya and Northern Tanzania. Christopher
Helm, London.

INDEX

Species are listed by their vernacular name (e.g. Red-billed Parrot) and by their scientific name. Specific scientific names are followed by the generic name as used in the book (e.g. *sordidus, Pionus*) and subspecific names are followed by both the specific and generic names (e.g. *antelius, Pionus sordidus*). Numbers in plain type refer to the first page of the relevant systematic entry. Numbers in bold type refer to the colour plate numbers.